Creative Uses
of Children's Literature

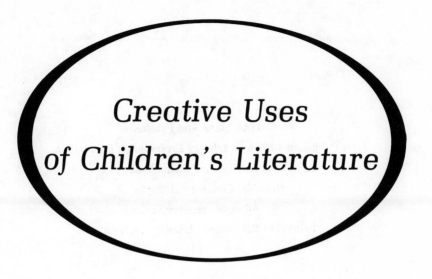

Creative Uses
of Children's Literature

by

MARY ANN PAULIN

with a foreword by
DR. MARILYN MILLER

LIBRARY PROFESSIONAL PUBLICATIONS
1982

© 1982 Mary Ann Paulin

First Published 1982 as a Library Professional Publication,

an imprint of The Shoe String Press Inc.

Hamden, Connecticut 06514

Printed in the United States of America

Library of Congress Cataloging in Publication Data

Paulin, Mary Ann, 1943-
Creative uses of children's literature.

Includes bibliographies and index.
1. Children—Books and reading.   2. Instructional materials centers.
3. Activity programs in education.   I. Title.
Z1037.P33   028.5   81-12405
ISBN 0-208-01861-1   AACR2

Contents

FOREWORD
by Dr. Marilyn Miller
11

PREFACE
13

Chapter One
INTRODUCING BOOKS IN ALL KINDS OF WAYS
15

Tree in the World; How the People Sang the Mountains Up and How the Valleys were Formed; Mountain Mists and Volcanoes; Stormalong, Sailor of the Seven Seas; Holiday Program; How Sweet Potatoes and Rice Came to Man; and Pecos Bill •

Chapter Two
EXPERIENCING ART THROUGH PICTURE BOOKS
167

Introduction • Drawings come to life • Lines become shapes • Art projects inspired by picture books • Names as artwork • Making outrageous hats • Creating unusual animals • Easter art projects • Egg trees, cookie trees, bird trees and more trees • Pinata and kite projects • Creating mood • Perception • Identifying the medium, technique and style of art in picture books • Variety in picture book illustration mediums • Watercolor and similar mediums used in picture books • Color in picture books • Books about color • Black and white picture books accented with color • Books about red • Little red, white or brown hen • Books about brown • Books about black • Books about white • Books about blue • Books about green • Books about yellow • Color and music • How and why stories about color from folklore • Spots and stripes in folklore • Spots, stripes and plaid in picture books • Collage in picture books • Cartoon illustrations in picture books • Photographs as illustrations • Alphabet photo books • Photography books • Photograms • Rubbings as illustrations • Woodcuts, linoleum blocks, vegetable prints • Lithography, a graphic technique • An awareness project • Identifying similar styles, techniques and mediums in illustrations • Books illustrated by one person that have simliar styles and techniques • Different styles or techniques used by one illustrator • Books by the same illustrator with different styles or techniques • Different artistic treatments of similar subjects • The sun—illustrated by many • How and why stories about the sun and moon • The moon—illustrated by many • Different styles, techniques or mediums within a single book • Comparing different illustrations for one story • Projects comparing illustrations • Art alternatives to book reports • Making murals and mosaics • Bread dough book figures • Papier mache book figures • Sculpture • Needlework in art • Toys from children's books • Coloring books • Comparing illustrations in books with similar subjects: a project • Projects for alphabets and counting books • Variety in alphabet books • Animal alphabet books • Alphabet books and science • Cities in alphabet books • Blacks in alphabet books • Nonfiction alphabet books • Alphabet books in verse • Parts of speech in alphabet books • Alphabet books introduce a favorite character • Alphabet books introduce an author or illustrator • Alphabet books and counting books by the same person • Counting books introduce an author or illustrator • Books with numbers • Counting out rhymes • Stories with numbers • Picture books: counting one to ten • Picture books: counting beyond ten • Nonverbal communication • Wordless picture books • Nonverbal scenes in picture books with words • Making a book •

• A variety of versions to read and play, live and with puppets •
Begin with a sound filmstrip • The Gingerbread Man—live action and with puppets • Stone soup—playing, live action or with
puppets • Three bears, pigs or goats—live action or with puppets • Playing Sendak's *Really Rosie* • Background reading on
puppetry • Books with chapters on puppetry • Making Marionettes • Puppet production—manipulation • Puppet production—
costume • Puppet production—scenery • Puppet production—
sound • Puppet production—lighting • Puppet stages • Puppet
patterns • Shadow puppets • Making and using finger puppets
• Hand puppets • Commercial hand and finger puppets • Making and using paper bag puppets • Papier mache puppets • Preparing a story for a puppet show • Puppet scripts • Puppet
plays based on children's literature • Building puppet plays from
folktales •

Chapter Six
USING RIDDLES, MAGIC, JOKES AND FOLK THEMES
461

The universal appeal of riddles • Easy-to-read riddle books •
Picture book riddles • Questions about books • Conundrums •
Puppet fun • Homonyms • Alphabet riddles • Tongue twisters
• Spelling riddles • Geography riddles • History riddles •
Science riddles • Math riddles • Universality of riddles in folk-
lore • Same riddle, different story • Same answer, different
riddles • Nursery rhyme riddles • Same riddle, different
answers • Same story, different title • Problem riddles •
Riddle songs • Using riddles to introduce a classroom unit on
salt • Using riddles to introduce a unit on library manners •
Similar riddle themes • The jealous king, emperor, mandarin • Different riddles in versions of the same story • Story
outline for the Red Etin, Red Ettin, or Red-Etin • Activities for the
Red Etin • The clever daughter: common elements • National
origins: common elements about the clever daughter • Questions
about the clever daughter story • Simpletons answer the riddles
• Similarities and differences between two simpleton stories •
Sequence in "the riddle" by Grimm • Answer the riddle and win
the princess • Riddle stories around the world • History riddle
stories • A riddle story to read aloud • Noodlehead stories •
Silly Finnish stories • Silly simpletons • Men of Gotham • Silly
counters • Mistaken reflections • Identifying themes of noodlehead stories • The riddle of communication • Introducing the
unit with a folktale • Objectives and activities • Topics (codes,
cyphers and symbols) • Encyclopedia references • History of
writing • Egyptian hieroglyphics • Japanese and Chinese calligraphy • American Indian picture writings, sign language and
smoke signals • Rebus writings • Cattle brands and tramp or
hobo signs • Codes and cyphers in literature • Codes and
cyphers • Pig latin • Morse code • The Braille alphabet •
Sign language for the deaf • Athletic signals • Flag signals •
Traffic signals • Music and mathematics • Magic numbers in
folklore—a program of stories to tell or read • Magic numbers in
children's literature • Magic numbers in children's literature—
one • Magic numbers in children's literature—two • Magic

Foreword

Reading guidance is the ecstasy and the agony of the literate librarian who works with children and young adults. It is ecstasy because it is fun to share good books with others who also find reading pleasurable. It is ecstasy because it is rewarding to find a good book for someone who has never really enjoyed reading. The look in a child's eyes during a story hour or the sincerity in a teenager's "thank you" for a title enjoyed are very warming. I must confess that of all of the experiences I had with students in our library and classrooms in Topeka (KS) many years ago, the ones I remember with the most pleasure are those moments after the booktalks had ended when I had to move back from the table as the students rushed to grab the titles that had just been presented.

Reading guidance is agony for the literate librarian because there are so many competing forces for the time young people have for reading for fun, for the enrichment of their studies, or for information about personal concerns. It is agony because we believe so strongly that reading is important as part of a lifetime interest and activity, and there seem to be so many who have to be convinced of this. In no school or public library are there ever enough of us to give each person the time we think is necessary to find and talk about books. Finding time to plan reading guidance programs is agony because it isn't the only thing most of us have to do. We are materials specialists who work with curriculum. We are organizers and retrievers of thousands of items of print and nonprint each year. We are managers who have to do budgets, performance appraisals, and revise selection policies.

Whether providing reading guidance is ecstasy, agony, or both at once, at any point in a librarian's program, it is hard work. There is a constantly growing number of books to know; our knowledge of children's interests and needs has expanded; the production of quality audiovisual materials has greatly increased; and the child is increasingly exposed to "media productions" that are well-designed, dramatic, colorful, and exciting. By the way, these challenges face all adults: teachers, parents, and librarians who want to introduce books to children so as to keep reading within a child's range of choices in a busy life.

This book, by an enthusiastic school librarian who is an avid reader and promoter of books and reading among students, is a rich resource of titles, ideas, techniques, and sources for all of those who want to know about good books to suggest to children, to select audiovisual materials appropriately, to plan good, creative reading guidance activities, to enhance mass media productions, and to enrich the curriculum.

Whether the author is suggesting where a limerick will lead, discussing how books of fantasy might be used with music, or advising how to enrich the curriculum in history, geography, literature, reading, art, music, and mathematics, creative ideas abound side by side with practical advice. For instance, in her section on "Preparing a Story for Playing" not only does she outline the guidelines for presentation but she advises on aspects of costumes (and their alternatives) from sources to acquisition and maintenance, with the reminder that here is a good project for volunteers.

Detailed guidelines and suggested activities to enrich subjects introduced by basal readers; sample storytelling programs for enriching sixth grade geography, and detailed ideas for enriching network television programs and the PBS National Geographic Television Specials add to a veritable compendium of ideas to increase the book's usefulness.

Television is not the only audiovisual medium included naturally in the ideas and suggestions for bringing children and books together. The author defines media other than books as "puppets, live storytellers, educational films, filmstrips, sound recordings in record or cassette format, video tapes, and entertainment movies shown in theaters or on television." Her suggestions for use of media other than books are so matter of fact that they lead easily to a logical integration of all the media including books. This integration and ease of suggestion results in the realization that approaching the best of all types of media with confidence and without prejudice can increase the creativity and relevance of reading guidance programs.

Today's children will read for pleasure, for personal growth and development, and for information when they know about good books and can get to them easily. Adults have the responsibility to help children in this important matter. This rich resource of ideas should help many adults, whether beginners or experienced with reading guidance techniques, who assume the responsibility for presenting books to children in a creative way.

MARILYN L. MILLER
SCHOOL OF LIBRARY SCIENCE
THE UNIVERSITY OF NORTH CAROLINA
AT CHAPEL HILL

Preface

The idea for this book was triggered by a four-hour workshop I was asked to organize for school library media specialists during one of our annual conferences. The workshop was planned for maximum audience participation from a group of about fifty practitioners to give them an opportunity to incorporate art, music, poetry, puppetry, and creative dramatics into literature and media programs for elementary school children.

The results were exciting and spin-offs were many. People asked that I develop a source book that could be used in staff development for sharing techniques with a wider audience of media specialists and classroom teachers.

While I took and taught creative dramatics courses at the university level, I became keenly aware that many creative dramatics students do not know where to go for help in selecting quality materials for dramatic activities. In my work with gifted education, I learned that parents and teachers have these needs also. I realized how much there was to share that is currently not found in textbooks for either the speech and language arts or the library media area.

So here is the book. I hope that other teachers and library media specialists, librarians serving children in public libraries, recreation directors and many others who work with children—and older young people, too—will enjoy, as much as I have, putting literature together with the other arts, looking at stories in new ways, comparing them, relating to them, and presenting them to students.

Access to the discussion and use of all titles mentioned in the text can be gained by author, title or subject, through:

1. a bibliography, divided into two categories, each numbered separately, with books in one and multimedia (nonprint) with the prefix M, in the other;

2. a comprehensive title index with nearly 6,000 entries (books and multimedia;)

3. a subject index with references to more than 2,000 subjects.

Access to the bibliographies is by author, with full bibliographic information for each of the author's titles. Page number references for each title can then be found in the title index. A desired item, known by title, will be found by consulting the title index directly.

The subject index runs from "abandonment" to "Zuni Indians." It contains references for ages ("ten-year-olds") and grade levels ("fourth grade,") as well as curricular relationships for some titles ("history").

At the end of each chapter, there are specialized subject categories of books discussed in that chapter, with titles listed by the numbers which will identify them in the bibliography.

To all teachers and library media specialists with whom I have worked in workshops, classes and programs, my thanks and appreciation for your responsiveness and encouragement. To the children and teachers of the elementary and middle schools of Michigan and Indiana where I have worked, and with fond memories of all the activities we have undertaken together, my deepest appreciation of all. May you always relish as you do now, listening, looking, thinking, planning, creating and reading.

1981   MARY ANN PAULIN

CHAPTER ONE

Introducing Books
in All Kinds of Ways

CHAPTER OBJECTIVES

1. To introduce students to a variety of books from which they can make meaningful selections for educational or recreational reading
2. To furnish teachers, public librarians, and school media specialists with techniques and samples of ways to present books to children in an interesting manner
3. To inspire adults who work with children to read more widely and share the results more often with children
4. To emphasize the importance of promoting reading through bulletin boards and displays, booktalks and panels, and reading aloud to children
5. To suggest books that have been successfully shared with students to teachers, librarians, and persons who work with children
6. To employ educational media (sound filmstrips, films, and recordings) to stimulate the use of print materials
7. To capitalize on movies and television to stimulate reading
8. To help students distinguish between fiction and nonfiction
9. To introduce children to various types of literature: fantasy, science fiction, adventure, biography, historical fiction, mystery and detective stories, and adventure
10. To expand students' vocabulary to include such terms as *series, sequel, pseudonym*
11. To enrich the basal reading program of the school by providing supplementary reading

TECHNIQUES FOR USING MEDIA INTRODUCED IN THIS CHAPTER

1. Correlate library instruction to basal reader topics.
2. Use picture books, whole chapters, and characters found in basal reader stories to establish a link between textbooks, nontextbooks, and other media.
3. Introduce nonfiction to students by way of articles found in basal readers.
4. Show filmstrips to introduce books in the categories of science fiction, fantasy, geography, adventure, historical fiction, realistic fiction, and geographical fiction.
5. Use booktalks to give group reading guidance.
6. Use subjects assigned by the teacher to introduce the many good book and nonprint materials on the subjects.

7. Group books with similar plots and introduce them together. Tell about one book to introduce the sequel, trilogy, or other books in a series.
8. Group books by themes and subthemes and introduce them by discussing several in depth, and briefly introduce others.
9. Explain the meaning of a title to stimulate interest in a book. Allow fascinating characters to introduce books by giving brief sketches that include both physical and mental characteristics.
10. Compare characters in different books to each other, so that students who liked one character will be able to find books with similar characters to enjoy.
11. Involve students in booktalks by referring to special interests or experiences of particular students, to someone who has just enjoyed reading a book being discussed, or to a television program based on the title or the characters.
12. Share personal experiences, especially reading experiences, as well as personal viewpoints about character, values, and ethics.
13. Incorporate current events or other experiences common to the group to establish rapport and common ground during a booktalk; read and refer to clippings from magazines or newspapers that relate to subjects found in the books that are being talked about.
14. Give booktalks that introduce types of literature: biography, historical fiction, mystery and detective stories, adventure, regional fiction, science fiction, and fantasy.
15. Introduce and define the vocabulary that goes with a particular genre, as, for instance, biography: autobiography, collective and individual biography, fictionalized biography, and biographical fiction.
16. Teach the use of indexes when introducing biographical data.
17. Follow up booktalks by providing bibliographies of the books discussed, as well as other titles.
18. Invite students to share books with each other on peer panels.
19. After similar books have been introduced to students, ask them to write their own stories using similar plot patterns or characters.
20. Introduce books by talking about authors of those books, showing sound filmstrips about the authors and their work, relating first hand information about them as well as that taken from book jackets, biographies, and conference and workshop speeches.
21. Allow birthday children to choose the story to be read to the entire class; give students paperback books as birthday gifts, and encourage them to give books as gifts to each other.
22. Encourage students to give books to family members for birthdays and special occasions. Provide purchase opportunities through book clubs and bookfairs.
23. Arrange displays of books by authors whose books were the basis of films or television.
24. Give as much advance publicity as possible to special television programs for which there are good related books, and follow up interests that

were stimulated by the programs by displays, discussions, bibliographies, and other projects. Encourage teachers to provide independent or group assignments that will take full advantage of the interest stimulated to encourage learning.

25. Develop multimedia bibliographies and projects related to ongoing series such as "The Little House on the Prairie."

26. Purchase materials to correlate with special educational or public broadcasting programs such as "Sesame Street," "The Electric Company," or "Mr. Roger's Neighborhood."

27. Encourage students to complete individual projects comparing movies or television programs made from books with the book itself.

28. Use a film or filmstrip based on a book to introduce or culminate a group project or experience with a particular title or group of titles.

29. Focus attention of students on book review and annotation techniques by viewing filmstrips which introduce books.

30. Read a chapter of a book, or a selection from it that appears in an anthology, to introduce that book, its characters, or its author.

31. Allow favorite cartoon characters like Charlie Brown or Superman to introduce books to read.

32. Provide short term loan collections of media from the library media center to the classroom on topics being introduced or studied.

33. Place books on display with a variety of related realia such as terrariums, snake skins, bird nests, and models of human body parts (available commercially).

34. Accent book display with student-made hobbies or projects such as photographs, model cars, handmade musical instruments, and collections of shells, coins, or mounted insects. Using student-made materials helps involve those students and their peers with the library media center and with reading, listening, and viewing.

35. Accent book displays with other media, study prints, newsclips, posters, and pictures. Include objects that figure prominently in the plot of the book in a display that promotes the book.

36. Use postcards, booklets, and prints featuring the work of children's authors and illustrators that may appear in exhibits, museums, or advertising to highlight their work. Example: children's book illustrator Beni Montresor has attained widespread recognition in the field of opera and theatrical design. A sketch or photograph from one of his sets might be obtained and used.

BOOKTALKS.   The books that children read and enjoy are usually books that have been recommended by others—by friends, librarians, teachers, and parents or other adults. Students may have seen a review or promotion of a book, or seen a version of a story or subject that sparked their interest at the movies or on television. Today's students *do* read when they know about good books, can get to them easily, and are presented with them in an exciting manner. After all, we live in a society in which we are accustomed to being *sold*—to being told what we will like, why we will want it, and where to get it.

Booktalks are one method of presenting books to students in a group, an occasion for talking about books and for arousing the desire to read a particular book in each child who is listening.

When students are assigned to read "a book," or a book on topic *x*, they often do not know how to select one that they will enjoy. Those who feel familiar and at ease with it can use the subject card catalog, but it doesn't tell enough to entice many students. Some will take the first, or even the shortest, book they find on a subject. If the whole class or even several sections of it are all looking for a book on the same topic, the card catalog user will find the books listed, and others will flounder. Some students will never ask the library media specialist for help, and so that specialist must figure out who needs help with individual reading guidance.

Booktalks provide some solutions. When the teacher notifies the library media specialist in advance, there is time to prepare with books and other media to meet the objectives of an assignment. Often these materials are not all listed under one or even two subjects in the card catalog, and advance preparation may include borrowing extra copies or titles from libraries or other sources outside of the school. The school library media specialist can also call the public library and tell the staff about the assignment, so that some books can be put aside for students to check out.

For example, a successful booktalk usually given to ninth grade English students can, with modifications, be given to seventh and eighth graders also. The goal is to introduce students to a variety of books with characters who are at or near their own ages and have similar problems, and thus help them to universalize their own experiences and put them in perspective, emphasizing that a lifetime habit of reading will always help them to do this at any age they happen to be. Specific objectives vary from teacher to teacher and might be to define characters, to judge the realism of situations, to share perceptions orally with classmates, or to discuss the problems presented and possible solutions. Fifty to a hundred junior novels may be included in the booktalk. Categories include: divorce, drugs, loneliness, rejection, mental illness, physical handicaps, dating problems, peer problems, parent problems, premarital pregnancy, or, on the brighter side, first love, developing a sense of identity, and the like. Not every book must be introduced in depth or even by title. A dozen "pregnant paperbacks" can be introduced by the armful. Two or three books might be introduced by giving the point of view from which the book was written: one, that of the pregnant girl's sister; another, that of the boy whose best girl is pregnant; and the third, that of a girl who is headed for adoption or a home for unwed mothers. Others can be introduced by author and title.

A sentence or two about a book that compares it with another or tells just enough about it to distinguish it from a thousand others is often just what a student needs to find the one that suits him or her best. A bibliography along with the talk provides students with the names of authors and titles they like the sound of, so they can check them. Students will come back months later to ask "Do you remember the books you told us about . . . ." Providing many titles fairly insures that a group of twenty-four to thirty students will find at least one title that speaks to each individually. A large selection also allows students to check out more than one book. After a booktalk, once the "eager beavers" (those who know exactly what they want) are out of the way, and checking out, the library media specialist can give individual reading guidance to students who are either making up their minds, can't find the book they decided upon, or aren't sure they want anything. Sometimes there must be a rule that a second or third book can be taken by one person only after everyone else has chosen a book. Since paperbacks are often chosen before hardbacks, encourage the eager readers to take a title in hardback if they will. Some enthusiastic readers will read three or four books before deciding which one they will use for a report. When teachers want each student to have a different title because reports are to be oral, each student should sign a list with the titles of books chosen. This should be done in the library media center as soon as the books are checked out.

The booktalk just described is just one example of one in which many titles are presented merely by mentioning title and subject. Only a dozen books were discussed in depth, because students would probably be doing that with each other as part of the assignment. The purpose was simply to give students an indication of what books there were and what they were about, so that they could make choices. Another booktalk that can be handled in this way is one that introduces biographies. Often the students don't know anything about the persons in a particular category or period, and so they don't know what to choose. It is helpful to tell why a person was famous. Booktalks featuring biographies are just as popular with fourth graders as they are with eleventh graders.

Booktalk themes are almost unlimited. They can focus on an occasion, a place, a group of characters, kinds of people or situations, the books of one author, or books on one subject.

Ideas for other booktalks can be found in books by Gillespie and Lembo: *Juniorplots: A Book Talk Manual for Teachers and Librarians* and *Introducing Books: A Guide for the Middle Grades*. The main purpose of the two books is to help teachers and librarians give reading guidance and booktalks to children and young adults between the ages of nine and fourteen. "The Book Talk" (pp. 1–6 of the first book) gives valuable hints about preparing booktalks.

For each book discussed there is bibliographic information and several pages of plot summary, thematic material, booktalk material, which includes page numbers and the names of other books on a similar topic.

Eight categories in *Juniorplots* are: Building a World View, Overcoming Emotional Growing Pains, Earning a Living, Understanding Physical Problems, Making Friends, Achieving Self-Reliance, Evaluating Life, and Appreciating Books.

Eleven categories in *Introducing Books* are: Getting Along in the Family, Making Friends, Developing Values, Understanding Physical Problems, Forming a World View, Respecting Living Creatures, Evaluating Contemporary Problems, Identifying Adult Roles, Learning to Think Abstractly, Appreciating Books, and Reading for Fun.

STEPS FOR PREPARING AND PRESENTING BOOKTALKS

1. Define the objectives for the booktalk. Are the students bent on free choice recreational reading or is the booktalk to provide them with help in selecting a book for an assigned project or report?

2. Let the size and age of the audience determine the theme and selections. While a wide variety of reading levels are needed, the format and approach of "easier" books on a given subject should not "talk down" to poorer readers. The age of the audience often determines themes.

3. Decide on a theme and subthemes. Locate books, filmstrips, and recordings on the subject and divide them into sub-categories. For instance, books about the Civil War mentioned in this chapter are fiction—those dealing with the underground railroad before the war and stories taking place during the war itself. Another category could have included biographies of such persons as Abraham Lincoln, Harriet Tubman, or Robert E. Lee. Poems and songs of the period could be introduced. Monjo's *The Drinking Gourd* is an easy-to-read book about the song that was a signal for slaves to leave the plantation to begin their trip on the underground railroad. Other categories could include spies, causes for the war, battles, and slavery.

4. Read as many of the books as possible and scan the others. Remember that it is difficult to enourage children to read books when you don't really know what's in them. Some of the books won't be suitable for inclusion in the group to be discussed and reading them is the only way to discover this.

5. Make a note card for each book, with author, title, place of publication, publisher, and copyright date. Sometimes reading levels and name of library (if more than one is used) are useful. An annotation for each book is a good idea, and it should include names and ages of characters, the setting (time and place), the situation in which the characters find themselves and page numbers of interesting incidents or especially quotable quotes. Reread these pages before the booktalk.

6. Prepare an annotated bibliography from the note cards. Suggestions for this bibliography are included in the section below called *Bibliographies with Booktalks.*

7. Choose the books to be discussed, if possible the ones especially enjoyed. It is easier to "sell" a book if you yourself are enthusiastic about it. Choose related filmstrips and recordings and one or two "lead" books in each sub-category to discuss in greatest detail. Line up other books to be mentioned with one or two sentences or merely by title and indicate that they are similar. Sometimes these are sequels or books by the same author. Remember that the books you talk about most are often the books that most of the group will want to read, and so be prepared to provide duplicate copies or talk about

more titles. Offering too few choices results in disappointments, and arouses interests without fulfilling them.

8. Choose your methods for presenting the particular book. You can select from the following: explain the title, paraphrase introduction and author's notes, tell about the author's personal life, give the author's purpose in writing the book, briefly describe the plot, read quotations, describe the characters, explain from whose point of view the story is told, describe the setting, relate the book to group and individual experiences, quote reviews, mention awards, tie the book to current events, emphasize the book with a prop or audio-visual aid, correlate the book with television and movies, compare the book with another book that is familiar to your audience. Samples of these methods are included in this chapter.

9. Establish the transitional books; bridges from one category to another. The books have already been organized into sub-themes and sub-categories. If the overall theme of the booktalk is animals, divide the books into stacks by type of animal. Books that include several kinds of animals can go in their own stack. Each stack can be divided into fiction and nonfiction. The books to be discussed in greatest detail are not necessarily the best bridge books. A book that is only mentioned by title and a one-sentence description might be the best bridge between the previous books introduced and the next category. Find common elements in the stories. Common elements could be authors, setting, special accomplishments, or plot similarities. The common elements help the person giving the booktalk decide which books logically follow one another within categories.

10. Prepare a short framework introduction for the booktalk. If the booktalk is strictly for pleasure, say so and explain that you are going to share books you have read and enjoyed or those that you know others have recommended. Or relate the introduction to the assignment. Tell students that their job in the library/media center today is to choose a book for their next book report (or other purpose). You have discussed this with their teacher and are prepared to help them. Relating to the theme makes for a short introduction. Books in the section below called *Television—The Holocaust* can be introduced simply by asking how many persons saw "The Holocaust" on television, or at another time how many persons saw the recently produced play or the movie *The Diary of Anne Frank*, or how many persons have heard of Adolf Hitler and Naziism.

11. Arrange the books in the order in which they are to be presented to eliminate the need for an outline. Notes for each book are included inside the book in case they need to be referred to. Books placed on a book truck can easily be reached when needed.

12. Hold up each book as it is presented so the entire group can see it, and give the author and title of the book loudly and clearly.

13. Discuss the books in a conversational manner suitable to sharing books

with good friends—which you are. Just remember that some of those
friends are sitting farther away from you than others.

14. Briefly show any sequels or other books in the series or similar books, and
place them with the book discussed in greater detail.

15. Place the book that has been discussed on a table so students can see the
front cover. Place similar books under or beside it. If many books
are to be discussed, place them on a table in piles according to
similarities so that students can find them.

16. Introduce the bibliography and invite students to check out books.

BIBLIOGRAPHIES WITH BOOKTALKS.   An annotated bibliography should
accompany a booktalk so that students can refer to the list at a later time to
choose additional books. The annotations will refresh their memories about
each title. The bibliography should include: (1) all books mentioned in the
booktalk; (2) related books which were not included for some reason in the
booktalk; (3) sequels or other books in a series that were briefly alluded to; (4)
reference books on the subject or those which contain brief references to it; and
(5) books on the subject of the booktalk outside the reading abilities of the
listeners at both high and low end of the ability spectrum.

Bibliographies should not be passed out to students until the end of the
booktalk, but when sharing books with teachers or library media specialists
they should be given the lists beforehand so that they can make notes. Sample of
bibliographies in this chapter includes: "If You Liked the Little House
Books. . . ."

Media specialists should keep a notebook of all bibliographies prepared,
enclosing them in plastic protectors when current, so that they can be used in
the library media center. Sometimes copies are given only to the teacher for
posting in the classroom instead of to each member of a class; students are invited to borrow and use a copy of a particular bibliography filed in the library
media center. Lists can be stapled into individual file folders where students
can easily find and carry them around as they search for wanted books. Large
labels on the front of folders will help identify subjects.

ESTABLISHING COMMON GROUND IN BOOKTALKS.   Several successful
techniques for involving booktalk audiences are: asking direct or rhetorical
questions; connecting the book to individual or group experiences; linking the
story to a familiar place; or drawing parallels to current events.

For instance, how would you feel if you woke up one morning and found
yourself in your mother's body? That's what happened to thirteen-year-old
Annabel Andrews in Rogers' *Freaky Friday*. If you have read Stolz's *The Dog on
Barkham Street* and know about the bully, Martin, you might wonder—Why is
Martin the way he is? Some answers are given in Stolz's *The Bully of Barkham
Street*.

Librarians sometimes ask questions and want a factual answer. How many
have ever seen a grizzly? How many have heard about grizzlies? David and his
father not only saw a grizzly when they were camping, but it ate or destroyed

their food and maimed David's father in *The Grizzly* by the Johnsons.

Don't be afraid to share personal experiences with students. You might ask how many of them are "middle children." As a middle child myself, I tell students that I can relate to the boys in Bach's *The Meat in a Sandwich* and Kingman's *Year of the Raccoon* who were middle children. I was a girl between two boys and Mike was a boy between two girls; he felt like *The Meat in a Sandwich*. Joey was one of three brothers who felt ordinary between the musical accomplishments of an older brother and the academic accomplishments of a younger brother. Jack, one of Cresswell's Bagthornes, was keenly aware of the talents of everyone else in the family in *Ordinary Jack*. Suzie's brother was the star of a rock group called "The Giraffes" and her parents were both unusual too—one was an artist and the other an author. So Suzie, like Jack, felt ordinary and decided to do something unusual in Campbell's *Why Not Join the Giraffes?* Tell students that at some time or other we have all felt like these characters.

Techniques employed in sharing these books are sharing personal information with the audience, asking a question, comparing characters in books and their experiences to universal feelings.

Sometimes relating books to group experiences could be as simple as asking students to remember a previous unit of study; perhaps it was the unit in U.S. History just before the Civil War when abolitionists were helping the slaves run away from plantations in the South through the United States to Canada. Ask students if they remember what the system for delivering slaves to Canada was called. When someone gives "the Underground Railroad" as the answer, explain that *By Secret Railway* by Meadowcroft is about a freed slave, Jim, who sent his friends to a family who would give them food and shelter. Students who live in or near Chicago will like to know that the story took place there in 1860, the year in which Abraham Lincoln was nominated by the first Republican Convention.

When reading through the books, mark pages with incidents or facts that can help you relate the story to a student. When introducing *Sidewalk Indian* by Ellis, share the feeling that the Wisconsin woods in which Charley was hiding were very much like the woods of the Michigan Upper Peninsula, or those of New York State. Mention that Mel Ellis is a free-lance journalist for the *Milwaukee Journal*, and talk about what a free-lance journalist is and what he does.

Share personal favorites. I always tell seventh graders during a general booktalk that I read Worth's *They Loved to Laugh* when I was their age, that it made me cry, and that I liked it so much that I read it every year until I was out of high school. Relate stories to the experiences of classmates whenever possible. Link the classmate who just moved from South Carolina with *Carolina Hurricane* by Rumsey, which tells of twelve-year-old Morgan's experiences when he was caught in a hurricane with his dog Tater. Ask for discussion of the most recent hurricane reported in the newspaper or on television. Make a transition to recent earthquakes, and after brief comments introduce Christopher's *Earthquake*.

Whenever books have been made into films shown in theaters or on television, ask students if they have seen the film, and invite comparison with the book from which it came. Why do they think changes were made? If a documentary contained information related to a book or books, make the connection.

Books introduced by using films, filmstrips, and television are discussed throughout this book, but especially later in this chapter.

INTRODUCING BOOKS BY TITLES.   Sometimes titles give valuable information about books. The title of an anthology may be the title of one of its poems, short stories, or folk or fairy tales, and can be used to introduce the collection.

Explaining the meaning of a title in an annotation or booktalk can introduce and describe the book. Titles can introduce the plot or a character in a book, or be names of places or of times. Titles are often the names of animals or one or more people, and sometimes of an inanimate object. Sometimes an explanation of the title can result in a sketch of the plot.

Several books included in this chapter could be introduced by telling about the *places* named in the title. *Rabbit Hill* is a country home where special animals, created by Lawson, live. Burnett's *Secret Garden* was a place through which two unhappy children transformed their lives. Mary Call lived in Appalachia *Where the Lillies Bloom;* Cleavers' *Trial Valley* is its sequel. O'Dell's *Island of the Blue Dolphins* was where the Indian girl Karana lived alone for eighteen years. Taylor's *The Cay* was a Caribbean Island or cay where a twelve-year-old boy and an old black man are marooned when their ship was torpedoed during World War II. Hill's *Ever-After Island* is a fantasy. Erwin's *Go to the Place of the Eyes* is a secret message, which the Evans children had to interpret in order to solve the mystery. Maple Hill is the place where ten-year-old Marly hopes a miracle will happen so that her father will recover his health and spirits in Sorensen's *Miracle on Maple Hill.*

A young girl lived in *The Upstairs Room* for two years to escape the Nazis, in a book by Reiss based on the author's own experience. Children enter another world in Key's *The Forgotten Door* and *Escape to Witch Mountain.* The wardrobe in Lewis's *The Lion, the Witch and the Wardrobe* is the passageway into a fantasy land. Meadowcroft's *By Secret Railway* tells of another kind of passageway, a real one to freedom, but not made of engines, cars, and rails but rather of people willing to risk helping black people escape slavery.

Several of the "Little House" books by Laura Ingalls Wilder have place names in the titles because the Ingalls family stopped along their way to the Dakota Territory. *The Little House in the Big Woods* was in Wisconsin. *On The Banks of Plum Creek* was in Minnesota. *By the Shores of Silver Lake, The Little House on the Prairie,* and *The Little Town on the Prairie* were in Dakota.

Titles of books can also refer to a special season in someone's life which helps to introduce them. One year, the animals of *Rabbit Hill* had an especially *Tough Winter.* Wilder's *The Long Winter* stretched from October to April. During George's *Summer of the Falcon,* June trained her sparrow hawk, and also grew up herself. Green's *The Summer of My German Soldier* was an unhappy time for twelve-year-old Patty during World War II, and Hunt's *Across Five Aprils* tells of five wartime springs during the Civil War.

Sometimes the period of the title is only a particular day, like Roger's

Freaky Friday, the day thirteen-year-old Annabel found herself in her mother's body. In Mazer's *Saturday, the Twelfth of October*, Zan thought she had spent months in prehistoric time when she had only been gone one Saturday, while *Time at The Top* refers to Susan's trip on the elevator of her apartment building past the top floor and into the Victorian Age. Ormondroyd's sequel to Susan's adventures is *All in Good Time*. Eleanor Estes's Melendy family pool their allowances to spend some special days in *The Saturdays*.

Sometimes a title tells of an eventful year in someone's life. Frazee's *Year of the Big Snow* concerns the fourth expedition of Fremont across the Rockies in 1848. Clifford's *Year of the Three-Legged Deer* was the year Jesse Benton lost his Indian wife and two children. Kingman's *Year of the Raccoon* tells of the unhappy year in which Joey, a middle child, thought his parents loved his older and younger brothers more than they did him. Brenner's *Year in the Life of Rosie Bernard* takes place during the depression of the 1930s when Rosie goes to live with her grandparents after her mother dies and she learns about her Jewish relatives. Steel called his story *The Year of the Bloody Sevens*, a nickname given to 1776 because of all the Indian massacres during that year, and tells of an eleven-year-old's brush with death. Fifteen-year-old Ben McLaren and his dog spent their year tracking a cougar in Dietz's *Year of the Big Cat*.

A period of several years gives a title to Wilder's *The First Four Years* which tells of the quick passing of time during the early time of Laura Ingalls's and Almanzo Wilder's marriage. *These Happy Golden Years* tell of the period when Laura was a teacher and Almanzo was courting her.

Sometimes the setting has the personality of a character and gives its name to the title, as with the old house in Hightower's *The Ghost of Follonsbee's Folly*. The house in Hamilton's *The House of Dies Drier* had also been used as a stop on the underground railroad. Unusual old houses are featured in Jackson's *Missing Melinda*, Little's *Look Through My Window*, and three books by Elizabeth Enright—*The Four-Storey Mistake, Gone-Away Lake*, and *Return to Gone-Away Lake*.

Books can be introduced by explaining the plot in terms of the title. Stone's *The Wooden River* is about Rosie MacClaren's winter at a lumber camp in the Saginaw Valley in the 1870s, where the solid mass of floating logs go downstream to the sawmill. In Bishop's *Twenty and Ten*, ten Jewish children are absorbed into the hideaway of twenty French children hidden in the country to escape the Nazis. Benery-Isbert's *Blue Mystery* is about a missing blue gloxinia. Clarke's *The Return of the Twelves* is about toy soldiers belonging to the Bronte children. De Jong's *The House of Sixty Fathers* is about a refugee boy who was adopted by sixty American servicemen in China. Other stories introduced by explaining the title are Bulla's *Down the Mississippi*, Estes's *The Hundred Dresses*, Dalgliesh's *The Courage of Sarah Noble*, Yates's *Carolina's Courage*, Day's *Landslide!*, Garfield's *Follow My Leader*, Jones's *The Edge of Two Worlds*, Wojciechowska's *Shadow of a Bull*, and Wuoiro's *Save Alice!*

Sometimes inanimate objects are characters in books. Beatty's *Nickle-Plated Beauty* is a stove that the oldest of seven Kimball children ordered COD from the Montgomery Ward catalog not realizing the COD meant "Collect on Delivery." The story took place in Washington Territory in 1886, as does another by Beatty, O The Red Rose Tree, about the making of a quilt.

In Kendall's fantasy, The Gammage Cup was the prize to be given to the most outstanding Minnipin village. McSwiggin's Snow Treasure was nine million dollars in gold bullion which was smuggled out of Norway under the noses of the Germans on the sleds of children.

The windmill in Von Stockhum's The Winged Watchman, Degen's Boxcar Transport 7-41-R, and Seraillier's Silver Sword, are all inanimate objects essential to their stories.

Sometimes the inanimate characters are dolls or toys, as in Bailey's Miss Hickory, Field's Hitty, Gage's Miss Osborne-the-Mop, and Bianco's The Velveteen Rabbit. Tolkien's The Hobbit was a make-believe character. Two books by Burton are about machines that seem real: the snowplow in Katy and the Big Snow and the Mary Ann in Mike Mulligan and His Steam Shovel.

Some titles feature the names of animals. Describing the animal(s) and one incident in its life will introduce the books. Kjelgaard's Big Red and Irish Red, Son of Big Red are Irish setters. Argess the collie is the star of Stolz's Dog on Barkham Street. Estes's Ginger Pye was a dog that the Pye children bought for a dollar they earned by cleaning the church. Bristle Face and Sputters, both books by Ball, are dogs of a mixed breed, and other dogs of mixed ancestry are Best's Desmond, Henry Higgins' dog Ribsy, Cone's Mishmash, and Gipson's Old Yeller and her son Savage Sam. Armstrong's Sounder was a mixture of Georgia redbone hound and bulldog, whose description appears on page 4. A description of Bawdon's The Peppermint Pig appears on p. 71. The wild ponies from Assateague and Chincoteague Islands in Virginia appear in Misty of Chincoteague, Sea Star, Orphan of Chincoteague and Stormy, Misty's Foal, all by Henry. Other horse books by Henry are descriptive of their titles except Brighty, who is a burro. The Black Stallion is the main character in Farley's books. Some animals are wild like Byar's Midnight Fox and George's Vulpes the Red Fox or Masked Prowler. Sharp's Miss Bianca, Ormondroyd's Broderick and White's Stuart Little are mice as well as book titles. Some titles name animals and people. Lawson's Ben and Me is about Ben Franklin and Amos the Mouse. Atwater's book Mr. Popper's Penguins stars the birds and Mr. Popper. Henry's Justin Morgan Had a Horse is about the real man who developed the Morgan horse.

Titles of books often include the names of people who have a prominent role in the book. Hamilton's Zeely looked like a Watusi Queen. Other black characters named in titles are Wagner's J.T., Walter's Lillie of Watts, Shotwell's Roosevelt Grady, Neufeld's Edgar Allan, and Jackson's Call Me Charley. Two books by Burchard are named for characters Bimby and Jed. Fritz's Brady lived during that same time and had something in common with Meader's Boy With a Pack, except that Brady had trouble keeping his mouth shut about the runaway slaves. DeAngeli's Thee, Hannah! is about a Quaker girl who was involved with the underground railroad.

Sometimes titles are groups of people: Wyss's Swiss Family Robinson,

Kastner's *Emil and the Detectives*, Winterfield's *Castaways in Lilliput* and *Detectives in Togas*, Suhl's *Uncle Misha's Partisans*, Estes's *The Moffats*, and Boston's *The Children of Green Knowe*. Cleary's *Mitch and Amy* is about twins.

Girls in titles include Burch's *Queenie Peavy*, Fitzhugh's *Harriet the Spy*, Cleaver's *Ellen Tebbits*, Cleary's *Ramona and Beezus*, Spyri's *Heidi*, and Greene's *A Girl Called Al* and the sequel *I Know You, Al*, and Haywood's *B is for Betsy*. Some boys are Haywood's *Little Eddie*, Cleary's *Henry Huggins* and *Otis Spofford*, Hoff's *Johnny Texas*, Robertson's *Henry Reed*, Sobol's *Encyclopedia Brown*, Barrie's *Peter Pan*, Allen's *Johnny Reb*, Forbes's *Johnny Tremain*, and Twain's *The Adventures of Tom Sawyer* and *The Adventures of Huckleberry Finn*. Three favorite characters of McCloskey are named in titles: *Burt Dow, Deep Water Man*, *Homer Price*, and *Lentil*.

INTRODUCING BOOKS BY THEIR CHARACTERS.   There are several ways that books can be introduced through their characters—those whose names appear in the title and others. Students like to read sequels and books in series because they like meeting the same favorite characters. They can be introduced in terms of their contribution to plot development, their relationship to the setting, their physical characteristics or mental capabilities as they and others perceive them. Sometimes book characters have talents, traits, or problems similar to those of persons in other books.

Kerby Maxwell from Corbett's *The Lemonade Trick* has a friend named Fenton Claypool who, according to the description of him, would probably enjoy knowing Leroy from *Encyclopedia Brown* and Tom Dennis Fitzgerald from *The Great Brain*. Tom and Encyclopedia Brown are very much alike except that Encyclopedia Brown uses the information he gains from reading in a more constructive manner. Students will enjoy comparing and contrasting the two boys and perhaps making up a tale in which they meet and try to best one another. Books about Encyclopedia Brown are included in the section of this chapter called "Using a Variety of Media."

Tom Dennis, the Great Brain, is a lot like Tom Sawyer and is of the same vintage. Tom, who had read everything he could lay his hands on, had at one time or another taken advantage of both his brothers, age twelve and eight, as well as the other children and some of the adults in the Aldenville, Utah, of 1897. In chapter 8 of *The Great Brain* there is a scene reminiscent of the whitewashing-the-fence scene pulled off by Tom Sawyer. Tom makes the neighborhood children pay to see the digging of the cesspool and later the first watercloset in town. His motives are not always of the purest, but he manages most of the time to do well for himself while doing good for others. A movie about Tom was released in 1978, and other titles about the Great Brain are available, most of them in paperback: *More Adventures of the Great Brain*, *The Great Brain Reforms*, *The Great Brain at the Academy*, *The Return of the Great Brain*, and *The Great Brain Does It Again*. Fitzgerald's adult book, also humorous, was *Papa Married a Mormon*.

Mrs. Graymalkin, the woman with magical powers who starts Kerby Maxwell on his adventurous way can introduce Mr. Mazzeeck who appeared to give a silver bottle to twelve-year-old Harry Houdini Marco in Snyder's *Black and Blue Magic*. The title refers to the colors Harry became from flying around in the dark and bumping into things, courtesy of his magic wings.

In picture books the physical appearance of the characters is shared pictorially with readers through the illustrations. Turkle not only created a precocious Quaker boy named Obadiah, but created his image in pictures for readers.

Physical descriptions of characters help readers "see" those people in their own minds. Perhaps that is why many audiovisuals based on books are best shown to students in intermediate grades and above as culminating activities rather than used to introduce the book. The audiovisuals create the character visually and the chance for the reader to create the image for himself is lost.

Pippi Longstocking, in the book by that title by Lindgren, is a very remarkable girl in actions and in looks. Students who have not seen the movies about Pippi can form their own picture of her by reading the description in the book about her. Readers learn that she has freckles, carrot red hair in braids, and wears a handmade blue dress with red patches and one brown and one black shoe, but each reader will create his own imaginary picture a little differently.

Sometimes the physical appearance of the main character is important to plot development. Fifth-grader Linda in Blume's *Blubber* and Marcus Rosenbloom of Mazer's *The Dollar Man* are both overweight. The lives of those two characters are affected more by their size than is Greene's *A Girl Called Al*, who, however, slimmed down in *I Know You, Al*.

A physical description of Neufeld's *Edgar Allan* appears in the story about him. That description is vital to the story because Edgar Allan is described as an attractive black child whose color made him unacceptable to the parishioners and friends of a white minister's family who wanted to adopt him. *Edgar Allan's* story is told from the point of view of twelve-year-old Michael Fickett.

Sometimes books can be introduced by telling about the point of view from which the story was written. Mary Call told her own story in the Cleavers' *Where the Lilies Bloom* and the sequel *Trial Valley*, whereas readers meet Burch's *Queenie Peavy* through the eyes of her principal.

Ox Olmstead himself insists that it isn't so wonderful to be a rich kid in *Ox: The Story of a Kid at the Top* and *Ox Goes North, More Trouble for the Kid at the Top* by Ney. Greene's *A Girl Called Al* and *I Know You, Al* are told by her friend. The Neuman divorce in Blume's *It's Not the End of the World* is described from the point of view of Karen Neuman. Blume's *Blubber* is told in the first person by Jill, another fifth grader, rather than by Linda, the overweight girl. Fourteen-year-old Tish's diary began in Johnston's *The Keeping Day* and ended in *Glory in the Flower*. Readers learn about Robertson's *Henry Reed* from his diary. Fitzgerald's *The Great Brain* is Tom Dennis Fitzgerald, but the eight stories are told by his younger brother, John. The point of view in Zindel's *The Pigman* changes from chapter to chapter. Alternate chapters are told from the point of view of John or Lorraine.

Nicknames given to book characters often reveal how others perceive them. Leroy "Encyclopedia" Brown and Tom "the Great Brain" Dennis Fitzgerald have nicknames that indicate their intellectual capacities. Greene's Paul, in *The Unmaking of Rabbit,* was timid and an easy mark for bullies, thus his nickname was "Rabbit." "Bugs Meany" from Sobol's book about Encyclopedia Brown sounds as rotten as he really is. Sometimes the nickname comes from a corruption of the character's name, as with eleven-year-old John Pickett Tracy, Jr., the "Dill Pickle" of Gage's *Miss Osborne-the-Mop.* "Tolly" is the nickname for Tolliver, the boy in Boston's books about Green Knowe.

Titles can give important clues about characters, and the problems that will create the plot. Three important facts about nine-year-old Manolo are given on page 1 in the first paragraph of Wojciechowska's *Shadow of a Bull.* The most important fact is that Manolo, although he was not brave, was expected to become a famous bullfighter like his father.

PEER BOOK PANELS.   The effective library media specialist knows which students are enthusiastic readers and what kinds of books each enjoys most. Such students can be most influential among their peers in encouraging reading by sharing books, telling which books they liked and why. Select five or six students of various intellectual and socioeconomic groups who are well liked and who are avid readers. The first time you prepare a panel, select at least one person who is really popular and is recognized as a leader by students—someone prominent in school activities. Also include someone bright who is a reader but not a favorite with teachers and administrators because of behavior patterns. This student can be very effective in a booktalk; his or her friends and followers are impressed that one of "theirs" has been asked to participate. This may be the first time that person was ever recognized publicly for positive behavior. Sometimes shy people blossom when asked to share what they have read in this type of activity. Not only should different types of students be represented, but a variety of types of books. A balanced book panel could include science fiction, animal books, mysteries, adventure, and books about real, contemporary situations. A range of topics presented by a variety of people helps insure success.

The process of organizing a panel is easier when students have listened to booktalks, and have an idea of what is to be accomplished. Help students select five or six books. You will need to know what these books are in order to provide transitions between speakers. This is best accomplished by telling about books that bridge two types of books.

Students are most comfortable when the panel is seated behind a long table, with books placed on the table in front of or beside each panel member. Students can pick up a book, discuss it, and then put it back on the table. The librarian can be seated in the middle, open the program with the purpose of the panel and introduce each student individually. After each panelist speaks, library media specialist thanks him or her, provides for transition by sharing several more books, and then goes on to the next panel member. The librarian can lengthen or shorten the program by varying the number of books used in the transition period. If six panel members each share five books and the librarian media specialist shares two between each presentation, some forty books will be presented.

Panel members could come from different sections of the same grade or from several grades. A panel could be composed of fifth and sixth graders, or all fourth graders, depending on the situation. One peer panel in a high school included students from grades nine through twelve. When students come from different classrooms, the library media specialist needs to arrange with each teacher to offer a special grade or reward for the student's participation. Arrangements must also be made with the teacher so the student can be released from the classroom during the book panel. Presentations may be given several times. If there are six panel members, the presentation might be given to each of the classes to which a panel member belongs. Or the panel might be presented to a totally different group of students.

Peer book panels are valuable for the participants as well as for the audience. They also reinforce the positive image of the library media center as an active generator of school activities.

READING ALOUD TO STUDENTS.   "Kids Who Read Were Read To." So says a bumper sticker distributed by the Michigan Reading Association and it is true. School media specialists and teachers need to make time to read to students to motivate reading. School library media specialists can schedule visits during which students in grades kindergarten through third can be read to in the media center. Small children love the stories and want to learn to read so they can read to themselves; older children who already read can be stimulated to read the same or similar stories. Teachers can set aside a half hour a week to read a whole book in installments or an entire short story or folk or fairy tale.

One technique is to read one or more chapters of a book to get students "into it" so they will want to read the rest to themselves. After reading the chapters, place the book (several copies) in the reading, viewing and listening area of the classroom. Jackson's *Missing Melinda* is a great book to do this with. Read chapters one through three which begins when the twins, Cordelia and Ophelia, find and name a doll, and ends when the doll is missing. Possible suspects are introduced in those chapters so students will be in suspense about who stole Melinda. From the first three chapters, listeners learn that Cordelia and Ophelia were named after characters in Shakespeare because their father knew all the plays by heart. Readers will learn how with the help of a new neighbor, Jimmy, and his family's heirloom doll as a decoy, the thief was captured. Students in grades three and four will love it.

Read chapter one to get into the story of Rogers' *Freaky Friday* for students in grades five through seven. This book was the basis of a movie made in 1977. A paperback edition makes it possible for several copies to be available to the classroom on long-term loan. Annabel's altered perspective on school and her classmates during the day she spends as her own mother are enlightening and can launch some good discussions about viewpoint.

Read a chapter or whole book that belongs to a series. This initial contact can introduce the setting and characters and students can read the sequels or other books in the series for themselves. Bond has three books about a Guinea pig named Olga da Polga: *The Tales of Olga da Polga, Olga Meets Her Match, More Tales of Olga da Polga,* and *Olga Carries On.* Chapters to read from *The Tales of Olga da Polga* are "Olga Sets Out," in which Olga is purchased from the pet shop; "The Naming of Olga da Polga," which tells how Olga wrote her name in sawdust with a stick so her new family would know her name; and "Olga's Story," a story Olga told about why guinea pigs have rosettes for tails. Before reading this part, hold up a guinea pig and let the group see the rosette tail. Children will throng to read more of Olga's adventures.

Another technique for reading aloud is to choose a short story or the shortest book in a series to introduce an author to students. Norton's *Poor Stainless, a New Story About the Borrowers* only has thirty-two pages, and the entire book can be read aloud to introduce the little people called "the borrowers" to students. The introduction to *Poor Stainless . . .* on page 8 can be read or paraphrased to introduce all of the books about the borrowers.

Hill's *Ever-After Island* is a good example of a book that can be introduced either by reading snatches from it accompanied by background information, or by reading the total book up to the most important point and then allowing students finish on their own. Ryan and Sara went on an expedition headed by Dr. Moody Murk to a remote island with their father, Professor Finney. The children wanted their father to marry Tracy Blair, the photographer-writer for *Nature's Secrets,* who was along on the expedition, and are almost thwarted by the sorceress Hepzibah.

When sharing this book, tell why the group went to *Ever-After Island,* and about the books that Dr. Moody Murk had hidden away in paper. Read page 24 beginning with "His heart thumping . . ." to the top of page 26 when he went back up on deck.

Another important part to read begins on page 39: "At last, yawning, they made sure the fire was out . . . ." to page 41 and the beginning of chapter 5. In chapter 5, two tiny elves, Garth and Finney, warned them to watch out for Hepzibah. The two boys, Ryan and Punky, met the mermaids Mer Blossom and Llura who explained that one was to have married a prince but the terrible Wizard of the Wind changed the prince into a flounder. Now only a human boy could break the spell by recovering the magic jewel from the Wizard. Stop reading chapter 5 on page 52.

Rumsey's *Lion on the Run* is an excellent book to read aloud to students in grades four through six. Jerry's dad, a lineman for the power company, brought home a tiny mountain lion which Jerry named Pepper. Jerry faithfully fed Pepper from a bottle, and they became friends. After Jerry returned to school, and Pepper scratched at the cupboards and sharpened her claws on the newel post of the bannister, Jerry had to build a house for her. But eventually, because it was against zoning laws to keep a mature nondomesticated animal, Pepper had to go. The adventures Jerry had when he took Pepper out to the wilds to train her to return to nature are exciting. Chapter 7, "The Protector" (pp. 127–42), is especially exciting.

Lion on the Run can be used to introduce other books about lions, especially

Adamson's books; *Born Free* is about teaching the African lioness, Elsa, to return to the wilds. Another book to introduce with this one is Dixon's *Lion on the Mountain*, about sixteen-year-old Jamie and hunting.

Other books about mountain lions or cougars or panthers that could be introduced are Aaron's *American Ghost*, Dietz's *Year of the Big Cat*, and Clive's *Weakfoot*. The last book, made into a movie, concerns a panther in the Great Okefenokee Swamp.

Ottley's *Boy Alone* is excellent for reading aloud. The sequel is *The Roan Colt*. The books could also be introduced by reading the author's note, or by reading one or more chapters. The author's notes at the back of each book explain that the setting is a cattle station called Yamboorah in Australia in the 1930s. The Dogman Kanga's job is explained. The explanation makes it easier for readers to understand why there is a conflict between the boy and Kanga for the dog Rags and his mother Brolga. Unfamiliar terms are explained.

Any teacher who reads *Boy Alone* to a class of fourth through sixth graders will be rewarded because students enjoy the characterization, the setting, and the incidents. As a follow-up they might be encouraged to read Wier's *The Loner* about another nameless boy who has no family. Or, the book could be used to stimulate nonfiction reading about Australia. Groups of related books should be placed in the classroom reading area as follow-up to all reading aloud activity. The first chapter of *Boy Alone* appears in Sutherland's *Arbuthnot Anthology of Children's Literature*.

Fleischman's *Mr. Mysterious and Company* is excellent for reading aloud to intermediate students. Because the book appears on the bibliography "If You Liked the *Little House* Books . . ." those books, too can be introduced through Mr. Mysterious and his family. This book can also be used to introduce other books by Fleischman, *Mr. Mysterious's Secrets of Magic*, and other books that explain magic tricks.

The Hackett family included Ma, Pa, Paul, Jane, and Madam Sweetpea the cow. Pa was Mr. Mysterious, a magician, and the family traveled in their wagon across the United States on their way to California where they planned to settle. Everyone in the family had a part in the magic shows they presented at every stop. The charge was twenty-five cents but anyone who did not feel the show was worth the price did not have to pay.

One of the exciting parts of the story is the capture of an outlaw, the Badlands Kid. Of special interest is Abracadabra Day which is explained on page 11. One day each year, the children were allowed to play a prank without worrying about a spanking. The only rule was that no one could be told in advance what day had been chosen. Students will want an Abracadabra Day of their own, and some teachers may be willing to try it, perhaps with a few rules of their own.

Read chapter 11, "Christmas Shopping" from *Mary Poppins* by Travers to students before the holidays, to interest them in other books about Mary Poppins.

Little's *From Anna* is another excellent book to read aloud to students in third or fourth grades at Christmas time so they can enjoy the warmth as well as ponder the friction that came to Anna's family during that season. Other books to recommend to students who enjoy this book are books about children with handicaps, other books by Little, or books about Nazi Germany. Books in the latter category appear in this chapter in a section called "Television—The Holocaust."

The children weren't allowed to sing a favorite song in school which contained the words "Thoughts Are Free," and had to sing "Deutschland, Deutschland Uber Alles" instead; neighbors began to disappear; and Papa wanted to remove his family from Germany. The move became a reality when Papa inherited his brother's store in Canada. Except for the first three chapters about difficult times in Germany in 1933, the story belongs to Anna, the youngest, called "Awkward Anna" because she was constantly stumbling or dropping things. It turned out that Anna couldn't see, but new friends and success greeted her after she got her glasses and attended a special school with other children who had sight problems. In chapters 15 through 20, Anna, with the help of Dr. Schumacher, made baskets as Christmas gifts for her family.

Chapters from Cleary's books about Henry Huggins, his friend Beezus, and pesty sister Ramona can be read aloud to introduce the characters. A selection from Henry Huggins called "Henry's Big Trouble" appears in the third grade reader Better Than Gold. Another selection "Henry and Ribs" appears in Fenner and McCrea's Stories for Fun and Adventure and Nelson's A Comparative Anthology of Children's Literature and explains how Henry found and named his dog Ribsy. Ribsy is introduced in the filmstrip Humor. Read page 25 of Henry and Ribsy to find out how Ribsy got into trouble with the police. The first two chapters of Henry and the Paper Route are excellent for reading aloud and tell how Henry got his job and how he offered kittens as premiums. In chapter two of Henry and the Clubhouse Henry learns about the perils of being a paperboy with a fierce new dog on the route. Chapter three should be read for Halloween.

The last chapter of Henry Huggins is about a dog show and can be used to introduce Beezus and Ramona Quimby and the book Ramona and Her Sister. The project in Henry and Beezus was to earn money for a bicycle. Beezus also called her sister Ramona the Pest and was embarrased by her. In Ramona the Brave, the first grader had to wrestle with the problem of being called a copycat or tattletale. In the 1978 Newbery honor book, Ramona and Her Father the second grader's father looses his job. Read Chapter 3 at Thanksgiving time and Chapter 7 at Christmas time. The book is followed by Ramona and Her Mother.

Mitch and Amy, twins, are almost in fourth grade. Introduce the book by telling students that Beverly Cleary and her husband have twins also. Use the book to introduce other books about bullies: Byars's The Eighteenth Emergency, Green's The Unmaking of Rabbit, "The Case of the Marble Shooter" from Sobol's Encyclopedia Gets His Man, and Stolz's two books about The Bully of Barkham Street.

Books by Carolyn Haywood can be introduced to third graders when they read "Eddie and the Doll" in Orbits, the Houghton-Mifflin reader or chapter 8 of Eddie and His Big Deals. Eddie and the Dog Holder is about one of Eddie and Anna Patricia's "Big Deals": Eddie held dogs while Anna Patricia painted them.

The "New Deal" in *Eddie's Green Thumb* is to sell seeds for the library fund. Read chapter 3 "I Hate Turnips" aloud. *Eddie's Valuable Property* and *Eddie's Happenings* are about the valuable property Eddie collects but which his family calls "junk." The second book tells about special days and months like National Pickle Week and National Pancake Month. There are chapters about real holidays like Thanksgiving, Christmas and Washington's birthday too. In chapter 1 of *Ever-Ready Eddie* the children plan what they will do when each becomes president of the student council. In *Annie Pat and Eddie*, he told her she couldn't be an actress because she didn't have red hair so she dyed it red. In *Eddie Makes Music*, Sid played the cello but all Eddie wanted to do was play ball until all his friends were in the new school orchestra and he was left out. Read chapter 7 for a Halloween treat.

All of *Eddie's Pay Dirt* can be read aloud to introduce books by Haywood. Ask students to guess what was in the packages marked "Snakes," "Dangerous! Atom Bomb!" and "Very Valuable! Pay Dirt!" Read how Eddie came to own his goat, Gardenia, when his class read *Heidi* in school in *Eddie and the Fire Engine*. Chapter 9 is excellent for reading aloud because Gardenia ate twenty-four pies.

Gruenberg's *Favorite Stories Old and New* contains a selection about *Little Eddie* when he was seven years old and forgot why he went to the store.

A related series by Haywood is about Betsy. In *B is for Betsy*, she wanted to buy a tea set for Ellen's sixth birthday. *Betsy and Billy* contains chapters for Halloween, Christmas, Valentine's Day and May Day suitable for reading by second graders. On page 73 there is a wonderful explanation why there are so many Santa Clauses at Christmas time. *Back to School with Betsy* contains holiday chapters for Christmas and Easter. During *Betsy's Busy Summer* the children learn about sharing and the results of exclusiveness. In *Betsy and Mr. Kilpatrick*, the children meet their new crossing guard when she comes to the Halloween party dressed in her working costume. In *Betsy and the Circus*, money is earned for a Mother's Day gift, a birthday gift for Mr. Kilpatrick the former crossing policeman, and Billy's Easter egg. Betsy and Billy are in the fourth grade in *Betsy and the Boys*. Chapter 8 is about Christmas and 9 and 10 are about valentines. In chapter 5, Billy and his friends organized a football team for which Betsy could be cheer leader if she kept little Eddie out of the way. In chapters 6 and 7 Betsy was allowed to play when she provided the football. *Betsy's Little Star* centers around unhappy Star all of whose friends were going to kindergarten without her, who wasn't invited to Billy's Halloween party (so she and Eddie Wilson dressed up and scared the partygoers), and whose birthday was on Christmas. Read chapter 2 of *Betsy's Winterhouse*, "Christmas Carols and the Birthday Tree." *Snowbound with Betsy* took place the week before Christmas when the family was without electricity or phone. Another family with children six and eight, were stranded with them. *Merry Christmas from Betsy* follows.

Since each chapter of *Away Went Balloons* is a story in itself, read one a day for eight days to first graders. First grader Jonathan has his first school bus ride in *Here Comes the Bus!* Read chapter 4 when someone has a birthday. In *Taffy and Melissa Molasses*, Taffy thought the fourth of July was George

Washington's birthday.

POSTERS TO USE WITH DISPLAYS.   Commercial posters provide instant decoration. Check in the card catalog for commercial sets. For example, in an elementary school the poster of *Madeline's Rescue* could be a background for a display including *Madeline, Madeline's Rescue, Madeline and the Bat Hat, Madeline and the Gypsies,* and *Madeline in London.* The sound filmstrip of *Madeline's Rescue* could also be included.

The poster *Madeline's Rescue* is one of four in Set no. 2 of the three picture sets of posters called *Horn Book Posters* from Caldecott Medal Books. Individual posters could be used with the book mentioned or with any other book by the same author. Several of the posters could be used with other Caldecott Medal Books.

Horizontal posters from the Horn Book posters, Set no. 1, are Keats's *Snowy Day,* Milhous's *Egg Tree,* Politi's *Song of the Swallows,* and Handforth's *Mei Li.* Poster Set no. 2 contains 24 x 27-inch vertical posters for Brown's *Cinderella,* Montresor's *May I Bring a Friend,* Bemelman's *Madeline's Rescue,* and Ets' *Nine Days to Christmas.* Set no. 3 contains horizontal and vertical posters for Chaucer's *Chanticleer and the Fox,* d'Aulaire's *Abraham Lincoln,* Thurber's *Many Moons,* and Langstaff's *Frog Went A-Courtin'.*

The posters for *Song of the Swallows* and *Frog Went A-Courtin'* could be used as background for a display case that included picture books that contained individual songs. A list of those books is included in the chapter on "Enhancing Books through Music."

COLLECTIONS WITH BOOK DISPLAYS.   Placing various collections of objects with books, filmstrips, posters, and vertical file pamphlets can provide interesting and easily put together displays which can motivate reading. When the collections belong to private individuals, good public relations can be achieved also. Don't forget to get pictures of the owner with his or her display for the local newspaper. Information about individuals in the school or community who have interesting collections to share should be part of the library media center's human resource file. The family who has lived in Japan may be able to talk to the sixth-grade class that is studying Japan, as well as provide materials for a display.

Interesting displays can be based upon collections of stamps, coins, model cars and airplanes, toy soldiers, and mounted insects and shells.

The following books can be displayed with a variety of seashells: Abbott's *Sea Shells of the World, a Guide to the Better-Known Species,* Buck's *Along the Seashore,* Clemons's *Shells Are Where You Find Them,* Cooper's *Science on the Shores and Banks,* Cutler's *Creative Shellcraft,* Goudey's *Houses from the Sea,* Hurd's *Starfish,* and Zim's *Seashores.*

Wherever there are counters in the library, place terrariums, aquariums, cages with hamsters, gerbils and other small pets up on the counters beside books on that subject. Be sure they are high enough to avoid being disturbed by viewers.

Place Hussey and Pessino's *Collection Cocoons* by some cocoons. A jar with a praying mantis can be accompanied by Earle's *Praying Mantis* and Huntington's *Praying Mantis*. Wong and Vessel's *Our Terrarium* can accompany a terrarium and Gans's *It's Nesting Time* can accompany one or more bird nests.

Display musical instruments or pictures of them with the following three books by Kettlekamp: *Flutes, Whistles and Reeds; Drums, Rattles, Bells;* and *Singing Strings.*

Sports displays can include several unusual chess sets with chess books, a baseball bat and glove with books or a football, shoes and helmet with football books. Basketball programs of local games and team pictures can accompany basketball books. A tennis racquet and balls can easily fit in a display case.

Mementos from a recent vacation to Paris can accompany Sasek's *This Is Paris,* or brochures, maps and McCloskey's *Time of Wonder* and Carpenter's *Maine* can accompany a written report on someone's vacation in Maine.

Persons who brought back artifacts from their visits to the Tutankhamen exhibit when it was in the United States might be persuaded to allow them to be placed in a display with books on Egypt and archeology.

Photos of neighborhood children with their pets can accompany books on dogs, cats, snakes, or the care of any pets.

Model Cars and Trucks and How to Build Them by Weiss can accompany a model car and truck collection.

Use clippings of newspapers and magazines from the vertical file as well as transparencies, filmstrips, and picture sets of earthquakes and volcanoes to accompany Lauber's *Earthquakes,* Brown's and Walter's *Historic Catastrophies: Earthquakes,* Marius's *First Book of Volcanoes and Earthquakes,* and Branley's *Shakes, Quakes and Shifts, Earth Tectonics.*

The following symbols can appear in objects or as flat pictures with these four books by Barth: lilies, rabbits and painted eggs with *The Story of Easter;* hearts, cupids, and red roses with *The Story of Valentine Symbols;* holly, reindeer, and colored lights with *The Story of Christmas Symbols;* witches, pumpkins and grinning ghosts with *The Story of Halloween Symbols.*

Sometimes just one object can accompany and add interest to a book. Display Tresselt's *The World in a Candy Egg* with a spun sugar egg that has a window. Display a Mexican clay pig with Morrow's *The Painted Pig.* The other things that the boy in the story did not want could be included—a straw horse, birds from gourds, puppets, and animals.

Cut out huge bright letters to spell "animal tracks" and print each letter with the black ink track of a different animal. Display with Kirn's *Let's Look at Tracks* and *Let's Look at More Tracks,* Mason's *Animal Tracks,* Murie's *A Field Guide to Animal Tracks,* and George's *Snow Track* (a cumulative book in which a white-footed mouse, weasel, skunk, cotton tail rabbit, raccoon, red fox, dog and bear follow the tracks of the others).

Plaster the back wall of the display case with pictures from magazines, newspapers, and posters of local, state, and national candidates. Cut out huge letters in dark blue to spell VOTE. Use red, white, and blue streamers to connect books with Lindop's *The First Book of Elections.* The background for books on various sports could use the same technique because clippings on that subject abound.

Displays using poems about snow, raindrops, kites, birds, insects and wildflowers appear in "Enjoying Poetry."

A large picture of Tico with gold foil for wings could accompany Lionni's *Tico and the Golden Wings*. Similar pictures could accompany other books.

In Stolz's easy reader, *Emmett's Pig*, Emmett always wanted a pig of his own but all he had was a collection of pigs. Place this book and other books about pigs in a display with all kinds of piggy banks or pig-shaped items. A stuffed Piglet from Milne's *Winnie-the-Pooh* might be included.

CHOOSING PICTURE BOOKS FOR READING ALOUD.   When choosing picture books to read to children, be sure that the books are large enough for a group of children to see easily.

Books by Crockett Johnson and Beatrix Potter are favorites, but their small formats make them unsuitable for reading just from the book itself to a group of children. However, since books by these authors are available on sound filmstrip, show the pictures to children while a narrator stands beside the screen and reads from the picture book. This allows children to experience the intimacy of being read to by the human voice while enabling them to see the illustrations. Be sure of coordination between the reader and the person changing the frames on the projector.

Mayer's *A Boy, a Dog and a Frog*, one of several by this author about these characters, is also too small for students to see the pictures. Seeing the pictures in Mayer's books is essential because they are wordless. Try showing groups of students illustrations in wordless books and have them tell the story. A bibliography of wordless picture books is included in the chapter, "Experiencing Art through Picture Books." Four wordless picture books available in filmstrip format are Krahn's *A Flying Saucer Full of Spaghetti*, Mayer's *Bubble Bubble*, Ward's *The Silver Pony*, and Winter's *The Bear and the Fly*.

Ola by the d'Aulaires had large illustrations that enable children to travel around Norway with Ola to a Lapp wedding and see, among other things, a fishing village before returning home. Picture books by Leo Politi, about children around the world, are good to read aloud and show to groups. *Song of the Swallows* is about the return of the swallows to the mission at Capistrano.

CONDUCTING PICTURE BOOK PROGRAMS.   *The Pleasure Is Mutual*, a 16mm film containing information on conducting effective picture book programs, should be seen by anyone who is planning to read picture books to children. The film can be of assistance to high school and college students as well as adults. Major areas covered are organization, preparation, presentation, and evaluation. Information is given on how to hold a book, characteristics of good stories, factors to consider when choosing stories, using volunteers, handling interruptions, introducing stories, and what to say when the story is finished. A booklet distributed by the Children's Book Council, *How to Conduct Effective Picture Book Programs*, includes scenes from the film and answers over fifty specific questions. A bibliography and suggestions on using the film and booklet for a workshop are included. Several persons are shown teaching fingerplays as well as reading books to children. The following books are shown in the film: Birnbaum's *Green Eyes*, Flack's *The Story About Ping*, Gay's *Look!*, Keats' *Whistle for Willie*, LaFontaine's *The Lion and the Rat*, Langstaff's *Over in the Meadow*, Lionni's *Inch by Inch*, *Old Mother Hubbard and Her Dog* from Mother Goose, Munari's *The Elephant's Wish*, Nodset's *Who Took the Farmer's Hat*, Rey's *Curious George Takes a Job*, Sendak's *Where the Wild Things Are*, Shaw's *It Looked Like Spilt Milk*, Slobodkina's *Caps for Sale*, and Brian Wildsmith's *ABC*.

HINTS FOR READING PICTURE BOOKS
1. Make sure that the books contain a worthwhile story and quality illustrations.
2. Coordinate the age level of the book with the age level of the listeners.
3. Be sure there is a balance between pictures and the story.
4. Include books with large enough illustrations to be seen by a group.
5. Enjoy the book yourself.
6. Know the story well enough so that you can read it while only glancing at the page.
7. Provide a space that is away from the traffic pattern.
8. Establish guidelines for the audience.
9. Provide a brief introduction to the book.
10. Hold the book so everyone in the audience can see the illustrations.
11. Provide stretching activities between stories.
12. Offer transitional information between activities.
13. End the session simply and with a bridge of anticipation for the next read aloud session.

READING PICTURE BOOKS TO STIMULATE ACTIVITIES.   Stories can be read to children for a variety of reasons. The reading may be an end in itself or it may serve as a springboard to other activities. Most of the time stories are read to children first and then other projects follow. Sometimes other books similar in content or design are introduced.

Some days it doesn't pay to get up in the morning and nobody understands or expresses that feeling better than Judith Viorst in *Alexander and the Terrible, Horrible, No Good, Very Bad Day*, and its sequel, *Alexander Who Used to be Rich Last Sunday*. Alexander knew the day wasn't going to be his best when all he found in his bowl was breakfast cereal, while his brothers found a Corvette Sting Ray car kit and a Junior Undercover Agent code ring. The story is a series of all the things that went wrong that day. It is ageless and universal in appeal. Listeners can change the events to reflect their own experiences to follow the reading with a creative writing experience.

Reading stories aloud is not just an activity for preschool and early primary students. Students in third and fourth grades enjoy hearing Holling's *Paddle-to-the-Sea* (a carved canoe traveled through the Great Lakes and reached the

Atlantic by way of the St. Lawrence River), Cooney's *Chanticleer and the Fox* (Chaucer's Nun's Priest's Tale about a cocky rooster), Alexander's *The King's Fountain* (about the only man brave enough to tell the King that his fountain was beautiful but was depriving the people of their water supply), and Charlip and Supree's *Harlequin and the Gift of Many Colors* (about how the harlequin costume originated).

Read Marcia Brown's *Stone Soup, an Old Tale* to children before they begin to play out the story. Directions for playing this and other stories are included in Chapter 5, "Playing Stories, Live Action and with Puppets."

Read *Jeanne Marie Counts Her Sheep* by François or Ipcar's *Brown Cow Farm* to students before they have an opportunity to look at the counting books listed in the chapter on "Experiencing Art through Picture Books," under the headings "Picture Books: Counting One to Ten," "Picture Books: Counting beyond Ten," and "Projects for Alphabet and Counting Books." Garten's *Alphabet Tale* is an alphabet book that invites students to participate, with three clues that help the audience guess which story is going to be next. The animals are listed, Alligator to Zebra, and the next animal begins with the next letter of the alphabet which is shown on the right-hand page; on the left-hand page a rhyme about the previous animal provides a rhyming clue to the identity of the next animal. Other alphabet books to read aloud appear in the chapter on art.

Other picture books written in rhyme that are especially good for reading aloud appear in the chapter on "Enjoying Poetry" in a section called *Stories in Rhyme*. Books about *Madeline* by Bemelmans and all the books by Kahl including *The Duchess Bakes a Cake*, books by Dr. Seuss such as *Horton Hatches the Egg*, and Lobel's *On the Day Peter Stuyvesant Sailed into Town*, come from that section.

Songs and poems as individual picture books can be read to students. Spier's seven-verse folk song *The Fox Went Out on a Chilly Night* and Ivimey's *The Complete Adventures of Ye Three Blind Mice* are only two of several songs included in the chapter on, "Enhancing Books through Music."

A section of this chapter entitled "Birthdays" includes many books to read aloud. Books with recurring phrases invite students to participate in reading the story. Three outstanding examples are Gag's *Millions of Cats*, Slobodkina's *Caps for Sale*, and Piper's *The Little Engine That Could*. In Gag's story, children will chime in when the phrase that begins "hundreds of cats, thousands of cats . . . ." is read. In Slobodkina's story, children have several opportunities to place themselves in the role of the peddler and ask for the caps. In Piper's story, the little red engine has positive thoughts and chugs to itself, "I think I can, I think I can" until it successfully hauls its cargo of children up over mountain. More books containing repetition are included in the chapter on "Playing Stories" in the sections on repetition and shadows.

Lipkind's Caldecott Medal book *Finders Keepers*, excellent for reading aloud, also contains repetition. Two dogs, Nap and Winkel, find a bone and fight over it. The dogs ask a farmer, a goat, an apprentice barber and a bigger dog which of them should own the bone—Nap who saw it first or Winkle who touched it first. The bigger dog makes them forget their differences by stealing their bone. Animal stories, especially those in which the animals are personified are good for reading aloud.

PICTURE BOOKS BY FAVORITE AUTHORS.   Some of the picture books that are still favorites are those about a snow plow, a steam shovel, and a tugboat. Gramatky's *Little Toot* is about a little tugboat who proved himself. After it has been read to students, they should be encouraged to examine it and other titles, *Little Toot on the Thames* and *Little Toot on the Grand Canal.* A story period might include telling two of the three stories about Little Toot. In *Little Toot on the Thames* the tugboat tried to tug a tramp steamer but instead it pulled him into the ocean and left him there. Eventually, Little Toot was escorted home by the huge *Queen Elizabeth.* In *Little Toot on the Grand Canal,* the tugboat went to Venice with Big Toot and became involved with pirates who were looting treasure. Again, Little Toot saved the day.

Virginia Lee Burton is a favorite author. *Katy and the Big Snow* is about a bulldozer-snowplow that belongs to the highway department of Geoppolis. During a big storm, Katy repeats "Follow me!" as she opens up the police station, post office, railway station, telephones, electrical repair station, water department, hospital, fire department, and airport. *Mike Mulligan and His Steam Shovel* is about a man and his shovel, Mary Ann. Mike's pride in Mary Ann was vindicated by a happy ending when Mary Ann was converted to become the furnace of the new town hall. *Maybelle the Cablecar* saw San Francisco outgrow cable cars until a citizen's committee to save cable cars provides a happy ending. Burton's *Little House,* the 1943 Caldecott Medal winner, saw changes occur as the countryside disappeared and the city grew around her. Children love the pictures of the changing seasons, and the additions on each successive page.

Picture books by Robert McCloskey are especially fun to share. The 1942 Caldecott book, *Make Way for Ducklings,* is perfect for reading aloud because the book has large clear illustrations and a simple, yet intriguing, story. Mr. and Mrs. Mallard built their nest on an island in Boston. After teaching her family how to swim and dive, Mrs. Mallard took them through traffic to another island in the middle of the Public Garden where Mr. Mallard was waiting for them. The Boston Police Department helped the family cross Beacon and other busy streets. *Blueberries for Sal* is about a little girl who went berry picking with her mother, a little bear cub who was berry picking with its mother, and how the two youngsters exchanged mothers for a short while. Sal appears three years older in *One Morning in Maine,* and has an adventure with her loose tooth. The 1958 Caldecott Medal book *Time of Wonder* is about a family at their vacation cottage on Penobscot Bay, Maine. Seasons and a hurricane are a *Time of Wonder,* as told in rhythmic prose and watercolor illustrations. *Burt Dow, Deep Water Man* is fun to read aloud because of words like "slish-cashlosh" and "cochety-doodly" and "klinkety-klink." When Burt, a retired seaman, and his pet gull caught a whale and put a Band-Aid on its tail where the hook caught it, Burt did not know that all the other whales would want a Band-Aid on their tails too.

McCloskey's *Homer Price* makes excellent reading aloud for intermediate students. If only one chapter is to be read aloud, then choose "The Doughnuts" (pp. 50–68).

Bright's *Georgie* is a special ghost friend of preschool and early primary children. Georgie helped out the New England family with whom he lived by squeaking the parlor door and the loose board on the stairs. Then the family knew when to go to bed, the cat knew when to prowl, and the owl knew when to hoot. Problems arose when Mr. Whittaker hammered the loose board firm and oiled the door hinges. In *Georgie's Halloween*, Georgie enters a village Halloween contest for the best costume. In *Georgie and the Robbers*, Miss Oliver the owl followed the thieves, Herman the cat went to get the police, while Georgie scared the robbers out of the barn into their waiting arms.

FAVORITE ANIMAL PICTURE BOOKS.   Duvoisin's *The Christmas Whale* took the place of Santa's sick reindeer so the children wouldn't be disappointed at Christmas.

Rey's *Cecily G and the Nine Monkeys* is about a giraffe who befriended nine monkeys. Payne's *Katy No-Pocket* is a mother kangaroo who had no pocket in which to carry her baby Freddy, and so she went to find out how other mothers carried their babies. A big blue apron, made for Katy, gave her enough pockets to carry other animal babies as well. Ungerer's *Crictor* is a boa constrictor who captured a burglar. *Albert's Toothache* by Williams is about an alligator who had a toothache in his big toe and no one except his grandmother has any sympathy for him. In Waber's *An Anteater Named Arthur*, Arthur (who is usually well-behaved) causes problems when he wants to change his name, has nothing to do but is not interested in helping, has a messy room, doesn't want to eat his breakfast, and is forgetful.

Waber's *A Firefly Named Torchy* lost friends because he was constantly aglow. Finally, he was shown a city where his light was just one of many. Another Waber book, *You Look Ridiculous Said the Rhinocerous to the Hippopotamus*, is described in the chapter "Experiencing Art through Picture Books," in a section called "Creating Unusual Animals." In Krasilovsky's *The Cow Who Fell in the Canal*, Hendrika, a Dutch cow, has enough adventures to talk about for a lifetime when she fell onto a raft in the canal and floated down to the city. Ferdinand the young bull in Leaf's *The Story of Ferdinand* wanted nothing more than to smell the flowers. Ferdinand was not interested in a career in the bull ring, but when a bee stung him and made him look ferocious, Ferdinand was taken away to fight. All he did was sit down in the middle of the ring and smell the flowers the ladies wore in their hair.

Conford's *The Impossible Possum* is Randolph who could not hang by his tail until his sister Geraldine used sap to make Randolph's tail stick to the branch. Freeman's *Dandelion* is about a lion who dressed up like a dandy. Freeman's *Norman the Doorman* is about a mouse, a doorman at a museum, who received recognition for his sculpture, and can be used to introduce other mice like *Anatole*, a favorite mouse from Paris created by Titus, who has several books about him.

Tompert's *Little Fox Goes to the End of the World* told his mother about all the places he plans to visit. When his mother suggested complications or asked questions, Little Fox had answers for her.

Flack's *The Story about Ping* is an all-time favorite. Ping, a duck who lives on a boat in the Yangtze River, was careful never to be the last duck to return at day's end, because the last duck would get a spank on its back. One day, when he knew he would be last, Ping did not go back to the boat. Later, after almost becoming duck dinner, Ping was so relieved to see his boat again he did not care if he was spanked. Even third graders enjoy Ping. However, Flack's *Angus and the Ducks, Angus and the Cat,* and *Angus Lost* are especially appropriate for preschool and early primary students. That same age group will enjoy the rhythmic prose of Tresselt in *Hi Mr. Robin!* and *Wake Up, Farm!* The first book introduces signs of spring and the second, farm animals.

The Happy Lion by Fatio lives in a zoo in a small French town and is visited often by a boy named Francois. One day Happy Lion walked out the open door of his cage and went to see the village, but was surprised that people who were friendly to him in the zoo were frightened of him. In *Happy Lion in Africa,* our friend is kidnapped and taken to Africa where he is frightened by the wild animals. A wildlife photographer, who recognized Happy Lion, rescues him. Happy Lion is lonesome in *Happy Lion Roars* so he is given a companion. In *Three Happy Lions,* the lions wonder what is to become of baby Francois—he was too big for a household pet and too mild for a circus lion. The message in *Happy Lion and the Bear* is that one should not roar at others until one knows them well.

The Happy Lion books are illustrated by Roger Duvoisin, the husband of Louise Fatio and creator of Petunia the goose and Veronica the hippo.

PICTURE BOOKS ABOUT PIGS.   Read to children groups of picture books that are on one theme about one animal, or by one author. For example, read Marshall's *Yummers!* about Emily Pig who went for a walk with Eugene Turtle so she could take her mind off food—but everything reminded her of it and the walk made her hungry. Pomerantz's *The Piggy in the Puddle,* illustrated by Marshall, makes an excellent companion book. The girl pig in the family won't come out of the mud puddle for her brother or parents so they join her. Words like "mooshy-squooshy" roll off the tongue and make the mud inviting. Oxenbury's *Pig Tale* could be another companion story. Bertha and Briggs, pigs, were bored with their life until they found a treasure. Farmer Palmer in Steig's *Farmer Palmer's Wagon Ride* is a pig. Farmer Palmer brought gifts home from market for his family. Pearl Piglet is the heroine of Steig's *The Amazing Bone.* Other books by Steig are excellent for reading aloud.

Wilbur is a famous pig from a book that is excellent for reading aloud—*Charlotte's Web* by E. B. White. A film about Charlotte the spider and her friends has been made from the book and is shown periodically on TV.

The Three Little Pigs are the most famous pigs in children's literature. Rayner's *Mr. and Mrs. Pig's Evening Out* is a story that can be read to children after they hear *The Three Little Pigs.* The fun begins when Mr. and Mrs. Pig hire a babysitter named Mrs. Wolf from an agency. Picture books are illustrated by Brooke and Du Bois. *Padre Porko, the Gentlemanly Pig* is the very wise pig from Spanish folklore. Eleven tales are included in that book illustrated by Eichenberg. *Coll and His White Pig* makes a good introduction to Alexander's fantasy trilogy that ends with *The High King*. Paddy Pork is the hero of Godall's two wordless picture books, *The Adventures of Paddy Pork* and *The Ballooning Adventures of Paddy Pork*. Children can visualize the story by following the half pages of these wordless books.

Rhymes from *This Little Pig-a-wig and Other Rhymes About Pigs* could be read between stories about pigs.

After one or two stories about pigs have been read to students, other books about pigs that are included in this section could be shared with students using the technique in this chapter in the section called *An Awareness Project*. Students could also be directed to a display of books about pigs.

A display of books about pigs should include easy readers so younger children can read to themselves. Lobel's beginning reader, *Small Pig*, is about a pig who wallowed in mud that was really cement. Stolz's *Emmett's Pig* is about a boy who got his wish for a pig of his own.

PICTURE BOOK FOLKTALES FROM AROUND THE WORLD. The following folktales in picture book format have not been identified elsewhere in this chapter. The books could be part of a display on folktales around the world, and could be introduced to students as the locations are pointed out on a map or globe.

Walker's *How the Hare Told the Truth about his Horse* comes from Italy. The hare told man that the lion was his horse so he had to trick the lion into being his horse.

Jacobs's tale *Buried Moon* is very English. Jeffers's illustrations add to the airiness of the moon in the bogs.

Shub adapted *Clever Kate* from a story of the Brothers Grimm. The easy reader is about a new wife who could not do anything right, but turned out to be smarter than she seemed.

Asbjornson's *The Squire's Bride* from Scandinavia fulfills the request for "a funny story." A rich old squire is almost tricked into marrying a mare dressed as a bride because a lassie is reluctant to become his wife.

Carlson's *We Want Sunshine in Our Houses* is a Finnish noodlehood story about men who build a house without windows and doors.

Schiller's *Audum and His Bear* and McGovern's *Half Kingdom, an Islandic Folktale* are both tales from Iceland. The first story is about the adventures of Audum who bought a white polar bear to give to King Sven of Denmark. King Sven gave Audum a ship and cargo, and a silver and gold bracelet. Audum had instructions to part with the bracelet only if he wanted to pay a great man for an obligation.

The King's Choice: a Folktale from India by Shivkumar extols the virtues of kindness. When the camel offered himself as food to the lion king to show that he was a loyal servant, the king showed his kindness in return.

Mosel's *Tikki Tikki Tembo* is about a Chinese boy who was given a long name because long names made a person seem important. However, the name was a handicap when he fell into a well and people had to say his long name before they could get someone to go for help.

Parry's *King of the Fish* is about a hare who was tricked into visiting the underwater kingdom where the King of Fish wanted his eyes. The hare said he had to go home to get his "farseeing" eyes, but he did not return. The tale comes from Korea.

Why the Sun and the Moon Live in the Sky: an African Folktale from Nigeria is retold by Dayrell. The how and why tale also includes the greed motif.

In Kirkpatrick's *Naja the Snake and Mangus the Mongoose, a Jamaican Folktale*, the mongoose was brought to Jamaica to kill snakes but instead they became friends, and now the snake protects the mongoose.

John Tabor's Ride, illustrated by Blair Lent, is a New England whaling tale about a man who rode a whale. McHargue's *The Mermaid and the Whale* comes from the same time period and concerns a mermaid who fell in love with a whale, and went for a ride on his back.

Credle's *Monkey See, Monkey Do* is about the mischief caused by the monkey that Uncle Bill brings to the Cullifer family in the Carolina lowlands.

Waupee, which means White Hawk, saw twelve sisters come from the sky in a basket and dance in *The Ring in the Prairie*. According to the Shawnee American Indian legend, Waupee caught one of them and married her. When the bride became homesick, she took her son up into the sky. Waupee later joined them and they were changed into white hawks.

Introduce two other picture books about American Indians at this time. Sleator's *Angry Man*, a Tlingit legend from Alaska, and McDermott's *Arrow to the Sun: a Pueblo Indian Tale*, the 1975 Caldecott Medal winner.

TALES FROM JEWISH TRADITION.   Several stories are about a rabbi. *The Golem*, written and illustrated by Beverly Brodsky McDermott, could be read at Passover time. In the story, a rabbi creates a Golem from dust to protect the Jews from the Gentiles who blame them for the hard times. The rabbi doesn't fully realize the extent to which the Golem will protect them in this Caldecott Honor book. Also at Passover, read Shulevitz's *The Magician* in which a mysterious visitor provides food for a poor couple. In Hirsh's *The Rabbi and the Twenty-Nine Witches: a Talmudic Legend*, witches shrink in the rain. A wise old rabbi rids the village of the witches that terrorize it whenever the moon is full.

Hirsh also wrote *Could Anything Be Worse*, the Yiddish version of a familiar folktale, about a man who finds his home too noisy and upon expert advice from the rabbi, adds relatives and animals so that later, when they are gone, he is satisfied with his original lot. The story is available in sound filmstrip format. Other stories on this theme are included in the chapter on "Playing Books."

Picture books by Singer include *Elijah the Slave: A Hebrew Legend* and *Mozel and Shlimazel*, which can be used to introduce Singer's two collections of Yiddish folklore. Singer's collections are *Zlateh the Goat & Other Stories* and

When Shlemiel Went to Warsaw & Other Stories.

In Elkin's *The Wisest Man in the World*, King Solomon of Israel lets a bee go and the bee promises to save the king sometime—much as the little mouse promises to return the favor to the lion in the famous Aesop fable. When the Queen of Sheba came, she posed a riddle that the bee helped Solomon solve by picking the one real flower from the ninety-nine false ones because the real flower had nectar. The essence of the story is summed up in a rhyme on the last page "Surely, wisdom is given/ to all living things," "And the tiniest creatures/ are teachers of kings." Ish-Kishor's *The Carpet of Solomon* is also about the wise king.

Simon Boom served only water at his daughter's wedding because he was looking for the best and learned that water was sweeter than sugar, clearer than honey, purer than oil, and better than all three of them. Margot Zemach illustrated Suhl's *Simon Boom Gives a Wedding*.

USING A VARIETY OF MEDIA.   A variety of media (puppets, live story-tellers, educational films, filmstrips, sound recordings in record or cassette format, videotapes, and entertainment movies shown in theaters or on television) have been recommended throughout this book. The purpose of using these media is to introduce books, and to show that ideas and words are the basis of all communication, audiovisual as well as printed, and complement rather than replace one another. When producers translate from one medium to another, there are some failures. Some entertainment films or even filmstrips distort books or destroy their meaning completely. Those media that are introduced in this book have been successfully used in classrooms or library media centers or are highly recommended by those who have carefully reviewed them.

Evaluation of audiovisuals is becoming more widespread. The following periodicals, subscribed to by many school and public libraries, review films: *Booklist, Hornbook, Library Journal, Learning Magazine,* and *Media and Methods.* Special awards for audiovisuals, especially filmstrips, are offered by all except *The Horn Book.* However, because *The Horn Book* is so selective, just the inclusion of an audiovisual means it is better than most. Numerous acceptable audiovisuals are included in *Elementary School Library Collection*, edited by Winkel.

Audiovisuals serve several unique purposes. They can provide access to master storytellers or expert readers of poetry. Although not all poets are excellent readers, hearing poems read by those who wrote them offers an extra dimension to poetry. Books which have music as an integral part of their content are enhanced by materials which include the music which might otherwise be missed. Some books that are meant to be discussed are not available in paperback so that everyone can read the book beforehand. Although some will have read the story, an audiovisual, especially a film or filmstrip, can provide the group with a reinforcing common experience on which to base the discussion. Some audiovisuals are appropriate for introducing books, others for culminating activities after a book has been read. Others have been prepared as "read-alongs" so that students can increase their skill while reading a selection. Many audiovisuals, especially documentary television and feature films and videotapes that may have nothing directly to do with books and are not based on them, can be used to stimulate reading.

The sound recording provides a unique opportunity to hear an author and storyteller, for example, Ruth Sawyer reading from her book *Joy to the World, Christmas Legends*. The book contains six carols and six stories and the recording called *Joy to the World* contains three stories and one carol. The carol is "A Carol from an Irish Cabin." The stories are "This Is the Christmas," "The Two Lambs," and "Precious Herbs of Christmas." Or listen to Virginia Hamilton read and sing her own edited version of her book *Zeely*. Ossie Davis and Ruby Dee read stories from Aardema's *Behind the Back of the Mountain* on the recording called *Zulu and Other African Folk Tales*.

One of the stories on the recording *Chinese Fairy Tales* read by actress Siobhan McKenna is called "The Chinese Red Riding Hoods." Listening to this story as a group could stimulate students to read other fairy tales on their own. *Moon Basket: An Indian Legend* was one of *Previews* best-of-the-year filmstrips for 1976. The filmstrip could provide a common experience that would introduce students to collections of books containing one or more Indian legends.

Listening to the recording of *Won't You Be My Neighbor* could introduce the PBS TV program, *Mr. Rogers' Neighborhood*. Students already familiar with the program might choose to sing along with Mr. Rogers. The sound filmstrip based on Byars's *The Lace Snail* in which the main character is made from a paper doily is one of several sound filmstrips and films that can stimulate art projects.

The recording *Poems and Songs of the Middle Earth* read by *Hobbit* author Tolkien himself, combines music and poetry. Other recordings are available in which Tolkien reads from his trilogy *The Lord of the Rings*.

Many sound recordings and filmstrips which use music as part of a book are included in the chapter on "Enhancing Books through Music." The recording of *Petunia* in which Julie Harris sings about Duvoisin's famous goose can be used to introduce all of the books about Petunia, but especially *Petunia and the Song*. The verses of Wells' *Noisy Nora* are read and sung by Nicole Frechette on the recording or sound filmstrip called *Noisy Nora*.

Two 16mm films can be used as culminating activities in which the books played a major role. *Paddle-to-the-Sea* is based on Holling's lovely book of the same title. *Rabbit Hill* can be used as a culminating activity but can also be used to introduce Lawson's *Rabbit Hill* and its sequel, *Tough Winter*.

Robert McCloskey's *Homer Price* is one of the American classics of children's books. One of the most famous scenes has been made into a film called *The Doughnuts*. Use this film to either introduce Homer or to enrich the second grade basal reader from Scott Foresman, *Hootenanny*. Barbara Sedgwick's "The Doughnut Machine That Wouldn't Stop" appears on pages 222–33 of *Hootenanny*. The story tells how the jelly-cinnamon-honey doughnut was accidentally invented. Photos on pages 234 to 248 of *Hootenanny* explain "How Doughnuts Are Made."

Some audiovisuals can be used to introduce concepts. The wordless filmstrip *Talking without Words* can be used to introduce students to a whole group of books included in the chapter "Experiencing Art in Picture Books" in sections called "Nonverbal Communication and Wordless Picture Books."

Economics can be introduced by showing the film *Clothing—A Pair of Jeans*. The book *Blue Jeans* by Rosenbloom can effectively be placed in the classroom reading area for students to learn more on the subject.

Sometimes media can be used as elementary guidance tools. The filmstrip based on Gaeddert's *Noisy Nancy Norris* can be shown and the concept of living and sharing in society discussed. An introduction to the filmstrip and book and a script as well as "Topics for Classroom Discussion" are included. Information on manners as well as identifying pleasant and annoying sounds are also included. A film of the book *Miss Esta Maude's Secret* based on a book by Cummings can be used to spark a discussion of stereotypes and how incorrect they can be. Miss Esta Maude was the schoolteacher who drove to school in an old black car but owned a red race car for her after work activities. No one knew she was the person in the flashy car who zoomed around helping people.

Numerous filmstrips are available for Parish's books about Amelia Bedelia. The filmstrips have been cited as being among the "Best Filmstrips of the Year." Filmstrips are available for each of the titles: *Amelia Bedelia, Thank You; Amelia Bedelia, Come Back; Amelia Bedelia;* and *Play Ball, Amelia Bedelia.* One or more of these filmstrips could introduce all titles. Use Amelia Bedelia to introduce riddles about homonyms included in the chapter "Using Jokes, Riddles, and Folk Themes" in a section called "Homonyms."

A film or filmstrip can be used to introduce a favorite book character. The Paddington and other Bear books could be introduced by the five-minute film based on Bond's *A Bear Called Paddington* called *Paddington Hits the Jackpot.* Paddington was a contestant on a quiz program and his category was math. The question was how many buns would he need to make five. Paddington answered two and a half and explained that because he always shared his buns two and a half really did make five.

The easy readers about Zion's dog named Harry can be introduced by showing one filmstrip. The filmstrips are *Harry, the Dirty Dog, Harry by the Sea, No Roses for Harry, Harry and the Lady Next Door.* Although Harry was very dirty, he ran away to avoid a bath, but later decided that he would rather have a bath than not to be recognized by his family. Show this filmstrip before the students play out the story. It is never to early to introduce the term "sequel." The sequel is *No Roses for Harry.* Grandma knitted Harry a sweater full of roses that he disliked. Every time Harry tried to lose the sweater, someone brought it back to him. Use any of those filmstrips to introduce other Zion books: *The Plant Sitter* and *Dear Garbage Man.*

Three sound filmstrips are available about Turkle's young Quaker boy who lived in Nantucket in the 1800s. Previewing and postviewing activities are included in the guide. All the books about Obadiah can lead in to books about whales, life in America in the nineteenth-century, and Quakers. In *Thy Friend Obadiah*, a seagull followed Obadiah everywhere, while they helped each other. *The Adventures of Obadiah* is about falsehoods, or suspected falsehoods, since no one in Obadiah's family believed all the stories he told. Telling tales could be discussed after seeing this filmstrip.

Books on filmstrip by Miller are *Mousekin's Golden House*, *Mousekin Finds a Friend*, and *Mousekin's Family*. Books about Mousekin *not* available in filmstrip format are *Mousekin's ABC's*, *Mousekin's Woodland Birthday*, and *Mousekin's Woodland Sleepers*. The Mousekin books could be used to introduce all the other picture books in this chapter under the heading "Mice Are Nice."

Although all of the following books about Curious George are available in sound filmstrip format, the one called *Curious George* can be used to introduce all the others: *Curious George Takes a Job*, *Curious George Gets a Medal*, *Curious George Goes to the Hospital*, and *Curious George Flies a Kite*. The last filmstrip could be used to introduce the books and stories about kites included in the chapter on "Experiencing Art Through Picture Books." A sound recording of *Curious George* is also available.

Lobel's *Frog and Toad Are Friends* and *Frog and Toad Together* were both honor books. There are five short stories in each and each story is available as a sound filmstrip. Directions for adapting those stories to puppet plays and creative dramatic exercises are included in the chapter on "Playing Stories, Live Action and With Puppets."

The books written and illustrated by the Hobans provide excellent spring-boards for discussion. They feature social concepts in simple terms made clear in the filmstrips: sibling rivalry, keeping your word, bedtime and rules, friendship, jealousy, and eating habits. The filmstrips and books available are *Baby Sister for Frances*, *Bargain for Frances*, *Bedtime for Frances*, *Best Friends for Frances*, *A Birthday for Frances*, and *Bread and Jam for Frances*. Introduce the book, then show the filmstrip. After the discussion, tell students that the book will be in the reading corner of the library media center for students to read on their own.

Another character for the same age group who has similar problems is Waber's crocodile, Lyle. These filmstrips can also be viewed to begin discussions of various social concepts. In *Lovable Lyle*, everyone seemed to love Lyle until he began to get nasty notes from a new little girl named Clover who was jealous. Other books about Lyle available in sound filmstrip format are *The House on East 88th Street*, *Lyle, Lyle Crocodile*, and *Lyle and the Birthday Party*. The last filmstrip can be used with *A Birthday for Frances* because both involve jealousy when it is someone else's birthday. Both filmstrips could be used to introduce all of the books about birthdays in this chapter in the section on "Introducing Books on Birthdays."

Attic of the Wind, based on Doris Lund's book of the same title, could be used to suggest to a class that they find and bring in samples of all the things the wind blew away. Place the articles in a showcase as they accumulate to advertise the book. Use this technique with MacGregor's *Theodore Turtle*, McClintock's *Pocketful of Cricket* and *The Wind Blew* and *Don't Forget the Bacon* by Hutchins. Commercial study prints about nonfiction subjects or about books can effectively be used in display cases with books on those subjects.

The MovieStrip developed by Films Inc. is one of the newest forms of media. Scenes from educational and entertainment films have been translated into filmstrip format to reduce costs so more individual schools can own them. One of these programs is the twelve filmstrip set that comes from the television program, "Roots," based on Alex Haley's book. A teacher's guide as well as copies of the script, ditto masters, and a read-along cassette are available for the first two MovieStrip sets. The four-part series, each unit of which can be purchased individually, are *Roots I: The Making of a Slave*, *Roots II: Adjusting to Plantation Life*, *Roots III: Masters and Slaves*, and *Roots IV: Civil War and Emancipation*. Some students may have seen the original television programs, first broadcast in 1977 and later repeated, but the filmstrips are understandable for those who did not see the series. There is much follow-up material in such categories as the black heritage, the Civil War, and books about the underground railroad that are included in this chapter in a section called "Introducing Historical Fiction." The Anansi folk tales from Africa make an effective follow-up which stresses an aspect of African culture. The MovieStrips for *Roots* are designed for grades seven and above and those students will find listening to a medley of African folktales a refreshing addition to a unit on slavery in the United States. The live storyteller provides another dimension to units of all types.

Another MovieStrip called *The Diary of Anne Frank* could be shown before conducting a booktalk to introduce the books in the section of the chapter called "Television—The Holocaust." The MovieStrip *Benji* could be used to introduce that personable dog and a booktalk introducing other dog or animal characters. The MovieStrip of *Dr. Doolittle* (a most successful movie starring Rex Harrison) is one way to introduce a series which has become controversial because of the British colonialist nineteenth-century view of Africa and Africans in some of its titles. The second title *The Voyages of Dr. Doolittle*, was awarded the first Newbery Medal for 1922, and the stories about the animal doctor who learned to talk with animals in their own language has given joy to generations of children. Self-contained incidents carefully chosen to avoid those with hurtful and harmful stereotypes, can be chosen for reading aloud.

EXPANDING BASAL READERS.   Most school systems in the United States still use a single basal reader or series of readers, and supplemental texts, and rely upon them as the basis for instruction. It is essential that the teachers and the library media specialist work together to widen the range of learning materials and opportunities for boys and girls. Increasingly, as the spectrum of abilities of children in every classroom grows larger and more diverse, especially with the mainstreaming of special learners into the classroom, a greater variety of print and nonprint media are required for individualized and small group learning that breaks out of lockstep patterns. The most important function of the school library media center and its program is to help teachers spin off from the basal texts to reinforce interests, facilitate independent learning, provide for individual pacing and practice, and motivate students to the habit of lifetime reading and learning.

Library media specialists can help youngsters follow up leads provided by the basal texts in several ways:

1. The library media specialist should know what basals or cobasals are being used in the classroom and become intimately familiar with the entire set for all grade levels. The examples following are just examples and may well be out of date for your school since new editions and new series are published all the time.

2. A complete set of teachers' editions should be part of the media center's professional reference collection. The library media specialist should examine the teachers' editions carefully for lists of suggested supplemental books to purchase.

3. If correlated lists are available for the basals in use, the library media specialist should consult them. For instance, there is the Spache Readability Projects booklet, *Correlation to Basal Readers* which correlates "library" books to several series and also grades the reading levels of the books. Eakin and Merrit's *Subject Index to Books for Primary Grades* indexed basals. Their list is outdated for basal reading series but the subject listings for supplementary books is still valuable. Library media specialists should consult individual textbook series for lists correlated to their basal readers.

4. The library media specialist should prepare a list of subjects included in the basal series and the grade levels at which they are introduced. The grade level is just a guide so that quantities of books about lions are not purchased for sixth graders when most of the articles or stories about lions appear in the first-grade reader. Of course a mixture of reading levels on any one subject is appropriate because the reading levels of students vary so greatly.

5. The list of subjects found in basals should be checked against the card catalog to see which books, filmstrips and other media on each subject are already in the collection.

6. The library specialist should provide analytic cards for materials which include the subject but for which there are no subject cards.

7. The library media specialist should check the list of subjects with the subject indexes of basic selection tools such as *The Children's Catalog*, Winkel's *Elementary School Library Collection*, NCTE's *Adventuring with Books*, *AAAS Science Book List for Children*, Huus's *Books to Enrich the Social Studies*, and Sutherland's *The Best in Children's Books*.

8. Library media specialists should keep subjects found in basal readers in mind when reading selection periodicals such as *Booklist*, *Bulletin of the Center for Children's Books*, *Elementary English*, *Horn Book*, *Kirkus Reviews*, *School Library Journal*, and *Science Books*.

9. All new related materials should be placed on bibliographies and given to the teachers using a particular basal. New materials ordered should be cataloged so the subjects found in the basals are reflected in the card catalog.

10. Library media specialists should make a list of all picture books or books in the library media center from which selections have been taken

for basal readers. Show the books when the class comes to that story so that students can see the relationship among pieces in basal readers and the whole books. If selections are parts of books, students can be encouraged to read the entire books or other books by that author.

11. Library media specialists should check poetry selections included in basals and, using the poetry indexes, find other poems about the same subject or by the same poet. Teaching intermediate students and middle school students to use these indexes is part of the library instruction program. Mary Ann Hoberman's poem, "I Like Old Clothes, " pages 37–39 of *Step Right Up,* the third-grade Scott Foresman reader, can be used to talk about pretending. A list of books about pretending is included in the chapter of this book, "Playing Stories: Live Action and with Puppets." Students could use the poetry indexes listed in this book under "Enjoying Poetry," to look up other poems by Hoberman. E. Y. Harburg's song "Somewhere Over the Rainbow" appears on page 87 of Bill Martin's fourth-grade Holt reader, *Sounds of Mystery,* 1967 edition. Send the book or recording of Baum's *The Wizard of Oz* to the classroom at that time.

12. Library media specialists should use basal reader topics to provide classroom collections on those subjects. Begin as early as first grade. When children read the first-grade Scott Foresman reader, *Calico Caper,* pages 92–97, "A Letter for Sako" they will learn about the post office. Place the three easy books about the post office in the classroom: Barr's *Mr. Zip and the U.S. Mail,* Greene's *Where Does a Letter Go,* and Meshover's *You Visit a Post Office/Telephone Company.* Read Keats's *A Letter to Amy* to students or show the sound filmstrip. Peter mailed a letter to Amy inviting her to his birthday party but he was afraid she wouldn't come. Materials for early primary grade reading corners in classrooms could be chosen by the library media specialist in collaboration with the teacher, but beginning in second and third grade, students can find those books by themselves from the card catalog.

13. Library media specialists should correlate library instruction to the curriculum and to basal reader assignments. For example, a group of the most advanced second graders could come to the library media center in small groups to learn how to locate materials by subject from the card catalog. The best time to begin this project would be when a subject from a story or article in the basal is being read. Make sure to choose a story on which there are many related subjects included in the card catalog. The library media specialist and the students could locate the materials together and the students could take them back to the classroom to share, view filmstrips and filmloops, or check out the books to take home. After third graders are given group instruction on using the card catalog, they can be

asked to locate the materials at various times as needed during the school year on their own. There is one potential problem: one third-grade class whose members came regularly to the media center to scour it for related materials amassed a huge pile of books, pictures, filmstrips, took the materials to their classroom, and forgot them. That class was treated to a special showing of the sound filmstrip of Duvoisin's *Petunia*. In that story, Petunia the goose walked around with a book tucked under her wing that she did not read, but carried because she wanted to have knowledge. A discussion of the filmstrip reinforced the correlation with what had been happening to the classroom collection, pointedly, but with humor.

14. Library media specialists should check lists of stories found in this chapter in a section called "Basal Readers and Storytelling." Although children like to hear favorite stories over and over, library media specialists should avoid introducing authors or telling stories from books which the children will meet the next year in their basal reader, if a special program is to be organized around that author or that story. With so many good selections from which to choose, it is best to introduce as many stories and authors as possible.

15. Basal reader stories written by outstanding authors of children's literature can stimulate students to investigate biographical information about those persons. Several authors are included in a section of this chapter called "Basal Readers Introduce Favorite Authors."

16. Basal reader subjects can inspire bulletin boards on special subjects. Allan Sommers's "A Fox Story," in the third-grade anthology, *Sounds of the Storyteller*, is a personal experience about how school children of Calvert County, Maryland, did not reveal the hiding place of a fox to fox hunters. Lew Sarett's "Four Little Foxes" follows on page 288. This would be a good time to have a display of "Foxy Books" of which a list is suggested in this chapter. Several of the titles are about children who watch or actively hide foxes from hunters. A poem called "The Fox," by a nine-year-old girl, Margaret Hannon, appears on page 191 of the Laidlaw primer, *The Blue-Tailed Horse*.

17. Materials to supplement the basal readers in use can become the nucleus of a classroom listening, reading and viewing corner. Library media specialists can provide long-term loans of individual filmstrip or 8mm projectors with or without sound to classrooms. Single earphones or complete listening posts insure that classmates will not be disturbed.

DOLPHINS, DINOSAURS, AND OTHER SUBJECTS INTRODUCED BY BASAL READERS. The 1978 edition of *Flying Hoofs*, the fourth-grade Scott Foresman reader, contains two selections about dolphins by Margaret Davidson, "The Dolphins Who Talked to Each Other" (pp. 431–34) and "About Dolphins" (pp. 424–30). The stories came from Davidson's *Nine True Dolphin*

Stories. Because the book is in paperback, several copies should be purchased for the classroom so students can be encouraged to read the other stories. Other dolphin books should be sent to the classroom or included in a display about dolphins. Many photos illustrate Moffett's *Dolphins*, which includes information on language, physical structure, senses, and social order. Goudey's *Here Come the Dolphins* is easy reading. A selection called "A Baby Is Born" from that book is found in Sutherland's *The Arbuthnot Anthology of Children's Literature*. Carter's *The Happy Dolphins*, available in paperback, is about Dal and Suwa, two bottlenose dolphins in the Florida Keys. Students may remember Flipper, the dolphin who had his own television series. Bridges's *The Playful Dolphins* is one of a set of four books from the National Geographic Society. The other three books include *Wonders of the Desert World, Animals Build Their Homes,* and *Camping Adventure*. In Edwards's *Isaac and Snow*, Isaac made friends with an albino porpoise.

Have students learn to use indexes and tables of contents of books about mammals. Chapter 5 of Waters's *Some Mammals Live in the Sea*, pages 44 and 45, is called "Dolphins, Porpoises and Small Whales." Check the index of Riedman's *Home Is the Sea: For Whales* to find a whole column devoted to dolphins.

Two Harper-I-Can-Read books that may be young for fourth graders but can be included in a dolphin display in the library media center are Benchley's *The Several Tricks of Edgar Dolphin* and Morris's *Dolphin*. The second book is a life cycle book; the first book is a story of a young dolphin who was trapped in a net by divers, put in a tank and figured out how to escape so that he could go home to his mother who had warned him not to get too close to the ship.

Another book that can be included with the display or could be read aloud is *Arion and the Dolphin*, by Alonzo Anderson, illustrated by Adrienne Adams. The story is based on an ancient Greek legend. On the way home from winning a music contest, the greedy crew wanted Arion's prize of gold and planned to steal it. Arion escaped overboard and was saved by dolphins. Four dolphin stories are listed in *Eastman's Index to Fairy Tales, 1949–1972*.

Glen Blough's "Discovering Dinosaurs" appears on pages 234 to 240 of the third-grade Harcourt basal reader, *Widening Circles*. Another article, "Reptiles in the Air," follows on pages 241 to 244. Wise's *Great Birds and Monsters of the Air* would be a suitable supplementary book to accompany the second article. Flying reptiles also appear in Ostrom's *The Strange World of Dinosaurs*, which is more difficult than the Wise book. Other prehistoric animals appear in Davidson's *When the Dinosaurs Disappeared, Mammals of Long Ago,* and the more difficult books, *Album of Prehistoric Animals,* and *Dinosaurs and Other Prehistoric Animals* by McGowen.

The easiest dinosaur books, the first of which are from the Let's-Read-and-Find-Out series, are Kaufman's *Little Dinosaurs and Early Birds* and Aliki Brandenberg's *My Visit to the Dinosaurs* and *Wild and Wooly Mammoths*. In the second book, the narrator, a small boy, saw dinosaurs in a museum. Parish's *Dinosaur Time* is a Harper-I-Can-Read book. Two other books are part of familiar easy reading series: Holsaert's *A Book to Begin on, Dinosaurs* and Clark's *True Book of Dinosaurs*. Jackson's *Days of the Dinosaurs* is one of a set of four National Geographic books which include *Dogs Working for People, Lion Cubs,* and *Treasures in the Sea. Dinosaur Days* by Knight and *Dinosaur Story* by Cole are also easy to read. Ipcar's *The Wonderful Egg* has illustrations that can be enjoyed by everyone. Zallinger's *Dinosaurs* and Knight's *Dinosaur Days* are for primary children. Selsam's *Tyrannosaurus Rex* and Cohen's *What Really Happened to the Dinosaurs?* are more difficult.

The Enormous Egg, found by a twelve-year-old, hatched into a Triceratops. Intermediate and middle school students will enjoy this humorous story which is written in the first person. *Narrow Passage* is the sequel. Two fiction books that are fun to read, yet provide information about dinosaurs, are Lampman's *The Shy Stegosaurus of Cricket Creek* and *The Shy Stegosaurus of Indian Springs.* Twelve-year-old twins moved to a run-down ranch their mother had inherited. Money was scarce, but Professor Harris, who was looking for fossils, boarded with them and provided needed money. While looking for fossils they met a friendly vegetarian Stegosaurus whom they named George, and with whom they had many adventures. In *The Shy Stegosaurus of Indian Springs,* the twins spent the summer with Auntie Casey while her brother, Professor Harris, and their mother were honeymooning. There they met a Klickitat Indian named Huckleberry, the only person besides them who could also see George. Read the first chapter of *The Shy Stegosaurus of Cricket Creek* to introduce both books.

The filmstrip, *The Search for Stegosaurus,* can be used to introduce the book *Riddle of the Stegosaurus* by Ipsen, which is about how paleontologists solved the riddle of the mysterious beast. Other books for intermediate students that stress paleontology and archeology are Asimov's *How Did We Find Out About Dinosaurs?,* Pringle's *Dinosaurs and Their World,* and Zim's *Dinosaurs.* The work of Dr. Barnum Brown and Dr. Roy Chapman Andrews is discussed in *Dodos and Dinosaurs* by Shuttlesworth, who also wrote *To Find a Dinosaur.* That book also talks about finding dinosaur remains and preparing them for museums. A girl named Mary Ann Anning discovered "The Mystery of Lyme Regis," which was the Ichthyosaurus, the first dinosaur to be discovered. Read the introduction to Blair's *Mary's Monster* to students because it tells about how Mary was born in 1799, the year George Washington died and Napoleon became First Consul.

Greene's *How to Know Dinosaurs* introduces the six major groups of dinosaurs in chronological order and gives pronunciations. Other general dinosaur books for intermediate students are Bloch's *Dinosaurs,* McGowen's *Album of Dinosaurs,* Matthews's *Wonders of the Dinosaur World,* Darling's *Before and After Dinosaurs,* and Ravielli's *The Rise and Fall of the Dinosaurs.*

An easy to understand sound filmstrip called *Dinosaurs* can be used as either an introductory or culminating activity. The ten study prints in the set called *Learning about Dinosaurs* can either be sent to the classroom or can be used as a background for a nice and easily made display of dinosaur books.

Pet books that provide more information for third graders who have read "Meet the Gerbils," in their Scott Foresman reader *Ride a Rainbow* are *Your First Pet and How to Take Care of It* by Stevens and *Gerbils and Other Small Pets* by Shuttlesworth. Other titles include Simon's *Discovering What Gerbils Do,* which includes experiments; Silverstein's *Gerbils: All About Them*, which is the most difficult book; and Dobrin's *Gerbils*. Herbert the gerbil was lost, and his replacement Max also disappeared in Dobrin's *Jillions of Gerbils*, until they were found later with babies. Weil's picture book *Fat Ernest* has a similar theme. Ernest and Erwin are gerbils but Ernest had to be renamed Ernestine. Place the filmstrip for *Sam Bangs and Moonshine*, by Ness, with the book on the back table of the classroom where headphones and a sound filmstrip projector are available. When students finish other work, they can view the filmstrip and make the connection between the filmstrip and the story they have just read. There is a gerbil in the book, although its main theme is that Samantha's "moonshine," or made up stories, almost cause the death of her cat and her friend, who believes them.

Whenever biographies or information about real people appear in basal readers, librarians and teachers should define the term and explain how biographies are found in the library media center. Individual and collective biographies can be explained when third graders read about the Wright Brothers on pages 711 to 723 of the Macmillan reader, *Better Than Gold*. Some titles students can find in the card catalog are Stevenson's *Wilbur and Orville Wright* and two books called *The Wright Brothers*, one by Reynolds and one by Thomas.

An article about Henry Ford appears on pages 39 to 41 of the Houghton-Mifflin third-grade reader, *Orbits*. Montgomery's *Henry Ford, Automotive Pioneer* makes easy supplementary reading. Library media specialists can take this opportunity to teach the use of "see" cards in the catalog to find related books and materials on "cars" or "automobiles."

How the Teddy Bear got its name is explained in the second-grade Scott Foresman reader, *Hootenanny*, in an article by Lisbeth Sanders called "The Teddy Bear Story." Introduce students to Judson's *Theodore Roosevelt, Fighting Patriot* and Monjo's *The One Bad Thing about Father*. The second book is written as if Teddy Roosevelt's son Quentin was wondering why his father decided to become president when he had held such other exciting jobs as police chief, cowboy, soldier, hunter, or could have been a boxer or a wrestler. The fact that Teddy bears are known around the world is shown by Nakatani's *My Teddy Bear*, about a Japanese boy. Second graders might enjoy listening to Ormondroyd's *Theodore's Rival*. Theodore, Lucy's teddy bear, felt dejected when Lucy received a birthday present—a stuffed panda bear she named Benjamin. Waber's story about the boy who went to sleep overnight at his friend's house and wondered whether or not to take his teddy bear, *Ira Sleeps Over*, is included in the Scott Foresman third-grade reader, *Ride a Rainbow*. Other stories about teddy bears are included in this chapter in the section on *Dolls* and can be found in the index under toy bears.

Two third-grade readers have articles on blindness. Articles on famous blind people, the Braille alphabet, and seeing eye dogs would be appropriate to introduce to students. The Braille alphabet appears on page 174 of Houghton Mifflin's *Orbits*, followed by "Seeing Eye Dogs," which came from McDonnell's *Stevie's Other Eyes*. Pages 55 to 69 of Macmillan's *More Than Words* also focuses on Braille, blindness and sight. Books about the Braille alphabet appear in chapter 6 of this book. These articles are especially useful for teaching students to look for several subjects in the card catalog, such as BLIND, BLIND-BIOGRAPHY, BLIND-EDUCATION, BLIND-FICTION, BRAILLE ALPHABET, EYE, LENSES, SEEING EYE DOGS, and VISION. Students may also look under the last names of persons who are blind.

Podendorf's *Touching for Telling*, which shows how blind people learn to use Braille, can be used with Neimark's *Touch of Light, the Story of Louis Braille* and *Seeing Fingers, the Story of Louis Braille*. Slow readers will enjoy Malone's *Annie Sullivan, Helen Keller's teacher*, and *Helen Keller: Toward the Light* by the Graffs. Bigland's *Helen Keller* and Peare's *Helen Keller Story* are more difficult to read. Hunter's *Child of the Silent Night* is about Laura Dewey Bridgman, a blind-deaf girl who paved the way for Helen Keller. *Light in the Dark: The Life of Samuel Gridley Howe* by Meltzer is about a Boston doctor who taught a blind, deaf, mute child. *Ray Charles* by Mathis is about a blind black boy who became totally blind when he was seven years old, learned to read music in Braille, and became a famous musician.

Triumph of the Seeing Eye by Putnam is about Frank Morris, a pioneer in training seeing eye dogs, and his dog Buddy. In Garfield's *Follow My Leader*, Leader is the name of the dog that leads eleven-year-old Jimmy who was blinded by a firecracker. Chipperfield's *Dog to Trust; the Saga of a Seeing Eye Dog* is about twenty-two-year-old Ralph and his dog Arno. Buddy, Leader and Arno are all German Shepherds, who in England are called Alsatians, and the next three seeing eye dogs are golden retrievers. The newest one is a photographic essay about Blythe, who became *Connie's New Eyes*. The other two books are more difficult to read. Rappaport's *Banner Forward! the Pictorial Biography of a Guide Dog* begins with Banner's education with its foster family and ends with his new mistress. Clewes's *Guide Dog* is about nineteen-year-old Roley Rolandson, who lost his sight in an accident.

Students interested in learning how the eye works should read Alder's *Your Eyes* and Elgin's *Human Body: the Eye*. The model of the eye may be borrowed from the library media center for the duration of the project. Books about the senses generally are Simon's *Find Out with Your Senses*, Scott's *Senses—Seeing, Hearing, Smelling, Tasting, Touching*, Schneider's *You and Your Senses*, and Gilmour's *Understanding Your Senses, Easy Experiments for Young People*.

Two adventure books about persons who are blind are Taylor's *The Cay* and Christopher's *Stranded*. Matt Christopher is known to boys who like to read sports fiction, a fact which should be mentioned when introducing *Stranded*. Blind Andy Cassett was washed overboard in the Caribbean and was marooned on an island with his dog Max. In Taylor's book, Philip and an old man are shipwrecked on a cay or island. When Philip was blinded, Timothy taught him survival skills. This book, also available as a sound filmstrip entitled *The Cay*, and as part of the sound filmstrip *Reading for the Fun of It: Adventure*, is set during World War II could be included among the books in this chapter under "Television—The Holocaust." In *Witch's Daughter* by Bawden, blind Janey saved her brother and the witch's daughter when they were trapped in a cave.

A blind author, Beverly Butler, wrote *Light a Single Candle* and *Gift of Gold* about girls who overcame their handicap.

Yolen's *The Seeing Stick* is a delightful book to read aloud to students and then place in the classroom reading corner with other books by Yolen. It has many of the characteristics of a folktale. The princess Hwei Ming was blind from birth and her father, the emperor, promised a fortune in jewels to whomever could help her. Monks, magician-priests and physicians failed, but an old man with a seeing stick succeeded. The old man carved each character and object he saw on his journey to the palace into his stick and then allowed the princess to trace the carvings with her fingers. Since the princess, the emperor and the old man were part of the story, he had her trace their faces as well. The old man told the princess his stories of the present and past, and the princess taught other blind children to see as she saw. In the spirit of a true folktale, the old man gave away the jewels. Students should be allowed to read the book on their own because the illustrations by Charlip and Maraslis, executed in wax crayon and pencil on vellum, must be experienced personally. The illustrations begin in black and white pencil but color is added as the princess is able to "see" more. To introduce the book, read "A note about Hwei Ming's name" at the back of the book, which tells about the poetic names given to Chinese children at birth. The blind princess's poetic name, Hwei Ming, meant "a darkened moon, with the hope of becoming bright and full in the future."

"The Beat of My Heart," an essay by Maryhelen Vannier, appears on pages 76–9 of the fourth-grade supplementary Holt reader, *Sounds of Mystery*. Some books to include in a classroom display are Zim's *Your Heart and How It Works*, Elgin's *The Human Body: The Heart*, and Silverstein's *Circulatory Systems: Rivers Within*. Schools that own the eight sound filmstrips *How Your Body Parts Function* I, should place the filmstrip about the heart and a combination filmstrip-tape player and earphones in the back of the room. Any other filmstrips on the heart should also be placed in that listening corner.

Third graders who have read about the Statue of Liberty and the American flag in the third-grade Macmillan basal, *More Than Words*, may enjoy viewing related filmstrips. The four filmstrips in *The Symbols of Democracy* series include *Our Flag*, *The National Anthem*, *The Statue of Liberty*, and *The Pledge of Allegiance*. The Peter Spier picture book and sound filmstrip in which the U.S. Military Academy glee club sings *The Star Spangled Banner* and related materials, are referred to in "Enhancing Books through Music," in the section called "History and Folklore." The four filmstrips in the series *American Flag in Music, Word and Deed* includes other symbols, the Pledge of Allegiance, and flags which have flown over the United States. Displaying flags is part of the two sound filmstrips called *Our Nation's Flag*. Other filmstrips to include in a listening corner of the classroom are *Betsy Ross*, *Francis Scott Key*, and *United States Flag*. Waller's *A Book to Begin on: Our Flag* and Freeman's *Stars and Stripes* can also be included. Ask students to find books about Betsy Ross, Francis Scott Key, and flags of the world in the card catalog.

Many free and inexpensive materials catalogs have listings of agencies providing pamphlets about flags. Leidy's *A Popular Guide to Government Publications* contains listings of sources from the U.S. Marine Corps, U.S. Post Office, Veterans Administration, House of Representatives, and Smithsonian on page 321 under "U.S.: The Flag." A display of actual flags could also be part of this study. The study of the flag or of Braille could introduce the unit on symbols suggested in chapter 6.

Besides the filmstrip *The Statue of Liberty* from the *Symbols of Democracy* series include the books *This Is New York* by Sasek, *The Story of the Statue of Liberty* by Miller, *Our Statue of Liberty* by Nason, *Meet Miss Liberty* by Patterson, and *The Statue of Liberty Comes to America* by Kraskein in a display. The last book contains the poem "New Colossus" by Emma Lazarus, with the famous "Give me your tired . . . ."

DOLLS. A privately owned doll collection, belonging to one or several persons, can be used with books about dolls for a special display in a locked showcase. Fiction and nonfiction books listed in this section can be interspersed with the dolls. Include the name of the collector, as well as interesting information about the collector and the doll. A picture of the owner, whether student or adult, could be included. Choosing the dolls might be the result of a doll contest with rules and judges, or dolls could be chosen by picking entries out of a hat. In a school, all entries could come from one classroom.

Nonfiction books to include in the display are Hoke's *First Book of Dolls*, Dow's *How to Make Doll Clothes*, Kahame's *Dolls to Make for Fun and Profit*, Jordan's *American Costume Dolls* and *Homemade Dolls in Foreign Dress*, Greenhowe's *Making Costume Dolls*, and Ackley's *Dolls to Make for Fun and Profit*. Young's *Here Is Your Hobby: Doll Collecting* is an essential title to include.

Two paperbacks include Roth's *Dressing Dolls* (which includes seventy patterns) and Jones's *Easy-to-Make Dolls with 19th-Century Costumes* (which includes patterns for dolls and clothes for ten dolls.)

Some books on dollhouses and furniture especially for children are Kahame's *There's a Decorator in Your Doll House*, Roche's *Dollhouse Magic, How to Make and Find Simple Dollhouse Furniture*, and Roth's *Making Dollhouse Accessories*. Paperbacks intended for older audiences are: Midkiff's *Colonial Furniture for Doll Houses and Miniature Rooms*, King's *The International Doll House Book*, Brann's *How to Build Dollhouses and Furniture*, Joyner's *Dollhouse Construction and Restoration*, Dickey's *How to Light a Doll House*, and three books of scaled plans by Dieber, *The Concord, Pepperwood Farm*, and *Wildflower Manor*. Dollhouses and books about making and furnishing them would also make an interesting display.

Soft toys made in home economics classes to be given with books as children's gifts can be included in a display. Friedericksen's *The Pooh Craft Book* includes patterns for all of Christopher Robin's animal friends. Greenhowe's *Making Costume Dolls* contains patterns for twenty-six figures. Roth's *The Art of Making Cloth Toys* includes patterns for the owl and the pussycat and the three bears. Books for making cloth and wooden toys appear in chapter 2 of this book, "Experiencing Art through Picture Books," in a section called "Toys from Children's Books."

A display called "Toys from Children's Books" could include Milne's *Winnie-the-Pooh* and other stories and stuffed toys about Christopher Robin and his friends, the paperbacks *Raggedy Ann Stories* and *Raggedy Andy Stories* by Gruelle, Williams's *The Velveteen Rabbit*, Young's *The Witch*, Waber's *Ira Sleeps Over*, Godall's *The Misadventures of Kelly, Dot and Esmeralda*, Collier's *Teddy Bear Habbit* and Jackson's *Missing Melinda*. Place *Missing Melinda* and *Caroline's Courage* next to a china doll. Place a teddy bear beside *Teddy Bear Habbit* and *Ira Sleeps Over*.

An entire display could be made using mobiles inspired by *The Witch Mobile*—a book about a little girl who is finally able to afford the little witch doll after the mobile is broken.

Other dolls can inspire projects. Beach's *Drusilla* is a cornhusk doll taken by her mistress to Minnesota in a covered wagon. Cornhusk dolls made by students can accompany the book in a display. Directions for making cornhusk dolls appear on pages 142 and 143 of Fiorotta's *The You and Me Heritage Tree*, chapter 6 of Rogowski's *Making American Folk Art Dolls*, Wendorff's *How to Make Cornhusk Dolls*, and chapter 13 of Pettit's *How to Make Whirligigs and Whimmydiddles and Other American Folkcraft Objects*. Twelve pages of step-by-step illustrations for making the dolls are given in the last book, while ten steps with explicit directions are given in Hoople's *The Heritage Sampler*. Displays provide a chance for students to "show off" projects they have made. Always be sure to display books which are useful in making the projects to reinforce the idea that books are valuable tools.

Another doll who traveled in a covered wagon from New Hampshire to Nebraska was Mary Lou, in Yates's *Caroline's Courage*. Mary Lou, like Jackson's *Missing Melinda*, was a china doll.

Bailey's *Miss Hickory*, which won the 1947 Newbery Medal, had a hickory nut for a head and an apple twig for a body, and could easily be recreated. Hickory nut dolls are included in Fiorotta's *The You and Me Heritage Tree* with directions for making apple head, wishbone, clothespin, chestnut, walnut head, prune, corn cob, cornhusk, potato, gourds and pine cone dolls. Heady's *Make Your Own Dolls* tells how to make cornhusk, corn cob, sock, flower, clothespin, chalk, bottle, stick, grass, bone, soap, spool, pipe cleaner, yarn, bread, magazine, and rag dolls.

Hitty: Her First Hundred Years by Fields was the 1930 Newbery winner. Like Bianca's *The Little Wooden Doll*, Hitty was made of wood, and became a world traveler during her first hundred years.

Another hundred-year-old doll was found and given a whole new wardrobe. Ayre's *Little Silk* takes place in Hong Kong.

Other dolls from around the world include Coatsworth's *The Noble Doll*, illustrated by Leo Politi. Rosita is Mexican and attends a posada and sees pinatas. Lownsbery's *Marta the Doll* depicts life in Poland. In Ishii's *The Dolls' Day*, Yoshiko wants special dolls of her own to celebrate Dolls' Day in Japan. In Parrish's *The Floating Island*, a doll family is shipwrecked on a tropical island.

Two books about dolls that would win a contest for the warmest books are *William's Doll* by Zolotow and *A Is for Annabelle* by Tudor. Everyone except his grandmother made fun of William when he asked for a doll because she knew it would be a good preparation for fatherhood. A song about the book appears in the book and film *Free to Be. . .You and Me* by Marlo Thomas. *A Is for Annabelle* is an alphabet book in rhyme illustrated in soft colors to give it a typical "old-fashioned" Tudor flavor. In another book by Tudor, *The Doll's Christmas*, two dolls entertain their friends at Christmas with a marionette show. *Miss Flora McFlimsey's Christmas Eve* is about an old forgotten and broken doll who came down on Christmas Eve to see the tree. In *Miss Flora McFlimsey's Easter Bonnet*, a rabbit made a hat just like the one in Miss Flora's dream. Those books are by Foster.

Did you know that all dolls come alive and speak on Christmas Eve? Besides Miss Flora, *Big Susan* by Jones also comes alive. Another personified doll appears in Carl Sandburg's picture book *The Wedding Procession of the Rag Doll and the Broom Handle Was in It*. That story comes from Sandburg's *Rootabaga Stories*.

Rumer Godden has written six books about dolls. *The Doll's House* is about Marchpane who disrupts life at the doll house. In *Candy Floss*, it is a little girl who isn't very nice. *Fairy Doll* is a doll given to a clumsy girl to be her good fairy. The story of *Holly and Ivy* is about a doll who was given to an orphan girl. *Miss Happiness and Miss Flower* is about dolls in a Japanese dollhouse and an unhappy little girl sent from India to live in England with cousins. *Impunity Jane* was played with by boys who had her steer boats and rocket ships. Another small doll is Johnston's *Sugarplum*.

McGinley's *The Most Beautiful Doll in the World* would be the first book to introduce when giving a book talk about dolls. Angela existed in the imagination of a girl named Dulcy. This story in rhyme is about how the first doll in the world might have been invented by a girl and her understanding mother. The same feelings are understood by William's grandmother when she understood why he needed a doll. Introduce *William's Doll* by Zolotow next.

Another book that is interesting to tell about is Jackson's *Missing Melinda*, whose story and suggestions for introducing it are described earlier in this chapter in the section on reading aloud to students. *The Teddy Bear Habbit* is a toy bear who became the carrier for stolen jewels. Although they are not the world's greatest pieces of children's literature, stories about Raggedy Ann and Andy are almost a folk tradition and the dolls appear on everything from curtains to planters. Students may be interested to know that the author was inspired to write the books because his daughter found a rag doll in an old trunk. The doll had been made by her great-grandmother for her grandmother. The first book was published in 1918 and over ten million books have been sold. "Raggedy Ann and the Kite" in *Raggedy Ann Stories* (pp. 33–42) could be read or retold. In that story, the rag doll was tied to the tail of a kite but broke loose, sailed away and landed near a robin's nest in a tree. The two letters in *Raggedy Ann Stories* (pp. 9–12) made an interesting introduction to the second book.

MEET THE MONSTERS.   Teachers and librarians can capitalize on the special interests of children that can lead to reading, listening, and viewing more materials on those subjects. Interest in monsters never seems to fade. Minotaurs and Gorgons come from classical mythology. Dragons abound in folklore. Television and newspapers periodically feature the Loch Ness Monster, the Abominable Snowman, and Big Foot or Sasquatch. Vampires and monsters from movies in theatres and on television and in comics include Dr. Frankenstein's monster, Dracula, and King Kong.

The sound filmstrip *Dracula* from the Folklore and Fable Series by *Scholastic* includes information about vampire lore from legend and literature. Eighth graders would enjoy seeing the filmstrip and carrying out the projects which include a radio play and the diary of a vampire. Scientific explanations for vampire bats, Dracula, and ghosts and zombies from around the world are given in Aylesworth's *Vampires and Other Ghosts*. Another book by the same author, *Movie Monsters*, gives more information about Frankenstein, King Kong, and Dracula.

The films *Frankenstein* and *Dracula* are both included in the "125 Feature Films" in Zornow and Goldstein's *Movies for Kids*. Dracula received two and a half stars in Scheuer's *Movies on TV* and three and a half out of four stars in Maltin's *TV Movies*. *Frankenstein* received three out of four stars in both Scheuer and Maltin's books. Both films were first released in 1931. Other films about the two monsters were not as well received. The book *Frankenstein* was written by Mary Shelley; the book about *Dracula* by Bram Stoker. Both books are available in numerous paperback editions. Books with pictures for reluctant readers by Thorne are *Godzilla, King Kong*, and *Frankenstein*. Also consider introducing Cohen's *The Greatest Monsters in the World*.

Interest is also high in the legendary Big Foot or Sasquatch of the Northwest. Place's *On the Track of Bigfoot* includes a bibliography of books and magazine articles about Bigfoot and information about where and when the monster has been seen. Byrne's *The Search for Big Foot, Monster, Myth or Man*, contains similar information. Two fiction books are *Rocky Mountain Monster* by Williams and *A Darkness of Giants* by Bosworth. In Williams's book, sixth-grader Martin Drosler made friends with Sasquatch. The most exciting part of the book is the twelve pages of facsimiles of news stories about Big Foot. In Bosworth's book, Greg was turned down for a photographer's job at a newspaper, decided that getting a picture of Bigfoot would be impressive, and set out to find him.

Bauman's *The Loch Ness Monster*, Cornell's *The Monster of Loch Ness*, and Benedict's *Mystery of the Loch Ness Monster*, contain information about that Scottish beast; a chapter is included in Buehr's *Sea Monsters*. Soule's *The Trail of the Abominable Snowman* tells of the beast that has supposedly inhabited the Himalayas for a hundred and forty years. A bibliography is included.

Giants, ogres, trolls, the Abominable Snowman and Loch Ness Monster are included in McHargue's *The Beasts of Never; a History Natural and Unnatural of Monsters Mythical and Magical*. Dragons, the basilisk, werewolfs, the

Phoenix, the Loch Ness Monster, and the Abominable Snowman are included in Krutch's *The Most Wonderful Animals That Ever Were*. Unicorns, dragons, beasts of the zodiac and heraldry, as well as the Loch Ness Monster and Abominable Snowman, are included in Jacobson's *First Book of Mythical Beasts*. The Loch Ness Monster, the Abominable Snowman, Sasquatch, the sphinx, the unicorn, and sea monsters are found in Quinn's *Land and Sea Monsters*.

Contemporary monsters can be used to introduce the classical ones—the Minotaur, Medusa, and Grendel. Several sources for Kingsley's version of the tale of the Minotaur and Theseus who killed him are *Theseus, a Greek Legend Retold* (pp. 100–06 of *A Golden Land* by Reeves, and pp. 163–212 of the Macmillan edition and pp. 125–165 of the Dutton edition of Kingsley's *The Heroes*). Stories of Theseus are told in *Book of Greek Myths* by the d'Aulaires, Colum's *The Golden Fleece and Heroes Who Lived before Achilles*, Hamilton's *Mythology*, and Gates's *The Lord of the Sky: Zeus*. Another book is Serrailler's *The Way of Danger: the Story of Theseus*. Theseus also appears in Evslin's *Heroes and Monsters of Greek Mythology* and in White's *The Golden Treasury of Myths and Legends*.

Stories of Icarus and his son Daedalus can also be introduced because Icarus built the labyrinth that held the Minotaur and built wings to escape from it. Stories of Icarus appear in this book's chapter 6 in a section called "Magic Numbers in Children's Literature—Two."

Perseus slew the Gorgon Medusa. Stories appear in Evslin's *Heroes and Monsters of Greek Mythology* and White's *The Golden Treasury of Myths and Legends*, as well as in Serraillier's *The Gorgon's Head: the Story of Perseus*. Stories also appear in Hamilton's *Mythology*, in the Macmillan edition and in the Dutton edition of Kingsley's *The Heroes*, Gates's *The Warrior Goddess: Athena*, Lang's *Blue Fairy Book*, and Johnson's *Anthology of Children's Literature*.

Beowulf, the hero of an old English saga, was involved with a monster called Grendel and his mother. Stories appear in Picard's *Tales of the British People*, Hazeltine's *Hero Tales from Many Lands*, White's *The Golden Treasury of Myths and Legends*, Johnson's *Anthology of Children's Literature*, and Gran's *A Cavalcade of Dragons*. Individual books are Serraillier's *Beowulf the Warrior* and Hosford's *By His Own Might, the Battles of Beowulf*. In introducing, paraphrase Beowulf from page 1 to 14, and then read pages 14 to 18 of Hosford's chapter "Beowulf's Encounter with Grendel." "How the Mother of Grendel Avenges His Death" appears on pages 23 to 38, and "How Beowulf Seeks Out Grendel's Mother in Her Lair Beneath the Sea" appears on pages 28 to 32. The recording *Beowulf and the Monsters* is narrated by Mabie Hamilton Wright and gives the story of Beowulf and Grendel on one side, and tells the history of Beowulf and the Anglo-Saxons on the other.

Gilgamesh and the Monster in the Wood is a recommended filmstrip, as are four silent captioned filmstrips called *Ghost Stories*, one of them called *The Vampires Die at Midnight*.

Monsters for little children are often more charming than frightening. A set of five sound filmstrips for little children is called *Monsters and Other Friendly Creatures*. "The Strawberry Monster's March" is sung off-key in *Andrew and* the Strawberry Monster. The whole filmstrip Emil the Tap Dancing Frog is told in song. Other titles are Monsters in the Closet, Monster Seeds, and Charlie and the Caterpillar. Suggested readings and correlation possibilities with other EB films are included.

Several rather tame books about monsters can be read or introduced to small children. Children find Viorst's My Mama Says There Aren't Any Zombies, Ghosts, Vampires, Creatures, Demons, Monsters, Fiends, Goblins, or Things funny when it is read to them. The boy wants to believe his mother, but he cites several humorous instances in which his mother had made a mistake. Children will enjoy looking at this book by themselves. Another monster one to enjoy by themselves is Mendoza's wordless book The Inspector. The Inspector and his hounds walk along swamps, cliffs, and other areas but do not see the monsters that are lurking there. Virginia Kahl's How Do You Hide a Monster? is best read aloud. The boy in Gackenback's Harry and the Terrible Watzit is positive that there is a terrible Watzit in his basement. Dorrie the little witch has nightmares in Dorrie and the Dreamland Monsters by Coombs. In Zion's Harry by the Sea, the dog Harry, covered with seaweed, is mistaken for a sea monster at the beach. Craig's Little Monsters contains eighteen color and black and white photographic close-ups and enlargements that make vampire bats, porcupine fish, the wolf spider, and other creatures look like monsters.

Several poetry anthologies contain poems about monsters. Brewton's Shrieks at Midnight, Macabre Poems, Eerie and Humorous is about all types of beasts, ghosts, and ghouls. According to the foreword, the ". . . macabre verses also have a touch of humor—grave humor." Prelutsky's The Snopp on the Sidewalk and Other Poems contains poems about Snopps, Wrimples, Wozzits, Splatts, and Flonsters. Another Prelutsky book is called Nightmares, Poems to Trouble Your Sleep. James Whitcomb Riley's poem "Little Orphant Annie," written in 1885, was made into the picture book The Gobble-uns'll Git You Ef You Don't Watch Out! Although Ciardi's anthology is entitled The Monster Den, or Look What Happened at My House—and to It, the fifteen poems are really about his children. The poem on page 15 is called "The Monster Den" in which Ciardi says he and his wife intended to have human children.

Monster jokes appear in Fox's Jokes and How to Tell Them. On page 79, readers learn why Frankenstein won't play baseball with Dracula. Sarnoff and Ruffins's The Monster Riddle Book is fun for all ages.

"Beauty is only skin deep" is the moral of several stories, the most famous of which is "Beauty and the Beast." Sources for that story appear in the chapter called "Playing Stories: Live Action and with Puppets," in a section of "Plays from Favorite Stories." Another version of the story comes from Africa. Gyerna's picture book Princess of the Full Moon is about a princess who scorned every suitor because he was not perfect, then married the "perfect" prince who was really a monster and was rescued by the love of a deformed shepherd. In a similar story, "Tola and the Sea Monster," in Haskett's Grains of Pepper, Folk Tales from Liberia (pp. 26–32), the girl is rescued by her ugly brother who could turn himself into a fly. See the index to Ireland's Index to Fairy Tales, 1949–72 for other stories to tell about beasts, monsters, and dragons.

One of the favorite dragon stories is Grahame's *The Reluctant Dragon*. Long ago, a boy made friends with an unusual dragon who wrote poetry, especially sonnets, instead of terrorizing people. Even so, he was a dragon—so St. George was asked to come and exterminate him. The boy arranged a mock fight and all ended well. Boris Karloff narrates the sound recording. Warburg has adapted Spenser's poem in the book *Saint George and the Dragon; Being the Legend of the Red Cross Knight from the Faerie Queen*. Plays about St. George appear in the chapter on "Playing Stories: Live Action and With Puppets." The story "St. George and The Dragon" appears on pages 82 to 86 of Green's *A Cavalcade of Dragons*.

Other anthologies to include in a monster display are Arnott's *Dragons, Ogres, and Scary Things, Two African Tales*; Elwood's *Monster Tales, Vampires, Werewolves and Things*, and Spicer's *Thirteen Monsters*. Books by Manning-Sanders are *A Book of Monsters, A Book of Dragons, A Book of Magical Beasts*, and *A Book of Devils and Demons*.

Monster books can be introduced through the display, captioned "Meet the Monsters," or through television, newspaper, and magazine accounts about Bigfoot, the Abominable Snowman, and the Loch Ness Monster. Films playing locally in theaters and on television can introduce classic monsters. Storytelling can include monsters, new and old. Other ways to encourage students to read is to provide them with captioned filmstrips, picture books, and poems about monsters.

MICE ARE NICE.   Over a hundred stories are listed under the heading "Mice" in Ireland's *Index to Fairy Tales, 1949–1972*, not including titles beginning with the word "mouse" or the subject "Dormice." Children, unlike most adults, love mice! A display of books about mice could appear in the library media center when stories about mice are being told. In addition to those stories in Ireland's index, there are stories that could be included because mice play an important role in the story, such as "Dick Whittington and His Cat," "Puss 'n Boots," "The Lion and the Mouse," "Why the Dog and Cat are Enemies," "How the Foxes Became Red," "Belling the Cat," "Cat and Mouse in Partnership," "The Flea," and "The Cock, the Mouse and the Little Red Hen."

A story hour program could include a story told and picture books read like Galdone's version of *The Town Mouse and the Country Mouse*, Gag's *Snippy and Snappy*. Participants could join in singing along with the sound filmstrip *The Complete Version of Ye Three Blind Mice* based on a picture book by Ivimey, and *Frog Went A-Courtin'* based on a picture book by Langstaff, since the young lady that frog courted was a Miss Mouse. The story "Snippy and Snappy" also appears in Greinberg's *Let's Read a Story*. Roach's *Two Roman Mice* includes Horace's original Latin text for the story of this town and country mouse. Belpre's *Perez and Martina* is a favorite folk tale from Puerto Rico about Senorita Martina, a Spanish cockroach who chose Perez Mouse from among many, many suitors.

Intermediate students will enjoy hearing the story "The Bee, the Harp, the Mouse and the Bum Clock." Have students act out the story according to the directions included in the chapter on "Playing Stories: Live-Action and with Puppets."

Shaw's The Mouse Book is a collection of stories and poems about mice illustrated by seventeen different artists including a six-year-old boy. Shimin and Duvoisin are among the artists featured. Unfortunately, the medium used by each illustrator is not given as it was for Shaw's The Fox Book. Included is a poem by Rose Fyleman which makes a good caption for a book display or bulletin board: MICE ARE NICE. Fyleman's poem begins "I think mice/Are rather nice." The poem goes on to tell why some people don't like mice. The typed poem might accompany the caption on the bulletin board. Students could be asked to find other poems about mice.

Another project about mice could be a festival featuring famous mouse characters like Miller's Mousekin, Cleary's Ralph, and two Titus characters, Anatole and Basil. Or, combine characters and have an author festival about Potter, Titus, Lionni, Oakley, Freeman, Steig, Sharp and Seldon—each of whom have written books about several mice or several books about one mouse.

The four small picture books for primary students about mice by Beatrix Potter have been loved by generations of children. There is The Story of Miss Moppet and The Tale of Mrs. Tittlemouse, and there is The Tale of Two Bad Mice. But best of all, perhaps, there is the story of The Tailor of Gloucester, and how the friendly little mice worked on Christmas Eve to finish the Mayor's elaborate coat while Simpkin the Cat's round and hungry face stared at them through the window. When they ran out, at the end, of cherry colored silk, they left a note in tiny, tiny mouse writing, "no more twist." The lovely porcelain figurine of Mrs. Tittlemouse, made in England, would be a great addition to the display case.

The most famous mouse is Anatole, the French mouse who earned his living tasting cheese in a Paris cheese factory. The book Anatole can introduce all of the other books because it tells how Anatole took the job so he could retain his dignity and not be accused of stealing cheese. In Anatole and the Cat, his job was made more difficult by a cat at the factory. In Anatole and the Thirty Thieves, Anatole helped catch thieves who are stealing from the factory. In Anatole and the Piano, Anatole was given a museum-piece minature piano for helping some orphans. Anatole's whole family was carried up and away over Paris when Anatole fixed a kite for his children in Anatole Over Paris. The family had further adventures when they were captured and forced to ride toy bicycles in a store window to promote business in Anatole and the Toyshop.

Another mouse created by Titus is introduced in Basil of Baker Street, a mouse version of Sherlock Holmes. Another title about the mouse detective is Basil and the Pygmy Cats.

Beverly Cleary's mouse Ralph has become almost as much a favorite as Henry Huggins or Beezus and Ramona. In The Mouse and the Motorcycle, Keith, the boy in Room 215 of the hotel where Ralph lived, had a toy motorcycle. Pages 23 to 27 tell how Ralph got the motorcycle to run and how he fell into the wastepaper basket. Read these pages to yourself and paraphrase or read them aloud to students. Then leave Ralph in the wastepaper basket and ask students if they think he ever got out. *Runaway Ralph* is the sequel to *The Mouse and the Motorcycle*. Read chapter one to review how Ralph got his motorcycle and to establish why he wanted to run away to the summer camp.

Mouse House by Rumer Godden is also a fantasy. Bonnie Mouse moved from the crowded flower pot in the basement to a jewelry box shaped like a house which held two cloth mice.

Another story containing a famous mouse has sequels. Children who saw or can be told about the television performance of the book *Cricket in Times Square* can be introduced to *Harry Cat's Pet Puppy* and *Tucker's Countryside*. In the first book, Tucker a mouse, Chester a cricket, and Harry a cat, live in the Times Square subway station and are friends with Mario Bellini, a boy whose parents own the newstand there. The cat acquired a puppy in the second story, and the animals moved to Connecticut in the third book. Much of the story *Cricket in Times Square* appears on the sound filmstrip *Fantasy*, and is used to help explain what fantasy is. Chester Cricket tours New York City in a picture book called *Chester Cricket's Pigeon Ride.*

Students may have seen the animated Disney movie *The Rescuers* based on a book that is a sequel to Sharp's *Miss Bianca*. In *Miss Bianca*, the mouse told the Prisoners' Aid Society about the girl named Patience who needed to be rescued from the evil Duchess who had kidnapped her and taken her to the Diamond Palace. In *The Rescuers*, the Prisoners' Aid Society freed a Norwegian poet who was held in Black Castle.

In Beskow's *The Astonishing Adventures of Patrick the Mouse*, an eight-year-old Swedish mouse is kidnapped and helps catch a gang of criminals. The book could be introduced to the same readers who enjoyed *Miss Bianca* and *The Rescuers.*

Miss Bianca was one of the mice that Broderick the mouse admired. Other mice about whom Ormondroyd's Broderick read and admired were Norman the Doorman, Amos of *Ben and Me*, and Anatole. A bibliography of titles about these other story mice appears in Ormondroyd's book and can be used to introduce these and other books about mice. After reading about these other famous mice, Broderick wanted to leave his mark on the world too, by doing something no mouse had ever done before. He did in another book. He sandpapered and waxed an old tongue depressor and, after much practice, mastered the art of surfing and caused a sensation. The vocabulary of surfing is included. After his world tour, Broderick made a documentary film, retired and wrote his memoirs, and sent an anonymous donation to the library to pay for chewing up bindings in his youth. The picture of Broderick on pages 2 and 3 reading a book is priceless.

Another mouse who curled up with books and read about mice in other times and other places was Victor, a city mouse. In Berson's *A Moose is Not a Mouse*, Victor saw a picture of a moose in a book and thought that moose was a strange way to spell mouse.

Freeman's *Norman the Doorman* is a mouse doorman at a famous museum. While Norman was an art lover, his cousin Petrini was a music lover. Petrini, *Pet of the Met*, lived in New York's Metropolitan Opera House, where during the

"The Magic Flute," he met a music-hating cat on stage.

Another favorite mouse of Broderick's was Amos the Mouse from Lawson's *Ben and Me.* (Who has been a favorite also of readers for nearly forty years.) Introduce Amos to third and fourth graders by asking them to list inventions of Ben Franklin. After students have listed lightning rods, spectacles, the Franklin stove, and other inventions, tell them that these items were really invented by Amos the Mouse. Answer the groans of disbelief by telling students to read *Ben and Me,* and they will understand the facts for themselves as they are written down by Amos. Also mention that Lawson's *Mr. Revere and I* was written by Paul Revere's horse, who was really responsible for the famous ride.

Another mouse figured in a great historical event. According to Wenning's *Christmas Mouse,* Kaspar Kleinmous chewed holes in the organ bellows so "Silent Night" was played for the very first time in 1818 in St. Nicholas Church by Father Joseph Mohr on a guitar.

Oakley's *The Church Mouse* concerns Arthur and his friends who did odd jobs for the parson in return for cheese. Sampson the cat and the mice caught a burglar. Sampson was the protector of the mice. The characters appear in *The Church Cat Abroad, The Church Mice Spread Their Wings,* and *The Church Mice Adrift.* These books are best read by someone to one or two children or by the child for himself, because often the words say one thing and the pictures say another, with hilarious results. For example, Sampson explained on one adventure that they were going through the Sahara Desert, when readers can plainly see in the pictures that they are merely walking through a sand and gravel pit.

Another story in which a cat is a friend of mice is Yeoman's *Mouse Trouble.* A miller did not want mice in his mill so he bought a cat. The miller treated the cat badly, and it wasn't successful at its job. The mice felt sorry for the cat and when the miller put him in a bag to drown, the mice rescued him.

In E. B. White's fantasy, *Stuart Little,* the second son of a human family was a mouse. Beautifully written by one of the most elegant prose stylists of our time, this story caused consternation and criticism among children's librarians when it first came out but children have loved it from the first and it has become a modern classic.

The same age group would enjoy Steig's *Abel's Island.* Abel mouse and his wife Amanda were swept from their home and left on an uninhabited island. In another Steig book, *Amos and Boris* are friends. Amos is a mouse and Boris is a whale.

Leo Lionni has written and illustrated three picture books in which the main character is a mouse. The illustrations of all three mice are very similar. In *Alexander and the Wind-Up Mouse,* Alexander wanted to be loved like Willie the toy mouse until he learned that Willie would be discarded as an old toy. Instead of being changed into a toy, Alexander asked that Willie be turned into a real mouse. Do you think he was? *Frederick* daydreamed during the summer while everyone else worked, but during the winter he kept everyone cheerful with his poetry. *Theodore and the Talking Mushroom* is about a mouse and his friends lizard, frog, and turtle who lived in an old stump. Because all three of the mice look similar, make a large mouse that looks like them and put it on a bulletin board and caption it "Is this Alexander, Frederick or Theodore?" A subheading could be "Read and find out," and list the titles.

Two books intended for individual enjoyment are Goodall's *Shrewbettina's Birthday* and Emberley's *A Birthday Wish*. In the first, a wordless book, a mouse helped the shrew have a wonderful birthday. In the second, also wordless, a mouse wished for an ice cream cone when he blew out his birthday candle, and a chain reaction was set in force that granted his wish.

Kumin's and Sexton's *Joey and the Birthday Present* is also about birthdays. Joey, a field mouse, made friends with Prince, a tame white mouse.

In Wahl's *Pleasant Fieldmouse*, fieldmouse, beaver, and tortoise rescued Mrs. Worry-Wind Hedgehog from a fox and an owl.

There are several mouse books especially for primary students. Six-year-old Jonathan took his jeep-driving mouse to show and tell in *School Mouse* by Harris. Hurd's *Come and Have Fun* and Lobel's *Mouse Tales* are both easy readers from the Harper I-Can-Read series. In the first, a cat wanted a mouse to come out and play, but the mouse knew why cat wanted him out of his house. There are seven separate *Mouse Tales*. *Whose Mouse Are You?* by Kraus is a story in rhyme about a mouse who felt left out until he had an opportunity to rescue his family. In *Something for Christmas* by Palmer Brown, a little mouse wanted to make a surprise Christmas present for his mother.

Eichenberg's *Dancing in the Moon, Counting Rhymes* contains fourteen mice skating on ice. Have children check alphabet and counting books for other pictures of mice.

Watercolors illustrate the Caldecott honor book *Mice Twice*, a cat and mouse tale written and illustrated by Low.

Edna Miller has many picture books about a mouse named Mousekin. Much information about the whitefoot mouse is included in these stories: *Mousekin's Christmas Eve*, *Mousekin's Golden House*, and *Mousekin's Woodland Sleeper* are seasonal books. The last one is about hibernation. *Mousekin's ABC* is a favorite alphabet book. *Mousekin Finds a Friend*, *Mousekin's Family*, and *Mousekin's Woodland Birthday* are about life in the woods. Display these books with a caged white foot mouse labeled "Mousekin."

Several nonfiction books to be included in a display of books about mice are by Hess, Freschet, and Earle. *Mouse and Company* by Hess contains large black and white photos. Most of the book concerns the female deer mouse who left home and began the life cycle. (A deer mouse is similar to a white-footed mouse.) Information about rats, gerbils, and hamsters and how to raise them is also included. Freschet's *Bear Mouse* is about a mother bear mouse who went out to get food for her week-old babies while other animals and birds such as the fox, owl, and bobcat are out to eat her. *Mice at Home and Afield* by Earle includes house mouse, Japanese waltzing mouse, Autumn harvest mouse, deer mouse, jumping mouse, rock mouse, pocket mouse, grasshopper mouse, scorpion mouse, and several kinds of mouse-like voles, one of which is the meadow vole—better known as field mice. Mice also are included in books about animals and mammals such as Zim and Hoffmeister's *Mammals, a Guide to Familiar American Species*.

FOXY BOOKS.   Foxes can be the subject of classroom study or the focus of a variety of activities radiating from the library media center. Gather together all of the books included in this section and place them on a counter display or in a showcase. Puppets and stuffed toy foxes can be included. "Foxy Books" makes a good caption. Use a large fox made by enlarging a picture on the opaque projector for the focus of the bulletin board. A unit on foxes could include folk tales told to or read by students, factual information about foxes, reading or listening to stories about foxes, drawing foxes, or comparing the conceptions of different artists. Project ideas will be suggested as books are introduced in this section.

Foxes abound in folktales and folk song. Peter Spier illustrated the folk song *Fox Went Out on a Chilly Night*, a beautiful picture book that is also available as a sound filmstrip. Another filmstrip and book is *Chanticleer and the Fox*, which is the "Nun's Priest's Tale" from Chaucer's *Canterbury Tales*. Barbara Cooney illustrated this 1959 Caldecott Medal winner. A fox caught Chanticleer by trickery—he flattered the rooster into singing with his eyes closed and grabbed him. But Chanticleer later "outfoxed" the fox. This picture book can be read to introduce Ginsberg's collection of nine stories *One Trick Too Many, Fox Stories from Russia*.

Three of the more famous Aesop tales concern foxes and are found in *Three Fox Tales* illustrated by Galdone. The stories are "The Fox and the Grapes," "The Fox and the Stork," and "The Fox and the Crow." Fox served soup to stork in shallow dishes so stork served soup to fox in a long-necked vase. The story makes an excellent introduction to the Anansi story "Anansi and His Visitor, Turtle," in Kaula's *African Village Folktales*. Compare the cleverness of crane and turtle. Another story which includes a fox that can be compared with an Anansi story is Merrill's *High, Wide and Handsome*. In Merrill's story, High (a monkey), Wide (a pig), and Handsome (a fox) and a visiting hound named Rolling Stone are the participants in a story contest in which the loser will become the slave of the winner. In "The Liar's Contest" (pp. 25–9) in Courlander's *Hat Shaking Dance*, a fly, moth and mosquito and Anansi the Spider tell similar stories in a contest.

Foxey Loxey is a familiar folk tale character who appears in many versions of Henny Penny. Sources for other versions are given in the chapter, "Playing Stories: Live-Action and With Puppets." Compare the illustrations in Galdone's picture book *Henny Penny* with the foxes in the Aesop's tales *Three Fox Fables*, illustrated also by Galdone.

Preston's *Squawk to the Moon Little Goose*, illustrated by Cooney, contains elements of Aesop's "The Boy Who Cried Wolf." A little gosling disobeyed its mother, was caught by the fox, bothered the farmer so many times that he thought her squawking was a false alarm, but was saved by the fox's greed.

According to Maria Leach's *Standard Dictionary of Folklore, Mythology and Legend* the epic of Reynard appeared in Europe in the eleventh century and achieved its height of popularity in the fourteenth and fifteenth centuries. The stories were written by unknown writers and satirized the church, knighthood, and lawyers. Some of those stories were connected with the literary fables of Aesop, others with the lore of the hunt. Reynard (which means "fox" in French) is the name used in many fox stories. Astrid Lindgren adapted a poem to produce *The Tompten and the Fox*. The Tompten, a small gnome-like denizen of Scandinavia, gave Reynard porridge each night so the fox wouldn't eat the hens. The illustrations are outstanding and can be enjoyed in sound filmstrip format.

Anita Lobel has retold a Danish folktale in an easy reader in the Read-Alone series called *King Rooster, Queen Hen*. The rooster and hen declared themselves king and queen and forced some mice to pull their carriage. "The Royal Couple" met, among other animals, a fox who invited them for dinner, but alert sparrow noticed the peculiar setting of the table and arranged an escape. Like Chaucer's Chanticleer, the rooster almost lost his life by puffing himself up to sing.

In LeFevre's *The Cock, the Mouse and the Little Red Hen*, the fox was bested at his own evil game by the Little Red Hen.

Hogrogian's Caldecott winning *One Fine Day* is an Armenian folk tale about a fox whose tail was chopped off, who sought help from a succession of animals and people in a fine repetitive tale.

Marcia Brown's *The Neighbors* is about a hare who made a house of bark and a fox who made a house of ice. When his house melted, fox chased hare out of his house and hare complained to wolf, bear, and a cock—the last of which succeeded in scaring fox out of hare's house.

Father Fox's Pennyrhymes by Clyde Watson are New England nonsense rhymes illustrated in watercolors by her sister Wendy. Clyde Watson's *Tom Fox and the Apple Pie* was also illustrated by Wendy. Tom Fox was one of fourteen little foxes, and his story can be used to reinforce the number 16, 8, 4, 2, and 1.

Many of William Steig's stories are like folktales. In *The Amazing Bone*, Pearl Pig found a magic bone that saved her from robbers. However, a fox abducted Pearl and the bone. Pearl made the fox grow smaller until he scurried into a mouse hole. In Tombert's engaging *Little Fox Goes to the End of the World*, the little fox told his mother all of the adventures he planned to go on. Harlequin disobeyed his parents and went to the valley where he was seen by the gamekeeper who told the squire who organized a hunt. However, Harlequin saved his family from the hunt by leading them into the swamp in Burningham's *Harlequin, the Fox Who Went Down the Valley*.

In Miles's *Fox and the Fire*, a fox had to give up chasing rabbits, mice, squirrels, and quail because of a forest fire. Instead, fox raided a henhouse. The blue-grey and red colors, along with black and white, provide a special mood for the book.

Fox in Socks by Seuss, a favorite easy reader, is also available as one of six filmstrips in a recommended set called *Beginner Books Filmstrips IV*.

Fox tracks which show running, walking, and loping gaits are a prelude and finale for Eberle's *Foxes Live Here*. Full-page black and white photos show a red fox family from two days old to maturity. The tracks of a red fox appear on pp. 64-65 of Mason's interesting *Animal Tracks*. Fox tracks in black ink could cover large red letters of a bulletin board caption. Photos also appear in Hess's *Foxes in the Woodshed*, which follows the growth of red foxes from birth to mating. Red, grey and Arctic foxes appear in Ripper's *Foxes and Wolves*. Pencil drawings and information about coyotes, wolves, wolverines and domestic dogs is also included.

Five stories for intermediate and middle school students focus on foxes. Betsy Byars's *The Midnight Fox* will interest even those who are not animal lovers because ten-year-old Tom is a likable and believable character. Tom did not want to leave his home and his friend Petie to spend the summer on a farm while his parents are bicycling through Europe, until he saw the black fox. Read aloud page 45 from the end of Tom's letter to the end of page 46 ". . . she was gone." to capture the excitement and to stimulate interest in the book.

Four children visiting from Paris saw foxes in Baudouy's *Old One-Toe*. Near the old mill a red fox was raising her recent litter and was teaching them to hunt their own food and avoid enemies.

Vulpes, The Red Fox is an outstanding story and authentic natural science, too, by Jean and John George.

Red Fox, written by Roberts in 1905, shows the life cycle of a red fox in Eastern Canada. The story began with the father fox giving up his life to keep the hunter and dogs away from the den where the vixen and still-blind pups were. Roberts, like the Georges, provides a book in which animals keep their own characteristics even though the world is seen through their eyes.

Burnkett's *Foxes Three* is about three ten-day old foxes and a wildlife center.

Dillon's *A Family of Foxes* is more difficult to read than the other fox stories, and includes the superstition that foxes are evil, bring bad luck, and can turn themselves into people. In China and Japan, foxes are also accused of transforming themselves. Foxes are included in Platt's *Magic Animals of Japan*. For folktales about foxes, consult Ireland's *Index to Fairy Tales, 1949–72*. Over 250 stories about foxes are listed.

These fox books provide a variety of styles and mediums. Ginsberg's *One Trick Too Many* is executed in woodcuts, which provide a different mood from the illustrations in Hutchins's *Rosie's Walk*. The illustrations fit the story and provide most of the humor. Rosie, a chicken, unwittingly leads the fox who is following her into one hilarious disaster after another. Nonverbal communication also characterizes *Foxie* by the d'Aulaires. A recap of the story in twelve cartoon episodes without words appears at the beginning and end of the book. *Basil's Brush at the Beach* for which Firmin used cartoon characters, is about a fox and a mole. The fox is the title character.

Acrylic, wash, watercolor, pen and ink, painted glass, ink wash and pencil, collage, and woodcuts are mediums used by the artists who provide illustrations for poems and stories in Shaw's *The Fox Book*. After studying a variety of foxes illustrated by various artists, students might be interested in creating their own. This project could be completed by intermediate, middle, high school, or college art students. Ed Emberley's *Drawing Book of Animals* would help. A very simple project for preschool and kindergarten students is explained in the section of chapter 2, "Experiencing Art through Picture Books," called "An Awareness Project."

OWLS.   Shaw's *The Owl Book* contains poems and prose about owls illustrated by sixteen artists including Galdone, Duvoisin and Shimin. The book provides an excellent opportunity to contrast artistic styles and different mediums.

Compare the treatment of owls in three picture books by one artist. Compare the owl in *Brian Wildsmith's ABC* with the two owls in "A Stare of Owls" in *Brian Wildsmith's Birds*, and the owl in *the Owl and the Woodpecker*. In the last Wildsmith book, an owl wanted to sleep all day and a woodpecker wanted to sleep all night. Compare that picture book with another picture book on a similar theme but by an artist with a completely different style. In Pat Hutchins's *Good-Night, Owl!*, the owl could not sleep because various birds and animals were making noise. Use the story for cumulative participation is explained in the chapter on, "Playing Stories: Live-Action and with Puppets."

Ernst's *Owl's New Cards* is executed with soft pencil drawings; Celestino Piatti's *Happy Owls* is an enjoyable book to browse through and is also available as a sound filmstrip.

The Owl and the Lemming, an Eskimo Legend is a recommended filmstrip in which owl's vanity lost him his prey. Children who are curious about lemmings should be given Newton's *The March of the Lemmings*, which tell how the hamster-like creatures from Northern climates are drawn towards the sea and swim until they sink beneath the waves. Along their way the lemmings are prey for Arctic foxes and snow owls.

Another representation of owls is provided by Aruego and Dewey in *Owliver* by Kraus. Owliver wanted to be a fireman, but his parents wanted him to be a lawyer. Line drawings illustrate *A Toad for Tuesday* by Erickson, which is really mostly about George Owl who decided not to eat Warton Toad for his birthday but to make friends with him instead. Part I of this story appeared in the children's magazine, *Cricket*, and readers were invited to enter a contest and write an ending to the story. Several entries were later published.

Eastman's beginning reader, *Sam and the Firefly*, provides an illustration of an owl. Include this book in the group given to preschool or kindergarten students to look through after they have had Hutchins's *Good-Night, Owl!* read to them. Gus the firefly made words in lights, caused problems with cars, planes, and owls but saved the day by stopping a train. The book is also available as one of the six filmstrips in *The Beginner Books Filmstrips IV* set.

Lobel's *Owl at Home* is another easy reader, and five separate stories are included in the book. In the last one "Owl and the Moon," owl thought the moon was following him home because it was always behind him in the sky. Owl, personified, wears a derby hat. Lobel also illustrated Benchley's *The Strange Disappearance of Arthur Cluck*, an easy reader, in which Ralph Owl helped find a missing chick named Arthur Cluck. One of the chapters in the easy-to-read *Father Bear Comes Home* by Minarik, illustrated by Maurice Sendak, is called "Little Bear and Owl."

Aliki Brandenberg illustrated *Birds at Night* by Gans. This easy reader is one of the Let's-Read-and-Find-Out science series. Zim's *Owls* offers simple information on eye function, food, feathers, and eggs of owls. Many well-placed illustrations show many types of owls: elf, pygmy, barn, long-eared, short-screech, horned, snowy, and burrowing. Further information about owls is provided in May's *About Owls.*

Block prints depict a mother screech owl from the time of her twenty-eight days on the eggs until her four owlets leave the nest. The format of *The Mother Owl* makes learning a pleasure for primary students. Primary and intermediate students will have similar pleasure finding out about a desert owl in *Elf Owl* by the Buffs. Other desert plants and animals are introduced in this book about the smallest owls in the world.

Jean and John George, excellent nature writers, have written about a particular owl in *Bulbo, the Great Horned Owl.* The life cycle book is illustrated by Jean, and is intended for intermediate students. Jean George's *The Moon of the Owls* shows a full moon and a great horned owl sleeping beneath its shadow in January. Some animals that appear in the other months are mink, skunk, red fox, mouse, rabbit, mole, and deer. Farley Mowat is another nature writer. Introduce his *Owls in the Family* to students by reading the note from the author in which he addresses the question of whether or not Wal and Weeps were real owls. In the story, the owls meet Mutt, the dog from Mowat's *The Dog Who Wouldn't Be,* and a boy who made pets of owls in Saskatoon, Saskatchewan. Another book to include is Gage's *The Ghost of Five Owl Farm.* The significance of the owls in this story is not revealed until the last pages when the mystery is solved.

Look for information about owls in bird books like Zim's and Gabrielson's *Birds.* Two books called *Birds and Their Nests* also provide information. Verbers' book shows the nest of the burrowing owl and the owl himself appears in Earle's book, as will as an elf owl and the great horned owl. The nests of these three owls are very different—one is a hole in the ground, another a tree hollow, and a third one is a nest. Owls can also be found in books about the animals they eat. Voight's *Little Brown Bat* was almost eaten by an owl in this easy-to-read book. Similarly an owl appears in Freschet's *Bear Mouse.*

Habits of snowy, burrowing, barn, and great horned owls are included in Lavine's *Wonders of the Owl World* for intermediate students. The book can be introduced by telling students about some of the superstitions about owls found in Leach's *The Standard Dictionary of Folklore* (pp. 838–39). Many symbolisms and legends surround owls. The owl was the bird of Athena in classical Greece, and had a connotation of wisdom, but in ancient Rome the owl was an omen of death. Owls meant death to Scots, the Welsh, and the Cherokee Indians. Owls were sorcerors to the Bantu, Zulu and Yoruba tribes of Africa. Kiowa American Indian medicine men became owls after death. Penobscot Indians believed that anyone who mocked a screech owl could expect the owl to come and burn him or her. To keep owls away, turn clothes inside out, knot handkerchiefs, and throw salt in the fire. In Newfoundland, owls are harbingers of bad weather. Jews consider owls unclean birds. The *Talmud* links bad dreams and owls, but the Pawnee Indians believed owls protected people in the night. A white owl was said to have saved Ghengis Kahn. The Buriats believed that owls protect children. Owl broth was said to cure whooping cough. Many people collect owls in various forms.

Introduce owls through music or poetry. In Slobodkin's *Wide-Awake Owl* the birds sang a song to owl, and owl sang herself to sleep. Music is given.

Read Lear's delightful nonsense poem to the class from Cooney's picture book, *The Owl and the Pussy Cat*, or show them the sound filmstrip. Three poems about owls from Shaw's *The Owl Book* can introduce owls: Kay McKemy's "Whooooo?" on pages 8 and 9, Aileen Fisher's "Who Says, Who Says" on pages 10 and 11, and Conrad Aiken's "The Owl" on pages 27 and 28. The shape and pattern of the words on the pages for Aiken's poem are interesting. Students could find other poems in Brewton's poetry indexes.

Raskin's *Who, Said Sue, Said Whoo?* is a cumulative story for which directions for playing are given in this book in the chapter "Playing Stories: Live-Action and with Puppets." Another book about owls included in that chapter is Freschet's *The Owl and the Prairie Dog*.

Place all of these books in a display case with various objects picturing owls. This should be easy to accomplish because owls are a popular motif and appear on plaques, bookends, paperweights, and a host of other objects. The caption for the display or for a bulletin board could be "Whooo Will Read These Books?" The display makes an interesting background for a story program at a public library, using various combinations of filmstrips and picture books. See chapter 2, "Experiencing Art through Picture Books," for a simple project for preschool and kindergarten students.

There are over fifty stories listed under the heading "Owls" in Ireland's *Index to Fairy Tales, 1949–72, Including Folklore, Legends and Myths in Collections*. Choose stories from that index for telling.

INTRODUCING BOOKS ON BIRTHDAYS.   A birthday is a special time in the lives of children and books can easily be made a part of that special day. A story in which there is a birthday can be read aloud. A book, which may or may not be about birthdays, can be dedicated to the birthday child when read to a whole class. In a family setting, the birthday child can sit on the parent's lap; in school or library media center, in the place of honor, such as on a special "birthday cushion." The birthday child might be asked to choose the book to be read. If the book read to the children contains a birthday of a favorite story character, the birthday child could choose another story from that series to be read. Several of the books in the following section are available in paperback. Library media specialists or classroom teachers may want to institute, as many have, a "birthday tradition." This might work so that each child will receive one paperback on his or her birthday; or the student might present a book to the library media center, with a gift plate. Students with summer birthdays would receive books at the end of the year.

BIRTHDAY STORIES ABOUT FAVORITE BOOK CHARACTERS   Babar the elephant is featured in *Babar's Birthday Surprise*. Read that book as well as *The Story of Babar* to students to celebrate someone's birthday. If they already know the original story, they will recognize a friend and appreciate the birthday even more. Sound filmstrips are available for *The Story of Babar*, *The Travels of Babar*, and *Babar the King*. 1981 was Babar's fiftieth birthday. From Miller's

Mousekin's Woodland Birthday readers learn how a white-footed mouse lives from birth to weaning and how other animal babies (fox, beaver, raccoon, wren, chipmunk, and box turtle) are taken care of by their mothers. The preschool birthday child could choose from among following books: *Mousekin's ABC, Mousekin's Woodland Sleepers, Mousekin's Christmas Eve, Mousekin's Golden House, Mousekin's Family,* and *Mousekin Finds a Friend.*

Filmstrips are available for four of Miller's books about Mousekin: *Mousekin's Golden House, Mousekin's Christmas Eve, Mousekin Finds a Friend,* and *Mousekin's Family*

Lyle the crocodile is a favorite with children in grades K-3. In Waber's *Lyle and the Birthday Party,* Lyle turned "mean green" with jealousy when Joshua, one of the children with whom he lived, had a birthday and got all the resulting attention. Although he did not want to be jealous, Lyle did things like step through one of the best presents, a drum. Lyle made himself so sick with jealousy that he had to go to the hospital, and when he went home, the family gave a party in Lyle's honor. There are four filmstrips available for *The House on E. 88th Street, Lovable Lyle, Lyle and the Birthday Party,* and *Lyle, Lyle Crocodile.*

Another beloved character, Frances the Badger, also has her nose "out of joint" over someone else's birthday. Frances was jealous because her younger sister Gloria was having a birthday in *A Birthday for Frances.* Frances bought Gloria a candy bar and bubble gum with her allowance, but chewed the bubble gum herself. Finally Frances was reconciled to the facts, and decided to behave properly. The story is available in paperback and sound filmstrip format. After having the book read to them or seeing the sound filmstrip, the birthday child could choose which other book or filmstrip about Frances is to be seen next. The following are also available as sound filmstrips: *Bedtime for Frances, Best Friends for Frances,* and *Bread and Jam for Frances.*

Another birthday story about jealousy is about a modern boy who was jealous of his brother. Finally Henry pulled himself together and wrote "Today is not my birthday," which is also the title of Rudolph's book.

Horatio the cat in Clymer's *Horatio's Birthday* is grumpy because he does not know it is his birthday and that the tuna fish pie and the company are for him. So while everyone gathered to visit, Horatio went seeking his own adventure. Other books about the grumpy cat are *Horatio, Leave Horatio Alone, Horatio Goes to the Country,* and *Horatio Solves a Mystery.*

Veronica, Duvoison's hippo, stars in *Veronica and the Birthday Present.* The present is Candy, the kitten who was intended for the farmer's wife, but ends up giving joy to Veronica. After hearing this birthday story, the kindergarten through third-grade birthday child could choose to have the following books about Veronica read to the group: *Lonely Veronica, Our Veronica, Veronica's Smile, Veronica,* and *Veronica Goes to Petunia's Farm.* The last two are available as paperback editions. The last book combines two favorite Duvoisin characters, Veronica and the goose, Petunia. The book *Petunia* is also available as a sound filmstrip.

Chapter 7 of *Paddington Marches On,* "An Unexpected Party," is about the bon voyage party held for Paddington before he set off to help his Aunt Lucy celebrate her one-hundredth birthday. Chapters 7, 1, 3, and 4 of *Paddington Marches On* are included on the same 16mm film. Use the film to introduce other books about Paddington: *A Bear Called Paddington* and *More About Paddington*. All three books are available in paperback.

The chapter "In Which Eeyore Has a Birthday and Gets Two Presents," in Milne's *Winnie-the-Pooh* tells how Pooh ate the honey he was going to give Eeyore for a present, and gave Eeyore just the jar. Children are asked to have friends and relatives sign their names on the date of their birthday in *Pooh's Birthday Book*. Each day contains a poem or quote from A. A. Milne. Students will enjoy getting signatures from their friends as well as enjoy having a record of their birthdays. Teachers could give the paperback to class members as a birthday gift. Class members could sign the book and present it to the birthday boy or girl. On the last day of school each child who has a summer birthday would receive a copy of the book. Parents or grandparents could give the birthday book at a birthday party and everyone there could sign their names. Names of aunts, uncles and cousins could be already signed in.

Show the sound filmstrip of *Jenny's Birthday Book* to a class and then read Averill's *Jenny's Bedside Book*. In the second book Jenny Linsky, the black cat, had the flu and eighteen other cats sang her to sleep. There is also a story within a story because Puss in Boots is told. After Averill's *The Fire Cat*, Pickles, was rescued from a tree by the fire department, he stayed on and was given a fire hat of his own.

Lindgren's unconventional Pippi Longstocking invited her friends Timmy and Anika to her birthday party and surprised them by giving each of them a present. This party appears as the last chapter of *Pippi Longstocking*, and also appears on pages 158–68 of Corrigan's *Holiday Ring*.

BIRTHDAY BOOKS BY FAVORITE AUTHORS.   A classroom project for grades two to four can be based on Goodall's picture books without words. Introduce first *Shrewbettina's Birthday*, a book that gives all of Shrewbettina's adventures for that special day.

Divide students into ten groups, one for each of Goodall's books. (If fewer titles are owned, have fewer groups.) Ask each group to write a script for their book. Complete bibliographic details for all of Goodall's books and other wordless stories are given in the bibliography called "Picture Books Without Words" from the chapter called "Experiencing Art through Picture Books." Emberley's *A Birthday Wish* is one of them.

There is a Dr. Seuss country where birthdays begin with a big blast on a Birthday Horn. *Happy Birthday to You!* explains what else happens to the birthday person, including action by the Happy Birthday Asso-see-eye-ation, birthday birds, and pets from the Official Katroo Birthday Pet Reservation. Children will enjoy hearing this story read by Hans Conreid on a recording called *Happy Birthday to You! And to Think That I Saw It on Mulberry Street* is one of the other four stories on the recording. Seuss paperback books could be given as prizes at a birthday party in which the recording was part of the entertainment.

A coloring book called Kate Greenaway's Birthday could be given to a birthday girl after selections have been read from Greenaway's *Birthday Book for Children.*

BIRTHDAYS—OTHER TIMES AND OTHER PLACES.   Tasha Tudor's warm birthday story, *Becky's Birthday,* is about a ten-year-old farm girl from horse and buggy days whose party included home-made ice cream and a hayride. On page 47 the group sang a verse of "Fox Went Out in a Hungry Plight." After reading Tudor's *Becky's Birthday* to children, the filmstrip of Spier's book, *Fox Went Out on a Chilly Night,* could be shown and that song sung as an example of how folk songs are altered to suit the people who sing them.

Spanish-speaking children will especially enjoy Politi's *Juanita.* The Mexican birthday song called "Las Mananitas" (little morning) is included. A five-year-old girl wanted a doll for her birthday in *Manuela's Birthday* by Bannon. The American Artists couldn't find a doll with blue eyes and gold hair like Manuela wanted, so they not only made one but painted a picture of Manuela holding the doll so she would have a remembrance of that day.

The Birthday Visitor by Uchida is about a seven-year-old Japanese-American boy who has visitors from Japan on his birthday. The boy thought the visitors dull until one prayed over his dead bird. *Taro and the Bamboo Shoot* by Matsuno concerns a nine-year-old Japanese boy and a bamboo shoot that grew tall and took Taro with it.

Teachers and library media specialists should check Price's *Happy Days, a UNICEF Book of Birthday Name Days and Growing Days* for international ideas and songs.

Nicole's Birthday by Frere, about a family birthday party, won the Prix Loisirs Jeunes of France.

Zolotow's *Over and Over* is about a preschool girl who had no concept of time or seasons and asked her mother "what comes next" and holidays unfold—Christmas, Valentine's Day, Easter, summer vacation at the seashore, Halloween, Thanksgiving, and a birthday party. The little girl wished on her birthday candles for "it all to happen again." The last sentence in the book is "And of course, over and over, year after year, it did."

Lillie, a sixth-grader in Walter's book *Lillie of Watts, a Birthday Discovery,* had a birthday May 17, the same date the Supreme Court had ruled that schools must be integrated, long before Lillie was born. Lillie's teacher, Mr. Knox, told them about birthday parties but no one in the class had ever had one. Mr. Knox always played "Happy Birthday" on his violin to the birthday child, and that was the nice part of the day, but it was followed by one small disaster after another. Finally, Lillie gets a gift that will last always—she learns how much her mother loves her.

Lexau's *Striped Ice Cream* can be introduced by its title. Becky, the youngest, and black like Lillie, worries that she won't get striped ice cream (Neapolitan) for her eighth birthday because her family is having hard times.

BIRTHDAY PARTIES.   Birthday parties are a high point for children in books or out of them!

Although Steven wished for snow on his early December birthday, he was disappointed when the farm was snowbound and none of his friends could come to his party. A traveler arranged for a horse and sleigh, so all ended well in Kay's *Snow Birthday*. In *Paul's Christmas Birthday* by the Carricks, a boy is unhappy with his day before Christmas birthday.

Another birthday takes place in summer. In Aliki Brandenburg's *June 7*, a family had just sat down to lunch when the doorbell rang. Eventually the whole family arrived and readers learn that it is the narrator's birthday party. Everyone sang "Happy Birthday" on the last page.

Krauss's *The Birthday Party* is about a boy who had never been to a birthday party until he came home and found a surprise party waiting for him.

In Keats's *A Letter to Amy*, Peter worried that Amy might refuse an invitation to his birthday party because he had accidentally knocked her down. Preschool and early elementary students would enjoy browsing through Keats's other books about him after they have heard this story or have seen the sound filmstrip.

Mary Tate remembered promises made to her that she thought had been forgotten until her birthday came and she realized that everyone had remembered. *Don't You Remember?* is written by Clifton.

There are several animal birthday parties in books. In "The Cunning Cat and His Company" from Untermeyer's *Aesop's Fables*, a cat invited neighbors to his birthday dinner and expected them to be the entertainment as well as the dinner.

In Watson's *Birthday Goat*, father goat promised his kid a birthday wish, and the birthday ended with a picnic.

In Niklewiczowa's *Sparrow's Magic*, Mrs. Quail wanted to invite Mr. Hamster to her birthday party as well as borrow flour from him for the cake, but Mr. Hamster selfishly refused.

Kumin's *Joey and the Birthday Party* is about a little field mouse who made friends with Prince, a tame white rat.

While Lisette went to the village, her animals prepared a surprise for her seventy-sixth birthday in Fischer's *The Birthday*.

Four and five year olds will identify with the protagonist in Iwasaki's *Birthday Wish*. Allison went to a friend's house for a birthday party the day before her own birthday, forgot whose birthday it was, and blew out Judy's candles. The next day Allison let Judy blow out the candles on her cake.

Peter in Kingman's *Peter's Long Walk* woke up early on his birthday and went to school, only to find out from a custodian that it was summer vacation and he would have to wait until fall to go to school.

In Lobel's *Birthday for a Princess*, the princess had a party but some of her friends, including the organ grinder, were not invited, so she let them climb up a rope to attend the party anyway.

BIRTHDAY PRESENTS.   There are several stories in which children wonder what to give someone—often their mother—for a birthday present. In Flack's

Ask Mr. Bear, a small boy asked several animals what they would give his mother. Preschoolers will love the repetition and the potential for adding to the story.

Kindergartners will enjoy hearing Beskow's *Peter's Adventures in Blueberry Land*. Father Blueberry, king of an area of the forest, saw Peter crying because he couldn't see any berries to give his mother for her birthday, so he helped him collect berries. Peter thought that he had imagined his adventure, but the berries were real.

Zolotow's *Mr. Rabbit and the Lovely Present* is another story about choosing birthday presents, and is also available on sound filmstrip. A little girl asked Mr. Rabbit what to get her mother for her birthday. When she told him that mother liked red, he enumerated objects that are red, and did the same for yellow, green, and blue. Finally the girl and the rabbit agreed on a basket of fruit that contained green pears, yellow bananas, red apples, and blue grapes. Other books about colors to share with students after the filmstrip has been presented are included in the chapter on "Experiencing Art through Picture Books."

Two I-Can-Read books are about birthday presents. Heilbroner's *The Happy Birthday Present* also includes colors. Peter and Davy try to decide what to get mother for her birthday. Davy wanted to get her a dump truck, but Peter sent him into a store to buy lipstick. The clerk listed all the shades of red and pink but children will chuckle when Davy asked for green. Finally after he went to several stores, the brothers collected a pinwheel, shell, flower pot, and lollipop. They fastened these objects together to make their mother a happy birthday tree. In Lowrey's *Six Silver Spoons*, Debby and Tim got six silver spoons from Mr. Paul Revere for their mother's birthday present and took them through the British lines to their mother just before the battle of Lexington and Concord that began the American Revolutionary War.

Prince's *Vanya and the Clay Queen* is about a sullen, arrogant and cold-hearted queen whose husband's unusual birthday present was to have her likeness done by artists in a contest. The contest was open to the common folk, not just flattering courtiers as judges and contestants. An old woman named Vanya worked with clay and received most of the votes for the best likeness because her portrait was sullen, arrogant, and cold-hearted. This is a good one for starting a discussion, perhaps with third graders, about seeing ourselves as others see us.

Bruno Munari's *The Birthday Present* could be read to nursery school children to honor a birthday child. Two other favorites, *Bruno Munari's ABC* and *Bruno Munari's Zoo*, could also be read or the filmstrips of the books shown. The first book could be kept in a special place and used only for birthdays. The birthday child could be asked to get the book from that special place.

The Secret Birthday Message by Carle contains a treasure hunt in which the clues led Tim to his birthday present—a puppy. Parents could leave messages for finding a birthday puppy, or some other gift. *The Secret Birthday Message* could also provide an activity for a birthday party. After the book is read, the guests could make up messages that the birthday child must follow in order to find each present. Guests could work in pairs and construct one message for two gifts.

Crictor, from a picture book of the same name by Ungerer, was the boa constrictor Madame Bodot received for a birthday present.

In *Benjamin's 365 Birthdays* by Barrett, nine-year-old Benjamin wanted his birthday to last, so he wrapped up the whole house as his present. *Big Cowboy Western* by Scott is about Martin, a five-year-old who received six shooters and a holster for his birthday but had to play with the peddler's horse because he didn't have one of his own.

Nicholas wanted a pet for his birthday in Sandberg's *Nicholas' Favorite Pet*. All Rafer wanted for his birthday in Lexau's *Me Day* was a letter from his father. In Lundgren's *Matt's Grandfather*, Matt visited his eighty-five-year-old grandfather in a rest home on his birthday but his grandfather did not recognize him.

One of the stories in Tompert's *Little Otter Remembers and Other Stories* is "Little Otter's Birthday Gift."

In Collier's *The Birthday Tree*, a farmer gave a little girl a tree for her birthday and she planted it, pressed the leaves, and dreamed of when it would be big enough for all her friends to sit under it.

BIRTHDAY POEMS.   Livingston's *O Frabjous Day! Poetry for Holidays and Special Occasions* contains a section entitled "Birth, Birthdays, and Christenings." A dozen poems by poets Countee Cullen, Robert Frost, Emily Dickinson, William Carlos Williams, David McCord, and others are included. There is a "Song for the Newborn" sung by Pueblo Indians as well as Japanese and Chinese poems.

David McCord's "Who Wants a Birthday" is found on page 157 of Corrigan's *Holiday Ring*. To find other poems about birthdays, check the subject index of poetry indexes. The newest Brewton index is *Index to Poetry for Children and Young People, 1970–75*. Finger plays for birthdays are included in Binder and Thompson's *Rhymes for Fingers and Flannelboards*.

BIRTHDAYS OF FAMOUS PEOPLE INCLUDING AUTHORS.   Olcott's *Good Stories for Great Birthdays* contains 200 stories about the birthdays of 23 people including Franklin, Lincoln, Jackson, Jefferson, Penn, and others. The stories could be read on the birth date of the famous person, to start a project of locating more information about that person in encyclopedias, history books, and individual and collective biographies.

There are several ways to celebrate birthdays of authors and illustrators: posting dates of birthdays with bibliographies; circulating displays for books; parties with cake and candles which represent the number of titles owned by the library; reading one or more chapters from an author's work; showing a film or filmstrip based on a book by or about that person; a booktalk to introduce several books by that author; researching the life and home environment of the author or illustrator; or sending a birthday card in care of the publisher. Creators of books for children usually love to get letters from readers, but classroom assignments lack spontaneity.

Author and illustrator birthdays are given for most entries in reference books entitled *Something About the Author* (Gale), and four volumes of the H. W. Wilson Company's *The Book of Junior Authors*, *More Junior Authors*, *Third Book of Junior Authors*, and *Fourth Book of Junior Authors and Illustrators*.

USING SEQUELS.   Sometimes it is easier to find "the best book someone has ever read" than it is to find *another* book that the person will enjoy just as well. Often the next book a librarian gives to a person who describes that "best book" is similar but not about the same character. However, when readers are curious about what happened to a character or want to read more about the same person or animal, then a sequel may be the answer.

Even though the sequels in this section are similar to their antecedents, the various books that have sequels are of many different types and are different from each other. These books can be used for individual reading guidance or could provide the theme for a booktalk. All of the titles in a booktalk could be introduced in pairs.

Most of the books in this section would be suitable to introduce to readers in grades four through six. Those who have read Harris's *The Moon in the Cloud* may wish to read the sequel, *The Shadow on the Sun* to find out what happened when Noah got off the ark. Read the author's note in each book to get background on Biblical, historical, and geographical placement for the stories. In the first book, Noah received word from God. Read pages 8 and 9 up until "For this is what you are to do. . . ." That section introduces Ham as a problem child whom God wasn't sure he wanted along on the ark.

It is difficult to tell very much about this book without spoiling the reading pleasure for students. The sequel tells about what happened to Reuben, Thamar, and Kemi, the cat, in the Black Land (Egypt) after they got out of the ark.

Dog lovers who enjoyed Kjelgaard's *Big Red* will also enjoy *Irish Red, Son of Big Red*. Rich Mr. Haggin owned Big Red, the champion Irish Setter, but the dog's heart belonged to Danny Pickett, whom Mr. Haggin had hired to help train the dog. When Red, the $7,000 dog, was injured by a bear, Danny bought Red from Mr. Haggin. In *Big Red*, Mr. Haggin had bought a spectacular female Irish Setter named Sheilah. In the book *Irish Red, Son of Big Red*, Sheilah and Big Red's fifth pup, Mike, was a runt and apparently untrainable. Finally, Ross and Danny had to prove that Irish Setters were better than English Setters, but could they?

Hard won, never-wavering friendship between man and dog in the wilderness occurred between *Silver Chief*, part husky and part wolf, and Jim Thorpe of the Royal Canadian Mounted Police. In the sequel, *The Return of Silver Chief*, the two friends captured escaped Nazi prisoners. These are wonderfully absorbing tales by Jack O'Brien who wrote about a life he knew and loved. These are among the best dog stories of all time for grades four through six.

Some books that follow Farley's *Black Stallion* are *Son of Black Stallion*,

Black Stallion and the Girl, Black Stallion Mystery, Black Stallion Returns, and *Black Stallion Revolts.* Boys and girls who have reached "the horsey period" will want to read all of them.

The animal in one of the books by Beatty is much more interesting to ride than a horse. Beulah Land Quincy rode a Texas longhorn named Travis in *How Many Miles to Sundown,* the sequel to *It's a Long Way to Whiskey Creek.*

In Beatty's *It's a Long Way to Whiskey Creek,* thirteen-year-old Parker Quincy was the family representative sent 400 miles from Cottonwood, Texas to Whiskey Creek in 1879 to bring his brother Jesse's body home for burial. His dog J.E.B. Stuart and his friend Nate went along. Both boys were glad to be on the road. The boys escaped a medicine show and an evangelist, but were aided by an old outlaw named "The Tonkawa Kid." Nate Graber appears in the sequel, *How Many Miles to Sundown.* Thirteen-year-old Beulah Land Quincy followed her brother Leo who accompanied Nate Graber in his search for his father in Texas, Mexico, and the Arizona Territories. The trio were accompanied by Travis, a longhorn steer.

Life in the Southwest in the 1880s was difficult and so is life in Appalachia today.

Before Roy Luther died, he made his fourteen-year-old daughter Mary Call promise several things: that she wouldn't tell anybody when he died, and secretly bury him on the mountain; and that she would keep a neighbor, Kaiser Pease, from marrying her older sister Devola who was "dreamy." When Roy Luther died, Mary Call buried him in secret and pretended that he was still alive so that the family wouldn't be separated and become wards of the county. The responsibility of finding money for food, keeping the house in repair, keeping all of them in school, keeping the neighbors from finding out their father was dead, and keeping Kaiser from marrying Devola was almost more than the spunky Mary Call could handle. *Where the Lilies Bloom* by the Cleavers was made into a film that has been seen in theaters and on television. Anyone who has read it or has seen the film will want to read the sequel, *Trial Valley.*

Mary Call is sixteen years old in *Trial Valley* and young men came courting. Thad Yancey was a son of a gentleman farmer from Virginia who raised horses and apples; Thad was an apprentice in the field of public services; Gaither Graybeal was a neighbor who couldn't see Mary Call's vision but tried hard to understand. At the end of the book readers do not learn which young man is for Mary Call; only which young man *isn't* right for her.

Continuing sagas about families are usually well-liked.

Mine for Keeps by Little is about Sarah Jane Copel who has cerebral palsy. Sal had trouble adjusting to life at home after being in a special school where she received more attention. Anyone who likes dogs will appreciate how a puppy helped Sal's adjustment. The sequel, *Spring Begins in March,* focuses on the problems of Sal's sister Meg who doesn't have many friends and poor grades in school.

Two other books by Little are *Look through My Window* and *Kate.* Emily Blair and her parents lived quietly together until one day her mother came home and said that Aunt Barbara was being hospitalized for TB and they were taking in the four cousins. That same night Emily's father came home with the news that he was being transferred. Read chapter one to establish personalities and situations.

The Blair family moved and bought a big old house next to an eccentric old lady. In the garret attic Emily chose for herself, she found a locked box with two notes which started friendships and adventures in her new hometown. Emily was an avid reader and chose the garret attic for her own room because it reminded her of Heidi's loft and Sara Crew's garret.

Look through My Window is mostly about Emily Blair. In the sequel, the emphasis is on her friend Kate. The character sketch about Kate that Emily had to write for class appears on pages 8 and 9, so readers learn about Kate through Emily's eyes. Kate, like Blume's Margaret from *Are You There God, It's Me Margaret*, is the child of a Jewish-Gentile marriage, and Kate learns more about her father's Jewish heritage. In Johnston's *The Keeping Days* and the sequel *Glory in the Flower*, readers learn about Letitia Sterling from her own diary. Tish began the diary on her fourteenth birthday in 1900.

The most popular sixth-grade girl in fiction after Judy Blume's Margaret is Fitzhugh's *Harriet the Spy*. Harriet wanted to be a writer so she observed and recorded life around her in her notebook. The things she said about her friends were true but were not necessarily the kinds of things people want said about themselves. When Harriet dropped her notebook and her friends read her candid remarks there was big trouble. Harriet and her friend became involved in a mystery during a summer vacation on Long Island in the sequel, *The Long Secret*. Harriet was a rich girl who received more attention from Ole Golly, the housekeeper than she did from her parents.

Another lonely child of rich parents is twelve-year-old Franklin Olmstead who is called Ox because he is big and fat and is only in the fourth grade. He is the "sort of" hero of *Ox: The Story of a Kid at the Top*. Ox, is fifteen in *Ox Goes North, More Trouble for the Kid at the Top*. Ox who lived in Palm Beach, was sent to a camp in Vermont for the summer. There Ox became involved in the life of his bunkmate Tommy whose scheming grandparents are trying to steal his trust fund. Stories that show that "rich kids have problems, too" are a long and honored tradition in children's literature.

Girls who enjoy Margaret and Harriet will also like Green's *A Girl Called Al* and its sequel, *I Know You, Al*, as well as Ellen in the Cleavers' *Ellen Grae* and the sequel, *Lady Ellen Grae*.

Sach's *Veronica Ganz* could and did beat up everyone at school but when the new boy, Peter, came she found herself thwarted at every turn. Some readers may object to the "secret weapon" Veronica used to finally beat Peter. In the sequel, *Peter and Veronica* became best friends. Peter took Veronica to eat knishes at his uncle's store and Veronica took Peter to her uncle's diner. Peter defied his whole family to invite Veronica to his Bar Mitzvah. The two friends quarrelled when Veronica did not come.

Another friendship between a boy and a girl occurs in books by Beverly Cleary. *Henry and Beezus* is the sequel to *Henry Huggins*. Although Henry and Beatrice or Beezus are not great buddies, they tolerate and respect each other.

There are numerous sequels with these characters. The friendship between Eddie Wilson and Anna Patricia or between Eddie and Sidney Stewart seem even stronger than the friendship between Henry and Beezus. The three characters appear in various books by Haywood.

The friendship in Enright's *Gone-Away Lake* and *Return to Gone-Away Lake* is between cousins. In *Gone-Away Lake*, eleven-year-old Portia and her seven-year-old brother Foster went alone to visit their Aunt Hilda, Uncle Jake, and their twelve-year-old cousin Julian. Portia and Julian were best friends and explored together. The two saw a rock that had the Latin inscription "Lapis Philosophorum Tarquin et Pindar, 15 July 1891." Those events are explained in chapter 2, "The Stone in the Swamp" which is a good chapter to read aloud, and Pindar himself told the story of the rock in chapter 6, "The Knife and the Buttonhook." One of the abandoned homes on the disappearing lake came into its own when the Blake parents bought the house filled with antiques and the previous owner's ghost in the sequel *Return to Gone-Away Lake*.

Sometimes stories about a family stretch into several books. Taylor's *All-of-a-Kind Family* was a family of five Jewish girls who lived in New York before World War I. The sequel, *More All-of-a-Kind Family* took place two years later. In *All-of-a-Kind Family Uptown* Ella, the oldest, had a boyfriend who went off to war. That book is followed by *All-of-a-Kind Family Downtown*. In *Ella of All-of-a-Kind Family*, Jules came back from the war but Ella had to share him.

Another famous family dominated by girls which provides many sequels is the Ingalls family of the "Little House" books. Descriptions of those stories appear in this chapter in an annotated bibliography called, "If You Liked the 'Little House' books. . ." Information about Laura Ingalls and her sisters is also included in the section called "Introducing Jo, Caddie, and Laura."

Numerous sequels in science fiction and fantasies that are included in this chapter are to books by Alexander, Dickinson, Cooper, LeGuin, Lewis, Norton, Slobodkin, Todd, Tolkien, and Travers.

Some books with sequels that are included elsewhere in this chapter that could also be included in a booktalk are Alcott's *Little Men*, the sequel to *Little Women*; Anckersvard's *Madcap Mystery*, sequel to *The Robber Ghost*; Best's *Desmond and the Peppermint Ghost*, sequel to *Desmond's First Case*; Brink's *Magical Melons*, the sequel to *Caddie Woodlawn*; Butterworth's *Narrow Passage*, sequel to *The Enormous Egg*; Cleary's *Runaway Ralph*, sequel to *The Mouse and the Motorcycle*; Enright's *The Four Story Mistake*, sequel to *The Saturdays'*; Estes's *The Middle Moffat*, sequel to *The Moffats*; Gipson's *Savage Sam*, sequel to *Old Yeller*; Henry's *Sea Star, Orphan of Chincoteague*, sequel to *Misty of Chincoteague*; Langton's *The Swing in the Summerhouse*, sequel to *The Diamond in the Window*; Lawson's *Tough Winter*, sequel to *Rabbit Hill*; Lovelace's *Betsy Tacy and Tib*, sequel to *Betsy-Tacy*; Mowat's *The Curse of the Viking Grave*, sequel to *Lost in the Barrens*; O'Dell's *Zia*, sequel to *Island of the Blue Dolphins*; Ormondroyd's *All in Good Time*, sequel to *Time at the Top*; Ottley's *The Roan Colt*, sequel to *Boy Alone*; Selden's *Tucker's Countryside*, sequel to *Cricket in Times Square*; Sharp's *The Rescuers*, sequel to *Miss Bianca*; and Winterfeld's *Mystery of the Roman Ransom*, the sequel to *Detectives in Togas*.

MOTIVATING READING THROUGH TELEVISION.   Television has been blamed for the decline in reading by children. However, experiments have shown that if parents, teachers, and school and public librarians make the effort to make connections and provide linkage with follow-up reading, TV can actually help stimulate reading.

Often a television series, television special, or movie shown on television can provide a common element of interests which can be expanded and extended with related books.

A bulletin board or a showcase featuring books correlated to a TV program can be captioned "Television and Books" or "What's New on TV." The format of the display could remain the same but the posters and books would change. The display might be on top of a counter in one place so that students will feel encouraged to check out the books, filmstrips, or cassettes. The purpose of the display is not so everyone in the school or public library has a chance to see and admire it but to flag attention and sell a product: a particular book. When displays are on countertops, a small easel that can easily handle a poster 20 x 20 inches could be provided for promotional material, which might include posters or clippings from television guides.

There are many types of programs that can be correlated with books. Displays of books can be prepared about animals to be featured on "Wild Kingdom," "Wild World of Animals," "The Wonderful World of Disney," and "National Geographic Specials." The display should be put up before and left up after the program. Most students will check out books after they have seen the program and their curiosity has been aroused. Displaying the books before the program serves to alert viewers so it won't be missed.

Correlating books with science programs on television is not new. Mr. Wizzard (Don Herbert) from the 1950's and 1960's performed many laboratory experiments which were then available in books. The high school science educational television program "NOVA" includes very complete study guides which contain multimedia lists for supplementary reading, viewing, and listening.

Television can provide children with cultural experiences they might otherwise not have: opera live from the stage of the Metropolitan Opera House, ballet, plays, interviews with famous people, and documentaries. Programs based on books, including children's literature, are seen more often than ever: *Little Women*, narrated by Joanne Woodward, appeared as a ballet on NBC; "The Little House" series is one of the most enduring and most popular on televison.

Teachers can give definite assignments correlating TV viewing with books, search skills, and independent study. Most of these projects would be enrichment opportunities for students who need to be challenged in intermediate classes, or they could be elective projects in English, social studies, or science for classes in middle, junior high, and high school. While watching a program about animals, for instance, students could make a list of facts stated about a particular animal and then check these in several sources to verify them. A group of students may want to read and discuss books about, whales, survival, or Nazism and the Jews after seeing the programs that relate to these subjects.

Individual students may wish to compare the movie and book versions, and list similarities and differences or explain why they liked one more than the other.

ADVANCE NOTICE OF TELEVISION PROGRAMS.   Teachers and librarians who want to correlate reading activites with television programs need time to gather together supplementary materials for displays or enrichment materials for classrooms. It is too late to start planning when *TV Guide* or other TV listings come out and often there is not enough time to promote viewing and gathering follow-up materials. Instead, use the guides included in this section. *Television Highlights*, a guide to worthwhile programs of interest to children for three months at a time, is issued from Television Information Office, 745 Fifth Avenue, New York, New York 10022. *Television Highlights* tells which programs to look for and gives approximate dates. Local guides will then give exact times and stations.

PTST or Prime Time School Television, 120 South LaSalle Street, Chicago, Illinois 60603, also produces guides to television programs and often includes a section called "PSTS Talking about TV" in local newspaper guides to television. One example was the guide for Tolstoy's *Anna Karenina* which first appeared in 1978 on Masterpiece Theatre for PBS. The guide, made possible by a grant, included a discussion guide, list of characters, bibliography, and discussion questions.

Program descriptions for *Sesame Street* and *The Electric Company* are available from the Children's Television Workshop, 1 Lincoln Plaza, New York, New York 10023. Use the same address when writing for information about setting up reading clubs. CTW has had Reading Reinforcement materials available since the beginning of the telecasts. Write to Community Education Services Division of the Children's Television Workshop, for; *Monthly Scripts Highlights*, $5.00, which include individual program summaries, suggested educational activities, and information about guest performers. *Sesame Street Activities*, $2.00, is a manual that includes activities for understanding individual differences in people, especially handicaps. *Muppet Gallery*, $1.00, emphasizes social skills and includes color photos of muppet characters. *The Electric Company Guide/Activity Book* is a sixteen-page handbook of listings and contains sixty ditto masters, crossword puzzles.

Program listings for *Mr. Rogers' Neighborhood* can be acquired from PBS, 475 L'Enfant Plaza, S.W., Washington D.C. 20024.

National Geographic specials are produced by the National Geographic Society and WQED, Pittsburgh. Special posters giving advance information about the programs are sent free from Metropolitan Pittsburgh Public Broadcasting, Inc., 4802 5th Avenue in Pittsburgh, Pennsylvania 15213. Posters are about 16 x 11 inches and are colorful. Information about the topic is included on the reverse side.

NOVA, a television program to enrich science, social science, and English in junior and senior high schools, appears several times a week on PBS and originates from WGBH, Boston. Each teacher's guide includes information about programs for two months, and contains a subject key that tells whether the programs fall in the realms of physical sciences, life and earth sciences, social sciences, related disciplines, or special topics. Also included is an annotated bibliography, synopsis, and comments for teachers, vocabulary, viewing goals, and suggested activities and discussion topics. A teacher's guide to NOVA is prepared in cooperation with the National Science Teachers Association, The National Council for the Social Studies, and the American Association of School Librarians.

Teachers Guides to Television, 699 Madison Avenue, New York, New York 10021, publishes viewer guides several times a year, as well as guides for special programs for children and young adults on the major networks.

A twenty-four-page viewer guide of Dickens' *Hard Times* was made available as a sponsored service. That guide was similar to those produced by Teachers Guides to Television, and included a letter to parents about discussing the film, why it is important to view with children, as well as a related film list and a bibliography. A synopsis of episodes and discussion topics were included.

Teachers Guides to Television also produced the guides which the sponsor of the NBC television program sent out as a special service to help in utilizing *The Hobbit* more effectively. These guides from Teacher Guides to Television include a related film list and a book list prepared by the Young Adult Services Division of the American Library Association. Other information includes the aim, suggested activities before viewing, synopsis, further explanation, and suggestions for after viewing.

Action for Children's Television (ACT), at 46 Austin Street, Newtonville, Massachusetts 02160, offers a variety of materials to help parents, teachers, and librarians promote good TV programming and eliminate violent, vulgar, and shoddy shows and exploitive advertising aimed at children and young people. Membership, which helps support their work, is $15.00 per year and includes a twice yearly newsmagazine, *re: ACT*. Publications include *The ACT Guide to Children's TV: How to Treat TV with TLC*, a revision of an earlier booklet by Evelyn Kaye now 226 pp. and published by the Beacon Press in Boston, in both paper and cloth editions. ACT has a poster available for $1.00 with the *Treat TV with TLC* slogan, explaining that TLC stands for the three things that adults must do to help children get the most good from TV: Talk, Look, and Choose. There is also a series, now comprising three volumes, available from Ballinger Publishing Co., also in cloth and paper: *Promise and Performance: ACT's Guide to TV Programming for Children*. Volume I is *Children with Special Needs* by Maureen Harmonay; Volume II is *The Arts*, also by Harmonay; and Volume III is *The Young Adolescents*, by Margaret Schwarz. Finally, late in 1981, ACT published *Editor's Choice*, edited by Peggy Charren, which describes a collection of books from more than thirty major publishers that the editors of those books believe, and ACT agrees, would make excellent TV programs. This is intended to inspire producers, but there are many ways in which library media specialists would find these suggestions useful.

Ratings of various shows from the National Association for Better Broadcasting are available from the NABB at P. O. Box 43640, Los Angeles, CA 90043.

Sample copies of a monthly paperback promotion calendar featuring TV and movie tie-ins is available from Julie Marshall, Ludington News Co., Inc., 1600 East Grand Boulevard, Detroit, Michigan 48211. A subscription for twelve issues is $10.

Subscribers to *Facts on File, the World News Digest* with index receive posters of forthcoming programs. Posters include program details, the issue, a synopsis, and background readings. The programs are programs on current or historical events that appear on network stations but are not necessarily prepared for children, although children may be part of the audience.

A number of attempts had been made over the years to get network television to cite a few related books following appropriate programs, and to prepare and distribute bibliographies, and urge viewers to "read more about it." The formation of the Center for the Book in the Library of Congress in 1977, however, sparked high-level collaboration from at least one network, CBS, and the "Read More About It" project was launched. During the 1979–80 season, thirty-second announcements connecting the content of ten TV specials with related books featured an actor or actress from the program who mentioned several selected titles and urged the huge audience to read more about the setting, the characters, or the historical incident of the program they have just viewed. Reading lists of titles linked to each special are prepared by the Library of Congress, and include popular titles that are often available in paper back editions. These lists, usually consisting of ten or twelve titles—of which only two or three can be mentioned on the broadcast—are published in advance of the telecasts and printed in the ALA *Booklist.* A second season of cooperation by CBS and the Center for the Book designed to "link the pleasure, power and excitement of books and television," featured among other programs a special about the last days of Hitler, a new adaptation of *A Tale of Two Cities,* and the fourteenth annual Country Music Association Awards—a good chance to show the diversity of books.

CHILDREN'S BOOKS ON NETWORK TELEVISION.   Many of the films based on children's books that have been shown in movie theatres and later on television or have been especially made for television are worth encouraging children to watch. Sometimes, as with the adaptation of Konigsburg's *From the Mixed-up Files of Mrs. Basil E. Frankweiler,* the result is disappointing. Sometimes the films are controversial as in *Willy Wonka and the Chocolate Factory* based on Dahl's book *Charlie and the Chocolate Factory.*

Teachers and school and public librarians can prepare themselves for these movies by winnowing the chaff from the wheat, and then by promoting the wheat. Once a movie has been scheduled and advertised in *TV Guide* or the television supplements to newspapers, teachers, librarians, and even parents can check in guides to see how the film was evaluated. Two adult guides are Scheuer's *Movie on TV* and Maltin's *TV Movies.* Four stars is the highest rating. It should be remembered that these guides are for adults, and films for children rank high only when they are for full family viewing. Persons who do not know about the paperback *Movies for Kids* will have to painstakingly go through thousands of movies in each guide and underline those based on children's books.

Movies for Kids was written by Edith Zarrow, the film producer of the Children's Television Workshop, and Ruth M. Goldstein, one of the first teachers of film appreciation in high schools. *Movies for Kids* contains a half to a full page of annotation for the main section of the book called "125 Feature Films." Another supplementary list is called "Not Prime but Choice." A third list is called "75 Short Films." The subtitle of the book explains the age range: *A Guide for Parents and Teachers on the Entertainment Film for Children 9 to 13.*

Movies for Kids is very readable and unlike most guides the entire book can be enjoyable. Read the book through the first time and then come back to it again and again as a reference book when specific movies appear on local stations. Each annotation is written with a flair and embodies tidbits of information that sell the movie just as similar pieces of information sell books in a booktalk. For example, children who love Marguerite Henry will be delighted to know that the burro seen in the film *Brighty of the Grand Canyon* is Henry's own pet. If the children in a family enjoyed the 1968 TV film of *Heidi* while the adult males roared because the spectacular finish to a football game was preempted, then readers will chuckle when reminded of that incident. Readers learn that Elizabeth Taylor's first major role in a movie was *Lassie Come Home* a year before she made *National Velvet.* Another gem is that *Wuthering Heights* with Laurence Olivier was chosen the best picture of 1938 by the New York Film Critics rather than *Gone with the Wind.*

Movies for Kids also helps teachers select the film to show a class after an entire class has read a book. Then the film can be ordered from library film networks, universities, other AV centers or film rental companies. For example, *Movies for Kids* provides the information that Selznick's *Adventures of Tom Sawyer* "as the most satisfactory available adaptation. . .", or that Errol Flynn is unequalled as Robin Hood in the 1938 film *The Adventures of Robin Hood* which includes in the cast Olivia de Haviland and Basil Rathbone.

Other useful features of *Movies for Kids* are the list of film distributors; a list of a hundred books about films; a list of about nineteen organizations concerned with films such as EFLA, the Educational Film Library Association, and a list of periodicals that review films. Some of these, usually found in schools, are *Booklist, Audio-Visual Instruction, Scholastic Teacher.*

Sometimes the networks select and promote special films that are appropriate for family viewing. A recent season of CBS "Family Film Classics" included films based on children's books. Each film was shown in several parts with a week intervening, and one of them was Marjorie Rawlings' Pulitzer Prize-winning novel *The Yearling,* a 1946 film that won three Academy Awards. The film has also been changed to filmstrip format by Films, Inc., so it can be shown on sound filmstrip equipment. *National Velvet,* based on Bagnold's book of the same title, was another in the CBS series as was *Where the Lillies Bloom.* Cleaver's book on which the film was based and its sequel, *Trial Valley,* could be promoted by showing the film.

Dr. Seuss doesn't usually need help to "sell" his books but the ABC television specials based upon his stories have surely exposed many potential readers to them. *How the Grinch Stole Christmas* and *Halloween is Grinch Night* were two Seuss specials. When *All Creatures Great and Small*, by a British veterinarian, based on a book of the same title appeared on TV, intermediate and middle school children read the book and found it fascinating even though it is considered a young adult or adult book. Some of those students even enjoyed the sequels *All Things Bright and Beautiful* and *All Things Wise and Wonderful*, *The Lord God Made Them All*, and *James Herriot's Yorkshire*. If all books were placed in rigid categories by age, many people would miss reading exciting books because it was not the "proper time." The only "proper time" to read a book is when the reader understands and enjoys it, regardless of age.

Other books that defy age limits are Tolkien's *The Hobbit* and the Lord of the Ring series which includes *The Fellowship of the Ring*, *The Two Towers*, and *Return of the King*. *The Hobbit* first appeared on NBC network television in November 1977, and undoubtedly the program will appear again. Sound recordings narrated by Tolkien himself are available: *The Hobbit* and the *Fellowship of the Ring* (includes chapter 5 of *The Hobbit*, "Riddles in the Dark";) *Lord of the Rings: The Two Towers and the Return of the King*; and *Poems and Songs of Middle Earth*. The song "The Road Goes Ever On" is a song cycle based on Tolkien's poetry. *The Hobbit* and the three Lord of the Rings titles are available in paperback. Commentaries on the books are Foster's *A Guide to Middle Earth*, Helms's *Tolkien's World*, and Tolkien's *The Tolkien Reader, Stories, Poems and Commentary*.

Another creation expressly for television for which *Teachers Guides to Television* sent out pre-program information was the ABC's *Children's Novel for Television* series. One of the most successful programs was based on Mildred Taylor's 1977 Newbery medal book *Roll of Thunder, Hear My Cry* which was shown in three consecutive segments. The program could be used to introduce that book as well as Taylor's *Song of the Trees* which was the first book about the Logan family. The book is called *Song of the Trees* because the pines, hickories, beeches and walnuts that stood on Logan land were special to Cassie who spoke to them and heard them singing in the wind in return. While Cassie's father was working in Louisiana laying tracks for the railroad, a white man threatened both the trees and her father. How Papa retained his dignity and self-respect makes an excellent story of life in rural Mississippi during the Depression. The story is short and easy enough for third graders yet the format and story are inviting enough for seventh graders. The Logan family—Cassie, Stacey, Christopher-John (Little Man), Ma, Big Mama, and Papa—also appear in *Roll of Thunder, Hear My Cry*. The television script remained amazingly true to the book, using Taylor's dialogue word-for-word in most instances. Very few stories have such realistic dialogue that can be easily translated from one medium to another.

Taylor helps readers, black and white, understand and feel with the Logan children when they walk to school while the white children ride a bus and when they have to use dirty, cast-off school books after the whites are finished with them. Readers feel with the Logans the pride of ownership in the land that had been purchased by the family during Reconstruction, feel the fear of what the night riders and their burnings can mean to family and friends. Both the film and the books can be viewed or read and then discussed or just internalized. All three will remain unsurpassed social vignettes that can be used and enjoyed for many years by many children.

TELEVISION—THE HOLOCAUST. In April 1978, hundreds of school children of all ages viewed a four-part program about a Jewish family in Nazi Germany during World War II entitled "The Holocaust." Teachers, school library media specialists, and public librarians who did not take advantage of the opportunity to talk about related books missed a marvelous opportunity, and should be alert for rebroadcasts. Another chance to talk about that period in history using the same books will occur when "The Diary of Anne Frank" reappears on television, or if the high school or community theatre produces the play. The play was based on the actual diary of a thirteen-year-old Jewish girl who, with her own and another family, went into hiding for two years in an old Amsterdam warehouse. Additional information about Anne can be found in two books: Schnabel's *Anne Frank: a Portrait in Courage* and *A Tribute to Anne Frank* edited by Steenmeijer. High school students or adults can read Schnabel's book for information about Anne's experiences in Auschwitz and Bergen-Belsen extermination camps, and her death. It is based on interviews with forty-two people who knew Anne. The second book is more valuable to upper elementary students because of the compact bits of information and the pictures. A section on historical background contains a chronology from 1919 to 1942 when the Frank family went into hiding. The number of victims who died in the fifteen concentration camps is given. Other information concerns the diary and how it was found; what happened to Anne and the others when they were captured; how Anne's handwriting was authenticated. There are photos of Anne; other writings by Anne; letters written by children and adults about the diary; statistics about visitors to Anne Frank's house; and the house and locations of various schools, homes for children and young people and other places, including Israel's Anne Frank Forest, which were named for Anne.

Some second-grade and most third-grade students will find it easier to read Reiss's *The Upstairs Room*, the story of another girl who hid from the Nazis in Holland from the time she was ten until the war's end. However, the book has appeal through the intermediate grades. This book grew out of the author's trip to Holland with her daughters to show them the false back in the closet where she and her sister hid. Annie, who was six in 1938, went into hiding in 1942. Events leading up to the occupation of Holland and the increasing persecution of Jews are related. Annie wasn't allowed to sit in her usual seat in school and later was not allowed to go to school at all; the family couldn't rent rooms in hotels or go to parks and beaches; the older sister Rachel lost her teaching job; father's cattle-buying business dropped off, and then Jews were forbidden altogether to engage in business. Later everyone had to wear a yellow star. Finally, when Annie's father learned that the Jews were to be taken away, he found places for his family to be hidden.

The introduction to *The Upstairs Room* could be read to introduce any of the books about the persecution of the Jews during World War II, the television program "The Holocaust," or as background for the play *The Diary of Anne Frank.*

Several other books written about the World War II period are based on actual events. De Jong's *The House of Sixty Fathers* is based on the author's experiences as part of Chennault's Fourteenth Air Force in China during that war. A Chinese orphan, Tien Pao, was adopted by De Jong, who was unable to bring the boy to the United States because of legal complications. Tien Pao has not been heard of since the communists took over China. De Jong has won the Newbery Medal, as well as the International Hans Christian Andersen Medal.

Sachs based *A Pocket Full of Seeds* on a notebook and discussions with Fanny Bienstock Krieger who was twelve when the Nazis occupied France. In the story, Nicole stayed overnight with her friend Francoise just before the Rostens, a wealthy Jewish family, left to escape to Switzerland, and when she returned to her own home she found that her own family had been taken. The book is short but may be complicated for readers who cannot make the adjustment to the flashbacks. The title is the last few words of a sonnet by Edna St. Vincent Millay.

Read the foreword of McSwigan's *Snow Treasure* to the whole class because it explains that the story is based on a true event. Norwegian children pulled gold bullion worth $9 million on their sleds thirty-five miles to the Norwegian freighter Bomma, which reached Baltimore June 28, 1940. Chapter two describes what led up to the plan to keep the gold from the Nazis. The fictitious characters are twelve-year-old Peter Lundstrom, his friend Michael, Helga Thomsen, and Peter's ten-year-old sister Leviske.

Arnold's *A Kind of Secret Weapon* is one of several stories about the Underground. The story takes place in Denmark in the winter of 1943, when the Nazis had already occupied Denmark for three and a half years. Chapter one, read aloud, establishes the background for the story. Peter Andersen came home to find his father and mother in the basement mimeographing an underground newspaper. Other chapters to read aloud are 11 and 12 when Peter delivered the papers to a Copenhagen kiosk where someone with the code name Anna took them. Another interesting part to read is about how Peter did not remember his country before the Nazi occupation. Read on page 105 beginning with "Lars listened . . ." and ending with ". . . tilted the empty glasses to each other." Another exciting scene is when Peter and his mother were hidden by the Pastor and later by Sister Gerda and the nuns at the hospital. Bits of information can be used in telling about the book: how, for instance, Peter's newspaper-man father used information he gained at the newspaper but wasn't allowed to print, or through BBC broadcasts from the hidden radio dropped to patriots by the RAF. Toward the end of the book Peter's father was picked up by the Gestapo, but when the last issue of his underground paper came out, it not only caused trouble for the German Commandant but came at just the right time to help save the lives of Peter and his mother—so the "secret weapon" had a double meaning.

Wuorio's *To Fight in Silence* offers the best possible explanation of the plight of the Danish people. The characters in the book can be introduced by reproducing the chart of the family tree printed in the prologue. The story emphasizes the strong family ties that bind the Scandinavian Countries together. Karen and Kristian's father was a newspaperman from Copenhagen and their cousin Thor's father was a shipowner from Oslo and Bergen. A connection could be made between this book and the previous one because Thor distributed underground newspapers. Thor and his cousins Karen and Kristian, although they are fictitious characters, took part in real events. When the Germans came to take away 8,000 Danish Jews, the Jews were warned and hidden so that only 200 were captured. This was very embarrassing to the German Plenipotentiary in Denmark, because he had already told Hitler that the Jews were purged from Denmark. One part to read aloud appears on page 174 when Kristian thought about how it would feel if it were his family who was told to leave their home on Christmas Eve. Read page 174 "As Kristian bicycled . . ." to ". . . to be a Dane." on page 175. Then read "What a dreadful message . . ." up to the last paragraph on page 175. Another part to read aloud when talking about the book are the pages on how messages were passed. Karen and Kristian received their first message in a bicycle pump and later in a sales slip and by shaking hands (pp. 125–128). Also read "One wintry night . . ." to the first sentence on page 136. The feelings of the time are conveyed by the fact that when the Danes were forbidden to light the traditional midsummer bonfires, the Swedes lighted them in their own nearby country so the Danes could see and enjoy them. Mention Rudi Dietl, a German boy who had lived with the family years ago, who now returned as a Nazi and caused trouble for them.

To Fight in Silence is an excellent book to read aloud to intermediate students, and use to introduce the other books, especially A Kind of Secret Weapon, to the class for independent reading.

Van Stockum's The Winged Watchman is another book about the Underground that can be explained by the title. The Winged Watchman was the windmill in which ten-year-old Joris, his older brother Dirk Jan, his sister Trixie, and his parents lived. In Holland where the story takes place, the position of windmill arms had had significance even before the war, but they were used as signals during the occupation. The Verhagen family was involved in the Dutch Underground— rearing as their own the six-month-old Jewish baby whose parents were taken away, saving the sheets of the underground newspaper from being captured, helping the British flyer, and taking messages. Enough clues are given so readers will figure out the favorite Uncle Cor is really the famous underground hero Kees Kip.

Dog lovers will love the collie pup Joris saved from being conscripted into the German army. Joris called the dog Freya after the Norse goddess, but did not tell his friend Hendrick why he named his dog that. Read pages 23–24 and ask students to investigate the Norse goddess. A funny incident occurred when the family was involved in smuggling the British flyer out in women's clothes.

Another exciting story of the underground takes place in the Zhitomir Forest in the Ukraine. Suhl's Uncle Miska's Partisans contains fictitious places, characters, and events, but was inspired by an actual event. Just after blowing up a German troop train, twenty-five-year-old Yoske and his partner Berek found a body sprawled on the ground, face down, clutching a violin case. That was how they met Mitek or Motelle, who was wandering from village to village looking for a place where the Jewish partisans lived. Mitek wanted to join them so he could avenge the death of his family. Chapter one (pp. 1–11) gives background for the story and can be read to introduce it. The rest of the book contains the action-packed adventures of *Uncle Miska's Partisans*. Motelle's assets are his excellent Ukrainian dialect (because he had never lived in a Jewish ghetto) and his fiddle. Motelle finally avenged his father and his sister Basha, with whom he carried on imaginary conversations. Another version of the story is *Motelle* by Samuels.

Cooper's *Dawn of Fear* is about three friends Derek, Peter, and Geoff who live twenty miles from London. Their fear is that the German planes that flew overhead on their way to bomb London might crash. Another problem was keeping their secret meeting place, their camp, from being destroyed by another gang of boys. The story has a sad ending. During the story, one of the boys and his younger brother listen to a broadcast of "The Children's Hour" when Kipling's *Just So* story "The Cat That Walked by Himself" was told. Students may wish to locate and read that story.

Carrie's War by Bawden is about a widow who took her children to the Welsh mining town to which she and her brother Nick had been evacuated during World War II. Carrie's own war was with herself and her fear that she was responsible for a fire which killed the people with whom she had stayed. The author herself was evacuated from London to a mining village in Wales during World War II.

Bishop's books *Twenty and Ten* and *Pancakes Paris* take the war to France. In *Twenty and Ten*, a class of French fifth graders and their teacher Sister Gabriele were sent to the country to escape the war. After ten Jewish children without ration cards become part of their group, two German officers come looking for them. Sister Gabriele was away getting the mail, the soldiers came but the children were hidden in caves and the twenty others refuse to speak. The story is easy to read and short. Read *Twenty and Ten* aloud to second or third graders. *Pancakes Paris*, which tells of hardships of living in Paris during the war, is even more suitable for reading to second graders. The stories are easily adapted for telling. One receptive group was a sixth-grade French class who enjoyed the retellings of both books.

A book for intermediate and middle school students is Walsh's *Fireweed*. This book is also about evacuating students from their homes. In this story, a boy and a girl who did not know each other before, both decide not to be evacuated and return to their bombed-out homes.

Zei's book *Petro's War* takes place when Greece went to war with Italy. Zei also wrote *Wildcat under Glass* about how fascism came to Greece in 1936 under the government of General Metaxas. In *Petro's War*, good looking Uncle Angelos left for the war a hero with flowers thrown at him and he came back in rags and with lice. Father had no job and quarreled with mother. Sotiris's grandmother was dumped into the cemetery at night so her ration coupons could be kept. Then Petro's grandfather, who had been dying, went out begging. Eventually, Petro met Achilles and Drossoula and became part of the Underground. Petro's code name was Pompom.

Seraillier's *The Silver Sword* takes the war to Poland, and concerns Joseph, the headmaster of a primary school in the suburbs of Warsaw. It is a story of separation, imprisonment, escape, and the efforts of Joseph to reunite with his Swiss wife and children. Use the title of the story explained on pages 33 to 35 to introduce this book.

Greene's *The Summer of My German Soldier* is very different from the other books. It deals with war and the lack of compassion for others. The story appeared on television in the fall of 1978. Students could also be introduced to the sequel, *Morning is a Long Time Coming*. When German prisoners of war came to Jenkinsville, Arkansas, life changed for twelve-year-old Patty. The young German POW Patty helped to escape was the only person except Ruth, the black cook, who treated her as a worthwhile person. In this story, it is the Jewish father who is the villain and the German POW who is the hero. Few books have such an unhappy plot and an unhappy ending.

There are two books in which the Jewish families escaped from Germany in time: Levitin's *Journey to America* and Kerr's *When Hitler Stole Pink Rabbit*. In the first book, twelve-year-old Lisa Platt's Uncle Benjamin and father left for America and the family were to go to Switzerland where father would send for them. When the family arrived in Zurich, mother became ill and the two older girls were sent to a camp where they experienced unpleasantness which they kept from their mother. Before leaving for New York, the girls and their mother learned that their Uncle Arnold and Aunt Helga had been shot and they also experienced passport problems but they got away. Their *Journey to America* took place in 1938. The family in *When Hitler Stole Pink Rabbit* also escaped to Switzerland. The father left first because he was a writer and expected to be imprisoned when Hitler gained power because he was anti-Nazi. Nine-year-old Anna thinks of all the possessions they have left in their own home— especially her stuffed Pink Rabbit. Beginning with "Anna tried to imagine it . . .," read that paragraph including Max's lament until the bottom of page 47 where Max tells his sister that they are lucky to be in Switzerland because the "Nazis came for all our passports the morning after the elections." After reading that much, explain to listeners that the rest of the book is devoted to how Anna and Max adjust to life in Switzerland, Paris, and finally London. In Paris, Max does well in school and Anna has trouble but finally succeeds. The author was the daughter of a distinguished writer who left Germany in 1933 to escape the Nazis. Both books could be used with *The Diary of Anne Frank* especially because the name Anne appears in all the books. Students could be asked to compare the Annes and Annies of several books with the experiences or personality of Anne Frank.

Degens's *Transport 7-41-R* is about a thirteen-year-old girl who is sent on a transport to Cologne, Germany, from the Russian Zone of Germany one year after World War II ended. The girl's mother bribed officials for a passport, saying her daughter was born in Cologne because she learned that more food was available in the western sector and she wanted her daughter to go to school there. Also, the father, who had returned from the war, abused his daughter. In the boxcar, the girl made friends with an old man and woman to whom the rest of the occupants were hostile because the woman's wheelchair took so much room. The interdependence of people in adversity is the message that comes through. A sound filmstrip of this story is available.

Holm's *North to Freedom* was a prize book in Scandinavia. David, a twelve-year-old boy, lived all of his life in a prison camp in Europe and did not understand when the guard told him where to get a bundle containing a water bottle and a compass with directions on how to get to Denmark. The boy lived in the camp with educated political prisoners and learned many languages but had never seen other children and knew nothing of the outside world. The plot has unbelievable elements but strange things do happen in wartime and *North to Freedom* is a book to read aloud and discuss, especially the reasons why persons are placed in concentration camps. Mature readers may be interested in reading Solzhenitsyn's *One Day in the Life of Ivan Denisovich.*

These books should be placed in a display with the caption "If You Liked Anne Frank" or with a poster introducing that film or the television program "The Holocaust." One possible poster would have been the "TV News Preview" which was sent to subscribers of *Facts on File.* A booktalk on this subject could be presented at any time using bits of information presented in this section. Teachers or librarians could read the parts suggested here. However, reading about books is no substitute for reading the books themselves.

CHILDREN'S BOOKS ON PBS TELEVISION.   The Public Broadcasting Service (PBS) is responsible for some exciting commercial-free programming for children. Two of the best known programs are produced by the Children's Television Workshop: "Sesame Street" and "Electric Company." A nine-part series based on the Narnia books of C.S. Lewis was produced by the Children's Television Workshop, and details about these books appear in this chapter in a section called "Time Travel." A series of the programs has been adapted to the languages and cultural nuances of other countries in programs called "Open Sesame." "Sesame Street" consists of an hour of forty or fifty separate segments for preschoolers about social concepts, perceptual skills, letters, and numbers. Top celebrities join the regular cast and add interest and importance to the show. "Big Bird," a regular, has become a celebrity himself. The muppets, who first appeared on "Sesame Street," now have their own prime-time show in the evenings and have become international favorites.

Sometimes the programs have a special theme. The Hawaiian program coincided with the two hundredth anniversary of Captain Cook's landing on the islands. While there are not many books about Hawaii written for preschoolers, it is still important for those children to know that there are books written about Hawaii. Pictures, including real objects like pineapples, also are useful to reinforce what the children saw on TV.

Children will especially enjoy *The Sesame Street Book of Letters, The Sesame Street Book of Puzzles, The Sesame Street Book of Shapes,* and *The Sesame Street Book of Numbers.* All four books are available in inexpensive paperbacks. Older children enjoy purchasing these books at book fairs to give as gifts to younger brothers and sisters. Book fairs before Christmas provide students with worthwhile gifts at a price they can afford. *The Sesame Street Song Book* by Raposo and Moss is available in hard cover edition. The songs "Sesame Street" and "The People in Your Neighborhood" are included. Other books to correlate with "Sesame Street" can be found in the chapter "Experiencing Art in Children's Books" in sections on alphabet books, on counting, on color, and a section called "Lines Become Shapes." Adults will be interested in background reading about the program in Feinstein's *All About Sesame Street* and Lesser's *Children and Television: Lessons from Sesame Street.*

"Electric Company," is the most widely viewed in-school program. The program for primary school children began in 1971; preschool targeted "Sesame Street" began in 1969. The cast includes Fargo North Decoder, Easy Reader, and Valerie the Librarian. Celebrities also appear. Schools and parents should subscribe to *Electric Company Magazine,* and parents consider purchasing *The Best of Electric Company, Electric Company Crazy Cut-Ups, The Electric Company Easy Reader's Activity Book, Electric Company Game Books,* and *The Electric Company Game Show Book.*

Books and recordings are available which reinforce concepts on the television series "Mr. Rogers' Neighborhood." Recordings include *Won't You Be My Neighbor?, Come On and Wake Up!, A Place of Our Own,* and *You are Special.* Some books are: *Mr. Rogers' Neighborhood, Mr. Rogers' Neighborhood: The Costume Party, Mr. Rogers' Songbook, Many Ways to Say I Love You, Tell Me, Mr. Rogers,* and *Mr. Rogers Talks About: The New Baby, Fighting, A Trip to the Doctor, Going to School, Haircuts, Moving.* Some books about social concepts are Anglund's *A Friend Is Someone Who Likes You,* Brown's *Noisy Book,* Flack's two books *Ask Mr. Bear* and *Angus Lost,* Hoban's *A Baby Sister for Frances,* Lipkind's *Finders Keepers,* Wells's *Noisy Nora,* and Zolotow's *Quarreling Book* and *The Hating Book.* Such feelings are explored on the program as sibling rivalry, jealousy, privacy, frustration, and happiness.

Background reading for adults includes the Spring 1977 issue of *School Media Quarterly* which is totally devoted to articles based on speeches given at the AASL Preconference on Children and Television at the 1976 American Library Association conference. One of the speakers was Hedda B. Sharapan, Associate Producer of "Mr. Rogers' Neighborhood." Other adult background reading about television includes Melody's *Children's TV: The Economics and Exploitation.* Chapter three is "A History of Children's Television," and chapter four is "The Unique Characteristics of Children's TV."

In "Mr. Rogers' Neighborhood," children can learn crafts like making puppets from socks and paper cups, see a marionette theatre, listen to various sounds made by musical instruments, see a model steam engine, visit a bakery, and meet pianist Van Cliburn or author-illustrator Ezra Jack Keats.

The trolley that takes viewers back and forth from reality to make-believe, and also puppets seen on "Mr. Rogers' Neighborhood" are available from Ideals, Inc. Since children are familiar with the trolley, use it or a prop with a book display or to introduce easy books about make-believe. A selection of stories could include folk and fairy tales like *The Three Billy Goats Gruff, Henny Penny,* or *Little Red Riding Hood,* and easy books like *Katy and the Big Snow* and *Mike Mulligan and His Steam Shovel* by Burton, *May I Bring a Friend* by DeRegniers, *Little Toot* by Gramatky, *The Mole Family's Christmas* by Hoban, *Tico and the Golden Wings* by Lionni and *Katy-No-Pocket* by Payne, *The Little Engine That Could* by Piper, and *Where the Wild Things Are* by Sendak.

"Once upon a Classic" has the largest PBS audience after "National Geographic Specials," "Masterpiece Theatre," and "Sesame Street." The programs originate from the BBC and Time-Life. Most of the programs run from six to twelve weeks, but several are contained in one hour. The one-hour presentation of *A Connecticut Yankee in King Arthur's Court* based on Mark Twain's story was a winner. In it a nineteenth-century boy is transported back to the court of King Arthur, and takes with him knowledge of advertising, gun-powder, and eating utensils, which he introduced, much to the agitation of Merlin. The television program could be used to introduce the books in this chapter in the section called "Time Travel." Other programs with from six to a dozen episodes were based on famous books, *The Prince and the Pauper* by Twain, *David Copperfield* by Dickens, *Lorna Doone* by Blackmoor, *Heidi* by Spyri, and *Robin Hood.*

"NOVA" is an educational series that coordinates science, social science, and English for junior and senior high school students. Some programs are suitable for intermediate grades. Often the topics are controversial, such as *Alaska: the Closing Frontier,* in which the debate between conservationists and land developers is presented. The guides include film and book lists. Other students may wish to read stories with Alaskan settings such as *Gentle Ben* or *Home is the North,* or books about Alaska such as Carpenter's *Alaska* or Pederson's *Alaska.* Books about conservation, ecology, and progress can also be included. Two "NOVA" programs were on whales and dolphins, for which books listed in the next section on "National Geographic Television Specials" could be used.

Whales, Dolphins and Men and *Dolphins and Men,* are available in video and 16mm format, as are other programs from NOVA, including *Hot-Blooded Dinosaurs, Bird Brain, Why Do Birds Sing?, Inside the Shark, Fusion: The Energy Promise, Will the Fishing Have to Stop?, The Sunspot Mystery, Hunters of the Seal, Secrets of Sleep, Strange Sleep, Lost World of the Maya, The Transplant Experience,* and *Across the Silence Barrier* (deafness).

NATIONAL GEOGRAPHIC TELEVISION SPECIALS.   One of the earliest National Geographic television specials, *The World of Jacques-Yves Cousteau,* aired in 1966. This special provided librarians an opportunity to arrange displays of books about Cousteau, underwater diving, and life in the sea. That program and subsequent programs are available from National Geographic as 16mm films or in video cassette format for nonbroadcast use. Special books to supplement *The World of Jacques-Yves Cousteau* are May's *Captain Cousteau, Undersea Explorer,* Cousteau and Diole's *Life and Death in a Coral Sea,* and two Cousteau books *The Ocean World of Jacques Cousteau* and *Jacques-Yves Cousteau's World without Sun.*

Two National Geographic specials that feature ecologists John and Frank Craighead are *Grizzly!* and *Wild River*. In *Wild River*, viewers travel down Idaho's Salmon River with the Craighead twins and their families. The unpolluted Salmon River is compared with the polluted Hudson and Potomac Rivers. In *Grizzly!* the twin brothers explain how bears are tranquilized so they can be studied to gain information that may prevent their extinction. Radio transmitters on the bear's collars allow them to be tracked. Viewers of the films will enjoy finding articles about the Craigheads in *National Geographic Magazine*.

The Craighead twins have a sister, Jean Craighead George, who is most famous for the book *My Side of the Mountain* which has appeared as a film in theaters and on television. Two of the many titles Jean has illustrated and written with her husband John are *Masked Prowler: The Story of a Raccoon*, and *Meph the Pet Skunk*.

Among the special interest maps available from National Geographic are *History Salvaged from the Sea, Whales of the World, Indians of North America, Traveler's Map of the British Isles*.

Some of the television specials complement books already produced by National Geographic. For example, the program *This Britain, Heritage of the Sea* complements the book *This England*. The book *The World of the American Indian* can be used with the television program *The New Indians* and the book *Undersea Treasures* can be used with the TV special *Treasure*. Whales can be found in Kellogg's *Wild Animals of North America* and Villiers's *Men, Ships and the Sea*. Persons who wish to correlate articles from the magazine with the television specials should check *The Handy Key to Your National Geographics; Subject and Picture Locator, 1915–1977*, or *National Geographic Index, 1947–1976*.

Book displays can be prepared to introduce and follow up National Geographic specials. The list of books about owls found in this chapter would be handy for promoting the TV program *Strange Creatures of the Night* because Minnesota barn owls were included. Other creatures in it were bats, hyenas and sightless cave-dwelling salamanders. Coyotes, rattlesnakes, and wild mustangs were included in the special *The Animals Nobody Loved*. The person who thinks that these animals do not appear in books for primary students should read Ryden's *The Wild Colt: The Life of a Young Mustang*, and *The Mustangs* by the Roevers.

The program that drew one of the largest audiences in the history of public television was National Geographic's 1975 *The Incredible Machine*. Included was information about the heart, blood vessels, inner ear, vocal chords, esophagus, trachea and lung, taste buds, bones, and joints. It is possible to rent or preview a condensed version of this program for nonbroadcast use. It would be very useful in connection with a variety of health and science units, and the library media center has a range of books and other media about the human body and how it works to correlate with it.

THE GREAT WHALES, A NATIONAL GEOGRAPHIC TV SPECIAL.   Viewers who expect National Geographic Specials to be informative, entertaining and first-class productions are not disappointed. Teachers and librarians can with complete confidence promote the programs. Promotional information appears in guides already mentioned in this chapter. Ads for National Geographic Specials, such as *Treasure*, about a Spanish Galleon off the Florida Keys, have appeared in Sunday supplements of newspapers. Use the poster sent from the originating PBS station to introduce books relating to all National Geographic Specials. Included in the program on *The Great Whales* were the birth of a whale, Oscar the killer whale, and the playful "singing" humpback whales. One book that could be used with the display is Fisher's *Namu, Making Friends with a Killer Whale*, which is one of a set of National Geographic Society books in a four-volume set called *Books for Young Explorers*. Set two includes *Honeybees, How Animals Hide, Namu,* and *Pandas*. The whale, caught by a salmon fisherman, was brought to an aquarium in Seattle where it was studied.

A modern fantasy about whales is similar to the Aesop fable of "The Lion and the Mouse." Steig's *Amos and Boris* is about a whale and a mouse who did good turns for each other. When Amos rolled off his ship into the water, he was saved by Boris the whale. Later, when Boris was flung ashore by Hurricane Yetta, Amos got two elephants to push him back into the water. Two folktales in picture-book format are *John Tabor's Ride* illustrated by Blair Lent and McHargue's *The Mermaid and the Whale*. Both are folktales from New England whaling days. The first book is also available as a film.

No feature on whales could fail to include Melville's American classic, *Moby Dick*. The movie *Moby Dick* surfaces on television regularly, or it can be borrowed or rented. The 1956 remake with Gregory Peck is recommended. Include the book *Moby Dick* in the display as well as other books about the whaling industry. The chapter called "Black Gold and Ambergris: Whale," in Forian and Wilson's *Animals That Made U.S. History*, includes Moby Dick, New Englanders, and illustrations of whales. Information about toothed whales including the killer whale, as well as the sperm and blue whales, are included. The sperm whale's contribution to U.S. history is also included in Cook and Wisher's *Warrior Whale*. Many maps and pictures of whaling vessels, equipment, disasters, the towns and people connected with the industry are included in American Heritage's *The Story of Yankee Whaling*. Information about Scrimshaw, the art of carving on bone and teeth, is included. Persons of any age can enjoy the pictures in *The Story of Yankee Whaling*. Giambarba's *Whales, Whaling and Whalecraft* is also about the industry. Meadowcraft's *When Nantucket Men Went Whaling* is an easier book.

Another book that appeals to all ages is Holling Clancy Holling's *Seabird* which is a picture-book work of art. In keeping with Holling's usual style, full-page colored illustrations appear on righthand pages and black and white drawings appear on the left. The Seabird was a gull carved by Ezra Brown from two walrus tusks and mounted on a whalebone when he was a boy on a whaler in 1832 to commemorate a gull that saved the ship. The good luck charm was poised over the cradle of Ezra's son Nathanial and, in turn, four generations of Browns, including James and Ken. The stories of the men and their occupations covers clipper ship days, steamers, ocean liners, and airplanes.

Information on whaling as well as about whales appears in Scheffer's *A Natural History of Marine Animals.* The humpback and killer whales appear in the book. Not all valuable information about the whaling industry appears in nonfiction. Three fiction books about whaling for intermediate and middle school students can provide similar information but within the framework of a story. Dave serviced a plane used to spot whales for a whaling fleet in Halacy's *Whale Spotters.* Fifteen-year-old Hugh was shanghaied by the step-uncle and step-cousin who also had appropriated his grandfather's inheritance. Besides learning whaling aboard the ship *Good Intent,* Hugh was washed ashore on a cannibal island in Sperry's *Danger to Downwind.* In Meader's *Whaler 'round the Horn,* a seventeen-year-old's boat was smashed by a white whale and he was washed ashore on an island inhabited by a Hawiian boy. Another seventeen-year-old boy, Alan from Scotland, was the only survivor of a whaler that hit an iceberg in 1757 near Greenland in Roth's *Iceberg Hermit. The Death of Evening Star; the Diary of a Young New England Whaler* was written and illustrated by Leonard E. Fisher. Although fiction, the story is told by a narrator who found the diary of the *Evening Star*'s cabin boy.

Various Indian tribes also depended upon the whale for food and oil. See pages 77 to 83 and 100 to 102 of Bleeker's *The Sea Hunters, Indians of the North West Coast,* and pages 89 to 191 of Bleeker's *The Eskimo,* for information on how those tribes hunted and cooked whales. Check whale hunting in the index for numerous pages about how the Makah Indians hunted whales in Kirk's *Hunters of the Whale, an Adventure in Northwest Coast Archaeology.* Information for the book came from an archaeological dig in Ozette, Washington. The Bleeker books are intended for intermediate students, and the Kirk book is for middle-school students. However, the format of all three books makes them acceptable to older students with reading problems.

Fisher also illustrated Conklin's *Journey of the Gray Whales.* Gray whales are a type of Baleen whale. The books with an exceptionally fine format, shows a mother whale and her baby from birth to their migration to the Pacific Coast in what is called "The Moby Dick Parade." Thousands of people gather to watch these whales move along the Pacific Coast.

Intermediate students will find information on whaling in chapter 7, "Large Whales and Whaling," of *Some Mammals Live in the Sea* by Waters. Chapter 5, "Dolphins, Porpoises and Small Whales"; chapter 6, "Killer Whales"; and chapter 8, "Marine Mammals in Captivity" provide information on specific types of whales. Photos and an index make this a useful source book. Graham's *Whale Watch* and Simon's *Killer Whale* are both for intermediate students. Over a hundred photos are included in Riedman and Gustafson's *Home Is the Sea: For Whales.* Especially useful is a table giving common name, scientific name, average and maximum length, where found, prevalence, and distinctive features of whales. Material is also included in McNulty's *Whales: Their Life in the Sea.* Evolution, physiology, senses, and the life cycle of whales are given. A glossary, bibliography, and index are included in Hoke and Pitt's *The First Book of Whales.*

Because whales are mammals, also check books like Williamson's *The First Book of Mammals* to find the twelve different pages where whales are mentioned. Earle's *Paws, Hoofs and Flippers* contains information about whales.

Young's *When the Whale Came to my Town* is told by a boy whose great-grandfather hunted whales. Photos help tell this experience of a dying whale that came to Provincetown, Massachusetts.

A display to introduce a whaling television feature such as "The Great Whales," and to induce follow-up should include books for primary readers. Behrens's *Look at the Sea Animals* shows a picture of a gray whale. Selsam's *Animals of the Sea* tells that the great blue whale is the largest animal in the world, weighs as much as forty elephants, and consumes ninety pounds of shrimp a day. Selsam and Hunt's *A First Look at Mammals* tells why whales are mammals. These three books are for students up to third grade. Zim's *The Great Whales* contains large print and can be read by late primary and early intermediate students. A chart shows that a whale is taller than ten elephants on top of each other. The size relationship among a cow, lion, man, dog, and other animals is also given. Clement Hurd's block prints illustrate Edith Hurd's *The Mother Whale* and show five years in the life of a mother sperm whale from one calf to the next. Sperm and little blue whales are included in Goudey's *Here Come the Whales!*

Mizumura's *The Blue Whale* is from the Let's-Read-and-Find-Out Science series for early primary students, and describes the birth of a blue whale, how it nurses, and other information about whales including how they swim and how they provide useful products which must not be over-exploited. Grosvenor's *The Blue Whale* for primary students is published by National Geographic Magazine. Two other books about the blue whale are for intermediate grades and above. Carrighar's *The Twilight Seas*, beautifully illustrated by Peter Parnall, takes the blue whale from birth to death and tells about natural enemies, hunters, voyages, and habitat. Cook's and Wisner's *Blue Whale; Vanishing Leviathan* includes photos, drawings, and old prints. Evolution, food, anatomy, behavior, and conservation are features.

The Right Whale: An Endangered Species is another National Geographic program which featured a zoologist in Argentina who was studying the right whales. *Portrait of a Whale*, another Geographic program, also discusses the right whale which is in danger of extinction. A special feature is listening to whales communicate. Students may enjoy listening to two sound recordings, *Songs of the Whale* and *Deep Voices, the Second Whale Record*. Because the recordings star actual whales —breathing, singing, snoring, and charging—the royalties are given to an organization dedicated to preserving whales. The records are fascinating because few persons have an opportunity to hear whale sounds. *The Right Whale: An Endangered Species*, *Portrait of a Whale*, and *The Great Whales* are available as 16mm films or on videocassettes.

A National Geographic map called *Whales of the World* is also available. Books to include in a display about whales just for fun are Benchley's easy reader *The Deep Dives of Stanley Whale*, McCloskey's *Burt Dow: Deep-Water Man*, and Duvoisin's picture book *The Christmas Whale*. In the last story, the whale takes the place of Santa's reindeer when they are too sick to travel.

INTRODUCING REALISTIC FICTION.   Before beginning a booktalk for students who are to be encouraged to read realistic fiction about life in the United States, teachers and librarians of students grades four through six should read the chapter on "Realistic Fiction," pp. 215–71 of Huck and Young's *Children's Literature in the Elementary School,* for its fine overview of realistic fiction. Numerous books are introduced in the following categories: happy home life, children without parents, relationships with one parent, finding acceptance by peers, life in a gang, racial differences, regional differences, different religious backgrounds, physical handicaps, migrant workers, poverty in many places, war, loneliness, death, gradual development of self, and moments of decision.

Another excellent source is chapter 11, "Realism in Children's Literature," of Georgiou's *Children's Literature,* which gives criteria for realistic fiction. The questions posed are excellent ones to use with students as they evaluate their books or as teachers and librarians evaluate the books they are to share with students. Criteria are in the following categories: theme, plot, characterization, style, and setting. Georgiou introduces books for three age groups in the categories: stories of animal life, stories of family life, stories of the sea, and sport stories.

"Criteria for Realistic Stories" are included also in chapter 10, "Modern Fiction," of Sutherland and Arbuthnot's *Children and Books.* Authors of books for children in grades four through six whose books are discussed are Estes, Enright, Sorenson, Lenski, Cleary, Robertson, Little, Fitzhugh, Fox, Snyder, Hamilton, Cleaver, Konigsburg, and Greene. Read this section, pages 311 to 328, for help in incorporating these books into a booktalk.

Problems encountered in the process of developing a sense of self identity include: Blume's *Are You There God? It's Me, Margaret* and *Then Again Maybe I Won't* (growing up physically), Burch's *Queenie Peavy* (antisocial behavior) and *Skinny* (orphaned), Byar's *The House of Wings* (abandonment) Campbell's *Why Not Join the Giraffes?* (misfit), Carlson's *Ann Aurelia and Dorothy* (friendship), Cleaver's *Ellen Grae and Lady Ellen Grae* (growing up), Fitzgerald's *Harriet the Spy* (peer relationships) and *The Long Secret* (mystery), Greene's *Unmaking of Rabbit* (peer relationships), Gripe's *The Night Daddy* (loneliness), Jackson's *Call Me Charley and Tessie* (interracial friendships), Stolz's *Bully of Barkham Street* (antisocial behavior), and Wagner's *J.T.* (loneliness).

All of those books are available as Dell Yearling paperbacks so it is inexpensive to order multiple copies. Exciting projects for each of these books are included in three books by Reasoner: *Releasing Children to Literature, Where the Readers Are,* and *When Children Read.*

Teachers who want to read chapters from realistic fiction to introduce certain books to students can find selections in several anthologies. Chapter 7, "Domestic Fiction," of Nelson's *Comparative Anthology of Children's Literature,* (pp. 441–505) includes selections from Cleary's *Henry Huggins,* Burch's *Skinny,* Wier's *The Loner,* Rabin's *False Start,* and Little's *Mine for Keeps.* An annotated bibliography of domestic and realistic fiction for children appears at the end of chapter 7.

Chapter 8, "American Minorities," of Nelson's *Comparative Anthology of Children's Literature* (pp. 506–75), includes selections from Waltrips's *Quiet Boy* (Indian), Jackson's *Call Me Charley* (Black), Sterling's *Mary Jane* (Black), Sorenson's *Plain Girl* (Quaker), Konigsburg's *About the B'Nai Bagels* (Jewish), Shotwell's *Roosevelt Grady* (migrant), Wier's *The Winners* (migrant), Lenski's *Cotton in My Sack* (regional poor), and Fitzhugh's *Harriet the Spy* (urban wealthy). Bibliographies at the end of chapter 8 are divided into topics: economic minorities, racial minorities, and religious minorities.

Some selections to read from "Life in the United States," which is a section of realistic fiction from part 3 of Sutherland's *Arbuthnot Anthology of Children's Literature*, are Cleary's *Ellen Tebbits* (pp. 611–17); Estes's *Middle Moffat* (pp. 627–32); Fox's *How Many Miles to Babylon* (pp. 632–38); Byar's *The Midnight Fox*, Sachs's *Peter and Veronica* (pp. 641–44); Konigsburg's *From the Mixed-Up Files of Mrs. Basil E. Frankweiler*; Burch's *Queenie Peavy* (pp. 666–69); Stolz's *A Dog on Barkham Street* (pp. 670–72); Cleaver's *Ellen Grae*, (pp. 684–87); Snyder's *The Egypt Game* (pp. 691–95); and Shotwell's *Roosevelt Grady* (pp. 695–98).

Numerous books that can be classed as realistic fiction and can be used in booktalks are included in this book. Several are included in the section called "Survival Books—A Booktalk" that are about modern American young people.

Books about people who are blind appear in a section of this chapter called "Dolphins, Dinosaurs and Other Subjects Introduced by Basal Readers." Realistic fiction from that section that can be included with these books are Butler's *Gift of Gold* and *Light a Single Candle*, Chipperfield's *A Dog to Trust*, Clewes's *Guide Dog*, Garfield's *Follow My Leader*, McDonnell's *Stevie's Other Eyes*, Putnam's *Triumph of the Seeing Eye*, and Rappaport's *Banner Forward*. Most of the books in this chapter in the section called "Using Sequels" would fall into the realistic category.

All of the books included in the sound filmstrip *Reading for the Fun of It: Realistic Fiction* introduce books about modern American children except Friis-Baastad's *Don't Take Teddy*, which was published in Norway. Books included in that filmstrip are Blume's *It's Not the End of the World* (divorce), Burch's *Queenie Peavy* (antisocial behavior), Byar's *The House of Wings* (abandonment), Cleary's *Ellen Tebbits* (friendship), Cleaver's *Where the Lilies Bloom* (responsibility), Cunningham's *Dorp Dead* (orphaned), Fitzhugh's *Harriet the Spy* (peer relationships), Friis-Baastad's *Don't Take Teddy* (retardation), Hamilton's *Zeely* (hero worship), Miles's *Annie and the Old One* (responsibility), and Weik's *The Jazz Man* (abandonment). Annotations for the following books appear in the "Bibliography for Students," in the teacher's guide: Burch's *Skinny* (orphaned), Byar's *Summer of the Swans* (retardation), Gage's *Big Blue Island* (orphaned), Konigsburg's *Jennifer, Hecate, MacBeth, William McKinley and Me, Elizabeth* (friendship, apprenticed witches), Krumgold's *Onion John* (friendship), and Neville's *It's Like This, Cat* (city life, boy's first date).

Another sound filmstrip that can be used to introduce a closely related type of realistic fiction (people living today in other countries), is *Reading for the Fun of It: Many Lands.* A pilot introduces the filmstrip which takes viewers on a trip around the world. The first book is Sommerfelt's *The Road to Agra* (India). Other books introduced are Buck's *The Big Wave* (Japan), Venable's *Hurry the Crossing* (Africa), O'Dell's *Sing Down the Moon* (U.S.-Navaho), Wojciechowska's *Shadow of a Bull* (Spain), Krumgold's . . . *And Now Miguel* (Mexico), DeJong's *The Wheel on the School* (Netherlands), and Watson's *The Mikhtar's Children* (Palestine and Israel). Books listed in the bibliography are Benary-Isbert's *The Ark* (Germany), Cunningham's *Burnish Me Bright* (France), Young Ik's *Blue in the Seed* (Korea), Schatz's *Bola and the Oba's Drummer* (West Africa), Seredy's *The Good Master* (Hungary), and Uchido's *Journey to Topaz* (U.S.-Japanese). Use this filmstrip to introduce other geographical fiction.

INTRODUCING BIOGRAPHIES.   Sometimes students are asked to read and report on a biography of their choice. However, many students find it difficult to identify a person about whom they would like to read. When students are looking for biographies on their own, they tend to look at books about people with whom they are familiar and don't expand their knowledge by learning about someone about whom they know nothing or very little. Many readers find that in adult life biography has become their favorite category of book and so the biography habit is one worth cultivating.

It is possible for students to be asked to search out their biographies from the card catalog by looking up subjects such as "U.S. History—Civil War—Biography," or "America, Discovery and Exploration—Biography." However, many students cannot think of a subject or look only at the subjects that were mentioned in class or crowd around the drawers containing books on sports. When the suggestion is made to look under the last name of someone they wish to read about, students often can't think of anyone or they choose a contemporary figure, usually someone in the entertainment field, about whom no individual biographies have been written.

Students need help with this. The library media specialist should gather a representative group of biographies, most of which are within the reading abilities of the average students in the class. Include some titles that are easier and some that are more difficult for other students in the class. Hold up the books, name the biographee, and tell that the person is an olympic star, explorer, naturalist, government leader, historical figure, scientist, inventor, author, or whatever. This introduces students to people they might otherwise not know about. Even if the student does not choose to read a book about Einstein, he or she has at least been exposed to his name and his accomplishment.

Library media specialists also need to introduce *vocabulary* to students: "biography," "autobiography," "anthology," "individual biography," "collective biography," "fictionalized biography," and "biographical fiction." Students should be told how biographies of different types are cataloged in the library. It is also important to point out that individual biographies are the only books in the library that do not include the first few letters of the author's last name under the call number. Instead, biographies include the first few letters of the person *about* whom the book is written. This procedure means that all the books about Abraham Lincoln will be together on the shelf.

One filmstrip which has been successfully used with students is *Biography, Literature for Children*. The teacher's guide contains content information, behavioral objectives, suggested discussion and activities, a script, a project for pupil follow-up, and bibliography. The main focus of the filmstrip is Benjamin Franklin as told by the d'Aulaires. Other books about Franklin mentioned are Lawson's *Ben and Me*, Judson's *Benjamin Franklin*, and Eaton's *That Lively Man, Ben Franklin*. One excellent project that could follow viewing the filmstrip, especially if the class is studying colonial America at the time, is to ask groups of students to locate other books about Franklin and compare the information found in those books. The library media specialist would have to be sure that books about Franklin by the following authors were in the library media center, either owned or borrowed for the project: d'Aulaire, C. Daugherty, J. Daugherty, Eaton, Fleming, Fritz, Meadowcroft, Merriam, Monjo, and Scarf.

Teachers and library media specialists who are preparing for a unit on biography should read the following chapters in children's literature anthologies. Chapter 6, "Biography and Historical Fiction," of Huck and Young's *Children's Literature in the Elementary School* (pp. 272–330), discusses criteria for juvenile biography, types of biographies and series. A bibliography is given. Chapter 12, "Biography," of Sutherland & Arbuthnot's *Children and Books* (pp. 400–43), explains biography as history and as literature. Fictionalized biography, biographical fiction, collective biographies, and series are introduced. The books that are introduced are divided into groups for different ages of readers.

Several anthologies include selections from biographies from which a teacher may choose to read. Selections about the lives of Ben Franklin, Paul Revere, Abe Lincoln, Louisa May Alcott, Harriet Tubman, Mark Twain, Crazy Horse, Emmeline Pankhurst, Teddy Roosevelt, Helen Keller, and Shirley Chisholm are included in Sutherland's *The Arbuthnot Anthology of Children's Literature* (pp. 776–852). Selections about Ethan Allen, Roger Williams, Chief Joseph, Louisa May Alcott, Mark Twain, Helen Keller, Benjamin West, Nathanial Bowditch, Lord Nelson, and Vasco Da Gama are included in chapter 12, "Biography" of Nelson's *A Comparative Anthology of Children's Literature*. Selections about Christopher Columbus, Amos Fortune, George Washington, Lafayette, Daniel Boone, John James Audubon, Abe Lincoln, Hans Christian Andersen, Louisa May Alcott, Clara Barton, Madame Curie, and Albert Schweitzer are included in a section called "Biography" in Johnson's *Anthology of Children's Literature* (pp. 767–824). Most of the famous people included in these anthologies are historical/traditional heroes or heroines. That is why that makes it even more important to include biographies of other people in a booktalk on biographies, so that children won't get the idea that *all* the great people have lived in the past.

One project suitable for third graders would be to introduce them to the biographies by Jean Fritz. Fritz's biographies, many of them, are about figures of the American Revolution, and Fritz's contribution is to present humorous and humanizing portraits of them. In *Why Don't You Get a Horse, Sam Adams?*, Sam is portrayed as not caring especially about his personal appearance. So when Sam went to a meeting in Philadelphia in 1774 as the representative of Massachusetts, his friends gave him gifts of clothing. The title alludes to the fact that when the British were coming, Sam Adams had to ride in a carriage because he couldn't ride a horse. John Adams finally appealed to Sam's vanity. When Sam imagined all the statues of everyone else on horseback but himself, he learned to ride a horse. During the first practices, Adams wore padded drawers. Fritz documents her information. In this book a postscript says information for this last fact came from a letter of John Adams to a friend, James Warren.

Will You Sign Here, John Hancock? explains that Hancock was a dandy who was vain and loved praise. Hancock's large signature on the Declaration of Independence is part of his image. Hancock was president of the Continental Congress but according to Fritz, Hancock did not do well as a general.

Where was Patrick Henry on the 29th of May? includes Henry's "Liberty or Death" speech. According to Fritz's book, Henry liked the out of doors and was not a successful planter or shopkeeper, but he loved to hear lawyers argue when court was in session so he decided to become a lawyer. Henry was shy at first but later became an articulate advocate for colonial independence, and was elected governor of Virginia five times.

Other biographies by Fritz are *Can't You Make Them Behave, King George?*, *And Then What Happened, Paul Revere?*, *What's the Big Idea, Ben Franklin?*, *George Washington's Breakfast*, and *Where do You Think You're Going, Christopher Columbus?* Fritz's biographies are excellent for students who are reluctant readers because the stories are funny, interesting, and readable. All of the titles except the last two are available in audio cassette format and are read by Fritz herself.

Monjo's humorous I Can Read biography of Teddy Roosevelt, *One Bad Thing about Father* is also interesting and easy to read. The book tells how Roosevelt read stories by Uncle Remus and poetry to his children. Quentin, the narrator, lists all the things father could have done instead of being president, all of which were actual accomplishments of Teddy Roosevelt. In an author's note, readers learn that Quentin died at the age of twenty in World War I.

INTRODUCING FANTASY.   Teachers and librarians can introduce fantasy to intermediate and middle school students by showing filmstrips about fantasy; by showing filmstrips based on books that are classified as fantasy; by organizing displays of books, bibliographies and booktalks; or combinations of all of these techniques.

The sound filmstrip *Fantasy, Literature for Children* introduces fantasy by discussing Selden's *Cricket in Times Square*. Other titles mentioned in the filmstrip are L'Engle's *A Wrinkle in Time*, Baum's *The Wizard of Oz*, Milne's *Winnie-the-Pooh*, Norton's *The Borrowers*, Lindgren's *Pippi Longstocking*, and Lofting's *Dr. Doolittle*. Three other authors are mentioned: C. S. Lewis, William Pene Du Bois, and Eleanor Cameron. Show the filmstrip to students and then let them discuss some of the suggested topics. After viewing the filmstrip, students can check out books from a group of fantasies that have been gathered for the purpose. Some are listed in the bibliography that accompanies the filmstrip.

The best article for background reading on fantasy is in Georgiou's *Children's Literature* (pp. 242–79). The "Criteria for Fantasy," included here are exceptionally helpful and an annotated bibliography provides excellent booktalk material. Another outstanding source is Hucks and Young's *Children's Literature in the Elementary School*, in which "Guides to Evaluating Modern Fantasy," pp. 338–39, provides teachers and library media specialists with four questions to ask in evaluating modern fantasy. Then Huck introduces fantasies in the following categories: strange and curious worlds, imaginary kingdoms, animal fantasy, the world of toys and dolls, Lilliputian worlds, fabulous flights, magical powers, overcoming evil, and time magic.

Chapter 8, "Modern Fantasy," in Sutherland and Arbuthnot's *Children and Books*, also offers information in the following categories: tales with folktale elements, tales of pure imagination, modern stories of talking beasts, personified toys and inanimate objects, and humorous fantasy. The bibliography of *Children and Books* (pp. 236–43) also includes science fiction.

An annotated bibliography (of fantasy) in the National Council of Teachers of English's *Adventuring With Books*. Also check the Index to *The Children's Catalog* under "Fantastic Fiction," and *Elementary School Library Collection* under "Fantasy."

Two bibliographies without annotations that appear in Lickteig's *An Introduction to Children's Literature* are "Personified Toys and Animals," and "Fantasy." Books from those lists as well as the above mentioned sources could provide a collection of books for students to check out after viewing the sound filmstrip *Reading For the Fun of It: Fantasy*. Books introduced in this one are Alexander's *The Book of Three*, Babbitt's *The Search for Delicious*, Boston's *Treasure of Green Knowe*, Butterworth's *The Enormous Egg*, Eager's *Half Magic*, Juster's *The Phantom Tollbooth*, Lewis's *The Lion, the Witch and the Wardrobe*, Lindgren's *Pippi Longstocking*, Norton's *The Borrowers*, Selden's *The Genie of Sutton Place*, and White's *Charlotte's Web*. Annotations for the following books appear in the "Bibliography for Students" of the teacher's manual: Cooper's *The Dark is Rising*, Dahl's *James and the Giant Peach*, Druon's *Tistou of the Green Thumbs*, Le Guin's *The Wizard of Earthsea*, and Travers's *Mary Poppins*.

Numerous recordings, filmstrips, or films of fantasies are available for Alexander's *The High King*, Atwater's *Mr. Popper's Penguins*, Du Bois's *The Twenty-One Balloons*, Kendall's *The Gammage Cup*, Lawson's *Rabbit Hill*, LeGuin's *The Tombs of Atuan*, Lofting's *The Voyages of Doctor Doolittle*, Norton's *The Borrowers*, Travers's *Mary Poppins*, and White's *Charlotte's Web*. All of *Charlotte's Web* is available as a recording or sound filmstrip, and Julie Harris reads from *Stuart Little* in a sound recording. The first twenty-four frames of the sound filmstrip *Humor* are devoted to *Mr. Popper's Penguins* by Atwater. Selections from that story and an article about the arctic appear in the third grade Macmillan reader *Better than Gold*. Maurice Evans reads from *Win-*

nie the Pooh on three recordings. Various chapters from Wind in the Willows are available on recordings by several different actors.

Besides appearing as a major part of the sound filmstrip Fantasy, Literature for Children, Selden's A Cricket in Times Square is also available as a separate two-part filmstrip. That title is also available as a recording and so are the sequels Harry Cat's Pet Puppy and Tucker's Countryside.

Other parts of this chapter can provide descriptions of books that can be used in displays and booktalks of fantasies. Descriptions of personified owls, mice, and dolls are included in sections on "Owls," "Mice," and "Dolls."

Information about audiovisuals to accompany Tolkien's Lord of the Rings trilogy and The Hobbit appear in the section of this chapter called "Children's Books on Network Television," as well as in the chapter on "Enjoying Poetry." Books about The Borrowers, outstanding fantasy created by Norton, appear in this chapter in the section "Reading Aloud to Children," and books about Mary Poppins by Travers are introduced by music in the chapter, "Enhancing Books through Music." Six phonograph records appear in the multimedia bibliography in this chapter. Three books by Dickinson take place in England when the Machine Haters or "Changes" have taken over the country and life has reverted back to the middle ages. The Weathermonger is about Geoff and Sally, a weathermonger and a witch. Heartease is the sequel to The Weathermonger in which Margaret and Jonathan rescued a witch and escaped across the Channel in an old tugboat. Devil's Children is the sequel to Heartease. Twelve-year-old Nicky Gore became a liaison between the villagers and a group of forty Sikhs who settled on an old farm.

LeGuin's The Wizard of Earthsea is the first book about Sparrowhawk who trained to be a master wizard at a school for wizards. While he was training to become a wizard, Sparrowhawk unleashed an evil force that could destroy the world. A selection from the Wizard of Earthsea appears in Nelson's A Comparative Anthology of Children's Literature. The Tombs of Atuan is the sequel to The Wizard of Earthsea. Sparrowhawk as the Wizard Ged became involved with Lenar (Arha) who had been serving the Nameless Ones as priestess in The Tombs of Atuan for eleven of her seventeen years. A recording based on The Tombs of Atuan is available. In The Farthest Shore, Prince Arren accompanied Ged in his search for the evil spirits.

TIME TRAVEL, A BOOKTALK.   Use the theme of time travel to introduce the following books to intermediate and middle school students. Ask students to name the three dimensions—height, length, and width. Then ask them if they know what is considered to be the fourth dimension. Explain that the books to be introduced all have a common element—characters that travel back and forth through time.

It should be noted that some of the books in this section are categorized as fantasy and some as science fiction. Sometimes the stories appear on both lists, depending upon the definition by the person making the list. Sources for definitions of these two genres occur in other sections of this chapter.

The thread that ties all these books together is how each person entered the fourth dimension. A variety of methods are utilized: a blue stone, a whispering shell, fog, toys, a mirror, an epileptic seizure, a picture on the wall, a portrait, a wardrobe, and a tesseract.

One of the earliest and most famous books about time travel was H. G. Wells's *The Time Machine*, a book that first appeared in 1895, in which the time traveler spent eight days in past time and had only been gone for four hours. Tell about this book or play the audio cassette to introduce the other stories about time. Playing the cassette in the classroom before coming to the media center for a booktalk would be an excellent introduction to the time travel theme. Or, the cassette and book could be made available to students to check out after the booktalk. To make it easier to follow the book while listening to the cassette, have someone underline the parts of the book that are recorded on the cassette. This can be an individual project of someone in the class.

Beckman's *Crusade in Jeans* is a recent book about a time machine. A twentieth-century teenager, Rudolf Hefting of Amsterdam, experimented with a time machine so that he could enter the middle ages and see knights and tournaments. Instead, a miscalculation set Rudolf down in the middle of ten thousand children who were part of the Children's Crusade headed for Jerusalem in the thirteenth century.

The subject of time travel appears more casually in numerous books for children. The rabbit in Carroll's *Alice in Wonderland* was late for a very important date and Alice followed him to another time and place. Barrie's *Peter Pan* found "Never Never Land" where children never grew old. Students who have not read the book have seen the play on television, and so many pupils know Wendy, John, and Michael as well as Peter, Tinker Bell, and Captain Hook.

In one of Lucy Boston's books about the children of Green Knowe, *Stranger at Green Knowe*, Tolly saw the portraits of the children who had lived at Green Knowe long ago, lived in their room, and saw their toys. When Tolly's great grandmother told him stories about those children, they became real to him. The stories in sequence are *The Children of Green Knowe, The Treasure at Green Knowe, The River at Green Knowe, The Stranger at Green Knowe, The Enemy at Green Knowe, Guardians at Green Knowe*. Another book, *The Stones of Green Knowe* takes the characters from a different perspective. That book begins in the eleventh century when the house was built and the boy of those times met the Children of Green Knowe of the future.

The house at Green Knowe is very important to all the books by Boston. Houses and castles are also important to several other stories. A ten year old orphan goes to live with his uncle, a wizard, in Bellaire's *The House With a Clock on Its Walls*. When Chris Fitton bought an antique miniature English inn, he and his stepsister Nan Mallory were transported into the time of James I of England. The house is pictured on the front cover of the book jacket, Norton's *Red Hart Magic*. A miniature china cottage provided Betony Dovewood the vehicle to travel over a hundred years back in time. The cottage was only five inches high, had a thatched roof, walls covered with roses and morning glories. The miniature cottage in Freeman's *The Other Face*, was also cracked. A picture of this miniature home also appears on the cover of the book jacket.

In Norton's *Lavender Green Magic*, some children went to live with their grandparents in a rundown house called "Dimsdale Place" in the country, and were transported to colonial days. A pillow caused Judy to dream and she was told to go into a maze.

There is a mystery in Langton's *The Diamond in the Window*. Eleanor and Edward, twentieth-century children, searched for a family secret involving Aunt Lily's lost love, Prince Krishna, and the aunt and uncle for whom they were named, Ned and Nora, who had disappeared as children. The search took the children back into the New England of Emerson, Thoreau, and the Alcotts. *The Swing in the Summerhouse* is the sequel to *The Diamond in the Window*.

Hold up Utley's *A Traveler in Time* and ask students how you would feel if you were taken back into time and had the hindsight of history to know that something terrible was going to happen but could find no one to believe you. That's what happened when Penelope walked through a door in her aunt and uncle's English manor house into the Elizabethan world of her ancestors and tried to use her knowledge of the future to change events involving Mary, Queen of Scots.

In Cameron's *The Court of the Stone Children* Nina, a twentieth-century girl, saw Dominique, a girl from Napoleon's era, near the carved stone children in the courtyard of a museum in San Francisco. "Dominique de Lombre with Her Cat, Lisabetta" was a painting by Jean Louis Baptiste Chrysastome in the museum. The museum also contained rooms from Dominique's chateau in France and the statues of six children came from her garden. Dominique came to life and begged Nina to help her. Dominique's father had been courtmartialed and shot for conspiring against the Emperor Napoleon in the early 1800s and for murdering Maurice, an old family retainer. Dominique wanted her father acquitted. One of the six statues in the museum courtyard held the key to the mystery.

Stone Griffins came to life in McHargue's *Stoneflight*, and might be introduced to students who enjoyed Cameron's book. Readers may be interested in Cresswell's *A Game of Catch* in which children from a painting in a museum come to life.

In Sleigh's *Jessamy*, Jessamy explored an old house and found herself back in 1914 during World War I, involved in a mystery regarding the theft of a rare book.

Hold up the book *Charlotte Sometimes* by Farmer and ask students if they ever wondered what it would be like to be trapped in another time. One morning Charlotte woke up to find that she had become Clare, a girl who lived during World War I.

Eleven-year-old Susie was on vacation at Merlin Castle which was famous for Merlin hawking. A mysterious boy named Bran could read the *Ancient Book of Merlin* about hawking by Dame Alip, in Williams's *Castle Merlin*.

In Dunlop's *Elizabeth, Elizabeth*, Elizabeth Martin was visiting her Aunt Kate who was researching the eighteenth-century Melville Family in a two-hundred-year-old house in Scotland, when a mirror transported Elizabeth back two hundred years in time. In Allan's *Romansgrove*, Claire and Richard moved back to the time seventy years before when Romansgrove had burned down.

Two books by Lively deal with time travel and houses. A seventy-year-old carved shield from New Guinea found in *The House in Norham Gardens* caused fourteen-year-old Clare Mayfield to have dreams. In *The Ghost of Thomas Kemp* an English boy, James Harrison, was claimed by Thomas Kemp, a seventeenth-century sorcerer, as his apprentice.

Rosemary went to visit her young vibrant aunt in an old house with a garden, and time stopped. Later Rosemary was transported into colonial times, in *Parsley, Sage, Rosemary and Time*, by Curry. Also by Curry, *Poor Tom's Ghost* is about a visit from a Shakespearean actor.

In *Tom's Midnight Garden* by Pearse, a Victorian garden materialized when the clock struck thirteen. The unusual grandfather clock along with Tom's situation was introduced in the first chapter, and in chapter two, the clock struck thirteen. Those chapters could be summarized and then chapter three read aloud. In that chapter, Tom had his experience in the hall and garden and later wondered if it were real or a dream. Often in fantasy, readers wonder how much of the story happened in the imagination of the main character.

In Eager's *The Time Garden*, the children went through time to Elizabethan age with the help of Natterjack, a small cockney monster. In another Eager book, *Half Magic*, it was a coin that looked like a nickel that caused magic things to happen, or to half happen. Their mother accidentally borrowed the coin to use for bus fare. While her aunt and uncle were showing her pictures of their vacation, mother wished she were home and found herself in the middle of nowhere, half way home, as the coin only granted half wishes. The coin allowed the children to go into the time of King Arthur and speak with Merlin and become involved with Sir Launcelot. In Eager's *Magic by the Lake*, Jane, Martha, Katherine, and Mark found a different kind of magic. They were transported to the South Pole where they could watch it being discovered. After snooping around in a cave, they hid only to find that thieves came and accused Ali Baba of disturbing their oil jars. The four had found their way into *The Arabian Nights*. In *Magic or Not?* Laura and James moved to Connecticut and met a friend, Lydia. Wishes seemed to be granted by a wishing well, or were they? In *Knight's Castle*, eight-year-old Ann and eleven-year-old Roger and their mother went to live with their aunt while their father was getting well. The toy soldier that belonged to their grandfather took them back into the storybook days of Ivanhoe, Rebecca, and Robin Hood.

As can be seen from the previously mentioned books, characters in books about time travel visit a variety of places and times. Mian's *Net to Catch a War* is about moving back to 1845 and the war with Mexico. Arthur's *On the Wasteland* is about moving back to when the Vikings ruled. *The Chalk Cross* by Amoss is about voodoo in New Orleans in 1832. Stephanie Martin, an art student at the Academie aux Bois in New Orleans, exchanged identities with the daughter of a Voodoo Queen. An American girl became a British peasant named Anne when she touched a strange girl in the woods in Anderson's *To Nowhere and Back*. In Oldenburg's *Potawatomi Indian Summer*, six modern children were part of a sad dream of a Manhagawa, the official dreamer of the

Potawatomis. Manhagawa dreamed a sad dream that there was no place in the future for his tribe, the forest, and animals. Pages 25–33 tells about the dream and how the children were transported into the past, and could be read aloud to introduce the story.

Portraits and pictures provide a frequent means of sending persons into the past. After seeing a portrait of a sixteenth-century Spanish girl, fifteen-year-old Willow dreamed about becoming that girl. Children saw a picture of an island and were transported there when they looked at it and said its name over and over. The cousins from Vermont and brother and sister from Paris met in Freydey's *Osprey Island*. Other books in which portraits played a major role are Boston's books about Green Knowe and Lewis' *The Voyage of the Dawn Treader*.

In *A Pattern of Roses* by Peyton, a boy has a counterpart in the past. A boy in a portrait showed a Danish boy that people, not time, are the most important factor in history in Holm's *Peter*.

A picture in an antique shop formed a bond between twentieth-century Katie and an ancestor who looked exactly like her in Shuburne's *Why Have the Birds Stopped Singing?* Katie, an epileptic, was allowed to go on a trip with a teacher and several friends if she promised to take her pills on schedule. When Katie saw a picture of a girl wearing the costume of another period in an antique shop, she was amazed that the girl looked exactly like her. In her rush to find out about the girl Katie forgot her pills, and as she said "The next thing I knew I had stepped off, literally, into thin air." Read the rest of page 34 and the beginning of page 35 which begins another chapter. During the brief time of Katie's seizure, she was transported into the time of her great, great, great grandmother Kathryn, who also had epilepsy, and was locked up by an uncle who wanted her inheritance. Katie lived Kathryn's life for several weeks during the brief period after Katie's fall. Use the paperback edition of this book when introducing it because the picture on the front cover shows Katie and her look-alike portrait.

A twentieth-century girl spent months in a primitive society in Mazer's *Saturday, the Twelfth of October*. As in this story time travel is often a form of escape for an unhappy adolescent.

The girl in Mary Stolz's *Cat in the Mirror* can be compared with the one in Mazer's *Saturday, the Twelfth of October* because both girls were unhappy and both entered another time by unhappily attaching themselves to an object. In *Cat in the Mirror*, Erin, a modern girl, and Irun, an ancient Egyptian girl, changed places. Both Erin and Irun had mothers they disliked, both had a cat, both were loved by a housekeeper or servant with similar names (Flora and Fl'ret), and they looked alike. Erin was not a member of any group at her exclusive school and made no friends except for a new Egyptian boy named Seti. When she overheard the "in-group" making fun of her at a museum, Erin flung herself sobbing against a glass wall panel holding an Egyptian exhibit. The glass reflected like a mirror and Erin became Irun. A mirror also aids Bethany's adventures in Murphy's *Grass Tower*.

In Mayne's *Hill Road*, Magra of Celtic Britain fled from pursuers who thought she was a witch because of her red hair, so she changed places with a modern British girl Sara who also had red hair.

In Mayne's *Earthfasts,* Modern Day David and Keith met eighteenth-century Nellie Jack John who had gone into the dungeon of a castle seeking King Arthur, his knights, and treasure. The drummer boy was the link between the two ages.

A bugler had a place in Lawson's *The Spring Rider.* Jacob and his sister Gray saw a Yankee bugler, a southern cavalry leader, and the Spring Rider (who was Abraham Lincoln) on their farm which had been the scene of a Civil War battle. The Spring Rider wanted the bugler to play taps so the ghosts of the battlefield could rest in peace. It is very difficult for some students to follow this book because the children themselves wonder what is real and what is not. Be sure to read the paragraph that follows the table of contents.

Callie, Harry and Lisa in Curry's *Daybreakers* moved between time zones by means of a small blue-green stone. In a companion book, *Beneath the Hill,* through the elf Kaolin and a door in the hillside, the children found themselves taken from modern times into ancient Wales.

While visiting her Aunt Esther in Wales, Carrie met the invisible Pontiflex family who traveled in time from 1921 to 1971, in Cresswell's *Up the Pier.* Conditions had to be just right to see them; the pierkeeper never did.

Three American children—twelve-year-old Peter, ten-year-old Becky, and fifteen-year-old Jen—went with their father David Morgan to the University of Wales where he taught for a year. Peter was taken back into time by a tuning key belonging to the harp of Taliesin, a famous sixth-century Welsh bard. After reading Bond's *A String in the Harp,* a student might be curious to learn more about Taliesin. Be sure to introduce Robbins's *Taliesin and King Arthur* which tells how the poet sang for King Arthur. Students may also be interested in reading Minnton's *Legends of King Arthur,* Pyle's *The Story of King Arthur and his Knights,* MacLeod's *The Book of King Arthur and his Noble Knights,* Picard's *Stories of King Arthur and his Knights,* and Williams's *The Sword of King Arthur.* Do not introduce these legendary books during the booktalk. Introduce them later to students who enjoyed *A String in the Harp* or Norton's *Steel Magic,* in which three children went through a magic door into King Arthur's time and each had to perform a feat of magic to return.

In Curry's *The Sleeper,* Jennifer and three others found a cave where King Arthur was sleeping until he was needed once again. The four children helped King Arthur save his treasure from the evil Fata Morgana.

In Grosser's *The Snake Horn,* Danny blew the Serpent Horn or Tartold and a visitor from seventeenth-century England appeared.

A whispering shell is the medium through which a boy and girl saw castles, knights, kings, and princesses in *The Twilight of Magic* by Hugh Lofting of Dr. Doolittle fame.

Ipcar's *The Queen of Spells* is based on the Scottish ballad "Tom Lin." The girl in the story wondered who Tom Lin was. Was he a horsethief, a madman, or someone who returned to earth from three hundred years ago. Had he really been taken to the Green World by the *Queen of Spells.* Was he going to return and marry her?

Several children wandered about the rubble of a demolished building in a Manchester, England, slum and found themselves in another world called Elidor where they became involved in a war between good and evil. The Unicorn's song was their hope for triumph over evil.

Twelve-year-old Greta of Nova Scotia in Sauer's *Fog Magic* found a secret village that had been lost for a hundred years through the medium of fog. Greta was the member of her family who loved the fog. "Fog had always seemed to her like the magic spell in the fairy tales—a spell that caught you up and kept you as safe, once you were inside it, as you would have been within a soap bubble." One day when walking by Blue Cove in the fog, Greta saw the secret village and talked with the people there. When her class voted to have their picnic at Blue Cove, Greta was upset because if it were a foggy day she might have to share her village with the other children.

Cutt's *Seven For the Sea* is another book in which fog transports people into an earlier time. Erchie and Mansie became lost in the fog, and when they followed a man back to their island, they found themselves in a time several hundred years earlier.

In Garner's *The Moon of Gomrath*, Susan and elves and dwarfs battled against the evil ones, Brollachan and Marrigan, who had awakened after centuries because of the power of a bracelet belonging to a twentieth-century girl.

Lloyd Alexander, who won the 1969 Newbery Medal for *The High King*, the fourth fantasy in the chronicle of Prydain, has written a book in which a cat moves about in time. In *Time Cat*, Gareth the cat took his owner Jason with him to travel in nine other lives which include Egypt, 2700 B.C.; Rome and Britain, 55 B.C.; Ireland, A.D. 411; Japan, A.D. 998; Italy, 1468; Peru, 1555; The Isle of Man, 1588; Germany, 1600; and America, 1775. Because the book is easy to read and understand for intermediate students and because it is available in paperback, several copies can be made available at the end of the booktalk on time travel. An easier book which can naturally accompany Alexander's book is *Danny Dunn, Time Traveler* by Williams and Abrashkin. The Professor, Danny, and three others traveled to 1763 where they saw Ben Franklin. Students will be familiar with Danny Dunn because of the numerous books in that series.

Perhaps the most famous book for young people concerning the dimension of time is Madeline L'Engle's *A Wrinkle in Time*, the 1963 Newbery Medal Winner. Its sequels are *A Wind in the Door* and *A Swiftly Tilting Planet*. Meg and her brother Charles Wallace looked for their scientist father who had been lost for four years in a time warp. Students are fascinated to know about a tesseract which is explained on pages 23, 62, and 75 to 79, of *A Wrinkle in Time*. A recording of the same name is available.

Ask students if they have read Cameron's *The Wonderful Flight to the Mushroom Planet* or *Stowaway to the Mushroom Planet*. Often someone in the group has read one of those popular stories. Address those students directly by saying "Then, of course, you already know Mr. Tyco Bass." Then lead into Cameron's *Time and Mr. Bass*. Read chapter 8, "At Stonehenge" (pp. 87–104), to hear the story Mr. Bass told David and Chuck about why they were in Wales.

Mr. Bass had second sight just like his ancestor who was the advisor and Royal Bard of Uther Pendragon in the fifth century. Pendragon was King Arthur's father. Mr. Bass not only inherited being Master of the Mycetian League, but also the second sight. Most of *Time and Mr. Bass* is about the search for the Thirteenth Scroll so its information could be transplanted and evil could be overcome.

Sometimes there is a fine line between science fiction and fantasy. *Time and Mr. Bass* could be either, but *The Wonderful Flight to the Mushroom Planet* and *Stowaway to the Mushroom Planet* are probably science fiction. The next few books about time are definitely in the science fiction category and are written by writers well known in that field. In Andre Norton's *The Time Traders*, Ross Murdock went back to the Bronze Age. In *Key Out of Time* by Norton, Ross Murdock and Gordon Ashe are time agents sent to investigate the past of a deserted planet called Hawaika. While setting up an underwater time gate, the two are separately taken back 10,000 years in the history of the planet. The book includes dolphins with telepathy, blue-suited hairless men who read minds, the Rovers or mechanized maritime people, or Foanna who were part of an occult civilization.

In Norton's *Operation Time Search*, Ray found himself back in the time of Atlantis where he became involved in a conflict between the people of Atlantis and the Mrians. After someone has read *Operation Time Search*, introduce him or her to *Kenny's Dear Dolphin* in which Ann is looking for the lost city of Atlantis. In *Walk Out of the World* by Nichols, Tobit and Judith walk into another world where they help the people of the Wanderer regain the capital city of Hagerrak which had been taken from them five hundred years before.

Heinlein's *Time for the Stars* utilizes time in another way. Thomas Paine Leonardo da Vinci Bartlett and his identical twin Patrick Henry Michelangelo Bartlett became involved in a project sponsored by the Long Range Foundation to find twins with telepathy to become part of Project Lebensraum. Eventually one twin would board the Torchship Lewis and Clark to find other planets that could support earth's growing population. The trip would last a century earth time but only a few years space time. The narrator is Tom who tells how he finally became the twin to go. Tom communicated telepathically and when Pat became too old to be Tom's partner for sending messages, his nieces Molly and Kathleen and later Vicky spoke with him and received the messages. When he returned to earth, Molly was in her sixties, Kathleen in her forties, and Vicky was his own age.

In John Christopher's trilogy *The White Mountains, The City of Gold and Lead,* and *The Pool of Fire,* the medieval past and the future world of the tripods existed simultaneously. Capping was a ceremony in which steel caps were implanted in the skulls of all fourteen-year-olds by the tripods to make humans docile and obedient. Will Parker did not want to be capped so he escaped to *The White Mountains* where he heard there were people who were free and uncapped. On the way, Will fell ill and was taken to the Castle of the Red Tower, and was cared for by the Comte and Comtesse and their daughter. At the castle, a tournament took place in which the winners would be given to the tripods. In the sequel to *The White Mountains*, *The City of Gold and Lead*, Will learned that there is another type of process besides the medieval French tournament by which the best athletes are given to the tripods. In the section of the world where Germany might have been, Olympic-like games selected persons to be given to the tripods. In the third book in the trilogy, *The Pool of Fire*, Will learned that in the land that was once Russia "The Hunt" on Execution Day provided humans for the tripods. On Execution Day men were turned loose and then hunted and killed for sport.

Time travel as we have said, works both ways. Townsend's *The Visitors* came from the future to the England of today.

Paramecia Foster lived in the fourth decade of the twenty-first century after the Eco War in which animals were destroyed and life as we know it now disappeared. It was not until Para visited a boy and an old woman in Kansas of the 1930s that she realized what led to the loss of animals on earth. A surprise in the ending linked Para and the boy Shandy.

In Parker's *Time to Choose* twentieth-century Stephen and Mary saw a utopian agricultural commune with young workers who looked exactly like themselves.

In Physson's *The Way Home*, three young Australians found themselves in another time. Prue, her small brother Peter, and older cousin Richard and his mother were in a car that overturned in a flood. Only the three children survived. The three Australians found themselves in a primitive village where aborigines lived. When they found the place where their own home had been, they found themselves in the future.

The seven books of C.S. Lewis are fantasy and begin with *The Lion, the Witch and the Wardrobe* in which Lucy walked through the back of a wardrobe into another land. Later, Peter, Susan, Edmund and Lucy went into the wardrobe to avoid the housekeeper who was taking a group of sightseers on a tour of the house. The children entered Narnia, met a dwarf, wicked witch, Father Christmas, and the good lion Aslan. Susan became queen of Narnia and Edmond became king, and they ruled for years and years; but when the children came back through the wardrobe, they had been gone less than an hour and the tour was just ending. The children were in a railroad station when they returned to Narnia a year later in *Prince Caspian, the Return to Narnia*.

The third book in the Narnia series is *The Voyage of the Dawn Treader*. To get a sense of time, read page 11 beginning with "Narnia time flows differently from ours." Chapter one is a good one to read aloud to children because it tells why Edmund and Lucy had to spend sixteen weeks with their Aunt Alberta and Uncle Harold and their despicable cousin Eustace Clarence Scrubb. That chapter explains how Lucy, Edmund and Eustace were in Lucy's room looking for something when the picture of the ship the *Dawn Treader* came alive and they found themselves in the water and then saved by Caspian, the boy king of Narnia whom they had placed on the throne during their last visit. Show students the diagram of the *Dawn Treader* opposite the title page and the picture of the children entering the picture on page 9.

The Silver Chair is the fourth book in the Narnia series. Because no one can go back to Narnia after three times, two other children went to Narnia instead of the original four. The children's cousin Eustace Scrubb explained to a classmate about Narnia and the two went there and reunited Prince Caspian with his son Rilian.

The Horse and His Boy is the fifth story in the chronicles of Narnia. As soon as listeners learn in the first chapter that Shasta was not really the son of the fisherman with whom he lived, everyone wonders who he really is. Ask students if they remember Paul Revere's talking horse in Lawson's *Mr. Revere and I.* Explain that this book also has a talking horse. After Shasta learned that the man with whom he lived wasn't really his father, he met the horse Breehy-hinny-brinny whom he called Bree. Bree had been kidnapped from Narnia and wanted to return, so he took Shasta with him. On the road they met Aravis Tarkeena, daughter of a lord, who was running away from a marriage she didn't want. Aravis's story is contained in chapter three on pages 29 to 35. If this section is read aloud, stop reading after ". . . next day all four of them . . . continued their journey together" on page 35.

The Magician's Nephew, the sixth Narnia book, tells how the wardrobe came to be built. During the days of Sherlock Holmes, a boy named Digary tried to live with his aunt and an uncle in London because his father was in India and his mother was ill. One day when he was crying he met a neighbor named Polly Plummer who made friends with him and showed him her secret cave. The children followed the cave's tunnel until it led to a room that was the study of Digary's uncle. All this is contained in the first chapter, as well as the information that Uncle Andrew's study was locked and that he was mysterious. The chapter ends when Uncle Andrew gave Polly one of the shiny yellow rings on the table and she vanished. If this chapter is read aloud, stop reading aloud at the end of chapter one and explain that Uncle Andrew offered Digary a yellow ring to follow Polly, and also two green rings with the power to bring them both back. Read the bottom of page 20 and part of page 21 to explain the green rings. Begin reading after "I was going to tell you . . ." to "His cheeks had gone very pale."

Jill and Eustace returned to Narnia in the seventh book, *The Last Battle.* An ape named Shift, a donkey named Puzzle, Aslan the lion, Reepicheep the mouse from *The Voyage of the Dawn Treader,* and Ginger the cat are all part of this final book in which the children helped King Tirian fight the evil Calormenes.

At the end of the booktalk, ask students if they noticed any common element in the stories besides the time theme and the way in which the characters moved in time. Listeners to the booktalk will notice that the people usually experienced days or years in another dimension during the space of a few hours.

Other books to include in a booktalk about time and space travel are Allen's *Spring on the Mountain,* Brandel's *The Mine of Lost Days,* Dagt's *Towers of February, a Diary by an Anonymous (for the time being) Author, with Added Punctuation and Footnotes,* F. Eager's *Time Tangle,* Jones's *Mural Master,* Juster's *Phantom Tollbooth,* Randall's *Watcher in the Woods,* and Steele's *First of the Penguins.*

Books for advanced readers are DeCamp's *Tales Beyond Time: From Fantasy to Science Fiction,* Elwood's *More Science Fiction Tales,* and Hildick's *Time Explorer.*

INTRODUCING SCIENCE FICTION.   Science fiction is one type of fantasy that is often considered almost realistic—the realism of the future perhaps—because interplanetary voyages, computers, and other robots have become a reality. These things were all projected originally in science fiction. The world could be taken over by life from other planets, as happened in Christopher's White Mountains trilogy when the tripods ruled people on earth. Descriptions of the trilogy appear in the previous section of this chapter called Time Travel. Sometimes the problem comes from within the human community on earth, as happened in Neufeld's Sleep Two, Three, Four! when a totalitarian government isolated people by groups according to race, handicaps, or whatever category they chose, or in Dickinson's books beginning with The Weathermonger in which people called "The Changes" wanted to ban machines and revert to the middle ages. A Wrinkle in Time by L'Engle and its sequels most frequently are found on both fantasy and science fiction lists. Books by Heinlein, L'Engle, Christopher, and Dickinson are described in Sutherland and Arbuthnot's Children and Books.

A bibliography of science fiction appears in Lickteig's An Introduction to Children's Literature (pp. 251–52) and an annotated list appears in Adventuring with Books. See the index to The Children's Catalog and Winkel's Elementary School Library Collection for other titles and annotations.

Use these bibliographies to find titles to supplement a booktalk on science fiction books. Begin the booktalk with Key's The Forgotten Door. When a shooting star crossed the sky, Jon fell through the forgotten door from another planet to a valley in the hill country in the southern United States. Jon could communicate with animals as well as read minds. Because he was a stranger, Jon was blamed for robberies that were occurring. Even the U.S. Government was interested in Jon's unusual abilities. There are several series of books that can be introduced in a booktalk by introducing one or two titles. There are numerous books about Miss Pickerell. In Miss Pickerell Goes to Mars, that fascinating lady climbed aboard a spaceship headed for Mars and brought back seven red rocks for her nieces and nephews. In Miss Pickerell on the Moon, she went there to find a cure for the animal epidemic that made her cow and cat sick. Three books about Todd's Space Cat named Flyball involve Flyball's adventures in flight with Col. Fred Stone to the moon. In Space Cat Meets Mars, Flyball met the only cat left on Mars and took her home with him as his wife. In Space Cat and the Kittens, Flyball, his wife and kittens, Tailspin and Marty, traveled in the spaceship Einstein to a land where the kittens found adventure among prehistoric animals.

Cameron's The Wonderful Flight to the Mushroom Planet is about David and Chuck who helped Mr. Bass build a spaceship so he could go to the planet Basidium. In the sequel, Stowaway to the Mushroom Planet, David, Chuck, and Mr. Bass' nephew Theo returned to the Mushroom Planet and the glory-seeking Horatio Peabody stowed away.

Slobodkin's The Space Ship under the Apple Tree and the sequel, The Space Ship Returns to the Apple Tree, are about Eddie who met a little man named Marty who came from another planet. Students who liked these easy books will enjoy Lord's *The Day the Spaceship Landed*. This easy reader is written as if Michael were writing an assignment for English class called "The Day the Spaceship Landed." Michael couldn't write the report because he really saw a spaceship and the man from the ship kept him from speaking or writing about it until they left. Michael took one of them with him to a Halloween party where the spaceman won a prize for being a "space witch" because he was wearing a witch mask.

Another easy book is *The Fat Men from Space*. In Pinkwater's book, the earth was invaded by spacemen who came to steal junk food. Read the news bulletins in italics on pages 45 to 49 to introduce the book, i.e., "A news flash—the White House has been invaded by the spacemen who have carried off the President's private store of frozen Milky Way bars," page 49.

The Danny Dunn books by Williams and Abrashkin can provide hours of reading enjoyment to anyone who liked the first book. Danny's mother was the housekeeper for Professor Bullfinch, and his laboratory provided many adventures for Danny, his friend Joe, and the girl next door. In *Danny Dunn and the Voice from Outer Space*, Danny was embarrassed because he gave Dr. Hubert Bodger, director of the Whipple Observatory in Boston, a "50-cent" lecture on astronomy because he thought he was a tramp. There are references in the book to Baum's *The Wizard of Oz* and Tolkien's *The Hobbit*. Danny became involved in Project Gnome, listening to messages by radio signals from other planets. In *Danny Dunn, Time Traveler*, the Professor, Danny, Irene, and two boys named Joe traveled back in time to colonial days to 1763 where they met Ben Franklin. In *Danny Dunn and the Homework Machine*, the children used Professor Bullfinch's computer Miniac or "Minnie" to program their homework assignments. In *Danny Dunn and the Smallifying Machine*, Danny, Joe, and Irene were trapped inside a machine that reduced them in size so they were only a quarter of an inch high. In *Danny Dunn, Scientific Detective*, Danny found a missing department store manager with the help of a bloodhound robot and discovered something very interesting about the missing Mr. Anguish.

The previously mentioned books are easy enough for third and fourth graders, and most of them are exciting enough to be used with older students who have reading problems. Pinkwater's *Fat Men from Space* is especially useful for reluctant readers. A story about two special forces are told to recruits to inspire them in Harrison's *The Men from P.I.G. and R.O.B.O.T.*, for intermediate readers.

Include these books with books from the previously mentioned bibliographies to form a collection of books for students to check out after viewing the sound filmstrip *Reading for the Fun of It: Science Fiction*. Be sure to introduce the whole science fiction project by introducing Key's *The Forgotten Door*, using that book as a key or door to the other science fiction books. Books that are introduced in the sound filmstrip are Christopher's *The White Mountains*, Clarke's *Dolphin Island*, Del Rey's *The Runaway Robot*, Engdahl's *Enchantress from the Stars*, L'Engle's *A Wrinkle in Time*, Morton's *Moon of Three Rings*, Nourse's *Star Surgeon*, O'Brien's *Mrs. Frisby and the Rats of NIMH*, and Verne's *Twenty Thousand Leagues under the Sea*. Annotations are given for the following books in the "Bibliography for Students" in the teacher's guide: Dickinson's *The Weathermonger*, Lightner's *Star Dog*, MacGregor's *Miss Pickerell Goes to Mars*, Martel's *The City Underground*, and William's *Danny Dunn and the Homework Machine*.

INTRODUCING HISTORICAL FICTION.   The filmstrip *Historical Fiction, Literature for Children* can be used with students in grades four through eight. The filmstrip tells about Steele's *Perilous Road* and O'Dell's *Island of the Blue Dolphins*. The filmstrip could be shown either before or after students have read paperback copies of each title. A bibliography of historical fiction is included. Those books and others could be shown to students after they have seen the filmstrip. Other suggested discussion and activities and a pupil follow-up sheet about historical fiction are part of the teacher's guide.

The filmstrip *Historical Fiction*, because it includes *Perilous Road*, could be used to introduce other Civil War books. Ten-year-old Chris lived in Tennessee during the war and helped the Confederates even though his brother was a Yankee. In Hunt's *Across Five Aprils*, the family is split, with one fighting for the Confederacy and two fighting for the Union. Kansas was one of several states in which neighbor fought against neighbor. In Keith's *Rifles for Watie*, Jefferson Davis Bussey was a Union soldier but when he and his companion accidentally fell into the camp of Stand Watie's Cherokee Rebels while spying, they decided to pretend they were recruits. Jeff's name gave credibility to their story, and after serving fourteen months with Watie, Jeff learned that there were good people on both sides, including Lucy Washbourne.

Have students compare the common theme of *Perilous Road, Across Five Aprils*, and *Rifles for Watie*. Keith's book was the 1958 Newbery Medal winner. Hunt won the medal for another book in 1967. *Across Five Aprils* was a 1965 Newbery Honor Book and Steele's book was a 1959 Newbery Honor Book. All three books are available as individual sound filmstrips, which could be shown after students have read the books. Perhaps a third of the class could read each title. Burchard's *Jed* has the same theme. Sixteen-year-old Jed, a young Yankee soldier from Wisconsin, was on guard duty in Mississippi when he saw a nine-year-old Confederate boy with a broken leg. When Jed took the boy home, he met Philip's mother and sister, and later became their protector. The book is shorter and easier to read than the other three.

Other books about soldiers in the Civil War to introduce to students after they have seen the filmstrip *Historical Fiction* are Allen's *Johnny Reb*, Hall's *Cyrus Holt and the Civil War*, Meader's *The Muddy Road to Glory*, and Norton's *Ride Proud Rebel*. Books to mention for their unusual elements are Edmond's *Cadmus Henry* and Haugaard's *Orphans of the Wind*. The part Cadmus Henry played in the Civil War was unique. Because he could read and write, Cadmus was assigned to General Magruder's staff. Cadmus flew over Northern lines in a basket under a balloon to spy on the Yankees. The Pizzini was shot at and drifted back and forth across Union and Confederate lines until it landed Cadmus in some other adventures. Twelve-year-old Jim in *Orphans of the Wind* was sent to work on the ship *Four Winds* and his uncle not only pocketed his hire but his aunt took the blanket supplied to him. On board, Jim made friends with the Norwegian ship's cook, Rolf, who told of his terrible experiences the one and only time he worked on a slaver. In chapter 7, "Captain Mathews Makes a Speech," the crew learned they were to get double pay because the run was not to Boston as they had supposed.

Burchard wrote *Rat Hell* and *North by Night*. Other books about the Underground Railroad are Fall's *Canalboat to Freedom*, Howard's *North Wind Blows Free*, Meader's *Boy with a Pack*, Monjo's *The Drinking Gourd*, Fritz's *Brady*, and Metzer's *Underground Man*. Monjo's book is very easy reading. De Angeli's *Thee, Hannah!* is short, beautifully written and illustrated, and is easy to read. Hannah, a young Quaker girl who lived in Philadelphia before the Civil War, had more trouble with "Old Spotty" than anyone in her family. Grandmother said "Old Spotty" was the devil. Hannah couldn't understand why the Friends or Quakers had to dress so plainly and she was always getting into trouble because of her desire for pretty clothes. It is difficult to talk about this book in terms of the Underground Railroad without giving away the story because the ending deals with how Hannah came to terms with her Quaker heritage—a runaway slave asked her for help because she knew that Hannah was a Quaker by her plain clothes. The other books are easier to discuss. The *Boy with a Pack*, Bill Crawford, was a peddler. Because Bill traveled, he was able to aid slaves in seeking freedom. Joshua Brown was the *Underground Man.*.

Introduce historical fiction to students in grades four through seven by showing the sound filmstrip *Reading for the Fun of It: Historical Fiction*. The filmstrip introduces historical fiction set in anything from ancient to modern times. Check through the lists of historical fiction included in the anthologies and bibliographies in this section to pinpoint books that could be included in a display to accompany the filmstrip. Students could check out the books in the display, those shown in the filmstrip as well as other historical fiction by the same authors. Merely mentioning the author, title, and the time period of the book may be enough to introduce the books to the students who have just seen the filmstrip.

The filmstrip *Reading for the Fun of It: Historical Fiction* introduces Coolidge's *The Maid of Artemis* (ancient Greece), Edwards's *When the World's on Fire* (American Revolution), Keith's *Rifles for Watie* (American Civil War), Kent's *He Went with Christopher Columbus* (discovery and exploration), Lawson's *Ben and Me* (Ben Franklin's inventions), Paterson's *Ancient Japan*, Steele's *Cherokees* and *Wayah of the Real People* (colonial Williamsburg), Sutcliff's *The Witch's Brat* (middle ages), Treece's *The Dream Time* (prehistoric times), and Wilder's *Little House in the Big Woods* (frontier and pioneer life). Annotations included in a "Bibliography for Students," pages 23-4 of the teacher's guide, are Baker's *Walk the World's Rim* (Spanish exploration in America, 1500s), Brink's *Caddie Woodlawn* (frontier and pioneer life in Wisconsin), Coolidge's *Egyptian Adventures* (Egypt, 1500 B.C.), Fritz's *Brady* (underground railroad), Kelly's *The Trumpeter of Krakow* (renaissance Poland), and Treece's *The Last Viking* (tenth-century Scandinavia).

Teachers and librarians who are planning units that include historical fiction may wish to read background information. The best part of chapter 6, "Historical Fiction," pages 295 to 330 of Huck and Young's *Children's Literature in the Elementary School* is the "Criteria for Historical Fiction." Books are introduced in three categories: prehistoric times, the new world, and the old world. In chapter 11, "Historical Books," pages 368 to 399 of Sutherland and Arbuthnot's *Children and Books,* historical fiction is introduced by three age groups rather than by historical time periods. A valuable bibliography is included. Two annotated bibliographies appear in *Adventuring with Books:* "Historical: United States," pages 77 to 97, and "Other Times and Places," pages 97 to 129.

Other sources of books to use in book talks featuring historical fiction are *Children's Books to Enrich the Social Studies* by Huus and *The Subject Index to Books for Intermediate Grades* edited by Eakin. Neither book is recent but still contain valuable information and many available titles. Two books by Metzner are invaluable: *American History in Juvenile Books; a Chronological Guide* and *World History in Juvenile Books; a Geographical and Chronological Guide.* Other readings include pages 233 to 264 of Egoff's *Only Connect* and pages 95 to 130 of Egoff's *The Republic of Childhood;* pages 137 to 150 of *Horn Book Reflections on Children's Books and Reading* and pages 219 to 237 of Townsend's *Written for Children;* chapter 9, "The Creative Use of History and Other Facts," of Haviland's *Children and Literature* includes articles by Hester Burton, Rosemary Sutcliff, and others.

Selections from historical fiction are included in two anthologies. A section called "Historical Fiction," in Sutherland's *The Arbuthnot Anthology of Children's Literature,* includes selections from historical fiction around the world. A selection from Burchard's *Jed* is included. Selections from *The Perilous Road* by Steele and *Island of the Blue Dolphins* by O'Dell are included in chapter 10, "Historical Fiction," of Nelson's *A Comparative Anthology of Children's Literature.* Selections from eleven other historical fiction books are also included.

INTRODUCING JO, CADDIE, AND LAURA. Two favorite pioneer girls of intermediate students are Laura Ingalls and Caddie Woodlawn. Selections from books by Wilder and Brink are well represented in anthologies. Middle and junior high students will also love Jo March from Alcott's *Little Women.* An acceptable abridged version of the book is also available. The setting for all of the stories is the United States in the 1860s. Laura was really Laura Ingalls (Wilder) and Jo was much like Louisa May Alcott. Both Alcott and Wilder introduced their sisters in their stories. The stories in *Caddie Woodlawn* and *Magical Melons* were told to Carol Brink by her grandmother.

A recording which presents highlights of *Caddie Woodlawn* could be used to introduce the book. Or, selections could be read from anthologies. Two selections from *Caddie Woodlawn* by Brink about pioneer life in Wisconsin are chapters 12 and 13: "Caddie and the Indian Chief," in Huber's *Story and Verse for Children,* and chapter 7, "Breeches and Clogs," in Johnson's *Anthology of Children's Literature.* "The Willow Basket," in Gruenberg's *All Kinds of Courage,* comes from *Magical Melons, More Stories About Caddie Woodlawn.*

Sound filmstrips called *Caddie Woodlawn* and one called *Meet the Newbery Author: Carol Ryrie Brink* are available.

"Indians in the House," in Gruenberg's *Favorite Stories Old and New* (pp. 116-122) was taken from chapter 2 of *The Little House on the Prairie*.

"*Little Women Plan Christmas*," in Huber's *Story and Verse for Children*, (pp. 609-11) comes from chapter 2 of Louisa May Alcott's *Little Women*. That selection, "A Merry Christmas," is one of three read by Julie Harris in a reading called *Little Women*. The other two are "Gossip" and "The First Wedding." "Playing Pilgrims," of Martignoni's *The Illustrated Treasury of Children's Literature*, (pp. 484-91) could be read at Thanksgiving time. Introduce Alcott's story *An Old-Fashioned Thanksgiving* at this time. Seven children in nineteenth-century New England got ready for Thanksgiving while their mother was away caring for grandmother. The menu for a New England Thanksgiving is given: turkey with bread and onion stuffing, cranberry sauce with raisins and onions in cream, baked acorn squash with sausage, Johnny cakes, Louisa Alcott's apple stump, Aunt Dotty's jam cake and plum pudding.

Meigs wrote a biography of Alcott called *Invincible Louisa*, which won the 1934 Newbery Medal. "Damask Roses," in Nelson's *A Comparative Anthology of Children's Literature*, and "Louisa as a Nurse," in Huber's *Story and Verse for Children*, come from that biography. Meigs also wrote the introduction to the centennial edition of *Little Women* illustrated by Tasha Tudor. Read the introduction to *Invincible Louisa* or introduce other Alcott books: *Little Men* (which is a sequel to *Little Women*), *Eight Cousins, Rose in Bloom*, and *An Old-Fashioned Girl*. A sound recording of *Invincible Louisa* is also available.

We Alcotts by Fisher and Rabe is the story of Louisa Alcott's life from the viewpoint of Louisa's mother, affectionately called "Marmee" in *Little Women*. The section from *We Alcotts* called "My Kingdom" appears in Sutherland's *The Arbuthnot Anthology of Children's Literature* (pp. 810-15). Esther Benson narrates an abridged recording of *Little Women*.

Farmer Boy by Laura Ingalls Wilder is about Almanzo Wilder, the boy Laura Ingalls married. That book begins when Almanzo was nine years old. Chapter 16, "Independence Day," is included in Sutherland's *Arbuthnot Anthology of Children's Literature*. Not included in any of the anthologies discussed in this section, is chapter 26, "Christmas of Farmer Boy," which could be read for the holidays. "Christmas," chapter 4 of *The Little House in the Big Woods*, is included in Nelson's *A Comparative Anthology of Children's Literature*. Aunt Eliza, Uncle Peter, and the cousins came for Christmas. Another selection from that book is "Summertime," which appears in Johnson's *Anthology of Children's Literature*. (pp. 881-85). "Summertime" is chapter 10 of *The Little House in the Big Woods*. In two selections condensed from chapters 4 and 31 of *On the Banks of Plumb Creek*, Laura disobeyed and went toward the forbidden swimming hole, but turned back when she was frightened by a badger in "Deep Water," in Gruenberg's *All Kinds of Courage* (pp. 95-105). "Surprise" appears on page 298 of Pannell and Cavanah's *Holiday Round Up*, and tells of the family receiving gifts sent by Rev. Alden's church back East. Chapter 41, "Christmas Eve," and the preceding chapters of *On the Banks of Plum Creek* tell about the blizzard in which Pa went to the store to get Christmas candy, oyster crackers, and oysters for stew on Christmas, but was lost in the blizzard for three days and ate the candy and crackers. The oysters were still frozen solid when he finally found home.

In chapters 20 and 21, "The Night before Christmas" and "Merry Christmas," of By the Shores of Silver Lake, the family reminisced about Pa's adventures when he was lost for three days in a blizzard on another Christmas. In these chapters, Mr. and Mrs. Boast were stuck in the snow and spent the holidays with the Wilders. The extra food was no problem—they had jack rabbit for Christmas dinner; but finding presents for the Boasts was a problem. In "Merry Christmas," chapter 18 of The Long Winter, there was little food because the supply train was late. There were no stockings and no oyster soup. Instead, a blizzard was on its way and a letter arrived saying that another Christmas barrel would soon arrive from the church back East. A recording called Little House in the Big Woods/Little House on the Prairie is available. A set of four records and eight paperbacks are available so students can read along with The Little House in the Big Woods.

The television series "The Little House on the Prairie" has caused a renewed interest in the pioneer stories of Laura Ingalls Wilder. The "Little House" books in chronological order are: Little House in the Big Woods, Little House on the Prairie, On the Banks of Plum Creek, By the Shores of Silver Lake, Long Winter, Little Town on the Prairie, and These Happy Golden Years. Farmer Boy is about Almanzo Wilder, Laura's husband, and his growing up years. Two other books are a diary and letters: On the Way Home, A Diary of a Trip from South Dakota to Mansfield, Mo. in 1894 and West from Home, Letters of Laura Ingalls Wilder, San Francisco 1915.

Rose Wilder was born to Laura and Almanzo in The First Four Years. As Rose Wilder Lane she wrote Let the Hurricane Roar, which has recently been reissued as The Young Pioneers and is the basis for a television series by the same name.

Use the two television series to introduce frontier and pioneer stories in a booktalk. You may wish to make the following bibliography available to students.

IF YOU LIKED THE "LITTLE HOUSE" BOOKS. . .

Alcott, Louisa May. Little Women, or Meg, Jo, Beth, and Amy. Illus by Tasha Tudor. New York: Collins, 1969.
> If you like reading about Laura Ingalls, you will like Jo March and her three sisters who lived in New England in the 1860s.

Alcott, Louisa May. An Old-Fashioned Thanksgiving. Illus by Holly Johnson. Philadelphia: Lippincott, 1974.
> Children plan for Thanksgiving dinner while mother is away in a story that is like the "Little House" books.

Anderson, Lonzo. Zeb. Illus by Peter Burchard. New York: Knopf. 1966. OP
> In 1680, Zeb went with his father and brother to clear land so

the family could join them. When his father and brother drowned, Zeb had to carry on alone.

Beatty, Patricia. *How Many Miles to Sundown*. New York: Morrow, 1974.

Thirteen-year-old Beulah Land Quincey followed her brother Leo and a friend Nate into Texas, Mexico, and Arizona to look for Nate's father during the 1800s.

Beatty, Patricia. *A Long Way to Whiskey Creek*. New York: Morrow, 1971.

Thirteen-year-old Parker Quincey, a Texan, was sent four hundred miles in 1879 to bring home his brother's body for burial.

Brink, Carol. *Caddie Woodlawn*. Illus by Kate Seredy. New York: Macmillan, 1935.

also *Caddie Woodlawn*. Illus by Trina Shart Hyman. New York: Macmillan, 1973. Macmillan Paperback.

Eleven-year-old Caddie, a tomboy, lived in frontier Wisconsin. Stories are based on those told by the author's grandmother and cover 1864-65. 1936 Newbery Medal Winner.

Brink, Carol. *Magical Melons, More Stories About Caddie Woodlawn*. Illus by Marguerite Davis. New York: MacMillan, 1954. Paperback.

Caddie was ten years old when the story "Magical Melons" took place. Other stories cover the Woodlawn family between 1863-1866. "The Author's Note" provides useful background information.

Bulla, Clyde Robert. *Down the Mississippi*. Illus by Peter Burchard. New York: Crowell, 1954. Scholastic Paperback.

Eric went down the Mississippi River on a raft in 1850. Easy reading.

Byars, Betsy. *Trouble River*. Illus by Rocco Negri. New York: Viking, 1969. Penguin Paperback.

Twelve-year-old Dewey Martin and his grandmother traveled forty miles down Trouble River on a raft to avoid Indians.

Carr, Mary Jane. *Children of the Covered Wagon, a Story of the Oregon Trail*. Illus by Bob Kuhn. New York: Crowell, 1934. OP

Jerry, Myra, and Jim went with the wagon train from Independence, Missouri in 1844 to the Willamette Valley in Oregon. Classic.

Clifford, Eth. *The Year of the Three-Legged Deer*. Illus by Richard Cuffari. Boston: Houghton, 1972. Dell paperback.

Jesse Benton's Indian wife and his half-breed children, Takawsu and Chilili, faced hatred and violence on the Indiana frontier.

Coatsworth, Elizabeth. *The Sod House*. Illus by Manning de V. Lee. New York: Macmillan, 1954, 1967.

Ilse Traubel, child of German Emmigrants, and her doll Thumbelina traveled by flatboat across the Missouri River on their way to Kansas so her father could settle there and vote Kansas a free state.

Dalgliesh, Alice. *The Courage of Sara Noble*. Illus by Leonard Weisgard. New York: Scribner, 1954. Scribner Paperback.

Eight-year-old Sarah Noble moved to the Connecticut wilderness to cook for her father in 1707 while he was clearing land. Sarah was especially brave when her father left her with Indians while he went to fetch the rest of the family.

Dickinson, Alice. *Taken by the Indians: True Tales of Captivity*. New York: Watts, 1976.

Mary Jemison's story is one of six experiences written by white persons, who were captured by Indians between 1676 and 1864.

Douglas, Emily Taft. *Appleseed Farm*. Illus by Anne Vaughan. New York: Abingdon, 1948, 1958.

Ada moved by covered wagon from Boston to Indiana when she was nine. On her tenth birthday Ada was given seeds by Johnny Appleseed.

Field, Rachel. *Calico Bush*. Illus by Allen Lewis. New York: Macmillan, 1931, 1966. Dell Paperback.

Marguerite Ledoux, a French indentured servant, saved the Maine settlers from an Indian massacre in a unique way.

Fleischman, Sid. *Mr. Mysterious and Company*. Illus by Eric von Schmidt. Boston: Little, 1962. Dell Paperback.

Mr. Mysterious took his traveling magic show and his family to California with him in the 1880s so they could settle there. Humorous.

Flory, Jane. *Golden Venture*. Boston: Houghton, 1976.

Eleven-year-old Minnie Weldon stowed away in her father's wagon headed for the California Gold Rush.

Fritz, Jean. *The Cabin Faced West*. Illus by Feodor Rojankovsky. New York: Coward, 1958.

Ten-year-old Ann Hamilton lived in colonial Pennsylvania in 1784 and met General Washington.

Gardner, Jeanne Le Mohunier. *Mary Jemison, Seneca Captive*. Illus by Robert Parker. New York: Harcourt, 1966.

A real girl was captured by the Indians during the French and Indian wars.

Garson, Eugenia, ed. *The Laura Ingalls Wilder Songbook, Favorite Songs from the "Little House" Books*. Illus by Garth Williams. Music by Herbert Haufrecht. New York: Harper, 1968.

Piano and guitar arrangements for sixty-two songs with page references and quotes from the books of Laura Ingalls Wilder.

Goble, Paul and Dorothy Goble. *Red Hawks' Account of Custer's Last Battle; the Battle of the Little Bighorn, 25 June 1876*. New York: Pantheon, 1969.

This account of Custer's Last Stand is told from the viewpoint of a fifteen-year-old warrior named Red Hawk. An overview of the battle appears in italics.

Heiderstadt, Dorothy. *Stolen by the Indians.* Illus by Carl Kidwell. New York: McKay, 1968. OP

Twelve experiences of children or young people who were captured by the Indians and survived.

Hoff, Carol. *Johnny Texas.* Illus by Bob Meyers. Chicago: Follett, 1950. Dell Paperback.

Ten-year-old Johann moved to Texas from Germany. Father went to fight with General Houston in the Mexican War. Johann was the man of the family when their servant Tobias also left for the war. Easy reading.

Howard, Elizabeth. *Peddler's Girl.* New York: Morrow, 1951. OP

Lucilla and Elijan went traveling with Uncle Adam after their mother died.

Hunt, Mable Leigh. *Better Known as Johnny Appleseed.* Philadelphia: Lippincott, 1950.

A classic story about John Chapman who believed in spreading good will and apple seeds on the midwestern frontier.

Lampman, Evelyn Sibley. *Half-Breed.* Illus by Ann Grifalconi. New York: Doubleday, 1967. OP

When Pale-eyes' mother chose a new husband from among her people—the Crows—Pale-eyes decided to look for his white father Jess Hollingshead whom he had not seen for six years.

Lane, Rose Wilder. *The Young Pioneers.* New York: McGraw, 1976. Bantam Paperback.

A young couple, Charles and Caroline, went West and settled on Wild Plum Creek in the Dakotas. Originally published as *Let the Hurricane Roar.* Rose is the daughter of Laura and Almanzo Wilder.

Lenski, Lois. *Indian Captive, the Story of Mary Jemison.* Illus by author. Philadelphia: Lippincott, 1941.

A real white girl was captured by the Senecas in 1758 from her home in Pennsylvania.

McGraw, Eloise Jarvis. *Moccasin Trail.* New York: Coward. 1952.

Ten-year-old Jim Keath was adopted by the Crow Indians after he was attacked by a bear. Six years later Jim was reunited with his family.

McMeekin, Isabel McLennon. *Journey Cake.* Illus by Nicholas Panesis. New York: Messner, 1942. OP

The six Shadrow children went on the Wilderness Road with a free Negro Juba to join their father in Kentucky in 1793. Johnny Appleseed appears in the story.

Mason, Miriam E. *Caroline and Her Kettle Named Maude.* Illus by Kathleen

Voute. New York: Macmillan, 1951.

Eight-year-old Caroline moved from Gray's Crossing to the woods of Michigan. Caroline wanted a gun but got a copper kettle instead. Easy reading.

———. *Little Jonathan.* Illus by George and Doris Hauman. New York: Macmillan, 1944.

Seven-year-old Jonathan Brown was the youngest of twelve brothers and sisters. When he fell into the spring his buckskin shrank and he thought he had grown bigger. Easy reading.

———. *Middle Sister.* Illus by Grace Paull. New York: Macmillan, 1947.

Eight-year-old Sarah Samantha Glossbrenner moved West to Minnesota and took her apple tree called Miss Appleseed with her. Easy reading.

———. *Susannah, the Pioneer Cow.* Illus by Maud and Miska Petersham. New York: Macmillan, 1941.

The Wayne family moved from Virginia to the Midwest and took along Susannah and her calves Rosey and Posey. Easy reading.

———. *Young Mr. Meeker and His Exciting Journey to Oregon.* Illus by Sandra James. Indianapolis: Bobbs, 1952.

Ezra and Eliza Jane Meeker and their baby went to Oregon by wagon train. Based on a real experience.

Meader, Stephen W. *Boy With a Pack.* Illus by Edward Shenton. New York: Harcourt, 1939.

Seventeen-year-old Bill Crawford peddled wares throughout Vermont, New York, Pennsylvania, and Ohio.

Meadowcraft, Enid La Monte. *By Wagon and Flatboat.* Illus by Ninon McKnight. New York: Crowell, 1938.

A family traveled by wagon train and flatboat from Pennsylvania to Ohio in 1789.

Meigs, Cornelia. *Willow Whistle.* Illus by E. Boyd Smith. New York: Macmillan, 1931.

Eric and Mary Ann made friends with the Chief Gray Eagle, a Dakota Indian.

Orton, Helen Fuller. *Treasure in the Little Trunk.* Illus by Robert Ball. Philadelphia: Lippincott, 1932.

Ten-year-old Patty Armstrong carried her prize beads given her by her grandmother in a little trunk when they moved from Vermont to Western New York in 1824. The story centers on the lost beads.

Rounds, Glen. *The Prairie Schooners.* Illus by author. New York: Holiday, 1968.

Life on a wagon train to Oregon in the mid 1800s.

Speare, Elizabeth. *Calico Captive.* Illus by W.T. Mars. Boston: Houghton, 1957. Dell Paperback.

Miriam Willard was captured by Indians during the French

and Indian War. Based on the diary of Susanna Johnson.

Steele, William O. *Buffalo Knife.* Illus by Paul Galdone. New York: Harcourt, 1968. Voyager Paperback.

Nine-year-old Andy Clark and his family came down the Tennessee River by flatboat in 1782. Andy became friends with Isaac Brown.

————. *Flaming Arrows.* Illus by Paul Galdone. New York: Harcourt, 1957. Voyager Paperback.

Tennesee pioneers, Chad Robun and his family, resented being in the fort with a traitor's family during a Chickamauga raid.

————. *Wilderness Journey.* Illus by Paul Galdone. New York: Harcourt, 1953.

Ten-year-old Flan traveled the Wilderness Trail to the French Salt Lick with a hunter to prove his mettle.

————. *Winter Danger.* Illus by Paul Galdone. New York: Harcourt, 1954.

Eleven-year-old Caje wandered with his father in the wilderness and then settled down in Tennessee in 1780, while his father continued to hunt and roam.

Walker, Barbara M. *The Little House Cookbook: Frontier Foods from Laura Ingalls Wilder's Classic Stories.* Illus by Garth Williams. New York: Harper, 1979.

Recipes from the "Little House" books and information about frontier cooking are included.

Wilder, Laura Ingalls. *By the Shores of Silver Lake.* Illus by Garth Williams. New York: Harper, 1953. Trophy Paperback.

Thirteen-year-old Laura moved to the new town of DeSmet in the Dakota Territory because Pa was working at a railroad camp in the fourth "Little House" book.

————. *Farmer Boy.* Illus by Garth Williams. New York: Harper, 1953. Trophy Paperback.

Nine-year-old Almanzo Wilder lived in Northern New York. In ten years he married Laura Ingalls.

Wilder, Laura Ingalls. *The First Four Years.* Illus by Garth Williams. New York: Harper, 1971. Trophy Paperback.

Laura and Almanzo Wilder's first four years of married life on the Dakota prairie, 1885-1889. Their daughter Rose, author of *The Young Pioneers,* was born.

————. *The Little House in the Big Woods.* Illus by Garth Williams. New York: Harper, 1953. Trophy Paperback.

The very first book about Laura Ingalls's family took place when the family lived in Wisconsin.

————. *Little House on the Prairie.* Illus by Garth Williams. New York: Harper, 1953. Trophy Paperback.

In this sequel to *The Little House in the Big Woods,* the Ingalls family moved to a homestead on the Kansas prairie which is the setting for the television series.

———. *Little Town on the Prairie.* Illus by Garth Williams. New York: Harper, 1953. Trophy Paperback.

In the sixth "Little House" book, the Ingalls family lived in DeSmet, South Dakota. Laura was fifteen and Almanzo Wilder saw her home from a school exhibition.

———. *The Long Winter.* Illus by Garth Williams. New York: Harper, 1953. Trophy Paperback.

In the fifth "Little House" book, the Ingalls family moved from the prairie to town. The long, hard winter lasted from October to April.

———. *On the Banks of Plum Creek.* Illus by Garth Williams. New York: Harper, 1963. Trophy Paperback.

The Ingalls family moved to Minnesota where crops were ruined by storms and grasshoppers in the third "Little House" book.

———. *On the Way Home.* Illus by Garth Williams. New York: Harper, 1962. Trophy Paperback.

This is the diary account of the Wilder family's trip by wagon from the Dakota Territory to Missoui in 1894.

———. *These Happy Golden Years.* Illus by Garth Williams. New York: Harper, 1953. Trophy Paperback.

The seventh and last book in the "Little House" series tells about Laura the schoolteacher and her coming marriage.

———. *West From Home: Letters of Laura Ingalls Wilder, San Francisco, 1915.* Roger MacBride, editor. New York: Harper, 1964. Trophy Paperback.

Letters written by Laura Ingalls Wilder.

Wormser, Richard. *The Black Mustanger.* Illus by Don Bolognese. New York: Morrow, 1971.

Will Mesteno, half Negro and half Apache/Mexican set thirteen-year-old Dan Riker's father's leg and then became Dan's partner so they wouldn't lose their brand in post Civil War Texas.

Worth, Kathryn. *They Loved to Laugh.* Illus by Marguerite DeAngeli. New York: Doubleday, 1942. OP

When her parents died in an epidemic in 1831, Martitia went home with Dr. David to his wife and father and family of five boys and one girl. Martitia learned to assume duties in the household.

Yates, Elizabeth. *Carolina's Courage.* Illus by Nora S. Unwin. New York: Dutton, 1964.

Carolina Putnam's doll Leddy-Lou traveled with her from New Hampshire to Nebraska in the 1850s and served a special purpose on the trip.

Zachert, Donald. *Laura, the Life of Laura Ingalls Wilder, the Author of the Little House on the Prairie.* New York: Regnery, 1976. Avon Paperback.

Photos of the Ingalls family and of Laura at various ages add to this biography of Laura Ingalls Wilder, author of the "Little House" books.

INTRODUCING MYSTERIES.   Use Sherlock Holmes to introduce two books edited by Haycraft: *The Boys' Book of Great Detective Stories* and *The Boys' Second Book of Great Detective Stories*. Each story in both books has an outstanding sleuth as a main character and the stories center on deduction, not the crime. The first book is arranged chronologically from Edgar Alan Poe to Arthur B. Reeve, or from 1840 to 1912, and contains thirteen stories. Auguste Dupin from Poe's "The Purloined Letter" is the first detective, and Sherlock Holmes from Doyle's "The Adventure of the Speckled Band" is the second detective in the first book. The second book contains stories from E.C. Bentley to Edgar Wallace, covering the years between 1912 and 1940. Hercule Poirot is one of the fourteen detectives and appears in the story "The Million Dollar Bank Robbery" by Agatha Christie.

Haycraft wrote the introduction to *The Boys' Sherlock Homes*. Three collections about Doyle's famous character are *The Adventures of Sherlock Holmes*, *The Complete Sherlock Holmes*, and *Tales of Sherlock Holmes*. Recordings of Doyle's stories about Sherlock Holmes read by Basil Rathbone are *Stories of Sherlock Holmes: A Scandal in Bohemia*; *Stories of Sherlock Holmes: Silver Blaze*; *Stories of Sherlock Holmes: The Adventure of the Speckled Band and the Final Problem*; and *Stories of Sherlock Holmes: The Redheaded League*.

A modern story in which Sherlock Holmes is a character is Newman's *The Case of the Baker Street Irregulars*. Andrew came to London from Cornwall with a tutor he disliked. Mr. Dennison, the tutor, got into a hansom cab driven by a cabby with a crooked nose and then disappeared. Later the same cabby tried to abduct Andrew. Adventures leading to Andrew's identity began when Andrew met Sara "Screamer" Wiggins, an urchin, and her brother Sam. Sam and his friends, Alf and Bert, did odd jobs for Sherlock Holmes and were called Baker Street Irregulars. Holmes became involved in a kidnapping, art theft, and bombing in this book, and his deductions are worthy of Doyle himself.

A large silhouette of Sherlock Holmes with the caption "Mysterious Books" or "Solve a Book" can include the previously mentioned books plus two by Titus, *Basil of Baker Street* and *Basil and the Pygmy Cats*. Read chapter 1 of the first book because it not only introduces Basil but also the case he solved in the book. Because Sherlock Holmes books were written from Dr. Watson's point of view, the books about Basil are written from the point of view of Dr. David Q. Dawson. Basil lived in London in 1885 and learned sleuthing by listening to Sherlock Holmes tell Dr. Watson how he solved his cases. Basil took down the information in shortpaw. Basil's tailor even copied Holmes's wardrobe and the picture on the front cover shows *Basil of Baker Street*, a mouse dressed like Sherlock Holmes. In Titus's *Basil and the Pygmy Cats*, Dr. Dawson listed several cases on page 11 that can be used to entice readers. Continue reading on page twelve and thirteen so listeners can learn that *The Adventure of the Pygmy Cats* was Basil's favorite case, especially because Basil was interested in archaeology.

Pages 1 to 15 of chapter 1 set the stage for the book.

Brooks's *Freddy the Detective* was a pig who, like Basil the mouse, was inspired by Sherlock Holmes. A description of Freddy appears on pages 2 and 3. The most important part of that definition is that Freddy could read and he had a library of books, magazines, and newspapers. Freddy's favorite author was Sherlock Holmes. Read chapter one to introduce students to Freddy and to explain how Jinx the cat brought Freddy his first case. Jinx became Freddy's Dr. Watson. The first chapter is called "Freddy's First Case." After reading *Freddy the Detective*, students may be interested in reading other books about Freddy.

Basil and Freddy are not the only animal detectives. Best's Desmond, a dog of mixed ancestry belonging to Gus, was called a private eye although he would rather be called a private nose. Desmond hated to bite anyone in solving a case because biting was rude. *Desmond's First Case* was finding Mr. Titus, the retired banker from next door, who was missing. Mr. Titus was an inventor in his spare time. Gus learned that Mr. Titus was missing because his overalls and some of his tools were missing. Then Gus saw a man selling household inventions and Desmond smelled Mr. Titus's scent in the man's truck. Desmond was sidetracked from solving the mystery when Gus prepared him for a dog show at the county fair. Desmond felt sorry for Bill the Boxer who had won the show for three years, because Bill was only one breed of dog. At the same time, Desmond had hurt feelings himself because he was entered as "no breed" when actually he had more breeds in him than any dog at the fair. Use *Desmond's First Case* to introduce the sequel, *Desmond and the Peppermint Ghost*. Numerous paperback copies could be placed in a classroom collection.

Pinkerton, a Great Dane, catches a burglar in Kellogg's *Pinkerton Behave*. Students in grades two to four will enjoy six books by Quackenbush: *Detective Mole, Detective Mole and the Halloween Mystery, Detective Mole and the Circus Mystery, Detective Mole and the Seashore Mystery, Detective Mole and the Secret Clues,* and *Detective Mole and the Tip Top Mystery*.

There are many easy readers that are mysteries. These books can be introduced to students with Platt's *Big Max*, who is a miniature Sherlock Holmes. A second title is *Big Max in the Mystery of the Missing Moose*.

Another detective for small readers is *Nate the Great*, created by Sharmat. Other stories are *Nate the Great Goes Undercover, Nate the Great and the Phony Clue, Nate the Great and the Sticky Case* and *Nate the Great and the Lost List*. In the last book Nate and his dog Sludge helped Nate's friend find his missing grocery list. Rosamond, it seems, was making cat pancakes and had found the grocery list and thought it was a recipe without directions because it included tuna, salmon, and liver. In Lexau's *The Homework Caper*, it is homework, rather than a grocery list, that is missing.

Wizard, Tubby, Skinny, and Snitch were friends. Wizard, a private eye, tried to find out who took Mrs. Meech's blueberry pie in Bonsall's *The Case of the Hungry Stranger*. Those same boys tried unsuccessfully to find Snitch's cat Mildred in *The Case of the Cat's Meow*. Don't tell students that Mildred was found when she came out to get food in the night and then went back to where she had hidden her kittens. In *The Case of the Scaredy Cats*, girls took over the

134 • INTRODUCING BOOKS

boys' private eyes' clubhouse and wouldn't let the boys in unless they allowed girls to join the club, and this led to a case for the private eyes. In *The Case of the Dumb Bells*, after some phones were hooked up, the doorbells kept ringing, so the boys had to solve the mystery. Another Bonsall mystery is *The Case of the Double Cross*.

The Binky brothers created by Lawrence provide other easy-to-read detective stories. The boys are introduced in *Binky Brothers, Detectives*. Dinky was little, and Dinky's big brother was called Pinky because of his red hair. The brothers had a detective agency and the problem to be solved involved a stolen catcher's mitt.

Also introduce Lawrence's *The Binky Brothers and the Fearless Four*. "The Fearless Four" is the name of the club to which Pinky belongs. Someone smashed their snow fort and the club members mistakenly thought it was the new boy they wouldn't let into their club, but the case was solved.

There are two ways to introduce these easy-to-read mysteries to first graders. The books could make a display that would include mysteries of all types at all reading levels, motivating students to make their choices individually. Or, first-grade students could be invited to the library media center for a booktalk. Be sure that a display of other mysteries which includes a large picture of Sherlock Holmes is up somewhere in the school. Allude to the displays, explain what a mystery is, and tell students about Sherlock Holmes and Dr. Watson. Explain Holmes' clothing by showing pictures of him and of his imitator Basil the mouse. Freddy the detective explained who Sherlock Holmes was to Jinx the cat and two ducks, Emma and Alice, on pages 8 and 9 of Brooks's book. Show a picture of Freddy wearing a Holmes-type hat. Introduce Platt's *Big Max* first because he is a miniature Sherlock Holmes. Then introduce Dinky and Pinky by telling how they got their nicknames, and the other books by introducing the characters in them. Hold up each book and give the author and title. Introduce the main characters in each story by giving a physical description or some interesting information about them. After the characters are introduced, give a one-sentence explanation of the mystery. The title often gives a clue so the title could be explained.

Sobol's *Encyclopedia Brown* is one of the best liked of all the detectives. Introduce Leroy Brown to the students by reading pages one through two-and-a-half to students. Listeners will learn that the fifth-grade boy was known as Leroy to his teachers and parents but was known as Encyclopedia Brown to his friends, because his head was filled with facts. Encyclopedia's father was chief of police in Idaville and everyone thought he was the best policeman in the world. What everyone didn't realize was that Encyclopedia gave advice to his father over the dinner table. There are numerous books in this series, each with the same format. There are ten cases in each book that Encyclopedia Brown is asked to solve. At the end of each case, readers are asked how Encyclopedia Brown figured out the answers to the mysteries. They can then turn to the back of the book where the solutions are given.

Encyclopedia Brown books are extremely popular with students and are useful for remedial reading because each case involves only five or six pages and those pages are interesting. Students are motivated to read carefully and see if they can figure out who was responsible for the mystery. The books can also be used by teachers for checking comprehension because the whole key to enjoying the stories is understanding the situation, guessing at a solution, and then checking the back of the book for Sobol's solution.

The following titles are available in paperback editions: *Encyclopedia Brown, Boy Detective, Encyclopedia Brown and the Case of the Dead Eagles, Encyclopedia Brown Finds the Clues, Encyclopedia Brown Keeps the Peace, Encyclopedia Brown Saves the Day,* and *Encyclopedia Brown Shows the Way.* Other titles are included in the bibliography.

One project for fourth or fifth grade teachers that can only be used once is a contest in which half of the class competes with the other half. First, the school library media specialist must be contacted so none of the books about Encyclopedia Brown by Sobol are available for students to check out and read. Ask the public librarian to temporarily withhold the Sobol books from circulation. If individual teachers have copies of the books in their own room collections ask them to take the books home for the duration of the project. Then, purchase at least six different paperback titles of Sobol's books. Buy at least three copies of each book. Take two copies of the same title and cut them up so there is a complete set of ten cases. Two paperback copies are needed because the back of the last page of each case is on the flip side of the beginning of the other case. Remember that photocopying the pages violates "fair use" of the copy-law. Scholastic paperbacks cannot be distributed in any other format than the paperback book so permission is needed to cut up and distribute individual copies.

Mark each case with the name of the book from which it came. Take all the solutions and mark each with the title of the book from which it came and carefully hide them so they are not available to students. Once all twelve paperback books have been cut up, there will be complete sets for sixty cases; there are ten cases in each book. Take five stories from each book for each of the two teams. Take every other story in each book and divide them between the two teams so each team has five stories from each book. This is just a precaution in case one team would find one of the books from another source to obtain the answers. Take the twenty-four, or more or less, students in the fourth or fifth grade classroom and divide them into teams so there is an even distribution of students by ability. Explain the project to the students and assign a captain for each team. Give each captain thirty different cases solved by Encyclopedia Brown and ask the captain to distribute them to team members. The team that correctly solves the most cases is the winner. Prizes might be paperback copies of the books.

Teachers can give overall suggestions to the teams, but discovering and recording solutions requires group cooperation, and group decision making and reading all the cases. Tell captains to make sure that everyone on the team has a chance to read each case. Whenever a student thinks he or she has figured out the solution to the case, a meeting of the team can be called to discuss the solution. If the group agrees with the person, then the captain can take the solution to the teacher for verification. Penalties given for wrong solutions keep students from bothering the teacher with wild guesses. (Penalties can be subtracted from the final score). Two penalties, however, will lose the team one correct answer. Reading can take place outside the classroom, but time must be given in class for teams to meet. Teachers should remember to keep the contest short to maintain interest and to keep students from finding other sources of Encyclopedia Brown books which contain the answers.

Encyclopedia Brown can also be introduced to students through a four filmstrip set called *The Best of Encyclopedia Brown*. The four cases from three different books are: "The Case of Natty Nat" and "The Case of the Scattered Cards" from *Encyclopedia Brown, Boy Detective;* "The Case of the Hungry Hitchhiker" from *Encyclopedia Brown Strikes Again;* and "The Case of the Whistling Ghost" from *Encyclopedia Brown Gets His Man.* Stop the projector at the end of each case and allow time for students to solve the mystery.

Another way to introduce Encyclopedia Brown to students is for the teacher to read one of the stories each day and allow time for students to guess the solution.

Intermediate and middle school students will enjoy a booktalk to introduce various mysteries to them. Begin the booktalk with books by Doyle, Haycraft and the book by Newman. Spicer's *The Humming Top* never fails to interest students because it combines ESP with a mystery. Dorcas Gray, an orphan, receives powers of extrasensory perception when she spins the top which is her only possession. In three instances her unusual talent causes Dorcas to be sent back to the orphanage. Dorcas gave information to the woman that she had learned after spinning her top—the husband had a girl friend. When she was eighteen, Dorcas was hired by a rich old lady to find her missing grandson after the police and private detectives failed to do so. Could Dorcas find the missing grandson?

In Hildick's *The Case of the Secret Scribbler,* Jack McGurk and his gang try to prevent a robbery they learned about from a message they found.

Bonham's *The Mystery of the Fat Cat* is another favorite. Ask students if they have ever heard of a situation in which a rich person left money in his will to an animal. Or, cut out information about such a situation from the newspaper and keep it to use when introducing *The Mystery of the Fat Cat.* In this story, a rich woman has left her money to a cat that is being taken care of by a guardian. When and if the cat dies, the money is to go to the Dogtown Boys' Club for needed repairs and a swimming pool. The boys suspect that the cat has died and that the guardian has substituted another cat. Proving their suspicions is another matter.

Erwin's *Go to the Room of the Eyes* is an exciting mystery that can be introduced to students in several ways. Chapter 1 can be read aloud to introduce the Evans family: Mom, Dad, and the six children. Susan, the oldest, goes to a private school, Katie and Dave are sixth graders, May is next, Jody is in second grade, and Dinky is four. Persons who are planning a booktalk will also wish to read that chapter to establish the family and learn about their move in order to paraphrase the information. Page 13 of chapter 1 describes the house to which the Evans family moved. The description of the house can be used in a booktalk.

Read from the middle of the page, "We hopped out. . . ." to the end of that chapter on page 15. To establish the mystery, begin when Susan jumped out of bed, three-quarters of the way down on page 18, until the bottom of page 19, when she saw the piece of paper that contained the clue, "Go to the Room of the Eyes," a clue that was left by children who lived in the house thirty years before.

The first half of page 23 is a thrilling description of the twins when they saw the mysterious man. Pages 26 and 27 contain a double picture of Susan and the twins checking up on the mysterious visitor; two eyes are shown on the floor in the right corner. If you read to the end of that chapter, listeners will know that the eyes belonged to the gingerbread man who was to play an inportant part in the mystery because someone kept trying to steal him. Chapter 6 is about the first day of school and how Jody and May had no trouble fitting in but how Kate and Dave had problems. Page 82 contains the letter written by the children of E. G. Stanhope telling about the treasure hunt. More clues are given on pages 83 and 84.

Raskin's *The Mysterious Disappearance of Leon (I Mean Noel)* is a word puzzle and deciphered message that is more sophisticated than the messages in Erwin's *Go to the Room of the Eyes*. The book is not meant for every child. However, those who get caught up in the mystery find it a rewarding experience. Introduce the story by the questions on the front blurb. Raskin's *The Tattooed Potato and Other Clues* is about a seventeen-year-old female named Dickory Dock who answered an ad for an artist's assistant. Dickory's employer, Garson, said that Dickory was haunted. Dickory was haunted by the robbery at Dock's Hock Shop when her parents were murdered. The mystery will keep readers intrigued throughout the book, as well as send students running to art dictionaries and encyclopedias to find out about Van Gogh, Fragonard, Degas, Gauguin, Toulouse-Lautrec, Matisse, Picasso, Sonneborg, Whistler's signature, and Piero della Francesca. In Raskin's 1979 Newbery Winner *The Westing Game*, all sixteen people invited to the reading of a millionaire's will have a motive for murdering him. All the heirs are given clues which will lead them to the money and the guilty person. The Raskin books should be included in a booktalk to provide reading for students who need to be challenged or who think they are too intellectual to read such "light fiction" as mysteries.

One category of mysteries that could be introduced to students in a booktalk is a category that includes mysteries from other countries, some of them translated from other languages.

Smith's *No Way of Telling* could also be included in a booktalk on survival. Amy Bowen lived with her granny at a cottage in Wales called Gwyntfa. Amy's father had sold their larger home after Amy's mother died and he went to Australia, where he remarried and started another family. Mr. Protheroe now owned the former Bowen homestead called Dintirion. Read pages 31 and 32 to learn about the huge man who burst in upon Amy and her granny without saying a word and took blankets, a leg of mutton and a jar of pickles, and then disappeared. Who was this desperate man? Were the two men on skis really policemen who were chasing him? Why did the policemen kick the dog, Mick?

Why did granny distrust the policemen instead of the thief?

Nina Bawden is also British. In *A Handful of Thieves*, thirteen-year-old Fred McAlpine and his friends tried to recover the money stolen from his grandmother by stealing it back from the thief.

Eva-Lis Wuorio was born in Finland but now lives on the Island of Jersey in the English Channel. Mystery came to English twins Fiona and James, their cousin and tutor Alaric, and an American friend, Davy Bjornson III in *Save Alice!* when they were on their way to Ibiza, Spain, for a vacation. An eighty-year-old woman forced a white cockatoo that was seventy years old on them and gasped, "Save Alice!" Was Alice the cockatoo? Did she have anything to do with the car that was following them?

The next few mysteries have been translated from other languages. One of the most famous that comes from Germany is Kastner's *Emil and the Detectives*. Use the illustrations on pages 14-33 to introduce all the main characters and places important to the story. When Emil Tischbein went by train to Berlin to visit his grandmother, aunt, and cousin, he fell asleep and his money was stolen. Emil and his newly acquired friends followed the thief and captured him only to find a big surprise.

Two books by Winterfeld were written in German: *Detectives in Togas* and the sequel, *Mystery of the Roman Ransom*. In the first book seven boys in ancient Rome were special students in a school run by the Greek, Xantippus. One day Rufus wrote "Caius is a dumbbell" on a slate, a fight ensued, and Rufus was expelled. That same night Xantippus was knocked out and tied up in his wardrobe and the slate and several mathematics books were stolen. Also that night, the words from the slate were written in the same handwriting in red letters on the Temple of Minerva and Rufus was imprisoned. The boys believed Rufus's plea that he was innocent and they tried to discover the real culprit. In *Mystery of the Roman Ransom*, the same boys became involved in an assassination plot. The boys bought a deaf and dumb slave as a birthday gift for their teacher, Xantippus, but he refused the gift. When the boys tried to take Udo back, the slave merchant had disappeared and an old slave said a one-eyed gladiator was looking for Udo and said he wouldn't rest until he had him dead or alive. Why?

Benary-Isbert's *Blue Mystery* was also written in German. Ten-year-old Annegret did not believe the apprentice Fridolin had stolen the priceless blue gloxinia from her father's experimental greenhouse. Annegret solved the mystery with the help of her great dane, Cara, and her best friend, Uschi.

Books written by Karin Anckärsvard were translated from Swedish. The main characters of *The Robber Ghost* are a clique of children who live in Nordvik, a suburb of Stockholm: Hans and Bengt, Knut, Ulla, Karin, Lars, Louise, Carl Axel, and especially Cecelia and Michael. On page 15 the clique discussed the new boy Bertil Dal, and he appeared on page 21. In chapter 2, the colonel is introduced. The colonel was looking out the wrong window the night of the robbery or he might have seen the light from the castle, the blast, or the figures moving about, and the story might have never been written. Later in the book the colonel helped to solve a dilemma.

The same gang from *The Robber Ghost* appears in *Madcap Mystery*, and

Cecelia and Michael are the heroes again. The question to be answered in this mystery is, What did the rich newcomer, Mary Beth, have to do with the thieves plaguing the region?

Bera's *The Horse without a Head* was translated from the French. Ten French children enjoyed riding a headless wooden horse on three wheels. One day the horse was smashed and the children laid it aside to give to Monsieur Douin to see if it could be fixed. Questions to ask students are: Why was the peddler Roublot snooping around the horse? Why did two strangers in lumberjack clothing try to buy it for ten thousand francs? And why was the horse stolen? Teachers and library media specialists won't tell that the horse literally held the key with the address for the location of the hundred million francs stolen from the Paris-Ventimiglia express.

Use the books beginning with Sherlock Holmes and *The Humming Top* and ending with *Save Alice!* as core books for a booktalk. Then read other mysteries from the annotated list on pages 129-42 of the NCTE list, *Adventuring with Books*. Include some of those books in the booktalk or on a bibliography of mysteries. Another list of mysteries appears on pages 366-67 of Sutherland and Arbuthnot's *Children and Books*. More suggestions are included on pages 518-28 of Huck and Young's *Children's Literature in the Elementary School*.

Instead of giving a booktalk for students in grades four through eight, use the books mentioned in the previous paragraphs for a display to accompany the filmstrip, *Reading for the Fun of It: Mystery*. The filmstrip introduces the following books: Aiken's *Night Fall*, Bellairs's *The House with a Clock in Its Walls*, Bonham's *A Dream of Ghosts*, Bonzon's *Pursuit in the French Alps*, Clapp's *Jane-Emily*, Derleth's *The Beast in Holger's Woods*, Hamilton's *The House of Dies Drear*, Hitchcock's *Alfred Hitchcock's Haunted Houseful*, books from the Tod Moran Mysteries by Pease, and Sobol's *Encyclopedia Brown Shows the Way*. Books in the annotated bibliography are Bonham's *Mystery in Little Tokyo*, Corbett's *Dead Man's Light*, Robertson's *The Money Machine*, Snyder's *The Egypt Game*, and Winterfield's *Detectives in Togas*.

The chief value of this filmstrip is that it introduces different types of mysteries, those that involve crimes and clues, those that involve ghosts and supernatural events, and those that involve secrets.

SURVIVAL BOOKS.   There could be several reasons for introducing books about survival to students. First of all, survival stories rank high in the "Adventure" category, and are popular with all ages. Students like to have action in the books they read. Survival stories usually have very defined plots; the main characters are faced with a definite dilemma and need all their wits to survive a shipwreck, earthquake, flood, or plane crash. The characters might be lost, trapped, snowbound, or injured. The way each problem is resolved provides for either a happy or unhappy ending. Students can be introduced to these stories purely so they can learn enough about them to make a selection to enjoy. Or, students could be introduced to survival books in preparation for a creative writing assignment.

Individually or in groups, students could be asked to read several of these books, preferably on the same theme or by the same author, be equipped with first aid and other books about emergencies, and then, asked to write a survival story. One useful title is Greenbank's *A Handbook for Emergencies, Coming Out Alive.* With information from it, students could provide the details of accurate life-saving techniques. This book offers recommendations for signaling for help, finding food and water, first aid, and making small emergency survival packs to take along on trips. Students would be asked to describe their characters, providing them with names, ages, interests, and home life. The setting for the story is related to the dilemma. Perhaps characters set out on a journey of some type and disaster befalls them: students must write about how the characters handled the situation and how they survived, if they did.

Begin the unit with one of the greatest survival stories of all time—Defoe's *Robinson Crusoe,* published in 1719. To provide a common experience for the entire class, show the sound filmstrip adaptation of the story called *Robinson Crusoe.* A teacher's guide and paperback book accompany the two sound filmstrips.

Robinson Crusoe is based on the actual adventures of Alexander Selkirk, but Defoe says it is an allegory of his own life. Defoe named his character "Crusoe" and had him shipwrecked on an island off the coast of South America. There Crusoe lived for more than thirty years, planted his crops, tamed goats, and read his *Bible.* Chapter 8 "In Which Is Given a Copy of My Journal" begins with September 30, 1659, through September thirtieth of the following year. Crusoe saved the native whom he named Friday during the twenty-fourth year. In the thirty-fifth year, Crusoe and Friday were rescued and returned home, but Friday was killed on the way to Brazil. Crusoe married, and he and his wife had three children. Later Crusoe returned to the island he had named "Despair" and visited the mutineers who elected to live there and marry natives.

Chapters from *Robinson Crusoe* appear in several anthologies: Huber's *Story and Verse for Children* (pp. 753–58); Johnson's *Anthology of Children's Literature* (pp. 976–81); and Martignoni's *The Illustrated Treasury of Children's Literature* (pp. 429–37). Ian Richardson reads from Crusoe's journal entries on a sound recording. Politzer's book, *My Journals and Sketchbooks, by Robinson Crusoe,* is an excellent book to introduce to students because Politzer puts Defoe's story in diary form beginning with the shipwreck and ending with the rescue.

Friday and Robinson; Life on Speranza Island by Tournier is another splendid book about Crusoe's adventures and is short enough and exciting enough to read aloud to students. The book is very readable and stresses psychological elements in the characters of the two men. Some events, such as the ending, are different. On September 23, 1759, the ship *The Virginia* was wrecked near the San Juan Fernandez Islands four hundred miles off the coast of Chile. In this version, Crusoe called the islands "Speranza" or "hope" instead of "despair," and proceeded to declare himself the governor, make rules, begin a diary, and devise a calendar. This book tells how Crusoe saved the native whom he named Friday, and how he taught Friday to be the model servant. Later in the story, after the explosion which wrecked Crusoe's carefully constructed civilization,

Friday became the teacher and Crusoe learned how to live from him. When Captain Hunter of *The Whitebird* came on December 22, 1787, 28 years, 2 months, and 22 days later, Crusoe was so disillusioned by the actions of these "so-called" civilized people that he chose not to return with them. When Friday opted to board the schooner, Crusoe found that life would have no purpose until he learned that the cabin boy had run away from the schooner and would provide him with companionship.

Swift's *Gulliver's Travels* is another classic from the eighteenth century. The book was published in 1726 as *Travels into Several Remote Nations of the World*, by Lemuel Gulliver as a political allegory. Gulliver sailed the South Seas in 1699 as the ship's doctor and was shipwrecked in a land where the people were six inches high. Swift's book includes four voyages, the first and most famous is about the little people of Lilliput. Two sound recordings of the story are available; narrators are Denis Johnston and Anthony Quayle. Johnston reads chapters 1, 3, and 5. Johnson's *Anthology of Children's Literature* includes chapters 1, 3, and 4. "The Emperor of Lilliput" appears in Martignoni's *Illustrated Treasury of Children's Literature* (pp. 491–97).

A children's classic based on the Crusoe theme, *A Swiss Family Robinson*, was written in 1813 by a Swiss Army chaplain. A father, mother, and sons—Fritz, Ernest, Franz, and Jack—were shipwrecked on an island and lived comfortably because they borrowed extensively from the wreck. Major events from each of the eighteen chapters appear in the table of contents of the edition published by World. Anthony Quayle reads an abridged version on a sound recording. "Our First Harvest" appears in Martignoni's *The Illustrated Treasury of Children's Literature*, and "Shipwreck" appears in Huber's *Story and Verse for Children*.

Winterfeld's *Castaways in Lilliput* is about three children—Ralph, son of the ranch superintendent, Peggy (eleven), and Jim (nine)— children of a wealthy sheep breeder in Australia. The children found a rubber raft and floated away to an island where they landed and found miniature towns, some of which looked as if people had left in haste. After hearing sirens and seeing helicopters and frightened people, the children realized they were part of a Lilliput village so they waved twigs to show the inhabitants they were peaceful. However, the people of Lilliput thought otherwise and believed that the strangers were invaders. After Mr. Krumps, a friendly farmer, helped them send a cable to their parents and convince the inhabitants they meant no harm, the children were welcomed celebrities until Jim messed up the amusement park. When the children returned home, no one would believe their experiences.

In a fantasy by Brink called *Andy Buckram's Tin Men*, a twelve-year old boy is stranded on an island with two girls. Andy makes robots, and one of the best ways to introduce this book is to describe the robots. Campbell was made from tin soup cans and looked like a baby; Bucket had hooks for hands which held buckets to carry food and water to feed the pigs, chickens, and cows; and Supercan was called "Rowboat" because he could row a boat. Supercan, Andy's masterpiece, was six feet tall, and could add and subtract, had a bell that rang, and rowed the boat to the island where the three children and the robots were marooned.

Island MacKenzie by Williams is another fantasy, in which Miss Pethifer and the Captain's cat were the only survivors of a shipwreck.

O'Dell's *Island of the Blue Dolphins*, the 1961 Newbery Medal winner, has become a new classic story of survival. The Indian girl Karana and her brother were accidentally left behind on the Island of St. Nicholas off the California coast in the 1800s. Karana's brother was killed by wolves and she lived for eighteen years alone. *Zia* is the sequel, in which Karana's niece Zia was responsible for rescuing Karana from the island. The story does not have a happy ending. Zornow and Goldstein include the film *Island of the Blue Dolphins* in their list of "125 Feature Films" in *Movies for Kids*.

Taylor's *The Cay*, another story about a shipwreck, is available as a sound filmstrip. Phillip Enright, Jr., lived on the island of Curacao, a Dutch island off the coast of Venezuela, because his American father was an expert in refineries and worked for Royal Dutch Shell. Phillip's mother was apprehensive because German submarines were patrolling, so she insisted on taking Phillip home with her to Virginia where he would be safe. April 2, 1942, two days after leaving Panama, their ship was torpedoed by the Germans. When Phillip came to, he and Timothy, an elderly black man, were on a raft together. They landed on a small cay or island, but Phillip was blind. Timothy later died of malaria, but not before he had taught Phillip how to survive. People will want to know that Phillip was rescued August 20, 1942.

Two on an Island by Bradbury has twelve-year-old Jeff and nine-year-old Trudy, a brother and sister, and Sarge their German shepherd dog marooned on an island. If this book is introduced at a time other than during a booktalk, read chapter 1 because it gives the circumstances under which the children became marooned. Arriving at their grandmother's house three days before she expected them, the children found her gone. So they took a snack and went out in the boat to their favorite island. While they were there, the boat drifted away and they were marooned with a few bananas, cookies, and a thermos of milk, knowing that they would not be missed for three days.

So far our survival books have been about people who were shipwrecked and left on an island, but there are other stories about trips on rivers with adventures just as dangerous and exciting. One concerns thirteen-year-old Christian Holm and his parents who lived on a one hundred-sixty acre homestead in the Canadian Wilderness. One day Chris overheard his father tell his mother that he was disappointed that his son wasn't "like other boys." Chris set out to prove himself with the four by eight-foot log raft he had secretly built. The raft drifted out of the inlet into the river, and Chris was struck on the head by a boulder and passed out. Chris was on the raft for days before it fell apart just short of a falls, which would have killed him if he had gone over it. Without any weapons, supplies, or tools, Chris began his hundred mile trip home. In Derleth's *The Moon Tenders*, Steve and Sim built a raft to float forty miles down the Wisconsin River where they planned to hunt for Winnebago buried treasure. The boys found counterfeiters instead.

In Dahlstedt's *Terrible Wave*, fifteen-year-old Megan Maxwell survived the

Johnstown Flood of 1889. The title of Aaron's *American Ghost* is explained in a paragraph after the title page: it is the mountain lion, sometimes called a cougar, puma, or panther. In the 1860s, twelve-year Albert was home alone when the flood floated his Wisconsin farmhouse down Willow Creek to the Redman and the Wisconsin Rivers. He was alone, that is, except for the mountain lion who was in a tree that crashed into his parent's bedroom.

Eric, in Bulla's *Down the Mississippi*, took the trip on a raft in 1850. Bart and Alic had their own experiences in Harnden's *Runaway Raft*. In Byars's *Trouble River*, twelve-year-old Dewey Martin and his grandmother set out on Trouble River on Dewey's raft to avoid Indians. At their neighbors', they found the cabin burned, and the family gone, and so Dewey and his grandmother had no choice but to travel forty miles to the nearest town where his parents were.

Many books about the westward movement concern survival. Drazier's *The Stout-Hearted Seven, the True Adventures of the Sager Children Orphaned on the Oregon Trail in 1844* is about six children who set out for Oregon with their parents on a wagon train. A seventh child was born on the trail, but the parents died of fever shortly after that, twenty-six days apart. The baby survived by being passed from one nursing mother to another. When the children reached Oregon, they were adopted by the Whitmans but still faced an Indian massacre.

Sometimes the Indians are depicted as victims. In Hickman's *Valley of the Shadow*, young Tobias and his family, peaceful Delaware Indians who lived in a Moravian settlement in the Ohio Valley in 1781, were caught in a fight between the warring Wyandots and the white settlers. Based on historical events, this is not a happy story. Hickman shows an empathy with the Indians similar to the feeling created by the books of Scott O'Dell.

Numerous accounts of white settlers captured by the Indians are the basis for books. Most of them hoped to escape initially, until they learned to respect the Indians and were assimilated into the tribe. Two fictional boys who had trouble adjusting to the white world when they returned appear in McGraw's *Moccasin Trail* and in Richter's *Light in the Forest*. Walt Disney's movie *The Light in the Forest* appears on the supplementary list of films in Zormon and Goldstein's *Movies for Kids*. A sound recording is also available.

Survival in snowstorms provides several exciting stories. Anderson's *Zeb* went with his father and brother in 1680 to clear wilderness for the family homestead. The second wagon bringing Grandpa, mother, the little children, and the farm animals would start in the spring. When father and Abel were drowned while fording a river, Zeb had to dry himself off before he froze. Then he and his dog Rash went ahead to clear the land so the family could begin to plant the next spring. This books tells how Zeb survived the winter.

George's *Julie of the Wolves* deals in part with being lost in the Alaskan snow. Thirteen-year-old Miyax, an Eskimo girl, also called Julie, is the heroine of the 1973 Newbery Medal book which is also available as a sound filmstrip or a recording. Another person who was lost in the Alaskan snow was fifteen-year-old Brad in Morey's *Home is the North*. Brad's trek across sixty miles of Alaska is included in chapter 12. Whereas Julie was saved by the wolves, Ben, the six-year-old boy in Eckert's *Incident at Hawk's Hill* who vanished from his frontier home, was adopted by a badger on the prairie. The prologue tells how Hawk's Hill received its name. A sound recording of the same name is available. A film called *The Boy Who Talked to Badgers* was made for television.

Runaway Tony picked up hitchhiker Cindy and they became sidetracked for eleven days in Mazer's *Snowbound.* The story appeared on television.

The best way to introduce Day's *Landslide!* is either to read or paraphrase the "Introduction to Laurent" on pp. 7 and 8. The passage is too long to read during a booktalk, but the paragraph on page 7 beginning "Laurent, I'm putting you in charge of this trip as a kind of test . . ." could be read. Laurent's father put him in charge of his brother and sister and the two Berthier children because he was off in his own world too much. An avalanche of snow buried the house where they were staying.

Sometimes people voluntarily go out into the snow. Bixby's *The Impossible Journey of Sir Ernest Shackleton* tells of the Imperial Trans-Antarctic Expedition of 1914–16 which involved twenty-eight men. The feat Shackleton wanted to accomplish—crossing the Antarctic continent from sea to sea—was finally accomplished in 1957–58 by Sir Vivian Fuchs. Shackleton and part of his group were shipwrecked in the Antarctic in three boats.

Frazee's *Year of the Big Snow* was about the fourth expedition of Col. John Charles Fremont who intended to prove that a railroad could be run along the 38th parallel from St. Louis to San Francisco. However, 1848 was a terrible winter in the Rockies for the thirty-five men, twenty-two of whom were veterans of western travel. The story is seen through the eyes of a mountain man's nephew. Fourteen-year-old Ted McNabb was the nephew of Alexis Godey. Read the "Author's Foreword" for historical background.

After finding a great stone house with a Viking tablet, Jamie and Awasin's canoe crunched in the rapids and Jamie's leg was bruised. The two boys lived all winter without fire or food in Mowat's *Lost in the Barrens.* In a sequel, Jamie, Awasin, his sister, and an Eskimo, Peetyuk, try to relocate the place where they found the Viking tablet in *The Cruise of the Viking Grave.*

Fourteen-year-old Torgeir, sometimes called Midge, and his eight-year-old twin brother and sister lived with their parents on an air base in Norway, until they stowed away on an airplane that was on its way to a deserted island where the children got off and were marooned. The book is Hamre's *Operation Arctic.*

Thirteen-year-old David stowed away on a plane that was wrecked in the Canadian wilderness. Hyde's book is called *Strange Companion: A Story of Survival,* and David's strange companion was a whooping crane. Catherall's *Strange Intruder* was a polar bear, in the story of a boat shipwrecked between Scotland and Iceland.

The survival-adventure books by Arthur Catherall are similar to those of Hamre. Introduce one or two books and then briefly mention the others. *Lost Off the Grand Banks* is about Geoff, an English boy, who paid a stranger for a trip on a Grand Banks cod schooner—only to find that he had been tricked. The whole story up to chapter 3 is summarized on pages 30 and 31 when Geoff explained to Captain Maclure how he had been tricked. Later, Geoff and Kinney the captain's son are lost in the fog, and caught on the shelf of an iceberg, the same iceberg that had trapped an American submarine. Don't tell students that Geoff communicated with the sub by making the engine stop and start to create a Morse Code. Compare the cod fishing adventures of Geoff with those of Jimmy in Bunting's *High Tide for Labrador.*

Jan and his uncles, and a friend named Erik went out seal hunting from their Norwegian village in Catherall's *The Arctic Sealer.* They met teams of Russians who descended from helicopters to hunt seals and later accused them of stealing their pelts. The peak adventure was Jan's discovery of forty freezing survivors of a transpolar airplane.

Catherall's *Prisoners in the Snow* is about two children and their grandfather who tried to rescue a pilot who crashed into their Austrian farmhouse and who was buried by an avalanche on the roof of their shed.

In Catherall's *Last Horse on the Sands,* Paula and Simon, English children, and an old horse tried to rescue victims of a plane crash before the tide came in.

Red Sea Rescue by Catherall is about two Arab children, Ibrahim and Saala, who tried to rescue their shipwrecked father and his group. In his *Camel Caravan,* Youba and Fedada joined a camel caravan to Timbuktu which was attacked by desert raiders, in *Kidnapped by Accident,* Mikael and Marjetta of Finland tried to rescue a yacht.

Roth's *Two for Survival* is about the hijacking and crash of an airplane in the Canadian woods, and Mark and John are faced with surviving.

Sometimes trouble arises when people go hunting or camping. In Jeffries' *Trapped,* Gary and Bert went duck hunting even though there were high tide warnings and a blizzard was forecast. In a book by the Johnsons, eleven-year-old David's parents were separated, but his father had the court's permission to take David on a wilderness camping trip. Most of David's memories of his father were frightening and David was uncomfortable with him. Then a grizzly came and destroyed their food and wounded his father, and they were really stranded when the truck became inoperable. How Mark and David survive brings the story to a conclusion that even includes hope of reconciliation between David's parents. The title of the Johnsons' book is *The Grizzly.* Sometimes such a book can be introduced by a question: What would you do if your food was eaten by a grizzly who wounded your father and you couldn't get away because your truck wouldn't start? Read *The Grizzly* by the Johnsons to find out.

Two outdoor survival books are Budbill's *Snowshoe Trek to Otter River* and its sequel *Bones on Black Spruce Mountain.* Harvey and Rocky tried to win the "Best Camper" prize on a three-day camping trip, but were caught in a thunderstorm in Cook's *Fish Heads and Fire Ants.* The book is especially interesting because the two boys have very different habits.

Jean George's *My Side of the Mountain* is a popular survival book and film. The film was included in Zornow and Goldstein's list of "125 Feature Films" in their book *Movies for Kids.* Sam Gribley went to live in a tree in the Catskills for a year just to prove that he could do it. The city boy left with only a penknife, a ball of cord, an axe, and forty dollars.

The Polynesian boy Mafutu had to prove himself so he went to a desert island to overcome his fears in Sperry's 1941 Newbery Medal winner *Call It Courage*. A selection of the book appears in Nelson's *A Comparative Anthology of Children's Literature* (pp. 614–18) and in Johnson's *Anthology of Children's Literature* (pp. 942–45). The book is available on sound filmstrip under two titles: *Adventure, Literature for Children* and *Call It Courage*.

Books about surviving natural disasters in the form of floods and snowstorms have already been mentioned. These next few books concern survival from other natural disasters—hurricanes, earthquakes, and forest fires.

Twelve-year-old Morgan went out to collect the crab traps before the hurricane hit, but was delayed because his dog Tater went off after two herons. Chapters 1 through 4 of Rumsey's *Carolina Hurricane* set the stage for the rest of the book as Morgan is forced to endure the brunt of the hurricane while lost in the middle of a marsh. To complicate matters, the boat's engine had a cracked head.

Mark and his horse Colonel survived a tornado in DeJong's *A Horse Came Running*, and Jeff Belno and his horse Red survived an earthquake in the Adirondack Mountains in Christopher's *Earthquake*.

Fires are also disasters that require surviving. Read the "Foreword" of Clark's *Wildfire* to see why fires are common in that part of Australia. Forest fires also occur in Scholefield's *Brian's Dog* and Ellis's *When Lightning Strikes*.

Another book by Clark, *If the Earth Falls In*, takes place in Australia. In it, fifteen-year-old Louise and two boys are trapped in an abandoned mine.

Those three did not plan to be caught in the tunnel. However, the boys in Church's *Five Boys in a Cave* prepared for two days for their adventure. Jim Culter and the twenty men who dug a tunnel out of Libby prison in Richmond, Virginia, prepared an escape route for a hundred Yankees to escape from the Confederate prison during the Civil War. Linfield adapted a book called *Lion of the Kalahari*, written in Afrikaans by the Hobsons which concerns Skankwan who lived alone in the desert of South Africa until he was sixteen and avenged the deaths of his father and grandfather.

David, the boy in Holm's *North to Freedom*, was allowed to escape from a prison camp in an unnamed country. David's travels to Denmark are further described in the section of this Chapter called *Television—The Holocaust*. Most of the books in that section deal with Jews who survived Hitler and Nazism, and would be suitable to include in a booktalk about survival books. Such a talk could include a discussion with students of the various types of dangers one might be called upon to survive—natural or man-made.

Thirteen-year-old Aremis Slake was hunted and hounded by a gang. He had used the subway token he kept for emergencies, so when he was chased out of the park he ran under the turnstile of the subway and remained there 121 days in *Slakes Limbo* by Holman.

Neufeld's *Sleep Two, Three, Four!*, published in 1971, concerns dreadful possible conditions in the United States of 1983. Six children flee from a totalitarian government that chased them with helicopters and bloodhounds because they wanted to save a small boy with a club foot from being sent to a camp where handicapped persons were isolated. This is a good entry to a discussion of fascism.

Don't Take Teddy by Baastad is about Mikkel who wanted to save his brother Teddy from a home for retarded children. His reason for running away is similar to that in Hamre's *Operation Arctic.* Chapter 5, beginning with "Mrs. Bredon understands. . ." on page 63 provides excellent information about retarded children.

Key's *Escape to Witch Mountain* was made into a movie which appeared in 1978. Tia and Tony were sent to an orphanage for problem children. The two communicated without words, but only Tony could speak to other people. Tia's only possession, her box with the unusual gold star on top, was their only link with their past life. But, who were their family members, where did they come from, and what gave them powers to open locks, communicate with animals, and make toys and broomsticks dance to the harmonica?

Sometimes people survive a journey, as in Corcoran's *Long Journey.* Thirteen-year-old Laurie had lived with her grandfather at his gold mine near Hawkins Dry Diggings in Montana since her parents died. When grandfather began going blind, he sent Laurie and her horse Hook to Butte to get her Uncle Arthur. Grandfather gave Laurie a deed for half ownership in the mine so she would be a property owner and would be treated with respect. Laurie took with her a hunting knife, matches, change of clothes, some food and a frying pan, and some silver dollars. Many exciting events marked Laurie's journey.

Sometimes animals are involved in survival. Two dogs and a cat traveled home together through the Canadian wilderness in Burnford's *Incredible Journey.* Rumsey's *Lion on the Run* is a baby mountain lion who had to learn to survive in the wilderness. Another lion that a boy would like to see remain free is in the book *Lion on the Mountain* by Dixon.

All of these books could be included in a booktalk. Information from this section could help interest students in reading the books. A useful book to conclude a booktalk of survival stories is Gannon's *Great Survival Adventures* which contains nine stories. The book is also good for students who could not finish a complete book but could finish one short story.

Two filmstrips can be used to introduce adventure stories to students. One is called *Reading for the Fun of It: Adventure,* and the other is called *Adventure.* The second filmstrip *Adventure* includes a guide which gives behavioral objectives, suggested discussion and activities, gives content, provides a follow-up activity, and includes a bibliography. The books introduced are for students in grades four through six. The book discussed in detail is Sperry's *Call It Courage.* After showing this filmstrip, describe other books that are full of action.

Additional adventure books can be placed on a display in the library media center or sent to the classroom after the filmstrip *Reading for the Fun of It: Adventure* is shown. This filmstrip introduces nine books and gives annotations for five more in the bibliography. The teacher's guide includes the filmstrip script, discussion questions and activities, a bibliography for students, suggestions for using the series, objectives of the series, an introduction to adventure stories, and a professional bibliography. This filmstrip, as well as the other filmstrips in the *Reading for the Fun of It* series, are excellent guides for people who are learning how to give booktalks because the filmstrip is really a booktalk of the nine books. Use this filmstrip to introduce titles of adventure books to students. Use the filmstrip *Adventure* for helping students to analyze elements in adventure books. If both filmstrips are to be used with a unit, show *Adventure* first.

The following books are included in the sound filmstrip *Reading for the Fun of It: Adventure:* Burnford's *The Incredible Journey* (animals), Fox's *The Slave Dancer* (kidnapping, slavery), George's *Julie of the Wolves* (survival, Eskimo), Hamilton's *The Planet of Junior Brown* (blacks, New York City), Jones's *Edge of Two Worlds* (old and new Indian customs), O'Dell's *Island of the Blue Dolphins* (survival, abandonment), Picard's *The Odyssey of Homer* (trip home from the Trojan War), Taylor's *The Cay* (shipwrecked, World War II), and Twain's *The Adventures of Tom Sawyer* (boy adventures). Annotations for the following books appear in the "Bibliography for Students," in the teacher's guide: Fox's *How Many Miles to Babylon?* (dognapping), Gipson's *Old Yeller* (dog, frontier), O'Dell's *The Black Pearl* (danger, Mexico), Pease's *The Secret Cargo* (South Seas), and Picard's *The Iliad of Homer* (epic of the Trojan War).

TELLING A STORY.   According to experts each person must learn the story to be told by his or her own method. The method outlined here is this author's own personal method. Persons who already have a large repertoire of stories may want to change the order in the process.

1. *Consider the purpose and objectives* for telling the story. Is the story intended to entertain, stimulate reading similar tales, introduce special characters, or provide an introduction to a literature program?
2. *Consider the audience* who will hear the story. What is their age, sex, situation, background, and sophistication? Are they part of a planned public library program, a classroom which will be provided enrichment for a social studies unit, a weekly storytelling session for elementary school students, a bonfire camping experience, high school mythology students, teachers or librarians at a professional conference, or high school forensic contestants enrolled in the storytelling individual event?
3. *Read many stories.* Sometimes selection is mainly a process of discarding unsuitable stories. Collect a list of a dozen stories that beg you to tell them.
4. *Select the story* that suits your objectives and audience from the stories which suit you best.
5. *Plan your introduction.* Decide how you will introduce the story. Relate the story to a universal experience or one that most of the audience has experienced. Now is the time to provide background information on the time and place of the story, or to define words that may be unfamiliar.

6. *Select companion pieces.* If poems, fingerplays, stretch times or follow-up activities are to accompany the program, plan them now. If the story is to be part of a medley, select the other stories. If the story is to be part of a series of programs, plan the sequence for telling the stories.

7. *Find other versions* of the story from *The Children's Catalog,* Cathon's *Stories to Tell to Children,* the list of the Carnegie Library of Pittsburgh, Ireland's *Index to Fairy Tales, 1949–72,* Nelson's *A Comparative Anthology of Children's Literature,* and this and other chapters of this book. Consult the card catalog for individual picture book listings for the stories. Choose the version you like best or combine elements.

8. *Record Bibliographic Sources* for all stories so they can be found later. Include authors, titles, publishers, dates, pages, and libraries where the book was found, as well as call numbers. Indicate if the book is part of a personal collection.

9. *Read the story aloud* to see how it sounds. Not all good stories are suited for oral presentation.

10. *Identify the six major parts of a story:* the introduction, conflict, rising action, climax, falling action, and conclusion. The story should end soon after the climax.

11. *List the characters* in the order of appearance and write a sentence about each one. The description of the character should include physical characteristics, mannerisms, attitudes. Separate major and minor characters. Try to see them in your mind.

12. *Visualize the setting.* Is the setting important to the story? List details about the setting that are important.

13. *List the major events in sequence.* Note repetition of events. Indicate which characters took part in the event.

14. *Copy phrases* from the story that need to be repeated word for word from the text. This usually includes rhymes, repetitive phrases, or descriptions. Or mark a Xeroxed copy with an accenting pen.

15. *Read the story* several times, then outline it from memory.

16. *Tell the story to yourself* without consulting the book or notes.

17. *Reread the original story,* the list of characters, outline, major events, and then the original story.

18. *Picture the story* in your mind. See the characters unfold the action in the proper setting.

19. *Time the story* while telling it aloud just as it will be presented to an audience.

20. *Record the story* on a tape recorder and listen for awkward phrases and pauses, or tell the story in front of a mirror.

21. *Check physical facilities.* If the story is to be told in a place new to you, visit the site ahead of time to visualize the room and plan for seating arrangements for the audience and yourself, so there will be no surprises.

22. *Choose clothing* that will not detract from the story but will make you feel physically and mentally comfortable.

SAMPLE STORYTELLING PROGRAMS TO ENRICH SIXTH-GRADE GEOGRAPHY

These programs were designed to enrich a middle school curriculum which requires that sixth graders study geography with emphasis on world geographical regions, vegetation, climate, and physical features.

The theme centers on geographical phenomena—mountains, rivers, canyons, lakes, oceans, islands, plains, deserts, forests, jungles, rock formations, and lava flows as well as representative vegetation. How these phenomena are explained by folklore from around the world establishes the universality of theme and accentuates the commonality of human nature—its imagination and creativity.

Recorded selections were chosen to accompany the programs for several reasons. First, they are either mood music to enrich the story or provide the setting for it; secondly, when the chosen recorded segments are finished, they become the signal that the program is ready to begin or resume.

Each program is designed to last fifty minutes. Although essential, browsing time and opportunity for checking out books is in addition to the program time.

Besides general objectives for the entire program, specific objectives accompany each program.

GENERAL OBJECTIVES OF THE PROGRAM

1. To provide the companionship created by a shared experience.
2. To introduce students to a unique body of literature.
3. To develop an acquaintance with regional and worldwide tales.
4. To provide a pleasurable library experience.
5. To reinforce the human relationship between the librarian and the students.
6. To develop imagination.
7. To develop the listening skills.
8. To provide enrichment for a curriculum unit.
9. To interpret literature to sixth graders.
10. To introduce students to books.
11. To deepen the student's aesthetic appreciation.
12. To cultivate the capacity for literary appreciation.
13. To counteract some of the hustle and bustle of modern life.
14. To show the universality of cultures around the world through common themes.

How the People Sang the Mountains Up
and Other Stories Explaining Geographical Phenomena

PAUL BUNYAN, GEOGRAPHICAL WIZARD. (First Program)

Specific Objectives of the Program
  1. To provide an overview of the accomplishments of Paul Bunyan for sixth graders
  2. To provide a legendary explanation for many American geographical formations
  3. To introduce books about Paul Bunyan to sixth graders

Advance Publicity
    A display in the library showcase featuring books about Paul Bunyan was featured for a week before this program.

Signal for the Story to Begin
    When the students enter the library, the song "Once More A-Lumbering Go," side 1, band 1, from Songs of *Michigan Lumberjacks* will be playing. The stopping of the record is the signal that the story is to begin.

The Program
  A. "How Ol' Paul Changed the Map of America" (Malcolmson, pp. 251–59).
        An explanation of how Paul Bunyan was responsible for the formation of the following geographical phenomena: Cascade River Falls, Yosemite geysers, Arkansas Red River, Kiamichi Mountains in Eastern Oklahoma, dinosaur tracks in North Dakota, the iron mines in Northern Michigan, the Bad Lands of the Dakotas, Pikes Peak, Old Faithful in Yellowstone, the Great Salt Lake, Oklahoma dust storms, Grand Canyon of the Colorado, Puget Sound, the Great Lakes, and the Mississippi River.

  B. *Stretch Time*
        "Turner's Camp on the Chippewa," a lumbering song (side two, band 5) from the above record will be played. The stopping of the record will signal that the program is ready to resume.

  C.   A brief introduction to books from the display case about Paul Bunyan which are on the bibliography.

Follow-Up Activities
    An opportunity to look over and perhaps check out other books on Paul Bunyan will be provided.

Program Sources
Malcolmson, Anne. *Yankee Doodle's Cousins*. Houghton Mifflin, 1941. 268 p. il.

Bibliography
Blair, Walter. *Tall Tale America; a Legendary History of Our Humorous Heroes.* Coward-McCann, 1944. 262p. il.
Carmer, Carl. *America Sings; Stories and Songs of Our Country's Growing.* Knopf, 1942. 243p. il.
Felton, Harold W. *Legends of Paul Bunyan.* Knopf, 1947. 418p. il.

Frost, Frances. *Legends of the United Nations.* McGraw, 1943. 323p. il. pp. 165–74.

Leach, Maria. *Rainbow Book of American Folk Tales and Legends.* World, 1958. 318p. il. pp. 19–22.

McCormick, Dell J. *Paul Bunyan Swings his Axe.* Caxton, 1936. 111p. il.

————. *Tall Timber Tales, More Paul Bunyan Stories.* Caxton, 1939. 155p. il.

Malcolmson, Anne. *Yankee Doodle's Cousins.* Houghton, 1941. 267p. il. pp. 229–60.

Rounds, Glen. *Ol' Paul, the Mighty Logger.* Holiday, 1949. 173p. il.

Shapiro, Irwin. *Tall Tales of America.* Simon and Schuster, 1958. 124p. il. p. 81–95.

Shephard, Esther. *Paul Bunyan.* Harcourt, 1952. 233p. il.

Stevens, James. *Paul Bunyan.* Knopf, 1947. 245p. il.

Wadsworth, Wallace. *Paul Bunyan and his Great Blue Ox.* Doubleday, 1926. 238p. il.

WHY THE SEA IS SALTY. (Second Program)

Specific Objectives of the Program

1. To introduce students to traditional tales from Norway and the Philippines.
2. To tell a complete Paul Bunyan Tale rather than an overview of his accomplishments.
3. To tell a Paul Bunyan Tale from a region of the country not our own.
4. To show the universality of themes.

Advance Publicity

The topic was given to the students at the previous storytelling session.

Signal for the Story to Begin

Victory at Sea, RCA LSC-2335, 2226, 2523 contains mood music to be played as the students enter. When the music stops, the program begins.

The Program

A. "Digging Puget Sound" (Shephard, pp. 191–202).

The story will be adapted to make it short enough. Mr. Ranier asked Paul to dig a sound for Seattle and the dirt Paul dug out was used to make a mountain for Tacoma named after Mr. Ranier. When he wouldn't pay Paul, he began throwing dirt back and the dirt became the San Juan Islands. The pork salt from his beans ran into the ocean to make it salty. The foam is the soapsuds from his dishes.

B. *Stretch Time*

Play further sections of *Victory at Sea.*

C. "Why the Sea is Salty" (Gruenberg, pp. 418–21).

The traditional Norwegian tale about a poor brother who had a magic hand mill which made food. His brother was jealous and bought it to make salt herring; however he couldn't get it to stop. He

SAMPLE STORYTELLING PROGRAMS • 153

gave it to a sea captain but his boat filled with salt herring and sank, leaving all that salt in the sea.

D. "Why the Ocean is Salty" (Belting, pp. 55–67).

The Goddess of Night wanted a house as white as snow so the Philippino god of building tried to find white bricks, stones, or clay. When he couldn't find any white enough he made bricks of salt. They were transported to her home on a bridge over the ocean, but the ocean didn't like the noisy workers carrying salt over him so he destroyed the bridge and the salt melted into the sea.

Follow-Up Activities

A Russian folk tale about salt will be shown. (Zemach. *Salt, A Russian Tale.* Follett, 1965. unp.). Students will be provided with an opportunity to check out books.

Program Sources

Belting, Natalia. *The Earth is on a Fish's Back, Tales of Beginnings.*Holt, 1965.
        91p. il.
Gruenberg, S.M. *Favorite Stories Old and New.* Doubleday, 1955. 507p. il.
Shephard, Esther. *Paul Bunyan.* Harcourt, 1952. 233p. il.

ISLANDS AND HOW THEY CAME TO BE. (Third Program)

Specific Objectives of the Program
    1. To introduce students to a folk literature of Ireland, the Philippines, and
        Samoa.
    2. To provide legendary explanations for the formation of islands.
    3. To show the universality of themes.

Advance Publicity

A special display in the library showcase since the last program has been devoted to islands of the world, including materials on Hawaii, Indonesia, Ireland, New Zealand, Cuba, Greenland, Australia, the Philippines, etc.

Signal for the Story to Begin

When the students enter the library, a selection from *Irish Ballads, Folksongs, and Lyrics* will be played. The stopping of the record is the signal that the story is to begin.

The Program
    A. "How the Giant Finn Made the Isle of Man" (Young, pp. 1–6).

A brief introduction of Finn should precede this story. Mac Mac-Cracken of Scotland said he wouldn't come to Ireland to fight Finn MacCool unless he could come without getting his feet wet. So, Finn built the "Giants' Causeway" which still reaches from Scotland to Ireland. The dirt Finn threw into the Irish Sea became the Isle of Man and the hole he took it from became the Lough Negh, an Irish Lake.

B. "Finn MacCool, the Greatest of Civil Engineers" (Miller, pp. 283–97).
   Portions of this story should be told to show how the Irish-Americans credited Finn with accomplishments already credited to Paul Bunyan: Rainbow Bridge in Utah, irrigated the desert, dug the Grand Canyon.

C. *Stretch Time*
   Selections from the above record, including the funny ballad "Brian O'Linn" will be played. The stopping of the record is the signal that the program is ready to resume.

D. (Holding, p. 11 is the source for the statement that Maui the Fisherman cast his enchanted hook deep into the Pacific Ocean and pulled up the Island of Samoa. Allude to how the San Juan Islands were formed by Paul Bunyan from the previous week's story. (Shepard, p. 202).

E. "Legend of the First Filipinos" (Sechrist, pp. 3–7).
   The Supreme One created sea, sky, and kite (a bird). Sea and sky were jealous of kite's attentions and sky showered sea with rocks and earth. This land, surrounded by water was known as the Philippine Islands. The people came out of the split bamboo.

Follow-Up Activities
Students will be provided with an opportunity to check out display case books, legend books or others.

Program Sources
Holding, James. *Sky-Eater and Other South Sea Tales.* Abelard-Schuman, 1965. 124p. il.
Irish Ballads, Folk Songs, and Lyrics retold by Siabhan McKenna. Spoken Arts, n.d.
Miller, Olive B. *Heroes, Outlaws, and Funny Fellows.* Doubleday, 1944. 332p. il.
Sechrist, Elizabeth H. *Once in the First Times, Folk Tales From the Philippines.* Macrae Smith, 1949. 215p. il.
Shephard, Esther. *Paul Bunyan.* Harcourt, 1952. 233p. il.
Young, Blanche Cowley. *How the Manx Cat Lost His Tail and Other Manx Folk Stories.* McKay, 1959. 114p. il.

NANABOZHO, GRANDSON OF NAKOMIS. (Fourth Program)

Specific Objectives of the Program
1. To provide an introduction to the literature of the American Indian.
2. To develop an acquaintance with stories that explain phenomena typical of our geography and climate.

Advance Publicity
A display in the library showplace featuring American Indians will be featured that week. The topic of Nanabozho was announced at the previous

storytelling session.

Signal for the Story to Begin
When the students enter the library, selections from the *Song of Hiawatha* will be playing. The fact that Longfellow based his poem on the Nanabozho stories can serve as an introduction to the tales. The stopping of the record is the signal that the story is to begin.

The Program
A. "The Coming of Nanabozho" (Reid, pp. 13–16).
This story should be shortened for the purpose of introducing the story of Nakomis and her daughter Wenonah who was married to the North Wind, bore twins, and died leaving Nanabozho to the care of Nakomis.

B. "Nanabozho and the Birches" (Reid, pp. 47–50).
Excellent for descriptive passages on chipmunks, birds leaving for the winter, colored leaves, etc. Explains why the white birch is scarred.

C. *Stretch Time*
Play band six of side one of *Indians of the Great Lakes Region* featuring the Ojibwa of Isabella Reservation, Michigan and the selection of the Ojibwa of Lac Du Flambean, Wisconsin from the same record. The stopping of the record is the signal to return to the program.

D. "Nanabozho Saves Nakomis" (Reid, pp. 65–69).
Nanabozho rewards the maple trees for saving his grandmother by giving them maple sap. The people were so thankful that spring became a feasting time.

E. "Nanabozho Falls Asleep" (Reid, pp. 122–24).
This story is adapted to become a conclusion to the program. Shows the passing of winter. Tells how Nanabozho was changed to stone because he forgot his promise to the Great Spirit that he wouldn't harm the white men. This explains the face-like rock island in Thunder Bay.

Follow-Up Activities
A brief book talk consisting of a sentence or so explaining the area of the country or tribe represented in collections of tales in the American Indian books listed in the bibliography below.

Program Sources
Indians of the Great Lakes Region. Ethnic Folkways Library, 1956, FE-4003. 12" 33-1/3 rpm.
Reid, Dorothy M. *Tales of Nanabozho.* Walck, 1963. 128p. il.
Song of Hiawatha. Folkways, n.d. LC-R-59-52. 12" 33-1/3 rpm.

Bibliography
Bell, Corydon. *John Rattling-Gourd of Big Cave, a Collection of Cherokee Legends.* Macmillan, 1955. 103p. il.
Belting, Natalie. *The Long-Tailed Bear.* Bobbs,
Fisher, Anne B. *Stories California Indians Told.* Parnassus, 1957. 110p. il.
Gilham, Charles E. *Beyond the Clapping Mountains.* Macmillan, 1943. 134p. il.
Harris, Christie. *Once Upon a Totem.* Atheneum, 1963. 148p. il.
Leach, Maria. *Rainbow Book of American Folk Tales and Legends.* pp. 275–90. World, 1958. 318p. il.
Leekley, Thomas. *The World of Nanabozho, Tales of the Chippewa Indians.* Vanguard, 1965. 128p. il.
Longfellow, H. W. *Song of Hiawatha.* Dutton, 1960. 214p. il.
Marriott, Alice. *Winter-Telling Stories.* Sloane, 1947. 84p. il. (Kiowa)
Martin, Frances G. *Nine Tales of Coyote.* Harper, 1950. 60p.
————. *Nine Tales of Raven.* Harper, 1951. 60p. il.
Penney, Grace J. *Tales of the Cheyennes.* Houghton-Mifflin, 1953. 117p. il.
Running, Corrine. *When Coyote Walked the Earth, Indian Tales of the Pacific Northwest.* Holt, 1949. 71p. il.
Rushmore, H. and W. R. Hunt. *Dancing Horses of Acoma and Other Indian Stories.* World, 1963. 163p. il.
Writers' Project. *Legends of the Mighty Sioux.* Whitman, 1941. 158p. il.
Walker, Louis Jean. *Green Sky Hill.* Eerdman's 1964. 204p. il.
North American Indian Songs. Bowmar Records. N.D. 12" 33-1/3 rpm.

WHY THERE ARE NO TREES IN THE DESERT AND OTHER TREE STORIES. (Fifth Program)

Specific Objectives of the Program
1. To introduce stories from Africa and South America.
2. To provide legendary explanations about the origin of trees typical to certain locales.
3. To provide variations of the same story.

Advance Publicity
A bulletin board featuring Joyce Kilmer's poem "Trees" shows the poem printed in primary type on a large outline of a full deciduous tree with shadows of other types, palms, evergreens, leafless trees in the background. The topic for this session was given to the students after they had heard the stories about maple trees and birches in the Nanabozho stories.

Signal for the Story to Begin
While the students enter the library a selection from *Lawrence of Arabia* will be played. The stopping of the record is the signal that the story is to begin.

The Program
A. "Why There Are No Trees on the Desert" (Rounds, pp. 87–102).
While Paul was trying to scientifically cross types of trees with each other to come up with a tree which would grow lumber on the

branches like apples, he came up with a tree as big as the Redwoods but covered with thorns. He planted these on the desert but the women of America petitioned to have them removed so the desert would look like a desert. While he worked to remove them, his sweat washed gullies in the desert and the streams hindered his work so he dug the Grand Canyon for it to drain into. It also tells of curling the duck's tail and the origin of Colorado Springs.

B. "The Baobab Tree" (Heady, pp. 59-61).

Why the large gray trunk of the Baobab tree in Africa has scraggly leaves. In early times all trees could choose their own location and the Baobab asked to be moved several times until the Great One planted it with its mouth in the earth so he wouldn't have to listen to the complaining.

C. *Stretch Time*

Selections from *Panorama of Latin American Folklore* will be played. The stopping of the record is the signal that the program is about to resume.

D. "Origin of the Balsam Tree" (U.N. pp. 241-43)

This legend from El Salvador tells of two children of rival chiefs who wanted to marry. A war was fought to prevent the marriage and the young man is killed. When the chief saw his daughter comforting her lover, the enemy, the chief killed her and her six maidens. She and her friends turned to Balsam trees, multiplied and spread and now the Pacific shores are known as the Balsam coast.

E. "How the Warm Springs of Tipitapa Came to Be." (Henius, pp. 38-42).

This variant of the above story comes from Nicaragua. It should be adapted to briefly tell that when the two lovers are killed, the blood from their two hearts made a pool. The next day a warm spring with vapor rose in filmy spirals to the sky.

Follow-Up Activities
Students will be provided with an opportunity to check out books.

Program Sources
Heady, Eleanor. *When the Stones were Soft, East African Fireside Tales*. Funk and Wagnalls, 1968. 94p. il.
Henius, Frank. *Stories from the Americas*. Scribners, 1944. 114p. il.
Panorama of Latin American Folklore, 24 Traditional Songs. RCA MKL-6001.
Rounds, Glen. *Ol' Paul, the Mighty Logger*. Holiday, 1949. 173p. il.
United Nations Women's Guild. *Ride With The Sun, an Anthology of Folk Tales and Stories from the U.N.* McGraw-Hill, 1955. 296p. il.

THE MOST USEFUL TREE IN THE WORLD AND OTHER TREE STORIES. (Sixth Program)

Specific Objectives of the Program
  1. To provide legendary explanations about trees of Central Africa, and the
       South Seas.
  2. To show the universality of themes.

Advance Publicity
  The same bulletin board on trees remains in the library. The titles for these
stories were given during the last storytelling session.

Signal for the Story to Begin
  When the students enter the library, the song representing Fiji will be
played from *Folk Songs of Pacific Neighbors*. The stopping of the record is the
signal that the story is about to begin.

The Program
  A. "Tuna's Gift" (Rust, pp. 55–63).
          A pretty girl of the South Seas befriended the King of Fiji who had
          been changed to an eel. He said she should bury his head when he
          died. A coconut tree grew on that spot.

  B. "How the Coconut Tree Was Saved" (Leach, p. 126).
          An Apayao tale about how the coconut tree floated during the
          flood.

  C. *Stretch Time*
          Selections from *Music of Equatorial Africa* which presents a
          cross section of music from Central Africa will be played. The stop-
          ping of the record is the signal that the story is about to begin.

  D. "The Most Useful Tree in the World" (Burton, pp. 56–59).
          To stop an argument over which was the most useful tree, the
          King said he would give his daughter to whomever could guess
          which tree he told his son was best. The muskrat loved her and
          listened to the King say it was the Mwabi, tree of unselfishness. The
          roots are affection, the trunk giving, the branches welcome, and the
          leaves work. An excellent description of kinds of tropical trees and
          uses of trees in Central Africa.

  E. "Why Some Trees are Evergreen" (Leach, p. 125).
          A Cherokee tale about when the Great Spirit asked the trees to
          stay awake the first seven days of the world and only the cedar,
          pine, spruce, fir, holly, and laurel managed to stay awake.

Follow-Up Activities
  Students will be provided with an opportunity to check out books. Collections from Africa and Polynesia as a group will be mentioned.

Program Sources
Burton, W. F. *The Magic Drum, Tales from Central Africa*. Criterion, 1961.
          127p. il.

Folk Songs of Pacific Neighbors. Bowamar, n.d. 12" 33 1/3 rpm.
Leach, Maria. *How the People Sang the Mountains Up, How and Why Stories.*
    Viking, 1967. 159p. il.
Music of Equatorial Africa. Folkways, n.d. 4402. 12" 33-1/3 rpm.
Rust, Doris. *Tales from the Pacific, adapted for Children.* Faber and Faber, 1965.
    63p. il.

HOW THE PEOPLE SANG THE MOUNTAINS UP AND HOW THE VALLEYS
WERE FORMED. (Seventh Program)

Specific Objectives of the Program
    1. To provide legendary explanations for the formation of mountains.
    2. To show the universality of themes.

Advance Publicity
    A bulletin board in the library which shows a mountain similar to the
Japanese Fujiyama, complete with mist, is blue-grey with a white top and mist.
The background and squares with the six mountain titles typed on them are
bright vermillion.

Signal for the Story to Begin
    When the students enter the library, a selection from *On Top of Old Smoky*
will be played. The stopping of the record is a signal that the story is to begin.

The Program
    A. "Building the Rockies" (Rounds, pp. 102–117).
                After logging the Great Plains to furnish grazing land for the buf-
                falo, Paul answered the call of the King of Sweden. The King wanted
                some mountains between the Dakotas and the Pacific to cut off
                winter winds from Siberia. Paul filled the prairie dog holes with
                sourdough which pushed up the range of mountains.

    B. *Stretch Time*
                A section from *Mountain Songs of the Alps* will be played. The
                stopping of the record will be a signal for the program to resume.

    C. "How the World Was Made" (Bell, pp. 4–7).
                When there was no land, the animals lived in the sky vault but
                they were too crowded. Buzzard was sent down to see if the land
                was dry enough. Wherever his weary wings struck the ground there
                were valleys, otherwise the rest was all mountains. The animals
                called him back so the world wouldn't be all mountains and valleys.

    D. "How the People Sang the Mountains Up" (Leach, pp. 23–25).
                An Apache legend about how the mountains were formed.

Follow-Up Activities
    Students will be provided with an opportunity to check out books. Japanese
folk and fairy tales will be displayed.

Program Sources
Bell, Corydon. *John Rolling-Gourd of Big Cove, a Collection of Cherokee Legends.* Macmillan, 1955.
Leach, Maria. *How the People Sang the Mountains Up; How and Why Stories.* Viking, 1967. 159p. il.
Mountain Songs of the Alps. Folkways, 1958. FW 8807. 12" 33-1/3 rpm.
Rounds, Glen. *Ol' Paul, the Mighty Logger.* Holiday, 1949. 173p. il.

MOUNTAIN MISTS AND VOLCANOES. (Eighth Program)

Specific Objectives of the Program
1. To introduce students to folk literature from Hawaii, and Japan.
2. To show legendary explanations for unusual rock formations and accompanying peculiarities.

Advance Publicity
The mountain bulletin board from the previous week remains. Titles for this week were announced at the previous program.

Signal for the Story to Begin
Band 2, side 1 of *Folk Music From Japan* has instrumental music representative of Japan. The stopping of the music will signal the beginning of the story.

The Program
A. "The Smoke of Fujiyama" (Williston, pp. 75–81).
   A moon princess cared for her earthly parents but when her duties were over, she rose from the top of the sacred mountain until she reached the moon. The soft white wreath of smoke seen there today is a floating bridge to the city in the sky.

B. "How the Devil's Tower Came to Be" (Writer's Project, pp. 115–16).
   Two Indian Children in the Black Hills were being attacked by a bear so the Great Spirit in his kindness made the ground under them rise.

C. *Stretch Time*
   Selections from *Hawaiian Chant, Hula, and Music* will be played. The stopping of the record will signal that the program is about to resume.

D. "The Strange Sled Race" (Thomson, pp. 28–32).
   A Hawaiian story explaining that one side of Mauna Kea is free of lava flows because of the skill of the goddess of snow, Poliaku's skill at sled-racing.

Program Sources
Folk Music From Japan. Columbia World Library, n.d. KL 214. 12" 33-1/3 rpm.
Hawaiian Chant, Hula, and Music. Folkways, 1962. FW 8750. 12" 33-1/3 rpm.
Thomson, Vivian L. *Hawaiian Myths of Earth, Sea, and Sky.* Holiday House, 1966. 84p. il.

Williston, Teresa P. *Japanese Fairy Tales, Second Series*. Rand McNally, 1911. 96p. il.

Writers' Project. *Legends of the Mighty Sioux*. Whitman, 1941. 158p. il.

STORMALONG, SAILOR OF THE SEVEN SEAS (Ninth Program)

Specific Objectives of the Program
1. To provide background information on and introduce students to Old Stormalong.
2. To provide a legendary explanation for the White Cliffs of Dover.
3. To introduce books about Old Stormalong to sixth grade students.

Advance Publicity
A display in the library showcase featuring books about Old Stormalong was featured for a week prior to this program.

Signal for the Story to Begin
The song "Blow the Man Down" from *Sea Shanties* was playing when the students entered the library. The stopping of the record is the signal that the story is to begin.

The Program
A.   Read the five stanza poem about Stormalong on p. 64 of Felton.

B.   Adapt information from Malcolmson pp. 63–70 and Leach pp. 23–24 to provide background on Stormalong's birth and accomplishments.

C. *Stretch Time*
      Play the selection "Stormalong John" from the record *Sea Shanties*. The stopping of the record will signal the resumption of the story.

D. "The Dark Cliffs of Dover" (Felton, pp. 49–57).
      Stormalong had to soap the sides of the Courser to get the ship through the Dark Cliffs. It was a tight squeeze but they got through, however, the soap rubbed off on the rocks and the cliffs are white to this day. The suds make white caps.

Follow-Up Activities
A group of books about Stormalong that are listed on the bibliography will be introduced. Students will have an opportunity to check out books.

Program Sources
Felton, Harold W. *True Tales of Stormalong: Sailor of the Seven Seas*. Prentice-Hall, 1968. 64p. il.

Leach, Maria. *Rainbow Book of American Folk Tales and Legends*. World, 1958. 318p. il. pp. 23–24.

Sea Shanties. RCA LSC-2551. 12" 33 1/3 rpm.

Malcolmson, Anne. *Yankee Doodle's Cousins*. Houghton, 1941. 267p. il. pp. 63–70.

Bibliography
Blair, Walter. *Tall Tale America; a Legendary History of Our Humorous Heroes.*
Coward-McCann, 1944. 262p. il. pp. 9–22.
Carmer, Carl. *America Sings; Stories and Songs of Our Country's Growing.*
Knopf, 1942. 243p. il.
Felton, Harold W. *True Tales of Stormalong: Sailor of the Seven Seas.* Prentice-
Hall, 1968. 64p. il.
Leach, Maria. *The Rainbow Book of American Folk Tales and Legends.* World,
1958. 318p. il. pp. 23–24.
Malcolmson, Anne. *Mister Stormalong.* Houghton, 1952. 136p. il.
————. *Yankee Doodle's Cousins.* Houghton, 1941. 267p. il. pp. 63–70.
Shapiro, Irwin. *How Old Stormalong Captured Mocha Dick.* Messner, 1942.
47p. il.
————. *Tall Tales of America.* Simon and Schuster, 1958. 124p. il. pp. 7–21.

HOLIDAY PROGRAM. (Tenth Program)

Specific Objectives of the Program
1. To provide a story which describes autumn in this geographic region
2. To introduce a story to the students which meets the requirements for inclusion in the total program as well as is indicative of autumn and
   Thanksgiving.

Advance Publicity
The titles of these stories were announced at the previous session. A
bulletin board that has poetry written on colored leaves includes the poem used
in today's program.

Signal for the Story to Begin
In order to set the mood for the first two stories, "Autumn Leaves" will be
played as the children enter the room. The stopping of the record will indicate
that the story is to begin.

The Program
A. "Autumn Color" a poem by T. Robinson (Hazeltine, p. 97).
This poem contains imagery of leaves which provides an introduc-
tion to the first story.

B. "The Origin of Birds" (Walker, pp. 181–86).
This beautiful description of autumn in the Northeast with images
of animals and vegetation tells of how the Frost King killed the
leaves. To save the leaves, the Great Spirit turned them into birds
which would return in spring. Reddish brown birds became
thrushes, yellow birds became goldfinches, red maple leaves
became scarlet tanagers, etc.

C. *Stretch Time*
"Now Thank We All Our God" from the record *A Mighty Fortress*
will be played. The stopping of the record will indicate that the pro-

gram is about to resume.

D. "How Indian Corn Came Into the World" (Olcott)

An Indian boy went off into the forest to prove his manhood. There he wrestled three times with the Great Spirit in human form. Although he was weak because of his fast, the Great Spirit promised that one time the boy would win and when he did, he was to bury the man and care for his grave. The boy followed the instructions and Indian Corn grew from the grave, a gift from the Great Spirit.

Follow-Up Activities

The poetry bulletin board will be alluded to, holiday books and Indian legends will be suggested. An opportunity to check out books will be provided.

Program Sources

Hazeltine, Alice I. and Smith, Elva S. *The Year Around, Poems for Children.* Abingdon, 1956. 192p. il.

A Mighty Fortress. by the Shaw Corale. RCA, n.d. LSC-2199. 12" 33-1/3 rpm.

Olcott, F. J. *Good Stories for Great Holidays.* Houghton, 1914. 461p. il.

Walker, Louise Jean. *Legends of Green Sky Hill.* Eerdmans. 204p. il.

HOW SWEET POTATOES AND RICE CAME TO MAN. (Eleventh Program)

Specific Objectives of the Program

1. To show examples of the legendary explanations for important plants.
2. To provide examples of folk tales from Indonesia, New Zealand, and Easter Island.

Advance Publicity

A bulletin board with a bright purple background will have the huge letters HOW & WHY in light pink letters. On these letters will be typed the titles and sources for various how and why stories, i.e. "How Coyote Brought Fire to Man."

Signal for the Story to Begin

The selection from New Zealand from the record *Maori Songs of New Zealand* will be played. The stopping of the record is the signal that the story is to begin.

The Program

A. "The Sweet Potato" (Rust, pp. 11–18).

How one of the first men in New Zealand paddled to another land to get the sweet potato or Kumara and was sent home by the flying moa. He arrived home later than he was told to and so the moa was killed by the ogre on his return trip so no one has seen one since except for fossils.

B. "How the Yams Got Their Eyes" (Leach, p. 129).

The legend of how Rapu, the great gardener of Easter Island

owned all plants but wanted to own a yam. The red bird that brought it to him had carried it in its long beak and poked holes in it that left the eyes we have today.

C. *Stretch Time*

A selection from *Music of Indonesia* which represents Java will be played. The stopping of the record is the signal that the story is to begin.

D. *Princess of the Rice Fields, an Indonesian Folk Tale* (Kimishima, total story is unpaged).

A celestial princess becomes a rice plant in Java and her earthly lover becomes the male plant in this story of how rice came to Java.

Follow-Up Activities

The picture book *Princess of the Rice Fields, an Indonesian Folk Tale* will be introduced because it is a delightful blend of story and illustration. Time to check out books will be provided.

Program Sources

Kimishima, Hisako. *Princess of the Rice Fields, an Indonesian Folk Tale.* Walker, 1970. unp. il.

Leach, Maria. *How the People Sang the Mountains Up, How and Why Stories.* Viking, 1967. 159p. il.

Maori Songs of New Zealand. Folkways, n.d. 4433. LC R-59-848. 12" 33-1/3 rpm.

Music of Indonesia. Folkways, 1959. 4406. SC R-59-198. 12" 33-1/3 rpm.

Rust, Doris. *Tales from the Pacific, adapted for Children.* Faber and Faber, 1965. 63p. il.

PECOS BILL. (Twelfth Program)

Specific Objectives of the Program
1. To provide an overview of Pecos Bill for sixth graders.
2. To provide a legendary explanation for the formation of Death Valley and Grand Canyon.
3. To introduce books about Pecos Bill to sixth graders.
4. To develop an appreciation of music which has grown out of a regional occupation.

Advance Publicity

A display in the library showcase featuring books about Pecos Bill was exhibited for the week preceding this program. This topic was also announced at the previous storytelling program.

Signal for the Story to Begin

When the students enter the library "The Old Chisholm Trail" from *Songs of the Frontier* will be playing. The stopping of the record is the signal that the story is to begin.

The Program
A. "Pecos Bill" (Shapiro, pp. 7-23).
An overview of the story of Pecos Bill from the time he fell off the wagon until his death. It tells of his achievements as the greatest cowboy, how he invented the lariat, rode the cyclone, composed the songs "Cowboy's Lament," "Bury Me Not on the Lone Prairie," and "Old Chisholm Trail." Also how he formed Grand Canyon and Death Valley.

B. *Stretch time*
Play the song "Lonesome Cowboy" and "Bury Me Not on the Lone Prairie" from the above record. The stopping of the record will signal that the program is ready to resume.

C.   A brief book-talk in which various books about Pecos Bill are introduced.

Follow-Up Activities
A chance to check out books about Pecos Bill from the display as well as time for selecting other books will be provided.

Program Sources
Shapiro, Irwin. *Tall Tales of America.* Simon and Schuster, 1958. 124p. il.
Songs of the Frontier. by the Wagner Corale. Capitol, n.d. P8332. 12" 33⅓ rpm.

Bibliography
Blair, Walter, *Tall Tale America; a Legendary History of Our Humorous Heroes.* Coward-McCann, 1944. 262p. il. pp. 185-202.
Bowman, James C. *Pecos Bill, the Greatest Cowboy of all Time.* Whitman, 1937. 296p. il.
Carmer, Carl. *America Sings; Stories and Songs of Our Country's Growing.* Knopf, 1942. 243p. il.
Felton, Harold W. *New Tall Tales of Pecos Bill.* Prentice-Hall, 1958. 164p. il.
————. *Pecos Bill, Texas Cowpuncher.* Knopf, 1949. 177p. il.
Leach, Maria. *Rainbow Book of American Folk Tales and Legends.* World, 1958. 318p. il.
Malcolmson, Anne. *Yankee Doodle's Cousins.* Houghton, 1941. 267p. il. pp. 211-28.
Peck, Leigh. *Pecos Bill and Lightning.* Houghton, 1940. 68p. il.
Shapiro, Irwin. *Tall Tales of America.* Simon and Schuster, 1958. 124p. il.

SPECIALIZED BIBLIOGRAPHIC CATEGORIES

At the back of this book are two numbered bibliographies, one of multimedia (nonprint material), and one of books. The numbers below refer to those indexes, with the entries preceded by "M" found in the Multimedia Index.

INDIVIDUAL FOLK AND FAIRY TALES

138, M688, 178, 206, 302, 465, M212, M213, 570, 584, 1315, 1422, 1502, 1566, 1798, 2018, 2028, 2029, 2030, 2035, 2036, 2037, 2038, 2039, 2040, 2050, 2051, 2052, 2967, 3202, 3548, 3551, 3732, M555, 3733, 3734, 3843, 3981, 4217, 4438, 4486, 4602, 4720, 4802, 4854, 5000, M185.

COLLECTIONS OF FOLKLORE AND MYTHOLOGY

187, 202, 203, 208, 209, 210, 229, 230, 263, 281, 285, 377, 384, 386, 412, 511, 643, 699, 806, 843, 910, 912, 924, 953, 1090, 1094 a & b, 1164, 1170, 1233, 1242, 1313, 1318, 1432, 1570, 1616, 1617, 1618, 1636, 1894, 1950, 1968, 1979, 2011, 2014, 2019, 2026, 2053, 2064, 2066, 2067, 2143, 2147, 2148, 2149, 2150, 2151, 2153, 2157, 2270, 2405, 2421, 2458, 2459, 2460, 2489, 2498, 2547, 2548, 2565, 2609, 2648, 2786, 2789, 2794, 2851, 2993, 2995, 3168, 3212, 3216, 3217, 3247, 3249, 3250, 3251, 3270, 3509, 3540, 3686, 3717, 3729, 3730, 3731, 3900, 3919, 4016, 4124, 4301, 4563, 4570, 4629, 4638, 4642, 4667, 4668, 4744, 4873, 4874, 4878, 4879.

CHAPTER TWO

Experiencing Art
Through Picture Books

CHAPTER OBJECTIVES

1. To help students understand the total process of book production from writing and illustrating to printing and distribution, and to encourage them to create books of their own.
2. To have students recognize artists as human beings, skilled craftspersons, and imaginative creators.
3. To foster the appreciation for, as well as the information necessary to produce, illustrations using the following mediums and techniques: watercolor, gouache, tempera, pastels, pen and ink, and pencil.
4. To provide samples and descriptions of how to make illustrations using the following printing techniques: woodblocks, vegetable and linoleum prints, and lithography.
5. To provide picture books which represent the following art styles: cartoon, photography, and collage.
6. To interpret the concept of nonverbal communication through picture books.
7. To suggest project ideas for book report alternatives.
8. To introduce ideas for using picture books to enrich classroom units from kindergarten through high school.

TECHNIQUES FOR USING MEDIA INTRODUCED IN THIS CHAPTER

1. Inspire students to create their own imaginary beasts, hats, or other objects after reading picture books or stories about unusual and interesting animals and other things.
2. Use coloring books based on stories as models for bulletin board characters, or as introductions to stories.
3. Have students illustrate a folktale or story that has been read aloud to them.
4. Show posters of books to students to stimulate creation of other posters, and use the posters to advertise the books and the enjoyment to others.
5. Encourage children to create book characters they like in papier mache, clay, plaster, or some other medium.
6. Have students interpret a book, including the action, by making a diorama, mobile, mosaic, mural, bulletin board, or display.
7. Collaborate with another teacher (an art teacher if there is a special one)

to provide materials so that students can make sculptures of wire, wood, stone, and soap to interpret book characters.

8. Introduce do-it-yourself books about processes through picture books about carved objects.

9. Allow students to interpret books through stitchery reproductions of characters or scenes, or through wooden or stuffed toys they make as expressions of a book. Use the objects to stimulate the interest of other students.

10. After seeing and discussing various styles of art in picture books and in nonfiction books, have students create illustrations using collage, cartoon, and photographic techniques.

11. Provide books on techniques along with books illustrated in those techniques and encourage students to illustrate their own stories with woodcuts, linoleum blocks and vegetable prints.

12. Show picture books by the d'Aulaires that are illustrated by lithography to introduce that process, and then show other books and films about the method to stimulate interest in students.

13. Teach students to recognize the differences among watercolor, gouache, and tempera in picture book illustrations by introducing picture books in those media and telling about them. Then share books describing how to create in each of these media.

14. Present a film or filmstrip about an illustrator and how he or she works to introduce information about both the artist's books and techniques.

15. Compare the works of an illustrator when the artist is working with different authors. Discuss the author-illustrator creative relationship.

16. Encourage preschoolers to find favorite characters in other books in the same series. Discuss how they would know from the pictures that a character is the same.

17. Discuss with students two unlike illustrations by the same artist working in different media.

18. Assign students the job of comparing award winning picture books with those of the same illustrator which did not win awards, and telling why the award book won rather than the others.

19. Have students compare treatments of the same subject or object by several illustrators, and talk about the differences. Which one does each child like best? Which illustrations come closest to his own ideas of what the "something" or "someone" looks like?

20. Have students draw their own concepts of the sun and the moon, and compare them with the perspectives and conceptions of artists in several different books.

21. Have students illustrate the how and why of the origins of the sun, moon, and stars from folklore, after related stories have been read and pictures shown.

22. Enhance a discussion of mood in the story and in the art by using examples of various picture book illustrations.

23. Help students investigate the connections between color and music, be-

tween music and mathematics.

24. Use picture books to reinforce learning about color, counting and words with preschool and primary students.

25. Use picture books with a specific color in the title so that children can match the word with the colors in the illustrations.

26. Introduce nonverbal communication through wordless picture books, then have students write their own narration or story to the pictures, or illustrate a famous story that they know without using words.

27. Introduce a book by making simple drawings, or putting key words or names of characters on the chalkboard or overhead projector or large pad of paper, while telling the story.

28. After examining samples of alphabet or counting books, have students create alphabet or counting books of their own. If some children can produce a *rhyming* alphabet or counting book they should be encouraged to do so.

29. Use counting books to introduce number concepts to preschoolers and primary children, and include counting out rhymes as part of early mathematics instruction.

30. Use picture books and stories containing numbers (three pigs, seven brothers) to enrich mathematics instruction.

31. Certain alphabet books can be used as vehicles for identifying parts of speech, and some which contain particular characters, animals or objects can be used to introduce books related in some way.

32. Give students twenty-five or thirty books in one of several categories (picture books with one rhyme, counting books,) and have the class choose five that they would like to have in their classroom reading corner.

INTRODUCTION.   A young child's first experience with art may be through the pages of a picture book. Color, shape, line, proportion, and the relationship of one object to another — they are all here to be studied intently and their nuances absorbed even before they have meaning or any known connection with the story that is being told.

In their *Books for the Gifted Child,* Baskin and Harris have this to say about the importance of picture books:

> Despite their humble status, picture books may comprise the most important of all literary genres. Most avid adult readers insist that their lifetime habit began in the nursery, where they first encountered books that irrevocably convinced them that such objects contained untold hours of delight and were of singular importance. Picture books have, in reduced and simplified form, all the essential ingredients of any literary experience. . . .
>
> . . . Children's beginning books teach them about the world they are learning to inhabit, articulating events they have experienced and expressing a broad range of reactions and feelings that provide

models for their own subsequent behavior.

Picture book illustrations are an essential and intrinsic part of all this discovery and habituation. A good picture book achieves just the right balance between text and illustrations; one enhances the other. In addition to learning to enjoy the illustrations for themselves, and as part of the story, children can become aware of the variety of methods used to illustrate books, and can learn to identify differences and special characteristics among these methods. They can also learn to "read" the meaning of the illustrations without any words. All of this exposure can inspire interest and appreciation as well as creativity, as children want to illustrate the ideas they have themselves, the images they have imagined, or stories they have made up.

Some picture books will lead to other art projects, while some projects, on the other hand, can lead into books, and also interpretations of books for children at many different grade levels.

DRAWINGS COME TO LIFE.   There are numerous picture books and several stories in which animals or people in illustrations come alive or people and animals step into pictures. Such books can be used to stimulate imaginative combinations of art and creative writing.

Harold and the Purple Crayon may be the name of a small picture book by Johnson for primary grade children, but it has possibilities also for stimulating an artistic or creative writing experience. Harold creates the action in the book by drawing scenes with his purple crayon. Harold is responsible for creating all the action in his books and even draws a small forest with only one tree because he doesn't want to get lost in the woods. Students may wish to create experiences with a purple crayon of their own. Other books about Harold are *Harold's ABC, Harold's Circus, Harold's Trip to the Sky, Harold's Fairy Tale,* and *A Picture for Harold's Room.* In the last story Harold deals with proportion—he crosses off his bird picture because it is too big. The first and the last two titles are available on sound filmstrip, and the last title is also available in paperback. Several copies of the paperback could be distributed to the class to stimulate activity as an exercise by itself or following the showing of one or more filmstrips. Students could create stories or books of their own in any color they wish.

Johnson's books are reminiscent of the type of folk tale called the "drawing tale." Folklorist Carl Withers gives background information on the drawing tale and gives sources for his story, *The Black Cat,* which is similar to one drawn by Lewis Carroll. In a drawing tale the storyteller makes lines as he is talking and the end result becomes a picture, in this case a cat. This book could be used to introduce the drawing tale to students and inspire them to do their own.

Charlip's *Where Is Everybody?* is somewhat similar to a drawing tale. A few lines and words are added on every page until there is a picture, an outdoor scene complete with animals. When it rains, everyone disappears and only the rain is left.

There are many stories in which animals or objects in a painting or drawing come to life. Willard's *The Well-Mannered Balloon* differs slightly from that theme. James paints a pirate face on a balloon. The balloon pirate eats a meal with James's family and is very polite at mealtime and when everyone is awake, but when the family is asleep he eats up everything. Students may be encouraged to create faces on balloons as a follow-up project.

In Martha Alexander's book Blackboard Bear, a bear comes down from a blackboard and has adventures with Anthony. Anthony drew the bear on his chalkboard and then took the bear outside with him. In And My Mean Old Mother Will Be Sorry, Blackboard Bear, Anthony runs away from home and takes Blackboard Bear with him. In I Sure Am Glad to See You, Blackboard Bear, Anthony calls upon the bear to help him when he gets in trouble.

The Boy Who Could Make Things, by Preston, illustrated by Kessler, is about a boy who made a little family with paper, scissors, and crayons. The family did not do what he wanted them to until he painted red hearts on them.

Gagliardi's Magic Fish jumps out of a picture into a fountain, has adventures, but returns to the picture because children who visit the museum would miss him.

A toy bear, a doll and a live mouse step into a boat in a painting on the nursery wall and have adventures in Goodall's The Midnight Adventures of Kelly, Dot, and Esmeralda, a wordless picture book.

In The Magic Wallpaper by Francis, eight animals talk and come to life. The animals included in the story are a zebra, lion, giraffe, parrot, hippo, giant tortoise, elephant, and several gibbons. A wallpaper sample book used with this story might inspire creative writing and drawing projects.

The drawing master in Zemach's The Tricks of Master Dabble paints pictures so lifelike and true that they look real. After extorting jewels and money from the royal family, the master is discredited when his realistic paintings are exposed as mirrors.

Ma Lien and the Magic Brush is a Chinese folktale adapted by Kimishima that has been translated by Tresselt. Ma Lien, a penniless peasant, turns things he paints into real objects to help other people. A greedy Mandarin promised to release him from prison if he would paint a mountain of gold. Ma Lien didn't want his talent used for evil purposes so he painted the gold on an island, painted the Mandarin in a boat and a storm to sink the boat.

Kirkegaard's Otto Is a Rhino is about Topper, who draws Otto on the wall with a magic pencil and finds that the rhino comes to life and must be fed. Use this book with Lindgren's Emil and Piggy Beast, which has a similar theme.

The Little Chalk Man in Ctvrtek's story makes wild things happen when he comes to life and steps down from the wall.

Freeman's Chalk Box Story is about how eight colorful sticks of chalk create a story about a boy stranded on an island. A turtle is drawn into the story to carry the boy to a boat so he is rescued.

"The Boy Who Had to Draw Cats," pages 195 to 203 of Carpenter's Wonder Tales of Dogs and Cats and pages 29 to 33 of Littledale's Ghosts and Spirits of Many Lands, is a Japanese boy who drew cats everywhere until everyone was upset. Finally he was redeemed when the ferocious cats he had drawn killed the giant rat and saved everyone.

Ballinger's Knitted Cat doesn't have a tail because he wasn't finished.

McHargue's *Stone Flight* is about a stone griffin who comes to life and Jamie who flies on its back in a full length book for intermediate students.

Two books written for intermediate students to read to themselves, but which adults can enjoy reading parts of aloud, contain people who can enter another world through a drawing: Travers's *Mary Poppins* and Hopp's *The Magic Chalk*.

In one episode Mary Poppins goes to visit the Match-Man Bert, who also draws chalk pictures on the sidewalk. The two hold hands, stand in the middle of the picture, and find themselves inside it. They are wearing fine clothes and are served tea royally. A ride on a merry-go-round completes their adventure.

In the Norwegian story *The Magic Chalk*, John draws another boy against a fence with a piece of magic chalk. The boy comes alive and the two of them open the gate in the fence and enter another land. In their travels they encounter animal cookies that begin to talk. Each cookie has the initial letter as part of its design. The animal cookies speak in tongue twisters: "Greedy goats gnaw green grass" (p. 80).

Books in which the drawings or the characters come to life can say a lot to children about their own fantasies and feelings, about the loneliness and the desire for companionship which even the youngest of us occasionally experience. They can say a good deal about the nature and the thrill of creation and are excellent springboards for either discussion or activities such as each child drawing the character he would most like to have step out of a story to play with him.

LINES BECOME SHAPES.   For children who want to create their own drawings that may or may not come to life, the following books can be used to follow up on stories in the preceding section and to show how simple dots and lines create drawings. Stacy's *The Runaway Dot, an Adventure in Line* shows how dots formed a line that whirled, looped, and created many pictures. Robert's *Start with a Dot* shows how a dot stretches to become a line. Kessler's *What's in a Line?* is part of the Easy Reader Series and introduces that concept to children. A more difficult book by Kessler, *Art is Everywhere*, begins with lines and shapes. Rauch's *The Lines Are Coming: A Book About Drawings* shows how lines become shapes and designs.

Kepe's *Beasts from a Brush* shows how lines become imaginary beasts. Palazzo's *Magic Crayon, Drawing from Simple Shapes and Forms* shows how simple lines and shapes plus imagination create pictures. Circles become suns and moons, tennis balls and bubbles. Three circles become a turtle. Curves become many animals and the letter *R* becomes a rabbit, *O* an owl, and *W* a walrus. Ed Emberley's *Wing on a Flea* is available on sound filmstrip. This very creative book is written in rhyme and features triangles, rectangles, and circles. The book can be introduced by its title by reading a selection from the book: "A triangle is the wing on a flea/and the beak on a bird/if you'll just look and see." *Ed Emberley's Drawing Book of Animals* takes a basic shape, adds a few more shapes here and there, and in six or eight basic additions has created an animal. Some of the shapes become owls, bats, elephants, sharks, and foxes, to name a few. A similar technique is used to create faces of people and animals in Ed Emberley's Drawing Book of Faces. For instructions on making cars, boats, trains, and furniture, see Ed Emberley's Drawing Book: Make a World. See also Ed Emberley's Book of Weirdos. Thumbprints are the basis for design in Ed Emberley's Great Thumbprint Drawing Book. Three paperbacks by the same artist are Ed Emberley's Birds, Ed Emberley's Farms, and Ed Emberley's Trains.

How to draw special subjects appears in Bolognese's Drawing Horses and Foals and in Ames's Draw Fifty Airplanes, Aircraft and Spacecraft and Draw Fifty Dinosaurs and Other Prehistoric Animals.

Borton's Do You See What I See shows many kinds of lines including zig zag and curved as well as circles, squares, and triangles. Hoban's Circles, Triangles and Squares is illustrated by black and white photos showing these shapes in everyday life. In Are You Square? the Kesslers ask, "Is the moon square?" The authors also discuss circles and triangles. Schlein's Shapes includes circles and squares. Ellison's Fun with Lines and Curves also includes polygons and other shapes. Lines, circles, and squares are shown in Hart's The Young Designer. Outline shapes appear in Design Is a Dandelion, which includes form and shape, texture, balance, rhythm and variety, and content. Use Downer's The Story of Design for historic perspective. Kohn's Everything Has a Shape and Everything Has a Size is illustrated by Aliki and is available in paperback.

In Eric Carle's The Secret Birthday Message, a boy is given a note partly written in rebus characters that tells him where to go to get his birthday present. Each clue and each page contains a different shape.

Reiss's brightly colored Shapes shows how squares become cubes, triangles become pyramids, circles make spheres, and how rectangles, ovals, pentagons, and hexagons are found in a variety of objects from musical notes to bricks.

Bendick's Shapes, a Science Experiences book, includes circles, loops, curves, plane shapes, dimensions, ovals, triangles, octagons, spheres, hemispheres, tetrahedrons, icosahedrons, three dimensions, symmetry, and the importance of shapes.

Sitomer's Circles is from the Young Math Books Series and provides a different perspective. The book is excellent to use in stimulating designs. Also from the same series is Froman's Venn Diagrams which shows overlapping circles.

Crews's We Read: A-Z uses each letter of the alphabet and shapes to introduce a concept. Bold bright colors are used to help illustrate the point being made.

ART PROJECTS INSPIRED BY PICTURE BOOKS.   Some books for children, by their very nature, inspire creative projects. When thirty-five kindergarteners give a librarian pictures of a rainbow so she will have "a rainbow of her own," it is more than ample thanks for having read Freeman's Rainbow of My Own to them the previous week. This project, as well as the book, are easy enough for preschoolers through second graders to enjoy. The picture book takes a small boy outside where he sees the rainbow reflected everywhere. When he returns home, he has his very own rainbow when the sun shines through the window and makes a rainbow in his goldfish bowl.

A girl who also wants to have a rainbow of her own appears in *Annie's Rainbow*. This Australian book won several awards in 1976: Children's Book Council of Australia Picture Book of the Year, Visual Arts Board of the Australian Council Award for Illustration, and Design Award of the Australian Book Publisher's Association. Annie finds her rainbow reflected in the waters of a fountain.

Rainbows also appear in Bollinger's *Noah and the Rainbow* and Spier's *Noah's Ark*.

Guggenmos and Lueht's *Wonder-Fish from the Sea* is useful for inspiring students to make fish. The fish in the book find their shapes from leaves. Other books that show fish are Lionni's *Fish Is Fish*, Wildsmith's *Fishes*, and Yolen's *The Spotted Fish*.

Two books illustrated by Ungerer, *Snail Where Are You?* and *One, Two, Where's My Shoe* can inspire children to use shoes and snails in creating other objects. In the two books, shoes and snails are parts of other objects. Students may be encouraged to use other shapes to create picture books similar to these two.

Ezra Jack Keats's *Dreams* is about a paper mouse Roberto made at school. While everyone was in bed dreaming, Roberto and the mouse were having an adventure. In the morning when everyone else was awake, Roberto was dreaming. During the night each window of the apartment building had a different colored dream inside. Use Wersba's *Amanda Dreaming* and Kraus's *Milton the Early Riser* with Keats's *Dreams* to inspire students to recreate their own dreams.

Many kinds of houses are featured in Montresor's *House of Flowers, House of Stars*. Have students create unusual houses of their own. Unusual houses in nursery rhymes are featured in Leht's *From King Boggins' Hall to Nothing at All, a Collection of Improbable Houses and Unusual Places Found in Traditional Rhymes and Limericks*.

Twenty students would each have to design five dresses to have enough dresses to fill a bulletin board to advertise Estes's *The Hundred Dresses*. The girls in this story tease Wanda because she wears the same faded but clean dress to school. When Wanda tells them that she has a hundred dresses there are doubters, but the girls learn that Wanda is telling the truth only after she moves away. This story is also appropriate for intermediate students.

Ellen Raskin introduces family members in a rhyme reminiscent of "The House That Jack Built" in *Ghost in a Four-Room Apartment*. Besides the introduction of the characters, there is another story that is wordlessly taking place simultaneously in the book. Horace the invisible ghost is at work. *Ghost in a Four-Room Apartment* is a book that can be introduced to children through drawing. The illustrator of over a thousand book jackets and now the author/illustrator of numerous award-winning books, Raskin suggests that leaders draw the family figures on a large chart while introducing them in the words of the text. Characters may be stick figures drawn with a magic marker, if necessary. Most of the characters have a distinguishing characteristic that students will recognize even in stick figures. This book is one of several that can be read and reread countless times. Freeman's *Chalk Box Story* can also be drawn with chalk on large boards.

In Peppe's *Circus Numbers, a Counting Book*, the one hundred elephants are all fingerprints with legs, trunk, and a tail added. Students can create other animals using fingerprints. More ideas are given in *Ed Emberley's Great Thumbprint Drawing Book*. Use Mary O'Neill's poem, Lisa's "Fingerprints" from *Fingers Are Always Bringing Me News* to introduce the project.

Children who read McKee's *Elmer, the Story of a Patchwork Elephant* may want to color elephants of wild designs and colors. Tired of his patchwork coat which stood out among the grays of the other elephants, Elmer covered himself with gray berry juice until he looked like the others. Sad because Elmer was missing his friends didn't recognize him until the rain washed off the berry stains. Now the elephants celebrate a special carnival every year, at which time Elmer becomes gray and the other elephants have fun painting themselves wild colors. The results, demonstrated by the children, can be displayed on the classroom bulletin board or in a display case with the book. Solthy's *A Lemon-Yellow Elephant* has a similar problem, and makes a good companion book.

There are several other books about dissatisfied animals that can be used with the two elephant books. Emberley's *Rosebud* is a turtle who wants to be furry or feathery. Caught and painted with a rosebud on its back, Rosebud is then taken to a pet shop and sold.

Simon's *The Armadillo Who Had No Shell* is also unhappy because he doesn't look like the other armadillos. Students can check encyclopedias and reference books on animals to find out what an armadillo really looks like. Mannelo's relatives each try to give him a shell, which include a shoebox, bathing cap, banana leaves, and a stovepipe. In the end Mannelo learns that there is an advantage to being different—his difference enables him to save the others and become a hero. A story similar in theme is Burningham's *Borka: The Adventures of a Goose with No Feathers*. And of course *Rudolph, The Red-Nosed Reindeer* which first saw life as a children's book, has become a famous variation on this classic theme.

NAMES AS ARTWORK. Books in this section include art projects utilizing letters and words that are inspired by picture books. In Tomi Ungerer's *Crictor*, the boa constrictor forms letters of the alphabet with his body. Give students a sheet of paper and have Crictor help them to write their names using his body. Then display the illustrations with the book. The paperback copy can be easily attached to a bulletin board, or pages can be taken from the paperback and attached throughout the children's exhibit.

In *Talking Words, a Unique Alphabet*, Davar illustrates a word by an expression of its meaning. D is for "Dots" which is spelled out with black dots on white paper. The word "feathers" is written in feathers, and "mirror" is mirrored backwards on the right as a reflection of the word on the left.

Another example occurs in *Pick a Peck of Puzzles* by Roth, on pages 22-3 of a section called "Pictures to Read." The letters of a word are used to create a picture of that word; the letters of "elephant" actually make a picture of one. Readers can be invited to try to create pictures from their own name.

Two picture books about names are *Andy, That's My Name* by dePaola and *I Wrote It* by Krauss. In the first book, bigger boys won't let Andy play with them. However, the boys make words out of the letters "A-N-D-Y" that Andy carries on his wagon. Children can try to find words from within their own names. Andy is a good example because there are many words using "an," "and," and "andy." In *I Wrote It*, a name can be written on paper, snow, air, on a looking glass or a sidewalk. The last page shows many names written on waves.

There are two picture alphabet books in which the letter takes on the shape of the object discussed. They are Barry's *A Is for Anything, an ABC Book of Pictures and Rhymes*, and Schmiderer's *Alphabeast Book; an abcdarium*. In the first book a C becomes a canoe and in the second, letters evolve into animals.

MAKING OUTRAGEOUS HATS.   Use Ezra Keats's *Jennie's Hat* to inspire students to create unique hats of their own. Students may choose to draw the pictures or actually make hats. Jenny received a plain white hat from her aunt and longed for an exciting one, so she tried on a variety of objects, a straw basket, lampshade, flower pot among others. On her way to church her wish was fulfilled because the birds she had fed trimmed her hat with a collage of swans, a valentine, real and paper flowers, and a nest of chirping birds, among others. Students could create collage hats of their choice.

The nonsense poetry of Edward Lear is illustrated by Helen Oxenbury, a Kate Greenaway award winner, in *The Quangle Wangle's Hat*. In this story unusual animals come to see the hat.

Belinda is another girl who tries on a lampshade, wastepaper basket, shopping basket, and flower pot as hats in Clymer's *Belinda's New Spring Hat*. Miss Selma Town Mouse is proud of her new daisy hat in Hurlimann's *The Mouse with the Daisy Hat*.

Another book that could inspire students to create hats is *Jasmine*. Jasmine is a cow created by Roger Duvoisin who lives in the same barnyard with the artist's Petunia and Veronica. One day Jasmine finds a hat but all the other animals are unhappy when she wears it because they don't want her to be different. So the animals all find hats, one more outrageous than the other. When Jasmine removes her hat the others follow suit. After several more turns of playing "copy-cow," the problem is resolved.

Toni Ungerer's *The Hat* is about the top hat of a rich man that lands on the penniless head of a veteran of the Crimean War. In Mendoza's *Herman's Hat*, Herman won't take off his hat. In Seuss's *The Five Hundred Hats of Bartholomew Cubbins*, Bartholomew tries to take off his hat, but each time he does so, another one appears.

Asch's *Yellow Yellow* can inspire a hat-making project for preschoolers and kindergarteners. After returning a yellow hard hat to a construction worker, a boy goes home to make his own hat.

Also read Wood's *Grandmother Lucy and Her Hats*, Wiseman's *The Hat*

That Grew, and Wakana's *The Magic Hat*, Foster's *Miss Flora McFlimsey's Easter Bonnet*, and Fuchshuber's *The Wishing Hat*.

CREATING UNUSUAL ANIMALS.   One art project that children of various ages can enjoy is that of creating an imaginary animal. These animals can be inspired by one or more of the picture books included in this section. They can be read aloud, or older students may wish to browse through a collection of these picture books on their own or the art teacher can paraphrase some of the stories. Seidelman and Mintanye's *The Fourteenth Dragon*, Mayer's *Everyone Knows What a Dragon Looks Like*, and Lionni's *Fish Is Fish*, described elsewhere in this chapter, can be included in this group. Monster and dragon books listed in the index or in the library card catalog can also be added to this collection.

Fuller's *Beasts, an Alphabet of Fine Prints* is an introduction to old masters and includes engravings, etchings, woodcuts, and lithographs of famous prints in an alphabetical survey. That book shows various art techniques used in creating famous works of art and could be included in a display for older students. Art teachers may or may not want to use the Zaidenberg books in the How to Draw series that includes *How to Draw Birds, Fish and Reptiles, . . . Dogs, Cats and Horses, . . . Farm Animals, . . . Wild Animals*, and *Drawing All Animals*. If only one of Zaidenberg's books is to be included, use *How to Draw Prehistoric and Mythical Animals*.

One of the most exciting art-related picture books is William Pene Du Bois's *Lion*. One hundred and four artists who work in the animal factory invented the animals. Readers will enjoy the problems faced by one artist related to color, size, and other details for the animal he calls "lion". Art teachers can use the book for lively discussions on techniques needed to recreate the lion. *Lion* can be used to stimulate students to create an animal of their own. Assigning the voice can be the best part.

In Waber's *You Look Ridiculous Said the Rhinoceros to the Hippopotamus*, hippo becomes worried when a rhino tells him he looks ridiculous because he doesn't have a horn. Changed seven times with the addition of items deemed necessary by others, the hippo dreams she has a horn like the rhino, a mane like the lion, spots like the leopard, ears like the elephant, a tail like the monkey, a neck like the giraffe, a shell like the turtle, and a voice like the nightingale. Finally she shouted, "I no longer look ridiculous." Readers will howl at the resulting animal pictured in the book and appreciate the conclusion that no one can please everyone and the best thing is to be yourself. Recreating the animal for a bulletin board or creating an animal even more absurd can be fun.

In Farber's *As I Was Crossing Boston Common*, a turtle tells readers, "As I was crossing Boston Common not very fast, not very slow, I met a man with a creature in tow. Its collar was labeled Angwantibo. I thought it rather uncommon." This is repeated as each animal brings another in tow until readers again see the first man looking very "uncommon." Children will have fun noticing that each successive unusual animal begins with the next letter of the alphabet until twenty-six animals including a Kiang, Pudu, Xenopus, and Zibet are introduced.

At the end the animals, all of them real, are presented with a small picture and their place of origin. It would seem that the book could stimulate a dictionary project, but the animals do not appear in a collegiate dictionary so might not be readily accessible. Another project would be to explore reference books like Compton's *Dictionary of the Natural Sciences* and find other animals unknown to students. Think of the challenge of trying to put together an alphabet using only animals that no one in the class has ever heard of.

Maestro's *One More and One Less* shows strange looking animals portrayed in line drawings. Lines also become imaginary beasts in Kepes's outstanding book *Beasts from a Brush*.

Pete's *Whingdingdilly* is about a witch who transforms a dissatisfied dog into a mixed-up animal with elephant feet, rhinoceros's snout, deerlike antlers, camel's hump, and giraffe's neck. Scamp is eventually put on display but the witch changes him back into a dog to his embarrassment.

In Schmid's *Horns Everywhere*, a boy and his grandfather see a strange animal in the woods. When the beast is described to others, each person has his or her own perception of it. Even after they find that the horned animal is only a wild boar, people prefer to retain their original version of the beast.

In an easy story by Balian called *The Animal* a boy tells about an animal who shares his picnic. As each person retells the story, the animal becomes bigger and more ferocious although actually it was just a turtle. The book is similar in theme and audience to Hutchins's *The Surprise Party*.

Unusual looking pets appear in McKee's *The Magician and the Petnapping*.

McBroom's Zoo by Fleischman is about a man who starts a zoo with animals dropped by a tornado. The mixed-up animals include a Desert Vamooser, Silver-tailed Teakettler, Silverhill Gouger (a jackrabbit with long legs) and a seventeen-toed Hairy Prairie Hidebehind.

Folklorist Alvin Schwartz tells illustrator Glen Rounds about critters from American folklore in *Kickle Snifters and other Fearsome Critters*. If the passages were read before the students saw the illustrations, students could create their own illustrations, with any preconceived ideas.

In Ungerer's *The Beast of Monsieur*, a retired tax collector sees huge footprints near his pear tree. The leader should stop reading the story before the end and have the children illustrate what they think the beast looks like. The end of the story reveals that two children are responsible for the pear theft and cover-up.

Edward Lear's nonsense poem *The Scroubilous Pip* was completed by Ogden Nash. The picture book has been illustrated by Burchert. The other animals can't tell if this new arrival is a beast, fish, bird or insect. The foreword gives the background of the poem and mentions that at least a hundred animals have become extinct since the poem was written.

The animals "urial" and "vari" are included in Rojankovsky's *Animals in the Zoo*.

The X in *Celestino Piatti's Animal ABC* stands for an xopiatti, a nonexistent monster that is part bird, fish, and leopard. Students may also want to name the animal they have created after themselves.

EASTER ART PROJECTS.   Easter provides splendid opportunities for displaying books and the art creations they encourage. A display of novelty Easter eggs and the books which show the techniques of making them can stimulate others to create them.

Purchase or make sugar eggs, using directions on pages 137–43 of Coskey's *Easter Eggs for Everyone*. These sugar eggs with windows for viewing the scene inside can be displayed with Easter, spring, and bunny books and Tresselt's *The World in the Candy Egg*. In contrast to this title is Flanagan's *Window into an Egg*, a photographic story of the twenty-one day incubation period before the chick hatches.

In Hay's *An Egg Is for Wishing*, Nicholas fears going to the henhouse to get an egg for his mother to decorate for Easter. Instead he found the eggs of a cuckoo, an owl, duck, goose, and stork. The book explains the Ukranian psanka and what the various symbols on the egg mean. The hens and roosters on the eggs mean that wishes will come true and Nicholas wishes not to be afraid any more. Display the book with some psanka eggs and stimulate a project in which the class makes its own eggs. Directions for making psanka eggs are found on pages 66–69 of the Blue Mountain Crafts Council's *The Joy of Crafts*.

Other types of eggs can also be made in the classroom. *Egg Craft* by Newsome and *Easter Eggs for Everyone* give directions for decorating eggs. Also check Patterson's *A Holiday Book* for directions. Chapter three, pages 75–106 of Fiarotta's *The You and Me Heritage Tree* gives step by step directions for blowing out an egg, as well as directions for making fourteen types of decorated eggs including psanka eggs. Coskey's *Easter Eggs for Everyone* gives legends, customs, directions for blowing out eggs, dye, directions for making dyes, egg trees, batik, and collage eggs. Also check Belves's *How Artists Work; an Introduction to Techniques of Art* and Matill's *Meaning in Crafts*. Chapter 12 of Rogonski's *Making American Folk Art Dolls* tells how to prepare eggshells, blow out the egg, dye, and paint or mount them to make heads and faces.

Armor's book, *Adventures of Egbert the Easter Egg*, is about a little boy who couldn't go on an Easter egg hunt and about Egbert, a hard-boiled egg with a face, that was missed at the Easter egg hunt. The story is told in rollicking rhyme and is excellent to read to primary students. Everyone will want to draw a face on an egg after this story is read.

There are other stories suitable for telling. Wiese's *Happy Easter* for preschool and early primary children is about colored chicks that hatch from rabbits. In Zolotow's *The Bunny Who Found Easter*, the bunny learned that Easter wasn't a place but was a time. This is a good first introduction to changes in seasons and springtime. Adams's *Easter Egg Artists* is about the Abbott family whose task is to decorate Easter eggs. They get carried away and decorate their car, house, a bridge, airplane, and flagpole. Orson even invents comic eggs, and after hearing the story, children will want to do the same.

Tekla's Easter by Budd is about an eight-year-old girl who lives on an island off the coast of Sweden where pagan and Christian customs exist side by side. On one hand firecrackers and bonfires scare away witches of darkness on Easter Eve, and on the other hand they treasure Easter eggs painted with Bible stories. One of the Easter customs is that mother paints a Bible story on each egg. Then at the Easter meal everyone chooses an egg and tells the Bible story pictured on the egg, and then keeps the egg as a souvenir.

The display of eggs that is the most fun to create is an egg tree that can accompany the Caldecott Winner *The Egg Tree* by Milhous. Whether or not they are decorated with the Pennsylvania Dutch designs featured in the book, the eggs may be made by the teacher, contributed from home collections, or made by the children in class. In the latter case, decorating the tree is an important part of the project. Instructions for making an egg tree are given in Milhous's book. Background information on egg trees can be found in several books. Fisher's *Easter* shows that the Germans were the first to make an egg tree and tells about outdoor egg trees; Patterson's *A Holiday Book: Easter* devotes chapter 4 to eggs and rabbits and mentions egg trees. Newall's *An Egg at Easter, A Folklore Study* has twelve pages about egg trees. The first two are easy for children to read; the last book is for older students or teacher references.

A poster of *The Egg Tree* is part of set no. 1 of Horn Book Posters of Caldecott Medal Books, and could be a background for a display of fiction and nonfiction books about Easter.

EGG TREES, COOKIE TREES, BIRD TREES AND MORE TREES.   It is possible to have a tree in the classroom that is trimmed in something different every six weeks, and relate the tree to picture books with each trimming. Christmas is of course an obvious time and two Christmas tree books are Hutchin's *Silver Christmas Tree* and Anrooy's *The Bird Tree*. In the latter story, there was no money to buy decorations for the tree so the birds brought berries and nuts and provided their own bodies for decorations. An evergreen tree trimmed with just bird ornaments could illustrate that book, which is translated from the Dutch.

An evergreen tree can become a cookie tree. Recipes appear in Sattler's *Recipes for Art and Craft Materials* and Benish's *Handprints: A Book of Recipes for Your Art Program*. Two books to read in conjunction with Christmas are Irion's *The Christmas Cookie Tree* or Hoban's *Arthur's Christmas Cookies*. In the latter story Arthur's Christmas cookies were hard as rocks, so ingeniously he painted them, put hooks on them and gave them to his parents as Christmas tree ornaments instead of the cookie presents he had intended!

Williams's *The Cookie Tree* appears on a sound filmstrip and has an excellent teacher's manual to stimulate discussion. The story is about a chocolate cookie tree that appeared mysteriously in the center of Owlgate. The adults argued about its purpose and experts were called in to check the reasons for its existence. Only the children accepted the tree at face value. The tree disappeared after it had served its function and the children had eaten the cookies.

Although they are not about cookie trees, there are two other stories that can be combined with a cookie baking project: Buckley's *The Wonderful Little Boy* and *The Gingerbread Boy*. Whenever the little boy felt like a thundercloud his grandmother made smiling gingerbread boys for him. In the traditional story, the gingerbread boy or man runs away from the person who made him and from other animals until he is devoured by a crafty fox. This story can be read from *Tall Book of Nursery Tales*, and there is a picture book edition illustrated by Galdone. The easy reader by Lobel is called *The Pancake*.

Ayer's *The Paper-Flower Tree, a Tale from Thailand* is about a girl who wished for a tree made of paper flowers. Use Temko's *Paper-Cutting* and *Paper Capers*, Alkema's *Tissue Paper Creations*, and Stephan's *Creating with Tissue Paper* for directions for making the paper flowers. Then decorate the tree and display it with the book. Decorate a tree with pigs to introduce the Lobels' *A Treeful of Pigs* about a lazy farmer and his ambitious wife.

In *For Pepita: An Orange Tree* by Oleson, seven-year-old Pepita wanted an orange tree for her birthday but nobody gave her one. Her friend Manolo gave her the seeds so she could plant her own. Display this title with a miniature orange tree or use it in a project in which children are planting seeds. Perhaps orange seeds could be planted as a class project to see what grows.

Two of the most famous picture books about trees are Udry's *A Tree Is Nice* and Yashima's *The Village Tree*. From Udry's 1957 Caldecott winner, also available as a sound filmstrip, we learn that trees are nice because you can climb them, make swings in them, play in the leaves, or just look at them. Yashima's Japanese story shares that universal relationship of trees to people. An adult tells about how each generation plays the same games and sings the same songs under the same village tree by the river bank. Ducks, turtles, trout, and eels come to the river bank *Under the Green Willow*, in a picture book by Coatsworth.

Carigiet's *The Pear Tree, the Birch Tree, and the Barberry Bush* is the winner of the 1966 Hans Christian Andersen International Book Award for illustration. The setting is the Swiss mountains. The barberry bush seems at first to be not as useful as the pear and birch trees, but eventually the bush gives a home to the sparrows when the other trees cannot.

Mr. Tamarin's Trees, in a picture book by de Groat, were a bother to him because they shed on his lawn. His campaign against the trees and his complete reversal are humorous but contain a moral for readers. Ichikawa's *A Child's Book of Seasons* shows trees and children's activities throughout the seasons. The book reads like poetry and is illustrated in Kate Greenaway's style. Ross's *The Pine Tree* is also like simple poetry and is enhanced by pen and ink drawings. Chaffin's *I Have a Tree*, illustrated by Alexander, shows trees during the four seasons. Delessert's Swiss picture book, *The Tree*, also shows the changing seasons.

Cocgnac's *The Three Trees of the Samurai* is about a soldier who has lost all his status and with it most of his trees. The three trees he had left, a plum, a cherry, and a pine tree, he cut down for wood to warm a traveler who turned out to be the prince he had served as a soldier.

Barry's *The Musical Palm Tree, a Story of Puerto Rico* strikes a lighter mood. Pepito wants to give his mother a mantilla for the Fiesta Patronal so he earns money by showing people around San Juan. Shades of brown, green, and purplish-pink enhance this story about the tourist who went to see the musical palm tree.

The great Ludwig Bemelmans, creator of *Madeline*, has written and drawn

Parsley, a deer who watches hunters through binoculars. Parsley makes his home under a pine tree which has not been lumbered because it is crooked. The furniture that appears in the book is New England pine furniture. Twenty-three wild flowers appear in the book and are identified at the end of the book.

There are several nonfiction books about trees that also show one type of tree. Selsam's *Maple Tree* shows the life of a Norway maple tree in forty photographs, seven of them in color. The leaves from other types of maple trees are shown, as well as reasons why trees are important. *Lives of an Oak Tree* by Hutchins has beautifully detailed drawings of the animals, birds, and insects that live in the trees, eat the leaves, and live or rest under the tree. Growth rings, lightning, roots and soil erosion, floods, humus and seasons are all carefully explained through this outstanding combination of art and science. The book reads like a story. George's *The Hole in the Tree* also tells about the wildlife that contributes to the hole in an apple tree—bark beetle, tenant ants, and a raccoon family. *The Big Tree* by Mary and Conrad Buff is a history of the redwoods in California. Adler's *Redwoods Are the Tallest Trees in the World* tells their story for second and third graders. *How the Forest Grew* by Jaspersohn tells how an abandoned farm became a forest.

An easy nonfiction book about trees that shows how to tell the difference among trees is Selsam's *Play with Trees.* A more difficult book, but beautifully done, is Dowden's *The Blossom on the Bough, a Book of Trees.* Trees are listed by the seven forest regions, and pictures of leaves, flowers, cones, and rings are included.

A collection of books about trees should be displayed, or laid out, on a table whenever stories about trees are read and discussed or whenever trees are studied in science. Students can use the card catalog to find books and help make the display.

PINATA AND KITE PROJECTS.   Even high school Spanish classes have used Brock's book, *Piñatas,* to make a piñata for Christmas. Besides directions for making eleven different piñatas, there is a glossary and pronunciation guide, information on how piñatas began, how to use them, and three piñata stories. Other sources for information on making piñatas can be found by looking at some books about papier mache. Page 170 of *The Joy of Crafts,* edited by the Blue Mountain Crafts Council, includes directions. Some high school students will enjoy rereading the Caldecott winner, *Nine Days to Christmas* and sharing the story with younger brothers and sisters or with an elementary class. Ets's book tells of a small Mexican girl, Ceci, who went to the market with her mother to choose a piñata for her first posada or party. The several pages on which the piñatas talk to Ceci, asking her to choose them, show a variety of piñata shapes. Only one piñata, a star, says nothing but only shines and turns about for Ceci to see, and she chooses it. When the piñata is broken, its spirit becomes a star in the sky and is never really lost. *Nine Days to Christmas* is featured, one of the four posters in set no. 2 of the Horn Book Posters of Caldecott Medal Books. The poster is vertical in shape, and can be used, with the book, for display of piñatas made by the students.

Elementary students may wish to make a piñata as a class project after reading *Nine Days to Christmas* or after having the story told to them.

Two books that give helpful background information on posadas and pinatas are: Chapter 3, "The Christmas Season," pages 31 to 52, of *Fiesta Time in Mexico* by the Marcuses, and pages 244 to 250 of Toor's *A Treasury of Mexican Folkways*. The first book is written for children and the other book is a resource for teachers or older students.

Anderson's *Hai Yin, the Dragon Girl* can be used with *Nine Days to Christmas* because it tells of a festival celebrated in another country, Taiwan. Hai Yin became the first girl to win the prize when she created her dragon lantern for the lantern festival.

Kites are as important to spring in some cultures as piñatas are to other cultures at Christmas time. In Kurt Wiese's *Fish in the Air*, also available on a sound filmstrip, a Chinese boy named Fish wanted the biggest possible kite shaped like a fish. When Fish flies his kite, Tai Fung (The Big Wind) pulls him into the air. In their travels the boy and kite have several adventures, until finally a fish hawk tears the kite to pieces. Fallen into the water and caught in a fish net, Fish is bought by his father for a dollar from the surprised fisherman. Now wiser, Fish asks for a smaller kite the second time.

Kites are as much fun to make as pinatas. If making a real kite is not possible, smaller ones could be made and displayed with books about kites on a bulletin board or in a display case. One book in the kite collection should be Jane Yolen's, *World on a String, the Story of Kites*. Teachers will find in it much background history on kites that can be shared with young children, and older students will read the book for themselves. The author is the daughter of famous kitesman Will Yolen, who has written *The Young Sportsman's Guide to Kite Flying*.

Books that show types of kites and how to make them are Bahadur's *Come Fly a Kite*, Brummitt's *Kites, a Practical Guide to Kite Making and Flying*, Dolan's *The Complete Beginner's Guide to Making and Flying Kites*, Downer's *Kites, How to Make and Fly Them*, Fowler's *Kites, a Practical Guide to Kite Making and Flying*, Kettlekamp's *Kites*, Neal's *The Story of a Kite*, and Saito's *High Flyers*. Kettlekamp's book is the easiest of these to read. The books by Brummitt and Downer have the best drawings and directions. Neal's book is similar in content to *World on a String* but it is easier reading. The Fowler section on launching and flying is excellent. The Saito book has many colored photos of Japanese kites. The books by Downer, Fowler, and Kettlekamp all discuss contests and tournaments and give rules and prize categories. The books could perk up a windy March day or complement a social studies unit on Japan.

Ayer's *Nu Dang and His Kite* are from Siam. When his kite disappears, Nu Dang asks everyone on the street and in the floating market if they have seen his kite. The list of persons he asks reads like a who's who of Siamese community helpers. After the teacher has read the book to first graders, they may wish to check out the easy reader by Schlein called *The Big Green Thing*.

While repairing his children's kite, Anatole and his family find themselves flying over the city in *Anatole over Paris*, by Titus. Anatole is the famous French mouse who works in the Duvall Cheese Factory and is the hero of many Titus books.

The setting for Uchida's *Sumi's Prize*, illustrated by Mizumura, is modern Japan.

The White Kite by Sipherd is about a boy who made up stories. When Paul was really carried by a kite string to the moon and then dropped into a pond, he couldn't tell anyone because he was sure that no one would believe him.

In Yolen's *The Emperor and the Kite*, the fourth daughter of the Emperor Djeow Seow uses her kite to send messages to her imprisoned father. Finally the emperor escapes prison by flying out the window on the tail of the kite.

A similar escape appears in Yolen's *The Girl Who Loved the Wind*. In this old Chinese legend, the emperor imprisoned his daughter in a tower and she escaped by weaving a rope of her own hair and attaching it to the tail of a kite. The oriental papercut technique by a Chinese artist gives the book the potential for an art spin off.

A poem and a song can add humor to any unit or storytelling session that features kites. See chapter 4 on poetry for poems and songs about kites.

CREATING MOOD. Picture books can be used as an aid to discussing *mood* in art or in creative writing. Mood can be created by using various color combinations or even by lack of color. Color, shades, and shapes make Meyer's *Vicki* an imaginative wordless picture book. Domanska's shades of green and yellow create a place to which wild life would naturally gravitate in *Under the Willow* by Coatsworth. Color is one of the factors in creating mood in Spilka's *Paint All Kinds of Pictures*. The filmstrip based on the book can be used effectively with groups of primary students or adults. Spilka shows how pictures can be pretty, scary, funny, or exciting. The artist also demonstrates that paintings are expressions of feelings about a subject. All of the simple pictures speak to the viewer about creating a mood in one way or another. Mood is also part of a sound filmstrip *Enjoying Illustrations* which could be used to introduce the concepts or the specific books shown in the filmstrip. Although designed for intermediate students, it can well be used for older groups, with the final frames suggesting projects omitted.

Often the pictures and the words work together to create a particular mood as in Harowitz's *When the Sky Is Like Lace*. A dreamy quality results from colored pencil, crayon, and watercolors combined with the text which begins, "On a bimulous night, the sky is like lace." It is quite different from the mood reinforced by the refrain, "Oh, you're just talking silly talk" which occurs throughout Scheer's *Rain Makes Applesauce*, illustrated by Bileck in fanciful pastel colors.

Note how illustrations help set the mood for Iwasaki's *Staying Home Alone on a Rainy Day*. Blues, blacks, and greens by Weisgard help show different parts of the world in moonlight in Garelick's *Look at the Moon*. In Zolotow's *Wake Up and Good Night*, Weisgard uses colors and imagery to create mood. Watercolors in black and blue with pink highlights make Shulevitz's *Dawn* a memorable experience. Tissue overlays suggest mist in Munari's *The Circus in the Mist*. A completely different feeling is portrayed by Turkle in Chardiet's *C Is for Circus*. Turkle's illustrations look like old-time circus posters, and his pages are of varied hues, textures and shapes.

Sometimes artists use colors or styles typical of a special time or place for creating mood. In *Merry Ever After, the Story of Two Medieval Weddings*, Lasker tells readers in the foreword that he has based his illustrations on the work of artists who painted in the 15th century. Bahti uses earth tones of tan, brown, and black to illustrate the prehistoric Indian pottery of America's Southwest in Baylor's Caldecott Honor Book, *When Clay Sings*. Everton illustrates Prieto and Hopper's folktale *Birdmen of Papantla* after the style of the sacred yarn paintings of the Huichal Indians. Rushmore's *The Dancing Horses of Acoma and Other Acoma Indian Tales* is illustrated by Hunt in the style of the Acoma Pueblo. Folk carvings of animals from India are used by Claudine to illustrate *Flight of the Animals*, an ancient Buddhist legend similar to the Chicken Little story.

Arnold Lobel used blue and yellow in designs based on Holland Dutch tiles to illustrate *One Day Peter Stuyvesant Sailed into Town*. Domanska creates the illusion of stained glass windows to illustrate *Din Dan Don, It's Christmas*, a picture book illustrating a traditional Polish carol.

Persian miniatures lend mood to Young's illustrations of Yolen's *The Girl Who Loved the Wind* and the Dillons' illustrations for Travers's *Two Pairs of Shoes*. An Oriental paper cut technique is used to illustrate Yolen's *The Emperor and the Kite*. Japanese calligraphy by Okamura heightens the feeling in Cassidy's *Birds, Frogs and Moonlight, Haiku*, and is also included in the folktale by Wakana that is to be read from back to front. Calligraphy also enhances Wyndham's *Chinese Mother Goose Rhymes*.

Domanska adopted an African motif when she illustrated Fournier's retelling of *Coconut Thieves*. In Musgrove's *Ashanti to Zulu*, the color and style of the illustrations by the Dillons express life in the twenty-six African cultures represented in the 1977 Caldecott Medal book. In contrast, Moselle Thompson illustrated *Lift Every Voice and Sing* by the Johnsons in heavy dark lines that bespeak oppression and bondage.

The flavor of Pennsylvania Dutch life comes through in *The Egg Tree* by Milhous and *The Christmas Cookie Tree* by Irion.

Unusual graphic treatment can help create a special mood for a book. The light mood of Eric Carle's *The Hungry Caterpillar* is heightened by pages of different sizes with holes where the caterpillar ate his way through the book.

Brown's *A Shepherd* illustrations look like an ancient scroll unfolding. The last page explains parchment, reed pens, and ink made of lampblack and resin. Lund's *I Wonder What's Under* is to be read sideways like a calendar. The illustrations show things Dudley found under his bed, and also all the building layers of his house.

Styles of drawings can also create moods. Cartoon-like illustrations usually create a light or comic mood. Check the section in this chapter called *Cartoon Illustrations in Picture Books*.

PERCEPTION.   No two people think exactly alike or view anything in the same way. If they did, this would be a dull world indeed. There are two types of stories that convey this concept. One type deals with different perceptions of the world in general, and the other deals with viewing art in particular.

Janina Domanska's picture book *What Do You See?* makes the point about perception through scratch painting and collage. A frog says the world is wet, a fly thinks the world is dry, a bat thinks the world is dark, and a fern thinks the world is green. The lark, who has seen the world as a whole, says that the world is all of those things. The same theme appears in *The Blind Men and the Elephant,* available in two picture books as well as a variety of formats. Check the index for all of the listings. In this traditional story, each of the seven blind men feels a different part of the elephant and describes the whole elephant in terms of his one section. The man holding the tail thinks an elephant is like a rope, and the man holding the ear thinks an elephant is like a fan. In Lionni's *Fish Is Fish* a frog visits earth and returns to tell the other fish of the unusual things he has seen. As birds, cows, and people are described, fish sees them all from his own perspective. Birds are fish with wings; cows are fish that have legs, horns, and carry pink bags of milk.

Two books about stone and rock also indicate differences in perception. Small pictures on the pages of Jean George's *All upon a Stone* show the lives of a male cricket, ground beetle, fresh water sponge, stone flies, as well as moss, lichens, and flowers. The end of the book shows that these details are merely part of a large painting three feet by four feet carried out in acrylics on canvas by Don Bolognese. In Bruno Munari's *From Afar It Is an Island* stones look different depending upon your perspective. Stones, like clouds, can look like a city, an island, or anything the viewer can imagine. In this book, a stone from a distance looked like an island. In Hoban's *Look Again!* viewers first see a small part of a black and white photo. Seeing the whole photo allows the viewer to be certain what the object really is.

Another story about perception is "The Speckled Hen's Eggs," found on pages 43 to 53 of Carlson's *The Talking Cat and Other Stories of French Canada.* The speckled hen laid an egg with pictures on it, and everyone saw something different in the pictures. Madame Roberge thought the crown meant that she had noble blood, but when she explored her background, she found out that rather than being descended from a duc or marquis, her greatgrandfather had been a thief. The crown was really the stolen silver bowl she kept her egg money in turned upside down. And so we learn, ". . . a turn of the egg can easily change a crown into a stolen bowl."

The small fish in Lionni's *Swimmy* use a trick in perception to save their lives. All the little red fish band together to form one large red fish with black Swimmy for the eye, so that the big fish who wants to eat them will think they are another large fish.

McDermott's retelling of an old folk tale called *The Crystal Apple* is about three Russian sisters who receive gifts from their father. One of the daughters was given a crystal apple and when she looked into it she saw Moscow, cathedrals, forests, and ships, but her sisters saw nothing because they had no imagination. There are people in this world who see things even without the help of a crystal apple.

The little lost girl in Reyher's adaptation of another Russian folktale shows that beauty is in the eye of the beholder. The child described her mother as *The Most Beautiful Woman in the World*, so a group of beautiful women are brought so the girl can identify one and be reunited with her mother. Instead, she is claimed by a fat ugly woman who says, "We do not love people because they are beautiful, but they seem beautiful because we love them."

In Abraham's *The Pigeon Man*, people accepted messages of good will by carrier pigeons from the recluse Barnaby, whom they had never seen. One day when Barnaby went out people glared at him, threw things at him, but did not recognize him as the Pigeon Man. Another person who was not recognized was the Great Cloud Dragon in *Everyone Knows What a Dragon Looks Like*, written by Williams and illustrated by Mayer. When the Mandarin learned that there was to be an invasion by the Wild Horsemen of the North, he decided there were four options available: stand and fight, run away, surrender, or pray to the Great Cloud Dragon for help. The last alternative was chosen, but when the Great Cloud Dragon appeared as a little old man, no one believed him because *Everyone Knows What a Dragon Looks Like*. Only the street sweeper Han, believed that the old man was the Great Cloud Dragon, and because of Han's faith and acts of friendship, the Dragon saved the city. The Dragon showed his true self only to Han; the others thought that now they really knew what a dragon looked like—he looked like a little old man. *The Fourteenth Dragon* is a picture book by two authors—Seidelman and Mintonye—and thirteen illustrators; each of the dragons in this picture book is the unique creation of a separate illustrator. The fourteenth dragon is the one that each reader draws for himself. The fact that no one need feel inferior about his drawing is pointed out in Pinkwater's *Bear's Picture*. No one else sees the same things in the picture that Bear sees and has painted, but Bear doesn't care because ". . . it is my picture." In the film *Ezra Keats*, that author/illustrator shares with viewers drawings of Peter's dog Willie that have been sent to him by children. Keats understands that each child saw and created Willie in his own way.

IDENTIFYING THE MEDIUM, TECHNIQUE AND STYLE OF ART IN PICTURE BOOKS. There are many different ways of interpreting a subject. The artist conveys his perception through his medium, techniques and personal style. There are several books and other sources of information about the techniques and styles of art in children's books. In *Illustrations in Children's Books*, Pat Cianciolo identifies representational art, expressionistic art, cubism, surrealism, collage, impressionistic art, pointillism, folk art, naive art, cartoon style, and photography. Cianciolo also gives examples of illustrations featuring watercolor, gouache and poster color, tempera, and pastel painting. The graphic techniques are discussed too, and examples are given of illustrations composed of woodcuts, cardboard cutouts, linocuts, wood engraving, scratchboard, stone lithography, color separations, and process printing for continuous art work. Teachers who are planning a unit on art in children's books should read this first.

Cianciolo's reviews of picture books include information about the artwork. *Picture Books for Children*, an annotated bibliography edited by her, reflects her interest in art. Most annotations of children's books stress the plot of the story rather than medium and techniques used in the artwork.

Information about the medium and printing processes for various Caldecott Medal winners is given in Miller and Field's *Caldecott Medal Books, 1938-57*, and *Newbery and Caldecott Books, 1956-65* and *Newbery and Caldecott Books, 1966-75*, both edited by Kingman.

Klemin's *The Art of Art for Children's Books, a Contemporary Survey* discusses each illustration shown in the book from the point of view of medium and technique. Representative samples of the work of sixty-three illustrators are shown and discussed. One learns that Marcia Brown's illustrations for Andersen's *The Wild Swans* was illustrated in lettering pen and ink and a one color wash in rose, and that *Lion* by William Péne du Bois was executed in line with color separations. A similar book by Klemin, *The Illustrated Book: Its Art and Craft*, does not focus on children's picture books although eight of the seventy-five artists discussed in the book also illustrate children's books.

Mahony's *Illustrators of Children's Books, 1774-1945*, Miller's *Illustrators of Children's Books, 1946-1956*, and Kingman's *Illustrators of Children's Books, 1957-1966 and 1967-1976* include hundreds of biographies that deal with illustrators and their craft as well as lists of books illustrated by them. These lists are useful in comparing many books illustrated by one person.

In *American Picturebooks from Noah's Ark to the Beast Within*, Barbara Bader discusses the picture book as an art form.

Chapter 8, "Materials and Techniques of the Artist," in Moore's *The Many Ways of Seeing, an Introduction to the Pleasures of Art* is excellent background reading. Samples of five drawing techniques are shown: pencil, pen line, red and black chalk, pencil and brush and India Ink, and pen ink and a bistre wash. Watercolor, fresco, tempera, and oil are discussed under painting. Samples of five printmaking techniques are given: etching, woodcut, lithograph, engraving, and etching and drypoint. Six types of sculpture are discussed: wood, sandstone, two types of bronze, steel brazed with copper, and terra cotta. The terms "relief," "intaglio," "lithography," "silk screen" and "monotype" are explained.

The special properties of various media are explained in Borten's *A Picture Has a Special Look*. The book and sound filmstrip, meant for primary students, make an effective overview for any age group. The sense of each medium—crayon, lead pencil, pen and ink, collage, pastel chalk, poster paints, and oil—is expressed as well as variations within the medium.

The above titles are essential background reading for elementary art teachers, teachers in self-contained classrooms, and high school art teachers who are preparing to teach students to identify and work in different mediums.

Another important source to consult, Belves and Mathey's *How Artists Work: an Introduction to Techniques of Art*, shows young children engaged in making projects. Over fifty techniques from pencil and charcoal to roof ornaments are described. Meyer has written an excellent teacher idea book which includes brief information on what is needed as well as how to accomplish *One Hundred Fifty Techniques in Art*. Stacey's *Experiments in Art* introduces basic principles and techniques. Teachers will find Mayer's *A Dictionary of Art Terms and Techniques* useful. Over 3,000 definitions of materials and methods are given.

VARIETY IN PICTURE BOOK ILLUSTRATION MEDIUMS.   The picture books discussed in this section may be displayed with tags noting the medium used to create the illustrations. In some instances a nonfiction book telling how to produce that type of illustration is listed. These practical how-to books, as well as student samples, could also accompany picture books created with the medium. The books can also be used in art classes to show other uses for a particular art form. Two books representing each type of illustration could be chosen. Students could be given one book and asked to match it with another book.

When creating batik, show students the picture book *The Magic Cooking Pot* written and illustrated by Towle. The Goddess Durga helps a man get back his magic pot of rice—it is never empty—after it is stolen by the wicked innkeeper in this folk tale from India. It took a year and a half for Towle to make the batiks which illustrate the book. Four nonfiction books about batik are Belfer's *Designing Batik and Tie Dye*, Martin's *Batik for Beginners*, Meliach's *Contemporary Batik and Tie Dye*, and Stein's *Batik as a Hobby*.

Sheaks's *Painting with Acrylics: From Start to Finish* includes the wet and dry method, glazing, paint combinations, relief painting, and collage making. A combination of acrylics and collage was used by Keats in *Apartment Three*. Keats used acrylics on canvas to illustrate *The King's Fountain* by Lloyd Alexander. In this parable a poor peasant is the only one who has the courage to tell the king that his fountain is taking away the source of drinking water for the people. Also executed in acrylics on canvas is Jean George's *All upon a Stone*. Barbara Cooney used acrylics to illustrate Belting's *Christmas Folk*, which shows Elizabethan mummers and other folk and their activities between November 30 (St. Andrew's Day) and January 5 (Twelfth Night). The 1973 Caldecott Medal winner, illustrated by Blair Lent, was painted in acrylics. *The Funny Little Woman* by Hearn and retold by Mosel is a Japanese folk tale in which a monstrous oni is outwitted by the funny little woman.

In *Pastels Are Great*, John Hawkinson not only defines pastel but he shows how to make different strokes, including flat, edge, diagonal, curved, shaded, molding, and texture. Hawkinson discusses how to hold the pastel, the types of paper to use, and values and color. Weiss covers the use of pastels in part two of *Paint, Brush and Pallet*. William Pene du Bois used pastels to illustrate *William's Doll*, a sensitive story about how a boy can love a doll in preparation for fatherhood.

Holmes's *Drawings to Live With* includes information about using pen, pencil, and chalk. The term "pen and ink," used to describe illustrations, sounds as if all the illustrations would be similar. However, there can be great variety depending on the medium used in adding the colors. Some picture books that show this to be true are Rockwell's *The Wonderful Eggs of Furucchia*, an Italian folktale about a woman who had magic eggs that would help anyone with a kind heart; Jeschke's *Sidney* about a chicken who pretends to be a fox; Jeffers's *Three Jovial Huntsmen*, an illustrated nursery rhyme; and Wells's *Benjamin and Tulip*, about raccoons. Garth Williams used pen and ink to illustrate Russell Hoban's *Bedtime for Frances*. The other books about the famous badger are illustrated by Lillian Hoban and include *A Baby Sister for Frances*.

Kay Chorao used pen and ink drawings to illustrate Schweninger's *The Hunt for Rabbit's Galosh* but she used pencil drawings to illustrate Williams's *Albert's Toothache*. Albert the alligator's family was skeptical when he told them that he had a toothache in his big toe. Martha Alexander illustrated *Nobody Asked Me if I Wanted a Baby Sister* in pencil. Colors are added with tempera. Pencil drawings are included in two wordless picture books: Krahn's *The Self-Made Snowman* and Ueno's *Elephant Buttons*. Halftone pencil drawings illustrate Barclay's *The Little Brown Gazelle* and *One Misty Morning: Rhymes from Mother Goose*.

As explained in Ness's *Do You Have the Time, Lydia*, pencil shading is only one of the mediums used. Pencil shadings and dark black pencil lines are evident in Tombert's colorful story about imagination, *Little Fox Goes to the End of the World*.

Brinton Turkle uses charcoal to illustrate *The Adventures of Obadiah* and *Thy Friend Obadiah*.

Barbara Garrison used etchings to illustrate Yolen's *The Sultan's Perfect Tree*. The Sultan wanted everything around him to be perfect. When he noticed that his tree was not perfect, he had a tree painted on his window. However, the tree did not change with the seasons, and then he realized that a real tree is better than perfect because it is living, growing, and changing. Domanska uses etchings to illustrate *Under the Green Willow*. Two other types of printmaking that have special sections in this chapter are woodcuts and lithography.

Two art mediums used in painting are watercolors and oil. Two nonfiction books about painting in oils are Zaidenberg's *How to Paint in Oils* and Weiss's *Paint, Brush and Pallet*.

WATERCOLOR AND SIMILAR MEDIUMS USED IN PICTURE BOOKS. The term "watercolor," includes tempera and gouache. Books by John Hawkinson, who enjoys sharing his techniques, can be used to introduce watercolor as well as to show techniques in using that medium. In *Paint a Rainbow*, Hawkinson instructs nine-year-old Larry in step-by-step basic strokes with two brushes to create a watercolor rainbow.

The books of John Hawkinson fall into two categories: picture books of which nature is an intrinsic part such as *The Old Stump*, *Where the Wild Apples Grow* and *Our Wonderful Wayside*; and two books which contain nature activities, *Collect, Print and Paint from Nature* and *More Collect, Print and Paint from Nature*.

The Old Stump is about a family of mice who live in a stump and about all the wild life around them. *More How to Print and Paint from Nature* tells how to create those animals in watercolors. Brush strokes are shown for a butterfly, insects, fish, birds, and squirrels. The last page lists names and pages of the animals so that the book can be used for identification. *How to Print and Paint from Nature* tells how to make leaves, trees, trunks, stems, and flowers. Trees from different regions are shown.

Four books on the techniques of painting with watercolors for older students are Brommer's *Transparent Watercolor; Ideas and Techniques*, Croney's *My Way with Watercolor*, Hilder's *Starting with Watercolor*, and Zaidenberg's *How to Paint with Watercolors*. Brommer's book is especially helpful for providing many watercolor techniques and has black and white photos and four bibliographies, one of which contains twenty-six titles on technique. Croney's book gives step-by-step demonstrations, shows four techniques, advantages and disadvantages of the medium, and explains materials and equipment. Zaidenberg discusses materials, brushes, color, wet and dry paper, strokes, flowing a wash, blends, landscapes, and water color pencils. Also consult chapter 5, "Paint with Water Colors," from *The Young Artist* by Mills and Weiss's *Paint, Brush and Palette*. Also read Mattil's *Meaning in Crafts* and Belves's *How Artists Work: An Introduction to Techniques of Art* and Patterson's *Exploring with Paint*.

The following Caldecott Medal books were illustrated in watercolors: *The Little House* by Burton, 1943; Field's *Prayer for a Child*, illustrated by Jones, 1945; *Big Snow* by the Haders, 1949; *The Biggest Bear* by Ward, 1953; *Madeline's Rescue* by Bemelmans, 1954; Udry's *A Tree Is Nice* illustrated by Simont, 1957; *Time of Wonder* by McCloskey, 1958; *Sylvester and the Magic Pebble* by Steig, 1970; and *Duffy and the Devil* by the Zemachs, 1974.

The following books illustrated in watercolors present a variety of styles and types of literature: Gaetano's illustrations of *Longhouse Winter, Iroquois Transformation Tales* by Jones; Grabianski's illustrations of Aesop's *Androcles and the Lion; Father Fox's Penny Rhymes* by the Watsons; Nonny Hogrogian's *Little Red Riding Hood*; Leslie Brooke's *Johnny Crow's Party*; and *The Tale of Peter Rabbit* and all the other Beatrix Potter stories.

Other animal stories done in watercolors are all the Miller books about Mousekin, among them *Mousekin's ABC* about life in the forest. Another alphabet is Tasha Tudor's rhymed *A Is for Annabelle*. *Machines* by the Rockwells shows pulleys, levers, and gears. In Keith's *Prra-ah*, Toad is caught by some children, called a frog, and is given turtle food. In *Will's Quills* by Freeman, a goose named Willoughby is rescued by Shakespeare, and gives Will a writing quill in return. Children can learn about such family relationships as those of grandson and brother-in-law in Charlip and Moore's *Hooray for Me*, illustrated by Williams.

There are four books that may be compared as to content and medium of illustration. *Time of Wonder*, McCloskey's 1958 Caldecott Medal Book, is about a storm on an island in Penobscot Bay off the coast of Maine. Baldwin's *The Sometimes Island*, illustrated by Robinson, is about a peninsula in Maine. Anderson's *The Day the Hurricane Happened* is illustrated by Ann Grifalconi. *Lost in the Storm* by the Carricks is also executed in watercolors.

There are several books which show tinting, shading, or washing with watercolor. Ardizzone uses wash in his books *Little Tim and the Brave Sea Captain*, *Tim in Danger*, and *Tim and the Lighthouse*. Wash drawings alternate with full color paintings in Mizumura's *If I Were a Cricket*. De Paola uses wash illustrations in *Andy, That's My Name*.

Klemin, in her book *The Art of Art for Children's Books, a Contemporary Survey*, features many artists who use the medium of watercolor. No differentiation is made between tempera or gouache. Cianciolo, however, has a separate section on gouache and poster color in her book *Illustrations in Children's Books*. Included in the section on gouache and poster color in her book are Duvoisin, Wildsmith, Brandenberg, and Weisgard. Illustrators using poster color include Piatti, Sidjakov, Sendak, and Munari.

While watercolors are transparent, gouache, made of the same materials, but with the addition of white, is opaque. Two Caldecott Medal books using this medium are McDermott's *Arrow to the Sun*, 1975, and Weisgard's illustrations of MacDonald's *The Little Island*, 1947. Brian Wildsmith's *ABC*, the 1963 Kate Greenaway Medal book, presents another example of gouache. McDermott's *The Stonecutter, a Japanese Folktale* is a collage made from cut-up pieces of paper colored with gouache. Barrets used gouache to illustrate Pearce's retelling of Grimm's *Beauty and the Beast*.

According to page 67 of Peterson's glossary in *Exploring with Paint*, tempera is "a water soluble paint which dries with a non glossy finish." This is because egg is added. Exceptional examples of picture books using tempera as a medium are three Caldecott winners: Politi's *Song of the Swallows* (1950), Milhous's *The Egg Tree* (1951), and Robbins's *Baboushka and the Three Kings* illustrated by Sidjakov. These books can be used in several ways. They can help students to identify the different mediums used in picture books, or the picture books can be used with children who are painting in watercolors, gouache, and tempera to enable them to see what the finished product looks like.

COLOR IN PICTURE BOOKS.   Because color is an important part of many picture books, books in this chapter can be used by teachers in various ways to introduce the concept of color to groups of all ages. Picture books can introduce the primary colors, importance of all colors, value and hue, color and mood, harmony, and color separation as a printing technique or color and poetry in folklore.

When colors are first introduced in the preschool or primary grades, gather together books in the following categories for students to examine and enjoy: books illustrated vividly with primary colors, books with colors in their titles, books about one or more colors, black and white books accented with one color. The children will enjoy recognizing the colors and naming them.

BOOKS ABOUT COLOR.   Tison and Taylor's *The Adventures of the Three Colors* is excellent for showing how primary colors in combination create other colors. This can be shown through the use of transparent overlays. The book shows two animals overlapping in such a way as to create a third animal of another color and shape. A blue elephant and a yellow dog overlap to create a green fish; a red pig and a yellow butterfly make an orange snail; and a blue seal and a red flamingo create a purple turtle.

Circles establish the concept of basic colors in Hoban's wordless book *Is it Red? Is it Yellow? Is it Blue? An Adventure in Color.*

In Duvoisin's *See What I Am*, each of the colors thinks that it is best and lists all of the objects that have its color. The attributes of each color are listed on the left side of the page, while a picture on the right shows the world as it would look in just that color. Eventually all of the colors agree that in harmony they can make the world beautiful, and the last page shows the same picture with all the colors together. The book is narrated by a cat named Max who appears in the left corner of the left page and changes color with the pages.

Preschool children will enjoy *Freight Train* by Crews in which each of the train's cars is a different color.

Margaret Wise Brown's *Color Kittens* is a picture book for primary children that shows kittens of many colors trying to create green by mixing red and white. After trying other combinations unsuccessfully they accidentally mix yellow and blue.

Hailstones and Halibut Bones contains poems about colors by O'Neill. A two-part film based on the book is narrated by Celeste Holm and is popular with age groups from elementary to adult. The point of the book and film is that colors convey feelings, and both are essential to any unit on color or poetry. Check the index for suggestions for dramatic presentation of the book.

In Lionni's *A Color of His Own*, a chameleon, unhappy because he has no color of his own but takes color from his surroundings, is finally satisfied when he can be the same color as another chameleon. In Spier's *Oh, Were They Ever Happy!*, three children paint the outside of their house in many colors.

Ann and Paul Rand's *Sparkle and Spin* shows the mood of words related to color.

> Some words are gay and bright
> and full of light
> like tinsel and silver
> and sparkle and spin . . .

Sparkle and Spin and *I Know a Lot of Things* are available on sound filmstrip. Those two books and *Listen Listen* are enjoyed for their simple concepts, bold designs, and bright colors.

Bold colors are used in the books of Jan Balet: *The Fence, The Gift,* and *Joanjo. Three Poor Tailors* by Ambrus, also colorful, won the 1966 Kate Greenaway Medal, the English counterpart of the Caldecott Medal.

Warburg's *Keep It a Secret* relates moods and colors. Some feelings expressed by color in this rhyming picture book are green is the smell of grass, blue is like wind, and red is the sound of someone you love giggling.

Emberley's *Green Says Go* also deals with colors and moods: purple with anger, cowardly yellow, jealously green, and embarrassed red. Examples of color in everyday life as in traffic signals, are given as well as colors and their relationships to holidays and weather. Primary and secondary colors and their combinations are given, with information on how to make them lighter and darker.

Reiss's *Colors* provides bold illustrations on contrasting backgrounds to show many shades of red, yellow, orange, blue, green, purple, brown, and black.

Crews's *We Read: A-Z* is an alphabet book using bright colors to explain terms such as "bottom," "corner," "horizontal," "equal," "under," "vertical," "whole," "only." The colors are part of the descriptions.

Three other nonfiction books about color in ascending order of difficulty are Paschel's *First Book of Color*, Adler's *Color in Your Life*, and Itten's *The Art of Color*. The Paschel book explains the relationship between light and color; the three different qualities of color (hue, brightness or value, and saturation or purity); complementary colors; color wheels; tints, tones, and shades; mixing primary colors; color separation; color and feelings; color preferences; color combinations and visibility; deceiving tones and colors; and how background influences color. In contrast to the first book, Adler's *Color in Your Life* actually contains little color except two color plates. Concepts included are light and color; how colors change in different kinds of light; refraction; transmission of color; colors in nature; dyes; color in printing, TV and photography; color and mood. Itten's oversized book, *The Art of Color*, includes a good history of color and color theory. Two approaches to understanding the art of color—subjective feelings and objective color principles—are used and color expression, color impression, and composition are covered. Color contrasts and hues are explained through famous paintings.

Birren's *Color: A Survey in Words and Pictures from Ancient Mysticism to Modern Science* is an important source of background information on color for teachers. Its three parts include the "Mystical Beginnings," a section about religion, mythology and superstition; the "Impact of Science and Culture," dealing with color in painting, color theory, and the harmony of music and color; the "Implications for Modern Life" section which includes color in nature, color and emotion, and personal color preferences.

Also for background, teachers will find useful chapter 3, "Color in the Classroom," (pp. 58-82) of Thompson's *Nonverbal Communication in the Classroom*.

BLACK AND WHITE PICTURE BOOKS ACCENTED WITH COLOR.
Children who are just learning to recognize colors will enjoy identifying the accent colors in otherwise black and white books.

Brinckloe's *Gordon's House* contains five stories illustrated in black and white with green accents. Aliki Brandenberg's *Keep Your Mouth Closed, Dear*, also accented in green, is about Charles, a crocodile, who swallowed things every time he opened his mouth. Mizumura's *The Way of An Ant* is accented in green and yellow. Grimm's *Rumpelstiltskin*, retold by Tarcov and illustrated by Garey, is very appropriately accented in yellow/gold.

The Little Red Flower by Tripps is about a dreary coal town where a man named Mr. Greenthumb has the only red and green plant in town.

Most of the black and white accented picture books are accented in red. Darrow's *Animal Etiquette* is one. Another is *By the Sea* by Amos, wordless and in black and white except for a kite, a boy's bathing suit, the dog's collar and a balloon. Another wordless picture book accented in red is *Who's Seen the Scissors* about a pair of tailor's scissors that fly through the air causing mischief. The illustrations are pencil drawings with the red scissors and the red-dotted trail they leave. Armstrong's *The Thump Bam Bump Mystery* for primary students is about a kangaroo on the top floor of an apartment building.

Two books with the accent color as part of their title are Kellogg's *The Mystery of the Red Mittens* and Bright's *My Red Umbrella*. *My Red Umbrella* is available on a sound filmstrip which could be used to introduce the story about the missing red mittens that finally show up when the snowman melts.

Also accented in red, an excellent companion book is Schweninger's *Hunt for Rabbit's Galosh*, in which Rabbit mailed a valentine to his mother and lost one of his galoshes in the mailbox.

BOOKS ABOUT "RED".   In Wolf's *Seeing Red*, the king of colors is called by several of its variations including magenta, crimson, scarlet, and vermillion. Gottlieb's *What Is Red?* also includes other colors. In Bright's *I Like Red*, Janey sees lots of things that are red, but finally finds another person, a boy, who has red hair like her dog and herself.

Lipkind's *The Two Reds* is about Red the cat and Red the boy who lived on the same street but weren't friends until they shared laughter over the confusion caused by both of them. The last line of the book reads, "Now the two Reds are together all the time."

Fatio's *Little Red Bantam*, illustrated by Duvoisin, becomes friends with a big rooster when the fox becomes a mutual enemy.

Mizumura illustrated Matsuno's *A Pair of Red Clogs*, about a grandmother, who remembers all the things she did as a girl with a new pair of red clogs as she prepares to give her granddaughter a pair. The scene at the market when she is deciding which clogs to buy may be compared with the choice made by Ceci when she chooses a piñata from among so many in *Nine Days to Christmas* by Ets.

Miss Esta Maude's Secret by Cummings is about a schoolteacher who sedately drives a black vintage car to school but secretly has a red racing car that she drives very fast at night. During one of her nightly adventures she rushes a young couple to the hospital to have a baby. The colors in the book are red, black, and gold, and the story is useful for stimulating discussion on mistaken judgments about people, made on the basis of appearances, as well as color connotations.

In McKee's *Mr. Benn—Red Knight*, Mr. Benn tries on a suit of armor for a costume party and finds that the fitting room door opens into a magic land. In *1 2 3 4 5 6 7 8 9 Benn*, Mr. Benn tries on a prison costume and finds himself in prison. Before he gets out, Mr. Benn changes all of the cells and the uniforms to bright colors.

Red Fox and His Canoe by Benchley, illustrated by Lobel, is an I-Can-Read book about an Indian boy who allows so many animals into his boat that it capsizes. The story can effectively be compared with Mr. Gumpy's Outing by Burningham which is designed for the same age group. The sound filmstrip of Mr. Gumpy's Outing could be used to introduce Red Fox and His Canoe to students. Or students who have already read about Red Fox could view the filmstrip and compare and contrast the events with Burningham's story.

Two other stories with "red" in the title that are available on sound filmstrip could be used to introduce the color red, other books with "red" in the title, or books accented with red. Swift's The Little Red Lighthouse and the Great Gray Bridge, illustrated by Ward, is about a little lighthouse (which actually exists) which thought it was overshadowed by the new bridge (New York City's George Washington Bridge) but finally realized that a traffic signal for boats on the Hudson was still needed too. The book is available in paperback.

In Parkin's The Red Carpet, the lovely red carpet of a large hotel rolled down the steps onto the street and down the road until the city was carpeted in red. When the police catch up with the carpet at the dock, the guest of honor has stepped onto it from the boat.

Red is a frequent color in folklore and fairy tales. The Little Red Hen is explained further on as is Snow White and Rose Red. Little Red Riding Hood is a favorite for children to illustrate themselves. Some children enjoyed listening to the story with earphones in a corner of the media center while coloring a ditto copy of the wolf dressed as a grandmother in bed, covered with a patchwork quilt that offered exciting possibilities for color expression. Some collections containing the story are De La Mare's Tales Told Again, Johnson's Anthology of Children's Literature, Lang's Blue Fairy Book, Rackham's Arthur Rackham Fairy Book, and Steele's English Fairy Tales and the Tall Book of Nursery Tales. Three illustrated picture book retellings include Nonny Hogrogian's, and The Renowned History of Little Red Riding Hood and Little Red Riding Hood, one illustrated by Galdone and the other by Pincus. The last book is available in paperback. Hogrogian's book has a moral at the end of the rhymed story that warns children about confiding in strangers.

THE LITTLE RED, WHITE, OR BROWN HEN.   The story of the Little Red Hen appears in several picture books. The most colorful and unusual is Domanska's The Little Red Hen. Galdone's Little Red Hen is available on sound filmstrip and in paperback. The two picture books are excellent for comparison with each other because they are in completely different styles. Collections containing the story are Haviland's The Fairy Tale Treasury, Hutchinson's Chimney Corner Stories, and The Tall Book of Nursery Tales. Two books that contain dramatizations are Sloane's Fun with Folktales and Ward's Stories to Dramatize.

A bilingual version by Williams is The Little Red Hen/La Pequena Gallina and contains a picture glossary, summary, and Spanish and English captions. Instead of making bread, the Little Red Hen makes a tortilla. The book is essential in areas that have Spanish-speaking children or in schools where Spanish is taught at any level. Such bilingual books should also be in schools where only

English is spoken to create an awareness for other languages and other cultures.

LeFevre's *The Cock, the Mouse and the Little Red Hen* is an old folk tale and is available in a reprint of the original 1907 edition as well as in an edition from another publisher. The story also appears in Arbuthnot's *Time for Old Magic,* Hutchinson's *Chimney Corner Stories,* and Sutherland's *Arbuthnot Anthology of Children's Literature.* In this version the two animals won't help the hen; the fox captures them all, and the Little Red Hen cuts a hole in the sack, substitutes stones, and sews it up so the fox falls into the water and is drowned. Naturally the cock and mouse never grumble again. The story is useful for comparing to the other versions. Then there is *The Little White Hen,* a folk tale adapted by Kijimima and Hane, a similar story.

BOOKS ABOUT "BROWN". In Barclay's *The Little Brown Gazelle,* the mother leaves her baby to rest under an acacia tree, where he sees all the jungle animals pass by including birds, lions, snakes, hedgehogs, gorilla, and jackals. The illustrations are executed in halftone pencil drawings.

The Little Brown Hen came whenever Willie called her. When Willie wanted duck eggs for his mother's birthday he found his hen sitting on some that she had hatched.

Ipcar's *Brown Cow Farm* is a favorite counting book which uses shades of brown in the illustrations. The last page actually does show 100 farm animals—the children counted just to be sure!

Kirn's *Tip for Tap* is illustrated in earth tones. When the jackal played a trick on the camel, the camel retaliated, saying "Tip for Tap."

In Wondriska's *Mr. Brown and Mr. Gray,* two men are asked by the King to define happiness, and one thinks possessions are the answer.

Brenner's *Mr. Tall and Mr. Small* is a story in rhyme about a short gray mouse and a tannish tall giraffe who reconciled themselves to their sizes. Another humorous story about size is Victor's imaginative *Bigger Than an Elephant.* The first sentence is, "What would you do if you could be the size of anything you see?" Animals in the pictures range from goldfish to elephant. The book is a good stimulator for discussion or for creative writing.

Adoff's *Black Is Brown Is Tan* pictures a white father and other family members who are various shades of brown. The author is married to Newbery Award winning author Virginia Hamilton.

Bond's book says *Brown Is a Beautiful Color.* The book, done in brown and white, discovers all of these objects in brown of some shade."

BOOKS ABOUT "BLACK". Some of the books in this section also indicate that black is beautiful. Fife's *Adam's ABC* and illustrated by Mozelle Thompson for city children that shows that many worthwhile city things are black in color and conveys the black is beautiful message without so many words. *Lift Every Voice and Sing, the Black National Anthem,* written by the Johnsons and illustrated conveys that message also. The book is completely illustrated in black and white. Music is given. Grossman, Grawn, and the pupils of PS 150 in the

Bronx created a book called *Black means . . .* Arkin's *Black and White* contains words and music that tell the story of school integration: "The ink is black/ The page is white/ Together we learn to read and write."

Two books about colors that have a message of racial acceptance are *People Are Like Lollipops* and Shire's *The Snow Kings.* The first describes the land of the Salizar people who, like lollipops, come in different sizes, shapes, colors, and wrappers and come from different places but, "When you come down to it, all lollipops are lollipops and all people are people." In *The Snow Kings* the yellow, brown, and pink kings and their people quarrel until an interlude during which the three Kings, fallen into a pit, become snow covered and indistinguishable and enjoy themselves until the snow melts.

Several books include animals that are black. Farley's *Little Black, a Pony* is an easy book written by the author of dozens of books about *The Black Stallion.* Bahrang's *The Little Black Fish* is swallowed by a pelican. In Buckley's *Josie's Buttercup,* illustrated by Evaline Ness, Buttercup is a black dog that is "bouncy, jouncy, pouncy and bouncy." In *A Rose, a Bridge and a Wild Black Horse* by Zolotow, one of the things a boy tells his sister he will do for her when he grows up is to tame a wild black horse for her to ride.

BOOKS ABOUT "WHITE."   Tresselt's *White Snow Bright Snow,* illustrated by Duvoisin, was the 1948 Caldecott winner. Scenes are in bright blues, reds, and yellows, and the book is also available in a sound filmstrip.

The imagery in Zolotow's *The White Marble* is full of color. The sunset at the beginning of the story—". . . folded its wings and the pink and orange plumage of the sunset was covered by the fleecy grey and purple sky." In the story the white marble is a symbol of friendship between a young boy and girl.

Charlotte and the White Horse by Kraus, illustrated by Sendak, is a small book that tells of a girl's love for a horse, and it is available on sound filmstrip.

Suho and the White Horse, a Legend of Mongolia by Otsuka is about a horse on the Steppes and a horserace in which Suho is cheated out of a prize.

Two famous artists have illustrated Grimm's *Snow White and Rose Red.* Adrienne Adams and Barbara Cooney have each illustrated the story of the two sisters who befriend a bear who is really a prince under an evil spell. The stories and illustrations are interesting for children to compare. A play is included in Bennett's *Creative Plays and Programs for Holidays* as well as in many Grimm collections, including *The Complete Grimm's Fairy Tales,* Hutchinson's *Chimney Corner Fairy Tales,* Lang's *The Blue Fairy Book,* Untermeyer's *The Golden Treasury of Children's Literature,* and Sutherland's *Arbuthnot Anthology of Children's Literature.*

Wanda Gag's *Snow White and the Seven Dwarfs* was a Caldecott Honor book in 1939 and Nancy Burkert's book of the same title was an honor book in 1973. The newest and most unusual version is translated by Paul Heins and illustrated by Trina Hyman. Gag's illustrations, in her own distinctive folk style, are black and white. Burkert's illustrations are lovely and the colors are pastel, giving the book a romantic flavor. The newest of the three reflects the artist's New England awareness of witchcraft: the gilt on the wicked stepmother's mirror is alive with demons and devils. The female devil on the frame changes and finally disappears when the stepmother is thwarted. The dwarfs in all three books have special characters that are very unlike those of the Disney creations. Very lively discussions on the the three books can and will result when the three are introduced with that intent.

A French fairy tale with "white" in the title is the Comtesse d'Aulnoy's *The White Cat*. The story appears in *The White Cat and Other French Fairy Tales*, Arbuthnot's *Anthology of Children's Literature* and *Time for Old Magic*, Sutherland's *Arbuthnot Anthology of Children's Literature*, and Lang's *The Blue Fairy Book*. The less familiar story concerns a princess who has been turned into a white cat by fairies; her mother it seems gave her to them in return for eating fruit from a special garden. The cat meets the youngest of three sons who must complete three tasks in order to be his father's successor. The first task is to find and bring in muslin that could pass through the eye of a needle, the most beautiful little dog, and the most beautiful princess in the world. The cat helps the youngest son to accomplish all three of these tasks. Impossible tasks and cleverness tests are of course basic to folk and fairy tales from many cultures.

BOOKS ABOUT "BLUE."   The first "blue" person to come to mind is the nursery favorite "Little Boy Blue." A favorite of small children is McCloskey's lovely *Blueberries for Sal*, available on sound filmstrip and in paperback. Sewall's *Blue Barns, the Story of Two Big Geese and Seven Little Ducks* is about two white geese who take the ducks under their wings and show them the sights of the farm. The leaves are red and yellow and the snow is white.

In Preston's humorous story *The Sad Story of the Little Bluebird* illustrated by Barbara Cooney, a hungry cat hops, skips, and jumps after a little bluebird until the bird flies away leaving the hungry and frustrated cat behind.

Lionni's *Little Blue and Little Yellow* is an abstraction. Blue's best friend is "yellow"; they hug each other until they are green. Their parents don't recognize or accept them until they have all hugged each other. Small children will grasp the concept that blue and yellow make green but will miss most of the acceptance message.

The Blue Jackal, a folktale from India, is about Long Howl who was despised for being a jackal. When he fell into a vat of blue dye and no one recognized him as a jackal, he was accepted. Taking advantage of people's fear of him as an unknown animal he makes himself king. Becoming proud and bossy he is found out when he can't resist howling with his brother and sister jackals. Versions are available illustrated by Marcia Brown and by Gabhai.

Everything in French's *The Blue Bird* is blue except Jade Lotus who owned a beautiful blue bird in a cage. When the bird stopped singing, she and Chaing Ti took the bird to the enchantress so she could tell them why the bird wasn't singing. On the way, they helped a tortoise, a cat, and a dragon. When the two arrived at the palace of the enchantress they noticed that there were many birds carved into the pillars and woven into the screens and carpets. When the enchantress demands their bird they are saved by the tortoise, cat, and dragon, who destroyed the enchantress, free the birds, and bring the book alive with color.

Wolf's *Feelin, Blue* gives shades, relationships to other colors, and feelings of colors.

May's *Blue River*, illustrated by Quackenbush, is an ecology book about the life and saving of a river. Indians lived along the bank; there was a lumber mill, a larger town, factories, pollution, algae, chemicals to kill insects, dead fish, garbage, sewage, and factory chemicals being dumped before hope for survival was restored.

BOOKS ABOUT "GREEN." Zacharias's *But Where Is the Green Parrot?* is a book that contains hidden pictures. A green parrot lurks among toy chests and other items in nine double-page spreads. Another book with hidden pictures is Livermore's *Find the Cat.*

Coatsworth's *Under the Green Willow*, illustrated by Domanska, is illustrated in dark olive green, yellow, light green, and bright yellow-green. A quiet book with more beauty than substance, it identifies a place, known to the sun, where ducks, turtles, trout, catfish, and eels can enjoy themselves.

Green Noses, translated and retold by Wiesner, tells of a rich and crafty farmer who proclaims that anyone who wants to marry his daughter must work on his farm for one year. He managed to trick each man out of staying a year until he met one young man he couldn't outmaneuver.

Birnbaum's *Green Eyes* is about the first year of a baby cat told in the first person.

The Green Christmas by Kroeber, illustrated by Larrecq, is about a boy and girl who have moved from Colorado to California and, about to experience their first green Christmas, are afraid Santa won't find them without snow.

Although Emberley's book is entitled *Green Says Go*, the other colors and their meanings are included in the book.

Two easy reading books are Hurd's *Last One Home Is a Green Pig* and Schlein's *The Big Green Thing* (a kite).

Lionni's *Greentail Mouse* is a picture book but the subject is too complex for preschool and early elementary students. The mice, getting costumes ready for Mardi Gras, become the ferocious animals of their costumes until hate and suspicion reign.

Blume's *The One in the Middle Is a Green Kangaroo* is about a middle child, a second grader, who receives recognition by playing a green kangaroo in his brother's fifth- and sixth-grade play at school.

Three stories which do not have green in the title but are concerned with green animals are Massie's *Komodo Dragon's Jewels*, Weber's *Lyle the Crocodile*, and Stevens's *Hooray for Pig!* The first story is about a green lizard who boarded the tourist boat to the mainland in pursuit of the lights he thought were jewels. The Komodo Dragons really do exist on an island in Indonesia. The *Lyle the Crocodile* books are carried out in green, orange, and yellow and include *Lovable Lyle, Lyle and the Birthday Party, Lyle Finds His Mother*, and *Lyle Lyle Crocodile*. Several of them are available in paperback. *Hooray for Pig!*, executed in green and brown, tells of Pig, who, with the help of raccoon, muskrat, and otter overcomes his fear of the water and learns to swim. The book is an easy reader.

BOOKS ABOUT "YELLOW".   Wolff's *Hellow Yellow!* is about shades of yellow and their relationship to orange and green, red and blue.

In Asch's *Yellow Yellow*, a small boy returns a yellow hard hat to a worker and then goes home to make his own hat. Making a paper hat so each child can have one to wear is a natural follow-up project.

There is a *Big Yellow Balloon* in Fenton's book of the same title. It's a "following" tale: a cat thought it was the sun so he stalked it, to catch it and assure that it would always be night and hunting time; a dog followed the cat; the dog catcher followed the dog; a little old lady with a purse followed the dog catcher to save the dog; a burglar followed the purse; and a policeman followed the burglar until . . . .

Soltly's *A Lemon-Yellow Elephant* is called "Trunk"; the other elephants were glad he was yellow because it was helpful when they were lost.

In Dalton's *Yellow Is a Duck*, readers learn what yellow is and that yellow is many things, including a brick road in *The Wizard of Oz*.

Remy Charlip's *Where is Everybody?* is in black and white but has a yellow sun. Line drawings are added page by page to create a completed book.

Lionni's *Tico and the Golden Wings* is about a bird that had no wings but dreamed of golden ones. When his dream came true Tico gave away golden feathers to help people in need, and as he did so, they were replaced with black silk feathers. The other birds were happy because he now looked like them, but Tico remembered that each person is different and has his own golden dreams.

Keeping's *Charley, Charlotte and the Golden Canary*, also on sound filmstrip, was the 1968 Kate Greenaway Medal winner given by the (British) Library Association for the best illustrated children's book of the year. The story is about two city children who were friends until Charlotte moved away, and the canary who brought them together again.

COLOR AND MUSIC.   Chapter 12 of Birren's *Color* . . . is called "The Harmony of Music and Color." Two picture books which express this idea are Ezra Keats's *Apt. 3* and Eric Carle's *I See a Song*. Keats captured the sound and color of music at the end of *Apt. 3*: "He played purples and grays and rain and smoke and the sound of night."

In Carle's *I See a Song*, the violinist says on the first page: "I see a song. I paint music. I hear color . . . . My music talks. My colors dance."

Maurice Sendak, author and illustrator, knows that music plays an important part in his work. Sendak believes that composers use different colors just as artists do. He regularly works to music and changes selections until he finds one that allows him to pick up the right color from the music. The interview appears in the film *Maurice Sendak*. Most of that interview appears in the film *The Lively Art of the Picture Book*.

HOW AND WHY STORIES ABOUT COLOR FROM FOLKLORE.   Most of the how and why stories about color concern birds. According to the story of "How the Birds Got Their Colored Feathers," a Venezuelan tale on pages 100 to 103 of Arnott's *Animal Folk Tales Around the World*, all birds were once grey. South American birds are so colorful because they took their colors from an intricately patterned snake skin. Another version comes from the Tahlton Indians of British Columbia, Canada, in "How the Birds Came to Have Their Many Colors," pages 37 and 38 of Belting's *The Long-Tailed Bear and Other Indian Legends*, which explains that during the war between Raven and Grizzly Bear, Raven painted the birds with war paint. In a North Carolina Negro tale about Noah's ark called "Why the Birds are Different Colors," pages 89 and 90 of Leach's *How the People Sang the Mountains Up*, the birds flew through the rainbow and took their colors from whichever stripe they passed through. Those with several colors flew around in the colors. On pages 3 to 8, "Why the Birds Wear Bright Plumage," from Palmer's *Why the North Star Stands Still and Other Indian Legends* is a Payute tale. There wasn't enough food on the new earth for both birds and animals so the birds flew away to get seeds, and were rewarded by bright plumage and the ability to sing songs, to make the earth a beautiful place. "The Origin of Birds," on pages 181 to 186 of Walker's *Legends of Green Sky Hill*, explains that when the Frost King killed the leaves, the Great Spirit changed them into birds that would return in spring. Red maple leaves became scarlet tanagers, yellow leaves became goldfinches, and so forth.

The title story in Spellman's *The Beautiful Blue Jay and Other Tales of India*, tells why the jay is blue and has an ugly voice, when originally he had a beautiful voice but was an ugly brown color. It seems that Princess Lakshmi was beautiful but had an ugly voice, and Prince Rama, whom she loved, was blind and only heard her voice. When the jay traded voices with the princess, he became a beautiful blue but had forever after the ugly voice of the princess.

The stories about how individual birds received their colors are predominantly about red and black birds. "How the Cardinal Got His Red Feathers" comes from a Cherokee legend retold on pages 62 to 66 of Belting's *The Long-Tailed Bear*: raccoon, playing a trick on wolf, covered his eyes with mud; when brown bird pecked off the mud wolf thanked him by painting his feathers with streaks of red mud from the rocks. A similar story called "How the Redbird Got His Color" is found on pages 62 to 64 of Mooney's *Cherokee Indian Tales*.

A story from the African Congo on page 95 of Leach's *How the People Sang the Mountains Up* tells "Why Robin Has a Red Breast." The male bird has a red breast and the female doesn't because when they were out of red camwood powder the male went to the village to get some, and while he carried it home in his mouth the powder melted and dribbled on his breast, making it red. Another version called "How Robin's Breast Became Red" is found on pages 181 and 182 of Cathon's *Perhaps and Perchance*: a boy trying to keep a fire going grew tired; polar bear tried to put it out but robin fanned the flame and so scorched his breast. A similar story "Why the Robin Has a Red Breast" begins on page 195 of Walker's *Legends of Green Sky Hill*.

The Miao tribe of West China in the mountains of Tibet tell "How the Cock

Got His Red Crown." The story which appears on pages 27 to 32 of Hume's *Favorite Children's Stories from China and Tibet*, explains that once there were six suns and the emperor wanted archers to shoot them. All failed until one person shot five reflections of the sun so even the sixth sun disappeared and sulked, and would not come out until the rooster crowed. As a reward, sun gave rooster a red crown which he still wears when he calls up the sun.

There are several stories about why ravens and crows are black. Crow originally had golden feathers in a story told by the Palungs of Burma on pages 77 to 81 of Belting's *The Earth Is on a Fish's Back*. In the story "Why the Crow Is Black and Men Find Precious Stones in the Earth," Princess Naga, one of the serpent-dragons, changed herself into a beautiful woman. The sun fell in love with her, left her when he found out that she had deceived him, but later relented and told crow to take Naga a bag of jewels. Crow hung the bag on a branch and when he went to get the jewels they had been replaced with stones. The sun was angry and cursed crow: "From this day . . . you will be the ugliest bird on earth. You will crow and not sing. Other birds will be afraid of you. Men will dislike you."

According to the story "How the Raven Got to Be Black," in Penney's *Tales of the Cheyenne*, white raven was tied over a green wood fire until all his feathers turned black and the smoke made his voice hoarse as punishment for scaring away the buffalo.

"Why Crows are Black" is found on pages 113 to 16 to De Leeuw's *Indonesian Legends and Folk Tales*. The crow, once white and called "The Bird of Paradise," was the messenger of Allah. Allah asked crow to bring water from the fountain of life so the clay person Allah had fashioned could come alive and be immortal. On the way home, Crow drank some water although he had promised not to do so. Therefore the man had life but there wasn't enough water to make him immortal. Crow then lied about why there wasn't enough water, but Magpie informed on him. Allah turned crow black and gave Magpie some black feathers for telling tales.

Ann Kirn took her story The *Peacock and the Crow* from an old Chinese fable. In that story a peacock and a crow were invited to Lord Tiger's wedding and they wanted to look nice so they decided to paint each other. After crow had painted peacock, peacock deliberately knocked the paints in the river so that only black was left for crow. Because peacock was a false friend, whenever sunlight strikes crow's feathers, they shine like a rainbow.

According to a Pima Indian tale from Carlsen's *Let's Pretend It Happened to You*, we learn "How the Bluebird and the Coyote Got Their Colors." Once all animals were ugly except the green coyote. When he saw a bird who was blue, he learned the secret of dipping in a special lake and chanting a song so he could become blue too. However, coyote would not share the secret. In his pride, he tripped and fell in the mud and has been that color ever since.

"Why Crane's Feathers Are Brown and Otter Doesn't Feel the Cold" is an Assiniboin Indian tale from the Dakotas. The story is found in Belting's *The Long-Tailed Bear*. Crane baby hatched too late to fly South for the winter so he stayed with otter but was stolen by Osni, the cold. Crane's beak became black and his feathers were singed when he fanned the coals with his wings to keep warm. "How Eagle Got Smoke in His Feathers," pages 46 to 51 of Palmer's *Why the North Star Stands Still . . .* tells how patient eagle waited until all the other animals got their colors. He got the color he wanted—pure white feathers and leggings with red trim. Once very sociable and vain because of his beauty, Eagle got dirty in a cave so he is no longer vain or sociable.

"How Mr. Crane's Eyes Became Blue" is found on pages 76 to 85 of Gilham's *Beyond the Clapping Mountains, Eskimo Stories from Alaska.* Mr. Crane took out his brown eyes and laid them by the sand to be a lookout for him while he picked salmonberries. After two false alarms, Mr. Crane paid no attention to the eyes until they were stolen. He tried using many different berries for substitute eyes until he finally settled on blueberries.

A Tewa Indian legend from the Pueblos of New Mexico, on pages 89 to 92 of Belting's *The Long-Tailed Bear,* is entitled "How Turkey Got His White Tail Feathers." During the flood, all animals fled to the mountains but they became so crowded, turkey's feathers hung down in the water and the color was washed out.

A Brazilian version of this tale called "Why the Fox Has a Dark Tail" is found in Fells's *Tales from the Amazon.* In this story it was a fox's tail that became discolored because it hung into the water during the time of the great flood. Pages 93 and 94 of Belting's *Long-Tailed Bear* tells "Why the Tip of Fox's Tail Is White." According to the Acomas, Pueblo Indians of New Mexico, the tip of fox's tail is white because mouse bit the color out of it. Mouse also took fur from fox's tail to make a nest, so to replace the fur, fox rolled in pitch and then stuck some fur on.

According to the Eskimos, foxes were white until Mr. Fox blushed in shame because he let Mrs. Mouse outwit him and escape. "How the Foxes Became Red" is found on pages 99 to 105 of Gilham's *Beyond the Clapping Mountains* and in the anthology of Cathon and Schmidt, *Perhaps and Perchance,* on pages 48 to 52. "How the Fox Was Outwitted" on pages 95 to 98 of Walker's *Legends of Green Sky Hill* tells that fox got his black nose from snapping at a burning stick. In the story from the Chippewas, fox wanted to learn woodpecker's song so he could fool the doves and eat them.

"How the Brazilian Beetles Got Their Gorgeous Coats" is found on pages 201 to 210 of *Fairy Tales from Brazil* by Fells. Grey rat challenged the little brown beetle to a race thinking the beetle was slow, but beetle won because she could fly. "After this . . . never judge any one by his looks alone," said brown beetle. Asked what color she wanted to be, she chose the green and gold of the parrot. One little beetle wished she were blue and was allowed to change color if she was willing to give up something. In return for her new blue coat she gave up her hard,firm shell and the chance to grow bigger, so she is not used in jewelry like green and gold beetles, and is smaller than they are. The flag of Brazil is green with a diamond of gold like the colors on the green beetle's back, but there is also a blue circle with stars that looks like the back of the blue beetle.

Other items in nature are the subject of legends. In Palmer's *Why the North*

Star Stands Still, (pp. 84-88) readers learn "How the Flowers Get Their Colors." The gods got colored earth from the mountains and put it in buffalo skins with seeds and then scattered the earth all over the world.

"Why Some Trees Are Evergreen" is a Cherokee legend found on page 125 of Leach's *How the People Sang the Mountains Up*. All plants and trees were asked to keep awake and keep watch for seven nights. Those who were able to endure were allowed to be forever green. A Chippewa version is found on pages 152 to 155 of Walker's *Legends of Green Sky Hill*, "Why the Evergreen Trees Never Lose Their Leaves." A little bird that had broken its wing was left behind in the snow. It asked many trees for help but was refused shelter until the spruce, pine and juniper gave it shelter and berries. The Great Spirit announced that all trees would lose their leaves for part of the year except the trees that were kind to the little bird.

SPOTS AND STRIPES IN FOLKLORE.   There are several stories that can stimulate discussion of striped and spotted animals and plants in nature, and the discussion in turn can stimulate illustration projects or creative stories by students themselves.

According to folklore, several animals have become spotted by being burned by hot coals. "How the Owl Got His Spots" is a Cherokee story found in Bell's *John Rattling Gourd*. The Great Spirit answered the request of the animals to have fire so lightning and fire were placed in a hollow tree on an island. Raven and snake were scorched black trying to get the fire. Screech owl nearly burned out his eyes, so they are red even today. Horned owl has rings about his eyes because ashes blew in his face. Owl hid because everyone said he was ugly. The curious people built a fire to see the owl's face and sparks flew up and burned spots in owl's coat. The Shawnee tell "How the Wildcat Got His Spots" on pages 71-73 of Belting's *Long-Tailed Bear*: Wildcat wanted to eat rabbit but rabbit scattered the fire while getting away and burned wildcat's fur in the process. "How the Speckled Hen Got Her Speckles" is explained in Fells's *Fairy Tales from Brazil*: a little white hen found a letter and took it to the king. On the way she met and carried a fox, a river, and a fire, in her brown basket. Her riders sat on the letter and damaged it so the king was infuriated and had her thrown into the poultry yard in preparation for being eaten. The three friends saved her but the ashes of the fire scattered over her, and so now she and her descendants are speckled.

According to "Why the Guinea-fowls Are Speckled," in *The Complete Tales of Uncle Remus* by Harris, guinea fowls were once all blue. The guineas saved the cow from a lion so the cow asked them what they wanted as a reward. The guineas said they did not want to be blue because they couldn't hide, so the cow put them in a row, put her tail in the milk bucket, and swished milk over the guineas and chanted an incantation for the guineas to become gray. They did, but white spots appeared on their feathers where the milk dried in the sun.

"How the Big Moth Got Fire in His Wings" on pages 41 to 45 of Palmer's *Why the North Star Stands Still* tells how the troublemaker Un-nu-pit destroyed the Chief of the Dancers, Ne-ab, who was vain and danced too close to the fire.

Ne-ab was revived as a red-winged moth whose back and wings are gray and sprinkled with ashes but red like fire underneath. In June Ne-ab's children dance around the fire.

Also in the Palmer collection is "How the Badger, the Skunk, and the Sage Hen Were Marked" (pp. 99-102). According to this story, Ksav and Shinava went out to hunt rabbits and Ksav bragged about his magic bow even though warned against doing so. The arrow flew around the world, creasing the skunk's back and badger's forehead. The sage hen's throat was burned black and Ksav was turned into a bullet hawk.

The Iroquois story "How the Chipmunk Got His Stripes" is found (pp. 75-76) in Leach's *How the People Sang the Mountains Up* and on pages 21 to 25 of Raskin's *Indian Tales*. Bear and chipmunk each sang for a different reason; bear wanted perpetual night and chipmunk wanted light to come. When the sun did come up, bear became angry and grabbed at chipmunk. Chipmunk got away but bear's claws made marks on his back that are still there today. A Chippewa legend found on pages 91 to 94 of Walker's *Legends of Green Sky Hill* tells "Why the Raccoon Has Rings on Its Tail." Manabozho heard raccoon bragging about how he stole meat from two blind men who accused each other of stealing, so Nanabozho made raccoon wear as many stripes as the pieces of meat he stole.

"How Packrat Got Its Patches" is found on pages 89 to 94 of Palmer's *Why the North Star Stands Still*. Packrat invited everyone to his house for a party. After he did tricks for his guests he sent them away with their eyes closed, but always ate those who had the honor to stand next to him. When the animals found out what Packrat was doing, they attacked him, and naturally he still carries the scars today.

"How Kingfisher Got His Necklace," page 96 of Leach's *How the People Sang the Mountains Up*, is a Chippewa story. Wenebojo was looking for his drowned nephew and stopped to talk to a bird who admitted he was waiting for the body to surface. Wenebojo put a string of beads around the bird's neck and intended to catch him, but the bird got away. Wenebojo named the bird "kingfisher" and said he would have to dive for food forever. Kingfisher still wears the necklace today and the ruffled head he got when he escaped from Wenebojo.

Mariott and Rachlin's *American Indian Mythology* contains "How and Why: The Painted Turtle" (pp. 124-27) a Sauk tale. According to the editors, this story shows a Christian moral influence: "This story is to be told to young men, as a warning of what might happen to them if they act like turtles." Turtle had painted himself and taken a girl into the woods to seduce her but she put him to sleep and ants bit him. The story draws chuckles from high school students.

STRIPES, SPOTS AND PLAIDS IN PICTURE BOOKS.   Ipcar's *Stripes and Spots* is about a little striped tiger and a little spotted leopard who became friends. The tiger ate leaves, flowers, striped bugs, and chipmunks, while the leopard ate leaves, flowers, spotted bugs, and turtles.

Horatio, a striped cat, appears in Clymer's *Horatio's Birthday* and of course the cat in *Alice in Wonderland* is striped. Balet's *Ladismouse* is about a mouse who growled at a blue-striped cat. *Stripe* is the title of McClung's life story of a chipmunk.

The *Old Witch and the Polka Dot Ribbon* by the Devlins is one of many polka dot books. Levitin's *A Single Speckled Egg* is a nonsense story about three farmers' wives who try to out-complain their husbands. Roselli's *The Polka Dot Child* wakes to find that she has measles after dreaming about tiger lilies, dalmations, speckled trout, and other animals with spots. *Spots are Special* by Galbraith is about a girl with chicken pox. When Sandy is sick she pretends she is a leopard, a spotted frog, a dalmation, or a giraffe. *The Little Spotted Fish* by Yolen is a British folktale about a fish who saves a boy's life twice and even a third time at risk to himself. Several kinds of unusual looking fish are shown. Students may wish to draw fish of their own that are even more colorful.

Leichman's *Shaggy Dogs and Spotty Dogs and Shaggy and Spotty Dogs* is a rhyming book that shows various types of dogs. Skaar's *Nothing But Cats and All About Dogs* is an easier book that contains many contrasting adjectives— striped and spotted, tall and short, fat and thin, nice and naughty, sad and happy, lazy and busy, hungry and full. All of the different kinds of cats say "meow" and all of the dogs say "bow-wow." Kumin's *What Color is Caesar?* asks: is Caesar a black dog with white spots or a white dog with black spots? Lopshire's *Put Me in the Zoo* is an easy reading book about a polka dot beast. *The Checker Players* is a funny book by Venable in which an alligator and bear meet on the water halfway between their homes to play checkers.

The Plaid Peacock by Alan was hatched just as some bagpipers marched by. The peacock later became their mascot. Another peacock story is Alexander's *Peacocks Are Very Special*.

Emberley's *The Wizard of Op* is a complicated story which is the vehicle for showing readers the techniques of optical art. Projects in optical illusion are given in the following two nonfiction books: *Experiments in Optical Illusion* by Beeler and Branley, and *Op Tricks, Creating Kinetic Art* by Marks.

COLLAGE IN PICTURE BOOKS.   Collage making is fascinating to groups of all ages. Marks, on page five of his book called *Collage*, explains that "The word collage comes from the French word *coller* which means to paste or glue." A brief history of collage and step-by-step instructions for making twelve collages are included in Marks's book. Mayer and Web also give step-by-step procedures and many illustrations in their book, *New Ways in Collage*. This excellent guide for teachers tells of the basic method and variations. Materials and tools are listed in this book, as well as in Beaney's *Adventures with Collage*. Gluing hints as well as fabric, relief, and junk collages are included. Group projects are discussed. Page 43 shows a collage inspired by a nonsense story by Edward Lear that was created by a ten- and an eleven-year-old girl. Page 30 shows a fabric collage of a horse done by a fourteen-year-old. Pages 34 to 38 show projects done by children. Weiss defines collage and tells about ingredients, tools, and searching for materials. The first section of his *Collage and Construction* is especially helpful because most projects for the classroom will not entail the construction that is explained in the last part. *Making Collages* by the Borjas gives eight examples of technique. Other sources such as Janitch's *Country Collage*, Priolo's *Ideas for Collage*, and Pellerson's and Gerring's *Exploring with Paint*, also present information for leaders.

Whenever anyone is working on a collage, it is useful to see examples. Many picture books provide these samples, and several famous artists use collage frequently in their books. The first one who comes to mind is a master of the technique—Ezra Jack Keats. *Snowy Day* was the 1962 Caldecott Medal winner, is available in paperback, on film and sound filmstrip, and expresses the excitement of a small boy for new snowfall. The author's *Whistle for Willie*, also available in paperback, has the same boy, Peter, learning how to whistle for the first time. In *Peter's Chair*, Peter has trouble realizing that he will have to share his chair, among other things, with a new baby. In *A Letter to Amy* Peter invites her to his birthday party. Peter and his dachshund Willie face neighborhood bullies who confiscate the goggles Peter has found in *Goggles*, a 1970 Caldecott Honor Book, which combines paint and collage. *Hi Cat* features Willie, Peter, and Archie as they plan a program for other children. Another project they have is in *Pet Show*. All three picture books are available in paperback editions. In *Jennie's Hat*, Keats uses cut-out pieces of watercolor. In *Dreams*, Keats combines collage and acrylics. In *Apartment 3*, two boys investigate sounds coming from that apartment and discover a blind man. Other books executed in collage by Keats are *John Henry*, *The Little Drummer Boy*, *Over in the Meadow*, *Louie* and *Louie's Search*.

Three commercially prepared posters showing Keats's art are available and could be posted in the art room when collages are being made or would enhance a classroom or library media center. When studying the collages by Keats, students might want to see a filmed interview called *Ezra Jack Keats*. The seventeen-minute film includes the book *A Letter to Amy*. Many of Keats's books are available on film, filmstrip, or in paperback.

One book illustrated by him is *In the Park; an Excursion in Four Languages*, written by Hautzig, which shows what one could expect to find in a park in New York, Paris, Moscow, and Madrid, and is written in English, French, Russian, and Spanish.

Roger Duvoisin is known best for his illustrations of *Veronica*, *Petunia*, and *Happy Lion*, none of which uses collage. But Duvoisin has again collaborated with Louise Fatio, this time using collages, in *Hector Penguin*. Hector is lost in a forest where none of the animals has ever seen a penguin. Everyone has an idea about Hector until crow finally identifies him as a penguin, even to his Latin name. Duvoisin also illustrated some of Freschet's nature books with collage. *The Old Bullfrog* lived a long time in the pond and successfully avoided being eaten by a heron. The animals seen on this summer day are shown in daily activities. Included are six different kinds of birds, a red squirrel, porcupine, deer, caterpillar, and others. *Web in the Grass*, also written by Freschet, shows a spider building a nest that catches a mosquito and a green fly. The nature cycle is portrayed pictorially when a blue jay finds a black beetle and a toad tries to catch the spider.

Peppe uses tissue paper and gingham and other items to create *Hey Riddle*

Riddle, a Book of Traditional Riddles that includes forty-five Mother Goose Rhymes. Other books by Peppe in the collage technique are *Alphabet Book, Circus Numbers,* and *The House That Jack Built.* Peppe's *Simple Simon* utilizes collage combined with paint.

Janina Domanska combines scratch painting and collage in *What Do You See?* in which four items in nature see the world differently.

Evaline Ness uses ink and collage to illustrate Black's *Woman of the Wood.* This variation on the Pygmalion-Galatea/My Fair Lady theme tells of a woodcarver, a tailor, and a teacher who created a woman from a branch, clothed her, and taught her to speak. Then the three men argued over who owned her. A wise man decided that no one can ever own anyone else.

Eric Carle uses painted tissue paper as part of his collage in Mendoza's *The Scarecrow Clock.* A drummer frog, butternut cat, jumpy puppy and blueberry bear all help tell time. Non-verbal books, discussed later in this chapter, which contain collage illustrations by Carle include *I See a Song* and *The Secret Birthday Message* and *1, 2, 3 to the Zoo.*

Barthelme uses collage illustrations taken from nineteenth-century engravings to enhance *The Slightly Irregular Fire Engine or the Hithering Thithering Djinn.* In the story, Mathilda sees a mysterious Chinese house in the yard and walks into it and adventure.

De Forest's *The Prancing Pony, Nursery Rhymes from Japan,* illustrated by Keiko Hida, uses collages on rice paper in a unique way. Oragami pasted into collage designs is called hari-e. Hida's new art of using raised paper is called kusa-e from the words picture and grass. An interesting article on that art is included in the book.

Luzzati's version of Grimm's *Punchinello* is *Punch and the Magic Fish.* This familiar story of the fish who can grant wishes uses collages in an unusual way. Another favorite, *Peter and the Wolf,* is carried out in collage by a Japanese artist. The collage techniques in two Bible stories can be compared with each other: Singer's *Why Noah Chose the Dove* illustrated by Carle, and Wynant's *Noah's Ark.*

Two books of collage ask a question. Fisher's poetry book illustrated by Carle shows twelve different animals' mothers in *Do Bears Have Mothers, Too?* for which Eastman's *Are You My Mother?* (not illustrated in collage) would be a good companion book. Graboff's *Do Catbirds Wear Whiskers?* is easy to read and is composed of nonsense collages.

Nicholas' Favorite Pet by the Sandbergs tells about a boy who asks for an elephant, rhino, hippo, lion, snake, crocodile, and cobra for his birthday. The family compromises on a dog. Steven Kellogg's *Can I Keep Him?* has the same theme. *The Hare and the Tortoise,* an excellent example of collage figures cut from fabric, is also available on sound filmstrip. *Sweet Betsy from Pike* by Abisch and Kaplan also uses fabric.

There are two picture books that are not illustrated in collage but which may inspire children to make collages. They are *Harlequin and the Gift of Many Colors* and *Pezzettino. Pezzettino* by Lionni is a little square piece of orange who wants to know what he is a piece of, until he finally learns that he is himself.

Collage pieces could be used to create a bulletin board figure of Pezzettino. Other Lionni books illustrated by collage are *Inch by Inch*, a simple story of how an inchworm cleverly escapes from a bird, and *Frederick*, a mouse who doesn't work gathering food in summer but earns his keep by entertaining the others in winter.

The story of *Harlequin and the Gift of Many Colors* is by Charlip and Supree, and is best read at Carnival or Mardi Gras time, the Tuesday before Ash Wednesday. The introduction to the book shows early drawings of the traditional figure, Harlequin, four hundred years ago wearing his patched suit of irregular pieces. It wasn't until later that pictures showed him in diamond-shaped patches. This particular story is found in a book published in 1865 called *Larousse's Dictionaire Universel du XIX Siecle*. The character of Harlequin comes from Bergamo, Italy. In the story, friends were talking about what they would wear to the carnival when they noticed that Harlequin wasn't contributing to the conversation. When they realized that it was because he was too poor to buy a costume, they all gave Harlequin scraps from their costumes but no one piece was enough for any one part of his garment. Harlequin had the idea of sewing the scraps on his trousers and his costume was really marvelous. According to the last page of the story, ". . . Harlequin was the happiest of them all on this happy night, for he was clothed in the love of his friends."

Read *Harlequin and the Gift of Many Colors* to the students and have them bring scraps from home to contribute to a bulletin board size costume for Harlequin, or students could each make one small painting and then the sheets could be cut into pieces and distributed to group members so they could each make a costume for their own individual Harlequin or for one large figure.

CARTOON ILLUSTRATIONS IN PICTURE BOOKS.   Students who might not otherwise be motivated to make a book for themselves could be interested in making a book illustrated with cartoons or comics. Consult the section about making a comic book in Weiss's *How to Make Your Own Book*. Cumming's *Make Your Own Comics for Fun and Profit* shows several professional artists and examples of work they did when they were in school. The book deals with planning, placement of figures, use of symbols, angles of viewing, and recommended materials. Also consult Zaidenberg's *How to Draw Cartoons: A Book for Beginners*.

One of the most famous cartoonists, Charles Schultz, comes to mind. Several hardbacks include *Snoopy and His Sopwith Camel*, *Snoopy and the Red Baron*, and *Charlie Brown's All-Stars*. Readers of the last title are not surprised to learn that Charlie Brown's team lost 123-0! Many titles are available in paperback: *Play It Again, Charlie Brown*, *Speak Softly and Carry a Beagle*, and *Win a Few, Lose a Few, Charlie Brown*. Teachers can also share the musical comedy *You're a Good Man, Charlie Brown* by Gesner and the biography *Charlie Brown and Charlie Shultz* by Mendelson with their students.

Two author-illustrators whose cartoon-like drawings have won them outstanding awards are William Steig and Raymond Briggs. Briggs won the 1973 Kate Greenaway Medal for *Father Christmas*, a book with few words whose cartoon-like illustrations show Santa's attitude on Christmas Eve. *Father Christmas Goes on Holiday* continues the tradition. Steig won the 1970 Caldecott Medal for *Sylvester and the Magic Pebble*. Sylvester, a donkey, when confronted by a dangerous lion, became a rock using a magic pebble, but, as a rock, found himself unable to hold the pebble to change himself back into a donkey. *Amos and Boris, Dominic, The Real Thief,* and *Farmer Palmer's Wagon Ride* are all cartoon illustrated, the first two having been nominated for the National Book Award. *Abel's Island* is a Newbery Honor book for 1977. The farmer in *Farmer Palmer's Wagon Ride* is a pig who, with his hired man, a donkey, must make use of all the presents they had planned to take home from market in order to get the wagon home. *The Amazing Bone,* a 1977 Caldecott honor book, is also about a pig named "Pearl" who found a talking bone that saved her from robbers.

Pomerantz's *The Piggy in the Puddle* has cartoon-like characters who use delightful words such as "squishy," "squashy," "wiggling," and "giggling." The little pig's family try to get her to use soap to get clean and the results are unexpected and hilarious. James Marshall's *Yummers!* is about another pig, Emily, who has a bad habit—she eats too much. When Eugene Turtle persuades Emily to go for a walk she sees only more things to eat.

Barton's illustrations in Venable's *The Checker Players* feature a bear and a crocodile who successfully build a boat together so they can play checkers in it.

Kantrowitz's *I Wonder If Herbie's Home Yet* is another book in which the cartoon-like drawings are perfect for the plot and the humor. Smokey's best friend has gone skating with someone else and Smokey thinks terrible thoughts about him until the misunderstanding is cleared up.

In Aliki Brandenberg's *June 7,* the family is at home when the doorbell rings and everyone comes in with baskets of food for a picnic that ends as a birthday party.

Some other picture books utilizing a variety of cartoon-like characters are Graham's *Be Nice to Spiders,* Zion's *Dear Garbage Man,* The Watsons's *Birthday Goat* and *Father Fox's Pennyrhymes,* Firmin's *Basil Bush at the Beach,* Krahn's *A Flying Saucer Full of Spaghetti,* Flora's *Sherwood Walks Home,* and Smaridge's *The Big Tidy-Up.*

PHOTOGRAPHS AS ILLUSTRATIONS.   Photographs have long been part of "language experience" activities in which a leader takes pictures of a field trip or children take their own pictures and write stories. These creations are then bound in a folder and become a "book" that might even be cataloged and placed in the school library-media center. There are books listed in this section that could provide models for projects.

For a beginning book simple concepts are best. One hilarious picture book that stresses this point is written by Willard and illustrated by de Paola and called *Simple Pictures Are Best*. A shoemaker and his wife keep adding items around them despite the photographer's admonition that "simple pictures are best." The following examples contain very simple concepts. Tana Hoban has used black and white photographs in *Circles, Triangles and Squares, Over, Under and Through and Other Spatial Concepts,* and *Push Pull, Empty Full: a Book of Opposites* to explain the concepts. Hoban's *Where Is It?* is a simple story in verse about a young rabbit who finds its own Easter basket full of carrots and cabbage. Hoban's *Count and See* is a very simple black and white photo counting book. Allen's *Numbers: A First Counting Book* is photographed in color.

De Regniers's *The Shadow Book* shows black and white photos of long and short shadows. Strong's *Glowing in the Dark* includes photos of all kinds of light: signs, candles, and lamps. Merriman's *Bam Zam Boom!* combines drawings and photos in showing the demolishing of an old building. Benzen's *Miguel's Mountain* shows city children playing in a park.

Brenner's two books show *Faces* and *Bodies* through black and white photos. The imagery in *Faces* is outstanding, and points out also that although everyone's face is different, all faces have as common elements eyes, mouth, nose, and ears. Older students will enjoy Brenner's more complicated *Snake-Lovers Diary* which uses photos profusely. Van Gelder's *Whose Nose Is This?* asks children to guess from a small photo of a nose to whom it belongs. Humphrey's *What Is It For?* shows black and white photos of manholes, gratings, conveyor belts, and fire escapes and asks, "What is it for?" Many more pictures could be taken to add a custom-made sequel to both *Whose Nose Is This?* and *What Is It For?* The latter book would be good to stimulate discussion of form and context. Hoban's *Look Again!* includes black and white nature photos and presents another guessing game. First a small part of the object is shown through a small square in the middle of the page. The second page reveals the total object and children will easily be able to guess what the object is. Again, there are follow-up possibilities.

Zoo City by Lewis has split pages. The top half has an object that resembles an animal. The bottom resembles an inanimate object. By flipping the pages, students can match the look-alikes.

Castle's *Face Talk, Hand Talk, Body Talk* portrays the theory of nonverbal communication through photography.

Busch's *A Walk in the Snow* builds on a simple activity to develop various projects. The book is accompanied by a leader's guide that relates ten activities to the book, such as identifying tracks made by patterned snowboot soles.

Black and white photos show Stecher and Kandell's *Max the Music Maker* finding music in his world.

Colored photographs accompany verses and provide descriptions in *Things* by the Dunns. Very ordinary activities like marching, running and hopping appear in black and white photos in Grant's *Hey Look at Me! Sometimes I Dance Mountains* by Baylor combines photos and drawings to translate words into motion.

A good example of photographs used to show a particular lifestyle is Ann Nolan Clark's *Along Sandy Trails*. The life of a Navajo Indian girl and her life in the desert is portrayed and is available also as a sound filmstrip.

Colored photos illustrate Atwood's *Haiku: The Mood of the Earth* and also *My Own Rhythm, an Approach to Haiku*. Students could read poems and take photographs to illustrate them, or better still write poems and then take the photographs. The photos and poems could either be featured on a bulletin board or compiled into a book. Atwood's *New Moon Cove* shows etchings, sculpture, watercolor and still life, all associated with nature. All three books are outstanding.

Hess's *Rabbits in the Meadow*, Eberle's *Fawn in the Woods*, and Ylla's *Two Little Bears* are stories about wild animals told in photographs. Other Ylla books are *Little Elephant* and *Animal Babies*. Hess's book portrays a family of cottontail rabbits from birth through their first summer. The Ylla book is a story about two bear cubs who, told by their mother not to get lost while she hunted for honey, forgot the warning. Once lost, they asked a calf, horse, chick, baby rabbits, raccoon, and crow where their mother was and, reunited by the crow, promised never to run away again. Eberle's book about the fawn is a life cycle book. Selsam's science books, like *The Harlequin Moth*, use color and black and white photographs and are often life cycle books. Another book by Selsam is *Hidden Animals*, a Science-I-Can-Read book with photos of animals camouflaged by nature followed by a second picture with a fainter background so the animal or insect is clearly visible.

There are three photo books about cats. *Kitten's Little Boy* by Wright is about a kitten who imagines himself a tiger, lion, and Egyptian statue among other things. Kaffler's *I'll Show You Cats* shares cats with readers. Stevens's *The Birth of Sunset's Kittens* shows pictures of the kittens during and after birth. Flannigan's *Window into an Egg: Seeing Life Begin* is a series of black and white photos showing various stages of development of a chick until it is hatched. Welch's *Just Like Puppies* shows a poodle who loses her puppies and adopts four baby raccoons. Selsam's *How Kittens Grow* and *How Puppies Grow* utilize photographs, and both are available in paperback.

Connie's New Eyes by Wolf is really a photographic essay about a twenty-two-year-old blind teacher and the fifteen-year-old 4-H club member who raises a puppy to be her seeing-eye dog. The book provides students with a good model for a photographic essay.

ALPHABET PHOTO BOOKS.   The first three books utilize black and white photos. Deasy's *City ABC's* is in rhyme with adults and children pictured in laundromats, manholes, and at newsstands. Grant's *Hey Look at Me, A City ABC* shows several activities of small children on each page. Reuben's *Apples to Zippers, an Alphabet Book* includes objects and animals. Matthiesen's *ABC, an Alphabet* is photographed in color and uses common objects. Carle's *All About Arthur* uses colored photographs of letters on boxcars, neon signs, and walls. That book is narrated by Arthur, an ape, who was created by woodcuts. Photo alphabets bring a quality of reality to picture books but also cause them to become dated quickly. Making a photo alphabet can lend a sense of immediacy; use black and white film and an Instamatic to create inexpensive, localized photo alphabet books, to be presented to local preschool and primary groups.

Criteria for good alphabet books, are found later in this chapter in a section called *Projects for Alphabet and Counting Books*.

PHOTOGRAPHY BOOKS.   Books on photography that are likely to be in the school library media center are Czaja's *Writing with Light, a Simple Workshop in Basic Photography*; Glubok's *The Art of Photography*; Holland's *How to Photograph Your World*; Noren's *Photography: How to Improve Your Technique*; and Weiss's *Lens and Shutter: an Introduction to Photography*. Beginning photographers will also wish to consult booklets published by the manufacturers of cameras. Scheffler's *Seeing Eye* contains experiments in nature. Very small children who need to know the importance of holding the camera steady and keeping fingers away from the lens should read Leen's *Taking Pictures*. Steinberg's *Photography* includes the following types of information: kinds of cameras, history, hints, field trips, darkrooms, and displaying photographs. Jacobs's *Instant Photography* gives a history of the technique as well as information on the technique. A glossary and bibliography are included.

See pages 20 to 29 of the August, 1977, issue of *National Geographic World* for the article "Make Your Own Pinhole Camera."

PHOTOGRAMS.   Hoban's book *Shapes and Things* uses the photogram technique of taking pictures without a camera. Objects are placed on photographic paper in darkroom conditions and then are exposed to light. They are then developed as photographic prints. An excellent book telling how to create photograms is Mirina's *Pictures Without a Camera*. Consult pages 18 to 20 of Halter's *Photography Without a Camera* for more information.

RUBBINGS AS ILLUSTRATIONS.   Rubbings can provide easy illustrations for picture books made by children. Ideas for illustrations using candle wax and a heelball of wax are given in Cross's *Simple Printing Methods*. All of the senses are involved in Kinn's *Full of Wonder*. Crayon rubbings using leaves, shells, coins, feathers, buttons, pea pods, bark, pine needles, twigs, and paper clips are some of the items used. Seidelman and Mintonye's *Rub Book* is easy reading.

WOODCUTS, LINOLEUM BLOCKS, VEGETABLE PRINTS.   Simon's *The Story of Printing* is a basic book to read before beginning any unit about woodcuts. Besides explaining what wood engraving and woodcuts are, an example of each is shown. An explicit drawing showing the grain of a block of wood used for each technique is included. Chapter 2 of Heller's *Printmaking Today* is called "Woodcuts and Wood Engravings" and is an excellent teacher source. Formulas, recipes, and sources of supplies are also given. Rockwell's *Printmaking* gives step-by-step directions that can be followed by intermediate students. Excellent photos enhance Sternberg's *Woodcut*, which explains the total process of making woodcuts. Another excellent book that begins with selecting the wood takes the reader through drawing, cutting, and printing is *Introducing Woodcuts* by Woods. A paper edition is available. *New Media in Printmaking* by Bickford includes extremely detailed information on woodcuts and linoleum blocks. The two previous titles also include linoleum prints.

In the sound filmstrip, *Gail Haley: Wood and Linoleum Illustration*, the

Caldecott winner discusses technique as well as sources for ideas for A Story, A Story and Go Away, Stay Away.

Also consult chapter 5, "Ornament and Block Printing," of Voss's Reinhold Craft and Hobby Book; pages 101-03 are on woodcuts. Another excellent source is chapter 3 of Mattil's Meaning in Crafts, "Try Making Prints." Chapter 4, "Printmaking," of Penn's Individualized Arts and Crafts Lessons for the Elementary School is also useful. Chapter 5, "Cutting," of Daniel's Simple Printmaking with Children deals with making woodblocks as well as blocks of other materials. Also consult the index to Harovitz's Understanding Children's Art for Better Teaching, Liberman's Printing as a Hobby, and Seidelman and Mintonye's Creating with Wood. Woodcuts are included in Rockwell's Printmaking. Also consult encyclopedias under "Printing" and "Graphic Arts." Let's Print by Tingle and Print Making by MacStravic are also helpful. Sattler's Recipes for Art and Craft Materials includes a recipe for printing ink on page 106.

Early examples of woodcuts and wood engravings are given in McMurtrie's The Book, The Story of Printing and Bookmaking. Chapter 8, "The Twentieth Century," of Bland's A History of Book Illustration shows examples of woodcuts and wood engravings. See also Holme's Drawings to Live With and More Shapes and Stories, a Book about Pictures by the Grigsons. Cole's The Birds and the Beasts Were There and Blake's Songs of Innocence are poetry illustrated by woodcuts.

Displays of modern picture books using woodcut illustrations are an important part of any project in which children make their own illustrations. Antonio Frasconi is an outstanding master of the art of creating woodcut illustrations. His See and Say, A Picture Book in Four Languages is written in English, Italian, French, and Spanish. A different color is used for each language and a guide to pronunciation is given. See and Say is also a sound filmstrip. The Snow and the Sun, La Nieve y el Sol is a South American folk rhyme written in English and Spanish. Another book written in Spanish and English, illustrated by Frasconi, is Crickets and Frogs, a Fable by Gabriela Minstral. In the story, crickets and frogs fight to see who can sing the loudest. Finally they decide that each will sing for half the night. Frasconi also illustrated sections from Walt Whitman's "Leaves of Grass" in Overhead the Sun, which honored the one hundred fiftieth birthday of Whitman. In 1960 the Grand Prix at the Venice Film Festival was won by a film called The Neighboring Shores, which contained one hundred woodcuts to illustrate poems by Whitman.

The House That Jack Built, a Picture Book in Two Languages is illustrated with woodcuts, written in English and French, and was a Caldecott Honor Book in 1959.

Ann Grifalconi used an orange and blue background for woodcuts in Clifton's Everett Anderson's Year, to illustrate twelve poems, one for each month of the year. Grifalconi also used woodcuts to illustrate Graham's David He No Fear, poems told in the words and thought patterns of a modern African boy, and Weik's The Jazz Man, a book for older children.

Marcia Brown won a Caldecott Medal for her woodcuts in Once a Mouse . . ., a fable from India about a mouse who becomes bigger and bigger until he is reduced to size again when he acts too proud. *How, Hippo*, about a little hippo who meets a crocodile the first time he is away from his mother, is available on sound filmstrip, and her *All Butterflies*, an alphabet book, is also a visual puzzle—find the butterflies in the pictures.

Another alphabet book executed in woodcuts is Falls's *ABC Book*, an over-sized book that uses bright colors in unusual shades. The book is also available in paperback.

Ed Emberley used woodcuts to illustrate his wife Barbara's *One Wide River to Cross* and also their 1968 Caldecott winner, *Drummer Hoff*. Both are available as sound filmstrips. Gail Haley's 1971 Caldecott winner *A Story A Story* tells how all the Anansi or Spider tales came to earth. The story is available as a film and as a sound filmstrip.

Nonny Hogrogian, also a Caldecott winner, used woodcuts to illustrate Fontane's *Sir Ribbeck of Ribbeck of Havelland*. The nineteenth-century poem translated by Shub is about a man who made sure that the children of his village, rather than his miserly son, would have pears from his tree.

Still another Caldecott winner, Evaline Ness, uses woodcuts to illustrate the Scottish song *Kellyburn Braes* and *Josefina February*, a girl of Haiti who has a terrible choice to make. Pen-and-ink drawings and woodcuts are combined in *The Girl and the Goatherd or This and That and Thus and So*. The heroine must perform three impossible tasks for a witch. *Tom Tit Tot*, a version of Rumpelstiltskin, was a 1966 Caldecott Honor Book.

The nine Russian folk stories in *One Trick Too Many, Fox Stories from Russia*, are illustrated by Helen Siegl, who also illustrated the nine stories in Walker's *The Dancing Palm Tree and Other Nigerian Folktales* and White's retelling of *Aesop's Fables*.

The following books, illustrated in woodcuts by different illustrators, show a variety of styles. Eric Carle combines photos and woodcuts in his alphabet book, *All about Arthur*. Allstrom's *Songs Along the Way* contains sixteen psalms from the Old Testament and is illustrated in woodcuts by Mel Silverman. Harris's *Once upon a Totem, a Book of North American Indian Legends* is illustrated by John Frazer Mills. Pink, gold, and orange provide a background for Rocco Negri's woodcuts of Hawkins' retelling of *Androcles and the Lion*. Four colors are used in Pratt and Kula's *Magic Animals of Japan, Twelve Folktales of Japan*.

In Klemin's *The Art of Art for Children's Books: A Contemporary Survey*, the woodcuts of Fritz Kredel, Seong Moy, Evaline Ness, Leona Pierce, and Antonio Frasconi are shown. Woodcuts of Evaline Ness, Antonio Frasconi, Ed Emberley, Gil Miretil, and Barbara Smucker are shown in Cianciolo's *Illustrations in Children's Books*.

Wood engravings are used by Boris Artzybasheff in illustrating *Aesop's Fables* and by Philip Reed in the 1964 Caldecott honor book *Mother Goose and Nursery Rhymes*.

Aliki illustrated *Hush Little Baby, a Folk Lullaby* by painting on woodblocks. The grain of the wood shows through and complements the eighteenth century background.

Printmaking from linoleum blocks is another way students can make illustrations for books of their own. *Print-making without a Press* by Erickson and Sproul, available also in paperback, is an important addition to the collection because it shows how to make woodcuts and linoleum prints. Also consult Daniels and Turner's *Explaining Printmaking for Young People. Introducing Woodcuts* by Woods shows a selection of children's linoleum prints.

Directions for making linoleum block prints are also given in Ritson and Smith's *Creative Teaching of Art in the Elementary School* and chapter 10, "Printing," of Gaitshell's *Children and Their Art, Methods for the Elementary School.* Consult chapter 5 of Daniels's *Simple Printmaking with Children* and Voss's *Reinhold Craft and Hobby Book.* Zaidenberg's *Prints and How to Make Them, Graphic Art for the Beginner* gives information about making linoleum blocks on pages 62-68.

Bland's *History of Book Illustration* gives examples of linoleum engravings and drawings on linoleum in chapter 8, "The Twentieth Century." Marcia Brown uses dark green and white linoleum blocks to illustrate *Backbone of the King; the Story of Paka'a and His Son Ku,* a Hawaiian hero legend about how Ku restores his father to his position as advisor to the king. Brown also uses linoleum blocks to illustrate *Dick Whittington and His Cat,* an English folk tale of an orphan boy who became Lord Mayor of London with the help of a mouse-catching cat. Eric Carle uses linoleum cuts to illustrate *Feathered Ones and Furry,* a book of fifty animal poems by Aileen Fisher. Blue, red and black are used in Clement Hurd's illustrations of Valen's *Wingfin and Topple* about a fish who was afraid because his fins were too long.

Younger children who cannot safely use knives in cutting linoleum and wood blocks are able to make effective prints from vegetables, styrofoam, and cardboard. Chapter 10 of Gaitshell's *Children and Their Art, Methods for the Elementary School* describes potato and other vegetables for printing as well as stick printing. Consult Wirtenberg's *All-Around-the-House Art and Craft Book* for information on vegetable printing. Also see page 104 of Carlson's *Make It Yourself, Handicraft for Boys and Girls* and Kurth's *Print a Book.*

A book for leaders is Lidstone's *Design Activities for the Elementary Classroom.* Cardboard printing is shown on pages 32 and 33 and potato printing is shown on pages 24 and 25. Good black and white illustrations are given. Larger explicit drawings on how to make potato prints are given in *Painting, Printing and Modeling,* a book in the Color Crafts Series. Rockwell's *Printmaking* gives directions for using styrofoam prints. Children will enjoy making illustrations for books of their own using these techniques.

LITHOGRAPHY, A GRAPHIC TECHNIQUE.   Use the books of Ingri and Edgar d'Aulaire to introduce lithography to students. In the film *Children of the Northlights* the d'Aulaires talk about the processes of lithography and how their art has changed over the years. Ingri learned to imitate the lithographic process on acetate for producing colors.

Biographies written and illustrated by the d'Aulaires includes the 1939 Caldecott Medal winner, *Abraham Lincoln, Leif the Lucky, Benjamin Franklin,*

Columbus, George Washington and *Pocahontas*.

Other books by the d'Aulaires include *d'Aulaires' Book of Greek Myths*, *d'Aulaires' Trolls, Norse Gods and Giants, Foxie: The Singing Dog*, and *Magic Meadow*. The book used in the film to show how a book is made is *The Terrible Troll Bird*. In it in addition to seeing Edgar draw on a stone, viewers see a lithographic print being made from a stone.

Use Hirsch's *Printing from a Stone, the Story of Lithography*, as a companion book and source of information about the technique. Many encyclopedias also contain articles on lithography. Chapter 9 of Simon's *The Story of Printing* contains a print by Currier and Ives and shows a picture of Senefelder, the inventor of lithography, and tells of three methods of lithography—the planographic method, offset lithography, and the new photo offset. Chapter 1 of Heller's *Printmaking Today* is an excellent teacher reference. Illustrations and directions are given in Zaidenberg's *Prints and How to Make Them, Graphic Art for the Beginner* (pp. 115-32). Other sources to consult are Dean's *Printing, Tool of Freedom, The First Book of Printing* by the Epsteins, Holme's *Drawings to Live With*, Kay's *Printing*, and Rogers's *Painted Rock to Printed Page*. Read chapter 9, "Offset Lithography—A Growing Giant," in Simon's *The Story of Printing from Wood Blocks to Electronics*.

Some books utilizing lithography are Robert McCloskey's *One Morning in Maine* and *Make Way for Ducklings*, and *Rapunzel, a Story by the Brothers Grimm* illustrated by Felix Hoffman.

AN AWARENESS PROJECT.   Preschool and kindergarten pupils will enjoy being made aware that many authors and illustrators have used the same animals or objects in their books, and comparing the perceptions presented by different artists. A half-hour session in a library media center can provide this awareness.

The group of children arrives and sits in the story corner to hear the library media specialist read Gag's *Millions of Cats*. When the story is finished, the children seat themselves at tables. One picture book (containing an illustration of a cat) has been placed on the table in front of each chair. Three picture books are placed in the middle of the table. As each student finishes looking at his book, he or she can trade with a book from the middle. This way, all of the children, whatever their rate of "reading," will be happily occupied and the pictures of cats can be shared and compared. Sharing books is an important concept that can be developed in this manner. Using words to define the differences or similarities among the cats is a prime opportunity to develop verbal skills.

Millions of Cats was used in this example because, while there are not millions of cats in picture books, there are certainly hundreds of them! Dogs appear in books even more frequently than cats. Even stories not directly about a dog often have a dog frisking about in the pages. After the initial session when all children are allowed to participate, another shorter session can be devoted to sharing some elephants, chipmunks, mice, penguins, or other animals that appeared in the story told that day. These animals can be found in the grouping of books previously laid out on the tables. If the books read were part of a series such as Miller's Mousekin books, other books in the series should be spread out among the tables, to provide for recognition and identification of a specific character.

This project was used in a kindergarten class in a school of disadvantaged children. During the session when the children looked at the picture books, they were shown how to turn pages, exchange books with those in the middle of the table, and learn general good library habits.

IDENTIFYING SIMILAR STYLES, TECHNIQUES AND MEDIUMS IN ILLUSTRA-TIONS. Children as early as first and second grade can learn to identify illustrations created by the same artist. The following lists contain pairs of books illustrated by the same person in which the artist used the same style and technique. The activity to be used with these books is best carried out in a library media center or other room with tables. Place three or four books from the list on a table with ten other books that are not on the list. One book from each matching pair is given to a student whose task is to match the book in hand with a book from the table. Each table will contain three or four books from the list. The books are divided into table groups to avoid the congestion that would result from all of the books being on one table.

Every effort was made to choose books that were of different shapes and about different characters so that the shape and characters would not give the children too many clues. Starred illustrators indicate the books that have the same format and/or characters. These books may be given to children who might otherwise be unable to match their book with one from the table. Teachers of first grade students might use the starred illustrators as a base for the project. To make the project easier, the first grade teachers can choose other illustrators from the list and find books from the same series so the format and characters are the same.

The teacher should choose the pages that the students are to compare. A marker may be placed in the book given to the student. Books placed on the table may be opened to the pages so students cannot read the name of the illustrator from the title page.

After the students have matched their books, discuss why they were able to do so. Some ideas that will surface are color, art technique, style, design, and format.

BOOKS ILLUSTRATED BY ONE PERSON THAT HAVE SIMILAR STYLES AND TECHNIQUES.

ADAMS, ADRIENNE	*Jorinda and Joringel*
	Woggle of Witches
ALEXANDER, MARTHA*	*Blackboard Bear*
	And My Mean Old Mother Will Be Sorry, Blackboard Bear
ANDERSON, C.W.	*Billy and Blaze*
	The Crooked Colt

ANGLUND, JOAN WALSH	A Friend Is Someone Who Likes You
	In a Pumpkin Shell
ANNO, MITSUMASA	Topsy-Turvies
	Upside-Downers
ARDIZZONE, EDWARD*	Little Tim and the Brave Sea
	Captain
	Tim All Alone
ARUEGO, JOSE	Look What I Can Do
	What Is Pink? (Rosetti)
AULAIRE D', INGRI & EDGAR	Don't Count Your Chicks
	Ola
BEMELMANS, LUDWIG	Madeline's Rescue
	Parsley
BRIGHT, ROBERT*	Georgie
	Georgie's Halloween
BROOKE, LESLIE	Johnny Crow's Garden
	Johnny Crow's Party
BROWN, MARCIA	How, Hippo
	Once a Mouse . . .
BRUNHOFF, JEAN DE*	Babar and Father Christmas
	The Story of Babar
BURTON, VIRGINIA LEE	Katy and the Big Snow
	Mike Mulligan and His Steam Shovel
CALDECOTT, RANDOLPH	Queen of Hearts
	Sing a Song for Sixpence
CARIGIET, ALOIS	A Bell for Ursli (Chonz)
	Florina and the Wild Bird (Chonz)
CHARLOT, JEAN	Timid Ghost (Brenner)
	Two Little Trains (Brown)
DENNIS, WESLEY*	Flip
	Flip and the Cows
DUVOISIN, ROGER	Petunia
	Veronica
EICHENBERG, FRITZ	Ape in a Cape
	Dancing in the Moon
ETS, MARIE HALL	Another Day
	In the Forest
FLACK, MARJORIE*	Angus and the Cat
	Angus and the Ducks
FRANÇOISE	Chouchou
	Noel for Jeanne Marie
FREEMAN, DON	Norman the Doorman

	Pet of the Met (Freeman, Don & Lydia)
GAG, WANDA	*Millions of Cats*
	Snow White and the Seven Dwarfs
CALDONE, PAUL	*The Little Red Hen*
	The Three Little Pigs
GEISEL, THEODORE SEUSS	*Five Hundred Hats of Bartholomew Cubbins*
	Green Eggs and Ham
GOODALL, JOHN*	*Adventures of Paddy Pork*
	Ballooning Adventures of Paddy Pork
GRAMATKY, HARDIE	*Bolivar*
	Little Toot
HUTCHINS, PAT	*Rosie's Walk*
	The Surprise Party
IPCAR, DAHLOV	*Brown Cow Farm*
	I Like Animals
JOHNSON, CROCKETT	*Harold and the Purple Crayon*
	Mickey's Magnet (Branley)
KAHL, VIRGINIA	*The Duchess Bakes a Cake*
	Maxie
KELLOGG, STEVEN	*Can I Keep Him?*
	Much Bigger Than Martin
LAWSON, ROBERT	*Ben and Me*
	Ferdinand (Leaf)
LENSKI, LOIS	*Little Auto*
	I Like Winter
MCDERMOTT, GERALD	*Anansi the Spider*
	Arrow to the Sun
MAYER, MERCER*	*Frog Goes to Dinner*
	Frog, Where Are You?
MILLER, EDNA	*Duck Duck*
	Mousekin's Golden House
MONTRESOR, BENI	*Cinderella*
	May I Bring a Friend?
NEWBERRY, CLARE T.	*Barkis*
	Kittens' ABC
PIATTI, CELESTINO	*Celestino Piatti's ABC*
	Happy Owls
POLITI, LEO	*Moy Moy*
	Song of the Swallows

Rey, H.A.	Curious George
	Pretzel (Rey, Margaret)
Rey, H. A.	Curious George Rides a Bike
	Katy No-Pocket (Emmy Payne)
Rockwell, Ann	The Awful Mess
	Cunningham's Rooster
Rojankovsky, Feodor	Frog Went A-courtin' (Langstaff)
	Over in the Meadow (Langstaff)
Rounds, Glenn	Blind Colt
	Casey Jones
Sasek, M.*	This Is London
	This is Paris
Steig, William	Amos and Boris
	Sylvester and the Magic Pebble
Tudor, Tasha	A Is for ANNABELLE
	1 Is One
Turkle, Brinton*	Adventures of Obadiah
	Obadiah the Bold
Ungerer, Tomi	One, Two, Where's My Shoe?
	Snail, Where Are You?
Waber, Barbara	An Anteater Named Arthur
	Lovable Lyle
Ward, Lynd	The Biggest Bear
	The Silver Pony
Wildsmith, Brian	Brian Wildsmith's ABC
	Brian Wildsmith's Wild Animals
Yashima, Taro	Crow Boy
	Umbrella

DIFFERENT STYLES OR TECHNIQUES USED BY ONE ILLUSTRATOR.   Illustrators sometimes vary their style for several reasons. Changes may be based on: (1) The technique or medium with which the artist is working, (2) the nature of the subject matter of the story and the mood to be projected, (3) the author and series with which the illustrator is working, (4) whether the artist is working alone or with another artist, (5) the growth and expansion as a creative artist of the illustrator through the years, and (6) desire by the artist to experiment.

Over forty pairs of books illustrated by one person were chosen because the books represent the different styles or mediums of one artist.

This project can be carried out in several ways. The pairs of books can be laid out together and individual class members may choose an illustrator based on the books or on their familiarity with the illustrator. After examining the books, students can list differences in style and medium with possible explanations for the differences. Group sharing is an important culminating project. Illustrations can be shared (in a smallish group) by holding them up and giving explanations, or in a larger one, by using the opaque projector.

In one case the only difference in the illustration is the addition of color, as in the books illustrated by Anita Lobel; both books were illustrated in pen and ink. Sometimes the differences result from the use of different mediums: Arnold Lobol illustrated one book in pen and ink and the other with pencil drawjngs; Shulevitz used pen and ink for one and water color for another. Marcia Brown, Roger Duvoisin, Ellen Raskin, and Maurice Sendak utilize a variety of styles or mediums in their books. Sendak seems to create different illustrations for the various authors with styles of whom he works: Joslin, Krauss, Minarik, Udry, and himself. Likewise, the illustrations of Duvoisin vary as he illustrated for Fatio, Tresselt, and himself.

This assignment takes individual differences into account. Some students may be able only to match the books and give one or two reasons to account for the differences. Others may wish to explore all of the books by an illustrator and identify all of the styles and mediums as well as biographies of the illustrators. To find other books students can look for illustrators in the card catalog, the *Children's Catalog,* and in the illustrator index, *Illustrators of Children's Boos* (in four volumes) edited by Mahony, Miller, and Kingman. Other books students can examine to discover art techniques are listed in this chapter.

BOOKS BY THE SAME ILLUSTRATOR WITH DIFFERENT STYLES OR TECHNIQUES

BRANDENBERG, ALIKI	*June 7* *The Story of Johnny Appleseed*
BRIGGS, RAYMOND	*Father Christmas* *Mother Goose Treasury*
BROWN, MARCIA	*Cinderella* *Once a Mouse* *Felice* *Stone Soup*
BURKERT, NANCY	*Scroobilous Pip* (Lear) *Snow White and the Seven Dwarfs* (Grimm)
CARLE, ERIC	*All About Arthur* *Do You Want to Be My Friend?* *Feathered Ones and Furry* (Fisher) *The Hungry Caterpillar*
CHARLIP, REMY	*Mother Mother I Feel Sick* (Charlip and Supree) *Thirteen*

COONEY, BARBARA	*Chanticleer and the Fox* (Chaucer)
	Wynken, Blynken and Nod (Field)
DE PAOLA, TOMI	*Charlie Needs a Cloak*
	Strega Nona
DILLON, LEO AND DIANNE	*The Hundred Penny Box* (Mathis)
	Why Mosquitos Buzz in People's Ears (Aardema)
DOMANSKA, JANINA	*Look There Is a Turtle Flying What Do You See?*
	If All the Seas Were One Sea
	Whizz (Lear)
DU BOIS, WILLIAM	*Lion*
	Otto in Texas
DUVOISIN, ROGER	*A for the Ark*
	Happy Lion
EMBERLEY, ED	*The Parade Book*
	Simon's Song (Emberley, Barbara)
GALDONE, PAUL	*Anatole* (Titus)
	Hereafter This (Jacobs)
HOGROGIAN, NONNY	*Apples*
	The Renouned History of Little Red Riding Hood
HUTCHINS, PAT	*Changes Changes*
	Surprise Party
KEATS, EZRA JACK	*The King's Fountain* (Alexander)
	Snowy Day
LENT, BLAIR	*The Wave* (Hodges)
	Why the Sun and the Moon Live in the Sky
LIONNI, LEO	*Inch by Inch*
	Pezzettino
LOBEL, ANITA	*Peter Penny's Dance* (Quinn-Harkin)
	Troll Music
LOBEL, ARNOLD	*Good Ethan* (Fox)
	Hildilid's Night (Ryan)
MCCLOSKEY, ROBERT	*Make Way for Ducklings*
	One Morning in Maine
MAYER, MERCER	*A Boy, A Dog and A Frog*
	Everyone Knows What a Dragon Looks Like (Williams)
MILHOUS, KATHARINE	*Appolonia's Valentine*
	Egg Tree

NESS, EVALINE	*Don't You Remember?* (Clifton) *Josefina February*
QUACKENBUSH, ROBERT	*She'll Be Comin' Round the Mountain* *Six Silver Spoons* (Lowrey)
RASKIN, ELLEN	*Ghost in a Four Room Apartment* *Who, Said Sue, Said Who*
SENDAK, MAURICE	*Charlotte and the White Horse* (Krauss) *A Hole Is to Dig* (Krauss)
SENDAK, MAURICE	*Little Bear* (Minarik) *Where the Wild Things Are*
SHIMIN, SYMEON	*Listen Rabbit!* (Fisher) *One Small Blue Bead* (Schweitzer)
SHULEVITZ, URI	*Dawn* *The Magician*
TUDOR, TASHA	*Around the Year* *Corgiville Fair*
TURKLE, BRINTON	*Adventures of Obadiah* *Boy Who Didn't Believe in Spring* (Clifton)
UNGERER, TOMI	*The Hat* *That Pest Jonathan* (Cole)
UNGERER, TOMI	*Crictor* *The Mellops*
WABER, BERNARD	*A Firefly Named Torchy* *Lovable Lyle*
WATSON, WENDY	*Father Fox's Pennyrhymes* (Watson, Clyde) *Tom Fox and the Apple Pie* (Watson, Clyde)
WEISGARD, LEONARD	*The Rabbit Story* (Tresselt) *When I Go to the Moon* (Lewis)
WIESE, KURT	*Fish in the Air* *The Thief in the Attic*
WILLIAMS, GARTH	*Bedtime for Frances* (Hoban) *Chicken Book*
ZEMACH, MARGOT	*Mommy Buy Me a China Doll* (Zemach, Harve) *Nail Soup* (Zemach, Harve)

DIFFERENT ARTISTIC TREATMENTS OF SIMILAR SUBJECTS.   John Langstaff, narrating the film *The Lively Art of Picture Books*, talked about how artists view and express the same objects in different ways. Examples relating to cats, towns, lions, and trees were given. Have the students, after viewing the film, compare books on those subjects as listed in the film, and then have them find others. Cited in the film were pictures of four cat books by Marcia Brown: *Dick Whittington and His Cat*, *Felice*, *Once a Mouse . . .*, and *Puss in Boots*. The styles and techniques of each differs from the others. Other cat books include Caldecott's *Hey Diddle Diddle Picture Book*, *Minou* by Francoise, *Millions of Cats* by Gag, Langstaff's *Frog Went a-Courtin'* illustrated by Rojankovsky, Lipkind's *The Two Reds* illustrated by Mordvinoff, Potter's *The Tale of Peter Rabbit*, and *I Know a Lot of Things* by the Rands. It is easy to find pictures of cats in picture books. First graders can do this. The section in the film about lions can be discussed along with the section about cats since lions are really big cats! Books about lions included are Brooke's *Johnny Crow's Garden*, Coatsworth's *The Peaceable Kingdom* illustrated by Eichenbert, Daugherty's *Andy and the Lion*, Du Bois's *Lion*, Fatio's *Happy Lion* illustrated by Duvoisin, Bruno Munari's *Zoo*, and Ungerer's *Crictor*.

Books showing different towns in *The Lively Art of Picture Books* are Ardizzone's *Little Tim and the Brave Sea Captain*, the d'Aulaire's *Ola*, Bemelmans's *Madeline's Rescue*, Burton's *The Little House*, Chonz's *A Bell for Ursli* illustrated by Carigiet, Frasconi's *See and Say*, Harris's *Little Boy Brown* illustrated by Francois, Politi's *Saint Francis and the Animals*, Rey's *Curious George Gets a Job*, Robbins's *Baboushka and the Three Kings* illustrated by Sidjakov, Sasek's *This Is Paris*, and Spier's *The Fox Went Out on a Chilly Night*.

Books showing various perceptions of trees include Fitch's *A Book About God* illustrated by Weisgard, Hoffman's *Rapunzel*, Keats's *Snowy Day*, Leaf's *The Story of Ferdinand* illustrated by Lawson, Lenski's *The Little Farm*, Lionni's *Inch by Inch*, Ness's *All in the Morning Early* illustrated by Sorche Nic Leodhas, Udry's *A Tree Is Nice* illustrated by Simont, and Yashima's *The Village Tree*.

The sound filmstrip *Enjoying Illustrations* includes among several subjects treated differently by illustrators—the Trojan Horse and Abraham Lincoln.

THE SUN—ILLUSTRATED BY MANY.   Instead of having students look up the books on cats, towns, lions, and trees after viewing the film *The Lively Art of Picture Books*, have students find different treatments of other subjects such as the sun and the moon.

There are many ways of drawing the sun. Small children often draw a circle with straight lines radiating from it all around. This type of sun has been drawn by Eric Carle in *The Tiny Seed*, Remy Charlip in *Where is Everybody?*, and by Max Velthuijs, one of Holland's best known painters. Velthuijs's *The Wolf and the Kid* was written by Domjan and is about Janco, the goatherd, who saved a kid from the wolf by playing his flute. More sophisticated rays emit from the sun in Domanska's *I Saw a Ship a-Sailing*.

In contrast, the sun is portrayed in eight different ways by Rubin in *Three by Three* by Kruss. Colors for the sun include bright yellow, turquoise, red, and fuchsia. In Merriam's *Funny Town*, Ness colored the sun green in a land where people slept by day and played at night, where snow and the sun were green and grass was pink and the people living there think *we* are funny. Ness illustrated the sun pink, orange, and yellow in *Do You Have the Time Lydia?*, and the same colors appear for the sun in Andersen's *The Snow Queen*, adapted by Lewis and illustrated by Bagdonovich.

In *Borka, The Adventures of a Goose with No Feathers*, Burningham created a yellow blob of a sun. Touches of orange and blue accent the book. Borka finally found a garden with so many birds that she wouldn't look conspicuous in her grey woolen jersey. Another Burningham sun appears in *Cannonball Simp*. The sun has rings around it in Anderson's *Mr. Biddle and the Birds*. Aichinger illustrated a yellow sun with orange rings around it in Bulla's *Jonah and the Great Fish*. Another book by Bulla is *What Makes a Shadow*, a scientific book illustrated by Adrienne Adams, and still another sun by Adams appears in Grimm's *Jorinda and Joringel*.

In *A Green Christmas* by Kroeber, Larrecq expresses the children's fear that Santa won't be able to come to sunny California as he did to snowy Colorado. The effect of the sun-burnt grass and Santa flying over the sun are fascinating.

Sometimes a change in medium changes illustration. John Hawkinson created an orange and yellow sun via watercolors in *Paint a Rainbow*. An unusual line drawing of the sun is illustrated by Gekiere in Bradbury's *Switch On the Night*, a story about a boy who didn't like night. A new twist to an old tale features the sun in woodcuts and etchings by Kaplan in Abish's *Around the House that Jack Built*, which begins "This is the sun that shines on the house that Jack built."

The following books can be added to a group of books showing suns: Bednorik's *Elefish*, Gordon's illustrations of MacBeth's *Jonah and the Lord*, Holling's *Paddle-to-the-Sea*, Montresor's *House of Flowers, House of Stars*, Levin's illustrations in Thaler's *The Smiling Book*, illustrations by Rounds in Freshet's *Lizard Lying in the Snow*, *All on a May Morning* written by Willard and illustrated by the Shekerjians, and Stone's illustrations of Simon's *A Tree for Me*.

Two stories about the sun are Fregosi's *Sun Grumble* and Wiesner's *The Constant Little Mouse*. A test of strength is the subject of the La Fontaine fable illustrated by Brian Wildsmith, *The North Wind and the Sun*, in which the sun and wind bet each other that they can get a traveler to take off his coat. The sun achieves through warmth and gentleness what the wind cannot achieve through strength and bluster. In the Mexican folktale *The Billy Goat in the Chile Patch*, a burro, dog, and cock couldn't get the goat to move, but a lowly ant was able to—he bit the goat and off it went. The sun illustrations in these books about strength can be compared.

HOW AND WHY STORIES ABOUT THE SUN AND THE MOON. Belting's *The Sun Is a Golden Earring* includes folk sayings about the wind, weather, rainbows, and storms. Students might like to make their own book jacket for this book.

"Why the Sun and the Moon Live in the Sky" appears in Arnott's *African Myths and Legends* (pp. 133-34) and in Leach's *How the People Sang the Moun-*

tains Up (pp. 20-21). Have students illustrate the story, then show them Blair Lent's illustrations in the picture book of the same title that was adapted by Dayrell. Display the illustrations with the book jacket on a bulletin board or with the book in a showcase. According to the story, water never came to visit sun, and his wife moon, because sun's house wasn't big enough. When sun built a new house, he invited water who flowed in and brought all the fish and life within him and forced sun and moon up into the sky where they are today.

Why the Sun Was Late was written by Elkin and illustrated by Snyder, and appears in book and sound filmstrip format. The sun was late because of problems caused by the fly. As punishment, the fly can now only say "buzz." The sun didn't come out for three days in Ginsburg's *How the Sun Was Brought Back to the Sky*, a Slovenian tale illustrated by Aruego and Dewey, because its face had to be cleaned before it could shine on the animals.

There are many stories explaining the marks on the moon. According to Lifton's story *The Rice-Cake Rabbit*, there is a warrior rabbit up there who is "Samurai of the Moon" because rabbits can't be Samurai on earth.

Wiesner's *Moon Stories* includes three stories. According to "Star Cookies," a tale that traveled from India via Finland to Czechoslovakia, the moon is a thoughtful little girl who shares her delicious cookies with Mother Sky. "The Tidy King" is an adaptation of a Persian tale in which the king collected books but had difficulty learning the letters of the alphabet. When the king noticed that the moon was covered with smudges he offered 1,000 gold pieces to anyone who could clean it. Boxes were piled up but did not reach the moon so the cleaner wanted to remove the bottom box and place it on top. In "Elephant and the Moon" a London astronomer, Dr. Pompus Bombastus, said he saw an elephant on the moon but it was really his assistant's pet mouse who was lost in the telescope.

An Indian girl, Lapowinsa, said the moon was ugly because of the marks on its face so she was taken away into the sky by a rainbow. Her brother Lupan shot arrows into the sky and made a chain ladder of the arrows and climbed up to rescue her. This story is *The Angry Moon* by Sleator, and Blair Lent won the Caldecott Medal for his illustrations. Compare the moon in this book with Lent's illustrations in Dayrell's *Why the Sun and Moon Live in the Sky*, which was a Caldecott honor book.

Withers's retelling of *Painting the Moon, a Folktale of Estonia*, is about how the devil tried to cover the moon with pitch because it made too much light for him to play his tricks at night. The story also appears on pages 7 to 16 of *The Moon Painters and Other Estonian Folk Tales* by Maas.

"Why the Moon Has Scars on Her Face," pages 62 to 65 of Belting's *The Earth Is on a Fish's Back* comes from India. Ashamed because she was so fair-skinned, the moon had a woman tattoo her face with a tortoise, a hare, a scorpion and two eggs. This is an excellent story for students to illustrate. A Tinguian version from the Philippines, called "Why There Are Shadows on the Moon," (on page 14 of Sechrist's *Once in the First Times*) explains that the sun was angry at the moon and threw sand in its face, leaving dark places. "Why There Is a Man in the Moon" is on pages 3 to 5 of Jablow's *Man in the Moon*.

"Why the Moon's Face Is Smutty" appears on pages 545 and 546 of *The Complete Tales of Uncle Remus* by Harris, and says that the moon tripped over a bag of charcoal as it was changing and still shows signs of that incident on his face.

Ungerer's *Moon Man* enviously watched people until he caught the tail of a fiery comet to come to earth and be with them. Instead he crashed to earth and was put in jail, but escaped because when the moon became thin, so did he, and he squeezed through the bars and escaped.

Two legends about the moon's size are "Why the Moon Wanes" and "Why the Moon Changes Size." The first is found (pp. 83–88) in Reed's *The Talkative Beasts* and is a Hindu story from India. In "Why the Moon Wanes," Parvati was married to Siva, the god of life and death. She wanted a child desperately and finally got one, but due to a curse the child Gamesha was given an elephant's head, threw his tusk at the moon, pierced it, and it became dark. Now the moon has to go through a process of getting smaller and larger. "Why the Moon Changes" appears on pages 94 to 98 of Palmer's *Why the North Star Stands Still and Other Indian Legends*. The sun grew tired so his son took over for him in the winter. The boy's youthful vitality carries him across the sky faster than his father moves, so that is why winter days are shorter. In *Moon Mouse* by Hall, Arthur thought the moon was cheese and that it became only a sliver because he ate some of it.

On pages 103 to 109 of Cathon and Schmidt's *Perhaps and Perchance*, we learn that when the sun went too quickly across the world, Ma-ui caught the sixteen legs of the sun in a noose and beat it until the sun promised to go slower. Winter is a compromise. Illustrating this story should produce some unusual pictures. A similar story appears in picture book format as *Legs of the Moon* by Jacobs. In this Hawaiian tale, the red-bearded people held the legs of the moon to make the night longer.

"How the Moon and Stars Came to Be" appears on pages 12 and 13 of Sechrist's *Once in the First Times*. This story from the Philippines tells how the woman hung her pearls on the sky while she was pounding rice. When she repeatedly struck the sky while pounding, the sky rose higher and higher to avoid the blows. The woman's pearls became the stars and her comb the moon.

"Why the Sun Is Brighter Than the Moon" is an American Indian tale found on pages 32 and 34 of Belting's *The Earth Is on a Fish's Back*. The sun wears a bright feather cloak made for a boy by his grandmother. An Ojibwa tale called "Why There Is Both Day and Night" appears in the same book. Owl and rabbit disagreed about whether or not there was enough light in the world. Also in Belting is the Kutenai Indian story from the Western United States called "How It Came About That There Is a Sun and a Moon." Animals took turns being the sun, but they weren't effective. Finally Elder Brother became the sun and Younger Brother became the moon.

Stories from collections about the sun and moon can be illustrated by students. Stories in picture books about the sun and moon or containing the sun and moon can be compared with each other in visual presentation of the same object.

Three farmers argued about everything in Levitin's noodle picture book,

Who Owns the Moon? The village teacher decided that each farmer would own it two days of the week but on Sunday it would belong to everyone. During the week each man sat home and admired his moon, but on Sunday they got together and argued again.

THE MOON — ILLUSTRATED BY MANY.   A white moon appears in Rockwell and Harlow's *Toad*. Witches make shadows in front of the moon illustrated by Adrienne Adams in Anderson's *The Halloween Party*. Adams created another moon in her own book, *A Woggle of Witches*. Another moon appears in her *Snow White and Rose Red* by Grimm. Students can compare the several moons drawn by one artist. The sun and the moon appear in Wildsmith's *What the Moon Saw*. Read Thurber's *Many Moons* to children and have them illustrate the story, before showing them Louis Slobodkin's Caldecott Medal-winning illustrations, about the spoiled princess Lenore who wanted to have the moon.

An orange moon against blue appears in Marc Brown's illustrations for Clymer's *Four Corners of the Sky: Poems, Chants and Oratory*. Blue and white illustrations by Cooney illustrate Field's poem *Wynken, Blynken and Nod*, which is also available on sound filmstrip. Brown's *Goodnight Moon* with illustrations by Garth Williams is told in verse.

Compare the moon in two books illustrated by Uri Shulevitz, *Oh What a Noise!* and *Soldier and Tsar in the Forest*. The second story was translated by Lourie. The first book is about putting off bedtime and the second is a Russian folk tale about a king who meets a runaway soldier who saves the king's life and is pardoned.

Hemling's *What's in the Dark?* can be used with Shulevitz's *Oh What a Noise!* and Bradbury's *Switch on the Night*.

Little John, retold from a nineteenth-century German story, is about a moon that peered through the window and laughed so hard she started to cry. There are several pages without words so the story can be used for verbal expression.

Pencil drawings shaded with blue were used in *Calendar Moon*, a 1963 Caldecott honor book, illustrated by Bryson and edited by Belting. Names for the months are taken from myths and legends. A Delaware Indian designation is "This-is-the-moon-when-the-juice-drips-from-the-trees." From Central Africa comes "The-month-in-which-men-throw-away-their-hoes," and from Northern Siberia "This-is-the-mosquito-month." Students can make up their own names for the months and illustrate them. The illustrations can be displayed on a bulletin board or compiled by students into a book of their own.

Please refer to the section of the chapter on "Enjoying Poetry" called "Introducing Books or Groups of Books with Poems" for poems about the moon.

DIFFERENT STYLES, TECHNIQUES, OR MEDIUMS WITHIN A SINGLE BOOK.   An artist does not always use the same medium or style of illustration within one book. Using the following as examples, students can find other picture books which present different styles or mediums within the same book.

Eric Carle used colored photographs and black wood block prints to illustrate *All about Arthur*. Both McKee and DuBois use line drawings without color in their books that have colored illustrations—*Mr. Benn-Red Knight* and *Lion*. In *Lazy Bear*, Brian Wildsmith includes a colorful grassy area that is different in style and color from the animal illustrations.

Each of the thirteen dragons in *The Fourteenth Dragon* by Seidelman and Mintonye are illustrated by a different person. The fourteenth dragon is to be illustrated by the reader.

Each page in Keeping's colorful *Joseph's Yard* seems to be a different experience, as style and medium varies. The story is about a boy who traded with a junk man for a plant. One year he picked it too soon and it died. The next year he protected it from birds, insects, and cats by covering it with his coat but it died from lack of sun and rain.

In *Design Is a Dandelion* by Lovoos, eleven different styles of trees are pictured.

Aiken's *Cats and Bats and Things with Wings* includes sixteen poems, each illustrated in a different medium. There are line drawings, water color, pencil, ink blots, colored ink, and pen and ink. This book would be useful in acquainting students with different mediums. Differences from page to page are found in famous paintings in MacAgy's *Going for a Walk with a Line, A Step into the World of Modern Art*.

The books in the Animal Art Anthology series show a variety of artistic interpretations of one animal. The stories and poems are illustrated so that many examples can be found in one book. Shaw's *Fox Book* presents fourteen artists, including Shimin, Duvoisin, Galdone, Mitshuhasi, and Grifalconi, working in eight different mediums, and can be used in several ways. Students can use the book simply for reveling in enjoyment of fox stories, or to identify the work of a particular artist or a specific medium, or to compare illustrations executed in the same medium. Other books about foxes can be compared. (A list of books about foxes, mice, and owls are included in the first chapter.) Other Shaw books in the same series are *The Bird Book, The Cat Book, The Frog Book, The Mouse Book,* and *The Owl Book*.

Many different art styles are included in the book and filmstrip of Spilka's *Paint All Kinds of Pictures*. Illustrations using several types of mediums are included in Barton's book and filmstrip, *A Picture Has a Special Look*.

COMPARING DIFFERENT ILLUSTRATIONS FOR ONE STORY.   Students can compare how two artists perceived the same story or characters. Lindgren's *Pippi Longstocking* was illustrated by Glanzman and by Kennedy. Frances the badger by Hoban was illustrated by Garth Williams in *Bedtime for Frances* and by Lillian Hoban in *Bread and Jam for Frances* and the other books in the series. Three illustrators of *Snow White and the Seven Dwarfs* have already been mentioned in this chapter in the section on "Books about White."

A variety of illustrators have interpreted the poems of Edward Lear. Check the section of the chapter on "Enjoying Poetry," called "The Nonsense of Lear." Over a hundred different artists and their interpretations of *Alice in Wonderland* are represented in *The Illustrators of Alice*, edited by Graham. Alice, as seen by seventeen different illustrators, including two filmmakers, is located in black and white plates in Doyle's *Who's Who in Children's Literature* following page 20. The article on "Alice" in Fisher's *Who's Who in Children's Books* shows six different book illustrations and one 1966 movie character. *Alice's Adventures under Ground, a Facsimile of the Original Lewis Carroll Manuscript* is a photo-reproduction of a manuscript handwritten and illustrated by Dodgson. The original manuscript was purchased for $50,000 and given to the British Museum in 1948. Charles Dodgson originally wrote the story for Alice Liddell, the daughter of a colleague, with no intention of publishing it, and used the pseudonym "Lewis Carroll" when it was published.

PROJECTS COMPARING ILLUSTRATIONS.   Compare the illustrations by Roger Duvoisin in the Tresselt books *The Frog in the Well* and *Hide and Seek Fog*, Fatio's *Happy Lion* books, Holl's *The Rain Puddle*, and Zolotow's *In My Garden* with books that he wrote himself such as *Day and Night, Spring Snow, Veronica,* and *Petunia.*

Compare the horses drawn by Wesley Dennis for Marguerite Henry's *Black Gold, Stormy,* and *White Stallion of Lipizza* with other horses Dennis drew for the Viking edition of Steinbeck's *Red Pony,* the World edition of Sewell's *Black Beauty,* Daly's *Ginger Horse,* and Dennis's own stories about *Flip, Flip and the Cows,* and *Flip and the Morning.* Or compare the illustrations of horses by Dennis with those of Anderson in C. W. Anderson's *Complete Book of Horses and Horsemanship, Twenty Gallant Horses,* and the books about *Billy and Blaze.*

Compare the illustrations of Helen Borten in her own books *Do You See What I See?* and *Do You Move as I Do?* with the ones she illustrated for Franklyn Branley in *The Moon Seems to Change* and *What Makes Day and Night.*

Compare John Burningham's illustrations in the Random edition of Fleming's *Chitty-Chitty-Bang-Bang* with those in the easy book *Mr. Gumpy's Outing,* which Burningham wrote himself.

Compare the illustrations by Warren Chappell in Richter's story, *Light in the Forest* (Knopf edition) with his illustrations in *The Nutcracker* and *The Magic Flute.*

ART ALTERNATIVES TO BOOK REPORTS.   Art projects provide good alternatives to book reports. Students can make book jackets, bookmarkers, dioramas, murals, mobiles, mosaics, posters, and models of book characters. Illustrations of projects are provided on pages 610–25, "Creative Reporting," of Huck and Young's *Children's Literature in the Elementary School.* More ideas appear in chapter 5, "Experiencing Literature Orally and through Writing," in Whitehead's *Children's Literature: Strategies for Teaching.*

For suggestions on dioramas, see pages 77 and 78 in *Meaning in Crafts* by Mattil. Models can be made in plaster, paper sculpture, papier-maché, or bread dough. Step-by-step directions for *Creating with Plaster* are given by Meilach in a book by that name. Also consult Slade's *Modeling in Clay, Plaster, and Papier-Maché.* Numerous sources for bread dough and papier-maché will be given in following sections.

Directions for making a medieval castle and people are given on pages 50 to 63 of Peterson's *Making Toys with Plywood*. The castle could be used with DeAngeli's *Door in the Wall*. Giblin's *The Scarecrow Book* includes the directions for making one.

Helfman's *Making Pictures Move* gives instructions for nine animated projects including a peep show, panorama from a shoebox, and flip book. Two sources for information on mobiles are Lynch's *How to Make Mobiles* and Shinagawa's *Charm in Motion: A Collection of Mobiles*. Leaders can obtain excellent patterns from the second book. The first book is intended for students of junior high age and up, and includes balance, materials, and tools. Cardboard, metal, and glass mobiles are shown. Patterns as well as ideas for children making their own are given. Although specific suggestions are not given for making mobiles based on scenes from children's books, scenes can easily be placed on mobile parts. Check Jensen's *Play with Paper* for information on paper mobiles.

MAKING MURALS AND MOSAICS.   Three books provide basic information for making murals. Randall's *Murals for Schools, Sharing Creative Expression* tells about murals in paper sculpture, newspaper, corrugated paper, relief, mosaic, and collage. Chapter 2, "Creating the School Mural," includes choosing a subject, planning, arranging committees, making the mural, and storage. Chapter 3, "Materials to Use," suggests tempera, chalk, crayon, poster paints, watercolors, and cleaners. Chapter 5, "Murals and the Three R's," gives suggestions for using murals in the curriculum. A bibliography, although dated, includes articles from *Arts and Activities* and many from *School Arts* magazines.

Children Make Murals and Sculpture by Rosenberg and Wittenberg includes colored photos of classroom and community projects. Consult pages 41-55 for school projects. Paper and cloth murals are covered.

Mural Manual: How to Paint Murals for the Classroom, Community Center and Street Corner by Rogovin et al. has explicit directions for painting murals on public buildings and ideas for getting permission, insurance, documentation, dedication, and copyright. More useful to schools is chapter 10, "The Classroom Mural" (pp. 55-66); chapter 11, "How to Do Portable Mural Panels," (pp. 67-74); and chapter 12, "How to Do a Mural on Cloth," (pp. 75-77). Information on the mural movement in the United States and Mexico is appended.

Murals can be a group project resulting from one or several books read by and to the class. The mural can be as simple as depicting Gag's *Millions of Cats* or a selection of Japanese folklore. Tombert's *The Little Fox Goes to the End of the World* is especially suitable for making a mural in primary grades. In the story a little fox tells her mother all the places she plans to go and all the adventures she will encounter. Ten groups of children can each work on drawing one of the adventures such as the little fox's encounters with bears, lions, the desert, winds, and one-eyed cats.

Mosaics can be used in creating murals or in creating smaller scenes. Information on planning, materials, subjects, sketches, and application are included in Seidelman's and Mintonye's *Creating Mosaics*. A glossary and background information are features of Currier's *Art of Mosaics*. Pebble sculpture is included in Kohn's *Beachcomber's Book* and Chernoff's *Pebbles and Pods*. The shapes of pebbles in Lionni's *On My Beach Are Many Pebbles* stress variety in pebbles. Ten kinds of mosaics are included in Meyer's *One Hundred Fifty Techniques in Art* (pp. 44–49). Tools and materials are included in McFee's *Preparation for Art*.

Rogowski's *Making American Folk Art Dolls* contains directions for making figures from wire, corn husks, nuts and seeds, wishbones, gourds, spools, yarn, socks, wood, styrofoam, soap, eggshells, bread dough, dried fruit, leather, papier-mâché, and felt. Patterns for clothing are given as well as directions for making the dolls themselves. Heady's *Make Your Own Dolls* offers suggestions for materials and techniques for making dolls from socks, flowers, clothespins, chalk, bottles, sticks, grass, bones, corncobs, soap, spools, pipe cleaners, yarn, cornhusks, bread, magazines, and rags. These dolls can be used in displays and dioramas to represent book characters. Stories about dolls appear in the chapter on "Introducing Books in All Kinds of Ways."

BREAD DOUGH BOOK FIGURES.   Both Rogowski's and Heady's books contain information on making dolls from bread dough. Chapter 13 in Rogowski's book is called "Bread Dough Characters." Sommer's *The Bread Dough Craft Book* includes recipes and ideas for molding dollhouses, furniture, games, and toys. Chernoff's *Clay-Dough-Play-Dough* has recipes and ideas for animals, robots, snakes, snails, Easter eggs, mobiles, and stained glass windows. Nichell's *This Is Baker's Clay* includes the recipe, directions, and many photos. Williamson's paperback *Baker's Clay* includes the recipe, directions, samples, and history. The Blue Mountain Crafts Council's *Joy of Crafts* (pp. 196–202) has recipes and ideas for sculpturing bread flowers. Bread dough for modeling is included in Sattler's *Recipes for Art and Craft Materials* (pp. 54–55). A recipe for baker's dough appears in Penn's *Individualized Arts and Crafts Lessons for the Elementary School* (pp. 143–67). A recipe for bread heads is given on page 51 of Price's *Concoctions*.

In Tomie de Paola's *Watch Out for the Chicken Feet in Your Soup*, Joey is embarrassed to take his friend Eugene to visit his old-fashioned Italian grandmother but finds to his surprise that Eugene thinks she is the greatest when they make bread-dough dolls. The recipe for the dolls is at the end of the book. A more unorthodox grandmother appears in *Kevin's Grandma* by Williams.

PAPIER-MACHÉ BOOK FIGURES.   Papier-maché is an easy and inexpensive way to make large book figures. Imagine large Mother Goose figures, Dr. Seuss characters such as *Cat in the Hat*, Browning's *The Pied Piper of Hamelin*, and the rats, du Bois's *The Hare and the Tortoise and the Tortoise and the Hare/La Liebre y la tortuga y la tortuga y la liebre* or *The Hare and the Tortoise* by La Fontaine, illustrated by Wildmark, Bond's *A Bear Called Paddington*, *Mr. Popper's Penguins* by the Atwaters, Anderson's *The Ugly Duckling* as a swan, or Lindgren's *The Tompten*, all in papier-maché figures.

Abish and Kaplan's *Art Is For You* is only one of several books that give directions for making objects of papier-maché. Wet and dry methods, armatures of bottles, boxes, and wires are shown with photos and directions for making people and animals in Seidelman's *Creating with Papier-Mâché*. Chapter 5, "Solid Papier-Mâché"; chapter 6, "Solid Birds and Animals"; chapter 7, "Hollow Paper People"; and chapter 8, "Hollow Birds and Animals" show materials and equipment in *Exploring Papier-Mâché* by Betts. See also Anderson's *Papier-Mâché and How to Use It*, chapter 7 of Penn's *Individual Arts and Crafts Lessons for the Elementary School*, and chapter 7 of Mattil's *Meanings in Crafts*. How to make a full rounded figure is given on pages 33 to 63 of Mohnson's *Papier-Mâché*. Information in determining body proportions is especially useful. Besides working with plaster of paris and paper sculpture, drawings and photos are given for making animals of papier-mâché in Kenny's *The Art of Papier-Mâché*. *Design of Papier-Mâché* is by Kenny and his wife Carla. Patterns are included for an elephant, lion, owl, whale, dragon and cat. Photos and directions are given. Slade's *Modeling in Clay, Plaster and Papier-Mâché* tells about the layer method, modeling on wire and over balloons.

The books by Abisch and Kaplan, Seidelman, and Slade all contain information for making puppets of papier-mâché. Books about making other types of puppets are included in the chapter of this book, "Playing Stories Live Action and with Puppets."

SCULPTURE. Pygmalion fell in love with a beautiful statue and asked Venus to give Galatea life so that he could marry her. This tale from mythology provided the base for George Bernard Shaw's *Pygmalion*, which in turn provided the story for Lerner's and Loew's musical, *My Fair Lady*. A picture book by Black, *Woman of the Wood*, is another variation of this tale.

Collodi's *Pinocchio* is perhaps the most famous figure carved from wood who comes to life. Carved objects are the theme of three books written and illustrated by Holling Clancy Holling. In *Paddle-to-the-Sea*, a carved Indian in a canoe traveled from the Great Lakes to the Atlantic via the St. Lawrence River. *Seabird* is a carved bird that brought luck to four generations of seamen. In *Tree in the Trail*, an oxen yoke is carved from a tree. Students who feel inspired to whittle can consult Hunt's *Whittling with Ben Hunt*, Leeming's *Fun with Wood*. Paine's *Looking at Sculpture* presents sculpture in stone, wood, clay, and bronze. The first twenty-four pages of Pettit's *How to Make Whirligigs and Whimmy Diddles and Other American Folkcraft Objects* gives diagrams. Seidelman and Mintonye's *Creating with Wood* gives instructions on pages 24–43. Weiss's *Carving: How to Carve Wood and Stone* gives step-by-step procedures from selecting the wood to the final product. Those who would rather carve in soap should consult Gabu's *Soap Sculpture*. Information on how to carve doll heads out of styrofoam, soap, and balsa wood are given in Rogowski's *Making American Folk Dolls*.

Brindze's *The Story of the Totem Pole* tells about early story-telling poles and offers another expression of woodcarving. Totem poles are included as one of Hunt's forty projects and are also part of Weiss's book. *Out of the Earth I Sing, Poetry and Songs of Primitive Peoples of the World* by Lewis shows pictures of primitive paintings, carvings, sculpture, and weaving.

Intuk's Friend by Morrow is illustrated by Ellen Raskin and is about a soapstone carving. Intuk learns that there are fewer seals so now his family must move to Point Barrow, Alaska, because the government needs carpenters. Soloquay and Intuk are friends and hate to part. Intuk gives his friend a boy carved from a walrus tusk and receives a soapstone for a carving.

Franklin Stein was written and illustrated by Ellen Raskin. Franklin made a friend he called Fred from mops, a coat hanger, a potato masher, a coffee pot, and other items. People at the show in which Franklin entered Fred called him gruesome, weird, and revolting, but the judge found Fred original, creative, artistic, and superb. At one time or another many people have wanted to create someone like Fred. Some of the illustrations in *Collage and Construction* by Weiss contain some basic elements. With *Franklin Stein* as inspiration, art classes may wish to create their own "friend." A note from the book jacket explains that Ellen Raskin actually created a Fred of her own in her studio before writing and illustrating *Franklin Stein*.

Two other books about crazy inventions are McHargue's *The Wonderful Wings of Harold Harrabescue* and Mayer's *Me and My Flying Machine*. In the first book, the children brought many items to Mr. Harrabescue to put into the wings he was making. One day the wings were missing but every so often the children would find some of their things on the ground and know that Mr. Harrabescue was happily flying around the world. *Me and My Flying Machine* could inspire invention also.

Gladstone's *A Carrot for a Nose; the Form of Folk Sculpture on America's City Streets and Country Roads* contains weathervanes, whirligigs, gravestones, carousel figures, snowmen, and scarecrows. McHargue's *Stone Flight* is a notable children's book and is about a stone griffin that comes to life. Slade's *Modeling in Clay, Plaster and Papier-Mâché* is a more traditional book about sculpturing. Johnson's *Sculpture, the Basic Methods and Materials* includes wood, stone, and metal carving and gives step-by-step instructions. Leyh's *Children Make Sculpture* includes a section called "Putting Things Together" that would be helpful when creating a character like Fred. It is an idea book, not a how-to-do-it book. Also included are carving, clay and plaster work.

Miller has written a book illustrated by the Hawkinsons called *The Statue of Liberty*, about our most famous statue. French sculptor Auguste Bartholdi created it and the head first appeared at the 1878 Paris world's fair. Later Eiffel (of tower fame) made the framework for the statue and it was finished in 1884. A description of how the statue was dismantled and moved to the United States is fascinating.

Another book that gives a step-by-step process is Macaulay's *Cathedral: the Story of Its Construction*. The thirteenth-century French cathedral in this story is imaginary, but the book authentically describes how a Gothic cathedral would have been constructed in 1252.

The story "The Stonecutter" appears on pages 101 to 105 of Lang's *The Crimson Fairy Book* and as a picture book, film, and filmstrip created by Gerald McDermott. In it a lowly stonecutter became a rich man, a prince, the sun, clouds, and finally a mountain as he became increasingly more powerful until his last wish was granted, and he became a stonecutter again. A similar theme about strength is found in Wiesner's The Constant Little Mouse.

Another tale about stonecutters and wishes is The Two Stonecutters by Titus, in which the goddess of the forest grants Japanese brothers seven wishes. All are wasted but the final wish which brings the brothers back to where they were in the first place.

Black and white photos from the Hirshhorn Museum and Sculpture Garden, at the Smithsonian Institution in Washington illustrate Horwitz's A Child's Garden of Sculpture.

NEEDLEWORK IN ART.   The Bayeux Tapestry, the Story of the Norman Conquest, 1066 is told in two parts. The first part, in large print, chronicles the events; the second part describes the background of the tapestry. The tapestry, ordered by Bishop Odo, isn't real tapestry but embroidery or needlework, and is located in the town hall of Bayeux, France. An illustration is also found on page 6 of Janson's The Picture History of Painting from Cave Painting to Modern Times.

Several books have illustrations that look like tapestry, needlework, or fabric. Domanska's The Turnip uses background illustrations that look like a needlework sampler. Towle's The Magic Cooking Pot contains illustrations created in batik. According to the illustrator and reteller, it took a year and a half to make the batik used in the book. This folktale from India is another version of the "Lad and the North Wind." See page 130 of Tritten's Art Techniques for Children for information on batik. Belves's How Artists Work: an Introduction to Techniques of Art includes information about embroidery, weaving, and tapestry.

Stitchery projects can provide an alternative to book reports. A scene from a book, captured and displayed in needlework, can outlast and give more enjoyment than a written report. Three basic books of stitches and techniques for making samplers and wall hangings are Christensen and Ashner's Cross Stitchery; Needlepointing with Yarn in a Variety of Decorative Stitches; Needlepoint Simplified by the same authors; and Miller's The Stitchery Book, Embroidery for Beginners, which includes forty-five different stitches. Other books include Hanley's Fun with Needlepoint, Lightbody's Introducing Needlepoint, and Wilson's Embroidery Book.

Needlepoint Designs after Illustrations by Beatrix Potter Charted for Easy Use by Weiss is a paperback that gives stitches, patterns, and captions for twenty-four designs of Beatrix Potter characters. The last page folds out to show how completed projects will look.

TOYS FROM CHILDREN'S BOOKS.   There are toys available commercially that represent book characters. It is possible to purchase Milne's Pooh Bear, Tigger and others, as stuffed toys, as well as china figurines of Beatrix Potter characters, Joan Walsh Anglund dolls, and Seuss's Cat in the Hat.

There are several books that give instructions for making toys based on literary characters. Toys from the Tales of Beatrix Potter by Hutchings includes patterns and instructions for materials and methods for making animals, furniture, and baskets. Friedericksen's *The Pooh Craft Book* gives patterns for all of the animals in Milne's books. Directions are given on how to make felt pictures and stuffed toys as well as a clay "honey pot." Smith's *Nursery Rhyme Toys* offers directions, full-scale patterns, and black and white photos of the finished products from fourteen nursery rhymes. Roth's *The Art of Making Cloth Toys* gives directions, materials, patterns, and color photos of the finished product for many animals including the Three Bears, a dragon, an elephant, a clown, a witch, and a wizard. Dyer's *Design Your Own Stuffed Toys* includes patterns for a kangaroo, cat, bear, dog, giraffe, horse, bird, and rag doll. *Eva's Animal Friends, Complete Instructions for Making the World-Famous Eva Soft Toys* by Paludan includes patterns and instructions for a bear, owl, goat, foal, monkey, elephant, lion, hippo, fish, rabbit, eel, and crab. Directions for making many toys appears in *One Hundred Sixty-Seven Things to Make for Children* issued by Better Homes and Gardens. Morton's *Do-It-Yourself Dinosaurs: Imaginative Toycraft for Beginners* includes patterns for stuffed dinosaurs. Stevenson's *The Art of Making Wooden Toys* and Peterson's *Making Toys with Plywood* offer instruction on other types of toys.

Stuffed toys, dolls, figurines, and wooden toys related to books make quick, effective displays.

COLORING BOOKS.   A paperback book of *Kate Greenaway's Birthday Coloring Book* is available as an actual coloring book. Several other famous picture books are also available as coloring books: *Edward Lear's Nonsense Coloring Book, Richard Scarry's Best Coloring Activity Book,* and *Mary Poppins Story for Coloring.* The *Frog and Toad Coloring Book* contains favorite pages from Arnold Lobel's *Frog and Toad All Year, Frog and Toad Together, Days with Frog and Toad,* and *Frog and Toad Are Friends. Beatrix Potter's Painting Book, Outline Pictures from the Peter Rabbit Books* contains Benjamin Bunny, Jeremy Fisher, Squirrel Nutkin, and others. The complete text as well as drawings by Nancy Perkins are included in *Beatrix Potter, the Tale of Peter Rabbit Coloring Book.* Both books are paperbound and inexpensive.

All of these coloring books can be used in the conventional way or individual pictures can be enlarged using the opaque projector for bulletin board use.

COMPARING ILLUSTRATIONS IN BOOKS WITH SIMILAR SUBJECTS: A PROJECT.   There is a picture book project that can be enjoyed by and benefit students at many levels: a fourth or seventh grade class, a high school art class, or a college children's literature class. Divided into four groups, students examine picture books of nursery rhymes or poetry, alphabet, or counting books. Each "committee" is assigned fifteen picture books from one category, and based on a list of criteria, chooses five outstanding ones. The purpose may be to choose five because the library can only afford to add that many books, or the purpose may be to choose books specifically for their artistic merit. Different purposes will naturally produce different results. If there is time, have two different committees evaluate the same books and compare the results. Even with the same purpose, the outcome could be different.

PROJECTS FOR ALPHABET AND COUNTING BOOKS.   Alphabet and counting books find themselves in this chapter on art and illustrations because it is essentially the art work that makes them different from each other, as well as the theme and execution of that theme. Illustrations and choice of objects should be in keeping with the theme and since they are the major purpose of the book, numerals and letters should be clearly represented.

Students can make their own alphabet and counting books. First graders can cut out pictures from catalogs and magazines (good for reading readiness). Older students may study the criteria for a good alphabet or counting book and prepare one on a localized school or community theme for use by younger students. An instamatic camera and a list of objects relating to one theme is the first step to preparing an alphabet or counting book.

Five alphabet books that feature photos are Deasy's *City ABC's*, Grant's *Hey, Look at Me! a City ABC*, and Reuben's *Apples to Zippers*, all photographed in black and white; Mattheisen's *ABC, an Alphabet Book* and Carle's *All About Arthur* are photographed in color. These books can be used as models for classroom-produced alphabet books.

Alphabet books are good for introducing the use of different mediums and techniques used by an illustrator. Among those which were illustrated in woodcuts for example, Brown's *All Butterflies, an ABC* and *The ABC Book* by Falls are easily picked out. Woodcuts and photos are used by Carle in *All About Arthur*, and *Beasts, an Alphabet of Fine Prints* by Fuller contains several art techniques, woodcuts among them. Some students may include *Anno's Alphabet* among the books illustrated by woodcuts, but close examination will show that the three dimensional letters are painted to look like wood. Ask students to find the lithographs in Fuller's book and compare them with Rojankovsky's *Animals in the Zoo*.

VARIETY IN ALPHABET BOOKS.   Alphabet books are as varied as the people who create them. Chwast's *Still Another Alphabet Book* is also a game or a puzzle, with scrambled letters in red at the bottom of the page including a word to describe something found in the picture. A brother and sister gain a new baby in Lord's *Our New Baby's ABC*. Mendoza's *Alphabet Boat, a Seagoing Alphabet Book* includes nautical terms like mainsail, and weather information. Crews's *We Read A-Z* emphasizes colors and shapes. Farber's *This Is the Ambulance Leaving the Zoo*, illustrated by de Paola, is a cumulative story and reads, "This is the BUS stopping to let the AMBULANCE whiz by. These are the CARS piling up behind the stopped BUS."

Kate Greenaway's classic alphabet book with its delicate drawings is called *A Apple Pie*. An alphabet rhyme that has not been illustrated but would be fun for students to draw is the one found on page 29 of Rackham's *Mother Goose Nursery Rhymes*, page 42 of *Marguerite DeAngeli's Book of Nursery and Mother Goose Rhymes*, and pages 214 and 215 of *The Mother Goose Treasury* by Briggs. The rhyme begins, "A was an Archer, and shot at a frog, B was a

Butcher, and had a great dog." Each class member could be given a letter to illustrate. Another source of alphabet rhymes to illustrate is Baldwin's *One Hundred Nineteenth-Century Rhyming Alphabets in English*, or students could create their own rhymes. An old rhyme is illustrated by the Provensens in *A Peaceable Kingdom: A Shaker Abecedarius*.

ANIMAL ALPHABET BOOKS.　　There are more animal alphabet books than any other type. Roger Duvoisin's *A Is for the Ark* shows all the animals parading two by two into Noah's Ark. There are several kinds of animals listed under each letter. Garten's *Alphabet Tale* gives a clue to the animal on the following page by showing its tail. Included in *Adam's Book of Odd Creatures* by Low are an Alewife, Basilisk, Cassowary, Dodo, Earwig, and Florinder, introduced by a passage from the Old Testament (Genesis II:19). Celestino Piatti's *Animal ABC* includes many animals, including the fictitious xopiatti. Circus animals are part of Chardiet's *C is for Circus*, illustrated by Brinton Turkle in a style reminiscent of old circus posters. Fuller's *Beasts, an Alphabet of Fine Prints* introduces animals by old masters in engravings, etchings, woodcuts and lithographs. In Eichenbert's *Ape in a Cape, an Alphabet of Odd Animals*, the animals are not unusual but their activities are—Owl on the prowl, Lizard with a wizard, Egret in a minuet, Bear in despair, Yak with a pack, Mouse in a blouse. In Farber's *As I Was Crossing Boston Commons*, it is the animal that is unusual and the activity that is common. Animals from an Angwantibo to a Zibet go for a walk.

Two books about familiar animals are Gag's *ABC Bunny* and Newberry's *Kittens ABC*. The latter book shows many breeds of kittens.

Animals from albatross to zebra are included in Sarosas's *ABC's of Origami, Paper Folding for Children*. Rojankovsky's *Animals in the Zoo* contains no text except letters and the names of the animals. Montresor's *A for Angel* uses arrows rather than words.

ALPHABET BOOKS AND SCIENCE.　　Besides being aesthetically pleasing, Marcia Brown's *All Butterflies, an ABC*, includes many varieties of butterflies. *Apricot ABC* by Miles shows bees, crickets, butterflies, inchworms, junebugs, Queen Anne's lace, turtles, and a titmouse among other plants and animals. Mitsumaso *Anno's Alphabet, an Adventure in Imagination* uses pen and ink drawings of entwined foliage to frame his pages. Each of the (plants identified at the back of the book) begins with the letter on the page—anemones and asters on the first pages and zinnias on the last page.

Asimov's *ABC's of Space* is really a science book using photographs and defining space terms. Milgram's *ABC of Ecology* does not deal with the whole spectrum of ecology but only with urban pollution.

CITIES IN ALPHABET BOOKS.　　Several alphabet books focus on cities. *A Big City* by Grossbart features antennas and garbage cans. *Big City ABC* by Staats begins with "alley." *City ABC's* by Deasy begins with "alley" and includes "bridges," "cranes," "fountains," "laundromats," "vendors," and "zoos." The illustrations are very modern and show adults and older children.

All Around the Town by McGinley is specifically about New York. Although Grant's alphabet book is called *Hey, Look at Me! A City ABC* the words are not necessarily city activities: "grinning," "hopping," "itching," "jumping," "waving," "yelling," and "zipping." Fife's *Adam's ABC* is about city life; of black city dwellers specifically.

BLACKS IN ALPHABET BOOKS.   Several alphabet books in fact relate particularly to blacks. As Adam, Arthur, and Albert tell what a day is like for black city children in *Adam's ABC*, there is focus on black objects throughout the alphabet. Clifton has compiled an alphabet of famous black Americans who have made contributions to our country in *The Black ABC's*. The Feelings give information on life in East Africa in their book *Jambo Means Hello*, utilizing the Swahili alphabet of twenty-four letters. Bond's *A Is for Africa* presents many aspects of African life while Musgrove's *Ashanti to Zulu: African Traditions* focuses on tribal customs. The latter book, illustrated by Leo and Diane Dillon, won the 1977 Caldecott Medal.

NONFICTION ALPHABET BOOKS.   There are several other nonfiction alphabet books. *Our American ABC* by the Petershams includes persons from history, biography, and legend. Sloane's *ABC Book of Early Americana, a Sketch-Book of Antiques and American Firsts* shows pencil sketches of antiques beginning with almanacs.

Charlip and others have created *Handtalk: An ABC of Finger Spelling and Sign Language* which shows colored photos of the signing alphabet for the deaf in use.

Black and white photo silhouettes of instruments appear in McMillan's *The Alphabet Symphony, An ABC Book*.

Russell's *A Is for Apple and Why, the Story of Our Alphabet* is a book about where the alphabet came from. Cave illustrations, pictograms, hieroglyphics, phonograms, and alphabets of the Phoenicians, Greeks, and Romans are given. It is included here because it is an easy to understand background book and can be used in conjunction with alphabet books.

ALPHABET BOOKS IN VERSE.   Many alphabet books include rhyme, alliteration, tongue twisters, and nonsense verse. Two books including nursery rhymes are those illustrated by Joan Walsh Anglund, *In a Pumpkin Shell, a Mother Goose ABC* and *Nuts to You and Nuts to Me; an Alphabet Book of Poems* by Hoberman. The second book contains a rhyme for each letter of the alphabet, nonsense verses, and tongue twisters. *The Sesame Street Book of Letters* by the Children's Television Workshop also includes tongue twisters. The best tongue twister book of all time is Marcia Brown's *Peter Piper's Alphabet* which gives a tongue twister for every letter of the alphabet. Alliteration also occurs in *Mary Poppins A-Z* by Travers. The page for the letter of the alphabet includes a story in words beginning with that letter. In Moore's *Certainly, Carrie, Cut the Cake, Poems A-Z* we find that "Eleven elephants emptied their trunks in front of Eliza and Ed. . . ." In *Bruno Munari's ABC* we find "Ant on an apple." *All about*

Arthur says that "In Cincinnati he came across a cool calico cat selling cotton candy on a corner. The Cat was called Cindy." Chardiet's *C Is for Circus* includes "E is for Elephants, who look extremely elegant, marching trunk to tail. . . ." Sendak's *Alligators All Around* has a family of alligators "doing dishes" as well as other activities. The book is one of the four miniature Nutshell Library books and is available in sound filmstrip format. Alliteration also occurs in Helen Oxenbury's *ABC of Things.*

Three of the books about cities are in rhyme: Deasy's *City ABC*, McGinley's *All Around the Town*, and Staat's *Big City ABC.* Other books in rhyme are *A Is for Alphabet* illustrated by Suyeaka and Barry's *A Is for Anything, an ABC Book of Pictures and Rhymes.* In the last book the letter takes on the shape of the object discussed. Rhyme also appears in Hosey's *Alphabet*, Gag's *ABC Bunny*, Miles's *Apricot ABC*, Fujikawa's *A to Z Picture Book*, and Eichenberg's *Ape in a Cape.* The latter book contains nonsense in internal rhyme: carp with a harp, Irish setter with a letter, and a vulture with culture. The best of the nonsense books, of course, is Edward Lear's *ABC, Lear Alphabet*, available in paperback called *Nonsense Alphabet.*

PARTS OF SPEECH IN ALPHABET BOOKS.   You can use alphabet books for identifying parts of speech. Use *Bruno Munari's ABC* in filmstrip or book format for identifying nouns and adjectives. *Apricot ABC* by Miles includes a mixture of common and proper nouns as well as adjectives. There are common and proper nouns in Asimov's *ABC's of Space*, with one of each given for each letter, beginning with "Apollo" and "astronaut." Newberry's *Kitten's ABC* contains proper nouns. *City ABC's* contains nouns. All of the animal books are excellent sources of nouns. Use *John Burningham's ABC* to have children list singular and plural nouns. Marcia Brown's *All Butterflies* uses nouns and verbs effectively. *We Read-AZ* is full of adjectives and adverbs. Grant's *Hey, Look at Me!* can be used to introduce gerunds and includes "jumping," "marching," "running," "splashing," and "tickling."

ALPHABET BOOKS INTRODUCE A FAVORITE CHARACTER.   Use the alphabet book to introduce a favorite character like Curious George. *Curious George Learns the Alphabet* can be used to introduce all of the Curious George books by H.A. Rey: *Curious George, Curious George Gets a Medal, Curious George Rides a Bike, Curious George Takes a Job*, and *Curious George Flies a Kite.* Or use *Mary Poppins A-Z* to introduce the other Travers books: *Mary Poppins, Mary Poppins Comes Back, Mary Poppins in the Park*, and *Mary Poppins Opens the Door.* Use *Little Bear Learns to Read the Cookbook* by Janice, illustrated by Mariana, to introduce the other books about Little Bear. In this book children think up food that begins with a particular letter of the alphabet. This encourages participation because listeners will wish to add other foods beginning with that same letter. In *Little Bear's Pancake Party*, Little Bear cries because the box he got from the grocer did not contain pancakes, until he learns that he has to *make* the pancakes from the mix. Other books about Little Bear include holiday books: *Little Bear's Christmas, Little Bear's Thanksgiving*, and *Lit-*

tle Bear Marches in the St. Patrick's Day Parade.

ALPHABET BOOKS INTRODUCE AN AUTHOR OR ILLUSTRATOR.   Students in small groups or individually can find other books by an alphabet book author or illustrator. *Bruno Munari's ABC, Pepe's An Alphabet Book, Helen Oxenbury's ABC of Things, Richard Scarry's ABC Word Book, John Burningham's ABC,* Duvoisin's *A for the Ark,* Brian Wildsmith's *ABC,* Celestino Piatti's *Animal ABC,* Asimov's *ABC's of Space,* Anno's *Anno's Alphabet: An Adventure in Imagination,* Brown's *All Butterflies, An ABC* and *Peter Piper's Alphabet,* Carle's *All about Arthur,* Ed Emberley's *ABC,* Feelings's *Jambo Means Hello,* Gag's *ABC Bunny,* McGinley's *All Around the Town,* Petersham's *An American ABC,* and Sloane's *ABC Book of Early Americana* can all be used to introduce their other books. Searchers will not be surprised to learn that other Asimov titles include *Building Blocks of the Universe, Realm of Numbers, Words of Science,* and others. They may be surprised to find that Asimov has also written a book called *Words from the Myths* and edited a collection of science fiction short stories called *I Robot.*

ALPHABET AND COUNTING BOOKS BY THE SAME PERSON.   The styles and quality of picture books about letters and about numbers can be compared with each other. Students can be given one and asked to find the other using the card catalog. The project is easy enough for some first and second graders. People who have written or illustrated both an alphabet and a counting book include Anno, Carle, Chwast, Duvoisin, Eichenberg, Feelings, Oxenbury, Pepe, Sendak, and Wildsmith. Use alphabet books to introduce counting books by the same author or illustrator.

COUNTING BOOKS INTRODUCE AN AUTHOR OR ILLUSTRATOR.   Counting books can be used to introduce children to other books by that person. *Jeanne Marie Counts Her Sheep* by Françoise can be used to introduce *The Big Rain, Jeanne Marie at the Fair, Noël for Jeanne Marie,* and *Springtime for Jeanne Marie.* Several of these books about the little French girl are also available in paperback. *Bears on Wheels* by the Berenstains can be used to introduce *The Bears Almanac,* which is about the seasons, and the others: *Bear Scouts, The Bears' Christmas, The Bears' Picnic, The Bears' Vacation,* and *Bears in the Night*—all easy readers. Clifton's *Everett Anderson's 1, 2, 3* can introduce other books about that character.

BOOKS WITH NUMBERS.   Two nonfiction books about numbers include *Counting Systems; the Familiar and the Unusual* by Luce and *Number Ideas through Pictures* by Charosh. These books are not really counting books but reach a step beyond counting books. The first includes hieroglyphics, Roman numerals and bases 2, 8, and 10 for computer use. Questions are posed and answers are given on pages 38 to 48. The second book is more like a counting book; numbers and their meanings are introduced in a colorful setting. The book is from the Young Math series. Another book from that series, also written by

Charosh, is *Mathematical Games for One or Two*. In the Third-Take-Away game, players learn that the second player can win only when there are 3, 6, 9, etc. items. Otherwise the first player will win. Another puzzle book is *Brian Wildsmith's Puzzles* which asks questions: how many teeth does the dragon have or how many chicks should the mother hen have based on the number of broken eggshells around her?

The *One to Fifty Book* by Anne and Alex Wyse provides stimulation for creating a number or alphabet book in the classroom. The illustrations are based on pictures drawn by children through the years in Anne's classroom. *One Old Oxford Ox* is an alliterative counting rhyme illustrated by Bayley.

Eric Carles's *1, 2, 3 to the Zoo* includes a train load of animals. Each car has animals in it: three giraffes, four lions, etc. As each car is added, the small train at the bottom of the page grows longer. The last page includes a fold-out to make three pages and shows all of the animals at the zoo. The train at the bottom is then empty. Children may wish to make a trainload full of animals to fit the bulletin board space on top of the blackboard that is narrow but long. This book won first prize as most outstanding at the 1970 International Children's Book Fair in Bologna, Italy.

COUNTING OUT RHYMES.   Counting rhymes and poems are popular with children and can be used to introduce number concepts. Grayson's *Let's Count and Count and Count Out!* contains over seventy rhymes. They are arranged in chapters by the number mentioned in the rhyme from 1-20. There are as many as eight rhymes for some numbers between 1 and 10, but only one rhyme was located for numbers 11 through 20. The rhymes were taken from literature or were written by the author. Most of them can be used to reinforce verb concepts, and the action makes them naturals as participation experiences. In "Five Tiny Toads" the words "first" through "fifth" are introduced. Some familiar rhymes include "Going to St. Ives" (7), "Higgledy Piggledy" (10), "Buckle My Shoe" (20), and "Over in the Meadow" (3).

Incidentally, two picture books contain the song "Over in the Meadow." Langstaff's book illustrated by Rojankovsky contains music. The version illustrated by Ezra Keats does not. The first book is available in paperback, the second in sound filmstrip.

Other sources of counting out rhymes are pages 107-112 of Johnson's *What They Say in New England, and Other American Folklore*, and Carl Withers's *Counting Out Rhymes*. Bolton's *Counting-Out Rhymes* is a reproduction of a book first published in 1888 and contains almost a thousand rhymes. There are twenty-two stories about counting and twenty rhymes listed in Ireland's *Index to Fairy Tales, 1949-72*.

STORIES WITH NUMBERS.   *One Two Three Going to Sea* by Alain is part of "an adding and subtracting" series and contains cumulative adding. Fishermen are added to a boat until there are ten. The overcrowded boat overturns and four swim home, three ride home on pelicans, two on seals, and one is caught in a net. The fishermen are subtracted as they are rescued. Alain's story and

Elkin's *Six Foolish Fishermen* make a good pair of stories to read aloud together.

In Mahy's *The Boy Who Was Followed Home,* illustrated by Steven Kellogg, Robert is followed home from school first by a single hippo and then by as many as seven. A witch gives Robert a pill to cure the problem and it worked—Robert was no longer followed by hippopotami but by giraffes instead.

In Carle's *The Rooster Who Set Out to See the World,* the rooster asks two cats, three frogs, four turtles, and five fishes to accompany him. They go along until they miss the comforts of home and group by group they abandon him. In another book by Carle, *The Very Hungry Caterpillar,* a caterpillar literally eats his way through the book until it becomes a butterfly. The holes in the book, the various page shapes and the food eaten add to the interest.

Baum's *One Bright Monday Morning* is about spring and begins "While on my way to school, I saw . . . flowers blooming, bees buzzing, ants crawling . . . ." The tale is cumulative and could suggest a class project for making a similar book about one or more of the other seasons.

Merriman's *Project 1-2-3* is about a housing project that takes up one block and has two front doors, two elevators, two mailboxes, seven maintenance men who fix seven stuffed toilets, seven stopped sinks, and seven broken door keys. The book begins with one and ends with ten workers in the basement. More than a counting book, it creates awareness of some of the frustrations of city life.

PICTURE BOOKS: COUNTING 1-10.   In Ann and Paul Rand's *Little One,* a lonely little "one" wasn't wanted by anyone until a hoop joined him to make "ten." In addition to the baby ducks in Duvoisin's *Two Lonely Ducks,* the days of the week and months are introduced. Someone who was not lonely enough is *One Was Johnny* by Sendak! Johnny decides that if the house isn't empty by the time he counts backwards from ten, he will eat everyone.

Several books introduce the concept of adding and subtracting. In *The Sesame Street Book of Numbers* compiled by the Children's Television Workshop, numbers are unfolded and an empty line fills up with spies peeking out from behind trench coats. After the spies are seen, they disappear one by one. Steiner's *Ten in a Family,* shows that Mr. and Mrs. Mouse are 1 + 1 = 2; the baby makes it 2 + 1 = 3. In Maestro's *One More and One Less,* strange looking animals take readers up to ten and then subtract one per page until the reader is back at one. *Ants Go Marching* up to number "10" in Freschet's book.

Bridgemen's *All the Little Bunnies* takes readers from one to ten and back again, in rhyme. Also in rhyme are *One Is the Sun* by the Blegvads and *The Chicken Book* by Garth Williams. The Williams book is based on an old counting-out rhyme and only goes up to three. In *Three by Three* by Kruss, three cats chase three mice, three foxes chase three cats, three hounds chase three foxes, and three hunters chase three hounds in rhyme. Another counting story told in verse is Gregor's *1, 2, 3, 4, 5.* The Gregor book and *Numbers: A First Counting Book* by Allen use photos to show numbers, and a localized photo number book could be made inexpensively with an instamatic and black and white film. Allen does not show the same items in a number category but mixes up types of items.

Linda asks her big brother *What Is One?* in a book of that name by Watson.

Linda's brother shows her one pine tree, four boots, ten fingers and other items from one to ten. The same question could be asked as children point out objects in the room.

Ten What? A Mystery Counting Book by Hoban and Selig contains a secret message.

Tom and Muriel Feelings show numbers one through ten with Swahili words which also introduce readers to life in East Africa in *Mojo Means One.*

Teddy Bears One to Ten by Gretz is about old dirty teddy bears who get rejuvenated at the cleaners and come back on the bus for tea. Another funny book is McLeod's *One Snail and Me,* in which some of the animals in the bathtub with the narrator include four seals with lunch pails, six kangaroos with bathing shoes, and ten little minnows who tickle.

PICTURE BOOKS: COUNTING BEYOND TEN.   Vogel's *One Is No Fun but Twenty Is Plenty* is written in verse and contains such zany items as eighteen meatballs. Eichenberg's *Dancing in the Moon* is also in rhyme with hilarity beginning with one raccoon dancing in the moon and going on with four pandas resting on verandas, seven baboons drawing cartoons, and ten cats trying on hats.

Tasha Tudor's *One Is One* is in her usual soft colors and provides a delicate and charming contrast. *Anno's Counting Book* has clusters of numbers scattered throughout country scenes. Colored cubes at the left show what number to look for on the page.

Nolan's *Monster Bubbles* is a wordless picture book that shows monsters blowing bubbles in quantities from one to twenty. Bishop's *Twenty-two Bears* tells of the antics of bears in the wilds of Wyoming, and the author's *Five Chinese Brothers* can be included with books about numbers.

Helen Oxenbury takes readers up to fifty in *Numbers of Things,* but also speculates about how many stars there are. The book can be used to introduce the concept of similar and different. There are seven chairs each of which is different and has someone sleeping in each. There are nine different kinds of birds and twenty different balloons and forty different fish, but the thirty penguins and fifty ladybugs all look the same. Another book that combines numbers and concepts is Slobodkin's *Millions and Millions and Millions!* Tall and thin, short and round, and woods and sea are some contrasts. Some of the many items explored are cards, dogs, cats, shells, ships, trees, flowers, ice cream cones, and telephones. The last two pages end with the following message: "But in the whole wide world there is only one *you* and one *me.*"

Pepe's *Circus Numbers* begins with one ringmaster and goes to one hundred elephants. Like Oxenbury, Pepe asks readers to speculate—this time about the number of people in the crowd.

Bright colors provide the background for *Numbers: A Book* by John J. Reiss. Numbers from one to twenty are represented and then skip to thirty, forty, and one hundred centipede legs. A thousand raindrops end the book. Other pictures include eleven kites, six birthday candles, nine baseball players, fifty candy kisses, and sixty lollipops. Six birthday candles are also shown in Hoban's *Count* and See. Photos of items and dots explain each number. Pictures and dots are shown from one to fifteen, beginning with one fire hydrant. After twenty watermelon seeds, pictures count by tens to one hundred peas in a pod.

Brown Cow Farm by Ipcar is a favorite counting book and shows animals from one horse to ten geese. The book is good for showing multiplying because each animal, beginning with two dogs, has ten babies until ten geese have one hundred goslings.

NONVERBAL COMMUNICATION.   Many new titles on nonverbal communication illustrate the growth of interest in this phenomenon. The two special areas of interest in these books are kinesics and proxemics. Birdwhistell's Kinesics and Context is the model for all the popular body-language books in print today. Among those books are hardback and paperback editions of Julius Fast's Body Language and Jane Howard's Please Touch: A Guided Tour of the Human Potential Movement. Another popular writer is Bernard Gunther, who in Sense Relaxation Below Your Mind addresses himself to sensory awareness. Edward Hall's area of interest, proxemics, is explained in The Silent Language. This pioneer in the field also wrote The Hidden Dimension. Ruesch and associates, in their early research, established three aspects of nonverbal communication: sign language, action language, and object language discussed in his Nonverbal Communication. He, Birdwhistell, and Hall are considered among the foremost authorities in this area. Also consult Knapp's Nonverbal Communication and Eisenberg's and Smith's Nonverbal Communication. Knapp addresses himself to space, physical appearance and dress, physical behavior, face and eyes, vocal cues, and observing and recording nonverbal behavior which include proxemic and kinesic analysis. Besides Ruesch's three categories, Eisenberg and Smith discuss paralanguage or nonverbal vocalization, body movements, illustrators, regulators, adaptors, kinesics, and proxemics.

For a concise overview of nonverbal communication read chapter 6, "Nonverbal Communication," on pages 101-118 or Brooks's Speech Communication. Morlan and Tuttle list functions and types on pages 35-56 of chapter 3, "Nonverbal Variables," in their book An Introduction to Effective Oral Communication. Chapter 6, "Nonverbal Communication, Nonverbal Behavior, and Animal Communication" in Steinfatt's Human Communication, an Interpersonal Introduction includes animal communication as well as human nonverbal communication. Chapter 6, "The Eloquence of Action: Nonverbal Communication," of Keltner's Interpersonal Speech-Communication, Elements and Structures, is also helpful.

Books containing helpful instructions to elementary and secondary teachers are Hennings's Smiles, Nods and Pauses, Activities to Enrich Children's Communication Skills and Thompson's Beyond Words, Nonverbal Communication in the Classroom. Check the bibliographies of these two books for other sources.

WORDLESS PICTURE BOOKS.   There are several picture books for children which do not contain words but tell the story through gestures, facial expression, the actions of the characters, and background scenery. Books without words can be used for reading readiness or can provide older students opportunities to verbalize orally or on paper. The easiest, least complicated books are given first.

Ruth Carroll illustrated four wordless picture books especially for preschool and primary aged children. *What Whiskers Did* is about a puppy who breaks his leash and follows a rabbit into its hole to avoid a fox. Children who enjoyed Whiskers will also appreciate the *Adventures of Witch Cat*. In *Rolling Downhill* a dog and a cat become entangled in a ball of yarn. The Chimp in *The Chimp and the Clowns* has adventures when he leaves the circus parade. In *The Dolphin and the Mermaid* the underwater creatures dislike being disrupted by people so they get even, much to the amusement of anyone who sees the book.

Another almost wordless book for preschoolers and early elementary students is Burningham's *Seasons*, which can be used to introduce other Burningham books that have more words but still have simple themes, i.e., *Mr. Gumpy's Outing*.

Noriko Ueno's *Elephant Buttons* is absolutely charming. The elephant unbuttons himself and out steps a horse who unbuttons himself and out steps a lion. Primary children and even adults will wonder who will come out next as a succession of seal, monkey, duck, and mouse appear. The last animal to appear is a total surprise.

Brinton Turkle's *Deep in the Forest* is a story of "Goldilocks and the Three Bears" in reverse—a bear invades Goldilocks's house. The story will delight children who have just heard "Goldilocks and the Three Bears." Another reversal appears in Ramage's *The Joneses*; the Mother operates a submarine while Dad stays at home.

In *Bobo's Dream* by Martha Alexander a daschund named Bobo loses his bone to a larger dog. When he dreams, he becomes a larger than life-sized hero and rescues his master's football. Freshly awakened from his dream, Bobo rescues his own bone. In Alexander's *Out! Out! Out!* a wild bird who flies into a room is enjoyed by the child but not by the adult. Other books by Alexander have fewer words than most books. The nonverbal books can be used to introduce the books about *Blackboard Bear* and *The Story Grandmother Told, No Ducks in Our Bathtub, Sabrina, We Never Get to Do Anything*, and *I'll Be the Horse if You'll Play with Me*.

Two other wordless books about boys are Lisker's *Lost* and Sugito's *My Friend Little John and Me*.

In Kjell Ringi's *The Magic Stick*, a boy picks up a stick that becomes, among other things, a magician's wand, riding quirt, spyglass and sword. He fantasizes a role for himself in each related scene but throws away the stick when he sees other children laugh at him. The book would be good to stimulate discussion in classes where children are shy about playing or expressing their feelings in dramatic play. *The Winner* is another book by Ringi that could be used for a similar purpose.

Symeon Shimin's *A Special Birthday* very simply and effectively shows a girl who wakes to find a ball of ribbon on her pillow, and follows the ribbon until she finds her wrapped presents. Emberley's *A Birthday Wish* is wordless.

The Secret Birthday Message by Eric Carle is another book about a hidden birthday present. A rebus note composed of words in pictures gives the birthday boy clues to finding the present, which is a puppy. The last page shows arrows to all places the boy looked. There is only a sentence on each page.

Apples by Caldecott winner Nonny Hogrogian begins when a boy throws away an apple core. Many animals also leave their cores and an orchard results. Pat Hutchins's *Changes, Changes* is for smaller children and shows the adventures of two wooden figures who live in a building block enclosure that catches fire.

The messages in Tana Hoban's books without words are expressed through photographs. Items in everyday life that include *Circles, Triangles and Squares* in their construction are shown. In *Big Ones, Little Ones*, there are black and white photos showing young and old, wild and domestic animals. The last page gives the fourteen pictures and the name of the animal and the name of the offspring, i.e., "pig" and "piglet," "horse" and "colt."

Peter Wetzel's two oversized books *The Good Bird* and *The Naughty Bird* also have simple themes. The good bird is a wild bird who shares a worm with a fish who is imprisoned in a goldfish bowl.

Fernando Krahn's *The Self-Made Snowman* is made from a small avalanche in the mountains and eventually becomes part of a parade for a local festival. *The Snowman* comes alive in Briggs's book. Another humorous wordless book by Krahn is *Who's Seen the Scissors*. A tailor's scissors cut through newspapers, a clothesline, instrument strings, and a politician's suspenders among other things before they return and are put in a cage by the tailor. Another wordless book by Krahn, *A Flying Saucer Full of Spaghetti*, is available as a filmstrip. Use the filmstrip to introduce other wordless books by Krahn: *April Fools, Catch That Cat!, A Funny Friend from Heaven, The Mystery of the Giant Footprints*, and *Sebastian and the Mushroom*.

Tomi Ungerer's book *One, Two, Where's My Shoe* contains only that sentence at the beginning and "three, four, on the floor!" on the last page. The rest of the book shows pictures in which shoe forms are integrated into birds, ships, fish, snakes, etc. The only sentences in *Snail, Where Are You?* are the title sentence and the answer at the end, "Here I am." As in Ungerer's very creative book, the repeated design is seen in over a dozen places including a tuba, waves, horns, smoke rings, and a pig's tail.

Brian Wildsmith's *Circus* has two sentences to the book, one at the beginning and one at the end. "The circus comes to town . . . and . . . the circus goes on to the next town." The illustrations are executed in Wildsmith's colorful style.

Pancakes for Breakfast by de Paola shows a woman searching for ingredients from the cow, hen and other sources. In *The Hunter and the Animals*, de Paola shows a hunter who is tricked by animals when he falls asleep in a forest.

Jose Aruego's *Look What I Can Do* is a humorous tale based on an old Philippine proverb. "A caribou who herds with fence jumpers becomes a fence jumper too." The book contains two sentences, one of which is repeated. One caribou says to the other, "Look what I can do!" The other says, "I can do it too!" For the rest of the book the two caribous cavort in unison while the other animals watch. When they return exhausted from their activities a third caribou repeats the title sentence and the other two caribous sit on him.

Beni Montresor's *ABC Picture Stories* has no words but contains the initial letters with arrows pointing out the pictures on the page that begin with those letters. The words then have to be supplied by the readers.

Anno's Alphabet has already been mentioned. The letters are painted to look three-dimensional, like wood. The black and white borders around each page contain flowers or herbs beginning with the same letter. Mitsumaso Anno is a delight! His *Topsy-Turvies, Pictures to Stretch the Imagination*, can be looked at and appreciated from all four sides of the book. People of all ages will enjoy trying to find out what is "wrong" with each picture. *Anno's Counting Book* and *Anno's Journey* are also wordless. *Upside-Downers: More Pictures to Stretch the Imagination* has words.

By the Sea by Amos is about a kite that takes a boy into the sky and a balloon that takes a dog into the sky. There are no words.

Angel's *The Ark* has an unusual fold-out format. The front and back are page 1 and 2. Six more pages fold out from the inside of the book. The illustrations show the animals going into the ark.

The books of John Goodall also have an unusual format. Goodall's books present problems to the printer because the color register of the pages must match each other perfectly to make the book effective. Each of almost a dozen titles, follows a similar format—half pages open like sideways dutch doors and change the scene enough to suggest action without relying on dialogue. The books are five by seven inches in size.

The only words in *The Adventures of Paddy Pork* are "Always Try to Be Good," stitched on a sampler above the little pig's bed that we see at the end of Paddy's adventures. While in town with his mother, Paddy leaves her to follow a circus and gets lost. Among the adventures he faces are being taken home by a "friendly" fox. A decade later, Goodall wrote *Paddy's Evening Out*, one of the funniest of his books. The expressions on the faces of the animals almost prove that pictures are worth a thousand words. Paddy attends the theater and falls into the orchestra pit from the balcony while trying to retrieve his companion's fan. He flees into a dressing room and hides in a trunk which finds its way onto stage in a magician's act in which Paddy succeeds in unleashing the magician's doves. After several other equally hilarious incidents, Paddy ends up on the stage during the curtain call and receives bouquets because the audience thought he was part of the show. Other books about Paddy are *The Ballooning Adventures of Paddy Pork*, *Paddy Pork's Holiday* and *Paddy's New Hat*.

Jacko is another mischievous animal. The sailor's monkey jumps into an open window and eats a pie and releases a parrot from a cage. Jacko has further adventures on board a ship that is attacked by pirates.

Shrewbetinna's Birthday is about a shrew who begins and ends her birthday in bed. During the day, Shrewbetinna's purse is snatched and then rescued by a handsome mouse, and a birthday party completes the story.

Kittens are the characters in *Surprise Picnic*. Exciting and unusual adventures happen to the kitten family as they row to an island for a picnic. In *The Midnight Adventures of Kelly, Dot, and Esmeralda*, a toy bear, doll, and live mouse wake up at midnight and go for a ride in a boat found in a picture on the nursery wall. Other books by Goodall that follow the same format are *Naughty Nancy*, *Creepy Castle*, and *Edwardian Summer*.

Split pages also occur in Oakley's *Magical Changes* so that "readers" create their own combinations of surrealistic paintings.

Mercer Mayer is another prolific producer of picture books without words. Four of Mercer's books are about *A Boy, A Dog and A Frog*. In the sequel, *Frog, Where Are You?* the frog escapes from the jar while the boy is sleeping so the boy and dog have to go and look for him. In *Frog on His Own*, frog leaves the boy and dog during a walk in the park and gets into trouble, eventually being saved from a cat by the boy and the dog. Two mischievious things the frog does are to hop into a picnic basket and to sink a sailboat by hopping onto it. The funniest book about the boy and the frog occurs when the boy smuggles the frog into a family dinner party at an expensive restaurant in *Frog Goes to Dinner*. Based on past knowledge of frog, no one is surprised to find him in such unwelcome places as a lady's salad and a couple's champagne glass, a disgrace to the family. The unrepentant boy is sent to his room where he and frog relive the evening's events for dog. *One Frog Too Many* and *A Boy, A Dog, and a Friend* are about the same characters.

Two favorite Mayer nonverbal books deal with uncontrollable body actions. In *Ah-Choo*, an elephant sneezes and destroys a house, court, and jail but wins the lady hippo from the rhino policeman. Facial expressions on the faces of the animals in *Ah-Choo* and *Hiccups* are outstanding. In *Hiccups* a hippo takes his girlfriend out in a boat but all she does is hiccup. Nothing he can do, including hitting her on the head and dumping her overboard, helps. The look in her eye when she has stopped but he begins to hiccup is priceless. Everyone who is clumsy will identify with the hippo in Mayer's *Oops*.

Children can begin at either end of two books by Mazer, *Two Moral Tales* and *Two More Moral Tales* because the two stories in each book are upside down from each other. Schweninger's *A Dance for Three* contains three stories and Fromm's *Muffel and Plume* contains nine.

There are five wordless picture books available in filmstrip format: Crews's *Truck*, Ward's *The Silver Pony*, Krahn's *A Flying Saucer Full of Spaghetti*, Mayer's *Bubble Bubble* about the marvelous shapes that a boy makes from a magic bubble machine, and Winter's *The Bear and the Fly* in which a bear creates havoc while attempting to kill a fly with a fly swatter. In another wordless book by Winter, *Sir Andrew*, a donkey, is conceited about his appearance. A class can add dialogue to the pictures shown on the screen or smaller groups can make tape recordings of the stories. The filmstrips also can be used to introduce the concept of communicating without words. Other filmstrips depicting favorite picture books with words can be shown without the accompanying record or cassette so that children can retell the story in their own words.

The longest of the nonverbal books is *The Silver Pony* which has 192 pages, half of them drawings by noted artist Lynd Ward. The page opposite each picture is blank and almost invites the viewer to supply the words. Eight episodes begin when a farm boy sees a silver winged horse while watching the cows. When the boy tells his father to come and look, the horse is gone and he gets spanked for lying. Later he rides the horse to various adventures until the horse shies at an exploding satellite and the boy falls off, and is found sleeping in the yard by his parents. When he awakes, the boy and viewer wonder if it all was a dream, until he finds a real silver pony waiting for him from his parents.

Another book that is longer than most of the nonverbal books is Steiner's *I am Andy, You-tell-a-story Book*. Titles are given for thirteen stories that are told only with pictures. The pictures are numbered and there are two or three per page. Most of the stories contain five or six pictures per story. Children can make up stories based on the titles, some of which are "Andy Plays George Washington," "Andy Plays the Trumpet," "Andy Goes Fishing," and "Andy Is a Baby Sitter."

There are also thirteen stories in a book by Remy Charlip and Jerry Joyner called *Thirteen*. This creative and unusual book can be enjoyed by persons of any age. There are thirteen stories that are carried on simultaneously on a double page spread. Viewers can follow one story through all of the pages of the book and then return to pick up the second story, or readers may read all thirteen of them straight through. For those viewers who choose this option, the preceding page is shown in one of the corners. The book has to be seen to be appreciated. Each story can be viewed many times.

Two 1980 Caldecott honor books are wordless: Bang's *The Grey Lady and the Strawberry Snatcher* about a blue monster who chases an old lady and Crews's *Truck* in which a red truck weaves in and out of traffic. Although there is no story, words appear on road signs and vehicles.

The books of Eric Carle are also very creative. Brightly colored collage forms represent the music played by the violin in Carle's *I See a Song*. The only words in the books are in a hand-lettered section at the beginning of the story letting each person enjoy his or her own song. The book can be used by music and art teachers for students of many ages because it expresses creativity.

In a note to parents and teachers in his *Do You Want to Be My Friend?* Eric Carle explains the importance of the book for prereading skills because the story is arranged so that it must be "read" from left to right. In the story, a little mouse is looking for a friend but the horse is too busy. Mouse sees the tail of another animal and turns the page to find an alligator. This process is repeated until mouse sees a lion, hippo, seal, monkey, peacock, fox, kangaroo, giraffe, and snake. The story reminds one of Garten's *Alphabet Tale* which leads readers through from page to page showing the tail and a rhymed clue of the next animal allowing the reader to guess which animal comes next. (*Alphabet Tale* has words.)

The friendship theme appears in Eleanor Schick's *Making Friends*. In this wordless picture book, a preschool child offers friendship to a bug, squirrel, worm, butterfly, bird, and others until he finally offers friendship to another child.

The books by Renate Meyer express a mood rather than tell a story. *Vickie* is excluded from a group of children and finds company in nature and eventually becomes part of the group. In *Hide-and-Seek* a boy and girl hide from each other.

Journey to the Moon by Fuchs is about the eight-day Apollo II mission. Two pages at the beginning of the book explain the importance of the mission and list events, but the illustrations are not accompanied by any narrative.

NONVERBAL SCENES IN PICTURE BOOKS WITH WORDS.   Besides picture books that are entirely wordless, there are three ways in which nonverbal messages are relayed in children's books. Some picture books have pages within them that are single or double-page spreads that do not have dialogue but add to the story and are designed to be "read." Other books depend on pictures at the end of the book to deliver the "punch line" instead of using words to convey the ending. Another category includes books that have a second story being told by pictures simultaneously with a story being told by words and even other illustrations, a story within a story.

This section contains examples of all three types.

Galbraith's *Spots Are Special* is an example of a book that depends on illustration to deliver the "punch line." Sandy has chicken pox and pretends she is various spotted animals. Her brother Eric wants to play with her but she won't let him. Finally, at the end of the book she relents. Then readers discover for themselves by the spots on his face that Eric has chicken pox too.

In Stevenson's *The Night After Christmas,* a bear and doll are discarded. The nonverbal last page is the only way to know that the story has a happy ending.

In Carrick's *Sleep Out* Christopher gets camping gear for his birthday. When they get to their cottage, Christopher's father is too busy to camp out with him so he strikes out alone and even discourages his dog from following him. After moving around several times because of "night noises," Christopher sleeps in an abandoned house. The wolf he imagines he hears following him turns out to be his dog Badger. With Badger as company, he finishes the night without incident. Christopher enthusiastically returns to the cottage and tells his parents that he plans to sleep out again the next night. The last page contains the nonverbal "punch line." Readers will chuckle when they see Christopher's tent pitched under a tree next to the cottage.

Another camping story is Mayer's *You're the Scaredy-Cat.* Two boys camp out in the yard and one of them tells the other about a garbage-can monster. The storyteller dreams his story and the monster gets bigger and bigger until he wakes to a noise. His friend is already sleeping in the house when he gets inside. As in his other books, Mayer relies on illustrations to help tell the story.

In *I Am a Hunter* by Mayer, there is a two-page spread in which a boy pretends he is killing a snake in the back yard. When the snake he was attacking turns out to be the garden hose, his father is not pleased.

Mayer, who has many wordless picture books to his credit, is very aware of nonverbal communication in his illustrations for picture books that contain some dialogue. The following three stories contain more dialogue than those just described.

In A Special Trick, Elroy, like the sorcerer's apprentice, is left alone by the magician to clean and dust the tent. Elroy's adventures begin when he finds an old magic dictionary and says some of the words aloud which produce a six-eyed monster called a galaplop. The story is told opposite colored illustrations that have much interesting detail. The story can be "re-read" by looking at the pictures. The pictures can also be the springboard for having children retell the story in their own words. The monsters, like the monsters in There's a Nightmare in My Closet and Sendak's Where the Wild Things Are, are ferocious but not menacing.

The troll in The Terrible Trolls follows that same pattern. The book shows life in medieval times as a modern boy imagines it. The two-page spread without words at the end of the book explains the phrase on the preceding page about the fight in the troll's castle. There is little dialogue but much to see in the illustrations.

Another book about the middle ages is Merry Ever After, the Story of Two Medieval Weddings by Lasker. Anne and Gilbert are nobility and the marriage is arranged and executed according to the customs of their class. Martha and Simon are peasants and their betrothal and wedding similarly reflect their class. The contrast in the activities in the illustrations offers another reason for viewing them carefully. There are also similarities in the customs. The illustrations are patterned on some paintings from the fifteenth century, and a sound filmstrip is available.

The contrasting expressions on the faces of the people in Mayer's The Queen Who Wanted to Dance as they show their disapproval of the king's law forbidding dancing and singing, adds to the story. Finally, when almost everyone is in jail for singing and dancing the king decides to join them.

Martha Alexander, who also has illustrated several wordless picture books, has published other books that have very little dialogue like We Never Get to Do Anything. In that story, Adam wants to go swimming but his mother is too busy. Finally rain solves his problem. No Ducks in Our Bathtub has dialogue but not on every page. The humorous story shows how a boy who wants a pet gets 103 fish eggs and puts them in the bathtub. When he returns from his vacation he finds that he has 103 frogs.

Sugita's Wake Up Little Tree, A Christmas Fantasy is a beautiful picture book that has few words. Another Christmas story won the Kate Greenaway Medal. Raymond Briggs's Father Christmas presents a Santa in cartoon style whose only noises are grumbles. Santa grumpily delivers his presents and goes home to soak in the tub.

Oxenbury's Pig Tale also utilizes cartoon-like illustrations. Two discontented pigs named "Bertha" and "Briggs" wanted money and riches. Their wish came true when they found a treasure and could buy everything they wanted. These possessions are shown in eight individual pictures in a two-page wordless spread. There are several similar groups of eight pictures throughout the book. The pages occur again when the car and other gadgets break down and the clothes get dirty. Like *Father Christmas*, *Pig Tale* is also British. Words like "bonnet" and "telly" may need to be interpreted for American children.

Elephant Girl by Cutler, illustrated by Oxenbury, has few words.

In Clymer's *Horatio's Birthday* Robert Quackenbush shows a cat named "Horatio" who is as grumpy as *Father Christmas*. Horatio is grumpy because visitors invade his house; he does not know that they have come to celebrate his birthday. While everyone is having a good time, Horatio gets outside through a pipe in the basement and joins some wild cats on escapades before he returns home with a pretty little yellow cat that he has saved. At the end of the story Horatio and his friend are fed and content. Anyone who sees Horatio's rounded tummy and sees him roll over on his back knows that he is content. Horatio winks at the readers on the last page because his family continues to speculate about how the yellow cat got inside and where Horatio went when he disappeared. Readers can tell by the expression on Horatio's face that he will keep his secret.

Expressions in Shulevitz's *Oh What a Noise!* reveal the attitude of a boy who puts off bedtime as long as he can.

There are two pages without words in *Wildfire* by Valens. Lightning strikes a forest and the animals are escaping.

In Schmid's *Horns Everywhere*, there are fifteen pages without words as people are looking for a strange beast loose in the woods.

There are five stories in *Gordon's House* by Brinckloe. In "One Rainy Day" (pp. 29-36), there are four pages without words in which Gordon Bear paints the rain.

In Shire's *The Snow Kings*, three kings live side by side in three kingdoms. The yellow, brown, and pink kings are always quarreling until they fall into a pit and become snow covered and colorless. The colorless kings have a good time together for four pages without words. Unfortunately, when the snow melts, they become their former selves again. The book is excellent for stimulating discussion.

Sometimes there are nonverbal stories that are being told simultaneously with the other words and pictures in a book. Trina Hyman's illustrations in Paul Heins's translation of Grimm's *Snow White* is an excellent example of this concept. The gilt on the mirror into which the wicked stepmother looks has, among other figures, a female devil. The mirror changes during the story and at the end, when the wicked queen meets her just reward, the devil figure is missing.

Ellen Raskin has two stories running simultaneously in her *Ghost in a Four-Room Apartment*. The written story introduces the immediate family members who live in the apartment as well as other family members who are guests. There are no words on the colorful double page spreads between these introductions. These are the pages in which Horace, the invisible ghost who also lives in the apartment, makes his mischief. The expressions on the faces of the family as they encounter disruptions by Horace are a delight. The book offers something each time it is "read" through.

In Barton's *Buzz Buzz Buzz*, a bee stings a bull who jumps and makes the cow kick the farmer's wife so she goes home and yells at her husband who hits the mule who kicks over the shed and scares a goat who butts a dog into a pond so it chases a goose who in turn bites a cat's tail who chases after a bird who sees a bee and dives at him. The last picture shows the bee taking after the bull with an angry look on the bee's face. The bee acts as if he were the injured party as he begins the chain reaction again. Although the expressions on the faces of the other people and animals are interesting, the look on the bee's face gives an added meaning to the story.

The ending of Alexander's *Blackboard Bear* also depends on reading the pictures. Anthony draws the four boys who wouldn't play with him on the blackboard next to a honey pot. When the four boys have a change of heart and ask Anthony and his bear to come fishing with them, Anthony says that the bear must finish lunch first. No words are necessary on the last page when Anthony wipes off the bear's mouth and the honey pot is empty on the floor. All that is left on the blackboard are the cap, feather, and mask worn by the boys.

The end of *Mexicali Soup* by Hitte and Hayes is told by the illustrations. A Mexican mother prepares a family favorite, Mexicali soup. When she lists the ingredients, each person asks that one of the ingredients be left out. The daughter says that potatoes are fattening and one son says that city people do not eat peppers. When the soup is served, everyone complained that it did not smell, taste, or look like Mexicali Soup. One of them even suggested it even tasted like water. Mama insisted that she made it exactly according to their specifications and listed the person and the ingredient they asked her to leave out. The last picture shows each person helping to dice or bring the left out ingredients to put into the pot.

In Lund's *You Ought to See Herbert's House*, illustrated by Steven Kellogg, Herbert tries to impress his new friend Roger with stories about his house. Among other things, Herbert tells Roger that his house has three towers, a moat, twin tepees, and a tree in the living room. When Herbert confesses to his mother she asks him to invite Roger to spend the night. Roger accepts and the last page shows them sleeping in a tent on a rug they pretend is a buffalo robe. The previous two-page spread shows the two boys having fun pretending to be Indians, eating cake, climbing trees, and hearing a bedtime story.

Discussing illustrations in children's books provides an opportunity for introducing and expanding the concept of nonverbal communication.

MAKING A BOOK.   The "Young Authors" movement has gained momentum in the last few years as teachers help students to write and illustrate books of their own. Several films and filmstrips that can help in this process are *How a Picture Book is Made, Creating a Children's Book,* and *Story of a Book.*

Story of a Book outlines the six steps Lucille and Holling Clancy Holling took to create the book *Pagoo*. The steps are 1—getting the idea for the book, 2—researching the idea in the library as well as first-hand observation, 3—writing and rewriting, 4—drawing the illustrations, 5—putting together a dummy, 6—printing the book. *Story of a Book* is available as a 16mm film or as a filmstrip. The impact of the film is greater but the filmstrip is less expensive and can be owned by individual schools. The accompanying worksheets and activities are helpful. Students may wish to investigate other books about hermit crabs or other books by the Hollings; check the bibliography.

How a Picture Books is Made is a filmstrip that shows how The Island of the Skog was created. A filmstrip of that book is an excellent companion. The steps for creating the book are: 1—how Steven Kellogg got the idea of writing about mice, 2—writing, 3—consulting with the editor, 4—rewriting, 5—creating the illustrations, and 6—preparing the dummy. Steps that were omitted in other films are 7—printing, 8—binding, and 9—distributing. Students will wish to look at other books by Kellogg; check the bibliography.

Creating a Children's Book is about a lesser known author-illustrator, Jolly Roger Bradfield and the creating of It's a Good Knight for Dragons.

McCloskey appears as one of three Caldecott winning author/illustrators in The Lively Art of Picture Books hosted by John Langstaff. Viewers visit the herb garden that appears in Barbara Cooney's Chanticleer and the Fox by Chaucer. Information about Cooney's The Owl and the Pussycat by Lear and Wynken, Blynken and Nod by Field is included. McCloskey tells how his summer home on an island provided inspiration for Time of Wonder which is also a sound filmstrip. Maurice Sendak's city apartment is the setting for telling about how an unpublished book eventually became Where the Wild Things Are, which is also a filmstrip. Individual films called Robert McCloskey and Maurice Sendak contain much of the same information.

Except for Andy and the Lion, a book and filmstrip, James Daugherty is best known for the biographies he has written and illustrated, including Carl Sandburg's Abe Lincoln Grows Up. Check the bibliography for biographies by Daugherty. In the film, Daugherty discusses how he came to write and illustrate Daniel Boone.

The filmstrip Evolution of a Graphic Concept: The Stonecutter can be used with McDermott's filmstrip and book The Stonecutter because it explains the process necessary to create the illustrations for that Japanese folktale. A Letter to Amy appears in iconographic form in the film about Ezra Jack Keats. In Tracing a Legend: The Story of the Green Man, Gail Haley tells how she created that picture book. A companion filmstrip is The Green Man. Other filmstrips are Gail E. Haley: Wood and Linoleum Illustration, Children of the North-Lights (about Ingri and Edgar D'Aulaire), and Mr. Shepard and Mr. Milne (about Winnie-the-Pooh).

Greenfeld's Books from Writer to Reader is an up-to-date book for intermediates and above about the writer, agent, decision to publish, editor, illustrator, copy editor, designer, jacket designer, production supervisor, compositor, proofreader, indexing, printing, color printing, and binding. Steps from the warehouse to bookstore and reader, as well as reviewing, are included.

Teachers will also wish to read chapter 11 of Pitz's Illustrating Children's Books for information about body, jackets, and title pages. Larrick used McCloskey's Make Way for Ducklings as an example of how a book is written, illustrated and published in chapter 14 of Teacher's Guide to Children's Books.

Foster's Pages, Pictures and Print: A Book in the Making is suitable for advanced intermediate students as well as teacher reference. Gordon 's *Making Picture Books, a Method of Learning Graphic Sequence* is written from the graphic arts viewpoint and is for teachers. Jennett's *The Making of Books* is divided into two parts, printing and design. Simon's *The Story of Printing from Wood Blocks to Electronics* begins with the birth of printing through platen and rotary presses, photogravure, rotogravure, lithography and other printing changes. Lehmann-Haupt's *The Life of the Book* is another classic for teacher use.

Sections of books for teachers to read are "Illustration and Production" from Colby's *Writing, Illustrating and Editing Children's Books* and "Graphic Processes in Children's Books" from Mahony's *Illustration of Children's Books, 1744-1945.* Also read pp. 59-103 and 113-22 of Karl's *From Childhood to Childhood* and pp. 129-34 of Yolen's *Writing Books for Children.*

Information on how individual books were written or illustrated appears in the acceptance speeches found in *Caldecott Medal Books, 1937-1957* and *Newbery Medal Books, 1922-1955* both edited by Miller and Field and *Newbery and Caldecott Medal Books, 1956-1965* and *Newbery and Caldecott Medal Books, 1966-1975* both edited by Kingman. There are filmstrips about many of the Medal Winners.

Instructions for making a first book in class are given in Kurth's *Print a Book.* Ingredients needed are a potato, knife, paper, needle and thread. Before starting a unit on book making, teachers should read *How to Make Your Own Book* by Weiss. Clear step-by-step line drawings show stapling, sewing, gluing, and making hard covers. Other styles of books included are Jack in the box, Japanese style, different shapes, double books, scrolls, comic books, flip books, and albums. Directions and photos telling about accordion books and sewn booklets are given on pages 224-29 of Penn's *Individualized Arts and Crafts Lessons for the Elementary School.* Tools, equipment, sequence of operations and sewing books are given in Corderoy's *Bookbinding for Beginners.* Consult Watson's *Hand Bookbinding, a Manual of Instruction* for more ideas.

SPECIALIZED BIBLIOGRAPHIC CATEGORIES

At the back of this book are two numbered bibliographes, one of multimedia (nonprint material), and one of books. The numbers below refer to those bibliographies, with the entries preceded by "M" found in the Multimedia list.

ALPHABET MEDIA
8, 98, 99, 181, 215, 216, 217, 218, 296, 662, M13, 672, 749, 804, 899, 902, 922, 933, 956, 1015, 1083, 1192, 1201, 1272, 1292, 1426, 1436, 1494, 1516, 1575, 1576, 1577, 1604, 1634, 1659, 1794, 1795, 1804, 1850, 1967, 1980, 1982, 2059, 2306, 2393, 2524, 2542, 2859, 2869, 2997, 3088, 3096, 3172, 3211, 3286, 3354, 3355, 3358, 3360, 3383, 3385, 3440, 3492, 3513, M104, 3515, M49, 3557, 3656, 3718, 3735, 3764, 3852, 3937, M162, 3978, 4007, 4042, 4050, 4051, 4072, 4103, 4105, 4118, 4201, M15, M16, M573, M574, 4227, M176, 4340, 4425, 4516, 4528,

4606, M412, 4622, 4831, 4846, 4850.

MEDIA ABOUT NUMBERS AND COUNTING
73, 134, 170, 182, 317, 329, 419, M63, 465, M212, M213, 491, M213, 519, 570, 621, 658, M719, M720, 811, 813, 814, 817, 819, 907, 908, 916, 937, 957, 1012, 1020, 1202, 1453, 1495, 1502, 1503, 1605, 1732, M329, 1771, 1806, M447, M448, 2007, 2008, 2291, M679, 2294, 2305, 2329, 2339, 2469, M103, 2605, 2627, 2659, 2754, 2808, M510, M511, 2943, 3030, 3105, 3199, 3204, 3208, 3223, 3224, 3231, 3359, 3370, 3309, 3586, 3657, 3719, 3884, 3930, 4104, 4208, M504, M505, 4210, M573, M574, 4240, M500, 4344, 4459, 4627, 4694, 4756, 4835, 4836, 4837, 4851, 4945, 4963, 5025.

PICTURE BOOKS WITHOUT WORDS
116, 122, 147, 175, 181, 182, 184, 207, 282, 625, 752, 805, 809, 815, 818, 847, 861, 862, 863, 864, 865, 866, 905, 1306, 1333, 1336, 1515, 1785, 1792, 1925, 1926, 1927, 1928, 1929, 1930, 1931, 1932, 1933, 1934, 1935, 1936, 2230, 2292, 2293, 2296, 2299, 2325, 2449, M119, M120 2657, 2728, 2729, 2730, M215, 2731, 2732, 2733, 2734, 2735, 2736, 3014, 3015, 3254, 3299, 3300, 3301, 3302, M106, 3303, 3304, 3305, 3306, 3307, 3308, 3310, 3311, 3312, 3317, 3318, 3378, 3379, 3440, 3511, 3586, 3616, 3881, 3957, 3958, 3978, 4113, 4155, 4282, 4417, M481, 4458, 4502, 4631, 4643, 4651, 4653, 4700, 4740, M611, 4785, 4786, 4833, M99, 4887, M58, 4888.

NONVERBAL COMMUNICATION
M677, 454, 656, 1497, 1594, 2071, 2089, 2090, 2236, 2398, 2649, 2705, 3466, 4043, 4461, 4562.

ART TECHNIQUES AND PROJECTS
M127, M155, M186, M192, M196, M198, M238a, M243, M301, M327, M384, M415, M435, M455, M518, M532, M584, M645, M707b, M747, 8, 96, 130, 142, 143, 144, 145, 146, 172, 173, 189, 194, 254, 284, 308, 338, 353, 365, 389, 438, 446, 451, 472, 479, 480, 498, 515, 553, 557, 558, M532, 572, 645, 648, 825, 868, 917, 919, 920, 928, 943, 944, 1052, 1105, 1116, 1156, 1159, 1195, 1197, 1200, 1207, 1216, 1222, 1235, 1236, 1282, 1284, 1326, 1327, 1409, 1492, 1507, 1517, 1518, 1519, 1520, 1521, 1522, 1523, 1524, 1529, 1530, 1542, 1545, 1607, 1626, 1661, 1714, 1768, 1797, 1799, 1818, 1836, 1837, 1876, 1885, 1886, 1902, 1937, 2001, 2004, 2005, 2010, 2055, 2074, 2108, 2123, 2139, 2146, 2164, 2165, 2167, 2168, 2169, 2217, 2218, 2228, 2229, 2236, 2267, 2273, 2317, 2345, 2352, 2356, 2359, 2362, 2364, 2366, 2367, 2388, 2389, 2390, 2423, 2437, 2445, 2446, 2447, 2515, 2526, 2527, 2536, 2547, 2548, 2552, 2553, 2599, 2606, 2610, 2655, 2656, 2662, 2665, 2672, 2673, 2688, 2689, 2690, 2691, 2695, 2703, 2704, 2717, 2759, 2762, 2764, 2783, 2812, 2813, 2844, 2890, 2895, 2899, 2970, 2971, 2972, 2973, 2974, 2977, 2979, 2980, 2995, 3115, 3121, 3124, 3125, 3169, 3213, 3220, 3229, 3230, 3233, 3257, 3258, 3259, 3267, 3287, 3298, 3321, 3340, 3341, 3342, 3380, 3388, 3390, 3402, 3403, 3436, 3445, 3454, 3456, 3479, 3547, 3565, 3579, 3580, 3588, 3653, 3659, 3661, 3663, 3667, 3670, 3676, 3716, 3745, 3752, 3753, 3775,

3777, 3807, 3845, 3849, 3853, 3855, 3880, 3886, 3897, 3963, 3968, 3993, 3996, 4005, 4006, 4013, 4032, 4179, 4180, 4181, 4182, 4183, 4276, 4283, 4314, 4334, 4349, 4359, 4360, 4390, 4391, 4393, 4423, M518, 4426, 4455, 4456, 4462, 4468, 4477, 4500, 4544, 4545, 4574, 4620, 4699, 4741, 4742, 4748, 4762, 4763, 4764, 4765, 4766, 4767, 4768, 4769, 4770, 4772, 4777, 4798, 4801, 4875, 4880, 4893, 4894, 4921, 4929, 4970, 4984, 4985, 4986, 4987, 4988, 4989, 4990, 4991, 4992, 4993, 4994

CHAPTER THREE

Enhancing Books through Music

CHAPTER OBJECTIVES

1. To provide examples which show how music can introduce books without musical themes to an audience.
2. To describe picture books which illustrate a single song and to suggest ways to use them creatively with groups of children.
3. To identify from songbook collections individual songs which can provide alternative verses, musical scores, and introductory information for stories, picture books, and nursery rhymes.
4. To show how books can introduce, explain, and provide for a greater appreciation of suites, operas, ballets, folksongs, and ballads.
5. To provide ideas on how to coordinate the use of paperback editions, sound filmstrips, 8mm and 16mm films, and phonograph records or cassettes with stories, picture books, and nursery rhymes.
6. To show how a variety of subject matter can be coordinated with music found in books.

TECHNIQUES FOR USING MEDIA INTRODUCED IN THIS CHAPTER

1. Picture books in this chapter should be read to the audience from the hardback edition (if there is a choice). Use the techniques suggested in chapter 1, "Introducing Books in All Kinds of Ways."
2. A recording or audio cassette tape of the song from the book may be used to introduce the book, and played to the group *before* the reading begins. Invite the group to sing along during the refrains and choruses only.
3. If the leader has a good enough singing voice, the song can be sung to the group instead of being read. Or the leader may sing while someone else plays the song on a musical instrument, such as a guitar or piano.
4. The leader may want to read the story from the picture book before individuals learn to play the song on various instruments. A "reading and performing program" could be worked out with the music teacher.
5. After reading the book and playing the song, the group may want to learn the lyrics. The group may then want to sing the story while following along in individual paperback copies.

6. The group may want to sing along while viewing the lyrics printed on a sound film strip, either accompanied or unaccompanied by sound.

7. The leader or one of the students may want to read from the book while the visual portion of the sound filmstrip is shown on the screen.

8. Once the picture book has been read, the audio portion of the sound filmstrip or the recording could be used while the leader turns appropriate pages of the book for the group.

9. Listening to a recording of the book or of songs from it may be a culminating activity after the book has been read aloud to the group.

10. After hearing and viewing a sound filmstrip of a book containing one or more songs, the group may want to make a cassette or cassettes which could be placed with the filmstrip in addition to the professional cassette which accompanies it.

11. Each class could be encouraged to make its own audio cassette to use with the filmstrip, and use its personalized rendition in its own classroom with the book and filmstrip and other materials.

12. Appropriate recorded music—not necessarily what is in the book or on an accompanying sound filmstrip—can be played softly in the background while the picture book is being read or the story from it told. Care must be taken to insure that this does not distract or prevent people from hearing.

13. Time should be provided after the book has been read or a media activity concluded, for the group to handle or check out the books or media introduced.

14. After the book has been read or the media activity completed, introduce other picture books with the same theme or subject so that the group will have a chance to choose from among a variety of similar books. Also, introduce other books with songs.

15. Use inexpensive paperback copies of books that are introduced to keep waiting lists short, and help meet the demand for holiday or other books of seasonal interest.

16. Use picture books with historical songs or ballads to introduce history or social studies units to many different grade levels. Also, use with ballads and songs that are related to history units in the curriculum.

17. Invite a local folksinger to perform live before, during, and at the end of a program of related readings from picture books.

18. Follow the presentation of a book, soundfilmstrip, or film or recording by having students search for other versions and further verses of the song or songs they have heard.

19. A 16mm film on folkmusic may be used to introduce books that contain some of the songs used as examples in the film.

20. Use a 16mm film or filmstrips or slides as background for the performance of a local music group, for an assembly or for an audience

outside the school. A multiscreen presentation, requiring several projectors and a mixed media format, can be effective and memorable, reinforcing the music with visual images.

21. A 16mm film of a picture book may effectively introduce the book.

22. Encourage children to make up additional verses to the songs in the books, which they may also have heard on recordings or audio cassettes.

23. Use recordings of songs to introduce books which may not have music or songs in them but which have themes similar to books that have.

24. Use music to help children to recreate a story in their imaginations and then talk about it together.

25. Use the picture book based on or including a song to clarify the meaning of the song's words.

26. Try playing out several songs, and setting the action to music.

INTRODUCING BOOKS WITH MUSIC.   Music may be used as a vehicle for introducing books which are not directly connected to music. Even if you can't sing, open your copy of Ellen Raskin's *Figgs and Phantoms* (Dutton, 1974) to p. 62 and sing the following verse to the tune of "Battle Hymn of the Republic."

> Mine eyes have seen the glory
>> of a tree so wild and free,
> That is standing on an island
>> that's surrounded by the sea;
> Whatsoever, howsoever,
>> wheresoever it may be,
> All Figgs go to Capri.
>> Glory, glory hallelujah,
>> Glory, glory hallelujah,
>> Glory, glory hallelujah,
>> All Figgs go to Capri.

Then hold up *Figgs and Phantoms*, a Newbery Honor Book, and explain to your audience that the Figg clan of Pineapple always sang this song sitting on the floor, with eyes closed while the eldest reverently read from the diary of Jonathan Figg about a "tree that grows wild and free and welcomed him with open arms and whispered 'Capri.'" After shouting "Capri" in unison, another member of the clan read Noah Figg's entry in the diary: ". . .The wild, free tree is only the key to the perfect dream. There are many wasps; there are many trees—each must find his own Capri."

Members of the Figg family can be introduced through the eyes of the heroine, Mona, whose mother is Sister Figg Newton, tap dancer and baton twirler; one uncle is Truman, the Human Pretzel; two others are Romulus the Walking Book of Knowledge and Remus the Talking Adding Machine; still another is Kadota and his Nine Performing Kanines. Mona's favorite was her Uncle Florence, the book dealer whom she was afraid would soon go to Capri, the Figg Family heaven.

Other books by Ellen Raskin written for this age level could also be introduced. They are *The Mysterious Disappearance of Leon (I Mean Noel)*, *The Tattooed Potato and Other Clues*, and her 1979 Newbery Medal winner *The Westing Game*.

Another fantasy, *Mary Poppins*, can also be introduced through music. Pamela Travers's books about Mary Poppins which were incorporated into a motion picture, can be ushered in with selections from the sound track of the film and by reading selections from the book *Mary Poppins A-Z*. Each letter of the alphabet in *Mary Poppins A-Z* is given two pages, one page for Mary Shepard's illustrations and the other for a story featuring Mary Poppins. One letter of the alphabet is used as much as possible on the pages featuring that letter. One could read the introduction to the story while the overture is playing softly in the background, or perhaps play the overture in full sound after reading the introduction. This can be followed by reading the story for the letter B, which tells about Admiral Boom and feeding the birds, tuppence a bag, and playing the third song on side two of the record. "Feed the Birds." Another song from the record, the fifth song on side two, is "Chim Chim Cheree" which can introduce, follow, or be played while reading the selection on the letter "L," "Let me in, Lords and Ladies. I'll Labor to Leave your Chimneys clear" (p. 23). The other Mary Poppins books could be introduced at that time, by title. These books are listed under "Travers, Pamela" in the bibliography at the end of this book.

Other fantasy books which can be introduced by music are *Chitty Chitty Bang Bang* and *The Wizard of Oz*. There are many other songs that could be used in addition to those from the sound tracks of the films.

Nineteen poems by Lewis Carroll from *Alice in Wonderland* and *Through the Looking Glass* are set to music in the book *Songs From Alice*, also available as a cassette.

Winnie the Pooh and Christopher Robin can be introduced against the background of three 20- by 31-inch "Scenes from Winnie the Pooh" posters to set the stage. The A.A. Milne books *When We Were Very Young* and *Now We Are Six* are the sources of poems read on a phonograph record *When We Were Very Young* by Dame Judith Anderson. Both these titles are contained also in *The World of Christopher Robin*. Children will then enjoy singing some of the songs from Fraser-Simson's arrangements in *The Pooh Song Book*. A. A. Milne's stories, *Winnie-the-Pooh* and *The House at Pooh Corner*, both included in *The World of Pooh*, can be introduced with the phonograph record *Winnie-the-Pooh* read and sung by Carol Channing. There is also a 16mm film, *Mr. Shepard and Mr. Milne*, a somewhat sentimental journey intended principally for adults which would appeal to all true Milne fans. In this Weston Woods color film, Christopher Robin Milne reads selections from his father's books and E. Shepard, the illustrator whose drawings helped make the characters so lovable, reminisces about his working relationship with A.A. Milne in the 1920s.

Of course, use of all these elements would make for too long a program for four to eight year olds (approximately the age of the audiences involved), but the presenter would select from these elements for a program of any desired length.

Two totally different books for different age groups can be introduced by the song, "Who Killed Cock Robin," "Cocky Robin," or simply "Cock Robin." The books are Jean George's *Who Really Killed Cock Robin?* and the Mother Goose rhyme made into a picture book, *The Courtship, Merry Marriage, and Feast of Cock Robin and Jenny Wren to Which Is Added the Doleful Death of Cock Robin.* The picture book, illustrated by Barbara Cooney, tells how all the animal friends help at the wedding and later the death of Cock Robin. The cock blew the horn, the rook was the parson, the lark sang, goldfinch gave the bride away, and linnet was bridesmaid. Later when Cock Robin is shot, owl dug the grave with a trowel, dove was chief mourner because of love. There is no music in the book but versions of the song are available in Bacon's *Forty-Six Two-Part American Folksongs*, Erdei and Komlos's *One Hundred Fifty American Folk Songs*, Fowke's *Ring Around the Moon*, Langstaff's *Hi! Ho! The Rattlin' Bog*, Langstaff's *Jim Along, Josie*, Winn's *Fireside Book of Children's Songs*, and Yolen's *Fireside Song Book of Birds and Beasts*. It is interesting to compare the versions and find that they do not list the same birds, and to note that some versions are longer than others.

George's book *Who Really Killed Cock Robin?* could be introduced by telling the story of the song. Sometimes an explanation of a book title is sufficient to interest children in reading the book. Students may never have heard the song or the old nursery rhyme. And so an explanation of the title and the song from which it came could be an introduction to a brief summary of the book. *Who Really Killed Cock Robin?* is an ecological mystery written for intermediate and junior high readers. Tony Isidoro has been watching a family of robins when suddenly, the robin he has called "Cock Robin" is dead. Tony and his friend Mary Alice then investigate the pollution in their community to find out what imbalance in the environment has killed Cock Robin.

The song "The Ants Go Marching One by One" could be used to introduce Freschet's picture book *Ants Go Marching*. The picture book doesn't attempt really to follow the song, but there is too close a connection to miss an opportunity to use it with the book. The song is familiar enough so that students could be asked to sing it after the story has been read. Music and lyrics for "The Ants Go Marching One by One" can be found in Larrick's *Wheels of the Bus Go Round and Round* and Glazer's *Do Your Ears Hang Low?*

Music doesn't always have to introduce the reading of books. Sometimes it is most effective when it is used *after* a story has been told or read. Herbert Donaldson has composed several suites available on the record *Nature and Make Believe* that can be played most effectively to help children recreate a story in their imaginations after it has been read or told to them. Three of these suites that have been used successfully with children are "The Three Billy Goats Gruff," "Chicken Little," and "The Hare and the Tortoise."

The "Three Billy Goats Gruff" has long been a favorite of children. Just as they are intrigued with the sizes of the three bears, small children are fascinated by the voices of the three billy goats and enjoy hearing the differences shown through changes in volume and pitch. After reading any of the picture book versions of the story children will enjoy listening to Donaldson's "Once Upon a Time Suite," in which the goats prance through the music with varying degrees of loudness and speed. The troll has an ominous sound that is easily recognized.

Children will also enjoy Donaldson's musical expression of the differences in speed between the hare and the tortoise. A reading of Brian Wildsmith's picture book *The Hare and the Tortoise* precedes the music.

A third suite is about Chicken Little who, when an acorn falls on his head, runs to tell the king that the sky is falling. On the way he spreads the alarm to other animals until in the confusion, the fox lures all of them into his den and they are not seen again. The reading of *Henny Penny* in paperback or hardback can precede this music. Donaldson's Chicken Little is a male; amusingly enough, the best picture book version includes a female chicken called Henny Penny.

The Three Billy Goats Gruff and *The Hare and the Tortoise* are also available on a Weston Woods sound filmstrip. *Henny Penny* is available in a paperback-record kit from Scholastic.

Lois Lenski's books belong to several series: books about "Mr. Small," "Davy Books," the "Read-and-Sing" series, and "Season Books." A phonograph record is available for the book *I Went for a Walk*, one of the books in the "Read-and-Sing" series. This music could be used to introduce other books in the same series or books from the "Mr. Small" series which also presents neighborhood people to children. One book from the "Read-and-Sing" series should be avoided: *When I Grow Up* is sexist and gives all assistant roles to females, i.e. male doctors and female nurses.

The most popular of all the Lenski books are the small-sized books about seasons: *I Like Winter, Now It's Fall, On a Summer Day*, and *Spring is Here*. Each book tells in verse the simple activities engaged in during each season. Music for the verses is given in *I Like Winter* and could be sung to introduce the series.

The Beatrix Potter stories are also found in small-sized books. *Songs of Peter Rabbit* can be used to introduce *The Tale of Peter Rabbit, The Tale of Benjamin Bunny, The Tale of Mr. Jeremy Fisher, The Tale of Tom Kitten, The Tale of Two Bad Mice* and others. These stories are also available as sound filmstrips from Weston Woods.

The cassette made to accompany Isadora's *Ben's Trumpet* could be used to introduce that picture book or Berger's *The Trumpet Book*, a history of trumpets.

Picture books by M. Sasek are enjoyed by diverse age groups because Sasek captures the atmosphere of major cities and countries of the world through illustrations accompanied by identifying text. The books could be introduced by showing the 16mm film *This is New York*. Or the books could be introduced by playing for each book in turn the appropriate selection from the recording, *National Anthems of the World*. All the available titles of Sasek's books could be displayed while selections from the recording were played and the audience guessed which book matches which music. Various countries and cities represented on the record include Israel, "Halikuah"; Venice and Rome,

"Inno Di Mameli"; Washington, "Star Spangled Banner"; Belfast, Edinburgh, and London, "God Save the Queen"; Paris, "La Marseillaise"; Munich, "Deutschland Uber Alles".

The audience could be invited to suggest appropriate sound effects or music for other books in the series, i.e., a countdown for *This Is Cape Kennedy,* "I Left My Heart in San Francisco" for *This Is San Francisco* and "The Eyes of Texas Are Upon You" for *This Is Texas.* This activity would probably be followed by time for browsing in the books. *This Is New York, This Is San Francisco,* and *This Is Washington, D.C.* are available in paperback, but it should be noted that the paperbacks are abridged versions.

Another book with a strong locational flavor is *Waltzing Matilda,* named the picture-book-of-the-year by the Childrens Book Council of Australia. In this instance, the book accents the music rather than the music accenting the book. Children as well as adults love to sing Patterson's song, but few really know that a swagman is a tramp, a matilda is his bundle or swag, and a jumbuck is a sheep. The illustrations in this picture book, which also has a glossary, explain the terms in the song. The only disadvantage in an otherwise flawless book is that no music is included. A musical score and lyrics appear, however, in *The Fireside Book of Folk Songs* by Boni, and a sound filmstrip is available.

For years children have been enjoying the "Little House" books of Laura Ingalls Wilder. Now a new generation has discovered those books through the television series "Little House on the Prairie." Children may not need to be *introduced* to these stories through the *Laura Ingalls Wilder Songbook,* since TV fans will probably be looking for any books they can find about Laura and her family. The songbook compiled and edited by Eugenia Garson will, however, be fun to coordinate with the books. This is easy to do because references to the Wilder book even to page number on which the song appears is given for each song. This songbook will be used and enjoyed wherever the "Little House" books are displayed, read, and enjoyed.

F.N. Monjo's book *The Drinking Gourd,* one of an I-Can-Read-History Series, tells of a Quaker boy who helps his father hide a slave during underground railroad days. The poem "Follow the Drinking Gourd" is listed on the first pages and provides an introduction to the story, with a one sentence explanation of the song or poem in the author's note at the end of the book. It is important to the story that readers know that the constellation known as the Big Dipper was the "drinking gourd" and that the end star in the handle was the North Star, symbol of freedom in the North for the escaping slaves. The song was often sung as a signal that the way was clear for escape. No music is given in the book but the musical score and lyrics can be found in Carmer's *America Sings,* Lomax's *Penguin Book of American Folk Songs,* and also under the title "Foller de Drinkin Gourd" in Lomax's *American Ballads and Folk Songs.* Background notes are given in each book. There are many versions of the "Drinking Gourd" song. Another version, which is different from the words in the Monjo book, is available on the phonograph record *American Negro Slave Songs,* and this music could be used to introduce the book.

The book, *The Drinking Gourd,* could be introduced a number of ways. The record could be played as an introduction to a brief history of the song and its use during underground railroad days. Or it could be played as background while the book is introduced. The poem in the front of the book could be read or sung by the presenter, and its meaning explained as an introduction. The song could be taught to the group after telling them about the book. This book need not be read to children. It is one that students can read for themselves and they should not be deprived of that pleasure.

HOLIDAY SONGS.   Holiday songs are always in demand. One of the most popular Thanksgiving poems set to music is "Over the River and Through the Woods." Lydia Child has caught the spirit of a bygone era through her soft illustrations which combine with the lyrics to form a charming picture book. The words and music for this traditional song are given at the end of the book. A paperback edition of this book helps supply extra copies to meet the heavy demand for this book in November. It can be used to introduce many Thanksgiving stories.

Quackenbush's collection, *The Holiday Song Book* is valuable for providing holiday songs around the calendar. Holiday songs that center on Christmas include Ehrets's *The International Book of Christmas Carols*, Harder's *On Christmas Day*, John's *The Great Song Book*, Simon's *Treasury of Christmas Songs and Carols*, Tasha Tudor's *Favorite Christmas Carols*, and two by Langstaff—*On Christmas Day in the Morning* and *The Season for Singing.*Varnum's *Play and Sing—It's Christmas!* contains instructions so people who have not studied the piano can play sixteen Christmas carols.

Three very different picture books illustrate the old favorite, "The Twelve Days of Christmas." This traditional song is found on most Christmas phonograph records and can be played to introduce any or all of the three books, which are illustrated respectively by Broomfield, Karasz, and Wildsmith. Two of the books have contrasting styles of illustration. Karasz's book is in soft pastels, while Wildsmith's is typically Brian Wildsmith—bright bold colors and shapes. The Broomfield book falls somewhere in between, for the artist combines whimsical line drawings and shaded colors. The Broomfield is also available on sound filmstrip or filmstrip with a text. The Broomfield and Karasz editions are each accompanied by separate musical arrangements for the song. No music accompanies the Wildsmith edition but the song is found in the following collections: Boni's *Fireside Book of Folk Songs*, Lomax's *Folk Songs of North America*, and Yolen's *Fireside Song Book of Birds and Beasts*.

A Scottish version of this song, which is a dance rather than a carol, is illustrated by Nonny Hogrogian in a picture book *The Thirteen Days of Yule*.

The famous Christmas carol, "We Three Kings of Orient Are" is found in most Christmas song books as well as is found in Horder's *On Christmas Day*. *Baboushka and the Three Kings*, the 1961 Caldecott winner, is a picture book based on a narrative song told in nine verses. The Russian legend which is its source is about an old woman who refused to follow the three kings when they were searching for the special child. Later she regretted it so now she searches endlessly because she missed her opportunity to follow the three kings to the

Christ Child.

In the Italian version, *Befana, A Christmas Story*, Befana also regrets not going with the three kings and follows after them, leaving gifts. No music is included in Rockwell's book. Tomi de Paola illustrated *The Legend of Old Befana: An Old Italian Christmas Story*. The kings or wise men also stopped at the home of a crippled boy, and when he gave them a gift, they gave him the gift of sound legs in the opera by Gian Carlo Menotti, *Amahl and the Night Visitors*, which appears on television during the Christmas season.

Christmas carols and the text from the Gospel according to St. Luke alternate in Slaughter's *And it Came to Pass: Bible Verses and Carols*. Leonard Weisgard illustrated this book which contains appropriate religious carols.

"Silent Night" is one of the most famous Christmas carols. How that famous song came to be written and sung in 1818 in a church in a little Austrian village is told in Hertha Pauli's *Silent Night, the Story of a Song*. Wenning's *The Christmas Mouse* is a lighter version based on actual fact, but focused on Kaspar Kleinmouse, who chewed holes in the bellows of the church organ in Oberndorf, Austria, on Christmas Eve, to the dismay of Father Joseph Mohr and organist Franz Gruber so that "Silent Night" was first played on the guitar at Midnight Mass. Lyrics are given in English and in German and music is provided.

Laura Baker adapted her story in song—*The Friendly Beasts*— from an old English Christmas carol in which a sheep, a cow, and a dove express in song the gifts they will give to the baby. When the donkey comes, he is asked what gift he will give and he proudly announces that he has brought Mary and Joseph to the stable. The Baker book is illustrated by Nicholas Sidjakov. Another book was illustrated by de Paola and the song with musical accompaniment is found in John Langstaff's collection *On Christmas Day in the Morning*. The song "The Friendly Beasts" appears on the phonograph record *Holiday Songs*.

Another picture book which expresses the nativity scene, but with two other carols, is *Away in a Manger, A Story of the Nativity*. This Swiss picture book is written by Mares Nussbaumer and illustrated by her husband Paul. The Nussbaumers have chosen their own country for the setting and have portrayed a forest with snow and Swiss costumes and personal characteristics. Music and lyrics for "Away in a Manger" and "O Come Little Children" are included in the book. Both songs are sung on the recording, *Christmas Carols*. Full-color illustrations opposite the text help tell how Mary and Joseph could find room only at the stable and how shepherds, wise men, and villagers came to visit. After Joseph thought everyone had gone home, he noticed that the village children and one shepherd had stayed behind because they couldn't bear to be parted from the baby. Joseph told them to go home to sleep after singing one more song. The song they sang was "Silent Night." Just one verse of the song, without music, is given.

Another beautifully illustrated Christmas carol about visiting the birthplace of the baby is the seventeenth-century carol illustrated in the picture book *Bring a Torch, Jeannette, Isabella*. The two girls are asked to hurry and bring a light with them so they can hasten with the others to the stable to see the baby

Jesus. Musical scores accompany the illustrations; music and lyrics are also given in a separate part of the book. "Un Flambeau, Jeannette, Isabelle" is given in English and French in Rockwell's *Savez-vous Planter Le Choux?*

Music and twelve verses are included for the traditional spiritual *Children, Go Where I Send Thee* illustrated by Shoemaker. The cumulative song begins "One for the itty bitty baby Born, born, born in Bethlehem" and continues with numbers through "twelve for the twelve disciples."

No music is included in a picture book based on a Polish Christmas carol called *Din Dan Don, It's Christmas*, which Janina Domanska illustrated to represent stained glass windows. In this carol, a duck, gander, turkey, rooster, nightingale, goldfinch, sparrows, and people find their way to the manger. The repetitive phrase "Din Dan Don" is reminiscent of the "rum pa pa pom" in the song "The Little Drummer Boy." This more recent Christmas song, introduced only in 1958, has become something of a classic itself. The song provides several opportunities for introducing and reading the picture book, the *Little Drummer Boy*, illustrated by Ezra Jack Keats. The hardback edition may be used by the reader at a picture book story program, after which the paperback edition can be handed out so that every two or three children have a book and can follow the singing. A piano would be helpful if one is available.

The children could sing along with or without the paperbacks, with the recording of the song, which is available on most Christmas albums. *The Little Drummer Boy* is available from Weston Woods in a sound filmstrip, in hardback format with record or cassette, or in a "hang-up library" which includes a paperback with record or cassette. Students could learn the song, record it on a blank cassette, and include the cassette in their own program package so it could be checked out by members of their own class or other classes in the school. The locally produced cassette could be played while a school assembly, class, or Sunday school audience views the filmstrip. The book is also represented iconographically (by which the book's original illustrations are used and made to appear to move) on a seven minute film by Weston Woods. The film guide suggests that live drummers can provide a background for the boys' choir and soloist. Either the filmstrip or the film could be shown at a musical concert while local musicians sing the song.

Good King Wenceslas; A Legend in Music and Pictures is illustrated in black and white by Newland.

An unusual book, *St. George and the Dragon*, is a folk or mummer's play that was acted out for Christmas during the middle ages. Illustrated with woodcuts, the book gives background for the play, lines, stage directions, costume suggestions, and information about the sword dance. The musical scores used in the play could help to introduce the book.

HISTORY AND FOLKLORE.   Folk heroes, events and historic institutions have found expression in songs, which are a part of oral history. Chapters on black heritage songs are found in the following collections: Boni's *Fireside Book of Folk Songs, Penguin Book of American Folk Songs* by A. Lomax, A. and J. Lomax's *American Ballads and Folk Songs*, Sandburg's book *American Songbag*, and Scott's *Ballad of America.* One of the most aesthetically pleasing collections of black American spirituals is Bryan's *Walk Together Children.* Each of the twenty-four songs is illustrated in beautifully stark black and white drawings. A three-part introduction explains the origin and legacy of the American spiritual. An equally stirring book contains just one song—*Lift Every Voice and Sing.* Mozelle Thompson's illustrations make the book a unique experience when it is read to an audience. In the book's introduction Augusta Baker, formerly the coordinator of children's services for the New York Public Library system and a famous storyteller, explains the background of the song and tells about James Weldon and J. Rosamond Johnson.

The 16mm film, *Discovering America's Folk Music,* depicts musical traditions, including spirituals, jazz, and rock, that have come to us from Africa. The interaction between European and African traditions is also shown.

The most famous folksongs and ballads written about a black man are those sung about John Henry. In *American Ballads and Folk Songs,* the Lomaxes have devoted thirteen pages to background information and music for several versions of stories about the legendary "steel drivin'" man who put his dignity on the line and faced death rather than give way to a heartless machine. One of the songs has twenty-two verses. In *America Sings,* Carmer devotes five pages to songs and background information and includes the tradition that John Henry did not die but lives on in the mountains. In the *Penguin Book of American Folk Songs,* Lomax tells the story of John Henry through thirteen verses which are different from those in previously, mentioned books. Stein begins his illustrated book, *Steel Driving Man, the Legend of John Henry,* with yet another five verses of the song. Stein's book takes each verse and weaves it into an explanation of the illustrated story. No music accompanies *Steel Driving Man.*

Ezra Jack Keats has illustrated a picture book for young children, *John Henry: An American Legend,* which tells the story of the hero but does not include music. Music and four verses are provided at the end of Felton's eighty-two page book of John Henry's life for intermediate and junior high readers, *John Henry's Hammer.*

Carl Sandburg sings a selection about John Henry on the record *American Songbag.* Pete Seeger also sings about John Henry on the record *Folk Songs for Young People.* Burl Ives sings of John Henry on the record *America's Musical Heritage,* (vol. 4, side 2). Nonmusical recordings include *American Tall Tales,* (vol. 1) and the poem read by John Randolph on *Famous American Story Poems.*

Another folksong about a railroad hero, the engineer Casey Jones, has been adapted to picture book format by Glen Rounds. The song is also sung on the Weston Woods filmstrip of Rounds's book, *Casey Jones.* Music and lyrics appear also in Boni's *Fireside Book of Folk Songs.* Twelve verses and background information about the song appear on pp. 366-69 of Sandburg's *The American Songbag.* Words for "John Henry" and "Casey Jones" appear on the second sound filmstrip, *Immigration and Industrialization,* of a set called *Folk Songs in American History.*

America Sings, Stories and Songs of Our Country's Growing by Carmer includes other folk heroes besides John Henry. Songs and background information about Stormalong, Mike Fink, Johnny Appleseed, Joe Jagarac, Tony Beaver, Daniel Boone, Pecos Bill, and Paul Bunyan are found in this volume. The songs and background information could be used to introduce and set the mood for story programs about a particular hero.

Although there is no music given or even hinted about in the picture book *The Story of Paul Bunyan* by Barbara Emberley and illustrated by Ed Emberley, music is an important part of the sound filmstrip created from the book by Teaching Resource Films, a division of the *New York Times*. On the record or cassette, Tom Glazer sings an introduction to the book; appropriate background music is also provided throughout the filmstrip.

The filmstrip *The Story of Paul Bunyan* could be used to introduce the book by the same name which is the easiest of the books about Paul Bunyan. *Paul Bunyan Swings His Axe* is the next easiest book. The folklore collections of Blair, Leach, Malcolmson, and Shapiro each contain a chapter devoted to Paul Bunyan. The Shepard book, *Paul Bunyan*, is a collection of tales about the famous logger taken from many sources. Two other phonograph records that could be used with the books are *Paul Bunyan in Story and Song* and *American Tall Tales*, (vol. 4).

Persons wishing background information on Paul Bunyan should consult Benet's *Reader's Encyclopedia*, Blair's *Tall Tale America*, Leach's *Funk and Wagnalls Standard Dictionary of Folklore, Mythology and Legend*, Leach's *Rainbow Book of American Folk Tales*, Malcolmson's *Yankee Doodle's Cousins*, Shapiro's *Tall Tales of America* and Stoutenburg's *America's Tall Tales*. Pecos Bill also appears in collections except the ones by Benet and Leach's *Rainbow Book*.

Pecos Bill is another special folk hero who can be introduced with songs of the West. The songs in *Texas Cowboy*, collected by Harold Felton, could be used to introduce two other books about Pecos Bill, who was a Texas cowboy. The Felton books are *Pecos Bill, Texas Cowboy* and *New Tall Tales of Pecos Bill*. Peck's *Pecos Bill and Lightning* could also be introduced. Songs of the American West with background information and music are included in all four Lomax books. The record *Tall Tales* (vol. 2) includes tales of Pecos Bill. On volume 6 of *America's Musical Heritage*, Burl Ives sings many cowboy songs.

In a section of *The American Songbag* called "The Great Open Spaces," Carl Sandburg includes fifteen songs of the American cowboy. Over a dozen songs with music are included in Sakett's *Cowboys and Songs They Sang*. Twenty songs are included in Felton's *Cowboy Jamboree: Western Songs and Lore*.

Pictures by Frederic Remington and Charles Russell provide background settings for two sound filmstrips called *The American Cowboy*. Songs included are "Night Herding Song," "Railroad Corral," "Git Along Little Dogies," "Old Chisholm Trail," "The Streets of Laredo," and "I Ride an Old Paint." In addition to the last four songs, "Down in the Valley," "Jesse James," and "Billy the Kid" are several of seventeen songs which appear on the cassette *Cowboy Songs*.

Music with guitar chords is included in a picture book illustrated by Glen Rounds which contains twenty-one verses about a cowboy who tried to tame an outlaw horse. The picture book *The Strawberry Roan* can be used with a unit on cowboys or could be sung to introduce books about horses.

U.S. History classes cannot study the expansion of our nation without hearing about the Erie Canal. Introducing stories about the canal through the famous folksong, "Erie Canal," is one way to approach the subject. Two verses of this folk song are charmingly illustrated by Peter Spier in a picture book which is as much good fun as it is good history. The music and the two verses of the song are presented opposite a page which shows a map and gives some background about the canal. The illustrations, words to the song, and the explanation make this song a valuable contribution to history classes at all levels. The explanation section gives answers to many questions including: How fast did the boats go?; How did canal children live?; and How high were the toll rates?

The Spier book is available on sound filmstrip and 16mm film from Weston Woods and in paperback format. The filmstrip is especially useful because the song is first sung while the pictures from the book are shown. Then the illustrations are shown while the audience is invited to sing along. The words appear on the filmstrip so the audience can fully participate.

More verses to the song are listed in Lomax's book *American Ballads and Folk Songs*. Other Erie Canal songs listed in that collection are "Ballad of the Erie Canal," "The Erie Canal Ballad," "Erie Canal," "A Trip on the Erie" and "The Raging Can-all." However, only the music to "The Erie Canal" and "E-R-I-E" have been provided in the Lomax book *American Ballads and Folk Songs*. Boni's *Fireside Book of Folk Songs* and Agay's *Best Loved Songs of the American People* include lyrics and music for "The Erie Canal." Carl Sandburg sings the song on his record or cassette of fifty songs taken from his book of the same title, *American Songbag*.

The song "E-R-I-E" has music and eight verses given in Boni's *Fireside Book of American Songs*, four verses in Lomax's *Penguin Book of American Folk Songs*, and three verses in Sandburg's *American Songbag*.

One way to approach this topic is by showing a 16mm film to intermediate through senior high school history classes. The film *E-R-I-E*, traces the history of the canal through old photographs and drawings as well as showing what it looks like today. The filmstrip *Building the Erie Canal* could be viewed individually or by a group. A natural outgrowth of the film or filmstrip would be researching for songs about the Erie Canal, as an individual or a group project. As they research, students will find the above mentioned versions. There are also several nonfiction books, among them *The Erie Canal* by Samuel Adams and *The Erie Canal* by the editors of American Heritage.

Picture books of patriotic songs can be used to explain the meaning of the songs and how they came to be part of our American traditions. Few people know, for example, that "Yankee Doodle" was written by a British surgeon. Rich Shakburg's book, illustrated with red, white, and blue woodcuts by Ed Emberley, and set in a typeface popular with colonial printers, tells the story in ten verses and a chorus. Interesting information such as the origin of the words "yankee" and "macaroni" and a recipe for Hasty Pudding is given. The book has been adapted as a color sound filmstrip from the Teaching Resource Films, a division of the *New York Times*. Music for the song appears at the end of Bang's *Steven Kellogg's Yankee Doodle*, a picture book. The song also appears in Browne's *The Story of Our National Ballads*. Background information also appears in Lyons's *Stories of Our American Patriotic Songs*. Both "Yankee Doodle" and "The Star Spangled Banner" appear in Agay's *Best Loved Songs of the American People*. Under the title *The Star Spangled Banner* there is a 16mm film as well as a sound filmstrip (cassette) and a super 8mm cartridge film loop, all based upon a book illustrated by Peter Spier and all available from Weston Woods. These have been shown as backgrounds for a bicentennial concert performed by a high school chorus, but could be used in a similar manner at any patriotic assembly. The local chorus sang while the filmstrips were being shown. These materials could be used at any level to give more meaning to the song lyrics. Since both "The Star Spangled Banner," and "Yankee Doodle" are so familiar, the book could be read and then the filmstrip shown while the audience sang the words. Both songs appear on the phonograph record *Favorite Songs, record 2*. Any combination of reading, viewing, and singing is possible. There are no limits to the imaginative ways these songs can be presented.

Each line of Peter Spier's book for verses 1, 2, and 4 is explained through one or two pages of illustrations. The music is given at the end of the book and all four verses are listed. Other information which makes the book useful as a reference book for history classes are the two pages about U.S. flags, a four-page explanation of the song including a photo of the original receipt for the song, and a portrait of Francis Scott Key. There are two other books about the "Star Spangled Banner" which are not as aesthetically pleasing but still usable, neither of which contains the music. Leisy's *Good Times Song Book* has it and it is included on the phonograph record *National Anthems of the World*.

The *Star Spangled Banner*, illustrated by Paul Galdone and listed under F. S. Key, is an illustrated picture book which uses as the text the original manuscript owned by the Maryland Historical Society. A photocopy of that manuscript and a replica of the earliest known photo of the "Star Spangled Banner," taken in 1874, are shown. Four pages of background information on the song's origin are included. *The Story of the Star-Spangled Banner* by Miller is not an illustrated picture book of the song. All four verses of Key's song are listed on one page with pictures of several American flags. The rest of the thirty-page book tells how Key came to write the song, how it became our national anthem, and why verse three is rarely sung. A biography of Key appears in Lyons's *Stories of Our American Patriotic Songs*. One can introduce other national anthems with Shaw's *National Anthems of the World*.

Several folksongs of historical significance have been illustrated to make picture books. In one, *Sweet Betsy from Pike*, illustrators Abish and Kaplan have captured America during the 1850s through collage. The ballad was written about Betsy and Ike who traveled to California by wagon to seek their fortunes during the gold rush. Music for the song as well as background information about the song's origin are given in this picture book. All three of the Lomax books provide music for the song but give different versions. *Folk Songs of North America* and *Penguin Book of America Folk Songs* list nine verses but the verses are different. Fourteen verses are given in A. and J. Lomax's *American Ballads and Folk Songs* and A. and J. Lomax's *Cowboy Songs and Other Frontier Ballads.* Music and lyrics are also given in Boni's *Fireside Book of Folk Songs* and Sandburg's book, *American Songbag.* Burl Ives sings the song on record 3 of *America's Musical Heritage.*

Another folk song of the same period which enjoys greater fame is "Oh Susannah!" the theme song of the gold rush. This song also is sung by Burl Ives on record 6 of *America's Musical Heritage.* Four verses and the chorus as well as the music are given in Boni's *Fireside Book of Folk Songs.* Because "Oh Susannah!" is more familiar than "Sweet Betsy from Pike," the first song could be read, sung or played from the phonograph record *Favorite Songs, Record 2* to introduce the picture book *Sweet Betsy from Pike.* Brief backgrounds of the two songs, emphasizing their similarity, could be given. Or "Oh Susannah!" could be sung after the story about Betsy was read. Another song of the gold rush era is "Clementine" which is included in the section entitled "Regional Folksongs" in this chapter. This song is incorporated into a melodrama written by Quackenbush in his book *Clementine*, which is also available on a Weston Woods filmstrip of the same name. The folksong "Clementine" is featured in the 16mm film *Folk Songs of the West.* Possibilities for using the three songs, all contained in Agay's *Best Loved Songs of the American People*, and related media are as limitless as your imagination.

It it interesting to students that folksongs were sung and passed along orally long before they were written down. Lyrics changed as they passed from one person or generation to another or as they moved from region to region, adapted to local customs, or were shaped by local history. A 16mm film, *Discovering American Folk Music*, explains the transformation of ballads and lyric songs after they reached America from Britain. The film also shows how musical traditions that came to us from Africa have interacted with those of Europe. The study guide for this film gives terminology and lists questions to be answered after viewing the film. If each two students in the class are given a question to answer, the film can be used as low as fifth and sixth grades. Berger's *The Story of Folk Music* which centers on American folk music should be available to students who have seen the film.

One folksong which has many versions and other titles is "Go Tell Aunt Rhody." Eleven verses and music are given in the picture book by Quackenbush which is told in rebus form and has hidden pictures within the illustrations. Aliki gives six verses in his brightly illustrated picture book also called *Go Tell Aunt Rhody.*

According to Yolen in *The Fireside Song Book of Birds and Beasts*, Aunt Rhody is called Aunt Nancy in the West and Aunt Patsy in the South. Other names include Dinah, Tabby, Tildy, and Phoebe. Yolen, Babon, and Erdei and Komlos have a song about Aunt Rhody while Fowke's main character in *Ring Around the Moon* is Aunt Abbie. Collections with music and lyrics under the title "Go Tell Aunt Rhody" are Engvick's *Lullabies and Night Songs*, Leisy's *Good Times Songbook*, and Winn's *Fireside Book of Children's Songs.* The same song is listed under the title "Old Grey Goose" or "Old Gray Goose" in the following collections: Langstaff's *Hi! Ho!, The Rattlin' Bog*, A. Lomax's *Penguin Book of American Folk Songs*, and J. and A. Lomax's *American Ballads and Folk Songs*. Fish's *Four and Twenty Blackbirds*, Langstaff's *Jim Along Josie*, and Poston's *Baby's Song Book* list the song under "Go Tell Aunt Nancy." Bertail's *Complete Nursery Song Book* lists the song as "Go Tell Aunt Rhodie."

Researching for many versions and verses of a song can be a study project growing naturally out of viewing the film *Discovering American Folk Music*.

The humorous lullaby "Mommy, Buy Me a China Doll" could be used to introduce the contributions of the early peddlers to American history. In the song, Eliza Lou sees a doll in the peddler's pack and asks her mother to buy her a doll, "Do, Mommy do!" The answer is "What could we buy it with, Eliza Lou," and Eliza gives her mother a succession of answers.

A sound filmstrip is also available or the music can be found in Erdei and Komlos's *One Hundred Fifty American Folk Songs* and Bacon's *Forty-Six Two Part American Folk Songs*.

Lullabies as well as ritual chants, dream songs, and medicine charms are included in *Songs of the Chippewa*. There have been books which have included Indian songs but none are as aesthetically pleasing as *Songs of the Chippewa*, which is illustrated in full color by Joe Servelle. John Bierhorst has arranged the songs for piano and guitar. *Songs of the Chippewa* could be used companionably with Sonia Blecker's *The Chippewa Indians: Rice Gatherers of the Great Lakes*. One of the songs, "Do Not Cry," appears on the phonograph record *North American Indian Songs* as "Do Not Weep."

Another song from the same collection of Great Lakes lore collected by Frances Densmore and Henry Rowe Schoolcraft is the song which was adapted into the poem "Hiawatha" by H. W. Longfellow. The 16mm film *Tales of Hiawatha* uses animated puppets to tell several episodes.

Another book by Bierhorst is *A Cry From the Earth: Music of the North American Indian*. Lullabies are included from the Cherokees, Kwokiutl and Tsimshian tribes. Other topics are life, death, love, war, and prayers. Chippewa and Cherokee lullabies are included on the sound filmstrip *North American Indian Songs* along with a Creek corn festival and Kiowa buffalo dance song. How Indian songs were part of their ceremonies is explained in Hoffman's book *American Indians Sing*.

REGIONAL FOLK SONGS.   "Billy Boy" is another folk song favorite available both in picture book and in filmstrip formats. Seventeen verses of "Billy Boy" were selected by folklorist Richard Chase for the book, illustrated by Glen Rounds. Of these seventeen verses, only three are similar to those in Langstaff's *Jim Along Josie* and only one, the verse about baking the cherry pie, is the same. In the Chase picture book and filmstrip, Billy's mother asks where he has been and sixteen other motherly questions and Billy responds to each with a different answer, followed by the familiar refrain, "She's a young thing and cannot leave her mother." It is very natural and not at all sexist for the boys to want to take Billy's part and the girls to take the part of the mother. Perhaps the leader can take the part of the mother and ask the questions to which the audience can respond in union; or each sixteen members of the audience could answer a question in turn while the other join in the refrain. "Billy Boy" is included in Fowke's *Ring Around the Moon* as an example of an "answer back" or dialogue song. A. and J. Lomax list twenty-three versions of this song in *American Ballads and Folk Songs*. Burl Ives sings it on a recording from *America's Musical Heritage*; the song also appears on a recording, *Favorite Songs*, record 1.

Two other picture books about songs that can be used with "Billy Boy" are Taylor's *Old Blue: You Good Dog You* and Langstaff's *Ol' Dan Tucker*. This second song is included in Agay's *Best Loved Songs of the American People*, and is a favorite for square dancing.

Use the picture book *The Swapping Boy* to introduce other Appalachian mountain swapping songs found in *Jean Ritchie's Swapping Song Book* which contains twenty-one songs from Kentucky's Cumberland mountains. "The Swapping Song" appears in Fowke's *Ring Around the Moon*. Use the song to introduce Shannon's swapping story, *The Piney Woods Peddler*.

Three other songs which are part of our American tradition are "Skip to My Lou," "She'll Be Coming Round the Mountain," and "Clementine." All three are illustrated and embellished by Quackenbush in individual picture books. The last two are also available in sound filmstrips.

The two filmstrips, *She'll Be Coming Round the Mountain* and *Clementine*, are useful beyond the elementary level because Quackenbush has created an old-fashioned melodrama around each song. There is much to be discussed, after reading the books and viewing the filmstrips, concerning the principles, elements, and background of melodramas and Wild West shows and their place in history. The two melodramas could be acted out by the group. The origin of the songs and their various versions and verses could be the impetus for a research project.

In *She'll Be Coming Round the Mountain*, the heroine is Annie O'Grady who is wardrobe mistress and tends the horses for Colonel Jack's Wild West Show. While sewing costumes aboard the train, Annie dreams of handsome Larry the engineer while Sneaky Pete, Rattlesnake Hank, and Crummy Joe, ornery train robbers, try to rob the train. Naturally Annie saves the day and Larry marries her when he sees how wonderful she is. Colorado Jack is eternally grateful and makes her the star of his show.

In the second book, a miner owes money to the villain who demands the miner's gold or the miner's daughter Clementine in marriage. While the father is desperately looking for gold to pay the debt, Clementine trips on a splinter and falls into the brine. Her father can't save her but a handsome hero does. They are married and the real happy ending is that the splinter Clementine tripped over is a lump of pure gold. The villain is unhappy until he meets Clementine's sister at the wedding, so all ends well.

Music for "She'll Be Coming Round the Mountain" is found in Agay's *Best Loved Songs of the American People*, Bley's *Best Singing Games for Children of All Ages*, Boni's *Fireside Book of Folk Songs*, Fowke's *Ring Around the Moon*, Leisy's *Good Times Songbook*, Lomax's *Folk Songs of North America*, Sandburg's *The American Songbag*, and Winn's *Fireside Book of Fun and Games*. "She'll Be Coming Round the Mountain" appears on record 1 of the album *Favorite Songs*, and is featured in the 16mm film *Folksongs of American History*. "Clementine" is also sung on the 16mm film *Folksongs of the Westward Movement*, and music and words appear in Boni's *Fireside Book of Folk Songs*, Leisy's *Good Times Songbook*, and Winn's *Fireside Book of Fun and Game Songs*.

Four folk songs from the British are also humorous. Sorch Nic Leodhas, the pseudonym of LeClaire Alger, has recreated an old Scottish song which Nonny Hogrogian illustrated to create the 1966 Caldecott Medal winner *Always Room for One More*. Even though he had a wife and ten bairns (children), Lachie MacLochlan hailed every traveler who passed his door and invited him or her in. There was room for everyone from the tinker and tailor and the peat cutters to the shepherd laddie and wee shepherd dog. They all rollicked and frolicked about until the house collapsed. A musical score, information about the song's background, and a glossary of terms complete this amusing tale.

Another folk song accompanied by music with a glossary and background notes was also adapted to picture book format by Sorche Nic Leodhas as *The Laird of Cockpen*, illustrated by Adrienne Adams. The Laird put on his finest clothes to woo the penniless lass with a long pedigree, but she surprises them both by refusing him. After thinking over her decision, a happy ending follows.

Music also accompanies Sorche Nic Leodhas's *Kellyburn Braes*. In this song, the auld laird in Kellyburn Braes had a wife who plagued him. He gave her to the Devil because they would be a good match, but the Devil couldn't handle her so he returned her to the laird.

Widdecombe Fair is a picture book illustrated by Price based on an old English folk song about ghosts on the moor. The singer asks Tom Pearce to lend him his grey mare so he and his friends could go to Widdecombe Fair. The recital of the names of his friends constitutes the chorus. When the horse doesn't return, Tom goes out looking for it. He finds his horse making out a will. The horse dies and Tom cries. Today the ghost still appears on the moor. Soft green and white illustrations contribute to the ghostliness of the book, which includes music. Burl Ives sings the song on record 1 of *America's Musical Heritage*.

Trina Schart Hyman has illustrated a picture book *On to Widdecombe Fair* written by Gauch. Both the author and illustrator traveled to Widdecombe in Devon, England, inspired by the song. Eight verses and music are included at the end of the book. Although seven men are listed as going to Widdecombe Fair, Gauch points out that the singer makes an eighth passenger, and that "and all" includes a dog as shown by a picture. Use Ritchie's *From Fair to Fair: Folk Songs of the British Isles* with this book. Ritchie's vehicle for linking songs from Ireland, Scotland, and England is a minstrel wandering from fair to fair.

The Derby Ram, A Ballad, illustrated by Rick Schreichter, is a picture book based on a ballad from the same part of England. Although there isn't any music in the book, ten verses and music are available in Erdei and Komlos's *One Hundred Fifty American Folk Songs*. The song is called "The Big Sheep" in Seeger's *Animal Folk Songs for Children*. Music for *The Derby Ram* also appears in Fowke's *Ring Around the Moon*.

Music for thirty English street cries are included in Langstaff's *Hot Cross Buns and Other Old Street Cries.*

ANIMAL SONGS.   The picture book *The Friendly Beasts* reminds us that some of the best songs to have been illustrated and presented in picture book format are about mankind's best friends—the animals.

Everyone knows that the three blind mice had their tails cut off by a carving knife, but few people realize that this verse is only verse ten out of a thirteen-verse song that has been retold, with illustrations by Corbould, by Ivimey, called *The Complete Version of Ye Three Blind Mice* in hardback and *Adventures of the Three Blind Mice* in the paperback edition. When reading the picture book, use the hardback edition because the illustrations are more exciting and colorful. The paperback edition illustrated by Langner is useful for providing multiple copies for group singing. Some of the words in the paperback edition have been simplified. The paperback is available separately or with a recording that combines singing and speaking.

A more expensive but preferred combination is the Weston Woods sound filmstrip in which all thirteen verses are sung on record or cassette, and the pictures are taken directly from the hardback edition. After hearing the story, children will wish to sing all verses of the song and can do so by reading the verses from the last frames of the filmstrip. Children may wish to make their own cassette. There are many possibilities for using the books, filmstrip, records, or cassettes as a springboard for games and other activities. A parody called "Three Myopic Rodents" appears in Winn's *Fireside Book of Fun and Game Songs.*

Music for "Three Blind Mice" is also available in Bertail's *Complete Nursery Song Book*, Poston's *Baby's Song Book*, and Yolen's and Green's *Fireside Song Book of Birds and Beasts*. Another song that could be used is "Hickory Dickory Dock," available in Langstaff's *Jim Along Josie* as well as in Mitchell and Poston. The Langstaff book also includes a song called "Creep Mouse Creep." These songs could be used with the picture books by Ivimey or could introduce other books that include famous mice: Freeman's *Norman the Doorman*, Gag's *Snippy and Snappy*, Titus's *Anatole and Basil of Baker Street*, and Potter's *Tale of Two Bad Mice* and *The Tailor of Gloucester.*

Frogs are even more popular than mice. Pete and Charles Seeger have created a book from a Firebrand film by Gene Deitch which is based on the old song "The Foolish Frog." Music is given in the book. The illustrations are bright and the story is lively. A farmer walking along a road was inspired by a bullfrog to sing a song. Soon his friends, their wives and children, the cows, chickens, barns, grass, and brook were all singing along and eating free strawberry pop and eating free soda crackers and stomping on the floor. The frog got so puffed up that he exploded in all directions; all that was left of him was his song. This rollicking story is also portrayed on a Weston Woods filmstrip.

Another song about a frog is one of the earliest folksongs adapted to picture book format, the 1956 Caldecott Medal winner, *Frog Went a Courtin'*. This well-known ballad has been adapted by John Langstaff and illustrated by Feodor Rojankovsky into a prize winning book that is available in paperback as well as in hardcover. The song has many versions and titles and has appeared in many parts of the country. One unusual title is "The Love-Sick Frog" which appears in *Mother Goose Treasury*. No music is given. Langstaff and Fish have included the musical scores and lyrics in their collections under the title "Frog Went a Courtin." The song is called "Frog He Would A-wooing Go" in the collections of Bertail, Mitchell, and Poston. The song is one of four in *Randolph Caldecott's John Gilpin and Other Stories*. The chorus in all four of these versions is "Heigh Ho! says Anthony Rowley." Winn's *Fireside Book of Children's Songs* and Sandburg's *American Songbook* have "Mr. Frog Went A-Courting" while Agay, Bley and Leisey's songs are titled "Froggie went A Courtin." Although the songs in Bley's *Best Singing Games for Children of All Ages* and Lomax's *Penguin Book of American Folk Songs* both have fourteen verses to the song, the lyrics are different. The Lomax version is a Texas variant. In it the guests are little black bug, gartersnake, and old tom cat. In this version Mr. Frog was lost because he jumped into the lake and was swallowed by a big black snake. In the Bley version the guests were a mealy moth, doodley bug, bumberly bee, cumberly cow, and pussily cat. The cat ate up the frog, the mouse, and the rat. The guests in the Langstaff picture book, were little white moth, big black bug, Mr. Coon, a spotted snake, bumblebee, nimble Flea, old gray goose, two little ants, little ol' fly, little chick, and old tom cat. The old tom cat chased away the guests. Then frog and mouse went to France on a honeymoon. The last lines of the various versions are the same or close to the same but the preceding line is different. In Lomax, the line is "The old hymn book lies on the shelf (twice) If you want any more you can sing it yourself, etc." Bley reads, "Cornbread and clabber milk settling on the shelf, mm-hmm. If you want any more you can sing it for youself, that's all (that's all)." Langstaff's picture book ends: "Frog's bridle and saddle are laid on the shelf. If you want anymore, you must sing it yourself."

The directions for making this song into an action game as directed by Bley on p. 63 and Leisey on pp. 106-07 are excellent.

Music is found on the Weston Woods sound filmstrip based on the picture book by Langstaff and is sung by Burl Ives on record 1 of *America's Musical Heritage*.

There are many ways to present this song, the books, and related material: (1) The book could be read in a lively dramatic maner; (2) the song could be played on the guitar and sung from the picture book by a live folksinger instead of being read; (3) the folksinger could sing the song while the Weston Woods filmstrip is being shown; (4) a phonograph record could be used as an introduction, or (5) ending, for the book; (6) the second time through the audience could sing the 'mm-hmm's" or chorus, or (7) informally sing along as much as they remember, or (8) sing along sharing paperback copies of the book; (9) the group could make its own cassette to be kept with the filmstrip; (10) an older group could research all the versions and prepare a tape to be checked out to students. (The tape could include several versions of the song sung or read by one or more persons.)

Another joint effort of Langstaff and Rojankovsky is the old counting song "Over in the Meadow." This version is also available in paperback edition and as a Weston Woods sound filmstrip. The Langstaff picture book includes music, but another picture book, also titled *Over in the Meadow* does not. The other version is illustrated by Ezra Jack Keats. Music is provided in Winn's *Fireside Book of Children's Songs*, Langstaff's *Hi! Ho! The Rattlin' Bog* and Glazer's *Do Your Ears Hang Low?* It is possible to count as high as you choose by making up verses which include other animals that live over in the meadow. The Keats book has one turtle, two fishes, three birdies, and ratties, honeys, crows, crickets, lizards, froggies, and ten fireflies. The Winn book only counts up to five and lists a frog, duck, bluebird, snake, and bees. The Langstaff editions, including the picture book, have one turtle, two foxes, three birdies, chipmunks, honeybees, beavers, polliwogs, owls, spiders, and ten bunnies. This book is a pleasurable way to identify animals and solidify number concepts.

Another old folk song that is available on sound filmstrip from Weston Woods is *The Fox Went Out on a Chilly Night*, illustrated by Peter Spier. The picture book, which is available in hardback and paperback, was a Caldecott honor book. Colored illustrations alternate with black and white line drawings in this seven-verse story about a fox who stole a goose and took it back to his den where his wife cut it up and they ate it. The "Fox's Foray," found in *Mother Goose Treasury*, is another version of the same story. No music is given.

One of the favorite nonsense songs that includes a fly, spider, bird, cat, dog, goat, cow, and horse is "I Know an Old Lady." The picture book by Bonne is available in hardback and paperback. The paperback edition, however, is not as colorful because it is printed in three colors while the hardback includes five colors. Music is given in the book and in Glazer's *Eye Winker Tom Tinker Chin Chopper*. Glazer gives directions for adding actions to the song. Music is also given in Winn's *Fireside Book of Children's Songs* and Yolen's *Fireside Song Book of Birds and Beasts*.

Another favorite, "Old MacDonald Had a Farm," is illustrated in picture book format by Quackenbush. Fish's *Four and Twenty Blackbirds* includes a British version of it. Music for the song is included in Bertail's *Nursery Song Book*. In Glazer's *Eye Winker Tom Tinker Chin Chopper* there is a cow, pig, duck, horse, donkey, and chicks, but in Winn's *What Shall We Do and Allee Galloo!* only ducks and chicks are mentioned. A paperback book illustrated by Graboff and accompanied by a phonograph record is available from Scholastic Books.

There is no music for Erskine's picture book *The Farmer in the Dell* but nine verses of the song are included in Fowke's *Sally Go Round the Sun*. Instead of the "cheese stands alone" as in the nine verses in Erdei and Komlos's *One Hundred Fifty American Folk Songs*, the last verse in Fowke's book is "We all take a bite." The verses include a farmer, wife, child, nurse, dog, cat, rat, and cheese. Another picture book is illustrated by Zuromskis.

It is possible to use songs about specific animals to introduce books about similar animals. For example, a song about lions could be sung in conjunction with Freeman's *Dandelion* or Fatio's *Happy Lion*. Two collections of animal songs, Zeitlin's *Castle in My City* and Seeger's *Animal Folk Songs for Children*, are good sources for these. The "Barnyard Song" found in Glazer's book could be used with any animal alphabet or farmyard book because it includes a bird, hen, duck, goose, pig, sheep, cow, and horse. Directions are given for actions to fit the singing. The title is not as familiar as the words, "I had a bird and the bird pleased me, I fed my bird on yonder tree. Bird goes fid-dle-de-fee." No music is included in a picture book of the song illustrated by Stanley called *Fiddle-i-fee: A Traditional American Chant*. This song, like "I Know an Old Lady Who Swallowed a Fly," is cumulative.

Barbara Emberley has adapted a song to produce the picture book *One Wide River to Cross*. Ed Emberley has created wood cuts of unusual animals against a background of bright reds, yellows, oranges, turquoises, greens, purples, and pinks in this Caldecott honor book. In the eleven verses, a basilisk, unicorn, maticore, griffin, alligator, ostrich, chickadee, hippopotamus and yak, among others, enter Noah's ark. A sound filmstrip of the book is available from the Educational Division of the *New York Times*. The same song appears in Leisey's *Good Times Songbook* under the title "One More River to Cross." A helpful program guide is included in the Leisey book. A paperback edition of the Emberley book is also available. Music from this paperback is sung on the same record as *Old MacDonald Had a Farm*.

Yurchenco's *A Fiesta of Folk Songs from Spain and Latin America* includes a chapter on animals and nature songs. Another book with a Latin flavor is Politi's Caldecott winner *Song of the Swallows*. This picture book tells about the migration of swallows to and from the mission at San Juan Capistrano. There are two songs; one is about swallows and the other is a welcome home song sung by the mission children when the swallows return. Children can listen to or sing the songs as they view and hear the Miller Brody sound filmstrip *Song of the Swallows*.

Another book about birds is *The Song of the Day Birds and the Night Birds*. Brightly colored illustrations, Ipcar style, accent this picture book which tells about day and night birds. Two songs begin this book: "The Song of the Day Birds" and "The Song of the Night Birds." The story is told in rhyme, "In a tree that was almost bare a partridge pecked at a golden pear."

Another folk song told in rhyme is a song adapted by John Langstaff and illustrated by Nancy W. Parker, *Oh, A-Hunting We Will Go*. No animals are killed because "We'll just pretend and in the end, We'll always let them go!" There are twelve verses to the song; some of them were made up by children. Children will love the humor of the verses and will want to make up additional ones. Each animal is caught and put in a container that rhymes with the name of the animal; the fox is put in a box, the lamb in a pram, goat—boat, bear—underwear, whale—pail, snake—cake, mouse—house, pig—wig, skunk—bunk, armadillo—pillow, fish—dish, and brontosaurus—chorus.

Another picture book, containing the same song *Catch a Little Fox*, by De Regniers and illustrated by Brinton Turkle, contains a fox, frog, cat, mouse, and dragon. This song is also found in Nelson's *Singing and Dancing Games for the Very Young* and in Langstaff's *Jim Along Josie* in a section called "Action Songs."

Rockwell's *El Toro Pinto* contains songs about a donkey, toad, monkey, and mosquito. *The Butterfly's Wedding*, (*Les Noces du Papillon*), includes a butterfly, snail, ant, honeybee, cicada, cricket, and glowworm. The song, from Rockwell's *Savez-vous Planter les Choux?*, is in English and French.

Nonny Hogrogian's watercolors illustrate *The Bears Are Sleeping*, a lullaby based on an old Russian melody. The notes and lyrics provide the text for the small-sized book. Bears, deer, and wolves are included.

Cononer's *Six Little Ducks* is about ducks who go to market and bake bread. Music for piano and guitar are included at the back of the book. See the chapter called "The Animal Fair" in Fowke's *Ring Around the Moon* for more songs about animals.

Animals and nature are featured in Crofut's *The Moon on the One Hand, Poetry in Song*, containing fifteen poems by famous poets set to music. Some of the nature poems in Crofut's book are "The Wind" and "The Cow" by Robert Louis Stevenson; "The Chipmunk's Day," "The Mockingbird," and "The Bird of Night" by Randall Jarrell; "The Eagle" by Alfred Lord Tennyson; and "Eletelephony" by Laura Richards. Other poets include John Clare, Hilaire Belloc, e.e. cummings, James Stephens, Elizabeth Fleming, and Thomas Moore. Use the picture book *The Pelican Chorus*, based on a Lear poem, with Crofut's book. Music as well as words are included.

Twenty-nine fables by La Fontaine have been set to music in Smith's collection *The Frogs Who Wanted a King and Other Songs from La Fontaine*. Some of the most familiar are "The Lion and the Rat," "The Hen Who Laid Golden Eggs," "The Tortoise and the Two Ducks," "The Hare and the Tortoise," "The City Rat and the Country Rat," and "The Ant and the Grasshopper."

NURSERY RHYMES.   Nursery rhymes also include animals. Originally, they were sung or chanted, but many of the tunes have been lost. However, recent interest in folk songs has unearthed many tunes while music for others has been created. Children just naturally join in when nursery rhymes are read or sung.

Wheeler's *Sing Mother Goose* includes fifty-two nursery rhymes, each of which is a favorite. Full-color illustrations accompany "Little Bo Peep," "Mary, Mary, Quite Contrary," "There Was a Little Girl," "Hot Cross Buns," "Old King Cole," "Seesaw, Margery Daw," "Bobby Shaftoe," "To Market, To Market," "Jack Be Nimble," and "Where, oh Where has my Little Dog Gone?"

Kapp's *Cock-A-Doodle Doo! Cock-A-Doodle Dandy!* includes piano and chords for the following rhymes and poems: "Owl and the Pussy Cat," "Solomon Grundy," "Jack Sprat, his Wife and Cat" (three verses), "Who Has Seen the Wind," "Wynken, Blynken, and Nod," and "Wee Willie Winkie."

Engvick has included a section of Mother Goose rhymes in his *Lullabies and Night Songs*. Some of them include "Little Miss Muffet," "Little Jack Horner," "Hickory Dickory Dock," "The Mulberry Bush," "Hey Diddle Diddle," and "Little Boy Blue." Naturally, "Wee Willie Winkie" in his night gown is included. Lullabies and nursery rhymes are included in John's *The Great Song Book*.

Fish's collection of nursery rhymes and stories, *Four and Twenty Blackbirds* has been reprinted several times. Thirteen of the rhymes have been set to simple music which is given at the end of the book.

Nelson's *Singing and Dancing Games for the Very Young* includes

"Rock'a'Bye Baby," "Twinkle, Twinkle, Little Star," and "Humpty Dumpty." A special feature of the book is the chart of age (ranging from two to eight years) at which children will most enjoy the activities presented.

Erdei and Komlos include "The Grand Old Duke of York" and "Bye Baby Bunting" in *One Hundred Fifty American Folk Songs to Sing, Read and Play.*

Bertail's *Complete Nursery Song Book* includes "Baa, Baa, Black Sheep," "Bye, Baby Bunting," "Ding Dong Bell," "Farmer in the Dell," "Georgie Porgie," "A Tisket, A Tasket," "Little Tommy Tucker," "Lucy Locket," "Muffin Man," "Old Mother Goose," and "Three Little Kittens."

"The Mulberry Bush" and "Drop the Handkerchief" are included in *Kate Greenaway's Book of Games.*

Glazer's *Do Your Ears Hang Low? Fifty More Musical Fingerplays* includes "Bye Baby Bunting," "I Had a Little Nut Tree," "A tisket, A tasket," "Little Bo-Peep," "Little Jack Horner," "London Bridge," and "Polly Put the Kettle On."

Kapp's *A Cat Came Fiddling* includes the following English and American nursery rhymes: "Hark Hark! the Dogs Do Bark!" "Goosey Goosey Gander," "There was a Crooked Man," "Cock-a-Doodle Doo (My Dame has lost her shoe)," "Tommy Snooks and Bessie Brooks." An informative introduction by Burl Ives is useful to leaders.

Barbara Emberley has adapted a nursery rhyme, "Simple Simon" and Ed Emberley has added woodcuts to create the picture book *Simon's Song*. The book has twelve verses, music for the piano, and red, blue, and green illustrations. It is also available in paperback. The paperback edition provides inexpensive multiple copies of the lyrics for singing and for children to look at individually after the book has been introduced. Music and lyrics are also available in Bertail's *Complete Nursery Song Book* and Wheeler's *Sing Mother Goose*. Lyrics only are available in the *Mother Goose Treasury* illustrated by Briggs.

Mitchell's *Every Child's Book of Nursery Songs* is an illustrated collection of ninety-one nursery rhymes set to music and includes the favorites: "Hey Diddle Diddle," "Little Miss Muffet," "Little Jack Horner," "Mary Had a Little Lamb," "Little Boy Blue," "Hickory Dickory Dock," and fourteen verses of "Old Mother Hubbard". The song "Old Mother Hubbard" can be used in connection with several picture books. The first one by Paul Galdone, is available on a Weston Woods sound filmstrip. His *Old Mother Hubbard and Her Dog* uses a traditional version of the rhyme and includes words like fishmonger, fruiterer, sempstress, and hosier. If the words in Galdone's book seem too archaic, consider using *Old Mother Hubbard and Her Dog* as illustrated by Evaline Ness, *The Comic Adventures of Old Mother Hubbard* illustrated by Arnold Lobel or *The Comic Adventures of Old Mother Hubbard and Her Dog* by de Paola. Music for "Old Mother Hubbard" is also available in Engvick's *Lullabies and Night Songs.*

Singing the song "Three Little Kittens" could introduce books about cats. One book called *Three Kittens* has nothing to do with lost mittens. It is translated from the Russian, and concerns three kittens, one black, one gray, and one white. They followed a mouse into a flour can and they all came out white; they followed a toad into a stovepipe and all came out black; then they followed a fish into the fish pond and all came out gray. When they dried off, the kittens returned to their original colors—black, gray, and white. The book is listed under Ginsburg in the bibliography. Several out of the hundreds of available cat books that could be introduced are Wanda Gag's *Millions of Cats*, four books by Newberry—*April's Kittens*, *Marshmallow*, *Mittens*, and *Smudge*—and *Puss in Boots* illustrated by Brown or Fischer. Music for "Three Little Kittens" is available in the collections by Bertail and Wheeler. Older children could be introduced to books about cats through Ipcar's *The Cat Came Back* which is based on an old folk song about the many lives of a cat.

Tom Tom the Piper's Son, illustrated by Paul Galdone, includes two of the many versions of that nursery rhyme. The most famous, the version about Tom stealing a pig, serves as an introduction to the book. This favorite nursery rhyme could be read or sung as an introduction to the story. Music and lyrics are available in Wheeler's *Sing Mother Goose*. The other version given in the picture book is "Tom he was a Piper's son, He learned to play when he was young, But the only tune that he could play was 'Over the hills and far away.'" (p. 5). This same version appears in "Tom, He Was a Piper's Son" in Kapp's *A Cat Came Fiddling*, which can be used in conjunction with the Galdone book, since it contains the music and the Galdone book does not.

May Justus's *Tale of a Pig* includes music for piano and guitar and could be used with the song and fingerplay "This Little Pig" from Glazer's *Eye Winker Tom Tinker Chin Chopper*, "The Three Little Pigs" from Fowke's *Ring Around the Moon*, or with *Other Rhymes about Pigs* by Lenore Blegvad illustrated by her husband which includes twenty-two nursery rhymes about pigs.

ROUNDS, RIDDLES, AND 'ROUND THE WORLD.   Thirteen animal rounds are included in Langstaff's *Sweetly Sings the Donkey*. Besides the title song, there are rounds about a snake, a woodchuck, cat, cuckoo, owl, bear, dormouse, and goose. Children can sing the songs or play them on recorders. "Sweetly Sings the Donkey" is also one of over fifty rounds in Yolen's *Rounds About Rounds About Rounds*. Others include "Merrily, Merrily," "White Coral Bells," "He Ho, Nobody's Home," "Frere Jacques," "Row, Row, Row Your Boat." and "Christmas is Coming." Twenty-one rounds are included in Fowke's *Ring Around the Moon*.

Riddle songs can be used to introduce riddle books found in the chapter on "Riddles, Magic, Jokes, and Folk Themes." "King Henry Has Set Me Free," a song about guessing riddles to release a captive princess is found on page 31 of Fowke's *Ring Around the Moon*. That book also includes forty-one riddles in rhyme. "The Riddle Song," p. 46 of Langstaff's *Jim Along Josie* and page 52 of Erdei and Komlos's *One Hundred Fifty American Folk Songs*, can also be used to introduce riddle stories for telling or reading.

Music can be used in geography and foreign language classes. Rockwell's *El Toro Pinto* contains thirty songs from Latin America, Spain, and the United States. Yurchenco's *A Fiesta of Folk Songs from Spain and Latin America* contains thirty-four songs. Rockwell's *Savez-vous Planter les Choux?* includes the French favorites "Au Clair de La Lune" and "Sur le Point d'Avignon."

ACTIVITY SONGS AND GAMES.   "London Bridge" is one of the most famous of the activity songs. Peter Spier has illustrated the song in London Bridge Is Falling Down, which is available in paperback and hardback. Spier's book begins with a quote from part of an old poem in which someone asks the way to London Town. A three-page section titled "London Bridge through the Centuries" gives background information. Spier effectively uses two-page illustrations to show his bridge, and Weston Woods has created a sound filmstrip.

Ed Emberley has illustrated the song in his picture book London Bridge Is Falling Down, the Song and the Game. Emberley has added a short history with notes about the guard's costume and directions on how to play the game. Eighteen verses are given.

Music is included in both these books but children may be interested in trying to find other verses to sing. Music and lyrics are given in Bertail's Complete Nursery Song Book, Engvick's Every Child's Book of Nursery Songs, and Poston's Baby's Song Book. Music for a parody in which the bridge falls up instead of down is found in Winn's Fireside Book of Fun and Game Songs.

There are several collections which include activity songs. These songs can be used as an interlude between stories in a story program. One example would be using the songs "Polly Put the Kettle On" and "I'm a Little Teapot" to follow a reading of Cameron's I Can't Said the Ant. In the story, a teapot is broken and when it is put back together again, Polly is asked to put the kettle on so "we'll all have tea." "I'm a Little Teapot" is even more valuable as a transition activity because it allows the audience to move around. "I'm a Little Teapot" can be found in Fowke's Sally Go Round the Sun and Winn's What Shall We Do and Allee Galoo. "Polly Put the Kettle On" is found in Bertail's Complete Nursery Song Book, Langstaff's Jim Along Josie, Engvick's Every Child's Book of Nursery Songs, Poston's Baby's Song Book, and Wheeler's Sing Mother Goose.

Activity songs included in Nelson's Singing and Dancing Games for the Very Young are "Sally Go Round the Moon," "I'm Very Small or I'm Very Very Tall," and "Clap Your Hands." "Where is Thumbkin?" is included in the fingerplays. Also included are clapping and guessing games, musical stories, question and answer songs, stretches and songs for coordination as well as eye contact.

Some activity songs found in Erdei and Komlos's One Hundred Fifty American Folk Songs to Sing, Read and Play are "Sally Go Round the Sun," "Ring Around the Rosy," "Tisket, a Tasket," "Farmer in the Dell," and "London Bridge."

A suggestion given in Winn's The Man Who Made Fine Tops is to substitute occupations like bricklayer to the tune of "Did You Ever See a Lassie."

Fingerplays can also be used as activities between stories. Glazer's Eye Winker Tom Tinker Chin Chopper and Do Your Ears Hang Low? each include fifty musical fingerplays. Musical fingerplays are also included in Fowke's Sally Go Round the Sun and Winn's What Shall We Do and Allee Galloo. More active songs and games are found in the following collections. Sally Go Round the Sun includes 300 songs for ball bouncing, clapping, foot tapping, as well as singing games that can be played in rings, bridges, and lines. Bley's Best Songs and

Games for Children of All Ages also includes jump rope jingles, counting and bouncing rhymes. Winn's *Fireside Book of Fun and Game Songs* has ten parts and has songs for motion, follow the leader, clapping, snapping, and peculiar noises. Langstaff's *Jim Along Josie* includes twenty singing games and twenty action songs. Larrick's *Wheel on the Bus Goes Round and Round* includes activity songs like "The Bear Went Over the Mountain," and clapping songs like "B-I-N-G-O" and "If You're Happy and You Know It." Winn's *Fireside Book of Fun and Game Songs* includes question and answer songs like "Hole in the Bucket," songs with improvised motions such as "Polly Wolly Doodle," and songs for arriving, cheering, waiting and leaving. The book concludes with lullabies.

Sometimes children are left with an emotional high after stimulating activities. At those times it is advantageous to provide a quieting activity.

One lullaby, "Mommy, Buy me a China Doll," has been mentioned earlier in this chapter. Two other folk song lullabies which have words and music that provide a soothing lull are "Hush Little Baby" and "All the Pretty Little Horses." Both songs have been made into picture books and the colors in each are subdued and add to the mood set by the words and music. Susan Jeffers used black pen-and-ink line drawings with overlays of yellow, gray-blue, and rust in *All the Pretty Little Horses* to create a soft effect; she provides lyrics but no musical score. Music for the song "All the Pretty Little Horses" is available in Lomax's *American Ballads and Folk Songs*, Engvick's *Lullabies and Night Songs*, and Winn's *Fireside Book of Children's Songs*. The song is also available under the title "Hush-you-bye" in Lomax's *Penguin Book of American Folk Songs*. The song is included on the record *Texas Folk Songs*. "Hushabye" is included in Bacon's *Forty-six Two-Part American Folk Songs* and Erdei and Komlos's *One Hundred Fifty American Folk Songs to Sing, Read and Play*.

Aliki has illustrated the song "Hush Little Baby" which includes the briefest of melodies—only twenty notes. More detailed music for "Hush Little Baby" is found in Engvick's *Lullabies and Night Songs*, Lomax's *Penguin Book of American Folk Songs*, and Winn's *Fireside Book of Fun and Game Songs*. Burl Ives sings the song on record 4 of *America's Musical Heritage*. The familiar lyrics of the song, "Hush little baby, don't say a word, Papa's gonna buy you a mockingbird," are also to be found in the Weston Wood sound filmstrip, and 16mm film version of the picture book which is also available in a paperback edition. The lyrics alone are given in *The Mother Goose Treasury* illustrated by Briggs. Music and lyrics for "Hush Little Baby" appear in Agay's *Best Loved Songs of the American People*. The song is called "Hush Little Minnie" in Bacon's *Forty-Six Two-Part American Folk Songs* and eight verses about Minnie also appear in a version called "The Mocking Bird" in Erdei and Komlos's *One Hundred Fifty American Folk Songs*.

If the program leader is also accomplished as a singer, it would be effective to quietly sing rather than tell both of these stories. If a recording of the songs is used, it could be played softly while the children are resting or could be used to introduce each story.

A Japanese lullaby, "Aizu Lullaby," is listed in Dietz's *Folk Songs of China*,

Japan, Korea, and on the accompanying record. This song could be used as a quieting activity after hearing a story with an oriental setting such as Flack's The Story of Ping.

Barbara Cooney has illustrated in soft blackish-blue and white, Eugene Field's Wynken, Blynken, and Nod. Music is not given in the book but the music can be found in Kapp's Cock-a-Doodle-Doo! Cock-a-Doodle-Dandy. A sound filmstrip of the picture book is available from Weston Woods.

OPERAS, BALLETS, AND OPERETTAS.   Some of our folksongs have come from operas and many operas and ballets are based on familiar folk and fairy tales. According to the notes in the unpaged Go Tell Aunt Rhody illustrated by Aliki, the music for this song was originally part of Jean Jacques Rousseau's opera The Village Soothsayer. Although the opera has been forgotten, the tune is still sung, one version being our American folksong "Go Tell Aunt Rhody."

There are other more enduring operas that have found their way into picture book format. Doris Orgel, with the cooperation of the Metropolitan Opera Guild, has retold the story of one of Richard Wagner's operas in The Story of Lohengrin, the Knight of the Swan. The well laid out illustrations help to tell the story which has fairy-tale qualities. A wicked count wishes to usurp the kingdom of the orphans Elsa and Godfrey. The Count's wife Ortud changes Godfrey into a swan and blames Elsa for his disappearance. When Elsa needs the knight of her dreams to fight for her honor, a mysterious knight comes in a boat drawn by a swan to rescue her. The knight and Elsa are married with the provision that she must never question his identity. They are happy until Ortud plants enough doubts in Elsa's mind so that Elsa begs her husband to tell her who he is. He explains that he is Lohengrin, son of Percival the Grail King who lives in the Castle Monsalvat where the Holy Grail is kept. Now Lohengrin must leave Elsa because "So mysterious is the power of the Grail that once its knights are known they must depart" (p. 53). Lohengrin gives Elsa three farewell gifts to give to her brother Godfrey when he returns to become the Duke of Barleant. The gifts are a horn for protection, a sword for victory, and a ring to remind Godfrey of Lohengrin. The swan boat comes for Lohengrin, who removes the chain from around one of the swan's necks and Godfrey appears. The boat disappears with Lohengrin who takes Elsa's soul with him.

This story and its background are also told by Clyde Bulla in his collection Stories of Favorite Operas. The Bulla version could easily be adapted for playing because the story is told in dialogue and action. Music to accompany some of the stories from Tannhauser, Tristan and Isolde, Die Meistersinger, and Lohengrin appears on the phonograph records Overtures and Music of the Drama by Wagner.

Bulla's collection The Fire, Stories from Wagner's Nibelungen Operas explains the four tales, Das Rheingold, Die Walkure, Siegfried, and Gotterdammerung. There is no music given, but musical themes are given in The Ring, retold by Updike and illustrated by Warren Chappell. The Ring is about the hero Siegfried and twenty-six musical themes are included in the picture book.

Chappell has similarly adapted Mozart's Magic Flute. The book The Magic

Flute is a retelling of the story accented with musical themes. A prose retelling without music is found in Bulla's *Stories of Favorite Operas.*

An opera by Rossini has been retold by Johanna Johnston and illustrated in black and white and color pen and ink drawings by Susan Perl. The picture book of *The Barber of Seville* is one of the most readable of the adaptations of operas. Information is given about the composer and about the opera itself. The phonograph recording of *The Barber of Seville* could be played after the story has been told. The version, without music, that is found in Bulla's collection *Stories of Favorite Operas* is suitable for playing.

Another fairy tale made into an opera by Rossini inspired a book available in paperback and hardback. Beni Montresor's *Cinderella* is very brightly illustrated and contains information about the composer. The phonograph record *Fantasy in Music* contains music from eight scenes of Prokofiev's *Cinderella Suite.* One of the most familiar of all picture books is Marcia Brown's 1955 Caldecott Medal winner, *Cinderella*, told without any connection with the opera.

Another fairy tale that has inspired an opera and many picture books is Grimm's *Hansel and Gretel.* Four of Engelbert Humperdinck's musical themes are included in Warren Chappell's retelling of *Hansel and Gretel.* A recording of Humperdinck's opera, *Hansel and Gretel*, is available. The *Hansel and Gretel* overture appears on the phonograph record *Stories in Ballet and Opera.* The story also appears in many collections; one of the easier to read collections is Virginia Haviland's *Favorite Fairy Tales Told in Germany.* A version suitable for playing is included in Bulla's *More Stories of Favorite Operas.* The picture book *Hansel and Gretel*, illustrated by Arnold Lobel, could also be used with these other versions.

The fairy tale "Sleeping Beauty" inspired Tschaikovsky to compose the music for one of his most famous works. Tschaikovsky's "Sleeping Beauty Waltz" appears on the phonograph record *Fantasy in Music.* Warren Chappell has used eight musical phrases of Tschaikovsky to help tell the ballet in his picture book, *Sleeping Beauty.* Samachson includes a synopsis and discussion of "Sleeping Beauty" in her book *The Russian Ballet, Three of Its Masterpieces.* Untermeyer includes the "Sleeping Princess" in his collection, *Tales from the Ballet.*

There are four individual picture book versions of the famous ballet, inspired by a Russian folktale, "Peter and the Wolf." The first two, those retold by Chappell and Voight explain how the characters are represented by instruments of the orchestra: Peter is represented by a string quartet, the bird by a flute, the duck by an oboe, the cat by a clarinet, the grandfather by a bassoon, the wolf by French horns, and the hunters by kettle or bass drums. One can read the story, picture book style, to children and then point out which instruments depict the characters before playing the Prokofiev music. Or the children could listen to the music first, then hear the story and decide which instruments are representing which characters. The Chappell book is available in a paperback edition.

The retelling by Ann Herring does not give any musical background. Children may enjoy looking at the bright collages. This version of *Peter and the*

Wolf is one of about a dozen books in the Fantasia Pictorial series called *Stories from Famous Music*. The quality of the series is uneven.

In Untermeyer's *Tales from the Ballet*, twenty ballets are illustrated and their stories told; no music accompanies the stories. Untermeyer is careful to emphasize that ballet is an expression of the story and that retelling pales by comparison. The "Nutcracker" is one of the ballets given in Untermeyer's collection, and there are two individual picture books based on this ballet.

M. Kushida has adapted the story from Tchaikovsky's ballet for the book *The Nutcracker* in the Fantasia Series. In his picture book, Warren Chappell has adapted and illustrated the story and has included six musical themes: "Harlequin and Columbine," "Waltz of the Snowflake," "The Mice," "Dance of the Reed Pipes," "Waltz of the Flowers," and "Chinese Dance." The records *Nutcracker* or *Stories in Ballet and Opera* could be used to identify the famous musical themes. The audience could close its eyes and imagine the "Waltz of the Flowers." A synopsis and discussion of "The Nutcracker" appears in Samochson's *The Russian Ballet, Three of Its Masterpieces*.

John Hosier has retold five stories, each of them connected with music, in his *Sorcerer's Apprentice and Other Stories*. Wanda Gag's *Sorcerer's Apprentice* is also available. "The Sorcerer's Apprentice" by the French composer Paul Dukas is based on a poem by Goethe. The film *The Sorcerer's Apprentice, a Musical Fantasy*, one of the best ways of expressing the story through music, pictures and words, uses animated puppets to tell the story. The book by Hosier should be made the basis of a discussion after the film is shown. Many students will wish to read the story for themselves. Anyone wanting to hear the music again may listen to the phonograph record *Legends in Music*.

The Italian composer, Rossini, composed an opera about William Tell, a Swiss historical hero. The overture is the only music which remains familiar, and can be used to introduce the story. The overture is available on many recordings, one of which is *William Tell*, played by the New York Philharmonic conducted by Leonard Bernstein. Two individual versions of the story which do not include music are Bettina Hurliman's picture book *William Tell and His Son* and, for intermediate and junior high readers, Mary and Conrad Buff's *The Apple and the Arrow*.

The three other musical tales told by Hosier include heroes of Russian, Hungarian, and German descent. Serge Prokofiev arranged five musical pieces to tell the Russian story of Lieutenant Kije. Music by Zoltan Kodaly tells about the Hungarian legendary hero Jary Janos. German composer Richard Strauss provides music for "Some Merry Pranks of Till Owglass." The phonograph record *Rogues in Music* contains musical selections about Lieutenant Kije and Jary Janos.

Ballets and operas cannot be mentioned without including a reference to operettas. The operettas of Gilbert and Sullivan come quickly to mind. *The Gilbert and Sullivan Song Book* listed in the bibliography under "Sullivan" contains twenty-six songs from seven of the most famous Gilbert and Sullivan operettas. Voice and piano arrangements are included for the following seven operettas: *HMS Pinafore, Pirates of Penzance, Patience, Iolanthe, The Mikado,*

Yeoman of the Guard, and *The Gondoliers.* A companion book by Bulla, *Stories of Gilbert and Sullivan Operas,* retells the stories of all seven mentioned above plus *Trial by Jury, The Sorcerer, Princess Ida,* and *Ruddigore.*

SPECIALIZED BIBLIOGRAPHIC CATEGORIES

At the back of this book are two numbered bibliographies, one of multimedia (nonprint material), and one of books. The numbers below refer to those bibliographies, with the entries preceded by "M" found in the Multimedia list.

INDIVIDUAL SONGS IN PICTURE BOOKS AND MULTIMEDIA
9, M32, M662, 19, 265, M291, 283, M205, M775, M776, 542, M216, M308, M309, 586, 587, M32, M306, M307, M369, 658, M719, M720, 896, M489, M636, 897, M521, 898, M201, M521, 909, M32, M85, M204, 923, 1103, 1342, 1345, 1391, 1512, M506, 1513, M612, 1526, 1550, 1787, M636, 1811, M354, M360, M625, 1855, M32, 2025, 2073, M521, 2253, M521, 2329, 2470, 2472, 2487, M8, M369, M370, 2488, M146, M147, 2532, M369, M680, 2551, 2558, M55, 2584, 2605, 2626, M367, M368, 2627, M510, M511, 2659, 2680, M205, M476, 2681, M630, M631, 2765, M489, M636, 2807, M32, M236, M237, 2799, 2800, 2805, 2806, 2808, M510, M511, 2874, 2906, 2912, M311, 3488, 3562, 3571, 3573, 3574, 3610, M132, 3691, M731, 3699, 3797, M620, M621, 3844, M32, 3870, M139, 3871, 3872, M369, 3873, M204, M607, 3874, 3966, 4038, M115, 4039, 4040, 4109, 4174, M221, M222, 4251, 4287, 4410, M193, M194, 4412, M225, M226, 4416, M386, 4428, 4453, M32, M217, M359, 4463, M32, M216, 4532, 4534, 4669, 4670, 4696, M521, 4778, 4837, 4980, 5002, M461, 5010, M32.

SONGBOOKS
61, 253, 432, 447, 449, 493, 540, 541, 695, 719, 837, 859, 1193, 1373, 1493, 1534, 1544, 1609, 1638, 1717, 1718, 1740, 1849, 1903, 1904, 2121, 2315, 2383, 2384, 2385, 2538, 2603, 2604, 2798, 2801, 2802, 2803, 2809, 2821, 2898, 2906, 2912, 3071, 3072, 3073, 3074, 3075, 3076, 3116, 3424, 3541, 3805, 3808, 3868, 3869, 3888, 3961, 3962, 3982, 3986, 4001, 4059, M151, 4069, 4162, 4175, 4206, M573, M574, 4226, 4267, 4313, 4355, 4506, 4626, 4679, 4787, 4788, 4884, 4885, 4886, 4960, 4965, 4978, 4999.

MUSIC IN MULTIMEDIA
M8, M15, M16, M21, M22, M23, M24, M25, M26, M27, M32, M41, M44, M45, M52, M55, M74, M85, M95, M107, M126a & b, M132, M139, M146, M147, M151, M175, M193, M194, M199, M201, M204, M205, M207, M216, M217, M218, M219, M221, M222, M225, M226, M236, M237, M262, M278, M291, M306, M307, M308, M309, M311, M315, M316, M337 M354, M358, M360, M361, M367, M368, M369, M386, M407, M420, M461, M470, M471, M472, M476, M486, M489, M504, M505, M506, M507, M510, M511, M512, M515,

M519, M521, M546, M573, M574, M585, M607, M612, M613, M620, M621, M622, M623, M625, M630, M631, M636, M648, M662, M680, M719, M720, M731, M757, M775, M776

CHAPTER FOUR

Enjoying Poetry

CHAPTER OBJECTIVES

1. To surround students with poetry in music, art, science, and social studies as well as in language arts classrooms.
2. To introduce several types of poetry (nursery rhymes, nonsense verse, limericks, rhyming and prose poems, hymns, haiku) to students in as many ways possible.
3. To stimulate students to read, write, and share poetry.
4. To present rhymes and poems to students through the mediums of sight and sound.
5. To use poetry as a vehicle for introducing books to students and to use fiction and nonfiction to introduce poems.
6. To meet poets through their lives and works.
7. To locate poetry through special indexes.
8. To suggest ideas for using print and nonprint sources of poems in reading, writing, and listening activities.
9. To furnish titles of books and audiovisuals containing individual poems, stories told in verse, anthologies containing many poets, collections of poems by one poet, and books introduced through poetry.
10. To develop verbal skills, discrimination, and taste in children and older students.

TECHNIQUES FOR USING MEDIA INTRODUCED IN THIS CHAPTER

1. Use nursery rhyme books on particular themes to introduce other books on similar themes.
2. Use nonsense verses to provide a bridge between nursery rhymes and poetry.
3. Use collections of nursery rhymes to compare and discuss with children the techniques and styles of outstanding artists.
4. Encourage students to illustrate poems that are read aloud to them, then compare their illustrations with those of several different artists' conceptions of the same subject.
5. Have children talk about single illustrated poems and compare the imagery of the words and the graphics. Do the two together convey the same mood? If not, why not?

6. Introduce classic poems through the picture book editions of those poems.
7. Use sound filmstrips of individual poems to introduce students to other poems by the same poet, or other poems on the subject.
8. Inspire students to write poems of their own by introducing published student poems to them. Read some poems written by famous poets when they were children.
9. Encourage students to add more verses to descriptive poems.
10. Share haiku poems with children and encourage them to write and illustrate some of their own.
11. Introduce the reading and writing of tanka poems through the more familiar haiku.
12. Encourage children to read poetry aloud, singly and in groups, to each other and to themselves.
13. Introduce poetry to students through choral reading.
14. Read one picture book in rhyme by an author to introduce other picture books by Slobodkin, Lenski, Hutchins, Chonz, Seuss, Kuhl, Bemelmans, Raskin, the Emberleys, Adoff, Sendak, Eichenberg, and Zemach.
15. Use poems, which although intended to introduce a section of book, do in fact introduce the entire book to students. Read the title poem of an anthology to introduce that anthology or a particular poet to students.
16. Introduce biographies of famous Americans such as Paul Revere, Martin Luther King, John Chapman, or others by reading poetry by or about those persons.
17. When individuals are reading biographies about a particular person, suggest that they locate a poem or poems about that person.
18. Encourage students to read biographies or biographical sketches of poets to better understand their work.
19. Remind students that psalms, hymns, and many prayers are poetry. Introduce the rhythmic prose of Bible stories by reading from the King James Version of the Bible.
20. Introduce limericks and limerick writers like Belloc, Lear, and Carroll by reading aloud from *The Limerick Trick* by Scott Corbutt.
21. Read published parodies of poems and rhymes to students and have them write their own parodies.
22. Use a lot of poetry to enrich curriculum units on the American Indian and Alaska.
23. Incorporate math and geography poems into classroom study of those subjects, through reading or displaying poems at appropriate times.
24. Choose lines from poems for bulletin board captions.
25. Use poems about snails, birds, fireflies, milkweeds, or dandelions to enrich and enliven science classes.

26. Have students match pictures of wildflowers, insects, birds, and animals with poems about these creatures.

27. Decorate science rooms with poems written on shapes of insects, birds, and wildflowers.

28. Display poems with related objects such as a vase of flowers, jars with cocoons, pussywillows, and the like.

29. Suspend poems from ceilings in the shape of autumn leaves, raindrops, kites, valentines, shamrocks, and snowflakes.

30. Teach students to find poems on these and any other subjects by author and title, by using the poetry indexes.

31. Display a group of books related to the subjects of the poems that are posted or hanging in mobile forms in various classrooms and display areas.

32. Read poems about food at a special feasting session featuring cookies, ice cream, jelly beans, etc.

33. Have students listen to recordings of poets reading from their own works, or of poetry read by professional actors.

34. Combine poetry and folklore to enrich classroom units in all subject areas.

ART IN NURSERY RHYME BOOKS.   Since nursery rhymes are often a child's first exposure to books, as well as to poetry, it is fortunate that so many collections are illustrated by fine artists. Providing children with several collections can show them that there are many ways to show any one idea, personage, or place.

The list of illustrators of nursery rhyme collections reads like a who's who of Caldecott and Kate Greenaway Medal winners. The Petershams won the 1946 Caldecott Medal for *The Rooster Crows*. Three collections were Caldecott honor books: 1945—Tasha Tudor's *Mother Goose*, 1955—Marguerite DeAngeli's *Book of Nursery and Mother Goose Rhymes*, and 1964—Philip Reed's *Mother Goose and Nursery Rhymes*. Individual rhymes that were Caldecott honor books are 1959—Frasconi's illustrations of *The House that Jack Built*, 1968—Emberley's *Drummer Hoff*, 1972—Domanska's *If All the Seas Were One Sea*, and 1974—Jeffers's *Three Jovial Huntsmen*. Two collections containing rhymes and music that were Caldecott honor books are Fish's *Four and Twenty Blackbirds* (1938) illustrated by Robert Lawson, and Wheeler's *Sing Mother Goose* (1946) illustrated by Marjorie Torrey. Individual songs that won the Caldecott Medal are Langstaff's *Frog Went a'Courtin'* (1956) illustrated by Feodor Rojankovsky, and Nic Leohodas's *Always Room for One More* (1956) illustrated by Nonny Hogrogian. Spier's *Fox Went Out on a Chilly Night* was an honor book in 1961. The Langstaff and Spier songs are available on sound filmstrips. Complete information on Mother Goose rhymes set to music is included in the chapter "Enhancing Books through Music."

Persons who have won the Caldecott Medal for other books and who have also illustrated nursery rhyme collections include Nonny Hogrogian—*One I Love, Two I Love and Other Loving Mother Goose Rhymes*, Blair Lent—*From*

King Boggin's Hall to Nothing at All, Feodor Rojankovsky—*Tall Book of Mother Goose*, Beni Montresor—*I Saw a Ship a-Sailing.* . ., Maurice Sendak—*Hector Protector and As I Went Over the Water*, Arnold Lobel—*Gregory Griggs and Other Nursery Rhyme People*, Latham—*Nursery Rhymes in French*, and Reid-Kerrigan—*Nursery Rhymes in Spanish*, (the last two illustrated by Barbara Cooney).

Persons who have had other books of theirs honored have illustrated nursery rhyme books: Marguerite DeAngeli's *A Pocket Full of Posies*, Joan Walsh Anglund's *In a Pumpkin Shell*, and four by Peter Spier—*Hurrah, We're Outward Bound, And So My Garden Grows, To Market! To Market!*, and *London Bridge is Falling Down*. The last book is available on sound filmstrip. Paul Galdone has illustrated numerous individual rhymes: *The House that Jack Built, Old Mother Hubbard and Her Dog, The Old Woman and Her Pig, Tom, Tom the Piper's Son, The History of Little Tom Tucker, The Life of Jack Sprat, His Wife and His Cat*, and *The Moving Adventures of Old Dame Trot and Her Comical Cat*. The first three books are also available on sound filmstrip.

Randolph Caldecott, for whom the Caldecott Award for the most outstanding American picture book is named, illustrated several nursery rhyme books. There are *Randolph Caldecott's Picture Books*, numbers one through four, with four rhymes in each book. These are also available as individual picture books. Filmstrips made from nursery rhymes illustrated by Caldecott are *Queen of Hearts, Sing a Song for Sixpence, Hey Diddle Diddle and Baby Bunting*, and *The Milkmaid*.

Kate Greenaway, for whom the British counterpart of the Caldecott Medal is named, has illustrated *Mother Goose: or, The Old Nursery Rhymes*, with forty-four rhymes. Three winners of the Kate Greenaway Medal have illustrated nursery rhyme collections: Helen Oxenbury who illustrated Anderson's *Cakes and Custards*; Raymond Briggs who illustrated *The Mother Goose Treasury, Fee Fi Fo Fum, a Picture Book of Nursery Rhymes, The White Land, a Book of Traditional Rhymes and Verses*, and *Ring-A Ring O'Roses*; and, of course, Brian Wildsmith's *Mother Goose*. A selection of about twenty rhymes from Briggs's *The Mother Goose Treasury* are available on sound filmstrip.

Other classic children's book artists are Leslie Brooke and Beatrix Potter. Brooke illustrated *Ring O'Roses* and Lang's *Nursery Rhyme Book*. Potter illustrated *Cecily Parsley's Nursery Rhymes*. Cecily, like Peter, is a rabbit. That book is included on the recording *Beatrix Potter Nursery Rhymes and Tales*.

A variety of techniques have been used in illustrating these nursery rhyme books. The golden age of woodcuts ran simultaneously with the career of Thomas Bewick who also revived the art of wood engraving. Some of the illustrations in Iona and Peter Opie's *Oxford Nursery Rhyme Book* are engravings by Thomas and John Bewick. Wood engravings by Philip Reed appear in *Mother Goose and Nursery Rhymes*. Harold Jones used stone lithography to create illustrations for Lines's *Lavender's Blue: A Book of Nursery Rhymes*. Watercolors are used by Potter, Spier, Tudor, Greenaway, DeAngeli, Wildsmith and others.

Preschool and primary grade children enjoy Mother Goose and other nursery rhymes, but it must be remembered that they can be enjoyed, compared, analyzed, and even parodied by older students on different levels of understanding and perception. It is important, too, for school library media staffs and teachers to realize that today's young children may not have been exposed *before* coming to school, to the extent earlier generations were, to the playing, singing, and reciting of these early childhood verses upon which a common heritage of language and allusion is based.

COMPARING ILLUSTRATIONS IN NURSERY RHYME BOOKS.

When introducing nursery rhymes to children, be sure to have as many different nursery rhyme books by as many illustrators as possible for the children to look through. Children might like to find the same rhyme in several collections to see how they are illustrated. Children may also wish to create their own illustrations.

One Misty Moisty Morning is the title of Miller's anthology of nursery rhymes. Compare the title rhyme with the same rhyme illustrated by Leslie Brooke in Lang's Nursery Rhyme Book, Rojankovsky's Tall Book of Mother Goose, Wright's Real Mother Goose, and Oxenbury's illustrations in Anderson's Cakes and Custards.

"Hark Hark the Dogs Do Bark" is found in Kate Greenaway's Mother Goose, Anglund's In a Pumpkin Shell, Brian Wildsmith's Mother Goose, and Mother Goose in Hieroglyphics. The last book contains rhymes in rebus form and could be used with Low's Mother Goose Riddle Rhymes. Students could put other nursery rhymes into rebus form.

Using an opaque projector to show the various illustrations is possible but the drawback is that the completely darkened room required tends to create behavior problems with young children. "The Old Woman Who Lived in a Shoe" is located in Briggs's Ring-a Ring O'Roses, Lines's Lavender's Blue, and Mother Goose in Hieroglyphics. The rhyme also appears in the collections illustrated and listed in the bibliography under Anglund, Greenaway, Montresor, Oxenbury, Reed, and Wildsmith. "Peter Peter Pumpkin Eater" is in Lavender's Blue, illustrated by Jones and edited by Lines, as well as in the collections illustrated by Anglund, Hogrogian, Lent, Montresor, Rojankovsky, Wildsmith, and Wright. The last page of Lines's book contains a full-page illustration. A large illustration appears in Wildsmith's collection and on the cover of Anglund's In a Pumpkin Shell.

Not all versions of a rhyme are the same. "To Market To Market to Buy a Fat Pig" is the most common version, but Kate Greenaway has the person buying a plum cake. Have students check the versions in Lines's Lavender's Blue and Spier's collection To Market! To Market!

The rhyme "Derby Ram" has nine verses in Briggs's Mother Goose Treasury, eight verses in Marguerite DeAngeli's Book of Nursery and Mother Goose Rhymes, and twelve verses as "I Was Going to Darby" in Tripp's Granpa' Grig Had a Pig (pp. 35-37). Compare these three with Schreiter's picture book The Derby Ram, a Ballad with its Old English illustrations in muted colors. The verses agree with the Briggs collection.

"Three Jovial Welshmen" is located in the Briggs and DeAngeli collections, as well as illustrated by Oxenbury in Anderson's *Cakes and Custards*. The rhyme "Three Jovial Huntsmen" is located in *Caldecott's Book Number Two* and as a separate book. "Three Jovial Huntsmen" is also an individual picture book illustrated by Susan Jeffers.

NURSERY RHYMES AS INDIVIDUAL PICTURE BOOKS.   There are many other nursery rhymes that are individual picture books. *I Saw a Ship A Sailing* is the title of Montresor's collection, as well as an individual picture book by Domanska. A full page is given opposite the text in Anderson's *Cakes and Custards*. The poem also appears in Rackham's *Mother Goose Nursery Rhymes*, Lines's *Lavender's Blue*, Marguerite DeAngeli's *Book of Nursery and Mother Goose Rhymes*, and Brian Wildsmith's *Mother Goose*.

Maurice Sendak illustrated two poems in *Hector Protector and As I Went Over the Water*. Compare Sendak's *Hector Protector* with Oxenbury's illustrations in Anderson's *Cakes and Custards*. The many asides spoken by Hector, as well as the nonverbal messages in the illustrations, add new dimensions to both nursery rhymes.

The House That Jack Built is available as four separate picture books as well as in a parody by Heilbroner (illustrated by Aliki) called *This is the House Where Jack Lives*. Frasconi illustrated his bilingual book with woodcuts for the English/French *The House That Jack Built; La Maison Que Jacques a Batie*. Two colorful editions are illustrated by Rogers and by Chwast and both are called *The House That Jack Built*. Paul Galdone also illustrated a book of the same title. The illustrations have an old-fashioned look in *The House That Jack Built and Other Favorite Jingles* designed by Anderson and Bradford. The poem "The House That Jack Built" also appears in the following collections: Briggs's *Mother Goose Treasury* (pp. 30-33); Marguerite DeAngeli's *Book of Nursery and Mother Goose Rhymes*, (pp. 18-20); Lines's *Lavender's Blue*, (pp. 139-143); Rackham's *Mother Goose Nursery Rhymes*, (pp. 37-41); and *The Oxford Nursery Rhyme Book* by the Opies (pp. 47-49). A parody for older students called "This Is the Pentagon Building" by G. E. Bates appears in Livingston's *Speak Roughly to Your Little Boy, a Collection of Parodies and Burlesques* (pp. 133-35).

Besides illustrating *The House That Jack Built*, Paul Galdone has illustrated many other individual rhymes as picture books. Galdone found all twenty-two stanzas of the famous four-line rhyme "Jack Sprat" in a 1920 chapbook, and they became the text for his book *The Life of Jack Sprat, His Wife and His Cat*. Persons interested in traditional endings for tales should check the last two lines of the book. An old chapbook was also the source for another rhyme about a cat, *The Moving Adventures of Dame Trot and Her Comical Cat*. Read that story with the more familiar *Old Mother Hubbard and Her Dog*, also illustrated by Galdone, Arnold Lobel's picture book *The Comic Adventures of Old Mother Hubbard and Her Dog* or de Paola's *The Comic Adventures of Old Mother Hubbard and her Dog*. In Evaline Ness's *Old Mother Hubbard and Her Dog*, the dog is a sheepdog. A cumulative untitled rhyme about a woman who bought a pig that would not go over the stile without the help of a cat, rat, rope, butcher, ox, water, fire, stick, and dog is found in Rackham's *Mother Goose Rhymes* (pp.

68-75), in Lines's *Lavender's Blue* (pp. 148-52), as well as in Galdone's *The Old Woman and Her Pig*. Two other familiar nursery rhyme picture books are about fellows named Tom—*Little Tom Tucker* and *Tom, Tom the Piper's Son*.

Burnie's Hill, A Traditional Rhyme has been illustrated by Erik Blegrad. The cumulative rhyme is from Scotland or Northern England.

The Mother Goose rhyme about Cock Robin is illustrated by Barbara Cooney in a picture book called *The Courtship, Merry Marriage, and Feast of Cock Robin and Jenny Wren to Which is Added the Doleful Death of Cock Robin*.

Langner's *Miss Lucy* is a picture book illustrating a nursery rhyme which is sometimes used as a jump rope jingle. The book can be used to introduce the collections of jump rope jingles, especially Worstell's *Jump the Rope Jingles*.

Nicola Bayley illustrated the nursery rhyme *One Old Oxford Ox* which has lots of alliteration, and can be most satisfactorily used with Brown's *Peter Piper's Alphabet*. *One Old Oxford Ox* is a counting rhyme that begins with one and goes to twelve. Other illustrated counting rhymes as well as alphabet books appear in the chapter "Experiencing Art through Picture Books."

"Three Blind Mice" is an interesting nursery rhyme to have children check for various illustrations. The illustration in *Charles Addams Mother Goose* is a satire on the painting "American Gothic" by Wood. Other interesting illustrations of the rhyme are to be found in Beatrix Potter's *Cecily Parsley's Nursery Rhymes*, Feodor Rojankovsky's *Tall Book of Mother Goose*, Blanche Wright's *Real Mother Goose*, L. Leslie Brooke's *Nursery Rhyme Book*, Anderson's *Cakes and Custards*, and Lang's *Nursery Rhyme Book*. The two individual books by Ivimey that contain thirteen verses to the song are illustrated by two different artists. *The Complete Version of Ye Three Blind Mice* is illustrated by Corbould. The paperback, *The Adventures of the Three Blind Mice*, is illustrated by Langner. Information about using the rhyme as a song is included in a section called Animal Songs in the chapter on "Enhancing Books through Music." Further information is found also in that chapter for the two picture books called *London Bridge is Falling Down*—one of them illustrated by Ed Emberley, the other by Peter Spier. The rhyme is also included in Briggs's *Mother Goose Treasury*, Lang's *Nursery Rhyme Book*, Lines's *Lavender's Blue*, and Rackham's *Mother Goose Nursery Rhymes*.

Rodney Peppe has illustrated *Simple Simon* in collage. Ed Emberley illustrated twelve verses of the same rhyme in *Simon's Song* with woodcuts and added music, which is available in paperback and sound filmstrip.

Nursery rhymes are meant to be read or said aloud and often take on a sing-song effect. Many have been set to music. Six collections of nursery rhyme songs that are discussed in the chapter on "Enhancing Books through Music," are Bertail's *Complete Nursery Song Book*, Engvick's *Lullabies and Night Songs*, Fish's *Four and Twenty Blackbirds*, Kapp's *Cock a Doodle Doo! Cock a Doodle Dandy!*, Poston's *Baby Song Book*, and Wheeler's *Sing Mother Goose*.

See pages 85 to 120 of Lang's *Nursery Rhyme Book* for a section entitled "Songs."

NURSERY RHYME BOOKS WITH SPECIAL THEMES.   Three nursery rhyme picture books by Peter Spiers are built upon special themes. *And So My Garden Grows* has rhymes about growing things like "Mary, Mary Quite Contrary," and is illustrated from sketches of actual Italian Gardens. *To Market! To Market!* includes rhymes like the one about going to get a fat pig. *Hurrah, We're Outward Bound* has rhymes from the sea. Cole's *The Sea, Ships and Sailors, Poems, Songs and Chanties* is also on the sea theme but for older students.

Blair Lent's *From King Boggins Hall to Nothing at All* presents fourteen unusual homes from nursery rhymes. Use it to introduce Anglund's *In a Pumpkin Shell* which shows "Peter Peter Pumpkin Eater" on the cover.

Lord's *The Days of the Week* includes "Monday's Child" and "Sneeze on Monday" and other rhymes about days of the week.

"Georgie Porgie" is one of the poems illustrated by Nonny Hogrogian in *One I Love, Two I Love and Other Loving Mother Goose Rhymes*.

Blegvad's *Mittens for Kittens and Other Rhymes about Cats* includes twenty-seven poems about cats. Eight of these are nursery rhymes including the St. Ives riddle, the cat who visited the queen, the cat who fell in the well, and Dame Trot and her cat. It is a great lead into the other poems or stories about cats.

Peppe's *Hey Riddle Riddle, A Book of Traditional Riddles* includes forty-five Mother Goose rhymes that are riddles.

Tucker's *Mother Goose Lost* contains lesser known Mother Goose rhymes.

NURSERY RHYMES AROUND THE WORLD.   South American folk rhymes in Spanish and English are included in *The Snow and the Sun, la Nieve y el Sol,* illustrated in woodcuts by Frasconi. The title rhyme is a cumulative one that discusses why either the snow or sun is bad. It is helpful for bilingual groups. Another Frasconi book that includes a bilingual cumulative rhyme is *The House That Jack Built,* written in English and French. Use it with Latham's *Mother Goose in French* illustrated by Barbara Cooney. Sixty French poems are included in DeKay's *Rimes de la Mere Oie, Mother Goose Rhymes Rendered into French.* Caldecott winner Cooney also illustrated Reid-Kerrigan's *Mother Goose in Spanish.*

Another Caldecott winner, Nonny Hogrogian, illustrated Morgenstern's *The Three Sparrows and Other Nursery Rhymes,* nonsense rhymes of German origin. DeForest's collection *The Prancing Pony, Nursery Rhymes from Japan* includes fifty-three nursery rhymes illustrated in collage. Wyndham's *Chinese Mother Goose Rhymes* are illustrated in watercolor. Cassedy's *Moon-Uncle-Moon-Uncle* includes forty-three rhymes from India. In Ross's *The Hungry Moon, Mexican Nursery Tales,* the thirteen tales are introduced by the original Mexican nursery rhymes. Mexico is one of twelve countries represented in Wolf's *Pojaro-cu-cu, Animal Rhymes from Many Lands.*

Bodecker's *It's Raining Said John Twaining* is a collection of Danish rhymes. *The Little Tuppen* is a cumulative nursery rhyme from Scandinavia. Little Tuppen is a chick whose mother approaches the spring for a cup of water to keep Little Tuppen from choking on a seed. A shoemaker, farmer, and blacksmith are among those approached for help. *The Speckled Hen* is a Russian nursery rhyme illustrated by Margot Zemach. Rhymes from France, Spain, Belgium, Holland, and Germany are included in Tucker's *Mother Goose Abroad.*

LONGER NURSERY RHYME ANTHOLOGIES.   Anyone who is looking for anthologies containing many rhymes should consult the following: *The Oxford Nursery Rhyme Book* by Iona and Peter Opie, which is the biggest collection and contains 800 rhymes; Briggs's *The Mother Goose Treasury* has 480 rhymes; the Marguerite DeAngeli's *Book of Nursery and Mother Goose Rhymes* has 376; Wright's *The Real Mother Goose* and Lang's *Nursery Rhyme Book* both have about 300 rhymes; Rackham's *Mother Goose and Nursery Rhymes* has somewhat fewer than 300; Alice and Martin Provensen's *Mother Goose Book* and Lines's *Lavender's Blue* contain between 130 and 150 rhymes; Anderson's *Cakes and Custards* has some 140; Rojankovsky's *Tall Book of Mother Goose* contains about 100 poems; Tudor's *Mother Goose*, Brian Wildsmith's *Mother Goose*, Philip Reed's *Mother Goose and Nursery Rhymes*, and DeAngeli's *Pocket Full of Posies* each contain about seventy.

Sechrist's *One Thousand Poems for Children* (pp. 3-41), contains at least 400 rhymes, none of them illustrated, and no illustrations accompany the 100 rhymes in the third edition of *Anthology of Children's Literature* by Johnson, Sickles, and Sayer. Check the table of contents to find nursery rhymes in Sutherland's *Arbuthnot Anthology of Children's Literature.*

Nursery rhymes are included in volume 1 of *Childcraft* which is called *Poems & Rhymes*, and in a section called "Mother Goose Rhymes" (pp. 53-66). Seventy-one rhymes as well as suggested grade levels and student activities are given.

See Martignoni's *The Illustrated Treasury of Children's Literature* (pp. 2-33), and Huber's *Story and Verse for Children* (pp. 53-65).

PARODIES.   Students who think they are "beyond" Mother Goose can still enjoy those same sounds and rhythmic patterns in nonsense verse parodies. Steven Vincent Benet's "A Nonsense Song" in Tudor's *Wings from the Wind* (pp. 112-13), is a perfect example of a poem that is one step away from Mother Goose yet can be enjoyed by adults. Parodies of Rapunzel and of Little Boy Blue are incorporated into the first two lines, "Rosemary, Rosemary, Let down your hair! The Cow's in the Hammock the Crow's in the chair!" It is interesting to readers to know that Benet's wife was named Rosemary. McCord's "Jack, Jill, Sprats, and Horner," page 39 of his collection *Away and Ago*, and Behn's "Mother Goose's Children," pages 22 and 23 of *The Wizard in the Well*, have similar themes.

"The Bargain," on page 77 of Nash's *You Can't Get There from Here*, is a parody of the riddle rhyme "Going to St. Ives." Over 100 parodies of nursery rhymes appear in Livingston's *Speak Roughly to Your Little Boy*. Among them are "Bye, Baby Bunting," "Little Bo-Peep," "Sing a Song of Sixpence," "Ring-a-ring-o'roses," and "The House That Jack Built." Jane Taylor's "The Star" whose first line is "Twinkle Twinkle Little Star" is a common poem that is easy to parody and would be a good poem to use when a whole classroom provides input into the parody. Remind them that no less a writer than Lewis Carroll used it "...like a tea tray in the sky."

Parodies are fun to listen to and children enjoy writing them.

The picture book *Three Poems of Edgar Allan Poe* can be used to introduce Livingston's *Speak Roughly to Your Little Boy*. Livingston's book contains parodies of both "Annabel Lee" and "The Bells." Read the parodies and invite students to write another parody of either of those poems or the third poem in the collection, "The Raven."

There is a parody of Clement Moore's "A Visit from St. Nicholas" by Gwendolyn Griswold on page 44 of Shaw's *The Mouse Book*. "The Thirteen Days" in *One's None, Old Rhymes for New Tongues* collected by Reeves, is another version of "The Twelve Days of Christmas."

Other famous poems for which parodies are given in Livingston's book are Edwin Arlington Robinson's "Miniver Cheevey," Percy Shelley's "Ozymandias," and William Wordsworth's "I Wandered Lonely as a Cloud."

The rhythm and meter of Longfellow's "Song of Hiawatha" is often imitated. There are two parodies given in Livingston's book. One of the parodies, "Hiawatha's Photographing," is by Lewis Carroll.

Nonsense poets Carroll, Nash, Belloc, and Lear are natural poets to parody. When reading the parodies aloud in class, teachers and students know that those poets would be laughing along with everyone else if they were listening. Lear's "How Pleasant to Know Mr. Lear" and Belloc's "Tarantella" are parodied in Livingston's *Speak Roughly to Your Little Boy*. There are nine parodies of poems of Lewis Carroll including "Jabberwocky" and "The Mad Hatter's Song."

Parodies of A. A. Milne's stories and verses appear in Crews's *The Pooh Perplex; a Freshman Casebook*. Music is included in Keller's *Glory, Glory, How Peculiar*, a book of parodies for early grades.

Two picture books that parody the song "The Twelve Days of Christmas" are Lobel's *A Small Sheep in a Pear Tree* and Mendoza's *A Wart Snake in a Fig Tree*.

Parodies can be created for Mother Goose rhymes as well as for more sophisticated poems so that parody writing can be interjected into the classroom experience from third grade through high school.

COLLECTIONS OF NONSENSE.   Some collections of nonsense rhymes to introduce to students in grades three through twelve are Blecker's *No End of Nonsense, Humorous Verses*; Brewton's *My Tang's Tungled and Other Ridiculous Situations, Humorous Poems* and *Quarks, Quasars and Other Quirks: Quizzical Poems for the Supersonic Age*; Ciardi's *The Man Who Sang the Sillies, The Reason for the Pelican,* and *Someone Could Win a Polar Bear*; Ets's *Beasts and Nonsense*; Green's *The Book of Nonsense*; Hughes's *Meet My Folks*; Hymes's *Oodles of Noodles and Other Rhymes*; Joslin's *Dear Dragon and Other Useful Letter Forms for Young Ladies and Gentlemen Engaged in Everyday Correspondence*; Lee's *Nicholas Knock and Other People Poems*; Livingston's *What a Wonderful Bird the Frog Are, an Assortment of Humorous Poetry and Verse*; Longman's *Would You Put Your Money in a Sand Bank?*; Love's *A Little Laughter*; Orgel's *Merry, Merry FIBruary*; Patrick's *Bug in a Jug and Other Funny Poems*; Prelutsky's *No End of Nonsense*; Richards's *Tirra Lirra*; Silverstein's *Where the Sidewalk Ends, the Poems and Drawings of Shel Silverstein*; Mr. *Smith and Other Nonsense* and *Laughing Time*, both by Smith; Tripp's *A Great Big Ugly Man Came Up and Tied his Horse to Me, a Book of Nonsense Verse*; Watson's *Father Fox's Penny Rhymes*; Wilbur's *Opposites*; and *A Rocket in My Pocket, the Rhymes and Chants of Young Americans* and *I Saw a Rocket Walk a Mile, Nonsense Tales, Chants and Songs from Many Lands*, both by Withers. The autograph verses of Lillian Morrison could also be included with the nonsense collections. They are: *A Diller a Dollar, Remember Me When This You See, Yours Till Niagra falls*, and *Touch Blue*.

INDIVIDUAL NONSENSE TITLES.   Polly Cameron's first book was *I Can't Said the Ant*. Equally funny are her *The Two-Ton Canary and Other Nonsense Riddles* and *The Green Machine* as well as Bodecker's *Let's Marry Said the Cherry and Other Nonsense Poems*. A special technique used by Heinig and Stillwell on page 191 of *Creative Dramtics for the Classroom Teacher* can be used to introduce those books.

Uncommon people and events occur in Scheer's *Upside Down Day* and *The Three Ladies Beside the Sea* by Levine, in which Edith of Ecstasy and Catherine of Compromise are conventional but Alice of Hazard likes to sit up in trees.

The best known as well as most beautiful nonsense picture book is Scheer's *Rain Makes Applesauce* illustrated by Bileck. The repetition of the title phrase connects the nonsense ideas with each other. "Do you know how it looks when it's bimulous and the sky is like lace?" Horwitz uses words like "bimulous," "swishing and swaying," and "gooseberry jam" in the beautifully executed *When the Sky Is Like Lace*. Rhyming nonsense words appear in Preston's Caldecott honor book, *Popcorn and Ma Goodness*. Blair Lent illustrated a Russian nonsense poem, Chukovsky's *The Telephone*. An old English tale, *Master of All Masters*, is not written in rhyme but the short picture book is included in this section because it is pure language nonsense. A man trained his maid to call items in his home by different names so she had trouble explaining that the cat's tail was on fire. Children can have fun making up nonsense words for articles in the classroom and then making up a very short story using those words. Noodle tales, about people who do nonsensical things are included in the chapter of this book titled "Using Riddles, Magic, Jokes, and Folk Themes."

LEAR'S NONSENSE.   Perhaps the most beautiful of all the picture books of individual nonsense is *The Scroobilous Pip*, illustrated by Nancy Ekholm Burkert, a poem written by Edward Lear and completed by Ogden Nash. The Pip is part bird, beast, insect, and fish and looks remarkably like a self-portrait of Lear that appears on pages 10, 13 and 50 of Lear's *Teapots and Quails and Other Nonsense* and on page 117 of Kelen's *Mr. Nonsense, A Life of Edward Lear*. The foreword to *The Scroobilous Pip* provides a good overview of Lear and his purpose in writing the story.

One of the most famous Lear poems is about "The Owl and the Pussy Cat." A French translation *Le Hibou Et La Poussiquette*, illustrated by Cooney, has the two animals sail off in a boat that is canary yellow instead of pea green. A glossary points out other differences and an English translation is provided at the end of the book. A sound filmstrip is available for an all-English edition illustrated by Barbara Cooney, and offers another avenue for introducing poems by Lear. Another picture book edition of *The Owl and the Pussy Cat* is illustrated by Gwen Fulton. Music for the poem is included in Kapp's *Cock-A-Doodle Do! Cock-A-Doodle Dandy!* The illustrations by Cooney and Fulton can be compared with those of Palazzo in *Edward Lear's Nonsense Book*. Patterns and directions for making an owl and a pussycat are included in Roth's *The Art of Making Cloth Toys*.

Galdone and Oxenbury have both illustrated editions of *The Quangle Wangle's Hat* about all the animals who come to see an unusual hat belonging to an unusual animal. Oxenbury won the 1970 Kate Greenaway Medal for her version. Claire Bloom reads the poem on the sound recording "Edward Lear's Nonsense Stories and Poems." This book can be used to introduce two more books by Lear, *The Popple* and *The Dong with a Luminous Nose* because these were two of the animals who came to see the Quangle Wangle's hat. One book contains two Lear poems, each of which is the first poem in the book depending upon which way the book is held. This "double feature" illustrated by Galdone is *Two Laughable Lyrics: The Popple Who Had No Toes* and *The Quangle Wangle's Hat*. Another Lear book illustrated by Galdone is the picture book *The Two Old Bachelors* who caught a muffin and a mouse, one of which ate the other. "The Popple Who Had No Toes" also appears in *Edward Lear's Nonsense Book*, illustrated by Palazzo, as well as in a picture book illustrated by Madison. The poem is also included on the sound recording *Nonsense Verse*.

Music appears at the end of *A Pelican Chorus*, illustrated by Berson. The same poem and others are illustrated by L. Leslie Brooke in *The Pelican Chorus and Other Nonsense Verses*. Another illustrated version appears in Palazzo's *Edward Lear's Nonsense Book*.

ABC: Lear Alphabet is a facsimile of the original handwritten book. Three pages at the end include the whole alphabet. "The Nonsense Alphabet" is one of eighteen poems in *Edward Lear's Nonsense Book*, and is also included in the ACEI anthology, *Sung Under the Silver Umbrella*. Palazzo has an illustrated version in *Edward Lear's Nonsense Book*. This should be contrasted with Eve Merriam's "Backwards" in her anthology *Catch a Little Rhyme* (pp. 32-33). In this nonsense rhyme, everyone says XYZ's instead of ABC's.

The Dong with a Luminous Nose and *The Jumblies* are two picture books of Lear poems illustrated by Gorey. The first poem is about the Dong who is in love with a Jumbly girl. Lear's own illustration of the long-nosed Dong appears in Lear's *Complete Nonsense Book* and Kelen's *Mr. Nonsense, A Life of Edward Lear*. "The Jumblies" is one of nineteen poems illustrated by L. Leslie Brooke that are included in *Nonsense Songs*. Included also in that collection is Lear's own drawing of "Calico Pie." Palazzo has also illustrated and included "The Jumblies" in his *Edward Lear's Nonsense Book*.

Arnold Lobel has illustrated the picture book *The Four Little Children Who Went Around the World.*

Since students are often fascinated with the lives of people, teachers may want to read Hoahes's *Edward Lear; the Life of a Wanderer* to get more information about Lear. Intermediate students can read Kelen's *Mr. Nonsense, A Life of Edward Lear* for themselves. A list of Lear's writings and a bibliography are included. The introduction to Lear's *Teapots and Quails and Other Nonsense* includes information about Lear's life taken from manuscripts in the Harvard College Library, and more information is found in the introduction to Palozzo's *Edward Lear's Nonsense Book.*

After reading and enjoying Lear's poems, students will appreciate the eight verse poem called "Mr. Lear" on page 118 of Tudor's *Wings from the Wind.* The funny poem was written by Mr. Lear, of course. The poem called "How Pleasant to Know Mr. Lear" is included on the recording *Nonsense Verse.* Other Lear poems included are "The Two Old Bachelors," "The Popple Who Has No Toes," "The Jumblies," "The Dong with a Luminous Nose," and "The Owl and the Pussycat." Carroll's "The Walrus and the Carpenter," "Jabberwocky," and "Humpty Dumpty's Song" are also on the same recording.

THE NONSENSE OF CARROLL, BELLOC, AND NASH.   Poems by Lear and Carroll appear in *Just for Fun, Humorous Stories and Poems* edited by Hazeltine and Smith. Nonsense poems of Lewis Carroll can be used to introduce *Alice in Wonderland* and *Through the Looking Glass.* Or teachers can be "name droppers" and use Alice to introduce the nonsense poems. The picture book *The Walrus and the Carpenter and Other Poems* contains eleven poems, nine of which were taken from those two famous books. The title poem, "Tweedledum and Tweedledee," and "Jabberwocky" all come from *Through the Looking Glass,* while "The Lobster Quadrille" comes from *Alice in Wonderland.* "Jabberwocky" and "The Walrus and the Carpenter" are found on the sound recording *Nonsense Verse.* "Tweedledum and Tweedledee" appears on the sound recording *Through the Looking Glass.*"Jabberwocky," Tweedledum and Tweedledee," and "The Walrus and the Carpenter" appear in the book and cassette *Songs from Alice.*

A poem on page 91 of Livingston's *Poems of Lewis Carroll* is an acrostic. The first letters of each line spell the name of Alice Pleasance Liddell, the girl for whom Carroll wrote *Alice in Wonderland.* The book also contains puzzles, riddles, and a cipher poem.

The Hunting of the Snark is available in two picture books, one illustrated by Oxenbury and one by Oechsli. *Jabberwocky* is a picture book illustrated by Zalben.

Wood's *The Snark was a Boojum; A Life of Lewis Carroll* should be read for background in Charles Dodgson. See also pages 49 to 57 of Benet's *Famous Poets for Young People.*

One of the funniest nonsense verses to read to students when they are well into the reading of nonsense verse is Belloc's poem in the introduction of *Cautionary Verses,* "Upon being asked by a reader whether the verses contained in this book were true."

The two favorite nonsense books by Belloc are *The Bad Child's Book of Beasts* and *More Beasts for Worse Children*. "The Lion," page 14, and "The Tiger," page 15, of the first book are especially funny. Three of the more famous poems often found in anthologies are illustrated by Steven Kellogg in the picture book *The Yak, The Python, The Frog*.

A favorite nonsense poem by Ogden Nash, found in picture book and sound filmstrip, is *Custard the Dragon*. Another funny picture book is about *The Cruise of the Aardvark* who thought he was going on a cruise when he entered Noah's ark.

Over one hundred Nash poems are to be found in *Parents Keep Out, Elderly Poems for Youngerly Readers*. Most of them are included on the sound recording by the same name. See page 39 for "The Trouble with a Kitten" and page 54 for information on how to tell the difference between a camel and a dromedary. Nash has collected humorous poems of others to add to some of his own in *The Moon Is Shining Bright as Day*. "The Germ" on page 164 is especially funny and could appropriately appear on a bulletin board in a science class.

One of Nash's poems for Christmas is about Jabez Dawes who didn't believe in Santa Claus and was turned into a jack-in-the-box and suffered an even worse fate in the last line of "The Boy Who Laughed at Santa Claus." The poem appears on two sound recordings— *Christmas With Ogden Nash* and Ogden Nash's *Parents Keep Out*. The poem also appears in Cole's *Story Poems Old and New* (the new edition is called *The Poets Tale: A New Book of Story Poems*).

Nash's narrative poem *Girls are Silly* makes a good companion book for Phyllis McGinley's *Boys are Awful* and Cole's *Beastly Boys and Ghastly Girls*.

Nonsense poetry including limericks by Cole, Ciardi, and Carroll are included in the sound filmstrip *A Pocketful of Poetry*.

LIMERICKS.   *Whizz!* is a picture book containing six limericks by Lear and illustrated by Janina Domanska that can be used to introduce limericks to children. The book can also be used to encourage students to verbalize. After looking at the illustrations, children can be encouraged to name all the things in the pictures that add to the information in the limericks. Twenty-one limericks are listed in *Limericks by Lear*, and over a hundred are included in Lear's *The Complete Nonsense Book*, and in Lear's *Teapots and Quails* (pp. 44-49). Sixty-one animal limericks are to be found in Jacobs's *Animal Antics in Limerick Land*. Advice on how to write limericks is included in *Laughable Limericks* by the Brewtons. David McCord is not above including a limerick on how to write limericks as well as a limerick about limericks in his introduction. His book of *Rhymes of the Never Was and Always Is* have limericks by McCord, Ciardi, Lear, De La Mare, Merriam, and Nash. Limericks can be used as an introduction to the other works by a poet. Humor does humanize and create interest.

Limericks are also included in Love's *A Little Laughter* and Livingston's *A Lollygag of Limericks*. Ross's *Illustrated Treasury of Poetry for Children* and Adshead and Duff's *An Inheritance of Poetry* all furnish limericks. The limericks about Beatrix Potter and Longfellow on p. 40 of Smith's *Mr. Smith and Other Nonsense* are too good to miss. Four limericks appear on page 22 of Livingston's *Four-Way Stop and Other Poems*.

Scott Corbett's *The Limerick Trick* is a good book to read aloud to intermediate students while you are studying nonsense verse and limericks. It seems that an English bike is the prize in the Third Annual City-Wide Elementary Schools Poetry Contest. Kerby wants to win the bike but doesn't want to write the poems so he goes to Mrs. Graymalkin for help. Mrs. Graymalkin's potion works wonders: Kerby writes a marvelous poem but as a side effect he begins to speak in limericks and later in couplets. The sassy manner in which Kerby spouts these poems gets him into trouble. Kerby can stop himself from spouting poetry only by hitting himself in the head, but since he cannot continue doing that, he needs to have Mrs. Graymalkin undo the spell. Teachers who do not wish to read the entire story may introduce the book to the students who are writing limericks by telling them just this much about it. Those who want to find out what happens will have to read the book! Reading the book to students can inspire a unit on limerick writing rather than being part of the project. If the teacher elects to read the entire book, then writing limericks and couplets is a natural activity which could begin any time after chapter 6 is finished. Once the students are beginning to enjoy *The Limerick Trick*, other books by Corbett can be put in the library corner of the classroom or displayed in the library media center flagged for a particular class's attention. Some of the books introduced could be Corbett mystery adventures such as *Dead Man's Light, Cutlas Island*, and *Diamonds are Trouble*. Less able readers will enjoy *Dr. Merlin's Magic Shop* and its sequel, *The Great Custard Pie Panic*. The favorites, however, will probably be the stories in which Mrs. Graymalkin gives Kerby directions for using the Feats O' Magic chemistry set. (Mrs. Graymalkin gives Kerby the set when he helped her out after she caught the heel of her shoe in the drain of the drinking fountain in the park.) The chemistry set helps Kerby play better baseball and street hockey in *The Baseball Trick, The Home Run Trick*, and *The Hockey Trick*. Kerby's dog Waldo becomes hairless at Halloween in *The Hairy-Horror Trick*. Waldo disappears during a city crackdown on loose dogs and Mrs. Graymalkin uses the chemistry set to produce Waldo as well as mischief in *The Disappearing Dog Trick*. Waldo is turned into a giant raccoon by Mrs. Graymalkin during a bicentennial caper in *The Black Mask Trick*. In *The Turnabout Trick*, the backfiring of Mrs. Graymalkin's ancient car Nostradamus is responsible for beginning a gunfight between the police and robbers. Kerby becomes a perfect gentleman and Waldo even gives up chasing Mrs. Pembroke's prissy cat Xerxes after they drink a magic potion in *The Lemonade Trick*. In *The Mailbox Trick*, Kerby is in trouble over some letters he has written. Reading the three letters to the students guarantees laughter especially if they already know the continuing cast of characters. If only two books are used, use this book with *The Limerick Trick* because both begin with a class assignment.

This just goes to show where a limerick may lead!

TITLE POEMS INTRODUCE ANTHOLOGIES.   Poems with unusual titles are often chosen as the title poem for a collection. Titles after all are designed to catch the interest of readers, and teachers can make use of them to introduce the collections to students by reading the title poem. Several of Kaye Starbird's collections can be used in this way: *A Snail's a Failure Socially and Other Poems, Mostly About People* and *The Pheasant on Route Seven.* The title poem of Hoberman's collection is *Hello and Good-By.* "The Golden Hive" by Behn is the first poem in his anthology of the same name. Other Behn collections that include the title poem are *The Little Hill, Windy Morning,* and *Wizard in the Well. Ragged Robbin* and *Blackbird in the Lilacs* are poems in collections of the poet James Reeves, Myra Livingston's collections that contain title poems are *Whispers and Other Poems, Wide Awake and Other Poems, The Way Things Are and Other Poems,* and *The Malibu and Other Poems.* Eve Merriam's *Catch a Little Rhyme* and *There Is No Rhyme for Silver* are both poems in the collections. A poem by Merriam is the title of Agree's anthology *How to Eat a Poem.* The title poem is the first one in Watson's collection *Blueberries' Lavender, Songs of the Farmer's Children.*

Two poems by Langston Hughes, "Dreams," page 19, and "I Dream a World," page 29, are included in Arna Bontemps's *Hold Fast to Dreams.* "Dreams" is also included in the collection of Hughes's poems called *The Dream Keeper and Other Poems.* Three dream poems are included in another Hughes anthology *Don't Turn Back.* Use these poems together with Martin Luther King's famous speech "I Have a Dream."

Sometimes the title of an anthology comes from *within* a poem that is included in the anthology. Milne's *Now We Are Six* takes its title from a line in the last poem in the book called "The End": "Now I am Six, I am clever as clever / I think I'll be six now forever and ever." Ogden Nash's anthology *The Moon Is Shining Bright as Day, an Anthology of Good-Humored Verse* takes its title from the second line of a Mother Goose rhyme that is included in the introduction to the book.

POEMS WITHIN BOOKS CAN INTRODUCE THE BOOK.   Collections of stories often include poems that can be used to introduce the whole book or its individual stories. Examples are Brown's *A Cavalcade of Sea Legends;* Hoke's *Witches, Witches, Witches;* Hope-Simpson's *A Cavalcade of Witches;* Farjeon's and Mayne's two collections *A Cavalcade of Kings* and *A Cavalcade of Queens.*

In Green's *A Cavalcade of Magicians,* a poem called "The Sorceror's Song" by W. S. Gilbert in the introduction can introduce the book.

Not only does a poem introduce Natalia Belting's *The Earth is on a Fish's Back, Tales of Beginnings,* but it has (on pages 9 and 10) the same title and makes an excellent introduction since it incorporates a related meaning.

Sometimes poems are used to introduce sections of a book as in Jacobs's *Is Somewhere Always Far Away?* The book contains forty-one poems and a poem introduces each of four sections—country, city, make believe, and home. A phrase of poetry introduces each of the twelve sections of Livingston's *A Tune beyond Us, a Collection of Poems.* The entire book is also introduced by a poem.

William Butler Yeats's poem "A Faery Song" is located in the front of Pilkington's *Shamrock and Spear, Tales and Legends from Ireland*. A portion of another poem by Yeats, "The Stolen Child," is used to introduce Myra Cohn Livingston's collection of poems *Come Away*. William Blake's "The Piper" is found in the introduction to Larrick's *Piper Pipe that Song Again*.

Poems by classic poets are often found in introductions to books of folklore and poetry.

Several books about Indians are introduced with poems. Hodge's *The Fire Bringer, a Payute Indian Legend* begins with a Chippewa poem. A ballad about the Haida Indians of Queen Charlotte's Island and the coming of the white man is used to introduce Harris's book *The Raven's Cry*.

Sometimes poems appear as an integral part of a book. Bran was given a poem as a sign so Will would trust him in the fantasy *The Grey King* by Cooper, the 1976 Newbery Winner. The third verse on page 37 can be read to introduce the book to students during a book talk. That verse contains the words "Cadfan's Way" and the "Grey King" which are important to the story and can be explained at the time the poem is read.

Several poems that are used to introduce books, or are titles of both poems and books, can provide springboards for persons starting to teach a unit about poetry or introduce poems to children. Eleanor Farjeon's poem "Poetry" introduces Doane's *A Small Child's Book of Verse*. The first line of the poem is "What is poetry?" "It doesn't always have to rhyme. . ." is the first line of a poem by Merriam entitled "Inside a Poem" found on page 3 of *It Doesn't Always Have to Rhyme*.

Use the poem "Hiding" by Dorothy Aldis found (pp. 104–105) in Untermeyer's *Rainbow in the Sky* with Livingston's book of poems *I'm Hiding*. Sixteen different pages in Livingston's book begin with "I'm Hiding" and each describes a different hiding place. Read some of the image-filled poems and have students continue with one or more hiding places in verse that they create themselves.

INTRODUCING BOOKS OR GROUPS OF BOOKS WITH POEMS.   The poem "Sugar Maples," in an unpaged collection of poems by Nancy Watson, can be used to introduce her book *Sugar on Snow*. Hoople's *The Heritage Sampler* gives information (pp. 125–28) on making maple sugar candy. Gemming's *Maple Harvest, The Story of Maple Sugaring* explains the process of making maple sugar and includes a visit to a sugarhouse.

Use Randall Jarrell's poem "Bats," in *Poetry of Earth* (pp. 10–11), edited and illustrated by Adrienne Adams, or on pp. 138–39 of Larrick's *Poems for Me and a Mountain Lion*, to introduce Jarrell's book *The Bat Poet*, illustrated by Maurice Sendak. It is about a sensitive bat who stayed awake in the daytime while all other bats slept, and then tried to tell the others in poetry what daytime was like. The poems by and about bats are included in the book. Two poems found in Cole's *The Birds and Beasts Were There* are called "The Bat." Pitter's poem is on pages 52 and 53, and Roethke's poem on page 45, and on the recording *Theodore Roethke Reads His Poetry*. Students can find other poems about bats by using the poetry indexes. Jarrell's recorded narration of *The Bat*

Poet can be used to stimulate students to find poems about bats.

David McCord's poem "Crows" is found on page 18 of *Poetry of Earth* and can be used to introduce folklore about why the crow is black. The poem begins "I like to walk / and hear the black crows talk."

Fisher's "The Old Man Moon," on page 59 of her *In the Woods, In the Meadow, In the Sky* makes a good introduction to a medley of tales and poems about the moon. According to the third Mother Goose rhyme in *One I Love, Two I Love*, there is a woman in the moon because "On Saturday night I lost my wife." Poems by Vachel Lindsay provide different answers for the riddle of the moon. In "The Man in the Moon," page 126 of Doane's *A Small Child's Book of Verse*, and in Larrick's *Piper Pipe That Song Again*, the "Moon's the North Wind's Cooky." On page 88 of Palmer's *Dragons, Unicorns and Other Magical Beasts*, Lindsay says that the moon is a griffin's egg in the poem "Yet Gentle Will the Griffin Be." Why the man in the moon is there is explained in an English verse called "The Man in the Moon" which introduces Jablow's and Withers's *The Man in the Moon, Sky Tales from Many Lands*. A "Moon Hare," page 78; "Moon-Ravens," page 52; and "The Moon-Bull," page 82, are only three of many poems in Hughes's *Moon-Whales and Other Moon Poems*. Twenty-one poems were collected and illustrated by Schweninger in *The Man in the Moon as he Sails the Sky and Other Moon Verse*.

A picture book in rhyme, Pape's *The First Doll in the World* can be used to introduce other books about dolls.

Livingston's poem "Tails," pages 28 and 29 of her book *Whispers . . .* can be used to introduce Garten's *The Alphabet Tale*, a picture book that introduces animals to viewers by showing them the tail before they turn the page to see the animal to which it belongs.

Aileen Fisher's poem "Whistling" can be used to introduce another picture book, Ezra Jack Keats's *Whistle for Willie*, about a boy who was trying to whistle for the first time. Fisher says "I never knew you had birds inside of you." The poem is found on page 7 of Fisher's collection *In One Door and Out the Other*. The poem "Whistling Willie," pages 16 and 17 of Starbird's *A Snail's a Failure Socially and Other Poems Mostly About People*, could also be introduced at this time.

Use the poem "How the Little Kite Learned to Fly," found (pp. 33-34) in Sechrist's *One Thousand Poems for Children*, with Piper's book *The Little Engine That Could* because both the engine and the kite had to think positively. The poet is unknown.

Aldis's poem "Inch-Worm," page 62 of her collection *Hello Day* is a perfect companion to Lionni's picture book *Inch by Inch*.

The poem "Crosspatch" on page 25 of Payne's *All the Day Long* can be used to introduce Viorst's *Alexander and the Terrible, Horrible, No Good, Very Bad Day*, or Lexau's *I Should Have Stayed in Bed*.

Use all nine stanzas or just the first five of "Chanticleer" to introduce Chaucer's *Chanticleer and the Fox*, the Caldecott award winning book illustrated by Barbara Cooney. Katherine T. Hickson's poem, found (pp. 421-422) in Sechrist's *One Thousand Poems for Children*, is very descriptive of Chanticleer's coloring as well as his morning duty. Another "Chanticleer" poem is found (pp. 61-62) in Brewton's *Under the Tent of the Sky.*

Use Behn's nonsense verse "Teaparty" on page 20 of his anthology *Windy Morning, Poems and Pictures* to introduce Ellen Raskin's *And It Rained,* a funny story about tribulations encountered while trying to have a perfect tea party.

Use the poem "What Did You Put in Your Pocket?" from deRegnier's *Something Special* to introduce Caudill's *Pocketful of Cricket* and Merriam's *What Can You Do With a Pocket?* A large and colorful pocket made of fabric or construction paper can be the focal point of a bulletin board. Slips of paper containing poems can be placed in the pocket and a student can be chosen each day to reach in and pull out a poem to be read aloud to the class.

Use Dixie Wilson's poem "Rainbows" on page 176 of Hubbard and Babbitt's *The Golden Flute;* Aldis's poem "Noah's Ark," page 2 of her collection *Hello Day;* or "Noah," a poem to dramatize on page 60 of Taylor's *Did You Fetch My Cow?* to introduce books about Noah's Ark such as Bellanger's *Noah and the Rainbow.* Hutton's picture book *Noah and the Flood* follows the King James version of the Bible. Duvoisin's *A for the Ark* is an alphabet book; Spier's *Noah's Ark* is a wordless book; and Farber's *Where's Gomer?* is a picture book about Noah's favorite grandson who was not to be found when the doors of the ark closed but appeared riding a dolphin at the end of the book. Haley's *Noah's Ark,* about a modern Noah who takes animals onto a barge to save them from extinction, is not written in rhyme. Nash's *Cruise of the Aardvark* is a humorous story poem about the famous trip. Reeves's *Ragged Robin* includes poems utilizing each letter of the alphabet. The poem about *N* is "Noah" and the poem about *R* is "Rain." Ciardi's "Why Noah Praised the Whale," in his collection *Fast and Slow,* can be used with Singer's book *Why Noah Chose the Dove.*

Joan Walsh Anglund's collection *A Year is Round* is so named because the astrological calendar is round. This collection and Eleanor Farjeon's poem "Zodiac," from her collection *Poems for Children* (or page 126 of her collection *Then Those Were There)* can be used to introduce Jagendorf's *Stories and Lore of the Zodiac* or the picture book *The Rat, the Ox and the Zodiac—a Chinese Legend* by Van Woerkom. There are twelve animals in the Chinese Zodiac and each of the twelve cycles is named for an animal. Van Woerkom's picture book tells how the clever and wise rat, rather than the big strong ox, came to represent the first year of the cycle.

The poem "Trading" on page 19 of Taylor's *Did You Feed My Cow?* can be used to introduce deRegniers's *Was It a Good Trade?* Another swapping song is Langstaff's *The Swapping Boy.* Other swapping songs can be found in Ritchie's *Swapping Song Book.*

Use every possible opportunity to introduce poetry into the content areas. Aliki Barnsoone's "Numbers," page 139 of Lueders's *Zero Makes Me Hungry,* is suitable for reading before a beginning math class. *Arithmetic in Verse and Rhyme* by Jacobs and Plotz's *Imagination's Other Place: Poems of Science and Mathematics* are other excellent sources of math poems. Another Plotz anthology is *Untune the Sky; Poems of Music and Dance.*

A poem about each of the great lakes can be found (pp. 48-53) in Downie's

The Wind Has Wings. The poems can be written on large blue shapes of each lake. Parker's *One Hundred Poems About Places* is also useful for geography classes.

Older students will enjoy being introduced to the following books. Use Dorothy Aldis's "I'm a Kitty" from page 12 of *Hello Day* to introduce Stolz's *Belling the Tiger*, a variation of the tale about putting a bell on a cat or tiger so the mice or other animals can keep track of it. "Oz," pages 43 and 44 of McCord's *All Day Long*, is a natural to introduce Baum's *The Wonderful Wizard of Oz*. *Poetry of Earth* by Addams includes Mary Austin's "Sandhill Crane" on page 39. The poem can be used to introduce Robertson's *In Search of a Sand Hill Crane*, a story about a boy who learns to become a wildlife photographer in Michigan's Upper Peninsula.

Tucker's *Mother Goose Abroad* includes a humorous German rhyme about a cuckoo and a donkey who quarreled about who could sing best. The rhyme ends ". . . screeching and then bawling, it was really quite appalling./ They sang this song together,/ cuck-hee, cuck-hoo, cuck-how." Use the rhyme to introduce the story "The Bremen Town Musicians." Paul Galdone illustrated a picture book by that title, Hans Fischer illustrated another version called *The Traveling Musicians* and 1981 Caldecott honor book, *The Bremen-Town Musicians*, was illustrated by Ilse Plume. The fairy tale is found in many collections, and is one of fifty found in *Grimm's Fairy Tales* with an introduction by Frances Clarke Sayers. Other sources include Haviland's *Favorite Fairy Tales Told in Germany* (pp. 72-85); Huber's *Story and Verse for Children* (pp. 229-230); Hutchinson's *Chimney Corner Stories* (pp. 27-34); De La Mare's *Tales Told Again* (pp. 25-32) and Rockwell's *The Old Woman and Her Pig and Ten Other Stories*. The Scottish tale "The Five Friends," in Belting's *Cat Tales*, is the same story but includes a bull, sheep, dog, cat, cock, and goose instead of the usual donkey, dog, cat, and rooster. Winifred Ward includes the story (pp. 43-46) in *Stories to Dramatize*.

Use Merriam's poem "Ululation" from her book of poems *It Doesn't Always Have to Rhyme* to introduce Spier's *Gobble, Growl, Grunt*. The three noises and many more are included in "Ululation." Each of fifteen lines of "Ululation" include three animal noises that can be said "line-a-child" fashion with each child saying one line. All children can say the last line together. Students can say each of the noises so that the sound expresses the noise.

Another Spier book, *Fast-Slow, High-Low: A Book of Opposites*, can be introduced by Ciardi's poem "Fast and Slow" from page 1 of his collection of thirty-four humorous and nonsense poems called *Fast and Slow*. The poem "Opposites" by Mary Ann Hoberman from page 12 of her anthology *Hello and Good-by* can be used with Spier's book or with Wilbur's small book of poems *Opposites*.

Use Robert Louis Stevenson's poem "The Wind" and Christina Rosetti's "Who Has Seen the Wind" to introduce other books about wind. The poems are found in Huber's *Story and Verse for Children*. Music for Rosetti's poem appears on page 25 of Kapp's *Cock-A-Doodle Doo!* Primary and preschool children will enjoy Hutchen's cumulative picture book in rhyme called *The Wind Blew*. More items blown away by the wind are collected in a special *Attic of the Wind*, a picture book poem by Lund also featured in a sound filmstrip. In Conger's *Who*

Has Seen the Wind? a small girl asks but no one has seen it until the girl herself sees the wind blowing a flag. Mizumura's *I See the Wind* is a lovely book of haiku-like poems illustrated in watercolor. Older students will enjoy Mary O'Neill's collection of poems called *Winds*. Bendick's *The Wind* is a scientific explanation; when used in a science class the book could be used to lead to poetry books about wind.

Frances the lovable badger sing-songs little poems throughout the Frances books by Hoban. Twenty-two poems are included in a separate book *Egg Thoughts and Other Frances Songs*, and can be used with other Frances books and sound filmstrips. "Gloria, My Little Sister," pages 24 to 26 of *Egg Thoughts*, is an especially appropriate poem to use with the picture book *Baby Sister for Frances*. During her period of adjustment to the new baby, Frances packs a knapsack and runs away even if it is only as far as under the dining room table. The pangs of jealousy as well as love come through in both the book and the poem. Frances is jealous of Gloria again during preparations for Gloria's birthday party in *A Birthday for Frances*. The poem "Brother" (pp. 22-23) in Hoberman's *Hello & Good-By* expresses a similar sibling relationship.

AESOP AND OTHER FABLES, IN AND OUT OF RHYME.   Ennis Reese has recreated almost two hundred fables in rhyme in his book *Fables from Aesop*. After a teacher has read one of the poems to a class, there are numerous projects that could follow. Students could be asked to illustrate the poem, find one or more prose versions and compare them, write their own prose version, or find a picture book illustrating a single fable. There are many sources of Aesop's fables. Boris Karloff narrates many of them on a recording called *Aesop's Fables*. Tales appear in Green's *A Big Book of Animal Fables*, Huber's *Story and Verse for Children*, Johnson's *Anthology of Children's Literature*, and Sutherland's *Arbuthnot Anthology of Children's Literature*. Many original works of art from the Metropolitan Museum of Art illustrate *Aesop: Five Centuries of Illustrated Fables*. One hundred illustrations by Randolph Caldecott illustrate twenty fables in *The Caldecott Aesop*. There are ninety fables edited and illustrated by wood engravings by Boris Artzybasheff in *Aesop's Fables* and eighty collected by Jacobs in *Fables of Aesop*. In a book of the same title, Anne Terry White has retold forty fables illustrated with woodcuts by Helen Siegl. The same number are illustrated by the Provensons in Untermeyer's adaptation, also called *Aesop's Fables*. Equally whimsical are the illustrations by Richard Scarry. Scarry's *Fables of LaFontaine* are mentioned here too because La Fontaine used Aesop as a source for many of his tales.

Individual picture books are available for several of the fables. Brian Wildsmith illustrated La Fontaine's versions of *The North Wind and the Sun*, *The Lion and the Rat*, *The Hare and the Tortoise*, and *The Miller, The Boy and the Donkey*. Roger Duvoisin also illustrated a version of this last story, which is available in sound filmstrip format. Another version, called "You Can't Please Everybody," appears in Gruenberg's *More Favorite Stories Old and New for Boys and Girls* (pp. 493-494). A version in which seven people or animals object to the way the man, boy, and donkey are traveling takes its title from what the donkey did not say—*Hee Haw*. Tomi Ungerer illustrated Showalter's version called *The Donkey Ride*, and one illustrated by Evans is called *The Man, The Boy and the Donkey*, who also retold and illustrated *The Boy Who Cried Wolf*. Paul Galdone illustrated a version of *The Hare and the Tortoise* and *The Town Mouse and the Country Mouse*, and a picture book called *Three Aesop Fox Fables* which includes "The Fox and the Grapes," "The Fox and the Stork," and "The Fox and the Crow." *Don't Count Your Chicks*, illustrated by the d'Aulaires, and Wahl's version *The Woman With the Eggs* are other versions of Reese's poem from Aesop called "The Little Milkmaid" (pp. 151-152). The d'Aulaires's version is available on sound filmstrip. Mary Stolz's *Belling the Tiger* is based on the Aesop fable put into poetry form by Reese and is called "The Mice in a Meeting." "The Ant and the Grasshopper," in *Fables from Aesop* (pp. 18-19) was expanded into a story poem by Ciardi called *John J. Plenty and Fiddler Dan*.

In beginning to study fables of Aesop, the teacher could read "The Silly Slave," pages 68-75 from *Trickster Tales* by Edmonds, to the students. The story is about slaves who tried to prove that they were clever except the silly one who decided to show the master his wisdom rather than tell him, and does so, using his wits. When the King Croesus heard of Aesop's wisdom, he bought him, but listeners do not find out until the last sentence that the slave is Aesop. Since one of the stories Aesop tells within this story is about the boy who cried "Wolf!" this would be one of the fables to start with; other familiar stories could follow. The picture books containing individual fables as well as the collection could be placed in a library corner of the classroom so students could read more fables on their own.

Arnold Lobel was asked by his publisher to illustrate a collection of fables by Aesop. Instead he created and illustrated twenty original *Fables* which won the 1981 Caldecott medal. *Fables* is enjoyed by adults as well as children.

POEMS INTRODUCE BIOGRAPHIES.   Biographies as well as fiction featuring real people as characters can be introduced by poems about people.

Use Myra Cohn Livingston's poem "Paul Revere Speaks" from page 24 of her collection *Four-Way Stop and Other Poems* to introduce Jean Fritz's *And Then What Happened, Paul Revere?*; Robert Lawson's *Mr. Revere and I*; several picture book editions of Longfellow's *Paul Revere's Ride*; Dorothy Canfield Fisher's *Paul Revere and the Minute Men*; and *America's Paul Revere* and *Johnny Tremain*, both by Esther Forbes—the last was the 1944 Newbery Medal winner.

Three poems in Adoff's *Black Out Loud* are about Martin Luther King: Gwendolyn Brooks's "Martin Luther King" (p. 28); Don Lee's "The Assassination" (p. 29); and Nikki Giovanni's "The Funeral of Martin Luther King" (p. 30). Music and verses to "We Shall Overcome" are found on page 79 of Clayton's biography of *Martin Luther King: The Peaceful Warrior*. Other biographies include two by Patterson: *Martin Luther King Junior* and *Martin Luther King, Jr.: Man of Peace*. The first of these as well as Bleiweiss's *Marching to Freedom* is available in paperback. Older readers will be interested in *The Life and Death of Martin Luther King* by Haskins.

Three poems about John Chapman can be used to introduce stories about Johnny Appleseed any time of the year or in May for Arbor Day. Vachel Lindsay's poem is the title of his anthology *Johnny Appleseed and Other Poems*; Helmer Oleson's "A Ballad of Johnny Appleseed" is found on page 27 of Sutherland's *The Arbuthnot Anthology of Children's Literature*; and Lydia Maria Child's "Appleseed John" is found in Sechrist's *One Thousand Poems for Children* (pp. 299-301). Chapman is a character in two fiction books and one easy book. They are, in order of reading difficulty, Aliki's *The Story of Johnny Appleseed*, Douglas's *Appleseed Farm*, and McMeekin's *Journey Cake*. Biographies include Le Sueur's *Little Brother of the Wilderness* and Hunt's *Better Known as Johnny Appleseed*. Tales about the legendary hero are found in Malcolmson's *Yankee Doodle's Cousins* and Leach's *Rainbow Book of American Folk Tales and Legends*. Music is found in Carmer's *America Sings*, and a play is included in Ward's *Stories to Dramatize*.

An assignment for intermediate grade students might be for them to find a biography written by James Daugherty or the d'Aulaires and then use the poetry indexes to see if poems were written about those persons. Another assignment for those students would be to find biographies to accompany the persons Eve Merriam wrote poems about in *Independent Voices*. Poems about Ben Franklin, Frederick Douglass, Henry David Thoreau, and Lucretia Mott, among others, are included.

There are poems about many famous Americans in *A Book of Americans* by the Benets, all of them available on a sound recording. Have students locate biographies about persons who appear in the poems.

STORY POEMS INTRODUCING HISTORY.   Many stories in rhyme can carry readers along with their rhythm to far-off places in other centuries and make them feel almost like eye witnesses to historical events, real or imagined.

One such story in rhyme takes place in the middle ages, in which a young girl asks the wizard to help her find her love. The title is the refrain to the song, *All on a May Morning*, and the flavor of the sixteenth century comes through quite clearly. In another book rhymes interpret twenty details of a painting from Brueghel the Younger's "Village Fair" in a picture book called *Pieter Brueghel's "The Fair"* by Craft. Then, there is a delightful rhyming picture book, featuring internal rhymes, *On The Day Peter Stuyvesant Sailed Into Town*, about the Dutch governor of the New World settlement of New Amsterdam which later became New York City, by Lobel.

There are three poems illustrated as picture books which take place during the American Revolution. The most famous of all is Longfellow's *Paul Revere's Ride*, illustrated by Low and Galdone. Also illustrated by Galdone is *The Battle for the Kegs* by Frances Hopkinson. The colonists sent kegs of gunpowder down the Delaware when the British held Philadelphia in 1778. The results damaged British pride more than anything else, but the episode and the ballad sung about it to the tune of Yankee Doodle had great propaganda value. The kegs were built in the cooperage owned by the author's family, which gives it added interest as an incident that really happened. Then, Carl Carmer, folklorist who loved

America's past and loved to make it live, wrote *The Boy Drummer of Vincennes*, a story poem about George Rogers Clark and the recapturing of Vincennes during the American Revolution. Historical background for the poem is given in the preface, and the poem is ideal for reading aloud when the revolutionary period is being studied because the cadence of drumbeats comes through the rhyme. (George Rogers Clark was the brother of William Clark of the Lewis and Clark expedition.) Other books about George Rogers Clark include De Leeuw's *George Rogers Clark, Frontier Fighter*, and, for older readers, *George Rogers Clark* by Nolan. There are several easy-to-read (as well as more demanding) biographies of William Clark, and a comparison of the two brothers and their contributions to a young America would make an interesting follow-up discussion and create an understanding of the closeness of the revolutionary period to the opening of the west.

Barbara Frietchie was immortalized by John Greenleaf Whittier for daring the rebels, "Shoot if you must this old gray head / but spare your country's flag, she said," as she hung out the union flag in defiance of rebel officer Stonewall Jackson in Maryland during the Civil War. She is the subject of a picture book by Galdone, called *Barbara Frietchie*.

RECOGNIZING POETS.   Children should be able to identify poets who are both exciting and prolific. One favorite is Christina Rossetti, born of Italian parents, who lived her life in London and gave us many memorable poems. Individual picture book editions of several of her books are popular. *What is Pink?* is illustrated by Jose Aruego, and *Goblin Market* was illustrated by Arthur Rackham and by Ellen Raskin.

Another favorite is Robert Louis Stevenson whose *A Child's Garden of Verses* is available in four illustrated editions, one of them by Tasha Tudor.

After reading "Paul Revere's Ride" or "Hiawatha" to intermediate students, introduce them to Peare's *Henry Wadsworth Longfellow, His Life*. Choose information from Benet's *Famous American Poets* (pp. 25-32) for background.

Use incidents from *Robert Frost* by Richards and from Benet's *Famous American Poets* (pp.129-132) to introduce Robert Frost's collections *You Come Too* and *The Road Not Taken*. Play the poem "The Road Not Taken" from the recording *Robert Frost Reads his Poetry*. Susan Jeffers's illustrated picture book of Frost's *Stopping By Woods on a Snowy Evening* is enjoyed by all ages.

Play "I Never Saw a Man" read by Julie Harris from the recording *Poems and Letters of Emily Dickinson*. Barth's biography of Emily Dickinson, *I'm Nobody! Who Are You?*, can also be used to introduce the collection of Dickinson poems, *Poems for Youth*. Dickinson also appears in Benet's book with biographies of Poe, Riley, Field, Sandburg, Lindsay, Holmes, and Lowell. Students will be especially interested in the chapter on Clement Moore, creator of "The Night before Christmas." Use information about Moore from pages 20 to 22 of Benet's *Famous Poems for Young People* before sharing the picture book editions of *The Night before Christmas* illustrated by de Paola, Rackham, Smith, Trimby, and Weisgard.

Several reference books found in many school media centers contain biographies that can be used in supplying background information on poets. Teachers can use the information when introducing poets or can ask students to prepare a short verbal sketch based on the information they find for themselves.

American Authors 1600-1900 by Kunitz contains information on Henry Wadsworth Longfellow, Edgar Allan Poe, and Walt Whitman. *Twentieth Century Authors* includes information about Hilaire Belloc, Stephen Vincent Benet, Gwendolyn Brooks, John Ciardi, e e cummings, Rachel Field, Robert Frost, Langston Hughes, James Weldon Johnson, Vachel Lindsay, Edna St. Vincent Millay, A. A. Milne, Ogden Nash, Carl Sandburg, and Sara Teasdale.

Easier to read information is found in the reference books on *Junior Authors and Illustrators* and *Something About the Author*. These are useful tools for teaching the skill of using an index to a reference set. The fourth Junior Author volume contains an index for all of the *Junior Author* books, and the latest volume of *Something About the Author* contains an index for the entire set. Many poets are included in general encyclopedias but the information is not as personal, does not contain quotes from the poets, and is generally not very interesting.

Benet's *Famous Poets for Young People* contains biographies of twenty-six poets. Mother Goose heads the list. The nonsense poets Lear, Carroll, and Belloc are included, as are Noyes, Frost, Sandburg, Longfellow, Lindsay, Blake, Kingsley, and Stevenson. Christina Rossetti, Laura Richards, Jane and Ann Taylor, Eleanor Farjeon, Rachel Field, and Rosemary Benet are also included, as well as Stephen Vincent Benet, A.A. Milne, Eugene Field, Walter De La Mare, James Whitcomb Riley, and Clement Moore.

RECORDED POEMS.   Poetry really comes into its own when it is read aloud, and, especially when read by expert readers or by the poets who created them, the poems have added meaning. Expert readers bring out nuances of meaning that may be missed by others and although poets themselves are not always the best readers, they bring another dimension to the poems—that of the creator's mind and spirit. Some recordings in which poets read their own poems have already been mentioned: *Ogden Nash Reads Ogden Nash, Christmas with Ogden Nash, Robert Frost Reads the Road Not Taken and Other Poems, Robert Frost Reads His Poetry, Theodore Roethke Reads His Poetry, Gwendolyn Brooks Reading Her Poetry, Carl Sandburg's Poems for Children,* and Eve Merriam's *Catch a Little Rhyme! Poems for Activity Time. The Poetry of Benet* read by the author and Joseph Wiseman includes Stephen Vincent Benet's "The Ballad of William Sycamore," "John James Audubon," and "Daniel Boone." *Poems and Songs of the Middle Earth* is read by Tolkien and two others. Tolkien reads from "The Adventures of Tom Bombadil," and William Elvin sings Donald Swann's "The Road Goes Ever On," a song cycle based on Tolkien's poetry. The poems from this recording can be used to introduce Tolkien's other works: *The Hobbit,* and the three Lord of the Rings books—*The Fellowship of the Ring, The Two Towers,* and *Return of the King.*

Selections from two poetry anthologies edited by Blanche Thompson, *Silver*

Pennies and *More Silver Pennies*, are both available as sound recordings. The poems are introduced and then read. Some of the poets included on the first recording are De La Mare, Fyleman, Conkling, Lowell, Roberts, Sandburg, and Morley. Vachel Lindsay's "The Little Turtle" and "The Mysterious Cat" are among the poems included. *More Silver Pennies* includes poems by Teasdale, Frost, Wylie, and Garland. Masefield's "Sea Fever" is among them, too.

Richard Lewis has edited three collections with the initial title *A Gathering of Great Poetry for Children* ... The subtitle of each recording includes the grade levels: kindergarten and up, second grade and up, fourth grade and up. Among those poems suggested for kindergarten and up are William Blake's "Spring," Langston Hughes's "Sea Calm," John Ciardi's "Please," Elizabeth Maddox Roberts's "The Firefly and the Rabbit," Hilda Conkling's "The Snail," and Edward Lear's "The Owl and the Pussycat." Poems suggested for second grade and up are Hilda Conkling's "Dandelion," Christina Rosetti's "The Caterpillar," Walter De La Mare's "Hide and Seek" and "Snowflake," Edna St. Vincent Millay's "Come Along in Then, Little Girl," Eve Merriam's "Metaphor," Theodore Roethke's "The Bat," and Sara Teasdale's "The Falling Star." Poems included on the recording *A Gathering of Great Poetry for Children Fourth Grade and Up* include, among others, Theodore Roethke's "The Heron," Emily Dickinson's "I'll Tell You How the Sun Rose," Walt Whitman's "Miracles," and Dylan Thomas's "Fern Hill."

LANGSTON HUGHES AND OTHER BLACK POETS.   Langston Hughes is one of the most fascinating of poets to study. Although he is more famous for his poetry, he has also written prose. Some of Hughes's nonfiction books are *The First Book of Jazz*, and three collective biographies—*Famous American Negroes*, *Famous Negro Heroes of America*, and *Famous Negro Music Makers*. Three biographies about Hughes are *Langston Hughes, Poet of His People* by Myers; *Langston Hughes, American Poet* by Walker; and *Always Movin' On* by Haskins. A shorter biography is located in volume 4 of *Something About the Author*. Students may be interested in reading more about Vachel Lindsay, the American poet who discovered Hughes's poems, and whose own poems appear in *Johnny Appleseed and Other Poems*. A chapter on Lindsay appears in Benet's *Famous American Poets*.

Woodcuts by Ann Grifalconi illustrated forty-five of Hughes's poems in *Don't Turn Back*. More poems by Hughes are included in *The Dream Keeper and Other Poems* and *Selected Poems of Langston Hughes*. Over fifty poems are included on the recording *The Poetry of Langston Hughes*. Several poems by Hughes appear in Arna Bontemps's *Hold Fast to Dreams* and poets in that anthology also include Shakespeare, Lindsay, Frost, Pound, Burns, Sandburg, Brooks, Cullen, and Johnson among others.

Once the study of Hughes has begun, there are countless spin-off projects. Phyllis Wheatley is one of the poets included in Hughes's *Famous American Negroes*, and there is an easy biography of her by Fuller, *Phyllis Wheatley, America's First Black Poetess*, or the more difficult biography, *The Story of Phyllis Wheatley* by Graham. Wheatley also appears in Rollins's *Famous*

American Negro Poets. Biographies of other black poets are featured in that collection: James Weldon Johnson, Arna Bontemps, Countee Cullen, Gwendolyn Brooks, and, of course, Langston Hughes. Poems by all of these poets are included in Bontemps's *American Negro Poems.* Poetry by Hughes, Johnson, and Cullen, as well as brief biographies, are included in Bontemps's poetry anthology, *Golden Slippers.*

There were twenty-three volumes of *Something About the Author* by 1981. Check the index of the entire set for names of black poets. Poems by all of the black poets in Rollins's *Famous American Negro Poets,* except Johnson, are included in *My Name is Black, an Anthology of Black Poets* edited by Ambrose. The poetess June Jordan is included in that collection; she is one of the editors of *The Voice of the Children, Writings by Black and Puerto Rican Young People.* Twenty-seven paintings by different artists illustrate Jordan's *Who Look At,* a lengthy poem covering the black American experience of the past hundred years. Jordan also wrote *Who Look at Me* and *His Own Where.* In *His Own Where,* sixteen-year-old Buddy loves a fourteen-year-old girl who has been taken from her parents because of her father's abuse. This book, as well as Steptoe's *Stevie,* is written in "black English." A combination of black and standard English is included, depending on who is speaking, in *A Hero Ain't Nothin' But a Sandwich* by Childress. Graham's *David He No Fear* is the story of David and Goliath told in dialect. Giovanni's picture book, *Spin a Soft Black Song,* includes poems about mommies, daddies, and other subjects close to a small child. These poems are written in black dialect. A poem about Martin Luther King by Giovanni appears in Adoff's *Black Out Loud. My Black Me* and *I am the Darker Brother* are other anthologies of black poets edited by Adoff, who is the husband of 1975 Newbery Award winner Virginia Hamilton. Adoff's harvest chant *Ma nda la* is a story poem that shows a black African family at work. Adoff's own poem, *Big Sister Tells Me That I'm Black,* includes the colors black, tan, and brown that are found in his picture book in rhyme, *Black Is Brown Is Tan.* Other books with the same theme are McGovern's *Black Is Beautiful,* a photo picture book told in rhyme that includes "without the night-black sky / could you see a firefly?" Use McGovern's book with Bond's *Brown Is Beautiful.* Arkin's *Black and White* contains a song. Clifton's *Black ABC's* can be enjoyed by older students as well as small children.

Grossman, Groom, and the children of P.S. 150 in the Bronx expressed their views in *Black Means.* Laurence illustrated the terse verse story *Harriet and the Promised Land* with stark bold illustrations, which help to tell the story of Harriet Tubman and what it meant to be black and a slave.

Clayton's *Martin Luther King: The Peaceful Warrior* includes music and verses to "We Shall Overcome." Students may also wish to read the picture book of Johnson's life, *Lift Every Voice and Sing,* illustrated in stark black and white. This book can be used to introduce the biography of Johnson in Rollins's *Famous American Negro Poets* as well as Johnson's poems in Bontemps's *American Negro Poetry.* Countee Cullen also appears in both of those books. Cullen's *The Lost Zoo* is a picture book poem about the animals who missed Noah's ark. Ruby Dee and Ossie Davis read Cullen's poetry on a recording called *The Poetry of Countee Cullen.*

Everett Anderson, created by Clifton, is a favorite character in picture book poems, and five books about him should be included in this section: *Everett Anderson's Christmas Coming, Everett Anderson's Year, Some of the Days of Everett Anderson, Everett Anderson's 1-2-3,* and *Everett Anderson's Friend.*

AMERICAN INDIAN AND ESKIMO POEMS.   Poetry is a natural addition to the study of the American Indian from the elementary through the high school grades. One of the most beautiful collections, also available in paperback edition, is *Trees Stand Shining, Poetry of the North American Indians,* edited by Jones. All ages will enjoy this beautiful book of thirty-two poems from fifteen tribes that includes lullabies, prayers, and war chants. Also available in paperback edition is Bierhorst's *In the Trail of the Wind: American Indian Poems and Ritual Orations.* Thirty tribes are represented in Bierhorst's book. Muted colors illustrate Hood's *The Turquoise House, Prose and Poetry of the American Indian.* Beltin's *Our Fathers Had Powerful Songs* should be included in this collection of Indian poems.

Houston's *Songs of the Dream People: Chants and Images from the Indians and Eskimos of North America* includes two color drawings of artifacts. Artifacts shown in photos are included in Lewis's *Out of the Earth I Sing; Poetry and Songs of Primitive Peoples of the World.* Eskimo and Indian poems are included.

Other Eskimo poetry books include ninety poems and chants in Lewis's *I Breathe a New Song* and *Eskimo Songs and Stories* translated by Field. The latter collection includes poems based on songs collected during the voyages of Rasmussen's fifth Thule expedition. The most beautiful collection of Eskimo poems, collected by Knud Rasmussen, is *Beyond the High Hills, a Book of Eskimo Poems.* Colored photos make this an exquisite book. Another enrichment book for use during a unit on Eskimos is Glubok's *The Art of the Eskimo* which features artifacts. Gillham's *Beyond the Clapping Mountain* contains thirteen animal folk tales and Melzeck's *The Day Tuk Became a Hunter* contains ten stories.

POETRY WRITTEN BY CHILDREN THEMSELVES.   Gather together a group of poetry books written by children as a temporary classroom collection to encourage students to write their own poetry. The same books might appear in a media center display, highlighted with poems written by children in that school. If possible, include the school's own poetry magazine or a state or national magazine that includes a poem written by a student in the school.

Anthologies written by urban children include Larrick's *I Heard a Scream in the Street;* Hopkin's *City Talk;* and Shaefer's and Mellor's *Young Voices,* which includes poems of fourth through sixth graders in the New York City schools. Anthologies of poems written by minorities include *Here I Am,* Jordan and Bush's *The Voice of the Children,* and Allen's *Whispering Wind, Poetry by Young American Indians.*

Anne Pellowski's *Have You Seen a Comet?* includes prose, poetry and art work of children from ages six to sixteen and from sixty-five different countries. Poems by children around the world are also included in Lewis's *Miracles,*

Poems by Children of the English Speaking World, and Lewis also edited *The Wind and the Rain. There Are Two Lives,* also edited by Lewis, includes poems of Japanese children, while Morton's *The Moon is Like a Silver Sickle* includes poems by Russian children. Behfel's *I Never Saw Another Butterfly* includes poems and drawings by children in the Terezin Concentration Camp during 1942–44, and includes a biography of each child with birth and death or departure date.

Adoff's *It is the Poem Singing into Your Eyes* includes poems written by children ages twelve and up. Larrick's *Green Is Like a Meadow of Grass* includes seventy-four poems by children ages six through thirteen.

Vanessa Howard's collection, *A Screaming Whisper* is included here because this seventeen-year-old had poems published in Jordan and Bush's *Voice of the Children* and in Larrick's *I Heard a Scream in the Street.* The collections of poems can be an inspiration to young poets.

Poems written by children from six to twelve years of age are included in Nelson's *Comparative Anthology of Children's Literature* (pp. 10006–09). Of special interest are four poems that Hilda Conkling wrote as a child. Students could be asked to find information about Conkling as well as search poetry indexes for other published poems. Students will be pleased to realize that this published poet began writing poetry as a child.

Conkling might serve as a lead into another project of discovering other major American poets who began writing and being published while they were still children. Edna St. Vincent Millay and Stephen Vincent Benet are two examples—both of them were published in the *St. Nicholas* magazine while they were children.

Students may also be inspired to write poetry for publication after they have examined student-written poems in several of the children's magazines. Teachers may wish to submit student poems to the following children's magazines: *Child Life, Cricket, Highlights for Children,* and *Jack and Jill.* The special sections in which child-written poems appear in these magazines are "Rhyme Time," "Poetry Contest," "Our Own Pages," and "Poetry by Our Readers."

Forty poems of award winners of the *Scholastic* Writing Awards from 1971 to 1974 are included in *grab me a bus . . .* edited by Joe Eaton and Malcolm Glass. Some of the poems have been included in *Junior Scholastic* and other Scholastic magazines. See the magazines published by Scholastic or this anthology for information on where to send student poems.

POEMS TO ILLUSTRATE.   Almost every anthology includes poems that are especially appropriate to use for art projects. Two poems that specifically talk about drawing are Myra Livingston's "If the Jay Would Stop I Would Paint Him," page 19 of her collection *A Crazy Flight and Other Poems,* and McCord's "How to Draw a Monkey," page 22 of his *The Star in the Pail.* After hearing Livingston's poem, the suggestions for painting the jay can be carried out by members of a class individually. Children can draw a monkey after McCord's poem is read to them.

A mobile with red fish hanging from it could include a copy of McCord's poem "Mobile" on one of the fish, inspired by the poem about a mobile with red fish on it on page 9 of McCord's collection, *All Day Long*. The poem "Fish" in Smith's *Laughing Time* (pp. 42–43) can be illustrated, too.

Aileen Fisher's *Skip Around the Year* includes thirty-nine poems about holidays. The first poem, "Almanac for the New Year," includes information about each month. Have one group of students make a collage showing scenes for each month and put a section of the poem on each corresponding collage. Another group in the class could be illustrating Sara Coleridge's "The Months" (page 145 of Sechrist's *One Thousand Poems for Children*), and Christina Rossetti's "The Months" (page 180 of Untermeyer's *Rainbow in the Sky*), at the same time.

Eleanor Farjeon's poem "The Riding of the Kings" in Hazeltine and Smith's *The Year Round* is about the three magi. Ask students to illustrate the poem using the three colors mentioned in the poem—red, gold and green. Details about the ages of the three wise men are given to provide added detail for the drawing. The poem could be introduced for Epiphany or Twelfth Night (January 6).

Clement Moore's "The Night before Christmas" is fun to illustrate. Poetry indexes will provide many sources. The children's illustrations could be displayed with the illustrated picture books of the poem. Moore's poem is found in Tudor's *Take Joy, The Tasha Tudor Christmas Book*, which also contains "Alphabet of Christmas." Read the poem, have the students illustrate it; then show them Tudor's illustrations. "The First Christmas Eve," in Behn's collection of poems *The Golden Hive* (pp. 42–43) is another appropriate Christmas poem to illustrate. Another Christmas poem to illustrate is Emilie Poulsson's "Santa Claus and the Mouse," of Brewton's *Under the Tent of the Sky* (pp. 178–180). "The Wonderful Christmas Tree" from Ipcar's *Whisperings and Other Things* is a counting rhyme that begins with one star and includes many animals as tree decorations until twelve chickadees are reached.

"The City Mouse and the Country Mouse" by Christina Rossetti is on pages 26 and 27 of Itse's *Hey Bug!* and on page 120 of Sechrist's *One Thousand Poems for Children*. The second mouse is called a garden mouse. The poem could be used to introduce the picture book *The Town Mouse and the Country Mouse* illustrated by Galdone, set in Elizabethton, England. The poem and the story are both found in Shaw's *The Mouse Book* along with about a dozen poems and five other tales or proverbs about mice. "The Elf and the Dormouse," page 31 of McFerron's *Poems to be Read Aloud to Children and by Children*, tells how the first umbrella was invented.

Ian Serraillier's poem "The Hare and the Tortoise," in Cole's *The Birds and Beasts Were There*, (pp. 88–90) is about Johnny the Hare and Sammy the Tortoise. Brian Wildsmith's illustrations of La Fontaine's story are also available in a sound filmstrip. Students may enjoy having the poem read to them before illustrating the story. Watching the filmstrip could be a culminating activity.

"The Sugar Plum Tree" by Eugene Field lends itself to a drawing project because of the description of all the "goodies." The poem is located in many anthologies besides Field's *Poems of Childhood*. Poetry indexes will provide other sources. Consider also Harry Behn's "The Fairy and the Bird" from page 33 of his anthology *Windy Morning*, or "Circles" from page 36 of Livingston's *Listen Children Listen*.

Eleanor Farjeon's poem "Circus" presents many images for drawing and could inspire a project culminating a unit on the circus or circus animals. The poem is found in Farjeon's book *Poems for Children*, (pp. 158–159). More animals to draw are inspired by Burgunder's "Zoo" from the anthology *From Summer to Summer*, a collection of fifty poems.

Colum's *Roofs of Gold, Poems to Read Aloud* is the source of several poems intermediate students can illustrate after the poem is read to them. These include John Masefield's "Cargoes"; Padraic Colum's "The Spider"; e e cummings's "The Little Tree"; and James Russell Lowell's "Aladdin."

Story poems are especially useful to inspire art projects. Cole's *Story Poems, Old and New* has over ninety poems from which to choose, and there is Parker's *One Hundred Story Poems*. The section of Untermeyer's *Rainbow in the Sky* called "I'll Tell You a Story," pages 263–318, and "Stories in Verse," pages 229–318, provide more stories to illustrate. Also see pages 169 to 198, "Stories in Verse," of Huber's *Story and Verse for Children*. Another source, Adhead's *Inheritance of Poetry*, includes many poems like Saxe's "The Blind Men and the Elephant" (pp. 97–98); Cowper's "John Gilpin" (pp. 157–167); and Holmes's "The Deacon's Masterpiece (pp. 168–171). Each of these stories is available as a separate picture book that students may enjoy seeing after they have drawn their own pictures.

ILLUSTRATED COLLECTIONS OF POETRY.   Some poetry anthologies are outstanding blends of art and poetry. Place these colorful anthologies on the special browsing shelf in the library media center or in the library corner of elementary classrooms, grades three through six, or in English classes in junior and senior high schools.

Students in senior high school English classes or special semester courses in poetry enjoy a project of comparing the imagery in the poems with the images created by the artist. Books from this section, as well as the illustrated editions of a single poem, are useful for this project.

Nature poetry divided into the four seasons is illustrated by Baskin in watercolors to make Hughes's *Season Songs* a beautiful book. Twenty-five nature poems by Margaret Wise Brown are illustrated by Leonard Weisgard in *Nibble Nibble*. Twenty-five poems are illustrated by Trina Schart Hyman in Moore's *Cinnamon Seed*. Poems about animals, the weather, and the seasons appear in Saunder's *Magic Lights and Streets of Shining Jet*. Poems about shadows appear in Moore's *Think About Shadows*.

A variety of art techniques were employed by Glaser in illustrating Aiken's *Cats and Bats and Things With Wings*, a collection of sixteen humorous animal poems. A variety of artists and their mediums are identified at the beginning of each of Shaw's books that include about eighteen poems and four stories by famous persons about one animal. The books are *The Bird Book*, *The Cat Book*, *The Fox Book*, *The Mouse Book*, and *The Owl Book*.

Two colorful animal books are *Run, Zebra, Run*, written and illustrated by Tony Chen, and Weiss's *A Paper Zoo*, illustrated by Ellen Raskin.

Richard Lewis has edited a collection of poetic images of Sir Rabindranath Tagore, Nobel poet of India, called *Moon, For What Do You Wait*. The poems are illustrated by Ashley Bryan, and the cobweb pages are especially memorable. The poems of Aileen Fisher, whether they are single poems or collections, are beautifully illustrated by a variety of artists. Collections of poems by Fisher that contain special illustrations are *Cricket in a Thicket*, a book of nature poems illustrated by Feodor Rojankovsky; *Feathered Ones and Furry*, animal poems illustrated in linoleum blocks by Eric Carle; forty-seven nature poems illustrated by Margot Tones in *In the Woods, In the Meadow, In the Sky*; and Lillian Hoban's illustrations of *In One Door and Out the Other* about ordinary things like whispers, food, and Christmas trees. *My Cat Has Eyes of Sapphire Blue* contains twenty-four poems about cats and *Skip Around the Year* contains poems about holidays. *Do Bears Have Mothers, Too?*, illustrated by Eric Carle, contains a dozen poems about animal mothers and their babies. Peter Parnall illustrated Fisher's *But Ostriches* which tells about habits, physical features, and eggs of ostriches and compares them with other birds.

POEMS AS DECORATIONS.   Poems can be written or typed on appropriate shapes by the teacher or student and suspended from the ceiling or attached to bulletin boards. Consider such shapes as autumn leaves, raindrops, kites, valentines, snowflakes, and shamrocks. Groups of related books can be displayed at the same time. Students can help find the poems to write on the shapes and learn how to use the poetry index at the same time. These indexes include *The Subject Index to Poetry for Children and Young People*; Granger's *Index to Poetry*, Sixth edition; Brewton's *Index to Children's Poetry* and its first and second supplements, and with others, *Index to Poetry for Children and Young People, 1964-69* and *1970-75*.

In January, have students take sheets of paper eight inches square, and cut out snowflakes. Then ask them to write or type short poems about snow or winter on pale blue construction paper using both sides of the "snowflake." No more than a third of the snowflakes should contain poems. A different poem could be on each side of a snowflake or different verses of the same poem. Hang the snowflakes from the ceiling of the classroom or the library media center. If the display is near a bulletin board, use three snowflakes as backgrounds for the words, "Books About Snow." A list of books you can use follows. In February, remove the snowflakes with snow poems and substitute shapes with red hearts and valentine poems.

The poem "Five More Days" is a good one for a snowflake. It is on the December twentieth page of Clifton's *Everett Anderson's Christmas Coming*. "First Snow" by Allen appears on page 7 of Allen's *A Pocketful of Poems*, and page 22 of Clithero's *Beginning-to-Read Poetry*. Dorothy Aldis's poem "Snow" also appears in the second collection.

Robert Frost's "Dust of Snow" appears in *Poetry of Earth*, a beautifully illustrated book by Adrienne Adams. Each of these poems is short and can appear on one side of a snowflake. Another poem from *Poetry on Earth* is too long, but you can use the first and fourth verses of Elinor Wylie's poem that begins "Let us walk in the white snow. . . ." Use the first two verses of "Falling Snow," by an unknown poet, from page 97 of Rasmussen's *Let's Say Poetry Together and Have Fun*. Another poem by an unknown poet is found on page 239 of Hubbard and Babbitt's *The Golden Flute*. The first line of "Winter" is "Whenever a snowflake leaves the sky." The poem has only four lines. Another short poem in the same anthology is "Snow" by Alice Wilkens from page 181. Tsuru's poem on page 160 of ACEI's *Sung Under the Silver Umbrella* begins "Willows in the snow. . . ."

Walter De La Mare's poem "The Snowflake" is included in several anthologies, including page 221 of Adshead's *Inheritance of Poetry* and Livingston's *Listen, Children, Listen*, page 80. Because the poem is long, use only the first three lines. Use the first six lines of Eastwick's "Winter in the Wood" on page 142 of Hazeltine and Smith's *The Year Round*. Another poem by Eastwick is found on page 61 of her *Cherry Stones! Garden Swings!* Although the poem has eight lines, all eight might appear on one side of a snowflake.

Use the first stanza of Dora Shorter's "A New Year," on page 167 of *The Year Round*. Use the first four lines of two poems from De La Mare's *Come Hither*; also see Eleanor Farjeon's "For Snow" and Eleanor Wylie's "Velvet Shoes."

McCord's poem "Snowflakes" from page 19 of his anthology *The Star in the Pail* is especially suitable when constructing a snowflake mobile. There are seven verses, each containing three lines. Each verse could be included on snowflakes dangling from a mobile. Mary Austin's "Rhyming Riddle" on page 193 of Cole's *A Book of Nature Poems* has snow for an answer, and will easily fit on a snowflake.

"Snow Flakes" by Mary Mapes Dodge appears in Stevenson's *Home Book of Verse for Young Folks* (pp. 318-19) and on page 139 of Sechrist's *One Thousand Poems for Children*. Any two of the three verses could be used. Or, using the verses as a pattern, a fourth verse could be added to provide verses for all four sides of two snowflakes. All of the poems on the snowflakes need not be published ones. Some of the poems could be written by students. The project could be a combination art, book display, practice using the poetry indexes, and creative writing assignment.

Students may wish to write their own valentine poems. Some of them may be no more than the "roses are red" variety. In fact working with valentine verse may provide a good chance to just be silly and write some verse such as that found in Lillian Morrison's autograph books, *Best Wishes, Amen, A New Collection of Autograph Verses; Remember Me When This You See, a Collection of Autograph Verses; Yours Till Niagra falls*, and *Who Would Marry a Mineral? Riddles, Runes, and Love Tunes*. Students will enjoy comparing the light autograph, greeting card or funny verse with "real" poems, and deciding what makes the difference.

The love poems selected and illustrated by Yaroslava from around the world for *I Like You and Other Poems for Valentine's Day* are diverse and unsentimental. Fisher's fifth poem "Valentines" in *Skip Around the Year* also

offers a fresh idea. The thousand valentines were "seeds for February birds."
Holiday poem books provide sources for valentine poems. Consult Sechrist's
Poems for Red Letter Days (pp. 52-55) and Hazeltine and Smith's *The Year
Round* (pp. 178-180) as well as other holiday collections. There are six Valentine
poems on page 21 of Doane's *A Small Child's Book of Verse*.

"I'll Wear a Shamrock" by Mary Carolyn Davies contains three verses, one
for each section of a shamrock. The poem is found on page 141 of *Bridled With
Rainbows* by the Brewtons. Monica Shannon's "The Four Leaf Clover" is found
on page 63 of the same collection. There are six couplets to the poem; use the
first four and place a couplet on each of the four sections of the clover leaf.
Another poem about a four-leaf clover is the four-line poem "I Found" on page
39 of Livingston's *Whispers and Other Poems*. Have students find other poems
about shamrocks and St. Patrick's Day and display them with appropriate
books. Another poem from Livingston's collection to be used on a bulletin board
is "Balloons. . .Balloons." Write one of the three verses of the poem on three colorful balloons. Bibliographic information could be on the shape of the person
holding the strings. A collection of poetry books could surround the bulletin
board. If bulletin board space near bookshelves or counters is lacking in the
classroom or library media center, cut the side of a huge cardboard box and
cover it with burlap. Items can be attached with masking tape from the back of
the item or with straight pins. Then place the new "bulletin board" on top of a
shelf or any flat place where books can be set up around it.

March is also the month for kite poems. Kite poems can easily be written or
typed on kites and kite tails and suspended or placed on bulletin boards. A collection of fiction and nonfiction books about kites can be arranged near the
bulletin board or perhaps the books and board can be part of the same display
case.

McCord's poem "Kite" on page 6 of his anthology *Take Sky* has three
stanzas, each with seven lines. Each stanza should be placed on a "yellow-
orangey" colored kite, since those colors appear in the poem. Use just the first
eight lines of a three-stanza poem "The Blue Kite" found on page 10 of Starbird's *Don't Ever Cross a Crocodile and Other Poems*. Again, the poem should be
placed on the color mentioned by the poem.

"The Kite," by Harry Behn, appears on pages 14 and 15 of his anthology of
thirty-five poems *Windy Morning, Poems and Pictures*, as well as in Arbuthnot's
Time for Poetry, third edition. All six lines of Brown's "My Kite" in Hubbard
and Babbitt's *The Golden Flute* (pp. 10-11) will fit on one kite. Two stanzas of
seven lines each are part of Dixie Willson's poem on page 123 of *The Golden
Flute*. Use only the first seven lines about what fun it would be to fly like a kite.
On page 193 of the same anthology is the famous poem of Robert Louis Stevenson, "The Wind" which begins "I saw you toss the kites on high. . . " It is found
in several anthologies.

"The Wind" on page 31 of Allen's *A Pocketful of Poems* is divided into three
parts. The first section has five lines and the two following stanzas each have
two lines. Place the five-line segment on a large kite and the two-line sections on
smaller kites. For variety, put all the bibliographic information for Rose Waldo's

"Kite Tales" on the kite and put the nine couplets on the nine tails. If only four couplets are to be used, use the first two and the last two stanzas. The poem appears on pages 8 and 9 of Hubbard and Babbitt's *The Golden Flute*. Ciardi's *You Know Who* contains a poem about kites on pages 12 and 13 called "Someone Asked Me." Place the poem on a kite body and put the last words, "flip, flip, flip, FLOP!" on the tail.

Aileen Fisher's poem "The Kite," page 62, is one of forty-seven poems from *In the Woods, In the Meadow, In the Sky*, and begins "What do you see where you ride, kite." There are three stanzas of different lengths. There are five lines in the first, two and six in the others. If this poem appears on the same bulletin board as Allen's "The Wind," make three kites of one color for one poem and three in another color for the other. Bibliographic information can be included on a seventh kite or divided to fit on pieces of the tail.

Issa has written two kite poems in haiku. The poem beginning "A beautiful kite" is in Behn's *Cricket Songs*. The fifty-ninth poem in that same unpaged book, about a loose kite that loses its spirit, is by Kubonta, and also appears on page 98 of Howard's *First Book of Short Verse*, as does "Kite Days" by Mark Sawyer. There are no page numbers in Joan Walsh Anglund's *Morning is a Little Child*, but there is a kite poem on the eighteenth page.

April is a good time to have students find or write poems on raindrops. The raindrops can be suspended on threads from a large umbrella that has the words "Tears From Out the Sky, Poems About Rain" on it. The phrase is a quote from Dixie Willson's poem "Rainbows" found on page 176 of Hubbard and Babbitt's *Golden Flute*. Another rainbow poem from the same collection is Christina Rossetti's "The Rainbow." Robert Louis Stevenson's four-line poem "Rain" is on page 189, and is found in other collections also. Isla Richardson's "Raindrops" is found on pages 176 and 177. Page 25 of Behn's *The Little Hill* contains seven couplets. Use the first couplet on a raindrop.

Robin Christopher's "Rain" on page 169 of Untermeyer's *Rainbow in the Sky* is suitable for raindrops that are part of a mobile. Another poem that can be used as a mobile of two strings of seven raindrops each is Langston Hughes's "April Rain Song" from page 73 of Livingston's *Listen, Children, Listen*. If large raindrops are used so that four lines can be accommodated, six raindrops are needed for Anne Hawkshaw's "Little Raindrops" from Stevenson's *The Home Book of Verse* (pp. 128-129). Robert Loveman's "April Rain" is found on page 295 of that same anthology. Longfellow's three-verse poem "Rain in Summer" begins "How beautiful is the rain!" and is found on pages 170 and 171 of Untermeyer's *Rainbow in the Sky*.

The nursery rhyme beginning "Rain, rain go away. . ." is found in many collections as well as Austin and Mills's *The Sound of Poetry*.

Farjeon's *A Prayer for Little Things* contains four lines about raindrops found under "Please God, Take Care of Little Things."

Use insects, birds, and flowers (found in the next section) as poems and shapes for May and June.

September is a time to have students create a bulletin board on poetry with a display of books about autumn and leaves while the class is studying the season in primary grades or while intermediate grades are working on it. The caption "Autumn Poetry" in large letters should be placed on large leaves of a contrasting color to the background; leaves of gold and orange on a tan background. Poems about leaves and autumn can be placed lower on the board on smaller colored leaves of various shapes. Emily Bronte's "Fall, Leaves Fall" on pages 210 and 211 of De La Mare's *Come Hither* is one such poem. Jacobs's *Poetry for Autumn* contains a variety of poems that have several verses that could be put on a cluster of leaves. Among them are Frank Sherman's "The Golden Rod" on page 6; Robert Louis Stevenson's "Autumn Fires" on page 10; and Elizabeth Ellen Long's "Autumn Song" on page 11. Each of the four verses of "Autumn" by Behn from page 33 of his collection *The Golden Hive* can be placed on a leaf. Two poems by Rose Burguner from her collection *From Summer to Summer* contain "Waltz of the Autumn Trees" on page 37, and "Look, the Leaves are Falling" on page 38. Use the first and third verses of Fisher's "Fall of the Year" from page 48 of her collection *Cricket in a Thicket*. Eleanor Farjeon's poem "Down Down" on page 325 of Austin Mills's *The Sound of Poetry* contains only three lines.

Livingston's *Whispers . . .* contains a poem called "October Magic" on page 40 that includes witches, goblins, bats, ghosts, and cats. Dorothy Thompson's "This is Halloween" from page 144 of *Bridled With Rainbows* by the Brewtons contains owls, goblins, cats, and jack-o-lanterns. Read the poems to the class and have them pick out the Halloween symbols. Then have students find other poems to fit the shape of each of the Halloween symbols mentioned in the poems. One example would be to use the last two lines of Theodore Roethke's "The Bat" across the wingspread of a bat shape. For visibility, type or write the poem on white paper and then attach the poem to the black bat. The poem is found on page 45 of Cole's *The Birds and Beasts Were There*. For more poems consult Prelutsky's *It's Halloween* and Hopkins's *Witching Time*. See chapter 2, "Experiencing Art through Picture Books," for books about Christmas, snow, kites, animals, and other subjects to use with poetry displays.

INSECTS, BIRDS AND WILDFLOWERS.   Poems can be used when identifying insects, birds and wildflowers. The poems can be put on the bulletin board and students can be asked to supply an appropriate photo or picture to go with each poem; or the shape of the insect, bird, or wildflower in appropriately colored paper can be put on the board and students can be asked to identify it and find a poem about that shape. Students will need to use the card catalog to locate identification books, as well as reinforcing skills in using poetry indexes and citing bibliographic sources.

To add zest to a unit on insects, decorate the room with insect poems. Two books to place in the chalk tray or in some other prominent place in the classroom are Itse's *Hey Bug! and Other Poems about Little Things* and Haberman's *Bugs: Poems*. In *Hey Bug!*, the scientific names are printed in small type beside the pictures so the book can be used for identification purposes. Ten of the thirty poems are about insects and include cocoons, crickets, grasshoppers, beetles, fireflies, and bees. The title poem on page 12, "Hey, Bug!" by Lilian

Moore, can introduce the book. For more insect poems, consult pages 99 to 110 of Brewton's *Under the Tent of the Sky*.

Some nonfiction books that identify insects are Blough's *Discovering Insects*, Lutz's *Field Book of Insects of the U.S. and Canada*, and Zim and Cottam's *Insects: A Guide to Familiar American Insects*.

McCord's poem "Cocoon" on page 28 of Petie's *Book of Big Bugs* could be pasted on a jar holding a cocoon. Hussey's book, *Collecting Cocoons*, could be placed beside the jar.

There are numerous poems about fireflies. Four of them are found in Brewton's *Under the Tent of the Sky*. The two poems called "Fireflies" are located on pages 102 and 103: one by Carolyn Hall, the other by Grace Wilson Coplen. "Firefly" by Elizabeth Madox Roberts is on page 102. "The Firefly" by John B. Tabb is on page 103. The poems by Hall and Coplen appear on page 130 of Hubbard and Babbitt's *The Golden Flute*, and the Roberts poem appears on page 131 of the same book. The poem by Roberts also appears on page 117 in Sechrist's *One Thousand Poems for Children*. "All About Fireflies" by McCord appears on page 11 of *Hey, Bug!*, and on page 3 of McCord's *The Star in a Pail*.

While studying fireflies in class, students could be asked to find poems about fireflies as well as fiction and nonfiction books. The beautifully illustrated *When Animals Are Babies* by Conklin shows fifteen insects in their natural settings, tells what they eat, and includes fireflies. The poems about fireflies could be used to introduce other books to small children: a delightful picture book, Waber's *A Firefly Named Torchy*; two books that tell how to take care of captured fireflies, *Fireflies in Nature and the Laboratory* by the Pooles and *Catch a Cricket; About the Capture and Care of Crickets, Grasshoppers, Fireflies and Other Companionable Creatures*. Ryder's *Fireflies* is a Science I Can Read book. Books to consult about fireflies are Earle's *Crickets*, Hogner's *Grasshoppers and Crickets*, George's *All upon a Stone*, Roberts's *You Can Make an Insect Zoo*, Stevens's *Catch a Cricket*, and Villiard's *Insects as Pets*.

There are five poems about snails in Ross's *The Illustrated Treasury of Poetry for Children* (pp. 234-237) and four poems on pages 91 to 94 in Cole's *The Birds and Beasts Were There*. Use these poems with a display of books about snails, or alternate reading poems and introducing the books to students. Two nonfiction books to introduce are Hess's *A Snail's Pace* and Hogner's *Snails*. The first book has excellent black and white photos. More photos, as well as information about food, enemies, and homes, are included in the Hogner book, which is more difficult reading. Rockwell's *The Story Snail* is an easy reader about a magic snail who tells a boy one hundred stories no one has ever heard before. When he has used up all the stories, John looks for the snail to find more stories. Lionni's picture book *The Biggest House in the World* is about a young snail who wants a bigger house until he realizes that he will lose his mobility. Ungerer's *Snail, Where Are You?* is a picture book in which all the objects in the illustrations include a hidden snail.

Poems set to music about ladybugs are located in the chapter "Enhancing Books through Music." In *Lady Bird Quickly* by Kepes, fourteen insects spread the word that ladybug should fly home at once. A ladybug is one of twelve creatures in Mizumura's *If I Were A Cricket.*

Bird shapes are especially adaptable for bird poems. Gwendolyn Reed's anthology, *Bird Songs*, contains 81 poems about birds. Chapter 1 contains poems about robins, and chapter 2 about wrens, and there are thirteen chapters altogether. Some of the poets included in the collection are Dickinson, de la Mare, Coleridge, Burns, Longfellow, Frost, Rossetti, Aiken, Blake, Sandburg, and Thoreau. Eighteen poems by Stevenson, Emerson, Hugo, Dickinson, Tennyson, Grahame, Blake, and others are each illustrated in Shaw's *The Bird Book.* One of the four tales about birds included in the book, "The Magpie's Nest," (pp. 33-35) is introduced by a poem "Once upon a Time When Pigs Spoke Rhyme."

Bird poems abound. Pages 83 to 95 of Brewton's *Under the Tent of the Sky* are about birds; also see the following anthologies: Cole's *The Birds and Beasts Were There* (pp. 231-268); Huffard's *My Poetry Book* (pp. 212-242); Untermeyer's *The Golden Treasury of Poetry* (pp. 58-67); Untermeyer's *Yesterday and Today* (pp. 22-25 and 184-188); Untermeyer's *Rainbow in the Sky* (pp. 217-229); Sechrist's *One Thousand Poems for Children* (pp. 105-117 and 403-434); and Gross's *Every Child's Book of Verse* (pp. 165-182). Stevenson's *Home Book of Verse for Young Folks* contains poems about a blackbird, bobwhite, sandpiper, nightingale, jackdaw, and skylark. Birds represented in Sechrist's *One Thousand Poems for Children* include the robin, bobwhite, brown thrush, chickadee, bluebird, hummingbird, linnet, swallow, crow, dove, owl, and lark. There are four bird poems in Swenson's *Poems to Solve* (pp. 19-22).

Beginner nonfiction bird books are Blough's *Bird Watchers and Bird Feeders* and Selsam and Hunt's *First Look at Birds.* Identification books include Audubon's *The Birds of America*, Dugdale's *Album of North American Birds*, Kieran's *An Introduction to Birds*, the National Geographic Society's *Song and Garden Birds of North America*, Austin's *Birds of the World*, and Zim and Gabrielson's *Birds, a Guide to the Most Familiar American Birds* and *A Field Guide to Western Birds.* These guides contain over two thousand pictures of birds, most of them in color.

Delicate wildflowers are well suited to poetry. Eastwick has included thirty-seven of her poems about wildflowers in *Traveler's Joy*, some of them about lady slipper, toothwort, daisy, anemone, and forget-me-not. The poems can be accompanied by drawings, pictures, or photos of wildflowers. Anno's *Alphabet* is a good companion book because a flower for each letter of the alphabet is entwined in the line drawing borders around each page, and a list to identify the flowers is at the back of the book. Edna Miller's picture book for small children, *Mousekin Finds a Friend*, includes cattails, foxgloves, dogtooth violets, and mouse-ear or forget-me-nots.

Three identification books are *The Macmillan Wild Flower Book* with 425 flowers pictured and 500 described, Stripska's *Wildflowers in Color* with 260 flowers, and Zim and Martin's *Flowers; a Guide to American Wildflowers* with 134 color paintings. Cavanna's *First Book of Wild Flowers* contains several sections: wildflowers that look like tame flowers; spring, summer, and fall wildflowers; seashore and water wildflowers. Illustrations are in black and white, with sixty variations included, and amusing nicknames are noted. Thirty-eight wildflowers are included in Busch's *Wildflowers and the Stories behind their Names*, such as milkweeds, dandelions, and Queen Anne's lace. Podendorf's *True Book of Weeds and Wild Flowers* is easy to read. Graham's *The Milkweed and Its World of Animals* discusses the milkweed from another angle. "In a Milkweed Cradle" the first line of a poem by an unknown poet, found on page 26 of Sechrist's *One Thousand Poems for Children*, can be attached to a vase or jar containing milkweed stems and pods. Selsam's book of black and white photos with little text, called *Milkweed*, can be placed beside the jar. The fourth couplet in Behn's "The Weed Seed" from *The Wizard in the Well*, on page 33, is about "milkweed purses."

The poem by M. L. Newton called "Queen Anne's Lace" is found in many anthologies including Brewton's *Bridled With Rainbows*, page 63; Huffard and Babbitt's *The Golden Flute*, page 93; Huffard's *My Poetry Book*, page 256; and Nash's *The Moon is Shining Bright as Day*, page 88. The poem is found in Thompson's book and recording *Silver Pennies*.

Use the six poems about dandelions found in *The Golden Flute* (pp. 88-91) with the bunches of real dandelions or illustrations of dandelions from the students. The life cycle book *Dandelions* by Svatos is a beautiful addition to any display. Also included in *The Golden Flute* are seven poems about pussywillows. Use the poems with Brown's picture book about the kitten named *Pussywillow*.

Kay Starbird's *The Pheasant on Route Seven* includes her poem "William Picked a Trillium," page 18, which warns readers in a humorous way about the dangers of picking wildflowers. "Spring Talk" in McCord's collection *All Day Long* includes violets, jack-in-the-pulpit, skunk cabbage, and other wildflowers. The poem "Lady's Slipper" is found on page 97 of Richard's anthology, *Tirra Lirra*. Moss's *Tiger and Other Lilies* includes poems about wild plants that contain names of animals such as toadstools and dogwood. "The Foxglove" appears on page 30 of Eastwick's *In and Out the Windows, Happy Poems for Children*. Nineteen of those poems have been set to music.

CLASSIC POEMS AS INDIVIDUAL PICTURE BOOKS.   Tennyson's *The Lady of Shalott*, a romantic poem first published in 1832, is in a book illustrated by Bernadette Watts. Other famous British poems published as individual picture books are Wordsworth's *Lucy Gray or Solitude*, Coleridge's *The Rime of the Ancient Mariner*, and Blake's *Songs of Innocence*. A Caldecott Medal winning picture book by Barbara Cooney, *Chanticleer and the Fox*, is an adaptation of Chaucer's *Nun's Priest's Tale*. Greenaway, Schwarz, and Hodges have all illustrated picture books of Browning's *The Pied Piper of Hamelin*, which students will enjoy illustrating themselves. One of many sources for the poem without illustration is Sechrist's *One Thousand Poems for Children* (pp. 294-299), and there are many prose versions of the story, among them, "The Pied Piper of Frenchville" found in Jacobs's *More English Folk and Fairy Tales* (pp. 1-6). Jacobs's *The Pied Piper and Other Fairy Tales* is a prose picture book version of the same story. The story in play form is found in Burack's *One Hundred Plays for Children* and Thane's *Plays from Famous Stories and Fairy Tales*. The Pied Piper is seen through the eyes of an orphaned baker's apprentice in Skurzynski's *What Happened in Hamelin.*

Theodor Fontain's poem *Sir Ribbeck of Ribbeck of Havelland,* translated from the German and illustrated by Nonny Hogrogian, concerns an old man who outwits his greedy son and makes sure that the neighborhood children will be able to eat pears from his tree even after he dies.

Christina Rosetti's *Goblin Market* is available in two very different editions. Arthur Rackham's picture book was originally published in 1862, and a brighter version has been illustrated and adapted by Ellen Raskin. Jose Aruego has illustrated Rosetti's *What is Pink?* Internal rhyme is a feature of the poem.

Saxe's *The Blind Men and the Elephant* has been illustrated by both Galdone and Quigley. The blind men describe the elephant differently because each has felt only a small part of the animal.

Eugene Field's *Wynken, Blynken and Nod,* a favorite poem with Barbara Cooney's illustrations in nighttime colors, is available on sound filmstrip. Another American favorite, also available on sound filmstrip, is Thayer's *Casey at the Bat.* Use the filmstrip to introduce other sports poems. Several collections of sports poems include Morrison's *Sprints and Distances,* Fleming's *Hosannah the Home Run, Sports Poems* by Knudson and Ebert, and *Sports and Games in Verse and Rhyme* by Jacobs.

John Ciardi has taken the fable of the grasshopper and the ant and put it into verse as *John J. Plenty and Fiddler Dan.* Another version is on page 211 of Arbuthnot's *Time for Fairy Tales Old and New.*

The Song of Hiawatha is a Longfellow favorite, and there is a fine illustrated version by Galdone. Key episodes are presented by puppets in an animated film called *Tales of Hiawatha.* Joan Kiddell-Monroe has illustrated *The Song of Hiawatha* as a single picture book. Use either of the picture books or the film to introduce children to other poems by Longfellow. The *Children's Own Longfellow* includes selections from "The Song of Hiawatha," "Paul Revere's Ride," "The Wreck of the Hesperus," and "The Village Blacksmith." Hal Holbrook reads all three poems and more on the recording *The Best Loved Poems of Longfellow.* Older students will enjoy the whole poem *Evangeline, a Tale of Acadia,* with two pages on Longfellow's life and an introduction to the poem by Mina Lewiton. Use Tallant's *Evangeline and the Acadians* with this book. Holbrook also narrates *Evangeline* on a recording of that name.

Clement Moore's *The Night before Christmas* is found in several separate picture books, illustrated by Tomi de Paola, Leonard Weisgard, Tasha Tudor, Edward Trimby, and Arthur Rackham. The same story under the name *T'was the Night before Christmas* is illustrated by Houghton, and *A Visit from St. Nicholas* is illustrated by Galdone.

Two of Walt Whitman's poems appear as picture books. Selections from "Leaves of Grass" are included and illustrated in woodcuts by Frasconi in *Overhead the Sun.* Krohn's *I Hear America Singing* has a red, white, and blue cover and includes mechanics, carpenters, boatmen, and mothers as well as others. The large print and cartoon-like drawings should make the book popular with primary students. High school teachers can even use the book successfully.

Oliver Wendell Holmes's *The Deacon's Masterpiece or the Wonderful One-*

Horse Shay, illustrated by Galdone, has a much-needed glossary to interpret terms from a hundred years ago.

Brinton Turkle illustrated Steven Vincent Benet's *The Ballad of William Sycamore* with charcoal sketches totally appropriate for the American pioneer story poem. Benet reads his own poem on a sound recording titled *The Poetry of Benet Read by the Author and Joseph Wiseman*.

ANIMAL STORIES IN VERSE.   Numerous books in rhyme feature animals. There are twelve different mothers in Fisher's *Do Bears Have Mothers, Too?* Almost thirty insects and animals are included in Hazen's *Where Do Bears Sleep? Bears on Wheels* and the *Bear's Almanac* by the Berenstains are written in rhyme. *Do Baby Bears Sit in Chairs?* by the Kesslers lists rhyming things that bears, lady bugs, seals, kangaroos, chicks, bees, goats, cats, kittens, and raccoons can't do. However, each animal has one accomplishment in common with the little boy who is the narrator.

Internal rhyme appears in *Timothy Turtle* by Palazzo which is excellent for reading aloud. Timothy, who wanted to be famous, is cheered by his friends when he does something no other turtle has done. Use Lindsay's famous poem "The Little Turtle," found on page 79 of Brewton's *Under the Tent of the Sky*, with this story.

Sixteen different animals are listed in Slobodkin's *The Friendly Animals*, and the names for male, female, and baby sheep are given. Twelve animals are included in Raskin's *Who, Said Sue, Said Whoo*, and twenty five in her *Twenty Two-Twenty-Three*. That story is reminiscent of *Johnny Crow's Garden* which includes eighteen different kinds of animals, *Johnny Crow's New Garden* which includes about thirty animals, and *Johnny Crow's Party* which includes over twenty. Six kinds of animals are introduced in DeRegnier's Caldecott Medal winner *May I Bring a Friend?* Five animals appear in her *Catch a Little Fox* which includes the same song as Langstaff's *Oh, A-Hunting We Will Go*, and tells of the capture of a dozen animals. In *Did You Ever See?* by Einsel, readers are asked "Did you ever see a shark bark?", and a similar question about fourteen animals. The last "Did you ever see" is guaranteed to make librarians chuckle!

A frog, fly, and bat each see the world differently in Domanska's *What Do You See?* A little tiger and a little leopard make friends in Ipcar's *Stripes and Spots*. Brenner's *Mr. Tall and Mr. Small*, illustrated by Tomi Ungerer, are a giraffe and a mouse.

Several humorous stories about pigs are told in rhyme. Oxenbury's *Pig Tale* is about Bertha and Briggs, who find a treasure, purchase many gadgets and fine clothes, and eventually throw them all away and revert back to their old ways. Pomerantz's *Piggy in the Puddle* likes to squish around in a mud puddle and ignores the pleas of her brother and parents to clean up. They offer her soap and she says "Nope!" Finally they join her. The alliteration makes it especially successful when read aloud. Children can almost feel the "mooshy-squooshy mud." Fourteen stanzas of an American folk song about an old woman and her prize-winning pig are included in *Tale of a Pig*. The melody as well as an arrangement for voice-piano are included.

Massie's *The Monstrous Glisson Glop*, who has red eyes and green teeth, ate all the lantern fish and electric eels before he realized that it would be dark without them in this rhyming ecology lesson. Rhyme appears throughout Young's *If I Rode a Dinosaur* in which a child fantasizes that he is riding different kinds of dinosaurs. A dinosaur appears in chapter 1 of the short rhyming book *Willy, Willy Don't Be Silly* by Vogel.

DOGS AND CATS IN POEMS AND STORIES. One of Eleanor Farjeon's *Poems for Children* is called "Dog." The poem appears to be written by a dog and listeners, no matter what breed (and many are mentioned) they own, will hear their dog saying "I'm your dog." That phrase could be a caption of a display of some famous storybooks starring dogs: Cleary's *Henry and Ribsy*; Estes's *Ginger Pye*, the dognapped dog; Gipson's *Old Yeller*; Kjelgaard's *Big Red*; Knight's *Lassie Come Home*; London's *White Fang*; O'Brien's *Silver Chief*; Stolz's *A Dog on Barkham Street*; and Terhune's *Lad: a Dog*. Also included could be books on dog care: Meek's *So-You're Going to Get a Puppy!*, Chrystie's *Pets*, and Morgan's *A Pet Book for Boys and Girls*. Smaller children enjoy Skaar's *Nothing but Cats and All about Dogs*. Naturally, *Hark! Hark! The Dogs Do Bark and Other Rhymes about Dogs* by Blegvad would be part of the display. Turner's *When It Rained Cats and Dogs*, a book with rhyming couplets, introduces many breeds of dogs and could be one of two dog stories told to children.

Nine dog poems are included in Untermeyer's *Golden Treasury of Poetry*. The heroic nature of collies is stressed by Edward Anthony in "The Collies" on page 43. Use it when introducing *Lassie Come Home* and *Lad: a Dog*. Also on the same page are "The Bloodhound" and "The Dachshund" by Anthony. "I've Got a Dog," page 75 of Howard's *The First Book of Short Verse*, is a humorous poem about dachshunds. Picture books about dachshunds to display with the last two poems include all of the books by Ezra Keats about Peter and his dachshund Willie, especially *Whistle for Willie*. Other books are Kahl's *Maxie*, Alexander's *Bobo's Dream*, Domanska's *Spring Is*, and Freeman's *Flash and Dash*. Five rhymes about dogs and six rhymes about cats appear in *The Oxford Nursery Rhyme Book* (pp. 34-35) by the Opies.

Two anthologies edited by Lee Bennett Hopkins are essential additions: *Pups, Dogs, Foxes and Wolves* and *Kits, Cats, Lions and Tigers*. Each book contains over twenty stories or poems. Stories, poems and riddles are included in Leach's *The Lion Sneezed; Folktales and Myths of the Cat*.

A book that contains both cat and dog stories (though more about cats) is *Wonder Tales of Dogs and Cats* by Carpenter. One tale in it about both is Latvian, "Why Dogs and Cats Are Not Friends." Two of the stories also appear in Belting's *Cat Tales*. "The Boy Who Drew Cats" appears on pages 83 to 89 and "Why Cats and Dogs Fight" appears on pages 34 to 36. This Rumanian version is different from the version found in the Carpenter collection. A third story "Why Dogs and Cats are Enemies" is found on pages 83 to 85 of Dobbs's *More Once-Upon-A-Time Stories*.

Chapter 3 of Gross's *Every Child's Book of Verse* called "Cats and Some

Dogs" includes poems on pages 67 to 86. Even primary students will enjoy the French story "The Kingdom Without a Cat" (pp. 25-34). The youngest son was left only a cat by his father but the cat brought him riches in a catless land infested with rats. The "The Cat with the Crooked Tail" (pp. 43-51), comes from Siam. "The Boy Who Had to Draw Cats" (pp. 195-203), is about a boy whose drawings of cats saved him and others from a giant rat.

Use poems about cats to introduce stories or books about cats. Three books that can serve as sources or be part of a display on cats are Blegvad's collection of twenty-seven cat poems, *Mittens for Kittens and Other Rhymes About Cats*; twenty-four cat poems in Fisher's *My Cat Has Eyes of Sapphire Blue*; and DeRegnier's own cat poems in a collection called *Cats, Cats, Cats, Cats, Cats*. One of the most famous rhymes about cats is "The Three Little Kittens." Two of the many sources are Brewton's *Under the Tent of the Sky* (pp. 152-153), and Sechrist's *One Thousand Poems for Children* (pp. 30-31). Another name for this rhyme is "The Careless Kittens," found in Untermeyer's *Rainbow in the Sky* on page 235. Eight other nursery rhymes about kittens are included in Blegvad's book.

Children who love the "Three Little Kittens" will also love F. E. Weatherby's "The Cat's Tea Party" about five little kittens whose manners at tea left something to be desired, found on pages 34 and 35 of Cole's *I Went to the Animal Fair*. Two other famous poems about cats are included in that collection: Lear's "The Owl and the Pussycat" and Vachel Lindsay's "The Mysterious Cat."

There are five cat poems in Swenson's *Poems to Solve* (pp. 14-18). Blishen's *Oxford Book of Poetry for Children* (pp. 104-112) contains poems about large and small cats and is entitled "He is of the Tribe of Tiger." Cat poems are found on pages 231 to 239 of *Rainbow in the Sky* and pages 44 to 55 of *The Golden Treasury of Poems*, both by Untermeyer; pages 48 to 59 of Kuskin's *Near the Window Tree*; and pages 117 to 140 of Cole's *The Birds and Beasts Were There*.

All of these stories and poems about cats could be introduced by Flanders's poem "THE CAT"—from his book *Creatures Great and Small* which ends,

> "But a Cat is a Cat
> And that is that
> And that's enough for me."

Shaw's *The Cat Book* is a compilation of eighteen poems and four stories about cats, each of which is illustrated by a different artist. Some of the poets included are Tolkien, Wordsworth, Farjeon, Nash, and Ciardi. One of the four folk stories is "Why Cats Always Wash Themselves after Eating."

If a storytelling program about cats is introduced by a poem and then folktales about cats, a display of books about cats would be especially suitable to draw attention to other cat stories that could be checked out. There are too many books about cats to mention all of them; however, a few for primary students as well as intermediate students should not be overlooked. The primary group should include the favorite folk-like story *Millions of Cats* by Wanda Gag. In *Hi, Cat!*, Ezra Keats provides a modern contrast when Archie is followed home by a cat. Beatrix Potter's *The Tale of Tom Kitten* is a classic. In the easy-to-read category is *The Cat in the Hat* by Seuss, and another easy reader is Averill's *Fire Cat* about Pickles the spotted cat who becomes the official fire department mascot. Eric Carle's *Have You Seen My Cat?* should be included because many kinds of cats including a lion, bobcat, and cheetah are uncovered while looking for a pet cat. These same cats and many more are included in Zim's *The Big Cats* and Zim's *Little Cat* includes housecats. Lemmon's *Junior Science Book of Big Cats* begins with the sabertooth and describes other big cats as well as gives information about paws, eyes, claws, and hunting habits. No display of books for primary students would be complete without Newberry's *Mittens* and *Marshmallow*. The second title is about a cat who was jealous of a bunny.

In Beverly Cleary's book for intermediate students, *Socks* is jealous of the new baby. Bailey's *Finnegan II, His Nine Lives* is about a cat who has lost more than nine already. Henry's *Benjamin West and His Cat Grimalkin* provides a story based on the biography of West, an artist, who used brushes made from cats' tails for his work. Todd's *Space Cat*, about Flyball, a feline astronaut, adds the dimension of science fiction to books for intermediate students. Marcia Brown's *Puss in Boots* is just one and a splendid one, of the many versions of the most famous of cat folk and fairy tales.

POETRY COLLECTIONS ON ONE SUBJECT.   Collections of poems on one subject may or may not be illustrated. In *Amelia Mixed the Mustard,* Evaline Ness collected and illustrated poems, all of which had a girl's name in the title, by Houseman, Keats, Farjeon, Nash, Stein, Millay, and other famous poets.

Lee Hopkins's poems in *This Street's for Me!*, illustrated by Ann Grifalconi, includes seventeen poems about such city life aspects as subway rides, water fountains, and fire hydrants.

Parker's *Here and There, One Hundred Poems About Places* is illustrated by Peter Spier, and could be used in connection with various social studies units, with students locating places on a map or globe after they have read the poem. Some of the more famous ones included are Emerson's "Concord Hymn," Sandburg's "Chicago," and Lindsay's "Kalamazoo."

Each of the anthologies of poems by Mary O'Neill is on one subject. *Hailstones and Halibut Bones* is about color and is available also as a 16mm film. Several poems on color are included in Barnstone's *The Real Tin Flower*. Soft colors illustrate McNeill's *Winds* and fourteen poems all about fingers are included in *Fingers Are Always Bringing Me News*. Some of these could be used to introduce books and activities based on fingerplays. Two other collections of O'Neill's are *Take a Number* and *Words Words Words*. The second of these includes a humorous poem on page 14 about Egyptian hieroglyphics, "If they chiseled / The wrong place / I wonder how / They could erase?"

POEMS ABOUT TIME.   It's always time to read poetry, so why not poems about time! They can be used to introduce books about time or to enrich a unit about clocks and time. There are fourteen poems by Phyllis McGinley in *Wonderful Time*. Harry Behn examines the concept of time from seconds, hours and seasons to centuries and forever in his collection, *All Kinds of Time*. One of the books to introduce by these poems is *The Riddle of Time* by the Bells, which includes the definition of time, the history of calendars, of clocks, the standardization of time, time in biology, the geologic calendar, and theories by Copernicus, Galileo, Kepler, Newton, and Einstein. Einstein's theory of relativity is also included in Bendick's *The First Book of Time*, which also tells of equator, light years, measuring time, the first clocks, atomic clocks, geologic time, and plant and animal clocks. Reck's *Clocks Tell the Time* tells about atomic and electric clocks, clockmaking, the stars, and U.S. time zones. The *Calendar*, by Bendick, tells about the history and invention of the calendar, uses, naming the day of the week, and many types of calendars. *Clocks and How They Go* by Gibbons is for primary students. Conrad Aiken's story poem, *Tom, Sue and the Clock*, shows the relationship between time and their daily activities. Children who are learning to tell time will enjoy Mendoza's *The Scarecrow Clock*, illustrated in collage by Eric Carle. McCord's poem, "Tick-Tock Talk" on page 24 of his *Away and Ago* is a humorous poem about the ticking of clocks. The most famous rhyme of all is "Hickory, Dickory Dock," found on page 58 of Brian Wildsmith's *Mother Goose*, as well as numerous other collections of nursery rhymes.

Pat Hutchins's *Clocks and More Clocks* can be introduced to students in sound filmstrip format.

POEMS ABOUT FOOD.   *Is Anybody Hungry?* by Dorothy Aldis contains twenty-seven poems about food. The poem "Hot Chocolate" on page 27 would be a perfect lead-in to serving that or some other treat after a story hour in a public library or day care center. Cocoa is also served in Christopher Morley's "Animal Crackers," found on page 81 of the Sechrist anthology, *One Thousand Poems for Children*, and also on the recording of Thompson's *Silver Pennies*. To serve up more breakfast items, read "Pancakes" from Paune's *All The Day Long*, or Virginia Kahl's *The Perfect Pancake*, in which a beggar tricks a good cook into giving him "just one more" pancake. Bacon goes well with pancakes, and in *Don't Forget the Bacon*, a boy's mother asks him to bring home "six farm eggs, a cake for tea, a pound of pears, and don't forget the bacon." He says it over to himself several times changing the words to others that sound similar. Gradually the words come around again to the original list, but readers or listeners can readily guess what he will forget to bring.

In *Seven Uncles Came to Dinner* by Auerbach, great-aunt Louise teaches Emile a rhyme so that he will remember what to bring from the store. Everything turns out all right even though he brings back things that rhyme but aren't quite the items he was supposed to get.

The best known book by a prolific storyteller in verse is Virginia Kahl's *The Duchess Bakes a Cake*. More of the duchess's culinary adventures are presented in *Plum Pudding for Christmas*, in which the duchess has every ingredient but plums for the king's pudding. Even the recipes for French Toast, apple pie, a yeast and a batter bread sound like poetry in Adoff's *Eats: Poems*. Ten poems "From the Kitchen" are found in McCord's *Away and Ago* (pp. 81-83), and include animal crackers, pistachio ice cream, fudge, macaroons, peanut butter, pickles, and more. There are marshmallows, gumdrops, peppermint canes, a chocolate cat, and a gingerbread dog in "The Sugar Plum Tree" from Field's *Poems of Childhood*.

Rose Agree's book, *How to Eat a Poem and Other Morsels, Food Poems for Children*, can be introduced with the title poem by Eve Merriam. Some of the other poets featured are de la Mare, Lear, Rossetti, McGinley, and Aldis. "Oodles of Noodles" on page 11 by Lucia and James Hyner is a delicious poem about a delicious casserole. Aileen Fisher's "Christmas Cookies," on page 24 of the same anthology can be used before beginning a cookie baking project, as can "Cookie Cutters" from Mary Ann Hoberman's *Nuts to You and Nuts to Me*, and alliterative adventure. See also, "What's to Eat?" in *Every Child's Book of Verse* (pp. 105-112), selected by Gross, which contains eleven poems about food.

The colors of all the jelly beans in "Jelly Beans" on page 45 of Fisher's *In One Door and Out the Other* can be used at the end of a lesson about colors. (You will find more books about colors in the chapter on "Experiencing Art through Picture Books.") Jelly beans make a fine and easy to handle treat after a session on colors. You can find a poem on "Bubble Gum" on page 23 of Payne's *One Thousand Poems for Children*, but samples need not be handed out! The Brewton's *Laughable Limericks* have some funny limericks about food on pages 81 to 90.

The people in Lard's *The Great Jam Sandwich* decided to make a huge jam sandwich to attract and trap the bothersome four million wasps that plagued them. Eight horses lift the giant loaf of bread, a dump truck lifts the jam, a tractor and a snow plow put on the butter, and the top slice of bread has to be put on by a helicopter. This story will evoke much delighted comment and some further suggestions from listeners when it is read aloud.

Food, some of it exotic, is a feature of many famous stories not in verse, for primary age children on up. Some of the food poems might be used to lead into a unit about nutrition, or to finding other books in which food got some of the characters into trouble. For example, Peter Rabbit was determined to nibble in Mr. MacGregor's garden, while Homer Price's doughnut machine gave him a hard time.

EASTER, CHRISTMAS AND OTHER SEASONS IN POETRY.   There are over thirty-five poems included in Hazeltine and Smith's *Easter Book of Legends and Stories*. Pages 3 to 5 also contain the story "Very Early in the Morning" taken from the Gospels. Poems including Marchette Chute's "Easter Parade," page 44, appear in Harper's *Easter Chimes, Stories for Easter and the Spring Season*. Also consult Sechrist and Woolsey's *It's Time for Easter* (pp. 103-137).

Poems, carols, and stories about Christmas appear in the following collections: Luckhardt's *Christmas Comes Once More*, Reeves's *The Christmas Book*, Sechrist and Woolsey's *It's Time for Christmas*, Smith and Hazeltine's *Christmas Book of Legends and Stories*, Spicer's *Forty-six Days of Christmas, a Cycle of Old World Songs, Legends, and Customs*, and Tudor's *Take Joy! The Tasha Tudor Christmas Book*.

Phyllis McGinley's picture book poem *The Year without a Santa Claus* can be used to introduce her collection of Christmas poems *Mince Pie and Mistletoe*. That book by McGinley in turn can be used effectively with her collection called *A Wreath of Christmas Legends*. Eaton's *Welcome Christmas!* is also a collection of Christmas poems. The Brewton's *Christmas Bells are Ringing, A Treasury of Christmas Poetry* takes its title from the second line of a four-line poem by Mary Jane Carr that appears as the foreword for the book. The line is "while Christmas Bells are ringing." Each chapter heading is also taken from a line of a poem. There are thirteen poems about Santa Claus in that book. Eleven poems about animals appear in a section called "Friendly Beasts Around Him Stood" (pp. 67-78). Page 73 contains the poem "Friendly Beasts" by an unknown poet. Another book about Christmas, Eaton's *The Animal's Christmas*, takes its title from a poem. Sechrist's *Christmas Everywhere a Book of Christmas Customs of Many Lands* is introduced by Phillip Brooks's "A Christmas Carol" which contains the line "Everywhere, everywhere Christmas tonight."

Seven poems, including Felicia Herman's "The Landing of the Pilgrim Fathers in New England" and Riley's "When the Frost is on the Pumpkin," are found in Harper's *The Harvest Feast, Stories of Thanksgiving, Yesterday and Today*. More Thanksgiving poems and stories are included in Luckhardt's *Thanksgiving; Feast and Festival* and Sechrist's *It's Time for Thanksgiving*.

Wallace's collection *Witch Poems*, illustrated by Trina Hyman, contains poems by Farjeon, L. Moore, and cummings. Another spooky collection edited by Wallace is *Monster Poems*. A four-line poem, "Witch Ways" by an unknown poet, is one of many poems in *Witches, Elves, and Goblins* edited by Jacobs. Another seasonal collection edited by Jacobs is *Poetry for Autumn* which includes poems by Stevenson and McCord. Poems are also included in Harper's *Ghosts and Goblins, Stories for Halloween*. McGovern's *Squeals and Squiggles and Ghostly Giggles* contains stories, games, and poems. Sechrist's *Heigh-Ho for Halloween* contains games, plays, and stories as well as poems. Poems by Ciardi, Sendak, Sandburg, Fisher, McCullers, and cummings are included in Hopkins's *Hey-how for Halloween*. Other books by Hopkins are *A-Haunting we will go: Ghostly Stories and Poems; Monsters, Ghoulies and Creepy Creatures;* and *Witching Time*.

Several collections that contain many different holiday poems are Hazeltine and Smith's *The Year Round*, Farjeon's *Around the Seasons*, Brewton's *Sing a Song of Seasons*, Fisher's *Skip Around the Year*, Larrick's *Poetry for Holidays*, and Sechrist's *Poems for Red Letter Days*. Check Corrigan's *Holiday Ring* for poems about New Year's, Valentine's Day, and Thanksgiving. Also check Oechsli's *Humpty Dumpty's Holiday Stories* for poems about Groundhog Day, spring, summer, and autumn. Lois Lenski has several little books about the seasons in rhyme: *Now It's Fall, I Like Winter,* and *Spring is Here*. These can be used in tandem with *Winter's Here* by Moncure, which describes winter activities and has music at the end of the book.

BOOKS AND FILMSTRIPS ABOUT SNOW.   The following books about snow can be included in the display: *White Snow, Bright Snow* by Tresselt, *The Big Snow* by the Haders, and *Snowy Day* by Keats. These three books are Caldecott

Medal winners. The first and last books are available as sound filmstrips. The first book shows how people cope with a large snowfall; the second shows how wild animals cope with a similar snowfall; and the third shows a small boy experiencing snow. For a book program, read *The Big Snow*, show the filmstrip *White Snow, Bright Snow*, and then read *Snowy Day*. The longest book is first; the filmstrip of the second book is an especially effective way to share that particular book; and the last book is short and more personal. The girl in *Josie and the Snow* by Buckley enjoys the snow just as much as Peter of *Snowy Day*. The two books make a good pair for reading aloud. Josie asks her dog and cat to come out and play, but they would rather sleep. Instead, Josie's mother, father, and brother join in outdoor fun.

White Snow, Bright Snow and *Katy and the Big Snow* by Burton also make a good pair to read together. In Burton's book, Katy the snowplow has the task of plowing out Megapolis. *Country Snowplow* by Shortall is an easy reader about Tom who helps the snowplow find the road after a big storm. Give the book to beginning readers after they have heard the other two stories.

Animal hibernation appears in Miller's picture book *Mousekin's Woodland Sleeper* and Kraus' *The Happy Day*, and in two nonfiction books, *When Winter Comes* by Fox and *All Ready for Winter* by Adelson. Reading animal tracks in the snow is included in Busch's *A Walk in the Snow* for primary readers and George's *Snow Tracks* for intermediate readers.

Bell's *Snow* discusses snowflake designs and tells how snowflakes are formed. Branley's *Snow Is Falling* explains what makes snow to beginning readers. Hoff's *When Will It Snow* is another easy reading book. Lenski's *I Like Winter* and Moncure's *Winter's Here* provide poems for small children.

Betsy is snowbound the week before Christmas in *Snowbound for Betsy*, a book for primary students to read to themselves. A boy is snowbound in Kay's *Snow Birthday* and is disappointed that no one can come for a party until the group arrives by sleigh! Another winter birthday is in Livingston's *Happy Birthday*. Cammie has a birthday during maple sugar time and looks forward to a party with *Sugar on Snow* in a story that explains the maple sugar process. A small boy creates his own party, a picnic of peanut butter and jelly outside in the snow, in Welber's *Winter Picnic*. The collection might include Knott's *Winter Cat*, about a wild gray cat that finally gets a home.

STORIES IN VERSE.   There are stories in verse about all manner of things and places that will please children of various ages and provide lead-ins to other poetry and to prose stories, too.

There are books about some of the problems that beset children— teeth, for one, messy rooms for another, feeling sick, or trying to quiet down at bedtime or when life becomes overly exciting. *Lucy McLockett* is a girl with a tooth problem: until she lost her front tooth she was fine and did everything just right, but afterwards she lost things and forgot to hang up her clothes. Posy in Pomerantz's *Mango Tooth* makes up rhymes about whatever causes each tooth to come out, accompanied by illustrations that show apartment living and life in a single parent family—a mother who is a writer. Lee Bennett Hopkins's collection, *Me! A Book of Poems,* has a poem on pages 15 and 16, called "This Tooth" that would go well with this story. Smaridge's *The Big Tidy Up* is written in verse, and can be paired with Rockwell's *The Awful Mess.* Louis Slobodkin has two books in rhyme about manners: the first is about Willie White who wasn't polite, but later changed his manners in *Excuse Me! Certainly*; the other is *Thank you, You're Welcome,* about Jimmy who, although usually very polite, has one bad day—as we all do now and then. It might be fun to use these to introduce a discussion about manners and different ways of encouraging children to develop good ones, now and in the past. Munro Leaf's books about the *Watchbirds,* first published in the 1940s, and, still further back, the titles about *The Goops* would make for interesting comparisons.

Mother, Mother I Feel Sick, Send for the Doctor Quick, Quick Quick by Charlip and Supree has an accompanying sound filmstrip. Ardizzone illustrated, in his inimitable fashion, Sicotte's *A Riot of Quiet,* a small book of quiet things like a minute turning into an hour, a bean sprouting, and other couplets. In contrast and comparison there are Margaret Wise Brown's wonderful noisy books—*The City Noisy Book, Country Noisy Book, Quiet Noisy Book, Summer Noisy Book,* and *Winter Noisy Book,* in which the little dog, Muffin, hears noises and wonders about them—great books for developing verbal skills in young children. Margaret Wise Brown also wrote the enduring sleepy thoughts book, *Goodnight Moon,* in which the little bunny says good night to the familiar things around him as the room gradually darkens. A book of poems, *Songs the Sandman Sings* compiled by Reed, is a perfect companion and could be accompanied by *Bedtime for Frances* by Hoban and *Clyde Monster* by Crane. Eleanor Farjeon's poem "Bedtime" and Leroy Johnson's "Hippity Hop to Bed," both on page 3 of the Reed compilation, are especially in tune with Brown's book.

Some stories in verse introduce very young children to other places, to themselves, and to other people. Selina Chonz's books illustrated by Alois Carigiet originated in Switzerland and are tales of the mountain people who speak one of the rare languages of the world, Romansh, derived from the language of ancient Rome. *A Bell for Ursli* and *Florina and the Wild Bird* open up the beauty and a bit of the life style of the people of the Grisons. Arnold Adoff has written *MA nDA LA* in which an African family's life is depicted against the background of a harvest chant; *Black Is Brown Is Tan* and *Big Sister Tells Me That I'm Black,* in which an older girl tries to instill in a younger sister the pride that goes with being black, brown, or tan. Bond's *Brown Is Beautiful* is also in verse, and all four books are intended to be read aloud.

And then there's *Madeline,* Ludwig Bemelmans's innocent and sophisticated convent school girl who lilts her way around Europe getting into and out of scrapes and funny situations. If there ever was a heroine or a series of stories in verse that prove that small children are not interested solely in the "here and now" of their familiar world, Madeline is it. The convent girls go walking two by two until Madeline gets appendicitis and everyone else wants to pretend she has it too! In *Madeline's Rescue,* she is rescued by the dog Genevieve from the Seine, and Genevieve is of course adopted. Readers tour

France with Madeline when she is accidentally left behind at a carnival in *Madeline and the Gypsies*. In *Madeline and the Bad Hat*, the heroine tangles with a neighbor, the son of the Spanish ambassador, and in *Madeline in London*, Madeline and her school mates see all the sights of London when they go to visit the ambassador's son. There is a recording of Carol Channing reading on *Madeline and the Gypsies and Other Stories* (which includes *Madeline in London*), and another recording, *Madeline and Other Bemelmans*, includes the other three titles.

There are two outstanding books in rhyme about shapes: Budney's *A Kiss is Round* and Ed Emberley's *Wing on a Flea*. Beginning readers will like *What Have I Got* in which a boy shows the contents of his pockets. McClintock's *Pocketful of Cricket*, read aloud, can lead into this last title.

And of course there are verse stories about animals—gentle or filled with hilarity or in between to suit every taste. There is Slobodkin's *The Friendly Animals* and de Regniers *May I Bring a Friend?*, illustrated by Beni Montresor, in which a small boy tells of the animals he will bring with him when he is invited to tea at the home of the king and queen. These include a giraffe, a hippo, monkeys, lions, an elephant, and a seal. Eleven animals are introduced in *Who, Said Sue, Said Whoo*, and introduction of the twelfth provides a little mystery and gives a surprise ending. Ellen Raskin's *Twenty-Two, Twenty-Three* is especially good to read at Christmas because page 24 takes place on Christmas Eve.

In *A Fly Went By*, six animals and a hunter are all chasing each other, and the creature which scares the hunter is a funny surprise. Harve Zemach's story, *The Judge*, illustrated by Margot Zemach can tickle the funny bone of preschoolers and primary grade children alike (not to mention adults): witnesses try to describe the creature they have seen but the judge won't listen, and justice is well served when the creature comes in and eats the judge!

And as for the funny, ridiculous, and infectious, Dr. Seuss may have had the longest run in versified story history. If Dr. Seuss's characters can't find a known word that rhymes when they want it to, they make one up. In *Horton Hatches the Egg*, a solemn elephant sits gingerly on an egg and keeps his promise; *Horton Hears a Who* in which the elephant meets a colony of little people, provided a sequel some years after the first book. Early on there was *To Think That I Saw It on Mulberry Street*, in which a small boy elaborates upon what he actually saw—not lying really, just stretching his imagination. *McElligot's Pool* features species of fish no marina ever saw, and unusual animals with even more unusual names populate *If I Ran the Circus* and *If I Ran the Zoo*. Then there is *Thidwick, the Big Hearted Moose* who has to shed his antlers to escape the hunters and which demonstrates as well as any of the Seuss titles one of the reasons for their enduring popularity with successive generations of children: these books have a point of view, they instill a sense of values for all their fun. Pictures and rhymes poke fun at the pompous, point scathingly at unfairness and hypocrisy, and extol the true and the just.

Many of the Dr. Seuss books are easy reading books and were written with the intent of luring not-so-enthusiastic readers into print. These include *The Cat* in the Hat, The Cat in the Hat Comes Back, Green Eggs and Ham, Fox in Sox, and One Fish Two Fish, Red Fish Blue Fish. Fox in Sox and The Cat in the Hat Comes Back are part of a six-filmstrip set called Beginner Books, filmstrip 4, which is highly recommended for lead in or follow up to the Seuss titles and other easy reader books.

INTRODUCING GIANTS.   There are several poems that can be used to introduce books and stories about giants. Read Charles Edward Carlyle's "Giant's Song" on page 189 of McFerran's Poems to Be Read Aloud to Children and by Children. Another poem, Joan Aiken's "Footprints" on page 29 of her collection The Skin Spinners is about cloud footprints that could be made by giants. Aiken suggests that perhaps they could have been made by abominable skymen. There are sixteen Giant Poems in Wallace's book illustrated by Tomes.

Everyone knows what giants say when they smell a person they would like to eat! "Fee Fie Fo Fum. . . ." Another rhyme, not as familiar, is the one found on page 4 of Ungerer's Zeralda's Ogre which begins "A Sniff! A Snuff! How Hungry I Feel!" The story about a girl named Zeralda who was taken home by an ogre, can be compared with the one about Scheherazade of the Arabian Nights. Zeralda cooked such marvelous meals for the ogre and his friends that they gave up eating people and when Zeralda grew up, the ogre shaved his beard and they were married. Five giants live on Fe-Fi-Fo-Fum Farm in Yolen's The Giants Farm.

Read Albert William Smith's poem "The Giant" in deRegniers's The Giant Book (pp. 126-130) to introduce the whole book to students. The book includes many famous giants including Goliath, Paul Bunyan, the beanstalk giant, and others. There are six stories about Jack the Giant Killer in deRegniers's book, as well as in Manning-Sanders's A Book of Giants. The best known story, a version from Joseph Jacobs which is included in William Mayne's Book of Giants, is taken from old chapbooks, and set during King Arthur's time. Jack tricks several giants and rescues a princess and other nobles who have been turned into animals. A rhyme spoken by the giant can be shared with the "Fee Fie Fo Fum" rhymes. The picture book based on Jacobs's version has Jack meeting King Arthur's son.

Jacobs's version of "Jack in the Beanstalk" is included also in the collections of deRegniers and Manning-Sanders, Fenner's Giants and Witches and a Dragon or Two, and De la Mare's Tales Told Again. Several picture book versions are available. Low illustrated de la Mare's Jack and the Beanstalk, and Wiesner wrote and illustrated a book of the same title. William Stobbs illustrated another Jack and the Beanstalk. Raymond Briggs wrote a story called Jim and the Beanstalk about a giant who couldn't eat Jack because he had no teeth. Jack also offers to get the giant glasses so he can read poetry. A giant with glasses, false teeth, and a wig provides a humorous contrast to the other stories. For other activities using this story, see Remo Bufano's Book of Puppetry (pp. 117-130) for "Jack and the Beanstalk, a Puppet Play" and Thane's Plays From Famous Stories and Fairy Tales (pp. 366-380) for "Jack and the Magic Beanstalk." Students can also compare any traditional tale about Jack with the story "The Bean Tree" included in Manning-Sanders's *Gianni and the Ogre*.

Paul Galdone illustrated an old verse version published in England in 1807. In *The History of Mother Waddle and the Marvelous Achievements of Her Son Jack*, the mother finds a coin and asks Jack to go and buy a goose at the fair but he brings home the magic bean. A maid instead of the giant's wife opens the door of the castle to Jack. Jack gives the giant too much wine, cuts off his head, and marries the young maid.

Eleven sources for varieties of Jack's story are listed in Ireland's *Index to Fairy Tales*. Students could be asked to find other stories of giants, about whom Ireland's index lists almost five columns of stories. deRegniers's *The Giant Book* contains the story of "Gianni and the Giant" on pages 60 to 68: "Gianni is my name, I'm the strongest in the land, I felled five hundred with a single hand." This theme of killing many pests is a familiar story in folklore. "The Brave Little Tailor," in Manning-Sanders's *A Book of Giants* (pp. 90-98) killed seven with one blow.

The American folk hero Paul Bunyan is a different sort of "New World" giant. A poem on page 171 of deRegniers's *The Giant Book* called "Paul Bunyan" could be used to introduce him in "Paul Bunyan Swings His Axe" found on pages 159 to 170 of the same book. See page 5 of Ratigan's *The Adventures of Paul Bunyan and Babe* for a poem to introduce stories about Samson, Goliath, and Hercules through a rhyme about Paul Bunyan. The entire book is made up of rhymes about Paul. Over a hundred poems and stories about Paul are to be found in Felton's *Legends of Paul Bunyan*. Use the poems in this book to introduce other Bunyan stories or to represent Bunyan when telling giant stories.

The Giant Book by deRegniers also includes giants from mythology, legend, and the Bible, and includes the story "David and Goliath." This story interestingly enough can be used when studying weights and measures since it mentions that the Bible gives Goliath's height as six cubits and a span. On page 21 of McHargue's *The Impossible People*, readers learn that a cubit is about 17 to 20 inches and a span is about 9 inches. Give students the information on cubits and spans and have them figure out how tall Goliath was. If the students calculate that Goliath was about 9-1/2 feet tall, tell them the story as a reward. Other stories about David are listed in this chapter under the heading "Children's Bibles and Bible Stories."

"Thor and the Giants" appears in deRegniers's book (pp. 94-105). A picture book of the same title rewritten by Feagles is also available, in which Thor, Loki, and Thailfe visit the land of the giants and are challenged to a contest by the giant Skymmer. When all three lose the contests, Skymmer explains how they were tricked by magic, for example, when Thor hit Skymmer three times on the head to wake him he was really hitting a mountain, and when Loki lost the eating contest, he lost to fire. Another Norse myth tells "How Loki Outwitted a Giant," retold by Picard and found on pages 35 to 41 of Mayne's *Book of Giants*.

The Cyclops is the most famous giant of Greek mythology. Read the story "The One-eyed Giant" in Green's *Tales of the Greeks and Trojans* (pp. 57-59), or Thompson's *One Hundred Favorite Folktales* (pp. 377-384) in a story called

"Polyphemus, the Cyclops." Also see pages 8 and 9 of McHargue's The Impossible People.

"Odysseus and the Land of the Giants" appears on pages 70 to 78 and "Gulliver and the Giant's Country" is found on pp. 136 to 158 of deRegniers's The Giant Book. A sound recording narrated by Anthony Quayle called Gulliver's Travels to Lilliput can be used with the last story.

Both Manning-Sanders and Mayne include the story "The Giant Who Had No Heart in His Body." DeRegniers and Manning-Sanders include a story about Fin M'Coul the Irish Hero and Cuchulain the Giant. March, especially St. Patrick's Day, is a good time to read or tell stories about the Irish giant.

Oscar Wilde's "The Selfish Giant" is included in William Mayne's Book of Giants. The story may prompt students to read Wilde's The Happy Prince and Other Stories which includes eight other fairy tales. A sound recording called The Happy Prince and Other Oscar Wilde Fairy Tales narrated by Basil Rathbone contains "The Selfish Giant," "The Happy Prince" and "The Nightingale and the Rose." A picture book illustrated by the Reiners, The Selfish Giant, is available as a sound filmstrip. Read the story at Easter time from Harper's Easter Chimes, (pp. 162-169) or from Sechrist's It's Time for Easter, (pp. 221-226).

Rhymes precede each of the three stories in Harrison's Book of Giant Stories. The "Little Boy's Secret" is that he has measles. "The Giant Who Was Afraid of Butterflies" was under a curse in which everything looked larger. The last story is about "The Giant Who Threw Tantrums."

When books about giants are gathered together, be sure to include Sarnoff and Puffins's Giants! A Riddle Book.

There are enough different types of giants so that each person in a classroom could find background information and stories about them. One useful background book is McHargue's The Impossible People. Chapter 1, "Big People," is introduced by a quote from Genesis of the King James Bible. McHargue lists and explains four characteristics of giants. Cousins of the giants are mentioned: ogres, Titans, Cyclops, and trolls. The d'Aulaire's Trolls makes a good companion book. McHargue mentions the Abominable Snowman and Beowulf and also golems. Beverly Brodsky McDermotts's The Golem, a Jewish Legend was a Caldecott honor book.

PRAYERS AND HYMNS. A list of books of prayers for children should begin with Prayers for a Child, the 1945 Caldecott Medal winner by Rachel Field, illustrated by Elizabeth Orton Jones. This book is now available in a paperback edition. Jones also illustrated Eleanor Farjeon's A Prayer for Little Things in which God is asked to take care of small things like seeds and raindrops.

Tasha Tudor's First Graces and First Prayers are small books. First Graces includes twenty-two graces and prayers; First Prayers selections from the New England Primer, St. Patrick, the Wesleys, and Martin Luther, including the Lord's Prayer and the Twenty-Third Psalm. The d'Aulaires have illustrated beautifully The Lord's Prayer. Barnhart's The Lord Is My Shepherd includes the Lord's Prayer as well as the Beatitudes. Table Graces for the Family by Ingzel, available in paperback edition, includes thirteen graces from the Revised Standard Version of the *Bible*, seven from the Book of Common Prayer, and hymns of Luther and Wesley. Elizabeth Yates's *Your Prayers and Mine* include prayers from the Old and New Testaments, from Socrates, the Navajos, St. Augustine, and St. Francis. *The Canticle of the Sun* after St. Francis of Assisi is illustrated by Jones and contains eight short songs of praise thanking God for the moon, stars, air, water, fire, earth, and all God's creatures. Many religions are represented in Jones's *This Is the Way, Prayers and Precepts from World Religions.* Huber's *Story and Verse for Children* includes religious items in a section called "Guideposts" (pp. 162-168), and includes a Navajo prayer, a grace by Robert Burns, "The Cradel Hymn" of Martin Luther, as well as Ceil Frances Alexander's "All Things Bright and Beautiful." Sechrist's *One Thousand Poems for Children* also has sections of religious poetry on pages 187-193 and 489 to 510 called "Poems of Praise" and "Poems of Reverence." Vipont's *Bless This Day* includes prayers of thanksgiving for work, bedtime and other blessings. A variety of religious prayers and poems are included in Plotz's *The Earth Is the Lord's, Poems of the Spirit.* Poems, Bible passages, and prayers are included in Herzel's *Christmas Is Today.* In Margaret Wise Brown's *A Child's Good Night Book,* readers see all the animal babies sleeping, and the child blessing family as well as ". . . small things that have no words." Wheeler's *Sing in Praise, A Collection of Best Loved Hymns* contains nineteen hymns, with many more in Marguerite DeAngeli's *Book of Favorite Hymns.*

PSALMS.   The Psalms are among the most beautiful and enduring poetry in the world. Several sources which include Psalms indicate which are most popular. Marguerite DeAngeli's arrangement and illustrations of *The Old Testament* include Psalms 23, 84, 24, 46, 42, 137, 126, 121, 100, 1, and 91. Nancy Barnhart's *The Lord Is My Shepherd* includes Psalms 23, 8, 46, 125, 48, 50, and 91. Background information about sixteen Psalms is given in *Songs Along the Way* illustrated with woodcuts by Mel Silverman. Psalms included are 19, 148, 121, 167, 118, 23, 99, 65, 100, 117, 13, 45, 84, 150, and 134. Thirty-three Psalms from the King James Version were selected by Elvajean Hall and illustrated by Charles Mozley in *The Psalms.* No illustrations accompany Psalms 37, 150, 100, 103, 147, 24, and 23 in a section called "Selections from the Psalms," in Sutherland's *Arbuthnot Anthology of Children's Literature* (pp. 134-135). A few proverbs from several chapters of the *Bible* are also included. The third edition of Johnson's *Anthology of Children's Literature* includes Psalms 1, 23, 24, 46, 91, 121, and 50. Psalms 23 and 100 are included in Huber's *Story and Verse for Children.*

  Songs of Joy from the Book of Psalms includes selections from the *Bible,* edited by Louis Untermeyer. The twenty-third Psalm is one of the most widely known and loved. Four books about just that Psalm are *The Twenty-Third Psalm* illustrated by Tasha Tudor, *The Twenty-Third Psalm: King James Version* illustrated by Marie Angel, and *The Shepherd's Psalm* illustrated by the Petershams. Tony Palazzo has made this favorite Psalm more understandable to children through his illustrations of animals and birds in *The Lord Is My Shepherd.* In a similar picture book, *A Time for All Things*, Palazzo explains Ecclesiastes 3: "There is a season, and a time to every purpose under the heaven." Also see *The Old Testament*, illustrated by DeAngeli, on pages 236 to 237 for the same verses. Palazzo also illustrated *Wings of the Morning, Verses from the Bible* which were selected by Robin Palmer.

Stories about David may be introduced when reading Psalms to children. Those stories are found in the next section of this chapter.

CHILDREN'S BIBLES AND BIBLE STORIES.   Three books that retain much of the flavor of the King James Version of the Bible are *The Golden Bible, from the King James Version of the Old Testament* selected by Elsa Jane Werner, illustrated by Feodor Rojankovsky, and Marguerite DeAngeli's abbreviated and illustrated *The Old Testament*. *The Golden Bible for Children, the New Testament* was also selected and arranged by Werner and illustrated by the Provensens.

Three collections of Bible stories that are faithful to the original language are Alvin Tresselt's *Stories from the Bible* illustrated with Lynd Ward's lithographs; Walter De la Mare's *Stories from the Bible* illustrated by Edward Ardizzone; and Nancy Burnhart's *The Lord Is My Shepherd, Stories from the Bible*. Marginal notes and references are part of the last book. Philip Turner's *Brian Wildsmith's Bible Stories* is beautifully illustrated; however, Turner's retellings have little poetic flavor and are just matter-of-fact statements of events.

Some picture books are simply illustrated Bible texts. Paul Galdone used the King James Version for his text when he illustrated the picture book *The First Seven Days, the Story of the Creation from Genesis*, while Jo Spier used the Jerusalem Bible as the text for *The Creation*. *And the Sun God Said: That's Good* is a poetic version of the creation told in black dialect by Ernest Gregg.

Many picture books are retellings of Bible stories. The story of Noah and his ark is a favorite, included in the collections of Bible stories already mentioned as well as Gruenberg's *Favorite Stories Old and New*. George Macbeth has retold the story in free verse in *Noah's Journey* while Lois Lenski's rhythmic text is her *Mr. and Mrs. Noah*. Other retellings include Wynant's *Noah's Ark* and Bollinger's *Noah and the Rainbow*. Hutton's *Noah and the Great Flood* is taken from the King James Version. One of those stories begins with a Bible quote from Genesis 9:2 " . . . Every beast of the earth, every fowl of the air," and Haley's modern version of Noah puts all the creatures into the ark to save them from extinction in our polluted land. The ostrich refused to come so there was no ostrich when survivors radioed from land to the barge that there were no animals left on earth and would Noah and his animals return to a special place provided for them. Margaret Wise Brown's book of animal poems, *The Fish with the Deep Sea Smile*, is introduced by Job 12:7 and 8 which also mentions "the beasts, fowls of the air and fishes of the sea." Use Macbeth's *Jonah and the Whale* which is a poem introduced by Jonah 1:17 with Brodsky's *Jonah; an Old Testament Story*. Each chapter of Shippen's *Moses* is introduced by a quote from the Bible.

The Tower of Babel is a beautiful picture book that can be used with the story of Noah's ark simply by introducing it as a story of the descendants of Noah. The 5,000-foot-high tower was built by the people as a show of power. When they wanted to build the tower even higher, God gave them many languages so they couldn't understand each other and work could not be completed. Eventually the people scattered by language groups all over the earth. This book is available in sound filmstrip format and could be used as part of a program of Bible stories as a change of pace. The filmstrip could also be used to introduce students to Wiesner's book so they could read it on their own.

Use the fifty-three animals which appear in Cole's *An Arkful of Animals* with Asimov's *Animals of the Bible.*

The Binding of Isaac by Cohen is for primary and intermediate students.

Isaac Singer and Elizabeth Shub translated the story of Lot's wife who was turned into a pillar of salt when she looked back at the wicked city of Sodom for the picture book *The Wicked City.*

Joseph and his coat of many colors is an interesting story for children to illustrate separately or in groups to prepare a large Joseph with his colorful coat for the bulletin board. There are two books for primary students and two for intermediate students. Primary students can read Bulla's easy reader, *Joseph the Dreamer,* to themselves but will enjoy having the picture book *Joseph and His Brothers* illustrated by the Petershams read to them. Intermediate students may read that book to themselves or may wish to read two books called *Joseph,* one written by Bollinger and the other written by Yates.

The Petershams also illustrated the picture book *Moses* which includes the childhood as well as the adulthood of Moses. Sappatta's *A Basket in the Reeds* is a book for primary students and uses the story of how Moses was found in the bullrushes as the basis for a story. Graham's *Road Down in the Sea,* which tells of how the Red Sea parted for the Israelites, is told in a Liberian-English dialect.

Since the historical chapter of Drucker's *Passover, a Season of Freedom* tells about Moses and the flight from Egypt, use it with Greenfield's *Passover.* Both authors and Hirsh have written books about Hanukkah or Chanukah. Since Drucker's book has recipes, crafts, puzzles and games, it could be used with Becker's *Jewish Holiday Crafts* and Lazar's *Jewish Holiday Book.*

One splendid picture book, *David and Goliath* by deRegniers, is excellent for reading aloud. Psalms of David are brought naturally into the story. David offered a Psalm when he was on his way to Saul's army and later sang one after he became king to remember the days when he was a shepherd boy. Two other books which include the story are Untermeyer's *The Firebringer and Other Great Stories* (pp. 109-112), and Greenberg's *Favorite Stories Old and New* (pp. 433-437). There are also several individual books containing the story. McClintock's *David and the Giant* is an easy reader and told in verse. The Petershams's *David* is a picture book intended to be read aloud and can be used with their other book *The Shepherd's Psalm.* Bollinger's *David* is written for intermediate students.

There are three picture books available about Jonah. Clyde Bulla's version is called *Jonah and the Great Fish* and includes several pages of illustrations without text. George MacBeth's *Jonah and the Lord* is an unrhymed poem. The newest version is Beverly Brodsky's *Jonah, an Old Testament Story.* The illustrations are similar to those she used in her Caldecott honor book, *The Golem, A Jewish Legend,* about a rabbi who created a golem from clay and magic and gave it life. Unfortunately, the golem bcame evil and had to be destroyed. The three books of Jonah are useful as examples of different styles of writing and different types of illustrations.

The story sometimes called "The Three Men in the Fiery Furnace" is about three Israelites who refused to bow down to the golden idol of King Nebuchadnezzar. When the three men, along with an angel, survived being thrown into a blazing furnace, the king accepted their God. The story taken verbatim from the King James Version of the Bible is illustrated by Galdone and is called *Shadrack, Meshack and Abednego,* from the Book of Daniel. The story is listed in *The Golden Bible, Stories from the Old Testament* as "The Statue of Gold." Other books that contain the story are Barnhart's *The Lord Is My Shepherd* and *The Old Testament* illustrated by DeAngeli.

An equally exciting story that takes place during the same period is also found in all of the Bible story books mentioned above: "Daniel in the Lion's Den." Instead of being thrown into a fiery furnace, Daniel is thrown to the lions and is saved. Bollinger has written a book called *Daniel* for intermediate students.

Bible stories about women are not as common as those with men as heroes. The Petershams's picture book called *Ruth* tells of Ruth's devotion to her mother-in-law. An abridgment of the Book of Ruth: 1 and 2 from the King James Version of the *Bible* is found on pages 703 to 705 of the third edition of Johnson's *Anthology of Children's Literature.* Mary, the mother of Jesus, appears, of course, in the stories of the nativity.

THE NATIVITY IN STORY AND VERSE.   The following books are listed in the bibliography under "Bible" because they follow the Revised Standard Version. *The First Christmas* from the Gospels according to St. Luke and St. Matthew was arranged by Barbara Neustadt and illustrated with medieval art. *The Christmas Story* from the Gospels of Matthew, Mark, and Luke was edited by Northrup and contains paintings from the Metropolitan Museum of Art. *The Christ Child* from Matthew and Luke was beautifully illustrated by the Petershams. The Provensens illustrated the story in *The Golden Bible for Children, the New Testament.*

Some very different versions of that familiar story are Graham's *Every Man Heart Lay Down* told in Liberian-English dialect. This poetic rendition of the nativity story begins with God being vexed with people "And Him heart no lay down." When the child was born everyone came . . . and every man heart lay down." Cajun dialect in a bayou setting provides the background for Rice's *Cajun Night before Christmas.* Caudill's *A Certain Shepherd* provides an Appalachian setting and a black child for the story. Trent's *The First Christmas* is told in rhythmic prose and includes the song "Away in the Manger" at the back of the book, and so it can be coupled with the picture book by the Nussbaumers

Away in the Manger. Luke is the source for Juchen's *The Holy Night* illustrated by Piatti in flat bold colors and also available on sound filmstrip. Another sound filmstrip, *Christmas in the Stable,* is based on a picture book by Astrid Lindgren. The poem "The Star" from *Lois Lenski's Christmas Stories* can be used to introduce *Marie Ets's Nine Days to Christmas* in which the Mexican Christmas celebration with posadas and pinatas is explained. Also included in Lenski's book are stories of six regional American Christmases. The play *A Visit of the Shepherds, a Nativity Play,* includes carols and verses and is included on pages 141-152 of Lenski's book.

Elizabeth Coatsworth in Harzel's *Christmas is Today* (pp. 69-71) tells the Christmas story using an animal mother as the narrator. When the colt complains because he is tired of sleeping in the barn in winter, the mare tells him a story of a barn where a miracle happened. That story can be used with Margaret Wise Brown's picture book rhyme *Christmas in the Barn* illustrated by Cooney or with Baker's poem/song *The Friendly Beasts.* Bible verses and carols are illustrated by Weisgard in Slaughter's *And It Came to Pass.* The Gospel of St. Luke is used and music for the piano and guitar are included. Hoffman's *The Story of Christmas* ends with the flight to Egypt and the return to Nazareth.

The life of Jesus after the nativity is included in the *Golden Bible for Children, the New Testament* and *Jesus' Story; a Little New Testament.*

HAIKU: AN INTERESTING WAY TO WRITE POEMS.   All ages enjoy the beautifully illustrated picture books of haiku that are available. *In a Spring Garden,* illustrated by Ezra Keats, features over twenty different garden creatures—grasshoppers, snails, owls, and skylarks are included. This outstanding book is also available in sound filmstrip format. The filmstrip could be used to introduce other haiku picture books. Twenty-one similar poems comprise Cassedy's *Birds, Frogs and Moonlight,* illustrated with Japanese calligraphy, which gives information about Basho and Issa, important haiku poets. Ellen Raskin's illustrations add much to Rebecca Caudill's haiku in *Come Along!* Colored photographs heighten the meaning of the poems in Atwood's *Haiku: The Mood of the Earth* and also *My Own Rhythm, an Approach to Haiku,* which includes poems by Basho, Issa, and Buson. *Don't Tell the Scarecrow and Other Japanese Poems* by Issa, Yayu, Kikoku and Other Japanese Poets includes thirty-four illustrated poems, and Issa is featured in *A Few Flies and I.*

Harry Behn translated two collections of Japanese haiku: *Cricket Songs* and *More Cricket Songs.* Pages 39 to 46 "On Haiku," from Behn's *Chrysalis, Concerning Children and Poetry,* gives helpful insights into haiku and inspiration for teachers. Henderson's book for teachers, *An Introduction to Haiku, An Anthology of Poems and Poets from Basho to Shiki,* not only discusses the characteristics of haiku but gives information on major poets, Basho, Buson, Issa, and Shiki, with samples of their poetry. Persons getting ready to teach students to write haiku will want to read this as well as chapter 11, "Haiku, Yes or No" of Livingston's *When You are Alone / It Keeps You Capone.* Chapter 3, "Dragons and Frogs—Oriental Culture and Poetry," of Ruth Carlson's *Enrich-*

ment Ideas, fulfills the promise of the title, provides an extensive bibliography of haiku books, and an historical overview of other types of Japanese poetry.

Forms are clearly explained and examples given in Johnson's *A Thousand Petals, Haiku and Tanka*, which contains three different poems about snow, fourteen about insects, and thirteen about animals. *The Seasons of Time, Tanka Poetry of Ancient Japan* includes poems on all the seasons. Tanka is a form older than haiku by about a thousand years and includes five lines with 5-7-5-7-7 syllables instead of the 4-7-5 pattern for haiku.

Some books include poems written in the spirit of haiku, and Kazue Mizumura's watercolors for the poems in *I See the Winds* heads the list. The seventeen poems each take a double page, one for the poem and the other for the illustration. Mizumura's newest book, *Flower Moon Snow*, provides woodcuts to accompany the haiku. Hannah Johnson's *Hello, Small Sparrow* also includes haiku-like poems.

Natalia Belting's *The Land of the Taffeta Dawn* is free-flowing poetry included here for its Eastern orientation. The story takes place during the eighth through tenth Century when the Vikings traded with China, and concerns the mad Empress Wu who ordered flowers to bloom in winter and decided that no one be appointed to high office unless he was a poet!

CHORAL READING. Choral speaking or reading is an exciting way to share poetry. Whitehead's *Children's Literature: Strategies for Teaching* summarizes several of its values. Four types are examined—refrain, line-a-child, antiphonal, and unison—with observations about each type. The hints on selecting voice groups are also helpful. Brown and Heltman's *Let's Read Together Poems, an Anthology of Verse for Choral Reading in Kindergarten and Primary Grades* includes simplified procedures and gives examples, and also a brief but valuable "A Word about Choral Reading" on page 2. The poems were tried in classrooms and are divided into nine categories, some of which are rhymes, nature and seasons, people, special days, wee folks, and magic. "Helpful Do's and Don'ts for the Director" are given in Abner and Abney and Rowe's *Choral Speaking Arrangements for the Lower Grades*. See pages 15 to 22 for samples of refrain, two-part, line-a-child, part-speaking, and unison. Pages 33 and 34 of Brown-Azarowicz's *A Handbook of Creative Choral Speaking* give thirteen suggestions called "Some Do's for the Beginning Teacher."

Examples of five types of choral speaking are included in Winifred Ward's *Playmaking With Children*, (pp. 255–65): rhythmic or activity, refrain, two-part, groups and solo parts, and unison. Raymond Ross uses a different approach in "Choral Reading: United We Stand," of *Storyteller* (pp. 75–98). Ross speaks of interpreting word pictures, acquiring fresh aural images, and using echoic verse. Six suggestions for successful programs, especially within the story-hour, are given. Keppie's *Speech Improvement through Choral Speaking*, as well as Gullan's *Poetry Speaking for Children and the Speech Choir*, are helpful also. The last book lists refrain, sequence, cumulative and individual as types of choral reading, and is a classic in the field.

There are three sources of poems with directions for choral speaking by

Abney: *Choral Speaking Arrangements for the Junior High School, Choral Speaking for the Lower Grades,* and *Choral Speaking Arrangements for the Upper Grades.* Three by Carrie Rasmussen are *Let's Say Poetry Together and Have Fun: For Intermediate Grades, Let's Say Poetry Together and Have Fun: For Primary Grades,* and *Poems for Playtime.* Brown and Heltman have seven books called *Read Together Poems.* Also consult Bamman's *Oral Interpretation of Children's Literature.*

Three chapters in Sikes's *Children's Literature for Dramatization* contain poems as well as instructions for playing. See chapter 1, "Poetry Inviting Action"; chapter 2, "Poetry Inviting Characterization"; and chapter 3, "Poetry Motivating Conflicts."

According to Martha Laurion, an emeritus member of the faculty of Northern Michigan University, there are seven types of choral speaking: unison, activity, refrain, dialogue or antiphonal, line-a-child, cumulative or sequential, and a combination thereof. The following poems and books can be used to demonstrate those types.

There are many poems which can be read by all students together. Reading in unison is really the most difficult to direct because all students must be together for the entire poem. One very suitable poem is "Whiskey Frisky," a poem about a squirrel by an unknown poet. One of the many sources for it is Sechrist's *One Thousand Poems for Children,* (pp. 120–21). Students could be taught the poem after the books *Hurry, Skurry and Flurry* by the Buffs or *The Tale of Squirrel Nutkin* by Potter are read to them. Another poem is "The Wise Old Owl" found on page 47 of *Brian Wildsmith's Mother Goose.* A list of books that include owls to use in connection with this is found in the index.

There are many poems that provide for children to complete simple *activities* while a poem is read to them. *Brian Wildsmith's Mother Goose* provides several excellent activity nursery rhymes: "One Two Buckle My Shoe," page 30; "Pat-a-Cake," page 43; "Jack and Jill," page 54; "O, The Grand Old Duke of York," page 76; and "Two Little Dicky Birds," page 21. "Jump and Jiggle" by Evelyn Beyer, found on page 117 of McCaslin's *Creative Dramatics in the Classroom,* is a favorite and provides for twelve separate animal actions and one human action. The poem can be played in unison or line-a-child. "Two Witches" by Alexander Resnikoff (p. 62 of the October, 1974, issue of *Cricket*) is a paired activity poem. Students can be divided into pairs with one person being the first witch and the second person being the other witch. The poem is suitable for introducing into a classroom where homonyms are being studied. Three exciting picture books about homonyms are Hansom's *Homonyms, More Homonyms: Steak and Stake and Other Words that Sound the Same but Look as Different as Chili and Chilly,* and *Still More Homonyms, Night and Knight and Other Words that Sound the Same but Look as Different as Ball and Bawl.*

Children's magazines are a source of favorite as well as new poems, and others that include poems are *Child Life, Highlights for Children, Jack and Jill, Children's Digest,* and *Humpty Dumpty.* For complete bibliographic information on these magazines, check the bibliography.

William Blake's "Spring" is found on page 142 of Sechrist's *One Thousand*

Poems for Children. The refrain is "Merrily, merrily to welcome in the year," and it follows each of the three verses. Students could be asked to find other poems about spring using the poetry indexes.

The chapter, "Enhancing Books through Music" cites songs in individual picture books that contain refrains and can be used for choral speaking, among them are *One Wide River to Cross* and *London Bridge is Falling Down* by Emberley; *Clementine, Go Tell Aunt Rhody* and *She'll Be Coming Round the Mountain* by Quackenbush; *The Foolish Frog* by the Seegers; *Yankee Doodle* by Shackburg; *The Erie Canal, Fox Went Out on a Chilly Night* and *London Bridge* by Spier. *Widdecombe Fair,* Monjo's *The Drinking Gourd* and *Frog He Would a-Wooing G.,* illustrated by either Caldecott or Stephens, also have refrains. "The Derby Ram" found on pages 29 and 30 of de la Mare's *Animal Stories,* is also found in a picture book with the same title.

Sometimes refrains are very brief as in *The Old Woman and the Peddlar;* students can say the refrain in unison after each line, "Fa la la la la la la."

"Halloween," in Hoberman's *Hello and Goodby,* (pp. 54–55) has four verses. At the end of each of the first three verses, students respond in unison "But I don't tell." At the end of the fourth verse the response is "But I run away fast and I still don't tell!" The cue for students is the word "well" which ends each verse.

Pages 20 to 22 of de la Mare's *Animal Stories* contains "The World Turned Upside Down" which also has a refrain for saying in unison. The poem is made up of nineteen couplets.

Carlson's *Picture That!* contains a poem on pages 70 and 71 called "It's Christmas!" At the end of each verse, the audience repeats the title of the poem but in a different manner, softly at first but with growing excitement. Directions are given in parenthesis after that two-word refrain in each verse.

Choral speaking can include two groups responding to each other in *dialogue* or antiphonally (the parts spoken in responsive, alternating parts). One example found on page 96 of Brewton's *Gaily We Parade* and on page 68 of *Brian Wildsmith's Mother Goose* is a rhyme whose first line is "Where are you going, my pretty maid?" The group can be divided into males and females, with the males asking the questions and the girls responding. The two talk about marrying. There are twenty-four response rhymes in Margaret Taylor's *Did You Feed My Cow?* in chapter 1, "Call and Response."

One of the easiest types of choral reading to identify and one of the most successfully used with children is *line-a-child,* in which each person says one line. Often the first or last lines or both are said in unison. "Solomon Grundy" has seven solo parts for the days of the week but the first and last two lines can be said in unison. In Rose Fyleman's "Mice" everyone says the first line "I think mice are rather nice," as well as the last line, and there are eight individual parts. Three of the many sources are ACEI's *Sung under a Silver Umbrella,* Huber's *Story and Verse for Children* and Thompson's *More Silver Pennies.* Jacobs's *Is Somewhere Always Far Away?* (p. 29) has a poem called "Wishing." There are six wishes to be spoken individually and then everyone says the last two lines together. Merriam's "Ululation," page 18 of *It Doesn't Always Have to*

Rhyme has fifteen lines for individual speaking with everyone saying the last line. The animal sounds can be said with feeling and gusto. The "Chant" on page 2 of McCord's *The Star in the Pail* has parts for eighteen animals and a narrator who says the last line of each of the six verses.

It's Raining Said John Twaining is the title rhyme in a book of Danish nursery rhymes. Eleven people stand in a line each with a slip of paper with short dialogue on it. The narrator identifies each person, who responds. Coats and one umbrella are needed to play this rhyme. One of the men is sent to buy some coats. The charm of the rhyme is in John Wett's answer because there were not enough coats to go around.

Alphabet rhymes are natural for line-a-child choral speaking. An example is "Tom Thumb's Alphabet" found in Sechrist under that name but in other sources often referred to as "A was an Archer." There are twenty-six lines to that rhyme. For more rhyming alphabet books, consult the section on "Alphabet Books in Verse" in chapter 2, "Experiencing Art through Picture Books."

Charles Causley's book *Figgie Hobbin* has several poems that can be spoken in line-a-child fashion. "Quack! said the Billy Goat" has twelve animals and a narrator. If they wish, each animal can wear a sign or a mask to show what he is. If there are no props, students can be lined up in the order in which they are to speak. Cues for students are the name of the animal in front of them. The billy goat begins. BILLY GOAT: "Quack!" NARRATOR: "said the billy goat." HEN: "Oink!" NARRATOR: "said the hen." This nonsense verse will make students laugh especially when they learn why all the animals are talking. This poem could be used to introduce other nonsense books. The same anthology contains "As I Went Down Zig Zag," which has twelve parts plus a narrator. The first line of each stanza is the same as the title. The second line is the same in each verse except for the time. The students, one at a time, say the second line and supply the missing time from 1 to 12. The narrator reads the second line "The clock striking . . . ," and the first student says "one," etc.

Another song is Zemach's *Mommy, Buy Me a China Doll*. This one is *cumulative*, as is Barbara Emberley's *Drummer Hoff*. The poem has six parts and a narrator. The narrator reads all of the story but pauses after each name so the student designated as that soldier can say his part. Example: NARRATOR: "Corporal Farrel," CORPORAL FARREL: "brought the barrel." NARRATOR: Private Parridge," PRIVATE PARRIDGE: "brought the carriage." EVERYONE: "But Drummer Hoff fired it off." Cumulative stories can also be shared by having the narrator pause and all the students say in unison what each soldier brought. Because the story is cumulative, students will learn to say the story as each segment is repeated and added to. Another favorite cumulative rhyme for which there are many sources is *The House that Jack Built*.

Like reading poems in unison, there are also many poems that are *combinations* of the types already mentioned. Suggestions for reading A. A. Milne's "Buckingham Palace" are given on pages 16 and 17 of Hughes's *Let's Enjoy Poetry*. The rhythm of the poems comes through clearly. "Five Little Rabbits" from *The Rooster Crows* by the Petershams can be spoken by six speakers and a narrator. The narrator says everything except the speaking parts of the five little rabbits who each say the brief sentence in quotation marks.

The poem "What Did You Put in Your Pocket?" from deRegniers's *Something Special* is an example of several types of choral reading. The first group asks the title question on Monday morning and the second group answers. Everyone has a chance to repeat part of the phrase's "slushy gushy pudding!" The first group repeats their chant for Tuesday and the second groups responds. Then everyone repeats the slushy phrase and adds Tuesday's phrase "icy icy water!" This poem combines dialogue or antiphonal, unison and cumulative choral reading.

"What's the Funniest Thing" also found in deRegniers's *Something Special* can inspire creative writing because children can parallel the writing by adding other adjectives. Each of the four verses is open ended and readers or listeners are asked what their funniest, saddest, noisiest or quietest things are. After the entire poem has been read, students can add their own ideas.

MAURICE SENDAK AND CHORAL SPEAKING.   Choral speaking can be effectively used to introduce Maurice Sendak's Nutshell library consisting of *Chicken Soup with Rice, Alligators All Around, Pierre,* and *One Was Johnny.* Each title is available in sound filmstrip format. Carole King also sings the song on a recording, *Really Rosie.* Music appears in the paperback *Maurice Sendak's Really Rosie Starring the Nutshell Kids.* If the 16mm film *Really Rosie* is shown first, using the books in choral reading could be a natural following.

For *Chicken Soup with Rice* the leader reads each verse plus the words "sipping once." This is the students' cue for saying in unison, "Sipping twice, sipping chicken soup with rice." In March the cue is "blowing once." The reader may wish to put each month on the board and beside the month put the cue word January—"sipping," February —"happy," etc. Then all the students can say the whole refrain together. A transparency with the month and cue on it, eliminates the need for writing the information on the board. In a class of twenty-four, two students could be assigned to answer for each month. The rhyming picture book provides an excellent example of choral speaking using a refrain.

Alligators All Around by Sendak has twenty-six parts (twenty-six letters in the alphabet.) Each student can be assigned a letter. Everyone says the last line together, which happens to be the title of the book.

In Sendak's *Pierre,* all students can say Pierre's line in unison "I don't care." Sendak's *One Was Johnny* is a counting book that goes from one to ten and from nine back to one. If only ten students are assigned, then the other children and the leader could say in unison the part between one and ten and nine and one.

SPECIALIZED BIBLIOGRAPHIC CATEGORIES

At the back of this book are two numbered bibliographies, one of multimedia (nonprint material), and one of books. The numbers below refer to those bibliographies, with the entries preceded by "M" found in the Multimedia list.

INDIVIDUAL RHYMES, STORIES AND POEMS
43, 44, 45, 64, 237, 265, 329, 330, 331, 332, 333, 334, 372, 382, 390, M394, M395, M401, 391, M396, 392, M397, M398, 393, M399, 394, M400, 409, 442, 443, 444, 445, 469, 487, 520, 542, M216, 602, 650, 651, M331, 652, 653, 677, 679, 689, 690, 691, 706, 773, 778, 779, 780, 781, 782, M216, 783, M283, 784, 785, 787, 788, 789, 858, M557, 790, 791, M613, 792, 799, 800, 801, 838, 855, 856, 857, 904, 940, 941, 958, 961, 1015, 1018, 1019, 1020, 1021, 1022, 1080, 1081, 1082, 1204, 1271, 1292, 1345, 1349, 1351, M416, 1352, 1353, 1356, 1358, 1359, 1391, 1392, 1393, 1398, 1494, 1495, 1496, 1511, 1512, 1513, 1526, 1529, 1631, M772, M773, 1641, 1646, 1647, 1649, 1652, 1655, 1657, 1708, 1727, 1737, 1739, 1789, 1804, 1823, 1824, 1826, 1827, 1828, 1829, M497, 1832, 1833, M300, 1834, M496, 1835, 1845, 1846, M738, 1939, 1940, 1949, 2007, 2216, 2226, 2300, 2301, 2305, 2344, 2357, 2378, 2451, 2456, 2473, 2487, M8, M369, 2488, M146, M147, 2530, 2532, M369, 2534, 2551, 2584, 2585, 2586, 2587, 2588, 2589, 2591, 2592, 2627, M510, M511, 2644, 2663, 2671, 2742, 2796, 2799, 2800, 2805, 2806, 2807, M236, M237, 2808, 2836, M514, M515, 2859, 2862, 2865, 2866, 2867, 2870, 2871, 2872, 2873, 2874, 2876, 2877, 2878, 2879, 2881, 2882, 2911, 2923, 2925, 2929, 2939, 3048, 3062, 3066, 3079, M195, 3080, M195, 3081, 3082, 3083, M676, 3085, 3089, 3109, 3119, 3120, 3127, 3128, M214, 3129, 3130, 3171, 3172, 3178, 3179, 3277, 3363, 3373, 3383, 3428, 3432, 3446, 3447, 3448, 3449, 3450, 3451, 3453, 3488, 3522, 3523, 3524, 3550, M495, 3557, 3570, 3571, 3573, 3574, 3609, 3658, 3669, 3688, M575, M576, 3722, 3723, 3800, 3801, 3893, 3897, 3899, 3921, 3956, 3992, 4004, 4026, 4027, 4028, 4101, 4107, 4108, 4109, 4155, 4156, 4201, M15, M16, M573, M574, 4202, M126 a & b, M573, M574, 4203, 4208, M504, M505, M573, M574 4209, M533, M534, M573, M574, 4210, 4220, 4223, 4224, M116, 4225, M117, 4227, M176, 4229, M224, 4230, M257, 4231, M175, 4232, M297, 4233, 4234, 4235, 4236, 4238, 4239, 4240, M500, 4241, 4242, 4243, 4300, 4331, 4342, 4425, 4532, 4535, 4546, 4547, 4556, M114, 4622, 4623, 4627, 4635, 4695, 4736, 4799, 4800, 4803, 4840, 4897, 4926, 5001, M338, 5005

COLLECTIONS OF POEMS AND RHYMES
M68, M118, M134, M200, M240, M241, M242, M261, M488, M491, M492, M546, M547, M548, M549, M550, M565, M600, 27, 31, 46, 47, 48, 49, 50, 62, 63, 65, 90, 91, 92, 93, 94, 95, 132, 135, 174, 177, 179, 229, 232, 233, 288, 290, 354, 356, 357, 358, 359, 360, 361, 362, 370, 371, 373, 374, 385, 408, M93, 447, 475, 481, 488, 489, 490, 494, 507, 508, 509, 549, 550, 607, 608, 609, 610, 611, 612, 613, 614, 615, 616, 617, 618, 619, 626, 627, 628, 629, 654, 680, 742, 753, 774, 775, 776, 777, 860, 869, 870, 871, 886, 900, 915, 925, 926, 927, 959, 960, 962, 963, 964, 965, 966, 967, 1023, 1065, 1066, 1067, 1068, 1069, 1070, 1071, 1072, 1073, 1074, 1075, 1076, 1077, 1078, 1079, 1093, 1287, 1288, 1289, 1303, 1312, 1314, 1316, 1344, 1354, 1357, 1360, 1372, 1382, 1383, 1410, 1429, 1430, 1470, 1471, 1472, 1473, 1474, 1475, 1476, 1479, 1559, 1579a, 1580, 1581, 1583, 1625, 1628, 1629, 1630, 1638, 1642, 1643, 1645, 1648, 1650, 1653, 1654, 1698, 1788,

1790, 1817, 1899, 1957, 1976, 1985, 1986, 1987, 2058, 2215, 2234, 2272, 2289, 2302, 2303, 2304, 2306, 2307, 2360, 2368, 2369, 2370, 2371, 2372, 2373, 2374, 2375, 2376, 2377, 2396, 2399, 2404, 2405, 2409, 2410, 2411, 2416, 2417, 2418, 2419, 2420, 2464, 2474, 2484, 2485, 2486, 2493a & b, 2494, 2505, 2506, 2507, 2508, 2509, 2510, 2511, 2512, 2513, 2514, 2549, 2568, 2572, 2603, 2604, 2710, 2756, 2766, 2791, 2814, 2815, 2816, 2817, 2818, 2819, 2820, 2824, 2860, 2861, 2863, M186, 2868, 2875, 2880, 2881, 2883, 2884, 2931, 2952, 2953, M312, 2954, 2955, 2956, 2957, 2958, 2989, 2990, 2992, 3032, 3033, 3034, 3035, 3036, 3037, 3038, 3039, 3040, 3041, 3042, 3043, 3045, 3046, 3047, 3078, M77, 3087, 3091, 3092, 3100, 3108, 3151, 3152, 3153, 3154, 3155, 3156, 3157, 3158, 3173, 3175, 3176, 3177, 3238, 3365, M118, 3366, 3368, 3369, 3372, 3406, 3408, 3409, 3413, 3415, 3424, 3426, 3427, 3437, 3455, 3457, 3458, 3465, 3469, 3470, 3471, 3472, 3473, 3474, 3475, 3476, 3481, 3485, 3486, 3587, 3488, 3489, 3490, 3491, 3492, 3493, 3494, 3495, 3496, 3497, 3498, 3499, 3500, 3501, 3502, 3503, 3504, 3527, M491, 3544, 3634, 3640, M261, 3641, 3642, 3643, 3644, 3645, 3683, 3684, 3685, 3695, 3701, 3714, 3721, 3741, 3782, 3783, 3784, 3792, 3806, 3830, 3831, 3832, 3833, 3834, 3835, 3901, 3908, 3912, 3913, 3914, 3917, 3920, 3923, 3924, 3948, 3961, 3962, 4015, 4023, 4025, 4066, M113, 4068, M113, 4168, 4169, 4206, M473, M474, 4226, 4248, 4252, 4310, 4364, 4365, 4414, 4419, 4422, 4430, 4431, 4432, 4433, 4434, 4435, 4474, 4478, M129, 4479, M129, 4480, M129, 4481, M129, 4482, M129, 4518, 4519, 4524, 2560, M610, 4561, M466, 4618, 4619, 4659, 4660, 4661, 4662, 4664, 4665, 4666, 4698, 4728, 4729, 4749, 4754, 4771, 4784, 4787, 4818, 4877, 4900, 4901, 4902, 4911, 4919, 4920, 4928, 4931, 4932, 4942, 4950.

CHAPTER FIVE

Playing Stories
Live Action and with Puppets

CHAPTER OBJECTIVES

1. To enrich the curriculum in history, geography, literature, reading, art, music, and mathematics with creative activities.
2. To show examples of activities that help children express creativity in a variety of ways: making puppets and masks, writing scripts, improvising, role playing, and playing out stories.
3. To increase communication skills through projects involving writing and speaking.
4. To encourage creative writing skills in teachers and students by having them create pantomimes, plays and puppet scripts.
5. To present projects in which students can make individual creative contributions yet work together to prepare a unified project.
6. To teach students the difference between reality and pretending.
7. To provide teachers, public librarians, school media specialists, and other persons who work with children with techniques and sources for playing stories.
8. To provide teachers, public librarians, school media specialists, and other persons who work with children with techniques and sources for writing and producing puppet shows.
9. To provide teachers, public librarians, school media specialists, and other persons who work with children with techniques and sources for pantomimes and fingerplays.
10. To identify and list sources of plays for children or puppets that are based on children's literature.

TECHNIQUES FOR USING MEDIA INTRODUCED IN THIS CHAPTER

1. Provide for quieting activities to precede special events during which children are to listen.
2. Introduce number concepts through finger plays.
3. Provide exercise times with action songs and games, finger plays and playing stories that involve motion.
4. Improve visual literacy for primary students by telling stories using shadows and flannel board images.
5. Ask intermediate students to make shadow outlines or flannel board figures to represent characters in stories, and encourage some of them to retell a story to younger children (at home or at school) using

the figures.

6. Pantomime poetry, songs, nonverbal picture books, and action sections of stories to introduce these to a group of children.

7. Introduce books to children by having them pantomime while selections from the book are read, in original or adapted form.

8. Have students develop characters and plot by introducing dialogue to go with the pantomime.

9. Permit students to express emotions while playing out, pantomiming or role playing stories.

10. Ask children to express emotions while playing or pantomiming characters in books: embarrassment, humiliation, joy, jealousy, anger, unhappiness, disappointment, surprise, excitement, dismay, worry, anticipation, happiness, accomplishment, puzzlement, and self-satisfaction.

11. Ask students to pantomime or play parts of a filmstrip they have seen that is based on a story from a book.

12. Use one book in a series by such authors as Alexander, Lobel, Minarik, Sharmat, and Zion in a creative way, with flannelboard, pantomime, or playing out, live or with puppets, as a means of introducing other books in the series, or by those authors.

13. Talk about the six major parts of a story before playing it, but after reading it aloud, and have students list all events in chronological order and see if all the parts are accounted for—that is, match up with the events.

14. Discuss the following character traits when developing a character to play live or project with puppets: physical appearance; how do others see him and how does he see himself; interests; occupation; personality quirks or mannerisms.

15. Encourage students to write plays for live actors or puppets in lieu of book reports.

16. Develop and encourage a sense of humor in students by having them create plays that are parodies of folklore or literary classics.

17. Improve student social and group work skills by having groups produce plays.

18. Introduce the universal concept of a circus with music, finger puppets, and pantomime.

19. Review parts of the orchestra by pantomiming various instruments while playing a recording of each instrument playing.

20. After reading stories of legendary heroes, have students create puppet shows or plays based on the characters, creating new legendary situations for the heroes or heroines.

21. Culminate a geography or history lesson by putting some of the historical figures or places into a play to act live or with puppets.

22. Prepare for creative experiences with warm-up exercises.

23. Find individual plays to introduce biographies and other study of historical characters such as Paul Revere or Harriet Tubman.

24. Have students read play scripts aloud to overcome self-consciousness and encourage expressive reading.
25. Encourage students to read several versions of a story before deciding upon one to play out. Relate other stories to those played.
26. Have students draw a picture of the character each is to play.
27. Establish a collection of commercial handpuppets and have them available to check out.
28. Integrate art and literature by having students make a variety of puppets, masks, drawings, and costumes for creative dramatic activities in the library media center or in the classroom.
29. Show students and explain the workings of and advantages of, the different types of puppets. Encourage puppet making from many kinds of materials.
30. Encourage students to use their math and science skills, as well as developing manual dexterity, by making stages with sound and lighting for puppet theatre.
31. Introduce a network of other stories every time a story is shared through puppets, pantomime, fingerplays, or live action.

FINGERPLAYS AND ACTION SONGS.   Fingerplays are rhymes or chants that involve children by allowing them to participate by clapping hands, wiggling fingers or toes, or moving other body parts. Scott and Thompson, in their collection *Rhymes for Fingers and Flannelboards*, list on pp. 2 and 3 six values of fingerplays which include (1) building vocabulary, (2) complementing reading, (3) aiding language development, (4) facilitating self-expression, (5) teaching number concepts, and (6) providing relaxation. Suggestions for teaching fingerplays appear on page 5, and also on pages 8 and 9 of Salisbury's *Finger Fun*.

Glazer, in his "Author's Introduction" to *Eye Winker, Tom Tinker, Chin Chopper, and Do Your Ears Hang Low?, 50 More Musical Fingerplays* includes information about Friedrich Froebel, the father of kindergarten, and Emily Poulsson, a pioneer in collecting fingerplays. Froebel and Poulsson are cited also in an introductory "For Mothers and Teachers" in *Fingerplays and Action Rhymes* by Jacobs.

Although Glazer calls all of his one hundred songs musical fingerplays, some of them are really action songs. The distinction between a fingerplay and an action song is not great. Fingerplays usually involve simple movements for preschoolers that can be accomplished without moving far from their chairs, desks, or seating pattern during story hours. Simple fingerplays can be done by just one child in bed or on a lap. Action songs require complicated actions and involve music. Heinig and Stillwell give definitions for fingerplays and for action songs on pages 23 and 24 of their book *Creative Dramatics for the Classroom Teacher*, and also examples of single-action poetry which involve a single movement. A definition of, and examples for, action *games* appear on pages 24 and 25, and action stories on pages 25 and 26.

Some of Glazer's fingerplays set to music are "I'm a Little Tea-Pot," "Where Is Thumbkin?" "Grandma's Spectacles," and "Pat-a-Cake." "The

Mulberry Bush" and "Old MacDonald," included in Glazer's books, are really action songs.

"The Bus" in Grayson's *Let's Do Fingerplays* is in fact an action song in which students pantomime simple actions like wheels going round and round, horns going beep, paying fare, bouncing over bumps, etc. The song appears in several books including Larrick's *The Wheels of the Bus Go Round and Round*. Numerous other books with action songs are included in the chapter, "Enhancing Books through Music." Books included are Bley's *Best Singing Games*; Fowke's *Sally Go Round the Sun*; Glazer's two titles; Wheeler's *What Shall We Do and Allee Galloo!*, *Play Songs and Singing Games for Young Children*; and two books by Winn, *The Fireside Book of Children's Songs* and *The Fireside Book of Fun and Games*.

"The Farmer in the Dell" is really an action game, also available as a picture book, and could be played after Duvoisin's *Petunia* is read aloud. Other books about Petunia and her farm animal friends are *Petunia; I Love You, Petunia's Treasure; Petunia's Christmas; Petunia and the Song; Petunia, Beware!; Petunia's Trip;* and *Our Veronica Goes to Petunia's Farm*.

Words but no music appear for seven action games on pages 100 and 101 of Moore's *Preschool Story Hour:* "Ring Around the Rosie" an action game, and "Did You Ever See a Lassie" and "Looby Loo."

Silverstein's poem "The Boa Constrictor" in *Where the Sidewalk Ends*, is an excellent example of an action poem, and can be used with Ungerer's picture book about the boa constrictor named *Crictor*.

There are many sources of fingerplays. *Rhymes for Fingers and Flannelboards* contains fingerplays by subject: seven on birthdays, eight on the circus and zoo, eleven on city sights, twenty-three about the farm, twenty-eight from other lands, fifteen fun with numbers, thirty-two holidays, eighteen home and family, twenty-one in fields and woods, five make-believe, twelve Mother Goose, nine rhymes for active times and nine rhymes for quiet times, twenty-two about seasons, and eleven on land.

Grayson's *Let's Do Fingerplays* contains twenty fingerplays about the child from top to toe, thirty about dressing up, seventeen things that go, twenty-three animal antics, one about the family, ten about the world outdoors, eighteen big people and little people, thirty counting and counting out, nineteen around the house, ten noise makers, and twenty-three holidays and special occasions.

Seventeen fingerplays are found in *Finger Rhymes* by the Taylors. Nine of the twenty rhymes in the Taylors's *Number Rhymes* include music. Nine fingerplays are included in Tashjian's *Juba This and Juba That!* and *With a Deep Sea Smile*.

Steiner and Pond's *Finger Play Fun* contains eleven "quiet down" fingerplays; twenty counting; twenty me, myself, and I; seventeen animals; twenty-three people; twenty-one the world; thirteen Halloween, and eight for Christmas.

Poulsson's *Finger Plays for Nursery and Kindergarten*, first published in 1889, contains eighteen fingerplays set to music. Twenty-two fingerplays, fourteen songs and three rhythms are included in Salisbury's *Finger Fun, Songs and*

Rhythms for the Very Young. Twenty-nine fingerplays with photos appear in *Finger Plays and Action Rhymes* by Jacobs.

Fingerplays are also included in Bauer's *Handbook for Storytellers* (pp. 300–06) and in *Partners in Play—A Step-by-Step Guide to Imaginative Play in Children,* (pp. 32–33) by the Singers. More fingerplays are included in Cole's *I Saw a Purple Cow and 100 Other Recipes for Learning,* and on two sound recording called *Finger Play.*

Yamaguchi's *Finger Plays,* available in a paperback edition, was designed so young children can look at the pictures and imitate the finger plays. The first sixteen pages are a rhyme about baby's activities. A rhyme about two black magpies occupies the next twelve pages. The last eight pages are about an apple tree.

There are over four hundred finger plays with some stories and games for preschoolers in *Ring a Ring O' Roses,* a booklet published by the Flint Michigan Public Library. Finger plays are arranged in categories: animal kingdom (in the water, in the woods, on the farm), around the house, child from top to toe (active time, dressing up, my family, quiet time), circus and zoo, holidays, insects, land of make believe, people we know (carpenters, cobblers, friends, Indians, soldiers), things that go, things that grow, toyland, wonders of the seasons. Suggestions for playing out each rhyme are given and a first line index is included. The list of forty-six stories to tell and play and another list of fourteen favorite folk tales makes this booklet, with its large number of finger plays, a necessity even without the inducement of its small price tag. Fourteen fingerplays taken from that collection have been illustrated by Marc Brown in *Finger Rhyme.*

Fingerplays are especially useful during preschool story hours. Children are expected to sit quietly and listen while stories are being told; however it's asking too much of preschoolers and primary children to sit for long without letting off steam. Fingerplays and action songs allow children to do this. Many of the action songs and games encourage children to move about the room and get rid of excess energy before listening to another story.

Fingerplays can have a direct relationship to the stories being told. Use the fingerplays "Snowflakes" or "Snow Men" on page 48 of Grayson's *Let's Do Fingerplays* to accompany a story program of picture books and filmstrips about winter and snow. Keats's *A Snow Day* is one of the stories which can be introduced as a book, filmstrip, or film.

"Five Little Firemen," page 25 of Scott and Thompson's book or page 53 of Grayson's book, can be used between the sharing of the non-fiction *What It's Like to Be a Fireman* by Shay and Green's *What They Do, Policemen and Firemen.* The same fingerplay would be used to bridge from the nonfiction books about firemen to the fiction books such as *The Little Fire Engine* by Lenski, *The Little Fire Engine* by Greene, or *Hercules* by Gramatky. *Hercules* is also available as a sound filmstrip. A story program could include Shay's book, followed by a visit from a fireman. Then Lenski's book could be read, followed by the fingerplay and the filmstrip by Gramatky. Any combination of the above stories could be used.

Greene's *What They Do, Policemen and Firemen* could be read in between two fingerplays found on page 25 of Scott and Thompson's book, "Five Strong Policemen" and "Five Little Firemen."

"Halloween Witches," and "Witch," found in Grayson's book or Steiner and Pond's *Finger Play Fun* (which has thirteen Halloween entries), could be used between Halloween stories. Also use *A Woggle of Witches* by Adams, or books about the ghost *Georgie* by Bright, or books about the witch *Dorrie* by Combs. Some of the Dorrie titles are *Dorrie and the Blue Witch, Dorrie and the Goblin,* and *Dorrie and the Haunted House.* Books about Georgie include *Georgie, Georgie to the Rescue,* and *Georgie and the Robbers.*

Giving students a change of pace between stories is only one way of using fingerplays during story hours. Some fingerplays can be used to "settle down" for the story hour: three "Fingerplays to Quiet" are included on page 93 of Moore's *Pre-School Story Hour;* "Grandma's Glasses" is a popular quieting fingerplay from the same book with two verses—one about grandma and one about grandpa. The fingerplay "I'm a Little Puppet Clown," page 132 of Scott and Thompson's book, lets students pretend they are marionettes becoming stiff, tall, or limp, and could be used between scenes of a puppet play or between two puppet shows. If several activities are planned between shows, use this fingerplay last because it has a quieting effect.

QUIETING ACTIVITIES.   Quieting activities can serve to calm a group and settle children to listen before beginning to read aloud, tell a story, etc. They are also good following strenuous and lively physical or mental exercise periods that leave children with a natural high, such as recess, gym, or even a lively creative dramatics session.

There are many types of quieting activities: fingerplays, relaxing exercises, listening to stories and poems that soothe by their rhythm or are about sleepy people or animals, or playing out a story that ends on a quiet note.

The last line of "Two Mother Pigs" is ". . . And squealed and squealed till they went to sleep." That fingerplay is found in Grayson's *Let's Do Fingerplays* and in *Ring a Ring O'Roses* published by the Flint (Michigan) Public Library. "Let Your Hands Clap," found on page 90 of Grayson's book ends with the words "Quiet Be" as do the following: "Quiet Be" on page 38 of Steiner and Pond's *Finger Play Fun;* and another version of "Clap, Clap, Clap" on page 35 of the Flint Public Library's booklet.

Fingerplays not included in the section "Quiet Time" of *Finger Play Fun* are also useful as quieters: "My Turtle," "Three Frogs," "If I Were a Bird," "Little Puppies and Kittens," "Naptime," "The Lambs," "This Little Cow," "Two Mother Pigs," "My House," "Animals," "We Can Jump," "Baby's Bath," "Baby's Nap," "Helping Hands at Home," "I'm a Little Puppet Clown," "Five Little Snowmen," "Gently Falling Leaves," "I Am a Snowman," "Melting Snowman," "The Snowman," "Quiet Time," "By Gum! By Gum!" "The Farmyard," "The Top," and "Ten Little Indians." Nine rhymes for quiet times appear in Scott and Thompson's *Rhymes and Fingers and Flannelboards.*

Children who act like falling leaves or melting ice can become relaxed! "I Am a Little Puppet Clown" is excellent for relaxing, because the marionette has its strings loosened so that its head, arms, legs, and body relax until it is asleep. It appears on page 132 of Scott and Thompson's book and page 63 of the Flint Public Library's booklet; when children loosen up like the puppet, this fingerplay becomes a relaxing exercise.

Pages 1 through 26 of Henricks and Roberts's *The Second Centering Book, More Awareness Activities for Children, Parents and Teachers,* contains activities to relax. Exercise four, "Centering Body and Mind," is especially useful.

In Kroll's *If I Could Be My Grandmother,* a little girl pretending to be her grandmother, reads two stories at bedtime to her granddaughter. Not all bedtime stories or stories that serve as quieting activities need to be about quiet subjects or children and animals that fall asleep, but here are some that do contain those elements.

Elkin's *The Loudest Noise in the World* is about Prince Hulla-Baloo who wanted the loudest noise in the world for his birthday. Everyone in the world agreed to yell at the same time to fulfull Prince Hulla-Baloo's request, but one woman said that she wouldn't be able to hear everyone else if she was yelling so she would open her mouth but not make a sound. The woman told her husband, and he told others until everyone in the kingdom decided to do the same thing. When it was time to make the noise, all two billion people listened for the loudest noise in the world—but heard only absolute silence. Unexpectedly, Prince Hulla-Baloo enjoyed the quiet. For the first time he heard birds sing, leaves whisper, and water ripple. The town of Hub-Bub changed from the noisiest city to become "The City of Quiet."

Seven separate stories are included in Lobel's easy reader, *Mouse Tales.* "Clouds" on pages 17 to 24, shows how clouds make pictures, and is a relaxing story. His *Owl at Home* includes "Owl and the Moon" in which the moon followed owl home and peeked in the window when owl went to sleep. Marshall's *What's the Matter with Carruthers?* is about an overtired animal who has forgotten to hibernate. *Twenty-Six Lively Letters: Making an ABC Quiet Book* by Williams and Grundmann could also be included.

Horatio, the cat in Clymer's *Leave Horatio Alone,* liked everything quiet. He ran away in anger, but learned from his experience with another family of children who dressed him in doll's clothes that his own family was not so bad after all.

There are several stories suitable for playing that end quietly. Eckert's *Tonight at Nine* is good to play before resting because in the last verse all the animal musicians are fast asleep after their concert. In Ginsburg's *Which Is the Best,* a rooster and a goose argue about the best place to sleep. Several other animals they consult have different opinions. The crow thought a tree was best; the pig liked a puddle; the mole his burrow; the squirrel a hollow of a tree; the carp a quiet brook; and the beetle likes to sleep under the bark of a tree. The kitty was asleep and didn't answer, so the other animals fell asleep also. The story can be played in groups of nine with actions to suit, and additional animals can be added so each class member is included. Research would be necessary to find out how and where the additional animals slept. Hazen's *Where Do Bears Sleep?* is also about places where various animals and children sleep.

Several stories for younger children are either about animals who are sleepy or tell how animals go to sleep. Warburg's *Curl Up Small* is a lullaby about a baby fish, bird, bear and child who set out to see the world but got sleepy. Brown's *The Sleepy Little Lion* met other animals but became very sleepy. Another book by Margaret Wise Brown is *A Child's Good Night Book*. Birds, fish, wild monkeys, sailboats, cars, trucks, and various animals all go to sleep. Even children "stop thinking and whistling and talking." Animals, insects, and children went to sleep in Zolotow's *Sleepy Book*, also available in sound filmstrip format. Coatsworth's *Good Night* is a prose poem, in which a star saw animal mothers and babies, including kittens, going to sleep. A little boy, tucked in for the night, left his bed to find one of the kittens to take to bed with him.

Animals and children fall asleep at the end of several books. The Fog Maiden tucked the children into bed and kissed them asleep after taking them adventuring in de Paola's *When Everyone Was Fast Asleep*. Sadie was asleep at the end of her song in *What Sadie Sang* by Rice. The chapter in Minarik's *Little Bear's Visit* called "Not-Tired" shows Little Bear exhausted from his visit with his grandparents and asleep by the time his parents came to get him.

Not all children or animals fall asleep that easily. The feelings of some children are reflected in Barrett's *I Hate to Go to Bed*. Two brothers have trouble getting to sleep in Sharmat's *Goodnight Andrew, Goodnight Craig*. Bedtime is also a problem for the famous badger Frances in Hoban's *Bedtime for Frances*. Introduce Montresor's *Bedtime* with a sound filmstrip.

Marzollo's *Close Your Eyes* has a father encouraging a reluctant child to go to sleep. The rhyme and the illustrations have a soothing effect. Jeffers also illustrated the picture book of the lullaby *All the Pretty Little Horses*. Sources of music for that song are given in the chapter on "Enhancing Books through Music" in a section called "Activity Songs and Games." Engvick's *Lullabies and Night Songs* illustrated by Sendak contains numerous lullabies and is one of several books containing lullabies.

Untermeyer's *Rainbow in the Sky* contains sixteen poems about quietness including "Little Sandman's Song" (pp. 431-32), adapted by Untermeyer from the German and "Days End" (page 433), by Henry Newbolt. "Cradle Songs," in Sechrist's *One Thousand Poems for Children* (pp. 43-53), has twenty-seven poems. "Rock-a-Bye, Baby" on page 46 contains two verses, the first of which is unfamiliar. Rossetti's "Lullaby" appears on page 49. Stevenson's "Bed in Summer" appears on page 82 and begins a section about bedtime.

There are two kinds of poems that can serve as a tranquilizing activity—those with a soothing rhythm and those with a quieting subject. Consult poetry indexes for poems with quieting subjects. Brewton's *Index to Poetry for Children and Young People, 1970-75*, has six poems listed under "quiet," two under "resting," and four under "good-night poems," There are poems about "night," about "bedtime," two and a half columns about "dreams," about "lullabies," and about "sleep." Other poetry indexes are listed in the chapter "Enjoying Poetry."

Dawn by Schulevitz, based on a Chinese poem, is about the beginning of day, but projects a tranquil mood through black and blue watercolors with pink highlights. Field's *Wynken, Blynken and Nod*, a favorite, is illustrated in sleepy blues. The picture book with Cooney's illustrations is also available as a sound filmstrip. "How Quiet?" on page 44 of Jacob and Johnson's *Is Somewhere Always Far Away?* could also be used.

"Susie's Sleepy Time" by Marsh, in *The Read-to-Me Storybook* (pp. 142-45) is a very good story to tell at bedtime.

WARMUPS.   A five-minute warm-up period with the whole group involved in the same activity is useful for breaking the ice before beginning a creative dramatic session. One good exercise has pairs of students playing catch with an object that changes in size, weight, and texture. "Playing tennis" also involves pairs. Players can become a knight in heavy armor, or a famous professional player, or a clown, or a bear, or an elephant. Or divide the group into three's and ask students to jump rope while you read rhymes from Worstell's *Jump the Rope Jingles*. Divide the entire group in half and ask them to play tug of war.

Another warm-up activity can be played by walking in a circle. Ask children to pretend they are walking in their bare feet on glass, hot sand, across a mucky-bottomed stream, or on freshly cut grass. Ask students to walk in shoes that are too tight, the last mile of a fifty mile trip, across a tightrope, on the narrow ledge of a building, down a pirate's plank, or through high grass and weeds.

Warm-up activities can be related to books. Ask primary students to go for a ride in Burt Dow's rowboat (McCloskey), or *Noah's Ark* (Spier), *Little Toot* (Gramatky), *The Little Engine That Could* (Piper), *The Christmas Whale* (Duvoisin), or in Miss Esta Maude's old black car or her new, shiny red car (Cummings). Intermediate students can be asked to ride with Miss Pickerell when she goes to Mars, the arctic, or underseas (MacGregor). Other space tours are available with Flyball the Space Cat (Todd) or with Mr. Bass on a *Wonderful Flight to the Mushroom Planet* (Cameron). Students can ride on James's Giant Peach (Dahl), on Pecos Bill's Cyclone (Felton), or on a flying carpet from the *Arabian Nights*. Flying on a broomstick with *A Woggle of Witches* is also exciting. One could fly up with Mary Poppins (Travers) and her umbrella or to go up in a basket held up with balloons, with Professor Sherman and his *Twenty-One Balloons* (DuBois). Children can also take the bumpy ride down into the Grand Canyon on a burro, *Brighty* by Henry. A favorite horse is Farley's *Black Stallion*. Riding horses is not the same, as the ride depends on the horse. Riding Pie as Velvet Brown winning the Grand Natonal (Bagnold) is very different from riding *Black Beauty* (Sewell) after she became a broken-down cart horse.

Students can try on imaginary hats belonging to book characters. They could pretend to be the monkeys trying on hats in Slobodkina's *Caps for Sale* or try on one of Bartholomew Cubbins's *Five Hundred Hats*, by Dr. Seuss. A hat that makes a person become a special character is worn in Rey's *Curious George* by the "Man in the Yellow Hat." A very different character in a yellow hat stole the Pye children's dog Ginger (Estes). Hats belonging to witches, such as *The Littlest Witch* (Massey), provide a character change. The Japanese *Magic Listening Cap* by Uchida allows people to understand the language of animals.

Passing objects from person to person can be played in a limited amount of space, even by children sitting at their desks, standing or sitting in a circle. The objects passed around in this exercise can come from children's books.

Primary students can pass around Cinderella's glass slipper (Perrault), the duck *Ping* (Flack), the mouse *Norman the Doorman* (Freeman), or an egg from *The Egg Tree* (Milhouse). The full honey pot from *Winnie the Pooh* by Milne provides a sticky object for passing carefully! Try handing around *Frog and Toad Together* (Lobel); *Timothy Turtle* (Davis) would be easier to handle.

Intermediate students could pass around *Harriet the Spy's* notebook (Fitzhugh), a pancake from *Pancakes Paris* (Bishop), or *The Enormous Egg* (Butterworth). One of Lassie's puppies (Knight) would be a lively handful as would Amos the mouse from *Ben and Me* (Lawson), or Uncle Analdis from *Rabbit Hill* (Lawson). *The Pet Skunk* (George) and Little Eddie's goat Gardenia (Haywood) might have special problems of acceptance. One of *Homer Price's* doughnuts might not make it all the way around the circle (McCloskey), but Robinson Crusoe's last meal (Defoe) would have a better chance. Tinkerbell (Barrie); *Thumbelina* (Andersen); the borrower, Arietty by Norton; or a friend of Gulliver's from Lilliput (Swift) would all probably be handled with care as would *Charlotte's Web* (White). Some objects that would require different handling would be Steele's *Buffalo Knife*, Tom Sawyer's whitewash brush (Clemens) John Henry's hammer (Felton), Shad's copper-toed boots (DeAngeli), Hans Brinker's silver skates (Dodge), seeds from Johnny Appleseed (Douglas), Janey Larkin's *Blue Willow* plate by Gates, the *Gammage Cup* (Kendall), the *Matchlock Gun* (Edmonds), and the doll *Hitty* (Field).

PRETENDING.   Pretending should be part of every child's life. Pretending is a healthy activity, but not being able to tell the difference between reality and make-believe is not. Fred Rogers of *Mr. Roger's Neighborhood* on PBS television rides a trolley back and forth between the real world and the world of make believe. The 1964 Caldecott winner, Evaline Ness's *Sam, Bangs and Moonshine* is the perfect story to use to discuss the difference between reality and make believe (moonshine) because its main character, Samantha, has a problem with it. Her inability to tell the difference between stories and fibs is almost responsible for the death of a young boy.

There are many books in which animals and children pretend they are someone or something else. It is a worthwhile activity for children to put themselves in someone else's role, to play out stories in which they are someone or something else—as long as they realize it is make believe.

In McKee's *123456789 Benn*, Mr. Benn put on a prison uniform in a costume shop and found himself in prison. In *Mr. Benn-Red Knight*, Mr. Benn, trying to find a costume for a fancy dress party, found that the door to the fitting room was a door to a magic land where Mr. Benn fought a dragon. Students pretending they are Mr. Benn can pantomime or play out what they will be when they come out the magical door of the dressing room.

Ask children to choose a way of entering a land of make believe as the first step in a creative writing experience. Or do this as an oral exercise. Ask one child in the room to choose the method of entering the magic land; ask a second child to decide who the characters are who enter the land; and so on through the same steps that individual students would follow in a written assignment.

Steps in building the story are (1) *Who* are the main characters? (2) *What* are these characters going to do? (3) *Where* are they going? (4) *When* are they going? (5) *How* are the characters going to get there? (6) *Why* are the characters going there? (7) *How long* will they be there? (8) *What happens* to them there? (9) *Why* do they leave? (10) *How* do the characters leave? These steps allow entry to a magic land via a special key, door, mirror, or other means. After the activity there, the characters return to the real world via the magical means which brings the story to its conclusion. Hardly realizing it, the students have constructed a story with an introduction, characters, setting, rising action, climax, falling action, and conclusion.

Intermediate students could begin their journey with the wardrobe through which Lucy, Susan, Peter and Edmund entered Narnia in Lewis's fantasy, *The Lion, the Witch and the Wardrobe*. The first chapter, on "Introducing Books" lists about twenty means of entering the fourth dimension such as a blue stone, a whispering shell, fog, toys, a mirror, a portrait, a tesseract, a time machine, an old house, a special garden, a pier, a harp, a horn, an elevator, statues in a museum, and, of course, the wardrobe.

Not all activities using books in which a character pretends to be someone else are that complicated. In Kellott's *Much Bigger Than Martin*, there are nonverbal scenes to discuss or act out, feelings and emotions to discuss. Martin's smaller brother felt that Martin got the best of everything because he was bigger. Four nonverbal scenes appear on two pages with the caption "Then he makes me play his stupid games," showing the younger brother with the least desirable part. Martin was the pirate captain or the Indian chief, while the younger brother walked the plank or was burned at the stake. When the tables are turned, the younger brother pretended he was a giant and bigger than Martin. The story can encourage students to talk about how they feel about their size, fairness, selfishness and other problems. Students can also pretend the games in the book.

In Willard's *The Well-Mannered Balloon*, Jason painted a face on a balloon and it came to life. The chapter "Experiencing Art through Picture Books," has a section called "Drawings Come to Life" with similar fantasies. Children can paint a face on a balloon and then carry on a make-believe conversation with whomever it becomes. Such conversations can be very liberating, especially for shy children.

Another book by Willard can stimulate discussion about the difference between reality and make believe. *Stranger's Bread* can also be played out. Anatole was sent to get bread, but met a fox, a rabbit, a sheep, and a bear who ate the bread. He was not believed when he returned.

The following books about animal characters can be used to initiate discussions about pretending. In McLeod's *The Bear's Bicycle* a make-believe bear accompanied a boy on a bicycle trip. While the boy observed the courtesy rules of bike riding, the invisible bear who did not met with disaster. In discussing safety and courtesy rules of bike riding, the children can identify with the boy and not the bear.

Ormondroyd's *Broderick*, a mouse who lived in a broomcloset, judged books by their cover—he ate the bindings. He read some of them too and found several heroes he could pretend to be.

Jeschke's *Sidney* was a chicken who was given a fox mask and straw ears and a tail by the fairy chicken. Sidney began to look more and more like a fox so the foxes did not try to eat him. However, when Sidney was homesick and wanted to go home, his family would not accept him. Henrietta Chicken in the same story pretended she was a lion, rabbit, a sheep, and a duck.

Victor Mouse read a book about a moose and thought it was a strange way to pronounce mouse, so he pretended to be a moose in Berson's *A Moose Is Not a Mouse*.

Hubert, a barn cat, is Annixter's *Cat That Clumped*. The other cats did not like his pretending to be a horse but the rats loved Hubert, gave him food, and felt safe because they knew when he was coming.

In Wright's *Kitten's Little Boy*, a kitten imagined himself to be a tiger, a lion, and an Egyptian statue, while Fischer's *Pitschi; the Kitten That Always Wanted to Be Something Else* pretended to be a rooster, goat, duck, and rabbit.

The rabbit in Zakhoder's *Rosachak* wondered what it would be like to be a bird, fox, hedgehog, bear and elk.

Kraus's *Owliver* liked to act. Emotions expressed in the book are joy, anger, fear, sadness, goodness, hate, and love.

A child in Paterson's *If I Were a Toad* wanted to be twelve birds or animals. His daddy wished he were a bear so he could give bear hugs.

Martha's friend Ivy pretended that she was a *Changeling* in Snyder's book of the same title. (A changeling is someone stolen by the fairies as an infant and placed in someone else's home.) Because Ivy came from a disreputable family, she wanted to pretend she really belonged to another one. In another book by Snyder, a migrant girl entered an old mansion and found *The Velvet Room* in which she imagined the girl who once lived there. The girl in Snyder's *The Princess and the Giants* imagined that she was a princess.

It was a six-year-old who pretended that he was a lion trainer, astronaut, clown, knight, Robin Hood, baseball star, cowboy, pilot, and horse in Cretan's *Me, Myself and I*, and later how it feels to fly like a plane, run like a horse, or to move inside music.

Christopher and Gray played they were pirates before Bodger the dog was *Lost in the Storm* in Carrick's book. Alec's *Sand Castle* (Russ) was built in the imagination of a small boy. In Taylor's *Henry Explores the Jungle*, Henry read a book on jungles, pretended he was on safari in the woods, and really did help catch a tiger and earn a free ticket to the circus. In Sharmat's *Rex*, a boy pretended he was a dog because his mother was angry with him. Tina put on a yellow dress and pretended to be a sunflower to make her grandmother laugh in Baldwin's *Sunflowers for Tina*.

In Kroll's *If I Could Be My Grandmother*, a little girl pretended she was her grandmother. Gaedert's *Noisy Nancy Norris* liked to pretend she was various animals or people—all of them noisy.

Loretta, in Fregosi's *The Mammoth, the Owl and the Crab*, pretended that she was three hibernating animals so she wouldn't have to get up in the morning.

Balet's *Joanjo, a Portugese Tale* is about the Sampaio family. Joanjo had a dream—he worked in a shop and made enough money to have his own store, and later was chosen mayor, governor, and then king. The real king sent Joanjo to prison and was ready to shoot him when Joanjo woke up.

In Fleisher's *Quilts in the Attic*, two small sisters, Rosie and Natasha went to the attic and imagined they were various characters when they draped themselves in quilts. Alexander's *I'll Be the Horse If You'll Play with Me* is another book in which siblings play together. Some of the activities pretended are cops and robbers and horse and wagon.

PANTOMIME—BACKGROUND READINGS.   Pantomiming can be one of the simplest of dramatic exercises or, as perfected by Marcel Marceau, high art. It is often the first type of dramatic exercises attempted by a group, and can be used as a warm-up exercise before playing out a story. *Marcel Marceau's Alphabet Book* by Mendoza shows Marceau pantomiming from Awakening to Zzzzz's.

There are many readings for those who wish to learn more about pantomime. Hunt's *Pantomime: the Silent Theatre* gives history, from Greek, Roman, and medieval times, and includes information about mysteries, clowns, magicians, silent movies, television, modern mime, and a picture of Marcel Marceau.

McCaslin's *Creative Dramatics in the Classroom* gives helpful information on such topics as class size, length of class period, playing space, imagination, concentration, sense images, performing an action, mood and feelings, characterization for pantomime, and improvisation, in which characters speak. "Improvisation" is also the title of the chapter that follows the chapter on "Pantomime," of Crossup's *Children and Dramatics*. The same idea of pantomimes preceding actions with sound appears in Hennings's *Smiles, Nods and Pauses, Activities to Enrich Children's Communication Skills*.

Heinig and Stillwell devote three chapters to pantomime in their book, *Creative Dramatics for the Classroom Teacher*. The chapter, "Designing Creative Pantomime Activities," defines creative pantomime and discusses the degree of elaboration, technique, and the participation of the leader. Heinig and Stillwell suggest that ideas be shared in unison first. Seven steps for planning the ideas are given on page 159 of chapter 9 of their book (this chapter also includes the important warning that having one child at a time pantomime an idea in front of a class should be avoided). Subjects included in this chapter are team pantomime, sequence games, continuous pantomime, small group pantomime, count-freeze pantomimes, and guiding nonverbal communication. Twenty simple activities and eleven pantomime skits and stories are also included.

Pantomime games are found in Carlson's *Act It Out*, as are pantomime plays and tableaux. There are over fifty ideas for pantomimes in Olfson's *You Can Act!* The best book for providing pantomime ideas is Howard's *Pantomimes*,

Charades and Skits. It is a gold mine of suggestions and contains over a thousand charade topics. There are forty "Handy Pantomimes" such as opening a drawer, removing an object, and closing the drawer or unscrewing a light bulb and replacing it with a new one. The list begins with pasting a stamp on a letter and ends up with saddling and bridling a horse. Other examples are eighteen animal actions (p. 30), sixty occupations (pp. 32-33), thirty sounds (p. 35), thirty words with similar spellings (pp. 66-67), fifty familiar similes (pp. 67-68), and twenty-five paired skits (p. 96). The paired skits include a dancer with an awkward partner and a lion tamer with a ferocious lion.

Six suggestions for developing the skills of pantomime are given in Ziskind's *Telling Stories to Children.* Steps for teachers to follow in teaching children to pantomime simple story dramatization are included in the *Creative Dramatics Handbook* prepared by the School District of Philadelphia.

A pamphlet, *A Prelude to Play-Acting,* by Lane and Hartelius includes information on expression and movement, exploring the senses, handling imaginary objects, experiencing different environments. The mime drama included in the book is a circus. There is also information about costumes, props, and an eleven-step outline of action. There are parts for thirty-two students and more can be added as needed.

PANTOMIMING PARTS OF CHILDREN'S BOOKS.   After reading a story to children, ask them to pantomime some parts of the book. One of the best to use is the picture book *How the Devil Got His Due* by Berson. The devil hired a servant to do his work for him with the understanding that whoever complained first would receive ten blows with a stick. The boy, without complaining, cut wood, pitched hay, fed animals, cleaned stables, repaired the roof, harvested the grapes, weeded the vegetable garden, and scrubbed the floors. When the boy went home for a vacation, his brother came to take his place, and cleverly followed all of the directions given to him in literal terms. Asked, for example, to sew up the holes in the devil's clothes, the boy sewed up the armholes, neckhole, as well as other functional openings. When the devil complained, he received ten blows with a stick. Children can have fun pantomiming all of the tasks performed.

Another story with activities to pantomime is de Paola's *Strega Nona.* Anthony had to sweep the house, wash dishes, weed garden, pick vegetables, feed and milk the goat, and fetch water, but he was told that he must not touch the pasta pot. Naturally, he did and the result was that pasta slithered all over the town. Children can pantomime with the Juggler of Notre Dame in de Paola's *The Clown of God: an Old Story* which is also available as a sound filmstrip.

No matter what the children said to their grandfather, he said "could be worse," the title of a picture book by Stevenson. Then grandfather told a tall tale to which the children retaliated by saying "could be worse." There's lots of action that could easily be pantomimed by a group of primary students. In one of his escapades, grandfather got stuck inside a snowball which rolled down a mountain, landed in a desert, and began to melt.

Poems can provide activities to be pantomimed. Sheldon Harnick's poem

"Housework" appears on pages 54 to 59 of Marlo Thomas's *Free to be . . . You and Me*. Smiling ladies on television commercials help with the housework. The actions are scrub, rub, wash, wipe, mop, clean. Similar actions appear in Adhead's *Brownies Hush!*

Several activities can be pantomimed in "My Legs and I" on page 43 of Jacobs's *Is Somewhere Always Far Away?* In another poem on page 142 of that same book, "My Feet," children can jump, stomp, run, romp, skip, stroll or hop. "What Witches do," page 32, also provides action to pantomime.

Pilots, cowboys, tigers, captains, and parents are included in the poem "Pretending" on page 28 of Jacobs's *Is Somewhere Always Far Away?*

The first sentence of Victor's rhyming story, *Bigger Than an Elephant*, is "What would you do if you could be the size of anything you see?" Children can pantomime swimming with three goldfish, playing hide-and-seek in a log, or riding in the pouch of a kangaroo.

Lund's picture book, *Did You Ever?*, invites students to pantomime in unison. One of the questions in the book is "Did you ever lift your face to a gentle rain and then . . . when the sun came out, feel like a daisy opening up to the sky?" Some of the other questions concern pretending to be a fish, turtle, jack-in-the-box, and an orchestra conductor.

After going to the zoo in Fenton's *Fierce John*, Johnny pretended he was a lion. He roared fiercely at everyone, but no one paid any attention, so Johnny dressed up with a rope tail, mop mane, and nail claws, to make his father, mother, grandmother, and brother afraid of him. Even grandmother stood still so the lion would think she was a broom. Johnny had to eat candy and undress so they would know him. A real lion in Freeman's *Dandelion* was invited to a come-as-you-are party, but instead bought new clothes and got a haircut, and wasn't allowed into the party because the hostess didn't recognize him.

"How Thunder and Lightning Came to Be" appears in Maher's *The Blind Boy and the Lion*. (pp. 99-105). In this Eskimo folktale, children who were hungry pretended they were wolves, bears, salmon, caribou, and then thunder and lightning. The brother and sister were changed into thunder and lightning.

Minarik's books about *Little Bear* are favorites of early readers. The first story, "What Will Little Bear Wear?," is appropriate for unison pantomiming. Each child can be Little Bear. Because it was snowing, Mother Bear gave Little Bear a hat, coat, and snow pants. When she offered him a fur coat and took away the other three items, Little Bear was happy. Children can help Little Bear in the second story, "Birthday Soup." Little Bear thought no one remembered his birthday so he made birthday soup. Children can help add carrots, potatoes, peas, tomatoes, and can play out the story in groups of five; characters include Mother Bear, Little Bear, hen, duck, and cat.

In "Little Bear Goes to the Moon" our hero made a space helmet and pretended that he went to the moon. When Little Bear returned, his mother gave him lunch and then promised him a nap. This story, and the next one, "Little Bear's Wish," provide their own quieting activity, for after wishing for several things he cannot have, Little Bear wished for a story. Mother Bear's story was an overview of all that had happened that day in this particular book, and when she had finished, she tucked Little Bear in bed.

Because this title is available in paperback, a classroom set or one copy per two students could be acquired and shared by all first grade classrooms. Children could read the story to themselves, and then each story could be pantomimed or played. A rest period is a natural culminating activity.

Use this story to introduce all the other books about this favorite character to children. Other books by Minarik are Little Bear, Little Bear's Friend, A Kiss for Little Bear, and Father Bear Comes Home. Sound filmstrips are available for A Kiss for Little Bear and Little Bear's Visit.

Songs can provide material for pantomimes. Song number 29 of Glazer's Eye Winker Tom Tinker Chin Chopper, Fifty Musical Fingerplays contains "The Musicians," in which children have the opportunity to pretend they are playing a trumpet, tuba, trombone, and piccolo or being the conductor. The pictures of those instruments could be shown to children from posters or books, placed in the listening/viewing/reading center of the classroom.

The easiest book of illustrations of instruments in an orchestra is Green's Let's Learn about the Orchestra. Sketches appear in Lackey's Picture Book of Musical Instruments. Posell's This Is an Orchestra contains photos of instruments in four sections: strings, woodwind, brass, and percussion, but the people in the photos date them. In Kupferberg's A Rainbow of Sound; the Instruments of the Orchestra and Their Music, the photos show modern children. The instruments are divided into the same four basic sections, with a section about the conductor. The phonograph records called Instruments of the Orchestra can be used with the twenty-two posters and teacher's guide. Another set of posters called Meet the Instruments is available from Bowmar.

Picture books without words provide students with material for pantomimes. Mayer's Hiccup and Ah-Choo provide children with the title action, as well as scene-by-scene development of the stories. Since both books are available in paperback editions, it is possible to have several copies spread among a group at one time.

The Chicken's Child by Hartelius can be played out by groups of three. The trio consists of a hen, the alligator she hatched from an egg she found, and the farmer who owned the hen. The story is also suitable for pantomiming in unison. Children will like being asked to be the alligator eating a bushel of apples, a ladder, four pies, a washtub, a pump and pail, or a tractor. There are emotions to be pantomimed: displeasure, long-suffering, surprise, happiness, contentment, recognition, guilt, pleasure, excitement, fright, anger, gratitude, and contentment. Most of the nonverbal books express emotion through the illustrations. Because there are no words, the books are best expressed dramatically through pantomime. A list of picture books without words is included in the chapter on "Experiencing Art Through Picture Books."

Nate the Great, a detective for the easy reader set, solved the case of the garbage snatcher in Nate the Great Goes Undercover. The book is available in paperback edition, and so provide copies for every other student and rotate the copies around to the other first grade classes. Ask students to read the entire book. Then the teacher or students can read aloud until page 26 where the action begins and Nate is on the trail of the garbage snatcher. There are many activities to pantomime: Nate crawling into Sludge's doghouse, climbing into the garbage can and peaking out, creeping down the street, looking to the front, back, left and right, creeping up to an animal and discovering a skunk. Pantomiming can stop at page 38 or can continue until the end of the book. Use this book to introduce the following books by Sharmat about the detective: *Nate the Great, Nate the Great and the Lost List,* and *Nate the Great and the Phony Clue.* Playing a section of *Nate the Great Goes Undercover* can introduce other easy readers that are mysteries. Those books are listed in the first chapter of this book, "Introducing Books in All Kinds of Ways" in a section called "Introducing Mysteries."

"A List," in Lobel's *Frog and Toad Together* (pp. 4-18) can be used to introduce the other four stories in the easy reader. Toad wrote nine things she had to do on a list; each of the items can be pantomined: wake up, eat breakfast, get dressed, go to frog's house, take a walk with frog, eat lunch, take a nap, play games with frog, eat supper, and go to sleep.

Part of Freschet's *The Owl and the Prairie Dog* can be pantomimed. When the prairie dog woke up, his nose twitched, he scratched his ear, shook his tail, and tidied himself by combing out the leaves and grass from his coat. This short exercise could introduce the story to the students.

During narrative pantomime, the action occurs while a story or poem is read or a song is sung. There are not very many stories in which such continuous action takes place that children can pantomime the entire work. Two examples are "Peter and the Wolf," from Kamerman's *Dramatized Folk Tales of the World* and "The Snow Maiden" from Bennett's *Creative Plays and Programs for Holidays.*

Sivulich's *I'm Going on a Bear Hunt* is about a small boy who proclaimed that he is going on a bear hunt and is not afraid. After walking, climbing, sliding, swimming, and rowing, the boy saw the bear in a cave and had to repeat the return actions at a much faster pace. Of course, after he was safe, the boy maintained that he hadn't been afraid. The artist indicates the proper actions by using a different style and color of type.

Olfson, in *You Can Act!* includes a narrative pantomime of "Hansel and Gretel" that is easy enough for primary students to mime while the story is read aloud. Suggested actions are placed within parentheses, and are set in different type from the rest of the story. There are parts for Hansel, Gretel, mother, father, and the witch, and several groups of five can be playing out at the same time. After children have played the story they can be encouraged to look at picture books placed at the back of the classroom or in the library media center. Second graders will be able to read Haviland's easy adaptation in *Favorite Fairy Tales Told in Germany.* Anglund's picture book, *Nibble, Nibble, Mousekin* contains charming illustrations, and children will also enjoy looking at *Hansel and Gretel: A Story of the Forest,* which is a book of the opera, illustrated by Chappell.

Old Mother Hubbard and Her Dog, illustrated by Galdone, has continuous action. The dog laughed, licked his dish, stood on his head, fed the cat, danced a jig, played the flute, rode a goat, and read a newspaper, among other activities. Another picture book illustrated by Galdone that can be pantomimed while the story is read aloud is *The Old Woman and Her Pig*. McGovern's *Too Much Noise* is also a good possibility.

Songs provide excellent material for pantomime, and the recordings of those songs can provide the narration. Keats's *Over in The Meadow* is a good example, in which the various animals are busy doing things and making noises. Keats's *The Snowy Day* and *Whistle for Willie*, both of which can be introduced via films or sound filmstrips, are both excellent for preschool and primary children to pantomime while the story is being read. They can make snow angels outside in the snow with Peter, and try to whistle along with Peter so he can call his dog. Peter pretends to be his father when he puts on his father's hat, and a prop box full of hats can spark follow up play as well as lead into other "hat" stories.

Spier's *Fast Slow, High Low, a Book of Opposites* is good for active pantomiming as well as being useful to help preschoolers and primary grades learn about "long," "short"—"up," "down"—"open," "close," —"heavy, "light"—etc.

Eckert's *Tonight at Nine* is a German poem made into a picture book. Each verse involves an animal orchestra member: a dog plays the drums, a goose plays the flute, a cow plays the accordian, and a bull is the conductor of the concert. The story can be made into an effective shadow production with the poem as script.

Ets's *In the Forest*, about a child pretending, is eminently well suited for narrative pantomime. The main character is a boy who goes for a walk in the forest, complete with horn and paper hat. There's a lot of action by all sorts of animals, including a game of "drop the handkerchief" and "hide and seek." A birthday organized around this story could use these two games as well as a film, a filmstrip, and the reading of Sendak's *Where the Wild Things Are*, about Max who visited the forest under less sunny circumstances.

PANTOMIMING OR PLAYING EMOTION.   Even though there has been recent emphasis placed on the affective domain, many teachers do not recognize or use opportunities or activities which require students to identify, examine, or understand attitudes and emotions. Activities of this type are presented in this section. Each project can be pantomimed or played, with discussion following. Students are asked to reflect the emotions of a book character in a given situation and to show changes of emotions in this character in relation to the plot. Given a book character, children can be asked to make up an emotional situation to which that character reacts. Pairs of students can play out simple situations involving two characters.

Sometimes a character experiences many emotions in a single story. One example is Andersen's *The Fir Tree*. The full range of emotions in this story can be either pantomimed, played with words, or discussed after the book has been read to the class. Ask students how the tree felt when younger and smaller trees were cut and taken away and it was still not chosen—when it was chopped down—when it was decorated, lighted and placed in a dark corner—when it was the center of attention—when it was thrown outside—when the children laughed at it and called it ugly—when the children tore off the gold star—when it was abandoned.

A story can also be pantomimed, played, or discussed after a filmstrip of the story is shown. Show the filmstrip of Burton's *The Little House*. Students can be asked to think about how the house felt when it lived in the country—when horseless carriages appeared—when roads and houses were built—when trolleys changed to elevated trains —when skyscrapers loomed on each side of the little house. Students may or may not express themselves orally, or they may be asked to pantomime feelings first and then give them verbal expression.

Bear experienced several emotions in Bond and Banberry's *Paddington Bear, a Picture Book*. Ask students to discuss, then pantomime or play out how Paddington felt when he couldn't see to turn off the water taps and the water began overflowing—when he was covered with cream and jam while eating—when he was near the lost property office—when he took his first taxi ride—when he was sitting in an armchair in front of the fire.

Unison pantomiming in which emotions are expressed can take place while students are sitting or standing. The teacher or leader can place the emotional situations regarding characters from folk and fairy tales or children's classics on an index card for each book and situation. Although the following examples are identified by one or more emotions here, do not tell students in advance which emotion should be expressed. The response may or may not be discussed after pantomiming. Students may pantomime the situation first and then add words to the actions to play out the story. Many of these books have been introduced in other chapters.

EMBARRASSMENT: You are one of a group of people watching the emperor pass by. You can see that he doesn't have any clothes on but you must pretend that he does. Suddenly a small boy is saying that the emperor isn't wearing anything. (Andersen); HUMILIATION: You are the princess who couldn't make up her mind which prince to marry so your father made you marry a beggar. Now you are working in the kitchen of the castle of King Thrushbeard, one of the suitors you rejected. (Grimm); LAUGHTER: You are a princess who never laughs. Now you see a man with a golden goose with seven people trailing along behind because they are stuck to each other. (Grimm); JEALOUSY, ANGER: You are the Wicked Queen and stepmother of Snow White. You have just looked into the mirror and learned that Snow White has not been killed as you ordered, but is alive and still more beautiful than you. (Grimm); ANGER, GREED: You are the fisherman's wife and your husband has just told you that he had caught a magic fish which offered to grant him a wish but that he threw the fish back. (Grimm); HOPELESSNESS AND CHAGRIN: After calling "wolf, wolf!" several times just to see how people would react, you really see a wolf among the sheep and call out for help but no one believes you. (Aesop).

There are various degrees of UNHAPPINESS, DISAPPOINTMENT OR SADNESS: Your name is Baboushka and you have just realized that three men who left your house are the three magi. (Robbins); Your name is Heidi and you just learned that you must leave the mountain, Peter, the sheep, and your beloved grandfather. (Spyri); Your name is Jo March and you have just learned that your sister Beth is going to die. (Alcott).

Surprise can change to excitement, happiness or fear. SURPRISE AND EXCITEMENT: A noise has awakened you and you go to the window, open it and see a chubby man in a red suit with a sleigh and seven reindeer flying through the air. (Moore); SURPRISE AND DISMAY: You are Rip Van Winkle waking up after a nap which was really a twenty-year sleep, and so everything in your town seems to have changed. (Irving); SURPRISE AND DISMAY: You are Pinocchio and you have just told a lie; your nose feels funny—it's growing longer! (Collodi); SURPRISE AND WORRY: Your name is Bartholomew Cubbins and the king has asked you to take off your hat, but every time you take off your hat, another one appears. The king begins to threaten you. (Seuss); SURPRISE AND EITHER WORRY OR EXCITEMENT: You are Robinson Crusoe and think you are alone on a desert island, until you discover footprints in the sand. (Defoe); SURPRISE THEN ANGER: You are a peddler just waking up from a nap and you discover that all the caps you had for sale are gone. (Slobodkina).

The following persons or animals experience various degrees of DISMAY OR FEAR: You are Henny Penny and something falls from the sky and hits you on the head. (Henny Penny); Your name is Harriet and your friends have just read your journal. (Fitzhugh); You are one of the "Borrowers" and are in the kitchen borrowing sugar from a glass cannister when you are "seen." (Norton).

In the next examples, the people feel either EXCITEMENT, ANTICIPATION OR HAPPINESS; sometimes the emotion changes as the story changes. EXCITEMENT: Your name is Wendy and a boy named Peter Pan has just taught you how to fly. (Barrie); ANGER, ANTICIPATION AND HUNGER: You are a giant and returning home after a hard day's work, you smell a human being in your house. (Weisner); ANTICIPATION THEN ACCOMPLISHMENT: You are young Arthur and are ready to pull the sword out of the stone. You are young Arthur and you have just pulled the sword from the stone. (White); SELF-SATISFACTION OR ANTICIPATION THEN DISMAY: You are a woman carrying eggs on your head, taking them to market. On the way you plan how you will spend your profits, but because your mind isn't on what you are doing, the basket falls and the eggs are broken. (Andersen); HAPPINESS THEN PUZZLEMENT: Your name is Happy Lion and you have walked out of your cage at the zoo and downtown for the first time. Your can't understand why people who normally smile at you are shouting and running away. (Fatio).

Sometimes emotions change in a story because of conflict or a new development in the plot. For example, Joel Chandler Harris's *Brer Rabbit* approached a funny-looking creature in the middle of the road and was friendly to it. When the creature did not reply to his greeting, Brer Rabbit hit it with his hand and stuck to the creature, and so on with other parts of his body and the same results. You are *Little Toot* in the harbor darting in and out among the big ships. *Conflict:* You are Little Toot alone in the storm. (Gramatky); You are Anansi the spider who is secretly eating food while the others are out in the field working. *Conflict:* You are Anansi and the others are returning from the field so you hide the hot beans on your head and cover them with your hat. (Courlander); You are a little bear and you have just discovered several unusual things in your home when you returned from your walk—your porridge is gone and your chair has been broken. *Conflict:* Now you discover a little girl sleeping in your bed. (Goldilocks); You are the farmer in *Gone Is Gone* who has just traded places with his wife and looks forward to an easier day. *Conflict:* As the day progresses things are beginning to go wrong. (Gag); You are the apprentice in *The Sorcerer's Apprentice* and you have been left alone after having learned the secret words to make the broom fetch water. *Conflict:* You don't remember the words to make the broom stop and the water is flooding the room. (Hosiers); You are Beauty and you think the Beast is dead. *Change:* You learn that he is alive, you promise to marry him, and he turns into a handsome prince. (Lang); Your stepsister has come back from the well and roses, pearls, and diamonds are coming from her mouth. *Conflict:* You go to the well too, but after being rude to a fairy, snakes and toads come from your mouth. (Grimm); You are Pandora and you are alone with the box which you have been told never to open. *Conflict:* You open the box anyway and all the evil spirits come tumbling out. You are an ugly duckling and you hate yourself. *Change:* You look into water and discover that you are a beautiful swan. (Andersen); You name is *Homer Price* and the doughnut machine won't stop. *Change:* You have just thought of an idea how to get the doughnuts sold and the diamond bracelet recovered at the same time. (McCloskey); Your name is Tom Sawyer and you are stuck with the job of whitewashing the fence when you would rather be fishing. *Change:* You have just discovered a way to get the fence whitewashed by others and have them pay for the privilege. (Twain); You are the boastful hare and are running a race which you are confident of winning. *Conflict:* You have just learned that the tortoise has beaten you in the race. (Aesop).

Sometimes several emotions are encountered. You are Horton the Elephant and you have been sitting and sitting and sitting on an egg waiting for it to hatch. The egg is hatching. Then mother bird comes back to claim her baby. (Seuss); You are a miller and you and your son are taking your donkey to market. When people make fun of you both for walking, you ask your son to ride the donkey. Now, an old man is shaming your son for riding while you walk. Now people are laughing at you and your son for carrying the donkey. (Aesop); Sometimes the emotion stays the same even though the plot does not, but it may or may not change in intensity. Your name is Ping and you know you will be the last duck to reenter the houseboat. *Change:* You are Ping and the houseboat has gone without you. (Flack).

Students can be paired; then pairs can act out situations simultaneously. Designate one person as A and the other as B. Tell A—"You are the town mouse visiting the country mouse." Tell B—"You are the country mouse and the town mouse is visiting you." Then reverse the situation. (Aesop); A—"You are Peter Rabbit and you have just eaten French beans, radishes and other goodies but while looking for parsley you see Farmer McGregor at the end of a cucumber frame." B—"You are Farmer McGregor working in your garden. All of a sudden a rabbit comes toward you, nibbling your vegetables." (Potter); A—"You are Rumpelstiltskin and you have come to ask the miller's daughter if she can guess your name." B—"You are the miller's daughter and you cannot guess the name of the little man." (Grimm); A—"You are Robin Hood, the proud outlaw, and you are ready to cross the bridge from the north." B—"You are Little John, a huge man of whom many are afraid. You are ready to cross the bridge from the south." (Pyle).

Books about the following characters are listed under the authors' names in the bibliography. Ask your intermediate students who are familiar with the characters to create new situations involving the characters. The situations should be suitable for pantomiming or playing and should begin with "You are . . . ." followed by the name of one character then "and" followed by the name of another character. Examples are as follows: "You are Kerby Maxwell and Mrs. Graymalkin has just . . . ." (Corbett); "You are Henry Huggins and Ribsy (or Ramona or Beezus) has just . . . ." (Cleary); "You are Caddie Woodlawn and . . . ."(Brink); "You are with Mary Poppins and . . . ." (Travers); "You are one of the Moffats and . . . ." (Estes); "You are Encyclopedia Brown and . . . ." (Sobel); "You are one of the Ingalls and . . . ." (Wilder); "You are one of the Borrowers and . . . ." (Norton); "You are Miss Pickerell and . . . ." (MacGregor); "You are Paddington Bear and . . . ." (Bond); "You are Pooh Bear and . . . ." (Milne); "You are a spider named Charlotte and . . . ." (White).

Ask primary students to create situations from the books involving these characters. The situations should be suitable for pantomiming or playing as described above. "You are Georgie and . . . ." (Bright); "Your name is Curious George and . . . ." (Rey); "You are Katie the Snowplow and . . . ." (Burton); "You are Madeline and . . . ." (Bemelmans); "You are Harold and you pick up your purple crayon and . . . ." (Johnson); "Your name is Jeanne Marie and . . . ." (Francoise); "Your name is Petunia and . . . ." (Duvoisin).

BACKGROUND READING FOR PLAYING STORIES.   Numerous books about creative dramatics give advice on how to prepare a story for playing. Many of them include examples of favorite tales to explain the process or to explain the elements of a story suitable for playing.

McCaslin's *Creative Dramatics in the Classroom* is valuable reading for anyone who plans to work with children to play out stories. Ten clues about characterization are given on pages 77 and 78. Information is also given about dialogue, plot, conflict, theme, climax, denouement, unity, dramatic irony, structure, comedy, tragedy, prologue, and epilogue. "The Three Wishes" on pages 83 to 91 is an example of a story that contains all the elements of a play and lists the seven elements. Chapter 6, "Building Plays from Simple Stories," pages 92 to 109, includes information about turning the following stories into plays: "The Boy Who Cried Wolf," pages 100 and 101; "Caps for Sale," pages 96 to 100; "The Tortoise and the Hare," pages 101 to 103; "Darby and Joan," pages 103 to 105; and "The Cobbler's Hump," pages 105 to 107. Six suggestions to precede the first playing and five discussion questions are given and five procedures for playing out a story are listed. Chapter 7, "Building Plays from Longer Stories," of the same title contains information for turning the following stories into plays: "The Golden Touch" (pp. 111-15); "The Stone in the Road" (pp. 116-19);

(pp. 116-19); "Prometheus" (pp. 119-23); "Blue Bonnets" (pp. 123-25); "A Legend of Spring" (pp. 125-28); and "The Coins of Lin Foo" (pp. 128-31). Information about characterization appears on page 132.

All the chapters in Heinig and Stillwell's *Creative Dramatics for the Classroom Teacher* build toward the last two chapters, "Story Dramatization and Project Work" and "The Leader in the Group." Information about narrating, creative pantomime, and dialogue is included, and a list of stories to dramatize is given as well as information about how a leader contributes to playing through ideas, participation, and acceptance or rejection. Information is given for playing "Why the Bear Has a Stumpy Tail" and "The Emperor's New Clothes."

Chapter 3, "How to Dramatize a Story," of Ward's *Stories to Dramatize* (pp. 8-15) includes advice to adults on helping children play out stories. Pointers are included in that chapter for setting the mood, presenting the story, planning the dramatization, choosing the casts, first playing, evaluation, praise and encouragement, and teacher participation. Seven aspects important for evaluation are given on page 13. Read chapters 6 through 9 of Ward's *Playmaking with Children*: "Presenting the Story," "Creative Plays Based on Stories," "Integration," and "Play Structure." Ward discusses whether to read or tell the story, and goes on to tell about setting the mood, making the story clear, planning the play, picking the scenes, and playing in small units. Eight vital aspects of story dramatization are given, similar to the seven aspects for evaluation in *Stories to Dramatize*. Several stories, including "The Sleeping Beauty" and "Snow White," are used to point out exposition, episodes, climax, characters, dialogue, and conclusion.

Geraldine Sikes, with Winifred Ward, is one of the foremost names in creative dramatics. Sikes's book, *Creative Dramatics, An Art for Children*, is an important source. Chapters 3, 4, and 6 are of special interest: "The Art of Drama," "The Creative Leader," and "How to Guide Children to Creative Drama." Sikes uses "Cinderella" as a model to analyze the fundamental drama elements, and explains the basic qualities in creative leadership. "A Tailor and a Bear" by the Brothers Grimm is used as the model for adding characterization, actions, plot, emotional conflict and dialogue. An analysis of basic models and appeals to children and an analysis of needs which the story might satisfy are included.

Read the first chapter of Fitzgerald's *World Tales for Creative Dramatics and Storytelling* for background information about motivation, the story, the playing of the story, dramatic knowledge, movement, characterization, dialogue, dramatic awareness, and developing the story into a play. Five ideas on which to base questions about playing out a story are given.

Although Carlson's *Let's Pretend It Happened to You* was intended for leaders of students from preschool age to grade three, the ideas are useful to anyone who plays out stories with children. The following information is contained on pages 16 to 23: choosing the tale (nine elements a story should have), introducing the activity (six guidelines), opening the activity (five guidelines for reading the story), discussing and planning the story (six guidelines on leader involvement), and evaluation.

Two famous stories are used as the basis for teaching leaders how to prepare a story for playing. Pages 88 to 91 of Ziskind's *Telling Stories to Children* tell how to create a dramatic situation from "The Three Billy Goats Gruff." A script for "The Hare and the Tortoise" is given and discussed on pages 205 and 206 of Huckleberry and Strothers's *Speech Education for the Elementary Teacher*. Sixteen stories suitable for playing are listed.

"The Emperor's New Clothes" is the example used for teaching playmaking in Kerman's *Plays and Creative Ways with Children*, which gives information also on selecting the story, preliminary discussion, finding the specific conflict, and building the structure. Categories under playmaking are storytelling, first playmaking, playmaking scene-by-scene, evaluation, and improvement.

The film *Stories in Motion* prepared by the Vermont Department of Libraries shows librarians using books creatively. One of the stories is Kahl's *The Duchess Bakes a Cake*.

After reading and viewing the sources suggested, check the following list of recommendations for "Preparing a Story for Playing." Those steps have successfully been used by this author.

PREPARING A STORY FOR PLAYING

1. *Select a worthwhile story* that has a laudable theme, lively characters, lots of action, crisp dialogue, and that appeals to the group who will be playing it.
2. *Seek a story with identifiable parts.* Be sure that the story has a suitable introduction, contains conflict, has a definite rising action, a recognizable climax, swift falling action and a just conclusion. Encourage participation in identifying the parts.
3. *Choose a story with many characters* so everyone in the group can have a part. Or choose a story that can be double cast and played simultaneously by two groups.
4. *Find other versions* of the story from *The Children's Catalog*, Cathon's *Stories to Tell to Children*, the list of the Carnegie Library of Pittsburgh, Ireland's *Index to Fairy Tales, 1949-72*, Nelson's *A Comparative Anthology of Children's Literature*. Consult the card catalog for individual picture book listings for the stories. Choose the version you like best or combine elements.
5. *Introduce the story to students* either by reading the version most suitable or by telling the story using the steps in *Telling A Story* found in chapter 1 of this book.
6. *List events chronologically* using a chalk board or overhead projector. Invite students to participate also in listing the characters in the order of their appearance.
7. *Identify the six major parts of the story;* the introduction, conflict, rising action, climax, falling action, and conclusion. Encourage participation.

8. *List the characters* in the order of appearance. Encourage participation.
9. *Assign characters to students.* Keep a record of which students have major parts so other students will have a chance for major parts in the next story.
10. *Assign character sketches* to students. Students should write a character sketch that includes a physical description, mental characteristics, motivation, and how he or she is viewed by himself or herself as well as by others.
11. *Avoid costumes.* Instead, assign students to bring a prop characteristic of their part and have them make a sign or mask representative of the character. Or have students play their parts without any props.
12. *Identify scenes and begin improvisation.* Each student should identify all scenes in which his character participates and then pantomime the actions within those scenes.
13. *Add dialogue* to the scenes, play them with others, and then link them together. Replay the story as many times as desired, consistent with avoiding overkill.
14. *Evaluate* the effectiveness of characters to plot development, actions, dialogue, and timing.

THE BEE, THE HARP, THE MOUSE, AND THE BUM CLOCK.   This Irish folktale is appropriate for telling and playing for St. Patrick's Day. Sources are MacManus's *Donegal Fairy Stories,* Fenner's *Princesses and Peasant Boys,* Hutchinson's *Chimney Corner Fairy Tales,* and Johnson's *Anthology of Children's Literature.* The story has elements of "Jack and the Beanstalk." Stories about unusual trades include "Hans in Luck," "Happy Go Lucky," "Gudbrand on the Hillside," and "What the Good Man Does Is Always Right." Make all of these other stories available to students at this time.

"The Bee, the Harp, the Mouse and the Bum Clock" is a favorite of children in grades one through five because of its humor, repetition, and the variety of interesting characters. There are fifteen people parts as well as parts for pots and pans, wheels and reels, men and women in the marketplace, and men and women of the court. The individual parts are Jack, his mother, three cows, man, bee, harp, mouse, bum clock (cockroach), wee woman, king, queen, princess, and soldier. If there are not enough students to fill all the extra parts, have one child play all the cows and have the men and women of the marketplace change at the end of the story to men and women of the court.

Tell the story to students and then follow the procedures in the previous section called *Preparing a Story for Telling.* "The Bee, the Harp, the Mouse and the Bum Clock" is used here as an example of placing the major events in proper sequence and identifying the six major parts of the story.

MAJOR EVENTS IN THE BEE, THE HARP, THE MOUSE, AND THE BUM CLOCK

1. Hard times befell the widow and her son Jack.
2. The widow sent Jack to the fair to sell the branny cow to get money for food.

3. Jack saw a man with a bee, harp, mouse, and bum clock at the fair.
4. Everyone at the fair sang and danced with the menagerie.
5. The man talked Jack into trading the branny cow for the bee and harp.
6. Jack used the bee and harp to make his mother laugh and dance.
7. Jack's mother was angry when she realized they had no money for food.
8. The widow sent Jack to the fair to sell the black cow to get money for food.
9. Jack saw the man with the mouse and the bum clock at the fair.
10. Everyone at the fair sang and danced with the mouse and the bum clock.
11. The man talked Jack into trading the black cow for the mouse.
12. Jack used the bee, harp, and mouse to make his mother laugh and dance.
13. Jack's mother was angry when she realized they had no money for food.
14. The widow sent Jack to the fair to sell the last cow to get money for food.
15. Jack saw the man at the fair with his bum clock.
16. Everyone at the fair sang and danced with the man and the bum clock.
17. The man talked Jack into trading the last cow for the bum clock.
18. Jack used the bee, harp, mouse, and the bum clock to make his mother laugh and dance.
19. Jack's mother was angry when she realized they had no money for food.
20. Jack met an old woman and learned that a princess as well as half a kingdom would be given to anyone who could make her laugh three times.
21. Jack took the bee, harp, mouse, and bum clock to the castle.
22. Jack learned that the heads on the spikes surrounding the castle were heads of those who had tried and failed to make the princess laugh.
23. Jack marched around the court with his menagerie on a string and the princess laughed.
24. Jack whistled and the bee, harp, mouse, and bum clock danced and so did the court, and the princess laughed a second time.
25. The mouse swished its tail in the mouth of the bum clock and it coughed, and so the princess laughed a third time.
26. Jack was washed and dressed in beautiful clothes, and he was so handsome that the princess fell in love with him.
27. Jack sent for his mother to come to the castle.
28. Jack and the princess were married.
29. The wedding feast lasted nine days and nights.
30. Jack and his princess lived happily ever after.

THE SIX MAJOR PARTS OF THE BEE, THE HARP, THE MOUSE, AND THE BUM CLOCK

    I INTRODUCTION
        A. *A widow*
            1. had only one son,
            2. was very poor; owned only three cows.
        B. *Jack*
            1. was an only child;

      2.   wasn't the brightest person.

II. CONFLICT
    A.   Hard times befell Jack and his mother.
    B.   The widow sent Jack to sell a cow at the market.

III. RISING ACTION
    A.   Jack saw a man with a dancing bee, harp, mouse and bum clock.
    B.   The man offered to trade the bee and harp for the cow.
        1.   Jack accepted the trade.
        2.   Jack returned home.
    C.   The widow was amused, then angry.
    D.   Jack traded the second cow for the mouse.
    E.   The widow was amused, then angry.
    F.   Jack traded the last cow for the bum clock.
    G.   The widow was amused, then angry.

IV. CLIMAX
    A.   Jack and his mother had no food to eat.
    B.   Jack learned about the King of Ireland's daughter.
        1.   a princess who hadn't laughed for seven years.
        2.   a princess who would be given in marriage with half the kingdom besides to anyone who could make her laugh three times.

V. FALLING ACTION
    A.   Jack set out for the castle.
    B.   The princess laughed
        1.   when she saw the ragged Jack with the bee, harp, mouse and bum clock on a string;
        2.   when the menagerie played and danced;
        3.   when the mouse's tail hit the bum clock in the mouth.

VI. CONCLUSION
    A.   Jack became handsome
        1.   when he was washed;
        2.   when he had beautiful clothes.
    B.   Jack married the princess.
    C.   Jack and the princess lived happily ever after.

STORIES FOR PLAYING.   "The Train Set" is one of three stories in Hutchins's *The Best Train Set Ever* (pp. 6–33), an easy reader book. The story is excellent for playing and gives students a chance to practice arithmetic skills as well. There are eight characters and two groups can easily play out the story.

Each person in the family had a limited amount of money to pay for a gift for Peter's birthday. Peter wanted a train set that cost thirty dollars, so each member of the family secretly bought part of the train from Mr. Mindy's store. Before playing, write on the blackboard or on an overhead projector "Peter wants a train set in Mr. Mindy's store that costs $30.00." Under the word "CHARACTERS" list Peter and Mr. Mindy as the first two characters, followed by the names of the other characters, as well as the piece of the train set they bought and how much they paid. Then add up the numbers and write $30.00 total. The characters and their gifts will also provide an outline for the children to follow when playing out the story. Much repetition of actions and phrases will make playing easy. The characters and their gifts and the amount they spent are: father and mother (engine for $10), Tony (track for $8), Ann (coach for $5), Frank (caboose for $4), and Maria (flat car for $3).

Waber's *You Look Ridiculous Said the Rhinocerous to the Hippopotamus* is excellent for playing with several groups of students. To aid in this playing story, a picture of each animal can be given to participants to pin or attach to his or her chest. The worried hippo, told by the rhino that he looked ridiculous because he did not have a horn, asked some other animals what additions he needed. All suggested their own best features: the lion said the hippo needed a mane; the leopard that he needed spots; the elephant, ears like fans; the monkey, a long tail; the giraffe, a long neck; the turtle, a shell; and the nightingale said he needed a beautiful voice. In the end the hippo dreams of having a horn like the rhino and all of the additions mentioned by the other animals so that he no longer looked ridiculous. At that point each student can finish touching up his original picture of hippo to show the very ridiculous looking composite animal, each one of which will be different according to the artist's conception.

There are seven characters in Hutchins's *The Surprise Party*, a picture book with the same theme as the old game of "Gossip" or "Whisper." One person whispers a message to another, and the message is then repeated through the group until the end result is not similar to the original message. Seven characters can play this story which begins with a message from rabbit who whispers to squirrel, "I'm having a party tomorrow. . . . It's a surprise." In the end, rabbit told them all about the party and they wondered why he didn't say so in the first place. The animals all agreed that the party was fun as well as a surprise. This story can be played by giving each student a picture of one of the animals. Or each student could draw his or her own animal. Paper bag puppets made by the children for use without a stage can also provide identities. Class members could make up additional animals and dialogue so that there would be enough parts for the story to be played using a double cast.

Fenton's *The Big Yellow Balloon* is another easy story to play. The cat thought Roger's big yellow balloon was the sun, so he wanted to kill it so he could hunt all the time—not just at night. The cat followed Roger and the balloon, the dog followed the cat, the dog catcher followed the dog, an old lady wanted to save the dog, a burglar was after the old lady's purse, and a policeman was after the burglar. The fun began when the cat broke the balloon.

Two stories by Ellen Raskin are excellent for playing. *And it Rained* is a hilarious story about a pig, a parrot, and a potto who have a tea party every afternoon at four. The three animals try to keep their tea party from being ruined. Groups of five students can take their scripts directly from the book.

Characters are a narrator, pig, parrot, potto and Sir Benjamin. (Since the last part is minimal, it can be dropped.) Raskin's *Who, Said Sue, Said Whoo?* contains parts for a polka dot cow, cross-eyed owl, shrew, goose, kangaroo, billy goat's ghost, gnu, two pigs, a chimp, a snake, Sue, a narrator, and a skunk. It is very effective to use a skunk puppet to enter at the end of the story. Assign parts to students by handing them a paper with the name of the animal on it. Students may wish to draw the animal on the paper and attach it to themselves while playing the story. The narrator reads the story while the animals stand in a line in the order in which they appear in the story. The only animal that needs to be modified is the kangaroo who may jump up and down while the narrator reads.

CASTING STORIES TO INCLUDE EVERYONE.   In order for playing to run smoothly, the leader must know how many parts are available before playing begins. It is advisable for leaders to list the characters in advance and attach the list to the story. It may be a good idea to place the name of a student opposite each character's name, so the list can also serve as a reference to insure that the same children are not always assigned a major role. The teacher need not always assign the roles. If a story has eight parts, the teacher can assign eight students to a group that will play it, but allow the students to decide who has which part within the group.

There are numerous ways to play a story so all students will be included. If there are twelve parts in the story to be played and a class consists of twenty-four players, it is possible for two groups to play the story simultaneously. The number of players in a story can also be condensed or expanded to include the correct number of players. Sometimes a character can be dropped or one person can play two parts. If there are crowd scenes, it is easy to assign all students who do not have a major part. A chorus serves the same purpose in a musical version. It is also easy to change the number of a small group of foxes, children, or pixies from the designated number to include one or two more players. Sometimes if another role is needed, a student can be assigned that of an inanimate object such as a clock, tree, squeaky door, or gateposts.

Sometimes it is possible for everyone to play each of the characters in a story. Have all of the children play a character in unison as the character is introduced. These characters can react to other imaginary characters. Another technique is to change roles during replay so that more children have a chance to play a major role. Some stories can be played by pairs of characters.

The stories that are included in this section have been chosen to demonstrate a variety of casting patterns. Some are flexible enough so that characters can be added or dropped. Some stories can accommodate an entire class in one cast or can be played by several groups of students simultaneously or by all students in unison. Although a story should not be chosen just because it can be conveniently played by everyone, it is a factor.

Read Rose's picture book *How Does a Czar Eat Potatoes?* to a class and then divide the students into pairs. One person is to pantomime or play the Czar and the other, the father. Or students can imitate both people eating potatoes, drinking tea, bathing, sleeping, crying, or being happy. Elkin's *How the Tsar*

Drinks Tea is a similar story.

Play the story "Barnyard Quarrel," found in Shecker's *Stone House Stories*, (pp. 14–21) in pairs. The story is about a chicken and rabbit who argue and call each other dumb cluck and dumb bunny. A good discussion of name calling can be opened up by this activity.

Children can pretend to be Birdwell's *Clifford the Big Red Dog* and sit up and beg, run after cars, chew shoes, dig in flowers. If children play in pairs, one can be Clifford's owner and they can play hide and seek, throw and fetch sticks, and give and get a bath and comb and be combed.

"Cookies," from Lobel's *Frog and Toad Together*, can be pantomimed or played in pairs. Frog put cookies in a box, tied a string around the box, got a ladder and put the box on a high shelf. Toad opened the box, cut the string, and ate more cookies. Many imaginary cookies are eaten in this story. A reward for good playing could be real cookies as a treat.

Maurice Sendak's illlustrations of the Grimm fairy tale in the picture book *King Grisley-Beard* make it different from the traditional story because two children play the parts of the dissatisfied princess and the poor musician who is really the king. The story is told with humor.

Show the class the filmstrip *Urashima Taro, a Japanese Folktale* and have them play out the story in pairs with one of the players as the tortoise princess and the other as Urashima Taro. Other characters can be imaginary.

Segal's *Tell Me a Mitzi* contains several stories. "Mitzi Takes a Taxi" can be played in pairs. Mitzi changed her baby brother Jacob's diapers, dressed him, took him with the stroller down in the elevator to a taxi, but had to get out when she didn't know her grandparent's address. There is humor in the story, and it can be pantomimed. Everyone in the class can play out "Mitzi and the President." The main characters are the president, Mitzi, Jacob, and father. Other class members can be people in the crowd.

Most of the fables of Aesop can be played out in pairs. After playing, the children could switch parts. After the story has been read to them from Johnson's *Anthology of Children's Literature*, children can create their own dialogue for "The Wind and the Sun," "A Lion and a Mouse," "The Shepherd Boy," "The Town Mouse and the Country Mouse," "The Crow and the Pitcher," "The Dog and His Shadow," "The Fox and the Crow," "The Hare and the Tortoise," and "The Fox and the Grapes." Twelve fables of Aesop appear also in Huber's *Story and Verse for Children*. In "The Cat and the Parrot," in Haviland's *Favorite Fairy Tales Told in India*, (pp. 27–34) a greedy cat ate five hundred cakes, a parrot, an old woman, old man and a donkey, king, queen, soldiers, elephants, and land crabs. The number of soldiers, elephants and land crabs can be changed to suit the number of students playing.

Coll and His White Pig can be used to introduce the other titles by Newbery winner Lloyd Alexander, because Dallben the Enchanter from *The Book of Three* is in this book and others in the cycle, including *The High King*. A cast of thousands could be used to play out this story; however, a classroom of third, fourth, or fifth graders would be sufficient. The action centers on Pig-Hen-Wen who was stolen. Other characters include Owl-Ash-Wing, King Arawn Annunin the Lord of the Land of the Dead, Oak-Horn-Stag, Star-Nose Chief Mole, and thousands of moles.

Lorenzo Bear and Company by Wahl is about Lorenzo and his friend Wolverine who found objects left behind by campers and traded them for items that would help them build a rocket ship to the moon. There are parts for Lorenzo, Wolverine, Mrs. Spotted Skunk, Mrs. Mink, muskrat, ground squirrel, and horned owl. Extras are red foxes, martens, hares, shrews, porcupines, beetles, opposums, and trader rats. This story can be effectively played out by a whole class. Research into the characters and habits of the various animals could be part of preparing the character sketches.

Simon's Soup by Komoda contains parts for everyone. Simon wanted to fly his new kite, but he had to make soup for the monkeys who were coming to supper. Ask children to help put the ingredients listed on the first page into the pot. Troubles started when Simon put his shoe through the kite and broke a chair getting the glue to mend it. Simon also had a series of animals knocking at his door, each saying an appropriate rhyme. Choose children to play the various parts: a beaver selling baked goods, a fox selling gadgets, a mother rabbit and children selling eggplants, a goat mowing lawns, and flowers from the monkeys. Extra children can be monkeys, baby rabbits, or even eggplants; or two people can be beavers, foxes, or goats.

The eight parts in "The Owl's Barn Sale," in Shecker's *Stone House Stories*, (pp. 4–10) can be played by duplicate groups. Fox bought a clock at owl's barn sale and sold it for twice as much to mouse, who gave it to rabbit who already had two clocks, so he gave it to the ladies' charity at the county fair. Raccoon won the clock at ring toss and laid it down when he went for a swim. Crow found the clock and lost it on a bet. Squirrel won the clock, and when raccoon saw it, the two argued. The clock was broken when they quarrelled, and the two animals went away leaving the clock behind. Owl found the clock and went home and put a "Barn Sale Over" sign on her barn. If needed, one person could be the clock.

Carlson's *Marie Louise's Heyday* has nine parts: Marie Louise, Mama, mother possum, Jake, John, Lucie, Lily, me and the witch toad. Marie Louise, the mongoose, babysat for five possum children. The children ate poisonous red berries instead of their boiled greens, so Marie Louise had to go to the witch toad for help. The toad saved the children in return for the boiled greens. The day was a tiring one for Marie Louise who went home to sleep. The next morning she was surprised when the five rascals brought her flowers and asked her to come and babysit with them again. Dialogue for the five possum children is given. Show the film strip to introduce the book.

Runaway Marie Louise by Carlson contains parts for twenty-three players. In the story, witch toad gave Marie Louise a new mama who turned out to be her own. Another book about these characters is *Marie Louise and Christopher*.

Holl's *The Rain Puddle* can involve everyone at one time. There are parts for as many animals as needed to involve an entire class. Ask students to name other farm animals in addition to those mentioned and then give those parts out to the students who name them. A wise old owl could be the narrator and another person could be the sun. This story could also be told with a flannelboard or with shadow puppets.

Aardema's *Who's in Rabbit's House?* is really a play. The Masai story originally appeared in Aardema's *Tales for the Third Ear*. There are parts for a rabbit, a voice, jackal, frog, leopard, elephant, and rhinoceros. Seven people can form a long green caterpillar. If there are twenty-eight in the class, two groups of fourteen can play or part of the class can be the observers seen in the story. The voice repeats the chant "I am the Long One. I eat trees and trample on elephants. Go Away! Or I will trample on You!"

Horwitz's *The Strange Story of the Frog Who Became a Prince* is different from the Grimm tale. In this story, a frog didn't want to be a prince because he wanted to be his own handsome frog self. The frog tried to say the magic words backwards, but he remained a prince. After becoming several other equally undesirable things, the frog was finally able to regain his original self. Everyone can be the prince in this story.

"How Boots Befooled the King" by Howard Pyle found in Fenner's *The Princess and the Peasant Boys*, (pp. 137–47) appeared orginally in Pyle's *Wonder Clock*. There are nine parts for King, Princess, Boots, etc., plus members of the court, so a whole class could be involved. Rockwell's *Poor Goose, a French Folktale* can be played by several groups of six players at the same time. A goose goes off to the castle to get some peppermint tea for her headache and overheard the old woman wish for a cat, lamb, cow, and goose, so she brought them to her. There is also a part for a wolf.

Zemach's *The Judge, an Untrue Tale* was a Caldecott honor book and is a favorite of children because it is a cumulative tale told in rhyme. Nine characters who need to learn lines are required. There are five prisoners or witnesses, two bailiffs, one judge, and one creature. Told that a creature with scary eyes and a hairy tail is creeping closer and closer, the judge threw the man in jail for telling an untruth. After four witnesses and more description, the "thing" appears. This story could be played simultaneously by several groups in a classroom or by stick puppets.

"Budulinek" appears in Haviland's *Favorite Fairy Tale Treasury* and Fillmore's *The Shepherd's Nosegay*. It is flexible enough to be played by seven, fourteen, twenty-one, or twenty-eight students if several groups play out the story simultaneously. The number of little foxes can be changed to add or subtract two characters from each group. The characters are Granny, Budulinek, a fox, three little foxes, and an organ grinder. A monkey for the organ grinder can be added if another part is needed.

Budulinek disobeyed Granny and let the fox come into the house three times because the fox promised to give Budulinek a ride on his tail. The first two times the fox merely ate up Budulinek's food and left. However, the third time the fox gave Budulinek a ride on his tail and took him to his den. Budulinek was later rescued by an organ grinder who got the foxes to sing a rhyme that went up to the number five. The teacher could be the organ grinder because of the verses that need to be chanted or sung. If the story is merely told, it can be treated as a participant story because the children can put up the appropriate number of fingers when the organ grinder sings.

Amahl and the Night Visitors is a Christmas story which has become familiar through TV. When the Wise men stopped at his house, crippled Amahl had nothing to give them except his crutch. When he did so, he was able to walk. The story is a retelling of the opera, and can be played with or without music.

"The Golden Goose" can be played with as few as thirteen characters or with as many as thirty or more. (Two groups can play out the story simultaneously.) There are fifteen characters, but people can be added as peasants or new characters created. Be aware of the magic number "seven"—there were seven people stuck to the goose. If there were twenty-six students in the class, the mother and innkeeper could be dropped and the story double cast with thirteen students in each group. The person playing the inkeeper can also play the king to eliminate one character.

In "The Golden Goose" two brothers, given a cake by their mother, had the opportunity to share it with an old man, but they refused. The third son, called "Dullhead" or "Simpleton," had only cinder cake but gladly shared it with the old man in the forest. A golden goose that appeared from the roots of a tree was his reward. The innkeeper's three curious daughters got stuck to the goose and each other when they tried to pluck a feather, and four other characters were also caught. This procession made the princess laugh so her father was bound to give her in marriage to the simpleton, but he had the boy accomplish three feats first—which the boy did with the help of the old man.

This classic tale from the Brothers Grimm has elements in common with many other fairy tales and can be used in conjunction with them. The princess to be given in marriage to whoever could make her laugh was like the princess in "The Bee, the Harp, the Mouse, and the Bumclock." The magic number "three" appears in many folktales with the third son or daughter the hero or heroine and with the third and youngest winning the prize. Greed and its punishment is often a theme: the two older brothers did not want to share their food with the old man and therefore missed out on a chance to win the princess.

Chapter 6, "Riddles, Magic, Jokes, and Folk Themes," lists other stories about a simple brother who wins the princess. There are heroes who will lose their heads if they fail in riddle contests, just as the simpleton will fail if he cannot make the princess laugh. In a similar story, "The Flea," from the Spanish, the boy won the princess with the help of an ant, beetle, and mouse for whom he did a favor, but at the end the princess in this story was unwilling to marry the boy.

Complete bibliographic information for the collections of fairy tales from the Brothers Grimm appear in the bibliography/index and include *About Wise Men and Simpletons, The Complete Grimms' Fairy Tales, Grimms' Fairy Tales* illustrated by Rackham, *Household Stories*, Haviland's *The Fairy Tale Treasury*, Johnson's *Anthology of Children's Literature*, Lang's *The Red Fairy Book*, and Sideman's *World's Best Fairy Tales*. Leslie Brooke illustrated *The Golden Goose Book . . .* , which also contains "The Three Bears," "The Three Little Pigs," and "Tom Thumb."

PLAYING STORIES FOR MANY PURPOSES.   Just as there are many types of stories, there can be several purposes for playing each story. When students play out easy books, they can reread the stories for a special purpose. Folktales and folk songs can be used to highlight a special area of the world or be organized around a specific theme. Stories are appropriate to times of the year because of their nature or theme. Curricular needs can be met and some stories included in this section support community helper awareness, number concepts, rhythm, and size relationships. Role playing can prompt discussion of many topics, including manners, habits, self concept, ethnic acceptance, or perception.

Adams's *A Woggle of Witches* provides a vehicle for allowing primary students to fly around the classroom at Halloween time. The children can pretend they are witches with or without props. Perhaps pointed black hats could be made in art class. In an ironic ending, the witches were frightened by children in Halloween costumes.

Carle's *The Secret Birthday Message* is really a treasure hunt in which a small boy found a secret message which led to his birthday gift.

Holl's *Small Bear's Name Hunt* is an easy reader, in which the repetition makes it suitable for both playing and puppetry. A small bear who wanted another name sought advice from Wee Willie, a tiny gray field mouse; Digger the woodchuck; Slim Jim, a snake; Croaker, a frog; and Buzzy, a bee, but found that none of the other names suited him as well as his own. Paper bag puppets could easily be made by first graders and then groups of eight could play the story.

The special attraction for the books by Holl, Benchley, and Lobel is that students in grades one and two can read the stories themselves before playing them.

Benchley's *The Strange Disappearance of Arthur Cluck* is an easy-to-read mystery. To play out the story, the characters are Arthur Cluck, his mother, a duck, rooster, cow, Ralph Owl, a fox, and Gus pack rat. Gus needs the following props: erasers, marbles, bottle tops, buttons, a tie clip, and an old tennis ball. Ralph is supposed to find Arthur.

Lobel's *King Rooster, Queen Hen* is an easy reader first graders can read before playing it. There are parts for a rooster, hen, many mice to pull the shoe, a sparrow maid, a duck cook, a crow butler, and a fox who invited them for supper. They escape the fox by asking him to sing. Another Lobel easy reader, *How the Rooster Saved the Day,* is also about animals.

The 1966 Caldecott winner, *Always Room for One More* based on a Scottish folk song by Nic Leodhas, can be played by an entire class. The characters are Lachie MacLachlan, his wife, ten children, a tinker, tailor, sailor, gallowglass, fishing lass, wife, four peat-cutters, a ranter, and a shepherd and his dog. The rest of the class can be the folks in the nearby town. The space in this story has to be defined so the group can leave when the rafters fall down. Playing this song can become noisy and physical.

Sewall's *The Wee Wee Mannie and the Big Big Coo, a Scottish Tale,* is the picture-book version of an old story about a cow that wouldn't stand still.

Two ways to utilize folktales are to attach them to specific areas of the world (by country or continent) or to link them together by theme or subjects. "The Straw Ox," in Haviland's *Favorite Fairy Tales Told in Russia* (pp. 53–56), is one version of the Tar Baby story. Characters needed are a bear, wolf, fox, hare, old man, old woman, and a straw ox. This can be paired with another Russian tale or a different version of Tar Baby.

"The Magic Sandals," in Newman's *Folk Tales of Latin America*, is suitable for playing. Haulachi was given the magic sandals because he had a kind heart. Use this activity with other stories about magic items.

Eecker's *Seven Little Rabbits* is a repetitious picture book that helps primary or kindergarten children grasp number concepts with their eyes. The rabbits drop off one by on one their way down the road to call on an old friend.

Eight players are needed to play out "The Seven Swabians," from Gag's *More Tales from Grimm*. The seven noodleheads are frightened by a monster who was really a hare. Playing out this story could follow a math lesson in the primary grades, or it could introduce other noodlehead stories.

Brenner's picture book *Mr. Tall and Mr. Small* is about a giraffe with enormous knobby knees and a mouse with whiskers. Both had fleas. The rhyming story can be played out live or as a puppet show. The person reading the story while two others play out the story could have fun with the voice changes for the two characters.

Being small is acceptable, but being small and lost is frightening. Raskin's *Moose, Goose, and Little Nobody* is about a goose and a moose who tried to find the mother and house of a mouse called Little Nobody.

Rhythms are part of playing in the next two books. *The Way the Tiger Walked* by Chaconas is about a tiger who went for a walk and was followed by a porcupine, zebra and elephant. The monkeys in the story howled, but the tiger taught all of them that they were marvelous in their own way. Vipont's *The Elephant and the Bad Boy*, illustrated by Raymond Briggs, is suitable for playing with a double cast. Students will enjoy pantomiming the ice cream man, butcher, baker, snackshop man, grocer, and candy store lady from whom the elephant took things. The story ends on a quiet note when the bad boy goes to bed. With some adaptation, this is suitable for narrative pantomime.

A variety of social concepts are introduced as some books are played. *As Right As Can Be* and *Dandelion* relate to an image concept. *An Anteater Named Arthur* had some bad habits and is especially good for role-playing, while the animals in *What Do You Say, Dear?* and *What Do You Do, Dear?* introduce manners. In *Alexander and the Terrible, Horrible, No Good, Very Bad Day*, children learn that everything does not always happen as we want it to and sometimes everything seems to go wrong. Before, during, and after stories are played is a good time to discuss feelings and relationships of characters and how their experiences relate to our lives. All of the following books can be used to promote such discussion.

Rose's *As Right As Can Be* begins when a man bought new shoelaces. They made his shoes look shabby, so he bought something else new. Eventually he acquired a whole new wardrobe including shoes, coat, trousers, and hat. His new self made his wife and home look shabby, so he changed them with borrowed money. Compare this story with Freeman's *Dandelion*.

Hitte's *Mexicali Soup* is fun for children to play because characterization is easy and it can spark discussion of many topics. Mother decided to fix a delicious soup for her family. The daughter Maria thought that potatoes were fattening, so she asked mother to leave them out; Antonio asked her to remove the hot peppers; Rosy wanted garlic left out; papa didn't like celery; Juan didn't want tomatoes; Manuel didn't like onions. So, mother fixed them all what they wanted and served plain water. There are parts for seven plus the baby. Compare this book to Aesop's "The Man, the Boy, and the Donkey," called *The Miller, the Boy and the Donkey* in a picture book and filmstrip illustrated by Duvoisin.

Students can also play out some hiliarious situations which call for good manners in *What Do You Say, Dear?* and *What Do You Do, Dear?* by Joslin. Use the sound filmstrips of both books to introduce them.

"I think I'll move to Australia" is the moan, in Viorst's *Alexander and the Terrible, Horrible, No Good, Very Bad Day*. Besides chiming in with the repetitive phrase, children will like to add things that happened to them on a bad day.

Use the filmstrip of Jeffers's picture book *Wild Robin* to discuss the actions of a wayward boy and a sister who loved him.

EXPANDING STORIES FOR PLAYING.   Some stories fall neatly into the six major parts of a story, have characters who are clearly defined, and have sequences of events with explicit actions that are often repeated. However, there are other stories that challenge students to use their imaginations and creative writing talents to adapt the stories for playing. These stories do not have ready-made dialogue or the repetitive action so perfectly exemplified by "The Three Billy Goats Gruff."

Flack's *Ask Mr. Bear* is an example of a story that is easy for primary students to play. Danny did not know what to get for his mother for her birthday, and so he asked his friends. Mrs. Hen said she would give an egg; Mrs. Goose, Mrs. Goat, Mrs. Sheep, and Mrs. Cow gave responses appropriate to them. Finally, Danny asked Mr. Bear who suggested a big birthday bear hug. This story can be played simply and effectively by several groups of eight students. To expand it, students can think of other animals Danny could ask for advice. They will have to identify some gift that could be expected from each animal. For example, a pig might provide a ham—depending on the group, they might discuss why this gift is of a different order from the others! Have students choose other animals and suitable gifts until each child in the class has participated.

Students will also have to develop their own characters and dialogue for deRegniers's *Little Sister and the Month Brothers*, one of several versions of a Russian folktale about the month brothers. This version is excellent for playing. Little sister had to do all of the work, but was still prettier and happier than her stepmother and stepsisters. They decided to get rid of little sister, so they sent her to look for fresh violets in the snowy forest, and later she was sent for fresh strawberries. She was aided by the month brothers, and eventually married a farmer. Students can make up their own story, and can have the little sister go out into the forest twelve times. The twelve month brothers could each be dressed like their month. There are seventeen parts to play, the twelve months, little sister, the stepmother, the stepsisters, and the farmer.

Van Woerkhom's *The Queen Who Couldn't Bake Gingerbread* needs additional parts written into it, especially parts for boys to play. King Pilaf was looking for a queen who was wise, beautiful, and knew how to bake gingerbread. He interviewed potential queens, but by the time he decided that one might be suitable she had married someone else. In order to give more parts to others, have several girls write scripts for additional prospects considered by the king.

Allow Joslin's etiquette books to introduce Hoban's *Dinner at Albertos*, which is excellent for discussing and playing etiquette. John Hippopotamus had two sons with good table manners, but because they lived at the bottom of the river they tracked mud all over the living room. No one would play with the Boa family anymore because they squeezed others in play and broke their ribs. The antics of Emma, Arthur Alberto, and Sidney are hilarious, and the situations in this story can be expanded to role playing.

Zion's *Harry the Dirty Dog*, an easy reader, is about a dog who ran away from home to avoid a bath and because he felt ignored. During his travels, Harry saw men fixing the street, and lots of other folk. Primary students can read the book themselves and play out the story, expanding it with more community helpers. Students can play out the tasks of various people in the community, and then his travels. Other books about Harry include *Harry by the Sea* or *No Roses for Harry!*

Tompert's *Little Fox Goes to the End of the World* can be played by all children at one time. Much freedom in choosing the actions of bears, lions, elephants, monkeys, crocodiles and one-eyed cats makes this a story with which primary students can let their imaginations run wild when they play out the things Little Fox told her mother she would see when she traveled to the end of the world. This story should be played out after students have had practice playing out more simple structured stories.

STORIES FOR PLAYING—BY AGES OF PLAYERS.   Persons who need guidelines in choosing stories and poems to play that are suitable for a particular age group can consult four books: Fitzgerald's *World Tales for Creative Dramatics and Storytelling*, Kase's *Stories for Creative Acting*, Sikes's *Children's Literature for Dramatization*, and Ward's *Stories to Dramatize*. Two of the books are arranged by age groups. Kase's *Stories for Creative Acting* contains fourteen stories for four to seven-year-olds, thirty stories for eight- to eleven-year-olds, and twenty stories for twelve- to fifteen-year-olds. Ward's *Stories to Dramatize* contains twenty-six stories for children five, six, and seven, years old, thirty-one stories for children eight and nine years old, twenty-four stories for children ten and eleven years old, and twenty-one stories for children twelve, thirteen, and fourteen years old.

Two of the books are not arranged in chronological order but include an index which arranges the stories and poems by age categories. Fitzgerald's *World Tales for Creative Dramatics* is arranged first by continent and then by country. An appendix in Fitzgerald's book on pages 318 to 25 is called "Suggested Age Levels" and is broken down into the following categories: six- and seven-year-olds, eight- and nine-year-olds, ten- and eleven-year-olds, and twelve- and thirteen-year-olds. Sikes's *Children's Literature for Dramatization* is organized by type of literature and type of action: "Poetry for Inviting Action," "Poetry Inviting Characterization," "Poetry Motivating Conflict," "Stories for Young Children," and "Stories for Older Children." One appendix has "Age Level Interests"; (ages 5-12); another appendix is arranged by seasons.

Not all authors agree about the age categories at which a story should be played. Sikes included her retelling of "The Peddler and the Monkeys" on all three of her lists, ages five through six, seven through nine, and ten through twelve. Ward used Sikes's story but gave it the title "The Peddler and His Caps" and placed it in the age category for eight- and nine-year-olds. Some stories that appear in both Kase's and Ward's books but in different age categories: "The Musicians of Bremen" (5-7 Ward) and "The Bremen Town Musicians" (8-11 Kase); "The Town Mouse and the Country Mouse" (4-7 Kase, 8-9 Ward); "King John and the Abbot of Canterbury" (8-11 Kase, 12-14 Ward), and "The Golden Goose" (8-11 Kase, 10-12 Fitzgerald). Teachers and librarians are reminded that these age categories are merely guides helpful for the novice or for comparison. Each teacher knows the abilities and interests of students in a particular classroom and whether or not they will play out the stories satisfactorily.

The books by Kase and Ward have the most stories in common. A few of these stories appear in the other two books. Stories in common for ages four through seven are "The Elf and the Dormouse" (Kase and Ward), "The Three Billy Goats Gruff" (Fitzgerald, Kase, and Ward), "Teeny Tiny" (Sikes and Ward), "Why the Evergreens Keep Their Leaves" (Kase and Ward). Stories in common for ages eight through eleven in Kase and Ward are: "The Emperor's New Clothes," "The Enchanted Shirt," "The Golden Touch" and "King Midas," "The Hurdy-Gurdy Man," "The Boy Who Cried Wolf" and "The Shepherd Boy," "The Clown Who Forgot How to Laugh," "The Old Market Woman," and "The Princess Who Could Not Cry." Stories Kase and Ward have in common for ages twelve through fourteen are "The Christmas Apple" and the ballad "Get Up and Bar the Door."

Sikes's *Children's Literature for Dramatization* contains the best selection of poetry: forty poems for five- and six-year-olds, over sixty poems for seven- through nine-year-olds, and thirty-seven poems for ten- through twelve-year-olds. Some poems appeared in more than one age category. Ward included seven Mother Goose rhymes for ages five through seven: "Hickory Dickory Dock," "Little Miss Muffet," "My Lady Wind," "Old King Cole," "The Queen of Hearts," "Sing a Song of Sixpence," and "Three Little Mice." Sikes included "Pat-a-Cake" and "To Market" for five and six-year-olds and "Humpty Dumpty," "Tom, Tom the Piper's Son," "Hey Diddle Diddle," and "I Had a Little Nut Tree" for ages five and six and seven through nine. Ward included some poetry besides nursery rhymes. A few of them are Dorothy Aldis's "Hiding" and Rachel Field's "Roads," both for eight- and nine-year-olds. Kase included Lear's "The Owl and the Pussycat" and Browning's "Pied Piper of Hamelin" for ages eight through eleven.

Six poems by Robert Louis Stevenson are included in Sikes's *Children's Literature for Dramatization*. "Marching Song," "My Shadow," and "The Swing" are included in the lists for both ages five and six and seven through nine. "The Wind" is listed for ages five through seven, and "Happy Thought" is listed for ages seven through nine. Some other favorite poems listed in Sikes's anthology and the appropriate age categories are: James Wendell Johnson's "The Creation" (7-9), Vachel Lindsay's "The Mysterious Cat" (7-9, 10-12), a selection from Longfellow's "Hiawatha's Childhood" (10-12), Clement C. Moore's "A Visit from St. Nicholas" (5-6, 7-9, 10-12), Ernest Laurence Thayer's "Casey at the Bat" (10-12) which is also available as a sound filmstrip, and Whittier's "Barbara Fritchie" (10-12). Three stories in rhyme from Aesop are included in Sikes's book for ages ten through twelve: Horace's "The Country Mouse and the Town Mouse," and "The Grasshopper and the Ant" and "The Turtle and the Rabbit," both from La Fontaine.

"The Town Mouse and the Country Mouse" as well as "The Boy Who Cried Wolf" and "The Shepherd Boy and the Wolf" also appear in the books by Kase and Ward. Kase's book contains two sections called "Aesop's Fables." One is for ages four through seven and the other is for ages eight through eleven.

Numerous legends appear in three of the books. Kase includes two legends for ages four through seven: "Why the Violet Slept So Late" and "Why the Evergreen Trees Keep Their Leaves." The last legend is also included in Ward's book for five-through seven-year-olds. Legends for eight-and nine-year-olds in Ward's book are "How the Robin's Breast Became Red" and "A Legend of Spring." For ten- and eleven-year-olds, Ward listed "The Sorcerer's Apprentice," "William Tell," "Johnnie Appleseed," and "Robin Hood's Merry Adventures with the Miller." Sikes included "The Prologue to the Merry Adventures of Robin Hood" for ages ten through twelve. "Our Lady's Juggler" was listed for ages twelve through fourteen by Ward.

Sikes and Ward include more myths than the other collections. Sikes listed the following myths for ages seven through twelve: "Prometheus," "Pandora," "Demeter and Persephone," and "The Death of Balder." Ward included "The Maid Who Defied Minerva" for ages eight and nine, and "The Quest of the Hammer" for ages twelve through fourteen. Hawthorne's "Golden Touch" is for ages ten and eleven in Ward's book, and "King Midas" is for ages eight through eleven in Kase's book.

Several Bible stories are categorized by ages in the anthologies by Sikes and Ward. The following stories are included in the collection by Sikes: "The Story of Christmas" (5-6, 7-9, 10-12), "David, the Shepherd Boy" (7-9, 10-12), "Psalm 150" (10-12), and "Joseph the Dreamer" (7-9, 10-12). Ward included "The Nativity" (10-11) and "The Good Samaritan" and "The Prodigal Son" (both 12-14).

Fitzgerald's *World Tales for Creative Dramatics* contains over a hundred folktales suitable for playing. The only folktale that is duplicated in another book is "Urashima Taro" (10-13 Fitzgerald and 7-12 Sikes). Sikes's *Children's Literature for Dramatization* contains five fairy tales for children seven through twelve: "The Snow Maiden," "Boots and His Brothers," "Snow White and Rose Red," "Molly Whuppie" and "Rapunzel." "The Frog Prince" is listed for ten- to twelve-year-olds.

The following traditional tales are appropriate for children ages four through seven: "Goldilocks and the Three Bears" (Ward), "The Little Red Hen" (Ward), "The Three Bears" (Kase), "The Three Billy Goats Gruff" (Fitzgerald, Kase and Ward), and "The Three Little Pigs" (Fitzgerald and Kase). "The Gingerbread Boy," "The Big Turnip," and "Henny Penny" are listed by Sikes for ages seven through nine.

Children's classics by favorite authors that have been included in the books by Kase, Sikes, and Ward are Hans Christian Andersen's "The Emperor's New Clothes" (8-11 Kase, 10-11 Ward), "The Princess and the Pea" (4-7 Kase) and "The Ugly Duckling" (7-9 Sikes); Charles Dickens's "A Christmas Carol" (12-14 Ward) and "Why the Chimes Rang" (10-12 Sikes); Kenneth Grahame's "Mr. Toad's Disguise" (10-11 Ward); Lucretia Hale's "Mrs. Peterkin Puts Salt in Her Coffee" (10-11 Ward); Joel Chandler Harris's "The Wonderful Tar Baby Story" (8-9 Ward); Washington Irving's "The Moor's Legacy" and "Rip Van Winkle" (12-14 Ward); A. A. Milne's "Tigger Has Breakfast" (8-9 Ward); Beatrix Potter's "The Tale of Peter Rabbit" (5-7 Ward); John Ruskin's "King of the Golden River" (10-12 Sikes); Dr. Seuss's "Five Hundred Hats of Bartholomew Cubbins" (8-11 Kase); William Shakespeare's "Macbeth," "A Midsummer Night's Dream," and "Taming of the Shrew" all retold by Mary MacLeod (12-14 Ward); Mark Twain's "The Jumping Frog of Calaveras County" (8-11 Kase), "The Prince and the Pauper" (12-14 Ward), and "Tom Sawyer Discovers a Law of Human Action" (10-11 Ward); and Oscar Wilde's "The Selfish Giant" (12-15 Kase).

PLAYS IN COLLECTIONS OR IN INDIVIDUAL BOOKS.   Numerous stories from folklore or children's classics have been made into plays that appear in individual books or anthologies. Reading a script written by others can help teachers and students to write plays based on other stories. The largest collections of stories from children's classics and from folktales that have been translated into dramas can be found in Thane's *Plays from Famous Stories and Fairy Tales* and two books by Kamerman, *Children's Plays from Favorite Stories* and *Dramatized Folk Tales of the World*.

Some students may choose to write parodies or spoofs on fairy tales. Boiko's *Children's Plays* contains three spoofs: "Cinder-Riley," "Cinder-Rabbit," and "Cupivac." The last play is about a computer that matches pairs from children's literature—like Sleeping Beauty and Rip Van Winkle. Fontaine's *Humorous Skits for Young People* contains "Androcles and His Pal," "Let Sleeping Beauties Lie," and "Another Cinderella." The Prince who woke up Sleeping Beauty did not find the romantic episode he expected, so he put the beauty back to sleep. The parody of Cinderella contains a pantomime scene involving Sophie, one of Cinderella's step-sisters. Humorous events in that story involve a chauffeur and a used sports convertible owned by a little old lady who drove only in the Indianapolis 500. At midnight the chauffeur changed into a mushroom and the car into a Hubbard squash. A squash was used because no pumpkin was available.

There are similar stories that are not parodies. Burack's *One Hundred Plays for Children* contains "A Chinese Rip Van Winkle." "A Small Crimson Parasol," which is a Japanese Little Red Riding Hood, appears in Boiko's *Children's Plays.*

Cullum's *Aesop in the Afternoon* contains sixty-six playlets from Aesop's Fables. Other fables from Aesop made into plays are "Androcles and the Lion," "Who Helped the Lion," "Androcles and His Pal," "Bell the Cat," "The Man, the Boy and the Donkey," and "The Tortoise and the Hare."

Sometimes a picture book can be correlated with a story that is played. Use Ginsburg's picture book *Mushroom in the Rain* with a similar play called "Under One Toadstool" found in Carlson's *Let's Pretend It Happened to You.*

Plays can be used to complement poetry. Burack's *One Hundred Plays for Children* contains two plays that can be used with Browning's poem "The Pied Piper of Hamelin," Grace Evelyn Mills's "Christmas Comes to Hamelin" and Lucy Kennedy's "The Pied Piper of Hamelin."

Sometimes plays include music. The six plays based on folktales included in Sloane's *Fun With Folk Tales, Six Plays in Verse with Music and Songs* are *King Thrushbeard, The Golden Goose, Rumplestiltskin, A Sprig of Rosemary, The Little Red Hen and the Grain of Wheat,* and *Who Laughs Last, Laughs Best.*

There are plays that can be related to a children's classic. Two plays to correlate with Alcott's *Little Women* are *Louisa Alcott's Wish,* and *Meg, Jo, Amy and Beth.* The second is a scene from the beginning of *Little Women* in which the sisters are knitting while they discuss Christmas. That scene and scenes from Spyri's *Heidi* and Carroll's *Alice in Wonderland and Through the Looking Glass* all appear in Cohen's *Scenes for Young Actors. Heidi, Clara,* a dialogue between the two girls in the parlor of Clara's home in Frankfort, was adapted by Lorraine Cohen. Eva Le Gallienne and Florida Friebus's adaptation called *Alice, The Red Queen* comes from act 2, scene 1. *The Lady Who Put Salt in Her Coffee* comes from Hale's *The Peterkin Papers.* Have children act out *Pirates* after they have read chapter 2 of Stevenson's *Treasure Island.* Other plays based on individual books are Dickens's *The Magic Fishbone,* Grahame's *The Reluctant Dragon,* Thurber's *The Great Quillow,* and Andersen's *The Swineherd.*

Eight plays were prepared for elementary students to perform for Shakespeare's four-hundredth birthday: *Hamlet, Macbeth, Romeo and Juliet, A Midsummer Night's Dream, Julius Caesar, The Comedy of Errors, The Taming of the Shrew,* and *The Tempest.* On pages 8 to 20 of *Shake Hands with Shakespeare, Eight Plays for Elementary Schools,* Cullum gives directions and suggestions for performing Shakespeare's plays. Complete lists of vocabulary, listed by scenes, are valuable for use when studying Shakespeare whether or not the plays are performed. The plays are also available individually from the publisher. Companion books are Nesbit's *Children's Shakespeare* and the Lambs' *Tales from Shakespeare.*

Several plays about children's classics appear in individual books. *Toad of Toad Hall* is a play written by A. A. Milne based on Grahame's *Wind in the Willows*. There are four acts, a prologue, and an epilogue. Twenty-four characters plus ten other parts allow for every member of a class to participate.

The seven plays in *Paddington on Stage* are based on *The Adventures of A Bear Called Paddington*.

Dahl's *Charlie and the Chocolate Factory, a Play* was adapted by Richard R. George. Five people have from twenty-five to fifty-eight lines. Other students can appear in the chorus.

There are six characters in *Squirrel Nutkin, a Children's Play*, adapted by Beatrix Potter herself. Music is included. That play is an individual book. *Peter Rabbit*, a play by Natalie Simonds, appears in Burack's *One Hundred Plays for Children* (pp. 757-61). The plays could be produced after books by Potter are read to or by primary children.

Intermediate students may like to read or play Joan Aiken's *Winterthing, a Play for Children*. The two-act fantasy/suspense play takes place in Scotland and includes music. Use the play with such books as *Nightbirds on Nantucket*, *Black Hearts in Battersea*, and *The Wolves of Willoughby Chase*.

There are three acts and parts for nineteen characters in Brink's play based on her own Newbery Award-winning *Caddie Woodlawn*. Brink explains the differences between the book and the play at the beginning of the book. One change is that many events are condensed into a short time span rather than spread out over a year.

Books about Harriet Tubman can be used with a play by Childress called *When the Rattlesnake Sounds*. There are three parts in this play about Harriet when she worked as a hotel laundress to raise money for the abolitionist cause. Books about Harriet Tubman are Laurence's *Harriet and the Promised Land*; Petry's *Harriet Tubman, Conductor on the Underground Railroad*; and Swift's *The Railroad to Freedom; a Story of the Civil War*. Similar stories can be found to accompany *Escape to Freedom: A Play About Young Frederick Douglass* by Ossie Davis.

PLAYS BASED ON CHILDREN'S LITERATURE.   Following is a list of plays derived or adapted from children's stories. The listing includes the title of the play, the number of characters in the play, and the short title of the anthology in which the play can be found. For the full name of the editor and title of each anthology, see the bibliography of this book.

African Trio: The Fierce Creature, When the Hare Brought the Sun, and The Princess Who Was Hidden from the World. 21 characters plus storytellers. Kamerman, *Dramatized. . .*, pp. 3-14.

Ali Baba and the Forty Thieves. 7 characters plus narrator. Durrell and Crossley, *Thirty Plays. . .*, pp. 45-53.

Alice, the Red Queen. (Carroll's *Alice in Wonderland*, act 2, scene 1). Number of characters variable. Cohen, *Scenes for. . .*, pp . 65-69.

Aladdin and His Wonderful Lamp. (*Arabian Nights*). 11 characters. Thane, *Plays from. . .*, pp. 38-57.

Androcles and the Lion. (Aesop's *Fables*). 4 characters plus spectators. Carlson, *Act It Out*, pp. 31-32.

Another Way to Weigh an Elephant. 7 characters plus narrator. Burack and Crossley, *Popular Plays*. . ., pp. 94-100.

The Apple of Contentment. 9 characters. Thane, *Plays from*. . ., pp. 153-168.

Arthur's Sword. 16 characters. Smith, *Plays*. . ., pp. 33-62.

The Baker's Neighbor. 10 characters plus villagers. Kamerman, *Dramatized*. . ., pp. 471-480.

Baron Barnaby's Box. 9 characters. Kamerman, *Dramatized*. . ., pp. 549-558.

Bell the Cat. (Aesop's *Fables*). 2 characters plus other mice. Carlson, *Act It Out*, p. 30.

Big Paul Bunyan. 14 characters plus lumberjacks and townspeople. Kamerman, *Dramatized*. . ., pp. 514-526.

The Brave Little Tailor. 12 characters and townspeople. Thane, *Plays from*. . ., pp. 397-413.

The Bridge to Killybog Fair. 16 players. Kamerman, *Dramatized*. . ., pp. 227-238.

Broom Market Day. 9 characters. Kamerman, *Dramatized*. . ., pp. 656-665.

The Builder of the Wall. 9 characters. Kamerman, *Dramatized*. . ., pp. 422-434.

The Child Who Was Made of Snow. 3 characters plus children. Bennett, *Creative Plays*. . .*Holidays*, pp. 283-287.

A Chinese Rip Van Winkle. 12 characters. Burack, *One Hundred*. . ., pp. 37-44.

A Christmas Carol. (Based on Dickens). 18 characters plus narrator and others. Burack and Crossley, *Popular Plays*. . ., pp. 337-353.

Christmas Comes to Hamelin. (Based on Browning's poem). 24 characters plus dolls and citizens. Burack, *One Hundred*. . ., pp. 528-539.

Christmas Every Day. 9 characters. Thane, *Plays from*. . ., pp. 216-230.

Cinder-Rabbit. 12 characters. Boiko, *Children's Plays*. . ., pp. 484-498.

Cinder-Riley. 7 characters plus dancers and prop boys. Boiko, *Childrens's Plays*. . ., pp. 239-248.

Cinderella. 26 characters. Burack, *One Hundred Plays*. . ., pp. 633-642.

Cinderella. 8 characters. Kamerman, *Little Plays*. . ., pp. 240-249.

Cinderella. 14 characters plus coachman's voice. Thane, *Plays from*. . . , pp. 430-499.

The City Mouse and the Country Mouse. 5 characters. Bennett, *Creative Plays . . . Holidays*, pp. 178-185.

The Comedy of Errors. (Based on Shakespeare). 16 characters plus citizens. Cullum, *Shake Hands*. . ., pp. 191-224.

The Covetous Councilman. 4 characters. Kamerman, *Dramatized*. . . , pp. 504-513.

Dame Fortune and Don Donkey. 14 characters plus villagers. Kamerman, *Dramatized*. . ., pp. 481-492.

David and Goliath. (Based on the Bible). 12 characters plus extra soldiers. Howard, *Complete*. . ., pp. 476-480.

Dick Whittington and His Cat. 7 characters plus voices and real cat. Thane, *Plays from*. . ., pp. 414-429.

Don Quixote Saves the Day. (Based on Cervantes). 14 characters plus extras. Howard, *Complete*. . . , pp. 525-535.

Dumling and the Golden Goose. 28 characters. Thane, *Plays from*. . . , pp. 105-119.

Elves and the Shoemaker. 16 characters. Thane, *Plays from*. . . , pp. 90-104.

The Emperor's Nightingale. 12 characters. Thane, *Plays from*. . ., pp. 3-19.

The Fierce Creature. 10 characters. Kamerman, *Dramatized*. . ., pp. 3-6.

Finn McCool. 11 characters. Kamerman, *Dramatized*. . ., pp. 218-226.

Fish in the Forest. 9 characters plus narrator. Burack and Crossley, *Popular Plays*. . ., pp. 45-56.

Fish in the Forest. 13 characters plus peasants and servants. Kamerman, *Dramatized*. . ., pp. 388-399.

The Five Brothers. 6 boys and narrator. Durrell and Crossley, *Thirty Plays*. . ., pp. 4-6.

The Floating Stone. 10 characters. Burack, *One Hundred*. . ., pp. 643-648.

A Gift for Hans Brinker. (Based on Dodge). 15 characters. Kamerman, *Dramatized*. . ., pp. 200-211.

A Gift from Johnny Appleseed. 10 characters. Kamerman, *Dramatized*. . ., pp. 537-548.

The Golden Goose. 15 characters plus lords and ladies. Sloane, *Fun with*. . ., pp. 59-79.

The Great Quillow. (Based on Thurber). 14 characters. Smith, *Plays and How*. . ., pp. 121-137.

The Great Samurai Sword. 12 characters. Kamerman, *Dramatized*. . ., pp. 306-316.

Gulliver Wins His Freedom. (Based on Swift). 15 characters and extras. Howard, *Complete Book*. . ., pp. 505-514.

Hans, Who Made the Princess Laugh. 13 characters. Burack, *One Hundred*. . ., pp. 726-733.

Hansel and Gretel. 5 characters. Burack, *One Hundred*. . ., pp. 751-756.

Hansel and Gretel. 6 characters plus voice and gingerbread children. Thane, *Plays from*. . ., pp. 335-351.

Hansel and Gretel. 5 characters plus narrator. Durrell and Crossley, *Thirty Plays*. . ., pp. 63-68.

Happy Christmas to All. (Based on Moore's *Night Before Christmas*). Burack, *One Hundred*. . ., pp. 540-554.

Happy Days for Little Women. 10 characters. Howard, *Complete Book*. . ., pp. 469-476.

The Happy Prince. (Based on Oscar Wilde). 14 characters plus narrator. Durrell and Crossley, *Favorite*. . ., pp. 150-163.

The Hare and the Tortoise. (Based on Aesop's *Fables*). 3 characters. Bennett, *Creative Plays*. . .*Holidays*, pp. 186-192.

Heidi. 11 characters. Thane, *Plays from*. . ., pp. 315-334.

Heidi, Clara. (Based on Spyri's *Heidi*). Cohen, *Scenes for*. . ., pp. 70-74.

Heidi Finds the Way. (Based on Spyri's *Heidi*). 10 characters plus narrator. Durrell and Crossley, *Favorite*. . ., pp. 181-195.

How the Bluebird and the Coyote Got Their Colors. Carlson, *Let's Pretend*. . ., pp. 67-70.

How Much Land Does a Man Need? (Based on Tolstoy). 8 characters. Burack and
 Crossley, *Popular Plays. . .*, pp. 284-299.
If Wishes Were Horses. 8 characters. Burack, *One Hundred. . .*, pp. 182-187.
The Indian Boy Without a Name. 8 characters. Kamerman, *Dramatized. . .*, pp.
 526-536.
Jack and Jill. 7 characters. Kamerman, *Dramatized. . .*, pp. 649-655.
Jack and the Magic Beanstalk. 9 characters plus farmers, wives, families, and
 two cows. Thane, *Plays from. . .*, pp. 366-380.
Jack Jouette's Ride. 13 characters plus chorus. Boiko, *Plays and. . .*, pp. 66-76.
Jenny-by-the-Day. 7 characters. Burack, *One Hundred. . .*, pp. 666-674.
Johnny Appleseed in Danger. 12 characters plus children and Indians. Howard,
 Complete. . ., pp. 458-462.
Julius Caesar. (Based on Shakespeare). 9 characters plus soldiers and Roman
 citizens. Cullum, *Shake Hands. . .*, pp. 165-189.
A Kettle of Brains. 4 characters. Burack, *One Hundred. . .*, pp. 790-795.
Kind Brother, Mean Brother. 3 characters. Carlson, *Let's Pretend. . .*, pp. 72-79.
King Alfred and the Cakes. 9 characters. Thane, *Plays from. . .*, pp. 143-152.
The King and the Bee. 6 characters. Kamerman, *Dramatized. . .*, pp. 250-257.
King Arthur and His Knights. 29 characters plus court. Kamerman, *Drama-
 tized. . .*, pp. 106-127.
King Horn. 6 characters. Kamerman, *Dramatized. . .*, pp. 447-457.
King Midas. 5 characters plus voices. Kamerman, *Dramatized. . .*, pp. 177-190.
King Thrushbeard. 18 characters plus court. Sloane, *Fun with. . .*, pp. 23-58.
The King Who Was Bored. 12 characters. Kamerman, *Dramatized. . .*, pp.
 334-345.
Lady Moon and the Thief: A Chinese Fantasy. 14 characters plus villagers.
 Boiko, *Plays and. . .*, pp. 19-26.
Lady Moon and the Thief: A Chinese Fantasy. 14 characters plus villagers.
 Kamerman, *Dramatized. . .*, pp. 23-31.
The Lady Who Put Salt in Her Coffee. 12 characters. Smith, *Seven Plays. . .*, pp.
 9-22.
Legend of the Christmas Rose. 5 characters. Carlson, *Act It Out*, pp. 82-84.
The Legend of the Christmas Rose. 10 characters plus narrator. Durrell and
 Crossley, *Favorite. . .*, pp. 92-98.
The Leprechaun Shoemakers. 12 characters. Kamerman, *Dramatized. . .*, pp.
 239-249.
The Lion and the Mouse. (Based on Aesop's *Fables*). 2 characters. Bennett,
 Creative. . ., pp. 193-197.
The Lion and the Mouse. (Aesop). 2 characters. Burack, *One Hundred. . .*, pp.
 605-608.
The Lion and the Mouse. (Aesop). 7 characters plus narrator. Durrell and
 Crossley, *Thirty Plays. . .*, pp. 11-17.
The Lion and the Mouse. (Aesop). 7 characters. Kamerman, *Little Plays. . .*, pp.
 249-255.
Little Hero of Holland. 9 characters. Burack, *One Hundred. . .*, pp. 577-586.
The Little Princess. 12 characters. Thane, *Plays from. . .*, pp. 283-302.

The Little Red Hen. 10 characters plus two narrators and chorus. Boiko, Plays and. . ., pp. 135-145.

The Little Red Hen and the Grain of Wheat. 5 characters plus chorus of four. Sloane, Fun with. . ., pp. 155-166.

Little Red Riding Hood. (See A Small Crimson Parasol.)

Little Red Riding Hood. 5 characters. Kamerman, Little. . ., pp. 277-285.

Little Snow White. 10 characters. Kamerman, Little. . ., pp. 285-291.

Louisa Alcott's Wish. 7 characters. Burack, One Hundred. . ., pp. 87-94.

Macbeth. (Based on Shakespeare). 22 characters plus banquet guests and servants. Cullum, Shake Hands. . ., pp. 63-74.

A Mad Tea Party. (Based on Lewis Carroll). 4 characters and narrator. Durrell and Crossley, Thirty Plays. . ., pp. 54-60.

The Magic Box. 14 characters. Kamerman, Dramatized. . ., pp. 258-277.

The Magic Cloak. 14 characters plus court and dancers. Kamerman, Dramatized. . ., pp. 435-446.

The Magic Cookie Jar. 4 characters. Burack, One Hundred. . ., pp. 706-717.

The Magic Fishbone. (Based on Dickens). 15 characters. Smith, Plays. . ., pp. 81-97.

Magic Goose. 17 characters plus narrator. Durrell and Crossley, Thirty Plays. . ., pp. 39-44.

The Magic Grapes. 9 characters. Kamerman, Dramatized. . ., pp. 258-264.

The Magic Nutmeg-Grater. 9 characters plus extras. Thane, Plays from . . ., pp. 198-215.

The Man, the Boy, and the Donkey. (Aesop's Fables). 6 characters plus extras. Carlson, Let's Pretend. . ., pp. 39-42.

Meg, Jo, Amy, Beth. (Based on Alcott's Little Women). Cohen, Scenes for. . ., pp. 78-84.

Merry Tyll and the Three Rogues. 25 characters plus villagers. Kamerman, Dramatized. . ., pp. 162-176.

A Midsummer Night's Dream. (Based on Shakespeare). 20 characters plus fairies. Cullum, Shake Hands. . ., pp. 125-164.

The Miniature Darzis. (Based on Grimms' The Elves and the Shoemaker). 7 characters. Smith, Seven plays. . ., pp. 45-60.

Miss Muffet and the Spider. 4 characters. Bennett, Creative. . ., pp. 359-362.

The Mixing Stick. 11 characters. Burack, One Hundred. . ., pp. 701-705.

A Most Special Dragon. 8 characters. Kamerman, Dramatized. . ., pp. 79-87.

Mother Goose Gives a Dinner. 12 characters. Kamerman, Little. . ., pp. 310-317.

Mother Goose's Christmas Surprise. 13 characters. Boiko, Children's. . ., pp. 155-163.

The Musicians of Bremen Town. 10 characters plus narrator. Kamerman, Dramatized. . ., pp. 155-161.

No Room at the Inn. 16 characters plus extras. Burack, One Hundred. . ., pp. 551-559.

The Ogre Who Built a Bridge. 10 characters. Kamerman, Dramatized. . ., pp. 278-287.

The Old Woman and the Tramp. 2 characters. Carlson, Act It Out, pp. 67-72.

The Return of Rip Van Winkle. (Based on Irving). Howard, *Complete Book.* . ., pp. 481–489.

Rip Van Winkle. (Based on Irving). 16 characters plus sailors, townspeople, and a voice. Thane, *Plays from.* . ., pp. 381–396.

Robin Hood Outwits the Sheriff. 19 characters. Kamerman, *Dramatized.* . ., pp. 61–78.

Robin Hood Tricks the Sheriff. 19 characters plus narrator. Durell and Crossley, *Favorite.* . ., pp. 280–288.

Romeo and Juliet. (Based on Shakespeare). 12 characters plus servants, guests, and chorus. Cullum, *Shake Hands.* . ., pp. 95–123.

Rumpelstiltskin. 6 characters plus extras. Bennett, *Creative.* . ., pp. 149–157.

Rumpelstiltskin. 9 characters. Burack, *One Hundred.* . ., pp. 587–595.

Rumpelstiltskin. 10 characters plus yeomen and peasants. Sloane, *Fun with.* . ., pp. 81–113.

The Salt in the Sea. 17 characters. Burack, *One Hundred.* . ., pp. 618–632.

Saucy Scarecrow. 14 characters plus extras. Thane, *Plays from.* . ., pp. 130–142.

Scheherazade. (From *Arabian Nights*). 10 characters plus narrator. Durrell and Crossley, *Favorite.* . ., pp. 237–245.

The Secret of the Wishing Well. 19 characters plus extras. Kamerman, *Dramatized.* . ., pp. 15–22.

Seven Simons. 8 characters or more. Carlson, *Funny Bone.* . ., pp. 64–69.

Sherlock Holmes and the Red-Headed League. (Based on Doyle). 6 characters plus narrator. Burack and Crossley, *Popular Plays.* . ., pp. 232–245.

Shirley Holmes and the FBI. 15 characters plus narrator. Burack and Crossley, *Popular Plays.* . ., pp. 118–131.

The Shoemaker and the Elves. 5 characters. Bennett, *Creative.* . ., pp. 228–236.

Shut the Door. 4 characters. Carlson, *Funny Bone.* . ., pp. 71–75.

Simple Olaf. 7 characters plus court. Kamerman, *Dramatized.* . ., pp. 413–421.

Sir Galahad and the Maidens. 15 characters plus extras. Howard, *Complete.* . ., pp. 463–469.

Sleeping Beauty. 17 characters. Burack, *One Hundred.* . ., pp. 596–604.

The Sleeping Beauty. 18 characters. Thane, *Plays from.* . ., pp. 303–314.

The Sleeping Mountains. 11 characters. Kamerman, *Dramatized.* . ., pp. 346–359.

A Small Crimson Parasol, Little Red Riding Hood Japanese Style. 10 characters. Boiko, *Children's.* . ., pp. 1–11.

Snow White. 10 characters plus narrator. Durrell and Crossley, *Thirty Plays.* . ., pp. 152–159.

Snow White and Rose Red. 8 characters plus attendants. Bennett, *Creative.* . ., pp. 158–177.

Snowflake. 14 characters plus 2 narrators, 2 prop boys, and dancing snowflakes. Boiko, *Plays and.* . ., pp. 181–192.

A Spouse for Susie Mouse. 8 characters, Kamerman, *Dramatized.* . ., pp. 318–323.

The Sprig of Rosemary. 20 characters plus soldiers. Sloane, *Fun with* . . ., pp.

COSTUMES AND ALTERNATIVES. Elaborate costumes for playing out stories are not necessary. Asking students to bring costumes to school or club meetings discriminates against parents who do not have the time, talent, or money to provide a suitable costume. Costumes for playing out stories suggests that the play will be performed for an audience, when in fact the main idea is playing for self-actualization and spontaneity.

There are several ways to provide for outward identification of characters without causing a hardship to participants. There can be a treasure chest of costumes in a classroom or library media center that will not embarrass students but will create additional fun: basic costumes that can be used over and over again by anyone. Costume elements for kings, queens, princes and princesses, court members, and a variety of animals are needed. Patterns that fit many sizes are contained in books such as Greenhowe's *Costumes for Nursery Tale Characters*. Specific costumes for various roles, Little Red Riding Hood and the wolf, for example, are included. Chernoff's *Easy Costumes You Don't Have to Sew* is less complicated and includes, among others, a dragon and a bat. No sewing is required for sixty costumes in Eisner's *Quick and Easy Holiday Costumes*.

The twenty-one costumes in Gilbreath's *Making Costumes for Parties, Plays and Holidays* include a ghost, scarecrow, gingerbread boy, octopus, dog, and other animals. Berk's *The First Book of Stage Costume and Make-Up* shows how to make costumes for various historical periods from the Romans to the American Civil War, as well as costumes from literature such as a prince, princess, and Robin Hood. A princess also appears in Lobley's *Making Children's Costumes*. Muzzles for wolves and dogs appear in Purdy's *Costumes for You to Make*. Parish's *Let's Be Early Settlers with Daniel Boone* includes frontier costumes, while her *Let's Be Indians* focuses on Indians. Ideas for making more Indian costumes appear in Hofsinde's *Indian Costumes* and Mason's *The Book of Indian Crafts and Costumes*. Ideas for costumes appear in Korty's *Plays from African Folktales*. Barnwell's *Disguises You Can Make* includes step by step directions for making twenty-four disguises. Included is a witch, elephant, monster, and a cat with variations for a tiger, leopard, and lion. The old man and old woman can be used for Gag's *Millions of Cats*. The robot can be used in playing Brink's *Andy Buckram's Tin Man*, the magician can be used with Fleischman's *Mr. Mysterious and Company*, the china doll can be used with the picture book or sound filmstrip of the Ozark folksong *Mommy, Buy Me a China Doll*, and the owl can be used with the books about owls discussed in the first chapter of this book.

There are some considerations involved with acquiring and maintaining a costume collection. Materials may be donated and care should be taken to utilize only washable (preferably drip-dry) fabrics. Help in creating the costumes could be found from retired persons who are handy with a needle or sewing machine. The only reward expected in these circumstances would be the feeling of being needed or a chance to see "live children" in the costumes. In this latter instance, an exception could be made to the non-performance rule, and children could visit a retirement center to share the excitement of the costumes. It is not necessary to prepare hours and hours for such a performance because spontaneity will be part of the audience appeal for persons who rarely have a chance to see children.

Costumes must be kept sanitary. That is why only washable and drip-dry fabrics should be used. It is possible to ask for volunteers to wash costumes, but quite another thing to expect volunteers to iron. Costumes should be washed after each wearing.

Usually it is enough just to identify characters by signs which show a picture of the character or just the character's name, or at the most a token element of costume—hats, crowns, etc. After a story has been read or told for the first time, give participants large self-sticking cards so each can identify his or her part. Eight by five cards with the name and picture of the characters can also be given to students as a way of distributing parts and for identification while playing. Laminated cards can be reused. Identifying tags may be pinned to the front bodice or the back, with safety pins.

Describing the character might be done by having each child draw a picture of that character. (Writing out the words can increase vocabulary.) One particular story that can be used as an example is Carl's picture book *The Rooster Who Set Out to See the World*. Fifteen or more children can play out the story. Each child, given the name of his character, can either draw it out freehand or use the opaque projector to reproduce the silhouettes that appear in the corner of each righthand page. Characters include one rooster, two cats, three frogs, four turtles, five fish, and as many fireflies as needed. The story is easily played with spontaneous dialogue. The rooster, out to see the world, met each group of animals, who decided to join him. When it began to get dark, the animals complained about hunger, fright, and the like—and group by group they departed in reverse order to that in joining the rooster. After this story is played, kindergarten and first graders will return again to the rich and colorful illustrations of the author/illustrator.

This project fulfills several objectives. It introduces an exciting picture book to children, in which words, as well as numbers from one to five are included. A numbers game of adding and subtracting is a possibility.

The use of props is one way to differentiate human characters. Crowns and scepters, hammers, mops, artificial patches and tatters, gloves, hats, musical instruments, bowls, and utensils are all indicators of who's who. Anyone wearing a pointed hat and carrying a broom must be a witch. The persons in "The Bee, the Harp, the Mouse and the Bum Clock" who represent the wheels and reels can cover themselves with all manner of artwork to depict wheels, gears, and bobbins. Persons depicting the pots and pans in the same story can find such objects in a prop chest in a classroom or draw their own.

Another artistic alternative is to provide students with sufficiently heavy paper sacks (about 8-lb weight) and ask them to create a paper bag puppet that can speak for the character. Paper bag puppets are successfuly used by children without requiring a stage.

Masks provide an alternative to costumes that is both sanitary and artistic. Development of a character demands investigation, and physical appearance is a major concern. Several worthwhile activities can come out of preparation. Research might be necessary before the authentic mask can be created; artistic talent as well as manual dexterity may be needed. The face mask is especially useful when an animal is played. The mask should not obstruct the view. Instructions for making masks appear in Hunt and Carlson's *Masks and Mask Makers*. Price's *Dancing Masks of Africa* shows West African ceremonial masks. More African masks appear in Kerina's *African Crafts*. Baylor's *They Put on Masks* contains authentic Southwest American Indian masks, and there are masks in Hofsinde's *Indian Arts* book. Twenty-one different kinds of masks are included in Lewis and Oppenheimer's *Folding Paper Masks*: owl, lion, dog, fox, deer, cat, elephant, eagle, rabbit, Satan, clown, and funny faces. Directions for making cardboard masks appear in Lidstone's *Building with Cardboard*.

Alkema's *Monster Masks* shows pictures of masks made from drinking straws, yarn and pipe cleaners, egg cartons, tinfoil, clay, and even a sand cast mask is included. Monsters can also be created with make-up although the process is messier and not as long lasting as a mask. Seventy-five photos and instructions for creating Frankenstein's bride, a mummy, and a werewolf are included in Cox's *Make-up Monsters*. Cox also has written a book called *Creature Costumes*.

PLAYS TO ENRICH GEOGRAPHY LESSONS. Winther's *Plays from Folktales of Africa and Asia* contains nineteen one-act royalty-free plays from African and Asian legends. Production notes at the end of the book include the number of characters, playing time, costumes, properties, setting, lighting, and sound. One play, *The First Talking Drum*, can be read as a story on pages 32 to 35 of Courlander's *The King's Drum and Other African Stories* before students execute the play.

Three plays from India can be used with the stories and background information about the *Ramayana* and the *Jatakas*. The bibliography contains several collections of folktales from India listed under their editors: Babbitt, DeRoin, Ghose, and Jacobs. The plays in Winther's book are *The Maharajah Is Bored* (pp. 83–95); *Prince Rama* (pp. 128–38); and *Pacca, the Little Bowman* (pp. 155–65). The first play is a Hindu folktale, the second comes from the Indian epic *The Ramayana*, and the third is a Jataka tale.

Bata's Lessons pages 69 to 79 of Winther's book, is based on an ancient Egyptian story called "The Tale of Two Brothers." This story could be used as a culminating activity after students heard or read stories from the section Magic Numbers in Children's Literature—Two.

The Arabian Nights is the source for *The Flying Horse Machine*, pages 115 to 26 of Winther's book. The play *Abu Nuwas*, pages 141 to 51, comes from the city of Baghdad, which is the setting for *The Arabian Nights*. Abu Nuwas a poet and storyteller who died in A.D. 810. Two stories included on those pages are "The Stolen Shoes" and "The Borrowed Cooking Pot."

There are three plays about Mexico included in Kamerman's *Dramatized Folk Tales of the World*. Additional information about them is found in the section of this chapter called "Plays Based on Children's Literature." The plays are: *Pepe and the Cornfield Bandit* by Boiko (which also appears in Boiko's *Plays and Programs for Boys and Girls*), *The King Who Was Bored* by Thane, and *The Sleeping Mountains* by Winther. Some books containing folktales of Mexico to use with these plays are Brenner's *The Boy Who Could Do Anything and Other Mexican Folktales*, Lindsey's *The Wonderful Chirrionera and Other Tales from Mexican Folklore*, and Lyons's *Tales People Tell in Mexico*.

Kamerman includes the numbers of male and female characters, playing time, costumes, props, setting, and lighting and is arranged by country so plays could easily be incorporated into social studies classes. There is at least one play for each of the following countries: Austria, China, Czechoslovakia, England, France, Germany, Greece, Holland, India, Ireland, Italy, Ancient Israel, Korea, Iran (Persia), Russia, Scotland, Spain, Switzerland, Turkey, the

United States, and Wales. There are also tales from Africa, Scandinavia, and South America.

There are a number of Japanese folktales that can be used with plays about Japan listed under the following compilers: Bang, Hearn, Marmur, McAlpine, Pratt, Sakade, Seki, and Uchida. Two plays about Japan by Boiko are *A Small Crimson Parasol* and *Honorable Cat's Decision*, and Kamerman's *Dramatized Folk Tales of the World* has Mapps's *The Ogre Who Built a Bridge*, Musil's *The Peach Tree Kingdom*, and Winther's *The Great Samurai Sword*.

Four plays from Japan included in Winther represent two styles of Japanese drama. *The Great Samurai Sword* (pp. 169–78) is an example of the Kabuki style and *Japanese Trio* (pp. 222–34), represents the Kyogen style. The three plays in the trio are *Paying the Eel Broiler*, *The Most Fearful Thing*, and *Why We Cannot Lend*. Related stories are *A Leak in an Old House* from Pratt and Kula's *Magic Animals of Japan* and the story from India by Lexau called *It All Began with a Drip, Drip, Drip*.

Follow the River Lai, pages 236–49 of Winther's book, is Vietnamese, a play about a mandarin who gave his possessions to a friend and went searching for the "Land of Bliss." Returning, he learned that his friend Le Vang, had died thirty years ago at the age of 92. Since a year on earth was a day in the "Land of Bliss," Tu Khiem had been gone a hundred years. This play could be the culminating activity of a unit which included such stories as "Sleeping Beauty," "Yarashima Taro," and "Rip Van Winkle," and others who had very long sleeps. The Vietnamese play can also be introduced and played after stories have been read from Graham's *The Beggar in the Blanket and Other Vietnamese Tales*, Robertson's *Fairy Tales from Viet Nam*, and Vo-Dinh's *The Toad Is the Emperor's Uncle, Animal Folktales from Viet-Nam*.

Read folktales from Aung and Trager's *A Kingdom Lost for a Drop of Honey and Other Burmese Folktales* in conjunction with the tale from Burma and Thailand called *The White Elephant*, which appears in Winther, on pages 181 to 93. Jewett's *Which Was Witch? Tales of Ghosts and Magic from Korea* contains stories to accompany the play in Winther, pages 196 to 207, *Fire Demon and South Wind*. *Ah Wing Fu and the Golden Dragon* pages 210 to 20, can accompany Chinese legends from Carpenter's *Tales of a Chinese Grandmother*, Hume's *Favorite Children's Stories from China and Tibet*, and Wyndham's *Tales the People Tell in China*. Read several stories to students from Kelsey's *Once the Hodja*, then ask them to perform *Listen to the Hodja* which appears on pages 99 to 111 of Winther's book.

PLAYS TO ENRICH HISTORY LESSONS.   Kamerman's *Patriotic and Historical Plays for Young People* contains twenty-five one-act royalty-free plays. These can be performed when a class is studying a particular historical event, and students can also read books from the library media center to gain insights into the motives of people involved. For example, intermediate students can read Mason's *The Winter at Valley Forge* for background information for Walter Hachett's play *Incident at Valley Forge*. A filmstrip called *Valley Forge* is part of a set called *War for Independence*. Read Galt's *Peter Zenger, Fighter* for Freedom, and pages 65 to 73 of Aymar and Sagarin's Laws and Trials That Created History with the play The Trial of Peter Zenger by Paul T. Nolan on pages 74 to 91. A filmstrip called Peter Zenger: The Struggle for a Free Press is a part of a series of six filmstrips called Colonial America.

Students can view the filmstrip The Boston Tea Party from the series called Founding of the Nation: The American Revolution, and/or read Thelan's The Story of the Boston Tea Party in conjunction with playing Lindsey Barbee's The Boston Tea Party (pp. 91–99). A filmstrip, The Boston Tea Party, is part of the War for Independence set.

Three books on the Constitution can accompany Carol J. Brown's The Constitution is Born (pp. 214–21): Commager's The Great Constitution, Morris's The First Book of the Constitution, and Peterson's The Making of the U.S. Constitution. A filmstrip called Framing the Constitution is part of a series called "Founding the Republic."

All plays are not found in collections. Behrens's book, called A New Flag for a New Country, the First National Flag, a Play, is about Betsy Ross and contains twelve parts. The filmstrip Betsy Ross is part of a set called American Patriots, and can be used with this book or the play 'Woof' for the Red, White and Blue, found on pages 163 to 67 of Kamerman's Patriotic and Historical Plays for Young People. A play about Betsy Ross by Catherine V. Schroll and Esther MacLellan called A Needle Fights for Freedom is found on pages 101 to 07 of Durrell and Crossley's Thirty Plays for Classroom Reading and on pages 31 to 35 of Kamerman's Little Plays for Little Players. Several of the Durrell and Crossley plays are suitable for reading aloud as well as playing.

Holiday plays found in collections may be about historical characters. Kamerman's Little Plays for Little Players contains two plays about Lincoln, two about Washington, and one about Columbus. A section called "Holiday Plays" in Burack's One Hundred Plays for Children also has two about Lincoln, two about Washington, and one about Columbus, and seven plays about Colonial life are in a section called "Historical Plays." Hark's and McQueen's Junior Plays for All Occasions contains two about Lincoln, two about Washington. Walsh's Six Plays in American History includes plays suitable for junior high school students.

Have students read books about the pilgrims before they make paper bag puppets of the pilgrim boy and girl and the Indian boy and girl from patterns in Williams's Paper Bag Puppets. The puppets can become the vehicles for discussing any event involving the pilgrims from the time they left England to the first Thanksgiving. Books to use as resources are Beck's Pilgrims of Plymouth, Daugherty's The Landing of the Pilgrims, Fritz's Who's That Sleeping on Plymouth Rock?, Groh's The Pilgrims: Brave Settlers of Plymouth, Hall-Quest's How the Pilgrims Came to Plymouth, McGovern's If You Sailed on the Mayflower, Richards's The Story of the Mayflower Compact, Smith's The Coming of the Pilgrims or Smith's Pilgrim's Courage, and Weisgard's Plymouth Thanksgiving. Some books could be fiction. Intermediate and middle school students will enjoy Clapp's story, Constance, about fourteen-year-old Constance Hopkins who was on the Mayflower, and was a friend of Priscilla Mullens, she who loved and married John Alden despite Captain Miles Standish's interest in her. Filmstrips include *Mayflower Experience* or *Plymouth Plantation* from the series *Life in the Early American Colonies* and *William Bradford: Leader of Plymouth Colony*, from the series *Colonial America*. A phonograph record called *Pilgrim Saga* can also be used.

This assignment about the pilgrims provides for individual differences because each student can read a book on his or her own level and then create appropriate dialogue for the puppets.

FLANNELBOARDS AND OVERHEAD PROJECTORS.   Some stories introduce a series of characters who are all involved in the same plot or even have the same lines. Henny Penny, Chicken Little, and the Timid Rabbit all thought the sky was falling and ran to tell the other animals. Sometimes the actions are not only repetitive but cumulative as well. Examples include a rhyme, a song and a story—"The House that Jack Built," "The Farmer in the Dell," and *The Old Woman and Her Pig*. In those examples, all previous characters and actions are repeated and new ones are added at the end.

Children love to play out those repetitive and cumulative stories or just recite along with a storyteller. Sometimes the children cannot help but memorize the lines after they have been repeated ten times, and visual reinforcement helps. Shadows provide this reinforcement and can be accomplished in several ways. An animal, person, or object cut from stiff paper and placed on the face of an overhead projector, transmits a shadow to the screen. Be sure the features are distinctive—profiles are best. A story can be told merely by adding or subtracting shapes from the face of the projector.

If more detail is required in physical features, clothing or color, the characters should be made for the flannelboard. They can be cut from magazines, or from paperback copies of the book, drawn from coloring book outlines, copied from the book using an opaque projector, or drawn freehand. The figures should be laminated and then dry-mounted to stiff cardboard. Attach sandpaper, velcro or any fabric to make the figure cling to the flannelboard. Similar figures, if attached to sticks, could become stick puppets to be used with a stage.

Some traditional tales that are suitable for telling using one or more of these techniques are "The Three Bears," "The Three Little Pigs," "The Little Red Hen," and "The Gingerbread Man." Three stories by the Brothers Grimm can be used: "The Shoemaker and the Elves," "The Golden Goose," and "Hans-in-Luck." Jacob's Jack and the Beanstalk" and Baker's "The Brahman, the Tiger and the Seven Judges" are both very satisfactory. Andersen's "The Little Fir Tree" and "What the Good Man Does Is Always Right" can also be used. Two Scandinavian stories by Asbjornsen and Moë that have repetition are "Gudbrand on the Hillside" and "The Three Billy Goats Gruff." Two similar stories, "Why the Bush Fowl Calls at Dawn and Why Flies Buzz" in Arnott's collection and Aardema's picture book *Why Mosquitoes Buzz in People's Ears*, can be told through the flannelboard. Other picture books that can be well adapted to flannelboards are Brown's *Stone Soup*, Burton's *The Little House*, Holl's *The*

Rain Puddle, Potter's *Peter Rabbit*, Tolstoy's *The Turnip*, and Wiesner's *Happy Go Lucky*.

Stories that follow are also suitable for telling using stick puppets, flannelboard characters, or shadows and silhouettes on the overhead projector.

Eastman's easy reader, *Are You My Mother?* is perfect for telling with silhouettes on the face of an overhead projector. A little bird, its mother, and a nest are the first silhouettes needed. A parade of other animals and machines (including a steam shovel) that are *not* the little bird's mother, plus the repetition, make it ideal.

The steam shovel can have a paper fastener to connect its boom and shovel to the machine so it can move when it lifts the little bird into the nest. If the shovel has a jagged edge, the bird can be wedged in for the trip. Cut the figures out of cardboard, laminate them on each side, and place them in a plastic bag to circulate with the book so that children can recreate the story for themselves.

Introduce the animals in Gay's *Look!* with flannelboard characters, which include a rabbit, lamb, brown bear cub, monkey, young deer, soft kitten playing with a ball, wild duckling swimming on the lake, a new chick, a plump puppy wagging its tail, a shell and snail, an elephant waving its trunk, a colt, and a small skunk.

Also by Gay is *What's Your Name?* The rhyme and illustrations provide clues, and a picture with the answer appears on the second page. The following animals are included: dog, donkey, pig, mouse, polar bear, penguin, squirrel, cat, frog, and rabbit. At the end of the book the animals ask the reader "What's your name?" Shadows can also be prepared for another guessing rhyme book, Garten and Batherman's *Alphabet Tale*. Show the letter "K" and the appropriate tail and say "Watch him hopping in the zoo. This tail is the tail of the ——." Then add the shadow or flannelboard character of the animal to the tail. You can remove each animal or letter from the flannelboard or allow your zoo to accumulate. Animals included are alligator, beaver, cat, donkey, elephant, fox, giraffe, horse, inchworm, jaguar, kangaroo, lion, monkey, newt, ostrich, porcupine, quail, raccoon, seal, tiger, unicorn, vulture, whale, xenerus, yak, and zebra. Insects, animals and birds appear in Teal's *The Little Woman Who Wanted Noise*, Ets's *Play With Me*, and Hazen's *Where Do Bears Sleep?*

DeRegnier's *It Does Not Say Meow and Other Animal Riddle Rhymes* contains clues in verse to the identity of nine well-known animals: cow, cat, bird, elephant, ant, mice, frog, dog, and bee. On the last page, readers are invited to make up their own riddles. The silhouette placed on the screen can provide the answer.

Memling's *Hi, All You Rabbits* is about animal noises. Place silhouettes of a rat, ducks, horses, birds, pigs, a cow, chicks, sheep, cats, and pups on the screen and ask students to make the appropriate noises.

William Cole selected hundreds of animal poems for his *The Birds and the Beasts Were There*. The collection is a sourcebook for shadows and flannelboard characters because there are poems about many animals and birds. Several poems that could be told with silhouettes are "Cat" (p. 13); "Centipede" (p. 223); and "Caterpillar" (p. 229). Fisher's *My Cat Has Eyes of Sapphire Blue* also contains poems that can be read while flannelboard or silhouettes are shown. "Kitten Talk" (p. 23) is an especially appropriate poem for using this technique. Langner's *Hi Diddle Diddle, a Book of Mother Goose Rhymes* includes many nursery rhymes that can be read or recited with leader and students while characters are seen on the screen or board. They include such favorites as "Little Jack Horner" and "Mary Had a Little Lamb." Anglund's *In a Pumpkin Shell* is a source for nursery rhymes to be recited with silhouettes.

Nodset's *Who Took the Farmer's Hat?* is a cumulative tale told through silhouettes. Place silhouettes of a squirrel, mouse, fly, goat, duck, and bird on the screen and repeat the phrase, "Who took the farmer's hat?" The story is especially suitable for a flannelboard presentation because of the hat.

Hutchins's *Good-Night Owl!* can be easily told with the flannelboard. Children will enjoy repeating the cumulative noises because bees buzz, a squirrel crunches, crows caw, woodpecker rat-a-tats, starlings twit, jays scream "ark ark," cuckoos cuckoo, the robin pips, the sparrows cheep, the doves coo, and the owl is unable to sleep. Each animal or bird appears on a different branch of a tree.

Holl's *The Remarkable Egg* also introduces birds to children as a boy tries to find out whose egg the red ball is. The following birds can be made into flannelboard characters: coot, chickadee, dove, meadow lark, cowbird, oriole, catbird, robin, hummingbird, cardinal, and owl.

"A Lost Button," in Lobel's *Frog and Toad are Friends, An Easy Reader* (pp. 28–39), can be told using silhouettes or flannelboard buttons. The buttons should be black or white, with two or four holes, small or big, round or square, thin or thick. Characters are frog, toad, sparrow, and raccoon.

Emberley's *The Wing on a Flea, A Book about Shapes,* is a fun way to learn about triangles, circles, and rectangles and can inspire children to create shapes of their own. The colorful shapes can be used for room decorations or on a shadow stage so children can guess what they are. Children can be asked to make characters of their own using those shapes.

The refrain in Hogan's *Eighteen Cousins* is catchy: "I looked at a lamb . . . But what did I see? EIGHTEEN COUSINS a-looking at me!," the refrain is changed to include a horse, pig, cow, lamb, chickens, baby ducklings, a gosling, a rooster, and dandelions. Silhouettes of the animals on a screen or flannelboard could cue children's responses.

Custard the Dragon is a poem and picture book by Ogden Nash which can be told with shadows or flannelboard characters. Shapes to include are Belinda and her house, a little yellow dog, little red wagon, little pet dragon, little black kitten, little gray mouse, stairs, and a pirate.

Sing "The Answers" by Robert Clairmont, pages 38 and 39 of Engvick's *Lullabies and Night Songs,* while sharing silhouettes of the animals. Because this song includes animal noises like "quack," "honk," "oink," and "moo," it can be used with other such books. The shapes are reminders to students as they learn the song.

"Over in the Meadow," pages 70 and 71 of Winn's *Fireside Book of Children's Songs,* requires the shapes of a frog, two ducks, three bluebirds, four snakes, and five little bees. A picture book by Ezra Jack Keats is also available. Langstaff's picture book, *Swapping Boy,* illustrated by Rojankovsky is also available as a sound filmstrip and can also be sung to silhouettes.

Animal shapes needed for Baker's Christmas song *The Friendly Beasts* are sheep, cow, two doves, a star, a donkey, and Mary, Joseph, and the babe.

The previous poems, as well as the following stories, are suitable for first and second graders.

The Billy Goat in the Chili Patch, a Mexican Folktale by Lazarus features a boy named Pepito, his mother, a goat, burro, dog, cock, and an ant. "Señor Billy Goat," pages 69 to 72 of Belpre's *Tiger and the Rabbit and Other Tales* can be told with the same silhouettes.

Flannelboard animals can help tell Tresselt's story *Frog in the Well:* frog, cow, blackbird, deer, fox, squirrel, and bear. Add raindrops and a group of frogs to complete the story about frog who lived in a well and thought it was the whole world until the well dried up and he found a new world above ground, including lots of other frogs.

The Magic Hat by Wakana could be told to second and third graders. Third graders could participate in making the silhouette characters from the story which begins at the back and includes Japanese characters. The hat allowed a man to hear what birds are saying about the princess, and it is featured also in Uchida's *The Magic Listening Cap,* (pp. 3–10). The moral of the story from Ceylon, "The Pearl Necklace," is that pride goeth before a fall. It is about a monkey who took a necklace, and is found in Tooze's *Three Tales of Monkey, Ancient Folk Tales from the Far East.* The story can be told with shadow puppets of a king, queen, maid, two monkeys, and others.

The following stories contain elements that make them suitable, not only for flannelboard or overhead presentations, but for playing out as well.

Gag's picture book *Nothing At All,* because of the repetition, is suited to flannelboard telling to first graders, and can also be played. The main characters are three dogs: Pointy, Curley, and Nothing-At-All, who was invisible as well as "...not very tall nor yet very small; He looked like nothing, Like nothing at all." A little boy and girl adopted Pointy and Curley but left Nothing-At-All behind because they couldn't see him. A jackdaw's advice and a magic formula helped him become a visible real dog.

Repetition of time is important to Carle's *The Grouchy Ladybug,* who asked insects, birds and animals of progressively larger sizes if they wanted to fight. A different animal or insect is challenged each hour until one becomes a friend. The story can be played out with the children using their hands as hands on the clock, or the story can be told with a flannelboard. As each animal (skunk, rhino, whale) is introduced, the hands on a clock at the left side of the flannelboard can be changed. Use this story with students who are learning to tell time.

"The Travels of a Fox," pages 91 to 98 of Hutchinson's *Chimney Corner Stories,* is suitable for playing by first through third graders with the aid of a flannelboard or with stick puppets. The four women in the story can be made from the same pattern, with clothing of a different color. A fox found a bumble bee and put it in a bag and asked a woman if she would keep the bag for him but not look inside. When the curious woman looked inside, the bee flew out and was eaten by the woman's rooster. When the fox came back and learned what had happened, he demanded the woman's rooster in payment for losing his bee. The same incidents are repeated as the fox works his way up through larger animals to a little boy.

Din Dan Don It's Christmas, an old Polish Christmas carol, can be introduced with shadows: a speckled duck playing the bagpipes, a turkey gander beating drums, a rooster blowing a trumpet, the star, and people who followed the parade to the manager. Because of the action, the story can also be played, with parts for everyone. Students of any age will enjoy this carol.

Another animals-in-action story is Eckert's *Tonight At Nine* which also features musical instruments, and could be played out to a musical background.

The following stories require more time, effort and imagination from the creator than some of the previous ones.

Byars's *The Lace Snail* can best be retold using the overhead projector with bits of lace from doilies or trimmings to make gifts given by the snail to bugs, snakes, turtles, a crocodile and hippo. This one is also available as a sound filmstrip.

Balian's *Humbug Witch,* about a little witch who took off all of her costume to reveal a little girl underneath, is told most effectively on a flannelboard.

Carle's *1, 2, 3 to the Zoo,* a counting book, can be told with shadows. Each railroad car in the story has animal shapes in it—three giraffes, four lions, etc. As each car is added, the small train at the bottom of the page grows longer.

Polushkin's *The Little Hen and the Giant* is about Kurochka, a brown hen who found a way to overcome the giant who ate every one of her eggs. There is plenty of action for flannelboard telling.

Red Chicken, hero of a story by the same name is Duvoisin's *The Three Sneezes and Other Swiss Tales,* is a similar character who went to get the money owed to him by a farmer. He is aided by a fox, a wolf, and a pond; the farmer and his wife eventually paid the debt because Red Chicken had such resourceful friends to help him.

Sometimes shadows on the overhead or flannelboard remind students of the sequence of events when they play out a story. Shadows of the ice cream man, the butcher, baker, grocer, and others could be shown as reminders when playing Vipont's *The Elephant and the Bad Boy.* The cat who, asked by a woman to watch the pot while she went to a neighbor's house, ate the gruel, the pot, the woman and everything else in sight, can be a splendid silhouette. The shadows of everything dispensed with can be placed behind the cat to make them disappear, and come forth again when they escape, as they do in Kent's *The Fat Cat, a Danish Folktale. The Snow and the Sun,* a cumulative folk tale in Spanish and English by Frasconi, is another good one with action and lots of characters.

Shadows of a dog, cat, bear, tiger, and dinosaur can help tell the story by Kellogg, *Can I Keep Him?,* in which Arnold asks his mother if he can keep them as pets. Others can be added, and used also with "My Very Own Pet" from Carlson's *Listen! And Help Tell The Story.* Animals who take refuge in a mitten in Tresselt's picture book *The Mitten, an Old Ukrainian Folktale,* can be made to disappear by placing them on top of the mitten on the overhead. Another version of this tale, "Five in a Glove," is found in Bamberger's *My First Big Story Book.*

Shadows from McClintock's easy reader, *A Fly Went By,* displayed on the overhead will help a class to reconstruct the simple sentences and dictate them to the teacher to put on the blackboard.

Glazer's *Eye Winker, Tom Tinker, Chin Chopper* has songs to be sung with prompting by the characters on an overhead or flannelboard. "The Barnyard Song," features a bird, hen, duck, goose, pig, horse, sheep, and a cow; "I Know an Old Lady," features a fly, spider, bird, dog, cat, cow, and horse.

Shadows on the overhead or flannelboard can be used to reinforce number and letter concepts as well as days of the week. Nic Leodhas's *All in the Morning Early* begins with one huntsman and ends with ten bonny lassies. Yolen's *An Invitation to the Butterfly Ball,* a counting rhyme, includes one mouse looking for a smaller dress so she can go to the butterfly ball. Students can be divided into groups of numbers from two to ten. Each group can recite the couplet which corresponds to their assigned number. Ten porcupines, nine frogs, can be shown on the screen or flannelboard as a cue. Another group of all students in unison can recite the four lines about the mouse. Livermore's *One to Ten Count Again* contains hidden pictures of animals. Shadows of the bull in the china shop, frogs, cows, camels, sheep, dogs, etc. can be shown to indicate to students the animals they need to find.

In *One Monday Morning,* a picture book by Shulevitz, the king, queen, and the prince came to visit the narrator but since he wasn't home, they had to return on other days of the week. By the time they returned on Sunday, the group also included a knight, guard, cook, baker, jester, and dog. The silhouettes can remind students of the story sequence as they retell or play out the story. DeRegniers's *May I Bring a Friend?* is an excellent companion book that includes royalty, animals, visits, and days of the week.

A VARIETY OF VERSIONS TO READ AND PLAY (LIVE AND WITH PUPPETS). Stories included in this section are available in variant versions around the world and can be linked or compared with similar stories. They are identified to provide students with projects in which reading or listening to many stories accompanies playing out the stories with live action, or with puppets, or telling the stories with flannelboard or silhouette characters.

Sources for a German story called "Hans in Luck" have been discussed before. In this story, Hans was given his wages in gold for seven years' work, but he traded the gold for a horse, the horse for a cow, the cow for a pig, the pig for a goose, and finally the goose for a grindstone which fell into the water. Hans was relieved to have nothing to carry home.

A similar character from Scandinavian folklore is called Gudbrand. Gudbrand took one of his cows to sell, but no-one would buy it so he traded until he had little left, but collected some money on a bet. The story, appears on pages 35 to 40 of Thorne-Thomsen's *East O' the Sun and West O' the Moon,* and other versions in Thompson's *One Hundred Favorite Folktales* (pp. 384-88); Sutherland's *Arbuthnot Anthology of Children's Literature* (pp. 44-46); and Arbuthnot's *Time* for *Fairy Tales, Old and New* (pp. 82-84). Versions by Asbjornsen and Moe appear on page 178 to 81 of *Norwegian Folk Tales*; pages 291 to 93 of Johnson's *Anthology of Children's Literature*; pages 377 and 78 of Nelson's *Comparative Anthology of Children's Literature*; and on pages 185 to 89 of Undset's *True and Untrue, and Other Norse Tales*. The story also appears in the d'Aulaires's *East of the Sun and West of the Moon.*

A picture book based on the Norwegian version is Wiesner's *Happy-Go-Lucky*. A farmer bet twenty gold crowns that his neighbor would be scolded by his wife because he traded the cow for a donkey, pig, goat, rooster, and then a restorative pill. The man won the money from his neighbor because his wife said that the important thing was to have her husband in good health. In Andersen's picture book *What the Good Man Does Is Always Right*, a man traded a horse, cow, sheep, goose, hen, and finally a bag of rotten apples. In this story, two Englishmen bet him that his wife would be upset when he got home but the man insisted that his wife would kiss him. The man won the bet because his wife found something good to say about every trade.

Students will see that Andersen based his story on the older folktales; this could be an inspiration for them to read several versions and make up one of their own. Olsen's "Jack and the Bean Futures" in Durell's *Just for Fun* (pp. 41-54), is a spoof on "Jack and the Beanstalk." Depending upon the abilities of the students, this project is suitable for students in grades two through six.

As a project for younger grades place the three picture books (Grimms's *Hans in Luck*, Wiesner's *Happy-Go-Lucky*, and Andersen's *What the Good Man Does Is Always Right*,) in the library media corner of the third grade classroom and ask students to make a list of the items that were traded in each story, or to list similarities and differences.

Some second graders and most third graders can read the stories for themselves and pick out the similarities. It is possible to ask them or even younger children to list items that were traded after a story about Gudbrand and one about Hans are told to them using flannelboard characters or silhouettes on the overhead projector. Tell them that they are about to participate in an exercise on how well they can listen. After the stories have been told, ask students to divide a sheet of paper in half lengthwise, and write the title "Hans in Luck" on one side and "Gudbrand on the Hillside" on the other (or this can be done on the overhead projector). Ask students to list the items each man traded and circle any animals that both men traded. Other similarities can be listed. After students have written their answers, place the flannelboard characters or the silhouettes for both stories back on the board or overhead so students can check their answers. Students might be given a prepared sheet listing animals traded or details from both stories, and then have to indicate from which story they came.

All of these stories can be easily played. In the German story, there is the employer (optional), Hans, a bag of gold (optional), horse, cow, pig, goose, grindstone (optional), Hans's mother (optional), as well as five people who trade with Hans. Optional parts can be omitted if there are not enough players. For example, if two groups of thirteen are playing the story, the story can either begin after Hans has received the gold from his employer or it can end before Hans has gone home empty handed to his mother so one character can be eliminated.

A maximum of sixteen characters can play "Gudbrand on the Hillside" in one group. Characters are Gudbrand, his cow, horse, pig, goat, sheep, goose, cock, friend, wife, and the six people with whom Gudbrand traded. If there are a few more students in the class, more animals and traders could be added, or several friends could bet Gudbrand rather than just one.

Characters needed for playing Andersen's story are: two men, the main character, his wife, horse, cow, sheep, goose, fowl (hen), a bag of rotten apples, and six people who traded with the man. The bag of apples could be imaginary or only one man could bet with the main character if two parts need to be eliminated. Then two groups of fourteen or twenty-eight students could play out the story at one time.

"The Brahman, the Tiger and the Seven Judges," in Baker's *Talking Tree* (pp. 236-41), is excellent for playing. In this story from India, a Brahman let a tiger out of his cage but then the tiger wanted to eat the Brahman. The tiger agreed to let the Brahman go if others would agree. The Brahman got opinions on why he shouldn't be eaten from a banyan tree, camel, bullock, eagle, alligator, jackal, and another man. The other man tricked the tiger back into the cage by asking him to reconstruct the situation so that he would understand it. This story can be played in groups of nine students. The more familiar version of this story is called "The Tiger, the Brahman and the Jackal." Groups of three students are needed for playing this version. There is a Mexican version called "Señor Coyote Settles a Quarrel" and an African version called "The Panther in the Pit." On pages 139 to 44 of her book *Puppet Shows Using Poems and Stories*, Ross suggests that students make masks and pantomime the story. All the versions are suitable for playing live, as well as for telling on the flannelboard or with silhouettes on the overhead projector. "The Tiger, the Brahman and the Jackal" would be the best version for a puppet show because it contains only three characters. After seeing it students could read one or more of the three other versions.

Another story from India that has several versions is called "The Flight of the Animals," "The Foolish Timid Rabbit," or "The Hare That Ran Away." In this familiar story, a coconut fell and hit a rabbit on the head and he went around shouting to other animals that the earth was falling in, until a lion heard the story and traced it to the rabbit and the coconut. The stories are excellent for playing because each can involve as many players as needed for one or more groups. Arbuthnot's "The Hare That Ran Away" has parts for the rabbit and lion, as well as for deer, sheep, a wild boar, buffalo, camel, tiger, and elephant. Several animals of each type can be used if needed. Johnson's "The Hare That Ran Away" has one rabbit telling hundreds of other rabbits that the earth is falling in. Carlson's version, called "The Timid Rabbit" includes a deer, fox, and elephant, besides the rabbit and the lion. In that version, a monkey dropped the coconut on the rabbit. Any version from India is suitable for telling via the flannelboard or overhead projector. The students could make paper bag puppets and play out the story without a stage. A puppet show using a stage and hand puppets is also easy to produce.

The English versions of this story are called "Chicken Little," "Chicken Licken," and "Henny Penny." A set of puppets from Nancy Renfro Studios called "Henny Penny Set" includes Henny Penny, Cocky Locky, Ducky Lucky, Goosey Loosey, Turkey Lurkey, and Foxy Loxy. Two tapes and scripts from the same source are available for six to eight year olds and for three to five year olds. "Henny Penny" is found in Arbuthnot's *Time for Old Magic* (pp. 9-10); De la Mare's *Animal Stories* (pp. 47-50); Haviland's *The Fairy Tale Treasury* (pp. 12-15); Hutchinson's *Chimney Corner Stories* (pp. 3-8); Jacobs's *English Folk and Fairy Tales* (pp. 118-21); Johnson's *Anthology of Children's Literature*; Martignoni's *The Illustrated Treasury of Children's Literature* (pp. 66-68); Montgomerie's *Twenty-five Fables* (pp. 22-25); Rackham's *The Arthur Rackham Fairy Book* (pp. 66-70); Rockwell's *The Three Bears and Fifteen Other Stories* (pp. 63-70); Sike's *Drama With Children* (pp. 236-39); and Sutherland's *The Arbuthnot Anthology of Children's Literature* (pp. 154-55). A picture book illustrated by Galdone is available in hardback as well as paperback version with a recording. In Jacobs's version, which appears in the Arbuthnot and the Johnson collections, Ducky Lucky is called "Ducky Daddles" and Foxy Loxy is called "Foxy-Woxy." "Chicken Little" is found in Sideman's *The World's Best Fairy Tales* (pp. 61-64). "Chicken Licken" is found in *The Tall Book of Nursery Tales* (pp. 55-61).

Another variation in which a lion tracked the problem to its source is the cumulative one Aardema uses in her 1976 Caldecott winning picture book, *Why Mosquitoes Buzz in People's Ears*. In that story, a mosquito caused a chain reaction involving an iguana, python, terrified rabbit, snake, crow, monkey, an owl baby, and a mother owl who was so unhappy that she didn't hoot to wake up the sun and night lasted and lasted. There are ten characters if the antelope who went to get the mother owl is counted. Another African version "Why the Bush-Fowl Calls at Dawn and Why Flies Buzz" appears on pages 56 to 63 of Arnott's *African Myths and Legends*. Arnott's version also appears on pages 411 to 413 of Nelson's *Comparative Anthology of Children's Literature*. A man dropped a knife while picking palm nuts, and the knife almost hit his wife who stepped away and stepped on a snake. This caused a chain reaction involving a rat, monkey, mango, elephant, creeper, until an ant heap fell on a bush-fowl's nest and broke all her eggs. The bush-fowl was so upset she did not call up morning so night did not end. Finally, the Great Spirit asked each participant for an explanation until the fault was traced to the black fly who bit the man and cause him to drop his knife. Because the fly refused to answer the Great Spirit's question and only said "buzz, buzz, buzz," that is all it can say today. This version requires eleven characters.

Both the Arnott and Aardema version can be told using silhouettes or flannelboard characters, or can be played out live by children.

Because *Why Mosquitoes Buzz in People's Ears* is available as a sound filmstrip, it is possible to show the filmstrip to students before they are asked to organize the story for playing. Similar projects that begin with a filmstrip are discussed in the next section.

Other filmstrips that could spark related activities are *Alligators All Around; Chicken Soup With Rice; The House That Jack Built; Journey Cake, Ho!; One Was Johnny; Pierre; Play With Me; Stone Soup; The Surprise Party; The Three Billy Goats Gruff;* and *Whose Mouse Are You?*

BEGIN WITH A SOUND FILMSTRIP.   There are numerous picture books that are also available as sound filmstrips. The projects in this section can all begin with a sound filmstrip. Sometimes the filmstrip can be a quieting activity as children view and listen in the dark after playing out a story.

Introduce the Russian folktale "The Turnip" by showing the sound filmstrip of Tolstoy's version illustrated by Kate Greenaway Medal winner Helen Oxenbury called *The Great Big Enormous Turnip.* Be sure to have a copy of the picture book available. Another picture book of the story is Domanska's *The Turnip* which is also available in paperback. A similar story also in paperback is Ets's picture book *The Elephant in the Well.* Other versions of the story appear in Sikes's *Children's Literature for Dramatization* (pp. 141-44), Haviland's *The Fairy Tale Treasury* (Tolstoy version, pp. 44-47), a choral-speaking version in Rasmussen's *Let's Say Poetry Together and Have Fun for Intermediate Grades* (pp. 18-19), Afanas'ev's *Russian Fairy Tales* (pp. 26-27), Fitzgerald's *World Tales for Creative Dramatics and Storytelling* (p. 133).

Preschool through first graders can view the sound filmstrip and play out the most famous version in which an old man planted seeds and a large turnip grew. When the old man could not pull up the turnip, he called his wife to come and help. The two of them could not pull up the turnip, so they called their granddaughter and eventually their dog, cat, and a mouse. It was the addition of the little mouse's strength that finally helped to pull the turnip out of the ground. Groups of six are needed to pull out the turnip. Teachers who want to project size relationships should tell the story using the flannelboard or with shadows so that the children can clearly grasp the size differences.

It is important to make copies available of the picture books by Tolstoy, Oxenbury, Domanska, and Ets for children to look at after they have played out the story or have seen it portrayed with shadows or on the flannelboard. Students in second and third grades can read the three stories from the picture books, or from the collections of Haviland and Fitzgerald. Students can compare the stories before choosing one of them to play. In the Domanska version, children can pantomime the grandfather planting the turnip and watering it every day, and of course take the parts of all the animals. A whole class can play out *The Elephant in the Well* which instead of being about a turnip is about an elephant with a clothesline on its trunk who tripped and fell into a well. Seven animals came along and tried to pull him out. When a mouse came along, all the animals laughed at it. However, the mouse's strength added to that of the horse, cow, goat, pig, lamb, and dog, and was all that was needed to pull the elephant out of the well. This cumulative story can be played with any size class; just add other animals to the list of seven until everyone in the class has a part. Be sure to place the additional animals in the proper order according to size. The fun in playing this version is that the children get to recite the names of all of the animals each time a new animal comes to help pull.

One project for first or second graders could be to divide the class into three groups and have each child make a mask or drawing to wear when playing out the version assigned to their group. Use the Domanska, Sikes, Fitzgerald, and Ets versions. Those four stories provide parts for thirty-three characters or thirty-six if three turnips are added. The culminating activity for this project also serves to quiet the group; show the sound filmstrip of the Tolstoy version, *The Great Big Enormous Turnip.*

Thirty-three or thirty-six third or fourth graders could read the versions by Domanska, Sikes, Fitzgerald, and Ets, and prepare shadows or flannelboard characters which could be used to tell the stories to kindergarten, first grade, or special education classes. The sound filmstrip of Tolstoy's *The Great Big Enormous Turnip* could be the introduction to the unit. The culminating activity could be a story told to the group by the teacher or librarian. This story is called "The Biggest Turnip in the World" and appears on pages 42 to 47 of Reeves's *The Secret Shoemaker and Other Stories*, and "The Turnip" on pages 483-85 of Grimms's *Tales for Young and Old* and pages 107-108 of De la Mare's *Tales Told Again.* In this story, a poor man found a turnip that was so huge that he decided to give it to the king. In return, the king gave gifts to the poor man. When the man's rich brother heard what had happened, he gave gifts to the king too, expecting a reward, but the reward he received was the turnip.

A project about greed and self-aggrandizement in which third or fourth grade students can be involved can follow the sound filmstrip *The Stonecutter.* In this Japanese folktale, a stonecutter wanted to be a prince until he learned that the sun was mightier. Other things that appeared to be mightier than the sun were a cloud and a mountain, so the spirit of the mountain changed the stonecutter into each of these. The story came full circle when a stonecutter began to chip away at the mountain. Ask students to compare that story with "A Mouse in Search of a Wife," from Green's *Big Book of Animal Fables* (pp. 88-89). This medieval fable was written by Marie de France who was also the source for Chaucer's "The Nun's Priest's Tale." In that story, a mouse went to the sun to ask him to marry his daughter because he wanted the mightiest for his daughter. The sun sent Mr. Mouse to a cloud, who sent him to the wind, who sent him to a great stone tower, who was angry because a mouse kept breaking through the mortar in the tower to build a nest. In "The Wedding of the Mouse" from Japan, a wall instead of a tower is nibbled.

Another story about a mouse is Wiesner's picture book *The Constant Little Mouse.* In this story, Sweetie Pie loved Count Hazelnut, but her parents wanted her to marry the sun. The chain of mighty persons here is a cloud, wind, and wall. Naturally, Sweetie Pie was able to marry her Count because a mouse was mightier than a wall. Another picture book features a rat, Schiller's *The White Rat's Tale.*

Two stories from Vietnam are "A Cat is a Cat is a Cat" and "Who is Mightiest." A cat is the mightiest in the first story, and a worm is mightiest in the second. A cat is also "The Greatest Person in the World" according to a story from Ceylon found on pages 16 to 20 of Belting's *Cat Tales.* A man wanted to marry his kitten to the greatest person in the world, so he went to the sun, who told him to go to the rain god, who sent him to the wind god. The chain in this story includes the king of the ants, a bull, and a leopard who said that a cat was its teacher to bring this story full cycle.

Two stories that begin with an animal slipping on the ice are a lamb in the picture book based on a Caucasian story *The Strongest One of All* and ice in the Italian story "The Inquiring Rabbit or the Strongest Thing in the World."

A project involving those stories could involve a viewing/listening/ reading center in the classroom. Provide copies of all books and filmstrips, and allow students to compare the various stories featuring mice, rat, cats and ice. After reading or viewing the stories, the student could indicate the similarities and differences. Students could also be given the choice of preparing shadows or flannelboard figures for the story of their choice. "The Wedding of the Mouse," in Uchida's *The Dancing Kettle*, is suitable for playing with hand puppets of papier-mache made by students, or telling with silhouettes.

Use the filmstrip *Fish in the Forest, a Russian Folktale* to introduce that story for playing to students in grades three through six. Everyone in the class can play it out because there are parts for Ivan, his wife Marya, the ruler and his court, and the villagers with whom Marya gossiped. Students can also take the part of the cakes, the rabbit, and the fish. Students may view the filmstrip, and create their own dialogue, but two versions of the story are already available as plays. There are nine characters plus a narrator in the one in Burack and Crossley's *Popular Plays for Classroom Reading*. There are parts for thirteen plus peasants and servants in Kamerman's *Dramatized Folk Tales of the World*. The version by Burack and Crossley is very suitable just for reading aloud. Have students read the play and then show the filmstrip.

Show the sound filmstrip called *Could Anything Be Worse?* based on a Yiddish tale illustrated by Hirsh. A man complained to the rabbi because his daughter didn't help around the house, his wife scolded and whined, the baby screamed constantly, the twins and the cat and dog fought. The rabbi's advice was to bring the chickens into the house. When the man complained a second time, the rabbi told him to bring the cow into the house. The third time the rabbi's advice was to bring in poor relations, and when the man complained again bitterly, the rabbi told him to get rid of the poor relations, the cow, and the chickens. When he did so, he found that his home was a paradise. There are fourteen main characters to the story; there are only two chickens, and the poor relations only include the brother and his wife. More characters can be added by adding more relatives and more chickens. If there are only twenty-eight students in the class, the story can be played with a double cast.

McGovern's *Too Much Noise* is a similar picture book. An old man named Peter lived in an old house where the bed creaked and the floor squeaked, and where the wind blew the leaves noisily through the trees and the tea kettle whistled. Peter went to the wise man of the village for advice and was told to get a cow. Each time Peter went to the wise man he was told to bring something else into the house that made more noise: the cow, donkey, sheep, hen, dog, and cat. Finally, when the wise man told him to let all of the animals go, Peter appreciated the quiet noises of his bed, the floor, the leaves, and the tea kettle. This story is excellent for playing with an entire class even though there are only eight main characters. The rest of the class can be the sound effects for the bed, floor, leaves, and tea kettle. The leaves can even move as they swish about.

In Dobbs's *No Room, An Old Story Retold* it is a selfish old peasant who was annoyed because his daughter, her husband, and child came to live. The peasant went to the wise man seven times, was given the advice about bringing in the barnyard, and learned to be satisfied with his lot. If the peasant is given a wife, there are parts for sixteen players. *A Cow in the House* by Watts and *The Wise Man on the Mountain* by Dillon have a similar theme.

The best projects involving these books would be for students in grades three and four to read McGovern's picture book *Too Much Noise* and involve the whole class in playing out the story. Then, as a quieting activity, show the filmstrip based on Hirsh's *Could Anything Be Worse?* Then introduce the other two picture books to the students and place them in the listening/viewing/reading center in the classroom. Ask students to read both stories and write a paragraph about which four main characters had the worst situation; students could also be asked to write about a situation in which they complained about something, that wasn't really as terrible as they made it out to be.

Follow-up activities for students in first and second grade would be to browse through the other books on the same theme, as well as other books about noise and quietness. One of those books could be Teal's *The Little Woman Who Wanted Noise*. In this story, the woman moved to the country which she found too quiet, so she acquired some animals and a noisy car. Another story, *Hattie Be Quiet, Hattie Be Good*, is an easy reader about someone who was so unusually quiet that her mother thought she was sick. Other books besides *Noisy and Quiet* are listed in the index to this book.

Bryant's "The Little Red Hen and the Grain of Wheat" appears on pages 32 to 35 of Haviland's *The Fairy Tale Treasury*. That same title appears on pages 64 and 65 of Hutchinson's *Chimney Corner Stories* and pages 41 and 42 of Ward's *Stories to Dramatize*. The story is called "The Little Red Hen" in *The Tall Book of Nursery Tales* (pp. 79-83). Picture books are illustrated by Domanska and Galdone.

There are many ways to introduce this favorite story to primary students. Two children with four puppets can easily play out this story. The story can also be played out on the flannelboard, with silhouettes or with stick puppets.

The Little Red Hen asked the duck, cat, and dog to help her to plant, cut, thresh, and bake the wheat into bread but they refused to help. Finally, when it was time, they offered to help eat the bread but the hen refused. In some versions, the hen shared the bread with her chicks. The addition of the chicks makes this story easy to play. The class can be divided into groups of six and any extra children can become additional chicks.

"The Little Red Hen" can become a choral speaking project. Divide the class into three groups—ducks, cats, and dogs. Then when the proper time comes, have all the ducks say in unison "Not I." The same can be done with the cats and dogs. At the end of the story the animals can all say that they will help eat the bread. The teacher can be the storyteller.

The Galdone picture book is available as a sound filmstrip. Show the filmstrip to students and then tell them that there is a similar story called "The Cock, the Mouse and the Little Red Hen," by LeFevre. Read the story from the picture book or from pages 13 to 15 of Arbuthnot's *Time for Fairy Tales Old and New*, pages 78 to 88 of Hutchinson's *Chimney Corner Stories*, pages 17 to 32 of Rockwell's *The Three Bears and Fifteen Other Stories*, or pages 155 to 57 of Sutherland's *Arbuthnot Anthology of Children's Literature*.

The other animals in this story also would not help the Little Red Hen gather sticks, fill the kettle, get or clear away the breakfast. Later, a fox caught the cock and mouse and put them in a sack to take to his children. The resourceful hen cut the others out of the sack and replaced them with stones. The weight of the stones dragged the fox into the water and he drowned. This story is excellent for playing out with groups of eight children. There are four little foxes in this story that want their father to get them something to eat.

One of the most delightful picture books for primary children, Slobodkina's *Caps for Sale*, is especially suitable for playing. The story can be introduced to children via the sound filmstrip. When a peddler fell asleep under a tree, his hats were taken by monkeys in the tree who would not give them back. Finally, the man threw his own cap down in exasperation and, of course, the monkeys followed suit and threw down their caps also. McCaslin used Sikes's version of the story as a sample of "Building Plays from Simple Stories" in chapter 6 of her book *Creative Dramatics in the Classroom*. Sikes included "The Peddler and the Monkeys" in her book *Children's Literature for Dramatization, an Anthology* (pp. 94-98). Other sources are "The Peddler and the Monkeys, an Indian Tale" in Bulatkin's *Eurasian Folk and Fairy Tales* (pp. 69-70); "The Monkeys and the Little Red Hats" in Carpenter's *African Wonder Tales* (pp. 71-76); "The Peddler and His Caps" in Tooze's *Storytelling* (pp. 81-83); and "Fifty Red Night-Caps," in Williams-Ellis's *Fairy Tales from the British Isles* (pp. 9-10).

Show students the sound filmstrip of *The Old Woman and Her Pig*, taken from the picture book by Galdone. One of the sources for this cumulative tale is *Lavender's Blue, A Book of Nursery Rhymes* compiled by Lines, and another is *The Old Woman and her Pig and Ten Other Stories*, illustrated by Rockwell.

Groups of eleven can play out this story. Assign students the following parts and ask each to make drawings of his part. The following players are needed: old woman, pig, dog, stick, fire, water, ox, butcher, rope, rat, and cat. A saucer of milk is optional.

In this traditional cumulative rhyme, the cat was asked to kill the rat because it wouldn't gnaw the rope which would hang the butcher who wouldn't kill the ox who wouldn't drink the water that wouldn't quench the fire that wouldn't burn the stick that wouldn't beat the dog that wouldn't bite the pig that wouldn't go over the stile. So the cat said that for a saucer of milk she would kill the rat, and when she began to do so a chain reaction began that eventually caused the pig to jump over the stile so the old woman could get home that night. In the version found in ACEI's *Told Under the Green Umbrella* (pp. 16-20), the woman got the milk for the cat from a cow.

One Fine Day, the 1972 Caldecott Medal winner, illustrated by Nonny Hogrogian, is a similar tale that is available as a sound filmstrip. A thirsty fox drank up all the milk in a woman's pail so she chopped off his tail. The woman said she would give the tail back only if the fox would give her back her milk. The fox went to a cow who asked for grass, the field of grass asked for water, the stream asked for a jug, a maiden with a jug asked for a blue bead. The fox told a peddler if he gave him a blue bead then the maiden would be pleased with him, but the peddler asked for an egg, the hen asked for some grain which the fox was finally able to get from a kind miller. Groups of nine students are needed to play out this story, and props that could be real or imaginary are a jug, blue bead, egg and grain. This Armenian folktale could be told with shadows or flannelboard characters.

"The Firefly," a tale from Italy that appears on pages 90 and 91 of Withers's I Saw a Rocket Walk a Mile is a similar story in which a firefly returned a boy's cap when he finally gave him some bread. "Why the Monkey Still has a Tail," pages 145 to 51 of Eels's Fairy Tales from Brazil began when a monkey played a trick on a rabbit so the rabbit had an armadillo roll a stone on monkey's tail. When the monkey tried to get away, the tail broke off and was taken by a cat. How the monkey got his tail back is very similar to Hogrogian's One Fine Day.

The Monkey's Whisker and "The Fig Tree" are also similar in style to The Old Woman and Her Pig and One Fine Day. Rockwell used Lang's Brown Fairy Book as the source for her picture book The Monkey's Whisker. In this cumulative Brasilian story, a barber shaved a monkey who was in a coconut tree so the monkey took the razor and gave it to a woman to clean a fish. When the woman dropped the razor in the water, she gave the monkey the fish. The monkey loaned the fish to a man for some bread but when he asked for the fish back, he was given coffee beans instead. Then a trade for flour with a young girl is transacted. Later the story came full circle when the barber wanted the razor. "The Fig Tree," pages 66 to 68 of Cothran's The Magic Calabash is a cumulative story from Puerto Rico. The story is best explained with a quote: "Ironing woman, give me my piece of wood. It was not mine. It was the woodcutter's. The woodcutter broke my axe. The axe was not mine. It was the fire's."

In Hoffman's A Boy Who Went Out to Gather Pears, a dog bit a boy to make him begin to gather pears so they would fall off a tree. The actions leading up to this event are very similar to The Old Woman and Her Pig: a butcher killed a calf to drink water to quench a fire to burn a stick to beat a dog so it would bite the boy.

Galdone's Little Tuppen, An Old Tale is a similar story. Cluck Cluck went to a spring to get water so Little Tuppen wouldn't choke while coughing. The chain of events included a blacksmith, farmer, cow, shoemaker, little boy, oak tree, and a spring. In "Munachar and Manachar," in Jacobs's Celtic Fairy Tales (pp. 170-74), an axe was needed to cut a rod to make a gag to hang Manachar who ate the raspberries. The cumulative story began when Munachar looked for the makings of a cake to give the threshers. Other parts of the chain included straw, cow, milk, butter, hounds, deer, water, a flag, and an axe.

"Drat the Wind," pages 22 and 23 of Withers's *I Saw a Rocket Walk a Mile*," is a cumulative tale from Missouri or Oklahoma in which a man tried to teach his dog to catch turtles. The chain reaction began when a man asked a stick to beat the dog. Numerous stories in Withers's book fit the same pattern. "Gaso The Teacher" (pp. 143-46) comes from Zanzibar. The chain reaction in this story led to the discovery of whoever threw the calabash that hit the teacher Gaso and killed him. In the Cuban story, "The Heron's Ball" (pp. 53-4), a rooster got his bill dirty and asked the grass to clean it. In the English story, "Titty Mouse and Tatty Mouse" (pp. 62-65), a three-legged stool asked Tatty Mouse why she was weeping to begin the chain reaction. "The Little Bird that Found the Pea," in Withers's book comes from India. A little bird took a pea to a miller to have it split but the pea caught in the socket of the mill. The chain reaction began when the chicken went to the carpenter to cut the mill handle. "How a Boy Got a Baboon," began when a boy caught a bird and asked his mother to roast it for him. This story comes from Sierra Leone or Liberia. The chain reaction began when a crow brought fire at the request of a louse and the louse decided to cook crow in "The Louse and the Crow" (pp. 108-09).

Burnie's Hill, A Traditional Rhyme is a picture book illustrated by Erik Blegvad that follows a similar pattern. In this cumulative rhyme a boy and girl talk about gold and money in a field taken by mousie whose home is in the wood burnt by fire, quenched by water drunk by a bull back of Burnie's Hill clad in snow melted by the sun up in the air.

THE GINGERBREAD MAN—LIVE ACTION AND WITH PUPPETS.   Versions of a story about a runaway gingerbread man or boy, pancake, bun, bannock, rice cake, or johnnycake can be found throughout the world. Some of them are better than others for playing, while some are more suited to puppetry or the flannelboard. Some of the stories include special parts for pantomiming, while others are excellent for storytelling.

"The Gingerbread Man," rewritten and illustrated by Anne Rockwell, appears on pages 33 to 44 of her book *The Three Bears and Fifteen Other Stories*. This story is excellent for reading aloud because it includes the famous refrain "Run, run, as fast as you can. You can't catch me! I'm the Gingerbread Man!" The story can be easily played out by students except for the part where the fox invited the pancake to sit on its tail, back, shoulder, and nose. There are enough parts for all children to participate in playing out the story, or it can easily be adapted to the flannelboard.

Another common version is the picture book illustrated by Galdone called *The Gingerbread Boy*. This version is suitable for both playing and the flannelboard. Characters are an old man, old woman, Gingerbread Boy, cow, horse, men threshing wheat in a barn, and mowers in a field. Because the fox invited the Gingerbread Boy to jump on his tail, head, shoulder, and nose, the story is not as suitable for puppetry as other versions. Shadows or flannelboard characters, however, could be cut out so that distinctive body parts would make this possible. The story includes the refrain and children will enjoy the threshing and mowing.

Ireson's picture book 'The Gingerbread Man provides the best incentive for making something to eat after the story has been read: the picture of the Gingerbread Man in the pan! All of the versions could be made available to students to read and sort into categories according to what animal or persons finally ate the main character as well as how it was accomplished. There are two versions of how the fox became the winner. Other winners were the mountain people, a pig, and a goat. Ireson's version offers opportunities for students to pantomime or could be played by a whole class because there are parts for everyone. Characters include the Gingerbread Man, the farmer's wife, butcher's wife, blacksmith, miller, tailor, cow, horse, and fox. Characters can be added to provide additional parts for a whole class.

Even more action appears in the Scottish version called "The Wee Bannock," pages 13 to 24 of Haviland's Favorite Fairy Tales Told in Scotland. Before parts are given out, students can work as a group or separately to establish what various characters do. This play is especially good for classroom playing because there are twenty-two parts. Additional children can be part of the shepherd's family. The original owners of the bannock (pancake) were a man and a woman. When they ate one bannock, the other one ran away, and encountered a tailor with two apprentices and a wife; a weaver and his wife; a housewife churning butter; a miller; a blacksmith; a man separating lint and his wife combing it; a cottage where a woman was stirring soup and her husband was braiding ropes; a cottage where a shepherd, his wife, and children were sitting down to eat; a house where a man threw his britches at the bannock; his wife; and a fox who welcomed the bannock. A similar version appears in Jacobs's More English Folk and Fairy Tales (pp. 73-77).

Jameson's easy picture book, The Clay Pot Boy, is about a childless couple from Russia who made a clay pot in the shape of a boy to be their son. The son proceeded to eat everyone up until he met his match—a billy goat who promised to make it easier for the clay pot boy by jumping into his mouth, but smashed the pot to pieces instead. This story is suitable for playing in first or second grade, and each of the students can be asked to read the story for himself or herself. There are thirty-two parts: the clay pot, the billy goat, the ten tubs of milk, five baskets of bread, an old woman and her spinning wheel, an old man and his hoe, the farmer's wife and her rake, a rooster, a hen and her egg, and a wooden barn. There are parts for twenty-five people if students do not take the part of utensils.

It is a pig that asked the pancake to sit on its snout to cross a river in a Norwegian version called "The Pancake," found on pages 238 and 239 of Sutherland's edition of the Arbuthnot Anthology of Children's Literature. That story was taken from Asbjornsen and Moe's Tales from the Field, as translated by Dasent, and is good for playing because it has sixteen characters: the pancake, a mother (Goody Poody), her seven children, Manny Panny, Henny Penny, Cocky Locky, Ducky Lucky, Goosey Poosy, Gander Pander, and Piggy Wiggy. Similar versions appear on pages 10 to 15 of ACEI's Told Under the Green Umbrella and pages 19 to 20 of Hutchinson's Chimney Corner Stories.

In Anita Lobel's easy reader, The Pancake, a pig eats the pancake.

Sawyer's picture book, *Journey Cake, Ho!*, placed the story "in a log cabin, t'other side of *Tip Top Mountain*." Two of the human characters, an old woman (Merry) and an old man (Grumble), have songs that make the book good for reading aloud. After hearing the story, children can be asked to pantomime the actions of the main characters. Merry's actions include, among others, carding, spinning, and knitting wool; Grumble's actions include, among others, shearing sheep and hoeing the garden. The actions of Johnny, the bound-out boy, include, among others, splitting kindling and lugging water. The two old people experience hardships when a fox carried off their hens, a wolf carried off their sheep, when their pig wandered off, and when their cow broke her leg. Since there was not enough food left, Johnny was sent on his way with a journey cake that got away from him. This story has a happier ending than most of the others because a cow, ducks, sheep, pig, hens, and a donkey follow the journey cake up the mountain back to the cabin where it is then reheated and eaten by the old man, old woman, and boy. The people and the animals then lived happily ever after.

Another American version found on pages 27 to 31 of Withers's *I Saw a Rocket Walk a Mile* is called "The Johnnycake." The characters are an old man, old woman, little boy, two well diggers, two ditch diggers, a bear, a wolf, and a fox.

Williams's *Paper Bag Puppets* contains patterns for making puppets for "The Gingerbread Man" characters (pp. 47-53). No story appears here with the puppets, but story and production notes which include techniques, action, and directions for making paper bag puppets appear in Ross's *Puppet Shows Using Poems and Stories* (pp. 150-155). The version included in Ross's book is called "Johnny-Cake" and is found in Jacobs's *English Folk and Fairy Tales* (pp. 162-165) and in Martignoni's *Illustrated Treasury of Children's Literature* (pp. 77-79). In this one the fox is able to eat the johnnycake by pretending that he couldn't hear what it was saying and asking it to come closer.

A clever fox also feigned deafness in "The Bun," in Hutchinson's *Candlelight Stories* (pp. 25-32). The song in this version would be fun for children to sing. Marcia Brown's picture book, *The Bun, A Tale from Russia*, is similar and well suited for a puppet show. In both versions, the bun was placed in the window to cool. A wall that has a window can be one of the props, and the bun, placed in the window, disappears from it. Then the bun can encounter the other animals in the forest, one at a time. Another Russian version found in Morton's *Harvest of Russian Children's Literature* (pp. 127-128) was written by Dorian Rottenberg and is called "The Doughnut." The characters are Grandpa, Grandma, a hare, a wolf, a bear, and a fox.

"The Rice Cake That Rolled Away," pages 123 to 31 of Uchida's *The Magic Listening Cap, More Folk Tales from Japan*, is about rice cakes made from sweet bean paste that rolled off the plate. The old man followed a rice cake to Ojizo-sama's shrine, captured it, and gave the clean half to Ojizo-sama. The statue in return invited the old man to climb up in its lap, on its shoulders, and then up on its head, and told the man that a group of ogres would come to gamble and drink in front of the statue and then the old man should beat a fan and crow like a cock. When he did so, the ogres rushed away leaving their gold behind. A nosey neighbor woman learned the story, so she and her husband forced a rice cake to go to the cave while they climbed up on Ojizo-sama to wait for the ogres. When one of the ogres caught his nose in a tree branch, the neighbor laughed and was beaten by them. This story could be told in conjunction with other stories about greed and its consequences.

Students could either play out this story or could make puppets to enact it for them. The statue in the live-action version could be a table, so the man could climb up on it. The story could be played out by two groups simultaneously with as many ogres as there are parts needed. Larger classes could have three groups playing the story simultaneously. When the story is played as a puppet show, there can be a papier-mache statue of Ojizo-sama that has a lap, shoulders, and head large and distinctive enough for the old man to sit on them. The number of ogres will have to be limited to four or less because two puppeteers will have to handle them. It may be possible to place the old man on the statue so that both pairs of hands will be free to manipulate the ogres. Students will enjoy making ogre puppets.

STONE SOUP—PLAYING, LIVE ACTION OR WITH PUPPETS. There are many versions of a folktale called "Stone Soup," "Nail Broth," or "The Old Woman and the Tramp." They come from many countries and fall into two categories—a version with many characters and one with only two characters. The versions in which several soldiers come to town and trick the villagers into providing meat, vegetables, and grain to add to their stone or nail is the best one for playing since it offers parts for a whole classroom of students. There can be four or five soldiers as well as several families of villagers, each of which can provide ingredients. Students can add a variety of vegetables from cabbage to carrots so that there will be parts for everyone. If the story is to be played with puppets, then the version in which a single soldier or a tramp comes to the door of the stingy old woman is best. Simple props include the kettle and the various ingredients.

Marcia Brown's picture book *Stone Soup* provides the best source if students are to play the story because three soldiers and numerous villagers appear in it. Another version for playing, by James Buechler, is "Stone Soup, a Russian Folk Tale," on pages 381 to 387 of Kamerman's *Dramatized Folk Tales of the World*, with eight characters and numerous villagers. Carlson includes a version called "The Old Woman and the Tramp" on pages 68 to 72 of *Act It Out*, which includes only two characters for pairs of students to play out. This version and others by the same name only have two characters, good for puppet shows. That particular title is of Swedish origin. Sources are "The Old Woman and the Tramp, a Swedish Folk Tale," pages 270 to 274 of Ward's *Stories to Dramatize*, and "The Old Woman and the Tramp" in Haviland's *Favorite Fairy Tales Told in Sweden* (pp. 15-28). Another version by Djurklo appears on pages 126 to 131 of Sechrist and Woolsey's *It's Time for Story Hour*. That same title appears on pages 149 to 154 of Greene's *Clever Cooks, A Concoction of Stories, Charms, Recipes and Riddles*, and includes a recipe for "Hearty Soup." Zemach illustrated a picture book called *Nail Soup, a Swedish Folk Tale* similar to the versions called "The Old Woman and the Tramp" except that a nail instead of a stone is used as a starter, as it is in "Nail Soup," in Curcija's *Yugoslav Folk-Tales* (pp. 153-154). The characters are a soldier and a granny.

The version from Belgium called "The Soup Stone" appears on pages 186 to 188 of Courlander's *Ride With The Sun, An Anthology of Folk Tales and Stories from the United Nations*, as well as on pages 17 to 20 of Leach's *The Soup Stone: The Magic of Familiar Things*. In this version, a single soldier stopped at a village and asked people to help him make stone soup. "Stone Soup in Bohemia," pages 17 to 25 of Morris's *The Upstairs Donkey and Other Stolen Stories*, is also about a single soldier. McGovern's *Stone Soup* is a paperback picture book in which a young man tricks an old lady into making soup from a stone.

An English version called "The Stone Stew" appears on pages 113-19 of Edmonds's *Trickster Tales*. In this version, one tramp helped another to learn how a master could get soup from a stingy old woman. An axe is used instead of a nail in "The Clever Soldier and the Stingy Woman," in Higonnet-Schnopper's *Tales from Atop a Russian Stove* (pp. 45-48).

Two other stories can accompany playing stone soup with puppets or by playing out the story. Hale's *The Glorious Christmas Soup Party* is about Mrs. Mouse who was able to provide a feast for her guests by putting together the simple gifts brought to her by guests. Hitte's *Mexicali Soup* is a turned around version of the tale, and would be fun for children to play in conjunction with the stone soup stories.

THREE BEARS, PIGS OR GOATS—LIVE ACTION OR WITH PUPPETS.   There are several versions of the story in which three bears came home from a walk to find that someone had eaten their porridge, sat upon their chairs, and slept in their beds. According to the story called "Scrapefoot," the bears found a fox by that name in one of their beds so the two biggest bears took hold of his feet and threw him out the window. In the version by Southey, the three bears found an old woman in the little bear's bed. In the most popular version by Steele, a little girl named "Goldilocks" was awakened by the three bears and was so frightened that she fled and was not seen again.

Because of the repetition, the story is easy enough to be played out by groups of four children in kindergarten and first grade. Any version with Goldilocks is recommended for playing, and is also suitable for adapting to a puppet show.

The version by Southey is about the old woman and is found under various titles in the following books: Arbuthnot's *Time for Old Magic* (pp. 5-7), which came from pages 96 to 101 of Jacobs's *English Folk and Fairy Tales*; Lang's *The Green Fairy Book* (pp. 234-37) Opie's *The Classic Fairy Tales* (pp. 201-05); Ross's *Puppet Shows Using Poems and Stories* (pp. 145-50); Rackham's *Arthur Rackham Fairy Book* (pp. 200-05); Sutherland's *Arbuthnot Anthology of Children's Literature* (pp. 150-52); and Ward's *Stories to Dramatize* (pp. 23-25).

The versions by Steele with Goldilocks appear under several titles in

Haviland's The Fairy Tale Treasury (pp. 36-43); Johnson's Anthology of Children's Literature (pp. 183-85); and Martignoni's The Illustrated Treasury of Children's Literature (pp. 69-73). Leslie Brooks illustrated the Steele version in his picture book, The Golden Goose Book. Galdone illustrated a picture book that features Goldilocks, and she is known as Golden Locks in Hutchinson's Chimney Corner Stories. Other sources for stories about the three bears are Kase's Stories for Creative Acting; Gruenberg's Favorite Stories Old and New; and The Tall Book of Nursery Tales.

Read or tell the story of "Scrapefoot" to children in kindergarten or first grade and ask them if they have ever heard of a similar story. Most of them will have heard the story of Goldilocks. Tell the children that there is a third version in which an old woman is found in the little bear's bed. Using an overhead or the chalkboard, list events of the story in chronological order. Divide the class into groups of four and tell them that they are to play out the story, each group deciding whether the visitor is to be a fox, little girl, or an old woman. If there is one group that does not have four persons, the teacher can fill in.

"The Three Bears" is also suitable for a puppet show. Production notes which include technique, cast, setting, and action for papier-mache hand puppets appear on pages 145 to 150 of Ross's Puppet Shows Using Poems and Stories, which features the old woman.

If the story "Scrapefoot" is to be acted with puppets, use four puppets from the Animal Fair Company—a fox, two bears, and a beaver that looks like a little bear. All four animals are of the same proportions. Commercial finger puppets of Goldilocks and her three friends are available from Trend Enterprises in a set called "Fairy Tales Finger Puppets." Directions or patterns for finger puppet bears appear in Hutchings's Making and Using Finger Puppets (pp. 80-82).

A cassette containing both Goldilocks and The Three Pigs, is available from Nancy Renfro Studios of Austin, Texas. The longer version is from twelve to fifteen minutes and is for children ages six to eight. The shorter version is available for children three to five years old. Scripts and ideas for making puppets and for performing the play are included with each script. One can order a set of hand puppets called "Goldilocks Set" from the same source. Another set called "The Three Piggies Set" includes three pigs, mama, the wolf, and a worm.

Acting out the play, The Three Pigs, involves more students than for The Three Bears or The Three Billy Goats Gruff, each of which only requires four characters. Eight players are needed to play The Three Pigs: a man with straw, a man with sticks, a man with bricks, three pigs, mother pig, and the wolf. If the group does not divide evenly into groups of eight, it is possible to have one person play the parts of several men to eliminate one or two characters. The mother could be imaginary if there is need to eliminate three characters.

Regardless of whether the story is called "The Three Pigs" or "The Three Little Pigs," the basic story is the same. A mother pig sent her three piglets off into the world where each of them purchased materials from a man to make a house. One house was made of straw; another of sticks; and a third of bricks. A wolf huffed and puffed the first two houses down, but could not blow down the house made of bricks. The wolf then tried to coax the pig from his home to get turnips, apples, and to go to the fair. However, the little pig outsmarted the wolf all three times. Finally, when the wolf decided to come down the chimney, the little pig had a boiling kettle waiting for the wolf—and ate him.

DuBois illustrated a picture book that is in rhyme, and another was written and illustrated by Galdone. "The Three Pigs" appears in Hutchinson's *Chimney Corner Stories* (pp. 54-60). "The Three Little Pigs" appears on pages 5 to 9 of ACEI's *Told Under the Green Umbrella*; pages 32 to 35 of Kase's *Stories for Creative Acting*; pages 100 to 05 of Lang's *The Green Fairy Book*; pages 81 to 91 of Rockwell's *The Three Bears and Fifteen Other Stories*; and pages 110 to 16 of *The Tall Book of Nursery Tales*. Another version appears in Williams-Ellis's *Fairy Tales from the British Isles* (pp. 39-43) and Sideman's *World's Best Fairy Tales* (pp. 459-64). "The Story of the Three Little Pigs" appears in Arbuthnot's *Time for Old Magic* (pp. 7-9); De la Mare's *Animal Stories* (pp. 16-19); Jacobs's *English Folk and Fairy Tales* (pp. 69-73); Johnson's *Anthology of Children's Literature* (pp. 185-86); and Lines's *Nursery Stories* (pp. 117-27). A southern mountain story called "The Old Sow and the Three Shoats" appears in Chase's *Grandfather Tales* (pp. 81-87).

Versions of the Scandinavian story, "The Three Billy Goats Gruff," are also similar to each other. The story could be introduced through the music as described in the chapter "Enhancing Books through Music," or it could be introduced with Marcia Brown's picture book in filmstrip format called *The Three Billy Goats Gruff*. Two other picture books with the same title are illustrated by Galdone and Blair. The story is used in Ziskind's *Telling Stories to Children* (pp. 88-91) as a sample of how to play out a story. Outlines of the goats to trace for stick puppets appear on pages 65 and 66 of Adair's *Do-It-In-a-Day Puppets for Beginners*. Four finger puppets of this story are available from Trend Enterprises in the set called "Fairy Tales Finger Puppets." See the section of this chapter called "Puppet Plays Based on Children's Literature."

Dasent was the source used by Fitzgerald in *World Tales for Creative Dramatics* (pp. 193-194) and by Ward in *Stories to Dramatize* (pp. 21-23). Thorne-Thomsen's version appears in ACEI's *Told Under the Green Umbrella* (pp. 21-23) and in Thorne-Thomsen's *East O' the Sun and West O' the Moon, with Other Norwegian Folk Tales* (pp. 17-19). Asbjornsen was the source for the story in the following collections: Arbuthnot's *Time for Old Magic* (pp. 115-16); Asbjornsen's *East of the Sun and West of the Moon, and Other Tales* (pp.16-18); Haviland's *The Fairy Tale Treasury* (pp. 56-57); Johnson's *Anthology of Children's Literature* (pp. 287-88); and Ross's *Puppet Shows Using Poems and Stories*. Other sources are the d'Aulaires' *East of the Sun and West of the Moon* (pp. 175-78); Haviland's *Favorite Fairy Tales Told in Norway* (pp. 45-49); Hutchinson's *Chimney Corner Stories* (pp. 35-39); Jones's *Scandinavian Legends and Folk Tales* (pp. 102-04); Kase's *Stories for Creative Acting* (pp. 30-32); Rockwell's *The Three Bears and 15 Other Stories* (pp. 81-91); Sideman's *The World's Best Fairy Tales* (pp. 361-64); *The Tall Book of Nursery Tales* (pp. 46-48); and Thompson's *One Hundred Favorite Folktales* (pp. 1-2).

PLAYING SENDAK'S REALLY ROSIE.   There are many ways to introduce Maurice Sendak's Nutshell library to students. Each of the four stories, *Alligators All Around, Chicken Soup with Rice, One Was Johnny,* and *Pierre* are available as separate sound filmstrips or 16mm films. All of them are part of a television program called "Really Rosie" in which music was provided by Carole King. That program is now available as a 16mm film and the songs appear on a recording called "Really Rosie." Music and lyrics for the songs are included in a paperback book called Maurice Sendak's *Really Rosie Starring the Nutshell Kids,* with music by Carole King.

Alligators All Around, an alphabet book, is perfect for pantomiming. The action includes bursting balloons, getting giggles, juggling jelly beans, riding reindeer, and throwing tantrums. Children will be challenged to find actions for some of the letters. Having headaches can be pantomimed by placing a hand on the brow but "ordering oatmeal" and "shockingly spoiled" will be more difficult but fun.

The choruses to *Chicken Soup with Rice* provide twelve different actions, one for each month. The more challenging actions are happy, oh my, whoopy, merry, and I told you. Easier activities to mime are sipping, blowing, mixing, sprinkling, selling, cooking, paddling, and spouting.

It is possible to designate groups of children to play the ten roles in *One Was Johnny* so as many as three groups could be playing at one time in a classroom. Designating players for *One Was Johnny* physically reinforces the concept of ten numbers. Some of the actions include a cat who chased the rat, a turtle who bit the dog's tail. If props are used, some interesting ones to include are mail, old clothes, an old shoe, and a banana.

Five characters are needed to play *Pierre;* Pierre, his mother, his father, a hungry lion, and the doctor. Students can sing the song or play out the story to the music or play the story using their own dialogue. With modification, the story can become a two-character puppet show, with the lion and Pierre.

BACKGROUND READING ON PUPPETRY.   It is important to read as much background information as possible before beginning a unit on puppetry. The following selections were chosen because they give help with making puppets, plays, and production.

Seven values to be found in puppetry are included on pages 182 and 183 of Huckleberry and Strother's *Speech Education for the Elementary Teacher.* Six good reasons for preferring puppets to playing out stories are included on page 18 of Adair and Patapoff's *Folk Puppet Plays for the Social Studies.* Reasons why a person might wish to be puppeteer are listed on pages 28 and 29 of Latshaw's *Puppetry, the Ultimate Disguise.* Lists of differences between actors and puppeteers are given on page 30. Six rules for puppetry are given on page 18 of Boylan's *How to Be a Puppeteer.*

Philpott's *Let's Look at Puppets* contains excellent background material on puppets and has an index of places and of puppet names. Also read chapter 2 of Currell's *Complete Book of Puppetry* and "The Puppets Tale—A Short History of Puppetry" from Bufano's *Book of Puppetry.* More information about the history of puppets can be found in the books by Batchelder, Beaumont, Finch, Jagendorf, Lewis, Reiniger, and Richter.

Five elements of good puppet theatre are included in Engler and Fijan's *Making Puppets Come Alive,* on pages 156 and 157. Nine "Qualities to Look for in Hand Puppetry" are also mentioned on those pages.

The "Appendix: An Outline for Lesson Plan" on pages 185 to 189 of Engler and Fijan's book tells what should be accomplished at each of the ten sessions. "Preparation of the End-of-Term Production" appears on pages 188 and 189. Ten sessions are also outlined for making a felt puppet.

Pages 17 to 20 of Rutter's *ABC Puppetry* list five types of puppets with an explanation of each: marionette, glove, rod, shadow, and flat figure. Philpott's *Modern Puppetry* classes puppets by type of manipulation: hand or glove, finger, string, stick, or rod.

Pages 34 to 37 of chapter 2 of Adair's *Do-It-in-a-Day Puppets* give indicators of character projected by exaggeration, voices, gestures, rhythm and mannerisms. A section called "Puppet Actions" appears on pages 68 and 69 of Olfson's *You Can Act.* Olfson invites puppeteers to practice hand movements that are typical of types of characters, and movements for glove puppets are also given. "Summary of Some Qualities to Look for in Hand Puppetry" appears on pages 156 and 157 of Engler and Fijan's *Making Puppets Come Alive.* Nine production tricks are included on pages 110 to 112 of Adair and Patapoff's *Folk Puppet Plays for the Social Studies.* Eight steps for turning a story into a play are listed on pages 16 and 17 of that same book. Six things to avoid are given on pages 74 and 75 of Curry and Wetzel's *Teaching with Puppets.*

Considerations in script writing are included by Hawes in *The Puppet Book* (pp. 130-132). Eleven steps to "Writing an Original Puppet Play" are listed in Ross's *Hand Puppets* (pp. 124-27). Six suggestions for creating stories are given in Curry and Wetzel's *Teaching with Puppets* (pp. 71-73). Read chapter 4 of Ross's *Hand Puppets* for information on adapting folktales, and information on adapting stories also appears in Snook's *Puppets.* Also see chapter 7 of Batchelder's *Puppet Theatre Handbook,* chapter 24 of Wall's *Complete Puppet Book,* chapter 3 of Bramall and Sommerville's *Expert Puppet Technique,* chapter 2 of Bodor's *Creating and Presenting Hand Puppets,* chapter 4 of Batchelder and Comer's *Puppets and Plays,* chapter 3 of Warrell's *Be a Puppeteer,* and chapter 1 of Boylan's *How to Be a Puppeteer.* Boylan's chapter is especially useful for writing dialogue. A list of stories suitable for adapting to puppet plays is included in Wall's *The Puppet Book.* The information on pages 16 and 17 of Adair and Patapoff's *Folk Puppet Plays . . .* called "Steps in Story Dramatization" can be used in puppetry or for playing out a story with live characters.

A "Production Checklist" of fourteen items appears in appendix 3, page 227 of Broadman's *Marionettes Onstage!* These same points apply to using any type of puppet, not just marionettes.

Numerous aids are provided in Latshaw's *Puppetry, the Ultimate Disguise.* Three time periods for a puppet show are listed on page 136. Information about casting, construction period, and technical and dress rehearsals appear on page 29.

BOOKS WITH CHAPTERS ON PUPPETRY.   Check language arts books for information about using puppets in teaching. Whitehead's *Children's Literature: Strategies for Teaching* gives "Suggestions for Using Drama, Puppetry and Art to Develop Creative Projects Based on Literature." Although chapter 3 (pp. 43-49) of Coddy's *Using Literature with Young Children* is called "Let's Act It Out, Literature for Dramatization," the chapter is mostly concerned with puppetry. Chapter 16 (pp. 225-43) of Bauer's *Handbook for Storytellers*, is called "Puppetry."

Art and craft books also include chapters on puppets. Chapter 10, of Montgomery's *Art for Teachers of Children*, "Materials Come Alive as Puppets," is a chapter teachers should read before working with stick puppets. Matil's *Meaning in Crafts* (pp. 44-57) chapter 4, "Puppets," lists types of puppets: paper bags, tubes, potato heads, finger and hand, marionettes, and stocking. Ideas for clothespin, finger, and other puppets are given in Vermeer and Lariviere's *The Little Kid's Four Seasons Craft Book*. Chapter 1, "Playful Puppets," of Sanderson's *Elementary Teacher's Art Ideas Desk Book* includes small and large bag puppets, shoe box, spool, and others. "Puppets Are Actors," chapter 2 of Carlson's *Act It Out*, includes information on movement of puppets: fist, ring, cardboard, blockhead, bag head, shadow, hand, rod, and marionette. Play production is included in chapter 6, "Puppet Shows," in Olfson's *You Can Put on a Show*. Mahlman and Jones's *Puppet Plays for Young Players* is basically a book of scripts, but a section called "How to Get the Most out of Your Rehearsals" (pp. 189-92) gives basics for having a good show, five rules for directors, and information about regular and dress rehearsals.

MAKING MARIONETTES.   Most people are surprised to know that a wide variety of puppets are classified as marionettes. Patterns for making a man and a dog cardboard marionette appear in Suib and Broadman's *Marionettes Onstage!* Patterns and directions for medieval characters (jester, knight, maiden, dragon, and king) appear in Roth's *The Art of Making Puppets and Marionettes* (pp. 143-64). Gates's *Easy to Make Puppets* includes directions for a one-string ghost and a three-string and a five-string witch. A basic man, woman, and children with a witch, fairy, king, and queen are included in Dean's *Wooden Spoon Puppets*. Directions for making Hansel and Gretel appear on pages 30 to 35. Instructions for making papier-mache balloon marionettes appear on page 206 of volume 11 of *Childcraft's* article "Puppets and Marionettes." Marionettes from cloth, papier-mache and wood are included in Fraser's *Introducing Puppetry*. A simple one-string puppet is included in Philpott's *Modern Puppetry* and a paper plate marionette is included in Currell's *Complete Book of Puppetry*.

The following books contain chapters on marionettes: part 1 of Broadman's *Marionettes on Stage!*, chapter 8 of Currell's *Complete Book of Puppetry*, chapter 2 of Finch's *Presenting Marionettes*, chapters 7, 8, 9, and 10 of Green's *Masks and Puppets*, chapter 4 of Green and Target's *Space Age Puppets and Masks*, chapter 4 of Mills and Dunn's *Marionettes, Masks, and Shadows*, chapter 7 of Mulholland's *Practical Puppetry*, chapters 3 and 4 of Rutter's *ABC*

Puppetry, chapter 4 of Tichnor's *Tom Tichnor's Puppets*, chapter 14 of Wall's *The Complete Puppet Book*, and chapter 14 of Wall's *The Puppet Book*.

Puppet books by the following authors should also be consulted: Batchelder, Batchelder and Comer, Cochrane, Jagendorf, Lewis, Snook, and Tuttle.

PUPPET PRODUCTION—MANIPULATION.   The following books include complete chapters devoted to manipulation: chapter 4 of Ackley's *Marionettes*, chapters 5 and 6 of Bramall and Somerville's *Expert Puppet Technique*, chapter 3 of Boylan's *How to Be a Puppeteer*, chapters 4, 5, 6, and 7 of Engler and Fijan's *Making Puppets Come Alive*, chapter 6 of Finch's *Presenting Marionettes*, and chapter 9 of McNamara's *Puppetry*. Page 190 of Mahlman and Jones's *Puppet Plays for Young Players* contains instructions. Also check sections of puppetry books by Batchelder and Comer, Bodor, Bufano, and Wall's *Complete Puppet Book*.

PUPPET PRODUCTION—COSTUME.   The following books on puppetry contain complete chapters devoted to costume: chapter 3 of Ackley's *Marionettes*, chapter 4 of Bodor's *Creating and Presenting Hand Puppets*, chapter 5 of Finch's *Presenting Marionettes*, and chapter 6 of Richter's *Fell's Guide to Hand Puppets*. Also check sections of puppetry books by Adair, Broadman, Bufano, Cochrane, Fraser, Green, Jagendorf, Mulholland, Philpott's *Modern Puppetry*, Ross's *Hand Puppets*, Rutter, Snook, Tuttle, Wall's *Complete Puppet Book*, and Worrell.

PUPPET PRODUCTION—SCENERY.   The following books on puppetry contain complete chapters about scenery: chapter 6 of Ackley's *Marionettes*, chapter 6 of Batchelder's *Puppet Theatre Handbook*, chapter 4 of Bodor's *Creating and Presenting Hand Puppets*, chapter 9 of Engler and Fijan's *Making Puppets Come Alive*, chapters 6 and 7 of Mills and Dunn's *Marionettes, Masks and Shadows*, and chapter 8 of Richter's *Fell's Guide to Hand Puppets*. Also read selections from the puppet books by Adair, Batchelder and Cormer, Broadman, Currell, Finch, Fraser, Jagendorf, Mahlman and Jones's *Puppet Plays for Young Players*, Rutter, Snook, Tuttle, and Worrell.

PUPPET PRODUCTION—SOUND.   "Music for Situations," pages 129 to 35 of Suib and Broadman's *Marionettes Onstage!*, lists titles and composers of music suitable for weddings; children, toys, and puppets; lullabies; animals, birds, and insects; activity, violence, and battle; military band music, bugle calls, seasons, night and day, and weather; and water. Mood music is included for peace, serenity, innocence; lightness, grace, charm; humor, wit, whimsy, and love; happiness, joy; eeriness, mystery, and impending doom; sadness, grief, and death. Phonograph record titles also appear on pages 193 and 194 of Mahlman and Jones's *Puppet Plays for Young Players*.

Check the indexes of puppetry books by the following authors for more information about sound: Adair, Jagendorf, Richter, and Rutter.

PUPPET PRODUCTION—LIGHTING.   The following books about puppetry contain chapters on lighting: chapter 6 of Batchelder's *Puppet Theatre Handbook*, chapter 8 of Bromall and Somerville's *Expert Puppet Technique*, chapter 10 of Currell's *Complete Book of Puppetry*, chapter 20 of Engler and Fijan's *Making Puppets Come Alive*, chapter 8 of Green and Targett's *Space Age Puppets and Masks*, chapter 10 of Richter's *Fell's Guide to Hand Puppets*, chapter 23 of Wall's *Complete Puppet Book*, and chapter 22 of Wall's *The Puppet Book*.

Further information about lighting can be found in the puppetry books by Adair, Batchelder and Comer, Blackman, Broadman, Bodor, Bufano, Fraser, Jagendorf, Hutchings, Ross's *Hand Puppets*, Rutter, and Worrell.

PUPPET STAGES.   There are many types of stages just as there are different types of puppets. Stages can be as informal as Pels suggests in *Easy Puppets*—desks, overturned tables, a screen, doorway, window, or box. Diagrams and measurements for a table screen are included on page 181 of Engler and Fijan's *Making Puppets Come Alive*. Figure 41 in Richter's *Fell's Guide to Hand Puppets* shows a full-length stage. A diagram for a marionette stage appears in chapter 22 and a portable glove puppet theatre in chapter 21 of Wall's *The Complete Puppet Book*. Sometimes stages can be purchased. Puppets of Seattle produces a cloth stage that can be folded called a "Portable Doorway Theatre." The stage is held in a doorway by a tension rod. Convenient pockets hold the puppets.

The following books about puppets contain chapters on puppet stages: chapter 5 of Ackley's *Marionettes*, chapter 5 of Batchelder's *Puppet Theatre Handbook*, chapter 5 of Boylan's *How to Be a Puppeteer*, part 2 of Broadman's *Marionettes on Stage!*, chapter 19 of Engler and Figan's *Making Puppets Come Alive*, chapter 7 of Finch's *Presenting Marionettes*, chapter 6 of Green's *Masks and Puppets*, chapter 1 of Green and Targett's *Space Age Puppets and Masks*, chapter 20 of McNamara's *Puppetry*, chapter 4 of Mills and Dunn's *Marionettes, Masks, and Shadows*, chapter 7 of Richter's *Fells Guide to Hand Puppets*, and chapter 5 of Worrell's *Be a Puppeteer!*

Also consult puppet books by the following authors: Adair, Batchelder and Comer, Blackman, Bodor, Bufano, Cochrane, Currell, Fraser, Lewis, Mulholland, Pels, Philpot, Reiniger, Snook, Tuttle, and Wall.

PUPPET PATTERNS.   Easy-to-follow directions and patterns for making various puppets appear in several books. These patterns are identified in this section for easy location of the information.

A basic costume pattern for a hand puppet appears on page 33 of Adair's *Do-It-in-a-Day Puppets for Beginners*. Patterns are also given for the following sock and glove puppets: a friendly sea dragon, sea monster, wise old bird, Wizard of Oz lion, Dutch boy, and little brown monster. A pattern for a cardboard goat for "The Three Billy Goats Gruff" appears on pages 65 and 66. Directions for making Punch and Judy and a clown out of felt appear on pages 74 to 79 of Hutchings's *Making and Using Finger Puppets*. A simple felt mouth pattern appears on pages 72 to 75 of Engler and Fijan's *Making Puppets Come*

Alive, which also includes patterns for eyes, noses and mouths on pages 166 and 167.

A hand puppet with a mouth can easily be made from the drawing on page 49 of Handford's *Complete Book of Puppets and Puppetry.* A basic head for moving mouth puppets appears in *Tom Tichenor's Puppets.* Patterns for a squirrel, rabbit and chipmunk appear on page 70, a mouse on 71, a basic head for a person on 56, and a basic body for a person on page 57.

Worrell's *Be a Puppeteer!* contains several excellent patterns: a puppet from a sleeve (p. 56) includes patterns for "Little Red Riding Hood"; a circle of cloth puppet (page 57) includes a Little Red Riding Hood and Grandmother; a talking mouth animal (page 58) includes a wolf and a bookworm; a sock with a mouth (page 59) includes a turtle, snake, goose, duck, chicken, cow, dog, wolf, worm, or reindeer; a half-circle of cloth (page 74) includes a mouse, pig, or woman.

Roth's *The Art of Making Puppets and Marionettes* contains patterns for making circus hand puppets in chapter 4. Animals included are a lion and dancing horse. Patterns for marionettes and costumes for a king, knight, maiden, jester, and dragon are included in chapter 5.

Snook's *Puppets* includes a pattern for a glove puppet on page 24 and a lion on page 28, puppet heads on pages 42 and 43, a string pig on page 72, and a string cat on page 68. Also included are a tennis ball head, a stocking toe head, and a balsa wood head with directions on how to create each one.

Lewis's *Making Easy Puppets* contains directions for folding a handkerchief over a hand to create a puppet (pp. 14-15), making a sock carrot (p. 23), a paper beak (pp. 38-39), and puppets from milk cartons and matchboxes. A Santa paper plate marionette appears on pages 48 and 49, and various paper bag puppet instructions appear in the section called "Making and Using Paper Bag Puppets."

A picture of a paper bird appears on page 53 of Carlson's *Play a Part.* Paper birds and flowers appear in Batchelder and Lee's *Puppets and Plays.* Plates 34 and 35 show a horse and a clown. Information about materials and construction directions for making a mitt penguin that looks like *Mr. Popper's Penguins* appears on pages 29 and 30 of Janvier's *Fabulous Birds You Can Make.*

Certain craft books contain brief information on making puppets. Sommer's *The Bread Dough Craft Book* contains information on making a finger puppet frog (pp. 59-60). Box puppets are included in the unpaged book *Just a Box* by Chernoff. Shadow puppets are included in Stephan's *Creating With Tissue Paper.* A ring puppet using bone curtain rings appears on pages 33 to 35 of Newsome's *Make It With Felt.* Patterns for a boy and girl hand puppet with legs are available in *Better Homes and Gardens' One Hundred Sixty-seven Things to Make for Children* (pp. 132-33).

SHADOW PUPPETS.   Shadow puppets are not seen directly by the audience but appear in silhouette on a screen of muslin, acetate, or parchment-like material—light from behind casting a shadow on the screen. Scenery consists of simple outlines of objects, and puppets are made of any stiff paper. Static puppets can be controlled from beneath the stage by a cardboard or stick. Threads, wires, rods, or cardboard strips can cause parts of puppets to move. Shadow puppets can be simply made by primary students or can be of the more complicated type in the Chinese tradition.

Reiniger's *Shadow Theatres and Shadow Films* contains illustrations of Chinese shadow theater and discusses the history of shadow theaters including Greek, Punch and Judy, and modern shadow play. A shadow stage is included. Theory and practice are given in Schonewolf's *Play with Light and Shadow, the Art and Techniques of Shadow Theatre*. Also read Blackham's *Shadow Puppets*.

There are patterns for characters, scenery and props in Cochrane's *Shadow Puppets in Color*. The first three chapters deal with technique: Simple Shadow Theatres; Color Shadow Puppets; and Scenery and Sound Effects. The last three chapters include shadow plays: *Moon Dragon, the Emperor's Horse*, a Chinese legend adapted for shadow puppets with three characters plus a crowd scene; *Karagiosis and the Dragon* is a Greek shadow play about Alexander the Great with six characters and a crowd scene; and *The Story of Rama and Sita*, based on a Hindu-Javanese legend that contains six characters and a monkey army.

Patterns as well as direction on how to make the puppets and conduct the performance are given in Young and Beckett's *The Rooster's Horns: A Chinese Puppet Play to Make and Perform*.

Hansel and Gretel, A Shadow Puppet Picture Book by Wiesner includes directions for making the theater and curtains, acetate sheets and shadows and how to fasten scenery to the screen. Five steps for making the stage from a grocery carton are included. Outlines for the puppets and diagrams for lighting are given, and the book contains dialogue as well as the silhouettes. The script can easily be modified to make the play shorter. This is one book to read before producing that first shadow play.

While one group is preparing the stage and silhouettes for scenery and puppets, another group can be making a Gingerbread House for everyone to eat after the production. Directions are given in *It's a Gingerbread House: Bake it, Build it, Eat it* by Williams.

The 16mm film *The Fisherman and His Wife* can be viewed for further ideas on using shadows.

Mendoza's *Shadowplay* shows twenty-six different kinds of animals, objects, and people to copy as hand exercises. The left page shows the hand position and the name of the object; the right page a photo of the silhouette. If only that page is shown to children, they could be asked to guess what it is. The foreword includes an ancient Chinese legend about the origin of the shadow.

Chapter 3, "Hand Exercises," of Severn's *Shadow Magic* contains eighteen illustrations for other hand shadows. Chapter 2, "Human Shadows," contains illustrations for body shadows. Human shadow plays appear on pages 29 to 34 of Kettlekamp's *Shadows*, and shadow animals shown are a dog, rabbit, alligator, or crocodile. Chinese shadow plays are mentioned on pages 23 to 28. Projected shadows appear on pages 57 to 59. Almaznino's *Art of Hand Shadows* contains twenty-three animals, thirteen people, four buildings, as well as plants and flowers of the desert. Also read chapter 8, "Shadows and Pictures," of Crosscup's *Children and Dramatics*. Shadow pantomimes are discussed on pages 33 and 34 of Carlson's *Act It Out*. A play, *Theseus and the Minotaur*, with three characters and a reader, is included on pages 34 to 37. Basic requirements for a shadow theater as well as the play "Jim Bridger and the Wolves" for six characters appears on pages 120 to 24. Information about making a shadow puppet appears in Stephen's *Creating with Tissue Paper*.

The following puppet books contain chapters on shadow puppets: chapter 7 of Currell's *Complete Book of Puppetry*, chapter 11 of McNamara's *Puppetry*, pages 205 to 225 of Mills and Dunn's *Marionettes, Masks and Shadows*, chapter 6 of Mulholland's *Practical Puppetry*, chapter 16 of Wall's *Complete Puppet Book*, and chapter 16 of Wall's *The Puppet Book*. Information on shadow puppets can also be found in puppet books by the following authors: Anderson, Batchelder, Batchelder and Comer, Cummings, Fraser, Philpott's *Modern Puppetry*, and in Ross's *Finger Puppets*.

The disastrous career of Etienne de Silhouette in the court of Louis XV before the French Revolution, as well as background on Augustin Edouart, the great American silhouette cutter, is included in Severan's chapter, "Silhouettes" (pp. 148-75). Information about Silhouette, Edouart, and Lavater is also included in Reiniger's *Shadow Theatres and Shadow Films*. Severan's book also includes information on how to make silhouettes, silhouettes as a party game, adapting Lavater's chair for making silhouettes, reducing silhouettes with a pantograph, using a sketching camera, finishing a silhouette, and mounting and framing are also included.

Silhouettes have been used as illustrations in several books. Fifty silhouettes illustrate the 1926 Newbery Medal-winning book, *Shen of the Sea* by Chrisman. Thompson's *Diary of a Monarch Butterfly* contains black and white silhouettes of the day-by-day life of a monarch butterfly from July 7 to August 2. Charlip and Supree's *Mother, Mother I Feel Sick, Send for the Doctor Quick, Quick, Quick* is a picture book with silhouettes for illustrations. All the images are silhouettes in Hoban's *Shapes and Things*. The background is black with white shapes. Schmiderer's *The Alphabeast Book, an Abecedarium* shows four silhouettes for each letter. The first silhouette is of the alphabet letter, the second picture fills in light spaces within the letter, the third image initiates the beginning of the fourth section, an animal or object beginning with that letter. For example, the stem of the lower case letter "b" makes the head and tail of a butterfly, and the rounded part of the letter is changed in shape to make the wide view of a butterfly's wings.

Elvira Everything by Asch is illustrated in stark black and white. A girl wanted a teddy bear but was given a doll named "Elvira Everything" who took over the girl's place in her own home.

Students can be introduced to books about shadows when they are making shadow puppets. Primary students will enjoy Keats's *Dreams*, a picture book which focuses on a paper mouse that fell from a window and made a shadow that grew larger and larger until it frightened a dog when he saw the outline on the building. Nonfiction books about shadows include Bulla's *What Makes a*

Shadow, deRegniers's *The Shadow Book*, Kettlekamp's *Shadows*, and Severan's *You and Your Shadow*.

MAKING AND USING FINGER PUPPETS.   Ross's *Finger Puppets, Easy to Make, Fun to Use* contains step-by-step directions for making nine kinds of finger puppets. Directions for making Thumbelina, the Farmer in the Dell, the Little Red Hen, and Chicken Licken are included. Patterns for making a paper finger puppet of Goldilocks and the three bears appear on pages 18 to 20 of Cummings's *101 Hand Puppets*. Patterns and step-by-step directions for making the Mother Goose characters Jack and Jill, the three little kittens and their mama, and Hey Diddle Diddle appear on pages 13 to 33 of Roth's *The Art of Making Puppets and Marionettes*. Directions and patterns for making a rabbit, squirrel, and mouse for one-finger puppets appear in Gates's *Easy to Make Puppets*, as does a pattern for a two-finger dancing bear. Finger mice appear in Philpott and McNeill's *The Know How Book of Puppets*. Patterns for ten little Indians (pp. 18-21) and a rooster (pp. 58-59) are included in Hutchings's *Making and Using Finger Puppets*. A paper doll-like puppet is shown on page 41 of Alkema's *Puppet-Making*. Sommers's *The Bread Dough Craft Book* contains information on making a finger puppet frog on pages 59-60. Finger puppets also appear in Batchelder's *Puppet Theatre Handbook*, Jagendorf's *Puppets for Beginners*, and Mulholland's *Practical Puppets*.

Commercial sets of finger puppets can be kept in the classroom or could be kept in boxes to be checked out from the library media center. Trend Enterprises offers four sets of these, each of them containing sixteen puppets. Although the puppets are printed on stiff cardboard, teachers and librarians may want to laminate them on both sides for extra durability. The puppets may be checked out from the library by adding a card and pocket and spine labels to the boxes. The *Fairy Tales Finger Puppets* contains four puppets for each of the following stories: "The Three Bears," "Little Red Riding Hood," "The Three Little Pigs," and "The Billy Goats Gruff." The sixteen puppets in the set called *Once Upon a Time Finger Puppets* include a giant, princess, cat, king, frog, four character dragon family, queen, girl, knight, horse, dog, butterfly, and boy. Sixteen animals included in the *Animal Brigade Finger Puppets* are tortoise, monkey, frog, rhinoceros, parrot, pelican, ostrich, alligator, octopus, penguin, lobster, kangaroo, spider, giraffe, walrus, and crab. Clowns, a lion, an acrobat, and an animal trainer are among the puppets included in the *Circus Time Finger Puppets*.

The following easy books can be used to create a circus mood for primary students: DeRegniers's *Circus*; Peppe's *Circus Numbers, A Counting Book*, containing illustrations like circus posters; and Wildsmith's *Brian Wildsmith's Circus*, containing almost no text except the writing on the circus posters. A sound filmstrip of that book is available. Shay's *What Happens at the Circus* contains black and white photos. Seuss's *If I Ran the Circus* is an easy reader told in nonsense verse. Prelutsky's *Circus* is a picture book based on a poem that also appears on pages 3 to 12 of Brewton's *Under the Tent of the Sky*. Hoff's *Barkley* is an easy reader about a dog who was retired from the circus because he was too old, but was asked back to teach tricks to the new dogs. The Petersham's *Circus Baby*, a book and a sound filmstrip, is about an elephant. Harriet, who went to the circus in Maestro's *Harriet Goes to the Circus*, was the elephant first in line until the line formed elsewhere so she became number ten. Use this book with Peppe's *Circus Numbers*. A sound recording called *Animals and Circus* can also set the mood for this experience. Verbs connected with the circus can be pantomimed from Maestro's *Busy Day: A Book of Action Words*.

Scholastic Book Services produced several sets of finger puppets that contain multiple sets of the same puppets so several groups of students can play out the story at the same time. Those sets include *Hansel and Gretel* as illustrated by Margot Tomes from a book retold by Ruth Cross. Grimm's *Rumpelstiltskin* finger puppets was illustrated by Edward Gorey and match the illustrations in his book published by Scholastic.

The set called *Famous Americans* contains over twenty-five finger puppets in duplicate sets. A teacher's guide lists biographies that are available about these persons as well as a brief sketch about their achievements and the times in which they lived. Thirty-eight different kinds of animals are included in the set called *Animal Finger Puppets*. The teacher's guide suggests that a copy of Spier's *Gobble Growl and Grunt* could be used to encourage kindergarten or first graders to make animal sounds with their puppets.

Another source of finger puppets is the coloring book and paper doll section of your favorite bookstore or discount store. Often punch-out finger puppets are available. Sometimes these finger puppets are about storybook characters like "The Three Bears" or contain knights, maidens, and dragons. The fabric section of a discount house or a fabric shop can yield small figures which can be laminated to make them stiff before cutting them out to make finger puppets. One special find included about twenty sets of Snow White and her seven dwarfs in one yard of flannel!

HAND PUPPETS.   Hundreds of different kinds of hand puppets can be made from egg cartons, cereal boxes, milk cartons, paper bags, paper cups, paper plates, papier-mache, styrofoam cups, envelopes, socks, plastic containers, sleeves, yarn, utensils, tubes and cylinders, fruits and vegetables, or any other imaginable source. The books which offer pictures and directions for the greatest variety of types of hand puppets are Alkema's *Puppet-Making*, Chernoff's *Puppet Party*, Cummings's *101 Hand Puppets*, Gates's *Easy to Make Puppets*, Philpott and McNeils's *Know-How Book of Puppets*, and Renfro's *Puppets for Play Production*.

If one of the objectives is to integrate art with writing and producing a puppet program, then teachers may wish to have students make their own puppets. However, when the emphasis is to be placed on writing and speaking, it is preferable not to have students spend time making their own puppets. Teachers and library media specialists should collect sets of puppets that can easily be used for a number of puppet shows. These puppets can be made by grandparents "adopted" by the school or could be made by students or staff members for the collection.

Puppets can also be purchased. A list of twenty-five companies that produce hand and finger puppets are included at the end of this section. Sets of puppets for a single story can be placed in a box with spine label and check-out card or in plastic bags with check-out cards for loan to classrooms or individual students. A Little Red Riding Hood set made from cloth and rubber is available from The Puppetmakers. Janice Kenagy Puppets has a Little Red Riding Hood set that is hand knitted. Both companies have a set for the three little pigs. Janice Kenagy specializes in sets of hand-knit washable puppets that are very sturdy. Some other stories for whom there are puppets are "The Little Red Hen," "Henny Penny," and "The Gingerbread Boy." Categories for Loan Bag Puppets from Nancy Renfro Studios are wildlife, birds, sealife, nature, insects, farm animals, people, pets, special puppets, and objects and clothing.

Some animals are found in puppet inventories of many companies, others are more difficult to find. Several exceptional puppets are the cow and mouse from Mazy Meyer; lamb from Princess Soft Toys; owl and pussy cat for Lear's poem; and a mother and baby kangaroo for introducing Payne's *Katy-No Pocket* from Dakin; a small rabbit from Character; a small knitted lion and mouse for playing Aesop's story from Dakin; frogs from Sheram, a large hare from Mighty Star Limited; a fox, skunk, and bears from Animal Fair; Sesame Street puppets from Child Horizon; Walt Disney characters including a large elephant from Walt Disney; a small elephant from Dakin; Snoopy and Woodstock from Determined; a donkey and hippo plus small knit animals from Possom Trot.

Use puppets to introduce picture books to children. One mouse from Mazy Meyer could introduce the picture book on the sound filmstrip *The Complete Version of Ye Three Blind Mice* by Ivimey. When the same mouse puts on a beret, he could introduce *Anatole*, the famous French mouse created by Titus. The donkey from Possom Trot could introduce the rounds selected by Langstaff in *Sweetly Sings the Donkey, Animal Rounds for Children to Sing or Play on Recorders*. The small Dakin elephant and a large Walt Disney elephant could introduce *The World's Worst Elephant Jokes* and *101 Elephant Jokes*. One of the best ice breakers for a group is to have them use puppets to tell jokes and riddles. One puppet can ask the question and the other can answer. Puppets with movable mouths work best.

Use Determined's Snoopy to introduce a dictionary unit to second or third graders using the *Charlie Brown Dictionary*. Students can play out Ellen Raskin's story, *Who, Said Sue, Said Whoo?* and add a puppet character. The surprise animal the others are all asking about is a skunk, and the teacher or librarian can surprise everyone by bringing out the Animal Fair skunk at the end of the story. Frogs by Sheram can introduce the picture book of the song *Frog Went A-Courtin'* retold by Langstaff. A fox from Animal Fair can introduce Spier's picture book of the song *Fox Went Out On a Chilly Night*.

A puppet from an amusement park in Minnesota (Valley Fair) can be used to introduce Gwynne's *A Chocolate Moose for Dinner*, a book of homonyms. Check the index to this book for other books about homonyms.

Handmade puppets can also introduce books. This author's Dutch Boy can introduce Green's *The Hole in the Dike* or be used with "The Leak in the Dike" from Ross's *Puppet Shows Using Poems and Stories*. Dorothy and Toto from Baum's *Wizard of Oz* was created out of stuffed paper bags by Kathryn Royce. The cucumber hand puppets by Paul Anderson represent Raggedy Ann and Andy. The three bears were created from a kit by Creations Limited by Nancy Hookwith. Karen Erva made Lady and the Tramp marionettes from styrofoam balls. Erva also made Little Bo Peep and the two sheep from cardboard tubes. Sheryl Daniels and Bev Harris created the stage, background, and puppets for "Hansel and Gretel" from directions found in Wiesner's *Hansel and Gretel, a Shadow Puppet Picture Book*.

COMMERCIAL HAND AND FINGER PUPPETS

Animal Fair, Inc., Chanhassen, MN. 55317
Dakin, San Francisco, California. (regular, knit-mitts)
Character Novelty Co., Inc., South Norwalk, CT.
Child Horizons, Inc., Bronx, N.Y. 10472 (Sesame Street puppets)
Creations Limited, Wee-Kin Works. 112-116 Park Hill Road, Harborne,
    Birmingham, England B179HD
Dan Dee Imports, Jersey City, N.J. 07305
Determined Productions, Inc., San Francisco, CA 94126
J and H Heart Company, 118 North Page St., Stroughton, WI 53589
Janice Kenagy Puppets, 706 Crest Dr., Papellion, Nebraska 68046
Mazy Meyer Puppets, Townsend, VT 05353
Mighty Star, Ltd., Montreal, Quebec, Canada
Nancy Renfro Studios, 1117 West Ninth Street, Austin, TX 78703
Poppets, 1800 East Olive Way, Seattle, WA 98102
Possum Trot, London, Kentucky 40741
Princess Soft Toys, Cannon Falls, MN 55009
The Puppetmakers, Princeton, WI 45968 (rubber)
Russ Bernie and Co., Oakland, NJ 07436
S and M Toy Co., Provo, Utah
Scholastic Books, Ind. 906 Sylvan Avenue, Englewood Cliffs, NJ 07632
Sheram Puppets, P.O. Box 1409, Columbus, OH 43216
Trend Enterprises, Inc., P.O. Box 43073, St. Paul, MN 55164
Valley Fair Entertainment Center, Shakopee, MN 55379
Von Seggen, Dale and Liz, 48250 Benham Avenue, Elkhart, IN 46514
Walt Disney Characters, California Stuffed Toys, 611 South Anderston
    Street, Los Angeles, CA 90023
Well-Made Toy Mfg. Co., 219 Sackman Street, Brooklyn, NY 11212

MAKING AND USING PAPER BAG PUPPETS. Several puppet books give directions for making flat or stuffed paper bag puppets. Chapter 1, "Paper Bag Puppets," of Ross's *Hand Puppets,* contains information on making and using empty or stuffed paper bags. A pattern for making a paper bag rabbit appears on pages 38 and 39 of Carlson's *Picture That!* Lewis's *Making Easy Puppets* has directions for making a rabbit paper bag puppet on pages 19 and 20, a fish on page 22, and a Jack in the bag marionette on page 21.

Information about paper bag puppets appears in puppet books by Alkema, Anderson, Cummings, Lewis, Pels, and Renfro. Paper bag puppets also appear in Adair's *Do-it-in-a-Day Puppets* and Batcheldor's *Puppet Theatre Handbook.*

Many patterns for making faces on 8-lb. weight paper bags appear in two books by Williams: *Paper-Bag Puppets* and *More Paper-Bag Puppets.* Patterns for animals and people in the section on the seasons from *More Paper-Bag Puppets* (pp. 16-39) are bear, turkey, Indian, snowflake, Eskimo girl, Christmas angel, Jack Frost, Easter bunny, Mrs. Easter Bunny, robin, goose, duck, lamb, father, mother, brother, sister, and baby.

After reading books, seeing filmstrips, studying prints, or hearing guest community helpers, students could make paper-bag puppets of community helpers. They could choose whichever one they wished or all children could make a fireman or policeman after they heard the stories included in a section of this chapter called "Fingerplays and Action Songs." Twelve community helpers that appear on pages 3 to 16 of *More Paper-Bag Puppets* are mailman, fireman, policeman, farmer, grocer, teacher, doctor, dentist, nurse, baker, bus driver, and librarian.

In *Paper-Bag Puppets,* patterns for puppets "On the Farm" include cat, cow, dog, duck, farmer, goat, goose, hen, horse, lamb, pig, and rooster. Puppet outlines for "At the Zoo" include bear, camel, elephant, giraffe, hippopotamus, lion, monkey, tiger, and zebra. Twelve outlines for making puppets for Halloween, Thanksgiving, and Christmas are also included.

A class of from sixteen to twenty students could be given a paper bag and the name of a character, then asked to find their character's pattern in Williams's *Paper-Bag Puppets,* and make a puppet. Next, students could be assigned to groups to make up a play about their characters. The following samples were given to college students in a creative dramatics class. Similar situations could be prepared for various levels of elementary students. The teacher could type the situations on a ditto and run off copies, so that four situations could be cut apart and distributed so each student has a set of directions.

HALLOWEEN: BLACK CAT, GHOST, JACK O'LANTERN, WITCH. You are sixth graders and your teacher has just given you this assignment: It is the day before Halloween and witch and ghost are planning some Halloween tricks that are not very nice. Black cat and Jack O'Lantern try to talk them out of the tricks and suggest alternatives. Plan a three to five minute puppet discussion on this theme.

INDIAN BOY, INDIAN GIRL, PILGRIM BOY, PILGRIM GIRL. It is mid-November and you are third graders who have just studied the pilgrims, and your teacher has given you this assignment: You are four children who have just finished the first Thanksgiving meal. You are not only getting to know each other better, but you are discussing what has happened during the past few days and especially the last few hours. Plan a three- to five-minute puppet discussion.

MRS. SANTA, SANTA, SNOWMAN, REINDEER. You are third graders and your teacher has given you this assignment: Today is December 20 and snowman has just learned that the father of the children who made him will be in the hospital having a very serious operation over the Christmas holidays. Plan a three- to five-minute puppet discussion on this theme.

ZOO ANIMALS: HIPPOPOTAMUS, GIRAFFE, ELEPHANT, MONKEY, TIGER, ZEBRA, LION, CAMEL, AND BEAR. You are second graders and your teacher has just given you this assignment: You are zoo animals who are concerned because there has been so much litter left in the zoo lately by visitors. You are gathering together to devise a plan to correct this situation. Nine zoo animals are included. Use as many zoo animals as necessary so each student can have a puppet part. The animals are listed in the order that they should be assigned; the most imaginative and interesting animals are listed first. Plan a three- to five-minute puppet discussion on this theme.

In *More Paper-Bag Puppets,* there are eighteen patterns on pages 39 to 60 in a section called "Children's Stories." Children can trace and color or cut out construction paper or cloth clothing for paper bag puppets for the four stories: "Little Red Riding Hood," "Jack and the Beanstalk," "The Little Red Hen," and "The Three Billy Goats Gruff." In a class of eighteen students, every student can have a part. If there are more than eighteen students, add one or two animals to the story of "The Little Red Hen" or use animals from *Paper-Bag Puppets* for three other stories. "The Three Little Pigs" and "Goldilocks" each contain four characters, while "The Gingerbread Man" contains six.

Other projects for relating paper bag puppets to books can also be established. Some possibilities are to read Dalgliesh's *The Thanksgiving Story* or Hays's *Pilgrim Thanksgiving* to students and have them make any of the four Thanksgiving puppets and create dialogue. The activity could follow a storytelling program in which students listened to stories told from Harper's *The Harvest Feast* or Sechrist's *It's Time for Thanksgiving.* This activity could be used with students in grades three to five.

Read any of Bright's picture books about *Georgie* the ghost to first grade students. Then give each student a ditto of the ghost face from Williams's *Paper-Bag Puppets* and ask them to make a puppet of Georgie. The children could keep the puppet to take home with them from the story-hour or a Halloween party. If the project is executed in a classroom, there may be time for the children to make up another story about Georgie.

Students will enjoy making paper bag puppets to play out Duvoisin's picture book, *Our Veronica Goes to Petunia's Farm.* Students can use the puppets without a stage. Outlines for tracing Veronica the hippo and all the farm animals except the donkey are available in Williams's *Paper-Bag Puppets* and *More Paper-Bag Puppets.* In the story, Veronica arrived at the farm but none of the animals would speak to her. Duvoisin's *Lonely Veronica* can be read to students so they can learn why Veronica was sent to the farm from the city, and *Veronica* explains how the hippo left the jungle to go to the city in the first place. Read all three stories before making paper bag puppets.

PAPIER-MÂCHÉ PUPPETS.   Many craft books contain information about making papier-mâché puppet heads. Consult page 158 of Tritten's *Art Techniques for Children;* pages 63 to 73 of Johnson's *Papier-Mâché;* page 66 of Carlson's *Make It Yourself!;* page 71 of Anderson's *Papier-Mâché and How to*

Use It; pages 64 to 66 of Larrimar's *Creative Papier-Mâché*. Sidelman's *Creating with Papier-Mâché* talks about molds for puppet heads. Meyer's *One Hundred Fifty Techniques in Art* includes information on solid and hollow heads, papier-mâché, and tells how to use balloons to make heads. Slades's *Modeling in Clay, Plaster and Papier-Mâché* explains two methods—layer (pp. 49-51) and pulp (pp. 54-55). Two chapters in *Exploring Papier-Mâché* by Betts include information on making puppets: "Guides for Hand Puppets" (pp. 53-58) and "Guides for Marionettes" (pp. 59-66).

"Papier-Mâché Puppets," pages 96 to 117 of Ross's *Hand Puppets,* contains eight "Things to Remember in Making Papier-Mâché Puppets." "Puppet-Heads of Papier-Mâché," pages 88 to 90 of Wall's *The Complete Puppet Book,* tells about materials, mixing the pulp, and modeling the head. Papier-mâché puppet heads are also included in Curry and Wetzel's *Teaching with Puppets* and Snook's *Puppets.* Alkema's *Puppet Making* includes information about papier-mâché over clay, crushed newspapers, light bulbs, or newspaper tubes. Recipes for adding sawdust and using tissue paper are included. Directions for making papier-mâché and sawdust mixtures for puppet heads appear in the 16mm film, *Puppets.* Remy Bufano's *Book of Puppetry* and Mills and Dunn's *Marionettes, Masks and Shadows* contain information about making papier-mâché marionettes. Directions for making a papier-mâché dragon marionette appear on pages 177 and 178. Authors of books on puppetry that also contain information about papier-mâché puppets are by Batchelder, Cummings, Frasier, McNamara, Pewls, and Philpott.

PREPARING A STORY FOR A PUPPET SHOW.*

1. *Select a worthwhile story* that has lively characters, lots of action, crisp dialogue, and appeal to those who will be performing it.
2. *Seek a story with identifiable parts,* a suitable introduction, conflict, definite rising action, a recognizable climax, swift falling action, and a just conclusion.
3. *Choose a story that has only four characters on stage at any one time.* Most puppet stages only have room for two puppeteers behind the scenes and manipulating with both arms at one time is a challenge. Any number of characters can appear in the story if puppets are available or there are students with enough time to make them.
4. *Choose the type of puppet* to be borrowed or made. Types of puppets by method of manipulation are glove or hand, finger, rod, shadow, or stringed. Hundreds of variations using a variety of materials can be chosen from a list called *Books on Puppetry.*
5. *Choose the stage* from among those available on loan or for purchase. The task of making a stage may be assigned to a custodian, parent, grandparent, teacher, or groups of students. The type of stage must

---

*These directions were written so that an entire class could be involved in a single production. If groups are producing separate puppet productions, the same steps need to be followed although the distribution of tasks may be different.

be compatible with the type of puppets being used. Check for curtains, outlets for sound and lighting, puppet books, and scenery fixtures.

6. *Find other versions* of the story in *The Children's Catalog,* Cathon's *Stories to Tell to Children,* the list of the Carnegie Library of Pittsburg, Ireland's *Index to Fairy Tales, 1949-72,* Nelson's *A Comparative Anthology of Children's Literature.* Consult the card catalog for individual picture book listings for the stories. Choose the version that is best suited for a puppet production or combine elements from each.

7. *Introduce the story to students* either by reading the version or by telling the story using the "Steps to Effective Storytelling" found in chapter 1 of this book.

8. *List the events chronologically* using a chalk board or overhead projector. Have students suggest the events to be dramatized.

9. *Identify the six major parts of the story* by having groups of students select what they think the six major parts are. Consolidate those lists using a chalk board or overhead projector.

10. *List the characters* in the order of appearance using suggestions by students. The characters can be listed on a chalk board or on a transparency. Decide which characters can be consolidated or eliminated.

11. *Begin making puppets.* Assign the puppet head to one person and the body with costume to another.

12. *Identify the scenes.* Change and consolidate the story so there are no more than three scenes. If possible, consider only one scene.

13. *Begin making scenery.* Assign committees to work on each scene. The students need to be familiar with the story as well as with the proportions of the stage and of the puppets.

14. *Gather props.* Limit the number of props to be handled by the puppets. Make sure that props can be easily handled by the puppets or can be securely attached to the scenery or stage. Props that fall or are badly manipulated are distracting.

15. *Assign character sketches* to students who will be manipulating the puppets. Have students examine various character indicators. Have students plot actions for their characters.

16. *Write the script* using the chronological events, major parts of the story, scenes, and characters and their actions to make a unified story.

17. *Decide whether to tape or have live dialogue.* Students may wish to read or speak the dialogue at the time of the show or may wish to prepare a tape so that all efforts during production are focused on manipulation. If a tape is to be made, assign a special group to practice reading the script and another to monitor the equipment.

18. *Assign a sound effects crew* to gather any recordings or objects needed to create believable sound effects. Background music might also be chosen. This committee works closely with the previous committee.

19. *Assign a lighting crew* to determine whether or not special lighting is needed for various scenes and how this can be accomplished during the production without distraction.
20. *Practice the scenes*, then tape the script with the help of the sound effects crew, writers and readers. If the show is to be performed live, link the scenes together.
21. *Evaluate* the effectiveness of characters to plot development, actions, manipulation, dialogue, timing, unity, puppets, costumes, props, scenery, lighting, and sound effects.
22. *Replay* the story and make the final tape or have a final rehearsal with live voices.

PUPPET SCRIPTS.   Before groups of any age write their own puppet plays, it is wise to read as many puppet plays as possible. Reading puppet scripts can be an activity for all ages and purposes. Teachers and school library media specialists may look for scripts to accompany a story from a basal reader or to complement a special unit. Public librarians may want to look for a play by title to accompany a story program. Parents may wish to select plays for groups such as scout troops or for informal groups of children. Several versions of one story can be analyzed to choose one or to decide that an original script would be best.

Beginning with third graders, students could be divided into groups of three or four to read scripts. Teachers could assign one or more parts to each elementary student. High school drama students and college students in creative dramatic classes who are preparing to write puppet plays could assign the parts to themselves. Groups of all ages could then read the plays aloud, with expression. Because students tend to become wrapped up in the play their own group is reading, it does not seem to bother them that about six other groups are reading aloud in the same room.

Fourty-four plays based on folk and fairy tales or classics in children's literature are available in three books by Mahlman and Jones—*Puppet Plays for Young Players* and *Puppet Plays from Favorite Stories* and *Folk Tale Plays for Puppets*. Sixteen stories based on folktales are available in Adair and Patapoff's *Folk Puppet Plays for the Social Studies*. Plays in those books may be presented without a royalty fee by amateur groups. An additional forty-five puppet shows based on stories and poems appeared in *Puppet Shows Using Poems and Stories* by Ross.

Production notes for the puppet plays given by Mahlman and Jones include number and type of puppet, characters, playing time, description of puppets, properties, setting, lighting and sound, and special effects. Adair and Patapoff include production pointers: stage, lights, scenery, and making your puppets. A list of characters and scenes is given at the beginning of the plays.

See Ross's *Puppet Shows Using Poems and Stories*, an outstanding source for forty-five sources for puppet shows. Numerous nursery rhymes are included. Some selections for Christmas are "Babushka" (pp. 78–80), "Christmas with the Cratchits" (pp. 168–76), "The First Christmas" (pp. 189–90), "The Little Drummer Boy" (pp. 71–73), "The Three Kings" (pp. 73–77), and "A Visit from St. Nicholas" (pp. 82–86). Folk heroes like Johnny Appleseed and Robin Hood are here. The following selections from Aesop are included: "Androcles and the Lion" (pp. 137–39), "The Crow and the Fox" (pp. 35–37), "The Fox and the Grapes" (pp. 133–34), "The Hare and the Tortoise" (pp. 131–33), and "The Lion and the Mouse" (pp. 134–37). Production notes given by Ross are technique, cast, setting, and action.

Persons seeking puppet scripts can find almost a hundred plays in those four books. However, these are all the work of only several authors and do not provide the variety to be found by reading plays by many different authors. You can choose from about seventy different titles from the following list.

PUPPET PLAYS BASED ON CHILDREN'S LITERATURE

Aesop's Fables: The Hare and the Tortoise, The Ant and the Grasshopper, The Lion and the Mouse. 11 characters. Mahlman and Jones, Puppet Plays from Favorite Stories, pp. 95–107.

Ali Baba and the Forty Thieves. (Arabian). 9 characters. Mahlman and Jones, Folk Tale Plays for Puppets, pp. 59–70.

Alice's Adventures in Wonderland. (Based on Lewis Carroll). 15 or more characters. Mahlman and Jones, Puppet Plays for Young Players, pp. 135–48.

Alice in Wonderland—A Mad Tea Party. (Based on Lewis Carroll). 4 characters. Wall, The Puppet Book, pp. 203–08.

Alice in Wonderland—The Mock Turtle's Story. (Based on Carroll). 3 characters. Wall, The Puppet Book, pp. 208–16.

Aladdin, or the Wonderful Lamp. (From The Arabian Nights). 7 characters. Mahlman and Jones, Puppet Plays from Favorite Stories, pp. 171–81.

Anansi and the Box of Stories. (African folktale). 5 characters Mahlmann and Jones. Folk Tale Plays for Puppets, pp. 51–58.

Anansi Finds a Fool. (African folktale). 6 characters plus villagers and storyteller. Adair and Patapoff, Folk Puppet Plays, pp. 41–47.

The Ant and the Grasshopper. (See Aesop's Fables).

Baba Yaga. (Russian). 7 characters. Mahlman and Jones, Folk Tale Plays for Puppets, pp. 13–24.

Beauty and the Beast. (French fairy tale, Perrault). 9 characters. Beaton, Marionettes, pp. 168–77.

Beauty and the Beast. 7 characters. Jagendorf, Penny Puppets, pp. 159–71.

Beauty and the Beast. 9 characters plus forest animals. Mahlman and Jones, Puppet Plays from Favorite Stories, pp. 153–62.

Blue Willow. (Chinese) 9 characters. Mahlmann and Jones. Folk Tale Plays for Puppets, pp. 123–30.

Cinderella or the Glass Slipper. (French folk tale, Perrault). 8 characters plus ladies and courtiers. Bufano, Book of Puppetry, pp. 131–56.

Cinderella or the Glass Slipper. 8 characters. Mahlman and Jones, Puppet Plays from Favorite Stories, pp. 1–13.

The City Mouse and the Country Mouse. (Aesop's Fables). 5 characters. Tichenor, Folk Plays . . . , pp. 49–61.

King of the Golden River. (Based on John Ruskin). 9 characters. Mahlman and Jones, *Puppet Plays from Favorite Stories*, pp. 193–204.

The Legend of Urashimo. (Japan). 7 characters. Mahlman and Jones, *Folk Tale Plays for Puppets*, pp. 80–88.

The Lion and the Mouse. (Aesop's *Fables*). 2 or 4 characters. Worrell, *Be a Puppeteer*, pp. 26–32.

The Lion and the Mouse. Mahlman and Jones, *Puppet Plays from Favorite Stories*.

Little Indian Brave. 10 characters. Mahlman and Jones, *Folk Tale Plays for Puppets*, pp. 25–36.

The Little Red Hen. 4 characters. Tichenor, *Folk Plays*. . . , pp. 80–96.

Little Red Riding Hood. (English or French fairy tale). 2 characters plus 5. Worrell, *Be a Puppeteer*, pp. 19–25.

Little Red Riding Hood. 6 characters. Cassette. The Puppet Tree.

Manora, the Blue Princess. (Siam). 10 characters. Mahlman and Jones, *Folk Tale Plays for Puppets*, pp. 109–122.

Moon Dragon, the Emperor's Horse. (Chinese legend). 3 characters plus crowd. Cochrane, *Shadow Puppets*. . . , pp. 18–25.

The Musicians of Bremen. (German fairy tale, Grimm). 7 characters. Boylan, *How to Be a Puppeteer*, pp. 34–59.

The Nutcracker Prince. (Tchaikovsky ballet). 7 characters plus snowflakes, candies, and dancers. Mahlman and Jones, *Puppet Plays from Favorite Stories*, pp. 183–191.

Perez and Martina. 7 characters. Mahlman and Jones, *Folk Tale Plays for Puppets*, pp. 71–79.

The Pied Piper of Hamelin. (Browning poem). 9 characters plus rats and children. Mahlman and Jones, *Puppet Plays from Favorite Stories*, pp. 15–22.

Pinocchio. (Carlo Collodi). 18 characters plus others. Bufano, (marionettes), pp. 157–232.

Pinocchio. 13 characters. Mahlman and Jones, *Puppet Plays for Young Players*, pp. 79–94.

The Princess and the Pea. (Hans Christian Andersen). 5 characters. Mahlman and Jones, *Puppet Plays for Young Players*, pp. 51–64.

The Princess Who Could Not Cry. 7 characters. Tichenor, *Folk Plays*. . . , pp. 32–48.

Punch and Judy. (Traditional European characters). 17 characters. Speaight, pp. 146–55.

Punch and Judy. 8 characters. Ross, *Hand Puppets*, pp. 164–83.

Punch and Judy, A Play for Puppets. A picture book by Ed Emberley. 11 characters.

Puss in Boots. (French fairy tale, Perrault). 8 characters. Mahlman and Jones, *Puppet Plays from Favorite Stories*, pp. 23–33.

The Rabbit Who Wanted Red Wings. (U.S.). 7 characters. Mahlman and Jones, *Folk Tale Plays for Puppets*, pp. 131–142.

Rapunzel. (German fairy tale, Grimm). 8 characters. Mahlman and Jones, *Pup-

The Tinderbox. (Hans Christian Andersen). 11 characters. Mahlman and Jones, Puppet Plays for Young Players, pp. 123–34.

Toads and Diamonds. (France). 7 characters. Mahlman and Jones, Folk Tale Plays for Puppets, pp. 89–97.

The Twelve Months. (Russian folk tale). 15 characters. Tichnor, Tom Tichenor's Puppets, pp. 179–89.

Uncle Remus Tales. (U.S.). 7 characters. Mahlman and Jones, Folk Tale Plays for Puppets, pp. 98–108.

Walk Tall, Talk Tall, Davy Crockett. (American folk hero). 8 characters plus speaker. Adair and Patapoff, Folk Puppet Plays, pp. 93–102.

Why Man Must Harvest His Crops. (Chinese folk tale). 3 characters plus crop voices. Adair and Patapoff, Folk Puppet Plays, pp. 78–81.

Why the Bear has a Stumpy Tail. (Scandinavian folk tale). 6 characters. Tichenor, Tom Tichenor's Puppets, pp. 104–12.

Why the Sea Is Salt. 9 characters. Mahlman and Jones, Puppet Plays for Young Players, pp. 37–50.

The Wizard of Oz. (Frank Baum). 19 characters. Mahlman and Jones, Puppet Plays for Young Players, pp. 149–68.

BUILDING PUPPET PLAYS FROM FOLKTALES.   Many folktales lend themselves to conversion to puppet plays because of a simple theme, a story with a repetition, economy of words, continuous action, and few characters. The following stories contain these elements. You can give them to students and ask them to create a puppet script based on the stories. The students can either make the puppets or use hand puppets from the library media collection.

"The Bremen Town Musicians" is easily adapted to create a puppet play. Chapter 6, "Backstage During a Puppet Play," of Boylan's How to Be a Puppeteer uses that story as an example for how to organize a puppet play in a version that uses six puppets, three puppeteers, scenery, props, and a narrator. Other titles for the story are "The Bremen Musicians" and "The Traveling Musicians." Students can read other versions of this story in the Crane edition of Household Stories by the Brothers Grimm (pp. 136–39); Grimms's About Wise Men and Simpletons (pp. 111–15); The Complete Grimms' Fairy Tales, illustrated by Kredel (pp. 144–47); Grimms' Fairy Tales illustrated by Rackham (pp. 114–18); 18); and Grimms' The House in the Wood (pp. 46–55). Haviland has included the story in Favorite Tales Told in Germany (pp. 72–85) and in The Fairy Tale Treasury (pp. 110–13). Three anthologies that include the story are Sutherland's Arbuthnot Anthology of Children's Literature (pp. 200–202); Johnson's Anthology of Children's Literature (pp. 128–30); and Martignoni's The Illustrated Treasury of Children's Literature (pp. 219–20). Other sources are ACEI's Told Under the Green Umbrella (pp. 67–73); Animal Stories (pp. 151–58) and Tales Told Again (pp. 25–32), both by De la Mare; Hutchinson's Chimney Corner Stories (pp. 127–34); and Ward's Stories to Dramatize (pp. 43–46). Available picture books are Grimms' The Bremen Town Musicians, illustrated by Galdone, and The Traveling Musicians, illustrated by Fischer. A version for choral speaking appears in Olfson's You Can Act! (pp. 107–115). This version has been successfully used as a script for a puppet show. A sound filmstrip is entitled *The Musicians of Bremen.*

"The Dog, the Cat, and the Mouse" appears in Mincieli's *Tales Merry and Wise* (pp. 65–71). In addition to the three animals there are two other characters—a mayor and a butcher. Many puppet collections contain two men who can be dressed for the part as well as having the three animals, and so no new puppets need be made. The script is easy to write because much of the dialogue can remain the same as in the story. A paper, entitling the dog to bones from the butcher during a famine, was given the dog by the mayor. The dog gave the paper to his friend the cat for safekeeping, and the cat in turn gave it to her friend the mouse. Unfortunately, the mouse chewed a hole in the paper during her sleep, changing the message so that the butcher beat the dog instead of giving it a bone. Three other versions of the story are listed in the chapter "Enjoying Poetry" in a section called "Dogs and Cats in Poems and Stories."

Eight puppet characters are needed for "The Cat Who Thought She Was a Dog," found in Singer's *Naftali the Storyteller and His Horse* (pp. 103–08). Characters include a peasant, his wife, three daughters, their dog, their cat, and a peddler. Problems arose when the peddler opened his pack and the wife bought a mirror. Children will have fun creating dialogue about the daughters discovering that one has a missing front tooth, another a broad nose, and another a narrow chin. Students will also enjoy scenes in which the dog and cat look into the mirror and each sees a ferocious animal. Until then each of them had thought they looked alike. Eventually, the peasant gets rid of the mirror.

Uchida's *Sea of Gold and Other Tales from Japan* contains a story that would make a good short puppet play, "The Foolish Cats." One cat was small and one was large, and both had rice cakes. However, the larger cat was jealous of the smaller cat's larger rice cake, and the two cats agreed to take their rice cakes to the monkey. The monkey placed the cakes on scales and took a bite of the bigger one to make them even. Finding his bite too large and the scales uneven, he took several bites out of each rice cake in turn until the scales were empty and the two cats realized their foolishness. Decorative scales could be borrowed from home, and blocks of cereal and marshmallow cakes could serve as rice cakes (if real rice cakes are not available). The puppeteer could take the monkey's bites of the cakes for him, and so practicing this play could be fun!

"Why the Cat Stares at the Moon" from Cormack's *Animal Tales from Ireland* tells of the cat who thought there was a mouse on the moon eating cheese. Puppets needed are a cat, dog, mouse, horse, and sheep, and this story could culminate a program of folktales about the moon. (See the chapter on "Experiencing Art through Picture Books.")

In Elkin's *The Wisest Man in the World, a Legend of Ancient Israel*, a bee was able to pick out the real flower from the artificial ones for wise King Solomon, and this would be a good choice for puppets.

"Casi Lampu's Lentemue" from Belpre's *The Tiger and the Rabbit and Other Tales* is a story with repetition suitable for a puppet show. The witch, angry because the boy guessed her name, had repeated the same rhyme to a cow, goat, pig, and finally to the crab who told the boy. Because the witch beat the crab with a stick, crabs to this day run away when they see humans. This puppet show could be played out with hand or shadow puppets as a culminating activity after reading versions of "Rumpelstiltskin."

An ogre, a father, mother, and three daughters are needed to create a puppet play from Kishi's picture book *The Ogre and His Bride*. An ogre, three feet tall, with a horn on top of his head, agreed to make rain for a farmer in return for one of the farmer's daughters. The youngest agreed to be the bride, and so her mother gave her a bag of mustard seed which trickled out along her path. By spring the seeds had grown into plants and the homesick girl followed the path home. The ogre followed, was given cooked beans, told to plant them and to claim his bride when the beans blossomed. Even today the custom of planting cooked beans to keep the devil away is followed by people in Japan.

"The Lame Dog," in Baker's *The Talking Tree and Other Stories*, (pp. 77–87), can be made into a puppet play. Because it has elements of several other fairy tales, those stories could be read by students in conjunction with this project. Other students in the class might choose to play out the other stories, "Beauty and the Beast" and the Scandinavian story, "East of the Sun and West of the Moon." Like Beauty, the princess in "The Lame Dog" was married to an animal who turned into a prince during the night while he slept, and similar events followed.

Three puppet scripts are included on the list in this chapter "Puppet Plays Based on Children's Literature" for the story "Beauty and the Beast." Picture books of that story are illustrated by Pearce and by the Mayers. Douglas Fairbanks reads the Mme. de Beaumont version on the recording called *Beauty and the Beast and Other Stories*. That same version is available in Arbuthnot's *Time For Old Magic* (pp. 93–102), Johnson's *Anthology of Children's Literature* (pp. 173–81), Lang's *The Blue Fairy Book* (pp. 100–19), and Sutherland's *Arbuthnot Anthology of Children's Literature* (pp. 216–24). Other sources include Berger's *Black Fairy Tales* (pp. 55–67), Haviland's *Favorite Fairy Tales Told in France* (pp. 38–59), Jacobs's *European Folk and Fairy Tales*, (pp. 34–41), Opie's *The Classic Fairy Tales* (pp. 139–50), Perrault's *Perrault's Complete Fairy Tales* (pp. 115–34), Rackham's *Arthur Rackham Fairy Book* (pp. 49–65), and Sideman's *The World's Best Fairy Tales*. After the students put on the puppet show the teacher could read an Irish version from Manning-Sanders's book *A Book of Sorcerers and Spells* and a similar story called "The Serpent and the Grape Grower's Daughter," in Delarue's *French Fairy Tales* (pp. 104–09).

Green's picture book *The Hole in the Dike* is available in hardback or paperback editions as well as on a sound filmstrip. Give students the book, show them the filmstrip, introduce them to other stories about the boy who kept his finger in the dike to save Holland, and ask them to write a puppet script. There can be as few characters as three; a mother, the boy, and one other person. Other characters could be added. Michael Lewis's version, "The Boy Who Kept His Finger in the Dike" appears on pages 522 to 25 of Untermeyer's *The Golden Treasury of Children's Literature*. A poem by Phoebe Cary appears on pages 171 and 172 of Huber's *Story and Verse for Children*, pages 179 to 85 of Parker's

One Hundred Story Poems and pages 51 to 62 of Ross's *Puppet Shows Using Poems and Stories.*

Students should look for the version of a story that best suits the medium. "Cinderella" is easier to play than it is to perform as a puppet show. However, a puppet show from "Cinderella" is possible. There are many versions of "Cinderella" stories from around the world. Another story is "The Princess on the Glass Hill." It is difficult to simulate a puppet on a horse climbing a glass hill but it is easier to play out that same activity. Belpre's picture book *Rainbow Colored Horse* would be more suitable for a puppet show and even for playing with a class. Be sure that students who write a puppet play from this story have the opportunity to read similar versions, hear recordings of other versions, or view filmstrips of those stories. Place these materials in a listening/viewing/reading corner of the classroom.

SPECIALIZED BIBLIOGRAPHIC CATEGORIES

At the back of this book are two numbered bibliographies, one of multimedia (nonprint material), and one of books. The numbers below refer to those bibliographies, with the entries preceded by "M" found in the Multimedia list.

PUPPETRY
5, 14, 15, 16, 129, 137, 162, 172, 205, 255, 261, 311, 312, 316, 322, 339, 347, 438, 452, 473, 510, 512, 573, 578, 710, 821, 825, 827, 919, 921, 1042, 1043, 1105, 1179, 1199, 1209, 1214, 1215, 1219, 1280, 1281, 1527, 1533, 1704, 1742, 1743, 1760, 1854, 1908, 1974, 2061, 2105, 2160, 2363, 2401, 2426, 2444, 2519, 2520, 2552, 2574, 2599, 2628, 2652, 2826, 2959, 2960, 2961, 2962, 3090, 3123, 3158, 3214, 3219, 3226, 3227, 3228, 3287, 3362, 3375, 3380, 3431, 3438, 3480, 3510, 3581, 3582, 3617, 3637, 3662, 3670, 3715, 3755, 3758, 3759, 3760, 3761, 3762, 3828, 3902, 3926, 3931, 3932, 3933, 3952, 4018, 4019, 4020, 4021, 4022, 4024, 4033, 4041, 4054, 4160, 4182, 4334, 4335, 4366, 4390, 4398, 4399, 4454, 4505, 4572, 4573, 4620, 4637, 4682, 4699, 4725, 4726, 4798, 4810, 4848, 4849, 4930, 4927, M211, M554.

PLAYS, INDIVIDUAL AND IN COLLECTIONS
71, 364, 411, 513, 514, 623, 640, 646, 729, 730, 731, 732, 821, 822, 828, 938, 1050, 1104, 1205, 1206, 1224, 1434, 1435, 1707, 2122, 2128, 2531, 2594, 2595, 2596, 2597, 2598, 2726, 2748, 3271, 3412, 3638, 3809, 3836, 4021, 4341, 4361, 4362, 4555, 4655, 4973, M637.

FINGERPLAYS
M207, 316, 661, 1053, 1705, 1903, 1904, 1971, 2220, 2494, 3460, 3826, 4062, 4164, 4460, 4525, 4526, 4527, 4529, 4530, 4949.

CHAPTER SIX

Using Riddles, Magic, Jokes, and Folk Themes

Teachers may choose to use all or parts of this chapter for any grade level. The difficulty of the assignments chosen and the depth to which they are pursued depends on the abilities of the students. There will be students with similar ability ranges at many grade levels. Student abilities may also vary from school to school. Activities range from stories to tell and share with preschool students to activities for high school English and mythology units.

CHAPTER OBJECTIVES

1. To introduce students to a form of literature comparable to myths, fables, folktales,and proverbs.
2. To identify types of jokes and riddles; i.e., conundrums, anticlimactics, teaching or verbal catches or sells, feeder jokes, anecdotes, riddles in rhyme, and riddle stories.
3. To stress the universality of mankind's experience by providing stories from around the world that contain similar themes, common riddles, or silly events common to human nature.
4. To provide examples of projects which employ the use of jokes and riddles and stories containing jokes and riddles.
5. To show how jokes and riddles can enrich a variety of subject matter including spelling, mathematics, science, history, and geography.
6. To provide examples of literature that stress mankind's desire to ask questions and find out about the world.
7. To provide projects to stimulate students who are usually unmotivated to read.
8. To provide projects in which language arts skills can be reinforced while students are introduced to folklore.
9. To provide an introduction to the study of communication.

TECHNIQUES FOR USING MEDIA INTRODUCED IN THIS CHAPTER

1. Use puppets who ask riddles or tell jokes to each other. These provide a good instrument for initial experiences in sharing information researched from many sources.
2. Prepare skits and programs using jokes and riddles to be presented to classmates or other groups.
3. Use riddles to introduce folklore, and also to introduce students to many worthwhile authors, including Zim, Milne, Doule, and Poe.

4. Read biographies of codemakers and codebreakers in connection with history and science units, for example, Morse, Champollion, and Braille.
5. Accumulate jokes and riddles on one theme for use in connection with a special holiday or event, or for an assembly program.
6. Search riddle books to find riddles that have a common answer, but spring from different questions, concerning needles, shadows, tongues, candles, or newspapers.
7. Search for particular kinds of riddles: conundrums, riddles in rhyme, homonyms, verbal catches or sells, or anticlimatic endings.
8. Look for riddles on particular topics and in subject areas: spelling, math, science, history, or geography, and correlate them with units in the classroom.
9. Have students create their own jokes and riddles based on the patterns they have found in books.
10. Practice speech skills by having students read or tell riddles and jokes to each other. Sharpen verbal skills with tongue twisters.
11. Riddles about books can be used to introduce them or describe them to others. Reading comprehension can be assessed by having students devise riddles about a book they have read instead of writing a book report.
12. Homonyms may be studied through conundrums, which can be used also to reinforce understanding of the multiple meaning of words.
13. Read noodle stories so that common elements in human nature can be better understood and discussed.
14. Emphasize the timeless qualities of human nature and how they cross time periods and cultures by pointing out the common riddles found in stories from all parts of the world.
15. Emphasize the important role of riddles in the folk literature of all peoples.
16. Enhance language projects emphasizing the skills of comparing and contrasting by working with the various versions of a story, both orally and in written form.
17. Use folktales containing riddles to introduce other classroom units. Use the picture book version of a riddle or noodle story to introduce other similar stories in an anthology.
18. After they have read several versions of a story, have students create their own version, and illustrate it.
19. Use parts of riddle stories to teach students the elements of footnoting and bibliography.
20. Have students list riddles that have been located in more than one story, and cite bibliographic references.
21. Have students share jokes and riddles through bulletin board and other displays of the jokes and riddles and related books.
22. Have students paraphrase a story orally and in writing.
23. Move geographically around the globe through riddle stories. Study a

story or group of stories in a context of its national or ethnic origin.
24. Use riddle stories from one locality to introduce other kinds of stories from that region and also its music and art.
25. Have students learn to encode and decode messages in several codes. Have a decoding contest, between classrooms or groups.
26. Have students learn at least one method of nonverbal communication.
27. Engage in the artistic experience of creating a personal brand, a rhebus story, or a story in picture writing or calligraphy.

THE UNIVERSAL APPEAL OF RIDDLES.   Jokes and riddle books have an appeal that is universal. Maria Leach says in *Riddle Me Riddle Me Ree* that "All we know is that everywhere, since the birth of language, the tongue of man has been asking for the answers. Man has always wanted to know all the answers!" Lillian Morrison spoke, in her preface to *Black Within and Red Without*, of ". . . the strangeness of the world, the wonder and surprise at one's first discovery of the objects in it."

Besides reflecting mankind's desire to know, riddles are part of our literature. The first statement in *Funk and Wagnall's Standard Dictionary of Folklore, Mythology and Legends'* article on riddles is about the place of riddles in literature: ". . . riddles rank with myths, fables, folktales and proverbs as one of the earliest and most widespread types of formulated thought . . . riddles are essentially metaphors, and metaphors are the result of the primary mental processes of association, comparison, and the perception of likenesses and differences."

Included in this chapter are a variety of riddles from around the world and throughout history with various activities introducing them to students. All types of riddles listed by Maria Leach are mentioned: riddles can be a prayer, sacred ritual, magic charm, test of cleverness, secret language, joke, pun, anecdote, trick, or lifesaver. In the beginning of *The American Riddle Book*, Withers and Benet talk about the riddles that have answers and list conundrums; anticlimatic, teasing, or verbal catches or sells; and feeder jokes or anecdotes. Some riddles, according to Morrison's preface to *Black Within and Red Without* are ". . . old nursery jingles but are also echoes of primitive chants, down home folk ballads, lovely Elizabethan lyrics . . . real poetry, of a playful, fresh, nonliterary kind to which people naturally respond."

Besides their universality and literary value, riddles and riddle stories make good vehicles for teaching because of their built-in motivation and the many activities that can spring from them.

EASY-TO-READ RIDDLE BOOKS.   Joke and riddle books contain built-in motivation for reading and can be used for older students who are poor readers. The books in this section are all written for the beginning reader.

Poet John Ciardi's book, *I Met a Man*, available in paperback, contains delightful read-it-yourself poetry. "This man lives at my house now" is a yo-yo; "I met a man that was all head" and "This man had six eyes" are both potatoes; "I met a man with three eyes" is a traffic light. This last riddle could be included in primary unit on safety.

Another literary person who appreciated jokes and riddles was Bennett Cerf. Cerf compiled four books in the Beginner Book series: *Bennett Cerf's Book of Animal Riddles, Bennett Cerf's Book of Laughs, Bennett Cerf's Book of Riddles, More Riddles* and *The Book of Riddles.* This last title contains thirty riddles and is typical of the other books. There is a question and picture on one page and the answer on the next page opposite a new riddle.

Ann Bishop has written nine riddle books that are easy reading and follow a similar format. Each book contains between eighty and one hundred twenty riddles, and answers are found at the bottom of each page in a section of a different color. The color for the answers in the *Riddle-Iculous Rid Alphabet* is red. This book is arranged with four or five riddles per page and has twenty-six pages, one for every letter of the alphabet from "Animated Amusements" to "Zany Zappers."

An example of Bishop's humor is *Noah Riddle* which contains riddles about Noah and his ark. "What was Noah's profession? He was an Ark-itect. (Architect)" Other titles by Bishop are *Chicken Riddle* (also about animals); *Riddle Raddle, Fiddle Faddle,* which is a sequel to *Hey Riddle Riddle; Merry-Go-Riddle* (107 riddles about amusement parks); *Wild Bill Hiccup's Riddle Book* and *The Ella Fannie Elephant Riddle Book.*

Gilbreath's *Beginning-to-Read Riddles and Jokes* contains simple concepts about letters and syllables, and is also available in paperback.

Also available in paperback is Chrystie's *Riddle Me This,* a small, compact unpaged book that contains approximately 160 riddles illustrated with line drawings. Primary students will identify with the one about the tooth: "You forget a tooth after it is pulled because it goes right out of your head."

Twenty-four riddles appear in Low's *A Mad Wet Hen and Other Riddles.*

Cole's *Book of Giggles* provides easy laughs. One of the newest read-it-yourself riddle books found its roots in television and was an instant success. The riddle from which *The Six Million Dollar Cucumber* takes its name is found on page 71. "What is green, has one bionic eye, fights crime?" Other titles that attract primary students are *The Electric Radish and Other Jokes* by Thorndike, *Keller's Ballpoint Bananas and Other Jokes for Kids* and *The Star Spangled Banana: and Other Revolutionary Riddles,* and Longman's *Would You Put Your Money in a Sand Bank?*

Jokes and riddles especially successful for story-hour programs for small children are found in Tashjian's *With a Deep Sea Smile, Story Hour Stretches for Large and Small Groups.* Hints on using the material and specific suggestions are given in the book.

PICTURE BOOK RIDDLES.   Several of the joke and riddle books are also artistic experiences. Peppe's *Hey Riddle Riddle,* which is also available in paperback, contains fifty Mother Goose riddles. Each riddle and solution are carried out in full-color collages. Answers are given at the end of the book.

Two other Mother Goose books that contain riddles and have artistic merit represent other countries. *Chinese Mother Goose Rhymes* edited by Hyndman is illustrated in soft blue with accents of orange, green, black, and pink. The book has to be read vertically like an oriental scroll. Rhymes, riddles, and games are included in Chinese and English. Ed Young selected the riddles for *High on a Hill: a Book of Chinese Riddles*. The songs, rhymes and riddles in *Moon-Uncle Moon-Uncle, Rhymes from India* were selected and translated by Cassedy and Thampi. Forty-three samples of the Mother Goose of an Indian child show that the tales are not told in the third person like English nursery rhymes but are addressed to the child directly by forces in nature. Some answers to riddles include a peacock, rainbow, the wind, and a cat.

De Regniers's book *It Does Not Say Meow and Other Animal Riddle Rhymes* is a picture book for preschool through kindergarten children. The book contains nine riddles about well known animals—cow, bird, elephant, ant, mice, frog, dog, and bee. The clues are in verse and the animal answers are shown on the following page. The last page invites students: "Penny for a penny, Stone for a stone, Do you want more riddles? . . . Make up you own." A project to write and illustrate other animal riddles in the same style would excite older students if they knew they were making the riddles for younger children. The project could be undertaken by intermediate students studying art or poetry or during any unit on jokes and riddles. Older students in art or childcare classes could also undertake the project for different objectives.

Humphrey's *What Is It For?* includes photographs of city scenes such as a ventilator, a night deposit box, and a fire escape. All fourteen close-up black and white photos ask in the caption, "What is it for?" and are followed by a picture of the article in the context of its surroundings with an explanation.

Hoban's *Look Again!* follows a similar format. A small part of an object is seen through a square hole in the page, and turning the page shows the whole object. No words are needed as the photos are self-explanatory. Both books could inspire students to take their own photos and collect them for a companion book. Photos are also used in Cole's *Find the Hidden Insect*.

Livermore's *Find the Cat* and *One to Ten Count Again* contain hidden pictures within the line illustrations. Less intricate are two books by Tomi Ungerer: *One, Two, Where's My Shoe?* and *Snail, Where are you?* In both books, the author-illustrator shows pictures in which shoe and snail forms are incorporated into the picture. The dialogue in both books is limited to a sentence or two.

Three books written by Sarnoff and illustrated by Ruffin provide an experience in color. They are *The Monster Riddle Book, WHAT? A Riddle Book* and *I Know! A Riddle*. The first book contains a surprisingly large number of riddles about monsters—139. The bright colors and garish illustrations fit the riddles. Read the riddle from the book jacket to a group of children, hold up the book and step quickly aside, or be prepared to be hurt in the rush to check out the book. Although the title should be included in all displays and lists of monster books, it is also enjoyed by non-monster fans. The book should be featured by any summer reading program at the public library that uses the monster theme. Some of the riddles can be used as captions for a bulletin board. For example, the first riddle in the book could be used with a collection of ghost books or short stories:

"What do ghosts eat for breakfast? Ghost Toasties and evaporated milk." WHAT? A Riddle Book includes five hundred riddles and according to the blurb the illustrations are prepared "in mixed media including dyes, acrylics, and sheet of flat transparent color over pencil or ink line. They are camera separated and printed in four colors. The two-color illustrations are pre-separated, prepared as black drawings with brown wash overlays, both reproduced as halftones." I Know! A Riddle Book is in a pocket-size format.

Low's Five Men Under One Umbrella and Other Ready-to-Read Riddles contains twenty-nine riddles. The riddles are given on one page with the answers on the reverse side. Illustrations are pen and ink drawings shaded with watercolors in pink, orange, yellow and brown. The title comes from a riddle featured on pages 7 and 8: the reason why the five men did not get wet was that it wasn't raining.

Joel and the Wild Goose, a picture book story by Sandburg, is about a boy who wants something of his own and finds his wish fulfilled when a wounded goose comes into his care. In the spring Joel finds the courage to let the goose go. Although the story is primarily a story about the love of a boy for a wild creature, Joel emerges as a real person, a boy who is constantly asking riddles of himself, his family, or no one in particular. At the end of the story when his heart is breaking Joel asks and answers a riddle he has posed to a mother goat. The story is excellent for reading aloud to primary students.

The Riddle Rat, by Don Hall, is an animal who uses his talent as a master riddler to amuse and rescue his family of nine brothers and ten sisters and other relatives. Kate's Secret Riddle Book can be used to introduce other books by Fleischman.

Rose Wyler's paperback The Riddle Kingdom is about a boy who was allowed into the Riddle Kingdom because he had three riddle gifts for the King's birthday. After living in the Riddle Kingdom, the boy wanted to marry the princess but first had to accomplish three tasks.

Other picture books included in various sections of this chapter are two titles by Bowman and Bianco—Seven Silly Wise Men and Who Was Tricked?; Carson and Wigg's We Want Sunshine in Our Houses; Chase's Jack and the Three Sillies; Cooney's Squack to the Moon, Little Goose; Elkin's Six Foolish Fishermen; Hall's Rain Puddle; Konopnicka's The Golden Seed; Quigley's Blind Men and the Elephant; Saxe's Blind Men and the Elephant; Wilkstein's 8,000 Stones, a Chinese Folktale; and two of Zemach's books, Salt, A Russian Tale and The Three Sillies. Teachers may want to provide a collection of picture books about riddles and nonsense stories in the back of the room along with some of the anthologies containing riddle and noodle stories.

QUESTIONS ABOUT BOOKS.   Harshaw and Evans wrote a book for teachers and library media specialists called In What Book? It is a source of over 400 questions about outstanding children's books divided into four parts: I. For the Very Young (ages 3–6); II. For Young Readers (ages 4–8); III. For Readers in the Middle Years (ages 8–12); and IV. For Older Readers (ages 12 up). There is an author-title index. The book was published some years ago but can still be a useful resource for the questions that can be treated as riddles. A good project would be for students to make up their own riddles about more recent favorite books and characters, and bring *In What Book?* up to date. Ruth Harshaw used many of the riddle questions in quizzes as part of a nationally syndicated radio program about children and books.

There is a section in Roth's paperback *Pick a Peck of Puzzles* called "Mother Goof" that includes a dozen mixed up Mother Goose sentences for students to unscramble. Pages 42 and 43 include a story called "Little Goldie Red Cape" that includes six famous fairy tale heroines. In another section of the book called "Whoo?" an owl asks fifteen questions which have answers in famous books.

CONUNDRUMS   According to Carl Withers on page 6 of *The American Riddle Book*, conundrums are a "type of riddle in which the solution generally depends upon a pun." In Leach's *Noodles, Nitwits, and Numskulls*, these conundrums are called "wordplay riddles." There are nine examples of wordplay riddles listed in Leach on pages 60 and 61. One example given on page 61 of Leach is "Why is a pencil like a riddle?" Because it is "No good without a point." Once children have seen and heard the riddles they should be able and eager to find other wordplay riddles or conundrums.

Wiesner's *The Riddle Pot* has over a dozen examples, for instance, "Why is a room full of married couples empty? Because there is not a single person in it." The third riddle in Gehrler's *A Pocket of Riddles* is "What happens when you give a cat lemonade? You get a sour puss." Another excellent example comes from Doty's unpaged *Puns, Gags, Quips and Riddles:* "Why do gardeners hate weeds? Because if you give them an inch, they'll take a yard." The fortieth riddle in Thaler's unpaged *Soup with Quackers* is "How many ants can fit in a boarding house? Tenants." Rees's *Pun Fun* contains several hundred puns in rhyme. Another book containing riddles in verse is Morrison's *Black Within and Red Without* which contains 200 riddles.

Wall's *Puzzles and Brain Twisters* contains seven conundrums. Students will be able to find conundrums in every riddle book they read.

PUPPET FUN.   Consult Carlson's *Funny-Bone Dramatics* for suggestions on how puppets can be the vehicle for using jokes and riddles. Some students may need the anonymity of puppets for telling their jokes and asking their riddles. Besides the joke skits listed in Carlson's book, the following books would be useful: Cerf's *Bennett Cerf's Book of Laughs*, Chrystie's *First Book of Jokes and Funny Things*, Clark's *Jokes, Puns and Riddles*, Cole's *Book of Giggles*, Doty's two books, *Puns, Gags, Quips and Riddles* and *Q's Are Weird O's*, Emrich's *The Hodgepodge Book*, Fox's *Funnier than the First One*, Gilbreath's *Beginning-to-Read Riddles and Jokes*, Hoke's six books—*The Big Book of Jokes*, Hoke's *Jokes, Cartoons and Funny Things, Jokes and Fun, Jokes, Giggles and Guffaws, Jokes, Jokes, Jokes*, and *More Jokes, Jokes, Jokes*, Kohn and Young's two books, *Jokes for Children* and *More Jokes for Children*, and Schwartz's *Tomfoolery, Trickery and Foolery with Words*.

These joke and riddle books can also be used as resources for a skit which employs the techniques developed on the television program "Laugh-In." Students could pop up or open doors to give their jokes, one liners, or one person could ask a riddle of another. To add variety to the program and to give students an opportunity to search for a specific type of riddle, the teacher could assign groups to find only one type of joke or riddle, i.e., conundrums, homonyms, anticlimactic, teasing or verbal catches or sells, or feeder jokes or anecdotes. The teacher could also assign groups to find jokes on only one topic, i.e. spelling, science, mathematics, history, or geography. Some students could go beyond this simple project and investigate famous teams of comedians to find out about their style and to see who was the "straight man."

On Page 57 of *Perplexing Puzzles and Tantalizing Teasers*, Gardner gives suggestions for students to make up their own "knock knock" jokes using five boys and five girls' names. A new book that includes 84 "knock knock" jokes about people is Cole's *Knock, Knock, the Most Ever*. A typical one: "Isabelle out of order? I had to knock." Cole's *Give Up? Cartoon Riddle Rhymers* and Bernstein's *Fiddle With a Riddle* are useful in helping students to write their own riddles.

HOMONYMS.   Some of the most prolific types of riddles are those which depend upon homonyms for the "punch line." When a class is studying homonyms, ask them a few riddles based on homonyms as examples. Then they can look through the books cited in the bibliography and list all the riddles that contain homonyms. Even second and third graders can list three pieces of basic bibliographic data, author, title, and page number of the book in which the riddle is found. Students may write the riddles on one side of a 3- by 5-inch card and the answer and the bibliographic data on the other side. Then the cards can be organized so that all riddles using the same homonym can be placed together. These cards can also be used on a riddle bulletin board, or students may just be asked to compile a list of homonyms. Leaders may wish to have a riddle contest in which the group is divided into two teams. Each team can ask the other team five homonym riddles per "round." Points are given for each riddle the other team cannot answer. Students may be able to answer the riddles because similar riddles may be found in several books, different riddles have the same answers, and practice with riddles makes it easier to solve them by thinking. According to Withers in his introduction to *Riddles of Many Lands*, riddle contest winners have been rewarded in many cultures. In the Fiji Islands the people chose sides and the losing side had to feast the winning side, while the Greek banquet guest who guessed the most riddles was crowned with laurel.

Another approach might be to give students a list of homonyms and have them find riddles that use those homonyms. A list of over 75 homonyms is given in the article on "homonyms" in Grolier's *New Book of Knowledge*. For example, Wiesner's *Riddle Pot* has riddles for "blew" and "blue" (p. 14) and "cell" and "sell" (16-17). Bishop's *Hey Riddle Riddle* is unpaged but has riddles for "choo-choo" and "chew," "hoarse" and "horse." Another book by Bishop, *Noah Riddle*, contains riddles for "meet" and "meat." In two other unpaged books by Doty and Gerber, *Puns, Gags, Quips and Riddles* contains "sense" and "cents," and *A Pack of Riddles* contains "pain" and "pane." Clark's *Jokes, Puns and Riddles* contains a riddle for "wine," "whine" on page 141.

Longman's book *Would You Put Your Money in a Sand Bank?* is a first choice for a unit on homonyms. "Why does a pine tree pine? Because it can never grow an ice-cream cone" (p. 9). "Why did the zookeeper run after the lady? Because she had a mole on her nose" (p. 10). The book is also a delight because of the bright colorful illustrations of Abner Graboff.

The book with the most homonym riddles is Carlson's *1001 Riddles for Children*. Since each riddle is numbered, the numbers of each riddle is given to help locate them:

11. tale-tail	355. week-weak	695. rain-rein
19. profit-prophet	361. knows-nose	753. maid-made
40. son-sun	389. leak-leek	806. right-write
58. chili-chilly	391. ware-wear	808. fore-four
66. yew-you	413. sew-so;seam-seem	819. bow-beau
88. horse-hoarse	422. peal-peel	846. scenter-center
145. deer-dear	429. beet-beat	847. reigns-rains
152. pain-pane	464. read-red	855. needs-kneads
173. beat-beet	466. read-reed	858. bore-boar
174. see-sea	486. wax-whacks	865. fur-fir
196. flea-flee	496. bolder-boulder	882. weak-week
207. adore-a door	501. rain-reign	889. foul-fowl
214. pain-pane	515. sealing-ceiling	891. pear-pair
223. patience-patients	521. bread-bred	907. presence-presents
250. so-sew	524. tied-tide	909. pairs-pears
258. deer-dear	542. made-maid	919. claws-clause;
		paws-pause
267. taught-taut	580. steak-stake	931. cell-sell
284. tail-tale	612. need-knead	959. blue-blew
299. leak-leek	642. night-knight	963. see-sea
311. soot-suit	656. weakly-weekly	968. fowl-foul
322. pain-pane	671. Greece-grease	973. pale-pail
338. sell-cell	682. red-read	975. close-clothes

MULTIPLE MEANINGS OF WORDS.   Students also learn that one word may have more than one meaning. Often words with double meanings provide the basis for a joke or riddle. Four of Bishop's books, all unpaged, provide riddles for primary students. *Hey Riddle Riddle* utilizes "cross," "date," "train," "mind," and "range." *Noah Riddle* uses "watch," "pine," and "cones." *Riddle Raddle, Fiddle Faddle* uses "channel" and "stir," and *Red Riddle* uses "crackers" and "pop." We find the following words used in Gerber's *A Pack of Riddles:* "blubber," "batter," "school," "serve," "butting," "channel," "racket," "horn."

Carlson's *1001 Riddles for Children* contains over forty-five words with double meanings. Because a number is assigned to each riddle, those numbers are listed with the words.

12. felt	333. leaves	648. march
24. nails	336. weigh	745. truck, brush
127. current	338. watches	747. train
131. date	376. strike	757. back
140. beats time	381. spring	762. drift
157. spring	423. light; watch	765. pants
164. dressing	426. conduct	781. train, mind
186. recovered	443. draw	784. boiling
193. stir	448. hail	822. powder
276. knit	458. squall	833. quarters
277. draft	483. lighter	850. scaled
279. face	487. bark	851. point
282. root	599. dough	920. shocked, ears
305. pull	620. key	933. knots
326. crab	630. toasted	952. spoke, saw
		990. station

Some of those riddles, like the riddle about "March" (no. 648), are found in other collections.

ALPHABET RIDDLES.   There are many riddles about letters of the alphabet. There are several motivational devices which could be used to spark students to collect these riddles. Large capital letters could be cut out the size of an 8½ by 11 inch sheet of colored construction paper and riddles could be written on the letters. The answers could be written on the back of the letter. Or riddle groups of four students could be assigned to see how many alphabet riddles they could find. They might be able to make a word from their letters. Even a nonsense word may be fun to make.

Listed here are some riddle books that contain riddles about letters. Wiesner's *A Pocketful of Riddles* contains riddles on the letters C and Y (p. 6); T (p. 7, 97, 118); G (p. 18); IC and IV (p. 106); MT (p. 97); U (p. 36, 65); D (p. 40); B (p. 180); and M (p. 116). Wiesner's *The Riddle Pot* contains the following letter riddles: KT, LN, and LC (p. 6); P (p. 50); D (p. 55); F (p. 55, 106); P (p. 67); NRG (p. 86); FOE (p. 89); and B and C (p. 94). On page 20 of Withers's *The American Riddle Book* there are many alphabet riddles: C, J. B, I, P, Q, T, L, U, O or G, IV, IC, LC, KT, KN, DK, XL, TT. R is on page 42 and on page 60 are T, A, B, C, E, G, IOCURMT and BLNDPG. On page 100 there are riddles for the letters D, H, A, N, C, W, L, Y and two for B and T. Emrich's *Nonsense Book of Riddles, Rhymes . . .* has riddles for E and M on page 66. The alphabet rhyme "A was Apple Pie" is found on page 233. This rhyme also appears on page 56 of Schwartz's *Tomfoolery, Trickery. . . .* The letters T and C appear in Carlson's *1001 Riddles for Children* as numbers 555 and 900. Gilbreth's *Beginning-to-Read Riddles and Jokes* contains riddles about the letters J, B, I, and C. Leeming's *Riddles Riddles Riddles* has a section on pages 89 to 92 called "Enigmas." Many of these enigmas are letter riddles. Bishop's *Riddle, Raddle, Fiddle Faddle* has three riddles on the same page about the letters in a post office.

TONGUE TWISTERS.   When students search for alphabet riddles, they will probably also find tongue twisters. Marcia Brown's *Peter Piper's Alphabet, Peter Piper's Practical Principle of Plain and Perfect Pronunciation* is an alphabet book with a tongue twister for every letter of the alphabet except *X, Y,* and *Z* which appear together.

Two books by Potter also concentrate on tongue twisters: *Tongue Tanglers* and *More Tongue Tanglers*. The first book contains forty-six tongue twisters. Wither's *A Rocket in My Pocket* also contains tongue twisters. For more tongue twisters consult Schwartz's *A Twister of Twists, a Tangler of Tongues* and Emrich's *Nonsense Book of Riddles, Rhymes, Tongue Twisters, Riddles and Jokes from American Folklore*, Brandreth's *The Biggest Tongue Twisters Book in the World*, Cricket's *Jokes, Riddles and Other Stuff*, and Rosenbloom's *Twist These on Your Tongue*.

SPELLING RIDDLES.   There are some days when spelling class needs a little levity. Gilbreath's *Beginning-to-Read Riddles and Jokes* is unpaged and contains a dialogue riddle about spelling "house" with two letters: *T - P*. This riddle is perfect for the puppet dialogue mentioned in Carlson's *Funny-Bone Dramatics*. Another unpaged book, Bishop's *Hey Riddle Riddle* asks three spelling riddles: how to spell "mousetrap" with three letters, which are *C-A-T*; what three letters make a man of a boy, *A-G-E*; what starts, ends, and is full of *T*, teapot. Another book by Bishop, *The Riddle-Iculous Rid-Alphabet Book* asks about a ten-letter word that starts with *G-A-S*, which is an automobile. The word in the English language that contains all the vowels is "unquestionably." Wiesner's *Riddle Pot* on page 72 asks students to spell "blackbird" in four letters. "Crow" is the answer. A three syllable word that combines the 26 letters is the alphabet (p. 103), and the word composed of five letters from which if you take away two, one remains is *ST-ONE* (p. 109). On page 118 *NOON* is a word spelled backwards and forwards.

Sarnoff's *Monster Riddle Book* on page 7 asks: "Why should someone giving a party look out for the letter G? Because it can turn a host into a ghost." The cover lists another riddle: "How can you make a witch scratch? By taking away the w." Reading one or two riddles from a book is one way to introduce it to students, Gilbreath's and Gerber's *Pack of Riddles* has three riddles about the keys—"turkey," "monkey," and "donkey." In *The American Riddle Book* by Withers, there are eight spelling riddles on page 60 and seven spelling riddles on page 96. There are twelve pages in the chapter "Spelling Trick Riddles" in Bernstein's *Fiddle With a Riddle*.

There are several riddles that follow a pattern of having letters "in the midst" of words. Riddle no. 555 in Carlson's *1001 Riddles for Children* has the riddle "Why is an island like the letter T? Because it's in the midst of water." A similar riddle appears in Bishop's *Noah Riddle* except that there is an ark instead of an island. After students have read many riddles, they can, through substitution, create their own riddles.

Riddle no. 893 in Carlson asks why the letter K is like a pig's tail? Naturally, because it's at the end of "pork." A riddle inspired by Carlson is: "Why is the letter N like a caboose? Because they are both at the end of a train." Creating a riddle from a pattern requires students to combine the processes of substitution, analogy and creation. On page 939 in the article entitled "Riddles" in volume 2 of the *Funk and Wagnalls Standard Dictionary of Folklore, Mythology and Legend* edited by Maria Leach we find that "Not only does interest in riddles wear off as civilization grows more complicated, the ability to solve riddles also disappears, just at the time when such skill is more needed than ever. Civilization demands specialists and the grooved, compartmented, and departmentalized education which is necessary for the production of experts in technical matters often neglects entirely the more fundamental pedagogy which educated children and adults by teaching them through riddles to look at every problem from all sides, and still keep a sense of humor."

GEOGRAPHY RIDDLES. Withers's *Riddles of Many Lands* is an excellent first choice for riddles to tie in with geography or social studies because the book contains 700 authentic folk riddles from over ninety countries, regions and tribal or ethnic units. The book is divided into seven major geographical areas. The universality of riddles is demonstrated by the different riddles from around the world that have "tongue" for an answer. Tongue riddles are found in Cuba (p. 30), Argentina (p. 41), Italy (p. 64), Norway (p. 79), Turkey (p. 100), Tibet (p. 139), and Hawaii (p. 151). There is also a riddle about the tongue listed in the section on Mother Goose in Withers's book. Walker's *Laughing Together; Giggles and Grins From Around the Globe* is by UNICEF.

Leach's *Riddle Me Riddle Me, Ree* lists the national origin for every riddle as well as giving background information in the notes section on pages 113 to 138.

Hubp's *Que Sera? What Can It Be, Traditional Spanish Riddles* could brighten up a Spanish class or any unit on Spanish-speaking countries.

Leeming's *Riddles Riddles Riddles* has riddles about geography on pages 39 to 42, 105 and 106, and 215 and 216.

Still's *Way Down Yonder on Troublesome Creek* is a regional riddle collection coming from the Appalachian Mountains. The section called "1923 Postoffices" is a three-page narrative that includes 100 places that existed in 1923. Students can consult maps of the Appalachian states or the Zip Code directory to see if any of those places still exist on state maps or have post office zip codes today. The nonexistence of many of these places today shows a continually changing world. Discovering the disappearance of these places requires map skills. The project offers a change of pace to students or an opportunity for a special individual or group project.

Bishop, Doty, Kohl, and Rees are also sources of geographic riddles. In Bishop's unpaged *Riddle Raddle, Fiddle Faddle,* there is one page that has several geographic riddles, three of them about Australia. Doty's *Puns, Gags, Quips, and Riddles,* also unpaged, has a riddle about four states beginning with the letter *I.* On page 24 of Rees's *Pun Fun* there is one riddle that includes puns about four states and one city. Kohl's *Jokes for Children* has a joke about Pennsylvania on page 43. There are nineteen geography riddles and ten about famous people in Bernstein's *Fiddle With a Riddle.*

HISTORY RIDDLES.   Keller and Baker's *The Star Spangled Banana and Other Revolutionary Riddles* is the perfect answer to a day (usually before the holidays) when no one can be serious about American history. Illustrations by Tomie de Paola add humor to the sixty-two riddles. One riddle guaranteed to get groans or cheers before February 22 from students at all levels is "What did George Washington's father say when he saw his report card? George, you're going down in history."

Two pilgrim riddles from page 247 of Clark's *Jokes, Puns and Riddles* are guaranteed to be as silly as any found in *The Star Spangled Banana.*

Pages 1 to 80 of Wyler's *Professor Egghead's Best Riddles* includes riddles from American and world history. Many riddles about history have the same answers because questions about where any document was signed will be the same: all are signed at the bottom. Where any famous person stood at any given historic occasion is of course on his feet.

Bishop's *Hey Riddle Riddle* has riddles about Paul Revere, the Pilgrims, Miles Standish, Columbus and Benjamin Franklin on the same unpaged page. One too good to pass by is "What did Benjamin Franklin say when he discovered electricity? He was too shocked to say anything."

One favorite president was fond of telling jokes and playing pranks. Beatrice Schenk de Regniers has collected many of those jokes in *The Abraham Lincoln Joke Book.* De Regnier's book could be used on or near February 12 with students in grades three through junior high school. All that is needed is one tall thin boy, a black coat, a stovepipe hat, a narrator (who can be the teacher), and one or two people to feed lines to the president because *The Abraham Lincoln Joke Book* is easily adapted to a dramatic situation. The program could begin with the teacher reading or retelling the information from the introduction to the book (p. 9-13). Then any parts of the book that tickle the fancy can be dramatized. Students will want to choose their selections. This tactic serves two purposes: they will have to read (and probably enjoy) the whole book; and the program will be improved because it is easier to tell stories which are personally enjoyed than those that are assigned.

One story called "The Big Stink" could easily be adapted to a dramatic situation. Narrator: "Some men came to Lincoln and told him, 'You got rid of your Secretary of War and you found a better man to put in his place. Why don't you get rid of *all* your old advisors in the same way.' Lincoln told these men they reminded him of a story. . . ." Then Lincoln, tall and thin and dressed in a black suit with a stovepipe hat tells the story found on pages 78 and 79 about a farmer who had trouble with his skunks so he went out to shoot them. He told his wife he saw seven skunks and when she inquired why he only shot one he said "Well, . . . the first skunk made such a big stink, I decided to leave the other six skunks alone." The paraphrasing here does not do justice to the story.

Another good story, about Abe as a boy, is found on pages 75 to 79 of Jagendorf's *Sand in the Bag and Other Folk Stories of Ohio, Indiana and Illinois*. It concerns an incident in which Abe held two boys with dirty feet upside down so they could make tracks on the ceiling and Abe's stepmother would think someone was walking on the ceiling. Incidentally, Abe re-whitewashed the ceiling after this prank, which also involved a riddle. Page 28 of Wyler's *Professor Egghead's Best Riddle* contains a Lincoln riddle. The answer on page 31 says "He used this riddle to explain that just saying a thing is so does not make it so."

For more serious information about Lincoln that would be suitable for a program consult the section on Abraham Lincoln's birthday on pages 27 to 39 of Carrigan's *Holiday Ring, Festival Stories and Poems*. Included are an introduction to Lincoln's life, the poems "Nancy Hanks and Abraham Lincoln 1809-1865" by Rosemary Carr and Stephen Vincent Benet and " 'Peculiarsome Abe' " by Carl Sandburg. Perusal of poetry anthologies and biographies will also add stories and poems to a Lincoln program.

SCIENCE RIDDLES.   Early folk riddles were about rivers, shadows, sky, weather, animals, and a variety of phenomena found in the universe. These riddles abound in all types of collections but especially in collections of authentic folk riddles. A riddle assignment in a science class might be to find ten riddles dealing with natural phenomena.

Riddles could provide the punch to a motivational bulletin board during the study of birds. The word "BIRDS" in large capital letters could be surrounded by many colored circles, with a riddle about a specific bird placed on each circle. The answer and bibliographic information about author, title, and page on which the riddle was found could be placed on the back. Primary teachers may want to place the riddles on colored paper the color and shape of the bird in the answer.

Page 28 of Withers's *The American Riddle Book* has a riddle about each of the following birds: gull, crane, cardinal, swift, lark, loon, goose, quail, swallow, lovebirds, gobbler, raven. Page 31 has two general bird riddles.

Leeming's *Riddles Riddles Riddles* contains "Bird Bafflers" on pages 213 and 214. Other subjects covered in the same book are trees (pp. 163–65), flowers (pp. 183–86), and animals (pp. 119–21).

Leach's *Riddle Me Riddle Me Ree* is divided into nine parts. Three of the divisions are universe, animals, and plants. Emrich's *The Hodgepodge Book* contains jokes and riddles about animals, birds, bugs and crawling things, weather, plants, and flowers. Morrison's *Black Within and Red Without* has a section on elements in nature such as snow, rain, sun, rivers. Another section in Morrison's book is devoted to animals.

Wyler has written two science riddle books: *Arrow Book of Science Riddles* and *Real Science Riddles*. A third, *Professor Egghead's Best Riddles*, has science riddles on pages 132 to 160; all three of these titles are available in paperback.

Riddles from the first group of books are folk riddles and are more serious in nature than some others. The Wyler riddles, although not folk riddles, are also serious. There are, however, some good and silly science riddles. Two from

Doty's unpaged *Puns, Gags, Quips and Riddles* are "What happens when an owl has laryngitis? He doesn't give a hoot." "What causes sun spots? Sun gravy." Bishop's unpaged *Noah Riddle* produced "What birds on the ark had four feet and yellow feathers? The pair of canaries." From Bishop's *Hey Riddle Riddle* comes "What fish have their eyes closest together? The smallest fish."

Finally, Rees' *Pun Fun* on page 112 contains this rhyme:

> As the tadpole said
> From under the log,
> "My tale is ended
> And now I'm a frog."

MATH RIDDLES.   Contrary to popular opinion, math riddles abound. Pages 88 to 132 of Wyler's *Professor Egghead's Best Riddles* contains math riddles. At the end of Bishop's *Hey Riddle Riddle* there are about a dozen riddles about several subjects which include silly addition, making change; two employ simple fractions. Reading these riddles to the math class could motivate students to find other math riddles to place on a bulletin board. Students who finish their math problems early may be allowed to look through the riddle books in the room to find other math riddles for the bulletin board.

There are many versions of the "how many feet" riddles. On page 18 of Sarnoff's *Monster Riddle Book* monsters have nine feet when there are three of them. The version in Gilbreath's *Beginning-to-Read Riddles and Jokes* has dogs and twelve legs, Chrystie's *Riddle Me This* asks about jack rabbits and eight feet. The riddle found on page 101 of Wyler's *Professor Egghead's Best Riddles* has counterparts in other riddle books. "How many times can seven be subtracted from 77?" The answer is once. Any number of riddles can be invented using these as a model.

More serious riddles are found in Wiesner's *A Pocketful of Riddles*. Page 48 askes what you add to 9 to make it less: the answer is add an *S* to the Roman numeral IX (six). On page 28 readers are asked to add five more lines to six lines to make nine. Page 33 has a riddle about a clock and another about addition. Pages 65, 77, and 89 contain riddles about division. Page 114 has a riddle about the numeral 8.

Page 70 of Withers's *The American Riddle Book* has ten number riddles and page 124 has eleven riddles about telling time.

Another riddle that can serve as a model is "Why is 2 + 2 = 5 like Noah's left foot?" is found in the unpaged *Noah Riddle* by Bishop. The answer is "It's not right." Another Bishop riddle that is found in *Riddle-Iculous Rid-Alphabet Book* concerns the question "If four men can build four boats in four days, how long will it take one man to build one boat?" The answer, of course, is four days. An old riddle joke found in the same book is what one arithmetic book said to the other, "I've got problems." Bishop's *Riddle Raddle, Fiddle Faddle* offers this gem, "If Mr. Ham, a butcher, is six feet tall, wears a forty-six inch belt and shoes that are size eleven, what does he weigh?" The answer is "meat." Doty asks which kind of snake doesn't multiply rapidly in his unpaged *Pun, Gags,*

Quips and Riddles. The answer is "an adder."

Math teachers should also keep a rotating collection of math puzzle books in the room for students who need the challenge. Books to be included in that collection are Adler's *Magic House of Numbers*; Adler's *Metric Puzzles*; Barr's *Entertaining with Number Tricks,* and *Fun and Tricks for Young Scientists*; Charosh's *Mathematical Games for One and Two*; three books by Fletcher, *Put On Your Thinking Cap, Puzzles and Quizzes, Puzzles, Puzzles and More Puzzles*; Gardner's *Perplexing Puzzles and Tantalizing Teasers*; Kettlekamp's *Puzzle Patterns*; Leeming's *Fun with Paper and Pencil*; Mosler's *The Puzzle School*; Roth's *Pick a Peck of Puzzles*; Wall's *First Book of Puzzles and Brain Twisters*; and Wyler's *Arrow Book of Science Riddles* and *Funny Number Tricks*.

UNIVERSALITY OF RIDDLES IN FOLKLORE.   Not only are riddles found in folklore around the world, but the same riddles appear in very different stories. The "Riddle of the Sphinx" is the oldest and most famous riddle in the world. How Oedipus solved the riddle and saved the city of Thebes from the Sphinx is reported on pages 45 and 46 of Leach's *Noodles, Nitwits and Numskulls* and pages 33 and 34 of Leach's *Riddle Me, Riddle Me, Ree.* Another easier-to-read source is pages 136 to 38 of Benson's *Stories of the Gods and Heroes.* Schwab's *Gods and Heroes, Myths and Epics of Ancient Greece* (pp. 234-5) has a more complicated story. Two standard mythologies which include it are *Bulfinch's Mythology* (pp. 123-24) and Hamilton's *Mythology* (pp. 375-82). Hamilton's book has the most extensive version and an illustration on page 377. Also see page 942 of the *Funk and Wagnalls Standard Dictionary of Folklore, Mythology and Legends,* edited by Leach.

Since this riddle is so famous, a large sphinx could be the focal picture on a bulletin board with the caption "Riddle of the Sphinx" in large letters surrounding it. Students could copy riddles on small cards with the riddle on one side and the answer on the other, and place them around the Sphinx. Elementary students would enjoy trying to answer riddles placed on the board by others. Junior and senior high school classes may be asked to list on the cards bibliographic information of books containing references to the Sphinx, Oedipus, or stories from folklore or riddle books that contain this riddle. This activity is suitable for high school mythology classes, Latin classes, or geography and history classes studying this time period.

The Sphinx makes a fascinating bulletin board focal point because of the head and face of a beautiful young woman and the body of a winged lion. The riddle of the Sphinx is: *What is it that goes on four legs in the morning, on two legs at midday, and on three legs in the evening?* The answer is: *Man crawls on all fours as a baby, walks on two legs as a man, and on three legs (with a cane) as an old man.* According to the ancient Greek story, anyone who passed near the rock on which the Sphinx sat outside the city of Thebes was asked the riddle. Anyone failing to answer correctly would be killed, anyone who could answer the riddle correctly could save the city. The riddle, which was so difficult for everyone, was easily answered by Oedipus.

The "Riddle of the Sphinx" appears in three of the folktales included in this chapter. One of them is the third riddle asked by the three-headed Red Ettin in Williams-Ellis's *Fairy Tales from the British Isles* in the story named after the red monster. The vain chief in "Riddler on the Hill" in Thompson's *Hawaiian Legends of Tricksters and Riddlers* asks the same riddle after he fails to beat his opponent in three physical contests. On page 70 of Brenner's *The Boy Who Could Do Anything and Other Mexican Folk Tales*, in the story "The Princess and Jose," Jose saves himself by asking the king the same riddle. The answer the king couldn't give correctly was "himself." Although the answer has a different twist, it is basically the same answer because the king is part of mankind.

SAME RIDDLE, DIFFERENT STORY.   Two other riddles which appear in more than one story appear here. The second riddle in "Outriddling the Princess" pages 50 to 53 of Leach's *Noodles, Nitwits and Numskulls* and the first question asked the abbot in "The Emperor's Questions" found on pages 15 to 20 of DeLeeuw's *Legends and Folk Tales of Holland* is "How deep is the sea?" The answer is that it is a stone's throw.

"Outriddling the Princess" also contains another riddle found in two stories. The boy knew that it was one step from this world to the next because his grandfather had had one foot in the grave for over a year. In "Hantsje and the Remarkable Feast" from Spicer's *Thirteen Devils* the first riddle is similar. Pieter had heard a priest say that one foot is in the grave and the other is in heaven so he knew how far it was from heaven to earth.

SAME ANSWER, DIFFERENT RIDDLES.   In "A Chiefess and a Riddle" in Thompson's *Hawaiian Legends of Tricksters and Riddlers* there are two different riddles in the same story that have the same answer. "Corner posts, cross pieces and thatching on a house" is the answer to two riddles. On page 63 the question is about men that stand, lie down, and are folded. On page 64 the question is about something that is plaited at the sides, back, and front but leaves an opening.

There are many "shadow" riddles. On page 77 of "The Riddling Prince of Puna," also in Thompson's book, there is the following shadow riddle:

My twin—
With me from the day I crawled
With me til the day I die
I cannot escape him,
Yet when storms come,
He deserts me.

On page 113 in "The Prince with the Golden Hand" from Saunders's *A Book of Dragons*, a shadow walks without feet, beckons without hands, and moves without a body. Leach's *The Soup Stone* on pages 109 and 110 lists five shadow riddles from around the world and explains several customs about shadows. There is a German shadow riddle on page 74 of Wither's *Riddles of Many Lands*. Also consult page 24 of Wiesner's *The Riddle Pot* and page 11 of Morrison's *Black Within and Red Without*.

Wither's book also lists tongue riddles from Cuba (p. 31), Argentina (p. 41), Mother Goose (p. 52), Italy (p. 64), Norway (p.79), Turkey (p. 100), Tibet (p. 139), and Hawaii (p. 151).

In *The Soup Stone, the Magic of Familiar Things,* Leach devotes pages 58 to 61 to riddles about needles. Needle riddles from Turkey, Jamaica, Serbia and Haiti are given, as well as customs from Hebrew, Irish, Aztec, Pueblo and Chinese tradition. On page 61 a brief noodle story explains the saying "looking for a needle in a haystack" and "needles and pins."

One of the most famous needle riddles is a rhyme called "Old Mother Twitchett" found on page 58 of Leach's *Soup Stone,* page 24 of Hoke's *Jokes and Fun* and page 30 of Wither's *American Riddle Book.*

> Old Mother Twitchett,
> She had but one eye
> And a long tail which she let fly.
> Every time she went over a gap
> She left a piece of her tail in the trap.

NURSERY RHYME RIDDLES.   Besides "Old Mother Twitchett," there are two other riddles that are found in nursery rhyme books—"St. Ives" and "Little Nancy Etticoat." Pepe's *Hey Riddle Riddle* illustrates all three rhymes. All three are also listed in Untermeyer's *Rainbow in the Sky* and *Mother Goose and Nursery Rhymes* illustrated with wood engravings by Philip Reed.

"Coming from St. Ives" has a two-page spread and is riddle no. 41 in Pepe's *Hey Riddle Riddle.* The rhyme is called "As I Was Going to St. Ives" found on page 24 of *Brian Wildsmith's Mother Goose.* Provensen's *Mother Goose* has a double spread showing eight people and 2,744 cats.

> As I was going to St. Ives,
> I met a man with seven wives,
> Each wife had seven sacks,
> Each sack had seven cats,
> Each cat had seven kits:
> Kits, cats, sacks and wives,
> How many were going to St. Ives?

The answer that is usually not given is that only one person is going to St. Ives. He met the others coming toward him.

In addition to the "St. Ives" riddle on page 89, Morrison's *Black Within and Red Without* contains two candle riddles. One is on page two, but the most famous candle riddle called "Little Nancy Etticoat" is listed on page 20.

> Little Nancy Etticoat,
> With a white petticoat,
> And a red nose;
> She has no feet or hands;
> The longer she stands
> The shorter she grows.

Assign students to see how many riddles they can find about shadows, tongues, needles and candles, and newspapers. There are probably more riddles than those listed in this chapter.

SAME RIDDLE, DIFFERENT ANSWERS.   Schwartz's *Tomfoolery, Trickery and Foolery with Words* lists one of the most common riddles that has several answers. Four answers, a chocolate sundae with ketchup on it, a sunburned zebra, a blushing zebra, and a skunk with diaper rash are all given as answers for what is black and white and red all over. The obvious answer, a newspaper, was not given. The newspaper was the answer for riddle no. 559 of Carlson's *1001 Riddles for Children*. Because there are so many answers, this riddle would make a simple skit or puppet presentation involving two or six characters.

The first riddle in "The Red Etin" in Pilkingham's *Shamrock and Spear*, Lines's *Tales of Magic and Enchantment*, and Steele's *English Fairy Tales* gives a bowl as the answer to a thing without an end. In the Williams-Ellis version in *Fairy Tales from the British Isles*, a thing without end is a ball. No national origin is given for the Williams-Ellis version but the story from Lines is Scottish and the story from Pilkingham is Irish. Another Irish version appears in Lang's *Blue Fairy Book* but the Lang version is closer to a Scottish version in Baker's *Golden Lynx*.

SAME STORY, DIFFERENT TITLE.   A very brief riddle story is found in two collections under two different titles. "A Riddle Story" found on page 129 of Fitzgerald's *World Tales for Creative Dramatics and Storytelling* and "A Riddling Tale" found on page 662 of Grimms' *Complete Grimms' Fairy Tales*. In the story, one of three women changed into flowers was allowed to visit her husband overnight. The woman begged her husband to break the spell by coming in the morning to the fields to pick her. The riddle in the story was how would the husband know his wife if all the flowers in the meadow looked alike? The answer was that because she spent the night in her home and not in the field, there was no dew on her so her husband was able to tell her from the other flowers.

PROBLEM RIDDLES.   Some riddles are posed in the form of problems. One of these problems is found in three versions. Leach on page 59 of *Noodles, Nitwits and Numskulls* calls this particular problem a "Transportation Problem." A man, who can only take one thing at a time with him, must cross a river. He has to take over a wolf, a goat, and a cabbage and keep them from eating each other. The man is Johnson's *What They Say in New England* has a similar problem but he is transporting a fox, a goose, and a bushel of corn. A version from Southern Russia has a man crossing a bridge with a hen, a walking stick, a copper kettle on his back, and a goat attached to his waist by a rope. A woman who wants his help in crossing the bridge tells him how to solve the problem. This version, found on pages 34 to 37 of Foster's *The Stone Horsemen, Tales from the Caucasus*, is called "The Ossete Riddle."

There are four similar problems posed in the Johnson book about New

England. Other problems also occur in Leach's *Noodles* book. The riddles in both of these books are brief paragraphs simply stating the situations. The Foster version is told in folk story form.

RIDDLE SONGS.   One folk riddle takes the form of a song. Song no. 113 in Leisy's *Good Times Song Book* is an English folk song called "The Riddle Song." The familiar song is about a cherry that has no stone, a chicken without a bone, a ring without an end, and a baby that doesn't cry. The answers are given in verse three. A parody is also given in the Leisy book.

The same song appears on page 13 of Leach's *Riddle Me, Riddle Me, Ree* but instead of a ring without end, this version says a story without end. This source also adds a "g" to the end of blooming, pipping, sleeping, and crying.

USING RIDDLES TO INTRODUCE A CLASSROOM UNIT ON SALT.

I threw it in the water, it changed into water,
It lives in the water, yet water kills it.
No feast, large or small, I don't attend.
The food of kings, but a dog won't eat it.

This riddle about salt found on page 117 of Leach's *The Soup Stone* as well as the three other proverbs on the same page can be used to introduce a unit on salt. Besides reading the usual nonfiction books, include folk stories about salt. Have the students locate various versions of the story explaining why the ocean is salty and then discuss scientific reasons for the salt. Talk about some of the customs and superstitions surrounding the use of salt.

On pages 114 to 117 Leach identifies about 25 superstitions, customs, and proverbs concerning salt, telling about bad luck, sacredness, being "worth one's salt," binding friendships, symbolizing eternity, securing covenants, magic charms, denoting rank, giving insults, antiseptic and healing powers, keeping awake, ceremonies, etiquette for eating, catching birds, foretelling weather, and magical powers. Other examples are given in Batchelor's *Superstitious? Here's Why* (pp. 4–12).

The salt riddle can be used to introduce other folk tales about salt such as "The Discovery of Salt" in Wyndham's *Tales the People Tell in China* (pp. 9–13). According to the law, all treasure must be reported to the emperor and according to tradition, the phoenix bird only perches on treasure. So when a man saw a phoenix perched on a mound of dirt he took part of the mound to the emperor. The emperor had the peasant beheaded for his insolence but later when moisture from the clods of dirt flavored his soup, he rewarded the peasant's son. The Russian story "Salt," found on pages 420 to 23 of Stith Thompson's *One Hundred Favorite Folktales*, is taken from Guterman's *Russian Fairy Tales*. In the story the third son, Ivan the Fool, begged to be allowed to have a cargo ship like his brothers. His father gave him a ship but winds blew him onto an island which had a mountain full of pure Russian salt. Ivan loaded his ship with salt. When Ivan stopped to trade with a kingdom that had never heard of salt, they scorned his white sand and would not trade until Ivan added salt to the King's food. The pleased king bought all his cargo and gave Ivan one measure of silver and one of gold for each, as well as the princess to take home with him. Ivan's jealous brothers seized his ship and threw Ivan into the sea. Ivan floated away on a board and was rescued by a giant who made him promise not to boast about him. When Ivan returns, the princess tells her father-in-law to be that she wished to marry Ivan and not his wicked brother. All ends well until Ivan boasts about the giant at his wedding feast. The angry and drunk giant then wrecks the hall. Three days later when the giant sees what he has done, he says that Ivan can boast all he wants to because now the giant knows what drunkenness can do. The moral about drunkenness at the end of the story would be quite suitable for today's students.

Another salt story is the "Queen's Question" found on pages 90 to 101 of Hodges's *Three Princes of Serendip*. The queen would marry the man who could eat the entire contents of a storage bin of salt in one day.

The story "Love Like Salt" is found on pages 118 and 119 of Leach's *The Soup Stone*. When a king returned home from a journey, each of his three daughters told him how good it was to have him home. The first said that having him home was like the return of the sun, the second daughter said his return was like light to her eyes, and the third daughter said having him home was as good as salt. The king did not understand how much his third daughter loved him until she arranged for a feast without salt to be served to him, and all ended well.

There are many versions of why the sea is salty. Stories appear in Belting's *The Earth Is on a Fish's Back* (pp. 55–57); Gruenberg's *Favorite Fairy Stories Old and New* (p. 418); Haviland's *Favorite Fairy Tales Told in Norway* (pp. 30–44); Leach's *How the People Sang the Mountains Up* (pp. 28–29); Sechrist's *Once in the First Times* (pp. 17–19); Sideman's *The World's Best Fairy Tales* (pp. 108–15); Simley's *Stories to Tell or Read Aloud*, volume 1 (pp. 39–42); and William-Ellis's *Round the World Fairy Tales* (pp. 130–44).

The following three nonfiction books about salt will also be useful. Buehr's *Salt, Sugar and Spice* includes information about and devotes a chapter to salt. Various expressions and customs concerning salt are listed on pages 12 and 13. The rest of the chapter is devoted to various types of salt and processing methods. Goldin's *Salt*, part of the Let's Read and Find Out Science series, is intended for beginning readers, and mentions salt as sodium chloride. Mauzey's *Salt Boy* is about ancient and modern methods of salt making and reads like a story in which an Egyptian boy, a foreign exchange student in Texas, goes on a field trip to a salt mine. The book describes the background research the boy did before going on the field trip. The book also tells about an Egyptian plant called "Halh el mansur" established in 1967 to use solar power to operate machinery and solar heat to boil salt brine. Other interesting sidelights found in the book include the story of Lot's wife and information on salt licks.

USING RIDDLES TO INTRODUCE A UNIT ON LIBRARY MANNERS. Several of the books listed in this chapter have jokes and riddles that could be used to introduce good library behavior. On page 135 of Clark's *Jokes, Puns and*

Riddles is the following joke: "SAUL: If your dog were eating your book what would you do? PAUL: I would take the words right out of his mouth." The following riddle is found in Bishop's unpaged *Riddle Red Riddle Book:* "Why did the doctor cut out part of his new book? It was marked appendix." Jane Sarnoff admonishes readers not to write in the book when they figure out the puzzles of the *Monster Riddle Book* or the monster may get them. The two books by Joslin, *What Do You Say, Dear* and *What Do You Do, Dear* are fun books on manners and the second book contains two items of library manners. "You are in the library reading a book when suddenly you are lassoed by Bad-Nose Bill. 'I've got you,' he says, 'and I'm taking you to my ranch, pronto. Now get moving.' What do you do, dear? Walk through the library quietly." Another situation in the book concerns using a book mark to save your place.

SIMILAR RIDDLE THEMES.   Sometimes a riddle theme appears in several stories. The king in "As Many As" on page 57 of Leach's *Noodles, Nitwits and Numskulls* asked a boy what his father was doing. The boy answered that the father was making much from little so the king knew that the father was sowing grain. This riddle is the central theme in the story "The Hidden Treasure of Khin" found on pages 29 to 32 of Courlander's collection, *The Tiger's Whisker and Other Tales and Legends from Asia and the Pacific.* In this Burmese tale, Khin left his father and their rice fields to go to the city to become rich. The advice his father gave him was that "only hidden treasure is worthwhile." Instead of gaining wealth, Khin became poorer and poorer. One day a man told Khin that his father had died and left him two bags of treasure, on the condition that Khin bury it. The bags contained rice and Khin thought his father was joking, until finally he realized what his father meant, and became a prosperous farmer.

Konopnicka's Polish folktale *The Golden Seed,* illustrated by Janina Domanska is a similar story. A king wished he had gold so his people would have clothes to wear, so an old merchant gave him a sack of seeds. The seeds sprouted, green shoots appeared, then blue flowers bloomed and turned into little balls on the stalks. The angry king had the stalks pulled out and thrown into the river, and the merchant imprisoned. While in prison, the old merchant combed out the silvery fibers of his weeds and the prison keeper's daughters spun the fiber called flax into linen. When the merchant presented the cloth to the king's daughter as a wedding gift, the king realized that the gift was better than gold, because now his people had something to wear.

THE JEALOUS KING, EMPEROR, MANDARIN.   The motif in which a king, emperor or mandarin questions a commoner because he is jealous is found in very different stories in England, Holland, and China. Each story involves a different twist to a riddle in which the ruler asks the other person to guess what he is thinking.

The story in De Leeuw's *Legends and Folk Tales of Holland* is called "The Emperor's Questions." Charles V, ruler of the Holy Roman Empire saw a sign on an abbey that said "Here one lives without a care." Charles V sent for the abbot saying he would give the monks something to worry about. The monks would answer three questions or they would find out what it meant to have trouble. The abbot was very worried until he met a shepherd who persuaded the abbot to let him take his place when he went before the emperor. The emperor asked and received answers to the first two questions: the sea is as deep as a stone's throw, and one cow tail could reach from the earth to the sun if it were long enough. For the last question, the emperor wanted the abbot to tell him what he was thinking. The shepherd answered that the emperor was thinking that he was talking to the abbot but he was not, he was talking to a shepherd. The emperor was so amused that he let the shepherd go and left the monks in peace.

There are two English versions of a similar story. Of the two versions, the one called "King John and the Abbot," found on pages 11 to 17 of Baldwin's *Favorite Tales of Long Ago*, is the better story. The other story is called "The Three Questions" and is found on pages 19 to 22 of Corcoran's *Folk Tales of England*.

In the English version, a jealous wicked King John heard that the Abbot of Canterbury had more money (Corcoran) or kept a better house (Baldwin) so the king threatened to execute the abbot if he could not answer three questions. The first question in the Corcoran version was about the worth—to the penny—of the king. The answer was that the king must be worth 25 shillings because the coin called a crown is worth 5 shillings and the coin called a sovereign is worth 20 shillings. The first question asked in the Baldwin version was how long the king would live. Naturally the king would live until the day he died and not a day longer. He would die when he took his last breath and not a moment longer.

The second riddles are the same in both stories. The king could ride around the world in 24 hours if he rode with the sun from sunrise to sunset. The last riddle was the same as in the De Leeuw version from Holland.

There are three Chinese stories: "A Beautiful Young Woman as the Head of the Family" in Hsieh, *Chinese Village Folk Tales* (pp. 58-62); "The Young Head of the Cheng Family" in Wyndham, *Tales the People Tell in China* (pp. 25-37); and "The Young Head of the Family" in Simley, *Folk Tales to Tell or Read Aloud* (pp. 1-4) that contain a situation similar to the one from Holland. The Chinese stories are essentially the same. A mandarin sees a sign over the door of a house reading "No Sorrow." Because he does not believe the sign, the mandarin asks the clever head of the household, a young girl, to complete two tasks and to answer one riddle. The riddle was about what the mandarin was thinking of doing, keeping and perhaps killing his pet quail, or letting it go. The girl's answer that saved her family was that if the mandarin could not guess her riddle, he had no right to ask her to answer his.

DIFFERENT RIDDLES IN VERSIONS OF THE SAME STORY.   There are six sources of the folktale "Red-Etin," "Red Ettin," or "Red Etin." Each version has three riddles but all riddles are common only in the versions by Lines, Pilkington, and Steele. This is unusual because the first is a Scottish version and the second is an Irish version. The third story is listed as English. As mentioned previously, the first riddle in the Lines, Pilkington, and Steele versions is the same as the first riddle in the Williams-Ellis version, but the answers are different. The second riddle in all four of these versions is the same. The answer is that a bridge is more dangerous the smaller it is. The third riddles, however, are different. The third riddle in the Williams-Ellis book is the "Riddle of the Sphinx" and the third riddle in the other books is a ship that sails with a live crew is an example of the dead carrying the living.

The Lang and Baker versions have two riddles in common, the first and third riddles. The first riddle, asking whether Scotland or Ireland was the first to be inhabited, is found on page 140 of Baker's *The Golden Lynx* and on page 387 of Lang's *The Blue Fairy Book*. It is interesting that neither version gives an answer for the riddle but only says that the boy answers the riddle correctly. Perhaps that is because the Baker version is of Scottish origin and the Lang version is of Irish origin, and if there is no answer then both groups can be happy. The third riddle in both books also does not have an answer. The question concerns which were made first: men or animals. The second riddle in the Lang book asks whether man was made for woman or woman made for man. The second riddle in the Baker version asks how old the world was when Adam was made.

Story Outline for the Red Etin, Red Ettin or Red-Etin

1. A poor widow has two sons or two widows have one or two sons.
2. The oldest son or two sons of one widow were given a journey cake ("bannock" in Lane and Baker versions) the size of which would depend upon how much water the son brought his mother from the well. Since the jar had a crack in it, the cake was small. The mother asked for half of the cake in return for her blessing, but the son or sons decided they needed the whole cake.
3. The boy leaves his knife with his family and tells them that if the blade turns red they will know he is in trouble.
4. The older brother or two brothers individually saw a shepherd watching over sheep. When asked whose sheep they were, the shepherd repeated a fourteen line verse that is the same in all four versions. In the verse we learn that the Red Etin of Ireland has stolen the daughter of King Malcolm of Scotland.
5. The boy encounters first an old man herding swine and then an old man herding goats. The old men each sing the same fourteen line verse to the boy.
6. The shepherd tells the boy to beware of the beasts. The boy sees them and runs to hide in the nearest place where an old man or woman hides him.
7. The Red Etin comes in and says a four-line verse reminiscent of the giant's "Fee fie foe fum" speech from "Jack and the Beanstalk."
8. The Red Etin finds the boy and asks him three riddles which he cannot guess, and so he is turned into a pillar of stone.
9. If the version has two widows, then the second son goes through all the same procedures and is turned to stone.

10. When the knife turns red, the younger son, or the only son of the second widow, goes off on a journey. The boy brings water to his mother so she can make a journey cake. In all of the versions except that of Williams-Ellis, a raven tells the boy about the crack and he fixes it. His journey cake is consequently larger and the boy chooses to share it with his mother in return for her blessing. In the Baker version the bannock actually becomes larger when he receives her blessing.
11. While on his way, the younger son meets an old woman and gives her half of his cake. In return she gives him a magic wand.
12. This last son meets a shepherd and asks whose sheep he is tending. The shepherd repeats the verse about the Red Etin. The shepherd warns the boy about the beasts.
13. The beasts are fearsome but the boy strikes them with his wand and they fall down dead.
14. The boy arrives at the castle; when the Etin comes out, he asks the boy three riddles which he answers correctly. A fight ensues and the Etin's strength wanes and the boy chops off all three of the Etin's heads.
15. The princess and other beautiful maidens are released from locked rooms and the two other brothers or the older brother are changed back from pillars of stone. The youngest boy marries King Malcolm's daughter and the other boy(s) marry noble young women.

Activities for the "Red Etin," "Red Ettin," or "Red-Etin."   All activities should be preceded by a discussion of why similar folk tales are found throughout the world and why versions vary.

1. Assign students to read one version of the story and write answers to questions 1-15 that follow in this section. Feel free to photocopy these questions so each student has a copy.
2. Assign students to read three versions of the story. They should read the Williams-Ellis version, either the Lang or Baker version, and one of either Lines, Pilkington, or Steele. Students should answer questions 1-18 for each story.
3. Assign students to read one version of the story and ask them the questions. Put answers on a chalkboard, large chart, or transparency. This will show differences between the versions.
4. Assign students to read any version but the Williams-Ellis version. Then read the Williams-Ellis version aloud. Have students interrupt whenever the version they read differs from this version. Or have students write down differences while the story is being read so students can make comments afterwards.
5. Assign students to read one version of the story. Assign them to discuss the story with two students, each of whom has read another version. Have students write down differences they found. Bring all students together for a brief overview. Avoid pairing Baker with Lang and be sure to separate those who have read Lines, Pilkington, or Steele.
6. Assign individual students to read two of the versions and make a list of

similarities and a list of differences in the versions. Avoid the pairings mentioned in question 5.

7. Assign students to read a version of this story. List all first riddles, second riddles, and third riddles with their editors on a chalkboard, large chart or transparency. Paraphrase questions 12 to 18 and read the section called "Different Riddles in Versions of the Same Story."

8. When studying bibliographies and footnotes, have all students read a version of the story. Include all riddles on a transparency. As a group, write a bibliography including information for each of the stories. At the direction of students, footnote each riddle on the chalkboard or on a transparency. Check the section in this chapter called "Footnotes for the 'Red Etin,' 'Red Ettin,' or 'Red-Etin.'"

9. Assign pairs of students to read the same two versions. Have one person record all the similarities and the other record all the differences. Avoid the pairings mentioned in question 5.

Questions to ask about the "Red Etin," "Red Ettin," or "Red-Etin."

1. What is the title of the story? (Be sure of the correct spelling and note any hyphens or special punctuation.)
2. Who is the editor or compiler of the collection in which the story is found?
3. What is the title of the collection in which the story is found?
4. What is the national origin of the story?
5. Is this version told in dialect? (Lang Version)
6. Does this version have one widow with two sons or two widows— one with two sons and one with one son?
7. Does the mother make a journey cake, cake, or bannock?
8. Does a raven tell the last boy that his jar is leaking or does he figure it out for himself?
9. Does the story say that the last boy is kinder?—more clever?
10. Does the bannock or journey cake grow larger when the boy shares it with his mother to get her blessing?
11. Does the last boy share his cake or bannock with an old woman, tell her his problems and receive the gift of a magic wand?
12. Does this story contain the "Riddle of the Sphinx"?
13. Are answers given to the riddles?
14. What are the riddles for which there are no answers?
15. What are the riddles for which there are answers? Give answers.
16. Does your version have any riddles that are the same as one found in another version? List them.
17. Do you have a riddle that does not appear in any other story? List it.
18. Do you have a riddle that is the same as one found in another version but the answer to that riddle is not the same?
19. Which three versions have exactly the same riddles and answers?

Footnotes for the "Red Etin," "Red Ettin" or "Red-Etin." Turabian's fourth edition of *A Manual for Writers of Term Papers, Theses, and Dissertations* is the source for the following footnote style.

¹Augusta Baker, "The Red-Etin," *The Golden Lynx and Other Tales* (Phila.: Lippincott, 1960), pp. 135-47.*

²Andrew Lang, "The Red Etin," *The Blue Fairy Book* (New York: Dover, 1965), pp. 385-88.**

³Kathleen Lines, "The Red Etin," *Tales of Magic and Enchantment* (London: Faber & Faber, 1966), pp. 118-126.*

⁴F.M. Pilkington, "The Red Etin," *Shamrock and Spear, Tales from Ireland* (New York: Holt, Rinehart & Winston, 1966), pp. 56-60.**

⁵Flora A. Steele, "The Red Ettin," *English Fairy Tales* (New York: Macmillan, 1946), pp. 221-226.***

⁶Amabel Williams-Ellis, "The Red Ettin," *Fairy Tales from the British Isles* (New York: Frederick Warne, 1960), pp. 292-301.

*Origin of story—Scotland   **Origin of story—Ireland   ***Origin of story—England.

THE CLEVER DAUGHTER.   Joseph Jacobs, international folklorist and a president of the English Folklore Society, included the story "The Clever Lass" in his book *European Folk and Fairy Tales*. According to his notes (pp. 256-59), the story is widespread and is found in eighty-six variants (12 German, 6 Teutonic, 13 Romance, 37 Slavic, 7 Finnish, Hungarian and Tartar, 6 Semitic, and 5 Indian).

The titles included for analysis are found in collections easily available and include variations from seven countries. See the section called "Common Elements about a Clever Daughter" for a listing by country of origin.

An assignment based on this story should contain four elements: (1) a discussion on the universality of theme and how and why versions are different from place to place; (2) an assignment to students to read individually one or more of the stories; (3) either activity A or B: A—List the nine elements in the story and have students identify, by number, which elements are found in their story, B—Ask students to answer the thirty questions about the story that follow in this section; (4) a total classroom discussion of which stories contain which elements or which stories answer which questions so everyone can share versions and see the totality of the project.

THE CLEVER DAUGHTER—COMMON ELEMENT NO. 1—A THREE-RIDDLE IN-TRODUCTION.   In the most frequent introduction to the story, a ruler must make a decision between a poor peasant and someone else. Instead of deciding for the peasant who is in the right, the ruler favors whichever person gives the best answer to a riddle. The peasant consults his clever daughter who gives him the best answer, and the other person consults his wife but his answers are inferior. Information about the riddles and answers for four sources are given below in the following order, (1) the riddle, (2) the wrong answer, and (3) the correct answer. Czech sources for Clever Manka are sweetest-honey-sleep, swiftest-mare-thought, richest-chest of golden ducats-earth; Jacobs's European version includes most beautiful-wife-spring, strongest-ox-earth, richest-himself-harvest; Ranke's German version includes quickest-heifer-sun, sweetest-sugar-sleep, fattest-sow-earth; and Ausubel's European Jewish version has swiftest-horse-thought, fattest-pig-earth, and dearest-wife-sleep.

The two Estonian versions collected by Mass and McNeill have very different riddles from those found in the other stories.

THE CLEVER DAUGHTER—COMMON ELEMENT NO. 2—THE MORTAR AND PESTLE INTRODUCTION.   In Grimms' German version called "The Peasant's Wise Daughter," the father finds a mortar on land the king has given him so he wishes to give the mortar to the king. The peasant's daughter insists that the mortar hasn't any value without the pestle. The king imprisons the peasant because he cannot produce the pestle. The peasant laments that he should have listened to his daughter; the king hears him and wants to see if the daugher is as clever as her father says. So the king sends her the "with and without" test. The Czech story called "A Clever Lass" in Fitzgerald's book has essentially the same introduction.

In the Italian version in Stith Thompson's book, the huntsman finds a mortar and gives it to the king even though the daughter advises him not to take the mortar without the pestle. The girl has already spoken in riddles with the prince and accepted his riddle gifts which were partially eaten by the messenger and which are part of common element no. 3.

THE CLEVER DAUGHTER—COMMON ELEMENT NO. 3—THREE RIDDLE PRESENTS.   The ruler sends the girl three presents by messenger and asks riddles to see if all of them arrived. Her answers indicate that the messenger ate some of the gifts, but she indicates by way of riddles that the messenger should be spared. In Wilson's Greek version the gifts were twelve loaves, a round cheese, and two wineskins. In Stith Thompson's Italian version the Prince sent a round cake, thirty patties and a cooked capon. In Jacobs's European version, the king sent a round cake, thirty small biscuits, and a roast capon. Leach's story, "The Full Moon," on page 49 of *Noodles, Nitwits and Numskulls* says the king sent a big round tart, thirty small cakes, and a roasted capon. This last version is typical of the interchange between the ruler and the girl. When the king asks if the moon were full, the girl replied that it was only a half moon. When he asked her if it were the thirteenth of the month, she said it was the fifteenth. She replied to his question about whether or not the cock crowed by saying that it had been through the mill. The final riddle was to "spare the pheasant for the sake of the partridge" which meant that the king should not punish the messenger.

THE CLEVER DAUGHTER—COMMON ELEMENT NO. 4—"WITH AND WITHOUT."   In the Estonian versions in collections of Maas and McNeill, the King asks the girl to come neither dressed nor undressed, neither by foot nor on horseback, neither by road nor foot path. So the clever girl came wearing a net, tied to a goat, who followed a track. When she arrived, the girl put one foot inside and kept the other outside.

Clever Manka was asked to come to the Burgomaster neither by day nor by night, neither riding nor walking, neither dressed nor undressed. So Manka arrived in the morning when night had not yet become day. Manka wrapped herself in a fishnet so she would not be dressed or undressed, and she traveled by goat with one leg on the goat's back and the other on the ground.

In Jacobs's European tale, the king tells the clever girl to come clothed yet unclothed, neither walking nor driving nor riding, neither in shadow nor sun, and with a gift and not a gift. The clever girl wrapped herself in her long hair and placed herself in a net which was attached to the tail of a horse. She held a sieve over her head to protect herself from the sun and platter covered by another platter to keep from having a shadow. She had a little bird between the platters and when the king took it for his gift, it flew away.

The Jewish version by Ausubel is very similar to that found in Jacobs, but has only three conditions instead of four. The girl is to come walking but riding, dressed but undressed, with a gift that is not a gift. She also wears a fishnet, rides a goat, and releases pigeons as gifts just as she is about to give them to the ruler.

The Czech story called "Clever Lass" is similar to the previous two stories. The girl is to come clothed but unclothed, neither riding nor walking, neither by day nor night, neither at noon nor morning, so she came at dusk, clothed in a fishnet, half riding a goat.

Grimms' German version has the girl come clothed but naked, not riding or walking, and not in the road nor off the road. So the girl wore a fishnet and tied it to the tail of an ass so that it dragged her along so she wasn't riding or walking. Since the ass walked through ruts she touched the ground only with her big toe so she was not on nor off the road. The German version by Ranke has the clever girl arriving not by day nor by night, not with an empty or satisfied stomach, not on the road nor beside it. The clever girl started early in the morning riding on a goat while she licked salt.

In leach's *Noodles, Nitwits and Numskulls* (p. 56), the story "With and Without" reports that a young girl came to the king with and without a present—a bird in her hands that flew away when she gave it to the young king.

THE CLEVER DAUGHTER—COMMON ELEMENT NO. 5—ANOTHER CLEVER-NESS TEST.   In three of the stories, the ruler is not satisfied with one test of the girl's cleverness but decides to test her again. In the first story the cleverness test comes after the capon test. In the last two stories, the clever girl has already helped her father answer the three riddles.

In Stith Thompson's Italian version, the prince asks the girl to make him a hundred ells of cloth out of four ounces of flax or he will hang the girl and her father. The girl sends her father to the prince with four small cords of flax and the message that she will weave the cloth if the prince makes a loom out of those cords.

In the Clever Manka stories of Czech origin the burgomaster sent Manka ten eggs and asked her to hatch them by tomorrow and bring him the chicks. Manka sent her shepherd father to the burgomaster with some millet. She agreed to bring him the ten chicks if the burgomaster can plant, grow, and harvest the millet so she can feed it to her chicks. The burgomaster then gives her the three "with and without" tests.

In Ranke's German version the judge sends the girl three hemp plants and she is to make a skirt, a sheet, and a towel from it. The girl sends the judge three small wooden pegs and says she will make the three items if the judge will make a flax brake, a spinning wheel, and a weaving loom from the three small pegs. After this, the judge gives her the three "with and without" tests.

Three Chinese tales about a clever girl who became head of a household are found in Hsieh, Simley, and Wyndham. The story in all three versions is essentially the same. The mandarin asks the girl to weave him a piece of cloth as long as the road; the clever girl retorts that she will do so if the mandarin finds the ends of the road and tells her how many feet long it is. The mandarin also said that he would fine the girl as much oil as there is water in the sea. The girl agreed to pay the fine as soon as the mandarin measured the sea and told her how many gallons the sea had in it. The mandarin asks the girl to divine his thoughts, whether or not he will squeeze to death, or let go the pet quail in his hands. The girl's reply is that if the mandarin doesn't know any more than she does, then he has no right to fine her. She countered with a riddle of her own. He had to guess what she was thinking, whether or not she meant to come in or go out when she stood with one foot on either side of the threshold, then she did not have to guess his riddle.

THE CLEVER DAUGHTER—COMMON ELEMENT NO. 6—THE COLT AND THE CART, OXEN, GELDING OR MARE.   Although the participants in ten stories differ slightly, the story is essentially the same. In the Manka Czech versions the colt went by a cart so the owner of the cart tried to claim the colt. These circumstances also prevail in the Russian picture book by Daniels. The Jewish version by Ausubel has a colt stand by a wagon instead of a cart while the Italian version has a cart but has a she-ass give birth. The other Czech version called "Clever Lass" has the colt run away from its mother and stand by a gelding. The Italian Stith Thompson and the two Estonian tales are similar but call the gelding a horse.

Although Grimms' German version has a colt or foal lie down near two oxen instead of a cart, wagon or gelding, the story is much the same as in the other versions. Two peasants dispute over the ownership of a foal that lies down between two oxen. The owner of the oxen claims the foal and when the two peasants bring the matter before the king the king says the colt should stay where it was found. The unhappy peasant told his troubles to the queen. Although she has promised not to meddle in the affairs of her husband, the queen tells the peasant to pretend he is fishing in the middle of the road. When the king asks him what he is doing the peasant should say that it is as easy to catch fish on dry land as it is for an ox to foal a colt. The king knew that only his wife could have thought up such a clever retort so she had broken her agreement not to meddle in his affairs. Before he banished her, the king told his wife she could take the one thing with her that she prized the most. So the queen drugged the king and took him with her as her most prized possession. When he awoke and saw how clever she had been, he relented and they returned home.

THE CLEVER DAUGHTER—COMMON ELEMENT NO. 7—THE MEDDLING WIFE IS BANISHED.   In all versions except the Ranke German version, the wife is banished because she gives the losing peasant advice which shows her husband that he has not made a wise decision. In the Ranke version, the disagreement came about over a matter of fish who could not understand peasant talk. Also in this version the wife was allowed to take three possessions with her instead of one.

In all of the Czech as well as Jacobs's European versions the wife tells the peasant to pretend he is fishing in the road. The Italian Stith-Thompson version has the peasant fishing in the square and the two Estonian and the Jewish version found in Ausubel have the peasant fishing in a sandheap. Otherwise the story is essentially the same, the peasant, when challenged about his foolishness by the king, retorts that his fishing in the sand, square or road is no sillier than a cart, gelding, horse, or ox giving birth to a colt. The ruler knows his wife has broken her agreement not to meddle so she is banished.

THE CLEVER DAUGHTER—COMMON ELEMENT NO. 8—THE MOST PRIZED POSSESSION.   In all versions except one that has an adult daughter in the cart-colt story, the wife is allowed to take her most prized possession with her so she chooses her husband. He of course admits to her cleverness, relents, and they happily return home. In the Ranke German version, the wife is allowed three possessions so she takes her purse, her father, and her husband. Otherwise the story ends the same as the others.

THE CLEVER DAUGHTER—COMMON ELEMENT NO. 9—TALKING IN RIDDLES.   All the stories with the "with and without" motif and the stories in which the king sends something round, small cakes, and a roasted bird and asks three riddles to see if the messenger has eaten any of the gifts, are examples of speaking in riddles.

The two Estonian stories edited by Maas and McNeill both contain conversation between the king and the peasant girl in which they speak in riddles. The king asked the whereabouts of the girl's father and she answered that her father was making better out of good (grinding grain at the mill). Her mother was hunting in the birch grove and killing what she caught and what she doesn't she brings home (fleas). The girl's sister was turning her back to the wind (burning rubbish), and her brother was neither in earth nor heaven because he was in a tree. The king then asked the girl to come to the palace using the "with and without" story.

There are several instances of speaking in riddles in "The Clever Bride of Tunisia" found in Nahmad's *The Peasant and the Donkey, Tales of the Near and Middle East.* The King of Tunisia met a peasant and asked his daughter for answers to the questions. She told her father that the question about whether or not the father was going to use the corn after harvesting it was to find out if he had any debts that needed to be paid with corn that might otherwise go to his household. The question about whether the people buried in the village cemetery were dead or not was to discover whether the dead had been of no account and forgotten or whether they lived in the people's memory.

The king gave a reward to the girl because he liked her answers. He sent her a loaf of bread every day for two weeks. Then one day he overheard the girl tell her father that the king was really not the son of a king because the loaves meant that he was a baker's son. The king was very surprised to learn from his mother that the girl was correct. The king banished the girl so she would not tell anyone of his humble origins.

While she was banished, the girl was seen and admired by the king of her new country. When he asked her to be his wife, she told him that he must have a meal with her. He did not eat the chicken and watermelon to her specifications so she refused his offer. When the king sent his messenger, the messenger also proposed so he had to eat the same meal, but he also did not eat to her specifications. The crown prince, however, shredded the pieces of chicken and threw them away so she knew that he would be able to keep the marriage a secret even if he were torn to pieces. He squeezed the watermelon juice to signify that even if his blood were shed, he would not divulge the secret. The shredding of the chicken is reminiscent of the dividing of the capon by the prince in Stith-Thompson's Italian version.

When the prince refused to divulge his marriage to the girl, he was thrown into prison. Before being executed he was granted his last wish, to travel to a certain part of town where, unbeknown to everyone else, his wife lived. As he passed she threw a bottle of perfume out the window as a sign to her husband that the news of their marriage could be spread just as perfume spreads.

In Leach's *Noodles, Nitwits and Numskulls*, the young king went to visit a girl and she said "The house has neither eyes nor ears" (p. 55). The young king knew from his answer that she wasn't ready because she did not see or hear him coming since there was no child in the house to look nor any dog in the yard to bark.

THE CLEVER DAUGHTER IN PICTURE BOOK FORMAT—COMMON ELEMENT NO. 10. Daniels's "The Tsar's Riddles or the Wise Little Girl," illustrated by Paul Galdone, has Russian origins. Two brothers disagree on possession of a new colt. One brother claimed the colt because it was found under his cart. The other brother said the colt belonged to his mare. The brothers took their disagreement to the tsar who gave them three riddles and asked them to come back in three days. The richer brother went to an old lady for his answers; the poorer brother who owned the mare was given the answers by his seven-year-old daughter.

When the tsar found out that the daughter had answered the riddles he gave the daughter three more riddles. The tsar was impressed so he gave the girl one last riddle—If your father is so poor, how do you manage to eat? The girl replied that her father catches fish on dry land and she carries them home in her apron and makes fish soup from them. Naturally the tsar said she was stupid, and the girl retorted that the tsar was not so smart either if he thought colts came from carts and not mares.

The picture book can be used during this unit in several ways. The teacher could read the picture book to the students and then assign them to read various versions and compare the versions with the nine common elements. Or the picture book could be given to one of the class members as one of the books to use in comparing a version of the story to the nine common elements.

COMMON ELEMENTS ABOUT THE CLEVER DAUGHTER

NATIONAL ORIGIN	EDITOR	TITLE	ELEMENTS
Czech	Arbuthnot	"Clever Manka"	1,4,5,6,7,8
Czech	Fillmore	"Clever Manka"	1,4,5,6,7,8
Czech	Sutherland	"Clever Manka"	1,4,5,6,7,8
Czech	Fitzgerald	"A Clever Lass"	2,4,6,7,8
Estonian	Maas	"The Farmer's Daughter"	1,4,6,7,8,9
Estonian	McNeill	"The Clever Peasant Girl"	1,4,6,7,8,9
European	Jacobs	"The Clever Lass"	1,3,4,6,7,8
Italian	Thompson	"The Clever Peasant Girl"	3,5,6,7,8,9
Jewish	Ausubel	"The Innkeeper's Clever Daughter"	1,4,6,7,8
Jewish	Nahmad	"The Clever Peasant Girl"	3
German	Grimm	"The Peasant's Wise Daughter"	2,4,6,7,8
German	Ranke	"The Farmer's Clever Daughter"	1,4,5,6,8
Greek	Wilson	"The Clever Peasant Girl"	4
Russian	Daniels	"The Tsar's Riddle or the Wise Little Girl"	1,6
Tunisian	Nahmad	"The Clever Bride of Tunisia"	1,10
Unknown	Leach	"The Full Moon"	3
Unknown	Leach	"With and Without"	4
Unknown	Leach	"As Many As"	5

QUESTIONS ABOUT THE CLEVER DAUGHTER STORY

1. What is the title of your story?
2. Who is the editor and what is the title of the collection in which it is found?
3. What is the national origin of the story?
4. Does the girl in the story have a name?

5. What is the occupation of her father?
6. If she is married, what is the occupation of her husband?
7. How does the girl meet her husband?
8. Does the prospective husband talk to the girl in riddles?
9. Does the ruler send the girl three gifts?
10. What are the gifts, what is the girl's explanation?
11. Is the father asked three riddles? What are they?
12. Is the father asked the three riddles to decide a question between the father and another man?
13. What is the occupation or a description of the other man?
14. What were the answers given by the girl to her father?
15. What were the answers of the other man?
16. What is the man called who has to decide who is the winner of the riddle contest?
17. Is there any mention of part of a gift that the father gives to the ruler?
18. Does the ruler ask the girl to come to him in an unusual manner?
19. Does the ruler test the girl with some unusual tasks?
20. Is there a dispute over the ownership of a colt?
21. Does the girl talk in riddles with anyone?
22. Does the judge or ruler marry the girl?
23. Does the husband ask his wife not to meddle in his affairs?
24. Does the wife meddle in one of her husband's affairs when she thinks he is wrong?
25. What is the situation in which the wife meddles?
26. Does the husband ask the wife to leave home because she has meddled?
27. Does the husband allow his wife to take anything with her?
28. What does the wife choose to take with her?
29. How does the wife outsmart her husband?
30. Do the husband and wife live happily ever after?

SIMPLETONS ANSWER THE RIDDLES.   Not all riddle stories are about clever persons. Sometimes, in folktales, it is the simple person who answers the riddle. Three such simple young men who answered riddles are Simple Peter, Juan Bobo, and Simple Ivan.

"Simpleton Peter" is found on pages 104 to 113 of Reeves's *English Folk and Fairy Stories*. "Juan Bobo and the Princess Answered Riddles" is found on pages 115 to 121 of Allegria's *The Three Wishes, a Collection of Puerto Rican Folktales*. Ivan the simpleton appears in the story "The Princess Who Wanted to Solve Riddles" on pages 345 to 347 of Stith Thompson's *100 Favorite Folk Tales* which was taken from Guterman's translation of *Russian Fairy Tales*. Incidentally, another "Ivan the Fool" appears on pages 420 to 423 of Stith Thompson's book in a story called "Salt." In that story Ivan succeeds in becoming rich and marries a princess.

Two of the stories—the Puerto Rican tale "Juan Bobo and the Princess Who Answered Riddles" and the Russian tale "The Princess Who Wanted to Solve Riddles"—provide an excellent vehicle for studying comparisons and contrasts.

Group or individual projects can be devised. The following four activities may be modified to suit individual objectives:

ACTIVITY 1—If the objectives are to practice listening skills and report information verbally, then the two stories could be read to the students. Then, using the chalkboard, flip chart or transparencies, make one list of similarities and another of differences in the stories. Students should participate in formulating the two lists.

ACTIVITY 2—If the objectives are to note similarities and differences by individual reading, then the students would read the stories to themselves. The findings could be shared orally or through individual written reports.

ACTIVITY 3—After completion of either project, but especially after completion of activity 1, students could compare either or both stories to a story from Grimm called "The Riddle." The easiest to read translation is found on pages 128 to 131 of Grimms' Complete Fairy Tales. Another translation is found on pages 300 to 303 of Lang's Green Fairy Book.

ACTIVITY 4—After completion of any of the other activities, introduce students to another but very different story called "Simpleton Peter." Students may just read for enjoyment or may be asked to list the events of the story in sequence. The story is as follows:

Simple Peter lived with his mother who asked him to go to the old woman's cottage to ask for more brains. The old woman told Peter he must bring her the heart of the thing he liked above all others. Then to test his choice, the old woman would ask Peter a riddle. Peter's mother suggested he take the heart of a pig because he loved fat bacon. The riddle the old woman asked Peter was, "What could run without feet?" Peter didn't know the answer so she sent him away. When Peter returned home, his mother was dead. He was sorrowful and wondered how he would get along without her because he liked her best of all creatures in the world. Peter decided to take her body to the old woman, and when he did, he was asked another riddle. Peter did not know the answer to "what is yellow, shines, and isn't gold?" On the way home Peter say down and cried in frustration. A pretty young woman came by and when Peter told her his troubles, she agreed to marry Peter and take care of him. Soon Peter decided he liked her best of all creatures, and so he took his wife to the old woman. The wife correctly answered the first two riddles—a river and the sun, and the last riddle as well: "A tadpole has first no legs, then two legs, then four legs." The old woman told Peter that he had all the brains he needed in his wife's head, because if a man has a clever wife, she is all the brains he needs.

The only similarity between "Simple Peter" and Juan Bobo and Ivan is that all three of them were simpletons.

SIMILARITIES AND DIFFERENCES BETWEEN TWO SIMPLETON STORIES. There are at least nine similarities and six differences to be found in "Juan Bobo and the Princess Who Answered Riddles" and "The Princess Who Wanted to Solve Riddles." These are answers to be found when completing activity 1 and 2.

Similarities

1. The hero is a simpleton.
2. A princess will marry whoever answers her riddle.
3. Anyone whose riddle is answered by the princess will have his head cut off.
4. Ivan and Juan make up riddles from experiences each has had on his trip to see the princess.
5. A parent does not want the son to go to the castle and possibly lose his head. (Juan's mother and Ivan's father)
6. The princess asks for more time before answering because she does not know the answer and because she does not want to marry the simpleton.
7. The princess sends her maid and then comes herself to get the answer from the hero.
8. The magic number "3" appears in both stories; Juan has three parts to his riddle and the princess has three days to solve it; Ivan has three riddles with one night each to solve each one, or a total of three days.
9. Both simple young men marry the princess.

Differences

1. Juan's mother provides him with a poisoned cake which provides the incident which gives him the idea for his riddle. Ivan simply sees something.
2. Juan's riddle was in rhyme; Ivan's was not.
3. Juan's and Ivan's riddles differed from each other.
4. Juan's payment for telling the princess the answer is her ring and shoe; Ivan's payment is that the princess must stand all night in his room without sleeping.
5. Juan tells the princess the answer and is kept from being beheaded only because he produces her ring and shoe as proof that she extracted the answer. Ivan is saved because the princess can't answer the last riddle because it was about her activities, and if she answered the riddle she would reveal to everyone how she coerced Ivan into giving her the answers to the other two.
6. Numbers 5 and 8 in the similarities could also be listed as differences.

SEQUENCE IN "THE RIDDLE" BY GRIMM.   Besides explaining the story, the following list provides proper sequence for the story. Each episode could be separated from the others and students could be asked to return them to their proper sequence. Grimms' "The Riddle" is found in collections of Grimm and Lang.

1. The king's son and a servant set out on a journey.
2. The prince sees a beautiful girl and asks her if he can have shelter for the night.
3. The young girl is not eager to invite the travelers in because her stepmother

is a witch.

4. The travelers spend the night but are careful not to eat or drink anything.
5. The next morning the prince leaves the house before his servant.
6. The witch tries to give the servant a drink to take to his master.
7. The drink is spilled and the poison in the drink kills the servant's horse.
8. The servant goes to tell his master what has happened.
9. The servant returns to his horse to get his saddle but finds a raven eating the dead horse.
10. Because he was hungry, the servant kills the raven, and takes it with him.
11. The prince and servant stop at an inn and give the raven to the cook to prepare.
12. The witch and robbers who were also at the inn eat soup made from the raven who was poisoned by eating the horse and they die.
13. The prince gives the robbers' gold to the young girl and they go on their way.
14. The prince and his servant arrive at a town where a princess has promised to marry anyone who can make up a riddle that she cannot guess. Anyone who cannot answer the riddle will be beheaded.
15. The prince makes up a riddle from his experiences. One slew none and yet slew twelve. The answer is the raven that ate the poisoned horse and killed the twelve murderers who ate the raven soup.
16. The princess cannot answer the riddle and asks for three days to think about the answer.
17. The first night the princess sends her maid to listen to the prince's dreams. The servant who had changed places with the prince snatches the girl's cloak from her.
18. The second night the princess sends another maid and the same thing happens again.
19. The third night the princess comes herself. She obtains the answer but loses her cloak.
20. The next day the princess answers the riddle and the prince asks for a hearing whereupon he produces the cloaks. The judge decides that the last cloak should be embroidered with gold and silver for a wedding cloak.
21. The prince and princess marry.

Those who compare "The Riddle" with "Juan Bobo and the Princess Who Answered Riddles" and "The Princess Who Wanted to Solve Riddles" will find "The Riddle" similar to the other two stories in numbers 2-4-6-7-9 as well as the differences for numbers 2-3-4-5.

ANSWER THE RIDDLE AND WIN THE PRINCESS. The Spanish story called "The Flea" is readily available in four sources. The Haviland version on pages 3 to 17 of *Favorite Fairy Tales Told in Spain* is almost word for word as the story found on pages 43 to 53 of Ross's *Buried Treasure and Other Picture Tales*. The main difference is that the animals in the story are called by their Spanish names in the Ross version. The Ross version is taken from Ruth Sawyer's *Picture Tales from Spain.* The story on pages 233 to 235 of Johnson's *Anthology of Children's Literature* is also taken from Sawyer's version.

When the king, who was fond of riddles, found a flea on his person, he laughed, had the flea fed until it was the size of a calf, and then had its skin made into a tambourine. His daughter Isabel, nicknamed Belita, danced with Felipa, the tambourine. Whichever suitor could answer the following riddle could have her for his wife: "Belita-Felipa-they dance well together-Belita-Felipa; now answer me whether you know this Felipa this *animalita*, If you answer right, then you marry Belita" (Haviland p. 6).

A shepherd heard about the contest and his mother reluctantly let him go, giving him a tortilla for his pocket. On the way the shepherd gave a ride and shared his tortilla with a little ant, a black beetle, and a little gray mouse.

When it came time for the shepherd to answer the riddle, the ant crawled over the tambourine and recognized it as a flea. The princess, however, refused to marry the shepherd who had answered correctly so the king granted any other favor instead of the hand of the princess. The shepherd asked for a cart drawn by two oxen and a pouch filled with gold. Because the mouse gnawed a hole in the bottom of the pouch, enough gold fell through the pouch to fill up the cart. The shepherd went his way and married a shepherd's daughter.

"The Flea" is easily understood and is a favorite of students. This is one of the easiest stories in this chapter for students to read and retell to others.

In "Outriddling the Princess" (Leach, *Noodles, Nitwits and Numskulls*, pp. 50-53) a princess named "Smarty" would marry no one except the person who answered her riddles. She even answered the riddles posed by an old riddler who knew a riddle for every day of the year. The riddles she answered are all on page 51 and include "How far is it across the earth?" ("A day's journey—the sun does it in a day."); "What has six legs, four ears, two faces, and is coming up the road?" ("A horse and rider coming, with four legs on the horse and two on the man—makes six. . .two ears on each one makes four—and each with his own face—makes two.") ". . .a head with seven tongues in it?" (A horse skull "with a bird's nest in it—seven young ones in the nest and a tongue in each bird").

A young boy came and the princess asked him three riddles: the boy guessed that the sun was a bird that sits on top of a cypress tree toward the East in the morning and on a tree toward the West at night. He also guessed that it was a stone's throw to the bottom of the sea. He also guessed that it was one step from this world to the next because his grandfather had one foot in the grave for over a year.

This story would be suitable for playing because of the princess's character. At the end of the story, the precocious princess gets a robin's egg popped in her mouth to silence her. Characters would be the princess, king, queen, old riddler, and the boy.

"The Prince with the Golden Hand" on pages 103 to 113 of Manning-Sanders's *A Book of Dragons* is about a princess who must be won from a dragon by riddles. The day before the princess was to choose a husband, a dragon took her away. Two princes set off to find her, but their horses returned without them. The hermit promised the princes' mother that she would have another son who within a month would wield a sword, within two months would ride horseback, and at three months be fully grown. Besides these accomplishments, his right hand and moustache were made of gold. The third son went off to find his brothers and the princess.

In order not to marry the dragon, the princess agreed to wed no one unless he could guess three riddles. Prince Golden Hand answered all three riddles and won the princess. He guessed that a shadow walks without feet, beckons without hands, and moves without a body. A bed has four legs but is not an animal, has feathers but is not a bird, has a body and gives off warmth but is not alive. Prince Golden Hand also guessed that a shoe when tied up goes a-roaming but loose it and it stays a-homing (p. 113).

Another riddle story in the same collection is "The Dragon and His Grandmother." A dragon saved three army deserters and gave them their freedom for seven years. Then if the soldiers answered a riddle they could have total freedom; if not, they would be the dragon's slaves forever. The three riddles asked of the men are reminiscen! of Hawaiian riddles.

"The Queen's Question" found in Hodges's *The Three Princes of Serendip* is a tale of ancient Ceylon. Before Queen Parvathi's father died, he said that she would marry a prince who could answer a question. The question concerned how a man could eat the contents of an entire storage bin of salt in one day.

Prince Rajahsingha had a goldsmith make a tiny golden box which held a storage bin no bigger than a pea. The prince filled the box with salt and ate the contents of the storage bin before her. When the Queen asked what the prince would do with a very large bin full of salt, the prince gave the correct answer to her ". . .whoever eats a pinch of salt with a friend and does not know his duty toward him, will never know it even though he eat all of the salt in all of the storage bins of the world. As for me, I shall always have for you the deepest sentiments of respect and love" (p. 97).

For the best effect, leaders should paraphrase or read parts of this story as an example of a riddle story to stimulate students to read other stories. For best results, the entire story should not be read aloud.

"The Queen's Riddles" found on pages 31 to 37 of Cothran's *The Magic Calabash* is one of many Hawaiian riddle tales. A chief on Oahu and a far-sighted man set out to see if the Lands of Wakea and Papa were larger and fairer. The two men met a fast runner named "Swift One," "Straight Shooter," "Man-Who-Could-Hear-Afar-Off," and two called "Man-Who-Dies-in-the-Cold" and "Man-Who-Dies-in-the-Fire." When the chief went to the queen to answer her four riddles, each of these men helped him to answer the riddles. Because he could answer all her riddles, the chief married the queen.

A story that may be compared to "The Queen's Riddles" is "The Three Tests" found in Fitzgerald's *World Tales for Creative Dramatics and Storytelling.* This story also includes a "Thirsty One" and a "Swift One."

RIDDLE STORIES AROUND THE WORLD.   "The Queen's Riddles" is just one of several riddle stories from Hawaii. There are four riddle stories in

Thompson's *Hawaiian Legends of Tricksters and Riddlers.* In most of the tales from other cultures, the person who cannot answer the riddle was beheaded, but in Hawaii, the person who fails is thrown into an oven. Sometimes, as with the father of "The Riddling Youngster" the remains become part of the "House of Bones" or the "Fence of Teeth." In this story Kai-paloosa goes to the riddling house to find his father. Even though Kai is very young, a contest is arranged between the boy and Kalani, the high chief. The contest consists of four rounds of chants about wonders found in their own islands, foods grown below the ground, foods grown above the ground, and canoe travels. They tie each round but Kai-paloosa won the last round, so he took his father's bones home. This story typifies a type of riddling in Hawaii that is not merely the asking and answering of riddles but includes quick-witted debate, complicated play on words, and the memorization of long chants.

On pages 72 to 79 of the Thompson collection, "The Riddling Chief of Puma" wanted to build the largest collection of riddles so he looked far and wide for them. If someone told the chief a riddle, he hated them because he wanted to be the only person to know the answer. Subsequently he had to ask them a riddle that they could not answer so that he could throw them in the oven and be the only one who knew the answers. The riddle found on page 73 is "Mo-ke-a-mo-ke-ki." Hoopai's brother has been consumed in the oven so Hoopai gathers three riddles and goes to avenge his brother. Hoopai presents his riddles to the chief, and the answers to the first two riddles are a shadow and an umbrella. The third riddle, found on page 76, is "My old man—He cries day and night, Through wind and sunshine, Through wet season and dry. Listen! You can hear him now." The answer is the surf.

Now that the chief has added Hoopai's riddles to his repertoire he must give Hoopai the unanswerable riddle so he can be rid of him. Hoopai did not know the answer and stalled for time saying that the answer to Mo-ke-ki-a-mo-ke-ki was in his head. The Riddling Chief was then burned in his own oven because the answer was the head. Because of this chief, even to this day the people of Puma won't tell you a riddle.

Because of the complexity of Hawaiian riddles, many of the riddle stories are unsuitable for younger students. "The Riddler on the Hill" (pp. 40-48) in Thompson's collection is an exception. A vain chief noticed that one of his warriors received attention from the young women and he was jealous. The chief challenged Mekila to a game of maika (bowling), sledding, and surfing and lost all three contests, so he challenged Mekila to a riddling contest. The riddle posed in the story was the "Riddle of the Sphinx." Mekila was able to answer the riddle only because he saw an old man who was hobbling with his cane, who was accompanied by his crawling grandson. The answer to the riddle, of course, is mankind; a child crawls on four legs, a young person walks on two legs, and an old person with a cane walks on three.

A class that is studying Hawaii may also wish to read the twelve stories in Thompson's *Hawaiian Myths of Earth, Sea and Sky.*

"The Princess and Jose" found in Brenner's *The Boy Who Could Do Anything* is a Mexican tale that also includes the "Riddle of the Sphinx." Jose was walking along a road when he was arrested because he looked like a thief and because the soldiers needed prisoners to build roads without pay. The princess felt sorry for Jose and took him food to eat; the soldiers teased her and said Jose would be the first one shot because he refused to build roads. Prisoners were always shot when the king was in a bad mood; he was in a bad mood now because he didn't have any new riddles. The princess persuaded her father to let Jose go if he could ask the king a riddle he could not answer. The king agreed. Jose asked the "Riddle of the Sphinx" but the king could not answer. The king was pleased when he found out that the answer was "himself," thought Jose was clever, and gave his daughter to Jose to marry.

Another king who was fond of riddles lived in Pakistan. In the story "The Four Riddles," pages 53 to 58 of Courlander's *Ride with the Sun, an Anthology of Folk Tales and Stories* from the United Nations, the king heard about a poor woodcutter who could answer any known riddle. The king sent his fakir to see if that was true. The fakir sat in a spot where the woodcutter's sons would pass. One at a time he told each of the sons of a vision or riddle. None of the sons could give the meaning of the visions so the fakir changed each one to stone. When the woodcutter went to look for his sons, he encountered the fakir and the four pillars of stone. The fakir said he would bring back the sons if the woodcutter could answer four riddles. The fakir repeated each riddle and as the woodcutter answered them correctly, a son reappeared.

From neighboring India comes the "Unsolved Riddle" in Ghose's *Folk Tales and Family Stories from Farther India.* A greedy man named Bako Delvyo collected food for a nonexistent man so he could get two portions. A white dog and his pack surrounded Bako and demanded a large meal. The dogs felt that the meal was owed to them because Bako, as a professional mourner, usurped the dogs' prerogative to howl. So Bako and the dogs howled at the sacrifice festival so that no one would eat. People thought it was unlucky to eat the food, so it went to the dogs. The riddle of whether Bako was clever or stupid is still debated today.

Another well known story from India is "The Blind Men and the Elephant," in which each of seven blind men feels a different part of an elephant and uses that part of the elephant to describe the entire creature. Two different picture books are available; one is by Quigley, the other is by Saxe. The story is available on pages 104 to 06 of Baldwin's *Favorite Tales of Long Ago*, page 112 of Johnson's *Anthology of Children's Literature* in the "Modern Fables" section, and on page 54 of Leach's *Noodles, Nitwits and Numskulls*. The poem by Saxe is also given on pages 37-39 of Ross's *Puppet Shows Using Poems and Stories.*

The story of the "Long-Nosed Giant" is based on an historical account of what happened when an elephant was sent to China from the ruler of Burma about A.D. 200. The story is found on pages 11 to 19 of Mar's *Chinese Tales of Folklore.* A picture book of that same story, retold by Diane Wolkstein, is called *8,000 Stones, A Chinese Folktale.* The riddle in the story was how much did the gift—the long-nosed giant—weigh? The reward to the person who answered the riddle would be a trip to Burma to give the ruler there a return gift. A young boy solved the problem by taking the elephant on a barge and marking the water line. Then after removing the elephant, he loaded the barge with stones until it sank to the same mark. Then the boy weighed each stone and added the weights together to arrive at the answer.

"Hantsje and the Remarkable Feast" from Spicer's *Thirteen Devils*, is a story of a greedy devil from the Netherlands. Pieter, a farmer, plowed up a crock with 303 gold pieces in it. The Devil Hantsje said the gold belonged to him because everything under the ground belonged to the devil. Hantsje said Pieter could have the gold if he accomplished three tasks. If not, the gold and Pieter's soul would belong to the devil. The first task was a riddle about how far it is from heaven to earth. Pieter remembered the priest talk about one foot being in the grave and the other in heaven, so Pieter correctly answered that it was one step. The second task was that the two would raise a crop on shares. Since the devil wanted what was under the ground, Pieter chose barley rather than onions, potatoes, carrots, or turnips so the devil got only roots. The third task was that by sunup Pieter was to "produce a beast the like of which I have never seen and the origin of which I cannot guess." Pieter's wife used pillows to make herself fat and rolled in honey and goose feathers. The devil couldn't guess what she was in three tries.

The last riddle from around the world comes from Italy and is called "The Clever Peasant." The story appears in Dobbs's *Once Upon a Time*. A king asked a peasant farmer how much he earned a day and how he spent the money. The peasant answered that he ate the first, put the second out to interest, gave the third back, and threw the fourth away. The king didn't understand because the peasant had spoken in riddles, so the king asked him to explain. The peasant explained that he fed himself first, then his children because some day they would have to care for him, and gave to his father for past support, and lastly to his wife because he received no profit from it. (Although the sexist overtones of the fourth item are offensive to today's raised awareness the tale could create a springboard for discussion of past traditions that need not be continued, and how deeply ingrained have been attitudes toward women, through many times and in many cultures.)

The king was pleased with the riddle and made the peasant promise not to tell anyone the answer until he had seen the king's face one hundred times. The king then asked his court if they could answer the riddle and of course no one could. One of the ministers, who knew that the king had spoken with a particular peasant the day before he made up the riddle about a peasant's earning went to find the peasant. The peasant when found was uncooperative and told the minister why he couldn't tell him the answers. The minister then produced one hundred coins, each of which showed a picture of the king on it. The peasant, tongue loosened by this tricky bribe, was able to tell the answers to the minister and the minister was able to tell the answers to the king.

HISTORY RIDDLE STORIES.   There are four riddle stories that have historic perspective. The best use of these particular stories is to paraphrase them briefly and to present them as examples of riddle stories in history. They are not the best stories for reading aloud to students.

"The Tale of the Riddle Sent to Bruce," pages 81 to 90 of Sorche Nic Leohdas's *Claymore and Kilt, Tales of Scottish Kings and Castles*, is about two claimants to the Scottish throne. It is said that the War for Scottish Independence began with the riddle of a spur and a coin. Here are the circumstances.

John Baliol, the King of Scotland, was a puppet of King Edward I of England. Robert Bruce, Earl of Carrick and Lord of Annandale, was trying to gain followers but was wary of the other claimant, Sir John Comyn, called "Red" Comyn because of his red hair. Bruce finally confided to Comyn that many Scottish earls were talking of forming a league to free Scotland and put a real Scottish king on the throne. Since the two of them were the logical choices, they agreed that one of them could be king and the other would own the property of both of them.

Bruce then went to London and while there, a servant of the Earl of Gloucester gave Bruce a deerskin pouch saying that Bruce had left it and that it might be important. Bruce knew that the contents of the pouch, which did not belong to him, had a hidden riddle message for him. The coin showed a picture of King Edward and the spur told him to get away quickly. Bruce learned that Comyn had told the king of their bargain, and on his return, met Comyn's messenger and killed him. Documents that the messenger was taking to the king proved Bruce's part in the plot.

After eight years of battles, Bruce became the best loved Scottish king.

The story "The Lothly Lady" by Chaucer is found in Westwood's *Medieval Tales*. King Arthur's queen spared the life of a knight condemned to die if the knight would answer the question found on page 26, "What is it that women most desire?" The knight was given his freedom and a year to find the answer. The knight heard many answers but finally he gave the correct one—"to gain mastery over men." The knight received this answer from an old hag who only gave him the answer if he would promise her whatever she asked. Horrified when she asked to marry him, he married her in secret. The hag gave the knight a choice—to have her old and true or young, fair, and faithless. The knight told her to choose and finally she had mastery over him. The hag chose to be young and true and changed herself into a beautiful maiden that the knight grew to love.

Another tale about knights is "The Riddle of the Black Knight," in Leekley's *The Riddle of the Black Knight, Tales and Fables from the Middle Ages*. The theory of innkeeper John of Wandlesbury was correct. The riddle of the Black Knight was that anyone who was a coward and still sought to defeat the Black Knight would win. Charles and Andrew had come to find the Black Knight who had killed their brother Albert and many others. Even though he was older, Charles let Andrew fight the Black Knight; when Andrew was wounded, Charles stood by paralyzed with fear. When Charles went back alone, he showed his courage and thus defeated the Black Knight. The story could be adapted for an action filled dramatic episode.

The last riddle does not come from the middle ages but from earlier sources of Jewish and Islamic tradition. The Queen of Sheba put three riddles to Solomon so he could show that he was wiser than all men. The three riddles reported in"King Solomon and the Queen of Sheba," found in Nahmad's *A Portion in Paradise*, are not necessarily the same as the riddles reported in other sources. For more information on Solomon and Sheba consult pages 942 and 943 of the article on riddles in the *Funk and Wagnalls Standard Dictionary of Folklore, Mythology and Legend*.

A RIDDLE STORY TO READ ALOUD.   If you have time to read only one riddle story aloud that would introduce students to all the other riddle stories listed in this chapter, the first choice would be A.A. Milne's "Prince Rabbit" found on pages 19 to 39 of Johnson's *The Harper Book of Princes*. The story is best enjoyed by children who know that seven times six is forty-two and not fifty-four.

In "Prince Rabbit" the king, who has no heirs, seeks one by putting several tests to anyone who is under twenty years of age, has a pedigree, and is ambitious to be the king's successor. The first test is a race which is won by a rabbit. The rabbit was allowed to enter the contest because he met the qualifications. The second place winner was Lord Calomel, so the next contest was between Lord Calomel and the rabbit. They fought with swords and rabbit gave Lord Calomel a broken arm and a sprained foot. Because Lord Calomel was in no shape for further physical contests, the next contest was a test of intelligence. Rabbit tricked the king in the first riddle even though the answer was given on a slip of paper to Lord Calomel. The next riddle was what was seven times six and Lord Calomel answered "54" so rabbit was in a predicament. If he gave the right answer, the king could declare him wrong, if he gave the wrong answer, he could also be declared wrong. The last contest includes excitement including Lord Calomel's being changed into a rabbit and a surprise ending that will be cheered by all listeners.

Reading this story to students could be an inducement to students to read other stories in *The Harper Book of Princes* or to read other stories containing riddles. This story could also be included in a festival of A.A. Milne's stories, especially *Winnie-the-Pooh*. Another selection to read aloud is Chapter 5 of *The Hobbit*, "Riddles in the Dark." Use that chapter to introduce other books by Tolkien.

NOODLEHEAD STORIES.   Librarians and media specialists are frequently asked by children and also by young adults for a story that is "funny." Such a story is very difficult to provide, for what seems humorous to one person may very well not seem humorous to another. However, there are some silly stories called "noodlehead stories" that often make people laugh. These stories are widespread because there are, and always have been, silly people throughout the world. Read Korty's *Silly Soup*, which includes plays and songs suitable for a unit that includes noodlehead stories.

SILLY FINNISH STORIES.   Sometimes these silly people live in an isolated part of the country as do the Finnish people from the nonexistent town of Holoma. "The Wise Men of Holoma" in Bowman's *Tales from a Finnish Tupa* (pp. 220-30) are also found in the picture book by Bowman and Bianca called

Seven Silly Wise Men. In these stories Matti was on the scene when the Hol-molaiset had nothing to eat but porridge. They needed a big kettle so they chopped a hole in the ice and poured the meal into the hole. When the cook slipped on the ice, fell into the hole and didn't return, the others followed one by one because they thought the greedy cook was down at the bottom of the lake eating up all the porridge. The story ends by saying that for all we know, they might be there arguing at the bottom of the lake even to this very day.

The second story in *Seven Silly Wise Men* and *Tales from a Finnish Tupa* can also be found in a picture book told by Carson and Wigg called *We Want Sunshine in Our Houses.* This picture book is told in the meter of the Finnish saga *Kalevala,* familiar because it is the same meter found in Longfellow's "Hiawatha." The story line is very simple. The people built their houses but the houses were dark inside because there were no windows. When the people saw that one window brought in some light, they decided that many windows would bring in much light. So the silly people knocked their houses down trying to make them all windows. Either of these picture books could be used to introduce other Finnish folklore or other tales about silly people.

Another picture book based on Finnish folklore is Bowman and Bianco's *Who Was Tricked?* based on the story "Pekka and the Rogues" also found in *Tales from a Finnish Tupa.*

There are stories listed under the heading of "Other Droll Stories" in Bowman's *Tales from a Finnish Tupa:* "Finland's Greatest Fisherman," "The Pig-Headed Wife," and "Stupid Peikko." In the last story, Peikko tricked Matti into staying to guard his gold while Peikko went to a wedding. Matti brought the door to the wedding because he swore he wouldn't leave the door out of his sight for a single instant. A similar incident occurs in the story "The Wise Men of Gotham" in Baldwin's *Favorite Tales of Long Ago.*

FINDING SOMEONE SILLIER.   A silly story about taking an animal to market is Chase's picture book *Jack and the Three Sillies.* Richard Chase, well-known folklorist of *Jack Tales* and *Grandfather Tales,* collected mountain stories of North Carolina, Virginia, and the Cumberlands. This picture book is the only story in which Jack is married.

Jack took a cow worth fifty dollars to market but traded it for a pig, goose, cat, and stone as each in turn grew unruly. His wife was angry with him for bringing home a stone, so she left home saying she was not coming back until she could find three men as silly as her husband and until she could get her money back. The wife found a man who wanted to get ropes to drag the moon out of the pond. She told him she would hire people to help him so he gave her ten dollars. The wife saw a woman who was using her husband for a plow mule and their mule for riding. For fifteen dollars she taught the couple how to hitch up the mule. The wife received twenty-five dollars from a man who was so grateful that she taught his wife how to make a neck hole in his shirt instead of beating his head through with a stick every time she made a shirt.

Another variation of this theme is about a young man who finds his fiance and her parents so silly that he goes away to find three others as silly before he will marry her.

Lang's story on pages 186 to 88 of *The Red Fairy Book* is called "The Six Sillies." The young man is disgusted because his girl friend and parents are crying and letting all the beer run out of the keg because all the names in the calendar are taken and they won't know what to name their child when they marry. The three silly people that the young man found were someone trying to load a cart with walnuts by knocking them down and trying to put them into the wagon with forks; a man trying to get his pig to climb a tree to eat acorns; and a man trying to jump into his trousers that were fastened to a tree. A similar story is on pages 177 to 181 of Sideman's *Anthology of the World's Best Fairy Tales*.

"The Three Sillies" found on pages 205 and 206 of Johnson's *Anthology of Children's Literature* is taken from Jacobs's *English Fairy Tales*. The girl and her parents were crying because a mallet might fall down and kill her unborn son if he should ever come down to the cellar to draw beer. The young man left to find three sillier—a woman who pastured her cow on the roof, a man who tried to jump into his trousers, and people who tried to get the moon's reflection out of the pond. This is the most common version and varies slightly in other versions. In "The Three Sillies" on pages 75 to 79 of Corcoran's *Folk Tales of England* the girl is crying because a hammer might fall and kill her unborn son when he went to the cellar for cider. Steele's "The Three Sillies" on pages 73 to 78 of *English Fairy Tales* includes a mallet and cider. In a story by the same name on pages 249 to 254 of Williams-Ellis's *Fairy Tales from the British Isles*, an axe might kill the son while he is in the cellar getting beer. The same incidents are included in Zemach's picture book *The Three Sillies*. Suggestions for vocabulary, questions, and activities for the paperback edition of this book are given for primary and intermediate students on pages 155 to 157 of Yeager's *Using Picture Books with Children*.

The story "The Three Great Noodles" found on pages 154 to 156 of Fitzgerald's *World Tales for Creative Dramatics and Storytelling* and originally found in Clouston's *The Book of Noodles* has a slightly different twist. The bride goes into the cellar to get wine during the wedding feast and does not return because she is afraid her unborn son named Bastianelo might die. The three sillies or noodles that the groom found were someone trying to fill a pail of water with a sieve, someone jumping into breeches, and a bride who was too tall for a gate so that they either had to cut off her head or the horse's legs.

SILLY SIMPLETONS.   Sometimes "Simpleton" stories can be used to introduce other stories about simpletons. The story "Simpletons" found in Mehdevi's *Persian Folk and Fairy Tales* could be used with stories from the section of this chapter called "Simpletons Answer the Riddles." Two other anthologies to introduce to a class are Clouston's *Book of Noodles: Stories of Simpletons* and Grimms' *About Wise Men and Simpletons*.

One silly story could be used to introduce students to other stories in a collection. For example, Howard Pyle's "The Simpleton and His Little Black Hen," pages 44 to 57 of Fenner's *Time to Laugh, Funny Tales from Here and There* could be used to introduce the other nineteen stories in the book. One of those other stories is "The Emperor's New Clothes."

In "The Simpleton and His Little Black Hen" Casper was the simple brother and John and James were greedy and clever. When the two greedy brothers divided up the family holdings, all they gave Casper was a little black hen. Casper took the hen to the fair to sell it and buy eggs so he could have more chicks to have more eggs and chicks. That part of the story reminds us of *Don't Count Your Chicks*, the picture book illustrated by the d'Aulaires. On the way to the fair, a landlord talked Casper into giving him the hen. In return the landlord promised Casper that if he tied his hen to a tree he could come back the next day for gold and silver. When Casper returned, there was no gold or silver until he chopped down the tree and accidentally found a robber's cache. Then the brothers and the landlord fought over the money. The money brought them all to the attention of the king. When the king and his daughter heard the story from Casper, the princess laughed and laughed. The king had promised her hand in marriage to anyone who made her laugh. Instead, they asked Casper what he would take instead of the princess. The king was insulted when Casper, who already had a girl friend, asked for ten dollars. Finally Casper outwits his brothers and the landlord and the king takes the culprits away and whips them.

MEN OF GOTHAM. Some other seemingly silly men who outwit a king were the men of Gotham. "The Wise Men of Gotham" only pretended they were stupid so the king wouldn't cut off their noses because they cut down trees to block the king's way. When the king sent his sheriff to investigate, the men of Gotham all pretended they were fools. Some rolled stones uphill to make the sun rise while others built a wall to keep the cuckoo bird from straying. One man carried a door on his back so robbers wouldn't break it open and get in and steal his money. This story is found on pages 21 to 27 of Baldwin's *Favorite Tales of Long Ago*.

Leach's *Noodles, Nitwits and Numskulls*, pages 30-37, includes the same background information about why the men of Gotham pretended to be fools. Their "proof" included building a wall to contain a bird. Another was that after twelve of them went swimming they each counted the others and found that there were only eleven. Another one-page story about these men is called "Drowning the Eel." The men threw the eel into the pond to drown him because the eel ate their fish.

In "A Fine Cheese" one of the men of Gotham saw a cheese in the pond so they tried to get it out with rakes. The cheese was the moon. In "Lightening the Load" the man riding a donkey with a sack of meal decided to lighten the load by putting the sack on his shoulders instead of across the donkey's back.

A four-line verse about three "Wise Men of Gotham" is found on page 22 of Johnson's *Anthology of Children's Literature*.

In Jagendorf's *Noodlehead Stories*, the wise men of Gotham argued whether or not sheep were to go over a bridge even though the men did not own any sheep. This is the first of five stories about the men of Gotham. Other stories that are the same as those already mentioned are "Of Hedging a Cuckoo," "Of Drowning Eels," and "Of Counting." Two stories that are different are "Of

Sending Cheeses" and "Of Sending Rent." In the first story a man of Gotham dropped a cheese and it rolled down the hill so he told his other cheeses to roll to the market and meet him there. He hasn't seen them since. In the other story, one of the men forgot to pay his landlord so he attached the money and a letter with directions to a hare. He also did not see his property again.

These stories could be compared to other stories about the men of Gotham or could be used to introduce the other sixty-four stories in Noodlehead Stories. The story about the sheep is also found on pages 203 to 208 of Steele's English Fairy Tales. Also see pages 88 and 89 of Fitzgerald's Tales of the World, A Collection of Fifty One-Act Plays for a play called "The Wise People of Gotham."

SILLY COUNTERS.   It has already been mentioned that Jagendorf's Noodlehead Stories contains the story "Of Counting" in which the men count to see if everyone is there but each forgets to count himself. A picture book by Elkin called Six Foolish Fishermen is available in paperback and hardback. Each edition has a different artist and the words in the paperback have been simplified. The six brothers decide to go fishing on a boat, raft, log, bridge, rock, and bank. When it is time to go, they count and recount but only count five. Finally a little boy counts six of them, and they are so delighted that they give him all their fish. This book provides easy reading with much practice in counting for beginning readers.

MISTAKEN REFLECTIONS.   The tale about the moon falling into the pond when people are really seeing its reflection is common to several stories. In Leach's Noodles, Nitwits and Numskulls, page 39, a man tried to drag the moon out of the pond with a net. This story could be used to introduce the sixteen other stories about silly peole that are found in Leach's book. The fifty-third story found on pages 249 to 252 of Jagendorf's Noodlehead Stories is a Spanish story about people who were afraid the donkey drinking from the pool had drunk up the moon when it was hidden behind a cloud. That story could be used to introduce the entire book of noodle stories.

In Holl's The Rain Puddle illustrated by Roger Duvoisin, a hen saw her reflection in a rain puddle and thought another hen had fallen in. While they were all excited, the sun came out and dried up the puddle.

Another picture book in which you could compare reflection scenes is a picture book illustrated by Barbara Cooney called Squawk to the Moon, Little Goose by Preston. The little gosling disobeyed his mother and went outside at night. He ran to the farmer first to tell the farmer that the fox had swallowed the moon and later to tell the farmer that the moon had fallen into the pond. Just as when the boy cried "Wolf! Wolf!" in another story, the farmer paid no attention when he heard the gosling crying out that the fox was abducting him. The fox was tricked into letting the gosling go when the gosling promised the fox a big round cheese. The cheese of course was the moon. See also Leach's "A Fine Cheese" in Noodles, Nitwits and Numskulls.

The four stories about reflections could be read and their similarities and differences could be discussed as a whole class or in smaller groups. If the small groups included four children, each one could tell his version to the others, and they could list differences and similarities.

IDENTIFYING THEMES OF NOODLEHEAD STORIES.   After students have read one or two stories or heard them told by their teachers or their peers, they can identify similar themes or motifs in these stories. Each student should be able to write the title of the story, the anthology from which it comes, the editor of the anthology, and the page numbers. Only the editor's names are mentioned here.

1. In which stories is a house built without any provision for light within the house? (Bowman *Seven*, Bowman *Tales*, Carlson)
2. In which stories does someone go out to sell an animal (cow or hen)? (Bowman *Who*, Chase, Fenner)
3. Which story had silly men jumping into their trousers? (Corcoran, Fitzgerald, Jacobs, Johnson, Lang, Steele, Williams-Ellis, Zemach)
4. In which stories is a cow pastured on the roof? (Corcoran, Jacobs, Johnson Steele, Williams-Ellis, Zemach)
5. In which stories was a moon or a reflection seen in a pond? (Chase, Corcoran, Holl, Jacobs, Jagendorf, Johnson, Leach, Preston, Steele, Williams-Ellis, Zemach)
6. In which stories did the persons return home richer than when they left? (Chase, Mehdevi)
7. In which stories was there a bride who was too tall? (Fitzgerald, Mehdevi)
8. In which stories does the cheese fall into the pond? (Leach, Preston)
9. In which stories do people who count to see if everyone is there forget to count themselves? (Elkin, Jagendorf, Leach)
10. In which stories does a man take a door with him so he doesn't let it out of his sight? (Baldwin, Bowman *Tales*)
11. In which stories do men argue about sheep they do not possess? (Jagendorf, Steele)
12. In which stories do men build a wall to keep in a bird? (Baldwin, Jagendorf, Leach)

THE RIDDLE OF COMMUNICATION.   Through the centuries, mankind has devised methods of communication and in each case the message must be encoded and decoded. To anyone who does not know the encoding and decoding procedures, the message is a mystery or riddle. Chapter 7 of Meadows's *Sounds and Signals: How We Communicate* addresses itself to the English language as a code.

Some of these communication methods include written alphabets, pictures, dots and dashes, flags, hand signals, raised dots, codes, ciphers, and symbols.

INTRODUCING THE UNIT WITH A FOLK TALE.   Folk tales can be interesting introductions to units of work, and "The Witless Imitator" makes an excellent introduction to a unit that includes hieroglyphics, rebus characters, Indian picture writing, Chinese and Japanese calligraphy, cattle brands, alphabets, codes and ciphers, Braille, deaf sign language, and Morse code, among others.

The story "The Witless Imitator" found on pages 18 to 20 of Hsieh's *Chinese Village Folk Tales* is about a teacher who deciphered a note written in hieroglyphic or rebus form. A young teacher who had been given his wages was on his way home to his wife and family when he saw a crying woman and an infant. The teacher gave them his money so he had to go out and get a job as a cooper during the holidays so he would have enough money for his own family. The teacher was mending a washtub at the home of an old illiterate couple who had a letter that he deciphered for them. The hieroglyphics depicted a goose beside a bed of lettuce, an old man watching the goose, a river with a plum tree on the bank, and four turtles under the plum tree. The interpretation given on page 19 is the symbol of humble acknowledgement of having been bought and reared, as one gets and feeds a goose on the products of one's garden. Then, you are expecting to hear from your son, since this old man looks toward the goose. You expect money from him, and may get it from the hands of Mr. Plum, who lives beside the river. That is shown by the plum tree depicted on the bank of the stream. He has received sixteen dollars for you, and this is indicated by the legs of the four turtles, four times four.

The old couple gave the teacher a boar's head as payment for deciphering the letter. The teacher then made up a poem about the head; the old couple enjoyed the poem so much that they gave him ten ounces of silver. When the regular cooper went to work the next day he decided to use the poem so he also could receive monetary rewards. However, the obese wife of his client did not enjoy the poem which read:

> Eyes sunk in fat; nose broad and flat;
> Cheeks that a pudgy width of jaw display;
> Ears standing out, hairy and stout;
> I'll take it home, and make a holiday. [p. 19]

The moral of the story is given in the last sentence on page 20. "We must learn to appreciate that the learned may ply the tools of the tradesman, but the illiterate cannot safely apply the wit of the wise."

OBJECTIVES AND ACTIVITIES.   The overall objective of a communication riddle unit is that students come to understand that there are various methods of communication. By the end of the unit students will be able to recognize the names and symbols for over a dozen of these methods. Each student will choose from a list of topics presented in the next section, research the topic, and bring back visual as well as verbal background information to the class. The visual can include showing relevant pages of books (using the opaque projector), one or more transparencies, or charts made by the students. In some instances, such as a report on the semaphore alphabet, a demonstration may be the most logical visual presentation.

The leader may ask students to transcribe the same sentence into their selected communication system. Possible sentences could be "I see three men on horses approaching" or "It will rain here today." If the messages were placed on 8-by-11-inch sheets of paper, then all the sheets could be bound together to form a booklet. However, not all students will be able to find the correct letters or symbols to encode the same message.

An important feature of this unit is that there is such a wide range of materials available so the students can cover the surface or conduct in-depth research. One student may be able just to identify what "hieroglyphics" means and provide a chart showing examples. Another student may complete a thorough researching of Champollion and how he solved the mystery of the Rosetta Stone or the deciphering of many codes such as Linear B. Enrichment activities such as reading a story about codes and ciphers by Doyle or Poe provide additional activities for advanced students.

Three books vital to the assignment are Dreyfuss's *Symbol Sourcebook*, Adkin's *Symbols: A Silent Language*, and Myller's *Symbols and Their Meaning*. Archen's *Symbols Around Us* is for teacher use.

TOPICS

1. Ancient alphabets (Sumerian, Phoenician, Greek, Roman)
2. Egyptian hieroglyphics
3. Breaking the Egyptian hieroglyphic code (Napoleon, Champollion, Young, Rosetta Stone)
4. Chinese and Japanese calligraphy
5. Transposition ciphers
6. Substitution ciphers
7. Caesar's cipher
8. Other ciphers
9. Multiplication codes
10. Position codes
11. Code machines
12. Other codes
13. Morse code
14. Indian sign language, smoke signals, and picture writings
15. Flag symbols, including the semaphore alphabet
16. Braille alphabet
17. Deaf sign language alphabet
18. Rebus
19. Cattle brands
20. Athletic signals
21. Hobo or tramp signs
22. International road signs, pictorial direction signs, traffic signals
23. Pig Latin
24. ITA—Initial Teaching Alphabet
25. IPA—International Phonetic Alphabet
26. Musical notes
27. Mathematical signs

28. Cave paintings
29. Religious, including Zodiac and astrology.
(If there are more students, have several persons work on numbers 2, 3, 5, 6, and 9.)

ENCYCLOPEDIA REFERENCES.   This project is excellent for reinforcing skills in using encyclopedias because the topics are found in a variety of places that require the use of indexes and see references. The following chart shows just four of the topics with the headings under which the illustrations of each are found.

	COMPTON'S 1976	NEW BOOK OF KNOWLEDGE 1977	WORLD BOOK 1976
Brands	Cattle Ranching	none	Ranching
Braille			
Alphabet	Blind	Blind	Braille
Hieroglyphics	Egyptian	Communication	Hieroglyphics
Morse Code	Telegraph	Radio, Amateur	Morse Code

HISTORY OF WRITING.   The easiest book on the history of writing is Taylor's *Wht's yr nm?* Excellent drawings, show cavemen pictures, pictographs, idea writings, rebus, Egyptian hieroglyphics, Phoenician alphabet, early Greek alphabet, classic Greek alphabet, early and classic Roman alphabet, and international signs. A time line at the end of the book enhances its value. Although the book was intended for intermediate students, it can also be understood by some primary students.

Regardless of the age of the students, leaders will wish to consult William and Rhoda Cahn's *The Story of Picture Writings from Cave to Computer* as a basic source. The book has a glossary, bibliography, and index as well as many drawings and diagrams. Diagrams are given for ideograms, picture writings of Egypt, Mesopotamia, China, cuneiform of the Sumerians, as well as hieroglyphics. Early alphabets of the Phoenicians, Greeks, Etruscans, and Romans are shown. A three-page colored diagram of the origin of the English alphabet and its relationship to other alphabetic scripts is given. Examples of the Bengali, Amharic, and Cyrillic alphabets are given. Writings in the middle ages, the development of printing, and computer printing are shown in photos and diagrams.

Helfman's *Signs and Symbols around the World* also gives a chart for seven words in the Sumerian, Egyptian, Chinese, and American Indian languages on page 50. On page 52 a chart of four words in Egyptian, Semitic, Phoenician, Greek, and Roman is given. Dugan's *How Our Alphabet Grew, the History of the Alphabet* is also a basic book. Ogg's *The 26 Letters* is a calligrapher's approach to the history of writing.

EGYPTIAN HIEROGLYPHICS.   Bauman says on page 51 of *The World of the Pharaohs* that ". . . hieroglyphics were alphabet scripts which had developed out of picture writing." Bauman includes colored illustrations throughout the book. Also, the names of the upper Egyptian provinces are written out on pages 72 and 73. In the chapter called "Decipher of the Hieroglyphics" on pages 47 to 56, thirteen-year-old Megdi and his father have a dialogue on how the riddle of hieroglyphics was solved.

Many sources besides Cahn and Bauman contain information about ancient Egyptian hieroglyphics. Asimov's *Egyptians* tells how Champollion cracked the secret of the Rosetta Stone early in the nineteenth century. Robinson's *First Book of Ancient Egypt* also tells about the Rosetta Stone. Chapter 2, "The-Not-So-Easy Task" of Mellersch's *Finding Out About Ancient Egypt* also tells how Young and Champollion deciphered the riddle of hieroglyphics. Pages 26 to 28 tell how Young and Champollion used the rebus idea to spell out the pictures and how they used the name of Ptolemy as a key. Other features of that book include how pictures developed into writing, and the index is very helpful. Pages 79 to 86 of Folsom's *The Language Book* is called "Detectives, Clues and Broken Codes" and gives the chronological steps in solving the riddle of hieroglyphics.

The main contribution of the Horizon book called *Pharaohs of Egypt* is the many pictures, including one of the Rosetta Stone. Many are in color and some include more than one page. Frimmer's book *The Stone That Spoke* shows the characters for Ptolemy's name on pages 43 and 44 but has few diagrams. The chief value of Frimmer's book is the first eight chapters, through page 72, which tells about deciphering hieroglyphics.

Scott's *Hieroglyphics for Fun* tells how to draw hieroglyphics and gives an adaptation of a tale written in hieroglyphics.

JAPANESE AND CHINESE CALLIGRAPHY.   The best explanation of Chinese calligraphy is given in Mars's *Chinese Tales of Folklore* in a chapter called "How Pictures Become Words." For pictures of Chinese characters note that Chinese characters are given lengthwise on the pages in Hyndman's *Chinese Mother Goose Rhymes*. Some of the rhymes in the book are riddles. Also consult Wolff's *Chinese Writing* and Wiese's *You Can Write Chinese*. Page 111 of Folsom's *The Language Book* shows numbers from 1 to 10. See also Colby's *Communication, How Man Talks to Man* and Hogben's *Wonderful World of Communication*. The *"Table of Contents"* in *Symbol Sourcebook* by Dreyfuss is written in eighteen languages, six of which use an alphabet other than ours. Japanese characters are often given in books of haiku poetry.

AMERICAN INDIAN PICTURE WRITINGS, SIGN LANGUAGE AND SMOKE SIGNALS.   The best book about picture writings of the American Indian is Hofsinde's book called *Indian Picture Writing*. There are 248 symbols and their meanings, including the Cree alphabet in the book. Pages 7 to 10 provide a useful introduction for leader and student. Pages 27 to 36 of Helfman's *Signs and Symbols Around the World* also includes information about Indian symbols. See the index of Cahns's *The Story of Writing* for information about North and

South American Indians.

The best book explaining the sign language of the North American Indian is Hofsinde's *Indian Sign Language*. Consult Coggins's *Flashes and Flags, the Story of Signaling* and Batchelor's *Communication: From Cave Writing to Television* for information about Indian smoke signals. This section could also be part of a unit on Indians. Goaman's *How Writing Began* includes information about picture writing and wampum. Many colored illustrations enhance Fronval & Dubois's *Indian Signs* and signals which includes feathers, blankets, trail signs, body paint, and smoke signals.

REBUS WRITINGS.   *Webster's New Collegiate Dictionary* defines "rebus" as follows: "A mode of expressing words and phrases by pictures or objects whose names resemble those words, or the syllables of which they are composed; hence, a form of riddle made up of such representations."

Making rebus stories or retelling stories in rebus form could be an interesting combined language arts and art project. Two picture books that could serve as models are Quackenbush's *Go Tell Aunt Rhody* and Low's *Mother Goose Riddle Rhymes*. The first book is a retelling of an old folk song; the second presents twenty-two Mother Goose rhymes in rebus form. Older students may wish to consult books on hieroglyphics in the section of this chapter called "Egyptian Hieroglyphics."

Wiesner's *Riddle Pot* contains rebus puzzles on pages 33, 36, 41, 51, 57, 71, 83, 93, and 100. Taylor's book *Wht's yr nm?* tells about picture writing but emphasizes sound or rebus writing. Helfman's *Signs and Symbols Around the World* gives examples on pages 53 and 45. Pages 32 and 33 of the Cahns' book *The Story of Writing* tell about the rebus or phonogram. Also consult Batchelor's *Communication: From Cave Writings to Televison.*

CATTLE BRANDS AND TRAMP OR HOBO SIGNS.   Besides the five cattle brands shown on page 11 of the Cahns' *The Story of Writing*, there are twenty brands in the Epsteins' *First Book of Codes and Ciphers*. The American Heritage book edited by Ward and Dykes called *Cowboys and Cattle Country* has several pages listed in the index. Twenty-four brands are shown on pages 134 and 135. Grant's *Cowboy Encyclopedia* shows 48 brands on page 30 and also tells about brands, branding irons, earmarks, mavericks, and rustlers.

Students could combine this topic with hobo and tramp signs. Three sources are the Epsteins' *First Book of Codes and Ciphers*, Goaman's *How Writing Began*, and Kohn's *Secret Codes and Ciphers*.

CODES AND CIPHERS IN LITERATURE.   The Epsteins' *First Book of Codes and Ciphers* refers to two famous stories about codes and ciphers: Sir Arthur Conan Doyle's "The Adventure of the Dancing Men" and Edgar Allen Poe's "The Gold Bug." Pallas's *Code Games* also refers to the fingerprinted words from the Sherlock Holmes adventure. Pallas mentions that the Gloria Scott System is named after Holmes. Both stories are found in Bond's *Famous Stories of Code and Cipher.*

The story about Sherlock Holmes is found in the following collections of Doyle: *Complete Sherlock Holmes, Return of Sherlock Holmes,* and *Treasury of Sherlock Holmes.* The first book is currently available in hardback or paperback edition, while the second is out of print in hardcover but available in paperback.

Poe's "The Gold Bug" is listed in twenty-six different editions of Poe in the main volume of *Short Story Index* as well as having at least one edition listed in each of the supplements. One edition that has an illustrated dictionary in the margin is Poe's *The Gold Bug and Other Tales and Poems,* published by Children's Press. A new Macmillan edition called *Tales and Poems of Edgar Allan Poe* is available. A paperback edition called *The Goldbug and Other Stories* is published by Branden. The Dutton edition illustrated by Arthur Rackham in the Children's Illustrated Classics series is called *Tales of Terror and Fantasy, Ten Stories from Mystery and Imagination. Tales of Mystery and Imagination* is available in both paperback and hard cover.

In Poe's "The Gold Bug," Legrand finds that a piece of parchment, when heated, shows a message in cipher language. The story tells how Legrand constructed a table to break the cipher, read the message and dig up Captain Kidd's treasure of coins and jewels.

Of the two stories, Doyle's "The Adventure of the Dancing Men" is the easiest to read silently to oneself. In the story, a man comes to Sherlock Holmes with some figures of men that look like a code. Readers learn that Holmes has written a monograph in which he analyzes 160 different ciphers. Holmes easily broke the code because *E* is the most common letter in the alphabet and the man's wife was named "Elsie." Watson and Holmes arrived too late to save the man but saved the wife from being accused of her husband's murder.

CODES AND CIPHERS.   Besides the Epstein and Pallas books there are others which include making and breaking codes. Kohn's *Secret Codes and Ciphers* includes eight different codes and ciphers, both dictionary and machine, and includes concealment, transportation, and substitution. A useful table in the appendix shows English letter and word frequency. Rothman's *Secrets and Ciphers and Codes* includes ten different codes, while Albert's *Secret Codes for Kids* includes twenty-nine different codes. Peterson's *How to Write Codes and Send Secret Messages* is available in paperback and hard cover. Pages 112 and 113 of Zarchy's *Using Electronics* contains cipher and telegraph codes. Chapter 8 of Kohl's *A Book of Puzzlements: Play and Invention with Language* is called "Codes and Ciphers."

Two highly respected authors of code books are Zim and Gardner. Zim's *Codes and Secret Writing* has a chapter called "Multiplication Table Codes." Pallas also includes problems for a math class on pages 79 to 86. Both Pallas and Zim include the Rail-Fence codes. Gardner includes a section on Interplanetary Communication in his books *Codes, Ciphers and Secret Writings* and *Games from Scientific American.* Gardner in the first of these two books has information on transposition, substitution, polyalphabetics, code machines, and historical methods. The books by the Epsteins, Gardner, Peterson, and Zim contain sections on invisible writing.

Books of interest to primary students are Peterson's *How to Write Codes and Send Secret Messages,* Taylor's *Wht's yr nm?* and Myrock's *The Secret Three.* Peterson's directions are easy enough to follow for second graders and include information on space codes, hidden word codes, Greek Code, Alphabet Codes, invisible ink, and ways to deliver the message. Many samples are included. Even the dedication is a message in Morse code to the radio men of the 127th Airborne Engineer Battalion 11th Airborne Division. There is a secret message on the cover that can be decoded by placing red cellophane over the title. Taylor's book contains excellent illustrations from cavemen pictures to modern international signs. Myrick's book is from the I Can Read series and is about a message in a bottle at the beach that is decoded by two boys who hold the message in front of a mirror. The boys answer the message in alphabet code. Several messages later they form a club with another boy and make up a secret club with a secret handshake and a name made up of parts of their names. The book contains excellent messages in code.

PIG LATIN.   Pig Latin is a simple code. Chapter 8, "Fun and Games with Words" from Kohn's *What a Funny Thing to Say,* contains information about Pig Latin. Other sources are pages 51 to 53 of Epstein's *First Book of Codes and Ciphers* and Folsom's *The Language Book,* page 182. Also consult Rothman and Tremain's *Secrets with Ciphers and Codes.*

MORSE CODE.   Three books which give the Morse Code are the Epsteins' *First Book of Codes and Ciphers* (pp. 29–30), Folsom's *The Language Book,* (p. 140), and the Cahns' *The Story of Writing* (p.116). A rough drawing of Morse's alphabet is given on page 33 of Hays's *Samuel Morse and the Telegraph.* Page 54 of that same book shows the first official telegraph message, "What Hath God Wrought." Another biographical source of information about Morse can be found on pages 228 to 238 of Cottler and Jaffee's *Heros of Civilization.* The second biographical reference is the more difficult. Also see Batchelor's *Communication: From Cave Writing to Television.*

THE BRAILLE ALPHABET.   Biographies of Louis Braille, the inventor of a system of reading for the blind, in the order of difficulty, include Davidson's *Louis Braille, the Boy Who Invented Books for the Blind,* Niemark's *Touch of Light,* DeGering's *Seeing Fingers,* and Kugelmass's *Louis Braille.* Encyclopedia listings under "Braille" or "Blindness" show the Braille system.

SIGN LANGUAGE FOR THE DEAF.   The complete alphabet and numbers in sign language are found on page 44 of Folsom's *The Language Book.* However, the most exciting book on sign language is Charlip's *Handbook, an ABC of Finger Spelling and Sign Language.* Colored photographs show each letter of the alphabet. Then at the bottom of the page, a word is given that begins with that letter and is made up of letters already used so far in the book. Check the bibliography to this book for more information on Charlip's book.

See Batchelor's *Communication: From Cave Writing to Television* for more information about sign language. Students may want to compare sign language for the deaf with Indian sign language.

ATHLETIC SIGNALS. Page 45 of Folsom's *The Language Book* shows coachs' and catchers' signals in baseball. Jackson's *How to Play Better Football* shows illustrations of football officials' signals. Liss's *Football Talk for Beginners* gives large diagrams of eighteen signals and violations on pages 50 to 58. Also, before the title page, symbols used in diagrams in the book are given, i.e. handoffs, blocks, and offensive and defensive plays.

Similar symbols are explained in Liss's *Basketball Talk for Beginners* in which nineteen signals are given on pages 56 to 65. Students should be encouraged to save the programs from athletic events because they often contain diagrams of referees' signals. Also consult Coggins's *Flashes and Flags, the Story of Signaling*.

FLAG SIGNALS. The semaphore alphabet contains twenty-six flag symbols that can be used in any language that uses the Latin alphabet. See pages 25 to 28 of the Epsteins' *First Book of Codes and Ciphers*, page 28 of Coggins's *Flashes and Flags, the Story of Signaling*, and pages 14 and 15 of Colby's *Communications, How Man Talks to Man*.

Also included in Colby's book is information about early signal flags and flags used in auto racing, storm warnings, and by the army. Consult boating manuals and free publications of state tourist councils for information on the use of flags in water safety. Consult page 138 of Folsom's *The Language Book* for information on international signal flags. Flag signals are also included in Batchelor's *Communication: From Cave Writing to Television*.

TRAFFIC SIGNALS. Lighthouses are discussed in Batchelor's book. Other light signals appear in Coggins's *Flashes and Flags, the Story of Signaling*. Coggins's book also contains a section on mirrors, air traffic lights, and railroad signals. International road signs appear on pages 143 to 148 of Helfman's *Signs and Symbols Around the World*. Chapter 3 of Meadow's *Sounds and Signals* is devoted to traffic signs. Consult driving manuals from individual states for hand signals used in driving automobiles, bicycles, and motorcycles.

MUSIC AND MATHEMATICS. Besides using a variety of music textbooks, use Craig's *The Story of Musical Notes*. The book gives the current system of whole, half, quarter, eighth, and sixteenth notes. Also included are early ways of writing music, square notes, Gregorian notation, diamond notes, syllables, and Fasola and Buckwheat notations.

Musical and mathematical notations are given on page 140 of Folsom's *The Language Book*. In addition to studying mathematical codes from the code books, students may wish to check mathematical textbooks and dictionaries for mathematical symbols. The following show numbers in several cultures, past and present: Jonas's *More New Ways in Mathematics*, Kenyon's *I Can Read About Calculators and Computers*, St. John's *How to Count Like a Martian*,

Simon's *The Day the Numbers Disappeared,* and Feravolo's *Wonders of Mathematics.* Feravolo's book also lists mathematical symbols on pages 61 and 62.

DeRossi's *Computers, Tools for Today* contains an excellent overview of computers. Simple symbols are given about computers in Spencer's *Story of Computers.* Cohen's *The Human Side of Computers* and Meadow's *The Story of Computers* contain two- and four-page bibliographies.

MAGIC NUMBERS IN FOLKLORE—A PROGRAM OF STORIES TO TELL OR READ.   This list of stories from anthologies or individual picture books provides a program for students from kindergarten to sixth grade. With the exception of poems and riddles for the number "eleven," most of the stories are traditional or modern folktales. The thirteen stories can be read or told on a planned daily or weekly schedule. The stories are divided into appropriate grade levels for better results, as well as to avoid repetition of stories from grade to grade. If the following plan were adopted in a school, it could be used for grades 1 and 3 and 6 or 5 or for grades K, 2, 4, or any combination which avoids duplication.

The program provides excellent motivation for students to read other stories containing a given number after the initial story is read or told to them. An entire network of stories is included in the number categories. Over a dozen stories containing the number seven are described and located. There are often variations of those stories. For example, stories about the Pleiades or *seven sisters* are included from the following traditions: Australia, Greece, Brazil, Cherokee, Iroquois, Cheyenne, Navajo, Wabonski, and Dyak. Each of the *Five Chinese Brothers* has an unusual talent. After reading the picture book or telling the story to students, have them read the ten other stories about persons with unusual talents that are mentioned in that section.

Although sources are given for the stories, teachers may want to give students only the names of the stories and have them locate the stories using story indexes. Or teachers may briefly tell about each story and hand out the anthologies or picture books containing those stories. The stories might be described and the books laid out on a special table at the back of the classroom. Teachers may wish to use the stories for individualized reading. Groups of students could be assigned to read other versions and then share them individually or in groups with the rest of the class. After reading about ten versions of a story, students may wish to write their own version. This network of stories has many possibilities for creative projects.

MAGIC NUMBERS IN CHILDREN'S LITERATURE

One	(K-1)	"Dick Whittington & His Cat"
	(2-3)	"Puss in Boots"
	(4-6)	"Ulysses & the Cyclops"
Two	(K-1)	"Elves & the Shoemaker"
	(2-3)	*Jorinda & Joringel*
	(4-6)	"Icarus & Daedalus"

Three   (K-1) "Three 3 Wishes"
           (2-3) "Rumpelstiltskin"
           (4-6) *The Flea*

Four   (K-1) "Brehman Town Musicians"
           (2-3) "Bee, Harp, Mouse & Bum Clock"
           (4-6) "Ali Baba & the Forty Thieves"

Five   (K-1) *Five Chinese Brothers*
           (2-3) *500 Hats of B C*
           (4-6) "The 5 Eggs"

Six   (K-1) *Six Foolish Fishermen*
           (2-3) "The Six Sillies"
           (4-6) "Thor Gains his Hammer"

Seven   (K-1) *The Wolf & the Seven Little Kids*
           (2-3) *Seven at One Blow*
           (4-6) (Pleiades)   (7 Stars)

Eight   (K-1) *8,000 Stones*
           (2-3) "8-Headed Dragon"
           (4-6) "Sleipnir & Degasus"

Nine   (K-1) "3 Bears," "3 Billy Goats," "3 Pigs"
           (2-3) "Princess on the Glass Hill"
           (4-6) 'Nine Muses & Orpheus"

Ten   (K-1) "Baby Moses"
           (2-3) "The Donkey's Tail"
           (4-6) "The Ten Plagues & the Ten Commandments"

Eleven   (K-1) Ask eleven riddles
           (2-3) Read eleven short poems
           (4-6) *The Wild Swans*

Twelve   (K-1) "The Twelve Dancing Princesses"
           (2-3) "The 12 Months"
           (4-6) "The 12 Labors of Hercules"

Thirteen   (K-1) *Dancing in the Moon, Counting Rhymes*
           (2-3) *The Luck Book*, pp. 95–100
           (4-6) "A Dozen is 13"

MAGIC NUMBERS IN CHILDREN'S LITERATURE—ONE.   One of the first that comes to mind when one thinks of stories that include the number one is the Greek giant, the one-eyed cyclops, Polyphemus. Two stories which could be read are "Polyphemus, the Cyclops," in Thompson's *One Hundred Favorite Folktales* (pp. 377–83) and "The One-Eyed Giant" in Green's *Tales of the Greeks and Trojans* (pp. 58–59). "No Man and the Cyclops," in Wilson's *Greek Fairy Tales* (pp. 98–102) is an excellent version for reading and/or telling, and stresses the play on words in the title. Also read "The Cyclops Cave," in Evslin's *The Adventures of Ulysses* (pp. 25–33). Three complete books about Odysseus or Ulysses are Column's *The Adventures of Odysseus and the Tale of Troy*, Church's *Odyssey of Homer*, and Lang's *The Adventures of Odysseus*.

A famous tale about one unique cat from England, and another from France, can introduce each other. Read the second story if only one is read because it is the more complicated and contains the most variations, while the first is easier for readers to follow on their own. Encourage the students to read the story by telling them that a cat changed the fortunes of his master from a poor lad into a rich man.

Dick Whittington, a cook's helper, married his employer's daughter, became Sheriff, and eventually Lord Mayor of London. Dick bought a cat for a penny, it went on a voyage, and was sold to a king and queen of a country plagued by rats and mice for an amount many times the value of the ship's cargo. Marcia Brown's picture book *Dick Whittington and His Cat* is an excellent source for the story and makes a good browsing book. Kathleen Lines retold a version that is illustrated by Ardizzone. Anthologies that include the story are Haviland's *Favorite Fairy Tales Told in England*, Johnson's *Anthology of Children's Literature*, Arthur Rackham's *Fairy Book*, Reeves's *English Fables and Fairy Stories*, Martignoni's *Illustrated Treasury of Children's Literature*, and Steele's *English Fairy Tales*. The story is one of four read by Claire Bloom on the recording *Dick Whittington and His Cat and Other English Fairy Tales*, in a version by Reeves.

Marcia Brown also illustrated *Puss in Boots*. This story from Perrault was also illustrated as a picture book by Hans Fischer and also by Paul Galdone. A retelling by Craig is illustrated by Jones. The play appears in Burack's *One Hundred Plays for Children*. Other sources include de la Mare's *Animal Stories*, Haviland's *Favorite Fairy Tales Told in France*, Haviland's *Fairy Tale Treasury*, Martignoni's *Illustrated Treasury of Children's Literature*, Arthur Rackham's *Fairy Book*, Sideman's *The World's Best Fairy Tales*, *The Tasha Tudor's Book of Fairy Tales*, and Williams-Ellis's *Round the World Fairy Tales*. Three collections of Perrault's stories that contain "Puss in Boots" are *Perrault's Classic French Fairy Tales*, *Perrault's Complete Fairy Tales*, and *Famous Fairy Tales*. The youngest son was given a cat as a legacy from his father. Through much scheming, the cat made arrangements for the king to believe that his master, the Marquis of Carabas, owned much land that really belonged to an ogre. The cat eliminated the ogre and set up his master in its place. The young man married the princess of course. A Lang version called "The Master Cat," pages 355 to 357 of Nelson's *Comparative Anthology of Children's Literature*, and pages 141 to 147 of Lang's *Blue Fairy Book*, is also about the cat who changed his master into the Marquis of Carabas. Claire Bloom narrates the Reeves retelling on a recording called *Dick Whittington and His Cat and Other English Fairy Tales*.

There are other versions of the story. One has a fox as the hero. "The

Miller-King" is found on pages 13 to 26 of Tashjian's *Once There Was and Was Not*. The readable story from Armenia is about a miller who caught a fox in his trap. The miller let the fox go and the fox helped him win the princess and vast estates by using the same tactics as Puss in Boots.

MAGIC NUMBERS IN CHILDREN'S LITERATURE—*TWO*.   Characters in folk and fairy tales come in threes more often than they come in pairs. The following pairs of characters are found in stories in other sections of this book. Two stories are about two people who outwit a witch. Read the less familiar Grimm story about *Jorinda and Joringel* and have the picture book by Anglund called *Nibble Nibble Mousekin*, a version of Hansel and Gretel, available for students to read. The picture-book version of *Jorinda and Joringel* can be used. There were two elves who helped the poor shoemaker in *The Elves and the Shoemaker*. The hare and the tortoise are a very famous pair. Read the story *The Hare and the Tortoise and the Tortoise and the Hare* by DuBois because it is longer and more involved. A tortoise outwits Anansi in "Anansi and His Visitor, Turtle," in Kaula's *African Village Folktales*. Another story about greed is the story of the kind unselfish daughter and the unkind selfish stepsister in versions of "Toads and Diamonds" or *Mother Holly*. Two similar characters appear in the versions of *The Month Brothers*. More greed appears in versions of *The Fisherman and His Wife* and *The Two Stonecutters*. "The Owl and the Pussycat" were another famous pair. The first part of Twain's *The Prince and the Pauper* in which a poor boy and a prince exchange places, could be read or, the story could be paraphrased for telling.

One unfamiliar tale for telling or reading aloud is found in Arnott's *African Myths and Legends*. "The Two Brothers" went out hunting and the youngest received bullocks, goats, cows, and sheep for his helpfulness to an old woman. The older brother, jealous, would not help when he fell over a cliff, but stole his animals and told their parents that he didn't know where the younger brother was. A honeybird spoils the older brother's plan. Two other brothers appear in the version about "The Turnip" that is similar in theme to the "Toads and Diamonds" stories.

Icarus and Daedalus, father and son pair from Greek mythology, were imprisoned in the labyrinth by King Minos with no way to escape except to fly out. Daedalus makes wings of wax for each of them but cautions his son not to fly too near the sun. Icarus disobeys and melts down. Two individual books are available: Seraillier's *A Fall from the Sky; the Story of Daedalus* illustrated by Stobbs, and Farmer's *Daedalus and Icarus* illustrated by Connor. The Peabody version is available in Nelson's *Comparative Anthology of Children's Literature*. The story is included also in Benson's *Stories of the Gods and Heroes*, Bullfinch's *A Book of Myth*, Coolidge's *Greek Myths*, Evslin's *Heroes and Monsters of Greek Myths*, Graves's *Greek Gods and Heroes*, Schreiber's *Stories of Gods and Heroes*, Shippin's *Bridle for Pegasus*, and Untermeyer's *World's Greatest Stories*.

There are two main characters in the story of "King Thrushbeard." The story appears on pages 208 to 212 of *Household Stories by the Brothers Grimm*, pages 64 to 69 of *Fairy Tales*, and pages 27 to 32 of *Grimms' Fairy Tales*, and also pages 91 to 98 of Grimms' *About Wise Men and Simpletons*. Individual picture books were illustrated by Felix Hoffman and Kurt Werth, and a modern version called *King Grisly-Beard* is illustrated by Maurice Sendak. The story is about a princess who was too proud and haughty, but who learned her lesson and lived happily ever after.

This next tale is about a husband who learned a lesson. "The Husband Who Was to Mind the House" is a Scandinavian tale about a man who thought his wife's job doing housework was easier than working in the fields so he traded for a day. The results are disastrous but funny. The story appears in Arbuthnot's *Time for Fairy Tales Old and New*, Asbjornsen and Moe's *East of the Sun and West of the Moon*, Hutchinson's *Candle-light Stories*, Martignoni's *Illustrated Treasury of Children's Literature*, Thorne-Thomsen's *East o'the Sun and West o'the Moon*, and Undset's *True and Untrue*. Picture books of the same story are Wiesner's *Turnabout*, McKee's *The Man Who Was Going to Mind the House*, and Gag's *Gone is Gone*. The Gag version also appears in Haviland's *Fairy Tale Treasury*, Fenner's *Fools and Funny Fellows*, and Johnson's *Anthology of Children's Literature*. A Russian version called "How the Peasant Kept House" appears in Daniels's *The Falcon Under the Hat*. Price's *The Rich Man and the Singer* contains "The Husband Who Wanted to Mind the House," an Ethiopian story. Another African story is "When the Husband Stayed Home," from Savory's *Lion Outwitted by Hare*.

MAGIC NUMBERS IN CHILDREN'S LITERATURE—*THREE*.   The most common number appearing in folk and fairy tales, as well as in contemporary children's literature, is three. When introducing this concept to students, ask them to name other tales besides "The Three Billy Goats Gruff" that contain three animals. They will probably mention "The Three Bears," "The Three Little Pigs," "The Three Little Kittens" and "The Three Blind Mice."

Explain that there are often three magic items, such as Loki was to bring back in "Thor Gains His Hammer" included in *How and Why Stories—Thunder, Lightning and Weather*. Often people in folk literature are given three wishes. The first sections of this chapter contain many stories that include three riddles: "The Flea," "Juan Bobo and the Princess Who Answered Riddles," "Outriddling the Princess," "The Prince with the Golden Hand," "Three Princes of Serendip," "The Riddling Chief of Puma," and "The Red Etin."

Or a person might be given three tasks to perform instead of three riddles. Often there are three characters in a story or three events. Stories in these categories include *Babushka and the Three Kings; Befano*; "The Bird, Mouse and the Sausage"; "The Cat, the Cook and the Lamb"; *Fish in the Forest; The Flying Carpet; High, Wide and Handsome; Hudden Dudden and Donald O'Neary; Jack and the Three Sillies*; "The Liar's Contest"; "The Little Red Hen"; "The Three Golden Oranges"; "The Three Ravens"; "The Three Sneezes"; and "The Tiger, the Brahman, and the Jackal."

There are often three brothers or three sisters in a story. Often the youngest is mistreated and thought to be dull, but in the end that person often triumphs. "Boots and His Brothers," "Ivan the Fool," "The Three Ivans," *Salt*, "The Firebird," and "The Princess on the Glass Hill" are all stories about three sons.

Beauty chose a rose for her gift from her father, but her two sisters chose frivolous gifts in "Beauty and the Beast." *Vasilisa the Beautiful* has two mean, lazy sisters and a wicked stepmother. The wicked stepmother theme is common in folk literature and appears most often in variants of *Cinderella*, of whom Vasilissa is the Russian counterpart.

According to Nelson, in *Comparative Anthology of Children's Literature*, there are over 500 recorded European and over one hundred recorded non-European versions of the Cinderella story. Nelson includes a dozen stories in his book which also include rags to riches stories about boys. Lang's "Cinderella" and Grimms' "Ashputtel" precede a dime-store variety story, and readers are asked to compare them. Also included are Jacobs' "Tattercoats" (pp. 190–192); Cushing's "The Poor Turkey Girl (Zuni-American Indian) (pp. 192–194); Hume's "The Chinese Cinderella" (pp. 195–196) (also pages 15 to 22 of Hume's *Favorite Children's Stories from China and Tibet)*; Green's "The Girl With the Rose-Red Slippers" (Egypt) (pp. 197–198); Filmore's "The Twelve Months" (Czechoslovakia) (pp. 199–203); Arnott's "The Snake Chief" (Xhosa-Africa) (pp. 203–206); "Boots and His Brothers" (Scandinavia) (pp. 207–209); Grimms' "The Water of Life" (Germany) (pp. 209–212); and "The Princess on the Glass Hill" (Scandinavia) (pp. 212–217).

Other sources of stories that are like Cinderella are to be found in Broadman's *Cinderellas Around the World*. About fourteen stories and parallels are listed in *Stories to Tell to Children* from the Carnegie Library of Pittsburgh. Over thirty titles called "Cinderella" or "Cinderellas" are listed in Ireland's *Index to Fairy Tales, 1949–1972*.

After Cinderella stories have been read to them or students have read the stories for themselves, encourage students to write their own versions of the story. Use *Nomi and the Magic Fish* from Africa as a student-written example. The picture book was written by Phumla, a fifteen -year-old Fingo Zula girl who speaks Xhosa. Nomi had a wicked stepmother who sent her without food to tend cattle in the veld. A magic fish heard Nomi crying and offered to give Nomi and her dog bread and milk each day. By beating the dog, the stepmother learned why Nomi was strong and healthy so she asked her unsuspecting husband to kill the fish. Nomi threw the bones of the fish in the chief's garden where no one was able to remove them. In true Cinderella fashion, the chief agreed to marry any girl who could pick up the bones and naturally only Nomi could do so. After reading some of the stories about male counterparts to Cinderella, stories with boys as heroes could also be included in the assignment.

Similar American Indian versions of "Cinderella" have different titles: "Little Scar Face," in ACEI's *Told Under the Green Umbrella;* "Little Burnt-Face" by Olcott, in Sutherland's *Arbuthnot Anthology of Children's Literature;* "Little Scarred One" by Cunningham, in the Child Study Association of America's *Castles and Dragons;* and "The Indian Cinderella" by Macmillan, in Fitzgerald's *World Tales for Creative Dramatics and Storytelling*. The Indian girl in these stories was chosen to marry an invisible brave. The maiden was named "Scar Face" or "Burnt-Face" because her sister threw ashes or cinders in her face to burn her.

Graham's *The Beggar in the Blanket and Other Vietnamese Tales* contains the title story, which is Cinderella-like. In "Cinder-Maid," in the Jacob's *European Folk and Fairy Tales*, the girl's clothes come out of a hazel nut from a tree on her mother's grave. In the versions of Ashputtel, the birds in the tree on her mother's grave give her the clothes. The story "Aschenputtel" in *Household Stories by the Brothers Grimm* is very gory. When the shoe came around for girls in the kingdom to try on, the other sisters cut off toes or a heel to fit into it. Later the birds pecked out the eyes of the false sisters. The version in Nelson is not as gory; neither are the "Ashputtel" stories in the Child Study Association of America's *Castles and Dragons* and De la Mare's *Animal Stories*.

"Ashpet," in Chase's *Grandfather Tales*, comes from the Southern hill country and has elements of the German story as well as the Russian. Ashpet, like Vasilissa, is sent to a witch woman to get a light. Because Ashpet is kind and polite to the witch, the old woman becomes her fairy godmother, washes her dishes for her and provides her with transportation and clothes for the dance—a horse and a red dress and slippers. Like the German versions, the sisters cut off part of their feet to fit into the slippers.

The girl in "Cat-skin," in de la Mare's *Animal Stories,* ran away from her father. The dying queen told her husband that he was to marry someone who had hair as beautiful as she. However, the king could find no one except his daughter who had hair as beautiful as his wife, so the king wanted to marry his daughter. The princess put off her father by asking for three dresses—gold like the sun, silver like the moon, and bright as the stars, as well as a mantle of a thousand kinds of fur. Unfortunately, the king gave his daughter all of these articles of clothing. So the princess sewed a ring, necklace, and broach of gold into the hem of her dress, put on the mantle of fur, packed her three dresses in a nutshell, put ashes on her face, and ran away. The girl was captured by huntsmen of a neighboring king, and was taken to work in his kitchen. The girl wore her three dresses at three balls given by the young king who was enchanted with the mystery girl. The princess also dropped the golden jewelry into his soup on three occasions. The young king recognized Cat-skin by slipping a ring onto her finger when they danced. A similar version is found in Reeves's *English Fables and Fairy Stories.*

The southern mountain story "Catskins," in Chase's *Grandfather Tales,* is also about a girl who wore cat skins for clothing. The girl was asked for her hand in marriage, but like the Russian heroine Vasilissa, she posed conditions. She wanted three dresses: one was to be the color of all the fish in the sea, the second the color of all the birds, and a third the color of flowers. When Catskins received the flying box, she flew away to a rich man's house where she got a job in the kitchen. Catskin appeared three times at the rich man's dances in her beautiful dresses. At the third dance, the rich man put a ring on her finger, and Catskin proved that she was the mystery girl by baking the ring into a cake.

Poor Tattercoats lived with a grandfather who despised her because his favorite daughter died when she was born. Tattercoat's nurse begged the grandfather three times to let her go to a ball given by the prince, but he refused. The prince accidentally met Tattercoats with the gooseboy, begged her to come to the ball, and said that he would dance with her in rags if only she would come. Tattercoats appeared at midnight at the ball, and the prince claimed her as his bride. When the goosepboy played his pipes, Tattercoat's garments became beautiful. The version in Sutherland's *Arbuthnot Anthology of Children's Literature* and Arbuthnot's *Time for Fairy Tales, Old and New* comes from Jacobs's *More English Fairy Tales*. Steele's story is also available as a picture book. "Tattercoats" also appears in Reeves's *English Fables and Fairy Stories* and Finlay's *Tattercoats and Other Folk Tales*.

Perrault's version of *Cinderella* is the most common. This is the one with the fairy godmother, pumpkin coach, and glass slipper. Perrault's version can be found in Arbuthnot's *Time for Fairy Tales, Old and New*, ACEI's *Told Under the Green Umbrella*, Baker's *The Talking Tree*, de la Mare's *Tales Told Again*, Grimms' *Fairy Tales*, *Tales from Grimm*, Gruenberg's *Favorite Stories Old and New*, Haviland's *Fairy Tale Treasury*, Haviland's *Favorite Fairy Tales Told in England*, Hutchinson's *Chimney Corner Stories*, Johnson's *Anthology of Children's Literature*, Lang's *Blue Fairy Book*, Perrault's *Classic French Fairy Tales*, Perrault's *Complete Fairy Tales*, Perrault's *Famous Fairy Tales*, Arthur Rackham's *Fairy Book*, Sideman's *The World's Best Fairy Tales*, Untermeyer's *Golden Treasury of Children's Literature*, and Williams-Ellis's *Fairy Tales from the British Isles*. Marcia Brown illustrated Perrault's *Cinderella* and received the Caldecott Medal for it in 1955. Other picture books of the Perrault version have been illustrated by Le Cain and Hughes. Evans and Langner have retold their own versions. The Evans version is illustrated by Rackham.

Colum's *The Girl Who Sat by the Ashes* and Farjeon's *The Glass Slipper* are both longer books by favorite authors who wished to create their own versions of the story. Numerous play versions appear in the chapter V, "Playing Stories: Live Action and with Puppets."

The male counterpart of Cinderella is called "Cinderlad" or "Boots." This youngest son of three is often thought to be dull, but during the story he outsmarts his brothers. Variants of the name "John" are also used—"Juan" in Spanish and "Ivan" in Russian. In the Norwegian "Boots and His Brothers," John is nicknamed "Boots," and succeeds in winning the princess and half the kingdom by performing three tasks which his brothers failed to accomplish. With the aid of a magic axe, spade and walnut, Boots felled a big oak, dug a well, and made water flow. The story is found in Arbuthnot's *Time for Fairy Tales, Old and New*, ACEI's *Told Under the Green Umbrella*, Huber's *Story and Verse for Children*, Hutchinson's *Chimney Corner Fairy Tales*, and Johnson's *Anthology of Children's Literature*.

"Boots and the Troll" appears in Thompson's *One Hundred Favorite Fairytales* and Haviland's *Favorite Fairy Tales Told in Norway*. "Cinderlad and the Troll's Seven Silver Ducks" is found in d'Aulaire's *East of the Sun and West of the Moon*. It is really bloodthirsty. The youngest of three brothers who was fit only to "sit and poke about in the ashes," had a job in the palace kitchen, but his

526 • RIDDLES, MAGIC, JOKES AND FOLK THEMES

two brothers got him in trouble by saying that Boots would bring the troll's seven silver ducks to the king. Boots outsmarts the troll's daughter by having her feel a nail rather than a finger to show her that he was not fat and juicy enough to eat. Later, Boots cut off the daughter's head while he was supposed to be sharpening the knife, then roasted the girl and served her to her father.

One of the most famous of all stories featuring a male counterpart for Cinderella is the Scandinavian "The Princess on the Glass Hill." The hero is called "Boots" in the story in Sutherland's *Arbuthnot Anthology of Children's Literature*, and Johnson's *Anthology of Children's Literature*, and "Cinderlad" in other versions. Other sources include Baker's *The Talking Tree*, Durham's *Tit for Tat and Other Latvian Folk Tales*, Kaplan's *Swedish Fairy Tales*, various versions of Asbjornsen and Moe's *East of the Sun and West of the Moon*, ACEI's *Told Under the Green Umbrella*, Haviland's *Favorite Fairy Tales Told in Norway*, Hutchinson's *Chimney Corner Fairy Tales*, Lang's *Blue Fairy Book*, Nelson's *A Comparative Anthology of Children's Literature*, Sideman's *The World's Best Fairy Tales*, Thompson's *One Hundred Favorite Folktales*. Each year one of the three brothers was asked by their father to stay awake all night on St. John's Night to see who was eating every root and blade of grass. The first two brothers were frightened off by the rumblings, but the youngest noticed the noise was caused by a horse with armor. The lad rode the horse in the armor of brass, silver and gold to ride up the glass mountain on three successive tries. The lad could claim the princess and half the kingdom, but he chose instead to collect the three golden apples that the princess threw at him as proof that he was the mysterious knight.

One story that has a similar name but is very different is a story called "The Glass Mountain," in Lang's *Yellow Fairy Book*, and comes from the Polish "Kletke." On the last day before seven years were up, a schoolboy caught a lynx, put the claws on his hands and feet and climbed the glass mountain. The eagle who protected the apple tree fought the boy and lifted him into the air. The boy cut off the eagle's feet and fell into branches of the tree. All those who perished on the mountain were then brought back to life.

The number "three" appears in a Scandinavian version of "Rumpelstiltskin" called "The Three Aunts." An industrious girl is resented by the other maids who told the queen that the girl could spin a pound of flax in twenty-four hours. She was required by the queen to do so. Three separate times three old women came to the girl and did the spinning in return for the girl's promise to call them "aunt" on the happiest day of her life. On the day the girl married the prince, the three women appeared and the girl called each of them "aunt." When the prince exclaimed over their ugliness, the women claimed that they had once been beautiful but that spinning was responsible for their red eyes, humped backs, and stretched noses. Naturally, the prince didn't want his bride to become ugly so she didn't have to spin ever again. The story in Fitzgerald's *World Tales for Creative Dramatics and Storytelling* comes from Dasent's *Popular Tales from the Norse*. The story in Martignoni's *Illustrated Treasury of Children's Literature* comes from d'Aulaire's *East of the Sun and West of the Moon*. See also Thompson's *One Hundred Favorite Folktales*, and McNeill's *The*

Sunken City. A play by Rowland appears in Burack's *One Hundred Plays for Children.*

Another husband decided to throw away his wife's spinning wheel. In this Scottish story, "Whippety Stourie," a woman's husband expected her to spin one hundred hanks of fine thread but she was able to produce only half a hank of coarse knotted thread. While her husband went on a journey, the woman saw six wee women—one of whom had a spinning wheel. Whippety Stourie spun the hanks of thread for the wife. After meeting the six women, the husband threw away her spinning wheel when he learned that their mouths were lopsided from too much spinning. The story "Whippety Stourie," found in Nelson's *Comparative Anthology of Children's Literature,* is taken from Wilson's *Scottish Folk Tales and Legends.* An introduction to this story, as well as "Tom Tit Tot" and Rumpelstiltskin," appears on page 281 of Nelson's book.

The number three also appears several times in the story "Rumpelstiltskin." According to the story, a king heard a miller brag that his daughter could spin straw into gold, so the king confined the girl and expected her to produce gold after which he would make her his queen. Rumpelstiltskin appeared to the girl three times and promised to spin the straw into gold in return for her ring, necklace, and first born. When Rumpelstiltskin later demanded the queen's child, the queen was given three days to guess the dwarf's name. A messenger overheard Rumpelstiltskin singing around his campfire and learned his name. Students will enjoy comparing the rhyme in the picture book *Rumpelstiltskin,* illustrated by Ayre, page 313 of Gruenberg's *Favorite Fairy Tales Old and New,* page 79 of Grimms' *About Wise Men and Simpletons,* and page 267 of *The Complete Grimms' Fairy Tales.* The story also appears in Nelson's *Comparative Anthology of Children's Literature, Household Stories by the Brothers Grimm,* Sutherland's revision of *Arbuthnot Anthology of Children's Literature* (which is the same as in *The Blue Fairy Book),* Johnson's *Anthology of Children's Literature* (which comes from Crane's *Household Stories),* Ward's *Stories to Dramatize,* Untermeyer's *Golden Treasury of Children's Literature,* Haviland's *Fairy Tale Treasury,* Haviland's *Favorite Fairy Tales Told in Germany,* and Martignoni's *Illustrated Treasury of Children's Literature.* Plays appear in Thane's *Plays from Famous Stories and Fairy Tales,* Bennett's *Creative Plays and Programs for Holidays,* and Burack's *One Hundred Plays for Children.* A puppet play appears in Ross's *Hand Puppets.* Three picture books listed under Grimm are illustrated by Tarcov, Stobbs, and Ayre.

A Cornish version of the story, written and illustrated by the Zemachs, is called *Duffy and the Devil.* The devil did the spinning for a servant girl named "Duffy," but did not tell her his name, and in three years planned to take Duffy away unless she guessed correctly. In the meantime, the squire married Duffy and he heard the devil laughing and chanting that his name was "Tarraway." When Duffy guessed Tarraway's name, all her spinning disappeared—even what the squire was wearing.

A Japanese story with similar elements is called *Oniroku and the Carpenter* by Matsui. Instead of spinning and weaving, the task was to build a bridge. The ogre asked the carpenter to guess his name or give him his eyes. The answer was provided by a voice in the enchanted woods.

An English version of "Rumpelstiltskin" called "Tom Tit Tot" contains the number five, as well as the number three. A woman's daughter ate five pies and her mother sang a song about it, but was ashamed to explain to the king what she was singing so she changed the words from "ate five pies today" to "spun five skeins today." Impressed, the king married the girl and demanded that on the last month of the year she would spin five skeins a day or lose her head. Tom Tit Tot agreed to spin for the queen in return for her guessing his name. The queen was to have three guesses a night for a month. The king overheard Tom Tit Tot's chant and told his wife. The story appears in Sutherland's *Arbuthnot Anthology of Children's Literature*, Baker's *Talking Tree*, De la Mare's *Animal Stories*, Hutchinson's *Chimney Corner Stories*, Jacobs's *English Folk and Fairy Tales*, Nelson's *Comparative Anthology of Children's Literature*, Reeves's *English Fables and Fairy Stories*, and Williams-Ellis's *Fairy Tales from the British Isles*. A picture book, *Tom Tit Tot*, is illustrated by Ness.

A spinning story with a different twist is "The Clever Peasant Girl," in Thompson's *One Hundred Favorite Folk Tales*. In this Italian story, a girl is asked by a prince to make a hundred ells of cloth out of four ounces of flax or she and her father will be hanged. The girl sent the prince four small cords of flax saying that she would weave the cloth if the prince made a loom of the cords. There are many such stories under the heading "The Clever Daughter" previously listed in this chapter.

A spinning wheel is the cause of Sleeping Beauty's one hundred years of sleep.

"The Three Figs" is a Puerto Rican tale found in Belpre's *The Tiger and the Rabbit*. When Fernando found three figs on one stem, he took them to the king. On the way, however, he tripped twice and spoiled two of the figs so he ate them. The king was pleased with the one huge fig and gave Fernando a basket full of gold coins. Fernando's friend Santiago decided to get some gold for himself so he took a whole cartful to the king and, because of his impatience and because the king realized his motives, Santiago was sent away while the guard pelted him with figs.

"The Three Ravens," is found in *Gianni and the Ogre* by Manning-Sanders. Giovanni could understand bird language and told his father that the birds said Giovanni would rise high in the world, be dressed in royal robes, and that his parents would kiss the hem of his garments. Giovanni's father hit him and knocked him overboard. Giovanni was rescued and, in turn, rescued a king from persecution by ravens, winning half the kingdom and the hand of the princess. When Giovanni became king his parents, having lost all their possessions through bad luck, came to that country as beggars and the prophecy was fulfilled.

Sometimes a story can be used to introduce another by the same author-illustrator or another tale of the same nationality. Aliki Brandenberg's *Three Gold Pieces, a Greek Folk Tale* can be used for both of these purposes. Yannas, a poor man, went to work as a servant for a rich man with the understanding that he would be given food and lodging but would get his pay in a lump sum. Finally, after ten years, Yannas was given three gold pieces, as well as three pieces of advice. The advice given to him saved his life, got him gold, and gave him a happy home. Another Greek folktale retold and illustrated by Aliki is *The Eggs*. A sea captain forgot to pay for his eggs at a restaurant. When he returned six years later and offered to pay for the meal, the innkeeper asked for 500 gold pieces because if he had put the eggs under a hen they would have multiplied until the innkeeper had a large chicken farm. The sea captain's lawyer won the case by saying that he had never heard of fried eggs hatching. Compare to Balet's *The Fence* and Daniels's *The Tsar's Riddles*. In the first story, a rich man wanted to make a poor man pay for smelling his food, so the poor man asked the rich man to pay for hearing his money jingle to show him the absurdity of his accusation. In the Russian story, a small girl is the only one wise enough to see the colt found under the wagon could not belong to the man who owned the wagon because a wagon cannot have a colt. (See riddle stories on this theme in earlier sections of this chapter.)

Ambros's *Three Poor Tailors* were tired of working so they went to town to have fun, but did not have money to pay their bill. They were put in jail until they mended the townspeople's clothes. Another folktale by Ambrus comes from Turkey. *The Little Cockerel* found a coin in a rubbish heap but the sultan took it. The cockerel shouted and shouted at the sultan, was punished, but came back again. Thrown into a beehive, the cockerel swallowed the bees and blew them into the sultan's room. Eventually, the golden coin was given back to him. *Brave Soldier Janosh* by Ambros is an old Hungarian tale about a boaster.

The title story, pages 3 to 7 of Duvoisin's *The Three Sneezes and Other Swiss Tales*, is a noodlehead story and can be used to introduce other silly stories found in earlier sections of this chapter. Jean-Marie is a Swiss who was impressed with a man who told him that the branch he was sitting on would fall to the ground when he finished sawing the branch. Jean-Marie followed the man and asked if he knew when Jean-Marie would die, and the man answered that it would be after the donkey sneezed three times. After the third sneeze, Jean-Marie lay down in the road because dead men do not stand up.

The title story of Boggs's *Three Golden Oranges and Other Spanish Folk Tales* concerns Diego who set off to find a wife. An old woman told him to pluck three oranges from a special tree he had to find. Three maidens came out of three oranges, but only the third maiden stayed because Diego was able to comply with her request for bread and water. Although the girl turned into a white dove to escape a witch, all ended well.

Spicer's "The Three Wishes" appear in *Long Ago in Serbia*. Three brothers who were guarding their father's pear tree shared pears with an angel disguised as a beggar. The angel gave each a wish: one brother wanted the river changed to wine so he could be a wine merchant; another wished the birds were boats and belonged to him; while the third wanted a good wife. When the angel reappeared after three years, the first two brothers had lost their kindness so the angel returned them to their former impoverished state. The third brother was hospitable so the angel blessed him and his wife.

The next story contains three wishes and could be used as a Halloween story. Barth's *Jack o'Lantern*, the story of the first jack o'lantern, is set in the hills of New England. Several parallels are mentioned at the end of the book in an author's note. Mean Jack the Blacksmith was very stingy. One night St. Peter came to Jack and Sairy's door disguised as a beggar, and Jack invited him in only because he thought he saw a gleam of gold. In return for lodging and food, St. Peter gave Jack three wishes. Jack wished that anyone who sat in his rocker in the blacksmith shop would stay there till he let them out, that anyone who touched his bellows would stick to it, and that anyone who climbed the apple tree would have to stay there until he let them down. When the devil learned that Jack was supposed to be as mean as he was, he sent his sons to fetch Jack—but the little devils were caught by the rocking chair and the bellows. When the devil himself came, he was caught in the tree and was let go only when he promised never to return. When Mean Jack died on All Hallows Eve, he went to heaven and hell but was refused at both places, and now wanders around in the marshes using a hollowed-out pumpkin with a candle in it for light.

A southern mountain version called "Wicked John and the Devil" appears in Chase's *Grandfather Tales*. John's three wishes are that anyone who sat in his rocking chair will have to stay there until he lets them out, that anyone who touched his sledge hammer would have to keep pounding until he told them to stop, and that anyone who touched his thorn bush would be held by it.

When mouse, spider, and fly went up to the Sky King to get light for lion and the world, they were asked to pass three tests. With the help of millions of ants, they cut all grass on the plain by the following day, mouse made a tunnel to bury all the roast cow that they had to eat. When the three were asked to choose from two boxes, they snatched the right one. The red box contained a rooster who called up the light when he crowed. The story appears in Bernstein and Korbin's picture book *The First Morning, an African Myth*.

MAGIC NUMBERS IN CHILDREN'S LITERATURE—*FOUR*.   "Ali Baba and the Forty Thieves," one of the tales of the *Arabian Nights*, can be included in the section on the number four because it is a multiple of that number. The story is about two brothers of ancient Persia, Kassim or Cassim (the rich brother) and Ali Baba (the poor brother). Ali Baba saw a group of men put goods into a cave; using the magic words "Open Sesame," Ali Baba went into the cave and took a small portion of the riches. Kassim found out about his brother's new wealth when Ali Baba's wife borrowed a measuring cup to measure the gold, and Kassim's wife put suet on the bottom of the cup to see what was being counted. When Ali Baba shared the secret with his brother, Kassim went to the cave, but in his greed Kassim spent too much time there and was found and quartered by the thieves. Eventually the thieves found Ali Baba's home but were foiled seven times by Ali Baba's slave girl, Morgiana, who eventually married Ali Baba's son. The story is found in Lang's *Arabian Nights*, Lang's *Blue Fairy Book*, Lines's *Tales of Magic and Enchantment*, Mozley's *First Book of Tales of Ancient Araby*, Arthur Rackham's *Fairy Book*, and Sideman's *The World's Best Fairy Tales*. Anthony Quayle reads from Williams-Ellis's version in a recording called *The Arabian Nights, Ali Baba and the Forty Thieves*.

The Round Sultan and the Straight Answer is another story that contains the number forty. This picture book by Walker is a tale from Turkey about a sultan who ate so much that he broke the scales and couldn't fit into the royal bathtub. When the sultan was told that he would be dead in forty days he worried himself down to a decent size.

"The Four Juans" appears in Newman's Folk Tales from Latin America and comes from Bolivia. The brothers went out to seek their fortunes and found oranges, peaches, and four Juanitas who gave each one a magic possession and asked the Juans to return in a year and marry them. The innkeeper told the king about the magic gifts but the four Juans used their magic oranges and peaches to hold on to the purse which was a constant source of gold, the silver tablecloth that provided food, the cloth that remained no matter how much was cut off, and the red cape that provided invisibility. Another Spanish story, "The Four Brothers Who Were Both Wise and Foolish," is found in Haviland's Favorite Fairy Tales Told in Spain. Each boy took a quarter of a peso and went out to seek his fortune. The first became a robber, the second a marksman, the third had marvelous eyesight, and the youngest was a coppersmith. Their talents were useful in rescuing a princess from a sea serpent.

The Four Clever Brothers by the Grimm brothers appears as a picture book illustrated by Felix Hoffman. As in the other story, four brothers went out to seek their fortune and agreed to meet in four years. Each of them learned a trade—one of them learned to steal things no one cared about; one had a telescope and could see everything on heaven and earth; one had a gun that hit everything he aimed at; and another could sew anything with his needle without leaving a noticeable seam. Their talents were put to use in bringing the princess to the king. The Five Chinese Brothers in the next section also have unusual talents.

A very famous story from the brothers Grimm is called "The Four Musicians," in Arbuthnot's Times for Fairy Tales Old and New, and "The Bremen Town Musicians" in Haviland's Favorite Fairy Tales Told in Germany. Additional sources appear in the chapter "Enjoying Poetry." A donkey, dog, cat and rooster are let go by their owners and meet and travel together toward Bremen, surprise a group of robbers, and take over their home.

Four talented creatures are featured in the Irish tale, "The Bee, the Harp, the Mouse and the Bumclock," in Fenner's Princesses and Peasant Boys, Haviland's Favorite Fairy Tales Told in Ireland, Hutchinson's Chimney Corner Fairy Tales, and Johnson's Anthology of Children's Literature. Use this story to encourage listeners to locate and read other stories about silly trades or swaps, especially "Jack and the Beanstalk," "Hans in Luck," and "Gudbrand on the Hillside." Activities related to this story are given in detail in chapter 5, "Playing Stories: Live Action and with Puppets."

MAGIC NUMBERS IN CHILDREN'S LITERATURE—FIVE.   Stories featuring the number five seem to be shorter than most of the other stories in this section. "The Five Swallow Sisters" appears in Martin's Nine Tales of Coyote. Coyote turns himself into a baby so he can be near the dam the sisters have built to trap salmon. Coyote wanted to destroy the dam and save the salmon, but the sisters pay him more attention than he wants and his plans fail. "Five Peas from the Same Pod" appears in Andersen's *Complete Fairy Tales and Stories*. A similar title for the story is included in Johnson's *Anthology of Children's Literature* and Harper's *Easter Chimes*. "The Five Eggs," in Courlander's tales from the United Nations called *Ride with the Sun* comes from Ecuador. This funy tale is about a man and wife who argue about how to divide the eggs. They cannot decide who should get three and who should get two.

The *Five Hundred Hats of Bartholomew Cubbins* by Seuss could be introduced with other stories about five.

Bishop's picture book illustrated by Wiese, *The Five Chinese Brothers*, is the great favorite, and is available in filmstrip format. Each of the five brothers had an unusual talent and when the look-alikes took each other's places, each unique talent kept them from being killed. The story is included in Tooze's *Storytelling*. The story that appears as "The Five Queer Brothers" in Nelson's *Comparative Anthology of Children's Literature* is taken from Sian Tek's *More Folk Tales from China*. Persons with unusual talents abound in folk and fairy tales, and this story could be used to introduce others. For example, various versions of the *Seven Simeons* appear in the section which follows under the number seven, as does "The Seven Stars," a Danish story. Friends with unusual talents help Noki in "The Ship that Sailed by Land and Sea," in Bowman and Bianco's *Tales from a Finnish Tupa*. McDermott's picture book *Anansi the Spider* tells about the talents of Anansi's six sons. Evaline Ness adapted and illustrated Lang's version of the story "Long, Broad and Quick-Eye." Long could stretch himself, Broad could inflate himself, and Quick-Eye's eyes could pierce anything he looked at. "Longshanks, Girth and Keen," a similar story, appears in Fillmore's *Shepherd's Nosegay*. "Broad Man, Tall Man with Eyes of Flame" appears in Manning-Sanders' *Book of Wizards*, and another story in Lang's *Gray Fairy Book*.

"Swift-as-the-Wind, Hold-fast and Hard-a-Iron" appears in Bamberger's *My First Big Story Book*. Three dogs helped to kill a dragon so a boy could win a princess.

The *Magic Feather Duster* by Will and Nicholas is a story that contains elements of folktales. The feather duster was obtained through the special talents of several brothers who could run like a greyhound, jump like a flea, eat much, pluck a branch and be quiet.

Include "The Four Clever Brothers" from the previous section, for each son had a special talent. The various versions of "How Six Traveled the Wide World" from the following section also includes six unusual talents.

MAGIC NUMBERS IN CHILDREN'S LITERATURE—SIX.   Stories that include the number six are not numerous. However, six is double three so two shorter stories involving the number three could be told or read to provide for this session. One story can qualify for a "sixes story" because the numbers in the title if added together total six! "Little One-Eye, Little Two-Eyes and Little Three-Eyes" is a tale that has elements of Cinderella and includes a magic tablecloth. Little Two-Eyes recites a rhyme to get the goat to bleat and a table to appear laden with food. The other sisters chided Little Two-Eyes because she was ordinary and looked like everyone else. Instead of a glass slipper, the prince's test was that he would marry whoever could get golden apples and silver twigs from a special tree. Naturally only Little Two-Eyes was able to satisfy the prince. The story appears in Lang's *Green Fairy Book*, Arbuthnot's *Time for Fairy Tales*, and *The Complete Grimms' Fairy Tales*. The most readable versions are translated from Grimm by May Sellar, and are found in *The World's Best Fairy Tales*, edited by Sideman, and in Hutchinson's *Chimney Corner Stories*.

"The Six Sillies" contains the same elements as the stories titled "The Three Sillies." Sources for those stories appear earlier in this chapter in the section of noodlehead stories called "Finding Someone Sillier." The basic story is that people are crying over something silly that has not yet happened and will probably never happen, and an onlooker, disgusted, declares that if he can find three other people who are just as silly he will return. He finds some even sillier. "The Six Sillies," found in Lang's *The Red Fairy Book* and Sideman's *Anthology of the World's Best Fairy Tales* is about a young man whose wife-to-be and future in-laws are letting all the beer run out of the keg while they cry because all the names in the calendar are taken and they won't know what to name their child when they marry. The version of Lang and Sideman is not as specific about this reason as the story in Lang's collection. Any version of "The Three Sillies" could be told simply by declaring that there were six silly persons in the story—the original family and the three silly people the young man found in his travels!

"The Six Hungry Beasts," in Lang's *Crimson Fairy Book*, comes from Finland. In the story listeners learn that the fox has a white tip on its tail because the bear threw a ladle after it and grazed the tip. This story is not for the beginning storyteller or for unsophisticated listeners because it is more difficult to follow than other fairy tales. A man tried to catch a marten but was caught and killed in his own trap. Six animals come to eat the man: the squirrel, the hare, the fox, the wolf, the bear, and the marten.

The picture book *The Six Foolish Fishermen* by Elkin is for very young children. Each fisherman tries to count to see how many of them there are but only counts five because he forgets to count himself. The story will especially appeal to children who are learning to count. These same children will enjoy the rhyme in Becker's *Seven Little Rabbits*.

Use *The Blind Men and the Elephant*, available in two picture books by Quigley and Saxe, to introduce other riddle stories. This story from India is about six blind men who feel a different part of the elephant and therefore have a different definition of the animal.

Singer's *The Fearsome Inn* is a picture book set in Poland. A witch named Doboshova and her husband, who is part devil, waylaid travelers on their way to Warsaw, Cracow and Leipzig. The couple held captive three beautiful girls—Reitze, Leitze, and Neitze—who were forced to be their servants. One winter three unsuspecting young men named Herchel, Velvel, and Leibel separately found themselves at Doboshova's inn. When Doboshova was about to feed them bread that would take away their human feelings, Lieibel pretended that he had lost a ring that could locate treasures and heal the sick. Then the greedy witch and her husband went to look for it, Leichel drew a circle around them with his magic chalk and the wicked couple could not get out until they signed an oath in blood that they would leave everything they owned to the six young people and that they and their offspring would never return. The three young men married the three young women they found at *The Fearsome Inn.*

"The Six Swans" found in Thompson's *One Hundred Favorite Folktales* is of Swedish origin. The wicked stepmother wanted to get rid of her husband's children so when he took his daughters on a trip the stepmother changed the six sons into six swans. Eventually the daughter learned how to change them back and the stepmother was changed into a black raven and she flew away. This story is so similar to Hans Christian Andersen's "The Wild Swans" in which there are eleven sons, that since that story is the only one in which the number eleven appears, the story should be saved until then, unless "six" stories are really needed.

MAGIC NUMBERS IN CHILDREN'S LITERATURE—*SEVEN.* "The Seven Ravens" is also included with stories about number eleven because a similar story contains six, seven, eleven, and twelve swans, ducks, and ravens.

The number seven appears frequently in folklore. Many of the famous folktales include the number in some versions. In the picture-book by de la Mare illustrated by Low of *Jack and the Beanstalk,* Jack received seven beans and his mother kissed him seven times. The King of Ireland has a daughter who had not laughed in seven years in "The Bee, the Harp, the Mouse, and the Bum-Clock," in *Donegal Fairy Tales* by MacManus.

In the version of "Sleeping Beauty" that appears in Haviland's *Favorite Fairy Tales Told in France,* there are seven place settings of gold encrusted with diamonds and rubies for the seven fairies that were invited to attend the christening. When the eighth fairy appears, she was upset that there was no place set and cursed the newborn princess. A similar version appears in Sideman's *The World's Best Fairy Tales.* In most versions there are twelve place settings, sometimes in golden caskets, or twelve plates.

There is a seven-headed serpent in "The Golden Phoenix" in Barbeau's collection of the same name. The story begins like "The Firebird" and has a glass mountain.

"The Brahman, The Tiger and the Seven Judges" is just one version of the "Tiger, the Brahman, and the Jackel." The version that appears in Baker's *Talking Tree* had the Brahman get seven opinions as to whether or not the tiger will eat him. The first six—the banyan tree, a camel, a bullock, an eagle, an alligator, and a jackal—all agree that the tiger should eat the Brahman because man is their enemy. The seventh, a man, disagrees and tricks the tiger into his cage. Sources for the version called "The Tiger, the Brahman, and the Jackal" appear in Arbuthnot's *Time for Fairy Tales Old and New,* Buck's *Fairy Tales of the Orient,* Haviland's *Favorite Fairy Tales Told in India,* Jacobs's *Indian Fairy*

Tales, and Johnson's *Anthology of Children's Literature*. A picture book by Steel, illustrated by Funai, is called *The Tiger, the Brahman and the Jackal*. In this version, it is the jackal who tricks the tiger back into his cage by having the tiger reconstruct the scene. The Spanish version taken from Storm's *Picture Tales from Mexico* is found in *The Buried Treasure* by Ross; in "Señor Coyote Settles a Quarrel," a rabbit helps a snake crawl out from under a rock. In an African version called "The Panther in the Pit," in Green's *The Big Book of Animal Fables*, the spider tricks the panther back into the pit after the kindly rat has released the panther.

"The Horse of Seven Colors," in Cothran's *The Magic Calabash*, has elements similar to "The Firebird" and "The Princess on the Glass Hill." In "The Glass Mountain," from Lang's *Yellow Fairy Book*, the princess waited in a castle seven years for someone to rescue her from the glass hill. This Polish version is different from the Scandinavian version called "The Princess on the Glass Hill." (See "Numbers in Folklore—Three," of this chapter.)

Felix Hoffman illustrated a picture book of the Grimms' tale *The Wolf and the Seven Little Kids*. Mother goat told her kids not to open the door to anyone, but the wolf put flour on his paws to make them white and the kids let him in. The wolf ate the kids but the mother goat cut open the wolf, replaced her kids with stones, and sewed the wolf up again. The version in *More Tales from Grimm* gives the place where each kid hid to escape the wolf. Other sources for the story are Bamberger's *My First Big Storybook*, Arbuthnot's *Time for Fairy Tales Old and New*, Grimms' *About Wise Men and Simpletons*, Grimms' *Fairy Tales*, illustrated by Kredel, *Household Stories by the Brothers Grimm*, and Martignoni's *Illustrated Treasury of Children's Literature*. The following stories follow Gag's version of the story: Haviland's *Fairy Tale Treasury*, Johnson's *Anthology of Children's Literature*, and Lines's *A Ring of Tales*.

Another version found in Huber's *Story and Verses for Children* is called "The Wolf and Seven Young Goslings." The mother in the story is a goose instead of a goat, but she also substitutes stones for her children and sews up the wolf. Compare this incident with a similar one found in "The Cock, the Mouse and the Little Red Hen." Sources are listed in the section on the color "red" in the chapter, "Experiencing Art through Picture Books."

"The Seven Swabians" is another tale from the Grimm brothers. The nonsense story about seven men who each took hold of a spear and chased an enemy that turned out to be just a little hare is found in *The Complete Grimms' Fairy Tales* and *Eric Carle's Storybook*.

"The Palace of the Seven Little Hills," in Manning-Sanders's *A Book of Sorcerers and Spells*, comes from Ireland. Michael and Rosa were hidden away in a palace among seven hills by their father to protect them from their wicked stepmother. The queen cast a spell on Michael which would cause him to be homeless unless he brought a red-mouthed cow, a self-playing dulcimer, and the princess Above All Measure Beautiful.

In the German story by the Grimms, "Hans in Luck," Hans served his master for seven years and was given a lump of gold which he traded until the seventh trade he had nothing left and thought himself lucky. The picture book was illustrated by Felix Hoffman. Other sources for the story include *The Complete Grimms' Fairy Tales, Household Stories by the Brothers Grimm,* Hutchinson's *Fireside Stories,* and *Eric Carle's Storybook.* "Gudbrand-on-the-Hillside," a Scandinavian story, has a similar theme.

"The Seven Foals" is from Scandinavia. The easiest version to read is the Dasent translation of Moe's story found in Manning-Sanders's *The Book of Magical Beasts.* Boots is the youngest of three brothers. The brothers were to watch the seven foals of the king and tell him what they ate and drank, and they would be rewarded with half the kingdom and the princess. Anyone who failed would have three red stripes cut into his back. The first two brothers rested with an old woman and did not see what the foals ate. Boots learned that they ate bread and drank wine. The foals told Boots to cut off their heads on his wedding day because they were really brothers of the princess. Other sources for the story are Arnott's *Animal Folk Tales Around the World,* Fenner's *Magic Hoofs,* Lang's *Red Fairy Book,* and Undset's *True and Untrue and Other Norse Tales.*

"The Seven Wishes" by Smedberg is found in *Great Swedish Fairy Tales* by Bauer. When the hero saved a frog from a snake, the snake turned into a princess who granted wishes. Some of the seven wishes that were not used wisely were that the firewood would walk home and that the bicycle he wished for would break into a hundred pieces. Since the sixth wish was a wise one, the hero was given another wish. The sixth wish was that the hero could read, and the seventh was that he become a good and useful person.

Two stories that contain the number seven are about seamen: Stormalong and Sinbad. Felton's *True Tall Tales of Stormalong, Sailor of the Seven Seas,* contains eight stories about Stormalong. There are five verses of a sea chanty about Stormalong at the end of the book. *The Seven Voyages of Sinbad the Sailor* is a whole book about Sinbad, as well as the title of a story in Lang's *Arabian Nights.* "The Story of Sinbad the Sailor" also appears in *Arthur Rackham's Fairy Book.* The Williams-Ellis version as narrated by Anthony Quayle on a recording is called *Sinbad the Sailor.*

Read one section of the story of Sinbad to students to interest them in reading the whole story. The selection called "Sinbad the Sailor," in Mozley's *The First Book of Tales of Ancient Araby,* is suitable for this purpose. This section tells how Sinbad was thrown into the sea by a huge whale and how he survived. Also included is "Sinbad and the Roc" in which Sinbad tied himself to the Roc's leg so when it flew away it would take Sinbad with it so he could escape from an island. Instead Sinbad became involved in a scheme to use the Roc to deliver diamonds.

One of the most famous stories containing the number seven is the Russian story "The Seven Simeons" or "The Seven Simons." In Artzybasheff's picture book, *The Seven Simeons,* the seven look-alike brothers each had a special talent. The first could build a tower to the sky, the second could see all kingdoms from the top of the tower, the third could make ships that could sail in one hour what another ship could travel in one day, the fourth could sail it and hide it under the water when necessary, the fifth, a blacksmith, made a gun that would never miss, the sixth would bring back whatever the gun shot. Nothing was beyond the power of the seventh Simeon. King Douda sent six of the brothers to bring him the Princess Helena, and locked up the seventh Simeon. "The Seven Simons," in Manning-Sanders's *The Glass Man and the Golden Bird*, is a Hungarian version. Several of the talents are different: the fifth brother made a cross-bow instead of a gun, and the seventh was a thief who could take anything. Two other versions with the same title are found in Lang's *The Crimson Fairy Book* and Sideman's *The World's Greatest Fairy Tales*. "The Seven Simeons Simeonovich" is found in McNeill's *The Double Knights*. "The Seven Simeons, Full Brothers" appears in Nelson's *A Comparative Anthology of Children's Literature*. (Other stories in which characters have unusual talents are listed under the number five in this chapter.)

"The Seven Stars," in Hatch's *More Danish Tales*, is similar to the Russian story "The Seven Simeons" except that six brothers instead of seven use their unusual talents to find the princess. Instead of being commissioned by a king to bring back the princess to be his wife, the brothers rescue a princess from the troll because her father promised half the kingdom and her hand in marriage. Compare this story with the six sons of Anansi who had unusual talents which helped to rescue their father. McDermott's picture book *Anansi the Spider* tells why the moon is in the sky. The moon was to have been the reward to the son who saved Anansi's life, but each of the sons helped and it couldn't be decided who should get it so it was placed in the sky.

In "The Seven Stars," the brothers argued about who was to marry the princess, and so a fairy placed all seven in the sky so they would not be parted. Those seven stars belong to the group called the Pleiades which are part of the constellation of Taurus. Six of the stars are easily visible but the seventh is not often seen without a telescope. The two most common legends about the Pleiades come from the Ancient Greeks and the American Indians. The Greeks called the stars "The Seven Sisters." According to Hamilton's *Mythology*, the Pleiades are the seven daughters of Atlas who were pursued by Orion. Finally Zeus placed them in the sky to escape Orion. The most famous of the Pleiades is Electra. According to *World Book Encyclopedia*, the reason one star is not as bright is because one of them hid in shame for marrying a mortal. "The Seven Sisters" has a slightly different story. It was the Goddess Diana instead of Zeus who saved the sisters from Orion. Diana changed the sisters into white doves which Orion continued to hunt until Diana placed them in the sky. Eventually Orion was placed in the sky beside them. Students may also wish to read about the constellation Orion which appears best in the autumn and winter. Lum's *The Stars in Our Heaven* tells various myths about Orion from around the world. For star charts and locations, have students read pages 50 to 53 of Freeman's *The Sun, the Moon and the Stars*, pages 114 to 116 of White's *All About the Stars*, and page 45 of Crosby's *Junior Science Book of Stars*. Peltier's *Guideposts to the Stars* gives factual information about Pegasus, Orion, the Pleiades, and Ursa Major and Minor. Mythological information about Ursa Major and Minor, the big and little dippers, appears on pages 27 to 38 of Gringhuis' *Giants, Dragons and Gods; Constellations and their Folklore*. Twelve major star groups are represented. More mythological information is given in Rey's *The Stars; a New Way to See Them.* Star charts are included in Zim and Baker's *Stars, a Guide to the Constellations, Sun, Moon, Planets and Other Features of the Heavens.*

According to the Daens, or blackfellow of Australia, the Pleiades or Seven Sisters are the Maya-mayi. "Maya-mayi the Seven Sisters" appears in Parker's *Australian Legendary Tales.* Wurrunna left his people and went to find a new country. In his travels he saw seven sisters take their yam sticks and go to work. Wurrunna stole their yam sticks and stuck them into the ground. Then he caught two girls as they tried to retrieve their sticks, and they became Wurrunna's wives. He asked them to cut pine bark but they refused, saying that if they did so Wurrunna would never see them again. Wurrunna would not listen and when the wives struck the trees, the trees grew taller, taking the wives up into the sky. The five other sisters reached down and took their sisters with them so that now all seven are in the sky.

A Cherokee version of the origin of the Pleiades is found in Leach's *How the People Sang the Mountains Up.* Seven boys played a game of rolling a stone wheel along the ground by sliding a stick under it. The boys decided to run away from home when their mothers boiled their stones with the corn. The boys danced faster and faster until they rose into the sky to become the Pleiades. Rockwell's version comes from the Iroquois and is illustrated in her picture book *The Dancing Stars.* Seven brothers are lured into the sky by the singing of the Bear (Ursa Major) and spent their nights dancing for the moon. Rockwell also explains why only six are easily visible. The youngest returned as a shooting star but did not change back to a boy. A pine tree sprang from his mother's tears and became the tallest tree in the forest so that the youngest brother could be near the other six. Many second graders will be able to read this book to themselves, but it can also be enjoyed by persons of any age level.

All stories about the Pleiades that come from the Iroquois are not the same. "The Dancing Brothers," in Belting's *The Moon is a Crystal Ball* is a different version. Indian brothers danced into the sky but one tripped and fell when he looked back at his weeping mother. The last son fell to the ground and a pine tree grew from his grave.

The Seven Little Stars is one of eight filmstrips on Canadian folklore produced by the Film Board of Canada. Another filmstrip from that series is *Glooscap and the Seven Wishes.*

"How the Seven Brothers Saved Their Sisters" is found in Penney's *Tales of the Cheyenne.* Seven orphan brothers became the adopted brothers of a young girl named Red Leaf who had no relatives except a grandmother. When Red Leaf was kidnapped by the Double-Teethed Bull, the brothers went to rescue her. When other plans failed, the youngest, Moksois, shot an arrow into the air that became a tall tree which they all used to climb into the sky to escape the bull. They are there today in the sky as stars. Red Leaf is the head star and Moksois stands off to one side.

Jablow and Withers report in *The Man in the Moon* that "The Pleiades," according to Indians of the Brazilian Amazon, are seven children who thought they weren't given enough to eat and went to their uncle's house in the sky. According to the fifth legend in Belting's *The Stars are Silver Reindeer*, the Dyaks of Sarawak say the "Pleiades" are rice stars in a bowl of rice and Pegasus is the storehouse. The thirteenth legend in Belting's book comes from the Indians of Mato Grosso in Brazil who say the Pleiades are a heap of grated manoic. According to the twelfth legend of Belting's book, there are star patterns of the Pleiades on the gourd rattles used by the Navajo Indians to heal the sick because the stars are inside the gourds.

A legend of the Wabanski Indians called "Glooscap and the Seven Wishes" is found in Hill's *More Glooscap Stories*. Glooscap tested the strength and courage of his people by moving to a distant and difficult-to-reach place and then promised one wish to anyone who could travel through dangerous territory to get to him. Seven of the strongest braves set out and finally reached Glooscap. Each of them were given something to open when they arrived home that would fulfill their wish. All but the first couldn't wait until reaching home and opened the parcel prematurely with disastrous results, showing that Pandora was not the only curious person. The only one who resisted was the first who wanted only to feed himself and his family. The others wished to be loved by many women, make others laugh, cure diseases, see enemies first, be taller, and outlive everyone else. Use this story to introduce other stories about the Micmac Indians of Eastern Canada. The picture book by Toye *How Summer Came to Canada* is one of the stories included in Macmillan's *Glooskap's Country and Other Indian Tales*.

Another American legend comes from pre-Colonial times. Anne Malcolmson's "The Golden Cities of Cibola," in McFerran's *Stories to be Read Aloud to Children and by Children* comes from the new world. The story is based on the experiences of De Vaca and the search for the golden cities by the Spanish explorer, Coronado.

"The Swan Maidens" is found in the Jacobs' *European Folk and Fairy Tales*. A hunter watched seven swans shed their clothes and become maidens. The hunter took the clothes of the youngest and married her. When their daughter accidentally found the clothes many years later, the mother flew away to rejoin her sisters in the land East o' the Sun and West o' the Moon at the top of the Crystal Mountain. In order to reclaim his wife, the hunter had to recognize her from among her identical sisters. The hunter recognized his wife because she had marks on her fingers from sewing.

The Seven Silly Wise Men is a picture book by Bowman and Bianco that contains three tales, some of which appear in their book *Tales from a Finnish Tupa*. In the stories, Matti comes across some silly people from an imaginary part of Finland. Use the story to introduce other Finnish stories or noodlehead stories.

One of Jane Yolen's stories that reads like a folktale has "seven" in the title. *The Seventh Mandarin* is about the mandarins who guarded and guided the king of an Eastern realm. One of their duties was to fly the king's dragon kite which carried the king's soul. The seventh or youngest mandarin lost the kite to the wind, which tore it beyond repair. On his return to the palace, the seventh mandarin noticed things—like the poverty of the people—that were not written in the scrolls of the kingdom. He learned that the king was ill and was dreaming that there were hovels in his kingdom. The other mandarins tried to keep the truth from the king, saying it could not be so because it wasn't in the scrolls; but the seventh mandarin could not remain silent. After that, a kite was sent up annually to remind the king of the folly of believing only what is written. The story is a good example of symbolism.

There are many titles for a story about a timid tailor who killed with one blow from seven to sixty flies who were eating the jam on his bread, and then made a belt proclaiming the feat. The most popular title is "Seven at One Blow." The stories are essentially the same. After making the belt, the tailor went off into the world where he met a giant. The tailor tricked the giant into thinking he squeezed water from a stone (which was really a cheese), he could throw an object (which was really a flying bird) and, further, could help to carry a tree (while he rested in the branches). The tailor even tricked the giants into fighting among themselves. A king promised his daughter and half the kingdom to anyone who could kill the giants but didn't want to give his daughter to a mere tailor, so he asked the tailor to secure a unicorn and a wild boar before he could marry the princess. When the princess heard her husband talk in his sleep about his days as a tailor, she was ashamed of his humble beginnings and plotted to get rid of him. The tailor learned of the plot and mumbled about his exploits in his sleep and threatened to do the same to anyone who might be hiding outside his door. Since everyone was afraid of him, he was left alone. Eventually the tailor became king and presumably lived happily ever after.

There are several individual picture books recounting the story. Price's *Sixty at a Blow, a Tall Tale from Turkey* is about a timid tailor named Mustafa. Mustafa's experience with the giants differs from other versions. *The Valiant Little Tailor*, illustrated by Jauss, is based on the Grimm version and is similar to the story told here. Pipkin is the tailor's name in Jay Williams's retelling of *Seven at One Blow*. Eric Carle chose "Seven at One Blow" as one of seven stories included in *Eric Carle's Storybook*. Tasha Tudor calls her hero "The Valiant Tailor," in *Tasha Tudor's Book of Fairy Tales*, and Eric Protter calls him a"Clever Little Tailor" in *The Child's Treasury of Folk and Fairy Tales*. "The Gallant Tailor" appears in *Household Stories by the Brothers Grimm*, and *Grimms' Fairy Tales* (Follett). Littledale's paperback picture book is called *Seven at One Blow*. The frequent title "The Brave Little Tailor" is found in Manning-Sanders's *Giants*, Martignoni's *Illustrated Treasury of Children's Literature*, Thompson's *One Hundred Favorite Folktales*, and Lang's *Blue Fairy Book*. The version by Wiggin and Smith found in Sideman's *World's Best Fairy Tales* is one of the best for telling.

Bloom narrates "The Brave Little Tailor" on Robert Southey's *Goldilocks and the Three Bears and Other Stories*, as well as "The Valiant Little Tailor" of Williams-Ellis on the recording *Snow White and Other Fairy Tales* by the brothers Grimm. All of the stories have the tailor kill seven flies except in Price's picture book *Sixty at a Blow*, "A Dozen at a Blow" which appears in *European Folk and Fairy Tales* by Jacobs, the Tashian version where Nazar kills a thousand, and "Lazarus and the Dragon," found in McNeill's *The Sunken City*. "Lazarus and the Dragon" is a Greek version of the story in which a cobbler kills forty at one blow. The cobbler stitched the motto "With one stroke I have taken forty lives" onto his scabbard and set off to seek his fortune. Dragons tried to kill Lazarus in his sleep but he put a log in his bed and the next morning he pretended that he had not slept well because fleas were biting him. The dragons were afraid of anyone who thought their blows were mere flea bites. He eventually bested everyone.

"Jack and the Varmints," in Chase's *Jack Tales* comes from the Carolina mountains. Jack killed seven little blue butterflies and made a sign saying "Strong-Man-Jack-Killed-Seven-at-a-Whack." Two very different versions come from Armenia and America. "Nazar the Brave" appears in Tashjian's *Once There Was and Was Not*. In Ancient Armenia a lazy peasant killed a thousand living things at one blow and attached a cloth to a long pole proclaiming his prowess. Seven giants are outwitted in the story, and Nazar accidentally rode a tiger like a horse and took troops into battle much like "Valiant Chattee-Maker."

"The Valiant Chattee-Maker" appears in Baker's *Talking Tree* and in Haviland's *Favorite Fairy Tales Told in India*, as well as is the title of a picture book by Price. Another picture book of the same story adapted by Lexau is *It All Began With a Drip, Drip, Drip*. "The Valiant Potter" appears in Courlander's United Nations anthology *Ride with the Sun*. During a storm, a chattee-maker (pottery-maker) hopped on a tiger, rode home, and tied it to a post, all the while thinking it was his donkey. The man became a hero the next day when everyone saw the tiger tied outside his house. The rajah made the chattee-maker commander-in-chief of his army. Later the chattee-maker's horse ran away with him into the enemy camp and again his mistake was taken for bravery and the people pleaded for mercy. The story is a Hindu tale from India.

Divide the class into fifths and assign each third person to read a version from Germany, Greece and Turkey, Armenia, and the United States. Assign the easiest of the German versions to students with the least ability, and have the students make a chronological list of events in the story. Another day divide the class into groups so that there will be a person representing each of the five versions of the story in each group. Have the students, using their lists of events, tell the other four about their story. Have students choose which person will tell their story first or arrange it so that the shy or reluctant student will be last. Students will enjoy hearing all the versions.

MAGIC NUMBERS IN CHILDREN'S LITERATURE—*EIGHT*.   Wolkstein's picture book of the Chinese folktale *8,000 Stones* tells how the gift elephant was weighed. The elephant was taken aboard the boat and a water line was marked on the boat. Then the elephant was removed and stones were piled on the boat until it sank to that line.

"The Eight-Headed Dragon" is found in Uchida's *The Dancing Kettle*. When Prince Susano played a prank on his sister the sun goddess, she punished him by shutting herself in a cave. Everyone pleaded with her to come out of the cave so there would be light, and she finally did. Everyone was so angry with the prince he ran away. In his travels Prince Susano saw a family whose eight daughters had been sacrificed to an eight-headed dragon. When the dragon drank poisoned wine, the prince cut off the heads, and later was forgiven and all ended well.

Odin is the Norwegian counterpart of Jupiter/Zeus. Sleipnir was the name of "Odin's Eight-Legged Steed," in a story found in the d'Aulaire's *Norse Gods and Giants.* Since the story is short, background information could be provided on the gods of Asgard and their fight with the jotuns. Or, the mythic Greek horse, Pegasus, could be introduced. In the story "Bellerophon," in Unter-meyer's *Firebringer,* Bellerophon is given a golden bridle he can use to ride the winged horse Pegasus to where the Chimaera lives. After Bellerophon killed the monster he forgot that Athena had helped him. In the version by Padraic Colum called "Bellerophon," found in Johnson's *Anthology of Children's Literature,* Pegasus left Bellerophon when the blood of the Chimaera was spilled on him. The story also appears in Cundiff and Webb's *Story-Telling for You* as "Pegasus, the Winged Horse" and in Carpenter's *Wonder Tales of Horses and Heroes.* A picture book called *Pegasus* has been retold and illustrated by Turska.

Small children will enjoy *Flip* the horse created and illustrated by Wesley Dennis who appears in several picture books, and dreamt that he had wings. Lynd Ward's *The Silver Pony* is a picture book without words about a boy's imaginary ride on a winged horse. Stories of Pegasus provide background infor-mation so students will really enjoy these two books to the fullest. Two adult sources are "Bellerophon," in Graves's *Greek Gods and Heroes,* and "Pegasus and Bellerophon," in Hamilton's *Mythology.*

MAGIC NUMBERS IN CHILDREN'S LITERATURE—*NINE.* Since nine is a multiple of three, it is possible to tell three brief stories involving three characters, and this may be especially appropriate for younger children. The three favorites to be told could be "Goldilocks and the Three Bears," "The Three Billy Goats Gruff," and "The Three Little Pigs." Another story that could be told in this category is "The Princess and the Glass Hill." There were three brothers, three magic horses, and three golden apples. Sources for this story are included in this chapter in the section called "Numbers in Folklore—Three."

"Okus-ool and His Nine Red Horses, a Tuvan Tale" is found in Ginsburg's *The Kaha Bird, Tales from the Steppes of Central Asia.* According to the story, the greedy Karaty-Kahn wanted the nine red horses of Okus-ool, who fled. When a wolf ate his horses, Okus-ool received a yellow dog, three yurt poles, three grains of gold, and a small iron box. Okus-ool had to hide from the Kahn three times and complete three tasks.

The story of Orpheus is included in the section "The Nine Muses," in *The d'Aulaire's Book of Greek Myths,* because he is the mortal son of Calliope, the muse of epic poetry. The specialties of the other eight muses are lyrics, music, comedy, tragedy, dance, astronomy, history, and hymns. Use this information as an introduction to other stories about Orpheus.

Two stories featuring the number nine come from Bowman and Bianco's *Tales from a Finnish Tupa*. Both of the stories contain elements that make them similar to the stories found in the section of this chapter called "Numbers in Folklore—Eleven" called *Seven Ravens, the Wild Swans, The Six Swans*, and *The Twelve Brothers*. These stories can be used in that section also.

"The Girl Who Sought Her Nine Brothers" is from *Tales from a Finnish Tupa*. The mother of nine sons was to set a spindle outside the door if the tenth child was a girl. If the child was another boy, an axe would be put outside the door and the sons would leave home. When the daughter was born, an ogress switched the spindle for an axe, and the boys left home. When the daughter grew up and learned about her lost brothers, she searched for them. The ogress pretended to help and together they found and worked for the nine boys. Vieno could not tell her brothers who she was because when she was with them she could not speak, but one day one of the brothers overheard her singing in the field and they learned who Vieno really was.

"Mielikki and Her Nine Sons" is found in *Tales from a Finnish Tupa*. A witch, disguised as a midwife, assisted at the birth of the king and queen's triplets, and replaced the boys with crows. The brothers were changed to their human shape when they ate bread made from their mother's milk.

Students may be reminded that one of the twelve labors of Hercules was to kill the nine-headed hydra. Sources are found in the section on the number twelve.

MAGIC NUMBERS IN CHILDREN'S LITERATURE—*TEN*.   The Bible provides a story in which there are ten plagues and ten commandments. Smaller children can be told the story of *Moses and the Bullrushes* and at the end, that this same man was involved later in the ten plagues and the ten commandments.

There are several sources of the story that can be read or paraphrased. Chapter 17, "Mount Sinai," and chapter 18, "The Covenant," can be read from Shippen's *Moses. The Children's Bible* contains several chapters about Moses: "The Birth of Moses" (pp. 96–98); "Moses in Midron" (pp. 100–102); "The Miraculous Signs" (pp. 104); "Moses Returns to Egypt" (p. 105); "Pharaoh and the Israelites" (p. 106); "God Speaks to Moses" (p. 107); "The Ten Plagues" (pp. 108–117); "The Night of the Passover" (pp. 118–119);"Crossing the Red Sea" (pp. 120–122); "The Bitter Well of Marah" (p. 124); "Mannah from Heaven" (p. 125); "Water from the Rock" (p. 129); "The Defeat of Amalek" (pp. 120–131); "Jethro Advises Moses" (pp. 132–133); and "The Ten Commandments" (pp. 134–136).

Part 2, "Stories About Moses and the Israelites," in Gwynne's *Rainbow Book of Bible Stories*, provides another source of stories. "The Baby Moses in His Strange Cradle," "Moses Call of God at the Burning Bush," "Moses and the Ten Plagues," "Moses Institutes the Passover," "Moses Leads the Israelites out of Egypt," "Moses and the Israelites Cross the Red Sea," and "Moses Receives the Ten Commandments." It is best to stop before the story of the golden calf.

"The Birth of Israel," in *The Old Testament* illustrated by De Angeli relates the story of Moses from birth to death.

Persian folklore has a story about the number "ten." Ten men went into a house to drink tea and left their shoes at the door. Hosen came out last to find that his new shoes had disappeared, so he went to the mullah or village judge to learn which of the others had played a trick on him. "The Donkey's Tail," in Kelsey's *Once the Mullah, Persian Folk Tales* contains the story of how the mullah learned which of the ten men had taken the shoes. The mullah asked each of the men to go into the stable and pull the tail of the donkey, because when the thief pulled the tail, the donkey would bray. However, all of the men went into the barn and came out and the donkey did not bray. The mullah knew that the man who was afraid to pull the donkey's tail was the man whose hands did not smell like the spearmint he had put on the donkey's tail.

Two cumulative stories for primary students involve ten people, animals, or objects. The picture book illustrated by Galdone of *The Old Woman and Her Pig* includes a cat, rat, rope, butcher, ox, water, fire, a stick, dog, and pig. An American version of the gingerbread man story called "The Johnnycake" is found in Withers's *I Saw a Rocket Walk a Mile*. The johnnycake escaped from an old man, old woman, little boy, two well diggers, two ditch diggers, a bear, a wolf, and was finally eaten by a fox.

MAGIC NUMBERS IN CHILDREN'S LITERATURE—ELEVEN. The story "The Wild Swans" by Hans Christian Andersen is the only story we could find containing the number "eleven." This story, however, is very similar to other stories containing other numbers and is called "The Six Swans," "The Seven Ravens," "The Wild Swans," "The Twelve Brothers" and "The Twelve Wild Ducks." Andersen's *The Wild Swan* appears in picture-book format and is illustrated by Marcia Brown. The Lucas translation of Andersen's story appears in Johnson's *Anthology of Children's Literature,* and Arbuthnot's *Time for Fairytales, Old and New.* Another translation appears in *Tales of Magic and Enchantment by Lines.* The eleven sons in the story were changed into swans to escape from the wicked queen. Their sister Eliza found them with the help of an old woman, and to break the spell, had to weave eleven shirts with long sleeves without speaking. This was complicated when she married a king. The archbishop accused her of being a witch, imprisoned her, and finally sentenced her to death. On the day she is to be burned at the stake, the girl is saved by the return of her brothers. One of the arms is not finished so one brother has a wing instead of an arm. It is unfortunate that this version is the only one that contains eleven princes because it is the least effective story. The story is not as concise as other versions which include different numbers. If the other stories up until this one have been read aloud rather than told, this would be a good story to tell to children. Read all of the versions and decide which version to tell. Explain to the children that the story is told in many countries with varying numbers of swans, ravens or ducks but that for this occasion there will be eleven brothers.

The most readable version is called "The Six Swans." The version in collections of Lang and the brothers Grimm are called by this title and are very similar. A lost king agreed to marry the daughter of a witch to get out of a forest.

The new queen changed the sons from the king's previous marriage into swans. Their sister searched for them and learned that she could change them back to human form if she worked on making shirts for them for six years without laughing or talking. The shirts were made of flowers of asters or stars. The sister married a king whose mother disliked her, so she is sentenced to death. As in the Andersen story, the sister is rescued from the stake at the last minute but one of the shirts is not finished. The story is found in de la Mare's *Animal Stories*. The Lang version is found in *The Yellow Fairy Book* and in *The World's Best Fairy Tales* by Sideman. Versions by Grimm appear in *More Tales from Grimm, Household Stories by the Brothers Grimm, Fairy Tales by Grimm, Grimms' Fairy Tales* (illustrated by Kredel), Grimms' *About Wise Men and Simpletons,* and *The Complete Grimms' Fairy Tales.* The last two versions do not contain as much detail as the others and are not preferred sources. The Thompson version, found in *One Hundred Favorite Folktales,* is a Swedish version in which the wicked stepmother is changed into a raven at the end of the story. There is a version by the Grimm brothers in which the brothers are changed into ravens instead of swans. In "The Seven Ravens," the sister goes to the Glass Mountain to get her brothers back. In the picture book *The Seven Ravens, a Story of the Brothers Grimm,* illustrated by Felix Hoffman, the sister is the cause for the brothers becoming ravens. The sister also goes to the Glass Mountain to seek her brothers. In the picture book, the father turns the sons into ravens as punishment for breaking the water jug containing water for the daughter's baptism.

A similar version of the same title, found in Bamberger's *My First Big Story Book,* is listed as being of Russian origin. The sister is also at fault in the Grimm and Lang versions called "Twelve Brothers." A king and queen had twelve sons and the king told the queen that if the thirteenth was a girl, the sons would have to be killed and everything would be given to the daughter. In this story the brothers are also ravens. In order for the brothers to be set free, their sister had to be dumb and not laugh for seven years. The sister was married to a king but was condemned to die when she would not talk. The seven years were up when she was to be burned at the stake, but the brothers swooped down and saved her. "The Twelve Brothers" is to be found in Lang's *Red Fairy Book, Household Stories by the Brothers Grimm, Grimms' Fairy Tales* illustrated by Kredel, *Grimms' Fairy Tales,* and *The Complete Grimms' Fairy Tales.* The last Grimm version is very sketchy and is not the best one for telling. "The Twelve Wild Ducks" is a Scandinavian version found in Thorne-Thomsen's *East o'the Sun and West o'the Moon.* In this version the king and queen had twelve sons but the queen wished for a daughter. In return for a daughter the queen promised a witch she would give her whatever came over the bridge. The queen saw a white dog coming and expected that she would be trading the dog for a daughter. However, the twelve sons came over the bridge instead and were turned into twelve ducks. When the daughter learned that it was her fault that her brothers were lost to them, she went to get them back and the rest of the story is much the same. The Dasent version appears in Fitzgerald's *World Tales for Creative Dramatics and Storytelling.* The story by the same title is found in

Asbjornsen and Moë's *Norwegian Folk Tales* and has a different beginning. The queen has a bloody nose, sees the red on the white snow and wishes for a daughter for whom she says she would even trade her sons. A troll-hag overhears her and changes the sons to ducks and gives the queen a daughter who is called "Snow White Rose Red." The story in Jones's *Scandinavian Legends and Folktales* is very similar but is called "The Wild Swans."

Two stories from Bowman and Bianco's *Tales from a Finnish Tupa* have elements similar to these stories. Information about the stories appears in the section of this chapter called "Numbers in Folklore— Nine." In "The Girl Who Sought Her Nine Brothers," a girl is responsible for her brothers leaving home. When she finds them she is unable to speak. In "Mielikki and Her Nine Sons," seven of nine sons are turned into black crows by a witch.

MAGIC NUMBERS IN CHILDREN'S LITERATURE—*TWELVE*.   "The Twelve Dancing Princesses" is a very popular fairy tale. Either a soldier or a cowboy discovers that the princesses wore out their shoes every night dancing with twelve princes. In return for finding out why his daughters wore out their shoes every night the king promised the hand of any of the princesses in marriage. In Walter de la Mare's version found in Colwell's *Storyteller's Second Choices* and in his *More Tales Told Again*, the soldier does not want to marry any of the princesses. Other versions of the story are found in Sideman's *The World's Best Fairy Tales*, Haviland's *Favorite Fairy Tales Told in France*, Lang's *Red Fairy Book*, Grimms' *Fairy Tales* illustrated by Kredel, and the *Complete Grimms' Fairy Tales*. The Lang version about *Star Gazer* the cowboy makes an individual picture book illustrated by Adrienne Adams. The Grimm version about the soldier is an individual picture book illustrated by Uri Shulevitz. The play is found in Thane's *Plays from Famous Stories and Fairy Tales*. "The Soldier and the Twelve Princesses" is found in Tarcov's *Three Princess Stories*.

Another princess would marry anyone who could hide from her. This princess from the story "The Twelve Windows" could see through anything in the castle as well as through her twelve windows. A young swineherder was given three chances to hide from the princess. The last time a fox helped him hide from the princess, in her own hairdo. Even the princess couldn't see the back of her own head! The story appears in de la Mare's *Tales Told Again*.

"The Twelve Months" is a popular Russian story about a Cinderella-type who is made to work hard by her stepmother and stepsister. When she is asked to find impossible things in the winter such as violets and strawberries, she is helped by the Month Brothers. When the lazy sister goes to find some of the treats for herself she becomes lost in the snow and her mother is also lost when she goes after her. DeRegniers's picture book is called *Little Sister and the Month Brothers*.

The Twelve Labors of Hercules is available as an individual book by Newman and another called *Heracles the Strong* by Seraillier. Gruenberg's *More Favorite Stories Old and New for Boys and Girls* contains the story under the first title. Adults and older students should read "The Labors of Heracles," in *Greek Gods and Heroes* by Graves. The labors were to kill the Nemean lion, the nine-headed Hydra, the boar of Erymanthia, the stag of Artemus, the Stymphalian birds, clean the Augean stables, catch the bull of Minos in Crete, capture the man-eating mares of King Dromedes of Thrace, secure the jeweled belt of the Amazon Queen Hippolyta, steal the cattle of the three-headed monster Geryon, give the apples of the Hesperides to Eurystheus, and see Cerberus the watchdog of the dead.

For information about Hercules in the stars, consult "The Kneeler's Twelve Tasks," in Gringhuis's *Giants, Dragons and Gods,* Lum's *The Stars in our Heavens,* and Joseph and Lippincott's *Point to the Stars.*

MAGIC NUMBERS IN CHILDREN'S LITERATURE—*THIRTEEN.* Leach's *The Luck Book* (pp. 95–100) contains four superstitions about "thirteen" being unlucky and six superstitions about thirteen being lucky. Also included is information about a baker's dozen. One origin of the term appears in *Tales Our Settlers Told* by the Raskins. Another appears in Cothran's *With a Wig With a Wag, Other American Folk Tales.* "A Dozen Is 13" comes from New Amsterdam in 1644 when Jan Pietersen Van Amsterdam was asked by an old hag for a dozen cookies. Jan gave her twelve and she asked loudly for a dozen. The baker only gave her twelve and he had bad luck all the following year. Finally the third time the old hag asked for a dozen cookies, Jan gave her 13.

For more information about superstitions and the number thirteen see *Superstitious!* by Heaps and *Superstitious? Here's Why!* by Batchelor and De Lys.

The Thirteen Days of Yule could be read or sung at this time. This Scottish version of "The Twelve Days of Christmas" is also a dance.

SPECIALIZED BIBLIOGRAPHIC CATEGORIES

At the back of this book are two numbered bibliographical indexes, one of multimedia (nonprint material), and one of books. The numbers below refer to those indexes, with the entries preceded by "M" found in the Multimedia Index.

JOKE AND RIDDLE BOOKS

RIDDLE STORIES

1167, 1168, 1169, 1170, 1234, 1278, 1324, 1386, 1504, 1636, 1716, 1879, 2014, 2064, 2072, 2096, 2153, 2157, 2309, 2403, 2498, 2517, 2518, 2540, 2556, 2787, 2789, 2790, 2849, 2852, 2855, 2885, 2995, 3117, 3216, 3245, 3252, 3338, 3411, 3519, 3520, 3766, 3771, 3854, 3887a, 3919, 4016, 4099, 4147, 4301, 4311, 4312, 4563, 4564, 4783, 4873, 4874, 4878, 4939, 4944.

THE RIDDLE OF COMMUNICATION

M197, 12, 29, 35, 75, 223, 298, 299, 300, 303, 304, 305, 306, 313, 323, 536, 637, 709, 772, 884, 902, 1045, 1048, 1051, 1097, 1178, 1273, 1274, 1305, 1363, 1411, 1412, 1413, 1414, 1415, 1416, 1417, 1418, M7, 1419, M638, M639, M640, 1416, 1418, 1426, 1427, 1541, 1624, 1706, 1786, 1842, 1843, 1909, 1966, 2055, 2173, 2227, 2320 a & b, 2322, 2386, 2403, 2465, 2490, 2561, 2562, 2661, 2714, 2715, 2755, 3016, 3017, 3252, 3332, 3333, 3343, 3517, 3518, 3539, 3631, 3664, 3747, 3787, 3788, 3789, 3790, 3791, 3934, 3976, 4036, 4060, 4073, 4163, 4315, 4402, 4531, 4738, 4807, 4814, 4815, 4912, 4929, 5012.

Bibliographical Indexes

* The Asterisk between the item number and the author denotes a Caldecott Medal winner.

M The Number preceded by "M" after the date is a related title in the Multimedia Index, which begins on page 645.

Books

1a Aardema, Verna. *The Riddle of the Drum; a Tale from Tizapan, Mexico.* Illus by Tony Chen. New York: Four Winds, 1979.

1b ———. *Tales for the Third Ear, From Equatorial Africa.* Illus by Ib Ohlsson. New York: Dutton, 1969

2 ———. *Who's in Rabbit's House?* Illus by Leo and Diane Dillon. New York: Dial, 1977.

3 *———. *Why Mosquitoes Buzz in People's Ears.* Illus by Leo and Diane Dillon. New York: Dial, 1975. Paperback. M751-M752.

4 Aaron, Chester. *American Ghost.* Illus by David Gwynne Lemon. New York: Harcourt, 1973.

5 Abbe, Dorothy. *The Dwiggins Marionettes: A Complete Experimental Theatre in Miniature.* Boston: Plays, 1970.

6 Abbott, R. Tucker. *Sea Shells of the World; a guide to the better-known species.* Illus by George and Marita Sandstrom. New York: Golden, 1962. Paperback.

7 Abisch, Roz. *Around the House that Jack Built: A Tale of Ecology.* New York: Parents, 1972.

8 Abisch, Roz and Boche Kaplan. *Art is For You.* New York: McKay, 1967.

9 ———. *Sweet Betsy From Pike.* New York: McCall, 1970. M32, M662.

10 Abney, Louise and Grace Rowe. *Choral Speaking Arangements for Lower Grades.* Magnolia, Mass: Expression, 1953.

11 Abraham, Jean-Pierre. *The Pigeon Man.* Illus by Alan E. Cober. New York: Harlin Quist, 1971.

12 Achen, Sven. *Symbols Around Us.* New York: Van Nostrand, 1978.

13 Ackley, Edith Flack. *Dolls to Make for Fun and Profit.* Illus by Tekla Ackley. Philadelphia: Lippincott, 1951.

14 ———. *Marionettes, Easy to Make! Fun to Use.* Phila.: Lippincott, 1929.

15 Adair, Margaret Weeks. *Do-it-in-a-day Puppets for Beginners, How to Make Your Puppets, Create Your Script, and Perform, all in One Day.* New York: Day, 1964.

16 ———. and Elizabeth Patapoff *Folk Puppet Plays for Social Studies.* New York: Day, 1972.

17 Adams, Adrienne. *Easter Egg Artists.* Illus by the author. New York: Scribner, 1976.

18 ———. *A Woggle of Witches.* Illus by the author. New York: Scribner, 1971. M768

19 Adams, Adrienne, illus. *Bring a Torch, Jeannette, Isabella, a provencial carol.* New York: Scribner, 1963.

20 Adams, Richard. *Watership Down.* New York: Macmillan, 1972. Avon paperback.

21 Adams, Samuel H. *The Erie Canal.* Illus by Leonard Vosburgh. New York: Random, 1953. M107, M193, M194.

22 Adamson, Joy. *Born Free.* New York: Random paperback, 1974. M95.

23 ———. *Born Free: A Lioness of Two Worlds.* New York: Pantheon, 1960.

24 ———. *Elsa.* New York: Pantheon, 1963.

25 ———. *Forever Free.* New York: Harcourt, 1963. Bantam paperback.

26 ———. *Living Free.* New York: Harcourt, 1961.

27 Addams, Charles. *The Charles Addams Mother Goose.* Illus by Charles Addams. New York: Harper, 1967.

28 Adelson, Lenore. *All Ready for Winter.* Illus by Kathleen Elgin. New York: McKay, 1952.

29a Adkins, Jan. *Symbols: A Silent Language.* New York: Walker, 1978.

29b Adler, Irving and Ruth Adler. *Your Eyes.* New York: Day, 1963.

30 Adshead, Gladys. *Brownies Hush.* Illus by Elizabeth Orton Jones. New York: Walck, 1930, 1966.

31 Adshead, Gladys and Annis Duff, ed. *An Inheritance of Poetry.* Illus by Mona S. Unwin. Boston: Houghton, 1948.

32 Adler, Bill. *The World's Worst Riddles and Jokes.* Illus by Ed Malsberg. New York: Grosset, 1976.

33 Adler, David A. *Redwoods are the Tallest Trees in the World.* Illus by Kazue Mizumura. New York: Crowell, 1978.

34 Adler, Irving. *Magic House of Numbers.* Illus by Ruth and Peggy Adler. New York: Day, 1974.

35 Adler, Irving and Joyce Adler. *Language and Man.* New York: Day, 1970.

36 Adler, Irving and Peggy Adler. *Adler Book of Puzzles and Riddles.* Illus by Peggy Adler. New York: Day, 1962.

37 Adler, Irving and Ruth. *The Calendar.* New York: Day, 1967.

38 ———. *Your Eyes.* New York: Day, 1963.

39 Adler, Peggy. *Geography Puzzles.* New York:

Watts, 1979.

40 ———. Second Adler Book of Puzzles and Riddles. New York: Day, 1963.

41 Adler, Peggy and Irving. Math Puzzles. New York: Watts, 1978.

42 ———. Metric Puzzles. New York: Watts, 1977.

43 Adoff, Arnold. Big Sister Tells Me That I'm Black. Illus by Lorenzo Lynch. New York: Holt, 1976.

44 ———. Black is Brown is Tan. Illus by Emily A. McCully. New York: Harper, 1973.

45 ———. Ma n Da la. Illus by Emily A. McCully. New York: Harper, 1971.

46 ———, ed. Black Out Loud, an Anthology of Modern Poems. Illus by Alvin Hollingsworth. New York: Macmillan, 1970. Dell paperback.

47 ———. I am the Darker Brother: An Anthology of Modern Poems by Black Americans. New York: Macmillan, 1968. Collier paperback.

48 ———. It is the Poem Singing Into Your Eyes: an Anthology of New Poets. New York: Harper, 1971.

49 ———. My Black Me, a Beginning Book of Black Poetry. New York: Dutton, 1974.

50 ———. The Poetry of Black America: An Anthology of the Twentieth Century. New York: Harper, 1973.

51 Aesop. Androcles and the Lion. Illus by Janusz Grabianski. New York: Watts, 1970.

52 ———. The Caldecott Aesop: Twenty Fables; a Facsimilie the 1883 edition of Alfred Caldecott. Illus by Randolph Caldecott. New York: Doubleday, 1978.

53 ———. Aesop: Five Centuries of Illustrated Fables. Selected by John H. McKendry. Illustrations from the Metropolitan Museum. New York: Graphic, 1964. (M10).

54 ———. Aesop's Fables. Edited and illustrated by Boris Artzybasheff. New York: Viking, 1933. (M10).

55 ———. Aesop's Fables. Retold by Anne Terry White and illustrated by Helen Siegl. New York: Random, 1964. (M10).

56 ———. Aesop's Fables. Adapted by Louis Untermeyer. Illus by A. and M. Provensen. New York: Golden, 1965. (M10).

57 ———. Fables from Aesop. Poems by Ennis Rees. Illus by J. J. Grandville. London: Oxford, 1966. (M10).

58 ———. The Fables of Aesop. Selected and retold by Joseph Jacobs. Illus by David Levine. Afterword by Clifton Fadiman. New York: Macmillan, 1964. (M10).

59 ———. The Lion and the Rat. Illus by Brian Wildsmith. New York: Watts, 1963.

60 ———. Three Aesop Fox Tales. Illus by Paul Galdone. New York: Seabury, 1971.

61 Agay, Dennes. Best Loved Songs of the American People. Illus by Reisie Lonette. Garden City, NY: Doubleday, 1975.

62 Agree, Rose H., ed. How to Eat a Poem and Other Morsels: A Collection of Food Poems for Children. New York: Pantheon, 1967.

63 Aiken, Conrad. Cats and Bats and Things with Wings. Illus by Milton Glaser. New York: Atheneum, 1965.

64 ———. Tom, Sue and the Clock. Illus by Julia Maas. New York: Crowell, 1966.

65 ———. Who's Zoo. Illus by John Vernon Lord. New York: Atheneum, 1977.

66 Aiken, Joan. Black Hearts in Battersea. Garden City, NY: Doubleday, 1964. Dell paperback.

67 ———. Go Saddle the Sea. Garden City, NY: Doubleday, 1977.

68 ———. Midnight is a Place. New York: Viking, 1974. Paperback.

69 ———. Night Fall. New York: Holt, 1969. Dell paperback.

70a ———. Nightbirds on Nantucket. Garden City, NY: Doubleday, 1966. Dell paperback.

70b ———. The Skin Spinners. New York: Viking, 1976.

71 ———. Winterthing, a Play for Children. Illus by Arvis Stewart. New York: Holt, 1972. Paperback.

72 ———. Wolves of Willoughby Chase. Garden City, NY: Doubleday, 1962, Dell paperback.

73 Alain. One, Two, Three, Going to Sea. Englewood Cliffs, NJ: Scholastic, 1969. Paperback.

74 Alan, Sandy. The Plaid Peacock. Illus by Kelly Oeshsli. New York: Pantheon, 1965.

75 Albert, Burton. Secret Codes for Kids. Chicago: Whitman, 1976.

76 Alcott, Louisa May. Eight Cousins. New York: Grosset and Dunlap, 1971.

77 ———. Eight Cousins. Illus by Hattie Longstreet Price. Boston: Little, 1874.

78 ———. Jo's Boys. New York: Grosset and Dunlap, 1949.

79 ———. Jo's Boys. New York: Macmillan, n.d. Collier paperback.

80 ———. Little Men. Illus by Douglas W. Gorsline. New York: Grosset and Dunlap, n.d.

81 ———. Little Men. Illus by Paul Hogarth. New York: Macmillan, 1963. Paperback.

82 ———. Little Women, or Meg, Jo, Beth and Amy. Illus by Tasha Tudor. New York: Collins, 1969. M381, M382, M383.

83 ———. Old Fashioned Girl. New York: Grosset and Dunlap, 1971.

84 ———. Old Fashioned Girl. Boston: Little, 1869.

85 ———. An Old-Fashioned Thanksgiving. Illus by Holly Johnson. Philadelphia: Lippincott, 1974.

86 ———. Rose in Bloom. New York: Grosset and Dunlap, 1971.

87 ———. Rose in Bloom. Boston: Little, 1876.

88 ———. Under the Lilacs. New York: Grosset and Dunlap, 1971.

89 ———. Under the Lilacs. Boston: Little, 1877.

90 Alderson, Brian. Cakes and Custard. Illus by Helen Oxenbury. New York: Morrow, 1975.

91 Aldis, Dorothy. All Together, a Child's Treasury of Verse. Illus by Helen Jameson, Marjorie Flack and Margaret Freeman. New York: Putnam, 1952.

92 ———. Hello Day. Illus by Susan Elson. New York: Putnam, 1959.

93 ———. Dum Stupid David. Illus by Jane Miller. New York: Putnam, 1965.

94 ———. Favorite Poems of Dorothy Aldis. Illus by Jack Lerman. New York: Putnam, 1970.

95 ———. *Is Anybody Hungry?* Illus by Arthur Markovia. New York: Putnam, 1964.

96 ———. *Nothing is Impossible; the Story of Beatrix Potter.* Illus by Richard Cuffari. New York: Atheneum, 1969.

97 Alegria, Ricardo E. *The Three Wishers, A Collection of Puerto Rican Folktales.* Illus by Lorenzo Homer. New York: Harcourt. 1969.

98 Alexander, A. *ABC of Cars and Trucks.* Illus by Ninon. Garden City, NY: Doubleday, 1956.

99 ———. *Boats and Ships from A to Z.* Illus by Will Huntington. Chicago: Rand, 1961.

100 Alexander, Lloyd. *The Black Cauldron.* New York: Holt, 1965. Dell paperback.

101 ———. *The Book of Three.* New York: Holt, 1964. Dell paperback.

102 ———. *The Castle of Llyr.* New York: Holt, 1966. Dell paperback.

103 ———. *The Cat Who Wished to be a Man.* New York: Dutton, 1973.

104 ———. *Coll and His White Pig.* Illus by Evaline Ness. New York: Holt, 1965.

105 ———. *The Foundling and Other Tales of Pyrdain.* New York: Holt, 1973.

106 ———. *The Four Donkeys.* Illus by Lester Abrams. New York: Holt, 1972.

107 ———. *The High King.* New York: Holt, 1968. Dell paperback. M285.

108 ———. *The King's Fountain.* Illus by Ezra J. Keats. New York: Dutton, 1971.

109 ———. *The Marvelous Misadventures of Sebastian; Grand Extravaganza, including a performance by the Entire Cast of the Gallimufry-Theatricus.* New York: Dutton, 1970.

110 ———. *Taran Wanderer.* New York: Holt, 1967. Dell paperback.

111 ———. *Time Cat.* Illus by Bill Sokol. New York: Holt, 1963. Camelot paperback.

112 ———. *The Truthful Harp.* Illus by Evaline Ness. New York: Holt, 1967. Paperback.

113 ———. *The Wizard in the Tree.* Illus by Laszlo Kubinyi. New York: Dutton, 1975.

114 Alexander, Martha. *And My Mean Old Mother Will be Sorry, Blackboard Bear.* Illus by the author. New York: Dial, 1972. Pied Piper paperback.

115 ———. *Blackboard Bear.* Illus by the author. New York: Dial, 1969.

116 ———. *Bobo's Dream.* New York: Dial, 1970. Scholastic paperback.

117 ———. *I Sure Am Glad to See You, Blackboard Bear.* Illus by the author. New York: Dial, 1976. Pied Piper paperback.

118 ———. *I'll Be the Horse if You'll Play with Me.* Illus by the author. New York: Dial, 1975.

119 ———. *I'll Protect You from the Jungle Beasts.* Illus by the author. New York: Dial, 1973. Pied Piper paperback.

120 ———. *No Ducks in our Bathtub.* New York: Dial, 1973. Pied Piper paperback.

121 ———. *Nobody Asked me if I Wanted a Baby Sister.* Illus by the author. New York: Dial, 1971.

122 ———. *Out!Out!Out!* New York: Dial, 1968.

123 ———. *Sabrina.* New York: Dial, 1971.

124 ———. *The Story Grandmother Told.* Illus by the author. New York: Dial, 1969.

125 ———. *We Never Get to Do Anything.* Illus by the author. New York: Dial, 1970. Pied Piper paperback.

126 ———. *We're in Trouble, Blackboard Bear.* Illus by the author. New York: Dial, 1980.

127 Alexander, Sue. *Peacocks are Very Special.* New York: Doubleday, 1976.

Aliki. See Brandenberg, Aliki.

128 Alkema, Chester J. *Monster Masks.* Photos by the author. New York: Sterling, 1973.

129 ———. *Puppet-Making.* New York: Sterling, 1971.

130 ———. *Tissue Paper Creations.* New York: Sterling, 1973.

131 Allen, Gertrude E. *Everyday Wildflowers.* New York: Houghton, 1965.

132 Allen, Marie Louise. *A Pocketful of Poems.* Illus by Sally Greenwold. New York: Harper, 1957.

133 Allen, Merrit P. *Johnny Reb.* Illus by Ralph Ray. New York: Longmans, 1952.

134 Allen, Robert. *Numbers: A First Counting Book.* New York: Platt, 1968.

135 Allen, Terry, ed. *The Whispering Wind, Poetry by Young American Indians.* New York: Doubleday, 1972. Paperback.

136 Allstrom, Elizabeth. *Songs Along the Way.* Illus by Mel Silverman. Nashville, Tenn.: Abingdon, 1961.

137 Almoznino, Albert. *The Art of Hand Shadows.* Photos by Y. Pinas. New York: Stravon, 1969. Paperback.

138 Ambrus, Victor G. *Three Poor Tailors.* Illus by the author. New York: Harcourt, 1965. M688.

139 Ambrus, Victor. *Brave Soldier Janosh.* New York: Harcourt, 1967. M585.

140 ———. *The Little Cockerel.* New York: Harcourt, 1968.

141 American Heritage. *The Erie Canal.* New York: American Heritage, 1964. M107, M193, M194.

American Heritage. See also, Ward, Don.

142 American Institute of Graphic Arts. *Catalog of Children's Book Shows.* 1941.

143 American Library Association. *Notable Children's Books, 1940–59.* Chicago: Children's Services Division, A.L.A., 1966. Paperback.

144 ———. *Notable Children's Books, 1940–70.* Chicago: Children's Services Division, A.L.A., 1976.

145 Ames, Lee J. *Draw Fifty Airplanes, Aircraft, and Spacecraft.* New York: Doubleday, 1977.

146 ———. *Draw Fifty Dinosaurs and Other Prehistoric Animals.* New York: Doubleday, 1977.

147a Amoss, Berthe. *By the Sea.* New York: Parents, 1969.

147b ———. *The Chalk Cross.* Boston: Houghton, 1976.

148 Anckarsvard, Karin. *Madcap Mystery.* Trans by Annabelle Macmillan. Illus by Paul Galdone. New York: Harcourt, 1957. Paperback.

149 ———. *The Mysterious Schoolmaster.* Trans by Annabelle Macmillan. Illus by Paul Galdone. New York: Harcourt, 1959. Voyager paperback.

150 ———. The Robber Ghost. Trans by Annabelle Macmillan. Illus by Paul Galdone. New York: Harcourt, 1961. Paperback.
151 Andersen, Hans Christian. Complete Fairy Tales and Stories. Trans. by Erik C. Haugaard. Foreward by Virginia Haviland. Garden City, NY: Doubleday, 1974.
152 ———. The Emperor's New Clothes. Illus and translated by Erik Blegvad. New York: Harcourt, n.d.
153 ———. The Emperor's New Clothes. Illus by Virginia Lee Burton. Boston: Houghton, 1949.
154 ———. The Fir Tree. Illus by Nancy Ekholm Burkert. New York: Harper, 1970.
155 ———. The Nightingale. Trans by Eva LaGallienne. Illus by Nancy E. Burkert. New York: Harper, 1965.
156 ———. The Snow Queen. Adapted by Naomi Lewis. Illus by Toma Bogdanovic. New York: Scroll, 1968.
157 ———. The Ugly Duckling. Illus by Adrienne Adams. New York: Scribner, 1965. Paperback.
158 ———. The Ugly Duckling. Trans by R. P. Keigwin. Illus by Toma Bogdanovic. New York: Scroll, 1971.
159 ———. What the Good Man Does is Always Right. Illus by Rick Schreiter. New York: Dial, 1968.
160 ———. The Wild Swans. Illus by Marcia Brown. New York: Scribner, 1963.
161 ———. The Woman with the Eggs. Adapted by Jan Wahl. Illus by Ray Cruz. New York: Crown, 1974.
162 Anderson, Benny E. Let's Start a Puppet Theatre. New York: Van Nostrand, 1973.
163 Anderson, Clarence W. C.W. Anderson's Complete Book of Horses and Horesmanship. New York: Macmillan, 1963.
164 ———. Billy and Blaze. New York: Macmillan, 1962.
165 ———. Twenty Gallant Horses. New York: Macmillan, 1965.
166 Anderson, Joy. Hai Yin, The Dragon Girl. Illus by Jay Yang.
167 Anderson, Lonzo. Arion and the Dolphins. Illus by Adrienne Adams. New York: Scribner, 1978.
168 ———. The Day the Hurricane Happened. Illus by Ann Grifalconi, Scribner, 1974.
169 ———. Mr. Biddle and the Birds. New York: Scribner, 1971.
170 ———. Two Hundred Rabbits. Illus by Adrienne Adams. New York: Viking, 1968. Seafarer paperback.
171a ———. Zeb. Illus by Peter Burchard. New York: Knopf, 1966.
171b Anderson, Margaret J. To Nowhere and Back. New York: Knopf, 1975.
172 Anderson, Mildred. Papier-Mâché-How to Use It. New York: Sterling, 1964. o.p.
173 ———. Papier Mâché Crafts. New York: Sterling, 1975.
174 Anderson, Robert L. and John Bradford. The House That Jack Built & Other Favorite Jingles. New York: Crown, 1964.
175 Angel, Marie. The Ark. New York: Harper, 1973.
176 Anglund, Joan Walsh. A Friend is Someone Who Likes You. Illus by the author. New York: Harcourt, 1958.
177 ———. Morning is a Little Child. Illus by the author. New York: Harcourt, 1969.
178 ———. Nibble Nibble Mousekin: A Tale of Hansel and Gretel. Illus by the author. New York: Harcourt, 1962. Voyager paperback.
179 ———. A Year is Round. Illus by the author. New York: Harcourt, 1966.
180 Annixter, Paul. Cat That Clumped. Illus by Brinton Turkle. New York: Holiday, 1966.
181 Anno, Mitsumasa. Anno's Alphabet, An Adventure in Imagination. Illus by the author. New York: Crowell, 1975.
182 ———. Anno's Counting Book. Illus by M. Anno. New York: Crowell, 1977.
183 ———. Anno's Journey. Illus by M. Anno. New York: Collins, 1977.
184 ———. Topsy-Turvies: Pictures to Stretch the Imagination. Illus by M. Anno. New York: Weatherhill, 1970.
185 ———. Upside-Downers: More Pictures to Stretch the Imagination. Illus. by M. Anno. New York: Weatherhill, 1971.
186 Anrooy, Frans Van. The Bird Tree. New York: Harcourt, 1966.
187a Arbuthnot, May Hill, comp. Time for Fairy Tales Old and New. Illus by John Averill. Glenview, Ill.: Scott Foresman, 1961.
187b ———. Time for Poetry. Glenview, IL: Scott Foresman, 1961.
188 Arbuthnot, May Hill and Zena Sutherland. Arbuthnot Anthology of Children's Literature, 4th ed. Glenview, Ill.: Scott Foresman, 1976.
189 ———. rev. by Sutherland. Children and Books. Glenview, Ill.: Scott Foresman, 1977.
190 Ardizzone, Edward. Little Tim and the Brave Sea Captain. Illus by the author. New York: Walck, 1955. M378, M379
191 ———. Tim in Danger. Illus by the author. New York: Walck, 1953.
192 ———. Tim and the Lighthouse. Illus by the author. New York: Walck, 1968.
193 ———. Tim All Alone. Illus by the author. New York: Walck, 1957. M697.
194 ———. The Young Ardizzone, an Autobiographical Fragment. New York: Macmillan, 1971. M186.
195 Arkin, David. Black and White. Music by Earl Robinson. Los Angeles, CA: Ward Ritchie, 1956, 1966.
196 Arkhurst, Joyce Cooper. Adventures of Spider. Boston: Little, 1964. Scholastic paperback.
197 Armour, Richard. Adventures of Egbert the Easter Egg. Illus by Paul Galdone. New York: McGraw, 1965.
198 Armstrong, Louise. The Thump, Bam, Bump Mystery. Illus by Ray Cruz. New York: Walker, 1975.
199 Armstrong, William H. Sounder. Illus by James Barkley. New York: Harper, 1969. M626
200 ———. Sour Land. New York: Harper, 1971.
201 Arnold, Elliott. A Kind of Secret Weapon. New York: Scribner, 1969.

202 Arnott, Kathleen. *African Myths and Legends*. Illus by Joan Kiddell-Monroe. New York: Walck, 1962.

203 ———. *Animal Folk Tales Around the World*. Illus by Bernadette Watts. New York: Walck, 1971.

204 ———. *Dragons, Ogres, and Scary Things: Two African Tales*. Champaign, IL: Garrard, 1974.

205 Arnott, Peter D. *Plays Without People; Puppetry and Serious Drama*. Bloomington: Indiana University, 1964.

206 Artzybasheff, Boris. *Seven Simeons: A Russian Tale*. Illus by the author. New York: Viking, 1961.

207 Aruego, Jose. *Look What I Can Do*. Illus by the author. New York: Scribner, 1971.

208 Asbjornsen, Peter and E. J. Moe. *East of the Sun and West of the Moon*. Illus by Tom Vroman. New York: Macmillan, 1953, 1963.

209 ———. *East of the Sun and West of the Moon and Other Tales*. New York: Nielsen, 1977.

210 ———. *Norwegian Folk Tales*. Trans by Pat Shaw Iversen and Carl Norman. Illus by Erik Werenskiold and Theodor Kittelsen. New York: Viking, 1960.

211 ———. *The Runaway Pancake*. Illus by Svend Otto S. Trans by Joan Tate. New York: Larousse, 1980.

212 Asch, Frank. *The Blue Balloon*. New York: McGraw, 1971.

213 ———. *Elvira Everything*. Illus by the author. New York: Harper, 1970.

214 ———. *Yellow Yellow*. New York: McGraw, 1971.

215 Asimov, Isaac. *ABC's of Earth*. New York: Walker, 1971.

216 ———. *ABC's of Ecology*. New York: Walker, 1972.

217 ———. *ABC's of Space*. New York: Walker, 1969.

218 ———. *ABC's of the Ocean*. New York: Walker, 1970.

219 ———. *Animals of the Bible*. Illus by Howard Berelson. New York: Doubleday, 1978.

220 ———. *Bloodstream: River of Life*. New York: Macmillan, 1966.

221 ———. *Building Blocks of the Universe*. New York: Abelard, 1961.

222 ———. *David Starr, Space Ranger*. Garden City, NY: Doubleday, 1951. Signet paperback.

223 ———. *The Egyptians*. Boston: Houghton-Mifflin, 1967.

224 ———. *How Did We Find Out About Dinosaurs?* Illus by David Wood. New York: Walker, 1973.

225 ———. *I Robot*. Garden City, NY: Doubleday, 1950. Fawcett paperback.

226 ———. *Realm of Numbers*. New York: Houghton, 1959.

227 ———. *Words from the Myths*. New York: Houghton, 1961. NAL paperback.

228 ———. *Words from Science*. New York: Houghton, 1959. NAL paperback.

229 Association for Childhood Education International. *Sung Under the Silver Umbrella, Poems for Younger Children*. New York: Macmillan, 1942.

230 ———. *Told Under the Green Umbrella*. New York: Macmillan, 1935, 1967.

231 Atwater, Richard and Florence. *Mr. Popper's Penguins*. Illus by Robert Lawson. Boston: Little, 1938.

232 Atwood, Ann. *Haiku: The Mood of Earth*. Photos by the author. New York: Scribner, 1971.

233 ———. *My Own Rhythm, an Approach to Haiku*. Photos by the author. New York: Scribner, 1973.

234 ———. *New Moon Cove*. Photos by the author. New York: Scribner, 1969.

235 ———. *The Wild Young Desert*. Photos by the author. New York: Scribner, 1970.

236 Audubon, John James. *The Birds of America*. New York: Macmillan, 1947.

237 Auerbach, Marjorie. *Seven Uncles Came to Dinner*. Illus by the author. New York: Knopf, 1963.

Aulaire, d' *see* d'Aulaire.

238 Ausubel, Nathan. *Treasury of Jewish Folklore, Stories, Traditions, Legends, Humor, Wisdom, and Folk Songs of the Jewish People*. New York: Crown, 1948.

239 Austin, Oliver L. *Birds of the World; a Survey of the Twenty-seven Orders and One Hundred Fifty-five Families*. Illus by Arthur Sing. New York: Golden, 1961.

240 ———. *Families of Birds*. New York: Western, 1971. Paperback.

241a Austin, Mary C. and Queenie Mills. *The Sound of Poetry*. Boston: Allyn and Bacon, 1963.

241b Averill, Esther. *The Fire Cat*. Illus by author. New York: Harper, 1960.

242 ———. *Jenny's Bedside Book*. Illus by the author. New York: Harper, 1959.

243 ———. *Jenny's Birthday Book*. Illus by the author. New York: Harper, 1954. M330

244 Ayer, Jacqueline. *Little Silk*. Illus by the author. New York: Harcourt, 1970.

245 ———. *Nu Dang and His Kite*. Illus by the author. New York: Harcourt, 1959.

246 ———. *The Paper-Flower Tree, a Tale of Thailand*. Illus by the author. New York: Harcourt, 1962.

247 Aylesworth, Thomas G. *Monsters from the Movies*. Philadelphia: Lippincott paperback, 1972.

248 ———. *Movie Monsters*. Philadelphia: Lippincott paperback, 1975.

249 ———. *Vampires and Other Ghosts*. Reading, Mass.: Addison-Wesley, 1972.

250 ———. *Werewolves and Other Monsters*. Reading, Mass.: Addison-Wesley, 1971.

251 Aymar, Brandt and Edward Sagarin. *Laws and Tricks that Created History*. New York: Crown, 1974.

252 Babbitt, Natalie. *The Search for Delicious*. New York: Avon, 1974. Paperback.

253 Bacon, Denise. *Forty-Six Two-Part American Folk Songs*. Wellesley, MA: Kodaly Musical Training Institute, 1973.

254 Bader, Barbara. *American Picturebooks from Noah's Ark to the Beast Within*. New York: Macmillan, 1975.

255 Bador, John. *Creating and Presenting Hand*

Puppets. New York: Reinhold, 1967.

256 Bagnold, Enid. *National Velvet.* Illus by Paul Brown. New York: Morrow, 1935, 1949. Archway paperback. M477

257 Bahadur, Dinesh. *Come Fly a Kite.* New York: Harvey, 1978.

258 Bahrang, Samuel. *The Little Black Fish.* Illus by Farsheed Meskali. Minneapolis: Carolrhoda, 1971.

259 Bailey, Carolyn S. *Finnegan Two, His Nine Lives.* Illus by Kate Seredy. New York: Viking, 1953.

260 ———. *Miss Hickory.* Illus by Ruth Gannett. New York: Viking, 1946. M451

261 Baird, Bill. *The Art of the Puppet.* New York: Macmillan, 1965.

262 Baker, Augusta. *The Golden Lynx and Other Tales.* Illus by Johannes Troyer. Philadelphia: Lippincott, 1960.

263 ———. *The Talking Tree, Fairy Tales from Fifteen Lands.* Illus by Johannes Troyer. Philadelphia: Lippincott, 1955.

264 Baker, Betty. *Walk the World's Rim.* New York: Harper, 1965.

265 Baker, Laura Nelson. *The Friendly Beasts.* Illus by Nicolas Sidjokov. Emeryville, CA: Parnassus, 1957. M291

266 Baldwin, Anne Morris. *The Sometimes Island.* Illus by Charles Robinson. New York: Norton, 1969.

267 ———. *Sunflowers for Tina.* Illus by Ann Grifalconi. New York: Four Winds, 1970. Paperback.

268 Baldwin, James. *Favorite Tales of Long Ago.* Illus by Lili Rethi. New York: Aladdin, 1955.

269 Baldwin, Gordon. *How the Indians Really Lived.* New York: Putnam, 1967.

270 ———.*Talking Drums to Written Word: How Early Man Learned to Communicate.* New York: Norton, 1970.

271 Baldwin, Ruth. *One Hundred 19th Century Rhyming Alphabets in English.* Carbondale: Southern Illinois Univ. Press, 1972.

272 Balet, Jan. *The Fence: a Mexican Tale.* Illus by the author. New York: Delacorte, 1967.

273 ———. *The Gift.* Illus by the author. New York: Delacorte, 1967.

274 ———. *Joanjo, a Portuguese Tale.* Illus by the author. New York: Delacorte, 1967.

275 ———. *The King and the Broom Maker.* Illus by the author. New York: Delacorte, 1969.

276 ———. *Ladismouse or the Adventures of Higher Education.* New York: Walck, 1971.

277 Balian, Lorna. *The Animal.* Illus by the author. Nashville: Abingdon, 1972.

278 ———. *Humbug Witch.* Illus by the author. Nashville: Abingdon, 1965.

279 Ball, Zachary. *Bristle Face.* New York: Holiday, 1962. Scholastic paperback.

280 ———. *Sputters.* New York: Holiday, 1963.

281 Bamberger, Richard. *My First Big Story Book.* Trans by James Thin. Illus by Emanuela Wallenta. Irvington-on-Hudson: Harvey, 1960. Penguin paperback.

282 Bang, Molly. *The Grey Lady and the Strawberry Snatcher.* New York: Four Winds, 1980.

283 Bangs, Edward. *Steven Kellogg's Yankee Doodle.* New York: Parents, 1976. M775, M776.

284 Bank-Jensen, Thea. *Play with Paper.* New York: Macmillan, 1962.

285 Barbeau, Marius. *The Golden Phoenix and Other French-Canadian Fairy Tales.* Illus by Arthur Price. New York: Walck, 1958.

286 Barclay, Gail. *The Little Brown Gazelle.* Illus by Kiyo Komoda. New York: Dial, 1968.

287 Barnhart, Nancy. *The Lord Is My Shepherd. Stories from the Bible Pictured in Bible Lands.* New York: Scribner, 1949.

288 Barnstone, Aliki. *The Real Tin Flower, Poems About the World at Nine.* Foreword by Anne Sexton. Illus by Paul Glovanopoulos. . New York: Macmillan, 1968.

289 Barnwell, Eve. *Disguises You Can Make.* Illus by Richard Rosenblum. New York: Lothrop, 1977.

290a Baron, Virginia Olsen. *Here I Am: Anthology of Poems Written by Young People in Some of America's Minority Groups.* New York: Dutton, 1969.

290b ———, ed. *The Seasons of Time, Tanka Poetry of Ancient Japan.* Illus by Yasuhide Kobashi. New York: Dial, 1968.

291 Barr, George. *Entertaining with Number Tricks.* Illus by Mildred Waltrip. New York: McGraw, 1971.

292 ———. *Fun and Tricks for Young Scientists.* Illus by Mildred Waltrip. New York: McGraw, 1968.

293 Barr, Jene. *Mister Zip and the U.S. Mail.* Illus by Helen Fulherson. Chicago: Whitman, 1964.

294 Barrett, Judi. *I Hate to Go to Bed.* Illus by Ray Cruz. New York: Four Winds, 1977.

295 Barrie, J.M. *Peter Pan.* Illus by Nora Unwin. New York: Scribner, 1950. Paperback.

296 Barry, Katharina. *A Is for Anything, an ABC Book of Pictures and Rhymes.* New York: Harcourt, 1961.

297 Barry, Robert. *The Musical Palm Tree, a Story of Puerto Rico.* New York: McGraw, 1965.

298 Barth, Edna. *A Christmas Feast: Poems, Sayings, Greetings, and Wishes.* Boston: Houghton, 1979.

299 ———. *Hearts, Cupids, and Red Roses, the Story of Valentine Symbols.* Boston: Houghton, n.d.

300 ———. *Holly, Reindeer, and Colored Lights, the Story of Christmas Symbols.* Illus by Ursula Arndt. Boston: Houghton, 1971.

301 ———. *I'm Nobody! Who Are You? The Story of Emily Dickinson.* Illus by Richard Cuffari. New York: Seabury, 1971.

302 ———. *Jack O'Lantern.* Illus by Paul Galdone. Boston: Houghton, 1974.

303 ———. *Lillies, Rabbits, and Painted Eggs; the Story of the Easter Symbols.* Illus by Ursula Arndt. Boston: Houghton, 1970.

304 ———. *Shamrocks, Harps, and Shillelaghs, the Story of St. Patrick's Day Symbols.* Illus by Ursula Arndt. Boston: Houghton, 1977.

305 ———. *Turkeys, Pilgrims, and Indian Corn, the Story of Thanksgiving Symbols.* Illus by Ursula Arndt. Boston: Houghton, 1975.

306 ———. *Witches, Pumpkins, and Grinning*

Ghosts, the Story of Halloween Symbols. Illus by Ursula Arndt. Boston: Houghton, 1972.

307 Barthelme, Donald. *The Slightly Irregular Fire Engine or the Hithering Thithering Djinn.* New York: Farrar, 1971.

308 Bartlet, Susan. *Books: A Book to Begin On.* Illus by Ellen Raskin. New York: Holt, 1968.

309 Barton, Byron. *Buzz Buzz Buzz.* New York: Macmillan, 1973.

310 Baskin, Barbara and Karen Harris. *Books for the Gifted Child.* New York: Bowker, 1980.

311 Batchelder, Marjorie H. *The Puppet Theatre Handbook.* New York: Harper, 1947.

312 ———— and Virginia Lee Comer. *Puppets and Plays; a Creative Approach.* New York: Harper, 1956.

313 Batchelor, Julie F. *Communication: From Cave Writing to Television.* New York: Harcourt, 1953.

314 Batchelor, Julie Forsyth and Claudia DeLys. *Superstitious? Here's Why!* Illus by Erik Blegvad. New York: Harcourt, 1954. Voyager paperback.

315 Baudouy, Michel-Aime. *Old One-Toe.* Trans by Marie Ponsot. Illus by Johannes Trayer. New York: Harcourt, 1959.

316 Bauer, Caroline Feller. *Handbook for Storytellers.* Chicago: American Library Association, 1977.

317 Baum, Arline and Joseph. *One Bright Monday Morning.* New York: Random, 1962. Random paperback.

318 Baum, L. Frank. *Wizard of Oz.* New York: Random, 1950. Rand paperback. M767

319 ————. *The Wizard of Oz.* Scholastic paperback, 1967. M767

320 ————. *The Wonderful Wizard of Oz.* New York: Dutton, n.d.

321 ————. *The Wonderful Wizard of Oz Coloring Book.* New York: Dover, 1974.

322 Bauman, Hans. *Caspar and His Friends: A Collection of Puppet Plays.* New York: Walck, 1969.

323 ————. *The World of the Pharaohs.* Illus by Hans Renner, photos by Albert Burges. New York: Pantheon, 1960. o.p.

324 Baumann, Elwood D. *Bigfoot: America's Abominable Snowman.* New York: Watts, 1975.

325 ————. *The Loch Ness Monster.* New York: Watts, 1972.

326 Bawden, Nina. *A Handful of Thieves.* Philadelphia: Lippincott, 1967.

327 ————. *Witch's Daughter.* Philadelphia: Lippincott, 1966.

328 ————. *Peppermint Pig.* Philadelphia: Lippincott, 1975.

329 Bayley, Nicola, illus. *One Old Oxford Ox.* New York: Atheneum, 1977.

330 Baylor, Byrd. *Coyote Cry.* Illus by Shimin Symeon. New York: Lothrop, 1972.

331 ————. *The Desert is Theirs.* Illus by Peter Parnall. New York: Scribner, 1975.

332 ————. *Everybody Needs a Rock.* Illus by Peter Parnall. New York: Scribner, 1974.

333 ————. *Guess Who My Favorite Person Is.* Illus by Robert Andrew Parker. New York: Scribner, 1977.

334 ————. *Hawk, I'm Your Brother.* Illus by Peter Parnall. New York: Scribner, 1976.

335 ————. *Sometimes I Dance Mountains.* Photos by Bill Sears. Drawings by Ken Longtemps. New York: Scribner, 1973.

336 ————. *They Put on Masks.* Illus by Jerry Ingram. New York: Scribner, 1974.

337 ————. *When Clay Sings.* Illus by Tom Bahti. New York: Scribner, 1972.

338 Beaney, Jan. *Adventures with Collage.* Photos by Alan Wysman. New York: Warne, 1970.

339 Beaton, Mabel and Less. *Marionettes, A Hobby for Every-one.* New York: Crowell, 1948.

340 Beatty, Patricia. *Blue Stars Watching.* New York: Morrow, 1969.

341 ————. *Hail Columbia.* Illus by Liz Dauber. New York: Morrow, 1964.

342 ————. *How Many Miles to Sundown.* Illus by Robert Quackenbush. New York: Morrow, 1974.

343 ————. *I Want My Sunday, Stranger.* New York: Morrow, 1977.

344 ————. *A Long Way to Whisky Creek.* Illus. by Franz Altschuler. New York: Morrow, 1971.

345 ————. *O the Red Rose Tree.* Illus by Rose Dauber. New York: Morrow, 1972.

346 ————. *The Nickel-Plated Beauty.* Illus by Liz Dauber. New York: Morrow, 1964.

347 Beaumont, Cyril W. *Puppets and Puppet Stages.* London: Studio Publications, 1938. Beaumont, de. *See* De Beaumont.

348 Beck, Barbara. *Pilgrims of Plymouth.* New York: Watts, 1972.

349 Becker, John. *Seven Little Rabbits.* Illus by Barbara Cooney. New York: Walker, 1973. Scholastic paperback.

350 Becker, Joyce. *Jewish Holiday Crafts.* New York: Bonim, 1977.

351 Bedford, Annie North. *Walt Disney's Mary Poppins.* Walt Disney Productions, 1964.

352 Bednarik, Rosi and Susan Bond. *Elefish.* Illus by Rosi Bednarik. New York: Scroll, 1971.

353 Beeler, Nelson F. and Franklyn Branley. *Experiments in Optical Illusion.* Illus by Fred Lyon. New York: Crowell, 1951.

354 Behn, Harry. *All Kinds of Time.* Illus by the author. New York: Harcourt, 1950.

355 ————. *Chrysalis, Concerning Children and Poetry.* New York: Harcourt, 1968.

356 ————. *Faraway Lurs.* Illus by the author. Cleveland: Collings, 1963; NY: Avon, 1976.

357 ————. *The Golden Hive.* Illus by the author. New York: Harcourt, 1966.

358 ————. *The Little Hill.* Illus by the author. New York: Harcourt, 1949.

359 ————. *Windy Morning.* Illus by the author. New York: Harcourt, 1953.

360 ————. *The Wizard in the Well.* Illus by the author. New York: Harcourt, 1956.

361 ————, ed. *Cricket Songs.* Illus by Japanese Masters. New York: Harcourt, 1964.

362 ————, ed. *More Cricket Songs.* Illus by Japanese Masters. New York: Harcourt, 1971.

363 Behrens, June. *Look at the Sea Animals.* Photos by Vince Streano. New York: Childrens Press, 1975.

364 ———. *A New Flag for a New Country, the First National Flag, A Play.* Illus by Lenny Meyer. Chicago: Childrens, 1975.

365 Belfer, Nancy. *Designing Batik and Tie Die.* New York: Davis, 1972.

366 Bell, Corydon. *John Rattling Gourd of Big Cave, a Collection of Cherokee Legends.* New York: Macmillan, 1955.

367 Bell, Thelma. *the Riddle of Time.* Illus by Corydon Bell. New York: Viking, 1963.

368 ———. *Snow.* Illus by Corydon Bell. New York: Viking, 1954.

369 Bellairs, John. *The House with a Clock on its Walls.* New York: Dial, 1973.

370 Belloc, Hilaire. *The Bad Child's Book of Beasts.* Illus by BTB. New York: Knopf, 1965. Dover Paperback.

371 ———. *Cautionary Verses.* Illus by BTB and Nicolas Bentley. New York: Knopf, 1968.

372 ———. *Matilda Who Told Lies and Was Burned to Death.* Illus by Steven Kellogg. New York: Dial, 1970

373 ———. *More Beasts for Worse Children.* Illus by BTB. New York: Knopf, 1966.

374 ———. *The Yak, the Python, the Frog: Three Beast Poems.* Illus by Steven Kellogg. New York: Parents, 1975.

375 Belpre, Pura. *Perez and Martina; a Portarican Folk Tale.* New York: Warne, 1960.

376 ———. *The Rainbow-colored Horse.* Illus by Antonio Martorell. New York: Warne, 1978.

377 ———. *The Tiger and the Rabbit, and Other Tales.* Illus by Tomie de Paola. Philadelphia: Lippincott, 1965.

378 Belting, Natalia. *Calendar Moon.* Illus by Bernarda Bryson. New York: Holt, 1964.

379 ———. *Cat Tales.* Illus by Leo Summers. New York: Holt, 1959.

380 ———. *Christmas Folk.* Illus by Barbara Cooney. New York: Holt, 1969.

381 ———. *The Earth is on a Fish's Back: Tales of Beginnings.* Illus by Esta Nesbitt. New York: Holt, 1965.

382 ———. *The Land of the Taffeta Dawn.* Illus by Joseph Low. New York: Dutton, 1973.

383 ———. *The Long-Tailed Bear and Other Indian Legends.* Illus by Louis F. Carea. Indianapolis: Bobbs, 1961.

384 ———. *The Moon is a Crystal Ball, Unfamiliar Legends of the Stars.* Illus by Anne Marie Jauss. Indianapolis: Bobbs, 1961.

385 ———. *Our Fathers Had Powerful Songs.* Illus by Laszlo Kubinyi. New York: Dutton, 1974.

386 ———. *The Stars Are Silver Reindeer.* Illus by Esta Nesbitt. New York: Holt, 1966.

387 ———. *The Sun is a Golden Earring.* Illus by Bernarda Bryson. New York: Holt, 1962. Owlet paperback.

388 ———. *Three Apples Fell from Heaven.* Indianapolis: Bobbs, n.d.

389 Belves, Pierre and Francois Mathey. *How Artists Work: an Introduction to Techniques of Art.* English adaptation by Alice Bach. New York: Lion, 1968.

390 Bemelman's, Ludwig. *Madeline.* Illus by the author. New York: Viking, 1939. Paperback. M394, M395, M401.

391 ———. *Madeline and the Bad Hat.* Illus by the author. New York: Viking, 1956. Paperback. M396.

392 ———. *Madeline and the Gypsies.* Illus by the author. New York: Viking, 1959. Paperback. M397, M398.

393 ———. *Madeline in London.* Illus by the author. New York: Viking, 1961. Paperback. M399.

394 *———. *Madeline's Rescue.* Illus by the author. New York: Viking, 1953. Paperback. M400.

395 ———. *Parsley.* Illus by the author. New York: Harcourt, 1953.

396 Benary-Isbert, Margot. *The Ark.* New York: Harcourt, 1953.

397 ———. *Blue Mystery.* Illus by Enrico Arno. Trans by Richard and Clara Winston. New York: Harcourt, 1957.

398 Benchley, Nathaniel. *Feldman Fieldmouse; a Fable.* Illus by Hillary Knight. New York: Harper, 1971. Paperback.

399 ———. *Red Fox and his Canoe.* New York: Harper, 1964. Scholastic paperback.

400 ———. *The Several Tricks of Edgar Dolphin.* Illus by Mamoru Tunai. New York: Harper, 1970.

401 ———. *The Strange Disappearance of Arthur Cluck.* Illus by Arnold Lobel. New York: Harper, 1967.

402 Bendick, Jeanne. *The First Book of Time.* New York: Watts, 1963.

403 ———. *Human Senses.* New York: Watts, 1968.

404 ———. *The Mystery of the Loch Ness Monster.* New York: McGraw, 1976.

405 ———. *The Wind.* Chicago: Rand, 1964.

406 Benet, Laura. *Famous American Poets.* New York: Dodd, 1950.

407 ———. *Famous Poets for Young People.* New York: Dodd, 1964.

408 Benet, Rosemary and Stephen. *A Book of Americans.* Illus by Charles Child. New York: Holt, 1933. M93.

409 Benet, Stephen Vincent. *the Ballad of William Sycamore.* Illus by Brinton Turkle. Boston: Little, 1972.

410 Benet, William, ed. *Reader's Encyclopedia.* New York: Crowell, 1965.

411 Bennett, Rowena. *Creative Plays and Programs for Holidays.* Boston: Plays, 1967.

412 Benson, Sally. *Stories of the Gods and Heroes.* Illus by Steele Savage. New York: Dial, 1940.

413 Bera, Paul. *The Horse Without a Head.* Trans by John Buchanan-Brown. Illus by Richard Kennedy. New York: Pantheon, 1958.

414 Berenstain, Stanley and Janet. *Bear Detectives.* New York: Beginner, 1975. M59

415 ———. *Bear Scouts.* New York: Beginner, 1967. M60.

416 ———. *Bear's Almanac.* New York: Random, 1973.

417 ———. *Bear's Christmas.* New York: Beginner, 1970. M61.

418 ———. *Bear's In the Night.* New York: Random, 1971. M62

419 ———. *Bears on Wheels.* New York: Ran-

dom, 1969. M63.

420 ———. *Bear's Picnic.* New York: Beginner, 1966. M64.

421 ———. *Bear's Vacation.* New York: Beginner, 1968. M65.

422 Berger, Melvin. *The Story of Folk Music.* New York: Phillips, 1976.

423 ———. *The Trumpet Book.* New York: Lothrop, 1978.

424 Berk, Barbara. *The First Book of Stage Costume and Make-up.* Illus by Jeanne Bendick. New York: Watts, 1954.

425 Bernstein, Joanne E. *Fiddle with a Riddle, Write Your Own Riddles.* Illus by Giulio Maestro. New York: Dutton, 1979.

426 Bernstein, Margery and Janet Kobrin. *The First Morning, an African Myth.* Illus by Enid Warner Romanek. New York: Scribner, 1976.

427 Berry, Erick. *Eating and Cooking Around the World; Fingers Before Forks.* New York: Day, 1963.

428 ———. *The Land and People of Finland.* Philadelphia: Lippincott, 1972.

429 ———. *The Land and People of Iceland.* Philadelphia: Lippincott, 1972.

430 Berson, Harold. *How the Devil Gets His Due.* Illus by the author. New York: Crown, 1972.

431 ———. *A Moose Is Not a Mouse.* New York: Crown, 1975.

432 Bertail, Inez. *Complete Nursery Song Book.* Illus by Walt Kelly. Music by I. Bertail. New York: Lothrop, 1954.

433 Beskow, Katja. *Astonishing Adventures of Patrick the Mouse.* Illus by Ylva Kallstrom-Eklund. New York: Delacorte, 1967. Dell Paperback.

434 Best, Herbert. *Desmond and the Peppermint Ghost.* New York: Penguin Paperback, 1968.

435 ———. *Desmond and the Peppermint Ghost: The Dog Detective's Third Case.* New York: Viking, 1965.

436 ———. *Desmond's First Case.* Illus by Ezra Jack Keats. New York: Viking, 1961.

437 ———. *Desmond the Dog Detective.* New York: Viking, 1962. Penguin Paperback.

438 Betts, Victoria B. *Exploring Papier-mâché.* Worcester, MA: Davis, 1955, 1966.

439 *Beyond the High Hills, a Book of Eskimo Poems.* Photos by Guy and Mary-Rouseliere. Cleveland: World, 1961.

440 Bianco, Margery. *Little Wooden Doll.* Illus by Pamela Bianco. New York: Macmillan, 1967.

441 Bible. *The Old Testament.* Illus by Marguerite De Angeli. Garden City, NY: Doubleday, 1960.

442 Bible. Old Testament. Daniel. *Shadrach, Meschack, and Abednego; from the Book of Daniel.* Illus by Paul Galdone. New York: McGraw, 1965.

443 Bible. Old Testament. Genesis. *The First Seven Days; the Story of the Creation from Genesis.* Illus by Paul Galdone. New York: Crowell, 1962.

444 Bible. Old Testament. Psalms. *Twenty-Third Psalm.* Illus by Marie Angel. New York: Crowell, 1970.

445 ———. *Twenty-Third Psalm.* Illus by Tasha Tudor. Worcester, Mass.: St. Onge.

446 Bickford, John. *New Media in Printmaking.* New York: Watson-Guptill, 1976.

447 Bierhorst, John. *A Cry from the Earth: Music of the North American Indians.* New York: Four Winds, 1979.

448 ———. *In the Trail of the Wind: American Indian Poems and Ritual Traditions.* New York: Farrar, 1971. Dell Paperback.

449 ———. *Songs of the Chippewa.* Illus by Joe Servello. Music by J. Bierhorst. New York: Farrar, 1974. Sixteen songs adapted from the collection of Frances Densmore and Henry Rowe Schoolcraft. Arranged for piano and guitar.

450 Biglund, Eileen. *Helen Keller.* Illus by Lili Cassel Wronker. New York: Phillips, 1967.

451 Billington, Elizabeth T., ed. *The Randolph Caldecott Treasury, an Anthology of the Illustrations of Randolph Caldecott.* New York: Warne, 1977.

452 Binyan, Helen. *Puppetry Today; Designing and Making Marionettes, Hand Puppets, Rod Puppets and Shadow Puppets.* New York: Watson-Guptil, 1966.

453 Binzen, Bill. *Miguel's Mountain.* New York: Coward, 1968.

454 Birdwhistell, Ray L. *Kinesics and Contest: Essays on Body Motion Communication.* Philadelphia: University of Pennsylvania, 1970. Paperback.

455 Birnbaum, A. *Green Eyes.* New York: Western, 1973.

456 Bishop, Anne. *Chicken Riddle.* Chicago: A. Whitman, 1972.

457 ———. *Ella Fannie Elephant Riddle Book.* Chicago: A. Whitman, 1974.

458 ———. *Hey Riddle Riddle.* Chicago: A. Whitman, 1968.

459 ———. *Merry-Go-Riddle.* Chicago: A. Whitman, 1973.

460 ———. *Noah Riddle?* Chicago: A. Whitman, 1970.

461 ———. *Riddle-Iculous Rid-Alphabet Book.* Chicago: A. Whitman, 1971.

462 ———. *Riddle Raddle, Fiddle Faddle.* Chicago: A. Whitman, 1966.

463 ———. *Riddle Red Riddle Book.* Chicago: A. Whitman, 1969.

464 ———. *Wild Bill Hiccup's Riddle Book.* Chicago: A. Whitman, 1975.

465 Biship, Claire H. *The Five Chinese Brothers.* Illus by Kurt Wiese. New York: Coward, 1938. Hale, 1938. M212, M213.

466 ———. *Pancake's Paris.* Illus by George Schreiber. New York: Viking, 1947.

467 ———. *Twenty and Ten.* Illus by William Pene DuBois. New York: Viking, 1952. Puffin paperback.

468 ———. *Twenty-two Bears.* New York: Viking, 1964.

469 Bishop, Elizabeth. *The Ballad of the Burglar of Babylon.* Illus by Ann Grifalconi. New York: Farrar, 1964, 1968.

470 Bixby, William. *The Impossible Journey of Sir Ernest Shackleton.* Boston: Little, 1970.

471 Black, Algernon D. *Woman of the Wood.* Illus by Evaline Ness. New York: Holt, 1973.

472 Blackburn, Henry. *Randolph Caldecott: A*

Personal Memoir of his Early Art Career. London: Sampson, Low, 1886.

473 Blackham, Olive. *Shadow Puppets.* New York: Harper, 1960.

474 Blackmoor, Richard A. *Lorna Doone.* New York: Dodd, n.d. Airmont paperback.

475 Blake, William. *Songs of Innocence.* Illus by Ellen Raskin. New York: Doubleday, 1966.

476 Blaire, Ruth. *Van Ness, Mary's Monster.* Illus by Richard Cuffari. New York: Coward, 1975.

477 Blair, Susan, illus. *The Three Billy Goats Gruff.* New York: Scholastic paperback, 1970.

478 Blair, Walter. *Tall Tale America, a Legendary History of Our Humorous Heroes.* Illus by Glen Rounds. New York: Coward, 1944.

479 Bland, David. *A History of Book Illustration.* Cleveland: World, 1958, 1969.

480 ———. *The Illustration of Books.* New York: Pantheon, 1952.

481 Blecher, Wilfred. *No End of Nonsense, Humorous Verses.* Translated by Jack Prelutsky. Illus by Wilfred Blecher. New York: Macmillan, 1968.

482 Bleeker, Sonia. *The Chippewa Indians; Rice Gatherers of the Great Lakes.* Illus by Patricia Boodell. New York: Morrow, 1955.

483 ———. *The Eskimo, Arctic Hunters and Trappers.* Illus by Patricia Boodell. New York: Morrow, 1959.

484 ———. *Navajo: Herders, Weavers and Silversmiths.* Illus by Pat Boodell. New York: Morrow, 1958.

485 ———. *The Sea Hunters, Indians of the Northwest Coast.* Illus by Althea Karr. New York: Morrow, 1951.

486 ———. *The Tuareg, Nomads and Warriors of the Sahara.* New York: Morrow, 1964.

487 Blegvad, Erik. *Burnie's Hill, a Traditional Rhyme.* New York: Atheneum, 1977.

488 Blegvad, Lenore, ed. *This Little Pig-a-wig and Other Rhymes About Pigs.* Illus by Erik Blegvad. New York: Atheneum, 1978.

489 ———. *Hark! Hark! The Dogs Do Bark and Other Rhymes About Dogs.* Illus by Erik Blegvad. New York: Atheneum, 1976.

490 ———. *Mittens for Kittens and Other Rhymes About Cats.* Illus by Erik Blegvad. New York: Atheneum, 1974.

491 Blegvad, Lenore and Erik. *One Is for the Sun.* New York: Harcourt, 1968.

492 Bleiweiss, Robert. *Marching to Freedom: The Life of Martin Luther King, Jr.* New York: NAL, 1971.

493 Bley, Edgar. *The Best Singing Games for Children of All Ages.* New York: Sterling, 1957.

494 Blishen, Edward, ed. *Oxford Book of Poetry for Children.* Illus by Brian Wildsmith. New York: Watts, 1964.

495 Bloch, Marie Halun. *Dinosaurs.* Illus by Mason. New York: Coward, 1955.

496 Blough, Glenn O. *Bird Watchers and Bird Feeders.* Illus by Jeanne Bendick. New York: McGraw, 1963.

497 ———. *Discovering Insects.* Illus by Jeanne Bendick. New York: McGraw, 1967.

498 Blue Mountain Crafts Council. *Joy of Crafts.* New York: Holt, 1975.

499 Blume, Judy. *Are You There God? It's Me, Margaret.* Scarsdale, NY: Bradbury, 1970. Dell paperback.

500 ———. *Blubber.* Scarsdale, NY: Bradbury, 1974. Dell paperback.

501 ———. *Deenie.* Scarsdale, NY: Bradbury, 1973. Dell paperback.

502 ———. *It's Not the End of the World.* Scarsdale, NY: Bradbury, 1972. Bantam paperback.

503 ———. *The One in the Middle is the Green Kangaroo.* Chicago: Reilly and Lee, 1969.

504 ———. *The One in the Middle is the Green Kangaroo.* Illus by Amy Aitken. Scarsdale, NY: Bradbury, 1981.

505 ———. *Tales of a Fourth Grade Nothing.* Illus by Roy Doty. New York: Dutton, 1972. Dell paperback.

506 ———. *Then Again, Maybe I Won't.* Scarsdale, NY: Bradbury, 1972. Dell paperback.

507 Bodeker, N. M. *Hurry, Hurry, Mary Dear! and Other Nonsense Poems.* New York: Atheneum, 1976.

508 ———. *Let's Marry Said the Cherry and Other Nonsense Poems.* Illus by N. M. Bodecker. New York: Atheneum, 1974. Aladdin paperback.

509 ———. *It's Raining Said John Twaining, Danish Nursery Rhymes.* Illus by N. M. Bodecker. New York: Atheneum, 1973. Aladdin paperback.

510 Bodor, John. *Creating and Presenting Hand Puppets.* New York: Reinhold, 1967.

511 Boggs, Ralph Steele and Mary Gould Davis. *Three Golden Oranges and Other Spanish Folk Tales.* Illus by Emma Brock. New York: McKay, 1936.

512 Bohmer, Gunther. *The Wonderful World of Puppets.* Boston: Plays, 1971.

513 Boiko, Claire. *Children's Plays for Creative Actors.* Boston: Plays, 1967.

514 Boiko, Claire. *Plays and Programs for Boys and Girls.* Boston: Plays, 1972.

515 Bolognese, Don. *Drawing Horses and Foals.* New York: Watts, 1977.

516 Bollinger, Max. *Noah and the Rainbow.* Trans. by Clyde R. Bulla. Illus by Helga Autringer. New York: Crowell, 1972.

517 Bollinger, Savelli Antonella. *The Knitted Cat.* New York: Macmillan, 1971.

518 ———. *The Mouse and the Knitted Cat.* New York: Macmillan, 1974.

519 Bolton, Henry C. *Counting-Out Rhymes of Children.* Detroit: Singing Tree, 1969.

520 Bond, Jean Careu. *Brown is a Beautiful Color.* Illus by Barbara Zuber. New York: Watts, 1969.

521 Bond, Michael. *A Bear Called Paddington.* Illus by Peggy Fortnum. Boston: Houghton, 1960. Dell paperback. M516.

522 ———. *More about Paddington.* Illus by Peggy Fortnum. Boston: Houghton, 1962. Dell paperback.

523 ———. *Olga Carries On.* Illus by Hans Helweg.New York: Hastings, 1977.

524 ———. *Olga Meets Her Match: More Tales of*

Olga da Polga. Illus by Hans Helweg. New York: Hastings, 1975. Puffin paperback.

525 ———. *Paddington Abroad.* Boston: Houghton, 1972. Dell paperback.

526 ———. *Paddington at Large.* Illus by Peggy Fortnum. Boston: Houghton, 1963. Dell paperback.

527 ———. *Paddington At Work.* Boston: Houghton, 1967. Dell paperback.

528 ———. *Paddington Goes to Town.* Illus by Peggy Fortnum. Boston: Houghton, 1968. Dell paperback.

529 ———. *Paddington Helps Out.* Illus by Peggy Fortnum. Boston: Houghton, 1961. Dell paperback.

530 ———. *Paddington Marches On.* Illus by Peggy Fortnum. Boston: Houghton, 1965. Dell paperback.

531 ———. *Paddington Takes the Air.* Boston: Houghton, 1971. Dell paperback.

532 ———. *Paddington Takes to TV.* Illus by Ivor Wood. Boston: Houghton, 1974. Dell paperback.

533 ———. *The Tales of Olga Da Polga.* Illus by Hans Helweg. New York: Macmillan, 1973. Puffin paperback.

534 Bond, Michael and Fred Banbery. *Paddington Bear, a Picture Book.* New York: Random, 1973.

535 Bond, Nancy. *A String in the Harp.* New York: Atheneum, 1976.

536 Bond, Raymond. *Famous Stories of Code and Cipher.* New York: Macmillan, n.d. Collier paperback.

537 Bonham, Frank. *A Dream of Ghosts.* New York: Dutton, 1973.

538 ———. *Mystery in Little Tokyo.* New York: Dutton, 1966.

539 ———. *Mystery of the Fat Cat.* Illus by Alvin Smith. New York: Dutton, 1968. Dell paperback.

540 Boni, Margaret. *Fireside Book of Favorite American Songs.* Illus by Auerlius Battaglia. Music by Norman Lloyd. New York: Simon and Schuster, 1952. S & S paperback.

541 ———. *Fireside Book of Folk Songs.* Illus by Alice and Martin Provensen. Music by Norman Lloyd. New York: Simon and Schuster, 1967.

542 Bonne, Rose. *I Know an Old Lady.* Illus by Abner Graboff. Music by Alan Mills. New York: Rand, 1961. Scholastic paperback. M216, M308, M309.

543 Bonsall, Crosby. *The Case of the Cats Meow.* New York: Harper, 1965.

544 ———. *The Case of the Double Cross.* New York: Harper, 1970.

545 ———. *The Case of the Dumb Bells.* New York: Harper, 1966.

546 ———. *The Case of the Hungry Stranger.* New York: Harper, 1963.

547 ———. *The Case of the Scaredy Cats.* New York: Harper, 1971.

548 ———. *I'll Show You Cats.* New York: Harper, 1964.

549 Bontemps, Arna. *Golden Slippers, an Anthology of Negro Poetry for Young Readers.* Illus by Henrietta Bruce Sharon. New York: Harper, 1941.

550 ———. *Hold Fast to Dreams, Poems Old and New.* Chicago: Follett, 1969.

551 Bonzon, Paul-Jacques. *Pursuit in the French Alps.* New York: Lothrop, 1963.

552 Borcher, Elizabeth. *There Comes a Time.* Trans. by Babbette Deutsch. Illus by Dietlind Blech. New York: Doubleday, 1965.

553 Borja, Robert and Corrine. *Making Collages.* Chicago: Whitman, 1972.

554 Borski, Lucia Merecha. *Good Sesee and Good Fortunes and Other Polish Folk Tales.* Illus by Erica Gorecka-Egan. New York: McKay, 1970.

555 Borton, Helen. *Do You Hear What I Hear?* Illus by the author. New York: Abelard, 1960.

556 ———. *Do You Move as I Move?* Illus by the author. New York: Abelard, 1963.

557 ———. *Do You See as I See?* Illus by the author. New York: Abelard, 1959.

558 ———. *A Picture Has a Special Look.* Illus by the author. New York: Abelard, 1961. M532.

559 Boston, Lucy. *The Children of Green Knowe.* Illus by Peter Boston. New York: Harcourt, 1967.

560 ———. *Enemy at Green Knowe.* Illus by Peter Boston. New York: Harcourt, 1964.

561 ———. *Guardians of the House.* Illus by Peter Boston. New York: Atheneum, 1975.

562 ———. *River at Green Knowe.* Illus by Peter Boston. New York: Harcourt, 1959. Voyager paperback.

563 ———. *Stones of Green Knowe.* Illus by Peter Boston. New York: Atheneum, 1976.

564 ———. *Stranger at Green Knowe.* Illus by Peter Boston. New York: Harcourt, 1961.

565 ———. *Treasure of Green Knowe.* Illus by Peter Boston. New York: Harcourt, 1958.

566 Bosworth, J. Allan. *A Darkness of Giants.* New York: Doubleday, 1972.

567 ———. *White Water, Still Water.* Illus by Charles W. Walker. New York: Doubleday, 1966. Archway paperback.

568 Bowman, James C. *Pecos Bill, the Greatest Cowboy of All Times.* Illus by Laura Bannon. New York: Whitman, 1937.

569 ———. *Who Was Tricked?* Illus by John Faulkner. Chicago: Whitman, 1936.

570 Bowman, James C. and Margery Bianco. *Seven Silly Wise Men.* Illus by John Faulkner. Chicago: Whitman, 1964.

571 ———. *Tales from a Finnish Tupa.* Illus by Laura Bannon. Chicago: Whitman, 1936, 1964.

572 Boy Scouts of America. *Bookbinding.* North Brunswick, NJ: Boy Scouts of America. 1969.

573 Boylan, Eleanor. *How to Be a Puppeteer.* Illus by Tomie de Paola. New York: Dutton, 1970.

574 Bradbury, Bianca. *Two on an Island.* Illus by Robert MacLean. Boston: Houghton, 1965.

575 Bradbury, Ray. *Switch on the Night.* Illus by Madeline Gekiere. New York: Pantheon, 1955.

576 Bradfield, Roger. *A Good Knight for Dragons.* New York: Young Scott, 1967.

577 Bradt, G. W. and Charles E. Schafer. *Michigan Wildlife Sketches, the Native Mammals of Michigan's Forests, Fields, and Marshes.*

Hillsdale, MI: Hillsdale Editorial Publications, 1971.

578 Bramall, Eric and Christopher C. Sommerville. *Expert Puppet Techniques, a Manual of Production for Puppeteers.* Boston: Plays, 1966.

579 Brandenberg, Aliki. *June Seven.* New York: Macmillan, 1972.

580 ———. *Keep Your Mouth Closed, Dear.* New York: Dial, 1973.

581 ———. *My Five Senses.* New York: Crowell, 1972. Paperback.

582 ———. *My Visit to the Dinosaurs.* New York: Crowell, 1969. Paperback.

583 ———. *The Story of Johnny Appleseed.* Englewood Cliffs, NJ: Prentice-Hall, 1963. P-H paperback. M30.

584 ———. *Three Gold Pieces.* New York: Pantheon, 1967.

585 ———. *Wild and Wooly Mammoths.* Illus by Aliki. New York: Crowell, 1977.

586 ———, illus. *Go Tell Aunt Rhody.* New York: Macmillan, 1967.

587 ———. *Hush Little Baby.* Englewood Cliffs, NJ: Prentice-Hall, 1968. M32, M306, M307, M370.

588 Brandreth, Gyles. *The Biggest Tongue Twisters Book in the World.* Illus by Alex Chin. New York: Sterling, 1978.

589 Branley, Franklyn M. *Age of Aquarius, You and Astrology.* Illus by Leonard Kessler, New York: Crowell, 1979.

590 ———. *Eclipse, Darkness in Daytime.* Illus by Donald Crews. New York: Crowell, 1973.

591 ———. *Mickey's Magnet.* New York: Scholastic, paperback, n.d.

592 ———. *Moon Seems to Change.* New York: Crowell, 1960.

593 ———. *Shakes, Quakes and Shifts; Earth Tectonics.* New York: Crowell, 1974.

594 ———. *What Makes Day and Night.* Illus by Helen Borten. New York: Crowell, 1961. Crocodile paperback.

595 Brann, Donald. *How to Build Dollhouses and Furniture.* Barcliff Manor, NY: Directions Simplified, 1976. Paperback.

596 Brenner, Anita. *The Boy Who Could Do Anything and Other Mexican Folk Tales.* New York: Wm. Scott, 1958.

597 ———. *The Timid Ghost.* Illus by Jean Charlot. New York: Young Scott, 1966.

598 Brenner, Barbara. *Bodies.* Photos by George Ancona. New York: Dutton, 1973.

599 ———. *Cunningham's Rooster.* Illus by Anne Rockwell, New York: Parents, 1975.

600 ———. *Faces.* Photos by George Ancona. New York: Dutton, 1970.

601 ———. *Snake-Lover's Diary.* Reading, MA: Addison-Wesley, 1970.

602 ———. *Mr. Tall and Mr. Small.* Illus by Tomi Ungerer. Reading, MA: Addison-Wesley, 1966.

603 ———. *Year in the Life of Rosie Bernard.* Illus by Joan Sandin. New York: Harper, 1971.

604 Brewton, John E. and Sara W. *Index to Children's Poetry.* New York: Wilson, 1942.

605 ———. *Index to Children's Poetry, first supplement.* New York: Wilson, 1954.

606 ———. *Index to Children's Poetry, second supplement.* New York: Wilson, 1965.

607 Brewton, John E., ed. *Under the Tent of the Sky, a Collection of Poems About Animals Large and Small.* Illus by Robert Lawson. New York: Macmillan, 1937.

608 Brewton, John E., et al, eds. *Index to Poetry for Children and Young People: 1946–69.* New York: Wilson, 1972.

609 ———. *Index to Poetry for Children and Young People: 1970–75.* New York: Wilson, 1978.

610 Brewton, Sara and John E. *Birthday Candles Burning Bright.* Illus by Vera Bock. New York: Macmillan, 1960.

611 ———. *Bridled with Rainbows: Poems About Many Things of Earth and Sky.* Illus by Vera Bock. New York: Macmillan, 1949.

612 ———. *Christmas Bells are Ringing, A Treasury of Christmas Poetry.* Illus by Decie Merwin. New York: Macmillan, 1964.

613 ———. *Gaily We Parade.* Illus by Robert Lawson. New York: Macmillan, 1964.

614 ———. *Sign a Song of Seasons; Poems About Holidays.* Illus by Vera Bock. New York: Macmillan, 1955.

615 Brewton, Sara and John E., eds. *America Forever New: A Book of Poems.* New York: Crowell, 1968.

616 ———. *Laughable Limericks.* Illus by Ingrid Fetz. New York: Crowell, 1965.

617 ———. *Shrieks at Midnight; Macabre Poems, Eerie and Humorous.* Illus by Ellen Raskin. New York: Crowell, 1969.

618 Brewton, Sara, et al. *Of Quarks, Quasars and Other Quirks, Quizzical Poems for the Supersonic Age.* Illus by Quentin Blake. New York: Crowell, 1977.

619 Brewton, Sara, et al, eds. *My Tang's Tungled and Other Ridiculous Situations: Humorous Poems.* Illus by Graham Booth. New York: Crowell, 1973.

620 Bridge, Linda McCarter. *The Playful Dolphins.* Photos by Lowell Georgia. Washington, D.C.: National Geographic Society, 1976.

621 Bridgman, Elizabeth. *All the Little Bunnies: A Counting Book.* New York: Atheneum, 1977.

622 Bridwell, Norman. *Clifford the Big Red Dog.* New York: Four Winds, 1963. Scholastic paperback.

623 Briggs, Elizabeth D., et al. *Subject Index to Children's Plays.* Chicago: American Library Association, 1940.

624a Briggs, Raymond. *Father Christmas.* New York: Coward, 1973.

624b ———. *Father Christmas Goes on Holiday.* New York: Coward, 1975.

625 ———. *The Snowman.* New York: Random, 1978.

626 Briggs, Raymond, ed. *Fee Fi Fo Fum, a Picture Book of Nursery Rhymes.* Illus by Raymond Briggs. New York: Coward, 1964.

627 ———. *The Mother Goose Treasury.* Illus by R. Briggs. New York: Coward, 1966.

628 ———. *Ring-O Ring O'Roses.* Illus by R. Briggs. New York: Coward, 1962.

629 ———. *The White Land, a Book of Traditional Rhymes and Verses.* Illus by R. Briggs. New York: Coward, 1963.

630 Bright, Robert. *Georgie.* Illus by the author. New York: Doubleday, 1958. Paperback. M244, M245.

631 ———. *Georgie and the Robbers.* Illus by the author. New York: Doubleday, 1963. Paperback.

632 ———. *Georgie to the Rescue.* Illus by the author. New York: Doubleday, 1956. Paperback.

633 ———. *Georgie's Halloween.* Illus by the author. New York: Doubleday, 1971. Paperback.

634 ———. *I Like Red.* Illus by the author. New York: Doubleday, 1955.

635 ———. *My Red Umbrella.* Illus by the author. New York: Morrow. 1959.

636 Brinckloe, Julie. *Gordon's House.* Garden City, NY: Doubleday, 1976.

637 Brindze, Ruth. *The Story of the Totem Pole.* Illus by Yeffe Kimball. New York: Vanguard, 1951.

638 Brink, Carol Ryrie. *Andy Buckram's Tin Men.* Illus by W. T. Mars. New York: Viking, 1966.

639a ———. *Caddie Woodlawn.* Illus by Kate Seredy. New York: Macmillan, 1935. M108.

639b ———. *Caddie Woodlawn.* Illus by Trina Schart Hyman. New York: Macmillan, 1973. Paperback.

640 ———. *Caddie Woodlawn, A Play.* New York: Macmillan, 1945.

641 ———. *Magical Melons: More Stories About Caddie Woodlawn.* Illus by Marguerite Davis. New York: Macmillan, 1944, 1963. Collier paperback.

642 Bro, Marguerite. *How the Mouse Deer Became King.* Illus by Joseph Low. New York: Doubleday, 1966.

643 Broadman, Muriel and Jack Leskoff. *Cinderellas Around the World.* Illus by Martin Ries. New York: McKay, 1976.

644 Brock, Emma. *Drusilla.* New York: Macmillan, 1937.

645 Brock, Virginia. *Pinatas.* Nashville, TN: Abingdon, 1966.

646 Brodley, Alfred and Michael Bond. *Paddington on Stage.* Illus by Peggy Fortnum. Boston: Houghton, 1974. Dell paperback.

647 Brodsky, Beverly. *Jonah; an Old Testament Story.* Philadelphia: Lippincott, 1977.

648 Brommer, Gerald F. *Transparent Watercolor; Ideas and Techniques.* New York: Sterling, 1973.

649 Brooke, L. Leslie. *The Golden Goose Book.* Illus by the author. New York: Warne, 1977.

650 Brooke, L. Leslie. *Johnny Crow's Garden.* Illus by the author. New York: Warne, 1903.

651 ———. *Johnny Crow's Garden.* Illus by the author. New York: Peter Possum Paperbacks, Watts, 1967. M331.

652 ———. *Johnny Crow's New Garden.* Illus by the author. New York: Warne, 1935.

653 ———. *Johnny Crow's party.* Illus by the author. New York: Warne, 1907.

654 ———. *Ring O'Roses.* Illus by the author. New York: Warne, 1922.

655 Brooks, Gwendolyn. *Selected Poems.* New York: Harper, 1963. Paperback. M260.

656 Brooks, William. *Speech Communication.* 2nd ed. Dubuque, Iowa: William C. Brown, 1974.

657 Brooks, Ron. *Annie's Rainbow.* New York: Collins, 1976.

658 Broomfield, Robert, illus. *Twelve Days of Christmas.* New York: McGraw-Hill, 1965. M719, M720.

659 Brown, Billye and Walter Brown. *Historic Catastrophes: Earth Quakes.* Reading, MA: Addison-Wesley, 1974.

660 Brown, Heywood. *A Shepherd.* Illus by Gilbert Riswold. Englewood Cliffs, NJ: Prentice-Hall, 1929, 1967.

661 Brown, Marc. *Finger Rhymes.* Illus by Marc Brown. New York: Dutton, 1980.

662 Brown, Marcia. *All Butterflies, an ABC.* New York: Scribner, 1974. M13.

663 ———. *Backbone of the King: The Story of Paka'a and his Son Ku.* New York: Scribner, 1966.

664 ———. *The Blue Jackal.* New York: Scribner, 1977.

665 ———. *The Bun: A Tale from Russia.* New York: Harcourt, 1972.

666 *———. Cinderella.* New York: Scribner, 1954. Book Fair paperback. M135, M136.

667 ———. *Dick Whittington and his Cat.* New York: Scribner, 1950.

668 ———. *Felice.* New York: Scribner, 1958.

669 ———. *How, Hippo!* New York: Scribner, 1969. Book Fair paperback. M302.

670 ———. *The Neighbors.* New York: Scribner, 1967.

671 *———. Once a Mouse. . .* New York: Scribner, 1961. M498.

672 ———. *Peter Piper's Alphabet.* New York: Scribner, 1959.

673 ———. *Puss and Boots.* New York: Scribner, 1952. M555.

674 ———. *Stone Soup.* New York: Scribner, 1947. Book Fair paperback. M634, M635.

675 ———. *Three Billy Goats Gruff.* New York: Harcourt, 1977. Voyager paperback. M687.

676 Brown, Margaret Wise. *A Child's Good Night Book.* Illus by Jean Charlot. New York: Young Scott, 1950.

677 ———. *Christmas in the Barn.* Illus by Barbara Cooney. New York: Crowell, 1952.

678 ———. *Color Kittens.* Illus by Alice and Martin Provensen. New York: Golden, 1949.

679 ———. *Goodnight Moon.* Illus by Clemont Hurd. New York: Harper, 1947.

680 ———. *Nibble Nibble.* Illus by Leonard Weisgard. New York: Young Scott, 1959.

681 ———. *The Sleepy Little Lion.* Illus by Ylla. New York: Harper, 1954. Trophy paperback.

682 ———. *Summer Noisy Book.* Illus by Leonard Weisgard. New York: Harper, 1951.

683 ———. *Two Little Trains.* Illus by Jean Charlot. New York: Young Scott, 1949.

684 ———. *Winter Noisy Book.* Illus by Leonard Weisgard. New York: Harper, 1947. Trophy paperback.

685 Brown, Michael. *A Cavalcade of Sea Legends.* Illus by Krystyna Turska. New York: Walck, 1971.

686 Brown, Palmer. *Something for Christmas.* Illus by the author. New York: Harper, 1958.

687 Brown-Azarovica, Marjorie Frances. *A Handbook of Creative Choral Speaking.* Minneapolis: Burgess, 1970.

688 Browne, C. C. The Story of our National Ballads. New York: Crowell, 1960.

689 Browning, Robert. The Pied Piper of Hamelin. Illus by Kate Greenaway. New York: Warne, n.d.

690 ———. The Pied Piper of Hamelin. Illus by Walter Hodges. New York: Coward, 1971.

691 ———. The Pied Piper of Hamelin. Illus by Lieselotte Schwarz. New York: Scroll, 1970.

692 Brummitt, Wyatt. Kites. Illus by Enid Kalschnig. New York: Western, 1971.

693 Bryan, Ashley. The Adventures of Aku. Illus by the author. New York: Atheneum, 1976.

694 ———. The Dancing Granny. New York: Atheneum, 1977.

695 Bryan, Ashley, Ed. Walk Together Children; Black American Spirituals. Selected and illus by A. Bryan. New York: Atheneum, 1974.

696 Bryant, Sara. How to Tell Stories to Children. Boston: Houghton, 1924. Gale Reprint, 1973.

697 Buck, Margaret Waring. Along the Seashore. Philadelphia: Abingdon, 1964. Paperback.

698 Buck, Pearl S. The Big Wave. New York: Day, 1947.

699 ———. Fairy Tales of the Orient. Illus by Jeanyee Wong. New York: Simon & Schuster, 1965.

700 ———. The Little Fox in the Middle. Illus by Rob Jones. New York: Macmillan, 1966. Macmillan paperback.

701 Buckley, Helen. Josie and the Snow. Illus by Evaline Ness. New York: Lathrop, 1964. M335.

702 Buckley, Helen E. Josie's Buttercup. Illus by Evaline Ness. New York: Lothrop. 1967.

703 ———. The Wonderful Little Boy. Illus by Rob Howard. New York: Lothrop. 1970.

704a Budbill, David. Bones on Black Spruce Mountain. New York: Dial, 1978.

704b ———. Snowshoe Trek to Otter River. New York: Dial, 1976. Bantam paperback.

705 Budd, Lillina. Tekla's Easter. Illus by Genia. Chicago: Rand, 1962.

706 Budney, Blossom. A Kiss is Round. Illus by Vladimir Bobri. New York: Lothrop, 1954.

707 Buehr, Walter. Salt, Sugar and Spice. New York: Morrow, 1969.

708 Buehr, Walter. Sea Monsters. Illus by the author. New York: Norton, 1966. Archway paperback.

709 ———. Sending the Word, The Story of Communication. New York: Putnam, 1959.

710 Bufano, Remo. Remo Bufano's Book of Puppetry. Edited by Arthur R. Richmond. New York: Macmillan, 1955.

711 Buff, Mary and Conrad. The Apple and the Arrow. Boston: Houghton, 1951. Sandpiper paperback. M358, M757.

712 ———. The Big Tree. New York: Viking 1946.

713 ———. Dash and Dart. New York: Viking 1942.

714 ———. Elf Owl. New York: Viking 1958.

715 ———. Forest Folk. New York: Viking 1962.

716 ———. Hurry Skurry Flurry. New York: Viking, 1954.

717 Bulatkin, I. F. Eurasian Folk and Fairy Tales. Illus by Howard Simon. New York: Criterion, 1965.

718 Bulfinch, Thomas. Bulfinch's Mythology. Illus by Elinor Raisdell. New York: Crowell, 1970. Dell paperback.

719 Bulla, Clyde R. I Went for a Walk, a Read-and-Sing Book. Illus by Lois Lenski. Music by C. R. Bulla. New York: Walck, 1958.

720 ———. Jonah and the Great Fish. Illus by Helga Aichinger. New York: Crowell, 1970.

721 ———. Joseph the Dreamer. Illus by Gordon Laite. New York: Crowell, 1971.

722 ———. More Stories of Favorite Operas. Illus by Joseph Low. New York: Crowell, 1965. M55, M472, M507, M512, M757.

723 ———. The Ring and the Fire, Stories from Wagner's Niebelungen Operas. Illus by Clare and John Ross. New York: Crowell, n.d. M472, M512.

724 ———. Song of Saint Francis. New York: Crowell, 1952.

725 ———. Stories of Favorite Operas. Illus by Robert Galster. New York: Crowell, 1959. M55, M472, M507, M512, M757.

726 ———. Stories of Gilbert and Sullivan Operas. Illus by James and Ruth McCrea. New York: Crowell, 1968. M470.

727 ———. What Makes a Shadow. Illus by Adrienne Adams. New York: Scholastic, 1962.

728 Bunting, Eve. High Tide for Labrador. Illus by Bernard Garbutt. Chicago: Childrens, 1975.

729 Burack, Abraham S., ed. One Hundred Plays for Children, an Anthology of Non-royalty One-act Plays. Boston: Plays, 1970.

730 Burack, Abraham and Alice Crossley. Favorite Plays for Classroom Reading. Boston: Plays, 1971.

731 ———. Popular Plays for Classroom Reading. Boston: Plays, 1974.

732 ———. Thirty Plays for Classroom Reading, a New Approach to the Reading Program in the Intermediate Grades. Boston: Plays, 1968.

733 Burch, Robert. Queenie Peavy. New York: Viking, 1966.

734 ———. Skinny. New York: Viking, 1964. Dell paperback.

735 Burchard, Peter. Bimby. New York: Coward, 1968.

736 ———. The Deserter: A Spy Story of the Civil War. New York: Coward, 1974.

737 ———. Jed: The Story of a Yankee Soldier and a Southern Boy. Illus by the author. New York: Coward, 1960.

738 ———. North by Night. Illus by the author. New York: Coward, 1962.

739 ———. Rat Hell. New York: Coward, 1971.

740 Burgess, Gelett. Goops and How to Be Them. New York: Dover, 1968.

741 ———. More Goops and How Not to Be Them. New York: Dover, 1968.

742 Burgunder, Rose. From Summer to Summer. Illus by Rita Faver. New York: Viking, 1965.

743 Burkett, Molly and John Burkett. Foxes Three. Illus by Pamela Johnson. Philadelphia: Lippincott, 1975.

744 Burnett, Frances Hodgson. The Secret Garden. Illus by Tasha Tudor. Philadelphia: Lippincott, 1962. Dell paperback.

745 Burnford, Sheila. The Incredible Journey. Il-

lus by Carl Burger. Boston: Little, 1960. Bantam paperback.

746 Burningham, John. Borka: The Adventures of a Goose With No Feathers. Illus by the author. New York: Random, 1964.

747 ———. Cannonball Simp. Illus by the author. Indianapolis: Bobbs-merrill, 1967.

748 ———. Harquin, the Fox Who Went Down to the Valley. Lawrence, MA: Merrimack, 1979.

749 ———. John Burningham's ABC. Illus by the author. Indianapolis: Bobbs, 1967.

750 ———. Mr. Gumpy's Motor Car. Illus by the author. New York: Crowell, 1976. Puffin paperback.

751 ———. Mr. Gumpy's Outing. Illus by the author. New York: Holt, 1971. M453.

752 ———. Seasons. Illus by the author. Indianapolis: Bobbs-Merrill, 1970.

753 Burns, Robert. Hand in Hand We'll Go, Ten Poems by Robert Burns. Illus by Nonny Hogrogian. New York: Crowell, 1965.

754 Burton, Virginia Lee. Katy and the Big Snow. Illus by the author. Boston: Houghton, 1943. Sandpiper paperback.

755 *———. The Little House. Illus by the author. Boston: Houghton, 1942. Paperback. M370.

756 ———. Mike Mulligan and his Steam Shovel. Illus by the author. Boston: Houghton, 1939. Paperback. M443, M444.

757 Busch, Phyllis S. A Walk in the Snow. Photos by Mary M. Thacher. Philadelphia: Lippincott, 1971.

758 ———. Wildflowers and the Stories Behind Their Names. Illus by Anne Ophelia Dowden. New York: Scribner, 1977.

759 Butler, Beverly. Gift of Gold. New York: Dodd, 1972. Archway paperback.

760 ———. Light a Single Candle. New York: Dodd, 1962. Archway paperback.

761 Butterworth, Olive. The Enormous Egg. Illus by Louis Darling. Boston: Little, 1956.

762 ———. Narrow Passage. Illus by Louis Darling. Boston: Little, 1973.

763 Byars, Betsy. The Eighteenth Emergency. Illus by Robert Grossman. New York: Viking, 1973. Avon paperback.

764 ———. Go and Hush the Baby. Illus by Emily A. McCully. New York: Viking, 1971.

765 ———. The House of Wings. Illus by Daniel Schwartz. New York: Viking, 1972.

766 Byars, Betsy. The Lace Snail. Illus by the author. New York: Viking, 1975. M347.

767 ———. The Midnight Fox. Illus by Ann Grifalconi. New York: Viking, 1968.

768 ———. Summer of the Swans. Illus by Ted Conis. New York: Viking, 1970. M657.

769 ———. Trouble River. Illus by Rocco Negri. New York: Viking, 1969. Puffin paperback.

770 Byfield, Barbara Nide. Haunted Churchbell. New York: Doubleday, 1971.

771 Byrne, Peter. The Search for Big Foot: Monster, Myth or Man. Acropolis, 1975.

772 Cahn, William and Rhoda. The Story of Writing from Cave Art to Computer. Illus by Anne Lewis. New York and Eau Claire, Wisconsin: Harvey House, 1963.

773 Caldecott, Randolph, illus. Babes in the Wood. New York: Warne, 1879.

774 Caldecott, Randolph. Caldecott Picture Book #1. New York: Warne, n.d.

775 ———. Caldecott Picture Book #2. New York: Warne, n.d.

776 ———. Caldecott Picture Book #3. New York: Warne, n.d.

777 ———. Caldecott Picture Book #4. New York: Warne, n.d.

778 ———. Come Lasses and Lads. New York: Warne, 1884.

779 ———. Elegy on a Mad Dog. New York: Warne, 1879.

780 ———. Farmer's Boy. New York: Warne, 1881.

781 ———. Fox Jumps Over the Parson's Gate. New York: Warne, 1883.

782 ———. Frog He Would a-Wooing Go. New York: Warne, 1883. M216.

783 ———. Hey Diddle Diddle with Baby Bunting. New York: Warne, 1882. M283.

784 ———. The House that Jack Built. New York: Warne, 1878.

785 ———. John Gilpin. New York: Warne, 1878.

786 ———. The Milkmaid. New York: Warne, 1882. M445.

787 ———. Mrs. Mary Blaize. New York: Warne, 1885.

788 ———. Queen of Hearts. New York: Warne, 1881. M557.

789 ———. Randolph Caldecott's John Gilpin and Other Stories; Containing: The Diverting History of John Gilpin; The House that Jack Built; The Frog he Would a-wooing go; The Milkmaid. New York: Warne, 1977.

790 ———. Ride a Cock Horse With a Farmer Went Trotting. New York: Warne, 1884.

791 ———. Sing a Song for Sixpence. New York: Warne, 1880. M613.

792 ———. Three Jovial Huntsmen. New York: Warne, 1880.

793 Cameron, Eleanor. Court of the Stone Children. New York: Dutton, 1973. Avon paperback.

794 ———. A Room Made of Windows. Illus by Trina Schart Hyman. Boston: Little, 1971. Dell paperback.

795 ———. A Spell is Cast. Illus by Beth and Joe Krush. Boston: Little, 1964. Archway paperback.

796 ———. The Terrible Churnadryne. Illus by Beth and Joe Krush. Boston: Little, 1959. Archway paperback.

797 ———. Time and Mr. Bass; a Mushroom Planet Book. Illus by Fred Meise. Boston: Little 1967.

798 ———. The Wonderful Flight to the Mushroom Planet. Boston: Little, 1954.

799 Cameron, Polly. The Green Machine. Illus by Consuelo Joerns. New York: Coward, 1969.

800 ———. I Can't Said the Ant. Illus by the author. New York: Coward, 1969.

801 ———. The Two Ton Canary and Other Nonsense Riddles. New York: Coward, 1965.

802 Carew, Jan. The Third Gift. Illus by Leo and Diane Dillon. Boston: Little, 1974.

803 Carigiet, Alois. The Pear Tree, the Birch Tree and the Barberry Bush. New York: Walck, 1967.

804 Carle, Eric. *All About Arthur: An Absolutely Absurd Ape.* Illus by the author. New York: Watts, 1974.

805 ———. *Do You Want to be my Friend?* New York: Crowell, 1971.

806 ———. *Eric Carle's Storybook: Seven Tales from the Brothers Grimm.* Retold and illus by E. Carle. New York: Watts, 1976.

807 ———. *The Grouchy Ladybug.* Illus by the author. New York: Crowell, 1977.

808 ———. *Have You Seen My Cat?* Illus by the author. New York: Watts, 1973.

809 ———. *I See a Song.* Illus by the author. New York: Crowell, 1973.

810 ———. *My Very First Book of Colors.* Illus by the author. New York: Crowell, 1974.

811 ———. *My Very First Book of Numbers.* Illus by the author. New York: Crowell, 1974.

812 ———. *My Very First Book of Shapes.* Illus by the author. New York: Crowell, 1974.

813 ———. *One, Two, Three to the Zoo.* Illus by the author. New York: Collins, 1968.

814 ———. *The Rooster Who Set Out to See the World.* Illus by the author. New York: Watts, 1972.

815 ———. *The Secret Birthday Message.* Illus by the author. New York: Crowell, 1972.

816 ———. *The Tiny Seed.* Illus by the author. New York: Crowell, 1970.

817 ———. *The Very Hungry Caterpillar.* Illus by the author. New York: Collins, 1970.

818 ———. *A Very Long Tail: A Folding Book.* Illus by the author. New York: Crowell, 1972.

819 ———. *A Very Long Train: A Folding Book.* Illus by the author. New York: Crowell, 1972.

820 Carle, Eric, retold and illus. *Twelve Tales fom Aesop.* New York: Philomel, 1980.

821 Carlson, Bernice Wells. *Act it Out.* Nashville, TN: Abingdon, 1956.

822 ———. *Funny-Bone Dramatics.* Nashville, TN: Abingdon, 1974.

823 ———. *Let's Pretend it Happened to You.* Illus by Rallph McDonald. Nashville, TN: Abingdon, 1973.

824 ———. *Listen! and Help Tell the Story.* Illus by Burmah Burns. Nashville: Abingdon, 1965.

825 ———. *Make It Yourself! Handicraft for Boys and Girls.* Nashville, TN: Abingdon, 1950. Paperback.

826 ———. *1001 Riddles for Children.* New York: Platt, 1949.

827 ———. *Picture That!* Illus by Delores Marie Rowland. Nashville, TN: Abingdon, 1977.

828 ———. *Play a Part.* Illus by Catherine Scholz. Nashville, TN: Abingdon, 1970.

829 Carlson, Bernice Wells and Ristiina Wigg. *We Want Sunshine in Our Houses.* Illus by David Stone. Nashville, TN: Abingdon, 1973.

830 Carlson, George. *Jokes and Riddles.* New York: Platt, n.d.

831 ———. *1001 Riddles for Children.* New York: Platt, 1949.

832 Carlson, Natalie. *Marie Louise and Christopher.* Illus by Jose Aruego and Ariane Dewey. New York: Scribner, 1974.

833 ———. *Marie Louise's Heyday.* Illus by Jose Aruego and Ariane Dewey. New York: Scribner, 1975. M406.

834 ———. *Runaway Marie Louise.* Illus by Jose Aruego and Ariane Dewey. New York: Scribner, 1977.

835 Carlson, Natalie S. *The Talking Cat and Other Stories of French Canada.* Illus by Roger Duvoisin. New York: Harper, 1952.

836 Carlson, Ruth Kearney. *Enrichment Ideas,* 2nd ed. Dubuque, Iowa: William C. Brown, 1976.

837 Carmer, Carl. *America Sings, Stories and Songs of Our Country's Growing.* New York: Knopf, 1942.

838 ———. *The Boy Drummer of Vincennes.* Illus by Seymour Fleishman. Irving-on-Hudson, New York: Harvey, 1972.

839 Carpenter, Allan. *Alaska: From Its Glorious Past to the Present.* Illus by Roger Herrington. Chicago: Childrens, 1968.

840 ———. *Enchantment of America; Maine.* Chicago: Childrens, 1966.

841 Carpenter, Frances. *Tales of a Chinese Grandmother.* Illus by Malthe Haoselriis. New York: Tuttle, 1972. Paperback.

842 ———. *Wonder Tales of Dogs and Cats.* Illus by Ezra Jack Keats. New York: Doubleday, 1955.

843 ———. *Wonder Tales of Horses and Heroes.* Illus by William D. Hayes. New York: Doubleday, 1962.

844 Carrick, Carol. *Lost in the Storm.* Illus by Don Carrick. New York: Seabury, 1974.

845 ———. *Paul's Christmas Birthday.* Illus by Donald Carrick. New York: Greenwillow, 1978.

846 ———. *Sleep Out.* Illus by Donald Carrick. New York: Seabury, 1973.

847 Carrick, Donald. *Drip, Drop.* New York: Macmillan, 1973.

848 Carrigan, Adeline. *Holiday Ring, Festival Stories and Poems.* Illus by Rainey Bennett. Chicago: Whitman, 1975.

849 Carrighar, Sally. *The Twilight Seas: A Blue Whale's Journey.* Illus by Peter Parnall. New York: Weybright and Falley, 1975.

850 Carroll, Lewis. *Alice in Wonderland.* Chicago: Rand McNally, 1944. Paperback. M12, M622.

851 ———. *Alice's Adventures in Wonderland and Through the Looking-Glass.* New York: Collins, 1975. M12, M622.

852 ———. *Alice's Adventures in Wonderland and Through the Looking-Glass.* New York: Dutton, 1954. M12, M622.

853 ———. *Alice's Adventures in Wonderland and Through the Looking-Glass.* Illus by John Tenniel. New York: Macmillan, 1963. Paperback. M12, M622.

854 ———. *Alice's Adventures Under Ground, a Fascimilie of the Original Lewis Carroll Manuscript.* Ann Arbor, MI.: University Microfilms, 1964.

855 ———. *The Hunting of the Snark.* Illus by Helen Oxenbury. New York: Watts, 1970.

856 ———. *The Hunting of the Snark, an Agony in Eight Fits by Lewis Carroll.* Illus by Kelly Oechsli. New York: Pantheon, 1966.

857 ———. *Jabberwocky.* Illus by Jane Breskin Zalben. New York: Warne, 1977.

858 ———. *Lewis Carroll's Jabberwocky.* Illus by Jane Breskin Zalben. New York: Warne, 1977.

859 ———. *Songs from Alice.* Music by Don Harper. Illus by Charles Folkard. New York: Holiday, 1978. Cassette. M622

860 ———. *The Walrus and the Carpenter and Other Poems.* Illus by Gerald Rose. New York: Dutton, 1969.

861 Carroll, Ruth. *The Chimp and the Clown.* New York: Walck, 1968.

862 ———. *Christmas Kitten.* New York: Walck, 1970.

863 ———. *Dolphin and the Mermaid.* New York: Walck, 1974.

864 ———. *Rolling Downhill.* New York: Walck, 1973

865 ———. *What Whiskers Did.* New York: Walck, 1965. Scholastic paperback.

866 ———. *The Witch Kitten.* New York: Walck, 1973.

867 Carter, Samuel. *The Happy Dolphins.* New York: Putnam, 1971. Archway paperback.

868 Cartner, William C. *The Young Calligraphers: A How-it-is-Done Book of Penmanship.* New York: Warne, 1969.

869 Cassedy, Sylvia and Suetake Kunihiro. *Birds, Frogs and Moonlight; Haiku.* Calligraphy by Koson Okamura. Illus by Vo-Dinh. Garden City, NY: Doubleday, 1967.

870 ———. *Moon-Uncle, Moon-Uncle; Rhymes from India.* Trans by Sylvia Cassedy and Parvathi Tempi. Illus by Susanna Suba. Garden City, NY: Doubleday, 1973.

871 Cassedy, Sylvia and Seutake Kunihiro. *Birds, Frogs, and Moonlight; Haiku.* Illus by Vo-Dinh. Calligraphy by Koson Okamura.Garden City, NY: Doubleday, 1967.

872 Castle, Sue. *Face Talk, Hand Talk, Body Talk.* Photos by Frances McLaughlin-Gill. Garden City, NY: Doubleday, 1977.

873 Catherall, Arthur. *Camel Caravan.* Illus by Joseph Papin. New York: Seabury, 1968.

874 ———. *Freedom for a Cheetah.* Illus by Shyam Varma. New York: Lothrop, 1971.

875 ———. *Kidnapped by Accident.* Illus by Victor G. Ambrus. New York: Lothrop, 1969. Scholastic paperback.

876 ———. *Last Horse on the Sands.* Illus by David Farris. New York: Lothrop, 1972. Tempo paperback.

877 ———. *Lone Seal Pup.* Illus by John Kaufman. New York: Dutton, 1965.

878 ———. *Night of the Black Frost.* New York: Lothrop, 1968.

879 ———. *Prisoners in the Snow.* Illus by Victor Ambrus. New York: Lothrop, 1967.

880 ———. *Red Sea Rescue.* Illus by Victor Ambrus. New York: Lothrop, 1969.

881 ———. *Strange Intruder.* New York: Lothrop, 1965. Archway paperback.

882 ———. *A Zebra Came to Drink.* New York: Dutton, 1967.

883a Cathon, Laura E. and Thursnelda Schmidt. *Perhaps and Perchance, Tales of Nature.* Illus by Anne Marie Jauss. New York: Abington, 1962.

883b Cathon, Laura E. et al, eds. *Stories to Tell to Children: A Selected List.* University of Pittsburg Press. 1974

884 Cottler, Joseph and Haym Jaffe. *Heroes of Civilization.* Boston: Little, 1969.

885 Caudill, Rebecca. *A Certain Small Shepherd.* Illus by William Pene DeBois. New York: Holt, 1965.

886 ———. *Come Along!* Illus by Ellen Raskin. New York: Holt, 1969. Paperback.

887 ———. *Pocketful of Cricket.* New York: Holt, 1964. Owlet paperback. M544.

888a Causley, Charles. *Figgie Hobbin.* New York: Walker, 1974.

888b Cavanna, Betty. *First Book of Wild Flowers.* Illus by Page Cary. New York: Watts, 1961.

889 Cavanah, Francis and Ruth Cromer Weir. *Twenty-four Horses: A Treasury of Stories.* Chicago: Rand McNally, 1950.

890 Cerf, Bennett A. *Bennett Cerf's Book of Animal Riddles.* New York: Random, 1964.

891 ———. *Bennett Cerf's Book of Laughs.* New York: Random, 1959.

892 ———. *Bennett Cerf's Book of Riddles.* New York: Random, 1960.

893 ———. *More Riddles.* New York: Random, 1961.

894 Chaconos, Doris. *The Way the Tiger Walked.* Illus by Frank Bozzo. New York: Scribner, 1970.

895 Chaffin, Lillie D. *I Have a Tree.* Illus by Martha Alexander. New York: David White, 1969.

Chappell, Warren. See also Updike, John.

896 Chapell, Warren, illus. *The Nutcracker.* New York: Knopf, 1958. M489, M636.

897 ———. *Peter and the Wolf.* by Serge Prokofieff. Foreword by Serge Koussevitzky. New York: Knopf, 1940. M521.

898 ———. *Sleeping Beauty.* Adapted and illus by W. Chappell from the Tales of Charles Perrault. Music by Peter Tschaikovsky. New York: Knopf, 1961. M201, M521.

899 Chardiet, Bernice. *C is for Circus.* Illus by Brinton Turkle. New York: Walker, 1971.

900 *Charge of the Light Brigade and Other Story Poems.* New York: Scholastic, paperback, 1970.

901 Charlip, Remy. *Where is Everybody?* New York: Young Scott, 1957.

902 Charlip, Remy and Mary Beth and George Ancona. *Handtalk: an ABC of Finger Spelling and Sign Language.* Illus by G. Ancona. New York: Parents, 1974.

903 Charlip, Remy and Burton Supree. *Harlequin and the Gift of Many Colors.* New York: Parents, 1973.

904 ———. *Mother Mother I Feel Sick, Send for the Doctor Quick Quick Quick.* Illus by R. Charlip. New York: Illus, 1966.

905 Charlip, Remy and Jerry Joyner. *Thirteen.* New York: Parents, 1975.

906 Charlip, Remy and Lillian Moore. *Hooray for Me!* New York: Parents, 1975.

907 Charosh, Mannis. *Mathematical Games for One or Two.* Illus by Lois Ehlert. New York: Crowell, 1972.

908 ———. *Number Ideas through Pictures.* Illus by Giulio Maestro. New York: Crowell, 1974.

909 Chase, Richard. *Billy Boy.* Illus by Glen Round. San Carlos, CA: Golden Gate, 1966. M32, M85, M204.

910 ———. *Grandfather Tales.* Illus by Berkley Williams. Boston: Houghton-Mifflin, 1948.

911 ———. *Jack and the Three Sillies.* Illus by Joshua Talford. Boston: Houghton-Mifflin, 1950.

912 ———. *Jack Tales.* Illus by Berkley Williams. Boston Houghton-Mifflin, 1943.

913 Chaucer, Geoffrey. *Canterbury Tales.* New York: Penguin, 1951. Puffin paperback.

914 *———. *Chanticleer and the Fox.* Illus by Barbara Cooney. New York: Crowell, 1958. M121, M122.

915 Chen, Tony. *Run, Zebra, Run.* Illus by the author. New York: Lothrop, 1972.

916 Cheng, Hou-Tien. *Six Chinese Brothers; an Ancient Tale.* Illus by the author. New York: Hold, 1979.

917 Chernoff, Goldie Taub. *Clay-Dough-Play Dough.* Illus by Margaret Hartelius. New York: Walker, 1974. Paperback.

918 ———. *Easy Costumes You Don't Have to Sew.* Costumes designed and illus by Margaret Hartelius. New York: Four Winds, 1977. Paperback.

919 ———. *Just a Box?* Illus by Margaret Hartelius. New York: Walker, 1973. Scholastic paperback.

920 ———. *Pebbles and Pods; a Book of Nature Craft.* Illus by Margaret Hartelius. Walker, 1973.

921 ———. *Puppet Party.* Illus by Margaret Hartelius. New York: Walker, 1971. Scholastic paperback.

922 Chess, Victoria. *Alfred's Alphabet Walk.* Illus by V. Chess. New York: Greenwillow, 1979.

923 Child, Lydia Maria. *Over the River and Through the Wood.* Illus by Brinton Turkle. New York: Coward, 1974. Schoastic paperback.

924 Child Study Association of America. *Castles and Dragons: Read-to-Myself Fairy Tales for Boys and Girls.* Illus by William Pene duBois. New York: Crowell, 1958.

925 ———. *Read Me Another Story.* Illus by Barbara Cooney. New York: Crowell, 1949.

926 ———. *Read Me More Stories.* Illus by Barbara Cooney. New York: Crowell, 1951.

927 ———. *Read-to-Me Story.* Illus by Lois Lenski. New York: Crowell, 1947.

928 Children's Book Council. *Children's Books: Awards and Prizes.* New York: Children's Book Council, 1975.

929 Children's Television Workshop. *The Best of Electric Company.* New York: Grosset and Dunlap, paperback, 1977.

930 ———. *The Electric Company Crazy Cut-Ups.* New York: Grosset and Dunlap paperback, 1977.

931 ———. *The Electric Company Easy Reader's Activity Book.* New York: Grosset paperback, 1977.

932 ———. *The Electric Company Game Show Book.* New York: Grosset paperback, 1977.

933 ———. *Sesame Street Book of Letters.* New York: Signet paperback, 1971.

934 ———. *Sesame Street Book of People and Things.* New York: Signet paperback, 1971.

935 ———. *Sesame Street Book of Puzzlers.* New York: Signet paperback, 1971.

936 ———. *Sesame Street Book of Shapes.* New York: Signet paperback, 1971.

937 ———. *Sesame Street Book of Numbers.* New York: Signet paperback, 1971.

938a Childress, Alice. *A Hero Ain't Nothin' but a Sandwich.* New York: Coward, 1973.

938b ———. *When the Rattlesnake Sounds: A Play About Harriet Tubman.* Illus by Charles Lilly. New York: Coward, 1975.

939 Chipperfield, Joseph. *Dog to Trust; the Saga of a Seeing Eye Dog.* Illus by Larry Toschik. New York: McKay, 1963.

940 Chonz, Selina. *A Bell for Ursli.* Illus by Alois Carigiet. New York: Walck, 1966.

941 ———. *Florina and the Wild Bird.* Illus by Alois Carigiet. Translated by Anne and Ian Serraillier. New York: Walck, 1966.

942 Chrisman, Arthur. *Shen of the Sea.* Illus by Else Hasselriis. New York: Dutton, 1925.

943 Christensen, Jo I. and Sonie S. Ashner. *Cross Stitchery; Needlepointing with Yarns in a Variety of Decorative Stitches.* New York: Sterling, 1973.

944 ———. *Needlepoint Simplified.* New York: Sterling 1971.

945 Christopher, John. *The City of Gold and Lead.* New York: Macmillan, 1967. Paperback.

946 ———. *The Pool of Fire.* New York: Macmillan, 1968. Paperback.

947 ———. *The White Mountains.* New York: Macmillan, 1967. Paperback.

948 Christopher, Matt. *Earthquake.* Illus by Ted Lewin. Boston: Little, 1975.

949 ———. *Stranded.* Illus by Gail Owens. Boston: Little, 1974.

950 Chrystie, Frances N. *First Book of Jokes and Funny Things.* New York: Watts, 1951.

951 ———. *Pets; a Complete Handbook on the Care, Understanding and Appreciation of All Kinds of Animal Pets.* Illus by Gillett G. Griffin. Boston: Little, 1974.

952a ———. *Riddle Me This.* New York: Walck, 1940. Walck paperback.

952b Chukovsky, Kornei, *The Telephone.* Trans from the Russian by William Smith. New York: Delacorte, 1977.

953 Church, Alfred J. *The Odyssey of Homer.* Illus by John Flaxman. New York: Macmillan, 1951.

954 Church, Richard. *Five Boys in a Cave.* New York: Day, 1950.

955 Churchill, Richard E. *The Six Million Dollar Cucumber.* Illus by Carol Nickolos. New York: Watts, 1976.

956 Chwast, Seymour. *Still Another Alphabet Book.* Illus by Martin Moskoff. New York: McGraw, 1969.

957 Chwast, Seymour and Martin Moskof. *Still Another Number Book.* New York: McGraw, 1971.

958 Chwast, Seymour, illus. *The House that Jack Built.* New York: Random, 1973.

959 Ciardi, John. *Fast and Slow.* Illus by Becky Gaver. Boston: Houghton, 1975.

960 ———. *I Met a Man*. Illus by Rob Osborn. Boston: Houghton, 1961.

961 ———. *John J. Plenty and Fiddler Dan*. Illus by Madeline Gekiere. Philadelphia: Lippincott, 1963.

962 ———. *The Man Who Sang the Sillies*. Illus by Edward Gorey. Philadelphia: Lippincott, 1961.

963 ———. *The Reason for the Pelican*. Illus by Madeline Gekiere. Philadelphia: Lippincott, 1959.

964 ———. *Someone Could Win a Polar Bear*. Illus by Edward Gorey. Philadelphia: Lippincott, 1970.

965 ———. *You Read to Me, I'll Read to You*. Illus by Edward Gorey. Philadelphia: Lippincott, 1961.

966 ———. *You Know Who*. Illus by Edward Gorey. Philadelphia: Lippincott, 1964.

967 ———. *The Monster Den and Look What Happened at MY House, and to It*. Illus by Edward Gorey. Philadelphia: Lippincott, 1966.

968 Clapp, Patricia. *Constance; a Story of Early Plymouth*. New York: Lothrop, 1968. Dell Paperback.

969 Clark, Ann Nolan. *All This Wild Land*. New York: Viking, 1976.

970 ———. *Along Sandy Trails*. Photos by Alfred Cohn. New York: Viking, 1969.

971 ———. *The Desert People*. Illus by Allan Houser. New York: Viking, 1962.

972 Clark, David Allen. *Jokes, Puns and Riddles*. Garden City, NY: Doubleday, 1968.

973 Clark, Mary Lou. *The True Book of Dinosaurs*. Illus by Chaucey Maltman. Chicago: Childrens Press, 1955.

974 Clark, Mavis Thorpe. *If the Earth Falls In*. New York: Seabury, 1975.

975 ———. *The Min-Men*. New York: Macmillan, 1969.

976 ———. *Wildfire*. New York: Macmillan, 1974.

977 Clarke, Arthur. *Dolphin Island*. New York: Holt, 1963. Berkley paperback.

978 Clarke, Pauline. *Return of the Twelves*. Illus by Bernarda Bryson. New York: Coward, 1963.

979 Claudine. *Flight of the Animals*. New York: Parents, 1971.

980 Clayton, Ed. *Martin Luther King: The Peaceful Warrior*. Illus by David Hodges. Englewood Cliffs, NJ: Prentice 1964, 1968.

981 Cleary, Beverly. *Beezus and Ramona*. Illus by Louis Darling. New York: Morrow, 1955. Paperback.

982 ———. *Ellen Tebbits*. Illus by Louis Darling. New York: Morrow, 1951. Dell paperback.

983 ———. *Emily's Runaway Imagination*. Illus by Joe and Beth Krush. New York: Morrow, 1961. Dell paperback.

984 ———. *Henry and Beezus*. Illus by Louis Darling. New York: Morrow, 1952. Paperback.

985 ———. *Henry and Ribsy*. Illus by Louis Darling. New York: Morrow, 1954. Dell paperback.

986 ———. *Henry and the Clubhouse*. Illus by Louis Darling. New York: Morrow, 1962. Paperback.

987 ———. *Henry and the Paper Route*. Illus by Louis Darling. New York: Morrow, 1957. Dell paperback.

988 ———. *Henry Huggins*. Illus by Louis Darling. New York: Morrow, 1950. Paperback.

989 ———. *Jean and Johnny*. Illus by Joe and Beth Krush. New York: Morrow, 1959.

990 ———. *Mitch and Amy*. Illus by George Porter. New York: Morrow, 1967. Dell paperback.

991 ———. *The Mouse and the Motorcycle*. Illus by Louis Darling. New York: Morrow, 1965. Archway paperback.

992 ———. *Otis Spofford*. Illus by Louis Darling. New York: Morrow, 1953. Dell paperback.

993 ———. *Ramona and Her Father*. Illus by Alan Tiegreen. New York: Morrow, 1977.

994 ———. *Ramona and Her Mother*. Illus by Alan Tiegreen. New York: Morrow, 1979. Dell paperback.

995 ———. *Ramona the Brave*. Illus by Alan Tiegreen. New York: Morrow, 1975 Scholastic paperback.

996 ———. *Ramona the Pest*. Illus by Louis Darling. New York: Morrow, 1968. Scholastic paperback.

997 ———. *The Real Hole*. Illus by Mary Stevens. New York: Morrow, 1960.

998 ———. *Ribsy*. Illus by Louis Darling. New York: Morrow, 1964. Archway paperback.

999 ———. *Runaway Ralph*. Illus by Louis Darling. New York: Morrow, 1970. Archway paperback.

1000 ———. *Socks*. Illus by Beatrice Darwin. New York: Morrow, 1973. Dell paperback.

1001 Cleaver, Vera and Bill Cleaver. *Ellen Grae*. Illus by Ellen Raskin. Philadelphia: Lippincott, 1967.

1002 ———. *Lady Ellen Grae*. Illus by Ellen Raskin. Philadelphia: Lippincott, 1968.

1003 ———. *Trial Valley*. Philadelphia: Lippincott, 1977. Bantam paperback.

1004 ———. *Where the Lilies Bloom*. Illus by Jim Spanfeller. Philadelphia: Lippincott, 1969. Signet paperback.

1005 Clemens, Samuel. *The Adventures of Huckleberry Finn*. New York: Dodd, 1953.

1006 ———. *The Adventures of Tom Sawyer*. New York: Dodd, 1958.

1007 ———. *A Connecticut Yankee in King Arthur's Court*. New York: Harper, n.d. M148.

1008 ———. *Prince and the Pauper*. New York: Tempo paperback, 1977. Paperbacks by Airmont, Collier, and NAL.

1009 Clemons, Elizabeth. *Shells Are Where You Find Them*. Illus by Joe Gault. New York: Knopf, 1960.

1010 ———. *Tide Pools and Beaches*. Illus by Joe Gault. New York: Knopf, 1964.

1011 ———. *Waves, Tides and Currents*. New York: Knopf, 1967.

1012 Cleveland, David. *The April Rabbits*. Illus by Nurit Karlin. New York: Coward, 1978.

1013 Clewes, Dorothy. *Guide Dog*. Illus by Peter Burchard. New York: Coward, 1965.

1014 Clifford, Eth. *The Year of the Three-Legged Deer*. Illus by Richard Cuffari. New York:

Houghton, 1971. Dell paperback.

1015 Clifton, Lucile. *Black ABC's.* Illus by Don Miller. New York: Dutton, 1970.

1016 ———. *Don't You Remember?* Illus by Evaline Ness. New York: Dutton, 1973.

1017 Clifton, Lucille. *The Boy Who Didn't Believe in Spring.* Illus by Brinton Turkle. New York: Dutton, 1973.

1018 ———. *Everett Anderson's Christmas Coming.* Illus by Evaline Ness. New York: Holt, 1971.

1019 ———. *Everett Anderson's Friend.* Illus by Evaline Ness. New York: Holt, 1976.

1020 ———. *Everett Anderson's 1-2-3's.* Illus by Evaline Ness. New York: Holt, 1974.

1021 ———. *Everett Anderson's Year.* Illus by Ann Grifalconi. New York: Holt, 1974.

1022 ———. *Some of the Days of Everett Anderson.* New York: Holt, 1970.

1023 Clithero, Sally, ed. *Begining-to-Read Poetry, Selected from Original Sources.* Illus by Erik Blegvad. Chicago: Follett, 1967.

1024 Clive, Linda. *Weakfoot.* New York: Lothrop, 1975. Bantam paperback.

1025 Cloudley-Thompson, J. L. *Animals of the Desert.* Illus by Colin Threadgall. New York: McGraw, 1969.

1026 Clouston, W. A. *Book of Noodles: Stories of Simpleton.* Detroit: Gale, 1969. Reprint.

1027 Clymer, Eleanor. *Belinda's New Spring Hat.* Illus by Giora Frammenghi. New York: Watts, 1969.

1028 ———. *The Big Pile of Dirt.* Illus by Robert Shore. New York: Holt, 1968.

1029 ———. *Horatio.* Illus by Robert Quackenbush. New York: Atheneum, 1974. Aladdin paperback.

1030 ———. *Horatio Goes to the Country.* Illus by R. Quackenbush. New York: Atheneum, 1978.

1031 ———. *Horatio Solves a Mystery.* Illus by R. Quackenbush. New York: Atheneum, 1980.

1032 ———. *Horatio's Birthday.* Illus by R. Quackenbush. New York: Atheneum, 1976.

1033 ———. *How I Went Shopping and What I Got.* Illus by Trina Schart Hyman. New York: Holt, 1972.

1034 ———. *Leave Horatio Alone.* Illus by R. Quackenbush. New York: Atheneum, 1974.

1035 ———. *Me and the Eggman.* Illus by David Stone. New York: Dutton, 1972.

1036 ———. *The Spider, the Cave, and the Pottery Bowl.* Illus by Ingrid Fetz. New York: Atheneum, 1971.

1037 Clymer, Theodore. *Four Corners of the Sky: Poems, Chants and Oratory.* Illus by Marc Brown. Boston: Little, 1975.

1038 Coatsworth, Elizabeth. *Good Night.* Illus by Jose Aruego. New York: Macmillan, 1972.

1039 ———. *The Noble Doll.* Illus by Leo Politi. New York: Viking, 1961.

1040 ———. *The Peaceable Kingdom.* Illus by Fritz Eichenberg. New York: Pantheon, n.d.

1041 ———. *Under the Green Willow.* Illus by Janina Domanska. New York: Macmillan, 1971.

1042 Cochrane, Louise. *Shadow Puppets in Color.* Illus by Kate Simunck. Boston: Plays, 1972.

1043 ———. *Tabletop Theatres.* Illus by Kate Simunek. Boston: Plays, 1974.

1044 Cocognac, C. *The Three Trees of the Samurai.* Illus by Alain LeFall. New York: Harlin Quist, 1969.

1045 Coggins, Jack. *Flashes and Flags, The Story of Signaling.* New York: Dodd, 1963.

1046 Cohen, Barbara. *The Binding of Isaac.* Illus by Charles Midolaycak. New York: Lothrop, 1978.

1047 Cohen, Daniel. *The Greatest Monsters in the World.* New York: Dodd, 1975.

1048 ———. *The Human Side of Computers.* McGraw, 1975.

1049 ———. *What Really Happened to the Dinosaurs?* Illus by H. Wells. New York: Dutton, 1977.

1050 Cohen, Lorraine. *Scenes for Young Actors.* New York: Avon, 1973.

1051 Colby, C. B. *Communications, How Man Talks Across the Land, Sea and Space.* New York: Coward, 1964.

1052 Colby, Jean Poindexter. *Writing, Illustrating and Editing Children's Books.* New York: Hastings, 1966. Paperback 1974.

1053 Cole, Ann, et al. *I Saw a Purple Cow and One Hundred Other Recipes for Learning.* Boston: Little, 1972. Paperback.

1054 Cole, Joanna. *Dinosaur Story.* Illus by Mort Kunstler. New York: Morrow, 1974. Scholastic paperback.

1055 ———. *Find the Hidden Insect.* Photos by Jerome Wexler. New York: Morrow, 1979.

1056 Cole, William. *An Arkful of Animals.* Illus by Lynn Munsinger. Boston: Houghton, 1978.

1057 ———. *Complete Book of Giggles.* New York: Collins, 1970.

1058 ———. *Give Up? Cartoon Riddle Rhymers.* Illus by Mike Thaler. New York: Watts, 1978.

1059 ———. *Knock, Knock, the Most Ever.* New York: Watts, 1976. Dell paperback.

1060 ———. *Knock Knocks You've Never Heard Before.* Illus by Mike Thaler. New York: Watts, 1977. Dell paperback.

1061 ———. *Oh, How Silly.* New York: Viking, 1970.

1062 ———. *Oh, That's Ridiculous.* New York: Viking, 1972.

1063 ———. *The Square Bear and other Riddle Rhymers.* New York: Scholastic paperback, 1977.

1064 ———. *That Pest Jonathan.* Illus by Tomi Ungerer. New York: Harper, 1970.

1065 ———. *What is Good for a Three-Year-Old.* Illus by Ingrid Fetz. New York: Holt, 1974.

1066 ———. *What is Good for a Four-Year-Old.* Illus by Ingrid Fetz. New York: Holt, 1967. Paperback.

1067 ———. *What is Good for a Five-Year-Old.* Illus by Ingrid Fetz. New York: Holt, 1969. Paperback.

1068 ———. *What is Good for a Six-Year-Old.* Illus by Ingrid Fetz. New York: Holt, 1965. Paperback.

1069 Cole, William, ed. *Beastly Boys and Ghastly Girls.* Illus by Tomi Ungerer. Cleveland: World, 1964.

1070 ———. *The Birds and the Beasts Were There.* Illus by Helen Siegl. Cleveland: World, 1963.

1071 ———. *A Book of Nature Poems.* Illus by

Robert A. Parker. New York: Viking, 1969.

1072 ———. Dinosaurs and Beasts of Yore; Verses. Illus by Susanna Natti. New York: Philomel, 1979.

1073 ———. Humorous Poetry for Children. Illus by Ervine Metzl. Cleveland: World, 1955.

1074 ———. I Went to the Animal Fair: a Book of Animal Poems. Illus by Colette Roselli. Cleveland: World, 1958.

1075 ———. Oh, What Nonsense. Illus by Tomi Ungerer. New York: Viking, 1966. Paperback.

1076 ———. Poems of Magic and Spells. Illus by Peggy Bacon. Cleveland: World, 1960.

1077 ———. The Poets Tale: A New Book of Story Poems. Illus by Charles Keeping. Cleveland: World, 1971.

1078 ———. The Sea, Ships and Sailors; Poems, Songs and Shanties. Illus by Robin Jacques. New York: Viking, 1967.

1079 ———. Story Poems Old and New. Illus by Walter Buehr. Cleveland: World, 1957.

1080 Coleridge, Samuel Taylor. The Rime of the Ancient Mariner. New York: Dover Paperback, 1970.

1081 ———. The Rime of the Ancient Mariner. Illus by Walter Hodges. New York: Coward, 1971.

1082 ———. The Rime of the Ancient Mariner. Illus by Howard Simon. New York: Hawthorn, 1966.

1083 Colletta, Irene. From A to Z; the Collected Letters of Irene and Hallie Colletta. Englewood Cliffs, NJ: Prentice-Hall, 1979.

1084 Collier, Ethel. The Birthday Tree. Illus by Honore Guilbeau. New York: Young Scott, 1961.

1085 Collier, James. The Teddy Bear Habit. New York: Grossett, 1967. Dell paperback.

1086 Collier, James and Christopher Collier. The Bloody Country. New York: Four Winds, 1976.

1087 ———. My Brother Sam Is Dead. New York: Four Winds, 1974. Scholastic paperback. M473.

1088 Collodi, Carlo. The Adventures of Pinocchio. Illus by Attillio Mussino. Trans by Carl Della Chiesa. New York: Macmillan, 1969. M537

1089 ———. Pinocchio: The Story of a Puppet. Illus by Charles Folkard. Trans by M. A. Murray and G. Tassinari. New York: Dutton, 1952. M537.

1090 Colum, Padraic. The Adventures of Odysseus and the Tale of Troy. Illus by Willy Pogany. New York: Macmillan, 1918.

1091 ———. The Girl Who Sat by the Ashes. Illus by Imero Gobbato. New York: Macmillan, 1968.

1092 ———. The Golden Fleece and the Heroes Who Lived Before Achilles. Illus by Willy Pogany. New York: Macmillan, 1921, 1962.

1093 Colum, Padraic, ed. Roofs of Gold, Poems to Read Aloud. New York: Macmillan, 1964.

1094a Colwell, Eileen. Second Storyteller's Choice. New York: Walck, 1965.

1094b ———. Storyteller's Choice. New York: Walck, 1964.

1095 Colver, Anne and Stewart Groff. The Wayfarer's Tree. New York: Dutton, 1973.

1096 Commager, Henry. The Great Constitution; a Book for Young Americans. Indianapolis: Bobbs, 1961.

1097 Compton's Encyclopedia, 26 volumes. Chicago: Compton's, 1976.

1098a Cone, Molly. Mishmash. Boston: Houghton, 1962.

1098b ———. Mishmash and the Substitute Teacher. Boston: Houghton, 1963.

1099a Conford, Ellen. The Impossible Possum. Boston: Little, 1971.

1099b Conger, Marian. Who Has Seen the Wind? Illus by Susan Perl. New York: Abingdon, 1959.

1100 Conklin, Gladys. If I Were a Bird. Illus by Artur Marbkvia. New York: Holiday, 1965.

1101 ———. Journey of the Gray Whales. Illus by Leonard Everett Fisher. New York: Holiday, 1974.

1102 ———. When Insects Are Babies. Illus by Artur Marokvia. New York: Holiday, 1969.

1103 Conover, Chris. Six Little Ducks. Illus by the author. New York: Crowell, 1976.

1104 Conrad, Edna and Mary Van Dyke. History on the Stage: Children Make Plays from Historical Novels. New York: Van Nostrand, 1971.

1105 Coody, Betty. Using Literature with Young Children. Dubuque, Iowa: Wm. C. Brown, 1973.

1106 Cook, Dorothy and Isabel Munro. Short Story Index. New York: Wilson, 1953. Annual Supplements.

1107 ———. 1950-54 Supplement. New York: Wilson, 1956.

1108 ———. 1955-58 Supplement. New York: Wilson, 1960.

1109 ———. 1959-63 Supplement. New York: Wilson, 1965.

1110 ———. 1963-68 Supplement. New York: Wilson, 1969.

1111 ———. 1969-73 Supplement. New York: Wilson, 1974.

1112 ———. 1974-78 Supplement. New York: Wilson, 1979.

1113 Cook, George S. Fish Heads and Fire Ants. Illus by H. B. Vestal. New York: Young Scott, 1973.

1114 Cook, Joseph and William Wisner. Blue Whale: Vanishing Leviathan. Illus by Jan Cook. New York: Dodd, 1973.

1115 ———. Warrior Whale. New York: Dodd, 1966.

1116 Cooke, David C. How Books Are Made. New York: Dodd, 1963.

1117 Coolidge, Olivia. Egyptian Adventures. Boston: Houghton, 1954.

1118 ———. Greek Myths. Illus by Edouard Sardoz. Boston: Houghton, 1949.

1119 ———. The Maid of Artemis. Boston: Houghton, 1969.

1120 Coombs, Patricia. Dorrie and the Blue Witch. Illus by the author. New York: Lothrop, 1964.

1121 ———. Dorrie and the Dream Yard Monsters. Illus by the author. New York: Morrow, 1964.

1122 ———. Dorrie and the Goblin. Illus by the author. New York: Lothrop, 1972.

1123 ———. Dorrie and the Haunted House. Illus by the author. New York: Lothrop, 1970.

1124 Cooney, Barbara. *Garland of Games and Other Diversions.* New York: Holt, 1969. Young Readers paperback.

1125 ———. *The Little Juggler.* Illus by the author. New York: Hastings, 1961.

1126 ———. *The Little Prayer.* Illus by the author. New York: Hastings, 1967.

1127 ———. *Snow White and Rose Red.* Illus by the author. New York: Delacorte, n.d.

1128 Cooper, Elizabeth. *Science On the Shores and Banks.* New York: Harcourt, 1960. Voyager paperback.

1129 Cooper, Elizabeth and Padraic. *A Tree is Something Wonderful.* San Carlos: Golden Gate, 1972.

1130 Cooper, Susan. *The Dark Is Rising.* Illus by Alan E. Cohen. New York: Atheneum, 1973. Paperback.

1131 ———. *Dawn of Fear.* Illus by Margery Gill. New York: Harcourt, 1970.

1132 ———. *Greenwitch.* New York: Atheneum, 1974.

1133 ———. *The Grey King.* Illus by Michael Heslop. New York: Atheneum, 1975.

1134 ———. *Over Sea, Under Stone.* Illus by Margery Gill. New York: Harcourt, 1965.

1135 ———. *Silver On the Tree.* New York: Atheneum, 1977.

1136 Corbett, Scott. *The Baseball Trick.* Illus by Paul Galdone. Boston: Little, 1965.

1137 ———. *The Black Mask Trick.* Illus by Paul Galdone. Boston: Little, 1976.

1138 ———. *Cutlass Island.* Boston: Little, 1962.

1139 ———. *Dead Man's Light.* Boston: Little, 1960.

1140 ———. *Diamonds Are More Trouble.* New York: Holt, 1967.

1141 ———. *The Disappearing Dog Trick.* Illus by Paul Galdone. Boston: Little, 1963.

1142 ———. *Dr. Merlin's Magic Shop.* Boston: Little, 1973.

1143 ———. *The Great Custard Pie Panic.* Boston: Little, 1974.

1144 ———. *The Harry Horror Trick.* Illus by Paul Galdone. Boston: Little, 1969.

1145 ———. *The Hateful Plateful Trick.* Illus by Paul Galdone. Boston: Little, 1971.

1146 ———. *The Hockey Trick.* Illus by Paul Galdone. Boston: Little, 1974.

1147 ———. *The Home Run Trick.* Illus by Paul Galdone. Boston: Little, 1973.

1148 ———. *The Lemonade Trick.* Illus by Paul Galdone. Boston: Little, 1960.

1149 ———. *The Limerick Trick.* Illus by Paul Galdone. Boston: Little, 1964.

1150 ———. *The Mailbox Trick.* Illus by Paul Galdone. Boston: Little, 1961.

1151 ———. *The Turnabout Trick.* Illus by Paul Galdone. Boston: Little, 1967.

1152 Corbin, William. *Golden Mare.* Illus by Pers Crowell. New York: Coward, 1955.

1153 ———. *Smoke.* New York: Coward, 1967.

1154 Cornell, James. *The Monster of Loch Ness.* New York: Scholastic, 1977.

1155 Corcoran, Jean. *Folk Tales of England.* Indianapolis: Bobbs-Merrill, 1963.

1156 Corderoy, John. *Bookbinding for Beginners.* New York: Watson-Guptill, 1967.

1157 Cormack, M. Grant. *Animal Tales from Ireland.* Illus by Vona Earle. New York: Day, 1955.

1158 Corrigan, Adeline. *Holiday Ring.* Chicago: Whitman, 1975.

1159 Corskey, Evelyn. *Easter Eggs for Everyone.* Illus by Giorgetta Bell. Photos by Sid Dorris. Nashville, TN: Abingdon, 1973.

1160 Cosgrove, Margaret. *Wonders of Your Senses.* Illus by the author. New York: Dodd, 1958.

1161 Cosgrove, Stephen. *The Muffin Muncher.* Illus by Robin James. Bothwell, WA: Serendipity, 1974.

1162 Cosman, Anna. *How to Read and Write Poetry.* New York: Watts, 1979.

1163 Cothran, Jean. *The Magic Calabash, More Folk Tales.* Illus by Clifford Geary. New York: McKay, 1956.

1164 ———. *With a Wig With a Wag and Other American Folk Tales.* Illus by Clifford N. Geary. New York: McKay, 1954.

1165 Courlander, Harold. *The Hat-Shaking Dance and Other Ashanti Tales from Ghana.* Illus by Enrico Arno. New York: Harcourt, 1957.

1166 ———. *Kantchil's Lime Pit and Other Stories from Indonesia.* Illus by Robert Kane. New York: Harcourt, 1950.

1167 ———. *The King's Drum and Other African Stories.* Illus by Enrico Arno. New York: Harcourt, 1962.

1168 ———. *Terrapin's Pot of Sense.* Illus by Elton Fax. New York: Holt, 1957.

1169 ———. *The Tiger's Whisker and Other Tales and Legends from Asia and the Pacific.* Illus by Enrico Arno. New York: Harcourt, 1959.

1170 Courlander, Harold, ed. and the United Nations Women's Guild. *Ride with the Sun, an Anthology of Folk Tales and Stories from the United Nations.* Illus by Roger Duvoisin. New York: Whittlesey House, 1955.

1171 Cousteau, Jacques-Yves. *Jacques-Yves Cousteau's World Without Sun.* New York: Harper, 1965.

1172 ———. *The Ocean World of Jacques Cousteau.* New York: Abrams, 1975.

1173 Cousteau, Jacques-Yves and Philippe Diole. *Life and Death in a Coral Sea.* New York: Doubleday, 1971.

1174 Cox, Marcia Lynn. *Creature Costumes.* New York: Grosset, 1977. Paperback.

1175 ———. *Make-Up Monsters.* New York: Grosset, 1977. Paperback.

1176 Craft, Ruth. *Pieter Brueghel's "The Fair."* Philadelphia: Lippincott, 1976.

1177 Craig, N. Jean. *Little Monsters.* Photos by the author. New York: Dial, 1977. Scholastic paperback.

1178 Craig, Jean. *The Story of Musical Notes.* Illus by George Overlie. Minneapolis: Lerner, 1962.

1179 Creative Educational Society, ed. *How to Have Fun Making Puppets.* Mankato, Minn.: Creative Educational Society, 1973.

1180 Credle, Ellis. *Big Fraid, Little Fraid.* New York: Nelson, 1964.

1181 ———. *Down, Down the Mountain.* New York: Nelson, 1934.

1182 Cresswell, Helen. *Absolutely Zero, Being the Second Part of the Bagthorpe Saga.* New York: Macmillan, 1978. Avon paperback.

1183 ———. *Bagthorpes Unlimited, Being the Third Part of the Bagthorpe Saga.* New York: Macmillan, 1978.

1184 ———. *The Bagthorpes vs the World: Being the Fourth Part of the Bagthorpe Saga.* New York: Macmillan, 1979. Avon paperback.

1185 ———. *A Game of Catch.* Illus by Ati Forberg. New York: Macmillan, 1977.

1186 ———. *The Night Watchmen.* Illus by Gareth Floyd. New York: Macmillan, 1969.

1187 ———. *Ordinary Jack, Being the First Part of the Bagthorpe Saga.* New York: Macmillan, 1977. Avon paperback.

1188 ———. *Up the Pier.* Illus by Gareth Floyd. New York: Macmillan, 1972.

1189 Cretan, Gladys. *Me, Myself, and I.* Illus by Don Bolognese. New York: Morrow, 1969.

1190 Crews, Donald. *Freight Train.* Illus by the author. New York: Greenwillow, 1978.

1191 ———. *Truck.* Illus by the author. New York: Greenwillow, 1978. M716.

1192 ———. *We Read: A–Z.* Illus by the author. New York: Harper, 1967.

1193 Crofut, William. *The Moon on the One Hand: Poetry in Song.* Music by Kenneth Cooper and Glenn Shattuck. Illus by Susan Crofut. New York: Atheneum, 1975.

1194 Crone, Robert L. *Clyde Monster.* Illus by Kat Charoa. New York: Dutton, 1976.

1195 Croney, Claude. *My Way with Watercolor, a Three-Value Approach.* Westport, Conn.: North Light Publications, 1973.

1196 Crosby, Phoebe. *Junior Science Book of Stars.* New Canaan, CT: Garrard, 1960.

1197 Cross, Jeanne. *Simple Printing Methods.* Springfield, MA: Phillips, 1972.

1198 Crossup, Richard. *Children and Dramatics.* New York: Scribner, 1966.

1199 Crothers, J. Frances. *The Puppeteers Library Guide; the Bibliographical Index to the Literature of the World Puppet Theatre.* Metuchen, N.J.: Scarecrow, 1971.

1200 Crouch, Marcus. *Beatrix Potter.* (Walck Monographs) New York: Walck, n.d.

1201 Crowther, Robert. *Most Amazing Hide-and-Seek Alphabet Book.* New York: Kestrel and Viking, 1978.

1202 ———. *The Most Amazing Hide-and-Seek Counting Book.* Illus by the author. New York: Viking, 1981.

1203 Ctvrtek, Vaclav. *The Little Chalk Man.* New York: Knopf, 1970.

1204 Cullen, Countee. *The Lost Zoo by Christopher Cat and Countee Cullen.* Illus by Joseph Low. Chicago: Follett, 1968.

1205 Cullum, Albert. *Aesop in the Afternoon.* New York: Citation, 1972. Paperback.

1206 Cullum, Albert, ed. *Shake Hands With Shakespeare.* New York: Citation, 1968. Paper.

1207 Cummings, Richard. *Make Your Own Comics: For Fun and Profit.* New York: Walck, 1975.

1208 ———. *One Hundred One Costumes.* Illus by Opal Jackson. New York: McKay, 1970.

1209 ———. *101 Hand Puppets, a Guide for Pup-

peteers of all Ages.* New York: McKay, 1962.

1210 Cummings, W.T. *Miss Esta Maude's Secret.* New York: Whittlesey, 1961. M450.

1211 Cundiff, Ruby and Barbara Webb. *Story-Telling for You.* Kent, OH: Kent State Univ. Pr., 1957.

1212 Cunningham, Julia. *Dorp Dead.* New York: Pantheon, 1965. Avon paperback.

1213 Curcija-Prodanovic, Nada. *Yugoslave Folktales.* Illus by Joan Kiddell Monroe. New York: Walck, 1957.

1214 Currell, David. *The Complete Book of Puppetry.* Boston: Plays, 1974.

1215 ———. *Puppetry for School Children.* Newton Center, MA: 1970.

1216 Currier, Richard L. *Art of Mosaics.* Minneapolis: Lerner, 1974.

1217 Curry, Jane Louise. *Beneath the Hill.* Illus by Imero Gobbato. New York: Harcourt, 1967.

1218a ———. *Daybreakers.* Illus by Chas. Robinson. New York: Harcourt, 1970.

1218b ———. *Parsley, Sage, Rosemary & Time.* New York: Atheneum, 1975.

1219 Curry, Louise H. and Chester M. Wetzel. *Teaching With Puppets.* Phila.: Fortress, 1966.

1220 Cutler, Katherine. *Creative Shellcraft.* Illus by Giulio Maestro. New York: Lothrop, 1971. Paperback.

1221 Cutler, Ivor. *Elephant Girl.* Illus by Helen Oxenbury. New York: Morrow, 1976.

1222 Czaja, Paul Clement. *Writing with Light, a Simple Workshop in Basic Photography.* Riverside, CT: Chatham, 1973.

1223 Dahl, Roald. *Charlie and the Chocolate Factory.* Illus by Joseph Schindelman. New York: Knopf, 1964. Paperback.

1224 ———. *Charlie and the Chocolate Factory; a Play.* New York: Knopf, 1976.

1225 ———. *James and the Giant Peach.* Illus by Nancy Ekholm Burkert. New York: Knopf, 1961.

1226 Dahlstedt, Marden. *The Terrible Wave.* Illus by Charles Robinson. New York: Coward, 1972.

1227 Dalgliesh, Alice. *The Bears on Hemlock Mountain.* Illus by Helen Sewell. New York: Scribner, 1952. paperback.

1228 Dalton, Arlene. *Yellow is a Duck.* New York: Rolton House, 1965.

1229 Daly, Kathleen. *Ladybug, Ladybug.* Illus by Susan Smith. New York: Am. Heritage, 1969.

1230 Daly, Maureen. *The Ginger Horse.* Illus by Wesley Dennis. New York: Dodd, 1964.

1231 Damjan, Mischa. *Little Green Man.* Illus by Maurice Kenelski. Trans by Alvin Tresselt. New York: Parents, 1971.

1232 ———. *The Wolf and the Kid.* Illus by Max Velthuijs. New York: McGraw, 1967.

1233 Daniels, Guy. *The Falcon Under the Hat, Russian Merry Tales and Fairy Tales.* Trans and sel by the author. Illus by Feodor Rojankovsky. New York: Funk and Wagnalls, 1969.

1234 Daniels, Guy. *Tsar's Riddles or the Wise Little Girl.* Illus by Paul Galdone. New York: McGraw, 1967.

1235 Daniels, Harvey and Silvie Turner. *Exploring

Printmaking for Young People. New York: Van Nostrand, 1972.

1236 ———. *Simple Printmaking with Children.* New York: Van Nostrand, 1972.

1237 Danziger, Paula. *The Cat Ate My Gymsuit.* New York: Delacorte, 1974. Dell paperback.

1238 Darbois, Dominique. *Hassan, Boy of the Desert.* Photos by the author. Chicago: Follett, 1961.

1239 Darling, Lois and Louis Darling. *Before and After Dinosaurs.* Illus by the authors. New York: Morrow, 1959.

1240 Darling, Louis. *Penguins.* New York: Morrow, 1956.

1241 Darrow, Whitney. *Animal Etiquette.* New York: Windmill, Simon and Schuster, 1969.

1242 Dasent, G.W. *Popular Tales from the Norse.* Detroit: Gale, 1971.

1243 Daugherty, Charles M. *Benjamin Franklin, Scientist-Diplomat.* Illus by John Falter. New York: Macmillan, 1965.

1244 Daugherty, James. *Andy and the Lion.* Illus by the author. New York: Viking, 1938. Paperback.

1245 ———. *Daniel Boone.* Illus by the author. New York: Viking, 1939. Paperback.

1246 ———. *Henry David Thoreau: A Man for Our Time.* Illus by the author. New York: Viking, 1967.

1247 ———. *The Landing of the Pilgrims.* Illus by the author. New York: Random, 1950.

1248 ———. *Of Courage Undaunted.* Illus by the author. New York: Viking, 1951.

1249 ———. *Poor Richard.* Illus by the author. New York: Viking, 1941.

1250 ———. *William Blake.* Illus by the author. New York: Viking, 1960.

1251 *d'Aulaire, Ingri and Edgar. *Abraham Lincoln.* Illus by the authors. Garden City, NY: Doubleday, 1957. M1.

1252 ———. *Animals Everywhere.* Illus by the authors. Garden City, NY: Doubleday, 1954. Paperback.

1253 ———. *Benjamin Franklin.* Illus by the authors. Garden City, NY: Doubleday, 1950.

1254 ———. *Buffalo Bill.* Illus by the authors. Garden City, NY: Doubleday, 1952.

1255 ———. *Children of the Northlights.* Illus by the authors. Garden City, NY: Doubleday, 1935. M127.

1256 ———. *Columbus.* Illus by the authors. Garden City, NY: Doubleday, 1955.

1257 ———. *d'Aulaire's Book of Greek Myths.* Illus by the authors. Garden City, NY: Doubleday, 1962. Paperback.

1258 ———. *d'Aulaire's Trolls.* Illus by the authors. Garden City, NY: Doubleday, 1972. Paperback. M127.

1259 ———. *Don't Count Your Chicks.* Illus by the authors. Garden City, NY: Doubleday, 1973. Paperback. M174.

1260 ———. *Foxie: The Singing Dog.* Illus by the authors. Garden City, NY: Doubleday, 1969.

1261 ———. *George Washington.* Illus by the authors. Garden City, NY: Doubleday, 1936.

1262 ———. *Leif the Lucky.* Illus by the authors. Garden City, NY: Doubleday, 1941.

1263 ———. *Magic Meadow.* Illus by the authors.

Garden City, NY: Doubleday, 1958.

1264 ———. *Nils.* Illus by the authors. Garden City, NY: Doubleday, 1948.

1265 ———. *Norse Gods and Giants.* Illus by the authors. Garden City, NY: Doubleday, 1967.

1266 ———. *Ola.* Illus by the authors. Garden City, NY: Doubleday, 1939. M473.

1267 ———. *Pocahontas.* Illus by the authors. Garden City, NY: Doubleday, 1939.

1268 ———. *The Terrible Troll Bird.* Illus by the authors. Garden City, NY: Doubleday, 1976.

1269 ———. *Two Cars.* Illus by the authors. Garden City, NY: Doubleday, 1955.

1270 d'Aulaire, Ingri and Edgar, eds. and illus. *East of the Sun and West of the Moon.* New York: Viking, 1969.

1271 d'Aulaire, Ingri and Edgar, illus. *The Lord's Prayer.* Garden City, NY: Doubleday, 1934.

1272a d'Aulnoy, Countess. *The White Cat and Other French Fairy Tales.* New York: Macmillan, 1967.

1272b Davar, Ashok. *Talking Words, a Unique Alphabet Book.* Indianapolis: Bobbs, 1969.

1273 Davidson, Jessica. *Is That Mother in the Bottle? Where Language Came From and Where It Is Going.* New York: Watts, 1972.

1274 Davidson, Margaret. *Louis Braille, the Boy Who Invented Books for the Blind.* Illus by Janet Compere. New York: Hastings, 1971.

1275 ———. *Nine True Dolphin Stories.* New York: Hastings, 1975. Scholastic paperback.

1276 Davidson, Rosalie. *When the Dinosaurs Disappeared: Mammals of Long Ago.* Illus by Bernard Barbutt. Chicago: Childrens, 1973.

1277a Davis, Ossie. *Escape to Freedom: a Play About Young Frederick Douglass.* New York: Viking, 1978.

1277b Davis, Robert. *Padre Porko, The Gentlemanly Pig.* New York: Holiday, 1948.

1278 Davis, Russell and Brent Ashabranner, eds. *The Lion's Whiskers, Tales of High Africa.* Illus by James G. Teason. Boston: Little, 1959.

1279 Day, Veronica. *Landslide!* Trans by Margaret Morgan. Illus by Margot Tomes. New York: Coward, 1961. Dell paperback.

1280 Dean, Audrey. *Puppets That are Different.* New York: Taplinger, 1973.

1281 ———. *Wooden Spoon Puppets.* Boston: Plays, 1976.

1282 Dean, Elizabeth. *Printing, Tool of Freedom.* Illus by Erwin Schachner. Englewood Cliffs, N.J.: Prentice-Hall, 1964.

1283 DeAngeli, Marguerite. *Black Fox of Lorne.* Garden City, NY: Doubleday, 1956.

1284 ———. *Butter at the Old Price.* Garden City, NY: Doubleday, 1971.

1285 ———. *Copper-Toed Boots.* Garden City, NY: Doubleday, 1938.

1286 De Angeli, Marguerite. *Door in the Wall: Story of Medieval London.* Illus by the author. Garden City, NY: Doubleday, 1949. Paperback.

1287 DeAngeli, Marguerite. *Marguerite DeAngeli's Book of Favorite Hymns.* Illus by Marguerite DeAngeli. Garden City, NY: Doubleday, 1963.

1288 ———. *Marguerite DeAngeli's Book of Nursery and Mother Goose Rhymes.* Illus by

Marguerite DeAngeli. Garden City, NY: Doubleday, 1954.

1289 ———. *A Pocket Full of Posies, a Merry Mother Goose.* Illus by Marguerite DeAngeli. Garden City, NY: Doubleday, 1954, 1961.

1290 ———. *Thee, Hannah!* Illus by the author. Garden City, NY: Doubleday, 1940.

1291 ———. *Yonie Wondernose.* Garden City, NY: Doubleday, 1944.

1292a Deason, Hilary, Comp. *AAAS Science Book List for Children,* 3rd Ed. Washington, D.C. American Association for the Advancement of Science, 1972, Supp., 1978.

1292b Deasy, Michael. *City ABC's.* Photos by Robert Perron. New York: Walker, 1974.

1293 deBeaumont, Marie. *Beauty and the Beast.* Illus by Erica Ducornet. New York: Knopf, 1968.

1294 ———. *Beauty and the Beast.* Trans and illus by Dianne Goode. New York: Bradbury, 1978.

1295 De Brunhoff, Jean. *Babar and Father Christmas.* Illus by the author. New York: Random, 1949.

1296 ———. *Meet Babar and His Family.* Illus by the author. New York: Random paperback, 1973. M419.

1297 ———. *The Story of Babar.* Illus by the author. New York: Random, 1937. M646.

1298 ———. *Travels of Babar.* Illus by the author. New York: Random, 1937, M709.

1299 De Brunhoff, Laurent. *Babar's Birthday Surprise.* Illus by the author. New York: Random, 1970.

1300 Defoe, Daniel. *The Life and Adventures of Robinson Crusoe.* Illus by Roger Duvoisin. New York: Watts, n.d. Large type edition. M582, M583.

1301 ———. *Robinson Crusoe.* Illus by Federico Castellon. New York: Macmillan, n.d. M582, M583.

1302 ———. *Robinson Crusoe.* Illus by N.C. Wyeth. New York: Scribner, 1957. M582, M583.

1303 DeForest, Charlotte, B. *The Prancing Pony, Nursery Rhymes from Japan.* Illus by Keiko Hida. New York: Weatherhill, 1968.

1304 Degens, T. *Transport 7-41-R.* New York: Viking, 1974. Dell paperback. M708.

1305 DeGering, Etta. *Seeing Fingers, the Story of Louis Braille.* New York: McKay, 1962.

1306 De Groat, Diane. *Alligator's Toothache.* New York: Crown, 1977.

1307 Deibler, Jacqueline Kerr. *The Concord.* Wildflower Manor, 1976.

1308 ———. *Pepperwood Farm.* Craft Publications, Inc., 1976.

1309 De Jong, Meindert. *The House of Sixty Fathers.* Illus by Maurice Sendak. New York: Harper, 1956. M299.

1310 ———. *A Horse Came Running.* New York: Macmillan, 1972. Collier paperback.

1311 ———. *The Wheel on the School.* Boston: Houghton, 1970.

1312 DeKay, Ormonde. *Rimes de la Mere Oie, Mother Goose Rhymes Rendered Into French.* Illus by Seymour Chwast, Milton Glasser and Barry Zaid. New York: Little, 1971.

1313 De La Mare, Walter. *Animal Stories.* New York: Scribner, 1940.

1314 ———. *Come Hither, a Collection of Rhymes and Poems for the Young of All Ages.* New York: Knopf, 1963.

1315 ———. *Jack and the Beanstalk.* Illus by Joseph Low. New York: Knopf, 1959.

1316 ———. *Peacock Pie.* Illus by Barbara Covey. New York: Knopf, 1961. Paperback.

1317 ———. *Stories from the Bible.* Illus by Edward Ardizzone. New York: Knopf, 1961.

1318 ———. *Tales Told Again.* Illus by Alan Howard. New York: Knopf, 1927, 1959.

1319 La Ramee, Louise. *A Dog of Flanders and Other Stories.* New York: Grosset and Dunlap, 1965. M177.

1320 Delarue, Paul. *French Fairy Tales.* Illus by Warren Chappel. New York: Knopf, 1968.

1321 Del Rey, Lester. *The Runaway Robot.* Philadelphia: Westminster, 1965.

1322 DeLeeuw, Adele. *George Rogers Clark, Frontier Fighter.* Illus by Russ Hoover. Scarsdale, N.Y.: Garrard, 1967.

1323 ———. *Indonesian Legends and Folk Tales.* Illus by Ronni Solbert. New York: Nelson, 1961.

1324 ———. *Legends and Folk Tales of Holland.* Illus by Paul Kennedy. New York: Nelson, 1963.

1325 Delessert, Etienne, and Eleanore Schmidt. *The Tree.* New York: Harlin Quist, 1966.

1326 DeMontreville, Doris and Elizabeth Crawford. *The Fourth Book of Junior Authors and Illustrators.* New York: Wilson, 1978.

1327 DeMontreville, Doris and Donna Hill. *The Third Book of Junior Authors.* New York: Wilson, 1972.

1328 Dennis, Wesley. *Flip.* New York: Viking, 1941. Puffin paperback.

1329 ———. *Flip and the Cows.* New York: Viking, 1942.

1330 Denny, Norman, and Josephine Filmer-Senkey. *The Bayeux Tapestry, the Story of the Norman Conquest, 1066.* New York: Atheneum, 1966.

1331 de Paola, Tomi. *Andy, That's My Name.* Illus by the author. Englewood Cliffs, NJ: Prentice-Hall, 1973.

1332 ———. *The Clown of God.* Illus by the author. New York: Harcourt, 1978. Voyager paperback, Scholastic paperback.

1333 ———. *The Hunter and the Animals, a Wordless Picture Book.* New York: Holiday, 1981.

1334 ———. *The Legend of Old Befana: An Italian Christmas Story.* Illus by the author. New York: Harcourt, 1980. Voyager Paperback.

1335 ———. *The Popcorn Book.* Illus by the author. New York: Holiday, 1978. Scholastic paperback.

1336 ———. *Pancakes for Breakfast.* New York: Harcourt, 1978.

1337 ———. *Strega Nona.* Illus by the author. Englewood Cliffs, NJ: Prentice-Hall, 1975. M650, M651.

1338 ———. *Things to Make and Do for Valentines Day.* Illus by the author. New York: Watts, 1976. Scholastic paperback.

1339 ———. *Watch Out for the Chicken Feet in*

Your Soup. Illus by the author. Englewood Cliffs, NJ: Prentice-Hall, 1974.

1340 ———. *When Everyone was Fast Asleep.* Illus by the author. New York: Holiday, 1976.

1341 de Paola, Tomi, illus. *The Comic Adventures of Old Mother Hubbard and Her Dog.* New York: Harcourt, 1981. Paperback.

1342 ———. *The Friendly Beasts, an Old English Christmas Carol.* New York: Putnam, 1981. Peppercorn paperback.

1343 De Regniers, Beatrice Shenk. *The Abraham Lincoln Joke Book.* New York: Random, 1965.

1344 ———. *Cats, Cats, Cats, Cats, Cats.* Illus by Bill Sokol. New York: Pantheon, 1958.

1345 ———. *Catch a Little Fox: Variations on a Folk Rhyme.* Illus by Brinton Turkle. New York: Seabury, 1970.

1346 ———. *David and Goliath.* Illus by Richard M. Powers. New York: Viking, 1965.

1347 ———. *The Giant Book.* Illus by William L. Cummings. New York: Atheneum, 1966.

1348 ———. *The Giant Book.* Illus by Maurice Sendak. New York: Harper, 1953.

1349 ———. *It Does Not Say Meow and Other Animal Riddle Rhymes.* Illus by Paul Galdone. New York: Seabury, 1972.

1350 ———. *Little Sister and the Month Brothers.* Illus by Margot Tomes. New York: Seabury, 1976.

1351 *———. *May I Bring a Friend.* Illus by Beni Montresor. New York: Atheneum, 1974. Aladdin paperback. M416.

1352 ———. *Red Riding Hood.* Illus by Edward Gorcy. New York: Atheneum, 1972.

1353 ———. *Willy O'Dwyer Jumped in the Fire.* Illus by Beni Montresor. New York: Atheneum, 1968.

1354 De Regniers, Beatrice S. and Al Giese. *Circus.* Illus by Al Griese. New York: Viking, 1966.

1355 De Regniers, Bernice S. and Isabel Gordon. *The Shadow Book.* Photos by Isabel Gordon. New York: Harcourt, 1960.

1356 De Regniers, Beatrice S. and Irene Haas. *A Little House of Your Own.* Illus by Irene Haas. New York: Harcourt, 1955.

1357 ———. *Something Special.* Illus by Irene Haas. New York: Harcourt, 1958.

1358 ———. *Was It a Good Trade?* Illus by Irene Haas. New York: Harcourt, 1956.

1359 De Regniers, Beatrice S. and Leona Pierce. *Who Likes the Sun?* Illus by Leona Pierce. New York: Harcourt, 1961.

1360 De Regniers, et al. *Poems Children Will Sit Still for: A Selection for the Primary Grades.* New York: Scholastic, 1969.

1361 Dereleth, August. *The Beast in Holger's Woods.* New York: Crowell, 1968.

1362 ———. *Moon Tenders.* New York: Duell, 1958.

1363 DeRossi, Claude J. *Computers, Tools for Today.* Chicago: Children's, 1972.

1364 Devlin, Wende and Harry. *The Old Witch and the Polka Dot Ribbon.* New York: Parents, 1970.

1365 Dickens, Charles. *A Christmas Carol.* New York: Dutton, 1963. Paperback. M131.

1366 ———. *David Copperfield.* Illus by N.B. Bodecker. New York: Macmillan, 1962.

M169.

1367 ———. *Great Expectations.* New York: Oxford, n.d. Paperbacks by Dutton, Macmillan, and New American Library. M254.

1368 ———. *The Magic Fishbone.* Illus by Faith Jacques. New York: Harvey, 1970.

1369 ———. *The Magic Fishbone.* Illus by Louis Slobodkin. New York: Vanguard, 1953.

1370 Dickens, Frank. *Fly Away Peter.* Illus by Ralph Steadman. New York: Scroll, 1963.

1371 Dickey, Jean. *How to Light a Doll House.* Craft Publications, 1975.

1372 Dickinson, Emily. *Poems for Youth.* Illus by George and Doris Hauman. New York: Little, 1934. M545.

1373 Dietz, Betty Warner. *Folk Songs of China, Japan, Korea.* New York: Day, 1964. Includes 7'' 33-1/3 rpm phonodisc.

1374 Dickinson, Peter. *Devil's Children.* Boston: Little, 1970.

1375 ———. *Heartsease.* Boston: Little, 1969.

1376 ———. *The Weathermonger.* Boston: Little, 1968.

1377 Dill, Barbara E., ed. *Children's Catalog,* 13th ed. New York: Wilson, 1976. Annual supplements.

1378 Dillon, Eilis. *The Wise Man on the Mountain.* Illus by Gaynor Chapman. New York: Atheneum, 1969.

1379 ———. *A Family of Foxes.* Illus by Vic Donahue. New York: Funk-Wagnalls, 1964. Paperback.

1380 Dines, Glen. *Pitidae the Color Maker.* New York: Macmillan, 1959.

1381 Dixon, Paige. *Lion on the Mountain.* Illus by J. H. Breslow. New York: Atheneum, 1972.

1382 Doab, Leonard. *A Crocodile Has Me by the Leg, African Poems.* Illus by Solomon Irlin Wanghoje. New York: Walker, 1966.

1383 Doane, Pelagie. *A Small Child's Book of Verse.* New York: Oxford, 1948.

1384 Dobbs, Rose. *More Once-Upon-A-Time-Stories.* Illus by Flavia Gag. New York: Random, 1961.

1385 ———. *No Room, an Old Story Retold.* Illus by Fritz Eichenberg. New York: McKay, 1944.

1386 ———. *Once Upon a Time, Twenty Cheerful Tales to Read and Tell.* Illus by Flavia Gag. New York: Random, 1950.

1387 Dobrin, Arnold. *Gerbils.* New York: Lothrop, 1970.

1388 ———. *Jillions of Gerbils.* Illus by the author. New York: Lothrop, 1970.

1389 Dodge, Mary Mapes. *Hans Brinker, or the Silver Skates.* Illus by Hilda van Stokum. New York: Collins, 1975.

1390 Dolan, Edward F. *The Complete Beginners Guide to Making and Flying Kites.* Illus by John Lane. New York: Doubleday, 1977.

1391 Domanska, Janina. *Din Dan Don, It's Christmas.* Illus by the author. New York: Greenwillow, 1975.

1392 ———. *I Saw a Ship a-Sailing.* Retold and illus by J. Domanska. New York: Macmillan, 1972.

1393 ———. *If All the Seas Were One Sea.* Retold and illus by J. Domanska. New York: Macmillan, 1971.

1394 ———. *The Little Red Hen.* Retold and illus by J. Domanska. New York: Macmillan, 1973.

1395 ———. *Look There is a Turtle Flying.* Illus by the author. New York: Macmillan, 1968.

1396 ———. *Spring Is.* Illus by the author. New York: Greenwillow, 1976.

1397 ———. *The Turnip.* Retold and illus by J. Domanska. New York: Macmillan, 1969. Collier paperback.

1398 ———. *What Do I See?* Illus by the author. New York: Macmillan, 1974.

1399 Domanska, Janina and Catherine Fournier. *The Coconut Thieves.* Illus by J. Domanska. New York: Scribner, 1964.

1400 Donovan, John. *I'll Get There, It Better Be Worth the Trip.* New York: Harper, 1969. Dell paperback.

1401 Dorian, Edith and W.N. Wilson. *Animals That Made U.S. History.* New York: McGraw, 1964.

1402 Doty, Roy. *Puns, Gags, Quips and Riddles, a Collection of Dreadful Jokes.* Garden City, NY: Doubleday, 1974.

1403 ———. *Q's Are Weird O's: More Puns, Gags, Quips and Riddles.* Garden City, NY: Doubleday, 1975.

1404 Douglas, Emily T. *Appleseed Farm.* Illus by Anne Vaughan. New York: Abingdon, 1948.

1405 Dow, Emily. *How to Make Doll Clothes.* New York: Coward, 1953.

1406 Dowden, Anne O. *The Blossom on the Bough, a Book of Trees.* New York: Crowell, 1975.

1407 ———. *Look at a Flower.* Illus by the author. New York: Crowell, 1963.

1408 Downer, Marion. *Kites, How to Make and Fly Them.* New York: Lothrop, 1959.

1409 ———. *The Story of Design.* New York: Lothrop, 1963.

1410 Downie, Mary Alice and Barbara Robertson. *The Wind Has Wings; Poems from Canada.* Illus by Elizabeth Cleaver. New York: Walck, 1968. Oxford paperback.

1411 Doyle, Sir Arthur Conan. *Adventures of Sherlock Holmes.* New York: Harper, 1892. Reprint. M7.

1412 ———. *Adventures of Sherlock Holmes.* New York: Collier paperback, 1962. M7.

1413 ———. *The Boys' Sherlock Holmes.* New York: Harper, 1961. M7.

1414 ———. *The Complete Sherlock Holmes.* New York: Doubleday, 1953. M7, M638, M639, M640.

1415 ———. *Complete Sherlock Holmes.* New York: Berkley, 1975. Paperback. M7, M638, M639, M640.

1416 ———. *Return of Sherlock Holmes.* New York: Berkley, n.d. Paperback. M7.

1417 ———. *Tales of Sherlock Holmes.* Illus by Harvey Dinnerstein. New York: Macmillan, 1963. M7.

1418 ———. *Treasury of Sherlock Holmes.* Hanover House, 1955. M7, M638, M639, M640.

1419a Dragt, Tonke. *Towers of February, A Diary by an Anonymous Author.* New York: Morrow, 1975.

1419b Dreyfuss, Henry. *Symbol Sourcebook, an Authoritative Guide to International Graphic Symbols.* New York: McGraw, 1972.

1420a Drucker, Malka. *Hanukkah, Eight Nights, Eight Lights.* New York: Holiday, 1980.

1420b ———. *Passover, a Season of Freedom.* New York: Holiday, 1981.

1421 Druon, Maurice. *Tistou of the Green Thumbs.* New York: Scribner, 1958.

1422 DuBois, William Pene. *The Hare and the Tortoise, and the Tortoise and the Hare/La Liebre y la tortuga y la tortuga y la liebre.* Garden City, NY: Doubleday, 1972. M268.

1423 ———. *Lion.* New York: Viking, 1956. Puffin paperback.

1424 ———. *Otto at Sea.* New York: Viking, 1958.

1425 ———. *Twenty-One Balloons.* Illus by the author. New York: Viking, 1947. M718.

1426 Dugan, William. *How Our Alphabet Grew, the History of the Alphabet.* Golden, 1972.

1427 Dunlop, Orrin E., Jr. *Communications in Space.* New York: Harper, 1970.

1428 Dunn, Judy. *Things.* Illus by Phoebe and Triss Dunn. New York: Doubleday, 1968.

1429 Dunning, Stephen, Edward Lueders & Hugh Smith, ed. *Reflections on a Gift of Watermelon Pickles and Other Modern Verse.* New York: Lothrop, 1966.

1430 ———. *Some Haystacks Don't Even Have Any Needles and Other Complete Modern Poems.* New York: Lothrop, 1969.

1431 Durell, Ann, ed. *Just for Fun.* New York: Dutton, 1977.

1432 Durham, Mae. *Tit for Tat and Other Latvian Folk Tales.* Illus by Harriet Pincus. New York: Harcourt, 1967.

1433 Durr, William, ed. *Fiesta.* Boston: Houghton-Mifflin, 1971.

1434 Durrell, Donald and Alice Crossley, eds. *Favorite Plays for Classroom Reading.* Boston: Plays, 1965, 1971.

1435 ———. *Thirty Plays for Classroom Reading.* Boston: Plays, 1968.

1436 Duvoisin, Roger. *A for the Ark.* Illus by the author. New York: Lothrop, 1952.

1437 ———. *The Christmas Whale.* Illus by the author. New York: Knopf, 1945.

1438 ———. *Day and Night.* Illus by the author. New York: Knopf, 1959.

1439 ———. *Jasmine.* Illus by the author. New York: Knopf, 1973. M328.

1440 ———. *Lonely Veronica.* Illus by the author. New York: Knopf, 1963.

1441 ———. *The Miller, His Son and Their Donkey.* Retold and illus by R. Duvoisin. New York: McGraw, 1962. M446.

1442 ———. *Our Veronica Goes to Petunia's Farm.* Illus by the author. New York: Knopf, 1962. Paperback. M509.

1443 ———. *Petunia.* Illus by the author. New York: Knopf, 1950. Paperback. M525, M526, M527.

1444 ———. *Petunia and the Song.* Illus by the author. New York: Knopf, 1951.

1445 ———. *Petunia, Beware!.* Illus by the author. New York: Knopf, 1958. Pinwheel paperback. M528.

1446 ———. *Petunia, I Love You.* Illus by the author. New York: Knopf, 1965.

1447 ———. *Petunia Takes a Trip.* Illus by the author. New York: Knopf, 1951. Pinwheel paperback. M529.

1448 ———. *Petunia's Treasure.* Illus by the author. New York: Knopf, 1975.

1449 ———. *Periwinkle.* Illus by the author. New York: Knopf, 1976.

1450 ———. *See What I Am.* Illus by the author. New York: Lothrop, 1974.

1451 ———. *Spring Snow.* Illus by the author. New York: Knopf, 1963.

1452 ———. *The Three Sneezes and Other Swiss Tales.* New York: Knopf, 1941.

1453 ———. *Two Lonely Ducks: A Counting Book.* Illus by the author. New York: Knopf, 1955.

1454 ———. *Veronica.* Illus by the author. New York: Knopf, 1961. Paperback.

1455 ———. *Veronica and the Birthday Present.* Illus by the author. New York: Knopf, 1971.

1456 ———. *Veronica's Smile.* Illus by the author. New York: Knopf, 1964.

1457 Eager, Edward. *Half Magic.* Illus by N.M. Bodecher. New York: Harcourt, 1954. Voyager paperback.

1458 ———. *Magic by the Lake.* Illus by N.M. Bodecher. New York: Harcourt, 1957.

1459 ———. *Magic or Not.* Illus by N.M. Bodecher. New York: Harcourt, 1959.

1460a ———. *The Time Garden.* New York: Harcourt, 1958.

1460b Eager, Frances. *Time Tangle.* New York Scholastic, 1979.

1461 Eakin, Mary, ed. *Subject Index to Books for Intermediate Grades,* 3rd ed. Chicago: A.L.A., 1963.

1462 Earle, Olive. *Birds in Their Nests.* Illus by the author. New York: Morrow, 1952.

1463 ———. *Crickets.* New York: Morrow, 1956.

1464 ———. *Mice at Home and Afield* Illus by the author. New York: Morrow, 1957.

1465 ———. *Paws, Hoofs, and Flippers* Illus by the author. New York: Morrow, 1954

1466 ———. *Praying Mantis.* New York: Morrow, 1969.

1467 Early, Margaret, et al. *Widening Circles.* New York: Harcourt, 1974.

1468 Eastman, Philip. *Are You My Mother?* Illus by the author. New York: Random, 1967.

1469 ———. *Sam and the Firefly.* Illus by the author. New York: Random, 1958. M591.

1470 Eastwick, Ivy O. *Cherry Stones! Garden Swings!* Illus by Robert A. Jones. New York: Abingdon, 1962.

1471 ———. *In and Out the Windows: Happy Poems for Children.* Illus by Gillian Barth. Rifton, N.Y.: Plough, 1969.

1472 ———. *Rainbow Over All.* Illus by Anne Siberell. New York: McKay, 1967.

1473 ———. *I Rode the Black Horse Far Away.* Illus by Robert A. Jones. New York: Abingdon, 1960.

1474 ———. *Traveler's Joy.* Illus by Decie Merwin. New York: McKay, 1960.

1475 Eaton, Anne Thaxter. *The Animals' Christmas, Poems, Carols and Stories.* Illus by Valenti Angelo. New York: Viking, 1944.

1476 ———. *Welcome Christmas! A Garland of Poems.* Illus by Valenti Angelo. New York: Viking, 1955.

1477 Eaton, Jeannette. *America's Own Mark Twain.* Illus by Leonard Everett Fisher. New York: Morrow, 1958.

1478 ———. *That Lively Man Ben Franklin.* Illus by Henry Pitz. New York: Morrow, 1948.

1479 Eaton, M. Joe and Malcolm Glass, ed. *grab me a bus . . . and other award wining poems from Scholastic writing awards.* New York: Scholastic, 1971. Paperback.

1480 Eberle, Irmengarde. *Bears Live Here.* New York: Doubleday, 1966.

1481 ———. *Fawn in the Woods.* Photos by Lilo Hess. New York: Crowell, 1962.

1482 ———. *Foxes Live Here.* New York: Doubleday, 1966.

1483 Eckert, Allan W. *Incident at Hawk's Hill.* Illus by John Schoenherr. Boston: Little, 1971. Dell paperback. M314.

1484 Eckert, Horst. *Tonight at Nine.* New York: Walck, 1967.

1485 Edelson, Edward. *Great Monsters of the Movies.* New York: Doubleday, 1973. Archway paperback.

1486 Edmonds, Walter D. *Cadmus Henry.* Illus by Manning de V. Lee. New York: Dodd, 1949.

1487 ———. *The Matchlock Gun.* Illus by Paul Lantz. New York: Dodd, 1941. M414.

1488 Edwards, Sally. *Isaac and Snow.* Illus by Michael Hampshire. New York: Coward, 1974.

1489 ———. *When the World's on Fire.* New York: Coward, 1972.

1490 Eells, Elsie. *Fairy Tales from Brazil, How and Why Tales from Brazilian Folk-Lore.* New York: Dodd, 1959. Kraus reprint.

1491 ———. *Tales from the Amazon.* New York: Dodd, 1956.

1492 Egoff, Sheila, G. T. Stubbs and I. F. Ashley. *Only Connect, Readings on Children's Literature.* New York: Oxford, 1969. Paperback.

1493 Ehret, Walter. *The International Book of Christmas Carols.* Trans. by George K. Evans. Music by W. Ehret. Illus by Don Martinetti. Foreword by Norman Luboff. Englewood Cliffs, NJ: Prentice-Hall, 1963.

1494 Eichenberg, Fritz. *Ape in a Cape: An Alphabet of Odd Animals.* Illus by the author. New York: Harcourt, 1952. Voyager paperback.

1495 ———. *Dancing in the Moon: Counting Rhymes.* Illus by the author. New York: Harcourt, 1956. Voyager paperback.

1496 Ensel, Walter. *Did You Ever See?* Illus by the author. Reading, MA: Addison-Wesley, 1962. Scholastic paperback.

1497 Eisenberg, Alene M. and Ralph R. Smith. *NonVerbal Communication.* Indianapolis: Bobbs, 1971. Paperback.

1498 Eisner, Vivienne. *Quick and Easy Holiday Costumes.* Illus by Carolyn Bentley. New York: Lothrop, 1977.

1499 Elgin, Kathleen. *The Eye.* Illus by the author. New York: Watts, 1967.

1500 ———. *The Heart.* Illus by the author. New York: Watts, 1968.

1501 Elkin, Benjamin. *Gillespie and the Guards.* Illus by James Daugherty. New York: Viking, 1957.

1502 ———. *Six Foolish Fishermen.* Illus by Katherine Evans. Chicago: Childrens, 1971.

1503 ———. *Why the Sun Was Late.* Illus by Jerome Snyder. New York: Parents, 1966.

1504 ———. *The Wisest Man in the World: A Legend of Ancient Egypt.* Illus by Anita Lobel. New York: Parents, 1968.

1505 Eller, William and Kathleen Hester, eds. *The Blue-Tailed Horse.* River Forest, IL: Laidlaw, 1976.

1506 ———. *Dots and Polka Dots.* River Forest, IL: Laidlaw, 1976.

1507 Ellison, Elsie. *Fun With Lines and Curves.* Illus by Susan Stan. New York: Lothrop, 1972. Paperback.

1508a Ellis, Mel. *When Lightning Strikes.* New York: Holt, 1970. Scholastic paperback.

1508b ———. *Sidewalk Indian.* New York: Holt, 1974.

1509 Ellison, Virginia. *The Pooh Cook Book.* Illus by Ernest Shepard. New York: Dutton, 1969. Dell paperback.

1510 Elwood, Roger. *Monster Tales, Vampires, Werewolves and Things.* Illus by Franz Altschuler. Chicago: Rand McNally, 1973. Paperback.

1511 *Emberley, Barbara. *Drummer Hoff.* Illus by Ed Emberley. Englewood Cliffs, NJ: Prentice-Hall, 1967. Paperback. M182, M183.

1512 ———. *One Wide River to Cross.* Illus by Ed Emberley. Englewood Cliffs, NJ: Prentice-Hall, 1966. M506

1513 ———. *Simon's Song.* Illus by Ed Emberley. Englewood Cliffs, NJ: Prentice-Hall, 1969. Paperback. M612.

1514 ———. *The Story of Paul Bunyan.* Illus by Ed Emberley. Englewood Cliffs, NJ: Prentice-Hall, 1963. M648.

1515 Emberley, Ed. *A Birthday Wish.* Boston: Little, 1977.

1516 ———. *Ed Emberley's ABC.* Illus by the author. Boston: Little, 1978.

1517 ———. *Ed Emberley's Little Drawing Book: Make a Word.* Boston: Little, 1972.

1518 ———. *Ed Emberley's Drawing Book of Animals.* Boston: Little, 1970.

1519 ———. *Ed Emberley's Drawing Book of Faces.* Boston: Little, 1975.

1520 ———. *Ed Emberley's Great Thumbprint Drawing Book.* Boston: Little, 1977.

1521 ———. *Ed Emberley's Little Drawing Book of Birds.* Boston: Little paperbacks, 1973.

1522 ———. *Ed Emberley's Little Drawing Book of Farms.* Boston: Little paperbacks, 1973.

1523 ———. *Ed Emberley's Little Drawing Book of Trains.* Boston: Little paperbacks, 1973.

1524 ———. *Ed Emberley's Little Drawing Book of Weirdos.* Boston: Little paperbacks, 1973.

1525 ———. *Green Says Go.* Boston: Little, 1968.

1526 ———. *London Bridge is Falling Down.* Englewood Cliffs, NJ: Prentice-Hall, 1967.

1527 ———. *Punch and Judy.* Boston: Little, 1965.

1528 ———. *Rosebud.* Boston: Little, 1966.

1529 ———. *Wing on a Flea: A Book About Shapes.* Boston: Little, 1961. M762.

1530 ———. *The Wizard of Op.* Boston: Little, 1975.

1531 Emrich, Duncan. *the Hodgepodge Book: An Almanac of American Folklore.* Illus by Ib Ohlsson. New York: Four Winds, 1972.

1532 Engdahl, Sylvia. *Enchantress from the Stars.* Illus by Rodney Shackell. New York: Atheneum, 1970. Aladdin paperback.

1533 Engler, Larry and Carol Fijan. *Making Puppets Come Alive; a Method of Learning and Teaching Hand Puppetry.* New York: Taplinger, 1973.

1534 Engvick, Alec. *Lullabies and Night Songs.* Illus by Maurice Sendak. Music by Alec Wilder. New York: Harper, 1965.

1535 Enright, Elizabeth. *The Four-Story Mistake.* Illus by the author. New York: Holt, 1942. Dell paperback.

1536 ———. *Gone Away Lake.* Illus by Beth and Joe Krush. New York: Harcourt, 1957. Voyager paperback.

1537 ———. *Return to Gone-Away.* Illus by Beth and Joe Krush. New York: Harcourt, 1961. Voyager paperback.

1538 ———. *The Saturdays.* Illus by the author. New York: Rinehart, 1941. Dell paperback.

1539 Epstein, Sam and Beryl. *All About the Desert.* Illus by Fritz Kredel. New York: Random, 1957.

1540 ———. *Baseball Hall of Fame: Stories of Champions.* Illus by Ken Wagner. Champaign, IL: Garrard, 1965.

1541 ———. *The First Book of Codes and Ciphers.* Illus by Laszlo Roth. New York: Watts, 1956.

1542 ———. *First Book of Printing.* New York: Watts, 1955, 1975.

1543 ———. *Harriet Tubman: Guide to Freedom.* Illus by Paul Frame. Champaign, IL: Garrard, 1968.

1544 Erdei, Peter and Katalin Komlos. *One Hundred Fifty American Folk Songs to Sing, Read and Play.* Selected and edited by Peter Erdei and the Staff of the Kodaly Musical Training Institute and collected by Katalin Komlos. New York: Boosey and Hawkes, 1974.

1545 Erickson, Janet D. and Adelainde Sproul. *Print-Making Without a Press.* New York: Van Nostrand, 1966. paperback 1974.

1546 Erickson, Russell. *A Toad for Tuesday.* Illus by Lawrence Di Fiori. New York: Lothrop, 1974.

1547 Ernest, Edward, ed. *The Kate Greenaway Treasury.* Intro. by Ruth Hill Viguers. Cleveland: World, 1967.

1548 Ernst, Kathryn. *Mr. Tamarin's Trees.* Illus by Diane de Groat. New York: Crown, 1976.

1549 Ernst, Kathryn and Diane De Groat. *Owls' New Cards.* New York: Crown, 1977.

1550 Erskine, Jim. *The Farmer in the Dell.* Illus by Diane Zuromskis. Boston: Little, 1978.

1551 Erwin, Betty K. *Go To the Room of the Eyes.* Illus by Irene Burns. Boston: Little, 1969.

1552 Estes, Eleanor. *Ginger Pye.* New York: Harcourt, 1951. Voyager paperback. M248.

1553 ———. *The Hundred Dresses.* Illus by Louis Slobodkin. New York: Harcourt, 1944. Voyager paperback.

1554 ———. *The Middle Moffat.* Illus by Louis Slobodkin. New York: Harcourt, 1942.

1555 ———. *The Moffats*. Illus by Louis Slobodkin. New York: Harcourt, 1941. Voyager paperback.

1556 ———. *Pinky Eye*. Illus by Edward Ardizzone. New York: Harcourt, 1958. Voyager paperback. M536.

1557 ———. *Rufus M*. Illus by Louis Slobodkin. New York: Harcourt, 1943.

1558 Ets, Marie Hall. *Another Day*. New York: Viking, 1953.

1559 ———. *Beasts and Nonsense*. New York: Viking, 1952.

1560 ———. *Elephant in a Well*. Illus by the author. New York: Viking, 1972. Penguin paperback.

1561 ———. *In the Forest*. Illus by the author. New York: Viking, 194. Penguin paperback. M313.

1562 ———. *Just Me*. New York: Viking, 1965. Penguin paperback. M341.

1563 ———. *Nine Days to Christmas*. Illus by the author. New York: Viking, 1959. M296, M480.

1564 ———. *Play With Me*. Illus by the author. New York: Viking, 1955. Penguin paperback. M542.

1565 ———. *Talking Without Words*. New York: Viking, 1968. M677.

1566 Evans, C. S. *Cinderella*. Illus by Arthur Rackham. New York: Viking, 1972.

1567 ———. *The Sleeping Beauty*. Illus by Arthur Rockham. New York: Viking, 1972. Dover paperback.

1568 Evans, Katherine. *The Boy Who Cried Wolf*. Retold and illus by K. Evans. Chicago: Whitman, 1960.

1569 ———. *The Man, the Boy and the Donkey*. Retold and illus by K. Evans. Chicago: Whitman, 1958.

1570 Evslin, Bernard. *The Adventures of Ulysses*. Illus by William Hunter. New York: Scholastic, 1969. Paperback.

1571 Evslin, Bernard and Dorothy and Ned Hooper. *Heroes and Monsters of Greek Myth*. Illus by William Hunter. New York: Scholastic, 1970.

1572 Eyerley, Jeannette. *The World of Ellen March*. Philadelphia: Lippincott, 1964.

1573 *Facts on File's News Reference Service*. Facts on File, Inc., 119W 57th Street, New York, NY 10019.

1574 Fall, Thomas. *Canalboat to Freedom*. Illus by Joseph Cellini. New York: Dial, 1966. Dell paperback.

1575 Falls, Charles B. *The ABC Book*. Illus by the author. New York: Doubleday, 1957. Doubleday paperback.

1576 Farber, Norma. *As I Was Crossing Boston Common*. Illus by Arnold Lobel. New York: Dutton, 1975.

1577 ———. *This Is the Ambulance Leaving the Zoo*. Illus by Tomi de Paola. New York: Dutton, 1975.

1578 ———. *Where's Gomer?* Illus by William Pene DuBois. New York: Dutton, 1974.

1579a Farjeon, Eleanor. *Around the Seasons*. Illus by Jane Paton. New York: Walck, 1969.

1579b ———. *A Cavalcade of Kings*. Illus by Victor Ambrus. New York: Walck, 1964.

1580 ———. *The Children's Bells*. Illus by Peggy Fortnum. New York: Walck, 1960.

1581 ———. *Eleanor Farjeon's Poems for Children*. Philadelphia: Lippincott, 1951.

1582 ———. *The Glass Slipper*. Illus by Ernest H. Shepard. New York: Viking, 1956.

1583 ———. *Then There were Three, Being Cherrystones, The Mulberry Bush, The Starry Floor*. Illus by Isabel and John Morton-Sale. Philadelphia: Lippincott, 1965.

1584 Farjeon, Eleanor and William Mayne. *A Cavalcade of Queens*. Illus by Victor Ambrus. New York: Walck, 1965.

1585 Farley, Walter. *Black Stallion*. New York: Random, 1941. Paperback.

1586 ———. *Black Stallion and the Girl*. New York: Random, 1971. Paperback.

1587 ———. *Black Stallion Mystery*. New York: Random, 1957. Paperback.

1588 ———. *Black Stallion Returns*. New York: Random, 1945. Paperback.

1589 ———. *Black Stallion Revolts*. New York: Random, 1953. Paperback.

1590 ———. *Little Black, a Pony*. Illus by James Schucker. New York: Beginner, 1961.

1591 ———. *Son of Black Stallion*. New York: Random, 1947. Paperback.

1592 ———. *Walter Farley's How to Stay Out of Trouble with your Horse*. Garden City, NY: Doubleday, 1980.

1593 Farmer, Penelope. *Charlotte Sometimes*. Illus by Chris Connor. New York: Harcourt, 1969

1594 Fast, Julius. *Body Language*. New York: Evans, 1970. Pocket Book paperback.

1595 Fatio, Louise. *Happy Lion*. Illus by Roger Duvoisin. New York: McGraw, 1954.

1596 ———. *Happy Lion and the Bear*. Illus by Roger Duvoisin. New York: McGraw, 1964.

1597 ———. *Happy Lion in Africa*. Illus by Roger Duvoisin. New York: McGraw, 1955.

1598 ———. *Happy Lion Roars*. Illus by Roger Duvoisin. New York: McGraw, 1957.

1599 ———. *Hector and Christina*. Illus by Roger Duvoisin. New York: McGraw, 1977.

1600 ———. *Hector Penguin*. Illus by Roger Duvoisin. New York: McGraw, 1973.

1601 ———. *Red Bantam*. New York: McGraw, 1963.

1602 ———. *Three Happy Lions*. Illus by Roger Duvoisin. New York: McGraw, 1959.

1603 Feagles, Anita. *Thor and the Giants, an Old Norse Legend Retold*. Illus by Gertrude Barrer-Russell. New York: Young Scott, 1968.

1604 Feelings, Muriel. *Jambo Means Hello: Swahili Alphabet Book*. Illus by Tom Feelings. New York: Dial, 1974.

1605 ———. *Moja Means One: Swahili Counting Book*. Illus by Tom Feelings. New York: Dial, 1971.

1606 ———. *Zamani Goes to Market*. Illus by Tom Feelings. New York: Seabury, 1970.

1607 Feelings, Tom. *Black Pilgrimage*. New York: Lothrop, 1972.

1608 Feinstein, Phyllis. *All About Sesame Street*. New York: Tower, 1971.

1609 Felton, Harold W. *Cowboy Jamboree,*

Western Songs and Lore. Music by Edward S. Breck. Illus by Aldren A. Watson. Foreword by Carl Carmer. New York: Knopf, 1951.

1610 ———. *John Henry and His Hammer.* Illus by Aldren A. Watson. New York: Knopf, 1950. M28, M32, M200, M353.

1611 ———. *Legends of Paul Bunyan.* Illus by Richard Bennett. New York: Knopf, 1947. M30.

1612 ———. *New Tall Tales of Pecos Bill.* Illus by William Mayers. Englewood Cliffs, NJ: Prentice-Hall, 1958. M29.

1613 ———. *Pecos Bill, Texas Cowpuncher.* Illus by Aldren A. Watson. New York: Knopf, 1949. M29.

1614 ———. *True Tall Tales of Stormalong: Sailor of the Seven Seas.* Illus by Joan Sandin. Englewood Cliffs, NJ: Prentice-Hall, 1968.

1615 Fenner, Phyllis, R. ed. *Fools and Funny Fellows.* Illus by Henry C. Pitz. New York: Knopf, 1947.

1616 ———. *Giants and Witches and a Dragon or Two.* Illus by Henry C. Pitz. New York: Knopf, 1943.

1617 ———. *Magic Hoofs, Horse Stories from Many Lands.* Illus by Henry C. Pitz. New York: Knopf, 1952.

1618 ———. *Princesses and Peasant Boys: Tales of Enchantment.* Illus by Henry C. Pitz. New York: Knopf, 1944.

1619 ———. *Time to Laugh, Funny Tales from Here and There.* Illus by Henry C. Pitz. New York: Knopf, 1942.

1620 Fenner, Phyllis and Mary McCrea. *Stories for Fun and Adventure, a Collection for All Boys and Girls Who Love Good Stories.* New York: Day, 1961.

1621 Fenton, Carroll Lane. *Wild Folks of the Desert.* Illus by Evelyn Carswell and the author. New York: Day, 1958.

1622 Fenton, Edward. *The Big Yellow Balloon.* Illus by Ib Ohlsson. New York: Doubleday, 1967.

1623 ———. *Fierce John.* Illus by William Pene DuBois. New York: Harper, 1959. Dell paperback.

1624 Feravolo, Rocco. *Wonders of Mathematics.* New York: Dodd, 1963.

1625 Ferris, Helen. *Favorite Poems Old and New.* Illus by Leonard Weisgard. New York: Doubleday, 1957.

1626 Fiarotta, Phyllis and Neol. *The You and Me Heritage Tree, Ethnic Crafts for Children.* New York: Workman, 1976.

1627 Fidell, Estelle A., ed. *Children's Catalog,* 12th ed. New York: Wilson, 1971. Annual supplements.

1628 Field, Edward, trans. *Eskimo Songs and Stories.* Illus by Kukshuk and Pudlo. New York: Delacorte, 1973.

1629 Field, Eugene. *Poems of Childhood.* Illus by Maxfield Parrish. New York: Scribner, 1904.

1630 ———. *Poems of Childhood.* Bridgeport, CT: Airmont paperback, 1969.

1631 Field, Eugene. *Wynken, Blynken, and Nod.* Illus by Barbara Cooney. New York: Hastings, 1970. M772, M773.

1632 *Field, Rachel. *Prayer for a Child.* Illus by Elizabeth Orton Jones. New York: Macmillan,

1944. Collier paperback.

1633 ———. *Hitty: Her First One Hundred Years.* New York: Macmillan, 1929, 1937.

1634 Fife, Dale. *Adam's ABC.* Illus by Don Robertson. New York: Coward, 1971.

1635 Fillmore, Parker. *The Laughing Prince.* Illus by Jan Van Everen. New York: Harcourt, 1921.

1636 ———. *The Shepherd's Nosegay: Stories from Finland and Czechoslovakia.* Ed. by Katherine Love. Illus by Enrico Arno. New York: Harcourt, 1958.

1637 Firmin, Peter. *Basil Bush at the Beach.* Illus by the author. New York: Parnassus, 1976.

1638 Fish, Helen Dean. *Four and Twenty Blackbirds, A Collection of Old Nursery Rhymes.* Illus by Robert Lawson. Philadelphia: Lippincott, 1965.

1639 Fischer, Hans. *The Birthday.* New York: Harcourt, 1954.

1640 ———. *Pitschi, the Kitten who Always Wanted to be Something Else.* New York: Harcourt, 1953.

1641 Fisher, Aileen. *But Ostriches.* Illus by Peter Parnall. New York: Crowell, 1970.

1642 ———. *Cricket in a Thicket.* Illus by Feodor Rojankovsky. New York: Scribner, 1963.

1643 ———. *Do Bears Have Mothers, Too?* Illus by Eric Carle. New York: Crowell, 1973.

1644 ———. *Easter.* Illus by Ati Forberg. New York: Crowell, 1968.

1645 ———. *Feathered Ones and Furry.* Illus by Eric Carle. New York: Crowell, 1971.

1646 ———. *Going Barefoot.* Illus by Adrienne Adams. New York: Crowell, 1960.

1647 ———. *I Like Weather.* Illus by Janina Domanska. New York: Crowell, 1963.

1648 ———. *In One Door and Out the Other, a Book of Poems.* Illus by Lillian Hoban. New York: Crowell, 1969.

1649 ———. *In the Middle of the Night.* Illus by Adrienne Adams. New York: Crowell, 1965.

1650 ———. *In the Woods, in the Meadow, in the Sky.* Illus by Margot Tomes. New York: Scribner, 1965.

1651 ———. *The Lantern in the Window.* Illus by Harper Johnson. Eau Claire, WI: Hale, 1957.

1652 ———. *Listen, Rabbit.* Illus by Symeon Shimin. New York: Crowell, 1964.

1653 ———. *My Cat Has Eyes of Sapphire Blue.* Illus by Marie Angel. New York: Crowell, 1973.

1654 ———. *Skin Around the Year.* Illus by Gioia Fiammenghi. New York: Crowell, 1967.

1655 ———. *Up, Up the Mountain.* Illus by Gilbert Resvold. New York: Crowell, 1968.

1656 Fisher, Aileen and Olive Rabe. *We Alcotts.* Illus by Ellen Raskin. New York: Atheneum, 1968.

1657 Fisher, Aileen Lucia. *We Went Looking.* Illus by Marie Angel. New York: Crowell, 1968.

1658 Fisher, Dorothy Canfield. *Paul Revere and the Minute Men.* Illus by Norman Price. New York: Random, 1950.

1659 Fisher, Leonard Everett. *Alphabet art, 13 ABC's from Around the World.* Illus by the author. New York: Four Winds, 1978.

1660 ———. *The Death of Evening Star; the Diary*

of a Young New England Whaler. Illus by the author. New York: Doubleday, 1972.

1661 Fisher, Margery. *Who's Who in Children's Books, a Treasury of the Familiar Characters of Childhood*. New York: Holt, 1975.

1662 Fisher, Ronald. *Namu; Making Friends with a Killer Whale*. Washington, D.C.: National Geographic Society, 1973.

1663 Fitch, Florence. *Book About God*. New York: Lothrop, 1953.

1664 Fitzgerald, Burdette S. *World Tales for Creative Dramatics and Storytelling*. Englewood Cliffs, NJ: Prentice-Hall, 1962.

1665 Fitzgerald, John D. *The Great Brain*. Illus by Mercer Mayer. New York: Dial, 1967. Dell paperback.

1666 ———. *The Great Brain at the Academy*. Illus by Mercer Mayer. New York: Dial, 1972. Dell paperback.

1667 ———. *The Great Brain Does it Again*. Illus by Mercer Mayer. New York: Dial, 1975.

1668 ———. *The Great Brain Reforms*. Illus by Mercer Mayer. New York: Dial, 1973. Dell paperback.

1669 ———. *Me and My Little Brain*. Illus by Mercer Mayer. New York: Dial, 1972. Dell paperback.

1670 ———. *More Adventures of the Great Brain*. Illus by Mercer Mayer. New York: Dial, 1969.

1671 ———. *Papa Married a Mormon*. Salt Lake City: Western Epics, 1976. Reprint.

1672 ———. *Return of the Great Brain*. Illus by Mercer Mayer. New York: Dial, 1974. Dell paperback.

1673 Fitzhugh, Louise. *Harriet the Spy*. Illus by the author. New York: Harper, 1964. Dell paperback.

1674 ———. *The Long Secret*. Illus by the author. New York: Harper, 1965. Dell paperback.

1675 Flack, Marjorie. *Angus and the Cat*. Illus by the author. Garden City, NY: Doubleday, 1971. Paperback.

1676 ———. *Angus and the Ducks*. Illus by the author. Garden City, NY: Doubleday, 1930. Paperback.

1677 ———. *Angus Lost*. Illus by the author. Garden City, NY: Doubleday, 1941. Paperback.

1678 ———. *Ask Mr. Bear*. Illus by the author. New York: Macmillan, 1932. Collier paperback.

1679 ———. *The Story About Ping*. Illus by Kurt Weise. New York: Viking, 1933. Puffin paperback. M643, M644.

1680 ———. *Walter the Lazy Mouse*. Garden City, NY: Doubleday, 1963. Paperback.

1681 Flanagan, Geraldine Lux. *Window Into an Egg: Seeing Life Begin*. New York: Young Scott, 1969.

1682a Flanders, Michael. *Creatures Great and Small*. New York: Holt, 1965.

1682b Fleischman, Sid. *By the Great Horn Spoon!* Illus by Eric von Schmidt. Boston: Little, 1963.

1683 ———. *Chancy and the Grand Rascal*. Illus by Eric von Schmidt. Boston: Little, 1966. Dell paperback.

1684 ———. *The Ghost in the Noonday Sun*. Illus

by Warren Chappell. Boston: Little, 1965. Dell paperback.

1685 ———. *Ghost on Saturday Night*. Eric von Schmidt. Boston: Little, 1974.

1686 ———. *Kate's Secret Riddle Book*. Illus by Barb Bollner. New York: Watts, 1977.

1687 ———. *McBroom and the Beanstalk*. Illus by Walter Lorraine. Boston: Little, 1978.

1688 ———. *McBroom and the Little Wind*. Illus by Kurt Werth. New York: Norton, 1967.

1689 ———. *McBroom Tells a Lie*. Illus by Walter Lord. Boston: Little, 1976.

1690 ———. *McBroom Tells the Truth*. Illus by Kurt Werth. New York: Tempo paperback, 1972.

1691 ———. *McBroom the Rainmaker*. New York: Grosset, 1973.

1692 ———. *McBroom's Ear*. Illus by Kurt Werth. New York: Norton, 1969.

1693 ———. *McBroom's Ghost*. New York: Grosset, 1971.

1694 ———. *McBroom's Zoo*. Illus by Kurt Werth. New York: Grosset, 1972.

1695 ———. *Mr. Mysterious and Company*. Illus by Eric von Schmidt. Boston: Little, 1972. Dell paperback.

1696 ———. *Mr. Mysterious's Secrets of Magic*. Illus by Eric von Schmidt. Boston: Little, 1975.

1697 Fleisher, Robbin. *Quilts in the Attic*. Illus by Ati Forberg. New York: Macmillan, 1978.

1698 Fleming, Alice. *Hosannah the Home Run! Poems About Sports*. Boston: Little, 1972.

1699 Fleming, Ian. *Chitty-Chitty Bang-Bang: The Magical Car*. Illus by John Burningham. New York: Random, 1964. Scholastic paperback, 1978.

1700 Fleming, Thomas J. *Benjamin Franklin*. New York: Four Winds, 1973.

1701 Fleming, Thomas and Francis Ronalds. *The Battle of Yorktown*. New York: American Heritage, 1968.

1702a Fletcher, Helen J. *Put On Your Thinking Cap*. New York: Abelard-Schuman, 1968.

1702b ———. *Puzzles and Quizzes*. New York: Abelard-Schuman, 1971.

1703 ———. *Puzzles, Puzzles and More Puzzles*. New York: Platt, 1969.

1704 Fling, Helen. *Marionettes: How to Make and Work Them*. Glouster, MA: Peter Smith, n.d. Dover paperback.

1705a Flint Public Library. *Ring A Ring O'Roses, Stories, Games and Finger Plays for Pre-School Children*. Flint, MI: Flint Board of Education, 1977.

1705b Flora, James. *Sherwood Walks Home*. New York: Harcourt, 1966.

1706 Folsom, Franklin. *The Language Book*. Illus by John Hull and Fran Mawicke. New York: Grosset and Dunlap, 1963.

1707 Fontaine, Robert. *Humorous Skits for Young People*. Boston: Plays, 1965, 1976.

1708 Fontane, Theodor. *Sir Ribbeck of Havelland*. Illus by Nonny Hogrogian. Translated by Elizabeth Shub. New York: Macmillan, 1969.

1709 Forbes, Esther. *America's Paul Revere*. Illus by Lynd Ward. Boston: Houghton, 1946.

1710 ———. *Johnny Tremain*. Illus by Lynd Ward.

Boston: Houghton, 1943. Dell paperback. M332, M333, M334.

1711 ———. *Paul Revere and the World He Lived In.* Boston: Houghton, 1942. Houghton paperback.

1712 Foster, Doris. *A Pocketful of Season.* Illus by Talivaldis Stubis. New York: Lothrop, 1961.

1713 Foster, G. Allen. *Communication: From Primitive Tom-Toms to Television.* New York: Criterion, 1965.

1714 Foster, Joanna. *Pages, Pictures and Print, a Book in the Making.* New York: Harcourt, 1958.

1715 Foster, Robert. *A Guide to Middle Earth.* Baltimore: Mirage Press, 1971. Ballantine paperback.

1716 Foster, Ruth. *The Stone Horsemen, Tales from the Caucasus.* Illus by Judith G. Brown. Indianapolis: Bobbs-Merrill, 1965.

1717 Fowke, Edith. *Ring Around the Moon.* Illus by Judith Gwyn Brown. Englewood Cliffs, NJ: Prentice-Hall, 1977.

1718 ———. *Sally Go Round the Sun, 300 Children's Songs, Rhymes, and Games.* Garden City, NY: Doubleday, 1970.

1719 Fowler, H. Waller. *Kites, a Practical Guide to Kite Making and Flying.* New York: A.S. Barnes, 1953, 1965.

1720 Fox, Charles Philip. *When Winter Comes.* Chicago: Reilly, 1962.

1721 Fox, Paula. *Good Ethan.* Illus by Arnold Lobel. Scarsdale, N.Y.: Bradbury, 1973.

1722 ———. *How Many Miles to Babylon.* Illus by Paul Giovanopolus. New York: White, 1967. Arch paperback.

1723 ———. *The Slave Dancer.* Illus by Eros Keith. Scarsdale, NY: Bradbury, 1973. Dell paperback.

1724 Fox, Siv Cedering. *The Blue Horse and Other Night Poems.* Illus by Donald Carrick. New York: Seabury, 1979.

1725 Fox, Sonny. *Funnier Than the First One.* New York: Putnam, 1972. Berkley Medalion paperback.

1726 ———. *Jokes and How to Tell Them.* Illus by Bob Gray. New York: Putnam, 1965.

1727 Frances of Assissi, Saint. *Song of the Sun; from the Chanticle of the Sun.* Illus by Elizabeth Orton Jones. New York: Macmillan, 1952.

1728 Francis, Frank. *Magic Wallpaper.* New York: Abelard, 1970.

1729 Francoise (Seignobosc). *The Big Rain.* Illus by the author. New York: Scribner, 1961.

1730 ———. *Chouchou.* Illus by the author. New York: Scribner, 1958

1731 ———. *Jean Marie at the Fair.* Illus by the author. New York: Scribner, 1959.

1732 ———. *Jeanne Marie Counts her Sheep.* Illus by the author. New York: Scribner, 1951. Scribner paperback. M329.

1733 ———. *Minou.* Illus by the author. New York: Scribner, 1962.

1734 ———. *Noel for Jeanne Marie.* Illus by the author. New York: Scribner, 1953.

1735 ———. *Springtime for Jeanne Marie.* Illus by the author. New York: Scribner, 1955. M628.

1736 Frank, Anne. *Anne Frank: The Diary of a* *Young Girl.* Garden City, NY: Doubleday, 1967. Pocket Books paperback. M171.

1737 Frasconi, Antonio. *The House that Jack Built, a Picture Book in Two Languages.* New York: Harcourt, 1958.

1738 ———. *See and Say, A Picture Book in Four Languages.* New York: Harcourt, 1955. Voyager paperback. M602.

1739 ———. *The Snow and the Sun: La Nieve y el Sol.* New York: Harcourt, 1961.

1740 Fraser-Simson, H. *The Pooh Song Book Containing the Hums of Pooh, The King's Breakfast and Fourteen Songs from When We Were Very Young.* Words by A. A. Milne, Music by H. Fraser-Simson. Illus by E. H. Shepard. New York: Dutton, 1958.

1741 Frazee, Steve. *The Year of the Big Snow, John Charles Fremont's Fourth Expedition.* New York: Holt, 1962.

1742 Frazer, Peter. *Introducing Puppetry.* New York: Watson-Guptill, 1968.

1743 ———. *Puppet Circus.* Boston: Plays, 1971.

1744 Frazier, Neta Lohnes. *Stout-Hearted Seven, the True Adventures of the Sager Children Orphaned on the Oregon Trail.* New York: Harcourt, 1973.

1745 Freedman, Russell. *Animal Fathers.* Illus by Joseph Cellini. New York: Holiday, 1976.

1746 Freeman, Don. *Beady Bear.* Illus by the author. New York: Viking, 1954. Penguin paperback.

1747 ———. *Chalk Box Story.* Philadelphia: Lippincott, 1976.

1748 ———. *Dandelion.* Illus by the author. New York: Viking, 1974. Puffin paperback. M168.

1749 ———. *Flash and Dash.* Illus by the author. Chicago: Children's, 1973.

1750 ———. *Norman the Doorman.* Illus by the author. New York: Viking, 1959. Puffin paperback. M484, M485.

1751 ———. *Penguins of all People.* New York: Viking, 1971.

1752 ———. *A Rainbow of My Own.* Illus by the author. New York: Viking, 1966. Puffin paperback. M562.

1753 ———. *Will's Quills.* Illus by the author. New York: Viking, 1975. Puffin paperback.

1754 Freeman, Lydia and Don. *Pet of the Met.* Illus by Don Freeman. New York: Viking, 1953. Puffin paperback.

1755 Freeman, Mae. *Stars and Stripes: the Story of the American Flag.* Illus by Larence Bjorklund. New York: Random, 1964.

1756 Freeman, Mae and Ira. *The Sun, the Moon and the Stars.* Illus by Rene Martin. New York: Random, 1979.

1757 Fregosi, Claudia. *Mammoth, the Owl, and the Crab.* New York: Macmillan, 1975.

1758 ———. *Sun Grumble.* New York: Macmillan, 1974.

1759 French, Fiona. *The Blue Bird.* New York: Walck, 1972.

1760 French, Susan. *Presenting Marionettes.* New York: Reinhold, 1964.

1761 Freschet, Bernice. *Ants Go Marching.* New York: Scribner, 1973.

1762 ———. *Bear Mouse.* Illus by Donald Carrick. New York: Scribner, 1973.

1763 ———. *Lizard Lying in the Sun.* Illus by Glen

Round. New York: Scribner, 1975.

1764 ———. The Old Bullfrog. Illus by Roger Duvoisin. New York: Scribner, 1968. M494.

1765 ———. The Owl and the Prairie Dog. Illus by Gilbert Riswold. New York: Scribner, 1969.

1766 ———. The Web in the Grass. Illus by Roger Duvoisin. New York: Scribner, 1972.

1767 Friedrich, Priscilla and Otto. The Easter Bunny That Overslept. New York: Lothrop, 1957.

1768 Friedricksen, Carol. The Pooh Craft Book. Illus by E. H. Shepard. New York: Dutton, 1976.

1769 Friis-Baastad, Babbis. Don't Take Teddy. Trans by Lise Somme McKinnon. New York: Scribner, 1967. Archway paperback.

1770 Frimmer, Steven. The Stone that Spoke and Other Clues to the Decipherment of Lost Languages. New York: Putnam, 1969.

1771 Friskey, Margaret. Chicken Little, Count-to-ten. Illus by Katherine Evans. Chicago: Childrens Press, 1946.

1772 ———. What is the Color of the Whole Wide World? Chicago: Children's Press, 1973.

1773 Fritz, Jean. And Then What Happened, Paul Revere? Illus by Margaret Tomes. New York: Coward, 1973. M36.

1774 ———. Brady. Illus by Lynd Ward. New York: Coward, 1960.

1775 ———. Can't You Make Them Behave, George Washington? New York: Coward, 1977. M110.

1776 ———. George Washington's Breakfast. Illus by Paul Galdone. New York: Coward, 1969.

1777 ———. What's the Big Idea, Ben Franklin? Illus by Margaret Tomes. New York: Coward, 1976. M736.

1778 ———. Where Do You Think You're Going, Christopher Columbus? Illus by Margot Tomes. New York: Putnam, 1980.

1779 ———. Where Was Patrick Henry on the 29th of May? Illus by Margret Tomes. New York: Coward, 1975. M741.

1780 ———. Who's that Stepping on Plymouth Rock? Illus by J. B. Handelman. New York: Coward, 1975.

1781 ———. Why Don't You Get a Horse, Sam Adams? Illus by Trina Schart Hyman. New York: Coward, 1974. M750.

1782 ———. Will You Sign Here, John Hancock? Illus by Trina Schart Hyman. New York: Coward, 1976. M756.

1783 Froman, Robert, The Great Reaching Out: How Living Beings Communicate. Cleveland: World, 1968.

1784 ———. Venn Diagrams. Illus by Jan Pyk. New York: Crowell, 1972.

1785 Fromm, Lilo. Muffel and Plums. Illus by L. Fromm. New York: Macmillan, 1973.

1786 Fronval, George and Daniel Dubois. Indian Signs and Signals. New York: Sterling, 1978.

1787 Frost, Frances. Gian-Carlo Menotti's Amahl and the Night Visitors. Illus by Roger Duvoisin. Music by Menotti. New York: McGraw, 1952. M636.

1788 Frost, Robert. The Road Not Taken. Introduction by Louis Untermeyer, illus by John O'Hara Cosgrove. New York: Holt, 1951. M581.

1789 ———. Stopping By Woods on a Snowy Evening. Illus by Susan Jeffers. New York: Dutton, 1978.

1790 ———. You Come Too, Favorite Poems for Young Readers. Illus by Thomas Nason. New York: Holt, 1959. M581.

1791 Fryatt, Norma R., ed. Hornbook Sampler on Children's Books and Readings, Selections from Twenty-five Years of the Horn Book Magazine 1929-1948. Introduction by Bertha Mahony Miller. Boston: Horn Book, 1959.

1792 Fuchs, Erich. Journey to the Moon. New York: Delacorte, 1969.

1793 Fuchshuber, Annegert. The Wishing Hat. Trans. by Elizabeth Crawford. New York: Morrow, 1977.

1794 Fujikawa, Gyo. A To Z Picture Book. Illus by the author. New York: Grosset and Dunlap, 1974.

1795 Fuller, Catherine L. Beasts, an Alphabet of Fine Prints. Boston: Little, 1968.

1796 Fuller, Miriam M. Phyllis Wheatley, America's First Black Poetess. Illus by Victor Mays. Scarsdale, N.Y.: Garrard, 1971.

1797 Fuller, Muriel, ed. More Junior Authors. New York: Wilson, 1963.

1798 Funai, Mamoru. The Tiger, the Brahman, and the Jackal. Illus by the author. New York: Holt, 1963.

1799 Gabu, Lester. Soap Sculpture. New York: Watts, 1969.

1800 Gackenback, Dick. Harry and the Terrible Watzit. New York: Seabury, 1977.

1801 ———. Hattie Be Quiet, Hattie Be Good. New York: Harper, 1977.

1802 Gaeddert, Lou Ann. Noisy Nancy Norris. Illus by Gioia Fiammenghi. Doubleday, 1965, 1971. paperback. M482.

1803 Gaffney, Maureen, ed. More Films Kids Like. Chicago: A.L.A., 1977.

1804 Gag, Wanda. The ABC Bunny. Illus by Howard Gag. New York: Coward, 1933. Paperback.

1805 ———. Gone is Gone or the Story of the Man Who Wanted to do Housework. Illus by the author. New York: Coward, 1935.

1806 ———. Millions of Cats. Illus by the author. New York: Coward, 1928. Paperback. M447, M448.

1807 ———. More Tales from Grimm. Trans and illus by W. Gag. New York: Coward, 1947.

1808 ———. Nothing at All. Illus by the author. New York: Coward, 1941.

1809 ———. Snippy and Snappy. Illus by the author. New York: Coward, 1931.

1810 ———. Snow White and the Seven Dwarfs. Retold and illus by W. Gag. New York: Coward, 1938.

1811 ———. The Sorcerer's Apprentice. Illus by Margot Tomes. New York: Coward, 1937. M354, M360, M625.

1812 ———. Tales from Grimm. Trans and illus by W. Gag. New York: Coward, 1936.

1813 Gage, Wilson. Big Blue Island. Illus by Glen Rounds. Cleveland: World, 1968. Archway paperback.

1814 ———. Ghost of Five Owl Farm. Illus by Paul Galdone. New York: Philomel, 1966.

1815 ———. *Miss Osborn-the-Mop.* Illus by Paul Galdone. New York: Philomel, 1963. Archway paperback.

1816 Gagliardi, Maria Francesca. *The Magic Fish.* Illus by Stepan Zavrel. New York: Putnam, 1966.

1817 Gagliardo, R., comp. *Let's Read Aloud, Stories and Poems.* Illus by Valenti Angelo. Philadelphia: Lippincott, 1962.

1818 Gaitskell, Charles D. *Children and Their Art, Methods for the Elementary School.* New York: Harcourt, 1958.

1819 Galbraith, Kathryn O. *Spots are Special.* Illus by Diane Dawson. New York: Atheneum, 1976.

1820 Galdone, Paul. *Cinderella.* Retold from Perrault and illus by P. Galdone. New York: McGraw, 1978.

1821 ———. *The Gingerbread Boy.* Retold and illus by P. Galdone. New York: Seabury, 1975.

1822 ———. *Henny Penny.* Retold and illus by P. Galdone. New York: Seabury, 1968.

1823 ———. *The History of Little Tom Tucker.* Retold and illus by P. Galdone. New York: McGraw, 1964.

1824 ———. *The Life of Jack Sprat, His Wife and Cat.* Retold and illus by P. Galdone. New York: McGraw, 1969.

1825 ———. *The Little Red Hen.* Retold and illus by P. Galdone. New York: Seabury, 1973. M375.

1826 ———. *Little Tom Tucker.* Retold and illus by P. Galdone. New York: McGraw, n.d.

1827 ———. *Little Tuppen.* Illus by the author. New York: Seabury, 1967.

1828 ———. *The Moving Adventures of Old Dame Trot and Her Comical Cat.* Illus by P. Galdone. New York: McGraw, 1973.

1829 ———. *The Old Woman and Her Pig.* Retold and illus by P. Galdone. New York: McGraw, 1960. M497.

1830 ———. *The Three Billy Goats Gruff.* Retold and illus by P. Galdone. New York: Seabury, 1973.

1831 ———. *The Three Little Pigs.* Retold and illus by P. Galdone. New York: Seabury, 1970.

1832 ———. *The Town Mouse and the Country Mouse.* Retold from Aesop by P. Galdone. New York: McGraw, 1971.

1833 Galdone, Paul, illus. *The House that Jack Built.* New York: McGraw, 1961. M300.

1834 ———. *Old Mother Hubbard and her Dog.* New York: McGraw, 1960. M496.

1835 ———. *Tom, Tom the Piper's Son.* New York: McGraw, 1964.

1836 Gale Research. *Contemporary Authors.* Detroit: Gale Research, 1971—.

1837 ———. *Something About the Author.* Detroit: Gale Research, 1971—.

1838 Galt, Tom. *Peter Zenger, Fighter for Freedom.* Illus by Ralph Ray. New York: Crowell, 1951.

1839 Gannon, Robert. *Great Survival Adventures.* Illus by Gil Cohen. New York: Random, 1973.

1840 Gans, Roma. *Birds at Night.* Illus by Aliki. New York: Crowell, 1968. Paperback.

1841 ———. *It's Nesting Time.* Illus by Kazue Mizumura. New York: Crowell, 1964. Paperback.

1842 Gardner, Martin. *Codes, Ciphers and Secret Writing.* New York: Simon and Schuster, 1972. Archway paperback.

1843 ———. *Martin Gardner's Sixth Book of Mathematical Games from Scientific American.* New York: Scribner's, 1975. Paperback.

1844 ———. *Perplexing Puzzles and Tantalizing Teasers.* Illus by Laszlo Kubinyi. New York: Simon and Schuster, 1969. Archway paperback.

1845 Garelick, May. *Look at the Moon.* Illus by Leonard Weisgard. New York: Young Scott, 1969.

1846 ———. *Where Does the Butterfly Go When It Rains?* Illus by Leonard Weisgard. New York: Young Scott, 1961. Scholastic paperback. M738.

1847 Garfield, J. B. *Follow My Leader.* Illus by Robert Greiner. New York: Viking, 1957. Scholastic paperback.

1848a Garner, Alan. *Elidor.* New York: Walck, 1965.

1848b ———. *The Moon of Gomrath.* New York: Walck, 1963.

1849 Garson, Eugenia. *The Laura Ingalls Wilder Songbook, Favorite Songs from the "Little House" Books.* Compiled and edited by E. Garson. Illus by Garth Williams. Music by Herbert Haufrecht. New York: Harper, 1968.

1850 Garten, Jan. *The Alphabet Tale.* Illus by Muriel Botherman. New York: Random, 1964.

1851 Gates, Doris. *Lord of the Sky: Zeus.* Illus by Robert Handville. New York: Viking, 1972.

1852 ———. *The Warrior Goddess: Athena.* Illus by Don Bolognese. New York: Viking, 1972.

1853 Gates, Frieda. *Easy to Make Costumes.* New York: Harvey House, 1978.

1854 ———. *Easy to Make Puppets.* New York: Harvey House, 1976.

1855 Gauch, Patricia Lee. *On to Widecombe Fair.* Illus by Trina Shart Hyman. New York: Putnam, 1978. M32.

1856 Gaver, Mary, ed. *The Elementary School Library Collection; a Guide to Books and Other Media, Phase 1-2-3,* 7th ed. Newark, N.J.: Bro Dart, 1972.

1857a Gay, Zhengy. *Look!* New York: Viking, 1952.

1857b ———. *What's Your Name.* New York: Viking, 1955.

1858 Geisel, Theodore Seuss. *The Cat in the Hat Song Book.* Music by Eugene Poddany. Illus by T. Geisel. New York: Random, 1967.

1859 Gemming, Elizabeth. *Maple Harvest, the Story of Maple Sugaring.* New York: Coward, 1976.

1860 George, Jean Craighead. *All Upon a Stone.* Illus by Don Bolognese. New York: Crowell, 1971. M14.

1861 ———. *Gull Number 737.* New York: Crowell, 1964.

1862 ———. *The Hole in the Tree.* New York: Dutton, 1957.

1863 ———. *Julie of the Wolves.* Illus by John Schoenherr. New York: Harper, 1972. Trophy paperback. M339.

1864 ———. *Moon of the Fox Pups.* New York: Crowell, 1968.

1865 ———. *The Moon of the Owls.* Illus by Jean Zullinger. New York: Crowell, 1967.

1866 ———. *The Moon of the Winter Bird.* Illus by Kazue Mizumura. New York: Crowell, 1969.

1867 ———. *My Side of the Mountain.* Illus by the author. New York: Dutton, 1959. Scholastic paperback. M475.

1868 ———. *Snow Tracks.* Illus by the author. New York: Dutton, 1958.

1869 ———. *Summer of the Falcon.* New York: Crowell, 1962.

1870 ———. *Who Really Killed Cock Robin.* New York: Dutton, 1973. Dutton paperback.

1871 George, John and Jean George. *Bubo, the Great Horned Owl.* Illus by Jean George. New York: Dutton, 1954.

1872 ———. *Masked Prowler: The Story of a Raccoon.* Illus by Jean George. New York: Dutton, 1950.

1873 ———. *Meph, the Pet Skunk.* Illus by Jean George. New York: Dutton, 1952.

1874 ———. *Vulpes, the Red Fox.* New York: Dutton, 1948.

1875 Georgiou, Constantine. *Children and Their Literature.* Englewood Cliffs, NJ: Prentice-Hall, 1969.

1876 Georgwin, Constantine. *Children and Their Literature.* Englewood Cliffs, NJ: Prentice-Hall, 1969.

1877 Gerler, William R. *A Pack of Riddles.* Illus by Ginlio Maestro. New York: Dutton, 1975.

1878 Gesner, Clark. *You're a Good Man, Charlie Brown.* Music and lyrics by the author. New York: Random, 1967.

1879 Ghose, Sudhin N. *Folk Tales and Fairy Stories from Further India.* Illus by Shrimati E. Carlile. New York: A. S. Barnes, 1966.

1880 Giambarba, Paul. *Whales, Whaling and Whalecraft.* New York: Scrimshaw, 1967.

1881 Gibbons, Gail. *Clocks and How they Go.* Illus by Gail Gibbons. New York: Crowell, 1979.

1882 Giblin, James and Dale Ferguson. *The Scarecrow Book.* New York: Crown, 1980.

1883 Gilbreath, Alice T. *Beginning-to-Read Riddles and Jokes.* Chicago: Follett, 1967. Follett paperback.

1884 ———. *Making Costumes for Parties, Plays and Holidays.* Illus by Timothy Evans. New York: Morrow, 1974.

1885 Gilbert, Nan. *See Yourself in Print: A Handbook for Young Writers.* Illus by Jacqueline Tower. New York: Hawthorn, 1968.

1886 Gillespie, Margaret C. and John W. Conner. *Creative Growth Through Literature for Children and Adolescents.* Columbus, Ohio: Charles Merrill, 1975.

1887 Gillham Charles E. *Beyond the Clapping Mountains, Eskimo Stories from Alaska.* Illus by Chanimum. New York: Macmillan, 1964.

1888 Gilmour, Ann. *Understanding Your Senses, Easy Experiments for Young People.* Photos by James Gilmour. Illus by Robin Collander. New York: Warne, 1963.

1889 Ginsburg, Mirra. *The Fox and the Hare.* Illus by Victor Nolden. New York: Crown, 1969.

1890 ———. *How the Sun was Brought Back to the Sky.* Illus by Jose Arrego & Ariane Dewey. New York: Collier, 1975.

1891 ———. *Mushroom in the Rain.* Illus by Jose Aruego and Ariane Dewey. New York: Macmillan, 1974. Paperback.

1892 ———. *One Trick Too Many; Fox Stories from Russia.* Illus by Helen Siegl. New York: Dial, 1973.

1893a ———. *The Strongest One of All.* Illus by Jose Aruego and Ariane Dewey. New York: Greenwillow, 1977.

1893b ———. *Which is the Best Place?* Adapted from the Russia of Pyotr Dhdochkin. New York: Macmillan, 1976.

1894 Ginsburg, Mirra, ed. *The Kaha Bird; Tales from the Steppes of Central Asia.* Illus by Rich Criffari. New York: Crown, 1971.

1895 ———. *The Lazies: Tales of the People of Russia.* Illus by Marian Parry. New York: Macmillan, 1973.

1896 Ginsburg, Mirra. *Three Kittens.* Illus by Giulio Maestro. Trans by V. Suteyev. New York: Crown, 1973.

1897 Ginsburg, Mirra, ed. *Three Rolls & One Doughnut.* New York: Dial, 1970

1898 Ginsburg, Mirra. *The Twelve Clever Brothers, and Other Fools; Folktales from Russia.* Philadelphia: Lippincott, 1979

1899 Giovanni, Nikki. *Spin a Soft Black Song.* Illus by Charles Bible. New York: Hill and Wang, 1971.

1900 Gipson, Fred. *Old Yeller.* Illus by Carl Burger. New York: Harper, 1956. Paperback.

1901 ———. *Savage Sam.* New York: Harper, 1962.

1902 Gladstone, M.J. *A Carrot for a Nose; the Form of Folk Sculpture on America's City Streets and Country Roads.* New York: Scribner's, 1974.

1903 Glazer, Tom. *Do Your Ears Hang Low? Fifty More Musical Fingerplays.* Illus by Mila Lazarevich. New York: Doubleday, 1980.

1904 ———. *Eye Winker Tom Tinker Chin Chopper, Fifty Musical Fingerplays.* Illus by Ron Himler. Garden City, NY: Doubleday, 1973.

1905 Glubok, Shirley. *The Art of Photography.* Designed by Gerard Nook. New York: Macmillan, 1977.

1906 ———. *The Art of the Eskimo.* Designed by Oscar Krauss. Photos by Alfred H. Tamarin. New York: Harper, 1964.

1907 Goaman, Muriel. *How Writing Began.* New York: Faber, 1966.

1908 ———. *Judy and Andrew's Puppet Book.* London: Faber and Faber, 1963. Boston: Plays, n.d.

1909 ———. *News and Messages.* David and Charles, 1973.

1910 Gobhai, Mehlli. *The Blue Jackal.* Englewood Cliffs, NJ: Prentice-Hall, 1968.

1911 ———. *Ramu and the Kite.* Englewood Cliffs, NJ: Prentice-Hall, 1968.

1912 * Goble, Paul. *The Girl Who Loved Wild Horses.* Illus by the author. Scarsdale, NY: Bradbury, 1978.

1913 Goble, Paul and Dorothy. *Red Hawk's Account of Custer's Last Battle.* Illus by P. Goble. New York: Pantheon, 1969.

1914 Godden, Rumer. *Candy Floss.* Illus by Adrienne Adams. New York: Viking, 1960.

1915 ———. *Dolls House.* New York: Viking, 1948.
1916 ———. *Fairy Doll.* Illus by Adrienne Adams. New York: Viking, 1956.
1917 ———. *Impunity Jane.* Illus by Adrienne Adams. New York: Viking, 1954.
1918 ———. *Miss Happiness and Miss Flower.* Illus by Jean Primrose. New York: Viking, 1961.
1919 ———. *Mouse House.* Illus by Adrienne Adams. New York: Viking, 1957. Paperback.
1920 ———. *The Story of Holly and Ivy.* Illus by Adrienne Adams. New York: Viking, 1958.
1921 Goetz, Delia. *Deserts.* Illus by Louis Darling. New York: Morrow, 1956.
1922 Goffstein, M.B. *My Noah's Ark.* New York: Harper, 1978.
1923 Goldin, Augusta. *Salt.* Illus by Robert Galster. New York: Crowell, 1965.
1924 Golding, William. *Lord of the Flies.* New York: Coward, 1962. Putnam paperback.
1925 Goodall, John S. *Adventures of Paddy Pork.* New York: Harcourt, 1968.
1926 ———. *Ballooning Adventures of Paddy Pork.* New York: Harcourt, 1969.
1927 ———. *Creepy Castle.* New York: Atheneum, 1975.
1928 ———. *An Edwardian Summer.* New York: Atheneum, 1976.
1929 ———. *Jacko.* New York: Harcourt, 1972.
1930 ———. *Midnight Adventures of Kelly, Dot & Esmeralda.* New York: Atheneum, 1973.
1931 ———. *Naughty Nancy.* New York: Atheneum, 1975.
1932 ———. *Paddy Pork's Holiday.* New York: Atheneum, 1976.
1933 ———. *Paddy's Evening Out.* New York: Atheneum, 1973.
1934 ———. *Paddy's New Hat.* New York: Atheneum, 1980.
1935 ———. *Shrewbetinna's Birthday.* New York: Harcourt, 1971.
1936 ———. *Surprise Picnic.* New York: Atheneum, 1977.
1937 Gordon, Stephen F. *Making Picture-Books, a Method of Learning Graphic Sequence.* New York: Van Nostrand, 1973.
1938 Gottlieb, Suzanne. *What Is Red?* Illus by Vladimer Bobri. New York: Lothrop, 1961.
1939 Goudey, Alice E. *Butterfly Time.* Illus by Adrienne Adams. New York: Scribner, 1964.
1940 ———. *The Day We Saw the Sun Come Up.* Illus by Adrienne Adams. New York: Scribner, 1961.
1941 ———. *Here Come the Dolphins!* Illus by Garry MacKenzie. New York: Scribner, 1961.
1942 ———. *Here Come the Raccoons!* Illus by Garry MacKenzie. New York: Scribner, 1959.
1943 ———. *Here Come the Whales!* Illus by Garry MacKenzie. New York: Scribner, 1956.
1944 ———. *Houses From the Sea.* Illus by Adrienne Adams. New York: Scribner, 1959. Paperback.
1945 Graboff, Abner. *Do Catbirds Wear Whiskers?* New York: Putnam's, 1967.
1946 Graff, Stewart and Polly Anne Graff. *Helen Keller: Toward the Light.* Illus by Paul Frame. Champaign, IL: Garrard, 1965.
1947 Graham, Ada and Frank. *The Milkweed and its World of Animals.* Photos by Les Line. New York: Doubleday, 1976.
1948 ———. *Whale Watch.* Illus by D. Tyler. New York: Delacorte, 1978.
1949 Graham, Al. *Timothy Turtle.* Illus by Tony Palazzo. New York: Viking, 1949. Seafarer paperback.
1950 Graham, Gail B. *The Beggar in the Blanket and Other Vietnamese Tales.* Illus by Bridgette Bryan. New York: Dial, 1970.
1951 Graham, Lorenz B. *David He No Fear.* Illus by Ann Grifalconi. New York: Crowell, 1971.
1952 ———. *Every Man Hear Lay Down.* Illus by Colleen Browning. New York: Crowell, 1970.
1953 ———. *Road Down in the Sea.* Illus by Gregario Prestopino. New York: Crowell, 1971.
1954 Graham, Margaret Bloy. *Be Nice to Spiders.* New York: Harper, 1967.
1955 Graham, Shirley. *The Story of Phyllis Wheatley.* New York: Messner, 1949.
1956 ———. *The Story of Phyllis Wheatley: The Poetess of the American Revolution.* Archway paperback.
1957 Grahame, Kenneth. *The Cambridge Book of Poetry for Children.* Illus by Gwen Raverat. New York: Putnam, 1933.
1958 ———. *The Reluctant Dragon.* Illus by Ernest H. Shepard. New York: Holiday, 1938, 53. M578.
1959 ———. *The River Bank: From Wind in the Willows.* Illus by Adrienne Adams. New York: Scribner, 1973.
1960 ———. *Wind in the Willows.* Illus by Ernest H. Shepard. New York: Scribner, 1933. Dell paperback. M759, M760, M761.
1961 ———. *Wind in the Willows.* Illus by Tasha Tudor. New York: Collins-World, 1966. M759, M760, M761.
1962 Gramatky, Hardie. *Bolivar.* Illus by the author. New York: Putnams, 1961.
1963 ———. *Hercules; the Story of an Old-Fashioned Fire Engine.* Illus by the author. New York: Putnam, 1940.
1964 ———. *Little Toot.* Illus by the author. New York: Putnam, 1939. M380.
1965 *Granger's Index to Poetry,* 6th edition. Edited by William Smith. New York: Columbia University, 1973.
1966 Grant, Bruce. *The Cowboy Encyclopedia, the Old and the New West from the Open Range to the Dude Ranch.* Illus by Jackie and Fiore Mastri. New York: Rand McNally, 1951. Paperback.
1967 Grant, Sandy. *Hey, Look at Me! A City ABC.* Photos by Larry Mulvehill. Scarsdale, N.Y.: Bradbury, 1973.
1968 Graves Robert. *Greek Gods and Heroes.* Illus by Dimitris Davis. New York: Doubleday, 1960.
1969 Graves, William, and National Geographic Society. *Hawaii.* National Geographic Society, 1970.
1970 Grayson, Marion F. *Let's Count and Count Out.* Illus by Deborah D. McClintock. Washington: Robert B. Luce, 1975.
1971 Grayson, Marion. *Let's Do Fingerplays.* Illus by Nancy Weyl. Washington, DC: Luce, 1962.

1972 Green, Margaret, ed. *A Big Book of Animal Fables.* Illus by Janusz Grabianski. New York: Watts, 1965.

1973 Green, Margaret. *The Big Book of Pets.* Illus by Janusz Grabianski. New York: Watts, 1966.

1974 Green, Michael Clifford and B.R.H. Targett. *Space Age Puppets and Masks.* Boston: Plays, 1969.

1975 Green, Norma. *The Hole in the Dike.* Illus by Eric Carle. New York: Crowell, 1974. Scholastic paperback. M289.

1976 Green, Roger L., ed. *The Book of Nonsense.* Illus by Charles Polkard. New York: Dutton, 1956.

1977 Green, Roger Lancelyn. *A Cavalcade of Dragons.* Illus by Krystyna Turkska. New York: Walck, 1970.

1978 ———. *Cavalcade of Magicians.* Illus by Victor Ambrus. New York: Walck, 1973.

1979 ———. *Tales of the Greeks and Trojans.* Illus by Janet and Anne Grahame Johnstone. London: Purnell, 1963.

1980 Greenaway, Kate. *A Apple Pie.* Illus by the author. New York: Warne, 1886.

1981 ———. *Birthday Book for Children.* New York: Warne, 1880.

1982 ———. *Kate Greenaway's Alphabet.* Illus by the author. New York: Warne, 1973. Paperback.

1983 ———. *Kate Greenaway's Birthday Coloring Book.* New York: Dover, 1974.

1984 ———. *Kate Greenaway's Book of Games.* Illus by the author. New York: Viking, 1976.

1985 ———. *Marigold Garden.* Illus by the author. New York: Warne, 1910.

1986 ———. *Under the Window.* Illus by Edmund Evans, and by the author. New York: Warne, 1879.

1987 Greenaway, Kate, ed. *Mother Goose; or The Old Nursery Rhymes.* Illus by the author. New York: Warne, n.d.

1988 Greenbank, Anthony. *A Handbook for Emergencies; Coming Out Alive.* Illus by Jerry Malone and Mel Klapholz. New York: Doubleday, 1976, paperback.

1989a Greene, Bette. *Summer of My German Soldier.* New York: Dial, 1973. Bantam paperback. M656.

1989b ———. *Morning is a Long Time Coming.* New York: Dial, 1977.

1990 Greene, Carla. *How to Know Dinosaurs.* Indianapolis: Bobbs, 1966.

1991 ———. *Let's Learn about the Orchestra.* Illus by Anne Lewis. New York: Harvey, 1967. M315.

1992 ———. *What They Do? Policemen and Firemen.* Illus by Leonard Kessler. New York: Harper, 1962.

1993 ———. *Where Does a Letter Go?* Illus by Leonard Kessler. New York: Harvey, 1966.

1994 Greene, Constance C. *A Girl Called Al.* Illus by Byron Barton. New York: Viking, 1969. Dell paperback.

1995 ———. *I Know You, Al.* Illus by Byron Barton. New York: Viking, 1975. Dell paperback.

1996 ———. *The Unmaking of Rabbit.* New York: Viking, 1972. Dell paperback.

1997 Greene, Ellin. *Clever Cooks; a Concoction of Stories, Charms, Recipes, and Riddles.* Illus by Trina Schart Hyman. New York: Lothrop, 1973.

1998 Greene, Ellin and Madalynne Schoenfeld. *A Multi-Media Approach to Children's Literature, A Selective List of films, filmstrips and recordings based on children's books.* Chicago: ALA, 1972.

1999 ———. *Recordings Based on Children's Books.* Chicago: ALA paperback, 1972.

2000 Greene, Graham. *Little Fire Engine.* Illus by Edward Ardizzone. New York: Doubleday, 1973.

2001 Greenfeld, Howard. *Books from Writer to Reader.* New York: Crown, 1976.

2002a ———. *Chanukah.* New York: Holt, 1976.

2002b ———. *Passover.* New York: Holt, 1978.

2003 ———. *Rosh Hashanah and Yom Kippur.* New York: Holt, 1979.

2004 Greenhow, Jean. *Costumes for Nursery Tale Characters.* Boston: Plays, 1975.

2005 ———. *Making Costume Dolls.* New York: Watson-Guptill, 1972.

2006 Gregg, Ernest. *And the Sun God Said: That's Hip.* Illus by Flacon Beaze. New York: Harper, 1972.

2007 Gregor, Arthur. *1, 2, 3, 4, 5 Verses.* Photos by Robert Doisneau. Philadelphia: Lippincott, 1956.

2008 Gretz, Susanna. *Teddy Bears, One to Ten.* Chicago: Follett, 1969.

2009 Grifalconi, Ann. *City Rhythms.* Illus by the author. Indianapolis: Bobbs, 1965.

2010 Grigson, Geofrey and Jane. *More Shapes and Stories, a Book About Pictures.* New York: Vanguard, 1967.

2011 Grimm, Jacob and Wilhelm. *About Wise Men and Simpletons: Twelve Tales from Grimm.* Trans by Elizabeth Shub and Nonny Hogrogian. New York: Macmillan, 1971.

2012 ———. *The Bremen Town Musicians.* Illus by Paul Galdone. New York: McGraw, 1963.

2013 ———. *Cinderella.* Illus by Otto S. Svend. Trans by Anne Rogers. New York: Larousse, 1978.

2014 ———. *The Complete Grimm's Fairy Tales.* Intro by Padraic Colum. Illus by Joseph Scharl. New York: Pantheon, 1972.

2015 ———. *The Fisherman and His Wife.* Illus by Madeline Gerkiere. New York: Pantheon, 1957. M211.

2016 ———. *The Fisherman and His Wife.* Illus by Elizabeth Shub. Trans by Monika Laimgruber. New York: Greenwillow, 1978. M211.

2017 ———. *The Fisherman and His Wife.* Illus by Margot Zemach. New York: Norton, 1966. M211.

2018 ———. *The Four Clever Brothers.* Illus by Felix Hoffman. New York: Harcourt, 1967.

2019 ———. *Grimm's Fairy Tales.* Trans by Mrs. E.V. Lucas, Lucy Crane and Miriam Edwardes. Illus by Fritz Kredel. New York: Grosset, 1945.

2020 ———. *Grimm's Fairy Tales.* Intro by Frances Clarke Sayers. Illus by children of 15 countries. Chicago: Follett, 1968.

2021 ———. *Grimm's Fairy Tales for Young and*

Old. Trans by Ralph Manheim. New York: Doubleday, 1977.

2022 ———. *Hans in Luck.* Illus by Felix Hoffman. New York: Atheneum, 1975.

2023 ———. *Hansel and Gretel.* Illus by Adrienne Adams. New York: Scribner, 1975. Paperback.

2024 ———. *Hansel and Gretel.* Illus by Arnold Lobel. New York: Delacorte, 1971.

2025 ———. *Hansel and Gretel; a Story of the Forest.* Illus by Warren Chappell. Music by Engelbert Humperdinck. New York: Knopf, 1944. M636.

2026 ———. *Household Stories from the Collection of the Brothers Grimm.* Trans by Lucy Crane. Illus by Walter Crane. New York: McGraw, 1964.

2027 Grimm Brothers. *Jorinda and Joringel.* Trans by Elizabeth Shub. Illus by Adrienne Adams. New York: Scribner's, 1968.

2028 ———. *King Grisley-Beard.* Illus by Maurice Sendak. New York: Farrar, 1973.

2029 ———. *King Thrushbeard.* Illus by Felix Hoffman. New York: Harcourt, 1970.

2030 ———. *King Thrushbeard.* Illus by Kurt Werth. New York: Viking, 1968.

2031 ———. *Little Red Riding Hood.* Illus by Bernadette Watts. Cleveland: World, 1968.

2032 Grimm. *The Musicians of Bremen.* Illus by Svend S. Otto. New York: Larousse, n.d. M469.

2033 ———. *Punch and the Magic Fish.* Retold and illus by Luzzati Emanuel. New York: Pantheon, 1972.

2034 ———. *Rapunzel.* Retold and illus by Felix Hoffman. New York: Harcourt, 1960.

2035 ———. *Rumpelstiltskin.* Illus by Jacqueline Ayer. New York: Harcourt, 1967.

2036 ———. *Rumpelstiltskin.* Translated by Edith Tarcov. Illus by Edward Gorey. New York: Four Winds, 1973. Scholastic paperback.

2037 ———. *Rumpelstiltskin.* Illus by William Stobbs. New York: Walck,1970.

2038 ———. *The Seven Ravens.* Illus by Felix Hoffman. New York: Harcourt, 1963.

2039 ———. *The Shoemaker and the Elves.* Illus by Adrienne Adams. New York: Scribner, 1960. Paperback. M609.

2040 ———. *Six Companions Find Their Fortune.* Illus by Lilo Fromm. Garden City, NY: Doubleday, 1969.

2041 ———. *The Sleeping Beauty.* Illus by Felix Hoffman. New York: Harcourt, 1960.

2042 ———. *Snow White and Rose Red.* Retold and illus by Barbara Cooney. New York: Delacorte, 1965.

2043 ———. *Snow White and Rose Red.* Translated by Wayne Andrews. Illus by Adrienne Adams. New York: Scribner's, 1964.

2044 ———. *Snow White and the Seven Dwarfs.* Trans and Illus by Wanda Gag. New York: Coward, 1939.

2045 ———. *Snow White and the Seven Dwarfs.* Translated by Paul Heins. Illus by Trina S. Hyman. Boston: Little, 1974.

2046 ———. *Snow White and the Seven Dwarfs.* Trans by Randall Jarrell. Illus by Nancy Ekholm Burkert. New York: Farrar, 1972.

2047 ———. *The Twelve Dancing Princesses.* Illus by Adrienne Adams. New York: Holt, 1966. Owlet paperback.

2048 ———. *The Twelve Dancing Princesses.* Illus by Elizabeth Shub. New York: Scribner, 1966.

2049 ———. *The Traveling Musicians.* Illus by Hans Fischer. New York: Harcourt, 1955.

2050 ———. *The Valiant Little Tailor.* Illus by Anne Marie Jauss. New York: Harvey, 1967.

2051 ———. *The Wolf and the Seven Little Kids.* Illus by Felix Hoffman. New York: Harcourt, 1959.

2052 ———. *The Wolf and the Seven Little Kids.* Illus by Otto S. Svend. New York: Larousse, 1977.

2053 Gringhuis, Dirk. *Giants, Dragons and Gods; Constellations and their Folklore.* Illus by the author. New York: Meredith, 1968.

2054 Groh, Lynn. *The Pilgrims; Brave Settlers of Plymouth.* Illus by Frank Vaughn. New York: Garrard, 1968.

2055 Grolier. *The New Book of Knowledge.* 20 Volumes. New York: Grolier, 1977.

2056 Grolier. *The Ocean World of Jacques Cousteau.* 20 Volumes. Danbury, CT: Danbury, 1974.

2057 Gross, Ruth. *Hansel and Gretel.* Illus by Margot Tomes. New York: Scholastic, 1974. Paperback.

2058 Gross, Sarah Chokla. *Every Child's Book of Verse.* Illus by Marta Cone. New York: Watts, 1968.

2059a Grossbart, Francine. *A Big City.* Illus by the author. New York: Harper, 1966.

2059b Grosser, Morton. *The Snake Horn.* Boston: Hall, 1973.

2060 Grossman, Barney and Gladys Groom and the Children of PS 150 Bronx. *Black Means...* Illus by Charles Bible. New York: Hill and Wang, 1970.

2061 Grossman, Jean. *How to Use Hand Puppets in Group Discussion.* New York: Play Schools Association, 1952.

2062 Grosvenor, Donna K. *The Blue Whale.* Illus by Larry Foster. Washington, D.C.: National Geographic, 1977.

2063 Gruenberg, Sidonie Matsner, ed. *All Kinds of Courage, Stories About Boys and Girls of Yesterday and Today.* Illus by James Lewicki. Garden City, NY: Doubleday, 1962.

2064 Gruenberg, Sidonie M. *Favorite Stories, Old and New.* Illus by Kurt Wiese. Garden City, NY: Doubleday, 1955.

2065 ———. *Let's Read a Story.* Illus by Virginia Parsons. Garden City, NY: Doubleday, 1957.

2066 ———. *More Favorite Stories Old and New for Boys and Girls.* Illus by Kurt Wiese. Garden City, NY: Doubleday, 1948, 1960.

2067 Grynne, Harold. *The Rainbow Book of Bible Stories.* Illus by Steele Savage. Cleveland: World, 1956.

2068 Guggenmos, Josef and Irmgard Lucht. *Wonder-Fish From the Sea.* Trans by Alvin Tresselt. New York: Parents, 1971.

2069 Guirma, Frederic. *Princess of the Full Moon.* Trans by John Garrett. New York: Macmillan, 1970.

2070 Gullan, Marjorie. *Poetry Speaking for Children.* Boston: Expression, 1973.

2071 Gunther, Bernard. *Sense Relaxation Below Your Mind.* New York: Macmillan, 1968. Collier paperback.

2072 Guterman, Norbert, trans. from Afanas Ev, Alexander. *Russian Fairy Tales.* New York: Pantheon, 1945, 1975.

2073 Haacken, Frans, illus. *Peter and the Wolf.* Music by Serge Prokofieff. New York: Watts, 1961. M521.

2074 Haddad, Helen R. *Potato Printing.* Illus by the author. New York: Crowell, 1981.

2075 *Hader, Berta and Elmer. *Big Snow.* Illus by the author. New York: Macmillan, 1948. Collier paperback. M82.

2076 Halacy, D.S., Jr. *Whale Spotters.* New York: Macmillan, 1958.

2077 Hale, Linda. *The Glorious Christmas Soup Party.* Illus by the author. New York: Viking, 1962.

2078 Hale, Lucretia. *The Peterkin Papers.* Illus by Harold Bratt. Boston: Houghton, 1924. Dover paperback.

2079 Haley, Alex. *Roots.* New York: Doubleday, 1976. Dell paperback. M586.

2080 Haley, Gail E. *Costumes for Plays and Playing.* New York: Methuen, 1978.

2081 ———. *Go Away, Stay Away.* Illus by the author. New York: Scribner, 1977. M249.

2082 ———. *The Green Man.* Illus by the author. New York: Scribner, 1980. M707b.

2083 ———. *Jack Jouette's Ride.* Illus by the author. New York: Viking, 1973.

2084 ———. *Noah's Ark.* Illus by the author. New York: Atheneum, 1971.

2085 *———. *A Story, A Story.* Illus by the author. New York: Atheneum, 1970. Aladdin paperback. M641.

2086 Hall, Anna Gertrude. *Cyrus Holt and the Civil War.* Illus by Dorothy Bayley Morse. New York: Viking, 1964.

2087 *Hall, Donald. *The Ox-Cart Man.* Illus by Barbara Cooney. New York: Viking, 1979.

2088 ———. *The Riddle Rat.* Illus by Mort Gerberg. New York: Warne, 1977.

2089 Hall, Edward. *The Hidden Dimension.* New York: Doubleday, 1966. Anchor paperback.

2090 ———. *The Silent Language.* New York: Doubleday, 1959. Anchor paperback.

2091 Hall, Lynn. *Careers for Dog Lovers.* Chicago: Follett, 1978. Paperback.

2092 ———. *Kids and Dog Shows.* Chicago: Follett, 1974.

2093 ———. *Shadows.* Illus by Joseph Cellini. Chicago: Follett, 1977.

2094 ———. *Sticks and Stones.* Chicago: Follett, 1972. Dell paperback.

2095 Hall-Quest, Olga. *How the Pilgrims Came to Plymouth.* Illus by James MacDonald. New York: Dutton, 1946.

2096 Hamilton, Edith. *Mythology.* Illus by Steele Savage. Boston: Little, 1942. NAL paperback.

2097 Hamilton, Hamish. *Secret Birthday Message.* London: Hamish Hamilton, 1971.

2098 Hamilton, Virginia. *The House of Dies Drier.* Illus by Eros Keith. New York: Macmillan, 1968. Paperback.

2099 ———. *M.C. Higgins the Great.* New York: Macmillan, 1974. Paperback.

2100 ———. *The Planet of Junior Brown.* New

York: Macmillan, 1971. Paperback. M540.

2101 ———. *Zeely.* Illus by Symeon Shimin. New York: Macmillan, 1967. Paperback. M782.

2102 Hamre, Leif. *Edge of Disaster.* New York: Harcourt, 1960.

2103 ———. *Leap Into Danger.* New York: Harcourt, 1966. Voyager paperback.

2104 ———. *Operation Arctic.* Trans by Dag Ryen. New York: Atheneum, 1973.

2105 Handford, Robert. *The Complete Book of Puppets and Puppeteering.* New York: Drake, 1975.

2106 *Handforth, Thomas. *Mei Li.* New York: Doubleday, 1938. M296

2107 *Handy Key to Your National Geographics; Subject and Picture Locater, 1915-1981,* 5th edition. Williamsville, NY: Charles S. Underhill, 1982.

2108 Hanley, Hope. *Fun with Needlepoint.* New York: Scribner, 1972.

2109 Hanson, Joan. *Antonyms, Hot and Cold and Other Words That Are as Different as Day and Night.* Minneapolis: Lerner, 1972.

2110 ———. *Homographic Homophones: Fly and Fly and Other Words That Look and Sound the Same But Are as Different in Meaning as Bat and Bat.* Minneapolis: Lerner, 1973.

2111 ———. *Homographs: Bow and Bow and Other Words That Look the Same But Sound as Different as Sow and Sow.* Minneapolis: Lerner, 1972.

2112 ———. *Homonyms, Hair and Hare and Other Words That Sound the Same But Look as Different as Bear and Bare.* Minneapolis: Lerner, 1972.

2113 ———. *More Antonyms, Wild and Tame and Other Words That Are as Different in Meaning as Work and Play.* Minneapolis: Lerner, 1973.

2114 ———. *More Homonyms: Steak and Stake and Other Words That Sound the Same But Look as Different as Chili and Chilly.* Minneapolis: Lerner, 1973.

2115 ———. *More Synonyms: Shout and Yell and Other Words That Mean the Same Thing But Look and Sound as Different as Loud and Noisy.* Minneapolis: Lerner, 1973.

2116 ———. *Similes: As Gentle as a Lamb, Spin Like a Top, and Other "Like" or "As" Comparisons Between Unlike Things.* Minneapolis: Lerner, 1976.

2117 ———. *Sound Words: Jingle, Buzz, Sizzle and Other Words That Imitate the Sounds Around Us.* Minneapolis: Lerner, 1976.

2118 ———. *Still More Antonyms: Together and Apart and Other Words That Are as Different in Meaning as Rise and Fall.* Minneapolis: Lerner, 1976.

2119 ———. *Still More Homonyms: Night and Knight and Other Words That Sound the Same But Look as Different as Ball and Bawl.* Minneapolis: Lerner, 1976.

Harcourt Reading Series. See Early, M.

2120 Hardendorff, Jeanne B., ed. *Just One More.* Illus by Don Bolognese. Philadelphia: Lippincott, 1969.

2121 ———. *Sing Song Scuppernong.* Illus by Jacqueline Chwast. New York: Holt, 1974.

2122 Hark, Mildred and Noel McQueen. *Junior*

Plays for all Occasions. Boston: Plays, 1955, 1969.

2123 Harkoven, Helen B. *Farms and Farmers in Art.* Minneapolis: Lerner, 1965.

2124 Harnden, Ruth. *Runaway Raft.* Illus by Marvin Friedman. Boston: Houghton, 1968.

2125 Harper, Wilhelmina. *Easter Chimes, Stories for Easter and the Spring Season.* Illus by Hoot von Zitzewitz. New York: Dutton, 1965.

2126 ———. *Ghosts and Goblins, Stories for Halloween.* Illus by William Wiesner. New York: Dutton, 1965.

2127a ———. *The Harvest Feast, Stories of Thanksgiving, Yesterday and Today.* Illus by W.T. Mars. New York: Dutton, 1965.

2127b Harris, Albert J. *Better Than Gold.* New York: Macmillan, 1974.

2128a ———. *More Than Words.* New York: Macmillan, 1974.

2128b Harris, Aurand. *Six Plays for Children.* Austin: University of Texas, 1977.

2129 Harris, Christie. *Once Upon a Totem.* Illus by John Frazer Mills. New York: Atheneum, 1963.

2130 ———. *Once More Upon a Totem.* New York: Atheneum, 1973.

2131 Harris, Christie. *Raven's Cry.* Illus by Bill Reid. New York: Atheneum, 1967.

2132 Harris, Dorothy J. *School Mouse.* New York: Warne, 1977.

2133 Harris, Joel Chandler. *Complete Tales of Uncle Remus.* Compiled by Richard Chase. Illus by Arthur B. Frost. Boston: Houghton, 1955.

2134 Harris, Louise Dyer and Norman Dyer. *Flash, the Life Story of a Firefly.* Illus by Henry B. Kane. Boston: Little, 1966.

2135a Harris, Rosemary. *The Moon in the Cloud.* New York: Macmillan, 1968.

2135b ———. *The Shadow on the Sun.* New York: Macmillan, 1970.

2136 Harrison, David L. *The Big Book of Giant Stories.* Illus by Philippe Fix. New York: McGraw, 1972.

2137 Harrison, Harry. *The Men From P.I.G. and R.O.B.O.T.* New York: Atheneum, 1978.

2138 Harshaw, Ruth and Hope H. Evans. *In What Book?* New York: Macmillan, 1970.

2139 Hart, Tony. *Young Designer.* New York: Warne, 1967.

2140 Haskett, Edythe Rance. *Grains of Pepper, Folk Tales from Liberia.* Illus by Musa Miatta. New York: Day, 1967.

2141 Haskins, James. *Always Movin' On, the Life of Langston Hughes.* New York: Watts, 1976.

2142 ———. *The Life and Death of Martin Luther King, Jr.* New York: Lothrop, 1977.

2143 Hatch, Mary C. *More Danish Tales.* Illus by Edgun. New York: Harcourt, 1949.

2144 Haugaard, Erik. *Orphans of the Wind.* Illus by Milton Johnson. Boston: Houghton, 1966. Dell paperback.

2145 Hautzig, Esther (Rudomin). *In the Park; an Excursion in Four Languages.* Illus by Ezra Jack Keats. New York: Macmillan, 1968.

2146 Haviland, Virginia. *Children and Literature. Views and Reviews.* Glenview, Ill.: Scott Foresman, 1973.

2147 ———. *Favorite Fairy Tales Told in England.* Illus by Bettina. Boston: Little, 1959.

2148 ———. *Favorite Fairy Tales Told in France.* Illus by Roger Duvoisin. Boston: Little, 1959.

2149 ———. *Favorite Fairy Tales Told in Germany.* Illus by Susanne Suba. Boston: Little, 1959.

2150 ———. *Favorite Fairy Tales Told in India.* Illus by Blair Lent. Boston: Little, 1973.

2151 ———. *Favorite Fairy Tales Told in Ireland.* Illus by Arthur Marokvia. Boston: Little, 1961.

2152 ———. *Favorite Fairy Tales Told in Italy.* Illus by Evaline Ness. Boston: Little, 1965.

2153 ———. *Favorite Fairy Tales Told in Norway.* Illus by Leonard Weisgard. Boston: Little, 1961.

2154 ———. *Favorite Fairy Tales Told in Poland.* Illus by Felix Hoffmann. Boston: Little, 1963.

2155 ———. *Favorite Fairy Tales Told in Russia.* Illus by Herbert Donska. Boston: Little, 1961.

2156 ———. *Favorite Fairy Tales Told in Scotland.* Illus by Adrienne Adams. Boston: Little, 1963.

2157 ———. *Favorite Fairy Tales Told in Spain.* Illus by Barbara Cooney. Boston: Little, 1963.

2158 ———. *Favorite Fairy Tales Told in Sweden.* Illus by Roni Solbert. Boston: Little, 1966.

2159 Haviland, Virginia, ed. *The Fairy Tale Treasury.* Illus by Raymond Briggs. New York: Coward, 1972.

2160 Hawes, Bill. *The Puppet Book.* San Diego: Beta, 1977.

2161 Hawes, Judy. *Fireflies in the Night.* Illus by Kazue Mizumura. New York: Crowell, 1963.

2162 Hawkins, Quail. *Androcles and the Lion.* Illus by Rocco Negri. New York: Coward, 1970.

2163 Hawkinson, John. *Let Me Take You on a Trail.* Illus by the author. Chicago: Whitman, 1972.

2164 ———. *Collect, Print and Paint from Nature.* Illus by the author. Chicago: Whitman, 1963.

2165 ———. *More Collect, Print and Paint from Nature.* Illus by the author. Chicago: Whitman, 1964.

2166 ———. *Old Stump.* Illus by the author. Chicago: Whitman, 1965.

2167 ———. *Our Wonderful Wayside.* Illus by the author. Chicago: Whitman, 1966.

2168 ———. *Paint a Rainbow.* Illus by the author. Chicago: Whitman, 1970.

2169 ———. *Pastels are Great!* Illus by the author. Chicago: Whitman, 1968.

2170 ———. *Where the Wild Apples Grow.* Illus by the author. Chicago: Whitman, 1967.

2171 Hay, Helen. *An Egg is for Wishing.* Illus by Yaroslava. New York: Abelard, 1966.

2172 Hays, Wilma Pitchford. *Pilgrim Thanksgiving.* New York: Coward, 1955.

2173 ———. *Samuel Morse and the Electronic Age.* New York: Watts, 1960.

2174 Haycraft, Howard, ed. *Boys' Book of Great Detective Stories.* New York: Harper, 1938.

2175 ———. *The Boys' Second Book of Great Detective Stories.* New York: Harper, 1940.

2176 Haywood, Carolyn. *Annie Pat and Eddie.* Illus by the author. New York: Morrow, 1960.

2177 ———. *Away Went Balloons.* Illus by the author. New York: Morrow, 1973.

2178 ———. *B is for Betsy.* Illus by the author. New York: Harcourt, 1939. Voyager paperback.

2179 ———. *Back to School with Betsy.* Illus by the author. New York: Harcourt, 1943.

2180 ———. *Betsy and Billy.* Illus by the author. New York: Harcourt, 1941.

2181 ———. *Betsy and Mister Kilpatrick.* Illus by the author. New York: Morrow, 1967.

2182 ———. *Betsy and the Boys.* Illus by the author. New York: Harcourt, 1945.

2183 ———. *Betsy and the Circus.* Illus by the author. New York: Morrow, 1954.

2184 ———. *Betsy's Busy Summer.* Illus by the author. New York: Morrow, 1956.

2185 ———. *Betsy's Little Star.* Illus by the author. New York: Morrow, 1950.

2186 ———. *Betsy's Play School.* Illus by the author. New York: Morrow, 1977.

2187 ———. *Betsy's Winterhouse.* Illus by the author. New York: Morrow, 1958.

2188 ———. *C is for Cupcake.* Illus by the author. New York: Morrow, 1974.

2189 ———. *A Christmas Fantasy.* Illus by the author. New York: Morrow, 1972.

2190 ———. *Eddie and Gardenia.* Illus by the author. New York: Morrow, 1951.

2191 ———. *Eddie's Big Deals.* Illus by the author. New York: Morrow, 1955.

2192 ———. *Eddie and Louella.* Illus by the author. New York: Morrow, 1959.

2193 ———. *Eddie and the Fire Engine.* Illus by the author. New York: Morrow, 1949.

2194 ———. *Eddie Makes Music.* Illus by the author. New York: Morrow, 1957.

2195 ———. *Eddie the Dog Holder.* Illus by the author. New York: Morrow, 1966.

2196 ———. *Eddie's Green Thumb.* Illus by the author. New York: Morrow, 1964.

2197 ———. *Eddie's Happenings.* Illus by the author. New York: Morrow, 1971.

2198 ———. *Eddie's Pay Dirt.* Illus by the author. New York: Morrow, 1953.

2199 ———. *Eddie's Valuable Property.* Illus by the author. New York: Morrow, 1975.

2200 ———. *Every-Ready Eddie.* Illus by the author. New York: Morrow, 1968.

2201 ———. *Here Comes the Bus.* Illus by the author. New York: Morrow, 1963.

2202 ———. *Here's a Penny.* Illus by the author. New York: Voyager paperback, 1965.

2203 ———. *Little Eddie.* Illus by the author. New York: Morrow, 1947.

2204 ———. *Merry Christmas from Betsy.* Illus by the author. New York: Morrow, 1970.

2205 ———. *Mixed-up Twins.* Illus by the author. New York: Morrow, 1952.

2206 ———. *Penny and Peter.* Illus by the author. New York: Morrow, 1946.

2207 ———. *Penny Goes to Camp.* Illus by the author. New York: Morrow, 1948.

2208 ———. *Robert Rows the River.* Illus by the author. New York: Morrow, 1966.

2209 ———. *Snowbound with Betsy.* Illus by the author. New York: Morrow, 1962.

2210 ———. *Taffy and Melissa Molasses.* Illus by the author. New York: Morrow, 1969.

2211 ———. *Two and Two are Four.* Illus by the author. New York: Harcourt, 1940.

2212 ———. *A Valentine Fantasy.* Illus by the author. New York: Morrow, 1976.

2213 Hazeltine, Alice I. *Hero Tales from Many Lands.* Illus by Gordon Laite. New York: Abingdon, 1961.

2214 Hazeltine, Alice I. and Elva S. Smith. *The Easter Book of Legends and Stories.* Illus by Pamela Bianco. New York: Lathrop, 1947.

2215 ———. *The Year Around, Poems for Children.* New York: Abingdon, 1956.

2216 Hazen, Barbara Shook. *Where Do Bears Sleep?* Illus by Ian E. Staunton. Reading, Mass.: Addison-Wesley, 1970.

2217 Headley, Frederick. *Light and Color.* Illus by Patricia Hamilton. New York: Day, 1962.

2218 Heady, Eleanor B. *Make Your Own Dolls.* Illus by Harold Heady. New York: Lathrop, 1974.

2219 Heaps, Willard A. *Superstitious!* New York: Nelson, 1972.

Heath Reading Series. See Witty, Paul A.

2220 Heinig, Ruth and Lyda Stillwell. *Creative Dramatics for the Classroom Teacher.* Englewood Cliffs, NJ: Prentice-Hall, 1974.

2221 Heinlein, Robert. *Citizen of the Galaxy.* New York: Scribner, 1957. Ace paperback.

2222 ———. *Have Space Suit, Will Travel.* New York: Scribner, 1977. Ace and Ballantine paperbacks.

2223 ———. *Rocket Ship Galileo.* New York: Scribner, 1947. Ace and Ballantine paperbacks.

2224 ———. *Starman Jones.* Illus by Clifford Gearu. New York: Scribner, 1953. Ballantine paperback.

2225 ———. *Time for the Stars.* New York: Scribner, 1956. Ace paperback.

2226 Heilbroner, Joan. *This is the House Where Jack Lives.* Illus by Aliki. New York: Harper, 1962.

2227 Helfman, Elizabeth S. *Signs and Symbols Around the World.* New York: Lothrop, 1967.

2228 Helfman, Harry Carmozin. *Making Pictures Move.* Illus by Willard Goodman. New York: Holt, 1969.

2229 Heller, Jules. *Printmaking Today; an Introduction to the Graphic Arts.* New York: Holt, 1958.

2230 Heller, Linde. *Lily at the Table.* New York: Macmillan, 1979.

2231 Hellman, Hal. *Communications in the World of the Future.* New York: Evans, 1969.

2232 Helms, Randel. *Tolkien's World.* Boston: Houghton, 1974. Paperback.

2233 Henderson, Harold G. *Haiku in English.* Rutland, VT: Tuttle, 1967.

2234 ———. *An Introduction to Haiku, An Anthology of Poems and Poets from Basho to Shiki.* New York: Doubleday, 1958. Anchor paperback.

2235 Hendricks, Gay and Thomas Roberts. *The Second Centering Book; More Awareness Activities for Children, Parents, and Teachers.* Englewood Cliffs, NJ: Prentice-Hall, 1977.

2236 Hennings, Dorothy. *Smiles, Nods and Pauses, Activities to Enrich Children's Communication Skills.* New York: Scholastic, 1974. Paperback.

2237 Henry, Marguerite. *Album of Dogs.* Illus by Wesley Dennis. Chicago: Rand McNally, 1970.

2238 ——. *Album of Horses.* Illus by Wesley Dennis. Chicago: Rand McNally, 1951.

2239 ——. *All About Horses.* Illus by Wesley Dennis. New York: Random, 1962.

2240 ——. *Benjamin West and His Cat Grimalkin.* Illus by Wesley Dennis. Indianapolis: Bobbs, 1947.

2241 ——. *Black Gold.* Illus by Wesley Dennis. Chicago: Rand McNally, 1957. Paperback.

2242 ——. *Born to Trot.* Illus by Wesley Dennis. Chicago: Rand McNally, 1950. Paperback.

2243 ——. *Brighty of the Grand Canyon.* Illus by Wesley Dennis. Chicago: Rand McNally, 1953. Paperback. M102.

2244 ——. *Justin Morgan Had a Horse.* Illus by Wesley Dennis. Chicago: Rand McNally, 1954. M342.

2245 ——. *King of the Wind.* Illus by Wesley Dennis. Chicago: Rand McNally, 1948. Paperback. M343.

2246 ——. *Misty of Chincoteague.* Illus by Wesley Dennis. Chicago: Rand McNally, 1947. Paperback. M456, M457.

2247 ——. *Mustang, Wild Spirit of the West.* Illus by Robert Lougheed. Chicago: Rand McNally, 1966. Paperback.

2248 ——. *Sea Star, Orphan of Chincoteague.* Illus by Wesley Dennis. Chicago: Rand McNally, 1949. Paperback. M598.

2249 ——. *Stormy, Misty's Foal.* Illus by Wesley Dennis. Chicago: Rand McNally, 1963. Paperback.

2250 ——. *White Stallion of Lipizza.* Illus by Wesley Dennis. Chicago: Rand, 1964.

2251 Henry, O. *The Ransom of Red Chief.* Illus by Paul Frame. New York: Hawthorn, 1970.

2252 Herbert, Don. *Mr. Wizard's Experiments for Young Scientists.* Illus by Dan Noonan. New York: Doubleday, 1959.

2253 Herring, Ann King. *Peter and the Wolf.* Illus by Kozo Shimizu. Photos by Yasuji Yajima. Music by Serge Prokofieff. Tokyo: Gakken, 1969. M521.

2254 Herriot, James. *All Creatures Great and Small.* New York: St Martin, 1972. Bantam paperback.

2255 ——. *All Things Bright and Beautiful.* New York: St. Martin, 1974. Bantam paperback.

2256 ——. *All Things Wise and Wonderful.* New York: St. Martin, 1977. Bantam paperback.

2257 ——. *James Heriott's Yorkshire.* New York: St. Martin, 1979. Paperback.

2258 ——. *The Lord God Made Them All.* New York: St. Martin, 1981.

2259 Herzel, Catherine. *Christmas Is Today.* Cleveland: World, 1971.

2260 Hess, Lilo. *Foxes in the Woodshed.* Photos by the author. New York: Scribner, 1966.

2261 ——. *Mouse and Company.* Photos by the author. New York: Scribner, 1972.

2262 ——. *Rabbits in the Meadow.* New York: Crowell, 1963.

2263 ——. *A Snail's Pace.* New York: Scribner, 1974.

2264 Hickman, Janet. *Valley of the Shadow.* New York: Macmillan, 1974.

2265 Hightower, Florence. *The Ghost of Follonsbee's Folly.* Illus by Ati Forberg. Boston: Houghton, 1958.

2266 Higonnet-Schnapper, Janet, Tr. *Tales from Atop a Russian Stove.* Illus by Franz Altschuler. Chicago: Whitman, 1973.

2267 Hilder, Rowland. *Starting with Watercolor.* New York: Watson-Guptill, 1966.

2268 Hildick, E.W. *The Case of the Secret Scribbler.* Illus by Lisl Weil. New York: Macmillan, 1978.

2269 Hill, Elizabeth Starr. *Ever-After Island.* New York: Dutton, 1977.

2270 Hill, Kay. *More Glooscap Stories, Legends of the Wabanaki Indians.* Illus by John Hamberger. New York: Dodd, 1970.

2271 Hilte, Kathryn. *When Noodlehead Went to the Fair.* Illus by Wendy Watson. New York: Parents, 1968.

2272 Hine, Al. *This Land is Mine; An Anthology of American Verse.* Illus by Leonard Vosburgh. Philadelphia: Lippencott, 1965.

2273 Hirsch, S. Carl. *Printing From a Stone, the Story of Lithography.* New York: Viking, 1967.

2274 Hirsh, Marilyn. *Could Anything Be Worse?* Illus by the author. New York: Holiday, 1974. M150.

2275 ——. *The Hanukkah Story.* New York: Bonim, 1977.

2276 ——. *How the World Got Its Color.* New York: Crown, 1972.

2277 Hitchcock, Alfred, ed. *Alfred Hitchcock's Haunted Houseful.* New York: Random, 1961.

2278 Hitte, Kathryn and William D. Hayes. *Mexicali Soup.* Illus by Ann Rockwell. New York: Parents, 1970.

2279 Hoban, Lillian. *Arthur's Christmas Cookies.* Illus by the author. New York: Harper, 1972.

2280 ——. *Arthur's Honey Bear.* Illus by the author. New York: Harper, 1974.

2281 ——. *Sugar Snow Spring.* Illus by the author. New York: Harper, 1973.

2282 Hoban, Russell. *A Baby Sister of Frances.* Illus by Lillian Hoban. New York: Harper, 1964. Trophy paperback. M53.

2283 ——. *A Bargain for Frances.* Illus by Lillian Hoban. New York: Harper, 1970. M56.

2284 ——. *Bedtime for Frances.* Illus by Garth Williams. New York: Harper, 1960. Trophy paperback. M71.

2285 ——. *Best Friends for Frances.* Illus by Lillian Hoban. New York: Harper, 1968. Trophy paperback. M76.

2286 ——. *Birthday for Frances.* Illus by Lillian Hoban. New York: Harper, 1968. Trophy paperback. M87.

2287 ——. *Bread and Jam for Frances.* Illus by Lillian Hoban. New York: Harper, 1964. Scholastic paperback. M97.

2288 ——. *Dinner at Alberto's.* Illus by James Marshall. New York: Crowell, 1975.

2289 ——. *Egg Thoughts, and Other Frances Songs.* Illus by Lillian Hoban. New York: Harper, 1972.

2290 ——. *The Mole Family's Christmas.* Illus by Lillian Hoban. New York: Parents, 1969. M460.

2291 Hoban, Russell and Sylvie Selig. *Ten What? A Mystery Counting Book.* New York: Scribners, 1974. M679.

2292 Hoban, Tana. *Big Ones, Little Ones.* New

York: Greenwillow, 1976.

2293 ————. Circles, Triangles and Squares. New York: Macmillan, 1974.

2294 ————. Count and See. New York: Macmillan, 1972. Paperback.

2295 ————. Is it Red? Is it Yellow? Is it Blue? An Adventure in Color. New York: Greenwillow, 1978.

2296 ————. Look Again. New York: Macmillan, 1971.

2297 ————. Over, Under, and Through and Other Spatial Concepts. New York: Macmillan, 1973.

2298 ————. Push, Pull, Empty Full, a Book of Opposites. New York: Macmillan, 1972. Paperback.

2299 ————. Shapes and Things. New York: Macmillan, 1970.

2300 ————. Where Is It? New York: Macmillan, 1974.

2301 Hoberman, Mary Ann. All My Shoes Come in Twos. Illus by Norman Hoberman. New York: Little, 1957.

2302 ————. Buggs: Poems. Illus by Victoria Chees. New York: Viking, 1976.

2303 ————. Hello and Good-by. Illus by Norman Hoberman. Boston: Little, 1959.

2304 ————. A Little Book of Little Beasts. Illus by Peter Parnall. New York: Simon and Schuster, 1973.

2305 ————. The Looking Book. Illus by Jerry Joyner. New York: Knopf, 1973.

2306 ————. Nuts to You and Nuts to Me: an Alphabet Book of Poems. Illus by Ronni Sobwrt. New York: Knopf, 1974.

2307 ————. The Raucous Auk: A Menagerie of Poems. New York: Viking, 1973.

2308 Hobson, Sam B. and George Carey. The Lion of the Kalahari. Trans and adapted by Esther Linfield. New York: Greenwillow, 1976.

2309 Hodges, Elizabeth J. Three Princes of Serendip. Illus by Jane Corwin. New York: Atheneum, 1964.

2310 Hodges, Margaret. The Fire Bringer, A Payute Indian Legend. Illus by Peter Parnall. Boston: Little, 1972.

2311 ————. The Wave. Illus by Blair Lent. Boston: Houghton, 1964.

2312 Hoff, Syd. Barkley. New York: Harper, 1975.

2313 ————. Dinosaur Do's and Don'ts. New York: Dutton, 1975.

2314 ————. When Will It Snow? Illus by Mary Chalmers. New York: Harper, 1971.

2315 Hoffman, Charles. American Indians Sing. Illus by Nicholas Amorosi. New York: Day, 1967.

2316 Hoffman, Felix. The Story of Christmas. Illus by the author. New York: Atheneum, 1975.

2317 Hoffman, Miriam S. and Eva A Samuels. Authors and Illustrators of Children's Books: Writing on their Lives and Work. New York: Bowker, 1972.

2318 Hofsinde, Robert. Indian Arts. Illus by the author. New York: Morrow, 1971.

2319 ————. Indian Costumes. Illus by the author. New York: Morrow, 1968.

2320a ————. Indian Picture Writing. Illus by the author. New York: Morrow, 1959.

2320b ————. Indian Sign Language. Illus by the author. New York: Morrow, 1956.

2321 Hogan, Carol. Eighteen Cousins. Illus by Beverly Komada. New York: Parents, 1968.

2322 Hogben, Lancelot. Wonderful World of Communication. Garden City, NY: Garden City Books, 1959.

2323 Hogner, Dorothy Childs. Grasshoppers and Crickets. Illus by Nils Hogner. New York: Crowell, 1960.

2324 ————. Snails. Illus by Nils Hogner. New York: Crowell. 1958.

2325 Hogrogian, Nonny. Apples. New York: Macmillan, 1972.

2326 ————. The Contest, an Armenian Folktale. Illus by the author. New York: Greenwillow, 1976.

2327* ————. One Fine Day. Illus by the author. New York: Macmillan, 1971. Collier paperback. M499.

2328 ————. The Renowned History of Little Red Riding Hood. Illus by the author. New York: Crowell, 1967.

2329 Hogrogian, Nonny, illus. The Thirteen Days of Yule. New York: Crowell, 1968.

2330 Hoke, Helen. The Big Book of Jokes. New York: Watts, 1971.

2331 ————. The First Book of Dolls. New York: Watts, 1954.

2332 ————. Hoke's Jokes, Cartoons & Funny Things. New York: Watts, 1976.

2333 ————. Jokes and Fun. New York: Watts, 1973.

2334 ————. Jokes, Giggles & Guffaws. New York: Watts, 1975.

2335 ————. Jokes, Jokes, Jokes. New York: Watts, 1963.

2336 ————. More Jokes, Jokes, Jokes. New York: Watts, 1975.

2337 Hoke, Helen, ed. Witches, Witches, Witches. Illus by W. R. Lohse. New York: Watts, 1958.

2338 Hoke, Helen and Valerie Pitt. Whales. Illus by Thomas R. Funderburk. New York: Watts, 1973.

2339 Holl, Adelaide. Let's Count. Illus by Lucinda McQueen. Reading, MA: Addison-Wesley, 1976.

2340 ————. Moon Mouse. Illus by Cyndy Szeheres. New York: Random, 1969. Paperback.

2341 ————. The Rain Puddle. Illus by Roger Duvoisin. New York: Lothrop, 1965.

2342 ————. The Remarkable Egg. Illus by Roger Duvoisin. New York: Lothrop, 1968.

2343 ————. Small Bear's Name Hunt. Drawings by Pat Bargielski. Champaign, IL: Garrard, 1977.

2344 Holland, Marion. A Big Ball of String. New York: Beginner, 1958.

2345 Holland, Viki. How to Photograph Your World. New York. Scribners, 1974.

2346 Holling, Holling Clancy. Book of Indians. Illus by the author and Lillian Holling. New York: Platt, 1935.

2347 ————. Minn of the Mississippi. Illus by the author. Boston: Houghton, 1951.

2348 ————. Paddle-to-the-Sea. Illus by the author. Boston: Houghton, 1941. M517.

2349 ————. Pagoo. Illus by the author and Lillian Holling. Boston: Harcourt, 1957. M645.

2350 ———. *Seabird.* Illus by the author. Boston: Houghton, 1948.

2351 ———. *Tree in the Trail.* Illus by the author. Boston: Houghton, 1942.

2352 Hollowell, Lillian, ed. *A Book of Children's Literature,* 3rd ed. New York: Holt, 1966.

2353 Holm, Anne. *North to Freedom.* Trans by L. W. Kingsland. New York: Harcourt, 1965. Paperback.

2354 ———. *Peter.* Trans by L. W. Kingsland. New York: Harcourt, 1968.

2355 Holman, Felice. *Slake's Limbo.* New York: Scribners, 1974. Dell paperback.

2356 Holme, Bryan. *Drawings to Live With.* New York: Viking, 1966.

2357 Holmes, Oliver Wendell. *The Deacon's Masterpiece of the Wonderful One-Horse Shay.* Illus by Paul Galdone. New York: McGraw, 1965.

2358 Holsaert, Eunice and Robert Gartland. *A Book to Begin on, Dinosaurs.* New York: Holt, 1959.

Holt Reading Series. See Martin, Bill, Jr. and Peggy Brogan.

2359 Holter, Patra. *Photography Without a Camera.* New York: Van Nostrand, 1972.

2360 Hood, Flora, ed. *The Turquoise Horse, Prose and Poetry of the American Indian.* Illus by Marylou Reifsnyder. New York: Putnam, 1972.

2361 Hooker, Ruth. *Kennaquhair.* Illus by Al Michini. New York: Abingdon, 1976.

2362 Hooney, F. Louis. *Art Activities for the Very Young from Three to Six Years.* Worcester, MA: Davis, 1961. Paperback.

2363 Hooper, Grizella H. *Puppet Making Through the Grades.* Worcester, MA: Davis, 1966.

2364 Hoople, Cheryl G. *The Heritage Sampler: A Book of Colonial Arts and Crafts.* Illus by Richard Cuffari. New York: Dial, 1975.

2365 Hope-Simpson, Jacynth. *A Cavalcade of Witches.* Illus by Krystyna Turska. New York: Walck, 1967.

2366 Hopkins, Lee B. *Books are by People: Interviews with 104 Authors and Illustrators of Books for Young Children.* Scholastic, 1969.

2367 ———. *More Books by More People: Interviews with 65 Authors of Books for Children.* New York: Scholastic, 1974. Paperback.

2368 ———. *This Street's for Me!* Illus by Ann Grifalconi. New York: Crown, 1970.

2369 Hopkins, Lee Bennett, ed. *A-Haunting We Will Go: Ghostly Stories and Poems.* Racine, WI: Whitman, 1977.

2370 ———. *City Talk.* Photos by Roy Aranella. New York: Knopf, 1970.

2371 ———. *Girls Can Too! A Book of Poems.* Illus by Emily McCully. New York: Watts, 1972.

2372 ———. *Hey-How for Halloween.* Illus by Janet McCaffery. New York: Harcourt, 1974.

2373 ———. *Kits, Cats, Lions and Tigers.* Illus by Vera Rosenberry. Chicago: Whitman, 1979.

2374 ———. *Me! A Book of Poems.* Illus by Talivaldis Stubis. New York: Seabury, 1970.

2375 ———. *Monsters, Ghoulies and Creepy Creatures.* Racine, WI: Whitman, 1977.

2376 ———. *Pups, Dogs, Foxes and Wolves.* Illus by Vera Rosenberry. Racine, WI: Whitman, 1979.

2377 ———. *Witching Time; Mischievous Stories and Poems.* Illus by Vera Rosenberry. Racine, WI: Whitman, 1977.

2378 Hopkinson, Francis. *The Battle of the Kegs.* Illus by Paul Galdone. New York: Crowell, 1964.

2379 Hopf, Alice L. *Biography of a Rhino.* Illus by Kiyo Komoda. New York: Putnam, 1972.

2380 ———. *Misunderstood Animals.* New York: McGraw, 1973.

2381 ———. *Pigs, Wild and Tame.* New York: Holiday, 1979.

2382 Hopp, Zinken. *The Magic Chalk.* Trans by Suzanne H. Bergendahl. Illus by Malvin Neset. New York: McKay, 1959.

2383 Horder, Mervyn. *On Christmas Day, First Carols to Play and Sing.* Illus by Margaret Gordon. Music by M. Horder. New York: Macmillan, 1969.

2384 ———. *The Season for Singing, American Christmas Songs and Carols.* Music by Seymour Barab. Garden City: NY: Doubleday, 1974.

2385 ———. *Sweetly Sings the Donkey; Animal Rounds for Children to Sing or Play on Recorders.* Illus by Nancy Winslow. New York: Atheneum, 1976.

2386 Horizon, editors of. *Pharaohs of Egypt.* New York: American Heritage, 1965.

2387 Horn, Geoffrey and Arthur Cavanaugh. *Bible Stories for Children.* Illus by Arvis Stewart. New York: Macmillan, 1980.

2388 Horovitz, Betty, Hilda Lewis and Mark Luca. *Understanding Children's Art for Better Teaching.* Columbus, Ohio: Merrill, 1967.

2389a Horwitz, Elinor Lander. *A Child's Garden of Sculpture.* Photos by Joshua Horwitz. Washington, D.C.: Washingtonian Books, 1976.

2389b ———. *When the Sky is Like Lace.* Philadelphia: Lippincott, 1975.

2390 ———. *Contemporary American Folk Artists.* Photos by Joshua Horwitz. Philadelphia: Lippincott, 1975.

2391 ———. *The Strange Story of the Frog who Became a Prince.* Illus by John Heinley. New York: Delacorte, 1971.

2392 ———. *When the Sky Is Like Lace.* Philadelphia: Lippincott, 1975.

2393 Hosea, Tobias and Lisa Baskin. *Hosie's Alphabet.* Illus by Leonard Baskin. New York: Viking, 1972.

2394 Hosford, Dorothy. *By His Own Might, the Battles of Beowulf.* Illus by Lazlo Matulay. New York: Holt, 1947.

2395 Hosiers, John. *The Sorcerer's Apprentice and Other Stories.* New York: Walck, 1961. M354, M360, M625.

2396 Houston, James, ed. *Songs of the Dream People; Chants and Images from the Indians and Eskimos of North America.* Illus by James Houston. New York: Atheneum, 1972.

2397 Howard, Elizabeth. *North Wind Blows Free.* New York: Morrow, 1949. Paperback.

2398 Howard, Jane. *Please Touch: A Guided Tour of the Human Potential Movement.* New York: McGraw, 1970. Dell paperback.

2399 Howard, Vanessa. *A Screaming Whisper.* Photos by J. Pinderhughes. New York: Holt, 1972.

2400 Howard, Vernon. *Pantomimes, Charades, and Skits.* Illus by Doug Anderson. New York: Sterling, 1974.

2401 ———. *Puppet and Pantomime Plays.* Illus by Doug Anderson. New York: Sterling, 1962.

2402 Howard, Vernon, ed. *The Complete Book of Children's Theatre.* Illus by Doug Anderson, et al. Garden City, NY: Doubleday, 1969.

2403 Hsieh, Tehayi, trans. and ed. *Chinese Village Folk Tales.* Boston: Bruce Humphries, 1948.

2404 Hubbard, Alice and Adeline Babbitt. *The Golden Flute, an Anthology of Poetry for Young Children.* New York: Day, 1932.

2405 Huber, Marian Blanton. *Story and Verse for Children.* Illus by Boris Artzybasheff. New York: Macmillan, 1940, 1965.

2406 Hubp, Loretta B., ed. *Que Sera? What Can It Be? Traditional Spanish Riddles.* Illus by Mircea Vasilus. New York: Day, 1970.

2407 Huck, Charlotte S. and Doris Y. Kuhn. *Children's Literature in the Elementary School.* New York: Holt, 1976.

2408 Huckleberry, Alan and Edward Strother. *Speech Education for the Elementary Teacher.* Boston: Allyn and Bacon, 1972.

2409 Huffard, Grace Thompson and Laura Mae Carlyle and Helen Ferris. *My Poetry Book, An Anthology of Modern Verse for Boys and Girls.* Illus by Willy Pogany. New York: Holt, 1956.

2410 Hughes, Langston. *Don't You Turn Back.* Selected by Lee Bennett Hopkins. Illus by Ann Grifalconi. New York: Knopf, 1969.

2411 ———. *The Dream Keeper and Other Poems.* Illus by Helen Sewell. New York: Knopf, 1932. M550.

2412 ———. *Famous American Negroes.* New York: Dodd, 1954.

2413 ———. *Famous Negro Heroes of America.* Illus by Gerald McCann. New York: Dodd, 1958.

2414 ———. *Famous Negro Music Makers.* New York: Dodd, 1955.

2415 ———. *The First Book of Jazz.* Illus by Cliff Roberts. Music by David Martin. New York: Watts, 1955.

2416 ———. *Selected Poems of Langston Hughes.* New York: Knopf, 1959. M550.

2417 ———. *Selected Poems of Langston Hughes.* New York: Random paperback, n.d. M550.

2418 Hughes, Ted. *Meet My Folks.* Illus by Mila Lazarerich. Indianapolis: Bobbs, 1973.

2419 ———. *Moon-Whales and Other Moon Poems.* Illus by Leonard Baskin. New York: Viking, 1976.

2420 ———. *Season Songs.* Illus by Leonard Baskin. New York: Viking, 1975.

2421 Hume, Lotta. *Favorite Children's Stories from China and Tibet.* Illus by Lo Koon Chiu. Rutland, VT: Tuttle, 1962.

2422a Humphrey, Henry. *What Is It For?* New York: Simon and Schuster, 1969.

2422b ———. *What's Inside?* New York: Simon and Schuster, 1972.

2423 Hunt, Ben. *Ben Hunt's Beginning Book of Whittling.* New York: Macmillan, 1970.

2424 Hunt, Douglas and Kari Hunt. *Pantomime: The Silent Theater.* Illus by the authors. New York: Atheneum, 1964.

2425 Hunt, Irene. *Across Five Aprils.* Illus by Albert John Pucci. Chicago: Follett, 1964. Tempo paperback. M2.

2426 Hunt, Kari and Bernice Carlson. *Masks and Mask Makers.* Nashville, Abingdon, 1961.

2427 Hunt, Mabel Leigh. *Better Known as Johnny Appleseed.* Illus by James Daugherty. Philadelphia: Lippincott, 1950.

2428 Hunter, Edith Fisher. *Child of the Silent Night.* Boston: Houghton, 1963. Dell paperback.

2429 Hunter, Molly. *Walking Stones, a Story of Suspense.* Illus by Trina Schart Hyman. New York: Harper, 1970. Trophy paperback.

2430 Huntington, Harriet E. *Let's Go to the Desert.* Photos by the author. Garden City, NY: Doubleday, 1949.

2431 ———. *Praying Mantis.* Garden City, NY: Doubleday, 1957.

2432 Hurd, Edith Thatcher. *Last One Home is a Green Pig.* Illus by Clement Hurd. New York: Harper, 1959.

2433 ———. *The Mother Kangaroo.* Illus by Clement Hurd. Philadelphia: Little, 1976.

2434 ———. *The Mother Owl.* Illus by Clement Hurd. Boston: Little, 1974.

2435 ———. *The Mother Whale.* Illus by Clement Hurd. Little: 1973.

2436 ———. *Starfish.* New York: Crowell, 1962.

2437 Hurlimann, Bettina. *Picture-Book World, Modern Picture-Books for Children from Twenty-five Countries.* Transl by Brian W. Alderson. Cleveland: World, 1969.

2438 ———. *William Tell and his Son.* Illus by Paul Nussbaumer. New York: Harcourt, 1967. M358, M757.

2439 Hurlimann, Ruth. *The Cat and Mouse who Shared a House.* Trans by Anthea Bell. Illus by the author. New York: Walck, 1973.

2440 ———. *The Mouse with the Daisy Hat.* New York: David White, 1971.

2441 Hurwitz, Johanna. *Busybody Nora.* New York: Morrow, 1976. Dell paperback.

2442 Huus, Helen. *Children's Books to Enrich the Social Studies.* National Council of Teachers of Social Studies, 1966.

2443 Hussey, Lois J. and Catherine Pessino. *Collecting Cocoons.* Illus by Isabel Sherwin Harris. New York: Crowell, 1953.

2444 Hutchings, Margaret. *Making and Using Finger Puppets.* New York: Taplinger, 1973.

2445 ———. *Making New Testament Toys.* New York: Taplinger, 1972. Hawthorn paperback.

2446 ———. *Making Old Testament Toys.* New York: Taplinger, 1972. Hawthorn paperback.

2447 ———. *Toys from the Tales of Beatrix Potter.* New York: Warne, 1973.

2448 Hutchins, Pat. *The Best Train Set Ever.* Illus by the author. New York: Greenwillow, 1978.

2449 ———. *Changes Changes.* New York: Macmillan, 1973. Collier paperback. M119, M120.

2450 ———. *Clocks and More Clocks.* Illus by the author. New York: Macmillan, 1970.

2451 ———. *Don't Forget the Bacon.* Illus by the author. New York: Greenwillow, 1976.

2452 ———. *Good-Night, Owl!* Illus by the author. New York: Macmillan, 1972. Paperback.

2453 ———. *Rosie's Walk.* Illus by the author. New York: Macmillan, 1968. Paperback.

M587, M588.

2454 ———. *The Silver Christmas Tree.* Illus by the author. New York: Macmillan, 1974.

2455 ———. *The Surprise Party.* Illus by the author. New York: Macmillan, 1969. Collier paperback. M661.

2456 ———. *The Wind Blew.* Illus by the author. New York: Macmillan, 1974.

2457 Hutchins, Ross E. *Lives of an Oak Tree.* Illus by Jerome P. Connally. Chicago: Rand, 1962.

2458 Hutchinson, Veronica S. *Candlelight Stories.* Illus by Lois Lenski. New York: Putnam, 1928.

2459 ———. *Chimney Corner Stories, Tales for Little Children.* Illus by Lois Lenski. New York: Putnam, 1925.

2460 ———. *Fireside Stories.* Illus by Lois Lenski. New York: Putnam, 1927.

2461 Hutton, Warwick. *The Sleeping Beauty.* Illus by the author. New York: Atheneum, 1979.

2462 Hyde, Dayton O. *Strange Companion: A Story of Survival.* New York: Dutton, 1975. Fawcett paperback.

2463 Hylander, Clarency. *The Macmillan Wild Flower Book.* Illus by Edith F. Johnston. New York: Macmillan, 1954.

2464 Hymes, James L. and Lucia. *Oodles of Noodles and Other Rhymes.* Illus by Leonard Kessler. New York: Young Scott, 1964.

2465 Hyndman, Robert Utley. *Chinese Mother Goose Rhymes.* Illus by Ed Young. Cleveland: World, 1968.

2466 Icenhower, Joseph. *The First Book of the Antarctic.* New York: Watts, 1956, 1971.

2467 Ichikawa, Satomi. *A Child's Book of Seasons.* New York: Parents, 1975.

2468 Ipcar, Dahlov. *The Biggest Fish in the Sea.* New York: Viking, 1972.

2469 ———. *Brown Cow Farm.* Illus by the author. New York: Doubleday, 1959. M103.

2470 ———. *The Cat Came Back.* Illus by the author. New York: Knopf, 1971.

2471 ———. *The Queen of Spells.* New York: Viking, 1973. Dell paperback.

2472 ———. *The Song of the Day Birds and the Night Birds.* Garden City, NY: Doubleday, 1967.

2473 ———. *Stripes and Spots.* Illus by the author. New York: Doubleday, 1961.

2474 ———. *Whisperings and Other Things.* New York: Knopf, 1967.

2475 ———. *The Wonderful Egg.* Illus by the author. New York: Doubleday, 1958.

2476 Ipsen, D. C. *The Riddle of the Stegosarus.* Reading, MA: Addison-Wesley, 1969.

2477 Ireland, Norma O., Comp. *Index to Fairy Tales, 1949-1972, Including Folklore, Legends and Myths in Collections.* Westwood, MA: Faxon, 1973.

2478 ———. *Index to Fairy Tales, 1973-1977 Including Folklore, Legends and Myths in Collection.* 4th Supplement. New York: Faxon, 1979.

2479 Irion, Ruth Hershey. *The Christmas Cookie Tree.* Philadelphia: Westminster, 1976.

2480 Irving, Washington. *Rip Van Winkle.* Illus by Arthur Rackham. Philadelphia: Lippincott, 1967.

2481 Irwin, Keith. *The Romance of Writing; from Egyptian Hieroglyphics to Modern Letters,* *Numbers and Signs.* New York: Viking, 1956.

2482 Isadora, Rachel. *Ben's Trumpet.* Illus by R. Isador. New York: Greenwillow, 1979. M74.

2483 Ishii, M. *The Dolls' Day for Yoshiko.* Trans by Yone Mizuta. Illus by Mamoru Funai. Chicago: Follett, 1966.

2484 Issa. *A Few Flies and I; Haiku.* Compiled by Jean Merrill and Ronni Solbert. Trans by R. H. Blyth and Nobuyuki Yuasa. Illus by Ronni Solbert. New York: Pantheon, 1969.

2485 ———. *Don't Tell the Scarecrow and Other Japanese Poems.* Illus by Talivaldis Stubis. New York: Four Winds, 1969. Scholastic paperback.

2486a Itse, Elizabeth M., ed. *Hey, Bug! and Other Poems About Little Things.* Illus by Susan Carlton Smith. New York: American Heritage, 1972.

2486b Itten, Johannes. *The Art of Color.* Stamford, CT: Van Nostrand. 1973.

2487 Ivimey, John W. *The Adventures of the Three Blind Mice.* Illus by Nola Langner. New York: Scholastic paperback, 1965. M8, M369.

2488 ———. *The Complete Version of Ye Three Blind Mice.* Illus by Walton Corbould. New York: Warne, 1928. M146, M147, M369.

2489 Jablow, Alta & Carl Withers. *The Man in the Moon: Sky Tales from Many Lands.* Illus by Peggy Wilson. New York: Holt, 1969.

2490 Jackson, C. Paul. *How to Play Better Football.* Illus by Leonard Kessler, New York: Crowell, 1972.

2491a Jackson, Jacqueline. *Missing Melinda.* Illus by Irene Burns. Boston: Little, 1967.

2491b Jackson, Jesse, *Call Me Charley.* New York: Harper, 1945.

2492a ———. *Tessie.* New York: Dell, 1969.

2492b Jackson, Kathryn. *Days of the Dinosaurs.* Illus by Jay H. Matternes. Washington, D.C.: National Geographic, 1973. Sold only in a set with *Dogs Working for People, Lion Cubs, Treasures in the Sea.*

2493a Jacobs, Allan D. and Leland B. *Arithmetic in Verse and Rhyme.* Illus by Kelly Oechali. Campaign, IL: Garrard, 1971.

2493b ———. *Sports and Games in Verse and Rhyme.* Champaign, IL: Garrard, 1975.

2494 Jacobs, Frances. *Finger Play and Action Rhymes.* Photos. New York: Lothrop, 1941.

2495 Jacobs, Francine. *Leggs of the Moon.* Illus by Rocco Negri. New York: Coward, 1971.

2496 Jacobs, Joseph. *English Fairy Tales.* Illus by John Batten. New York: Dover, 1898. Paperback.

2497 ———. *English Fairy Tales.* New York: Schocken paperback, 1967.

2498 ———. *European Folk and Fairy Tales.* Illus by John D. Batten. New York: Putnam, 1967.

2499 ———. *Indian Fairy Tales.* Illus by John D. Batten. New York: Putnam, n.d. Children's Literature Reprint Series, 1976.

2500 ———. *Jack the Giant Killer.* Illus by Fritz Wegner. New York: Walck, 1970.

2501 ———. *More English Folk and Fairy Tales.* Illus by John D. Batten. New York: Putnam, n.d.

2502 ———. *More English Fairy Tales.* New York: Schocken, 1968.

2503 ———. *The Pied Piper and Other Fairy Tales of Joseph Jacobs.* Illus by James Hill. New York: Macmillan, 1963.

2504 ———. *Tom Tit Tot.* Illus by Evaline Ness. New York: Scribners, 1965.

2505 Jacobs, Leland B. *Animal Antics in Limerick Land.* Illus by Edward Malsberg. Champaign, IL: Garrard, 1971.

2506 ———. *Funny Folks in Limerick Land.* Champaign, IL: Garrard, 1971.

2507 ———. *Holiday Happenings in Limerick Land.* Champaign, IL: Garrard, 1972.

2508 ———. *Is Somewhere Always Far Away?* Illus by John Johnson. New York: Holt, 1967. Owlet paperback.

2509 ———. *Poems About Fur and Feather Friends.* Champaign, IL: Garrard, 1971.

2510 ———. *Poetry for Autumn.* Illus by Stina Nagel. Champaign, IL: Garrard, 1968.

2511 ———. *Poetry for Bird Watchers.* Champaign, IL: Garrard, 1970.

2512 ———. *Poetry for Summer.* Champaign, IL: Garrard, 1970

2513 ———. *Poetry for Winter.* Champaign IL: Garrard, 1970.

2514 ———. *Poetry for Witches, Elves and Goblins.* Illus by Frank Aloise. Champaign, IL: Garrard, 1970.

2515a Jacobs, Joseph. *Master of All Masters.* Illus by Ann Rockwell. New York: Grosset, 1972.

2515b Jacobs, Lou. *Instant Photography.* New York: Lothrop, 1976.

2516 Jacobson, Helen. *The First Book of Mythical Beasts.* New York: Watts, 1960.

2517 Jagendorf, Moritz A. *The Merry Men of Gotham.* Illus by Shane Miller. New York: Vanguard, 1950.

2518 ———. *Noodlehead Stories from Around the World.* New York: Vanguard, 1957.

2519 ———. *Penny Puppets, Penny Theatre, and Penny Plays.* Illus by Fletcher Clark. Indianapolis: Bobbs, 1941.

2520 ———. *Puppets for Beginners.* Illus by Jean Michener. Boston: Plays, 1966.

2521 ———. *Sand in the Bag and Other Folk Stories of Ohio, Indiana and Illinois.* New York: Vanguard, 1952.

2522 ———. *Stories and Lore of the Zodiac.* New York: Vanguard, 1976.

2523a Jameson, Cynthia. *The Clay Pot Boy.* Illus by Arnold Lobel. New York: Coward, 1973.

2523b Janice. *Little Bear's Christmas.* New York: Lothrop, 1964.

2524a ———. *Little Bear Learns to Read the Cookbook.* Illus by Mariana. New York: Lothrop, 1969.

2524b ———. *Little Bear Marches in the St. Patrick's Day Parade.* New York: Lothrop, 1973.

2525a ———. *Little Bear's Pancake Party.* Illus by Mariana. New York: Lothrop, 1960.

2525b ———. *Little Bear's Thanksgiving.* New York: Lothrop, 1967.

2526 Janitch, Valerie. *Country Collage.* Radnor, PA: Chilton, 1975. Paperback.

2527 Janson, Horst and Dora J. *The Picture History of Painting, from Cave Painting to Modern Times.* New York: Abrams, 1957.

2528 Janvier, Jennine. *Fabulous Birds You Can Make.* Photos by Jean-Pierre Lesson. New York: Sterling, 1976.

2529 Jarrell, Randall. *The Bat Poet.* Illus by Maurice Sendak. New York: Macmillan, 1964. M57.

2530 ———. *A Rat is Born.* Illus by John Schoenker. New York: Doubleday, 1977.

2531 Jarvis, Sally. *Fried Onions and Marshmallows and Other Plays for Little People.* Illus by Franklin Luke. New York: Parents, 1968.

2532 Jeffers, Susan. *All the Pretty Horses.* Illus by the author. New York: Macmillan, 1967. Scholastic paperback. M369, M680.

2533 ———. *Wild Robin.* Illus by the author. Dutton, 1976. M755.

2534 Jeffers, Susan, illus. *Three Jovial Huntsmen: A Mother Goose Rhyme.* Scarsdale, N.Y.: Bradbury, 1973. Puffin paperback.

2535 Jeffries, Roderic. *Trapped.* New York: Harper, 1972. Trophy paperback.

2536 Jennett, Sean. *The Making of Books,* 4th ed. New York: Praeger, 1967.

2537 Jeschke, Susan. *Sidney.* New York: Holt, 1975.

2538 John, Timothy. *The Great Song Book.* Music by Peter Hankey. Illus by Tomi Ungerer. Garden City, NY: Doubleday, 1978.

2539 Johnson, Annabel & Edgar. *The Grizzley.* New York: Harper, 1946. Trophy paperback. Scholastic paperback.

2540 Johnson, Clifton. *What They Say in New England and Other Folklore.* New York: Columbia University Press, 1963.

2541 Johnson, Crockett. *Harold and the Purple Crayon.* Illus by the author. New York: Harper, 1958. M269, M270.

2542 ———. *Harold's ABC.* Illus by the author. New York: Harper, 1963.

2543 ———. *Harold's Circus.* Illus by the author. New York: Harper, n.d.

2544 ———. *Harold's Fairy Tale.* Illus by the author. New York: Harper, 1956. M271, M272.

2545 ———. *Harold's Trip to the Sky.* Illus by the author. New York: Harper, 1957.

2546 ———. *A Picture for Harold's Room.* Illus by the author. New York: Harper, 1960. Scholastic paperback. M530, M531.

2547 Johnson, Edna, et al. *Anthology of Children's Literature,* 4th edition. Boston: Houghton, 1970.

2548 ———. *Anthology of Children's Literature,* 5th edition. Boston: Houghton, 1976.

2549 Johnson, Hannah. *Hello, Small Sparrow.* Illus by Tony Chen. New York: Lothrop, 1971.

2550 Johnson, Ilse and Nika. *Cookies and Bread, the Baker's Art.* Photos by Ferdinand Boesch. New York: Bonanza, 1967.

2551 Johnson, James Weldon and J. Rosamond. *Lift Every Voice and Sing.* Illus by Moselle Thompson. New York: Hawthorn, 1970.

2552 Johnson, Lillian. *Papier-mâché.* New York: McKay, 1958.

2553 ———. *Sculpture, the Basic Methods and Materials.* New York: McKay, 1960.

2554 Johnson, M. S., et al. *Each and All.* New York: American Book Co., 1971.

2555 ———. *Gold and Silver*. New York: American Book Co., 1971.

2556 Johnson, Sally Patrick. *The Harper Book of Princes*. Illus by Janina Domanska. New York: Harper, 1964.

2557 Johnson, Sylvia A. *Animals of the Desert*. Illus by Alcuin C. Dornisch. Minneapolis: Lerner, 1976.

2558 Johnston, Johanna. *The Story of the Barber of Seville, Based on the Opera by Gioacchino Rossini*. New York: Putnam, 1966. M55.

2559 ———. *Sugerplum*. New York: Knopf, 1955.

2560a Johnston, Norma. *Glory in the Flower*. New York: Atheneum, 1974.

2560b ———. *The Keeping Days*. New York: Atheneum, 1973.

2561 Jonas, Arthur. *New Ways in Math*. Illus by Alihi. Englewood Cliffs, NJ: Prentice-Hall, 1962.

2562 ———. *More New Ways in Math*. Illus by Alihi. Englewood Cliffs, NJ: Prentice-Hall, 1964.

2563 Jones, Elizabeth. *Big Susan*. New York: Macmillan, 1967.

2564 Jones, G.P. *Easy-to-Make Dolls with 19th Century Costumes*. New York: Dover, 1974.

2565 Jones, Gwyn. *Scandinavian Legends and Folk-Tales*. Illus by Joan Kiddell-Monroe. London: Oxford, 1965.

2566 Jones, Hettie. *In Search of the Castaways*. New York: Pocket Books, 1978.

2567 ———. *Longhouse Winter, Iroquois Transformation Tales*. Illus by Nicholas Gaetano. New York: Holt, 1972.

2568 Jones, Hettie, ed. *Trees Stand Shining, Poetry of the North American Indians*. Illus by Robert Andrew Parker. New York: Dial, 1971. Pied Piper paperback.

2569 Jones, Weyman. *Edge of Two Worlds*. Illus by J.C. Kocisis. New York: Dial, 1968. Dell paperback.

2570 Jordan, June. *His Own Where*. New York: Crowell, 1971. Dell paperback.

2571 ———. *Who Look at Me*. New York: Crowell, 1969.

2572 Jordan, June and Terri Bush. *The Voice of the Children: Writings by Black and Puerto Rican Young People*. New York: Holt, 1970. Pocket Books paperback.

2573a Jordan, Nina R. *American Costume Dolls*. New York: Harcourt, 1941.

2573b ———. *Homemade Dolls in Foreign Dress*. New York: Harper, 1939.

2574 Joseph, Helen Haiman. *A Book of Marionettes*. New York: Viking, 1936.

2575 Joseph, Joseph Maron and Sara Lee Lippincott. *Point to the Stars*. New York: McGraw, 1977.

2576 Joslin, Sesyle. *What Do You Do Dear*. Illus by Maurice Sendak. Reading, Mass.: Addison Wesley, 1961. M734.

2577 ———. *What Do You Say, Dear*. Illus by Maurice Sendak. Reading, Mass.: Addison-Wesley, 1958. Scholastic paperback. M735.

2578 Joyner, Nina Glenn. *Dollhouse Construction and Restoration*. New York: Chilton, 1977. Paperback.

2579 Juchen, Aurel von. *The Holy Night: the Story of the First Christmas*. Illus by Celestino Piatti. Trans by Cornelia Schaeffer. New York: Atheneum, 1968. M292.

2580 Judson, Clara Ingram. *Benjamin Franklin*. Illus by Robert Frankenberg. Chicago: Follett, 1957.

2581 ———. *St. Lawrence Seaway*. Illus by Lorence F. Bjorklund. Chicago: Follett, 1959.

2582 ———. *Theodore Roosevelt, Fighting Patriot*. Illus by Lorence F. Bjorklund. Chicago: Follett, 1953.

2583 Juster, Norton. *The Phantom Tollbooth*. Illus by Jules Feiffer. New York: Random, 1961. Paperback.

2584 Justus, May. *Tale of a Pig, Adaptation of an American Folk Song*. Illus by Frank Aloise. Nashville: Abingdon, 1963.

2585 Kahl, Virginia. *Baron's Booty*. Illus by the author. New York: Scribners, 1963.

2586 ———. *The Duchess Bakes a Cake*. Illus by the author. New York: Scribners, 1955. Paperback. M184.

2587 ———. *Gunhilde and the Halloween Spell*. Illus by the author. New York: Scribners, 1975.

2588 ———. *Habits of Rabbits*. Illus by the author. New York: Scribner, 1957.

2589 ———. *How Do You Hide a Monster*. Illus by the author. New York: Scribner, 1971.

2590 ———. *Maxie*. Illus by the author. New York: Scribner, 1956.

2591 ———. *The Perfect Pancake*. Illus by the author. New York: Scribner, 1960.

2592 ———. *Plum Pudding for Christmas*. Illus by the author. New York: Scribner, 1956.

2593 Kahane, Melani. *There's a Decorator in Your Doll House*. New York: Atheneum, 1968.

2594 Kamerman, Sylvia, ed. *Children's Plays from Favorite Stories*. Boston: Plays, 1970.

2595 ———. *Dramatized Folk Tales of the World*. Boston: Plays, 1971.

2596 ———. *Fifty Plays for Junior Actors*. Boston: Plays, 1966.

2597 ———. *Little Plays for Little Players*. Boston: Plays, 1969.

2598 ———. *Patriotic and Historical Plays for Young People*. Boston: Plays, 1975.

2599 Kampmann, Lothar. *Creating with Puppets*. New York: Van Nostrand, 1972.

2600 Kantrowitz, Mildred. *I Wonder if Herbie's Home Yet*. Illus by Tony DeLuna. New York: Parents, 1971.

2602 Kaplan, Irma. *Swedish Fairy Tales*. Chicago: Follett, 1953, 67.

2603 Kapp, Paul. *A Cat Came Fiddling and Other Rhymes of Childhood*. Illus by Irene Haas. Music by Paul Kapp. New York: Harcourt, 1956.

2604 ———. *Cock-A-Doodle-Doo!* Illus by Anita Lobel. Music by Paul Kapp. New York: Harper, 1965.

2605 Karasz, Ilona, illus. *The Twelve Days of Christmas*. New York: Harper, 1949.

2606 Karl, Jean. *From Childhood to Childhood, Children's Books and their Creators*. New York: Day, 1970.

2607 Kastner, Erich. *Emil and the Detective*. Trans by May Massee. Illus by Walter Frier. New

York: Doubleday, 1955.

2608 Kaufman, John. *Little Dinosaurs and Early Birds*. Illus by the author. New York: Crowell, 1977.

2609 Kaula, Edna Mason. *African Village Folktales*. Illus by the author. New York: World, 1968.

2610 Kay, Evelyn. *The Family Guide to Children's Television, What to Watch, What to Miss, What to Change and How to Do It*. New York: Pantheon, 1974.

2611 Kay, Helen. *Snow Birthday*. Illus by Barbara Cooney. New York: Farrar, 1955.

2612 Kay, George. *Printing*. New York: Roy, 1968.

2613 Keats, Ezra Jack. *Apartment Three*. Illus by the author. New York: Macmillan, 1971. M44, M45.

2614 ———. *Dreams*. Illus by the author. New York: Macmillan, 1974. Paperback.

2615 ———. *Goggles*. Illus by the author. New York: Macmillan, 1969. Paperback. M350, M351.

2616 ———. *Hi Cat!* Illus by the author. New York: Macmillan, 1970. Collier paperback.

2617 ———. *Jeannie's Hat*. Illus by the author. New York: Harper, 1966.

2618 ———. *John Henry, an American Legend*. Illus by the author. New York: Pantheon, 1965. M28, M32, M200, M353.

2619 ———. *Letter to Amy*. Illus by the author. New York: Harper, 1968. M360, M361.

2620 ———. *Louie*. Illus by the author. New York: Greenwillow, 1975. Scholastic paperback.

2621 ———. *The Pet Show*. Illus by the author. New York: Macmillan, 1974. Collier, paperback.

2622 ———. *Peter's Chair*. Illus by the author. New York: Harper, 1967. M523, M524.

2623 *———. *Snowy Day*. Illus by the author. New York: Viking, 1962. Puffin paperback. M617, M618, M619.

2624 ———. *The Trip*. Illus by the author. New York: Greenwillow, n.d. Scholastic paperback.

2625 ———. *Whistle for Willie*. Illus by the author. New York: Viking, 1964. Puffin paperback. M743, M744.

2626 Keats, Ezra Jack, illus. *The Little Drummer Boy*. New York: Macmillan, 1968. Collier paperback. M367, M368.

2627 ———. *Over in the Meadow*. New York: Four Winds, 1971. Scholastic paperback. M510, M511.

2628 Keene, Donald. *Bunraku; the Art of the Japanese Puppet Theatre*. Photos by Kaneko Hiroshi. Tokyo: Kodansha, 1965.

2629 Keeping, Charles. *Charley, Charlotte and the Golden Canary*. London: Oxford University Press, 1967.

2630 ———. *Joseph's Yard*. New York: Watts, 1969.

2631 Keith, Eros. *Prra-ah*. Englewood Cliffs, NJ: Bradbury, 1969.

2632 Keith, Harold. *Rifles for Watie*. New York: Crowell, 1957. M579.

2633 Kelen, Emery. *Mr. Nonsense, a Life of Edward Lear*. Illus by Edward Lear. New York: Nelson, 1973.

2634 Keller, Charles. *Ballpoint Bananas and Other Jokes for Kids*. Englewood Cliffs, NJ: Prentice-Hall, 1973. Paperback.

2635 ———. *Star Spangled Banana and Other Revolutionary Riddles*. Englewood Cliffs, NJ: Prentice-Hall, 1974. Paperback.

2636 Kellog, Remington, et al. *Wild Animals of North America, Fifth Edition*. Washington, DC: National Geographic, 1971.

2637 Kellogg, Steven. *Can I Keep Him?* Illus by the author. New York: Dial, 1971.

2638 ———. *Island of the Skog*. Illus by the author. New York: Dial, 1973. Pied Piper paperback. M321, M322.

2639 ———. *Much Bigger than Martin*. Illus by the author. New York: Dial, 1976.

2640 ———. *Mystery Beast of Ostergeest*. Illus by the author. New York: Dial, 1971.

2641 ———. *Mystery of the Missing Red Mitten*. Illus by the author. New York: Dial, 1974.

2642 ———. *Orchard Cat*. Illus by the author. New York: Dial, 1972.

2643 ———. *Pinkerton, Behave!* Illus by the author. New York: Dial, 1979.

2644 ———. *There Was an Old Woman*. Illus by the author. New York: Parents, 1974.

2645 ———. *Won't Somebody Play With Me?* Illus by the author. New York: Dial, 1972.

2646 Kelly, Eric P. *Trumpeter of Krakow*. Illus by Janina Domanska. New York: Macmillan, 1966. Collier paperback.

2647 Kelly, Regina. *Paul Revere: Colonial Craftsman*. Illus by Harvey Kidder. Boston: Houghton, 1963.

2648a Kelsey, Alice Geer. *Once the Mullah; Persian Folk Tales*. Illus by Kurt Werth. New York: Longmans, 1954.

2648b ———. *Once the Hodja*. NY: Longmans, 1951.

2649 Keltner, John W. *Interpersonal Speech-Communication, Elements and Structure*. Belmont, CA: Wadsworth, 1970.

2650 Kendall, Carol. *The Gammage Cup*. Illus by Erik Blegvad. New York: Harper, 1959. Voyager paperback. M239.

2651 Kendall, Lace. *Houdini: Master of Escape*. New York: Macrae, 1960.

2652 Kennard, Joseph Spencer. *Masks and Marionettes*. Port Washington, N.Y.: Kennikat, 1967.

2653 Kennedy, X.J. *The Phantom Ice Cream Man; More Nonsense Verse*. Illus by David McPhail. New York: Atheneum, 1979.

2654 Kenny, Herbert. *Dear Dolphin*. Illus by Kelly Oechsli. New York: Pantheon, 1967.

2655 Kenny, John B. and Carla. *The Art of Papier Mâché*. Philadelphia: Chilton, 1968. Chilton paperback.

2656 ———. *Design in Papier Mâché*. Philadelphia: Chilton, 1971. Chilton paperback.

2657 Kent, Jack. *The Egg Book*. New York: Macmillan, 1975.

2658 ———. *Jack Kent's Happy Ever After*. Illus by the author. New York: Random, 1976.

2659 Kent, Jack, illus. *Jack Kent's Twelve Days of Christmas*. New York: Parents, 1973. Scholastic paperback.

2660 Kent, Louise. *He Went With Christopher Columbus*. Boston: Houghton, 1940.

2661 Kenyon, Raymond G. *I Can Learn about Calculators and Computers. New York: Harper, 1961.

2662 Kepes, Juliet. Beasts from a Brush. New York: Pantheon, 1955.

2663 ———. Lady Bird Quickly. Illus by the author. Boston: Little, 1964.

2664 Keppie, Elizabeth E. Speech Improvement through Choral Speaking. Boston: Expression, 1973.

2665 Kerina, Jane. African Crafts. Illus by Tom Feelings and Marylyn Katzman. New York: Lion, 1970.

2666 Kerman, Gertrude. Creative Ways With Children. Illus by Margaret Zimmerman. New York: Harvey, 1961.

2667 Kerr, Judith. When Hitler Stole Pink Rabbit. Illus by the author. New York: Coward, 1971. Dell paperback.

2668 Kerr, Laura J. Comp. Who's Where in Books, An Index to Biographical Material. Ann Arbor: Michigan Association of School Librarians, 1971.

2669 Kerr, M. E. Dinky Hocker Shoots Smack. New York: Harper, 1972. Dell paperback.

2670 Kessler, Ethel and Leonard. Are You Square? New York: Doubleday, 1966.

2671 ———. Do Bears Sit in Chairs? Illus by Leonard Kessler. New York: Doubleday, 1961. Paperback.

2672 Kessler, Leonard. Art is Everywhere, a Child's Guide to Drawing and Painting. New York: Dodd, 1958.

2673 ———. What's in a Line. New York: Grosset and Dunlop, 1962.

2674 Kettlekamp, Larry. Drums, Rattles, Bells. New York: Morrow, 1960.

2675 ———. Flutes, Whistles, and Reeds. New York: Morrow, 1962.

2676 ———. Kites. New York: Morrow, 1959.

2677 ———. Puzzle Patterns. New York: Morrow, n.d.

2678 ———. Shadows. Illus by the author. New York: Morrow, 1957.

2679 ———. Singing Strings. New York: Morrow, 1958.

2680 Key, Francis Scott. The Star Spangled Banner. Illus by Paul Galdone. New York: Crowell, 1966. M205, M476.

2681 ———. The Star Spangled Banner. Illus by Peter Spier. Garden City, NY: Doubleday, 1973. M205, M476, M630, M631.

2682 Key, Alexander. Escape to Witch Mountain. Illus by Leon Wisdom, Jr. New York: Westminster, 1968.

2683 ———. The Forgotten Door. New York: Westminster, 1965.

2684 Kieran, John. An Introduction to Birds. Illus by Don Echelberry. Garden City, NY: Doubleday, 1965.

2685 Kijima, Hajime. The Little White Hen, a Folk Tale. Illus by Setsuko Hane. New York: Harcourt, 1969.

2686 Kimishima, Hisako. Ma Lien and the Magic Brush. Trans by A. Tresselt. Illus by Kei Wakana. New York: Parents, 1968. M393.

2687 King, Stanley. The International Dolls House Book. New York: Crown, 1977. Paperback.

2688 Kingman, Lee, ed.. Newbery and Caldecott Medal Books: 1956-1965. Boston: Horn Book, 1975.

2689 ———. Newbery and Caldecott Medal Books, 1966-1975. Boston: Horn Book, 1975.

2690 Kingman, Lee, Joanna Foster and Ruth Giles Lontoft. Illustrators of Children's Books; 1957-1966. Boston: Horn Book, 1968.

2691 Kingman, Lee, Grace Allen Hogarth and Harriet Quimby, eds.. Illustrators of Children's Books 1967-1976. Boston: Horn Book, 1978.

2692 Kipling, Rudyard. Just So Stories. New York: Walker, 1972.

2693 Kirk, Ruth. Desert Life. Photos by Ruth and Louis Kirk. New York: Natural History Press, 1970.

2694 Kirk, Ruth and Richard Daugherty. Hunters of the Whale, an Adventure in Northwest Coast Archaeology. Photos by Ruth and Louis Kirk. New York: Morrow, 1974.

2695 Kirn, Ann. Full of Wonder. Cleveland: World, 1959.

2696 ———. Let's Look at More Tracks. New York: Putnam, 1969.

2697 ———. Let's Look at Tracks. New York: Putnam, 1970.

2698 ———. Peacock and the Crow. New York: Four Winds, 1969. Scholastic paperback.

2699 ———. Tip for Tap; From an Old Folk Tale. New York: Norton, 1970.

2700 Kishi, Nami. The Ogre and His Bride. Trans by Alvin Tresselt. Illus by Shasuke Fukuda. New York: Parents, 1971.

2701 Kjelgaard, Jim. Big Red. Illus by Bob Kuhn. New York: Holiday, 1954. Scholastic paperback. M81.

2702 ———. Irish Red, Son of Big Red. New York: Holiday, 1951. Scholastic paperback.

2703 Klemin, Diana. The Art of Art for Children's Books. New York: Potter, 1966.

2704 ———. The Illustrated Book: It's Art and Craft. New York: Potter, 1970.

2705 Knapp, Mark. Nonverbal Communication in Human Interaction. New York: Holt, 1972.

2706 Knight, Daniel. Dinosaur Days. Illus by Joel Scheck. New York: McGraw, 1977.

2707 Knight, David. Earth's Arid Lands. New York: Watts, 1964.

2708 Knight, Eric. Lassie Come Home. New York: Holt, 1971. Dell paperback. M349, M350.

2709 Knotts, Howard. The Winter Cat. New York: Harper, 1972.

2710 Knudson, Bozanne R. and P.K. Ebert. Sport Poems. New York: Dell paperback, 1971.

2711 Kohl, Herbert. A Book of Puzzlements: Play and Invention with Language.

2712 Kohl, Marguerite. Games for Children. Illus by Frederica Young. New York: Cornerstone Library, 1963.

2713 Kohn, Bernice. Fireflies. Illus by Erwin Schachner. Englewood Cliffs, NJ: Prentice-Hall, 1966.

2714 ———. Communications Satellites, Message Centers in Space. Englewood Cliffs, NJ: Four Winds, 1975.

2715 ———. Secret Codes and Ciphers. Illus by Frank Albise. Englewood Cliffs, NJ: Prentice-Hall, 1968. Paperback.

2716 ———. What a Funny Thing to Say. Illus by R.V. Blechman. New York: Dial, 1974.

2717 ———. Beachcomber's Book. Illus by

Arabelle Wheatley. New York: Viking, 1970.

2718 ———. Everything has a Shape and Everything has a Size. Illus by Aliki. Englewood Cliffs, NJ: Prentice-Hall, 1964.

2719 Kohn, Marguierite and Frederic Young. Jokes for Children. New York: Hill and Wang, 1963.

2720 ———. More Jokes for Children. New York: Hill and Wang, 1966.

2721 Komoda, Beverly. Simon's Soup Illus by the author. New York: Parents, 1978.

2722 Konigsburg, E. L. About the B'nai Bagels. Illus by the author. New York: Atheneum, 1967. Aladdin paperback.

2723 ———. From the Mixed-up Files of Mrs. Basil E. Frankmeiller. Illus by the author. New York: Atheneum, 1967. Aladdin paperback.

2724 ———. Jennifer, Hecate, Macbeth, William McKinley and Me, Elizabeth. New York: Atheneum, 1967. Aladdin paperback.

2725 Konopnicka, Maria. The Golden Seed. Adapted by Catherine Fournier. Illus by Janina Domanska. New York: Scribner, 1962.

2726 Korty, Carol. Plays for African Folktales: With Ideas for Acting, Dance, Costumes, and Music. Illus by Sandra Cain. New York: Scribner, 1975.

2727 ———. Silly Soup; Ten Zany Plays With Songs and Ideas for Making them Your Own. Music by Mary Lynn Solot. Photos by Majie Cope. New York: Scribners, 1977.

2728 Krahn, Fernando. April Fools. New York: Dutton, 1974.

2729 ———. Catch That Cat! New York: Dutton, 1978.

2730 ———. A Flying Saucer Full of Spaghetti. New York: Dutton, 1970. M215.

2731 ———. A Funny Friend from Heaven. Philadelphia: Lippincott, 1977.

2732 ———. How Santa Had a Long and Difficult Journey Delivering His Presents. New York: Delacorte, 1970.

2733 ———. The Mystery of the Giant Footprints. New York: Dutton, 1977.

2734 ———. Sebastian and the Mushroom. New York: Delacorte, 1976.

2735 ———. The Self-Made Snowman. Philadelphia: Lippincott, 1974.

2736 ———. Who's Seen the Scissors? New York: Dutton, 1975.

2737 Kraske, Robert. The Statue of Liberty Comes to America. Illus by Victor Mays. Champaign, IL: Garrard, 1972.

2738 Kraus, Robert. Ladybug, Ladybug. New York: Dutton, 1977. Windmill paperback.

2739 ———. Littlest Rabbit. Illus by the author. New York: Scholastic paperback, 1975.

2740 ———. Owliver. Illus by Jose Aruego and Adrianne Dewey. New York: Dutton, 1974. Windmill paperback.

2741 ———. Whose Mouse Are You? Illus by Jose Aruego. New York: Macmillan, 1970. Collier paperback. M748.

2742 Krauss, Ruth. Bears. Illus by Phyllis Rowand. Harper, 1948. Scholastic paperback.

2743 ———. Charlotte and the White Horse. Illus by Maurice Sendak. New York: Harper, 1955. M123.

2744 ———. Happy Day. Illus by Marc Simont. New York: Harper, 1949, M263.

2745 ———. A Hole is to Dig. Illus by Maurice Sendak. New York: Harper, 1952. M290.

2746 ———. I Write It. Illus by Mary Chalmero. New York: Harper, 1970.

2747 ———. A Very Special House. Illus by Maurice Sendak. New York: Harper, 1953.

2748 Kreider, Barbara. Index to Children's Plays in Collections. 2nd ed. Mutuchen, NJ: Scarecrow, 1977.

2749 Kroeber, Theodora. A Green Christmas. Illus by John Larrecq. Berkeley: Parnassus, 1967.

2750 Kroll, Steven. If I Could Be My Grandmother. Illus by Lady McCrady. New York: Pantheon, 1977.

2751 Krumgold, Joseph. And Now Miguel. New York: Crowell, 1953. Apollo paperback. M35.

2752 ———. Onion John. New York: Crowell, 1959. Apollo paperback.

2753 Kruss, James. My Great-Grandfather, the Heroes, and I. New York: Atheneum, 1973.

2754 ———. Three by Three, a Picture Book for Children Who Can Count to Three. Illus by Eva Johanna Rubin. New York: Macmillan, 1965. Collier paperback.

2755 Kugelmass, J. Alvin. Louis Braille; Windows for the Blind. New York: Messner, 1951.

2756 Kumin, Maxine W. No One Writes a Letter to the Snail; Poems. Illus by Bean Allen. New York: Putnam, 1962.

2757 ———. What Color is Caesar? Illus by Evaline Ness. New York: McGraw, 1978.

2758 Kumin, Maxine and Anne Sexton. Joey and the Birthday Present. Illus by Evaline Ness. New York: McGraw, 1971.

2759 Kunitz, Stanley and Vineta Colby. Twentieth Century Authors, First Supplement. New York: Wilson, 1955.

2760 Kunitz, Stanley and Howard Haycraft. American Authors 1600Z-1900. New York: Wilson, 1938.

2761 ———. Junior Book of Authors, 2nd ed. New York: Wilson, 1951.

2762 ———. Twentieth Century Authors, a Biographical Dictionary of Modern Literature. New York: Wilson, 1942.

2763 Kupferberg, Herbert. A Rainbow of Sound; the Instruments of the Orchestra and their Music. Illus by Morris Warmon. New York: Scribners, 1973. M316.

2764 Kurth, Heinz. Print a Book. New York: Viking, 1976. Puffin paperback.

2765 Kushida, Magoichi, Adaptor. The Nutcracker. Trans by Ann King Herring. Illus by Fumiko Hari. Tokyo: Gakken, 1971. M489, M636.

2766a Kuskin, Karla. Any Me I Want to Be; Poems. New York: Harper, 1972.

2766b ———. Near the Window Tree. New York: Harper, 1975.

2767 Kyle, Elizabeth. Song of the Waterfall; the Story of Edward and Nina Grieg. New York: Holt, 1970.

2768 La Beau, Dennis. Children's Authors and Illustrators: an Index to Biographical Dictionaries. Detroit: Gale, 1976.

2769 Lacey, Marion. Picture Book of Musical Instruments. Illus by Leonard Weisgard. New York: Lathrop, 1942.

2770 LaFontaine. Fables of LaFontaine. Illus by

Richard Scarry. New York: Doubleday, 1963.

2771 ———. The Hare and the Tortoise. Illus by Paul Galdone. New York: McGraw, 1962. M268.

2772 ———. The Hare and the Tortoise. Illus by Brian Wildsmith. New York: Watts, 1967. M267, M268.

2773 ———. The Lion and the Rat. Illus by Brian Wildsmith. New York: Watts, 1963. M365.

2774 ———. The Miller, the Boy and the Donkey. Illus by Brian Wildsmith. New York: Watts, 1963. M446.

2775 ———. The North Wind and the Sun. Illus by Brian Wildsmith. New York: Watts, 1964. M487.

2776 ———. The Rich Man and the Shoe-Maker; a Fable. Illus by Brian Wildsmith. New York: Watts, 1965. M101.
Laidlaw Reading Series, See Eller, William.

2777 Lamb, Charles and Mary. Favorite Tales fom Shakespeare. Ed. by Morris Schreiber. New York: Grosset, 1956.

2778 ———. Tales from Shakespeare. New York: Dutton, 1960. Paperback.

2779 ———. Ten Tales from Shakespeare. Illus by Grabranski. New York: Watts, 1969.

2780 Lamorisse, Albert. The Red Balloon. New York: Doubleday, 1957.

2781 Lampman, Evelyn. The Shy Stegosaurus of Cricket Creek. Illus by Herbert Buel. New York: Doubleday, 1955.

2782 ———. The Shy Stegosaurus of Indian Springs. Illus by Paul Galdone. New York: Doubleday, 1962.

2783 Lane, Margaret. The Tale of Beatrix Potter: A Biography. New York: Warne, 1968.

2784 Lane, Rusdi. Pantomime; a Prelude to Play-Acting. Illus by Margaret Harlelius. New York: Scholastic, 1974.

2785 Lanes, Selma. Down the Rabbit Hole; Adventures and Misadventures in the Realm of Children's Literature. New York: Atheneum, 1971.

2786 Lang, Andrew. Arabian Nights. Illus by Vera Bock. New York: Watts, 1946, 67.

2787 Lang, Andrew. The Blue Fairy Book. New York: Dover, 1965. Paperback.

2788 Lang, Andrew. The Crimson Fairy Book. Illus by Ben Kutcher. New York: Dover paperback, 1966.

2789 ———. The Green Fairy Book. New York: Dover, 1965. Paperback.

2790 ———. The Grey Fairy Book. New York: Dover, 1967. Paperback.

2791 ———. Nursery Rhyme Book. Illus by L. Leslie Brooke. New York: Warner, 1898. Dover paperback.

2792 ———. Pink Fairy Book. Dover Paperback, 1966.

2793 ———. Red Fairy Book. New York: Dover, 1966.

2794 ———. The Yellow Fairy Book. Glouster, MA: Peter Smith, n.d. Dover paperback.

2795 Langner, Nola. Cinderella. Illus by the author. New York: Scholastic paperback, 1974.

2796 ———. Miss Lucy. Illus by the author. New York: Macmillan, 1969.

2797 Langseth, Marcus and Lillian. Apollo Moon Rocks. Illus by Richard Criffari. New York: Coward, 1972.

2798 Langstaff, John. Hot Cross Buns and Other Old Street Cries. Illus by Nancy Winslow Parker. New York: Atheneum, 1978.

2799 ———. Oh, A-Hunting We Will Go. Illus by Nancy Winslow Parker. New York: Atheneum, 1974.

2800 ———. Soldier, Soldier, Won't You Marry Me? Garden City, NY: Doubleday, 1972.

2801 Langstaff, John, ed. Hi! Ho! The Rattlin' Bog and Other Folk Songs for Group Singing. New York: Harcourt, 1969.

2802 ———. On Christmas Day in the Morning. Illus by Anthony Groves-Raines. Music by Marshall Woodbridge. New York: Harcourt, 1959.

2803 ———. Sweetly Sings the Donkey; Animal Rounds for Children to Sing or Play on Recorders. Illus by Nancy Parker. New York: Atheneum, 1976.

2804 Langstaff, John, compiled by. St. George and the Dragon: A Folk Play. New York: Atheneum, 1963.

2805 Langstaff, John, et al. The Swapping Boy. Illus by Beth and Joe Krush. New York: Harcourt, 1960.

2806 Langstaff, John and Joe Krush. Ol' Dan Tucker. New York: Harcourt, 1963.

2807 *Langstaff, John and Feodor Rojankovsky. Frog Went a-Courtin'. New York: Harcourt, 1967. Voyager paperback. M32, M236, M237.

2808 ———. Over in the Meadow. New York: Harcourt, 1973. Voyager paperback. M510, M511.

2809 Langstaff, Nancy and John M., eds. Jim Along, Josie, a Collection of Folk Songs and Singing Games for Young Children. New York: Harcourt, 1970.

2810 Langton, Jane. The Diamond in the Window. Illus by Erik Blegvad. New York: Harper, 1962. Trophy paperback.

2811a ——— . The Swing in the Summerhouse. Illus by Erik Blegvad. New York: Harper, 1967.

2811b Lard, John V. The Giant Jam Sandwich. Boston: Houghton, 1973.

2812 Larkin, David, ed. The Art of Nancy Ekholm Burkert. Introduction by Michael Danoff. New York: Harper, 1977.

2813 Larrick, Nancy. Teacher's Guide to Children's Books. Columbus, Ohio. Merrill, 1963. Paperback.

2814 Larrick, Nancy, ed. Green is Like a Meadow of Grass; an Anthology of Children's Pleasure in Poetry. Illus by Kelly Oechsli. Champaign, Ill.: Garrard, 1968.

2815 ———. I Heard a Scream in the Street, Poems by Young People in the City. New York: Evans, 1970.

2816 ———. More Poetry for Holidays. Champaign, Ill.: Garrard, 1973.

2817 ———. On City Streets, an Anthology of Poetry. Illus by David Sagarin. New York: Evans, 1968.

2818 ———. Piper Pipe That Song Again. Illus by Kelly Oechsli. New York: Random, 1965.

2819 ———. Poetry for Holidays. Illus by Kelly Oechsli. Champaign, Ill.: Garrard, 1966.

2820 ———. *Room for Me and a Mountain Lion: Poetry for Open Space.* New York: Bantam paperback, 1975.

2821 ———. *The Wheels of the Bus Go Round and Round: School Bus Songs and Chants.* San Carlos, CA: Golden Gate, 1972.

2822 Larris, Ann. *People are Like Lollipops.* New York: Holiday, 1971.

2823 Lasker, Joe. *Merry Ever After, the Story of Two Medieval Weddings.* New York: Viking, 1976. Puffin paperback. M441.

2824 Latham, Hugh, transl. *Mother Goose in French.* Illus by Barbara Cooney. New York: Crowell, 1964.

2825 *Lathrop, Dorothy P. *Animals of the Bible.* Philadelphia: Lippincott, 1937.

2826 Latshaw, George. *Puppetry.* New York: Rosen, 1977.

2827 Lauber, Patricia. *Clarence and the Butcher.* New York: Coward, 1973.

2828 ———. *Clarence and the Cat.* Illus by Paul Galdone. New York: Coward, 1977.

2829 ———. *Clarence and the TV Dog.* New York: Coward, 1965.

2830 ———. *Clarence Goes to Town.* New York: Random, 1967.

2831 ———. *Earthquakes: New Scientific Ideas About How and Why the Earth Shakes.* New York: Random, 1972.

2832 ———. *Friendly Dolphins.* New York: Random, 1963.

2833 ———. *Great Whales.* Champaign, IL: Garrard, 1975.

2834 Lavine, Sigmund. *Wonders of the Owl World.* New York: Dodd, 1971.

2835 Lawrence, Harriet. *H. Philip Birdsong's ESP.* Illus by Sandy Huftaker. New York: Scott, 1969.

2836 Lawrence, Jacob. *Harriet and the Promised Land.* Illus by the author. New York: Simon & Schuster, 1968.

2837 Lawrence, James. *The Binky Brothers and the Fearless Four.* Illus by Leonard Kessler. New York: Harper, 1970.

2838 ———. *Binky Brothers, Detectives.* Illus by Leonard Kessler. New York: Harper, 1968. Trophy paperback.

2839 Lawson, John. *The Spring Rider.* New York: Crowell, 1968.

2840 Lawson, Robert. *Ben and Me.* Boston: Little, 1939. Dell paperback.

2841 ———. *The Great Wheel.* New York: Viking, 1957.

2842 ———. *Mr. Revere and I.* Illus by the author. Boston: Little, 1953. Dell paperback.

2843 ———. *Rabbit Hill.* Illus by the author. New York: Viking, 1944. Dell paperback. M560, M561.

2844 Lawson, Robert. *Robert Lawson, Illustrator: A Selection of his Characteristic Illustrations.* Introduction by Helen L. Jones. Boston: Little, 1972.

2845 *Lawson, Robert. *They Were Strong and Good.* Illus by the author. New York: Viking, 1940. M684.

2846 ———. *Tough Winter.* New York: Viking, 1954. Dell paperback.

2847 Lazar, Wendy. *Jewish Holiday Books.* New York: Doubleday, 1977.

2848 Lazarus, Keo Felner. *The Billy Goat in the Chili Patch, a Mexican Folktale.* Illus by Carol Rogers. Austin, Texas: Steck-Vaughan, 1972.

2849 Leach, Maria. *How the People Sang the Mountains Up, How and Why Stories.* Illus by Glen Rounds. New York: Viking, 1967.

2850 ———. *The Lion Sneezed; Folktales and Myths of the Cat.* Illus by Helen Siegl. New York: Crowell, 1977.

2851 ———. *The Luck Book.* Illus by Kurt Werth. Cleveland: World, 1964.

2852 ———. *Noodles, Nitwits and Numskulls.* Illus by Kurt Werth. Cleveland: World, 1961. Scholastic paperback.

2853 ———. *Rainbow Book of American Folk Tales and Legends.* Illus by Marc Simont. Cleveland: World, 1958.

2854 ———. *Riddle Me, Riddle Me, Ree.* New York: Viking, 1970. Puffin paperback.

2855 ———. *The Soup Stone: The Magic of Familiar Things.* Illus by Mamie Harmon. New York: Funk & Wagnalls, 1954.

2856 ———, ed. *Standard Dictionary of Folklore, Mythology and Legend.* New York: Funk & Wagnalls, 1950. 1972.

2857 Leaf, Munro. *The Story of Ferdinand.* Illus by Robert Lawson. New York: Viking, 1936. Seafarer paperback. M647.

2858 ———. *Wee Gillis.* Illus by Robert Lawson. New York: Viking, 1968. Seafarer paperback.

2859 Lear, Edward. *ABC.* Illus by the author. New York: McGraw, 1965.

2860 ———. *The Complete Nonsense Book.* New York: Dover paperback, n.d.

2861 ———. *The Complete Nonsense Book.* Edited by Lady Strachey. Intro. by the Earl of Cromer. New York: Dodd, 1948, 1964.

2862 ———. *The Dong With a Luminous Nose.* Illus by Edward Gorey. New York: Young Scott, 1959.

2863 ———. *Edward Lear's Nonsense Book.* Selected and illus by Tony Palazzo. New York: Garden City, 1956. M186.

2864 Lear, Edward. *Edward Lear's Nonsense Coloring Book.* New York: Dover paperback, 1971.

2865 ———. *The Four Little Children Who Went Around the World.* Illus by Arnold Lobel. New York: Macmillan, 1968.

2866 ———. *Le Hibou et la Poussiquette.* Trans by Francis Steigmuller. Illus by Barbara Cooney. Boston: Little, 1961.

2867 ———. *The Jumblies.* Illus by Edward Gorey. New York: Young Scott, 1968.

2868 ———. *Limericks by Lear.* Illus by Lois Ehlert. Cleveland: World, 1965.

2869 ———. *Nonsense Alphabet.* Illus by the author. New York: Watts. Pepter Possum paperback, 1975.

2870 ———. *The Owl and the Pussy Cat.* Illus by Gwen Fulton. New York: Atheneum, 1977.

2871 ———. *The Owl and the Pussycat.* Illus by William Pene DuBois. New York: Doubleday, n.d.

2872 ———. *The Owl and the Pussy Cat.* Illus by Barbara Cooney. Boston: Little, 1969. M514, M515.

2873 ———. *The Owl and the Pussy Cat.* New

York: Warne, 1975.

2874 ———. *The Pelican Chorus.* Illus by Harold Berson. New York: Parents, 1967.

2875 ———. *Pelican Chorus and Other Nonsense Verses.* Illus by L. Leslie Brooke. New York: Warner, 1954.

2876 Lear, Edward. *The Popple Who Has No Toes.* Illus by Kevin W. Madison. New York: Viking, 1977.

2877 ———. *The Quangle Wangle's Hat.* Illus by Paul Galdone. New York: Putnam, 1966.

2878 ———. *The Quangle Wangle's Hat.* Illus by Helen Oxenbury. New York: Watts, 1970.

2879 ———. *The Scroobilous Pip.* Illus by Nancy Ekholm Burkert. Completed by Ogden Nash New York: Harper, 1968.

2880 ———. *Teapots and Quails and Other Nonsense.* Cambridge, MA: Harvard University, 1954.

2881 ———. *Two Laughable Lyrics: The Popple Who Had No Toes, the Quangle Wangle's Hat.* Illus by Paul Galdone. New York: Putnam, 1966.

2882 ———. *The Two Old Bachelors.* Illus by Paul Galdone. New York: McGraw, 1962.

2883 ———. *Whizz: Six Limericks.* Illus by Janina Domanska. New York: Macmillan, 1973.

2884 Lee, Dennis. *Nicholas Knock & Other People Poems.* Illus by Frank Newfeld. Boston: Houghton, 1977.

2885 Leekley, Thomas B. *The Riddle of the Black Knight, and Other Tales and Fables Based on the Gesta Romanorum.* Illus by Johannes Troyer. New York: Vanguard, 1957.

2886 Leeming, Joseph. *Fun with Pencil and Paper.* Philadelphia: Lippincott, 1955.

2887 ———. *Fun with Puzzles.* Philadelphia: Lippincott, 1946.

2888 ———. *Riddles, Riddles, Riddles.* New York: Watts, 1953.

2889 Leen, Nina. *The Bat.* New York: Holt, 1976.

2890 ———. *Taking Pictures.* New York: Holt, 1976.

2891 Le Fevre, Felicite. *The Cock, the Mouse, and the Little Red Hen, an Old Tale Retold.* Illus by Tony Sarg. New York: Macrae, 1947.

2892 Le Guin, Ursula. *The Farthest Shore.* Illus by Gail Garraty. New York: Atheneum, 1972. Bantam paperback.

2893 ———. *The Tombs of Atuan.* Illus by Gail Garraty. New York: Atheneum, 1971. Bantam paperback. M702.

2894 ———. *The Wizard of Earthsea.* Illus by Ruth Robbins. New York: Parnassus, 1968. Bantam paperback.

2895 Lehmann-Haupt, Hellmut. *The Life of the Book.* Illus by Fritz Kredel. New York: Abelard, 1957.

2896 Leichman, Seymour. *Shaggy Dogs and Spotty Dogs and Shaggy and Spotty Dogs.* New York: Harcourt, 1973.

2897 Leidy, Philip. *A Popular Guide to Government Publications Fourth Edition.* New York: Columbia University, 1976.

2898 Leisy, James. *Good Times Song Book, 160 songs for Informal Singing with Resources for Song Leaders, Accompanists, and Singers.* Illus by David Dawson. Music by J. Leisy. Nashville: Abingdon, 1974. Singer's paper-

back edition by Abingdon.

2899 Lemming, J. *Fun With Wood.* Illus by Charles E. Pont. Philadelphia: Lippincott, 1942.

2900 Lemmon, Robert. *Junior Science Book of Big Cats.* Illus by Jean Zollinger. Champaign, IL: Garrard, 1962.

2901 L'Engle, Madeline. *Meet the Austins.* New York: Vanguard, 1960. Dell paperback.

2902 ———. *A Swiftly Tilting Planet.* New York: Farrar, 1978. Dell paperback.

2903 ———. *A Wind in the Door.* New York: Farrar, 1973. Dell paperback. M758.

2904 ———. *A Wrinkle in Time.* New York: Farrar, 1962. Dell paperback. M771.

2905 Lenski, Lois. *Animals for Me.* Illus by the author. New York: Walck, 1941.

2906 ———. *At Our House.* (Read-and-Sing Book). Illus by the author. New York: Walck, 1959.

2907 ———. *Davy and His Dog.* Illus by the author. New York: Walck, 1957.

2908 ———. *Davy Goes Places.* Illus by the author. New York: Walck, 1961.

2909 ———. *Davy's Day.* Illus by the author. New York: Walck, 1943.

2910 ———. *A Dog Came to School.* Illus by the author. New York: Walck, 1955.

2911 ———. *I Like Winter.* Illus by the author. New York: Walck, 1950.

2912 ———. *I Went for a Walk.* (Read-and-Sing Book). Music by C. R. Bulla. New York: Walck, 1958. M311.

2913 ———. *Let's Play House.* Illus by the author. New York: Walck, 1944.

2914 ———. *The Little Auto.* (Little Small) Illus by the author. New York: Walck, 1934. i.t.a. edition.

2915 ———. *The Little Airplane.* (Mr. Small). Illus by the author. New York: Walck, 1938.

2916 ———. *The Little Family.* Illus by the author. Garden City, NY: Doubleday, 1932.

2917 ———. *Little Farm.* Illus by the author. New York: Walck, 1942. i.t.a. edition. Walck paperback.

2918 ———. *Little Fire Engine.* (Mr. Small) Illus by the author. New York: Walck, 1946.

2919 ———. *Little Sailboat.* (Mr. Small). Illus by the author. New York: Walck, 1937.

2920 ———. *Little Train.* (Mr. Small). Illus by the author. New York: Walck, 1940. Walck paperback.

2921 ———. *Lois Lenski's Christmas Stories.* Philadelphia: Lippincott, 1968.

2922 ———. *Mr. and Mrs. Noah.* Illus by the author. New York: Crowell, 1948.

2923 ———. *Now It's Fall.* Illus by the author. New York: Walck, 1948.

2924 ———. *On a Summer Day.* (Season Books) Illus by the author. New York: Walck, 1953.

2925 ———. *Pappa Pequeno: Pappa Small.* Illus by the author. Translated by Maria D. Lado. New York: Walck, 1961.

2926 ———. *Pappa Small.* (Mr. Small). Illus by the author. New York: Walck, 1951.

2927 ———. *Policeman Small.* (Mr. Small) Illus by the author. New York: Walck, 1962.

2928 ———. *Songs of Mr. Small.* (Mr. Small) Illus by the author. New York: Walck, 1954.

2929 ———. *Spring is Here.* (Season Books). Illus by the author. New York: Walck, 1945.

2930 ———. *Surprise for Davy.* Illus by the author. New York: Walck, 1947.

2931 Lent, Blair. *From King Boggen's Hall to Nothing-at-All. A Collection of Improbable Houses and Unusual Places Found in Traditional Rhymes and Limericks.* Illus by Blair Lent. Boston: Little, 1967.

2932 ———. *John Tabor's Ride.* Illus by Ernest Small. Boston: Little, 1966.

2933 ———. *Why the Sun and the Moon Live in the Sky, an African Folktale by Elphinestone Dayrell.* Boston: Houghton, 1968.

2934 Leonard, Marcia and the Editors of *Cricket Magazine. Cricket's Jokes, Riddles and Other Stuff.* Designed by John Grandit. New York: Random, 1977.

2935 Leopold, A. Starker. *The Desert.* New York: Time-Life, 1967.

2936 Lerner, Alan J. *My Fair Lady.* New York: Signet paperback, n.d.

2937 Lesser, Gerald. *Children and TV: Lessons from "Sesame Street."* New York: Random, 1974.

2938 Lester, Julius. *To Be A Slave.* Illus by Tom Feelings. New York: Dial, 1968. Dell paperback.

2939 Levine, Rhoda. *Three Ladies Beside the Sea.* New York: Atheneum, 1963.

2940 Levitin, Sonia. *Journey to America.* Illus by Charles Robinson. New York: Atheneum, 1970. Aladdin paperback.

2941 ———. *A Single Speckled Egg.* Illus by John Larrecq. New York: Parnassus, 1976.

2942 ———. *Who Owns the Moon?* Illus by John Larrecq. New York: Parnassus, 1973.

2943 Lewin, Betsy. *Cat Count.* New York: Dodd, 1981.

2944 Lewis, C. S. *Horse and His Boy.* Illus by Pauline Baynes. New York: Macmillan, 1954. Collier paperback.

2945 ———. *Last Battle.* Illus by Pauline Baynes. New York: Macmillan, 1956. Collier paperback.

2946 ———. *Lion, the Witch, and the Wardrobe.* Illus by Pauline Baynes. New York: Macmillan, 1950. Collier paperback.

2947 ———. *Magician's Nephew.* Illus by Pauline Baynes. New York: Macmillan, 1955. Collier paperback.

2948 ———. *Prince Caspian; the Return to Narnia.* Illus by Pauline Baynes. New York: Macmillan, 1951. Collier paperback.

2949 ———. *Silver Chair.* Illus by Pauline Baynes. New York: Macmillan, 1953. Collier paperback.

2950 ———. *Voyage of the Dawn Treader.* Illus by Pauline Baynes. New York: Macmillan, 1952. Collier paperback.

2951 Lewis, Claudia. *When I go to the Moon.* Illus by Leonard Weisgard. New York: Macmillan, 1961. Collier paperback.

2952 Lewis, Richard, ed. *I Breathe a New Song: Poems of the Eskimo.* Illus by Oonark. New York: Simon and Schuster, 1971.

2953 ———. *In a Spring Garden.* Illus by Ezra Jack Keats. New York: Dial, 1965. M312.

2954 ———. *Miracles, Poems by Children of the English-Speaking World.* New York: Simon and Schuster, 1966.

2955 ———. *The Moment of Wonder: A Collection of Chinese and Japanese Poetry.* Illus by Chinese and Japanese masters. New York: Dial, 1963.

2956 ———. *Out of the Earth I Sing, Poetry and Songs of Primitive Peoples of the World.* New York: Norton, 1968.

2957 ———. *There are Two Lives: Poems by Children of Japan.* Trans. by Kimura Haruna. New York: Simon and Schuster, 1970.

2958 ———. *The Wind and the Rain, Children's Poems.* Photos by Helen Butterfield. New York: Simon and Schuster, 1968.

2959 Lewis, Roger. *Puppets and Marionettes.* New York: Knopf, 1952.

2960 Lewis, Shari. *Making Easy Puppets.* Illus by Larry Lurin. New York: Dutton, 1967.

2961 Lewis, Shari and Lillian Oppenheimer. *Folding Paper Masks.* New York: Dutton, 1965.

2962 ———. *Folding Paper Puppets.* New York: Stein and Day, 1963.

2963 Lewis, Stephen. *Zoo City.* New York: Greenwillow, 1976.

2964 Lexau, Joan. *Archimedes Takes a Bath.* Illus by Salvatore Murdocca. New York: Crowell, 1969.

2965 ———. *The Homework Caper.* Illus by Syd Hoff. New York: Harper, 1966.

2966 ———. *I Should Have Stayed in Bed.* Illus by Syd Hoff. New York: Harper, 1965.

2967 ———. *It All Began With a Drip, Drip, Drip.* Illus by Joan Sandin. New York: McCall, 1970.

2968 ———. *The Rooftop Mystery.* Illus by Syd Hoff. New York: Harper, 1968.

2969 ———. *Striped Ice Cream.* Illus by John Wilson. Philadelphia: Lippincott, 1968. Scholastic paperback.

2970 Leyh, Elizabeth. *Children Make Sculpture.* New York: Van Nostrand, 1972.

2971a Lickteig, Mary T. *An Introduction to Children's Literature.* Columbus: Merrill, 1975.

2971b Lidstone, John. *Building with Balsa Wood.* New York: Van Nostrand, 1965.

2972 ———. *Building with Cardboard.* Photos by Roger Kerkham. New York: Van Nostrand, 1968.

2973 ———. *Design Activities for the Elementary Classroom.* Worcester, MA: Davis, 1964. Paperback.

2974 Lieberman, J. Ben. *Printing as a Hobby.* New York: Sterling, 1965.

2975 Life. *The World We Live In.* Young Reader edition adapted by Jane W. Watson. New York: Golden, 1956.

2976 Lifton, Betty Jean. *The Rice Cake Rabbit.* Illus by Mitsui. New York: Norton, 1966.

2977 Lightbody, Donna M. *Introducing Needlepoint.* New York: Lothrop, 1973.

2978 Lightner, A. M. *Star Dog.* New York: McGraw, 1973.

2979 Linder, Leslie L. *The Art of Beatrix Potter.* New York: Warne, 1972.

2980 ———. *A History of the Writings of Beatrix Potter.* New York: Warne, 1971.

2981 Lindgren, Astrid. *Christmas in the Stable.* Illus by Harald Wilberg. New York: Coward,

1962. Paperback. M133.

2982 ————. *Pippi Goes on Board.* Illus by Louis S. Glanzman. Trans by Florence Lamborn. New York: Viking, 1957. Penguin paperback.

2983 ————. *Pippi In the South Seas.* Illus by Louis S. Glanzman. Trans by Gerry Bothmer. New York: Viking, 1959. Penguin paperback.

2984 ————. *Pippi Longstocking.* Illus by Louis S. Glanzman. Trans by Florence Lamborn. New York: Viking, 1950, 63. M538.

2985 ————. *Pippi On the Run.* Photos by Bo-Erik Gyberg. New York: Viking, 1976.

2986 ————. *The Tompten.* Illus by Harald Wiberg. New York: Coward, 1961. Paperback. M703.

2987 ————. *The Tompten and the Fox.* Illus by Harald Wiberg. New York: Coward, 1965. Paperback. M704.

2988 Lindop, Edmund. *First Book of Elections.* Illus by Gustave Nebel. New York: Watts, 1972.

2989 Lindsay, Vachel. *Johnny Appleseed and Other Poems.* Illus by George Richards. New York: Macmillan, 1928.

2990 ————. *Selected Poems of Vachel Lindsay.* Edited by Mark Harris. New York: Collier paperback, 1967.

2991 Lindsey, David. *The Wonderful Chirronera and Other Tales from Mexican Folklore.* Austin, TX: Heidelberg, 1974.

2992 Lines, Kathleen. *Lavender's Blue; A Book of Nursery Rhymes.* Illus by Harold Jones. New York: Watts, 1954.

2993 ————. *Nursery Stories.* Illus by Harold Imes. New York: Watts, 1960.

2994 ————. *A Ring of Tales.* Illus by Harold Jones. New York: Watts, 1959.

2995 ————. *Tales of Magic and Enchantment.* Illus by Alan Howard. London: Faber & Faber, 1966.

2996 Lionni, Leo. *Alexander and the Wind-Up Mouse.* Illus by the author. New York: Pantheon, 1969. Pinwheel paperback. M11.

2997 ————. *Alphabet Tree.* Illus by the author. New York: Pantheon, 1973. Paperback.

2998 ————. *The Biggest House in the World.* Illus by the author. New York: Pantheon, 1968. M84.

2999 ————. *A Color of His Own.* Illus by the author. New York: Pantheon, 1975. M143.

3000 ————. *Fish is Fish.* Illus by the author. New York: Pantheon, 1970. Pinwheel paperback. M209, M357.

3001 ————. *Frederick.* Illus by the author. New York: Pantheon, 1967. Pinwheel paperback. M229, M357.

3002 ————. *Greentail Mouse.* Illus by the author. New York: Pantheon, 1973.

3003 ————. *In the Rabbitgarden.* Illus by the author. New York: Astor-Honor, 1975.

3004 ————. *Inch by Inch.* Illus by the author. New York: Astor-Honor, 1962.

3005 ————. *Little Blue and Little Yellow.* Illus by the author. New York: Astor-Honor, 1959. M366.

3006 ————. *On My Beach There Are Many Pebbles.* Illus by the author. New York: Astor-Honor, 1961.

3007 ————. *Pezzettino.* Illus by the author. New York: Pantheon, 1975.

3008 ————. *Swimmy.* Illus by the author. New York: Pantheon, 1963. Pinwheel paperback. M357, M663.

3009 ————. *Theodore and the Talking Mushroom.* Illus by the author. New York: Pantheon, 1971. M357, M682.

3010 ————. *Tico and the Golden Wings.* Illus by the author. New York: Pantheon, 1964. Pinwheel paperback.

3011 *Lipkind, William and Nicholas Mordinoff. *Finders Keepers.* Illus by N. Mordinoff. New York: Harcourt, 1951. M206.

3012 Lipkind, William. *The Magic Feather Duster.* Illus by Nicholas Mordvinoff. New York: Harcourt, 1958.

3013 ————. *The Two Reds.* New York: Harcourt, 1950.

3014 Lisker, Sonia O. *The Attic Witch.* New York: Four Winds, 1973.

3015 ————. *Lost.* New York: Harcourt, 1975.

3016 Liss, Howard. *Basketball Talk for Beginners.* New York: Messner, 1970.

3017 ————. *Football Talk for Beginners.* New York: Messner, 1970. Archway paperback.

3018 List, Ilka Katherine. *Questions and Answers About Seashore Life.* Illus by the author. New York: Four Winds, 1971.

3019 Little, Jean. *From Anna.* New York: Harper, 1972. Trophy paperback.

3020 ————. *Home From Far.* Illus by Jerry Lozare. Boston: Little, 1965.

3021 ————. *Kate.* New York: Harper, 1971. Trophy paperback.

3022 ————. *Look Through My Window.* Illus by Joan Sandin. New York: Harper, 1970. Trophy paperback.

3023 ————. *Mine for Keeps.* Illus by Lewis Parker. Boston: Little, 1962. Archway paperback.

3024 ————. *Spring Begins in March.* Illus by Lewis Parker. Boston: Little, 1966.

3025 ————. *Take Wing.* Illus by Jerry Lozare. Boston: Little, 1968.

3026
3027 Littledale, Freya. *The Elves and the Shoemaker.* Illus by Brinton Turkle. New York: Four Winds, 1975. Paperback.

3028 ————. *Ghosts and Spirits of Many Lands.* Illus by Stefan Martin. New York: Doubleday, 1970.

3029 Livermore, Elaine. *Find the Cat.* Boston: Houghton-Mifflin, 1973.

3030 ————. *One to Ten, Count Again.* Boston: Houghton, 1973.

3031 Livenskii, Aleksandr M. *An Old Tale Carved Out of Stone.* New York: Crown, 1973.

3032 Livingston, Myra Cohn. *Come Away.* Illus by Irene Haas. New York: Atheneum, 1974.

3033 ————. *I'm Hiding.* Illus by Erik Blegvad. New York: Harcourt, 1961.

3034 ————. *A Crazy Flight and Other Poems.* Illus by James J. Spanfeller. New York: Harcourt, 1969.

3035 ————. *A Lollygag of Limericks.* New York: Atheneum, 1978.

3036 ————. *The Malibu and Other Poems.* New York: Atheneum, 1972.

3037 ————. *Poems of Christmas.* New York:

Atheneum, 1980.

3038 ———. *The Way Things Are and Other Poems.* New York: Atheneum, 1974.

3039 ———. *Wide Awake and Other Poems.* Illus by Jacqueline Chwast. New York: Harcourt, 1959.

3040 ———. *Whispers and Other Poems.* Illus by Jacqueline Chwast. New York: Harcourt, 1958. M742.

3041 Livingston, Myra Cohn, ed. *Calloah! Callay! Holiday Poems for Young Readers.* New York: Atheneum, 1978.

3042 ———. *Listen, Children Listen, an Anthology of Poems for the Very Young.* Illus by Trina Schart Hyman. New York: Harcourt, 1972.

3043 ———. *O Frabjous Day! Poetry for Holidays and Special Occasions.* New York: Atheneum, 1976.

3044 ———. *Poems of Lewis Carroll.* Illus by John Tenniel and others. New York: Crowell, 1973.

3045 ———. *Speak Roughly to Your Little Boy, A Collection of Parodies, Burlesques, Together With Original Poems, Chosen and Annotated for Young People.* Illus by Joseph Low. New York: Harcourt, 1971.

3046 ———. *A Tune Beyond Us, a Collection of Poems.* Illus by James J. Spanfeller. New York: Harcourt, 1968.

3047 ———. *What a Wonderful Bird the Frog Are, an Assortment of Humorous Poetry and Verse.* New York: Harcourt, 1973.

3048 Lobel, Adrienne. *A Small Sheep in a Pear Tree.* Illus by the author. New York: Harper, 1977.

3049 Lobel, Anita. *King Rooster, Queen Hen.* Illus by the author. New York: Greenwillow, 1975.

3050 ———. *The Pancake.* Illus by the author. New York: Greenwillow, 1978.

3051 ———. *Troll Music.* New York: Harper, n.d.

3052 Lobel, Arnold. *Days With Frog and Toad.* Illus by the author. New York: Harper, 1979.

3053 *———. *Fables.* Illus by the author. New York: Harper, 1980.

3054 ———. *Frog and Toad All Year.* Illus by the author. New York: Harper, 1976.

3055 ———. *Frog and Toad Are Friends.* Illus by the author. New York: Harper, 1970. Trophy paperback. M531, M532, M533.

3056 ———. *The Frog and Toad Coloring Book.* Illus by the author. New York: Harper, 1981. Paperback.

3057 ———. *Frog and Toad Together.* New York: Harper, 1972. Trophy paperback. M233, M234, M535.

3058 ———. *The Great Blueness and other Predicaments.* Illus by the author. New York: Harper, 1968.

3059 ———. *Gregory Griggs and Other Nursery Rhyme People.* Illus by the author. New York: Greenwillow, 1978.

3060 ———. *How the Rooster Saved the Day.* Illus by Anita Lobel. New York: Greenwillow, 1977.

3061a ———. *Mouse Soup.* Illus by the author. New York: Harper, 1977.

3061b ———. *Mouse Tales.* Illus by the author. New York: Harper, 1972. Trophy paperback.

3062 ———. *On the Day Peter Styvesant Sailed Into Town.* Illus by the author. New York: Harper, 1971.

3063 ———. *Owl at Home.* Illus by the author. New York: Harper, 1975.

3064 ———. *Small Pig.* Illus by the author. New York: Harper, 1969.

3065 ———. *A Treeful of Pigs.* Illus by Anita Lobel. New York: Greenwillow, 1979.

3066 Lobel, Arnold, illus. *The Comic Adventures of Old Mother Hubbard and Her Dog.* Scarsdale, NY: Bradbury, 1968.

3067 Lobley, Priscilla. *Making Children's Costumes.* New York: Taplinger, 1972.

3068 Lofting, Hugh. *The Story of Dr. Doolittle.* Philadelphia: Lippincott, 1920. Dell paperback. M173.

3069 ———. *The Twilight of Magic.* Illus by Lois Lenski. Philadelphia: Lippincott, 1967.

3070 ———. *Voyages of Doctor Doolittle.* Philadelphia: Lippincott, 1922. Dell paperback. M730.

3071 Lomax, Alan. *Folk Songs of North America, in the English Language.* Illus by Michael Leonard. Music by Peggy Seeger and Matyos Seiter. Garden City, NY: Doubleday, 1960.

3072 ———. *Penguin Book of American Folk Songs.* Music by Elizabeth Poston. Baltimore: Penguin, 1966.

3073 Lomax, Alan and John A. *American Ballads and Folk Songs.* New York: Macmillan, 1934.

3074 ———. *Cowboy Songs and Other Frontier Ballads.* New York: Macmillan, 1938.

3075 Lomax, John. *Folk Song U.S.A.* New York: New American Library paperback, 1975.

3076 Lomax, John and Alan. *Songs of the Cattle Trail and Cow Camps.* New York: Granger, 1979. Reproduction of 1920 edition.

3077 London, Jack. *White Fang.* New York: Macmillan, 1935. Scholastic paperback. Airmont paperback.

3078 Longfellow, Henry Wadsworth. *The Children's Own Longfellow.* New York: Houghton, 1920. M77.

3079 ———. *Evangeline. A Tale of Acadie.* Introduced by Mina Lewiton. Illus by Howard Simon. New York: Meredith, 1966. M195.

3080 ———. *Evangeline.* New York: Washington Square paperback, n.d. M195.

3081 ———. *Paul Revere's Ride.* Illus by Paul Galdone. New York: Crowell, 1963.

3082 ———. *Paul Revere's Ride.* Illus by Joseph Low. New York: Windmill, 1973.

3083 ———. *Song of Hiawatha.* Illus by Joan Kiddell-Monroe. New York: Dutton, 1960. M676.

3084 Longman, Harold. *Would You Put Your Money in a Sand Bank?* Illus by Abner Graboff. Chicago: Rand McNally, 1968.

3085 Lopshire, Robert. *Put Me in the Zoo.* New York: Beginner, 1960.

3086 Lord, Beman. *The Day the Spaceship Landed.* Illus by Harold Berson. New York: Walck, 1967.

3087 ———. *The Days of the Week.* Illus by Walter Erhard. New York: Walck, 1968.

3088 ———. *Our New Baby's ABC.* Illus by Velma Ilsley. New York: Walck, 1964.

3089 Lord, John Vernon and Janet Burroway. *The*

Giant Jim Sandwich. Boston: Houghton, 1973.

3090 Lorrimar, Betty. *Creative Papier Mâché.* New York: Watson, 1971.

3091 Love, Katherine. *A Little Laughter.* Illus by Walter Lorraine. New York: Crowell, 1957.

3092 ———. *A Pocketful of Rhyme.* Illus by Henrietta Jones. New York: Crowell, 1946.

3093 Lovelace, Maud Hart. *Betsy-Tacy.* Illus by Lois Lenski. New York: Crowell, 1940. Paperback.

3094 ———. *Betsy-Tacy and Tib.* Illus by Lois Lenski. New York: Crowell, 1940. Paperback.

3095 Lovoos, Janice. *Design is a Dandelion.* San Carlos, Calif.: Golden Gate, 1966.

3096 Low, Joseph. *Adam's Book of Odd Creatures.* New York: Atheneum, 1975.

3097 ———. *Five Men Under One Umbrella and Other Ready-to-Read Riddles.* New York: Macmillan, 1975.

3098 ———. *A Mad Wet Hen and Other Riddles.* Illus by J. Low. New York: Greenwillow, 1977.

3099 ———. *Mice Twice.* Illus by J. Low. New York: Atheneum, 1980.

3100 Low, Joseph and Ruth. *Mother Goose Riddle Rhymes.* New York: Harcourt, 1953.

3101 Lowe, Tracy, trans. *Alexander Pushkin's The Tale of Czar Saltian or the Princess and the Swan Princess.* Illus by I. Bilibin. New York: Crowell, 1975.

3102 ———. *Alexander Pushkin's The Tale of the Golden Cockerel.* Illus by I. Bilibin. New York: Crowell, 1975.

3103 Lownsbery, Eloise. *Marta the Doll.* Boston: Houghton, 1927.

3104 Lowrey, Janette S. *Six Silver Spoons.* Illus by Robert Quackenbush. New York: Harper, 1971.

3105 Luce, Marnie. *Counting Systems, the Familiar and the Unusual.* Minneapolis: Lerner, 1969.

3106 Luckhardt, Mildred. *Christmas Comes Once More, Stories and Poems for the Holiday Season.* Illus by Griska Dotzenko. New York: Abingdon, 1962.

3107 ———. *Thanksgiving; Feast and Festival.* Illus by Ralph McDonald. New York: Abingdon, 1966.

3108 Lueders, Edward and St. John Prunus. *Zero Makes Me Hungry, a Collection of Poems for Today.* Illus by John Reuter-Pacyna. New York: Lothrop, 1976.

3109 Lund, Doris H. *Attic of the Wind.* Illus by Ati Forberg. New York: Parents, 1966.

3110 ———. *Did You Ever?* Illus by Denman Hampson. New York: Parents, 1965.

3111 ———. *I Wonder What's Under.* Illus by Janet McCaffery. New York: Parents, 1970.

3112 ———. *You Ought to See Herbert's House.* Illus by Steven Kellog. New York: Watts, 1973.

3113 Lukashok, Alvin. *Communication Satellites: How They Work.* New York: Putnam, 1967.

3114 Lutz, Frank E. *Field Book of Insects of the U.S. and Canada.* New York: Putnam, 1935.

3115 Lynch, John. *How to Make Mobiles.* New York: Viking, 1953. Compass paperback.

3116 Lyons, John Henry. *Stories of our American Patriotic Songs.* Illus by Jacob Landau. New York: Vanguard, 1958. Words and music for ten American patriotic songs.

3117 Maas, Selve. *The Moon Painters and Other Estonian Folk Tales.* Illus by Laszlo Gal. New York: Viking, 1971.

3118 MacAgy, Douglas and Elizabeth. *Going for a Walk With a Line, a Step into the World of Modern Art.* Garden City, NY: Doubleday, 1959. Paperback.

3119 Macbeth, George. *Jonah and the Lord.* Illus by Margaret Gordon. New York: Holt, 1970.

3120 ———. *Noah's Journey.* Illus by Margaret Gordon. New York: Viking, 1966.

3121 MacCann, Donnarae and Olga Richard. *Child's First Books.* New York: Two Continents, 1975.

3122 McCaslin, Nellie. *Creative Dramatics in the Classroom,* 2nd ed. New York: McKay, 1975. Paperback.

3123 ———. *Puppet Fun.* New York: McKay, 1977.

3124 Macaulay, David. *Cathedral: The Story of its Construction.* Boston: Houghton, 1973.

3125 ———. *Pyramid.* Boston: Houghton-Mifflin, 1975.

3126 McCormick, Dell. *Paul Bunyan Swings His Axe.* Caldwell, Idaho: Caxton, 1936. Scholastic paperback.

3127 McClintock, Mike. *David and the Giant.* Illus by Fritz Siebel. New York: Harper, 1960.

3128 ———. *A Fly Went By.* Illus by Fritz Siebel. New York: Beginner, 1958. M214.

3129 ———. *Stop that Ball.* Illus by Fritz Siebel. New York: Beginner, 1958.

3130 ———. *What Have I Got?* Illus by Leonard Kessler. New York: Harper, 1961.

3131 McCloskey, Robert. *Blueberries for Sal.* Illus by the author. New York: Viking, 1948. Puffin paperback. M91, M92.

3132 ———. *Burt Dow Deep-Water Man.* Illus by the author. New York: Viking, 1963.

3133 ———. *Centerburg Tales.* Illus by the author. New York: Viking, 1951. Puffin paperback.

3134 ———. *Homer Price.* Illus by the author. New York: Viking, 1943. Puffin paperback. Scholastic paperback. M293, M294.

3135 ———. *Lentil.* Illus by the author. New York: Viking, 1940. Puffin paperback. M355, M356.

3136 *———. Make Way for Ducklings.* Illus by the author. New York: Viking, 1941. Puffin paperback. M403, M404.

3137 ———. *One Morning in Maine.* Illus by the author. New York: Viking, 1952. Puffin paperback. M503.

3138 *———. Time of Wonder.* Illus by the author. New York: Viking, 1957. M700, M701.

3139 McClung, Robert M. *Blaze, the Story of a Striped Skunk.* New York: Morrow, 1969.

3140 ———. *Ladybug.* New York: Morrow, 1966. Paperback. M348.

3141 ———. *Major, the Story of a Black Bear.* New York: Morrow, 1956.

3142 ———. *Redbird: The Story of a Cardinal.* New York: Morrow, 1968.

3143 ———. *Ruby Throat: The Story of a Hummingbird.* New York: Morrow, 1950. Paperback. M589.

3144 ———. *Scoop: The Last of the Brown*

Pelicans. New York: Morrow, 1972.

3145 ————. *Spike, the Story of a Whitetail Deer.* New York: Morrow, 1952.

3146 ————. *Spotted Salamander.* New York: Morrow, 1964.

3147 ————. *Stripe, the Story of a Chipmunk.* New York: Morrow, 1951. M652.

3148 ————. *Tiger: The Story of a Swallowtail Butterfly.* New York: Morrow, 1953. M694.

3149 ————. *Vulcan: The Story of a Bald Eagle.* New York: Morrow, 1955.

3150 ————. *Whitefoot, the Story of a Wood Mouse.* New York: Morrow, 1961. M746.

3151 McCord, David. *All Day Long, Fifty Rhymes of the Never Was and Always Is.* Illus by Henry B. Kane. Boston: Little, 1965. Dell paperback.

3152 ————. *Away and Ago.* Illus by Leslie Morrill. Boston: Little, 1968.

3153 ————. *Every Time I Climb a Tree.* Illus by Marc Simont. Boston: Little, 1967.

3154 ————. *Far and Few: Rhymes of the Never Was and Always Is.* Illus by Henry B. Kane. Boston: Little, 1952.

3155 ————. *For Me to Say, Rhymes of the Never Was and Always Is.* Illus by Henry B. Kane. Boston: Little, 1970.

3156 ————. *The Star in the Pail.* Illus by Marc Simont. Boston: Little, 1975.

3157 ————. *Take Sky, More Rhymes of the Never Was and Always Is.* Illus by Henry B. Kane. Boston: Little, 1962. Dell paperback.

3158 McCrea, Lilian. *Puppets and Puppet Plays.* Oxford: Oxford University, 1949.

3159 McDermott, Beverly Brodsky. *The Crystal Apple, a Russian Tale.* Illus by the author. New York: Viking, 1974. M156.

3160 ————. *The Golem, a Jewish Legend.* Illus by the author. Philadelphia: Lippincott, 1976. M253.

3161 McDermott, Gerald. *Anansi the Spider, a Tale from the Ashanti.* Illus by the author. New York: Holt, 1974. Puffin paperback. M34.

3162 *————. *Arrow to the Sun.* Illus by the author. New York: Viking, 1974. Puffin paperback. M48.

3163 ————. *The Stonecutter.* Illus by the author. New York: Viking, 1975. Puffin paperback. M632, M633.

3164 ————. *Sun Flight.* Illus by the author. New York: Four Winds, 1979.

3165 Mace, Elizabeth. *The Ghost Diviners.* New York: Nelson, 1977.

3166 *MacDonald, Golden. *The Little Island.* Illus by Leonard Weisgard. New York: Doubleday, 1946. M374.

3167 McDonnell, Lois Eddy. *Stevie's Other Eyes.* Friend Press, 1962. Paperback.

3168 McFarlan, Allan A. *Fireside Book of North American Indian Folktales.* Illus by Paulette McFarlan. Harrisburg, PA: Stackpole, 1974.

3169 McFee, June King. *Preparation for Art.* Illus by Jean Ray Laury. Belmont, Calif.: Wadsworth, 1966.

3170 McFerran, Ann. *Poems to be Read Aloud to Children and by Children.* Illus by Roberta Lewis Clark. New York: Nelson, 1965.

3171 McGinley, Nancy. *Lucy McLockett.* Illus by Helen Stone. Philadelphia: Lippincott, 1958.

3172 McGinley, Phyllis. *All Around the Town.* Illus by Helen Stone. Philadelphia: Lippincott, 1948.

3173 ————. *Mince Pie and Mistletoe.* Illus by Harold Berson. Philadelphia: Lippincott, 1961.

3174 ————. *The Most Wonderful Doll in the World.* Philadelphia: Lippincott, 1950.

3175 ————. *Wonderful Time.* Illus by John Alcorn. Philadelphia: Lippincott, 1965.

3176 ————. *Wonders and Surprises: A Collection of Poems.* Philadelphia: Lippincott, 1968.

3177 ————. *A Wreath of Christmas Legends.* Illus by Leonard Weisgard. New York: Macmillan, 1967.

3178 ————. *The Year Without a Santa Claus.* Illus by Kurt Werth. Philadelphia: Lippincott, 1957.

3179 McGovern, Ann. *Black is Beautiful.* Photos by Hope Wurnfeld. New York: Four Winds, 1969. Scholastic paperback.

3180 McGovern, Ann. *HeeHaw.* Illus by Eric von Schmidt. Boston: Houghton, 1969.

3181 ————. *Squeals and Squiggles and Ghostly Giggles.* Illus by Jeffrey Higginbottom. New York: Four Winds, 1973.

3182 ————. *Stone Soup.* Illus by Nola Langner. 1971. Scholastic paperback.

3183 ————. *Too Much Noise.* Illus by Simon Taback. Boston: Houghton, 1967. Scholastic paperback.

3184 McGowen, Tom. *Album of Dinosaurs.* Illus by Rod Ruth. Chicago: Rand McNally, 1972.

3185 ————. *Album of Prehistoric Animals.* Illus by Rod Ruth. Chicago: Rand McNally, 1974.

3186 ————. *Dinosaurs and Other Prehistoric Animals.* Illus by Rod Ruth. Chicago: Rand McNally, 1978.

3187 ————. *Spirit of the Wild.* Boston: Little, 1976.

3188 McGraw, Eloise. *Moccasin Trail.* New York: Coward, 1952. M459.

3189 MacGregor, Ellen. *Miss Pickerell and the Geiger Counter.* Illus by Paul Galdone. New York: McGraw, 1953. Paperback.

3190 ————. *Miss Pickerell Goes to Mars.* Illus by Paul Galdone. New York: McGraw, 1951. Archway paperback.

3191 ————. *Theodore Turtle.* Illus by Paul Galdone. New York: Whittesey, 1955.

3192 MacGregor, Ellen and Dora Pantell. *Miss Pickerell Goes on a Dig.* Illus by Charles Geer. New York: McGraw, 1966. Archway paperback.

3193 ————. *Miss Pickerell on the Moon.* Illus by Charles Geer. New York: McGraw, 1966. Archway paperback.

3194 McHargue, Georgess. *The Beasts of Never; a History Natural and Unnatural of Monsters Mythical and Magical.* Illus by Frank Bozzo. Indianapolis: Bobbs, 1968.

3195 ————. *The Impossible People, a History of Natural and Unnatural Beings, Terrible and Wonderful.* Illus by Frank Bozzo. New York: Holt, 1972. Dell paperback.

3196 ————. *The Mermaid and the Whale.* Illus by Robert and Andrew Parker. New York: Holt, 1973.

3197 ———. *Stoneflight*. Illus by Arvis Stewart. New York: Viking, 1975. Camelot paperback.

3198 ———. *The Wonderful Wings of Harold Harrabescu*. New York: Delacorte, 1971.

3199 Mack, Stan. *Ten Bears in my Bed*. New York: Pantheon, 1974.

3200 McKee, David. *Elmer, the Story of a Patchwork Elephant*. Illus by the author. New York: McGraw, 1968.

3201 ———. *The Magician and the Petnapping*. Illus by the author. Boston: Houghton, 1976.

3202 ———. *The Man Who Was Going to Mind the House: A Norwegian Folktale*. Illus by the author. New York: Abelard-Schuman, 1972.

3203 ———. *Mr. Benn—Red Knight*. Illus by the author. New York: McGraw, 1968.

3204 ———. *One, Two, Three, Four, Five, Six, Seven, Eight, Nine, Benn*. Illus by the author. New York: McGraw, 1970.

3205 McKillip, Patricia. *The House on Parchment Street*. New York: Atheneum, 1973.

3206 McKinley, Robin. *Beauty: A Retelling of the story of Beauty and the Beast*. New York: Harper, 1978.

3207 McLeod, Emilie. *The Bear's Bicycle*. Illus by David McPhail. Boston: Little, 1975.

3208 ———. *One Snail and Me, a Book of Numbers and Animals and a Bathtub*. Illus by Walter Lorraine. Boston: Little, 1961.

3209 McLeod, M. *The Book of King Arthur and His Noble Knights*. Illus by Henry C. Pitz. Philadelphia: Lippincott, 1949.

3210 McMeekin, Isabel M. *Journey Cake*. Illus by Nicholas Panesis. New York: Messner, 1942. Macmillan Reading Series. See Harris, Albert J.

3211 McMillan, Bruce. *An Alphabet Symphony, an ABC Book*. New York: Greenwillow, 1977.

3212 MacMillan, Cyrus. *Gooskap's Country and Other Indian Tales*. Illus by John A. Hall. New York: Walck, 1956.

3213 McMurtrie, Douglas C. *The Book, the Story of Printing and Book-Making*. London: Oxford, 1943.

3214 MacNamara, Desmond. *Puppetry*. Illus by Jack Stoddart. New York: Horizon, 1966.

3215 McNeer, May. *America's Mark Twain*. Illus by Lynd Ward. Boston: Houghton, 1962.

3216 McNeill, James. *The Double Knights, More Tales from Round the World*. Illus by Theo Dimson. New York: Walck, 1964.

3217 ———. *The Sunken City and Other Tales from Round the World*. Illus by Theo Dimson. New York: Walck, 1959.

3218 McNulty, Faith. *Whales: Their Life in the Sea*. Illus by John Schoenherr. New York: Harper, 1975.

3219 McPharlin, Paul. *The Puppet Theatre in America—A History 1924–1948*. Including Supplement. Boston: Plays, 1969.

3220 MacStravic, Suellen. *Print Making*. Illus by G. Overlie. Minneapolis: Lerner, 1973.

3221 McSwigan, Marie. *Snow Treasure*. Illus by Mary Reardon. New York: Dutton, 1942. Scholastic paperback.

3222 McWhirter, Morris and Ross, eds. *The Guinness Book of World Records*, 19th ed. New York: Sterling, 1981. Bantam paperback.

3223 Maestro, Betsy Giulio. *Harriet Goes to the Circus*. Illus by Giulio Maestro. New York: Crown, 1977.

3224 Maestro, Giulio. *One More and One Less*. Illus by the author. New York: Crown, 1974.

3225 Maher, Ramona. *The Blind Boy and the Loon and Other Eskimo Myths*. New York: Day, 1969.

3226 Mahlman, Lewis and David Cadwalader Jones. *Folk Tale Plays for Puppets*. Boston: Plays, 1980.

3227 ———. *Puppet Plays for Young Players; Twelve Royalty-free Plays for Hand Puppets, Rod Puppets or Marionettes*. Boston: Plays, 1974.

3228 ———. *Puppet Plays from Favorite Stories*. Boston: Plays, 1977.

3229 Mahon, Julie C. *First Book of Creative Writing*. Illus by Gustave E. Nebel. New York: Watts, 1968.

3230 Mahony, Bertha E., Louise Pauson Latimer and Beulah Folmsbee. *Illustrators of Children's Books: 1744–1945*. Boston: Horn Book, 1947.

3231 Mahy, Margaret. *The Boy Who Was Followed Home*. Illus by Steven Kellogg. New York: Watts, 1975.

3232 Major, Charles. *The Bears of Blue River*. New York: Macmillan, 1963.

3233 "Make Your Own Pinhole Camera." *National Geographic World*, August, 1977.

3234 Malcolmson, Anne. *Song of Robin Hood*. Illus by Virginia Lee Burton. Music by Grace Castagnetta. Boston: Houghton, 1947.

3235 ———. *Yankee Doodle's Cousin*. Illus by Robert McCloskey. Boston: Houghton, 1969.

3236 Malone, Mary. *Annie Sullivan*. Illus by Lydia Rosier. New York: Putnam, 1971.

3237 Maltin, Leonard. *TV Movies*. New York: Signet paperback, 1974.

3238 Mannheim, Grete. *Feather or Fur, a Collection of Animal Poems*. New York: Knopf, 1967.

3239 Manning, John, Ed'l. Consultant. *Calico Caper*. Glenview, IL: Scott-Foresman, 1978.

3240 ———. *Flying Hoofs*. Glenview, IL: Scott-Foresman, 1978.

3241 ———. *Hootenanny*. Glenview, IL: Scott-Foresman, 1978.

3242 ———. *Ride a Rainbow*. Glenview, IL: Scott-Foresman, 1978.

3243 ———. *Step Right Up*. Glenview, IL: Scott-Foresman, 1978.

3244 Manning-Sanders, Ruth. *A Book of Devils and Demons*. Illus by Robin Jacques. New York: Dutton, 1970.

3245 ———. *A Book of Dragons*. Illus by Robin Jacques. New York: Dutton, 1964.

3246 ———. *A Book of Giants*. Illus by Robin Jacques. New York: Methuen, 1962.

3247 ———. *A Book of Magical Beasts*. Illus by Raymond Briggs. New York: Nelson, 1970.

3248 ———. *A Book of Monsters*. Illus by Robin Jacques. New York: Dutton, 1976.

3249 ———. *A Book of Sorcerers and Spells*. Illus by Robin Jacques. New York: Dutton, 1973.

3250 ———. *Gianni and the Ogre*. Illus by Wm. Stubbs. New York: Dutton, 1970.

3251 ———. *The Glass Man and the Golden Bird, Hungarian Folk and Fairy Tales.* Illus by Victor Ambrus. New York: Roy, 1968.

3252 Mar, S. Y. Lu. *Chinese Tales of Folklore.* Illus by Howard Simon. New York: Criterion, 1964.

3253 Marcus, Rebecca and Judith. *Fiesta Time in Mexico.* Champagne, Ill.: Garrard, 1974.

3254 Mari, Dela. *The Magic Balloon.* New York: Philips, 1969.

3255 Mariana. *Miss Flora McFlimsey's Christmas Eve.* New York: Lathrop, 1949.

3256 ———. *Miss Flora McFlimsey's Easter Bonnet.* Illus by Miriam C. Foster. New York: Lathrop, 1951.

3257 Marino, T.J. *Pictures Without a Camera.* New York: Sterling, 1974.

3258 Marks, Mickey Klar. *Collage.* New York: Dial, 1968.

3259 ———. *Op-tricks: Creating Kinetic Art.* Kinetics by Edith Alberts. Photos by David Rosenfeld. Philadelphia: Lippincott, 1972.

3261 Markus, Rebecca B. *The First Book of Volcanoes and Earthquakes.* New York: Watts, 1972.

3262 Marriot, Alice and Carol K. Rachlin. *American Indian Mythology.* New York: Crowell, 1968. New American Library paperback, 1972 in print; Appollo paperback, 1972 in print.

3263 Marshall, James. *What's the Matter with Carruthers?* Illus by the author. Boston: Houghton, 1972.

3264 ———. *Yummers!* Illus by the author. Boston: Houghton, 1973.

3265 Martel, Suzanne. *The City Underground.* New York: Archway, 1964, 75. Paperback.

3266 Martignoni, Margaret E., ed. *The Illustrated Treasury of Children's Literature.* New York: Grosset and Dunlap, 1955.

3267 Martin, Beryl. *Batik for Beginners.* New York: Scribner, 1971.

3268 Martin, Bill Jr. and Peggy Brogan, eds. *Sounds of Mystery.* New York: Holt, 1972.

3269 ———. *Sounds of the Storyteller.* New York: Holt, 1972.

3270 Martin, Fran. *Nine Tales of Coyote.* Illus by Dorothy McEntee. New York: Harper, 1950.

3271 Martin, Judith. *Little Plays for Little People.* Illus by Alse Margaret Vogel. New York: Parents, 1965.

3272 Martin, Patricia Miles. *The Little Brown Hen.* Illus by Harper Johnson. New York: Crowell, 1960.

3273 ———. *The Rice Bowl Pet.* Illus by Ezra Jack Keats. New York: Crowell, 1962.

3274a Marzollo, Jean. *Close Your Eyes.* New York: Dial, 1980.

3274b Mason, Bernard. *The Book of Indian Crafts and Costumes.* Illus by Frederic Rock. New York: Wiley, 1946.

3275 Mason, George F. *Animal Tracks.* Illus by the author. New York: Morrow, 1943.

3276 Massie, Diane Redfield. *Komodo Dragon's Jewels.* New York: Macmillan, 1975.

3277 ———. *The Monstrous Glisson Glop.* New York: Parents, 1970.

3278 Mathis, Sharon Bell. *The Hundred Penny Box.* Illus by Les & Dianne Dillon. New York:

Viking, 1975.

3279 ———. *Ray Charles.* Illus by George Ford. New York: Crowell, 1973.

3280 Matsui, Tadashi. *Oniroku and the Carpenter.* Illus by Suekicki Akaba. Trans by Masako Matsuno. Englewood Cliffs, NJ: Prentice-Hall, 1963.

3281a Matsuno, Masako. *A Pair of Red Clogs.* Illus by Kazue Mizumura. Cleveland: World, 1960. Peppercorn paperback.

3281b ———. *Taro and the Bamboo Shoot.* Illus by Kazue Mizumura. New York: Pantheon, 1974.

3282 Matsutani, Miyoko. *The Crane Maiden.* Illus by Chihiro Iwasaki. Trans by Alvin Tresselt. New York: Parents, 1968.

3283 Matthews, Thomas. *Stories of the World's Great Operas.* Illus by Robert Shore. New York: Golden, 1968.

3284 Matthews, William W. *Story of Volcanoes and Earthquakes.* New York: Harvey House, 1969.

3285 ———. *Wonders of the Dinosaur World.* New York: Dodd, 1963.

3286 Matthiesen, Thomas. *ABC, an Alphabet Book.* Photos by the author. New York: Platt & Munk, 1966.

3287 Mattil, Edward L. *Meaning in Crafts.* Englewood Cliffs, NJ: Prentice-Hall, 1971.

3288 Mauzey, Merritt. *Salt Boy.* New York: Abelard-Schuman, 1963.

3289 Max, Peter. *Land of Blue.* New York: Watts, 1970.

3290 ———. *Land of Red.* New York: Watts, 1970.

3291 ———. *Land of Yellow.* New York: Watts, 1970.

3292 May, Julian. *Blue River.* Illus by Robert Quackenbush. New York: Holiday, 1971.

3293 ———. *Captain Cousteau, Undersea Explorer.* Illus by Phero Thomas. Mankato, Minn.: Creative Educational, 1972.

3294 ———. *The Land Beneath the Sea.* Illus by Leonard Everett Fisher. New York: Holiday, 1971.

3295a ———. *Living Things and Their Young.* Chicago: Follett, 1969.

3295b May, Robert. *Rudolph, the Red-Nosed Reindeer.* Chicago: Follett, 1980.

3296 Mayer, Marianna. *Beauty and the Beast.* Illus by Mercer Mayer. New York: Four Winds, 1978. Scholastic paperback.

3297 Mayer, Marianna and Mercer. *Me and My Flying Machine.* New York: Parents, 1971.

3298 Mayer, Mary Jane and Mary Webb. *New Ways in Collage.* New York: Van Nostrand, 1973.

3299 Mayer, Mercer. *Ah-Choo.* New York: Dial, 1976. Pied Piper paperback.

3300 ———. *A Boy, a Dog and a Friend.* New York: Dial, 1978. Pied Piper paperback.

3301 ———. *A Boy, a Dog and a Frog.* New York: Dial, 1967. Pied Piper paperback.

3302 ———. *Bubble, Bubble.* New York: Parents, 1973. Scholastic paperback. M106.

3303 ———. *Frog Goes to Dinner.* New York: Dial, 1974. Pied Piper paperback.

3304 ———. *Frog on His Own.* New York: Dial, 1973. Pied Piper paperback.

3305 ———. *Frog, Where Are You?* New York: Dial, 1969. Pied Piper paperback.

3306 ———. *The Great Cat Chase.* New York: Four Winds, 1975. Scholastic paperback.

3307 ———. *Hiccup.* New York: Dial, 1977. Pied Piper paperback.

3308 ———. *I Am a Hunter.* New York: Dial, 1969.

3309 ———. *Little Monster's Counting Book.* New York: Western. 1978. Paperback.

3310 ———. *Mine.* New York: Dial, 1970.

3311 ———. *One Frog Too Many.* New York: Dial, 1975. Pied Piper paperback.

3312 ———. *Oops.* New York: Dial, 1977. Pied Piper paperback.

3313 ———. *The Queen Always Wanted to Dance.* New York: Simon and Schuster, 1971.

3314 ———. *A Special Trick.* New York: Dial, 1970.

3315 ———. *A Terrible Troll.* New York: Dial, 1968.

3316 ———. *There's a Nightmare in my Closet.* New York: Dial, 1962. Pied Piper paperback.

3317 ———. *Two Moral Tales.* New York: Four Winds, 1974.

3318 ———. *Two More Moral Tales.* New York: Four Winds, 1974.

3319 ———. *What Do You Do With a Kangaroo?* New York: Four Winds, 1974. Scholastic paperback.

3320 ———. *You're the Scaredy-Cat.* New York: Parents, 1974.

3321 Mayer, Ralph. *A Dictionary of Art Terms and Techniques.* New York: Crowell, 1969. Crowell paperback.

3322 Mayne, William. *Earthfasts.* New York: Dutton, 1966.

3323 ———. *A Game of Dark.* New York: Dutton, 1971.

3324 ———. *Hill Road.* New York: Dutton, 1968.

3325 ———. *William Mayne's Book of Giants.* Illus by Raymond Briggs. New York: Dutton, 1968.

3326 Mazer, Harry. *The Dollar Man.* New York: Delacorte, 1974. Dell paperback.

3327 ———. *Snow Bound.* New York: Delacorte, 1973. Dell paperback.

3328 Mazer, Norma Fox. *Saturday, the Twelfth of October.* New York: Delacorte, 1975. Dell paperback.

3329 Meader, Stephen W. *Boy with a Pack.* Illus by Edward Shenton. New York: Harcourt, 1939.

3330 ———. *The Muddy Road to Glory.* Illus by George Hughes. New York: Harcourt, 1963.

3331 ———. *Whaler 'round the Horn.* Illus by Edward Shenton. New York: Harcourt, 1950.

3332 Meadow, Charles T. *Sounds and Signals: How We Communicate.* Philadelphia: Westminster, 1975. Paperback.

3333 ———. *The Story of Computers.* New York: Harvey, 1970.

3334 Meadowcroft, Enid L. *Benjamin Franklin.* New York: Scholastic paperback, 1973.

3335 ———. *By Secret Railway.* Illus by Henry C. Pitz. New York: Crowell, 1948.

3336 ———. *The First Year.* Illus by Grace Raull. New York: Crowell, 1946.

3337 ———. *When Nantucket Men Went Whaling.* Illus by Victory Mays. Champaign, IL: Garrard, 1966.

3338 Mehdevi, Anne Sinclair. *Persian Folk and Fairy Tales.* Illus by Paul Kennedy. New York: Knopf, 1965.

3339 Meigs, Cornelia. *Invincible Louisa.* Boston: Little, 1933. M324.

3340 Meilach, Dona. *Contemporary Batik and Tie Die.* New York: Crown, 1973. Crown paperback.

3341 ———. *Creating Art With Bread Dough.* Photos by the author. New York: Crown, 1976. Paperback.

3342 Meilach, Dona and Lee Erlin Snow. *Creative Stitchery.* Chicago: Reilly and Lee, 1970.

3343 Mellersh, H.E.L. *Finding Out About Ancient Egypt.* New York: Lothrop, 1962.

3344 Melody, William H. *Children's TV: The Economics of Exploitation.* New Haven, CT: Yale, 1973.

3345 Meltzer, M. *Light in the Dark; the Life of Samuel Gridley Howe.* New York: Crowell, 1964.

3346 Meltzer, Milton. *Underground Man.* Scarsdale, NY: Bradbury, 1972. Dell paperback.

3347 Meltzer, Seymour. *American History in Juvenile Books; a Chronological Guide.* New York: Wilson, 1966.

3348 ———. *World History in Juvenile Books, a Geographical and Chronological Guide.* New York: Wilson, 1973.

3349 Melville, Herman. *Moby Dick; or the White Whale.* Illus by Mead Schaeffer. New York: Dodd, 1923. M458.

3350 Melzock, Ronald. *The Day Tuk Became a Hunter and Other Eskimo Stories.* Illus by Carol Jones. New York: Dodd, 1967.

3351 Memling, Carl. *Hi, All you Rabbits.* Illus by Myra McGee. New York: Parents, 1970.

3352 ———. *What's in the Dark.* Illus by John Johnson. New York: Parents, 1971.

3353 Mendelson, Lee. *Charlie Brown and Charlie Schulz; in Celebration of the Twentieth Anniversary of Peanuts.* Cleveland: World, 1970.

3354 Mendoza, George. *Alphabet Boat, a Seagoing Alphabet Book.* Illus by Laurence Di Fiori. New York: American Heritage, 1972.

3355 ———. *Christmas Tree Alphabet Book.* Cleveland: World, 1971.

3356 ———. *Herman's Hat.* Illus by Frank Bozzo. New York: Doubleday, 1969.

3357 ———. *The Inspector.* Illus by Peter Parnall. New York: Doubleday, 1970.

3358 ———. *Marcel Marceau Alphabet Book.* Photos by Milton Greene. Garden City, NY: Doubleday, 1970.

3359 ———. *Marcel Marceau Counting Book.* Garden City, NY: Doubleday, 1971.

3360 ———. *Norman Rockwell's Americana ABC.* Illus by N. Rockwell. New York: Abrams, 1975. Nelson, 1979.

3361 ———. *The Scarecrow Clock.* Illus by Eric Carle. New York: Holt, 1971. Owlet paperback.

3362 ———. *Shadowplay.* New York: Holt, 1974.

3363 ———. *A Wart Snake in a Fig Tree.* Illus by Etienne Delessert. New York: Dial, 1968.

3364 Merriam, Eve. *Bam Zam Boom!* Photos by William Lightfoot. New York: Walker, 1972.

3365 ———. *Catch a Little Rhyme.* Illus by Imero Gobbato. New York: Atheneum, 1966. M118.

3366 ———. *Finding a Poem.* Illus by Seymour Chevost. New York: Atheneum, 1970.

3367 ———. *Funny Town.* Illus by Evaline Ness. New York: Crowell, 1963.

3368 ———. *Independent Voices.* Illus by Arvis Stewart. New York: Atheneum, 1968.

3369 ———. *It Doesn't Always Have to Rhyme.* Illus by Malcolm Spooner. New York: Atheneum, 1964.

3370 ———. *Project 1-2-3.* Illus by Harriet Sherman. New York: McGraw, 1971.

3371 ———. *The Story of Ben Franklin.* Illus by Brinton Turkle. New York: Four Winds, 1965. Scholastic paperback.

3372 ———. *There is No Rhyme for Silver.* Illus by Joseph Schidelman. New York: Atheneum, 1962.

3373 ———. *What Can You Do With a Pocket?* New York: Knopf, 1964.

3374 Merrill, Jean and Ronni Solbert. *High Wide and Handsome and Their Three Tall Tales.* New York: Young Scott, 1964.

3375 Merten, George. *The Hand Puppets.* New York: Nelson, 1957.

3376a Meshover, Leonard. *You Visit a Post Office/ Telephone Company.* Illus by Eve Hoffman. New York: Benefic, 1970.

3376b Metzner, Seymour, *World History in Juvenile Books.* New York: Wilson, 1973.

3377 Meyer, Carolyn. *The Bread Book, All About Bread and How to Make It.* New York: Harcourt, 1976. Paperback.

3378 Meyer, Renate. *Hide-and-Seek.* Scarsdale, N.Y.: Bradbury, 1972.

3379 ———. *Vicki, a Picture Book.* New York: Atheneum, 1968.

3380a Meyers, Hans. *One Hundred Fifty Techniques in Art.* New York: Reinhold, 1961.

3380b Mian, Mary. *Net to Catch A War.* Boston: Houghton, 1975.

3381 Midkiff, Pat. *Colonial Furniture for Doll Houses and Miniature Rooms.* New York: Drake, 1977.

3382 Miles, Miska. *Annie and the Old One.* Illus by Peter Parnall. Boston: Little, 1971.

3383 ———. *Apricot ABC.* Illus by Peter Parnall. Boston: Little, 1969.

3384 ———. *Fox and the Fire.* Illus by John Schoenherr. Boston: Little, 1966.

3385 Milgrom, Harry. *ABC of Ecology.* Photos by Donald Crews. New York: Macmillan, 1972. Collier paperback.

3386 Milhous, Katharine. *Appolonia's Valentine.* Illus by the author. New York: Scribner, 1954.

3387 ———. *The Egg Tree.* Illus by the author. New York: Scribner, 1950. M187.

3388 Miller, Bertha Mahony, and Elinor Whitney Field, eds.. *Caldecott Medal Books; 1938-1957.* Boston: Horn Book, 1957.

3389 ———. *Newbery Medal Books, 1922-1955.* Boston: Horn Book, 1955.

3390 Miller, Bertha Mahony, and Ruth Hill Viguers and Marcia Dalphin, eds.. *Illustrators of Children's Books: 1946-1956.* Boston: Horn Book, 1958.

3391 Miller, Edna. *Duck Duck.* Illus by the author. New York: Holiday, 1971.

3392 ———. *Mousekin's Close Call.* Illus by the author. Englewood Cliffs, NJ: Prentice-Hall, 1978. Paperback.

3393 ———. *Mousekin Finds a Friend* Illus by the author. Englewood Cliffs, NJ: Prentice-Hall, 1967. Paperback.

3394 ———. *Mousekin's ABC.* Illus by the author. Englewood Cliffs, NJ: Prentice-Hall, 1972. Paperback.

3395 ———. *Mousekin's Christmas Eve.* Illus by the author. Englewood Cliffs, NJ: Prentice-Hall, 1965. Paperback.

3396 ———. *Mousekin's Family.* Illus by the author. Englewood Cliffs, NJ: Prentice-Hall, 1969. Paperback.

3397 ———. *Jumping Bean.* Illus by the author. Englewood Cliffs, NJ: Prentice-Hall, 1979. Paperback.

3398 ———. *Mousekin Takes a Trip.* Illus by the author. Englewood Cliffs, NJ: Prentice-Hall, 1976. Paperback.

3399 ———. *Mousekin's Golden House.* Illus by the author. Englewood Cliffs, NJ: Prentice-Hall, 1964. Paperback.

3400 ———. *Mousekin's Woodland Birthday.* Illus by the author. Englewood Cliffs, NJ: Prentice-Hall, 1974.

3401 ———. *Mousekin's Woodland Sleepers.* Illus by the author. Englewood Cliffs, NJ: Prentice-Hall, 1970. Paperback.

3402 Miller, Irene Preston and Winifred Lubell. *The Stitchery Book; Embroidery for Beginners.* Garden City, NY: Doubleday, 1965.

3403 Mills, John Fitmaurice. *The Young Artist.* New York: Sterling, 1968.

3404 Miller, Natalie. *The Story of the Star Spangled Banner.* Illus by George Wilde. Chicago: Children's Press, 1965.

3405 ———. *The Story of the Statue of Liberty.* Illus by Lucy and John Hawkinson. Chicago: Chiildren's Press, 1965.

3406 Milne, A. A. *The Christopher Robin Book of Verse.* Illus by Ernest H. Shepard. New York: Dutton, 1967.

3407 ———. *The House at Pooh Corner.* Illus by Ernest Shepard. New York: Dutton, 1961. Dell paperback.

3408 ———. *Now We are Six.* Illus by Ernest H. Shepard. New York: Dutton, 1961. Dell paperback.

3409 ———. *The Pooh Song Book Containing the Hums of Pooh, The King's Breakfast and Fourteen Songs from When We Were Very Young.* Illus by E.H. Shepard. Music by H. Fraser-Simson. New York: Dutton, 1958.

3410 ———. *Pooh's Birthday Book.* New York: Dutton, 1963. Dell paperback.

3411 ———. *Prince Rabbit and the Princess Who Could Not Laugh.* Illus by Mary Shepard. New York: Dutton, 1966.

3412 ———. *Toad of Toad Hall; a Play from Kenneth Grahame's Book.* New York: Scribner, 1957.

3413 ———. *When We Were Very Young.* Illus by Ernest H. Shepard. New York: Dutton, 1961. Dell paperback.

3414 ———. *Winnie the Pooh.* Illus by Ernest Shepard. New York: Dutton, 1954. Dell paperback. M763, M764.

3415 ———. *The World of Christopher Robin: The Complete When We Were Very Young and Now We Are Six.* Illus by Ernest H. Shepard. New York: Dutton, 1958. M551, M763, M764.

3416 ———. *The World of Pooh, The Complete Winnie-the-Pooh and The House at Pooh's Corner.* Illus by E.H. Shepard. New York: Dutton, 1957. M63, M551, M574, M593.

3417 Milne, Lorus and Margerie. *The Crab that Crawled Out of the Past.* Illus by Kenneth Gosner. New York: Atheneum, 1965.

3418 Minarik, Else Homelund. *Father Bear Comes Home.* Illus by Maurice Sendak. New York: Harper, 1959.

3419 ———. *A Kiss for Little Bear.* Illus by Maurice Sendak. New York: Harper, 1968. M346.

3420 ———. *Little Bear.* Illus by Maurice Sendak. New York: Harper, 1957.

3421a ———. *Little Bear's Friend.* Illus by Sendak. New York: Harper, 1960

3421b ———. *Little Bear's Visit.* Illus by Maurice Sendak. New York: Harper, 1960. M365.

3422a Mincieli, Rose. *Tales Merry and Wise.* Illus by Kurt Werth. New York: Holt, 1958.

3422b Minnton, Janyce L. *Legends of King Arthur.* Illus by Bruno Frost. New York: Hart, 1965.

3423 Mistral, Gabriela. *Crickets and Frogs, a Fable.* Illus by Antonio Frasconi. Trans by Doris Dana. New York: Atheneum, 1972.

3424 Mitchell, Donald. *Every Child's Book of Nursery Songs.* Illus by Alan Howard. Music by Carey Blyton. New York: Crown, 1969.

3425a Mizumura, Kazue. *The Blue Whale.* Illus by the author. New York: Crowell, 1971.

3425b ———. *Emperor Penguins.* Illus by the author. New York: Crowell, 1969.

3426 ———. *Flower Moon Snow.* Illus by the author. New York: Crowell, 1977.

3427 ———. *I See the Winds.* Illus by the author. New York: Crowell, 1966.

3428 ———. *If I Were a Cricket.* Illus by the author. New York: Crowell, 1973.

3429 ———. *If I Were an Ant.* Illus by the author. New York: Crowell, 1970.

3430 Moffett, Martha and Robert. *Dolphins.* New York: Watts, 1971.

3431 Moloney, Joan. *Making Puppets and Puppet Theatres.* New York: Fell, 1973.

3432 Moncure, Jane Belk. *Winter is Here.* Illus by Frances Hook. Elgin, Ill.: Child's World, 1975.

3433 Monjo, F.N. *The Drinking Gourd.* Illus by Fred Brenner. New York: Harper, 1970.

3434 ———. *The One Bad Thing About Father.* Illus by Rocco Negri. New York: Harper, 1970.

3435 ———. *Poor Richard in France.* Illus by Brinton Turkle. New York: Holt, 1973. Dell paperback.

3436 Montebello, Mary S. *Children's Literature in the Curriculum.* Dubuque, Iowa: Wm. C. Brown, 1972.

3437 Montgomerie, Norah and William, ed. *A Book of Scottish Nursery Rhymes.* Illus by Ritchie and N. Montgomerie. New York: Oxford, 1964.

3438 Montgomery, Chandler. *Art for Teachers of Children; Foundations of Aesthetic Expression.* Columbus, Ohio: Merrill, 1968.

3439 Montgomery, Elizabeth Rider. *Henry Ford, Automotive Pioneer.* Illus by Russell Homer. Champaign, IL: Garrard, 1969.

3440 Montresor, Beni. *A for Angel; Beni Montresor's A.B.C. Picture Stories.* Illus by the author. New York: Knopf, 1969.

3441 ———. *Bedtime.* Illus by the author. New York: Harper, 1978. M70.

3442 ———. *Cinderella: from the Opera by Rossini.* New York: Knopf, 1965. Knopf paperback.

3443 ———. *House of Flowers, House of Stars.* New York: Knopf, 1962.

3444 Mooney, James. *Cherokee Animal Tales.* Illus by Robert Frankenberg. New York: Holiday, 1968.

3445 Moore, Anne Carroll. *A Century of Kate Greenaway.* New York: Warne, 1946.

3446 Moore, Clement C. *The Night Before Christmas.* Illus by Tomie dePaola. New York: Holiday, 1970. Paperback.

3447 ———. *The Night Before Christmas.* Illus by Arthur Rackham. Philadelphia: Lippincott, 1954.

3448 ———. *The Night Before Christmas.* Illus by Elisa Trimby. New York: Doubleday, 1977.

3449 ———. *The Night Before Christmas.* Illus by Tasha Tudor. New York: Rand, 1923.

3450 ———. *The Night Before Christmas.* Illus by Leonard Weisgard. New York: Grosset, 1961.

3451 ———. *'Twas the Night Before Christmas.* Illus by Jessie W. Smith. Boston: Houghton, 1912.

3252 ———. *A Visit from St. Nicholas.* Illus Paul Galdone. New York: McGraw, 1968.

3453 Moore, Janet Gaylord. *The Many Ways of Seeing, an Introduction to the Pleasures of Art.* Cleveland: World, 1968.

3454 Moore, John Travers. *Cinnamon Seed.* Illus by Trina Schart Hyman. Boston: Houghton, 1967.

3455 Moore, Lamont. *First Book of Paintings, an Introduction to Appreciation.* New York: Watts, 1960.

3456 Moore, Lilian. *I Thought I Heard the City.* Illus by Mary Jane Dutton. New York: Atheneum, 1969.

3457 ———. *Sam's Place, Poems from the Country.* Illus by Taliavauldis Stubis. New York: Atheneum, 1973.

3458 ———. *Think of Shadows.* Illus by Deborah Robinson. New York: Atheneum, 1980.

3459 Moore, Vardine. *Pre-School Story Hour.* Metuchen, NJ: Scarecrow, 1966.

3460 Morey, Walter. *Gentle Ben.* Illus by John Schoenherr. New York: Dutton, 1965. Avon paperback.

3461 ———. *Home is the North.* Illus by Robert Shore. New York: Dutton. Avon paperback.

3462 ———. *Kavik, the Wolf Dog.* Illus by Peter Parnall. New York: Dutton, 1968. Paperback.

3463 Morgan, Alfred. *A Pet Book for Boys and Girls.* Illus by Alfred Morgan and Ruth King. New York: Scribner, 1948.

3464 Morgan, Shirley. *Rain, Rain Don't Go Away.* Illus by Edward Ardizzone. New York: Dutton, 1972.

3465 Morgenstern, Christian. *The Three Sparrows and Other Nursery Poems.* Illus by Nonny Hogrogian. Trans by Max Knight. New York: Scribner, 1968.

3466 Morlan, Don B. and George E. Tuttle. *An Introduction to Effective Oral Communication.* Indianapolis: Bobbs-Merrill, 1976.

3467 Morris, Robert A. *Dolphin.* Illus by Mamoru Funai. New York: Harper, 1975.

3468 Morrison, Lillian. *Black Within and Red Without, a Book of Riddles.* New York: Crowell, 1953.

3469 ———. *A Dillar a Dollar, Rhymes and Sayings for the Ten O'Clock Scholar.* Illus by Marjorie Bauernschmidt. New York: Crowell, 1955.

3470 ———. *Remember Me When This You See, a Collection of Autograph Verses.* Illus by Marjorie Bauernschmidt. New York: Crowell, 1961.

3471 ———. *The Sidewalk Racer and Other Poems of Sports and Motion.* New York: Lothrop, 1977.

3472 ———. *Sprints and Distances, Sports in Poetry and Poetry in Sports.* Illus by Clare and John Ross. New York: Crowell, 1965.

3473 ———. *Best Wishes, Amen: A New Collection of Autograph Verses.* Illus by Loretta Lustig. New York: Crowell, 1974.

3474 ———. *Touch Blue, Signs and Spells, Love Charms and Chants, Allergies and Old Beliefs in Rhyme.* Illus by Doris Lee. New York: Crowell, 1958.

3475 ———. *Who Would Marry a Mineral? Riddles, Runes, and Love Tunes.* Illus by Rita F. Leydon. New York: Lathrop, 1978.

3476 ———. *Yours Til Niagra Falls.* Illus by Marjorie Bauernschmidt. New York: Crowell, 1950.

3477 Morrow, Elizabeth. *The Painted Pig.* Illus by Rene D'Harnoncourt. New York: Knopf, 1930.

3478 Morrow, Suzanne Stark. *Inatuk's Friend.* Illus by Ellen Raskin. Boston: Little, 1968.

3479 Morton, Brenda. *Do-it-yourself Dinosaurs: Imaginative Toycraft for Beginners.* New York: Taplinger, 1973.

3480 ———. *Needlework Puppets.* Illus by Irene Hawkins. Boston: Plays, 1967.

3481 Morton, Miriam. *The Moon is Like a Silver Sickle, a Celebration of Poetry by Russian Children.* New York: Simon and Schuster, 1972.

3482 *Mosel, Arlene. *The Funny Little Woman.* Illus by Blair Lent. New York: Dutton, 1972. Paperback. M238.

3483 ———. *Tiki Tiki Tembo.* Illus by Blair Lent. New York: Holt, 1968. M695, M696.

3484 Mosler, Gerald. *The Puzzle School.* Illus by Frank C. Smith. New York: Abelard-Schuman, 1977.

3485 Moss, Howard. *Tiger and Other Lilies.* Illus by Frederick H. Belli. New York: Atheneum, 1977.

3486 Mother Goose. *Animal Parade, Mother Goose Rhymes.* Illus by Sheila Waters. New York: Doubleday, 1970.

3487 ———. *Brian Wildsmith's Mother Goose: A Collection of Nursery Rhymes.* Illus by B. Wildsmith. New York: Watts, 1964. Paperback.

3488 ———. *The Courtship, Merry Marriage and Feast of Cock Robin and Jenny Wren in Which is Added the Doleful Death of Cock Robin.* Illus by Barbara Cooney. New York: Scribner, 1965.

3489 ———. *Hi Diddle Diddle, a Book of Mother Goose Rhymes.* Illus by Nola Langner. New York: Scholastic paperback, 1966.

3490 ———. *I Saw a Ship a-sailing, or the Wonderful Games that Only Little Flower-Plant Children can Play, as shown by Beni Montresor.* New York: Knopf, 1967.

3491 ———. *If Wishes were Horses and Other Rhymes.* Illus by Susan Jeffers. New York: Dutton, 1979.

3492 ———. *In a Pumpkin Shell, a Mother Goose ABC.* Illus by Joan Walsh Anglund. New York: Harcourt, 1960.

3493 ———. *Mother Goose and Nursery Rhymes.* Illus by Philip Reed. New York: Atheneum, 1963.

3494 ———. *Mother Goose Book.* Illus by Alice and Martin Provenson. New York: Random, 1976.

3495 ———. *Mother Goose in Hieroglyphics.* Boston: Houghton, 1962. Dover paperback.

3496 ———. *Mother Goose Nursery Rhymes.* Illus by Arthur Rackham. New York: Watts, 1969.

3497 ———. *Mother Goose, Seventy-seven Verses.* Illus by Tasha Tudor. New York: Walck, 1944.

3498 ———. *The Mother Goose Treasury.* Illus by Raymond Briggs. New York: Coward, 1966.

3499 ———. *One I Love, Two I Love and Other Loving Mother Goose Rhymes.* Illus by Nonny Hogrogian. New York: Dutton, 1972.

3500 ———. *One Two Buckle My Shoe, A Book of Counting Rhymes.* Illus by Gail E. Haley. New York: Doubleday, 1964.

3501 ———. *One Misty Moisty Morning.* Illus by Mitchell Miller. New York: Farrar, 1971.

3502 ———. *The Real Mother Goose.* Illus by Blanche F. Wright. New York: Rand, n.d.

3503 ———. *Sing-Song, a Nursery Rhyme Book for Children.* Illus by Marguerite Davis. New York: Macmillan, 1924.

3504 ———. *Tall Book of Mother Goose.* Illus by Feodor Rojankovsky. New York: Harper, 1942.

3505 Mowat, Farley. *Curse of the Viking Grave.* Boston: Little, 1966.

3506 ———. *The Dog Who Wouldn't Be.* Boston: Little, 1957. Pyramid paperback.

3507 ———. *Lost in the Barrens.* Illus by Charles Geer. Boston: Little, 1956.

3508 ———. *Owls in the Family.* Illus by Robert Frankenberg. Boston: Little, 1961.

3509 Mozley, Charles. *The First Book of Tales of Ancient Araby.* New York: Watts, 1960.

3510 Mulholland, John. *Practical Puppetry.* New York: Arco, 1961.

3511 Muller, Jorg. *The Changing Countryside.* New

York: Atheneum, 1977.
3512a Munari, Bruno. *Bruno Munari's Zoo*. Cleveland: World, 1963. M105.
3512b ———. *The Circus in the Mist*. Cleveland: World, 1968.
3513 ———. *Bruno Munari's ABC*. Illus by the author. Cleveland: World, 1960. M104.
3514 Murie, Olaus. *A Field Guide to Animal Tracks*. Boston: Houghton, 1975.
3515 *Musgrove, Margaret. *Ashanti to Zulu: African Traditions*. Illus by Leo and Diane Dillon. New York: Dial, 1976. Paperback. M49.
3516 Myers, Elizabeth P. *Langston Hughes, Poet of His People*. Illus by Russell Hoover. Champaign, Ill.: Garrard, 1970.
3517 Myller, Rolf. *Symbols and Their Meaning*. New York: Atheneum, 1978.
3518 Myrick, Mildred. *The Secret Three*. Illus by Arnold Lobel. New York: Harper, 1963.
3519 Nahmad, H.M. *The Peasant and the Donkey, Tales of the Near and Middle East*. Illus by William Papas. New York: Walck, 1968.
3520 ———. *A Portion in Paradise and Other Jewish Folktales*. New York: Norton, 1970. Schocken paperback.
3521 Nakatani, Chiyoko. *My Teddy Bear*. Illus by author. New York: Crowell, 1976.
3522 Nash Ogden. *The Cruise of the Aardvark*. Illus by Wendy Watson. New York: Evans, 1967.
3523 ———. *Custard the Dragon and the Wicked Knight*. Illus by Linell Nash Smith. Boston: Little, 1959. M166, M167.
3524 ———. *Girls are Silly*. Illus by Laurence B. Smith. New York: Watts, 1961.
3525 ———. *Parents Keep Out, Elderly Poems for Youngerly Readers*. Illus by Barb Carrigan. Boston: Little, 1951. M492.
3526 ———. *You Can't Get There from Here*. Illus by Maurice Sendak. Boston: Little, 1957.
3527 Nash, Ogden, ed. *The Moon is Shining Bright as Day: an Anthology of Good-Humored Verse*. Philadelphia: Lippincott, 1953. M491.
3528 Nason, Thelma. *Our Statue of Liberty*. Chicago: Follett, 1969.
3529 National Council of Teachers of English. *Adventuring with Books*. Urbana, IL: NCTE, 1973.
3530 National Geographic Society. *Books for Young Explorers, Set 1. Lion Cubs, Days of the Dinosaurs, Treasures in the Sea, Dogs, Working for People*. Washington, DC: National Geographic.
3531 ———. *Books for Young Explorers, Set 2. Honeybees, How Animals Hide, Namu, Pandas*. Washington, DC: National Geographic, 1973.
3532 ———. *Books for Young Explorers, Set 6. Camping Adventure, Animals that Build Their Homes, the Playful Dolphins and Wonders of the Desert World*. Washington, DC: National Geographic.
3533 ———. *National Geographic Index, 1947-1976, Inclusive*. Washington, DC: National Geographic, 1977. Supp. 1977-80.
3534 ———. *Song and Garden Birds of North America*. edited by Alex Wetmore. Book and

six phonograph records. Washington, DC: National Geographic, 1975.
3535 ———. *This England*. Washington, DC: 1967.
3536 ———. *Undersea Treasures*. Washington, DC: National Geographic, 1974.
3537 ———. *The World of the American Indian*. Washingon, DC: National Geographic, 1974.
3538 Neal, Harry Edward. *The Story of the Kite*. New York: Vanguard, 1954.
3539 Neimark, Anne E. *Touch of Light, the Story of Louis Braille*. Illus by Robert Parker. New York: Harcourt, 1970.
3540 Nelson, Mary Ann. *A Comparative Anthology of Children's Literature*. New York: Holt, 1972.
3541 Nelson, Esther L. *Singing and Dancing Games for the Very Young*. Illus by Minn Matsuda. Photos by Shirley Zerberg. New York: Sterling, 1977.
3542 Nesbit, E. *The Children's Shakespeare*. Illus by Roy Klep. New York: Random, 1938.
3543 Nesbit, Troy. *The Diamond Cave Mystery*. New York: Whitman, 1956.
3544 Ness, Evaline. *Amelia Mixed the Mustard*. Illus by the author. New York: Scribner, 1975.
3545 ———. *Do You Have the Time, Lydia?* New York: Dutton, 1971. Dutton paperback.
3546 ———. *The Girl and the Goatherd or This and That and Thus and So*. Illus by the author. New York: Dutton, 1970.
3547 ———. *Josefina February*. Illus by the author. New York: Scribner, 1973.
3548 ———. *Long, Broad, and Quick Eye*. New York: Scribner, 1969.
3549 *———. *Sam, Bangs and Moonshine*. Illus by the author. New York: Holt, 1966. Holt paperback. M592
3550 Ness, Evaline, illus. *Old Mother Hubbard and her Dog*. New York: Holt, 1972. Owlet paperback. M495.
3551 ———. *Tom Tit Tot*. New York: Scribner, 1965.
3552 Neufeld, John. *Edgar Allan*. New York: Philipps, 1968. NAL paperback.
3553 ———. *Sleep Two Three Four*. New York: Harper, 1972. Avon paperback in print.
3554 Neville, Emily. *It's Like This Cat*. Illus by Emil Weiss. New York: Harper, 1963. Paperback.
3555 Newberry, Clare T. *April's Kittens*. Illus by the author. New York: Harper, 1940.
3556 ———. *Barkis*. Illus by the author. New York: Harper, 1938.
3557 ———. *Kitten's ABC*. New York: Harper, 1964.
3558 ———. *Marshmallow*. Illus by the author. New York: Harper, 1942.
3559 ———. *Mittens*. Illus by the author. New York: Harper, 1936.
3560 ———. *Smudge*. Illus by the author. New York: Harper, 1948.
3561 Newell, Venetia. *An Egg at Easter, a Folklore Study*. Bloomington, Ind.: Indiana University Press, 1971.
3562 Newland, Mary Reed. *Good King Wenceslas; a Legend in Music and Pictures*. New York: Seabury, 1980.
3563a Newman, Robert. *The Case of the Baker

Street Irregulars, a Sherlock Holmes Story. New York: Atheneum, 1978. Bantam paper.

3563b ———. *Twelve Labors of Hercules.* Illus New York: Crowell, 1972.

3564 Newman, Shirlee Petkin. *Folk Tales from Latin America.* Indianapolis: Bobbs, 1962.

3565 Newsome, Arden J. *Egg Craft.* New York: Lothrop, 1973. Lothrop paperback.

3566 Newton, James R. *The March of the Lemmings.* Illus by Charles Robinson. New York: Crowell, 1976.

3567 Ney, John. *Ox Goes North, More Trouble for the Kid at the Top.* New York: Harper, 1973.

3568 ———. *Ox: The Story of a Kid at the Top.* Philadelphia: Little, 1970. Bantam paperback.

3569 ———. *Ox Under Pressure.* Philadelphia: Little, 1976.

3570 Nic Leodhas, Sorche. *All in the Morning Early.* Illus by Evaline Ness. New York: Holt, 1963. Paperback.

3571 *———. *Always Room for One More.* Illus by Nonny Hogrogian. New York: Holt, 1965. Owlet paperback.

3572 ———. *Heather and Broom; Tales of the Scottish Highlands.* Illus by Consuella Joerns. New York: Holt, 1960.

3573 ———. *Kellyburn Braes.* Illus by Evaline Ness. New York: Holt, 1968.

3574 ———. *The Laird of Cockpen.* Illus by Adrienne Adams. New York: Holt, 1969. Owlet paperback.

3575 ———. *Thistle and Thyme.* Illus by Evaline Ness. New York: Holt, 1962.

3576 Nichols, Ruth. *Walk Out of the World.* Illus by Trina Schart Hyman. New York: Harcourt, 1969.

3577 Nicholson, Margaret E. *People in Books, A Selective Guide to Bibliographical Literature Arranged by Vocations and Other Fields of Reader Interest.* New York: Wilson, 1969.

3578 ———. *People in Books, First Supplement.* New York: Wilson, 1977.

3579 Nickel, Mildred. *Let's Find Out About a Book.* Illus by Tod Krumeic. New York: Watts, 1971.

3580 Nickell, Mollie. *This is Baker's Clay: A New Sculpture Craft.* Illus by Marlo Johansen. Photos by the author. New York: Drake, 1973.

3581 Niculescu, Margaret. *Marionettes of the World.* Boston: Plays, 1969.

3582 Niculescu, Margaret, ed. *Puppet Theatre of the Modern World.* Boston: Plays, 1967.

3583 Niklewiczowa, Maria. *Sparrow's Magic.* Illus by Fruyuji Yamanaka. Trans by Alvin Tresselt. New York: Parents, 1970.

3584 Noahes, Vivien. *Edward Lear: The Life of a Wanderer.* Boston: Houghton, 1969.

3585 Nodset, Joan L. *Who Took the Farmer's Hat?* Illus by the author. New York: Harper, 1963. Scholastic paperback.

3586 Nolan, Dennis. *Monster Bubble.* New York: Prentice-Hall, 1976.

3587 Nolan, Jeannette, C. *George Rogers Clark.* New York: Messner, 1954.

3588 Noren, Catherine. *Photography: How to Improve Your Technique.* New York: Watts, 1973. Paperback.

3589 Norris, Gunilla. *Green and Something Else.* Illus by Charles Robinson. New York: Simon and Schuster, 1971.

3590 North, Sterling. *Rascal.* New York: Dutton, 1963. Avon paperback. M563.

3591 ———. *Rascal: A Memoir of a Better Era.* New York: Dutton, 1963.

3592 ———. *Mark Twain and the River.* Illus by Victor Mays. Boston: Houghton, 1961.

3593 Norton, Andre. *Key Out of Time.* Cleveland: World, 1963. Ace paperback in print.

3594 ———. *Lavender Green Magic.* Illus by Judity Gwyn Brown. New York: Crowell, 1974.

3595 ———. *Moon of Three Rings.* New York: Viking, 1966. Ace paperback in print.

3596 ———. *Operation Time Search.* New York: Harcourt, 1967. Ace paperback.

3597 ———. *Postmarked the Stars.* New York: Harcourt, 1969. Ace paperback in print.

3598 ———. *Red Hart Magic.* Illus by Donna Diamond. New York: Crowell, 1976.

3599 ———. *Steel Magic.* Illus by Robin Jacques. Cleveland: World, 1965.

3600 ———. *Time Traders.* Cleveland: World, 1958. Ace paperback in print.

3601a ———. *Uncharted Stars.* New York: Ace paperback, 1975.

3601b ———. *The Zero Stone.* New York: Viking, 1968.

3602 Norton, Mary. *Bed-knob and Broomstick.* Illus by Erik Blegvad. New York: Harcourt, 1957. Voyager paperback.

3603 ———. *The Borrowers.* Illus by Beth and Joe Krush. New York: Harcourt, 1953. Voyager paperback.

3604 ———. *The Borrowers Afield.* Illus by Beth and Joe Krush. New York: Harcourt, 1955. Voyager paperback.

3605 ———. *The Borrowers Afloat.* Illus by Beth and Joe Krush. New York: Harcourt, 1961. Voyager paperback.

3606 ———. *The Complete Adventures of the Borrowers.* Illus by Beth and Joe Krush. New York: Harcourt, 1967.

3607 ———. *Poor Stainless: A New Story about the Borrowers.* New York: Harcourt, 1971.

3608a Nostlinger, Christine. *Konrad.* Trans by Althea Bell. Illus by Carol Nicklaus. New York: Watts, 1977.

3608b Nourse, Alan. *Star Surgeon.* New York: McKay, 1962.

3609 Noyes, Alfred. *The Highwayman.* Illus by Gilbert Riswold. Englewood Cliffs, NJ: Prentice-Hall, 1969.

3610 Nussbaumer, Mares. *Away in a Manger, a Story of the Nativity.* Illus by Paul Nussbaumer. New York: Harcourt, 1965. M132.

3611 Oakley, Graham. *The Church Mice Abroad.* Illus by author. New York: Atheneum, 1973.

3612 ———. *The Church Mice Adrift.* Illus by author. New York: Atheneum, 1977. Aladdin paperback.

3613 ———. *The Church Mice and the Moon.* Illus by the author. New York: Atheneum, 1974. Aladdin paperback.

3614 ———. *The Church Mice Spread their Wings.* Illus by author. New York: Atheneum, 1976.

3615 ———. *The Church Mouse.* Illus by the author. New York: Atheneum, 1972. Aladdin paperback.

3616 ———. *Graham Oakley's Magical Changes.* New York: Atheneum, 1980.

3617 Obraztsov, Sergei. *The Children's Puppet Theatre.* Trans. by J.T. MacDermott. London: Faber and Faber, 1961.

3618 O'Brien, Jack. *The Return of Silver Chief.* Illus by Kurt Wiese. New York: Winston, 1943.

3619 ———. *Silver Chief: Dog of the North.* Illus by Kurt Wiese. New York: Winston, 1933.

3620 O'Brien, Robert and Zena. *Mrs. Frisby and the Rats of NIMH.* Illus by Zena Berstein. New York: Atheneum, 1971. Paperback. M452.

3621 O'Dell, Scott. *The Black Pearl.* Boston: Houghton, 1967. Dell paperback.. M89.

3622 ———. *Carlota.* Boston: Houghton, 1977. Dell paperback.

3623 ———. *Child of Fire.* Boston: Houghton, 1974. Dell paperback.

3624 ———. *Dark Canoe.* Boston: Houghton, 1968.

3625 ———. *Island of the Blue Dolphins.* Boston: Houghton, 1960. Dell paperback. M320.

3626 ———. *The King's Fifth.* Illus by Samuel Bruant. Boston: Houghton, 1966. Dell paperback. M344.

3627 ———. *Sing Down the Moon.* New York: Houghton, 1970. Dell paperback. M614.

3628 ———. *Zia.* Boston: Houghton, 1976. Dell paperback. M783.

3629 Oechsli, Kelly. *Humpty Dumpty's Holiday Stories.* New York: Parents, 1973.

3630 Office of Early Childhood Programs, the School District of Philadelphia. *Creative Dramatics Handbook.* Philadelphia: School District of Philadelphia, 1974. Distributed by the National Council of Teachers of English.

3631 Ogg, Oscar. *The Twenty-six Letters.* New York: Crowell, 1948.

3632 Olcott, F.J. *Good Stories for Great Birthdays.* Boston: Houghton, 1922.

3633 ———. *Good Stories for Great Holidays, Arranged for Story-Telling and Reading Aloud and for the Children's Own Reading.* Boston: Houghton, 1914. Folcroft Reproduction.

3634 ———. *Story-Telling Poems.* New York: Arno Reprint, n.d.

3635 Olenius, Elsa. *Swedish Fairy Tales.* Illus by John Bauer. Trans by Holger Lundberg. New York: Delacorte, 1973.

3636 Oleson, Claire. *For Pepita—An Orange Tree.* Illus by Margot Tomes. New York: Doubleday, 1967.

3637 Olfson, Lewy. *You Can Put on a Show.* New York: Sterling, 1975.

3638 ———. *Classics Adapted for Acting and Reading.* Boston: Plays, 1970.

3639 O'Neill, Mary. *Fingers Are Always Bringing Me News.* Illus by Don Bolognese. New York: Doubleday, 1969.

3640 ———. *Hailstones and Halibut Bones.* Illus by Leonard Weisgard. New York: Doubleday, 1961. M261.

3641 ———. *Take a Number.* Illus by Al Nagy. New York: Doubleday, 1966.

3642 ———. *Winds.* Illus by James Barkley. New York: Doubleday, 1973.

3643 ———. *Words, Words, Words.* Illus by New York: Doubleday, 1966.

3644 Opie, Iona and Peter, ed. *Oxford Nursery Rhyme Book.* Illus by Joan Hassall. Engravings by Thomas and John Bewick. New York: Oxford, 1955.

3645 ———. *The Oxford Book of Children's Verse.* New York: Oxford, 1973.

3646 Orgel, Doris. *The Story of Lohengrin, the Knight of the Swan.* Illus by Herbert Danska. New York: Putnam, 1966.

3647 Ormondroyd, Edward. *All in Good Time.* Illus by Ruth Robbins. Berkeley, CA: Parnassus, 1975.

3648 ———. *Broderick.* Illus by John Larrecqu. Berkeley, CA: Parnassus, 1971.

3649 ———. *Theodore's Rival.* Illus by John Larrecqu. Berkeley, CA: Parnassus, 1969.

3650 ———. *Time at the Top.* Illus by Peggy Bach. Berkeley, CA: Parnassus, 1963.

3651 Osmond, Edward. *From Drumbeat to Tickertape.* Criterion, 1960.

3652 Ostrom, John H. *The Strange World of Dinosaurs.* Illus by Joseph Sibal. New York: Putnam, 1964.

3653 Ota, Koski. *Printing for Fun.* New York: Obolensky, 1960.

3654 Otsuka, Yuzo. *Suho and the White Horse, a Legend of Mongolia.* Illus by Suekichi Akaba. Indianapolis: Bobbs, 1969. M655.

3655 Ovenden, Graham and John Davis, ed. *The Illustrators of Alice and Through the Looking Glass.* New York: St. Martins, 1973.

3656 Oxenbury, Helen. *Helen Oxenbury's ABC of Things.* Illus by the author. New York: Watts, 1972.

3657 ———. *Numbers of Things.* Illus by the author. New York: Watts, 1968.

3658 ———. *Pig Tale.* Illus by the author. New York: Morrow, 1973.

3659 Paine, Roberta M. *Looking at Sculpture.* New York: Lothrop, 1968.

3660 Paine, Albert Bigelow. *The Boys' Life of Mark Twain; the Story of a Man Who Made the World Laugh and Love Him.* New York: Harper, 1916.

3661 *Painting, Printing and Modeling.* New York: Watts, 1969, 1972.

3662 Paladan, Liz. *Playing With Puppets.* Boston: Plays, 1975. Paperback.

3663 Palazzo, Tony. *Magic Crayon, Drawings from Simple Shapes and Forms.* New York: Lion Press, 1967.

3664 Pallas, Norvin. *Code Games.* New York: Sterling, 1971.

3665 Palmer, Robin. *Dragons, Unicorns, and Other Magical Beasts.* Illus by Don Bolognese. New York: Walck, 1966.

3666 Palmer, William R. *Why the North Star Still Stands and Other Indian Legends.* Illus by Ursula Koering. Englewood Cliffs, N.J.: Prentice-Hall, 1946.

3667 Paludan, Liz. *Eva's Animals Friends, Complete Instructions for Making the World-famous Eva Soft Toys.* Transl by Ellen Goldman-Berrington. Photos by J. Buusmann. New York: Crown, 1973.

3668 Pannell, Lucile and Frances Cavanah. *Holiday Round Up.* Illus by Manning de V. Lee. Philadelphia: Macrae, 1950, 1968.

3669 Pape, Lee. *The First Doll in the World.* Illus by Leonard Weisgard. New York: Lothrop, 1961.

3670 *Papier Mache, Dying and Leatherwork.* New York: Watts, 1972.

3671 Parish, Peggy. *Amelia Bedelia.* Illus by Fritz Siebel. New York: Harper, 1963. Scholastic paperback. M19.

3672 ———. *Amelia Bedelia and the Surprise Shower.* Illus by Fritz Siebel. New York: Harper, 1966. Trophy paperback.

3673 ———. *Beginning Mobiles.* Illus by Lynn Sweat. New York: Macmillan, 1979.

3674 ———. *Come Back, Amelia Bedelia.* Illus by Wallace Tripp. New York: Harper, 1971. Trophy paperback. M144.

3675 ———. *Costumes to Make.* Illus by Lynn Sweat. New York: Macmillan, 1970.

3676 ———. *Dinosaur Time.* Illus by Arnold Lobel. New York: Harper, 1974.

3677 ———. *Good Work, Amelia Bedelia.* Illus by Lynn Sweat. New York: Greenwillow, 1976.

3678 ———. *Let's Be Early Settlers with Daniel Boone.* Illus by Arnold Lobel. New York: Harper, 1967.

3679 ———. *Let's Be Indians* Illus by Arnold Lobel. New York: Harper, 1962.

3680 ———. *Play Ball, Amelia Bedelia.* New York: Harper, 1972. Trophy paperback.

3681 ———. *Teach Us, Amelia Bedelia.* New York: Greenwillow, 1977.

3682 ———. *Thank You, Amelia Bedelia.* Illus by Fritz Siebel. New York: Harper, 1964. M681.

3683 Parker, Elinor. *Here and There One Hundred Poems About Places.* Illus by Peter Spier. New York: Crowell, 1967.

3684 ———. *One Hundred Story Poems.* Illus by Henry C. Pitz. New York: Crowell, 1951.

3685 ———. *One Hundred More Story Poems.* Illus by Peter Spier. New York: Crowell, 1960.

3686 Parker, K. Langloh. *Australian Legendary Tales.* H. Drake-Brockman, ed. Illus by Elizabeth Durack. New York: Viking, 1966.

3687 Parker, Richard. *A Time to Choose: A Story of Suspense.* New York: Harper, 1974.

3688 Parkin, Rex. *The Red Carpet.* Illus by the author. New York: Macmillan, 1948. Collier paperback. M575, 576.

3689 Parrish, Anne. *Floating Island.* New York: Harper, 1930.

3690a Pascal, Fran. *Hangin' Out With Cici.* New York: Viking, 1977. Arch paperback.

3690b Paschel, Herbert P. *First Book of Color.* New York: Watts, 1959.

3691 Paterson, A.B. *Waltzing Matilda.* Illus by Desmond Digby. New York: Holt, 1970. M731.

3692 Paterson, Diane. *If I were a Toad.* New York: Dial, 1977.

3693 Paterson, Katherine. *Bridge to Terabithia.* Illus by Donna Diamond. New York: Crowell, 1977. Avon paperback.

3694 ———. *Of Nightingales that Weep.* New York: Crowell, 1974. Avon paperback.

3695 Patrick, Gloria. *Bug in a Jug and Other Funny Poems.* New York: Scholastic paperback, 1973.

3696 Patterson, Lillie. *Martin Luther King, Jr.: Man of Peace.* Champaign, Ill.: Garrard, 1969.

3697 ———. *Martin Luther King, Jr.* Dell paperback, 1972.

3698 ———. *Meet Miss Liberty.* New York: Macmillan, 1962.

3699 Pauli, Hertha. *Silent Night, the Story of a Song.* Illus by Fritz Kredel. New York: Knopf, 1944.

3700 Payne, Emmy. *Katie No Pocket.* Illus by H.A. Rey. Boston: Houghton, 1969. Paperback.

3701 Payne, Nina. *All the Day Long.* Illus by Laurel Schindelman. New York: Atheneum, 1973.

3702 Peare, Catherine Owens. *The Helen Keller Story.* New York: Crowell, 1959.

3703 ———. *Henry Wadsworth Longfellow, His Life.* Illus by Margaret Ayer. New York: Holt, 1954.

3704 ———. *Mark Twain: His Life.* Illus by Margaret Ayer. New York: Holt, 1954.

3705 Pearce, Philippa. *Beauty and the Beast.* Illus by Alan Barrett. New York: Crowell, 1972.

3706 ———. *Tom's Midnight Garden.* Illus by Susan Einzig. Philadelphia: Lippincott, 1958.

3707 Pease, Howard. *The Secret Cargo.* Garden City, NY: Doubleday, 1946.

3708 ———. *The Tod Moran Mysteries.* Garden City, NY: Doubleday, 1930's.

3709 Peck, Leigh. *Pecos Bill and Lightning.* Illus by Kurt Wiese. New York: Houghton, 1940.

3710 Peck, Richard. *Ghosts I have Been.* New York: Viking, 1977. Dell paperback.

3711 Pederson, Elsa. *Alaska.* New York: Coward, 1968.

3712 Peet, Bill. *The Whingdingdilly.* Boston: Houghton, 1970

3713 Pelitier, Leslie. *Guideposts to the Stars: Exploring Stars Throughout the Year.* New York: Macmillan, 1972.

3714 Pellowski, Anne, ed. *Have You Seen a Comet? Children's Art and Writing from Around the World.* New York: Day, 1971.

3715 Pels, Gertrude. *Easy Puppets, Making and Using Hand Puppets.* New York: Crowell, 1951.

3716 Penn, Elizabeth Hall. *Individualized Arts and Crafts Lessons for the Elementary School.* W. Nyack, New York: Parker, 1975.

3717 Penny, Grace Johnson. *Tales of the Cheyenne.* Illus by Walter R. West. Boston: Houghton, 1953.

3718 Peppe, Rodney. *An Alphabet Book.* Illus by the author. New York: Four Winds, 1968.

3719 ———. *Circus Numbers, a Counting Book.* Illus by the author. New York: Delacorte, 1969.

3720 ———. *Odd One Out.* Illus by the author. New York: Viking, 1974. Seafarer paperback.

3721 Peppe, Rodney, illus. *Hey Riddle Riddle, a Book of Traditional Riddles.* New York: Holt, 1971. Owlet paperback.

3722 ———. *The House that Jack Built.* New York: Delacorte, 1970.

3723 ———. *Simple Simon.* New York: Holt, 1972.

3724 Perrault, Charles. *Cinderella.* Illus and trans. by Marcia Brown. New York: Scribners, 1954.

3725 ———. *Cinderella.* Illus by Paul Galdone. New York: McGraw, 1978.

3726 ———. *Cinderella, or the Little Glass Slipper.*

Illus by Shirley Hughes. New York: Walck, 1970.

3727 ———. Cinderella. Illus by Nola Langner. New York: Scholastic paperback, 1972.

3728 ———. Cinderella, or the Little Glass Slipper. Trans, adapted, and illus by Errol le Cain. New York: Bradbury, 1973.

3729 ———. Famous Fairy Tales. Trans by Sarah Chokla Gross. Illus by Charles Mozley. New York: Watts, 1959.

3730 ———. Perrault's Complete Fairy Tales. Trans by A.E. Johnson, et al. Illus by W. Heath Robinson. New York: Dodd, 1961, 1971.

3731 ———. Perrault's Classic French Fairy Tales. Illus by Janusz Grabinanski. New York: Meredith, 1967.

3732 ———. Puss in Boots. Illus by Marcia Brown. New York: Scribner, 1952. Scribner paperback. M555.

3733 ———. Puss in Boots. Illus by Paul Galdone. New York: Seabury, 1976.

3734 ———. Puss in Boots. Illus by Hans Fisher. New York: Harcourt, 1959.

3735 Petersham, Maud and Miska. An American ABC. Illus by the authors. New York: Macmillan, 1941.

3736 ———. The Christ Child. Illus by the authors. New York: Doubleday, 1931.

3737 ———. Circus Baby. Illus by the authors. New York: Macmillan, 1950. M137, M138.

3738 ———. David. Illus by the authors. New York: Macmillan, 1967.

3739 ———. Joseph and His Brothers. Illus by the authors. New York: Macmillan, 1958.

3740 ———. Moses; From the Story Told in the Old Testament. Illus by the authors. New York: Macmillan, 1958.

3741 *———. The Rooster Crows; a Book of American Rhymes and Jingles. New York: Macmillan, 1945. Paperback.

3742 ———. Ruth. Illus by the authors. New York:.

3743 ———. The Shepherd's Psalm.Illus by the authors. New York: Macmillan, 1962.

3744 ———. The Story of Jesus. Illus by the authors. New York: Macmillan, 1967.

3745 Peterson, Grete. Making Toys with Plywood. New York: Reinhold, 1967.

3746 Peterson, Helen. The Making of the U.S. Constitution. Champaign, IL: Garrard, 1974.

3747 Peterson, John. How to Write Codes and Send Secret Messages. Illus by Bernice Myers. Englewood Cliffs, NJ: Four Winds, 1970. Scholastic paperback.

3748 Peterson, Roger T. A Field Guide to the Birds, Giving Field Marks of All Species East of the Rockies. Boston: Houghton, 1947. Paperback.

3749 ———. A Field Guide to Western Birds; Field Marks of All Species Found in North America West of the 100th Meridian . . . . Boston: Houghton, 1968. Paperback.

3750 Petie, Haris. Book of Big Bugs. Englewood Cliffs, NJ: Prentice-Hall, 1977.

3751 Petry, Ann. Harriet Tubman, Conductor of the Underground Railroad. New York: Crowell, 1955.

3752 Petterson, Henry and Ray Gerring. Exploring with Paint. New York: Reinhold, 1964.

3753 Pettit, Florence H. How to Make Whirligigs

and Whimmy Diddles and Other American Folkcraft Objects. Illus by Laura L. Foster. New York: Crowell, 1972.

3754 Peyton, Kathleen. A Pattern of Roses. Illus by the author. New York: Crowell, 1973.

3755 Pflug, Betsy. Funny Bags. New York: Van Nostrand, 1968.

3756 Phelan, Mary Kay. Midnight Alarm: The Story of Paul Revere's Ride. Illus by Leonard Weisgard. New York: Crowell, 1968.

3757 ———. The Story of the Boston Tea Party. Illus by Frank Aloise. New York: Crowell, 1973.

3758 Philpott, Alexis Robert. Dictionary of Puppetry. Boston: Plays, 1969.

3759 ———. Eight Plays for Hand Puppets. Boston: Plays, 1968.

3760 ———. Let's Look at Puppets. Chicago: Whitman, 1966.

3761 ———. Let's Make Puppets. New York: Van Nostrand, 1972. Paperback.

3762a Philpott, Violet and Mary Jane McNeil. Know How Book of Puppets. New York: Sterling, 1976.

3762b Phipson, Joan. The Way Home. New York: Atheneum, 1973.

3763 Phumla. Nomi and the Magic Fish. Garden City, NY: Doubleday, 1972.

3764 Piatti, Celestino. Celestino Piatti's Animal ABC. Illus by the author. New York: Atheneum, 1966.

3765 ———. Happy Owls. Illus by the author. New York: Atheneum, 1964. M264, M265.

3766 Picard, Barbara Leonie. Celtic Tales: Legends of Tall Warriors of Old Enchantments. Illus by John G. Galsworthy. New York: Criterion, 1965.

3767 ———. The Iliad of Homer. New York: Walck, 1960.

3768 ———. The Odyssey of Homer. London: Oxford, 1952.

3769 ———. Stories of King Arthur and His Knights. Illus by Roy Morgan. New York: Walck, 1955.

3770 ———. Tales of the British People. Illus by Eric Fraser. New York: Criterion, 1961.

3771 Pilkington, F.M. Shamrock and Spear, Tales and Legends from Ireland. Illus by Leo and Diane Dillon. New York: Holt, 1968.

3772 Pinkwater, Daniel M. Fat Men from Space. Illus by the author. New York: Dodd, 1977.

3773 Pinkwater, Manus. Bear's Picture. Illus by the author. New York: Holt, 1972.

3774 Piper, Watty. The Little Engine That Could. Illus by George and Doris Hauman. New York: Platt, 1961. Scholastic paperback.

3775 Pitz, Henry. Illustrating Children's Books: History, Technique, Production., New York: Watson-Guptill, 1963.

3776 Place, Marian Templeton. On the Track of Bigfoot. New York: Dodd, 1974.

3777 Plagemann, Bentz. How to Write a Story. New York: Lothrop, 1971.

3778 Platt, Kin. Big Max. Illus by Robert Lopshire. New York: Harper, 1965.

3779 ———. Big Max in the Mystery of the Missing Moose. New York: Harper, 1977.

3780 ———. The Boy Who Could Make Himself Disappear. Philadelphia: Chilton, 1968. Dell paperback.

3781 ———. *Hey, Dummy.* Philadelphia: Chilton, 1971. Dell paperback.

3782 Plotz, Helen. *Earth is the Lord's: Poems of the Spirit.* Illus by Clare Leighton. New York: Crowell, 1965.

3783 ———. *Imagination's Other Place: Poems of Science and Mathematics.* Illus by Clare Leighton. New York: Crowell, 1955.

3784 ———. *Untune the Sky; Poems of Music and Dance.* Illus by Clare Leighton. New York: Crowell, 1957.

3785 Podendorf, Illa. *Touching for Telling.* Illus by Florence Frederick. Chicago: Children's, 1971.

3786 ———. *True Book of Weeds and Wild Flowers.* Illus by Mary Gehr. Chicago: Children's, 1955.

3787 Poe, Edgar Allan. *The Gold Bug and Other Stories.* Boston: Branden, 1962. Paperback.

3788 ———. *The Gold Bug and Other Tales of Mystery.* Illus by Al Davidson. Chicago: Children's Press, 1969.

3789 ———. *Tales and Poems of Edgar Allan Poe.* New York: Macmillan, 1953.

3790 ———. *Tales of Mystery and Imagination.* New York: Oxford University Press, n.d. Dutton paperback.

3791 ———. *Tales of Terror and Fantasy, Ten Stories from Mystery and Imagination.* New York: Dutton, 1972.

3792 ———. *Three Poems of Edgar Allan Poe.* Illus by Paul Galdone. New York: McGraw, 1966. M565.

3793 Politi, Leo. *Juanita.* Illus by the author. New York: Scribner, 1968.

3794 ———. *Moy Moy.* Illus by the author. New York: Scribner, 1960.

3795 ———. *Pedro, Angel of Olivera Street.* Illus by the author. New York: Scribner, 1946.

3796 ———. *Saint Francis and the Animals.* Illus by the author. New York: Scribner, 1959.

3797 *———. *Song of the Swallows.* Illus by the author. New York: Scribner, 1949. Paperback. M620, M621.

3798 Politzer, Annie. *My Journals and Sketchbooks, by Robinson Crusoe.* Illus by Michael Politzer. New York: Harcourt, 1974.

3799 Polushkin, Maria. *The Little Hen and the Giant.* Illus by Yuri Salzman. New York: Harper, 1977.

3800 Pomerantz, Charlotte. *The Mango Tooth.* Illus by Marilyn Hafner. New York: Greenwillow, 1977.

3801 ———. *The Piggy in the Puddle.* Illus by James Marshall. New York: Macmillan, 1974.

3802 Pond, Alonzo W. *Deserts: Silent Lands of the World.* New York: Norton, 1965.

3803 Pope, Elizabeth. *The Sherwood Ring.* New York: Houghton, 1958.

3804 Posell, Elsa. *This is an Orchestra.* Boston: Houghton, 1973. M316.

3805 Poston, Elizabeth. *Baby's Song Book.* Illus by William Stobbs. Music by Elizabeth Poston. New York: Crowell, 1971.

3806 Potter, Beatrix. *Cecily Parsley's Nursery Rhymes.* Illus by the author. New York: Warne, 1922.

3807 ———. *Letters to Children, Letters Written by Beatrix Potter during the 1890's.* New York: Walker, 1966.

3808 ———. *Songs of Peter Rabbit.* Music by Dudley Glass. New York: Warne, 1952.

3809 ———. *Squirrel Nutkin, a Children's Play.* New York: Warne, 1967.

3810 ———. *The Story of Miss Moppett.* Illus by the author. New York: Warne, 1906. Watts paperback.

3811 ———. *The Tailor of Gloucester.* Illus by the author. New York: Warne, 1968. Dover. paperback.

3812 ———. *Tale of Benjamin Bunny.* Illus by the author. New York: Warne, 1904. Dover paperback. M667, M668.

3813 ———. *Tale of Flopsy Bunnies.* Illus by the author. New York: Warne, 1909.

3814 ———. *Tale of Jemima Puddle-Duck.* Illus by the author. New York: Warne, 1908. i.t.a. edition.

3815 ———. *Tale of Johnny Townmouse.* Illus by the author. New York: Warne, 1918.

3816 ———. *Tale of Little Pig Robinson.* Illus by the author. New York: Warne, 1930.

3817 ———. *Tale of Mrs. Piggy-Winkle.* Illus by the author. New York: Warne, 1905. Dover paperback.

3818 ———. *Tale of Mrs. Tittlemouse.* Illus by the author. New York: Warne, 1910.

3819 ———. *Tale of Mister Jeremy Fisher.* Illus by the author. New York: Warne, 1906. Dover paperback. M669.

3820 ———. *Tale of Peter Rabbit.* Illus by the author. New York: Warne, 1902. Dover paperback. Scholastic paperback. M671, M672.

3821 ———. *Tale of Squirrel Nutkin.* Illus by the author. New York: Warne, 1903. Dover paperback. M673.

3822 ———. *Tale of Tom Kitten.* Illus by the author. New York: Warne, 1938. M674.

3823 ———. *The Tale of Two Bad Mice.* Illus by the author. New York: Warne, 1904. Dover paperback. M675.

3824 Potter, Charles Francis. *More Tongue Tanglers and a Rigmarole.* Cleveland: World, 1964.

3825 ———. *Tongue Tanglers.* Cleveland: World, 1962.

3826 Poulsson, Emilie. *Finger Plays for Nursery and Kindergarten.* New York: Hart, 1977.

3827 Pratt, Davis. *Magic Animals of Japan.* Illus by Elsa Kola. Berkeley, CA: Parnassus, 1967.

3828 Pratt, Lois. *Puppet Do-it-Yourself-Book.* Hicksville, N.Y.: Exposition, 1957.

3829 Prelutsky, Jack. *Circus.* Illus by Arnold Lobel. New York: Macmillan, 1978.

3830 ———. *A Gopher in the Garden and Other Animals Poems.* Illus by Robert Leydenfrost. New York: Macmillan, 1967.

3831 ———. *It's Halloween.* Illus by Marilyn Hafner. New York: Greenwillow, 1977.

3832 ———. *Nightmares, Poems to Trouble Your Sleep.* Illus by Arnold Lobel. New York: Greenwillow, 1976.

3833 ———. *The Snoop on the Sidewalk and Other Poems.* Illus by Byron Barton. New York:

Morrow, 1977.

3834 ———. *Toucans Two and Other Poems.* Illus by Jose Aruego. New York: Macmillan, 1970.

3835 Prelutsky, Jack, trans. *The End of Nonsense, Humorous Verses Translated from the German.* Illus by Wilifred Blecher. New York: Macmillan, 1968.

3836 Preston, Carol. *A Trilogy of Christmas Plays for Children.* New York: Harcourt, 1967.

3837 Preston, Edna Mitchell. *The Boy Who Could Make Things.* Illus by Leonard Kessler. New York: Viking, 1970.

3838 ———. *Popcorn and Ma Goodness.* Illus by Robert Andrew Parker. New York: Viking, 1959.

3839 ———. *The Sad Story of the Little Bluebird and the Hungry Cat.* New York: Four Winds, 1975.

3840 ———. *Squawk to the Moon, Little Goose.* Illus by Barbara Cooney. New York: Viking, 1974.

3841 Price, Christine. *Dancing Masks of Africa.* New York: Scribner, 1975.

3842 ———. *The Rich Man and the Singer.* Edited and illus by C. Price. New York: Dutton, n.d.

3843 ———. *Sixty at a Blow: A Tall Tale From Turkey.* Illus by the author. New York: Dutton, 1968.

3844 Price, Christine, illus. *Widdecombe Fair, an Old English Folk Song.* New York: Warne, 1968.

3845 Price, L. and Wronsky, M. *Concoctions.* New York: Dutton, 1976.

3846a Prieto, Mariana and Grizella Hopper. *The Birdmen of Papantla.* Illus by Macduff Everton. Pasadena, CA: Ward Ritchie Press, 1972.

3846b Prince, Gary M. *Vanya and the Clay Queen.* Minneapolis: Cariorltodo, 1975.

3847 Pringle, Laurence. *Dinosaurs and Their World.* New York: Harcourt, 1968. Voyager paperback.

3848 ———. *Into the Woods: Exploring the Forest Ecosystem.* New York: Macmillan, 1973.

3849 Priolo, Joan B. *Ideas for Collage.* New York: Sterling, 1972.

3850 Protter, Eric. *The Child's Treasury of Folk-Fairy Tales.* Great Neck, NY: Channel Press, 1961.

3851 Proudfit, Isabel. *River Boy, the Story of Mark Twain.* Illus by W.C. Nims. New York: Messner, 1940.

3852 Provensen, Alice and Martin. *A Peaceable Kingdom: the Shaker abecedarius.* New York: Viking, 1978.

3853 ———. *What is Color?* New York: Golden, 1967.

3854 Pugh, Ellen. *Tales from the Welsh Hills.* Illus by Joan Sandin. New York: Dodd, 1968.

3855 Purdy, Susan. *Books for You to Make.* Philadelphia: Lippincott, 1973.

3856 ———. *Costumes for You to Make.* Philadelphia: Lippincott, 1971.

3857 Putnam, Peter. *Triumph of the Seeing Eye.* Illus by Walter Lord. New York: Harper, 1963.

3858 Pyle, Howard. *Men of Iron.* New York: Harper, 1891. Airmont paperback.

3859 ———. *The Merry Adventures of Robin Hood of Great Renown in Nottinghamshire.* Illus by the author. New York: Scribner, 1946.

3860 ———. *The Story of King Arthur and His Knights.* Illus by the author. New York: Scribner, 1903. Dover paperback.

3861 ———. *Wonder Clock.* Illus by the author. New York: Harper, n.d.

3862 Quackenbush, Robert. *Detective Mole.* Illus by the author. New York: Lothrop, 1976.

3863 ———. *Detective Mole and the Circus Mystery.* Illus by the author. New York: Lothrop, 1980.

3864 ———. *Detective Mole and the Halloween Mystery.* Illus by the author. New York: Morrow, 1981.

3865 ———. *Detective Mole and the Seashore Mystery.* Illus by the author. New York: Lothrop, 1979.

3866 ———. *Detective Mole and the Secret Clues.* Illus by the author. New York: Lothrop, 1977.

3867 ———. *Detective Mole and the Tip-Top Mystery.* Illus by the author. New York: Lothrop, 1978.

3868 Quackenbush, Robert, ed. *The Holiday Song Book: 100 Songs! 27 Holidays!* Illus by R. Quackenbush. Music by Harry Buch. New York: Lothrop, 1977.

3869 ———. *The Gambit Book of Children's Songs.* Illus by Errol Le Cain. Music by D.M. and Roderick Bliss. Ipswich, MA: Gambit, 1970.

3870 Quackenbush, Robert, illus. *Clementine.* Philadelphia: Lippincott, 1974. M139.

3871 ———. *Go Tell Aunt Rhody.* Philadelphia: Lippincott, 1973.

3872 ———. *Old MacDonald Had a Farm.* Philadelphia: Lippincott, 1972. M369.

3873 ———. *She'll Be Comin' Round the Mountain.* Philadelphia: Lippincott, 1973. M204, M607.

3874 ———. *Skip to my Lou.* Philadelphia: Lippincott, 1975.

3875 Quigley, Lillian. *The Blind Men and the Elephant; an Old Tale from the Land of India.* Illus by Janice Holland. New York: Scribner, 1959. Scribner paperback. M90.

3876 Quin-Harkin, Janet. *Peter Penny's Dance.* Illus by Anita Lobel. New York: Dial, 1976.

3877 Quilici, Falco. *The Great Desert.* Adapted by Margaret V. Hyde. New York: McGraw, 1969.

3878 Quinn, Daniel. *Land and Sea Monsters.* Northbrook, IL: Hubbard, 1971.

3879 Rackham, Arthur. *The Arthur Rackham Fairy Book, a Book of Old Favorites.* Philadelphia: Lippincott, 1950.

3880 Rackow, Leo. *Postercraft.* New York: Sterling, 1971.

3881 Ramage, Corrine. *The Joneses.* Philadelphia: Lippincott, 1975.

3882 Rand, Ann and Paul. *I Know a Lot of Things.* New York: Harcourt, 1956. M310.

3883 ———. *Listen Listen.* New York: Harcourt, 1970.

3884 ———. *Little One.* New York: Harcourt, 1962.

3885 ———. *Sparkle and Spin, a Book About Words.* New York: Harcourt, 1957. M627.

3886a Randall, Arne W. *Murals for Schools, Sharing Creative Experiences.* Worcester, MA:

Davis, 1956.

3886b Randall, Florence. *Watcher in the Woods.* New York: Atheneum, 1976.

3887a Ranke, Kurt, ed. *Folktales of Germany.* Trans. by Lotte Ranke. Chicago: University of Chicago Press, 1966. Paperback.

3887b *Ransome, Arthur. *The Fool of the World and the Flying Ship.* Illus by Uri Shulevitz. New York: Farrar, 1968.

3888 Raposco, Jo and Jeffrey Moss. *The Sesame Street Song Book.* Illus by Loretta Trezzo. Music by Sy Oliver. New York: Simon and Schuster and the Children's Television Workshop, 1971.

3889 Rappaport, Eva. *Banner, Forward! The Pictorial Biography of a Guide Dog.* New York: Dutton, 1969.

3890 Raskin, Ellen. *And It Rained.* Illus by the author. New York: Atheneum, 1969.

3891 ———. *Figgs and Phantoms.* Illus by the author. New York: Dutton, 1974. Paperback.

3892 ———. *Franklin Stein.* Illus by the author. New York: Atheneum, 1972. Aladdin paperback.

3893 ———. *Ghost in a Four Room Apartment.* Illus by the author. New York: Atheneum, 1978. Aladdin paperback.

3894 ———. *The Mysterious Disappearance of Leon (I Mean Noel).* Illus by the author. New York: Dutton, 1973, Paperback.

3895 ———. *Nothing Ever Happens on My Block.* Illus by the author. New York: Atheneum, 1966. Scholastic paperback.

3896 ———. *The Tatooed Potato and Other Clues.* Illus by the author. New York: Dutton, 1975.

3897 ———. *Twenty-Two, Twenty-Three.* Illus by the author. New York: Atheneum, 1976.

3898 ———. *The Westing Game.* Illus by the author. New York: Dutton, 1978. Camelot paperback.

3899 ———. *Who, Said Sue, Said Who?* Illus by the author. New York: Atheneum, 1973. Aladdin paperback.

3900 Raskin, Joseph and Edith. *Tales Our Settlers Told.* Illus by William Sauts Back. New York: Lothrop, 1971.

3901 Rassmussen, Carrie. *Let's Say Poetry Together and Have Fun.* Illus by Morris Lundin. Minneapolis: Burgess, 1964.

3902 Rassmussen, Carrie and Caroline Storck. *Fun-Time Puppets.* Chicago: Childrens, 1952.

3903 Rau, Margaret. *The Penguin Book.* Illus by John Hamberger. New York: Hawthorn, 1968.

3904 Rauch, Hans-Georg. *The Lines are coming: A Book About Drawings.* New York: Scribners, 1978.

3905 Ravielli, Anthony. *The Rise and Fall of the Dinosaurs.* Illus by the author. New York: Parents, 1963.

3906 Rawlings, Marjorie K. *The Yearling.* Illus by N.C. Wyeth. New York: Scribner, 1939. Paperback. M777, M778.

3907 Rayner, Mary. *Mr. and Mrs. Pig's Evening Out.* New York: Atheneum, 1976. Aladdin paperback.

3908 Read, Herbert. *This Way Delight, A Book of Poetry for the Young.* Illus by Juliet Kepes. New York: Pantheon, 1956.

3909 Reck, Alma K. *Clocks Tell the Time.* Illus by Janina Domanska. New York: Scribner, 1960.

3910 Reed, Gwendolyn, ed. *Bird Songs.* Illus by Gabriele Margules. New York: Atheneum, 1969.

3911 ———. *Songs the Sandman Sings.* Illus by Peggy Owens Skillen. New York: Atheneum, 1969.

3912 Reed, Gwendolyn. *The Talkative Beasts, Myths, Fables and Poems of India.* Photos by Stella Snead. New York: Lothrop, 1969.

3914 Reed, Philip. *Out of the Ark, An Anthology of Animal Verse.* Illus by Gabrielle Margules. New York: Atheneum, 1968.

3915 Rees, Ennis. *Pun Fun.* New York: Abelard-Schuman, 1965.

3916 ———. *Riddles, Riddles Everywhere.* New York: Abelard-Schuman, 1964.

3917 Reeves, James. *Blackbird in the Lilac.* Illus by Edward Ardizzone. New York: Dutton, 1959.

3918 ———. *The Christmas Book.* Illus by Raymond Briggs. New York: Dutton, 1970.

3919 ———. *English Fables and Fairy Stories.* Illus by Joan Kiddell-Monroe. New York: Walck, 1954. Reproduction, Oxford University, 1968.

3920 ———. *Ragged Robin.* Illus by Jane Paton. New York: Dutton, 1961.

3921 ———. *Rhyming Will.* Illus by Edward Ardizzone. New York: McGraw, 1968.

3922 Reeves, James, ed. *A Golden Land; Stories, Poems, Songs, New and Old.* Illus by Gillian Conway, et al. New York: Hastings, 1958.

3923 ———. *One's None, Old Rhymes for New Tongues.* Illus by Bernadette Watts. New York: Watts, 1969.

3924 Reid, Alastair and Anthony Kerrigan, trans. *Mother Goose in Spanish.* Illus by Barbara Cooney. New York: Crowell, 1968.

3925 Reinecke, Esther. *Tim and the Green-Eyed Monster.* Illus by Lamese Skaff. Minneapolis: Denison, 1959.

3926 Reiniger, Lotte. *Shadow Puppets, Shadow Theatres and Shadow Films.* Boston: Plays, 1970.

3927 Reiss, Johanna. *The Upstairs Room.* New York: Crowell, 1972. Bantam paperback. M725.

3928 Reiss, John H. *Colors.*, Scarsdale, NY: Bradbury, 1969.

3929 ———. *Shapes.* Scarsdale, NY: Bradbury, 1974.

3930 ———. *Numbers.* Illus by the author. Scarsdale, NY: Bradbury, 1971.

3931 Renfro, Nancy. *Puppet Corner in Every Library.* Austin, TX: Renfro Studios, 1977. Paperback.

3932 ———. *Puppetry and the Art of Story Creation.* Austin, TX: Renfro Studios, 1979. Paperback.

3933 ———. *Puppets for Play Production.* New York: Funk and Wagnalls, 1969.

3934 Ress, Etta S. *Signals to Satellites in Today's World.* Mankato, MN: Creative Educational Society, 1965.

3935 Rey, H.A. *Curious George.* Illus by the author. Boston: Houghton, 1941. Sandpiper paperback. M157.

3936 ———. *Curious George Gets a Medal.* Illus by

the author. Boston: Houghton, 1957. Sandpiper paperback. M160.

3937 ———. *Curious George Learns the Alphabet.* Illus by the author. Boston: Houghton, 1963. Sandpiper paperback. M162.

3938 ———. *Curious George Rides a Bike.* Illus by the author. Boston: Houghton, 1952. Sandpiper paperback. M163.

3939 ———. *Curious George Takes a Job.* Illus by the author. Boston: Houghton, 1947. Sandpiper paperback. M165.

3940 ———. *The Stars; a New Way to see Them.* Boston: Houghton, 1967. Paperback.

3941 Rey, Margaret. *Curious George Flies a Kite.* Illus by H.A. Rey. Boston: Houghton, 1958. Paperback. M159.

3942 ———. *Curious George Goes to the Hospital.* Illus by H.A. Rey. Boston: Houghton, 1966. Paperback. M161.

3943 ———. *Pretzel.* Illus by H.A. Rey. New York: Harper, 1944.

3944 Reyner, Becky. *My Mother is the Most Beautiful Woman in the World: a Russian Folktale.* Illus by Ruth Gannett. New York: Lothrop, 1945.

3945 Reynolds, Quentin. *The Wright Brothers.* New York: Random, 1950.

3946 Rice, Eve. *What Sadie Sang.* Illus by the author. New York: Greenwillow, 1976.

3947 Rice, Susan. *Films Kids Like.* Chicago: A.L.A., 1973.

3948 Richards, Laura. *Tirra Lirra; Rhymes Old and New.* Illus by Margaret Davis. Forward by May Hill Arbuthnot. Boston: Little, 1955.

3949 Richards, Norman. *Robert Frost.* Chicago: Childrens', 1968.

3950 ———. *The Story of the Mayflower Compact.* Illus by Darrell Wiskur. Chicago: Childrens Press, 1967.

3951 Richter, Conrad. *The Light in the Forest.* New York: Knopf, 1953. Bantam paperback.

3952 Richter, Dorothy. *Fell's Guide to Hand Puppets. How to Make and Use Them.* New York: Fell, 1970.

3953 Richter, Hans Peter. *Friedrich.* Trans by Edith Kroll. New York: Holt, 1961. Dell paperback.

3954 ———. *I Was There.* Trans by Edith Kroll. New York: Holt, 1962. Dell paperback.

3955 Riedman, Sarah R. and Elton T. Gustafson. *Home is the Sea: For Whales.* New York: Abelard, 1971.

3956 Riley, James Whitcomb. *The Gobble-uns 'll Git You Ef You Don't Watch Out!* Illus by Joel Schick. Philadelphia: Lippincott, 1975.

3957 Ringi, Kjell. *The Magic Stick.* New York: Harper and Row, 1968.

3958 ———. *The Winner.* New York: Harper and Row, 1969.

3959 Rinkoff, Barbara. *Elbert, the Mind Reader.* New York: Lothrop, 1967. Scholastic paperback.

3960 Ripper, Charles L. *Foxes and Wolves.* Illus by the author. New York: Morrow, 1961.

3961 Ritchie, Jean. *From Fair to Fair: Folk Songs of the British Isles.* Photos by George Pickow. Music by Edward Tripp. New York: Walck, 1966.

3962 ———. *Jean Ritchie's Swapping Song Book.* Photos by George Pickow. Music by A.K. Fossner and Edward Tripp. New York: Walck, 1964.

3963 Ritson, Joh E. and James A. Smith. *Creative Teaching of Art in the Elementary School.* Boston: Allyn and Bacon, 1975.

3964 Roach, Marilynne K. *The Mouse and the Song.* Illus by Joseph Low. New York: Parents 1974.

3965 ———. *Two Roman Mice.* New York: Crowell, 1975.

3966 *Robbins, Ruth. *Baboushka and the Three Kings.* Illus by Nicolas Sidjakov. Parnassus, 1960.

3967 ———. *Taliesin and King Arthur.* Illus by the author. Berkeley, CA: Parnassus, 1970.

3968 Roberts, Cliff. *Start with a Dot.* New York: Watts, 1968.

3969 Roberts, Hortense R. *You Can Make an Insect Zoo.* Photos by Francis Munger. Chicago: Children's, 1974.

3970 Robertson, Keith. *Henry Reed, Inc.* Illus by Robert McCloskey. New York: Viking, 1958. Dell paperback. M280.

3971 ———. *Henry Reed's Baby Sitting Service.* Illus by Robert McCloskey. New York: Viking, 1966. Dell paperback.

3972 ———. *Henry Reed's Big Show.* Illus by Robert McCloskey. New York: Viking, 1970. Tempo paperback.

3973 ———. *Henry Reed's Journey.* Illus by Robert McCloskey. New York: Viking, 1963. Dell paperback.

3974 ———. *In Search of a Sandhill Crane.* Illus by Richard Cuffari. New York: Viking, 1973. Puffin paperback.

3975 ———. *The Money Machine.* Illus by George Porter. New York: Viking, 1969.

3976 Robinson, Charles Alexander. *First Book of Ancient Egypt.* Illus by Lili Rethi. New York: Watts, 1961.

3977 Roche, P.K. *Dollhouse Magic, How to Make and Find Simple Dollhouse Furniture.* Illus by Richard Cuffari. New York: Dial, 1977.

3978 Rockwell, Anne. *Albert B. Cub and Zebra, an Alphabet Storybook.* New York: Crowell, 1977.

3979 ———. *The Awful Mess.* Illus by the author. New York: Parents, 1973.

3980 ———. *Befana: A Christmas Story.* Illus by the author. New York: Atheneum, 1974.

3981 ———. *The Dancing Stars, an Iroquois Legend.* Illus by the author. New York: Crowell, 1972.

3982a ———. *El Toro Pinto and Other Songs in Spanish.* New York: Macmillan, 1971.

3982b ———. *Machines.* New York: Macmillan. 1972.

3983 ———. *The Monkey's Whisker: A Brazilian Folktale.* Illus by the author. New York: Parents, 1971.

3984 ———. *The Old Woman and her Pig and Ten Other Stories.* Illus by Anne Rockwell. New York: Crowell, 1979.

3985 ———. *Poor Goose: A French Folktale.* Illus by the author. New York: Crowell, 1976.

3986 ———. *Savez-vous Planter Les Choux?* and

Other French Songs. New York: World, 1969.
3987 ———. *The Story Snail.* Illus by the author. New York: Macmillan, 1974.
3988 ———. *The Three Bears and Fifteen Other Stories.* Illus by the author. New York: Crowell, 1975.
3989 ———. *The Wolf Who Had a Wonderful Dream.* Illus by the author. New York: Crowell, 1973.
3990 ———. *The Wonderful Eggs of Furucchia; a Picture Story from Italy.* Cleveland: World,1969.
3991 Rockwell, Anne and Harlow. *Machines.* New York: Macmillan, 1972.
3992 ———. *Toad.* New York: Doubleday, 1972.
3993 Rockwell, Harlow. *Printmaking.* Garden City, NY: Doubleday, 1973.
3994 Roethke, Theodore. *Roethke: Collected Poems.* Garden City, NY: Doubleday, n.d. Paperback. M683.
3995 Roever, J.M. and Wilfried. *The Mustangs.* Illus by J.M. Roever. Austin, TX: Steck-Vaughn, 1971.
3996 Rogers, Frances. *Painted Rock to Printed Page.* Philadelphia: Lippincott, 1960.
3997 Rogers, Frances and Alice Beard. *Heels, Wheels and Wire: The Story of Messages and Signals.* Philadelphia: Lippincott, 1967.
3998 Rogers, Fred. *Many Ways to Say I Love You.* Valley Forge, PA: Judson Paperback, 1977.
3999 ———. *Mr. Rogers' Neighborhood.* New York: Western, 1974.
4000 ———. *Mr. Rogers' Neighborhood: The Costume Party.* New York: Western, 1967.
4001 ———. *Mr. Rogers' Songbook.* Illus by Steven Kellogg. Music by John Costa. New York: Random, 1970.
4002 ———. *Mr. Rogers Talks About: The New Baby, Fighting, A Trip to the Doctor, Going to School, Haircuts, Moving.* Bronx, New York: Platt, 1974.
4003 ———. *Tell Me, Mr. Rogers.* Bronx, New York: Platt, 1975.
4004 Rogers, Joe. *The House that Jack Built.* New York: Lothrop, 1968.
4005 Rognowski, Gini and Gene DeWeese. *Making American Folk Dolls.* Radnor, PA: Chilton, 1975.
4006 Rogovin, Mark and Marie Burton and Holly Highbill. *Mural Manual: How to Paint Murals for the Classroom, Community Center and Street Corner.* Intro by Peter Seeger. Boston: Beacon Press, 1975. Paperback.
4007a Rojankovsky, Feodor. *Animals in the Zoo.* Illus by the author. New York: Knopf, 1962. Knopf paperback.
4007b ———. *Tall Book of Nursery Tales.* New York: Harper, 1944.
4008 Rollins, Charlemae. *Famous American Negro Poets.* New York: Dodd, 1965. Apollo paperback.
4009 Rose, Anne. *As Right as Can Be.* Illus by Arnold Lobel. New York: Dial, 1976.
4010 ———. *How Does a Czar Eat Potatoes?* Illus by Janosch. New York: Lothrop, 1973.
4011 Roselli, Luciana. *Polka Dot Child.* Greenwich, CT: N.Y. Graphic Society, 1964.
4012 Rosenberg, Judith K. *Young People's Litera-ture in Series: Fiction, Non-Fiction and Publisher's Series, 1973-75.* Littleton, Colorado: Libraries Unlimited, 1977.
4013 Rosenberg, Lilli Ann. *Children Make Murals and Sculpture.* Photos by Ken Wittenberg. New York: Reinhold, 1968.
4014 Rosenbloom, Joseph. *Twist These on your Tongue.* Illus by Joyce Behr. New York: Nelson, 1978.
4015 Ross, David, ed. *The Illustrated Treasury of Poetry for Children.* Intro by Mark Van Doren. New York: Grosset, 1970.
4016 Ross, Eulalie Steinmetz. *The Buried Treasure and Other Picture Tales.* Illus by Josef Cellini. Philadelphia: Lippincott, 1958.
4017 Ross, George Maxim. *The Pine Tree.* New York: Dutton, 1966.
4018 Ross, Laura. *Finger Puppets: Easy to Make, Fun to Use.* New York: Lothrop, 1971. Paperback.
4019 ———. *Hand Puppets: How to Make and Use Them.* New York: Lothrop, 1969. Paperback.
4020 ———. *Holiday Puppets and Plays.* New York: Lothrop, 1974.
4021 ———. *Puppet Shows Using Poems and Stories.* New York: Lothrop, 1970.
4022 ———. *Scrap Puppets; How to Make and Move Them.* Illus by Frank Ross, Jr. Photos by George Der. New York: Holt, 1978.
4023 Ross, Patricia Fent. *The Hungry Moon; Mexican Nursery Tales.* Illus by Carlos Merida. New York: Knopf, 1946.
4024 Ross, Ramon R. *Storyteller.* Columbus, Ohio: Merrill, 1972.
4025 Rossetti, Christina. *Doves and Pomegranates.* Illus by Margery Gill. New York: Macmillan, 1971.
4026 ———. *Goblin Market.* Illus by Ellen Raskin. New York: Dutton, 1970.
4027 ———. *Goblin Market.* Illus by Arthur Rackham. New York: Watts, 1969.
4028 ———. *What is Pink?* Illus by Jose Aruego. New York: Macmillan, 1971.
4029 Roth, Arnold. *Pick a Peck of Puzzles.* New York: Norton, 1966. Scholastic paperback.
4030 Roth, Arthur. *Iceberg Hermit.* New York: Four Winds, 1974. Scholastic paperback.
4031 ———. *Two for Survival.* New York: Scribner, 1976.
4032 Roth, Charlene Davis. *The Art of Making Cloth Toys.* New York: Radnor, PA: Chilton, 1974.
4033 ———. *The Art of Making Puppets and Marionettes.* Radnor, PA: Chilton, 1975.
4034 ———. *Dressing Dolls.* Photos by James A. Davis. New York: Crown, 1976. Paperback.
4035 ———. *Making Dollhouse Accessories.* New York: Crown, 1977. Paperback.
4036 Rothman, Joel and Ruthven Tremain. *Secrets with Ciphers and Codes.* New York: Macmillan, 1969. Collier paperback.
4037 Rounds, Glen. *The Blind Colt.* New York: Holiday, 1960.
4038 ———. *Casey Jones: The Story of a Brave Engineer.* San Carlos, CA: Golden Gate, 1969. M115.
4039 ———. *The Strawberry Roan.* Illus by the author. San Carlos, CA: Golden Gate, 1970.

4040 ———. *The Swapping Boy.* Illus by Beth and Joe Krush. New York: Harcourt, 1960.

4041a Rudolph, Marguerita and Dorothy H. Cohen. *Kindergarten: A Year of Learning.* Englewood Cliffs, NJ: Prentice-Hall, 1964.

4041b Rudolph, Marguerite. *Today is Not My Birthday.* Illus by Linda Edwards. New York: McGraw, 1973.

4042 Rueben, Patricia. *Apples to Zippers, an Alphabet Book.* New York: Doubleday, 1976.

4043 Ruesch, Jurgen and Weldon Kees. *Nonverbal Communication: Notes on the Visual Perception of Human Relations.* Berkeley: University of California Press, 1956.

4044 Rumsey, Marian. *Carolina Hurricane.* Illus by Ted Lewin. New York: Morrow, 1977. Scholastic paperback.

4045 ———. *Lion on the Run.* Illus by Ted Lewin. New York: Morrow, 1973. Tempo paperback.

4046 Rushmore, Helen. *The Dancing Horses of Acoma and other Acoma Indian Tales.* Cleveland: World, 1963.

4047 Ruskin, John. *The King of the Golden River or the Black Brothers.* Illus by Fritz Kredel. Cleveland: World, n.d.

4048 ———. *King of the Golden River or the Black Brothers.* Illus by Charles Stewart. New York: Watts, 1958. Dover paperback.

4049 Russ, Lavinia. *Alec's Sand Castle.* Illus by James Stevesson. New York: Harper, 1972.

4050 Russell, Solveig P. *A Is for Apple and Why, the Story of Our Alphabet.* New York: Abingdon, 1959.

4051 ———. *Bible ABC Book.* St. Louis: Concordia, 1967. Paperback.

4052 Russo, Susan, Comp. *The Moon's the North Wind's Cooky; Night Poems.* Illus by S. Russo. New York: Lothrop, 1979.

4053 Rutgers, Van Der Leoff. *Avalanche!* Illus by Gustav Schrotter. New York: Morrow, 1957.

4054 Rutter, Vicki. *ABC Puppetry.* Boston: Plays, 1969.

4055 Ryden, Hope. *The Wild Colt; the Life of a Young Mustang.* Photos by the author. New York: Coward, 1972.

4056 Ryder, Joanne. *Fireflies.* Illus by Don Bolognese. New York: Harper, 1977.

4057 Sachs, Marilyn. *Peter & Veronica.* Illus by Louis Glanzman. New York: Doubleday, 1969. Dell paperback.

4058a ———. *A Pocket Full of Seeds.* Illus by Ben Stahl. New York: Doubleday, 1973.

4058b ———. *Veronica Ganz.* Illus. New York: Doubleday, 1968. Dell paperback, 1977.

4059 Sackett, S.J. *Cowboys and Songs They Sang.* Illus by Walter Einsel. Music by Lionel Nowak. New York: Scott, 1967. M151.

4060 St. John, Glory. *How to Count Like a Martian.* New York: Walck, 1975.

4061 Saito, Tadao. *High Flyers, Colorful Kites from Japan.* San Francisco: Japan Publications, 1969.

4062 Salisbury, Helen Wright. *Finger Fun, Songs and Rhythms for the Very Young.* Los Angeles: Cowman, 1955.

4063 Samachson, Dorothy. *The Russian Ballet and Three of its Masterpieces.* New York: Lothrop, 1971.

4064 Samuels, Gertrude. *Motelle.* New York: Harper, 1976. Signet paperback.

4065 Sandberg, Inger and Lasse. *Nicholas' Favorite Pet.* New York: Delacorte, 1967.

4066 Sandburg, Carl. *Early Moon.* Illus by James Daugherty. New York: Harcourt, 1958. M113.

4067 ———. *Rootabaga Stories.* 2 Vols. Illus by Maude and Miska Petersham. New York: Harcourt, 1936. Voyager paperback.

4068 ———. *Wind Song.* Illus by William A. Smith. New York: Harcourt, 1960. M113.

4069a Sandburg, Carl, ed. *The American Songbag.* New York: Harcourt, 1927.

4069b Sandburg, Carl. *The Wedding Procession of the Rag Doll and the Broom Handle and Who Was In It.* New York: Harcourt, 1978.

4070 Sandburg, Helga. *Joel and the Wild Goose.* Illus by Thomas Daly and Peter Max. New York: Dial, 1963.

4071 Saporta, Raphael. *A Basket in the Reeds.* Illus by J. Hechthopf. New York: Lerner, 1965.

4072 Sarasas, Claude. *ABC's of Origami, Paper Folding for Children.* Rutland, Vt.: Tuttle, 1964.

4073 Sarnoff, Jane. *The Code and Cipher Book.* Illus by Reynold Ruffins. New York: Scribner, 1975. Paperback.

4074 ———. *Giants! a Riddle Book.* Illus by Reynold Ruffins. New York: Scribner, 1977.

4075 ———. *I Know! A Riddle Book.* Illus by Reynold Ruffins. New York: Scribner, 1974.

4076 ———. *Monster Riddle Book.* Illus by Reynold Ruffins. New York: Scribner, 1974. M462.

4077 ———. *What? A Riddle Book.* Illus by Reynold Ruffins. New York: Scribner, 1974.

4078 Sasek, Miroslav. *This is Australia.* Illus by the author. New York: Macmillan, 1971.

4079 ———. *This is Cape Kennedy.* Illus by the author. New York: Macmillan, 1965.

4080 ———. *This is Edinburgh.* Illus by the author. New York: Macmillan, 1961.

4081 ———. *This is Greece.* Illus by the author. New York: Macmillan, 1966.

4082 ———. *This is Historic Britain.* Illus by the author. New York: Macmillan, 1974.

4083 ———. *This is Hong Kong.* Illus by the author. New York: Macmillan, 1965

4084 ———. *This is Ireland.* Illus by the author. New York: Macmillan, 1965.

4085 ———. *This is London.* Illus by the author. New York: Macmillan, 1959.

4086 ———. *This is Munich.* Illus by the author. New York: Macmillan, 1961.

4087 ———. *This is New York.* Illus by the author. New York: Macmillan, 1960. Collier paperback, abridged. M686.

4088 ———. *This is Paris.* Illus by the author. New York: Macmillan, 1959.

4089 ———. *This is Rome.* Illus by the author. New York: Macmillan, 1960.

4090 ———. *This is San Francisco.* Illus by the author. New York: Macmillan, 1962. Collier paperback, abridged.

4091 ———. *This is Texas.* Illus by the author. New York: Macmillan, 1967.

4092 ———. *This is the United Nations.* Illus by the

author. New York: Macmillan, 1968.

4093 ———. *This is Venice.* Illus by the author. New York: Macmillan, 1961.

4094 ———. *This is Washington, D.C.* Illus by the author. New York: Macmillan, 1969. Collier paperback, abridged.

4095 Saunders, Dennis, ed. *Magic Lights and Streets of Shining Jet.* Photos by Terry Williams. New York: Greenwillow, 1978.

4096 Sauer, Julia L. *Fog Magic.* Illus by Lynd Ward. New York: Viking, 1943. Archway paperback.

4097 Savory, Phyllis. *The Lion Outwitted the Hare and Other African Tales.* Chicago: Whitman, 1971.

4098 Sawyer, Ruth. *Journey Cake, Ho!* Illus by Robert McCloskey. New York: Viking, 1953. Paperback. M336.

4099 ———. *Picture Tales from Spain.* Philadelphia: Lippincott, 1936.

4100 ———. *Roller Skates.* Illus by Valenti Angelo. New York: Viking, 1936. Dell paperback.

4101 Saxe, John Godfrey. *The Blind Men and the Elephant.* Illus by Paul Galdone. New York: McGraw, 1963.

4102 Scarf, Maggi. *Meet Benjamin Franklin.* Illus by Harry Beckhoff. New York: Random, 1968.

4103 Scarry, Richard. *Richard Scarry's ABC Word Book.* Illus by the author. New York: Random, 1971.

4104 ———. *Richard Scarry's Best Counting Book Ever.* Illus by the author. New York: Random, 1975.

4105 ———. *Richard Scarry's Find Your ABC's.* Illus by the author. New York: Random paperback, 1973.

4106 Scharen, Beatrix. *Gigen and Till.* New York: Atheneum, 1968.

4107 Scheer, Julian. *Upside Down Day.* Illus by Kelly Oeshsli. New York: Holiday, 1968.

4108 ———. *Rain Makes Applesauce.* Illus by Marvin Bileck. New York: Holiday, 1964.

4109 ———. *The Derby Ram, a Ballad.* Illus by Richard Schrecter. Garden City, NY: Doubleday, 1970.

4110 Scheffer, Victor B. *A Natural History of Marine Mammals.* Illus by Peter Parnall. New York: Scribner, 1976.

4111 ———. *The Seeing Eye.* New York: Scribner, 1971.

4112 Scheuer, Steven. *Movies on TV.* New York: Bantam, 1977.

4113 Schick, Eleanor. *Making Friends.* New York: Macmillan, 1969.

4114 Schiller, Barbara. *The White Rat's Tale.* Illus by Adrienne Adams. New York: Holt, 1967.

4115 Schlein, Miriam. *The Big Green Thing.* New York: Grosset, 1963.

4116 ———. *Shapes.* Illus by Sam Berman. New York: Scott, 1952. Hale, 1952.

4117 Schmid, Eleanore. *Horns Everywhere.* New York: Crown, 1968.

4118 Schmiderer, Dorothy. *Alphabeast Book; an abcdarium.* New York: Holt, 1971. Paperback.

4119 Schnabel, Ernest. *Anne Frank: A Portrait of Courage.* Trans by Richard and Clara Winston. New York: Harcourt, 1958. Harper paperback.

4120 Schneider, Leo. *You and Your Senses.* Illus by Gustav Schrotter. New York: Harcourt, 1956, 60.

4121 Scholefield, Edmund O. *Bryan's Dog.* Illus by Ned Butterfield. Cleveland: World, 1967.

4122 Schoenwolf, Herta. *Play With Light and Shadow, the Art and Techniques of Shadow Theatre.* New York: Reinhold, 1968.

4123 *School Media Quarterly, Journal of the American Association of School Libraries.* Vol. 5, Number 3, Spring, 1977.

4124 Schreiber, Morris. *Stories of Gods and Heroes.* Illus by Art Seiden. New York: Grosset, 1960.

4125 Schulz, Charles. *Bonjour Peanuts.* Illus by the author. New York: French and English Publications, n.d.

4126 ———. *Be My Valentine, Charlie Brown.* Illus by the author. New York: Random, 1976. Scholastic paperback.

4127 ———. *A Boy Named Charlie Brown.* Illus by the author. New York: Holt, 1969. Fawcett paperback. M96.

4128 ———. *Ca Ne Va Pas, Charlie Brown.* Illus by the author. New York: Holt, 1970. Paperback.

4129 ———. *A Charlie Brown Christmas.* Illus by the author. New York: Signet paperback, 1971.

4130 ———. *The Charlie Brown Dictionary.* Illus by the author. New York: Random, 1974. Scholastic paperback.

4131 ———. *The Charlie Brown Dictionary.* Illus by the author. Englewood Cliffs, NJ: Prentice-Hall, 1973.

4132 ———. *A Charlie Brown Thanksgiving.* Illus by the author. New York: Random, 1974. Signet, 1975.

4133 ———. *Charlie Brown's All-Stars.* Cleveland: World, 1962.

4134 ———. *Hay Que Avudarte, Charlie Brown.* Illus by the author. New York: Holt, n.d. Paperback.

4135 ———. *How Long, Great Pumpkin, How Long?* Illus by the author. New York: Holt, 1977. Paperback.

4136 ———. *It's Arbor Day, Charlie Brown.* Illus by the author. New York: Random, 1977. Scholastic paperback.

4137 ———. *It's the Easter Beagle, Charlie Brown.* Illus by the author. New York: Random, 1976. Scholastic paperback.

4138 ———. *It's the Great Pumpkin, Charlie Brown.* Illus by the author. New York: Signet paperback, 1971.

4139 ———. *Peanuts Classics.* Illus by the author. New York: Holt, 1970.

4140 ———. *Peanuts Treasury.* Illus by the author. New York: Holt, n.d.

4141 ———. *Snoopy and His Sopwith Camel.* Illus by the author. New York: Holt, 1969. Fawcett paperback.

4142 ———. *Snoopy and the Red Baron.* Illus by the author. New York: Holt, 1966. Fawcett paperback.

4143 ———. *Play It Again, Charlie Brown.* Illus by the author. New York: NAL paperback, 1972.

4144 ———. *Win a Few Lose a Few, Charlie Brown.* Illus by the author. New York: Holt, 1974.

4145 ———. *You're a Good Sport, Charlie Brown.* Illus by the author. New York: Random, 1976. Scholastic paperback.

4146 Schuman, Benjamin N. *The Human Eye.* Illus by Michael Meyers. New York: Atheneum, 1968.

4147 Schwab, Gustav. *Gods and Heroes, Myths and Epics of Ancient Greece.* New York: Pantheon, 1946.

4148 Schwartz, Alvin. *Chin Music: Tall Talk and Other Talk.* Philadelphia: Lippincott, 1979.

4149 ———. *Cross Your Fingers, Spit in Your Hat.* Philadelphia: Lippincott, 1974. Paperback.

4150 ———. *Flapdoodle: Pure Nonsense from American Folklore.* Philadelphia: Lippincott, 1980. Paperback.

4151 ———. *Kickle Snifters and Other Fearsome Critters.* Illus by Glen Rounds. Philadelphia: Lippincott, 1976. Bantam paperback.

4152 ———. *Tomfoolery, Trickery and Foolery with Words.* Illus by Glen Rounds. Philadelphia: Lippincott, 1973. Bantam paperback.

4153 ———. *A Twister of Twists, a Tangler of Tongues.* Philadelphia: Lippincott, 1972. Bantam paperback.

4154 ———. *Witcracks, Jokes & Jests from American Folklore.* Philadelphia: Lippincott, 1973. Bantam paperback.

4155 Schweitzer, Byrd Baylor. *Amigo.* Illus by Garth Williams. New York: Macmillan, 1963. Collier paperback.

4156 ———. *One Small Blue Bead.* Illus by Symeon Shimin. New York: Macmillan, 1965.

4157 Schweninger, Ann. *A Dance for Three.* New York: Dial, 1979.

4158 ———. *Hunt for Rabbit's Golosh.* Illus by Kay Chorao. New York: Doubleday, 1976.

4159 Schweninger, Ann, ed. and illus. *The Man in the Moon as He Sails the Sky and Other Moon Verse.* New York: Dodd, 1979.

4160 Scott, Adolphe Clarence. *The Puppet Theatre of Japan.* Rutland, Vt.: Tuttle 1963. Paperback.
Scott Foresman Reading Series. See Manning, John.

4161 Scott, John. *Senses and Seeing, Hearing, Tasting, Touching and Smelling.* Illus by John E. Johnson. New York: Parents, 1975.

4162 Scott, John Anthony. *The Ballad of America, the History of the U.S. in the Stories, the Words, the Music of More than 125 Songs.* New York: Grosset and Dunlap, 1967.

4163 Scott, Joseph and Lenore. *Hieroglyphs for Fun: Your Own Secret Code Language.* New York: Van Nostrand, 1974.

4164 Scott, Louise Binder and Jesse J. Thompson. *Rhymes for Fingers and Flannelboards.* Illus by Jean Flowers. New York: McGraw, 1960.

4165 Sechrist, Elizabeth H., ed. *Christmas Everywhere; a Book of Christmas Customs of Many Lands.* Illus by Guy Fry. New York: Macrae, 1936.

4166 ———. *Heigh-ho for Halloween!* Illus by Guy Fry. New York: Macrae, 1948.

4167 ———. *Once in the First Times, Folk Tales from the Philippines.* Illus by John Sheppard. Philadelphia: Macrae, 1949, 1969.

4168 ———. *One Thousand Poems for Children.* Illus by Henry Pitz. New York: Macrae, 1946.

4169 ———. *Poems for Red Letter Days.* Illus by Guy Fry. New York: Macrae, 1951.

4170 Sechrist, Elizabeth H. and Janette Woolsey. *It's Time for Christmas.* Illus by Reisie Lonette. New York: Macrae, 1959.

4171 ———. *It's Time for Easter.* Illus by Elsie Jane McCorkell. New York: Macrae, 1961.

4172 ———. *It's Time for Story Hour.* Illus by Elsie Jane McCorkell. New York: Macrae, 1964.

4173 ———. *It's Time for Thanksgiving.* Illus by Guy Fry. New York: Macrae, 1957.

4174 Seeger, Peter and Charles. *The Foolish Frog.* Illus by Miroslav Jagr. New York: Macmillan, 1973. M221, M222.

4175 Seeger, Ruth C. *Animal Folk Songs for Children.* Illus by Barbara Coon Cooney. Garden City, NY: Doubleday, 1950.

4176 Segal, Lore. *All the Way Home.* Illus by John Marshall. New York: Farrar, 1973.

4177 ———. *Tell Me a Mitzi.* Illus by Harriet Pincus. New York: Farrar, 1970. Scholastic paperback.

4178 ———. *Tell Me a Trudy.* Illus by Rosemary Wells. New York: Farrar, 1977.

4179 Seidelman, James E. and Grave Montonye. *Creating Mosaics.* Illus by Harriet Sherman. New York: Crowell, 1967.

4180 ———. *Creating with Paint.* Illus by Peter Landor. New York: Crowell, 1967.

4181 ———. *Rub Book.* Illus by Lynn Sweat. New York: Crowell, 1968.

4182 ———. *Creating with Papier-Mâché.* New York: Collier, 1971.

4183 ———. *Creating with Wood.* Illus by Lynn Sweat. New York: Crowell, 1969.

4184 Selden, George. *Chester Crickets Pigeon Ride.* Illus by Garth Williams. New York: Farrar, 1981.

4185 ———. *The Cricket in Times Square.* Illus by Garth Williams. New York: Farrar, 1960. Dell paperback.

4186 ———. *The Genie of Sutton Place.* New York: Farrar, 1973.

4187 ———. *Harry Cat's Pet Puppy.* Illus by Garth Williams. New York: Farrar, 1974. Dell paperback.

4188 ———. *Tucker's Countryside.* Illus by Garth Williams. New York: Farrar, 1969. Avon paperback.

4189 Sell, Violet, et al. *Subject Index to Poetry for Children and Young People.* Chicago: ALA, 1957.

4190 Selsam, Millicent, E. *Animals of the Sea.* Illus by John Hamberger. New York: Four Winds, 1975.

4191 ———. *The Harlequin Moth.* Photos by Jerome Wexler. New York: Morrow, 1975.

4192 ———. *Hidden Animals.* New York: Harper, 1947, 1969.

4193 ———. *How Kittens Grow.* New York: Four Winds, 1975. Scholastic paperback.

4194 ———. *How Puppies Grow.* New York: Four Winds, 1972. Scholastic paperback.

4195 ———. *Maple Tree.* Photos by Jerome Wexler. New York: Morrow, 1968.

4196 ———. *Milkweed.* Photos by Jerome Wexler. New York: Morrow, 1967.

4197 ———. *Play with Trees.* New York: Morrow, 1950.

4198 ———. *Tyrannosaurus Rex.* New York: Harper, 1978.

4199 Selsam, Millicent and Joyce Hunt. *A First Look at Birds.* Illus by Harriet Springer. New York: Walker, 1973.

4200 ———. *A First Look at Mammals.* Illus by Harriett Springer. New York: Walker, 1973.

4201 Sendak, Maurice. *Alligators All Around.* Illus by the author. New York: Harper, 1962. M15, M16, M573, M574.

4202 ———. *Chicken Soup With Rice, a Book of Months.* Illus by the author. New York: Harper, 1962. Scholastic paperback. M126, M573, M574.

4203 ———. *Hector Protector and As I Went Over the Water.* Illus by the author. New York: Harper, 1965.

4204 ———. *Higglety Pigglety Pop: Or There Must be More to Life.* Illus by the author. New York: Harper, 1967.

4205 ———. *Kenny's Window.* Illus by the author. New York: Harper, 1956.

4206 ———. *Maurice Sendak's Really Rosie Starring the Nutshell Kids.* Music by Carole King. Design by Jane Byers Bierhorst. New York: Harper, 1975. M573, M574.

4207 ———. The Nutshell Library: *Alligators All Around, Chicken Soup With Rice, One Was Johnny, and Pierre.* Illus by the author. New York: Harper, 1962. M15, M16, M126, M504, M505, M533, M534, M573, M574.

4208 ———. *One Was Johnny, a Counting Book.* Illus by the author. New York: Harper & Row, 1962. M504, M505, M573, M574.

4209 ———. *Pierre.* Illus by the author. New York: Harper, 1962. M533, M534, M573, M574.

4210 ———. *Seven Little Monsters.* Illus by the author. New York: Harper, 1977.

4211 ———. *The Sign on Rosie's Door.* Illus by the author. New York: Harper, 1960. M573, M574.

4212 ———. *Very Far Away.* Illus by the author. New York: Harper, 1960.

4213 *———. *Where the Wild Things Are.* Illus by the author. New York: Harper, 1963. M739, M740.

4214 Seredy, Kate. *The Good Master.* New York: Viking, 1935. Dell paperback.

4215 ———. *The Singing Tree.* New York: Viking, 1939. Dell paperback.

4216 Serraillier, Ian. *Beowulf the Warrior.* Illus by Severin. New York: Walck, 1961

4217 ———. *A Fall from the Sky: The Story of Daedalus.* Illus by William Stobbs. New York: Walck, 1966.

4218a ———. *The Gorgon's Head: The Story of Perseus.* Illus by William Stobbs. New York: Walck, 1961.

4218b ———. *Heracles the Strong.* New York: Walck, 1970.

4219 ———. *The Silver Sword.* Illus by C. Walter Hodges. New York: Philips, 1959.

4220 ———. *Suppose You Met a Witch.* Illus by Ed Emberley. Boston: Little, 1973.

4221 ———. *The Way of Danger: The Story of Theseus.* Illus by William Stobbs. New York: Walck, 1962.

4222 Seuling, Barbara. *The Teeny Tiny Woman; an Old English Ghost Tale.* Illus by the author. New York: Penguin, 1978. Puffin paperback.

4223 Seuss, Dr. (Theodore Geisel). *And to Think That I Saw it on Mulberry Street.* Illus by the author. New York: Vanguard, 1937. Scholastic paperback.

4224 ———. *The Cat in the Hat.* Illus by the author. New York: Beginner, 1947. Paperback. M116.

4225 ———. *The Cat in the Hat Comes Back.* Illus by the author. New York: Beginner, 1958. M117.

4226 ———. *The Cat in the Hat Song Book.* Illus by the author. Music by Eugene Poddany. New York: Random, 1967.

4227 ———. *Dr. Seuss' ABC.* Illus by the author. New York: Beginner, 1963. M176.

4228 ———. *The Five Hundred Hats of Bartholomew Cubbins.* Illus by the author. New York: Vanguard, 1938. Eau Claire, WI: E.M. Hale, 1938. Scholastic paperback.

4229 ———. *Fox in Socks.* Illus by the author. New York: Beginner, 1965. M224.

4230 ———. *Green Eggs and Ham.* Illus by the author. New York: Beginner, 1960. M257.

4231 ———. *Happy Birthday to You!* Illus by the author. New York: Random, 1954. M175.

4232 ———. *Horton Hatches the Egg.* Illus by the author. New York: Random, 1940. M297.

4233 ———. *Horton Hears a Who!* Illus by the author. New York: Random, 1954.

4234 ———. *How the Grinch Stole Christmas.* Illus by the author. New York: Random, 1957.

4235 ———. *If I Ran the Circus.* Illus by the author. New York: Random, 1956.

4236 ———. *If I Ran the Zoo.* Illus by the author. New York: Random, 1950.

4237 ———. *The King's Stilts.* Illus by the author. New York: Random, 1939.

4238 ———. *McElligot's Pool.* Illus by the author. New York: Random, 1947.

4239 ———. *On Beyond Zebra.* Illus by the author. New York: Random, 1955.

4240 ———. *One Fish Two Fish Red Fish Blue Fish.* Illus by the author. New York: Beginner, 1960. M500.

4241 ———. *Sneetches and Other Stories.* Illus by the author. New York: Random, 1961.

4242 ———. *Thidwick, the Big Hearted Moose.* Illus by the author. New York: Random, 1948.

4243 ———. *Yertle the Turtle and Other Stories.* Illus by the author. New York: Random, 1958.

4244 Severn, Bill. *You and Your Shadow.* New York: McKay, 1961.

4245 Severn, David. *The Girl in the Grove.* New York: Harper, 1974.

4246 Sewall, Marcia. *The Wee Mannie and the Big Big Coo., a Scottish Folk Tale.* Illus by the author. Boston: Little, 1977.

4247 Sewall, Marcia, illus. *Master of all Masters.* Boston: Little, 1972.

4248 Seward, Prudence. *The First Book of Nursery Rhymes.* New York: Watts, 1970.

4249 Sewell, Anna. *Black Beauty.* Illus by Wesley Dennis. Cleveland: World, n.d. M88.

4250 Sewell, Helen. *Blue Barns, the Story of Two Big Geese and Seven Little Ducks.* New York: Macmillan, 1961.

4251 Shackburg, Richard. *Yankee Doodle.* Illus by Ed Emberley. Englewood Cliffs, NJ: Prentice-Hall, 1965.

4252 Shaefer, Charles E. and Kathleen C. Mellor. *Young Voices: The Poems of Children.* New York: Macmillan, 1971. Collier paperback.

4253 Shannon, George. *The Piney Woods Peddler.* Illus by Nancy Tafuri. New York: Greenwillow, 1981.

4254 Shapiro, Irwin. *Tall Tales of America.* Illus by Al Schnidt. New York: Simon and Schuster, 1958.

4255 Shapiro, Irwin and Edouard A. Stackpole. *The Story of Yankee Whaling.* New York: American Heritage, 1959.

4256 Sharmat, Marjorie, E. *Goodnight Andrew; Goodnight Craig.* Illus by Mary Chambers. New York: Harper, 1969.

4257 ———. *Nate the Great.* Illus by Marc Simont. New York: Coward, 1972. Dell paperback.

4258 ———. *Nate the Great and the Lost List.* Illus by Marc Simont. New York: Coward, 1975. Dell paperback.

4259 ———. *Nate the Great and the Phony Clue.* Illus by Marc Simont. New York: Coward, 1977. Dell paperback.

4260 ———. *Nate the Great and the Sticky Case.* Illus by Marc Simont. New York: Coward, 1978. Dell paperback.

4261 ———. *Nate the Great Goes Undercover.* Illus by Marc Simont. New York: Coward, 1974. Dell paperback.

4262 ———. *Rex.* Illus by Emily McCully. New York: Harper, 1967.

4263 Sharp, Margery. *Miss Bianca.* Illus by Garth Williams. Boston: Little, 1962. Dell paperback.

4264 ———. *The Rescuers.* Illus by Garth Williams. Boston: Little, 1959. Dell paperback.

4265 Shaw, George Bernard. *Pygmalion.* New York: Washington Square paperback, 1973.

4266 Shaw, Geroge Bernard and Alan J. Lerner. *Pygmalion and My Fair Lady.* New York: Signet paperback, 1975.

4267 Shaw, Martin, et al. *National Anthems of the World.* New York: Arco, 1975. M476.

4268 Shaw, Richard, ed. *The Bird Book.* New York: Warne, 1974.

4269 ———. *The Cat Book.* New York: Warne, 1974.

4270 ———. *The Fox Book.* New York: Warne, 1971.

4271 ———. *The Frog Book.* New York: Warne, 1972.

4272 ———. *The Mouse Book.* New York: Warne, 1975.

4273 ———. *The Owl Book.* New York: Warne, 1975.

4274 Shay, Arthur. *What Happens at the Circus.* New York: Regnery, 1972. Contemporary paperback.

4275 ———. *What It's Like to be a Fireman.* New York: Reilly and Lee, 1971.

4276 Sheaks, Barclay. *Painting with Acrylics from Start to Finish.* Worcester, MA: Davis, 1972.

4277 Shecker, Ben. *Stone House Stories.* Illus by the author. New York: Harper, 1973.

4278 Sheldon, William D. et al. *The Reading of Poetry.* Boston: Allyn & Bacon, 1966.

4279 Shelley, Mary Wolstonecraft. *Frankenstein.* New York: Collier paperback, 1961.

4280 Shephard, Esther. *Paul Bunyan.* Illus by Rockwell Kent. New York: Harcourt, 1941.

4281 Sherburne, Zoa. *Why Have the Birds Stopped Singing?* New York: Morrow, 1974. Dell paperback.

4282 Shimin, Symeon. *A Special Birthday.* New York: McGraw, 1976.

4283 Shinagawa, Takumi. *Charm in Motion: A Collection of Mobiles.* Photos by Yoshio Takemi. San Francisco: Japan Publications, 1970.

4284 Shippin, Katherine B. *A Bridle for Pegasus.* Illus by C.B. Falls. New York: Viking, 1951.

4285 ———. *Moses.* New York: Harper, 1949.

4286 Shire, Ellen. *The Snow Kings, Story and Pictures.* New York: Walker, 1969.

4287 Shoemaker, Kathryne E., illus. *Children Go Where I Send Thee.* Minneapolis: Winston, 1980.

4288 Shortall, Leonard. *Country Snowplow.* New York: Morrow, 1960.

4289 Shotwell, Louise R. *Roosevelt Grady.* New York: Collins, 1963. Dell paperback.

4290 Showalter, Jean B. *The Donkey Ride.* Illus by Tomi Ungerer. New York: Doubleday, 1967.

4291a Showers, Paul. *Look at Your Eyes.* Illus by Paul Galdone. New York: Crowell, 1962.

4291b Shub, Elizabeth, adaptor. *Clever Kate.* Illus by Anita Lobel. New York: Macmillan, 1973.

4292 Shulevitz, Uri. *Dawn.* Illus by the author. New York: Farrar, 1974.

4293 ———. *The Magician.* Illus by the author. New York: Macmillan, 1973.

4294 ———. *Oh What a Noise.* Illus by the author. New York: Macmilllan, 1971.

4295 ———. *One Monday Morning.* Illus by the author. New York: Scribner 1967. M501, M502.

4296 ———. *Soldier and the Tzar in the Forest, a Russian Tale.* Illus by the author. New York: Farrar, 1972.

4297 Shuttlesworth, Dorothy. *Dodos and Dinosaurs.* New York: Hastings, 1968.

4298 ———. *Gerbils and Other Small Pets.* New York: Dutton, 1970.

4299 ———. *To Find a Dinosaur.* New York: Doubleday, 1973.

4300 Sicotte, Virginia. *A Riot of Quiet.* Illus by Edward Ardizzone. New York: Holt, 1969.

4301 Sideman, Belle B. *The World's Best Fairy Tales.* Illus by Fritz Kredel. Pleasantville, NY: Reader's Digest Assn., 1967.

4302 Sikes, Geraldine. *Children's Literature for Dramatization, an Anthology.* New York: Harper, 1964.

4303 ———. *Creative Dramatics, an Art for Children.* New York: Harper, 1958.

4304 Sikes, Geraldine Brain and Hazel Brain Dunnington. *Children's Theatre and Creative Dramatics.* Seattle: University of Washington Press, 1961.

4305 Silverberg, Robert. *Time of the Great Freeze.* New York: Holt, 1964.

4306 Silverman, Judith, comp. *An Index to Young Readers' Collective Biographies,* 3rd ed. New

York: Bowker, 1979.

4307 Silverstein, Alvin and Virginia. *Circulatory Systems: Rivers Within.* Illus by George Bakacs. Englewood Cliffs, NJ: Prentice-Hall, 1969.

4308 ———. *Gerbils; All About Them.* Photos by Frederick J. Breda. Philadelphia: Lippincott, 1976. Paperback.

4309 Silverstein, Shel. *The Giving Tree.* New York: Harper, 1964.

4310 ———. *Where the Sidewalk Ends, the Poems and Drawings of Shel Silverstein.* New York: Harper, 1974.

4311 Simley, Anne. *Folk Tales to Tell or Read Aloud, Vol. II.* Minneapolis: Burgess, 1963. Paperback.

4312 ———. *Stories to Tell or Read Aloud, Vol. I.* Minneapolis: Burgess, 1962.

4313 Simon, Henry W. *A Treasury of Christmas Songs and Carols.* Illus by Rafello Busoni. Music by Rudolph Fellner. New York: Houghton, 1973. Paperback. M132.

4314 Simon, Irving B. *The Story of Printing, from Wood Blocks to Electronics.* Illus by Charles E. Pont. Irvington-on-Hudson, NY: Harvey House, 1965.

4315 Simon, Leonard and Jeanne Bendick. *The Day the Numbers Disappeared.* Illus by Jeanne Bendick. Whittlesey, 1963.

4316 Simon, Norma. *A Tree for Me.* Illus by Helen Stone. Philadelphia: Lippincott, 1956.

4317 ———. *What Do I Say?* Illus by Joe Lasher. Chicago: Whitman, 1967.

4318 Simon, Seymour. *Discovering What Gerbils Do.* Illus by Jean Zollinger. New York: McGraw, 1971.

4319 ———. *Finding Out With Your Senses.* Illus by Emily McCully. New York: McGraw, 1971.

4320 ———. *Killer Whales.* Philadelphia: Lippincott, 1978.

4321 Simon, Sidney B. *The Armadillo Who Had No Shell.* Illus by Walter Lorraine. New York: Norton, 1966.

4322 Singer, Isaac Bashevis. *The Fearsome Inn.* Trans by the author and Elizabeth Shub. Illus by Nonny Hogrogian. New York: Scribner, 1967.

4323 ———. *Mazel and Shlimazel; or the Milk of a Lioness.* Illus by Margot Zemach. Trans by Elizabeth Shub. New York: Farrar, 1967. M417.

4324 ———. *Naftali the Storyteller and His Horse, Sus.* Illus by Margot Zemach. New York: Farrar, 1973.

4325 ———. *When Shlemiel Went to Warsaw and Other Stories.* Trans by the author and Elizabeth Shub. Illus by Margot Zemach. New York: Farrar, 1968. M753.

4326 ———. *Why Noah Chose the Dove.* Illus by Eric Carle. New York: Farrar, 1973. M753.

4327 ———. *The Wicked City.* Illus by Everett Fisher. New York: Farrar, 1972.

4328 ———. *Zlatah the Goat and Other Stories.* Trans by Singer and Elizabeth Shub. Illus by Maurice Sendak. New York: Harper, 1966. M785.

4329 Sipherd, Ray. *The White Kite.* Illus by June Goldsborough. Scarsdale, New York: Brad-

bury, 1972.

4330 Sivulich, Sandra Stroner. *I'm Going on a Bear Hunt.* Illus by Glen Rounds. New York: Dutton, 1973.

4331 Skaar, Grace. *Nothing But Cats and All About Dogs.* Illus by the author. New York: Young Scott, 1947.

4332 Skorpen, Leslie Moak. *Mandy's Grandmother.* New York: Dial, 1975.

4333 Skurzynski, Gloria. *What Happened in Hamelin.* New York: Four Winds, 1979.

4334 Slade, Richard. *Modeling in Clay, Plaster, and Papier Mâché.* New York: Lothrop, 1967. Paperback.

4335 ———. *You Can Make a String Puppet.* Boston: Plays, 1957.

4336 Sleator, William. *The Angry Moon.* Illus by Blair Lent. Boston: Little, 1970.

4337 ———. *Blackbriar.* New York: Dutton, 1972.

4338 Sleigh, Barbara. *Jessamy.* Indianapolis: Bobbs, 1967.

4339 Sloan, Carolyn. *Penguin and the Strange Animal.* Illus by Jill McDonald. New York: McGraw, 1974.

4340 Sloane, Eric. *ABC Book of Early Americana, a Sketchbook of Antiques and American Firsts.* Illus by the author. New York: Doubleday, 1963.

4341 Sloane, Gertrude Larned. *Fun with Folktales, Six Plays in Verse with Music and Songs.* Illus by Marian Dormer. New York: Dutton, 1942.

4342 Slobodkin, Louis. *The Friendly Animals.* Illus by the author. New York: Vanguard, 1944.

4343 ———. *Magic Michael.* Illus by the author. New York: Macmillan, 1944. M402.

4344a ———. *Millions and Millions and Millions.* Illus by the author. New York: Vanguard, 1955.

4344b ———. *Spaceship Returns to the Apple Tree.* New York: Macmillan, 1972.

4345a ———. *Spaceship Under the Apple Tree.* New York: Macmillan, 1971.

4345b ———. *The Wide-Awake Owl.* New York: Macmillan, 1958.

4346 Slobodkina, Esphyr. *Caps for Sale: A Tale of a Peddler, Some Monkeys and Their Monkey Business.* Reading: MA: Addison-Wesley, 1947. Scholastic paperback. M111, M112.

4347 Small, Ernest. *Baba Yaga.* Illus by Blair Lent. Boston: Houghton, 1966.

4348 Smaridge, Norah. *The Big Tidy-Up.* Illus by Les Gray. New York: Western, 1970.

4349 Smaridge, Norah. *Famous Author-Illustrators for Young People.* New York: Dodd, 1973.

4350 Smith Dodie. *101 Dalmations.* New York: Viking, 1957. Avon paperback.

4351 ———. *Starlight Barking.* New York: Simon and Schuster, 1967.

4352 Smith, Dorothy B.F. and Eva L. Andrews. *Subject Index to Poetry for Children and Young People 1957-75.* Chicago: ALA, 1977.

4353 Smith, E. Brooks and Robert Meredith. *The Coming of the Pilgrims; Told from Governor Bradford's Firsthand Account.* Illus by Leonard Everett Fisher. Boston: Little, 1964.

4354 ———. *Pilgrim Courage; from a First Hand Account by William Bradford, Governor of Plymouth Colony.* Illus by Leonard Everett

Fisher. Boston: Little, 1962.

4355 Smith, Edward. *The Frogs Who Wanted to be King and Other Stories from La Fontaine.* Illus by Margot Zemach. New York: Four Winds, 1977.

4356 Smith, Elva. S. and Alia Hazeltine. *The Christmas Book of Legends and Stories.* New York: Lothrop, 1944.

4357 ———. *Just for Fun, Humorous Stories and Poems.* Illus by Leonard Weisgard. New York: Lothrop, 1948.

4358 Smith Emma. *No Way of Telling.* New York: Atheneum, 1974.

4359 Smith, Evelyn. *Nursery Rhyme Toys.* New York: Drake, 1973.

4360 Smith, Irene. *A History of the Newbery and Caldecott Medals.* New York: Viking, 1957.

4361 Smith, Moyne Rice. *Plays and How to Put Them On.* Illus by Don Bolognese. New York: Walck, 1961.

4362 ———. *Seven Plays and How to Produce Them.* Illus by Don Bolognese. New York: Walck, 1968.

4363 Smith, William James. *Granger's Index to Poetry, 1970-77.* New York: Columbia, 1978.

4364 Smith, William Jay. *Laughing Time.* Illus by Juliet Kepes. Boston: Little, 1955.

4365 ———. *Mr. Smith and Other Nonsense Verses.* New York: Delacorte, 1968.

4366 Snook, Barbara. *Puppets.* Newton Center, MA: Branford, 1966.

4367 Snyder, Zilpha. *Black and Blue Magic.* Illus by Gene Holtan. New York: Atheneum, 1966. Scholastic paperback.

4368 ———. *Below the Root.* Illus by Alton Raible. New York: Atheneum, 1975.

4369 ———. *The Changeling.* Illus by Alton Raible. New York: Atheneum, 1970. Aladdin paperback.

4370 ———. *The Egypt Game.* Illus by Alton Raible. New York: Atheneum, 1967. Aladdin paperback. M188.

4371 ———. *The Headless Cupid.* Illus by Alton Raible. New York: Atheneum, 1971. Aladdin paperback.

4372 ———. *The Princess and the Giants.* Illus by Beatrice Darwin. New York: Atheneum, 1973.

4373 ———. *The Truth About Stone Hollow.* Illus by Alton Raible. New York: Atheneum, 1974.

4374 ———. *The Velvet Room.* Illus by Alton Raible. New York: Atheneum, 1965.

4375 ———. *The Witches of Worm.* Illus by Alton Raible. New York: Atheneum, 1972. Aladdin paperback.

4376 Sobol, Donald. *Encyclopedia Brown and the Case of the Dead Eagles.* Illus by Leonard Shortall. New York: Nelson, 1975. Scholastic paperback. M189.

4377 ———. *Encyclopedia Brown and the Case of the Moonlight Visitor.* Illus by Leonard Shortall. New York: Nelson, 1977. M189.

4378 ———. *Encyclopedia Brown and the Case of the Secret Pitch.* Illus by Leonard Shortall. New York: Nelson, 1965. M189.

4379 ———. *Encyclopedia Brown, Boy Detective.* Illus by Leonard Shortall. New York: Nelson, 1963. Scholastic paperback. M189.

4380 ———. *Encyclopedia Brown Finds the Clues.* Illus by Leonard Shortall. New York: Nelson, 1966. Scholastic paperback. M189.

4381 ———. *Encyclopedia Brown Gets His Man.* Illus by Leonard Shortall. New York: Nelson, 1967. M189.

4382 ———. *Encyclopedia Brown Keeps the Peace.* New York: Nelson, 1969. Scholastic paperback. M189.

4383 ———. *Encyclopedia Brown Lends a Hand.* Illus by Leonard Shortall. New York: Nelson, 1974. M189.

4384 ———. *Encyclopedia Brown Saves the Day.* Illus by Leonard Shortall. New York: Nelson, 1970. Archway paperback. M189.

4385 ———. *Encyclopedia Brown Shows the Way.* New York. Archway paperback. M189.

4386 ———. *Encyclopedia Brown Solves Them All.* Illus by Leonard Shortall. New York: Nelson, 1977. Scholastic paperback. M189.

4387 ———. *Encyclopedia Brown Tracks Them Down.* Illus by Leonard Shortall. New York: Nelson, 1971. M189

4388 Softly, Barbara. *A Lemon-Yellow Elephant Called Trunk.* Illus by Tony Veale. Irvington-on-Hudson, NY: Harvey House, 1970.

4389 Solzhenitsyn, Alexander. *One Day in the Life of Ivan Denisovich.* Trans by Ralph Parker. New York: Dutton, 1971. Signet and Bantam paperbacks.

4390 Sommer, Elyse. *The Bread Dough Craft Book.* Illus by Giulio Maestro. New York: Lothrop, 1972.

4391 ———. *Designing with Cutouts, the Art of Decoupage.* Illus by Giulio Maestro. New York: Lothrop, 1973.

4392 Sommerfelt, Aimee. *The Road to Agra.* New York: Criterion, 1961.

4393 Soper, Gill and Monica Stuart. *Come, Hear and See Creative Activities for Use with Bible Stories.* London: Faber and Faber, 1976.

4394 Sorensen, Virginia. *Miracles on Maple Hill.* Illus by Beth and Joe Krush. New York: Harcourt, 1956. Voyager paperback. M449.

4395 ———. *Plain Girl.* Illus by Charles Geer. New York: Harcourt, 1955. Voyager paperback.

4396 Soule, Gardner. *The Trail of the Abominable Snowman.* New York: Putnam, 1961.

4397 Spache, George D. *Correlation to Basal Readers.* Chicago: Follette, 1969.

4398 Speaight, George. *The History of the English Puppet Theatre.* New York: John deGraff, 1955.

4399 ———. *Punch and Judy: A History.* Boston: Plays, 1970.

4400 Speare, Elizabeth. *The Witch of Blackbird Pond.* Boston: Houghton, 1958. Paperback. M766.

4401 Spellman, John W., ed. *The Beautiful Blue Jay and Other Fables of India.* Illus by Jerry Pinkney. Boston: Little, 1967.

4402 Spencer, Donald D. *The Story of Computers.* Ormond Beach, Fla.: Abacus Computer Corporation, 1975. Abacus New York:

4403 Sperry, Armstrong. *Call it Courage.* Illus by the author. New York: Macmillan, 1940. Paperback. M109.

4404 ———. *Danger to Downwind.* New York:

Winston, 1947.

4405 Spicer, Dorothy G. *Forty-Six Days of Christmas, a Cycle of Old World Songs, Legends and Customs.* Illus by Anne Marie Janus. New York: Coward, 1960.

4406 ———. *The Humming Top.* New York: Phillips, 1968. Paperback.

4407 ———. *Long Ago in Serbia.* Illus by Linda Ominsky. Philadelphia: Westminster, 1968.

4408a ———. *Thirteen Devils.* New York: Coward, 1967.

4408b ———. *Thirteen Monsters.* New York: Coward, 1964.

4409 Spier, Peter, illus. *Crash Bang Boom.* Garden City, NY: Doubleday, 1972. Zephyr paperback.

4410 ———. *The Erie Canal.* Garden City, NY: Doubleday, 1970. Paperback. M193, M194.

4411 ———. *Fast-Slow High-Low, a Book of Opposites.* Garden City, NY: Doubleday, 1972. Zephyr paperback.

4412 ———. *Fox Went Out on a Chilly Night.* Garden City, NY: Doubleday, 1961. Paperback. M225, M226.

4413 ———. *Gobble, Growl, Grunt.* Garden City, NY: Doubleday, 1971. Zephyr paperback.

4414 ———. *Hurrah, We're Outward Bound!* Garden City, NY: Doubleday, 1968.

4415 ———. *The Legend of New Amsterdam.* Garden City, NY: Doubleday, 1979.

4416 ———. *London Bridge is Falling Down.* Garden City, NY: Doubleday, 1969. Paperback. M386.

4417 *———. *Noah's Ark.* Garden City, NY: Doubleday, 1977. M481.

4418 ———. *Oh, Were They Ever Happy.* Garden City, NY: Doubleday, 1978.

4419 ———. *And So My Garden Grows.* Garden City, NY: Doubleday, 1969.

4420 ———. *The Star Spangled Banner.* Garden City, NY: Doubleday, 1973. M630, M631.

4421 ———. *Tin Lizzie.* Garden City, NY: Doubleday, 1975. Paperback.

4422 ———. *To Market, To Market.* Garden City, NY: Doubleday, 1967. Paperback.

4423 Spilka, Arnold. *Paint All Kinds of Pictures.* New York: Walck, 1963. M518.

4424 Spyri, Johanna. *Heidi.* Illus by Leonard Weisgard. New York: Collins, 1972. Paperbacks in print: Airmont, Penguin, Scholastic. M279.

4425 Staat, Sara R. *Big City ABC.* Illus by Robert Keys. Chicago: Follett, 1968.

4426 Stacy, Donald. *Experiments in Art.* New York: Four Winds, 1975.

4427 ———. *The Runaway Dot, an Adventure in Line.* New York: Bobbs, 1969.

4428 Stanley, Diane, illus. *Fiddle-i-fee: A Traditional American Chant.* Boston: Little, 1979.

4429 Stecher, Miriam B. and Alice S. Kandell. *Max, the Music-Maker.* New York: Lothrop, 1980.

4430 Starbird, Kaye. *The Covered Bridge House and Other Poems.* Illus by Jim Arnosky. New York: Four Winds, 1979.

4431 ———. *Don't Ever Cross a Crocodile.* Illus by Kit Dalton. Philadelphia: Lippincott, 1966.

4432 ———. *The Pheasant on Route Seven.* Victoria de Larrea. Philadelphia: Lippincott, 1968.

4433 ———. *A Snail's a Failure Socially; and Other Poems, Mostly About People.* Illus by Kit Dalton. Philadelphia: Lippincott, 1966.

4434 ———. *Speaking of Cows.* Illus by Rita Fava. Philadelphia: Lippincott, 1960.

4435 ———. *Watch Out for the Mules.* New York: Harcourt, 1968.

4436 Stearns, Pamela. *Into the Painted Bear Lair.* Boston: Houghton, 1976.

4437 Steele, Flora Annie. *English Fairy Tales.* Illus by Arthur Rackham. Afterword by Clifton Fadiman. New York: Macmillan, 1946.

4438 ———. *Tattercoats, an Old English Tale.* Illus by Diane Goode. New York: Bradbury, 1976.

4439 ———. *The Tiger, the Brahman and the Jackal.* Illus by Mamoru Funai. New York: Holt, 1963.

4440 Steele, Mary Q. *First of the Penguins.* Illus by Susan Jeffers. New York: Macmillan, 1973.

4441 ———. *Journey Outside.* Illus by Rocco Negri. New York: Viking, 1969.

4442 Steele, William O. *The Perilous Road.* Illus by Paul Galdone. New York: Harcourt, 1958. Voyager paperback. M520.

4443 ———. *Wayah of the Real People.* New York: Holt, 1964.

4444 ———. *Year of the Bloody Sevens.* Illus by Charles Beck. New York: Harcourt, 1963.

4445 Steenmeijer, Anna S., ed. with the help of Otto Frank. *A Tribute to Anne Frank.* New York: Doubleday, 1971.

4446 Steffens, Lincoln. *Boy on Horseback.* New York: Harcourt, 1931, 1935, 59, 63.

4447 Steig, William. *Abel's Island.* Illus by the author. New York: Farrar, 1976.

4448 ———. *The Amazing Bone.* Illus by the author. New York: Farrar, 1976. Puffin paperback. M18.

4449 ———. *Amos and Boris.* Illus by the author. New York: Farrar, 1971. Puffin paperback.

4450 ———. *Dominic.* Illus by the author. New York: Farrar, 1972. Dell paperback.

4451 ———. *Farmer Palmer's Wagon Ride.* Illus by the author. New York: Farrar, 1974. M203.

4452 *———. *Sylvester and the Magic Pebble.* Illus by the author. New York: Simon and Schuster, 1969. Windmill paperback.

4453 Stein, Conrad. *Steel Driving Man, the Legend of John Henry.* Chicago: Children's Press, 1969. M32, M217, M359.

4454 Stein, Susan, M. and Sarah T. Lottick. *Three Four, Open the Door, Creative Fun for Young Children.* Chicago: Follett, 1971.

4455 Stein, Vivian. *Batik as a Hobby.* New York: Sterling, 1969.

4456 Steinberg, Phil. *Photography.* Illus by George Overlie. Minneapolis: Lerner, 1975.

4457 Steinbeck, John. *The Red Pony.* Illus by Wesley Dennis. New York: Viking, 1959.

4458 Steiner, Charlotte. *I Am Andy, You-Tell-a-Story-Book.* New York: Knopf, 1961.

4459 ———. *Ten in a Family.* New York: Knopf, 1960.

4460 Steiner, Violette and Roberta Evatt Pond. *Finger Play Fun.* Columbus, OH: Charles E.

Merrill, 1970.

4461 Steinfatt, Thomas M. *Human Communication, an Interpersonal Introduction.* Indianapolis: Bobbs, 1977.

4462 Stephan, Barbara. *Creating with Tissue Paper; Design, Technique, Decoration.* New York: Crown, 1973. Paperback.

4463 Stephens, Henry L., illus. *Frog He Would A Wooing Go.* New York: Walker, 1967. M32, M216.

4464 Steptoe, John. *Daddy is a Monster ... Sometimes.* Illus. New York: Lippincott, 1980.

4465 ———. *Stevie.* New York: Harper, 1969.

4466 Sterling, Dorothy. *Freedom Train, the Story of Harriet Tubman.* Illus by Ernest Crichlow. Garden City, NY: Doubleday, 1974.

4467 ———. *Mary Jane.* Illus by Ernest Crichlow. Garden City, NY: Doubleday, 1959. Scholastic paperback.

4468 Sternberg, Harry. *Woodcut.* Photos by Ted Davis. New York: Pitman, 1962. Pitman paperback.

4469 Stevens, Carla. *The Birth of Sunset's Kittens.* Photos by Leonard Stevens. New York: Young Scott, 1969.

4470 ———. *Catch a Cricket, About the Capture and Care of Crickets, Grasshoppers, Fireflies and Other Companionable Creatures.* Photos by Martin Inger. New York: Scott, 1961.

4471 ———. *Hooray for Pig!* Illus by Rainey Bennett. New York: Seabury, 1974.

4472 ———. *Your First Pet and How to Take Care of It.* New York: Macmillan, 1974.

4473 Stevenson, Augusta. *Wilbur and Orville Wright.* Indianapolis: Bobbs, 1959.

4474 Stevenson, Burton Egbert. *The Home Book of Verse for Young Folks.* New York: Holt, 1929, 1958.

4475 Stevenson, James. *Could be Worse!* Illus by the author. New York: Greenwillow, 1977. Puffin paperback.

4476 ———. *The Night After Christmas.* Illus by the author. New York: Greenwillow, 1981.

4477 Stevenson, Peter. *The Art of Making Wooden Toys.* Radnor, PA: Chilton, 1971. Chilton paperback.

4478 Stevenson, Robert Louis. *A Child's Garden of Verses.* Illus by Alex Dobkin. Cleveland: Collins, n.d. M129.

4479 ———. *A Child's Garden of Verses.* Illus by Alice and Martin Provensen. New York: Golden, 1951. M129.

4480 ———. *A Child's Garden of Verses.* Illus by Mary Shillabeer. New York: Dutton, n.d. M129.

4481 ———. *A Child's Garden of Verses.* Illus by Jessie Wilcox Smith. New York: Scribner, 1955. M129.

4482 ———. *A Child's Garden of Verses.* Illus by Tasha Tudor. New York: Walck, 1947. M129.

4483 ———. *Treasure Island.* Illus by N.C. Wyeth. New York: Scribner, 1939. M711, M712.

4484 Stewart, John. *The Key to the Kitchen.* Illus by Robert Quackenbush. New York: Lothrop, 1970.

4485 Stewig, John Warren. *Sending Messages.* Photos by Richard D. Bradley. Boston: Houghton, 1978.

4486 Still, James. *Jack and the Wonder Beans.* New York: Putnam, 1977.

4487 ———. *Way Down Yonder on Troublesome Creek, Appalachian Riddles and Rusties.* Illus by Janet McCaffery. New York: Putnam, 1974.

4488 Stobbs, William. *Jack and the Beanstalk.* Illus by the author. New York: Delacorte, 1965.

4489 Stoker, Bram. *Dracula.* New York: Doubleday, 1959. Paperbacks in print: Airmont, Dell, Scholastic, Tempo. M180, M181.

4490 Stolz, Mary. *Belling the Tiger.* New York: Harper, 1967.

4491 ———. *The Bully of Barkham Street.* Illus by Leonard Shortall. New York: Harper, 1963. Dell paperback.

4492 ———. *A Dog on Barkham Street.* Illus by Leonard Shortall. New York: Harper, 1960. Dell paperback.

4493 ———. *Emmett's Pig.* Illus by Garth Williams. New York: Harper, 1959.

4494 Stone, Nancy. *The Wooden River.* Illus by Betty Beely. Grand Rapids: Eerdmans, 1973.

4495 Storm, Theodor. *Little John.* Retold by Doris Orgel. Illus by Anita Lobel. New York: Farrar, 1972.

4496 Stoutenburg, Adrien. *American Tall-Tale Animals.* Illus by Glen Rounds. New York: Viking, 1968.

4497 ———. *American Tall Tales.* Illus by Richard Powers. New York: Viking, 1966. M28, M29, M30.

4498 Strong, Joanna. *Favorite Folktales and Fables.* Illus by Hubert Whatley. New York: Harcourt, 1950.

4499 Strong, Arline. *Glowing in the Dark.* New York: Atheneum, 1975.

4500 Strong, Leonard. *Sixteen Portraits of People Whose Houses Have Been Preserved by the National Trust.* Illus by Joan Hassall. London: Naldrett, 1951.

4501 Stupka, Arthur and the Eastern National Parks and Monument Association. *Wildflowers in Color.* New York: Harper, 1965.

4502 Sugita, Yutaka. *My Friend, Little John and Me.* New York: McGraw, 1973.

4503 ———. *Wake up, Little Tree, A Christmas Fantasy.* New York: Nelson, 1971.

4504a Suhl, Yuri. *Simon Boom Gives A Wedding.* New York: Four Winds, 1972.

4504b ———. *Uncle Misha's Partisans.* New York: Four Winds, 1973. Scholastic paperback.

4505 Suib, Leonard and Muriel Broadman. *Marionettes Onstage.* New York: Harper, 1975.

4506 Sullivan, A.S. *The Gilbert and Sullivan Song Book.* Selected by M. Hyatt and W. Fabell. Illus by M. Ayer. Music by I Shannon. New York: Random, 1963. M470.

4507 Sutcliff, Rosemary. *The Capricorn Bracelet.* Illus by Richard Cuffari. New York: Walck, 1973.

4508 ———. *Dawn Wind.* Illus by Charles Keeping. New York: Walck, 1962.

4509 ———. *The Knight's Fee.* Illus by Charles Keeping. New York: Walck, 1960.

4510 ———. *The Lantern Bearers.* Illus by Charles Keeping. New York: Walck, 1959.

4511 ———. *The Shield Ring.* New York: Walck, 1972.

4512 ———. *Warrior Scarlet.* New York: Walck, 1966.

4513 ———. *The Witch's Brat.* Illus by Richard Lebenson. New York: Walck, 1970.

4514 Sutherland, Zena, ed. *The Arbuthnot Anthology of Children's Literature,* 4th edition. Glencoe, IL: Scott Foresman, 1976.

4515 ———. *Children and Books.* 6th edition. New York: Glenview, IL: Scott Foresman, 1981.

4516 ———. *The Best in Children's Books: The University of Chicago Guide to Children's Literature, 1973-1978.* Chicago: University of Chicago Press, 1980.

4517 Suyeaka, George, illus. *A Is for Alphabet.* New York: Lothrop, 1968.

4518 Svatos, Ladislav. *Dandelion.* New York: Doubleday, 1976.

4519 Swanson, May. *More Poems to Solve.* New York: Scribner, 1970.

4520 ———. *Poems to Solve.* New York: Scribner, 1966.

4521 Swift, Hildegard. *Little Red Light House and the Great Gray Bridge.* Illus by Lynd Ward. New York: Harcourt, 1942. Voyager paperback. M376, M377.

4522 ———. *The Railroad to Freedom; A Story of the Civil War.* Illus by James Daugherty. New York: Harcourt, 1932.

4523 Swift, Jonathan. *Gulliver's Travels.* Illus by Arthur Rackham. Dutton, n.d. Paperback. M258, M259.

4524a Tagore, (Sir Rabindranath). *Moon For What Do You Wait?* Illus by Ashley Bryan. Edited by Richard Leras Leros. New York: Atheneum, 1967.

4524b Tarcov, Edith. *Three Famous Stories.* New York: Scholastic, 1979.

4525 Tashjian, Virginia A. *Juba This and Juba That.* Boston: Little, 1969.

4526 ———. *Once There Was and Was Not, Armenian Tales.* Illus by Nonny Hogrogian. Boston: Little, 1966.

4527 ———. *With a Deep Sea Smile; Story Hour Stretches for Large or Small Groups.* Illus by Rosemary Wells. New York: Little, 1974.

4528 Tallon, Robert. *Zoophabets.* Indianapolis: Bobbs, 1971.

4529 Taylor, Dorothy and John. *Finger Rhymes.* Illus by Brian Price Thomas. Photos by John Mayes. Loughborough, England: Ladybird, 1976.

4530 ———. *Number Rhymes.* Illus by Brian Price Thomas. Photos by John Mayes. Loughborough, England: Ladybird, 1976.

4531 Taylor, Margaret C. *Wht's Yr Nm?* New York: Harcourt, 1970.

4532 Taylor, Mark. *Bobby Shafto's Gone to Sea.* Illus by Graham Booth. San Carbos, Calif.: Golden Gate, 1970.

4533 ———. *Henry Explores the Jungle.* Illus by Graham Booth. New York: Atheneum, 1968.

4534 ———. *Old Blue: You Good Dog You.* Illus by Gene Holtan. San Carlos, CA: Golden Gate, 1970.

4535 ———. *The Old Woman and the Peddler.* Illus by Graham Booth. San Carlos, CA: Golden Gate, 1969.

4536 Taylor, Mildred. *Roll of Thunder Hear My Cry.* Illus. New York: Dial, 1976.

4537 ———. *Song of the Trees.* Illus. New York: Dial,1975.

4538 Taylor, Sydney. *All-of-a-Kind Family.* Illus by Mary Stevens. Chicago: Follett, 1951. Dell paperback.

4539 ———. *All-of-a-Kind Family Downtown.* Illus by Mary Stevens. Chicago: Follett, 1972. Dell paperback.

4540 ———. *All-of-a-Kind Family Uptown.* Illus by Mary Stevens. Chicago: Follett, 1958. Dell paperback.

4541 ———. *Ella of All-of-a-Kind Family.* Illus by Gail Owens. New York: Dutton, 1978.

4542 ———. *More All-of-a-Kind Family.* Illus by Mary Stevens. Chicago: Follett, 1954. Dell paperback.

4543 Taylor, Theodore. *The Cay.* New York: Doubleday, 1969. Avon paperback.

4544 Temko, Florence. *Paper Capers: All Kinds of Things to Make with Paper.* New York: Scholastic, 1975.

4545 ———. *Papercutting.* New York: Doubleday, 1973.

4546 Tennyson, Alfred Lloyd. *The Charge of the Light Brigade.* Illus by Alice and Martin Provence. New York: Golden, 1964.

4547 ———. *The Lady of Shalott.* Illus by Bernadette Watts. New York: Watts, 1968.

4548 Terhune, Albert Payson. *Lad: A Dog.* Illus by Sam Savutt. New York: Dutton, 1959.

4549 ———. *Lad of Sunnybank.* New York: Tempo paperback, 1968.

4550 Thaler, Mike. *Magic Letter Riddles.* Englewood Cliffs, NJ: Scholastic, 1975.

4551 ———. *Oinkers Away! Pig Riddles, Cartoons and Jokes.* New York: Archway paperback, 1981.

4552 ———. *The Smiling Book.* Illus by Arnie Levin. New York: Lothrop, 1971.

4553 ———. *Soup with Quackers, Funny Cartoon Riddles.* New York: Watts, 1976.

4554 ———. *The Yellow Brick Road: Funny Frog Cartoons, Riddles and Silly Stories.* Garden City, NY: Doubleday, 1978. Archway paperback.

4555 Thane, Adele. *Plays from Famous Stories and Fairy Tales: Royalty-Free Dramatizations of Favorite Children's Stories.* Boston: Play, 1975.

4556 Thayer, Ernest Lawrence. *Casy At the Bat.* Illus by Paul Frame. Englewood Cliffs, NJ: Prentice-Hall, 1964. M114.

4557 Thomas, Allison. *Benji.* From the screenplay by Joe Camp. New York: American Broadcasting Co., 1975. Pyramid paperback.

4558 Thomas, H. *The Wright Brothers.* New York: Putnam, 1960.

4559 Thomas, Marlo. *Free To Be . . . You and Me.* New York: McGraw Paperback, 1974.

4560 Thompson, Blanche Jennings. *Silver Pennies; A Call of Modern Poems for Boys and Girls.* Illus by Winifred Bromhall. New York: Macmillan, 1925. M610.

4561 ———. *More Silver Pennies.* Illus by Pelagie Doane. New York: Macmillan, 1938. M466.

4562 Thompson, James. *Beyond Words, Nonverbal Communicaiton in the Classroom.* Scholastic, 1973.

4563 Thompson, Steth. *One Hundred Favorite Folktales.* Illus by Franz Altschuler. Bloomington, Ind.: Indiana University, 1968. Paperback.

4564 Thompson, Vivian L. *Hawaiian Legends of Tricksters and Riddlers.* Illus by Sylvie Selig. New York: Holiday, 1969.

4565 ———. *Hawaiian Tales of Heroes and Champions.* New York: Holiday, 1971.

4566 Thorndike, Susan. *Electric Radish and Other Jokes.* New York: Doubleday, 1973.

4567 Thorne, Ian. *Frankenstein.* Mankato, Minn.: Crestwood, 1977.

4568 ———. *Godzilla.* Mankato, Minn.: Crestwood, 1977.

4569 ———. *King Kong.* Mankato, Minn.: Crestwood, 1977.

4570 Thorne-Thomsen, Gudrun. *East o' the Sun and West o' the Moon.* New York: Row, 1946.

4571 *Thurber, James. *Many Moons.* Illus by Louis Slobodkin. New York: Harcourt, 1943. M405.

4572 Tichenor, Tom. *Folk Plays for Puppets You Can Make.* Nashville, Abingdon, 1959.

4573 ———. *Tom Tichenor's Puppets.* Nashville, Abingdon, 1971.

4574 Tingle, Roger. *Let's Print.* New York: Van Nostrand, 1972. Paperback.

4575 Tison, Annette and Talus Taylor. *The Adventures of the Three Colors.* Cleveland: World, 1971.

4576 Titus, Eve. *Anatole.* Illus by Paul Galdone. New York: McGraw, 1956.

4577 ———. *Anatole and the Cat.* Illus by Paul Galdone. New York: McGraw, 1957.

4578 ———. *Anatole and the Piano.* Illus by Paul Galdone. New York: McGraw, 1966.

4579 ———. *Anatole and the Pied Piper.* Illus by Paul Galdone. New York: McGraw, 1979.

4580 ———. *Anatole and the Thirty Thieves.* Illus by Paul Galdone. New York: McGraw, 1969.

4581 ———. *Anatole Over Paris.* Illus by Paul Galdone. New York: McGraw, 1961.

4582 ———. *Basil and the Pygmy Cats.* Illus by Paul Galdone. New York: McGraw, 1971. Archway paperback.

4583 ———. *Basil of Baker Street.* Illus by Paul Galdone. New York: McGraw, 1958. Archway paperback.

4584 ———. *The Two Stonecutters.* Illus by Yoko Mitsuhashi. Garden City, NY: Doubleday, 1967.

4585 Todd, Ruthven. *Space Cat.* Illus by Paul Galdone. New York: Scribner, 1952.

4586 ———. *Space Cat and the Kittens.* Illus by Paul Galdone. New York: Scribner, 1958.

4587 ———. *Space Cat Meets Mars.* Illus by Paul Galdone. New York: Scribner, 1957.

4588 Tolkien, J.R.R. *Fellowship of the Ring.* Illus by the author. Boston: Houghton, 1967. Ballantine paperback. M288.

4589 ———. *The Hobbit; or There and Back Again.* Illus by the author. Boston: Houghton, 1938. Ballantine paperback. M288.

4590 ———. *Return of the King.* Illus by the author. Boston: Houghton, 1967. Ballantine paperback. M546.

4591 ———. *Simarillion.* Boston: Houghton, 1977.

4592 ———. *The Tolkien Reader.* New York: Ballantine, 1976.

4593 ———. *The Two Towers.* Illus by the author. Boston: Houghton, 1967. Ballantine paperback. M546.

4594 Tolstoy, Alexei. *The Great Big Enormous Turnip.* Illus by Helen Oxenbury. New York: Watts, 1969. M256.

4595 Tompert, Ann. *Little Fox Goes to the End of the World.* Illus by John Wallner. New York: Crown, 1976.

4596 ———. *Little Otter Remembers and Other Stories.* New York: Crown, 1977.

4597 Toor, Frances. *A Treasury of Mexican Folkways.* New York: Crown, 1947.

4598 Tooze, Ruth. *Storytelling.* Englewood Cliffs, NJ: Prentice-Hall, 1959.

4599 Tournier, Michel. *Friday and Robinson; Life on Speranza Island.* Trans by Ralph Manheim. New York: Knopf, 1972.

4600 Towle, Faith M. *The Magic Cooking Pot.* Boston: Houghton, 1975.

4601a Townsend, John R. *The Visitors.* Philadelphia: Lippincott, 1977.

4601b ———. *Written for Children.* Philadelphia: Lippincott, 1975.

4602 Toye, William. *How Summer Came to Canada.* Illus by Elizabeth Cleaver. New York: Walck, 1969.

4603 Travers, P.L. *Mary Poppins.* Illus by Mary Shepard. New York: Harcourt, 1934, 1962. Voyager paperback. M407, M408, M409.

4604 ———. *Mary Poppins and Mary Poppins Comes Back.* Illus by Mary Shepard. New York: Harcourt, 1963. M409, M410, M411.

4605 ———. *Mary Poppins Comes Back.* Illus by Mary Shepard. New York: Harcourt, 1963. Voyager paperback. M409, M410, M411.

4606 ———. *Mary Poppins from A to Z.* Illus by Mary Shepard. New York: Harcourt, 1962. M412

4607 ———. *Mary Poppins in the Park.* Illus by Mary Shepard. New York: Harcourt, 1952.

4608a ———. *Mary Poppins Opens the Door.* Illus by Mary Shepard and Agnes Sims. New York: Harcourt, 1943. M410.

4608b ———. *Two Pairs of Shoes.* New York: Viking, 1980.

4609a Treece, Henry. *The Dream Time.* New York: Meredith, 1967.

4609b ———. *The Last Viking.* New York: Pantheon, 1964.

4610 Trent, Robbie. *The First Christmas.* Illus by Marc Sinont. New York: Harper, 1948.

4611 Tresselt, Alvin R. *Frog in the Well.* Illus by Robert Duvoisin. New York: Lothrop, 1958.

4612 ———. *Hide and Seek Fog.* Illus by Roger Duvoisin. New York: Lothrop, 1965. M284.

4613 ———. *Rain Drop Splash.* Illus by Leonard Weisgard. New York: Lothrop, 1946. M564.

4614 ———. *Stories from the Bible retold by Alvin Tresselt.* Illus by Lynd Ward. New York: Coward, 1971.

4615 ———. *Sun Up.* Illus by Roger Duvoisin. New York: Lothrop, 1949.

4616 *———. *White Snow, Bright Snow.* Illus by

Roger Duvoisin. New York: Lothrop, 1947. M745.

4617 ———. *The World in a Candy Egg*. Illus by Roger Duvoisin. New York: Lothrop, 1967.

4618 Tripp, Wallace, ed. *Granfa' Grig Had a Pig and Other Rhymes Without Reason from Mother Goose*. Illus by Wallace Tripp. Boston: Little, 1976. Paperback.

4619 ———. *A Great Big Ugly Man Came Up and Tied His Horse to Me, a Book of Nonsense Verse*. Boston: Little, 1973. Paperback.

4620 Tritten, Gottfried. *Art Techniques for Children*. New York: Reinhold, 1964.

4621a Trosclair. *Cajun Night Before Christmas*. Edited by Howard Jacobs. Gretna, La.: Pelican, 1973.

4621b Tucker, Nicholas. *Mother Goose Abroad: Nursery Rhymes*. Illus by Trevor Stubley. New York: Crowell, 1973.

4622a ———. *Mother Goose Lost, Nursery Rhymes*. Illus by Trevor Stubley. New York: Crowell, 1971.

4622b Tudor, Tasha. *A is for Annabelle*. Illus by the author. New York: Walck, 1954. Paperback.

4623 ———. *Around The Year*. Illus by the author. New York: Walck, 1957.

4624 ———. *Corgiville Fair*. Illus by the author. New York: Crowell, 1971.

4625 ———. *The Dolls Christmas*. Illus by the author. New York: Walck, 1950. Paperback.

4626 ———. *Tasha Tudor's Favorite Christmas Carols*. Illus by T. Tudor and Linda Allen. New York: McKay, 1978.

4627 ———. *One Is One*. Illus by the author. New York: Walck, 1956. Walck paperback.

4628 ———. *Take Joy! The Tasha Tudor Christmas Book*. Illus by the author. Cleveland: World, 1966.

4629 ———. *The Tasha Tudor Book of Fairy Tales*. Illus by the author. New York: Platt, 1961.

4630 Turkle, Brinton. *The Adventures of Obadiah*. Illus by the author. New York: Viking, 1972. Puffin paperback. M4.

4631 ———. *Deep in the Forest*. New York: Dutton, 1977.

4632 ———. *Obadiah the Bold*. Illus by the author. New York: Viking, 1969. Puffin paperback. M490.

4633 ———. *Thy Friend Obadiah*. New York: Viking, 1972. Puffin paperback. M693.

4634 ———. *Mooncoin Castle; or Skullduggery Rewarded*. New York: 1970.

4635 Turner, Nancy Byrd. *When It Rained Cats and Dogs*. Illus by Tibor Gergley. Philadelphia: Lippincott, 1946.

4636 Turner, Philip. *Brian Wildsmith's Illustrated Bible Stories*. Illus by B. Wildsmith. New York: Watts, 1969.

4637 Tuttle, Florence P. *Puppets and Puppet Plays*. Illus by George Overlie. Mankato, MN: Creative Educational Society, 1962.

4638 Uchida, Yoshika. *The Dancing Kettle and Other Japanese Folk Tales*. Illus by Richard C. Jones. New York: Harcourt, 1949.

4639a ———. *The Magic Listening Cap, More Folk Tales from Japan*. Illus by the author. New York: Harcourt, 1955. Voyager paperback.

4639b ———. *Sea of Gold and Other Tales of Japan*. Boston: Gregg, 1980.

4640a ———. *Sumi's Prize*. Illus by Kazue Mizumura. New York: Scribner's, 1964.

4640b Udry, Janice. *Let's be Enemies*. Illus by Maurice Sendak. New York: Harper, 1961. M359.

4641 *Udry, Janice May. *A Tree is Nice*. Illus by Mark Simont. New York: Harper, 1956. M713.

4642 Undset, Sigrid. *True and Untrue and Other Norse Tales*. Illus by Frederick C. Chapman. New York: Knopf, 1945, 1958.

4643 Ueno, Noriko. *Elephant Buttons*. New York: Harper and Row, 1973.

4644 Ungerer, Tomi. *The Beast of Monsieur*. Illus by the author. New York: Farrar, 1971.

4645 ———. *Christmas Eve at the Mellops*. Illus by the author. New York: Harper, 1960. o.p.

4646 ———. *Crictor*. Illus by the author. New York: Harper, 1958. Scholastic paperback.

4647 ———. *Emile*. Illus by the author. New York: Harper, 1960.

4648 ———. *The Hat*. Illus by the author. New York: Parents, 1970.

4649 ———. *The Mellops Go Diving for Treasure*. Illus by the author. New York: Harper, 1957.

4650 ———. *Moon Man*. Illus by the author. New York: Harper, 1967.

4651 ———. *One, Two, Where's My Shoe?* Illus by the author. New York: Harper, 1964. Hale, 1964.

4652 ———. *Rufus*. Illus by the author. New York: Harper, 1961.

4653 ———. *Snail Where are You?* Illus by the author. New York: Harper, 1962.

4654 ———. *The Three Robbers*. Illus by the author. New York: Atheneum, 1962. Aladdin paperback. M690, M691.

4655 ———. *Zeralda's Ogre*. Illus by the author. New York: Harper, 1967.

4656 Unkelback, Kurt. *Albert Payson Terhune, the Master of Sunnybank*. New York: Charterhouse/McKay, 1972.

4657 Untermeyer, Louis. *Aesop's Fables*. Illus by A. and M. Provensen. New York: Golden, 1965.

4658 ———. *The Firebringer and Other Great Stories: Fifty-five Legends That Live Forever*. Illus by Mae Gerhard. New York: M. Evans, 1968.

4659 ———. *The Golden Treasury of Poetry*. Illus by Joan Walsh Anglund. New York: Golden, 1959.

4660 ———. *The Magic Circle: Stories and People in Poetry*. Illus by Beth and Joe Krush. New York: Harcourt, 1952.

4661 ———. *Rainbow in the Sky*. Illus by Reginald Birch. New York: Harcourt, 1935.

4662 ———. *Stars to Steer By*. Illus by Dorothy Bayley. New York: Harcourt, 1941.

4663 ———. *Tales from the Ballet*. Illus by A. and M. Provensen. New York: Golden, 1968.

4664 ———. *This Singing World, an Anthology of Modern Poetry for Young People*. Illus by Florence W. Ivins. New York: Harcourt, 1923.

4665 ———. *This Singing World, Junior Edition*. New York: Harcourt, 1926.

4666 ———. *Yesterday and Today: a Collection of Verse Designed for the Average Person*. New

York: Harcourt, 1927.

4667 ———. *The World's Greatest Stories; Legends that Live Forever.* Illus by Mae Gerhard. New York: Evans, 1964.

4668 Untermeyer, Louis and Bryna, eds. *The Golden Treasury of Children's Literature.* New York: Golden, 1966.

4669 Updike, John and Warren Chappell. *The Magic Flute.* Adapted and illus by John Updike and Warren Chappell. Music by Wolfgang Mozart. New York: Knopf, 1962.

4670 ———. *The Ring.* Adapted and illus by John Updike and Warren Chappell. Music by Richard Wagner. New York: Knopf, 1964.

4671 Uttley, Alison. *A Traveler in Time.* Illus by Christine Price. New York: Viking, 1964.

4672 Van Gelder, Richard. *Whose Nose is This?* New York: Walker, 1974.

4673 Van Leeuwen, Jean. *Tales of Oliver Pig.* Illus by Arnold Lobel. New York: Dial, 1979. Paperback.

4674 Van Orden, Phyllis, ed. *The Elementary School Library Collection: A Guide to Books and Other Media, Phase 1-2-3.* Newark, NJ: Bro Dart, 1977.

4675 Van Stockum, Hilda. *The Winged Watchman.* Illus by the author. New York: Farrar, 1963.

4676 Van Woerkom, Dorothy O. *The Queen Who Couldn't Bake Gingerbread.* Illus by Paul Galdone. New York: Knopf, 1975. M558.

4677 ———. *The Rat, the Ox, and the Zodiac, a Chinese Legend.* Illus by Errol le Cain. New York: Crown, 1976.

4678a ——— *Tit for Tat.* Illus by Douglas Florian. New York: Greenwillow, 1977.

4678b Valens, Evans G. *Wildfire.* New York: World, 1963.

4679a ——— *Wingfin and Topple.* New York: World, 1962.

4679b Varnum, Brooke Minarik. *Play and Sing—It's Christmas! A Piano Book of Easy-to-Play Carols.* Illus by Emily Arnold McCully. New York: Macmillan, 1980.

4680 Venable, Alan. *Checker Players.* Illus by Byron Barton. Philadelphia: Lippincott, 1973.

4681 ———. *Hurry the Crossing.* Philadelphia: Lippincott, 1974.

4682 Vermeer, Jackie and Marian Lariviere. *The Little Kid's Four Seasons Craft Book.* New York: Taplinger, 1974.

4683 Verne, Jules. *Around the World in 80 Days.* New York: Dodd, 1979. M47.

4684 ———. *Around the World in 80 Days.* New York: Viking, 1980. M47.

4685 ———. *Around the World in 80 Days.* Paperbacks by Airmont and Dell. M47.

4686 ———. *Twenty Thousand Leagues Under the Sea.* New York: Dodd, 1952.

4687 Vevers, Gwynne. *Birds and Their Nests.* Illus by Colin Threadgall. New York: McGraw, 1973.

4688 Victor, Joan Berg. *Bigger Than an Elephant.* New York: Crown, 1968.

4689 Villiers, Alan John, et al. *Men, Ships and the Sea.* Washington, DC: National Geographic, 1962, 1973.

4690 Viorst, Judith. *Alexander and the Terrible, Horrible, No Good Very Bad Day.* Illus by the author. New York: Atheneum, 1972. Aladdin paperback.

4691 ———. *Alexander Who Used to be Rich, Last Sunday.* Illus by the author. New York: Atheneum, 1980. Aladdin paperback.

4692 ———. *My Mama Says There Aren't Any Zombies, Ghosts, Vampires, Creatures, Demons, Monsters, Fiends, Gobblins, or Things.* Illus by Kay Chorao. New York: Atheneum, 1973. Paperback.

4693 Vipont, Elfrida. *The Elephant and the Bad Boy.* Illus by Raymond Briggs. New York: Coward, 1969.

4694 Vogel, Ilse-Margaret. *One Is No Fun, But Twenty Is Plenty.* New York: Atheneum, 1965. Aladdin paperback.

4695 ———. *Willy, Willy Don't Be Silly.* Illus by the author. New York: Atheneum, 1965.

4696 Voigt, Erna, Illus. *Peter and the Wolf.* Music by Serge Prokofieff. Boston: David R. Godine, 1979. M521.

4697 Voigt, Virginia Frances. *Little Brown Bat.* Illus by Earl Thollander. New York: Putnam, 1969.

4698 Volakova, H., ed. *I Never Saw Another Butterfly.* New York: McGraw, 1964.

4699 Voss, Gunther. *Reinhold Craft and Hobby Book.* New York: Reinhold, 1963.

4700 Vreuls, Diane. *Sums: A Looking Game.* New York: Viking, 1977.

4701 Waber, Bernard. *An Anteater Named Arthur.* Illus by the author. Boston: Houghton, 1967. Paperback.

4702 ———. *A Firefly Named Torchy.* Illus by the author. Boston: Houghton, 1970.

4703 ———. *The House on East 88th Street.* Illus by the author. Boston: Houghton, 1962. Paperback. M392.

4704 ———. *How to Go About Laying an Egg.* Illus by the author. Boston: Houghton, 1963.

4705 ———. *Ira Sleeps Over.* Illus by the author. Boston: Houghton, 1972. Sandpiper paperback.

4706 ———. *Lovable Lyle.* Illus by the author. Boston: Houghton, 1969. Paperback. M392

4707 ———. *Lyle and the Birthday Party.* Illus by the author. Boston: Houghton, 1966. Sandpiper paperback. M392.

4708 ———. *Lyle Finds His Mother.* Illus by the author. Boston: Houghton, 1969. Paperback.

4709 ———. *Lyle, Lyle, Crocodile.* Illus by the author. Boston: Houghton, 1965. Sandpiper paperback. M392.

4710 ———. *The Snake.* Illus by the author. Boston: Houghton, 1978.

4711 ———. *You Look Ridiculous, Said the Rhinoceros to the Hippopotamus.* Illus by the author. Boston: Houghton, 1966. Paperback.

4713 Wagner, Jane. *J.T.* Photos by Gordon Parks, Jr. New York: Van Nostrand, 1969. Dell paperback.

4714 Wahl, Jan. *Lorenzo Bear and Company.* Illus by Fernando Krahn. New York: Putnam, 1971.

4715 ———. *Pleasant Field Mouse.* New York: Harper, 1964. Dell paperback.

4716 Wakana, Kei. *The Magic Hat.* New York: Scroll, 1970.

4717 Walker, Alice. *Langston Hughes, American Poet.* Illus by Don Miller. New York: Crowell,

1974.

4718 Walker, Barbara K. *The Dancing Palm Tree and Other Nigerian Folktales.* Illus by Helen Seigl. New York: Parents, 1968.

4719 ———. *New Patches for Old.* Illus by Harold Berson. New York: Parents, 1973. M479.

4720 ———. *The Round Sultan and the Straight Answer.* New York: Parents, 1970.

4721 Walker, Barbara K., et al. *Laughing Together: Giggles and Grins from Around the Globe.* Illus by Simms Taback. New York: Four Winds and UNICEF, 1977.

4722 Walker, Barbara M. *The Little House Cookbook, Frontier Foods from Laura Ingalls Wilder's Classic Stories.* Illus by Garth Williams. New York: Harper, 1979.

4723 Walder, Louise Jean. *Green Sky Hill.* Grand Rapids, MI.: Eerdmans, 1964.

4724 Walker, Mildred Pitts. *Lillie of Watts; a Birthday Discovery.* Illus by Leonora E. Price. Los Angeles: Ward Ritchie, 1969.

4725 Wall, Leonard Vernon. *The Complete Puppet Book; a Book on Educational Puppetry.* New York: Crowell, 1951.

4726 Wall, Leonard V. et al. *The Puppet Book, a Practical Guide to Puppetry in Schools, Training Colleges and Clubs.* Boston: Plays, 1950.

4727 Wallace, Daisy, ed. *Giant Poems.* Illus by Margot Tomes. New York: Holiday, 1978.

4728 ———. *Monster Poems.* Illus by Kay Chorao. New York: Holiday, 1976.

4729 ———. *Witch Poems.* Illus by Trina S. Hyman. New York: Holiday, 1976.

4730 Wallechinsky, David and Irving and Amy Wallace. *The Book of Lists.* New York: Morrow, 1977. Bantam paperback.

4731 Waller, Leslie. *A Book to Begin On: Our Flag.* Illus by Shannon Stirnweis. New York: Holt, 1960.

4732 Walls, Fred. *First Book of Puzzles and Brain Twisters.* New York: Watts, 1970.

4733a Walsh, Jill Paton. *Fireweed.* New York: Farrar, 1969. Avon paperback.

4733b Walter, Mildred. *Lillie of Watts.* Illus by L. E. Price. Los Angeles: Ward Ritchie Press, 1969.

4734 Waltrip, Lela and Rufus. *Quiet Boy.* New York: McKay, 1961.

4735 Warburg, Sandal Stoddard. *Curl Up Small.* Illus by Trina Schart Hyman. Boston: Houghton, 1964.

4736 ———. *Keep It a Secret.* Illus by Ivan Chermayeff. Boston: Little, 1961.

4737 ———. *Saint George and the Dragon; Being the Legend of the Red Cross Knight from the Faerie Queene,* by Edmund Spenser, Adapted by Warburg. Illus by Pauline Boynes. Boston: Houghton, 1963.

4738 Ward, Don and J.C. Dykes. *Cowboys and Cattle Country.* New York: American Heritage, 1961.

4739 *Ward, Lynd. *The Biggest Bear.* Boston: Houghton, 1952. Sandpiper paperback. M83.

4740 ———. *The Silver Pony.* Boston: Houghton, 1973. M611.

4741 Ward, Martha and Dorothy Marquardt. *Authors of Books for Young People.* Metuchen, N.J.: Scarecrow, 1971.

4742 ———. *Illustrators of Books for Young People,* 2nd edition. Metuchen, N.J.: Scarecrow, 1975.

4743 Ward, Winifred. *Playmaking with Children from Kindergarten through Junior High School,* 2nd ed. New York: Appleton, 1957.

4744 ———. *Stories to Dramatize.* Anchorage, Ky.: Children's Theatre Press, 1952.

4745 Warner, Sunny B. *Tobias and His Big Red Satchel.* New York: Knopf, 1961.

4746 Water, John F. *Some Mammals Live in the Sea.* New York: Dodd, 1972.

4747 Watson, Aldren A. *Hand Bookbinding, a Manual of Instruction.* New York: Reinhold, 1963.

4748 Watson, Clyde. *Father Fox's Pennyrhymes.* Illus by Wendy Watson. New York: Crowell, 1971. Scholastic paperback.

4749 ———. *Tom Fox and the Apple Pie.* Illus by Wendy Watson. New York: Crowell, 1972.

4750 Watson, Jane Werner. *The Niger: Africa's River of Mystery.* Maps by Henri Fluchers. Champaign, IL: Garrard, 1971.

4751 Watson, Jane Werner and Clara Louise Grant. *Mexico, Land of the Plumed Serpent.* Champaign, IL: Garrard, 1968.

4752 Watson, Nancy Digman. *Birthday Goat.* Illus by Wendy Watson. New York: Crowell, 1974.

4753 ———. *Blueberries Lavender, Songs of the Farmer's Children.* Illus by Erik Blegvad. Reading, MA: Addison-Wesley, 1977.

4754 ———. *Sugar on Snow.* Illus by Aldren A. Watson. New York: Viking, 1964.

4755 ———. *What Is One?* Illus by Aldren Watson. New York: Knopf, 1954.

4756 ———. *Whose Birthday is it?* Illus by Aldren A. Watson. New York: Knopf, 1954.

4757 Watson, Sally. *The Mikhtar's Children.* New York: Holt, 1968.

4758 Watts, Mabel. *A Cow in the House.* Illus by Katherine Evans. Chicago: Follett, 1956.

4759 Weik, Mary Hays. *The Jazz Man.* Illus by Ann Grifalconi. New York: Atheneum, 1966.

4760 Weil, Lisl. *Fat Ernest.* Illus by the author. New York: Parents, 1973.

4761 Weisgard, Leonard. *Plymouth Thanksgiving.* Illus by the author. New York: Doubleday, 1967.

4762 Weiss, Harvey. *Carving: How to Carve Wood and Stone.* New York: Young Scott, 1976.

4763 ———. *Collage and Construction* New York: Young Scott, 1970.

4764 ———. *Clay, Wood and Wire.* New York: Young Scott, 1956.

4765 ———. *How to Make Your Own Books.* New York: Crowell, 1974.

4766 ———. *Lens and Shutter, an Introduction to Photography.* New York: Young Scott, 1971.

4767 ———. *Model Cars and Trucks and How to Build Them.* New York: Crowell, 1974.

4768 ———. *Paint, Brush and Pallett.* New York: Young Scott, 1966.

4769 ———. *Paper, Ink and Roller.* New York: Young Scott, 1958.

4770 ———. *Pencil, Pen and Brush.* New York: Young Scott, 1961. Scholastic paperback.

4771 Weiss, Renee Karal. *A Paper Zoo, A Collection of Animal Poems of Modern American*

Poets. Illus by Ellen Raskin. New York: Macmillan, 1968.

4772 Weiss, Rita. *Needlepoint Designs after Illustrations by Beatrix Potter Charted for Easy Use.* New York: Dover, 1976. Paperback.

4773 Welber, Robert. *Winter Picnic.* Illus by Deborah Ray. New York: Pantheon, 1970.

4774 Welch, Martha McKeen. *Just Like Puppies.* New York: Coward, 1969.

4775 Wells, H.G. *The Time Machine and the Invisible Man.* Illus by Dick Cole. Chicago: Childrens, 1969.

4776 Wells, Rosemary. *Noisy Nora.* Illus by the author. New York: Dial, 1973. Scholastic paperback. M483.

4777 Wendorff, Ruth. *How to Make Cornhusk Dolls.* New York: Arco, 1973.

4778 Wenning, Elisabeth. *The Christmas Mouse.* Illus by Barbara Remington. New York: Holt, 1959.

4779 Wersba, Barbara. *Amanda Dreaming.* Illus by Mercer Mayer. New York: Atheneum, 1973.

4780 Werth, Kurt and Mabel. *Molly and the Giant.* Illus by Kurt Werth. New York: Parents, 1973.

4781 West, Dorothy Herbert and Rachel Shor. *The Children's Catalog,* 10th ed. New York: Wilson, 1961. Annual supplements.

4782 Westall, Robert. *The Wind Eye.* New York: Greenwillow, 1977.

4783 Westwood, Jennifer. *Medieval Tales.* New York: Coward, 1968.

4784 Weygant, Neomi. *It's Winter.* Photos by the author. Philadelphia: Westminster, 1969.

4785 Wezel, Peter. *The Good Bird.* New York: Harper and Row, 1964.

4786 ———. *The Naughty Bird.* Chicago: Follett, 1967.

4787 Wheeler, Opal. *Sing in Praise, A Collection of Best Loved Hymns.* Illus by Marjorie Torrey. New York: Dutton, 1946.

4788 ———. *Sing Mother Goose.* Illus by Marjorie Torrey. New York: Dutton, 1945.

4789 White, Anne Terry. *All About the Stars.* New York: Random, 1954.

4790 ———. *The Golden Treasury of Myths and Legends.* Illus by Alice and Martin Provensen. New York: Golden, 1959.

4791 White, E.B. *Charlotte's Web.* Illus by Garth Williams. New York: Harper, 1952. Paperback. M124, M125.

4792 ———. *Stuart Little.* Illus by Garth Williams. New York: Harper, 1945. Paperback. M653.

4793 ———. *Trumpet of the Swan.* Illus by Edward Frascino. New York: Harper, 1970. Paperback.

4794 White, Robb. *Flight Deck.* New York: Doubleday, 1956. Scholastic paperback.

4795 ———. *Torpedo Run.* New York: Doubleday, 1962. Scholastic paperback.

4796 ———. *Up Periscope.* New York: Doubleday, 1956. Scholastic paperback.

4797 White, T.H. *The Sword in the Stone.* New York: Putnam, 1939. Dell paperback.

4798 Whitehead, Robert. *Children's Literature: Strategies for Teaching.* Englewood Cliffs, NJ: Prentice-Hall, 1968.

4799 Whitman, Walt. *I Hear America Singing.* Illus by Fernando Krahn. New York: Delacorte. 1975.

4800 ———. *Overhead the Sun: Lines from Walt Whitman.* Illus by Antonio Frasconi. New York: Farrar, 1969.

4801 Whitney, Phyllis. *Writing Juvenile Fiction.* Boston: Writer, 1947, 1960.

4802 Whitney, Thomas. *Vasilisa the Beautiful.* Illus by Nonny Hogrogian. New York: Macmillan, 1970.

4803 Whittier, John Greenleaf. *Barbara Frietchie.* Illus by Paul Galdone. New York: Crowell, 1965.

4804 Wier, Esther. *The Loner.* Illus by Christine Price. New York: McKay, 1967. M387.

4805 ———. *The Winners.* New York: McKay, 1967.

4806 Wiese, Kurt. *Fish in the Air; Story and Pictures.* New York: Viking, 1948. M208.

4807 ———. *You Can Write Chinese.* New York: Viking, 1945. Paperback.

4808 Wiesner, William. *The Constant Little Mouse.* Illus by the author. New York: Four Winds, 1971.

4809 ———. *Green Noses.* New York: Four Winds, 1969.

4810 ———. *Hansel and Gretel, a Shadow Puppet Picture Book.* Illus by the author. New York: Seabury, 1971.

4811 ———. *Happy-go-Lucky.* Illus by the author. New York: Seabury, 1970.

4812 ———. *Jack and the Beanstalk.* Illus by the author. New York: Scholastic paperback, 1973.

4813 ———. *Moon Stories.* New York: Seabury, 1973.

4814 ———. *A Pocketful of Riddles.* New York: Dutton, 1966.

4815 ———. *The Riddle Pot.* New York: Dutton, 1973.

4816 ———. *The Tower of Babel.* Illus by the author. New York: Viking, 1968. M707.

4817 Wiggin, Kate Douglas. *Rebecca of Sunnybrook Farm.* New York: Grosset and Dunlap, 1903. Tempo paperback.

4818 Wilbur, Ricard. *Opposites.* Illus by the author. New York: Harcourt, 1973.

4819 Wilde, Oscar. *The Happy Prince and Other Stories.* New York: Dutton, 1968. M266.

4820 Wilder, Laura Ingalls. *By the Shores of Silver Lake.* Illus by Garth Williams. New York: Harper, 1953. Paperback.

4821 ———. *Farmer Boy.* Illus by Garth Williams. New York: Harper, 1953. Paperback.

4822 ———. *The First Four Years.* Illus by Garth Williams. New York: Harper, 1971. Trophy paperback.

4823 ———. *Little House in the Big Woods.* Illus by Garth Williams. New York: Harper, 1953. Paperback. M371, M372.

4824 ———. *Little House on the Prairie.* Illus by Garth Williams. New York: Harper, 1953. Paperback. M373.

4825 ———. *Little Town on the Prairie.* Illus by Garth Williams. New York: Harper, 1953. Paperback.

4826 ———. *Long Winter.* Illus by Garth Williams.

New York: Harper, 1953. Paperback.

4827 ———. *On the Banks of Plum Creek.* Illus by Garth Williams. New York: Harper, 1953. Paperback.

4828 ———. *On the Way Home.* Rose W. Lane, ed. New York: Harper, 1962. Trophy paperback.

4829 ———. *These Happy Golden Years.* Illus by Garth Williams. New York: Harper, 1953. Paperback.

4830 ———. *West From Home: Letters of Laura Ingalls Wilder, San Francisco, 1915.* Roger MacBride, ed. New York: Harper, 1964. Trophy paperback.

4831 Wildsmith, Brian. *Brian Wildsmith's ABC.* Illus by the author. New York: Watts, 1962.

4832 ———. *Brian Wildsmith's Birds.* Illus by the author. New York: Watts, 1967. M98.

4833 ———. *Brian Wildsmith's Circus.* Illus by the author. New York: Watts, 1968. M99.

4834 ———. *Brian Wildsmith's Fishes.* Illus by the author. New York: Watts, 1968. M100.

4835 ———. *Brian Wildsmith's One, Two, Three.* Illus by the author. New York: Watts, 1965.

4836 ———. *Brian Wildsmith's Puzzles.* Illus by the author. New York: Watts, 1971.

4837 ———. *Brian Wildsmith's the Twelve Days of Christmas.* New York: Watts, 1972. Paper.

4838 ———. *Brian Wildsmith's Wild Animals.* Illus by the author. New York: Watts, 1967. M101.

4839a ———. *Lazy Bear.* New York: Watts, 1974.

4839b ———. *The Owl and the Woodpecker.* Illus by the author. New York: Watts, 1972.

Will and Nicholas, see Lipkind & Morduinoff

4840 Willard, Nancy. *All On a May Morning.* Illus by Haig and Regina Skekerjian. New York: Putnam, 1975.

4841 ———. *Simple Pictures Are Best.* Illus by Tomie DePaola. New York: Harcourt, 1976.

4842 ———. *Stranger's Bread.* Illus by David McPhail. New York: Harcourt, 1977.

4843 ———. *The Well-Mannered Balloon.* Illus by Haig and Regina Skekerjian. New York: Harcourt, 1976.

4844 Williams, Barbara. *Albert's Toothache.* New York: Dutton, 1974.

4845 ———. *Kevin's Grandma.* Illus by Kay Chorao. New York: Dutton, 1975.

4846 Williams, Barbara and Carol Grundmann. *Twenty-six Lively Letters; Making an ABC Quiet Book.* New York: Taplinger, 1977.

4847 Williams, Bert. *Rocky Mountain Monster.* New York: Nelson, 1972.

4848 Williams, DeAtna M. *Paper Bag Puppets.* Palo Alto, CA: Fearon, 1966.

4849 ———. *More Paper Bag Puppets.* Palo Alto, CA: Fearon, 1968.

4850 Williams, Garth. *Big Golden Animal ABC.* Illus by the author. New York: Golden, 1954.

4851 ———. *The Chicken Book: A Traditional Rhyme.* Illus by the author. New York: Delacorte, 1970.

4852 Williams, Jay. *The Cookie Tree.* Illus by Blake Hampton. New York: Parents, 1967. M149.

4853 ———. *Everyone Knows What a Dragon Looks Like.* Illus by Mercer Mayer. New York: Four Winds, 1976. Scholastic paperback.

4854 ———. *Seven at one Blow.* Illus by Frisco Henstra. New York: Parents, 1972.

4855 ———. *The Sword of King Arthur.* Illus by Louis Glanzman. New York: Crowell, 1968.

4856 ——— and Raymond Abrashkin. *Danny Dunn and the Anti-Gravity Paint.* Illus by Ezra Jack Keats. New York: McGraw, 1956.

4857 ———. *Danny Dunn and the Automatic House.* Illus. New York: McGraw, 1956.

4858 ———. *Danny Dunn and the Fossil Cave.* Illus by Brinton Turkle. New York: McGraw, 1961.

4859 ———. *Danny Dunn and the Homework Machine.* Illus by Ezra Jack Keats. New York: McGraw, 1958.

4860 ———. *Danny Dunn and the Smallifying Machine.* Illus by Paul Sagsoorian. New York: McGraw, 1969.

4861 ———. *Danny Dunn and the Universal Clue.* Illus. New York: McGraw, 1977.

4862 ———. *Danny Dunn and the Voice from Space.* Illus by Leo Summers. New York: McGraw, 1967.

4863 ———. *Danny Dunn and the Weather Machine.* Illus by Ezra Jack Keats. New York: McGraw, 1974.

4864 ———. *Danny Dunn, Invisible Boy.* Illus by Paul Sagsoorian. New York: McGraw, 1974. Archway paperback.

4865 ———. *Danny Dunn on the Ocean Floor.* Illus by Brinton Turkle. New York: McGraw, 1960.

4866 ———. *Danny Dunn: Scientific Detective.* Illus by Paul Sagsoorian. New York: McGraw, 1975. Archway paperback.

4867 ———. *Danny Dunn, Time Traveler.* Illus by Owen Kampen. New York: McGraw, 1963.

4868 Williams, Letty. *The Little Red Hen/La Pequena Gullina Roja.* Illus by Herb William. Englewood Cliffs, NJ: Prentice-Hall, 1969. Paperback.

4869 Williams, Margery. *The Velveteen Rabbitt; or How Toys Become Real.* Illus by William Nicholson. Garden City, NY: Doubleday, 1926. Avon paperback.

4870 Williams, Ursula. *Castle Merlin.* New York: Nelson, 1972.

4871 ———. *Island Mackenzie.* Illus by Edward Ardizzone. New York: Morrow, 1960.

4872 Williams, Vera B. *It's a Gingerbread House: Bake it, Build it, Eat it.* New York: Greenwillow, 1978.

4873 Williams-Ellis, Amabel. *Fairy Tales from the British Isles.* Illus by Pauline Baynes. New York: Warne, 1960.

4874 ———. *Round the World Fairy Tales.* Illus by William Stobbs. New York: Warne, 1966.

4875 Williamson, Ethie. *Baker's Clay.* New York: Van Nostrand, 1976.

4876 Williamson, Margaret. *The First Book of Mammals.* Illus by the author. New York: Watts, 1957.

4877 Wilner, Isabel. *The Poetry Troupe, an Anthology of Poems to Read Aloud.* New York: Scribner, 1977.

4878 Wilson, Barbara. *Greek Fairy Tales.* Illus by Harry Toothill. Chicago: Follett, 1966.

4879 ———. *Scottish Folk-Tales and Legends.* Illus by Joan Kiddell-Monroe. New York: Walck, 1954.

4880 Wilson, Erica. *Erica Wilson's Embroidery Book.* New York: Scribners, 1973.

4881 Wilson, Holly. *Snowbound in Hidden Valley.*

Illus by Dorothy Bayley Morse. New York: Messner, 1957.

4882 Winkle, Lois, ed. *The Elementary School Library Collection: A Guide to Books and Other Media, Phase 1-2-3,* 12th ed. Newark, NJ: Bro Dart, 1979.

4883 Winn, Marie. *The Man Who Made Fine Tops, a Story About Why People do Different Kinds of Work.* New York: Simon and Schuster, 1970.

4884 Winn, Marie, ed. *Fireside Book of Children's Songs.* Illus by John Alcorn. Music by Allan Miller. New York: Simon and Schuster, 1966.

4885 ———. *Fireside Book of Fun and Game Songs.* Illus by Whitney Darrow, Jr. Music by Allan Miller. New York: Simon and Schuster, 1974.

4886 ———. *What Shall We Do and Alle Galloo! Play Songs and Singing Games for Young Children.* New York: Harper, 1972.

4887 Winter, Paula. *The Bear and the Fly.* New York: Crown, 1976. M58.

4888 ———. *Sir Andrew.* New York: Crown, 1980.

4889 Winterfeld, Henry. *Castaways in Lilliput.* Trans by Kyrill Schabert. Illus by William M. Hutchinson. New York: Harcourt, 1960.

4890 ———. *Detectives in Togas.* Trans by Richard and Clara Winston. New York: Harcourt, 1956. Voyager paperback.

4891 ———. *Mystery of the Roman Ransom.* Trans by Edith McCormick. Illus by Fritz Biermann. New York: Harcourt, 1971.

4892 Winthrop, Elizabeth. *Walking Away.* Illus by Noelle Massina. New York: Harper, 1973.

4893 Wintle, Justin and Emma Fisher. *The Pied Pipers: Interviews with the Influential Creators of Children's Literature.* New York: Two Continents, 1975.

4894 Wirtenberg, Patricia. *All-Around-the-House-Art and Craft Book.* Boston: Houghton, 1968.

4895 Wise, William. *Great Birds and Monsters of the Air.* Illus by Joseph Sibol. New York: Putnam, 1969.

4896 Wiseman, Bernard. *The Hat that Grew.* EauClaire, WI: Hale, 1967.

4897 ———. *Little New Kangaroo.* Illus by Roberg Lopshire. New York: Macmillan, 1973.

4898 Withers, Carl. *Painting the Moon, a Folktale from Estonia.* Illus by Adrienne Adams. New York: Dutton, 1970.

4899 ———. *The Tale of a Black Cat.* Illus by Alan Cober. New York: Holt, 1969. Holt Owlet.

4900 Withers, Carl. Comp. *I Saw a Rocket Walk a Mile, Nonsense Tales, Chants and Songs from Many Lands.* Illus by John E. Johnson. New York: Holt, 1965.

4901 ———. *Favorite Rhymes from a Rocket in My Pocket.* New York: Scholastic, paperback, 1967.

4902 ———. *A Rocket in My Pocket, the Rhymes and Chants of Young Americans.* Illus by Susanne Suba. New York: Holt, 1948.

4903 ———. *Treasury of Games, Riddles, Stunts, Tricks, Tongue-Twisters, Rhymes, Chanting, Singing.* New York: Grosset and Dunlap, 1969.

4904 ———. *World of Nonsense, Strange and Humorous Tales of Many Lands.* New York: Holt, 1968.

4905 Withers, Carl, and Sula Benet. Comp. *American Riddle Book.* New York: Abelard, 1954.

4906 ———. *Riddles of Many Lands.* New York: Abelard, 1956.

4907 Withers, Carl and Alta Jablow. Comp. *The Man in the Moon, Sky Tales from Many Lands.* Illus by Peggy Wilson. New York: Holt, 1969.

4908 Witty, Paul A. and Alma Moore Freeland, eds. *Peacock Lane.* Boston: Heath, 1964.

4909 Wojciechowska, Mia. *Shadow of a Bull.* Illus by Alvin Smith. New York: Atheneum, 1965. Paperback. M606.

4910 Wolf, Bernard. *Connie's New Eyes.* Photos by the author. Philadelphia: Lippincott, 1976.

4911 Wolf, Ingrid. *Pajaro-cu-cu, Animal Rhymes from Many Lands.* Illus by I.W. and Gertraut Fuchs. New York: Atheneum, 1967.

4912 Wolff, Diane. *Chinese Writing.* New York: Holt, 1975.

4913 Wolff, Robert J. *Feeling Blue.* New York: Scribner, 1968.

4914 ———. *Hello, Yellow!* New York: Scribner, 1968.

4915 ———. *Seeing Red.* New York: Scribner, 1968.

4916 Wolkstein, Diane. *Eight Thousand Stones: A Chinese Folktale.* Illus by Edward Young. New York: Doubleday, 1972.

4917 Wood, James P. *The Snark Was a Boajum: A Life of Lewis Carroll.* Illus by David Levine. New York: Pantheon, 1966.

4918 Wood, Joyce. *Grandmother Lucy and Her Hats.* Illus by Frank Francis. New York: Atheneum, 1968.

4919 Wood, Ray. *The American Mother Goose.* Illus by Ed Hargis. Foreword by John A. Lomax. Philadelphia: Lippincott, 1952.

4920 ———. *Fun in American Folk Rhymes.* Illus by Ed Hargis. Philadelphia: Lippincott, 1952.

4921 Woods, Gerald. *Introducing Woodcuts.* New York: Watson-Guptill, 1968.

4922 Wondriska, William. *Mr. Brown and Mr. Gray.* New York: Holt, 1968. Owlet paperback.

4923 Wong, Herbert H. *My Ladybug.* Illus by Marie N. Bohlen. Reading, MA: Addison-Wesley, 1969.

4924 Wong, Herbert H. and Matthew F. Vessel. *Our Terrariums.* Illus by Aldren Watson. Reading, MA: Addison-Wesley, 1969.

4925 Worburg, Sandal S. *Keep it a Secret.* Ivan Chermayeff. Boston: Little, 1961.

4926 Wordsworth, William. *Lucy Gray or Solitude.* Illus by Gilbert Riswold. Englewood Cliffs, NJ: Prentice-Hall, 1964.

4927 World Book-Childcraft. *Childcraft, Make and Do,* Vol. 11. Chicago: World Book-Childcraft, Int'l., 1976.

4928 ———. *Childcraft, Poems and Rhymes,* Vol. 1. Chicago: World Book-Childcraft, Int'l., 1977.

4929 ———. *World Book Encyclopedia.* Chicago: World Book-Childcraft, Int'l., 1978.

4930 Worrell, Estelle Ansley. *Be a Puppeteer! The Lively Puppet Book.* New York: McGraw, 1969.

4931 Worstell, Emma, ed. *Jump Rope Jingles.* New York: Macmillan, 1967. Collier paperback.

4932 Worth, Valerie. *More Small Poems*. Illus by Natalie Babbitt. New York: Farrar, 1976.

4933 Wright, Dave. *Kitten's Little Boy*. New York: Four Winds, 1971.

4934 Wuorio, Eva-Lis. *Save Alice!* New York: Holt, 1968.

4935 ———. *To Fight in Silence*. New York: Holt, 1973.

4936 Wyler, Rose. *Arrow Book of Science Riddles*. Englewood Cliffs, NJ: Prentice-Hall, 1969. Paperback.

4937 ———. *Professor Egghead's Best Riddles*. New York: Simon & Schuster, 1973. Arch paperback.

4938 ———. *Real Science Riddles*. New York: Hastings, 1971.

4939 ———. *The Riddle Kingdom*. Englewood Cliffs, NJ: Scholastic paperbacks, 1967.

4940 Wyler, Rose and Gerald Ames. *Funny Number Tricks, Easy Magic with Arithmetic*. Illus by Talivaldis Stubis. New York: Parents, 1976.

4941 Wynants, Miche. *Noah's Ark*. New York: Harcourt, 1965.

4942 Wyndham, Robert, ed. *Chinese Mother Goose Rhymes*. Illus by Ed Young. New York: Collins, 1968.

4944 ———. *Tales the People Tell in China*. Illus by Jay Yang. New York: Messner, 1971.

4945 Wyse, Anne and Alex. *The One to Fifty Book*. Toronto, Canada: University of Toronto Press, 1973. Paperback.

4946 Wyss, Johann D. *The Swiss Family Robinson*. Illus by Charles Folkard. New York: Dutton, 1949. M666.

4947 ———. *The Swiss Family Robinson*. Illus by Jeanne Edwards. New York: Collins, 1972. M666.

4948 ———. *The Swiss Family Robinson*. Paperback books in print: Airmont, Dell, and Scholastic abridged. M666.

4949 Yamaguchi, Marianne. *Fingerplays*. Illus by the author. New York: Holt, 1972. Holt paperback.

4950 Yaroslava. *I Like You and Other Poems for Valentine's Day*. Illus by the author. New York: Scribner, 1976.

4951 Yates, Elizabeth. *Amos Fortune, Free Man*. New York: Dutton, 1967. M33.

4952 ———. *Carolina's Courage*. Illus by Nora Unwin. New York: Dutton, 1964.

4953 Yashima, Taro. *Crow Boy*. New York: Viking, 1955. Puffin paperback.

4954 ———. *The Golden Footprints*. Illus by Muku Hatoju. Cleveland: World, 1960.

4955 ———. *Umbrella*. New York: Viking, 1958. Puffin paperback. M723.

4956 ———. *The Village Tree*. New York: Viking, 1953. Puffin paperback.

4957 Yeager, Allan. *Using Picture Books with Children, a Guide to Owlet Books*. New York: Holt, 1973. Paperback edition.

4958 Yeoman, John. *Mouse Trouble*. Illus by Quentin Blake. New York: Macmillan, 1972. Collier paperback.

4959 Yolen, Jane. *The Emperor and the Kite*. Cleveland: World, 1967.

4960 ———. *The Fireside Song Book of Birds and Beasts*. Music by Barbara Green. Illus by Peter Parnall. New York: Simon and Schuster, 1972.

4961 ———. *The Giants Farm*. Illus by Tomi dePaola. New York: Seabury, 1977.

4962 ———. *The Girl Who Loved the Wind*. Illus by Ed Young. New York: Crowell, 1972.

4963 ———. *An Invitation to the Butterfly Ball, a Counting Rhyme*. Illus by Jane Breskin Zolben. New York: Parents, 1976.

4964 ———. *The Little Spotted Fish*. Illus by Frisco Henstra. New York: Seabury, 1975.

4965 ———. *Rounds About Rounds About Rounds*. Music by Barbara Green. Illus by Fail Gibbons. New York: Watts, 1977.

4966 ———. *The Seeing Stick*. Illus by Remy Charlip and Demetra Maraslis. New York: Crowell, 1977.

4967 ———. *The Seventh Mandarin*. Illus by Ed Young. New York: Seabury, 1970.

4968 ———. *The Sultan's Perfect Tree*. Illus by Barbara Garrison. New York: Parents, 1977.

4969 ———. *The World on a String, the Story of Kites*. Cleveland: World, 1968.

4970 ———. *Writing Books for Children*. Boston: Writer, 1976.

4971 Yolen, Will. *The Young Sportsman's Guide to Kite Flying*. New York: Nelson, 1963.

4972 Young, Ed. *High on a Hill: a Book of Chinese Riddles*. Illus by the author. New York: Collins, 1980.

4973 Young, Ed and Hilary Beckett. *The Rooster's Horns: A Chinese Puppet Play to Make and Perform*. New York: Collins, 1978.

4974 Young, Helen. *Here is Your Hobby; Doll Collecting*. New York: Putnam, 1964.

4975 Young, Jim. *When the Whale Came to My Town . . .* Photos by Dan Bernstein. New York: Knopf, 1974.

4976 Young, Miriam. *If I Rode a Dinosaur*. Illus by Robert Quackenbush. New York: Lothrop, 1974.

4977 ———. *The Witch Mobile*. Illus by Victoria Chess. New York: Lothrop, 1969.

4978 Yurchenco, Henrietta. *A Fiesta of Folk Songs from Spain and Latin America*. Illus by Jules Maidoff. New York: Putnam, 1967.

4979 Ylla. *Bears are Sleeping*. Illus by Nonny Hogrogian. New York: Scribners, 1967.

4980 ———. *Two Little Bears*. New York: Harper, 1954. Trophy paperback.

4981 ——— and Arthur Gregor. *Animal Babies*. New York: Harper, 1959. Trophy paperback.

4982 ———. *The Little Elephant*. New York: Harper, 1956. Trophy paperback.

4983 Zacharias, Thomas and Wanda. *But Where is the Green Parrot?* New York: Delacorte, 1968.

4984 Zaidenberg, Arthur. *Drawing All Animals*. New York: Funk and Wagnalls, 1974.

4985 ———. *How to Draw Birds, Fish and Reptiles*. New York: Abelard, 1962.

4986 ———. *How to Draw Cartoons: A Book for Beginners*. New York: Vanguard, n.d.

4987 ———. *How to Draw Dogs, Cats and Horses*. New York: Abelard, 1959.

4988 ———. *How to Draw Farm Animals*. New York: Abelard, 1959.

4989 ———. *How to Draw Prehistoric and Mythical Animals.* New York: Abelard, 1967.

4990 ———. *How to Draw Wild Animals.* New York: Abelard, 1958

4991 ———. *How to Draw with Pen and Brush.* New York: Vanguard, 1965.

4992 ———. *How to Paint in Oil: A Book for Beginners.* New York: Vanguard, 1957.

4993 ———. *How to Paint with Watercolors.* New York: Vanguard, 1968.

4994 ———. *Prints and How to Make Them, Graphic Arts for the Beginner.* New York: Harper, 1964.

4995 Zakhoder, Boris. *Roschak, a Russian Story.* Trans by Marguerita Rudolph. Illus by Yaroslava. New York: Lothrop, 1970.

4996a Zallinger, Peter. *Dinosaurs.* New York: Random, 1977.

4996b Zarchy, Harry. *Using Electronics.* New York: Knopf, nd.

4997 Zei, Alki. *Petro's War.* Trans by Edward Fenton. New York: Dutton, 1972.

4998 ———. *Wildcat Under Glass.* Trans by Edward Fenton. New York: Holt, 1968.

4999 Zeitlin, Patty. *Castle in My City, Songs for Young Children.* Illus by the children. San Carlos, CA: Golden Gate Junior Books, 1968.

5000 *Zemach, Harve. *Duffy and the Devil.* Illus by Margot Zemach. New York: Farrar, 1973. M185.

5001 ———. *The Judge; an Untrue Tale.* Illus by Margot Zemach. New York: Farrar, 1969. M338.

5002 ———. *Mommy Buy Me a China Doll.* Illus by Margot Zemach. Chicago: Follett, 1966, 1975. M461.

5003 ———. *Nail Soup.* Illus by Margot Zemach. Chicago: Follett, 1964.

5004 ———. *Salt, a Russian Tale.* Illus by Margot Zemach. Chicago: Follett, 1965. M590.

5005 ———. *The Speckled Hen; a Russian Nursery Rhyme.* Illus by Margot Zemach. New York: Holt, 1966. Owlet paperback.

5006 Zemach, Margot. *It Could Always Be Worse.* Illus by the author. New York: Farrar, 1976. Scholastic paperback. M323.

5007 ———. *The Three Sillies.* Illus by the author. New York: Holt, 1963. Owlet paperback.

5008 ———. *Too Much Nose: An Italian Tale.* Illus by the author. New York: Holt, 1967. Owlet paperback.

5009 ———. *The Tricks of Master Dabble.* Illus by the author. New York: Holt, 1965. Owlet paperback.

5010 ———. *Hush Little Baby.* Illus by the author. New York: Dutton, 1976. M32.

5011 Zim, Herbert S. *The Big Cats.* Illus by Gardell S. Christensen. New York: Morrow, 1955.

5012 ———. *Codes and Secret Writing.* New York: Morrow, 1948.

5013 ———. *Dinosaurs.* Illus by James Gordon Irving. New York: Morrow, 1954.

5014 ———. *The Great Whales.* Illus by James Gordon Irving. New York: Morrow, 1951.

5015 ———. *Little Cat.* Illus by Jean Zallinger. New York: Morrow, 1978.

5016 ———. *Our Senses and How They Work.* Illus by Herschel Wartik. New York: Morrow, 1956.

5017 ———. *Owls.* Illus by James Gordon Irving and Rene Martin. New York: Morrow, 1977.

5018 ———. *Your Heart and How it Works.* Illus by Gustav Schrotter. New York: Morrow, 1959.

5019 ——— and Robert H. Baker. *Stars, a Guide to the Constellations, Sun, Moon, Planets and Other Features of the Heavens.* Illus by James Gordon Irving. New York: Golden, 1956.

5020 ——— and Clarence Cottaw. *Insects; A Guide to Familiar American Insects.* New York: Western, 1951. Golden paperback.

5021 ——— and Ira N. Gabrielson. *Birds, A Guide to the Most Familiar American Birds.* Illus by James Gordon Irving. Wester, 1949, 1956. Golden paperback.

5022 ——— and Donald Hoffmeister. *Mammals, A Guide to Familiar American Species.* Illus by James Gordon Irving. Racine, WI: Western, 1955. Paperback.

5023 ——— and Lester Ingle. *Seashores.* Illus by Dorothea and Sy Barlowe. Racine, WI: Western, 1955. Paperback.

5024 ——— and Alexander C. Martin. *A Guide to American Wildflowers.* New York: Golden, 1950.

5025a Zindel, Paul. *The Pig Man.* New York: Harper, 1968.

5025b Ziner, Feenie and Paul Galdone. *Counting Carnival.* Illus by Paul Galdone. New York: Coward, 1962.

5026 Zion, Gene. *Dear Garbage Man.* Illus by Margaret Bloy Graham. New York: Harper, 1957.

5027 ———. *Harry and the Lady Next Door.* New York: Harper, 1960. M273, M277.

5028 ———. *Harry by the Sea.* Illus by Margaret Bloy Graham. New York: Harper, 1965. Trophy paperback. M274, M277.

5029 ———. *Harry the Dirty Dog.* Illus by Margaret Bloy Graham. New York: Harper, 1956. Trophy paperback. M276, M277.

5030 ———. *Hide and Seek Day.* Illus by Margaret Bloy Graham. New York: Harper, 1954.

5031 ———. *No Roses for Harry!* Illus by Margaret Bloy Graham. New York: Harper, 1958. Trophy paperback. M277.

5032a ———. *The Plant Sitter.* Illus by Margaret Bloy Graham. New York: Harper, 1959. Scholastic paperback.

5032b Ziskind, Sylvia. *Telling Stories to Children.* New York: Wilson, 1976.

5033 Zolotow, Charlotte. *The Bunny Who Found Easter.* Illus by Betty Peterson. Berkeley, CA: Parnassus. 1959.

5035 ———. *The Hating Book.* Illus by Ben Shecter. New York: Harper, 1969.

5936 ———. *Mr. Rabbit and the Lovely Present.* Illus by Maurice Sendak. New York: Harper, 1962. M454.

5037 ———. *Over and Over.* Illus by Garth Williams. New York: Harper, 1957.

5038 ———. *The Quarreling Book.* Illus by Arnold Lobel. New York: Harper, 1963.

5039 ———. *A Rose, a Bridge, and a Wild Black Horse.* Illus by Uri Shulevitz. Eau Claire, WI: Hale, 1964.

5040 ———. *The Sky Was Blue*. Illus by Garth Williams. New York: Harper, 1963.

5041 ———. *The Sleepy Book*. Illus by Vladimir Bobri. New York: Lothrop, 1958. M616.

5042 ———. *Wake Up and Good Night*. Illus by Leonard Weisgard. New York: Harper, 1971.

5043 ———. *The White Marble*. Illus by Lilian Obligado. New York: Abelard, 1963.

5044 ———. *William's Doll*. Illus by William Pene duBois. New York: Harper, 1972.

5045 Zornow, Edith and Ruth M. Goldstein. *Movies for Kids, a Guide for Parents and Teachers on the Entertainment Film for Children Nine through Thirteen*. New York: Avon paperback, 1973.

Multimedia (Nonprint)

M1   *Abraham Lincoln.* (Poster) Horn Book Poster Set #3. Boston: Horn Book, n.d. From a book by Ingri and Edgar Parin d'Aulaire.

M2   *Across Five Aprils.* (2 filmstrips with record or cassette; individual cassette) Westminster, MD: Miller-Brody/Random House, n.d. Based on a book by Irene Hunt.

M3   *Adventure Literature for Children.* (Filmstrip with record and guide) Verdugo City, CA: Pied Piper, 1971. 12 min.

M4   *Adventure of Obadiah.* (Filmstrip with record or cassette and guide) New York: Viking, 1972. Narrated by Brinton Turkle from his book.

M5   *Adventures of Robin Hood.* (16mm film) Burbank, CA: Warner Bros., 1938. 102 min. Live action. Color.

M6   *Adventures of Robinson Crusoe.* New York: United Artists, 1954. 90 min. Live action. Color. Based on a book by Daniel Defoe.

M7   *Adventures of Sherlock Holmes.* (16mm film) Los Angeles, CA: Twentieth Century Fox, 1939. 85 min. Live action. Black and white. Based on a story by Sir Arthur Conan Doyle.

M8   *Adventures of Three Blind Mice and Henny Penny.* (Phonograph record and paperbacks) Englewood Cliffs, NJ: Scholastic, n.d.

M9   *Adventures of Tom Sawyer.* (16mm film) United Artists, 1938. 93 min. Live action. Color. Based on a book by Samuel Clemens.

M10   *Aesop's Fables.* (Phonograph record or cassette) New York: Caedmon, n.d. Narrated by Boris Karloff. Based on fables of Aesop.

M11   *Alexander and the Wind-up Mouse.* (Filmstrip with record or cassette; individual cassette) Westminster, MD: Random, n.d. Based on a book by Leo Lionni.

M12   *Alice in Wonderland.* (Phonograph record or cassette) Caedmon, 1958. Narrated by Stanley Holloway. Based on a book by Lewis Carroll.

M13   *All Butterflies.* (Posters) New York: Scribner, 1974. A portfolio of reproductions from the book by Marcia Brown.

M14   *All Upon a Stone.* (Filmstrip with cassette) Miller-Brody, n.d. Based on a book by Jean Craighead George.

M15   *Alligators All Around.* (16mm film) Weston, CT: Weston Woods, 1978. 2 min. Animated. Color. Based on a book by Maurice Sendak.

M16   _____. (Filmstrip with cassette or test booklet; individual cassette) Weston Woods, n.d. 39fr. 4 min. Based on a book by M. Sendak.

M17   *Along Sandy Trails.* (Filmstrip with record or cassette) Viking, 1969. Based on a book by Ann Nolan Clark.

M18   *The Amazing Bone.* (Filmstrip with cassette; individual cassette) Miller-Brody, n.d. Narrated by Tammy Grimes. Based on a book by Williiam Steig.

M19   *Amelia Bedelia.* (4 filmstrips with records or cassettes) Bedford Hills, NY: Teaching Resource Films, an Educational Division of the New York Times, n.d. Based on the books *Amelia Bedelia; Thank You, Amelia Bedelia; Come Back, Amelia Bedelia;* and *Play Ball, Amelia Bedelia.* Based on books by Peggy Parish.

M20   *The American Cowboy.* (2 filmstrips with cassettes) North Hollywood, CA: Bowmar, 1970. 26 min. 102 fr.

M21   *American Favorite Ballads, Vol. 1-5.* (5 Phonograph records) Englewood Cliffs, NJ: Folkways/Scholastic, n.d. Sung by Pete Seeger.

M22   *American Flag in Music, Word, and Deed.* (4 filmstrips with record or cassette) Englewood Cliffs, NJ: Prentice-Hall Media, 1973.

M23   *American Folk Songs for Children.* (Phonograph record) Folkways, 1953. Sung by Pete Seeger.

M24   *American History in Ballad and Song, Vol. I, II.* (6 phonograph records) Pleasantville, NY: Educational Audio Visual, n.d. Sung by Pete Seeger and others.

M25   *American Negro Slave Songs.* (Phonograph Record) Los Angeles, CA: Everest, 1973.

M26   *American Songbag.* (Phonograph record or cassette) Folkways, n.d. Sung by Carl Sandburg.

M27   *American Songfest.* (16mm film) Weston Woods, 1977. 42 min. Live action. Color.

M28   *American Tall Tales, Vol. I.* (Phonograph record or cassette) Caedmon, n.d. Narrated by Ed Begley. John Henry and Joe Magarac. Based on a book by Adrien Stoutenburg.

M29   *American Tall Tales, Vol. II.* (Phonograph record or cassette) Caedmon, n.d. Narrated by Ed Begley. Davy Crockett and Pecos Bill. Based on a book by Adrien Stoutenburg.

M30   *American Tall Tales, Vol. IV.* (Phonograph record or cassette) Caedmon, n.d. Narrated by Ed Begley. Johnny Appleseed and Paul Bunyan. Based on a book by Adrien Stoutenburg.

M31   *Americans Who Shaped History.* (6 filmstrips) Mahwah, NJ: Troll Associates, 1968. Includes: The Washingtons, America's First Family; The Jeffersons of Monticello; Robert E. Lee, Soldier of the South; Dolly Madison in the White House; Paul Revere, Patriot and Craftsman; Betsy Ross: Flagmaker for America.

M32 *America's Musical Heritage,* Vol. 1-6. (Phonograph Records) New York: Watts, 1963. Sung by Burl Ives.

M33 *Amos Fortune, Free Man.* (2 filmstrips with record or cassette; individual cassette) Miller-Brody, n.d. Based on a book by Elizabeth Yates.

M34 *Anansi the Spider.* (Filmstrip with cassette or text booklet; individual cassette) Weston Woods, n.d. 43 fr. 10 min. Based on a book by Gerald McDermott.

M35 *And Now Miguel.* (16 mm film) Los Angeles, CA: Universal, 1966. 95 min. Live action. Color. Based on a book by Joseph Krumgold.

M36 *And Then What Happened, Paul Revere?* (Cassette) Weston Woods, n.d. 24 min. Read by Jean Fritz from her book.

M37 *Andy and the Lion.* (16mm film) Weston Woods, 1955. 10 min. Iconographic. Color. Based on a book by James Daugherty.

M38 ———. (Filmstrip with cassette or text booklet; individual cassette) Weston Woods, n.d. 42 fr. 7 min. Based on a book by J. Daugherty.

M39 *Angus and the Cat.* (Filmstrip with cassette or text booklet; individual cassette) Weston Woods, n.d. 43 fr. 6 min. Based on a book by Marjorie Flack.

M40 *Angus and the Ducks.* (Filmstrip with cassette or text booklet; individual cassette) Weston Woods, 1961. 35 fr. 6 min. Based on a book by Marjorie Flack.

M41 *Animals and Circus* (Phonograph record) Bowmar, n.d.

M42 *Animals Nobody Loved.* (16mm film or videocassette) Washington, D.C. National Geographic, 1975. 52 min. Live action. Color.

M43 *Anne Frank: The Dairy of a Young Girl.* (2 records or cassettes and 12 paperbacks) Miller-Brody, n.d. Narrated by Julie Harris. Based on Anne Frank's diary.

M44 *Apartment 3.* (16mm film) Weston Woods, 1977. 8 min. Iconographic. Color. Based on a book by Ezra Jack Keats.

M45 ———. (Filmstrip with cassette or text booklet; individual cassette) Weston Woods, n.d. 37 fr. 8 min. Based on a book by E.J. Keats.

M46 *Are You My Mother?* (Filmstrip with record or cassette; individual cassette) Random, n.d. Based on a book by P.D. Eastman.

M47 *Around the World in Eighty Days.* (16mm film) United Artists, 1956. 168 min. Live action. Color. Based on a book by Jules Verne.

M48 *Arrow to the Sun.* (Filmstrip with cassette or text booklet; individual cassette) Weston Woods, 1975. 36 fr. 9 min. Based on a book by Gerald McDermott.

M49 *Ashanti to Zulu: African Traditions.* (Filmstrip with cassette or text booklet; individual cassette) Weston Woods, n.d. 32 fr. 17 min. Illus by Leo and Diane Dillon. Based on a

book by Margaret Musgrove.

M50 *Attic of the Wind.* (16mm film) Weston Woods, 1974. 6 min. Iconographic. Color. Based on a book by Doris Lund.

M51 ———. (Filmstrip with cassette or text booklet; individual cassette) Weston Woods, n.d. 21 fr. 6 min. Including In a Spring Garden. Illus by Ati Forberg. Based on a book by D. Lund.

M52 *An Audio Visual History of American Folk Music.* (5 filmstrips and 5 phonograph records) Pleasantville, NY: Educational Audio Visual, 1975. 90 min. 317 fr.

M53 *A Baby Sister for Frances.* (Filmstrip with record or cassette) BFA Educational Media, 1971. Based on a book by Russell Hoban.

M54 *Bambi.* (Record or cassette) Caedmon, n.d. Narrated by Glynis Johns. Based on a book by Felix Salten.

M55 *The Barber of Seville and William Tell.* (Phonograph record) Columbia, n.d. New York Philharmonic conducted by Bernstein. From operas by Rossini.

M56 *A Bargain for Frances.* (Filmstrip with record or cassette) BFA Educational Media, 1971. Based on a book by Russell Hoban.

M57 *The Bat Poet.* (Phonograph record or cassette) Caedmon, n.d. Written and narrated by Randall Jarrell.

M58 *The Bear and the Fly.* (Filmstrip). Weston Woods, 1977. 31 fr. Based on a book by Paula Winter.

M59 *The Bear Detectives.* (Filmstrip with record or cassette) Random House, n.d. Based on a book by Stan and Jan Berenstain.

M60 *The Bear Scouts.* (Filmstrip with record or cassette) Random House, n.d. Based on a book by Stan and Jan Berenstain.

M61 *The Bears' Christmas.* (Filmstrip with record or cassette) Random House, n.d. Based on a book by Stan and Jan Berenstain.

M62 *Bears in the Night.* (Filmstrip with record or cassette) Random House, n.d. Based on a book by Stan and Jan Berenstain.

M63 *Bears on Wheels.* (Filmstrip with record or cassette) Random House, n.d. Based on a book by Stan and Jan Berenstain.

M64 *The Bears' Picnic.* (Filmstrip with record or cassette) Random House, n.d. Based on a book by Stan and Jan Berenstain.

M65 *The Bears' Vacation.* (Filmstrip with record or cassette) Random House, n.d. Based on a book by Stan and Jan Berenstain.

M66 *The Beast of Monsieur Racine.* (16mm film) Weston Woods, 1957. 9 min. Animated. Color. Based on a book by Tomi Ungerer.

M67 ———. (Filmstrip with cassette or booklet) Weston Woods, 1957. 52 fr. 14 min. Based on a book by Tomi Ungerer.

M68 *Beatrix Potter Nursery Rhymes and Tales.* (Phonograph record or cassette) Caedmon, n.d. Based on works by B. Potter.

M69 *Beauty and the Beast and Other Stories.* (Phonograph record or cassette) Caedmon, 1972. Narrated by Douglas Fairbanks. Based on the version by Mme de Beaumont.

M70 *Bedtime.* (Filmstrip with cassette or booklet) Weston Woods, 1980. 28 fr. 5 min. Based on a book by Beni Montresor.

M71 Bedtime for Frances. (Filmstrip with record or cassette) BFA Educational Media, 1971. Based on a book by Russell Hoban.

M72 Beginner Books Filmstrip No. 4 (6 filmstrips with records or cassettes with guides) Random House, 1975. Includes: Robert the Race Horse, Mr. Brown can Moo! Can You?, Sam and the Firefly, Cat in the Hat Comes Back, Babar Loses His Crown, and Fox in Socks.

M73 Benji. (2 MovieStrips with cassettes and guide) Wilmette, IL: Films, Inc., 1976. Based on the Mulberry Square film

M74 Ben's Trumpet. (Filmstrip with cassette) Miller-Brody, 1980. Based on a book by Rachel Isadora.

M75 Beowulf and the Monsters. (Phonograph record or cassette) Children's Classics on Tape, 1973. 60 min. Based on an Old English hero tale.

M76 Best Friends for Frances. (Filmstrip with record or cassette) BFA Educational Media, 1971. Based on a book by Russell Hoban.

M77 Best Loved Poems of Longfellow. (Phonograph record or cassette) Caedmon, n.d. Narrated by Hal Holbrook. Based on poems by Longfellow.

M78 The Best of Encyclopedia Brown. (4 filmstrips with cassettes) Miller-Brody, 1977. 50 fr. each. Includes: "The Case of Natty Nat," "The Case of the Scattered Cards," "The Case of the Hungry Hitchhiker," and "The Case of the Whistling Ghost." Stories from books by Donald Sobol.

M79 ———. (4 cassettes and 24 paperbacks) Miller-Brody, n.d. Stories from books by D. Sobol.

M80 Betsy Ross (Filmstrip) Encyclopedia Britannica, 1954. (American Patriots Series).

M81 Big Red. (16mm film) Burbank, CA: Walt Disney Productions, 1962. 93 min. Live action. Color. Based on a book by Jim Kjelgaard.

M82 The Big Snow. (Filmstrip with cassette or booklet; individual cassette) Weston Woods, n.d. 53 fr. 11 min. Based on a book by Berta and Elmer Hader.

M83 The Biggest Bear. (Filmstrip with cassette or booklet; individual cassette) Weston Woods, 1958. 48 fr. 7 min. Based on a book by Lynd Ward.

M84 The Biggest House in the World. (Filmstrip with cassette or booklet; individual cassette) Random House, n.d. Based on a book by Leo Lionni.

M85 Billy Boy. (Filmstrip with cassette or text booklet; individual cassette) Weston Woods, n.d. 38 fr. 6 min. Illus. by Glen Rounds. Based on a book by Richard Chase.

M86 Biography, Literature for Children. (Filmstrip with record or cassette and guide) Verdugo City, CA: Pied Piper, 1970. 12 min.

M87 A Birthday for Frances. (Filmstrip with record or cassette) BFA Educational Media, 1971. Based on a book by Russell Hoban.

M88 Black Beauty. (Record or cassette) Caedmon, n.d. Narrated by Claire Bloom. Based on a book by Anna Sewell.

M89 The Black Pearl. (2 filmstrips with record or cassette; individual cassette) Miller-Brody, n.d. Based on a book by Scott O'Dell.

M90 The Blind Men and the Elephant. (Filmstrip with record or cassette; individual cassette) Miller-Brody, n.d. Based on a book by Lillian Quigley.

M91 Blueberries for Sal. (16mm film) Weston Woods, 1967. 9 min. Iconographic. Color. Based on a book by Robert McCloskey.

M92 ———. (Filmstrip with cassette; individual cassette) Weston Woods, n.d. 47 fr. 9 min. Based on a book by R. McCloskey.

M93 A Book of Americans. (Phonograph record or cassette) Caedmon, n.d. Narrated by Maureen Stapleton and Pat Hingle. Based on a book by Rosemary and Stephen Vincent Benet.

M94 Booklist. (Periodical) American Library Association. 50 E. Huron St., Chicago, IL 60611.

M95 Born Free. (16mm film) Toronto, Ontario, Canada: Columbia, 1966. 95 min. Live action. Color. Based on a book by Joy Adamson.

M96 A Boy Named Charlie Brown. (16mm film) CFF, 1969. 85 min. Animated. Color. Based on a character by Charles Schulz.

M97 Bread and Jam for Frances. (Filmstrip with record or cassette) BFA Educational Media, 1971. Based on a book by Russell Hoban.

M98 Brian Wildsmith's Birds. (Filmstrip with cassette or text booklet; individual cassette) Weston Woods, n.d. 18 fr. 4 min. (Also includes The North Wind and the Sun) Based on books by Brian Wildsmith.

M99 Brian Wildsmith's Circus. (Filmstrip with cassette or text booklet; individual cassette) Weston Woods, n.d. 20 fr. 4 min. (Also includes Brian Wildsmith's Fishes) Based on books by B. Wildsmith.

M100 Brian Wildsmith's Fishes. (Filmstrip with cassette or text booklet; individual cassette) Weston Woods, n.d. 21 fr. 5 min. (Also includes Brian Wildsmith's Circus) Based on books by B. Wildsmith.

M101 Brian Wildsmith's Wild Animals. (Filmstrip with cassette or text booklet; individual cassette) Weston Woods, n.d. 19 fr. 6 min. (Also includes The Rich Man and the Shoe-maker) Based on books by B. Wildsmith.

M102 Brighty of the Grand Canyon. (16mm film) Feature Film Corp. of America, 1967. 89 min. Live action. Color. Based on a book by Marguerite Henry.

M103 Brown Cow Farm (Filmstrip with cassette) Weston Woods, 1964. Based on a book by Dahlov Ipcar.

M104 Bruno Munari's ABC. (Filmstrip with cassette or text booklet; individual cassette) Weston Woods, 1964. 30 fr. 4 min. Based on a book by B. Munari.

M105 ———. Bruno Munari's Zoo. (Filmstrip with cassette or text booklet; individual cassette) Weston Woods, n.d. 25 fr. 3 min. Based on a book by B. Munari.

M106 Bubble Bubble. (Filmstrip) Weston Woods, n.d. 30 fr. Based on a book by Mercer Mayer.

M107a Building the Erie Canal. (Filmstrip) Encyclopedia Britannica Corp., 1967. (Growth of the Nation: 1790–1860).

M107b Bulletin of the Center for Children's Books. (Periodical) University of Chicago Graduate Library School, 5801 Ellis Avenue, Chicago, Ill. 60637

M108 Caddie Woodlawn. (2 filmstrips with record or cassette; individual cassette) Miller-Brody, n.d. Based on a book by Carol Ryrie Brink.

M109 Call it Courage. (2 filmstrips with record or cassette; individual cassette) Miller-Brody, n.d. Based on a book by Armstrong Sperry.

M110 Can't You Make Them Behave, King George? (Cassette) Weston Woods, n.d. 29 min. Narrated by Jean Fritz from her book.

M111 Caps for Sale. (16mm film) Weston Woods, n.d. 5 min. Iconographic. Color. Based on a book by Esphyr Slobodkina.

M112 ———. (Filmstrip with cassette or text booklet; individual cassette) Weston Woods, 1958. 34 fr. 5 min. Based on a book by E. Slobodkina.

M113 Carl Sandburg's Poems for Children. (Phonograph record or cassette) Caedmon, n.d. Narrated by C. Sandburg from his poems.

M114 Casey at the Bat. (Filmstrip with record or cassette; individual cassette) Weston Woods. 1967. 35 fr. 5 min. Illus by Paul Frame. Based on a poem by Ernest Thayer.

M115 Casey Jones. (Filmstrip with record or cassette; individual cassette) Weston Woods, 1968. Based on a book by Glen Rounds.

M116 The Cat in the Hat. (Filmstrip with record or cassette; individual cassette) Random House, n.d. Based on a book by Dr. Seuss.

M117 The Cat in the Hat Comes Back. (Filmstrip with record or individual cassette) Random House, 1975. Based on a book by Dr. Seuss.

M118 Catch a Little Rhyme! Peoms for Activity Time. (Record or cassette) Caedmon, n.d. Narrated by Eve Merriam from her poems.

M119 Changes, Changes. (8mm or 16mm film) Weston Woods, n.d. 6 min. Animated. Color. Based on a book by Pat Hutchins.

M120 ———. (Filmstrip with cassette or text booklet; individual cassette) Weston Woods, 1971. 30 fr. 6 min. Based on a book by Pat Hutchins.

M121 Chanticleer and the Fox. (Filmstrip with cassette or text booklet; individual cassette) Weston Woods, 1959. 47 fr. 10 min. Illus by Barbara Cooney. Based on a book by Geoffrey Chaucer.

M122 ———. (Poster) Horn Book Poster Ser # 3, n.d. Illus by B. Cooney. Based on a book by G. Chaucer.

M123 Charlotte and the White Horse. (Filmstrip with cassette or text booklet; individual cassette) Weston Woods, n.d. 22 fr. 5 min. (Also includes Mr. Rabbit and the Lovely Present) Illus by Maurice Sendak. Based on a book by Ruth Krauss.

M124 Charlotte's Web. (18 filmstrips with 6 records, chart and poster) Santa Monica: Stephen Bosustow Productions, n.d. 7-14 min. each. Narrated by E. B. White from his own book.

M125 ———. (4 records) Pathways of Sound, n.d.

Narrated by E. B. White from his own book.

M126a Chicken Soup With Rice. (16mm film) Weston Woods, 1978. 5 min. Animated. Color. Based on a book by Maurice Sendak.

M126b ———. (Filmstrip with cassette or text booklet; individual cassette). Weston Woods, 1977. 26 fr. 5 min. Based on a book by M. Sendak.

M127 Children of the Northlights. (16 mm film) Weston Woods, n.d. Color. Interview with Ingri & Edgar d'Aulaire.

M128 Children's Digest. (Periodical) Parents' Magazine Enterprises, Inc., 52 Vanderbilt Ave., New York, NY 10017.

M129 A Child's Garden of Verses. (Phonograph record or cassette) Caedmon, n.d. Narrated by Dame Judith Anderson. Based on Poems by Robert Louis Stevenson.

M130 Chinese Fairy Tales. (Phonograph record or cassette) Caedmon, n.d. Narrated by Siobhan McKenna.

M131 A Christmas Carol. (Phonograph record or cassette) Caedmon, n.d. Performed by Sir Ralph Richardson, et al. Based on a story by Charles Dickens.

M132 Christmas Carols. (Phonograph record) Bowmar, n.d.

M133 Christmas in the Stable. (Filmstrip with cassette or text booklet; individual cassette) Weston Woods, n.d. 20 fr. 6 min. (Also includes The Tomten). Illus by Harald Wiberg. Based on books by Astrid Lindgren.

M134 Christmas with Ogden Nash. (Phonograph record or cassette) Caedmon, n.d. Narrated by Ogden Nash from his poems.

M135 Cinderella (2 filmstrips with cassettes; individual cassettes) Miller-Brody, n.d. Based on a book by Marcia Brown.

M136 ———. (Poster) Horn Book Poster Set #2, Horn Book, n.d. From a book by Marcia Brown.

M137 Circus Baby. (16mm film) Weston Woods, n.d. 5 min. Iconographic. Color. Based on a book by Maud and Miska Petersham.

M138 ———. (Filmstrip with cassette or text booklet; individual cassette) Weston Woods, 1958. 35 fr. 6 min. Based on a book by M. and M. Petersham.

M139 Clementine. (Filmstrip with cassette or text booklet; individual cassette) Weston Woods, 1924. 40 fr. 10 min. Based on a book by Robert Quackenbush.

M140 Clocks and More Clocks. (Filmstrip with cassette or text booklet; individual cassette) Weston Woods, 1970. 29 fr. 5 min. Based on a book by Pat Hutchins.

M141 Clothing—A Pair of Jeans. (16mm film) LAA, 1971. 13 min. Live action. Color.

M142 The Clown of God. (Filmstrip with cassette or text booklet; individual cassette) Weston Woods, n.d. 53 fr. 15 min. Based on a book by Tonie de Paola.

M143 A Color of His Own.. (Filmstrip with record or cassette; individual cassette) Random House, n.d. Based on a book by Leo Lionni.

M144 Come Back, Amelia Bedelia. (Filmstrip with record or cassette) Teaching Resource Films, an Educational Division of the New York Times, n.d. 54 fr. Based on a book by

Peggy Parish.

M145 *Come On and Wake Up!* (Phonograph record) Woodbury, N.Y.: Pickwick International, Inc.; n.d. Sung by Fred Rogers.

M146 *The Complete Version of Ye Three Blind Mice.* (Filmstrip with cassette or text booklet; individual cassette) Weston Woods, n.d. 34 fr. Illus by Walton Courbould. Based on a book by John Ivimey.

M147 *The Complete Version of Ye Three Blind Mice and Henny Penny.* (Phonograph record and paperbacks) Scholastic Companion Series. Based on a book by J. Ivimey.

M148 *A Connecticut Yankee in King Arthur's Court.* (16mm film) Paramount, 1949. 107 min. Live action. Color. Based on a book by Mark Twain.

M149 *The Cookie Tree.* (Filmstrip with record or cassette) A-V International Corporation, n.d. Reading Motivation Set II. Based on a book by Jay Williams.

M150 *Could Anything Be Worse?* (Filmstrip with cassette or text booklet; individual cassette) Weston Woods, 1974. 33 fr. 9 min. Based on a book by Marilyn Hirsh.

M151 *Cowboy Songs.* (Cassette) National Geographic, 1976.

M152 *Cricket, The Magazine for Children.* (Periodical) Open Court Publishing Company. Box 599, La Salle, IL. 61301.

M153 *The Cricket in Times Square.* (2 filmstrips with record or cassette; individual cassette) Miller Brody, n.d. Based on a book by George Selden.

M154 ———. (Listening Library; 3 records or cassettes) Miller Brody, n.d. Includes The Cricket in Times Square, Tucker's Countryside, and Harry Cat's Pet Puppy by George Selden.

M155 *Creating a Children's Book.* (16 mm film) New York, ACI, 1971. 12 min. Live Action. Color.

M156 *The Crystal Apple.* (Filmstrip with cassette or text booklet; individual cassette) Weston Woods, 1974. 25 fr. 6 min. Based on a book by Beverly Brodsky McDermott.

M157 *Curious George.* (Filmstrip with record or cassette) Teaching Resource Films, an Educational Division of the New York Times, n.d. 53 fr. Based on a book by H. A. Rey.

M158 ———.(Phonograph record or cassette) Caedmon, n.d. Narrated by Julie Harris. Based on a book by H. A. Rey.

M159 ———.*Curious George Flies a Kite.* (Filmstrip with record or cassette) Teaching Resource Films, an Educational Division of the New York Times, n.d. 63 fr. Based on a book by H. A. Rey.

M160 *Curious George Gets a Medal.* (Filmstrip with record or cassette) Teaching Resource Films, an Educational Division of the New York Times, n.d. 63 fr. Based on a book by H. A. Rey.

M161 *Curious George Goes to the Hospital.* (Filmstrip with record or cassette) Teaching Resource Films, an Educational Division of the New York Times, n.d. 67 fr. Based on a book by H. A. Rey.

M162 *Curious George Learns the Alphabet.* (Phonograph record or cassette) Caedmon, n.d. Narrated by Julie Harris. Based on a book by H. A. Rey.

M163 *Curious George Rides a Bike.* (8 mm and 16mm film) Weston Woods, 1958. 10 min. Iconographic. Color. Captioned film available. Based on a book by H. A. Rey.

M164 ———. (Filmstrip with cassette or text booklet; individual cassette) Weston Woods, n.d. 58 fr. 10 min. Based on a book by H. A. Rey.

M165 *Curious George Takes a Job.* (Filmstrip with record or cassette) Teaching Resource Films, an Educational Division of the New York Times, n.d. 62 fr. Based on a book by H. A. Rey.

M166 *Custard the Dragon.* (16 mm film) Weston Woods, n.d. 6 min. Live action. Color. Based on a poem by Ogden Nash.

M167 ———. (Filmstrip with cassette or text booklet; individual cassette) Weston Woods, 1967. 30 fr. 5 min. Illus by Linell Nash Smith. Based on a poem by Ogden Nash.

M168 *Dandelion.* (Filmstrip with record or cassette) Viking, n.d. Based on a book by Don Freeman.

M169 *David Copperfield.* (16mm film) New York: MGM, 1935. 133 min. Live action. Black and white. Based on a book by Charles Dickens.

M170 *Deep Voices, the Second Whale Record.* (Phonograph record) Capitol Records, 1977. Voices by whales.

M171 *The Diary of Anne Frank.* (3 MovieStrips with cassettes and guide) Films, Inc., n.d. Taken from the movie which was based on Anne Frank's diary.

M172 *Dinosaurs.* (Filmstrip with cassette) National Geographic, 1978. 12 min.

M173 *Dr. Doolittle.* (3 MovieStrips with cassettes, guide, activity cards and paperback) Films, Inc., 1976. Taken from the Twentieth Century Fox movie based on *The Story of Dr. Doolittle* by Hugh Lofting.

M174 *Don't Count Your Chicks.* (Filmstrip with cassette or text booklet; individual cassette) Weston Woods, 1962. 38 fr. 6 min. Based on a book by Ingri and Edgar Parin d'Aulaire.

M175 *Dr. Seuss: Happy Birthday to You.* (Phonograph record or cassette) Caedmon, n.d. Narrated by Hans Conried. Based on a book by Dr. Seuss.

M176 *Dr. Seuss's ABC.* Filmstrip with record or cassette; individual cassette) Random House, n.d. Based on a book by Dr. Seuss.

M177 *Dog of Flanders.* (16mm film) Twentieth Century Fox, 1959. 97 min. Live action. Color. Based on a book by De La Ramee.

M178 *Dolphins and Men.* (16mm film or videocassette-discussion guide) BBC and Time-Life Films, 1973. 25 min. Live action. Color. Produced for the TV program NOVA.

M179 *Doughnuts.* (16mm film) Weston Woods, 1967. 25 min. Live action. Color. Based on the book *Homer Price* by Robert McCloskey.

M180 *Dracula.* (16mm film) Universal Studios, 1931. 76 min. Live action. Black and white. Based on a book by Bram Stoker.

M181 ———. (Filmstrip with record or cassette). Scholastic Literature Filmstrips, 1975. Based on a book by B. Stoker.

M182 *Drummer Hoff.* (8 or 16mm film) Weston Woods, 1969. 6 min. Animated. Color. Illus by Ed Emberley. Based on a book by Barbara Emberley.

M183 ———. (Filmstrip with cassette, text booklet; individual cassette) Weston Woods, 1967. 33 fr. 4 min. Based on a book by E. and B. Emberley.

M184 *The Duchess Bakes a Cake* (Filmstrip with record or cassette; individual cassette) Miller-Brody, n.d. Based on a book by Virginia Kahl.

M185 *Duffy and the Devil.* (2 filmstrips with cassette; individual cassette) Miller-Brody, n.d. Based on a book by Harve and Margot Zemach.

M186a *Edward Ardizzone.* (16mm film) Weston Woods, n.d. 13 min. Live action. Color.

M186b *Edward Lear's Nonsense Stories and Poems.* (Phonograph record or cassette) Caedmon, n.d. Narrated by Claire Bloom. Based on poems by Edward Lear.

M187 *The Egg Tree.* (Poster) Horn Book Poster Set #1. Horn Book, n.d. Based on a book by Katherine Milhous.

M188 *The Egypt Game.* (Phonograph record or cassette) Miller-Brody, n.d. Based on a book by Zilpha Snyder.

M189 *Encyclopedia Brown Solves Them All.* (4 filmstrips with cassettes) Miller-Brody, 1977. 50 fr. each. Includes "The Case of Sir Biscuit-Shooter," "The Case of the Missing Clues," "The Case of the Super-Secret Hold," "The Case of the Muscle Maker." Stories from Books by Donald Sobol.

M190 ———. (Read-Alongs with 4 cassettes and 8 paperbacks) Miller-Brody, n.d. Based on stories by D. Sobol.

M191 *English Journal.* (Periodical) National Council of Teachers of English, 111 Kenyon Rd., Urbana, IL 61801.

M192 *Enjoying Illustrations.* (Filmstrip with cassette) Pied Piper, 1971. 12 min. color.

M193 *The Erie Canal.* (8mm and 16mm film) Weston Woods, 1976. 7 min. Iconographic. Color. Based on a book by Peter Spier.

M194 ———. (Filmstrip with cassette, text booklet; individual cassette) Weston Woods, 1974. 29 fr. 5 min. Based on a book by P. Spier.

M195 *Evangeline.* (Phonograph record or cassette) Caedmon, n.d. Narrated by Hal Holbrook. Based on a poem by Henry Wadsworth Longfellow.

M196 *Evolution of a Graphic Concept: The Stonecutter.* (Filmstrip with cassette) Weston Woods, 1977. Interview with Gerald McDermott.

M197 *The Eye.* (Model) Chicago: Denoyer-Geppert, n.d.

M198 *Ezra Jack Keats.* (16mm film) Weston Woods, 1970. 17 min. Live-action. Color. Interview with E.J. Keats.

M199 *Fairy Tales in Music.* (Phonograph record) Bowmar, n.d.

M200 *Famous American Story Poems.* (Phonograph record) n.d. Read by John Randolph and Paul Sparer.

M201 *Fantasy in Music.* (Phonograph record) Bowmar, n.d.

M202 *Fantasy, Literature for Children.* (Filmstrip with record or cassette, guide.) Pied Piper, 1970. 12 min.

M203 *Farmer Palmer's Wagon Ride.* (2 filmstrips with cassette; individual cassette) Miller-Brody, n.d. Based on a book by William Steig.

M204 *Favorite Songs, Record 1.* (Phonograph record) Bowmar, n.d.

M205 *Favorite Songs, Record 2.* (Phonograph record) Bowmar, n.d.

M206 *Finders Keepers.* (Filmstrip with cassette or text booklet; individual cassette) Weston Woods, 1960. 40 fr. 7 min. Illus by Nicolas Mordvinoff. Based on a book by William Lipkind.

M207 *Finger Play.* (2 phonograph records and guide) Miller-Brody, n.d.

M208 *Fish in the Air.* . (Filmstrip with cassette or text booklet; individual cassette) Weston Woods, 1967. 33 fr. 7 min. Based on a book by Kurt Wiese.

M209 *Fish in the Forest: A Russian Folktale.* (Filmstrip with cassette) New York: Guidance Associates (Harcourt Brace), 1974. 76 fr.

M210 *Fish is Fish.* (Filmstrip with record or cassette; individual cassette) Random House, n.d. Based on a book by Leo Lionni.

M211 *The Fisherman and His Wife.* (16mm film) Weston Woods, n.d. 20 min. Animated. Color. Based on a Grimm tale retold by Wanda Gag.

M212 *The Five Chinese Brothers* (8mm and 16mm film) Weston Woods, 1958. 10 min. Iconographic. Color. Illus by Kurt Wiese. Based on a book by Claire Bishop.

M213 ———. (Filmstrip with cassette or text booklet; individual cassette) Weston Woods, 1959. 56 fr. 10 min. Illus by K. Wiese. Based on a book by C. Bishop.

M214 *A Fly Went By.* (Filmstrip with record or cassette; individual cassette) Random House, n.d. Based on a book by Mike McClintock.

M215 *A Flying Saucer Full of Spaghetti.* (Filmstrip with study guide) Weston Woods, 1977. 25 fr. Based on a book by Fernando Krahn.

M216 *Folk Songs for Young Folk—Animals, Vol. 1.* (Phonograph Record) Folkways, 1958. Sung by Alan Mills. Includes: "Who Killed Cock Robin?" "A Frog He Would a-Wooing Go," and "I Know an Old Lady."

M217 *Folk Songs for Young People.* (Phonograph record) Folkways, n.d. Sung by Pete Seeger.

M218 *Folk Songs in American History.* (6 filmstrips and records) Pleasantville, NY: Warren Schloat, 1967. 60 or 70 fr. each.

M219 *Folk Tales in Song.* (Phonograph record) Old Greenwich, CT: Listening Library, n.d.

M220 *Folklore and Fable Unit: Magic and Superstition, Pecos Bill, Dracula, Folkmusic.* (4 filmstrips with records and guide) Scholastic Literature Filmstrips, 1975.

M221 *The Foolish Frog.* (16 mm film) Weston Woods, n.d. 8 min. Animated. Color. Illustrated by Miloslav Jagr. Based on a book by Pete and Charles Seeger.

M222 ———. (Filmstrip with cassette or text

booklet; individual cassette) Weston Woods, 1955. Illus by M. Jagr. Based on a book by P. and C. Seeger.

M223 Founding of the Nation: The American Revolution. (4 filmstrips with record or cassette) Encyclopedia Britannica, 1973. Includes The Boston Tea Party, The Shot Heard Round the World, Valley Forge, and Yorktown.

M224 Fox in Socks. (Filmstrip with record or cassette; individual filmstrip) Beginner Books Filmstrip, 4, 1975. Based on a book by Dr. Seuss.

M225 Fox Went Out on a Chilly Night. (8mm and 16mm film) Weston Woods, 1968. 8 min. Iconographic. Color. Based on a song illustrated by Peter Spier.

M226 ———. (Filmstrip with cassette or text booklet; individual cassette) Weston Woods, 1965. 40 fr. 8 min. Based on a song illus by P. Spier.

M227 Francis Scott Key. (Filmstrip) Encyclopedia Britannica, 1954. 45 fr. (American Patriots Series)

M228 Frankenstein. (16mm film) Universal Studios, 1931. 71 min. Live action. Black and white. Based on a book by Mary Wollstonecraft Shelley.

M229 Frederick. (Filmstrip with record or cassette; individual cassette) Random House, n.d. Based on a book by Leo Lionni.

M230 Freight Train. (Filmstrip with cassette; individual cassette) Random House—Miller-Brody, 1980. Based on a book by Donald Crews.

M231 Frog and Toad are Friends. (5 filmstrips with records or cassettes) Miller-Brody, n.d. Includes the stories: "Spring," "The Story," "A Lost Button," "A Swim," "The Letter." In English or Spanish. Based on a book by Arnold Lobel.

M232 ———. (Paperback with record) Scholastic Records, 1976. Includes the stories: "Spring," "A Swim," and "A Lost Button." Narrated by Arnold Lobel from his book.

M233 Frog and Toad Read-Alongs. (2 phonograph records or cassettes and 16 paperbacks) Miller-Brody, n.d. Includes all stories from Frog and Toad are Friends and Frog and Toad Together by Arnold Lobel.

M234 Frog and Toad Together. (5 filmstrips with records or cassettes) Miller-Brody, n.d. Includes: "A List," "The Garden," "Dragons and Giants," "The Dream." In English or Spanish. Based on a book by Arnold Lobel.

M235 ———. (Paperback with record) Scholastic Records, 1973. 6½ min. Includes the stories: "The Garden," "Cookies," and "The Dream." Narrated by Arnold Lobel from his book.

M236 Frog Went-A-Courtin'. (16mm film) Weston Woods, n.d. 12 min. Iconographic. Color. Illus by Feodor Rojankovsky. Based on a book by John Langstaff.

M237 ———. (Filmstrip with cassette or text-booklet; individual cassette) Weston Woods, 1955. 34 fr. 13 min. Illus by F. Rojankovsky. Based on a book by J. Langstaff.

M238a The Funny Little Woman. Filmstrip with cassette or text booklet; individual cassette) Weston Woods, 1973. 38 fr. 9 min. Illus by Blair Lent. Based on a story retold by Arlene Mosel.

M238b Gail E. Haley: Wood and Linoleum Illustration. (Filmstrip with cassette) Weston Woods, n.d. 71 fr. 17 min. Includes Go Away, Stay Away by G.E. Haley.

M239 The Gammage Cup. (2 filmstrips with record or cassette; individual cassette) Miller-Brody, n.d. Based on a book by Carol Kendall.

M240 A Gathering of Great Poetry for Children, Fourth Grade and Up. (Phonograph record or cassette) Caedmon, n.d. Narrated by Julie Harris, Cyril Ritchard, David Wayne, Dylan Thomas, Robert Frost, Robert Graves, Elizabeth Biship, e.e. cummings. Edited by Richard Lewis.

M241 A Gathering of Great Poetry for Children, Kindergarten and Up. (Phonograph record or cassette) Caedmon, n.d. Narrated by Julie Harris, Cyril Ritchard, David Wayne, Robert Frost and Carl Sandburg. Edited by Richard Lewis.

M242 A Gathering of Great Poetry for Children, Second Grade and Up. (Phonograph record or cassette) Caedmon, n.d. Narrated by Julie Harris, Cyril Ritchard, David Wayne, Robert Frost, Carl Sandburg, Robert Graves, e.e. cummings, and T.S. Eliot. Edited by Richard Lewis.

M243 Gene Deitch, the Picture Book Animated. (16mm film) Weston Woods, n.d.

M244 Georgie. (16mm film) Weston Woods, 1965. 6 min. Iconographic. Color. Based on a book by Robert Bright.

M245 ———. (Filmstrip with cassette or text booklet; individual cassette) Weston Woods, n.d. 40 fr. 6 min. Based on a book by R. Bright.

M246 Ghost Stories. (4 filmstrips and guide) Wayne, NJ; Leonard Peck Productions, 1974. 45 fr. Includes: The Vampires Die at Midnight, Icy Finger of Dawn, Ghost of Count Lorenzo, and Curse of the Pirate Gold.

M247 Gilgamesh and the Monster in the Wood. (Filmstrip and Cassette) New York: Acorn Films, n.d.

M248 Ginger Pye. (2 filmstrips with record or cassette; individual cassette) Miller-Brody, n.d. Based on a book by Eleanor Estes.

M249 Go Away, Stay Away. (Filmstrip with cassette or text booklet; individual cassette) Weston Woods, n.d. 38 fr. 10 min. Based on a book by Gail Haley.

M250 Goggles. (16mm film) Weston Woods, 1974. 6 min. Iconographic. Color. Based on a book by Ezra Jack Keats.

M251 ———. Filmstrip with cassette or text booklet; individual cassette) Weston Woods, n.d. 30 fr. 6 min. Based on a book by Ezra Jack Keats.

M252 Golden Slumbers. (Phonograph record or cassette) Caedmon, n.d. Songs by Pete Seeger and Oscar Brand.

M253 The Golem. (Filmstrip with cassette or text booklet; individual cassette) Weston Woods, n.d. 61 fr. 10 min. Based on a book by Beverly Brodsky.

M254 *Great Expectations*. (16mm film) Britain, 1946. 118 min. Live action. Black and white. Based on a book by Charles Dickens.

M255 *The Great Whales*. (16mm film or video-cassette) National Geographic, 1978. 59 min. Live action. Color. Produced for TV.

M256 *The Great Big Enormous Turnip*. (Filmstrip with cassette or text booklet; individual cassette) Weston Woods, 1972. 24 fr. 4 min. Illus by Helen Oxenbury. Based on a story by Alexei Tolstoy. (Includes *The Three Poor Tailors*.

M257 *Green Eggs and Ham*. (Filmstrip with record or cassette; individual cassette) Random House, n.d. Based on a book by Dr. Seuss.

M258 *Gulliver's Travels*. (Phonograph record) New Rochelle, NY: Spoken Arts, n.d. Narrated by Denis Johnston. Based on a book by Jonathan Swift.

M259 *Gulliver's Travels: A Voyage to Lilliput*. (Phonograph record or cassette) Caedmon, n.d. Narrated by Anthony Quayle. Based on a book by J. Swift.

M260 *Gwendolyn Brooks Reading Her Poetry*. (Phonograph record or cassette) Caedmon, n.d. Narrated by Gwendolyn Brooks from her poems.

M261 *Hailstones and Halibut Bones, Pt. I and II*. (16 mm films) Sterling Educational Films, 1964, 1967. Pt. I 6 min. Pt. II 7 min. Animated. Color. Narrated by Celeste Holm. Based on a book by Mary O'Neill.

M262 *Hansel and Gretel*. (Phonograph Record) New York: RCA, n.d. Excerpts from the opera by Humperdinck.

M263 *The Happy Day*. (Filmstrip with cassette or text booklet; individual cassette) Weston Woods, n.d. 18 fr. 2 min. Illus by Marc Simont. Based on a book by Ruth Krauss.

M264 *The Happy Owls*. (8mm and 16mm film) Weston Woods, 1969. 7 min. Animated. Color. Based on a book by Celestino Piatti.

M265 ———. (Filmstrip with cassette or text booklet; individual cassette) Weston Woods, 1968. 21 fr. 4 min. Based on a book by C. Piatti.

M266 *The Happy Prince and Other Oscar Wilde Fairy Tales*. (Phonograph record or cassette) Caedmon, n.d. Narrated by Basil Rathbone. Based on a book by Oscar Wilde.

M267 *The Hare and the Tortoise*. (Filmstrip with cassette or text booklet; individual cassette) Weston Woods, n.d. 20 fr. 4 min. (Including *The Lion and the Rat*) Illus by Brian Wildsmith. Based on a fable by La Fontaine.

M268 *The Hare and the Tortoise*. (Filmstrip with record or cassette) Chicago: Coronet, 1972. Based on a fable by La Fontaine.

M269 *Harold and the Purple Crayon*. (8mm and 16mm film) Weston Woods, 1969. 8 min. Animated. Color. Based on a book by Crockett Johnson.

M270 ———. (Filmstrip with cassette or text booklet; individual cassette) Weston Woods, 1962. 64 fr. 7 min. Based on a book by C. Johnson.

M271 *Harold's Fairy Tale*. (16mm film) Weston Woods, 1974. 8 min. Animated. Color. Based on a book by Crockett Johnson.

M272 ———. (Filmstrip with cassette or text booklet; individual cassette) Weston Woods, 1971. 61 fr. 9 min. Based on a book by C. Johnson.

M273 *Harry and the Lady Next Door*. (Filmstrip with cassette; individual cassette) Miller-Brody, 1977. Based on a book by Gene Zion.

M274 *Harry by the Sea*. (Filmstrip with cassette; individual cassette) Miller-Brody, 1977. Based on a book by G. Zion

M275 *Harry Cat's Pet Puppy*. (Phonograph record or cassette) Miller-Brody, n.d. Based on a book by George Selden.

M276 *Harry the Dirty Dog*. (Filmstrip with cassette; individual cassette) Miller-Brody, 1977. Based on a book by G. Zion.

M277 *Harry the Dirty Dog Read-Alongs*. (4 cassettes with 32 paperbacks) Miller-Brody, 1977. Includes: *Harry the Dirty Dog, Harry by the Sea, No Roses for Harry!* and *Harry and the Lady Next Door*.

M278 *Henny Penny and the Adventures of Three Blind Mice*. (Phonograph record and paperbacks) Scholastic Books, n.d. Based on a book by Paul Galdone and J. W. Ivimey.

M279 *Heidi*. (16mm film) New York: NBC-TV, 1968. 120 min. Live action. Color. Based on a book by Johanna Spyri.

M280 *Henry Reed, Inc.* (Phonograph record or cassette) Viking/Live Oak, n.d. 45 min. Based on a book by Keith Robertson.

M281 *Hercules*. (16mm film) Weston Woods, 1960. 11 min. Iconographic. Color. Based on a book by Hardie Gramatky.

M282 ———. (Filmstrip with cassette or text booklet; individual cassette) Weston Woods, 1957. 52 fr. 11 min. Based on a book by H. Gramatky.

M283 *Hey Diddle Diddle and Baby Bunting*. (Filmstrip with cassette or text booklet; individual cassette) Weston Woods, 1962. (Also includes *The Milkmaid*) Based on books illustrated by Randolph Caldecott.

M284 *Hide and Seek Fog*. (Filmstrip with cassette or text booklet; individual cassette) Weston Woods, n.d. Illus by Roger Duvoisin. Based on a book by Alvin Tresselt.

M285 *The High King*. (4 filmstrips with records or cassettes) Miller-Brody, n.d. Based on a book by Lloyd Alexander.

M286 *Highlights for Children* (Periodical) Highlights for Children, Inc., 2300 W. 5th Ave., P.O. Box 269, Columbus, OH

M287 *Historical Fiction, Literature for Children*. (Filmstrip with record or cassette) Verdugo City, CA: Pied Piper, 1971. 12 min.

M288 *The Hobbit and the Fellowship of the Ring*. (Phonograph record or cassette) Caedmon, n.d. Narrated by J. R. R. Tolkien from his books.

M289 *The Hole in the Dike*. (Filmstrip with cassette or text booklet; individual cassette) Weston Woods, n.d. 24 fr. 7 min. Illus by Eric Carle. Based on a book by Norma Green.

M290 *A Hole is to Dig*. (Filmstrip with cassette or text booklet; individual cassette) Weston Woods, 1968. 69 fr. 13 min. Illus by Maurice

Sendak. Based on a book by Ruth Krauss.

M291 *Holiday Songs.* (Phonograph record). Bowmar, n.d.

M292 *The Holy Night.* (Filmstrip with cassette or text booklet; individual cassette) Weston Woods, 1970. 19 fr. 4 min. Illus by Celestino Piatti. Based on a book by Aurel von Juchen.

M293 *Homer Price.* (16mm film or cassette) Weston Woods, n.d. 66 min. Live-action. Color. Based on a book by Robert McCloskey.

M294 *Homer Price.* (Phonograph record or cassette) Viking, n.d. 45 min. Based on a book by Robert McCloskey.

M295 *Horn Book Magazine.* (Periodical) Horn Book, Inc. Park Square Bldg. 31 St. James Ave. Boston, MA 02116.

M296 *Horn Book Posters from Caldecott Medal books.* (3 sets of 4 posters) Boston: Horn Book, n.d. Set #1—Keats's *Snowy Day,* Milhous's *The Egg Tree,* Politi's *Song of the Swallows,* Handforth's *Mei Li.* Set #2—Brown's *Cinderella,* DeRegniers's *May I Bring a Friend,* Bemelman's *Madeline's Rescue,* and Ets's *Nine Days to Christmas.* Set #3—Chaucer's *Chanticleer and the Fox,* the d'Aulaires' *Abraham Lincoln,* Thurber's *Many Moons,* and Langstaff's *Frog Went A-Courtin'.*

M297 *Horton Hatches the Egg.* (2 filmstrips with records or cassette) Random, 1967. Based on a book by Dr. Seuss.

M298 *Hot-Blooded Dinosaurs.* (16mm film or video cassette) BBC and WGBH, 1978. 52 min. Color. Produced for TV, NOVA.

M299 *The House of Sixty Fathers.* (2 filmstrips with record or cassette) Miller-Brody, n.d. Based on a book by Meindert DeJong.

M300 *The House that Jack Built.* (Filmstrip with cassette or text booklet; individual cassette) Weston Woods, n.d. 27 fr. 4 min. Based on a book by Paul Galdone.

M301 *How a Picture Book is Made.* (Filmstrip with cassette and guide) Weston Woods, 1977. Tells about *The Island of the Skog* by Steven Kellogg.

M302 *How, Hippo!* (Filmstrip with record or cassette) Miller-Brody, n.d. Based on a book by Marcia Brown.

M303 *How Your Body Parts Function, 1.* (8 filmstrips and 4 cassettes) Jamaica, NY: Eye Gate, 1974.

M304 *Humor, Literature for Children.* (Filmstrip with record or cassette; guide) Verdugo City, CA: Pied Piper, 1970. 12 min.

M305 *Hunters of the Seal.* (16mm or video cassettes and discussion guide) WGBH, 1976. 30 min. Color. Produced for TV, NOVA.

M306 *Hush Little Baby.* (16mm film) Weston Woods, 1976. 5 min. Iconographic. Color. Based on a song illustrated by Aliki Brandenburg.

M307 ———. (Filmstrip with cassette or text booklet; individual cassette) Weston Woods, 1970. 17 fr. 3 min. Based on a song illustrated by Aliki Brandenburg.

M308 *I Know an Old Lady.* (Filmstrip with cassette or text booklet; individual cassette) Weston Woods, 1965. 46 fr. 7 min. Illus by Abner Graboff. Based on a book by Rose Bonne and Alan Mills.

M309 *I Know an Old Lady/ Teeny Tiny Woman.* (Phonograph record and paperbacks) Scholastic, n.d. Based on a book by R. Bonne and A. Mills.

M310 *I Know a Lot of Things.* (Filmstrip with cassette or text booklet; individual cassette) Weston Woods, n.d. (Including *Sparkle and Spin*) Based on a book by Ann and Paul Rand.

M311 *I Went for a Walk.* (Phonograph record) Walck, 1958. Based on a book by Lois Lenski.

M312 *In a Spring Garden.* (Filmstrip with cassette or text booklet; individual cassette) Weston Woods, n.d. (Also includes Attic of the Wind) Illus by Ezra Jack Keats. Based on a book by Richard Lewis.

M313 *In the Forest.* (Filmstrip with cassette) Viking/Live Oak, n.d. Based on a book by Marie Hall Ets.

M314 *Incident at Hawk's Hill.* (Phonograph record or cassette) Miller-Brody, 1975. Based on a book by Allan Eckert.

M315 *Instruments of the Orchestra.* (22 posters and teacher's guide) New York: RCA, n.d.

M316 *Instruments of the Orchestra.* (2 phonograph records) New York: RCA, n.d.

M317 *Inside the Shark.* (16mm or video cassette) BBC and WGBH, 1976. 50 min. Live action. Color. Discussion guide. Produced for TV.

M318 *Instructional Innovator.* (Periodical) Formerly *Audiovisual Instruction.* Association for Educational Communications and Technology. 1126 16th St., N.W. Washington, D.C. 20036.

M319 *Instructor.* (Periodical) Instructor Publications, Inc. 7 Bank Street. Dansville, NY 14437.

M320 *Island of the Blue Dolphins.* (16mm film) Universal, 1964. 101 min. Live action. Color. Based on a book by Scott O'Dell.

M321 *The Island of the Skog.* (16mm film) Weston Woods, n.d. 13 min. Iconographic. Color. Based on a book by Steven Kellogg.

M322 ———. (Filmstrip with cassette or text booklet; individual cassette) Weston Woods, n.d. 50 fr. 11 min. Based on a book by S. Kellogg.

M323 *It Could Always Be Worse.* (Filmstrip with cassette; individual cassette) Miller-Brody, n.d. Based on a book by Margot Zemach.

M324 *Invincible Louisa.* (Phonograph record or cassette) Miller-Brody, n.d. Based on a book by Cornelia Meigs.

M325 *Jack and Jill.* (Periodical) Curtis Publishing Co., *Saturday Evening Post.* 1100 Waterway Blvd. P.O. 567B. Indianapolis, IN 46206.

M326 *Jack Jouette's Ride.* (Filmstrip with cassette or text booklet; individual cassette) Weston Woods, 1975. 34 fr. 7 min. Based on a book by Gail Haley.

M327 *James Daugherty.* (16mm film) Weston Woods, n.d. 19 min. Live-action. Color. Interview with J. Daugherty.

M328 *Jasmine.* (Filmstrip with record or cassette; individual cassette) Random House, n.d. Based on a book by Roger Duvoisin.

M329 *Jeanne-Marie Counts Her Sheep.* (Filmstrip

with record or cassette; individual cassette) Miller-Brody, n.d. Based on a book by Francoise.

M330 Jenny's Birthday Book. (Filmstrip with cassette or text booklet; individual cassette) Weston Woods, 1959. 33 fr. Based on a book by Esther Averill.

M331 Johnny Crow's Garden. (Filmstrip with cassette or text booklet; individual cassette) Weston Woods, 1959. 28 fr. 4 min. Based on a book by L. Leslie Brooke.

M332 Johnny Tremain. (16mm film) Walt Disney, 1957. 80 min. Live action. Color. Based on a book by Esther Forbes.

M333 ———. (Phonograph record or cassette) Miller-Brody, 1970. 21 min. Based on a book by E. Forbes.

M334 ———. (Phonograph record or cassette) Caedmon, n.d. Performed by E. G. Marshall, et al. Based on a book by E. Forbes.

M335 Josie and the Snow. (Filmstrip with cassette or text booklet; individual cassette) Weston Woods, 1968. 29 fr. 3 min. Illus by Evaline Ness. Based on a book by Helen Buckley.

M336 Journey Cake, Ho! (Filmstrip with cassette or text booklet; individual cassette) Weston Woods, 1967. 36 fr. 11 min. Illus by Robert McCloskey. Based on a book by Ruth Sawyer.

M337 Joy to the World. ((Phonograph record or cassette) Weston Woods, n.d.

M338 The Judge. (Filmstrip with cassette) Miller-Brody, n.d. Based on a book by Harve and Margot Zemach.

M339 Julie of the Wolves. (2 filmstrips with record or cassette; individual cassette) Miller-Brody, n.d. Based on a book by Jean George.

M340 Junior Scholastic, a National Magazine for Junior High School and Upper Elementary Grades. (Periodical) Scholastic Magazines. 50 W. 44th St. New York, NY 10036.

M341 Just Me. (Filmstrip with cassette or text booklet; individual cassette) Weston Woods, n.d. 32 fr. 8 min. Based on a book by Marie Hall Ets.

M342 Justin Morgan Had a Horse. (2 filmstrips with record or cassette; individual cassette) Miller-Brody, n.d. Based on a book by Marguerite Henry.

M343 King of the Wind. (2 filmstrips with record or cassette; individual cassette) Miller-Brody, 1971. Based on a book by Marguerite Henry.

M344 The King's Fifth. (2 filmstrips with record or cassette; individual cassette) Miller-Brody, n.d. Based on a book by Scott O'Dell.

M345 Kirkus Reviews. (Periodical) 200 Park Avenue, South. New York, NY. 10003.

M346 A Kiss for Little Bear. (Filmstrip with cassette or text booklet; individual cassette) Weston Woods, 1972. 35 fr. 4 min. Illus by Maurice Sendak. Based on a book by Else Holmelund Minarik.

M347 The Lace Snail. (Filmstrip with cassette) Viking, n.d. Based on a book by Betsy Byars.

M348 Ladybug. (4 paperbacks with cassette) Morrow, n.d. Based on a book by Robert McClung.

M349 Lassie Come-Home. (16mm film) New York,

NY: MGM, 1943. 90 min. Live action. Color. Based on a book by Eric Knight.

M350 ———. (Phonograph record or cassette) Caedmon, 1973. Narrated by David McCallum. Based on a book by E. Knight.

M351 Learning About Dinosaurs. (10 study prints) Encyclopedia Britannica Educational Corp., n.d.

M352 Learning, the Magazine for Creative Teaching. (Periodical) Education Today Co., Inc. 530 University Ave. Palo Alto, CA 94301.

M353 The Legend of John Henry. (16mm) Santa Monica, CA: Pyramid, 1974. 11 min. Color.

M354 Legends in Music. (Phonograph record) Bowmar, n.d.

M355 Lentil. (16mm film) Weston Woods, 1956. 9 min. Iconographic. Color. Based on a book by Robert McCloskey.

M356 ———. (Filmstrip with cassette or text booklet; individual cassette) Weston Woods, 1958. 41 fr. 9 min. Based on a book by R. McCloskey.

M357 Leo Lionni Read-Along Library. (4 cassettes and 4 books). Random House, n.d. Based on Frederick, Swimmy, Fish is Fish, and Theodore and the Talking Mushroom by L. Lionni.

M358 Leonard Bernstein Conducts for Young . . . (Phonograph Record) Columbia, n.d. Bernstein conducting the New York Philharmonic.

M359 Let's Be Enemies. (Filmstrip with cassette or text booklet; individual cassette) Weston Woods, 1970. 32 fr. 3 min. Illus by Maurice Sendak. Based on a book by Janice May Udry.

M360 A Letter to Amy. (16mm film) Weston Woods, 1970. 7 min. Iconographic. Color. Based on a book by Ezra Jack Keats.

M361 ———. (Filmstrip with cassette or text booklet; individual cassette) Weston Woods, 1970. 38 fr. 6 min. Based on a book by E. J. Keats.

M362 Library Journal. (Periodical) R. R. Bowker. 1180 Avenue of the Americas. New York, NY 10036.

M363 Life in the Early American Colonies. (6 filmstrips and 3 cassettes) Troll Associates, 1971. Includes Mayflower Experience, Plymouth Plantation, Colonial Shelter and Defence, Colonial Food, Religion, Education, Recreation, Colonial Crafts.

M364 The Lion and the Rat. (Filmstrip with cassette or text booklet; individual cassette) Weston Woods, 1969. 18 fr. 3 min. (Including The Hare and the Tortoise) Illus by Brian Wildsmith. Based on a fable by La Fontaine.

M365 Little Bear's Visit (Filmstrip with cassette; text booklet; individual cassette) Weston Woods, 1967. 62 fr. 14 min. Illus by Maurice Sendak, Based on a book by Else Holmelund Minarik.

M366 Little Blue and Little Yellow. (16mm film) Contemporary Films, n.d. 9 min. Animated. Color. Based on a book by Leo Lionni.

M367 The Little Drummer Boy. (8mm or 16mm film) Weston Woods, n.d. 7 min. Iconographic.

Color. Illus by Ezra Jack Keats. Based on a song by Katherine Davis, Henry Onorati, and Harry Simeone.

M368 ————. (Filmstrip with cassette or text booklet; individual cassette) Weston Woods, 1971. 24 fr. 7 min. Illus by E. J. Keats. Based on a song by K. Davis, H. Onorati, and H. Simeone.

M369 *Little Favorites.* (Phonograph record) Bowmar, n.d. Includes: *All the Pretty Little Horses, Eency Weency Spider, Hush Little Baby, Old MacDonald Had a Farm,* and *Three Blind Mice.*

M370 *The Little House.* (Filmstrip with cassette or text booklet; individual cassette) Weston Woods, 1973. 55 fr. 13 min. Based on a book by Virginia Lee Burton.

M371 *The Little House in the Big Woods.* (Phonograph record or cassette) Miller-Brody, n.d. Based on a book by L. I. Wilder.

M372 *The Little House in the Big Woods.* (4 phonograph records and 8 paperbacks) Super Reading Starter, a Read Along Unit. Educational Reading Service, n.d. Based on a book by Laura Ingalls Wilder.

M373 *The Little House on the Prairie.* (Phonograph record or cassette) Miller-Brody, n.d. Based on a book by L. I. Wilder.

M374 *The Little Island.* (Filmstrip with cassette or text booklet; individual cassette) Weston Woods, 1961. 39 fr. 6 min. Illus by Leonard Weisgard. Based on a book by Golden MacDonald.

M375 *The Little Red Hen.* (Filmstrip with cassette or text booklet; individual cassette) Weston Woods, 1973. 31 fr. 8 min. Based on a story illus by Paul Galdone.

M376 *The Little Red Lighthouse..* (8mm and 16mm film) Weston Woods, 1955. 9 min. Iconographic. Color. Illus by Lynd Ward. Based on a book by Hildegarde Swift.

M377 ————. (Filmstrip with cassette or text booklet; individual cassette) Weston Woods, 1958. 42 fr. 9 min. Illus by L. Ward. Based on a book by H. Swift.

M378 *Little Tim and the Brave Sea Captain.* (8mm and 16mm film) Weston Woods, 1976. 11 min. Iconographic. Color. Based on a book by Edward Ardizzone.

M379 ————. *Little Tim and the Brave Sea Captain.* (Filmstrip with cassette or text booklet; individual cassette) Weston Woods, 1962. 58 fr. 9 min. Based on a book by E. Ardizzone.

M380 *Little Toot.* (Filmstrip with cassette or text booklet; individual cassette) Weston Woods, 1958. 52 fr. 10 min. Based on a book by Hardie Gramatky.

M381 *Little Women.* (16mm film) RKO, 1933. 107 min. Live action. Black and white. Based on a book by Louisa May Alcott.

M382 ————. (Phonograph record or cassette) Caedmon, 1975. 60 min. Narrated by Julie Harris. Based on a book by L. M. Alcott.

M383 ————. (2 phonograph records or cassettes) Listening Library, 1974. Narrated by Ester Benson. Based on a book by L. M. Alcott.

M384 *The Lively Art of the Picture Book.* (16mm film) Weston Woods, n.d. 57 min. Live action.

Color.

M385 *The Living Sands of Namib.* (16mm film or videocassettes) National Geographic, 1978. 59 min. Live action. Color. Produced for TV.

M386 *London Bridge is Falling Down!* (Filmstrip with cassette or text booklet; individual cassette) Weston Woods, 1976. 22 fr. 6 min. Based on a song illustrated by Peter Spier.

M387 *The Loner.* (2 filmstrips with record or cassette; individual cassette) Miller-Brody, n.d. Based on a book by Ester Wier.

M388 *Look What I Can Do.* (Filmstrip with cassette) Miller-Brody, n.d. Based on a book by Jose Aruego.

M389 *The Lord of the Rings: The Two Towers and the Return of the King.* (Phonograph record or cassette) Caedmon, n.d. Narrated by J.R.R. Tolkien from his books.

M390 *A Lost Button.* (Filmstrip with record or cassette) Miller-brody, n.d. From the book *Frog and Toad are Friends* by Arnold Lobel.

M391 *The Loudest Noise in the World.* (Filmstrip with cassette or text booklet; individual cassette) Weston Woods, 1967. 40 fr. 11 min. Illus by James Daugherty. Based on a book by Benjamin Elkin.

M392 *Lyle, the Crocodile.* (4 filmstrips with 2 records or cassettes) Teaching Resource Films, an Educational Division of the New York Times, n.d. 1 hr. 296 fr. Based on four books by Bernard Waber: *The House on East 88th Street, Loveable Lyle, Lyle and the Birthday Party,* and *Lyle, Lyle Crocodile.*

M393 *Ma Lien and the Magic Brush.* (Filmstrip with record) New York, NY: Learning Corp. of Am., 1972. 11 min. Based on a book by Hisako Kimishima.

M394 *Madeline.* (Filmstrip with cassette) Viking, n.d. Based on a book by Ludwig Bemelmans.

M395 *Madeline and other Bemelmans.* (Phonograph record or cassette) Caedmon, n.d. Narrated by Carol Channing. Based on a book by L. Bemelmans.

M396 *Madeline and the Bad Hat.* (Cassette and 8 paperbacks) Viking Seafarer Reading Chest, n.d. Based on a book by L. Bemelmans.

M397 *Madeline and the Gypsies.* (Cassette and 8 paperbacks) Viking Seafarer Reading Chest, n.d. Based on a book by L. Bemelmans.

M398 *Madeline and the Gypsies and Other Stories.* (Phonograph record or cassette) Caedmon, n.d. Narrated by Carol Channing. Based on books by L. Bemelmans.

M399 *Madeline in London.* (Cassette and 8 paperbacks) Viking Seafarer Reading Chest, n.d. Based on a book by L. Bemelmans.

M400 *Madeline's Rescue.* (Filmstrip with record or cassette) Weston Woods, 1960. 53 fr. 6 min. Based on a book by L. Bemelmans.

M401 ————. (Poster) Horn Book Poster Set #2. Horn Book, n.d. Based on a book by L. Bemelmans.

M402 *Magic Michael.* (Filmstrip with cassette or text booklet; individual cassette) Weston Woods, 1959. Based on a book by Louis Slobodkin.

M403 *Make Way for Ducklings.* (Cassette) Viking, n.d. Based on a book by Robert McCloskey.

M404 ———. (Filmstrip with cassette or text booklet; individual cassette) Weston Woods, 1958. 47fr. 11 min. Based on a book by R. McCloskey.

M405 *Many Moons.* (Poster) Horn Book Poster Set #3. Horn Book, n.d. Illus by Louis Slobodkin from a book by James Thurber.

M406 *Marie Louise's Heyday.* (Filmstrip with cassette; individual cassette) Miller-Brody, n.d. Based on a book by Natalie Savage Carlson.

M407 *Mary Poppins.* (Phonograph record) Buena Vista, 1964. Sound track of the movie by Walt Disney Productions. Written by R.M. and R.S. Sherman, arranged and conducted by I. Kostat, and sung by Julie Andrews, Dick Van Dyke et al. Based on a book by Pamela Travers.

M408 ———. (Phonograph record or cassette) Caedmon, n.d. Narrated by Maggie Smith, et al. Based on a book by P. Travers.

M409 *Mary Poppins and the Banks Family.* (Phonograph record or cassette) Caedmon, n.d. Narrated by Maggie Smith, et al. Based on the book *Mary Poppins Comes Back* by P. Travers.

M410 *Mary Poppins: Balloons and Balloons.* (Phonograph record or cassette) Caedmon, n.d. Narrated by Robert Stephens et al. Based on the books *Mary Poppins Opens the Door* and *Mary Poppins Comes Back* by Pamela Travers.

M411 *Mary Poppins Comes Back.* (Phonograph record or cassette) Caedmon, n.d. Narrated by Maggie Smith et al. Based on a book by P. Travers.

M412 *Mary Poppins from A to Z.* (Phonograph record or cassette) Caedmon, n.d. Narrated by Robert Stephens. Music by Leslie Pearson. Based on a book by P. Travers.

M413 *Mary Poppins Opens the Door.* (Phonograph record or cassette) Caedmon, n.d. Narrated by Maggie Smith, et al. Based on a book by Pamela Travers.

M414 *The Matchlock Gun.* (2 filmstrips and record or cassette; individual cassette) Miller-Brody, n.d. Based on a book by Walter Edmonds.

M415 *Maurice Sendak.* (16mm film) Weston Woods, 1966. 14 min. Live action. Color. Interview with M. Sendak.

M416 *May I Bring a Friend?.* (Filmstrip with cassette or text booklet; individual cassette) Weston Woods, 1973. 32 fr. 7 min. Illus by Beni Montresor. Based on a book by Beatrice S. DeRegniers.

M417 *Mazel and Shlimazel.* (Filmstrip with record or cassette; individual cassette) Miller-Brody, n.d. Based on a book by Isaac Bashevis Singer.

M418 *Media and Methods.* (Periodical) North American Publishing Co. 401 N. Broad St. Philadelphia, PA 19108.

M419 *Meet Babar and his Family.* (Filmstrip with record or cassette; individual cassette) Viking, n.d. Based on a book by Jean De Brunhoff.

M420 *Meet the Instruments.* (25 posters) Bowman, n.d. Color. 14x22.

M421 *Meet the Newbery Author: Lloyd Alexander.* (Filmstrip with record or cassette) Miller-Brody, n.d.

M422 *Meet the Newbery Author: William H. Armstrong.* (Filmstrip with record or cassette) Miller-Brody, n.d.

M423 *Meet the Newbery Author: Natalie Babbitt.* (Filmstrip with record or cassette) Miller-Brody, n.d.

M424 *Meet the Newbery Author: Carol Ryrie Brink.* (Filmstrip with record or cassette) Miller-Brody, n.d.

M425 *Meet the Newbery Author: Betsy Byars.* (Filmstrip with record or cassette) Miller-Brody, n.d.

M426 *Meet the Newbery Author: Beverly Cleary.* (Filmstrip with record or cassette) Miller-Brody, n.d.

M427 *Meet the Newbery Author: James Lincoln Collier and Christopher Collier.* (Filmstrip with record or cassette) Miller-Brody, n.d.

M428 *Meet the Newbery Author: Susan Cooper.* (Filmstrip with record or cassette) Miller-Brody, n.d.

M429 *Meet the Newbery Author: Eleanor Estes.* (Filmstrip with record or cassette) Miller-Brody, n.d.

M430 *Meet the Newbery Author: Bette Greene.* (Filmstrip with record or cassette) Miller-Brody, n.d.

M431 *Meet the Newbery Author: Virginia Hamilton.* (Filmstrip with record or cassette) Miller-Brody, n.d.

M432 *Meet the Newbery Author: Marguerite Henry.* (Filmstrip with record or cassette) Miller-Brody, n.d.

M433 *Meet the Newbery Author: Jamake Highwater.* (Filmstrip with record or cassette) Miller-Brody, n.d.

M434 *Meet the Newbery Author: Madeleine L'Engle.* (Filmstrip with record or cassette) Miller-Brody, n.d.

M435 *Meet the Newbery Author: Arnold Lobel.* (Filmstrip with record or cassette) Miller-Brody, n.d.

M436 *Meet the Newbery Author: Scott O'Dell.* (Filmstrip with record or cassette) Miller-Brody, n.d.

M437 *Meet the Newbery Author: Isaac Bashevis Singer.* (Filmstrip with record or cassette) Miller-Brody, n.d.

M438 *Meet the Newbery Author: Laura Ingalls Wilder.* (Filmstrip with record or cassette) Miller-Brody, n.d.

M439 *Meet the Newbery Author: Elizabeth Yates.* (Filmstrip with record or cassette) Miller-Brody, n.d.

M440 *Meet the Newbery Author: Laurence Yep.* (Filmstrip with record or cassette) Miller-Brody, n.d.

M441 *Merry Ever After.* (Filmstrip with Cassette) Viking, n.d. Based on a book by Joe Lasker

M442 *The Mighty Volga.* (16mm film or videocassette) National Geographic, 1977. 25 min. Live action. Color. Produced for TV.

M443 *Mike Mulligan and his Steam Shovel.* (8mm and 16mm film) Weston Woods, 1956. 11

min. Iconographic. Color. Based on a book by Virginia Lee Burton.

M444 ———. (Filmstrip with cassette or text booklet; individual cassette) Weston Woods, n.d. 59 fr. 11 min. Based on a book by V.L. Burton.

M445 The Milkmaid. (Filmstrip with cassette or text booklet; individual cassette) Weston Woods, n.d. Based on a book by Randolph Caldecott.

M446 The Miller, His Son and Their Donkey. (Filmstrip with cassette or text booklet; individual cassette) Weston Woods, 1962. 25 fr. 5 min. Based on a fable illustrated by Roger Duvoisin.

M447 Millions of Cats. (8mm or 16mm film) Weston Woods, 1955. 10 min. Iconographic. Color. Based on a book by Wanda Gag.

M448 ———. (Filmstrip with cassette or text booklet; individual cassette) Weston Woods, 1956. 44 fr. 10 min. Based on a book by W. Gag.

M449 Miracles on Maple Hill. (Phonograph record or cassette) Miller-Brody, n.d. Based on a book by Virginia Sorenson.

M450 Miss Esta Maude's Secret. (16mm film) McGraw Hill, 1964. 10 min. Color. Based on a book by W.T. Cummings.

M451 Miss Hickory. (Phonograph record or cassette) Miller-Brody, n.d. Based on a book by Carolyn Bailey.

M452 Mrs. Frisby and the Rats of NIMH. (2 filmstrips with record or cassette; individual cassette) Miller-Brody, n.d. Based on a book by Robert C. O'Brien.

M453 Mr. Gumpy's Outing. (Filmstrip with cassette or text booklet; individual cassette) Weston Woods, n.d. 33 fr. 5 min. Based on a book by John Burningham.

M454 Mr. Rabbit and and the Lovely Present. (Filmstrip with cassette or text booklet; individual cassette) Weston Woods, 1965. 26 min. 7 min. Illus by Maurice Sendak. Based on a book by Charlotte Zolotow.

M455 Mr. Shepard and Mr. Milne. (16mm film) Weston Woods, n.d. 28 min. Live action. Color. Christopher Robin Milne reads from his father's works and Ernest Sheperd tells about illustrating When We Were Very Young, Winnie-the-Pooh, The House at Pooh Corner, and Now We are Six by A. A. Milne.

M456 Misty. (16mm film) Twentieth Century Fox, 1961. 92 min. Live action. Color. Based on a book by Marguerite Henry.

M457 Misty of Chincoteague. (2 filmstrips and record or cassette; individual cassette) Miller-Brody, n.d. Based on a book by Marguerite Henry.

M458 Moby Dick. (16mm film) Warner Bros., 1956. 116 min. Live action. Color. Based on a book by Herman Melville.

M459 Moccasin Trail. (Phonographic record or cassette) Miller-Brody, n.d. Based on a book by Eloise McGraw.

M460 Mole Family's Christmas. (Filmstrip with record or cassette) Learning Corporation of America, n.d. 15 min. Based on a book by Russell Hoban.

M461 Mommy Buy Me a China Doll. (Filmstrip with cassette or text booklet) Weston Woods, 1970, 23 fr. Illus by Margot Zemach. Based on a book by Harve Zemach.

M462 The Monster Riddle Book. (Filmstrip with cassette; individual cassette) Miller-Brody, 1981. Based on a book by Jane Sarnoff and Reynold Ruffins.

M463 Monsters and Other Friendly Creatures. (5 filmstrips with records or cassettes and bibliography) Encyclopedia Britannica, 1974. Titles include: Monsters in the Closet, Monster Seeds, Andrew and the Strawberry Monster, Charlie and the Caterpillar, Emil, the Tap-dancing Frog.

M464 Monsters and Other Science Mysteries. (8 filmstrips with cassettes and guides) Miller-Brody, 1977. Includes: The Mystery of the Loch Ness Monster, The Mystery of the Abominable Snowman, The Mystery of the Bermuda Triangle, The Mystery of Witchcraft, The Mystery of ESP, The Mystery of Astrology, and The Mystery of Life on Other Worlds.

M465 Moon Basket; An Indian Legend. (Filmstrip with record or cassette and guide) Stanford, CA: Multi-Media Productions, 1974. 6 min.

M466 More Silver Pennies. (Phonograph record or cassette) Caedmon, n.d. Narrated by Claire Bloom and Cyril Ritchard. Based on a book edited by Blanche Jennings Thompson.

M467 More Winnie-the-Pooh. (Phonograph record) Pathways of Sound, n.d. Narrated by Maurice Evans. Based on a book by A.A. Milne.

M468 Mousekin. (4 filmstrips with 2 records or 4 cassettes) Teaching Resource Films, an Educational Division of the New York Times, n.d. 30 min. 157 fr. Based on four books by Edna Miller: Mousekin Finds a Friend, Mousekin's Christmas Eve, Mousekin's Family and Mousekin's Golden House.

M469 The Musicians of Bremen. (Filmstrip with cassette or text booklet; individual cassette) Weston Woods, 1980. 39 fr. 9 min. Illus by Svend S. Otto Based on a tale by the brothers Grimm.

M470 Music of Gilbert and Sullivan. (Phonograph record) Westminster, n.d. Johnson Orchestra.

M471 Music of the Black Man in America. (2 phonograph records or cassettes) Bowmar, n.d.

M472 Music of the Drama, by Wagner. (Phonograph record) Bowmar Orchestral Library, n.d.

M473 My Brother Sam is Dead. (Phonograph record or cassette) Miller-Brody, 1976. Based on a book by James and Christopher Collier.

M474 My Red Umbrella. (Filmstrip with cassette or text booklet; individual cassette) Weston Woods, n.d. Based on a book by Robert Bright.

M475 My Side of the Mountain. (16mm film) Hollywood, CA: Paramount, 1969. 100 min. Live action. Color. Based on a book by Jean Craighead George.

M476 *National Anthems of the World.* (Phonograph record) Everest, n.d. Played by the Vienna State Opera Orchestra.

M477 *National Velvet.* (16mm film) MGM, 1944. 123 min. Live action. Color. Based on a book by Enid Bagnold.

M478 *Nature and Make Believe.* (Phonograph record) Bowmar Orchestral Library, 1965.

M479 *New Patches for Old.* (Filmstrip with cassette or text booklet; individual cassette) Weston Woods, 1974. 46 fr. 11 min. Illus by Harold Berson. Based on a story by Barbara K. Walker and Ahmel E. Usyal.

M480 *Nine Days to Christmas.* (Poster) Horn Book Poster Set #2. Horn Book, n.d. From a book by Marie Hall Ets.

M481 *Noah's Ark.* (Filmstrip with cassette individual filmstrip or individual cassette) Weston Woods, n.d. 67 fr. 11 min. Based on a book by Peter Spier.

M482 *Noisy Nancy Norris.* (Filmstrip with record or cassette) Guidance Associates (Harcourt Brace), n.d. Based on a book by Lou Ann Gaeddert.

M483 *Noisy Nora.* (Filmstrip with text booklet; individual cassette) Weston Woods, 1975. 28 fr. 10 min. Narrated and sung by Nicole Frechette. Based on a book by Rosemary Wells.

M484 *Norman the Doorman.* (16mm film) Weston Woods, n.d. 15 min. Iconographic. Color. Based on a book by Don Freeman.

M485 ————. (Filmstrip with cassette; text booklets; individual cassette) Weston Woods, 1965. 55 fr. 11 min. Based on a book by D. Freeman.

M486 *North American Indian Songs.* (2 filmstrips with record or cassette) Bowmar, 1972.

M487 *The North Wind and the Sun.* (Filmstrip with cassette or text booklet; individual cassette) Weston Woods, 1970. 20 fr. 2 min. Including *Brian Wildsmith's Birds.* Illus by Brian Wildsmith. Based on a fable by La Fontaine.

M488 *Nonsense Verse.* (Phonograph record or cassette) Caedmon, n.d. Narrated by Bea Lillie, Cyril Ritchard and Stanley Holloway. Based on poems by L. Carroll and E. Lear.

M489 *Nutcracker and Peter and the Wolf.* (Phonograph record) Columbia, n.d. Music by Tschaikovsky and Prokofief. Conducted by Leonard Bernstein with the New York Philharmonic orchestra.

M490 *Obadiah the Bold.* (Filmstrip with record or cassette) Viking, 1970. 33 fr. Read by Brinton Turkle from his book.

M491 *Ogden Nash Reads Ogden Nash.* (Phonograph record or cassette) Caedmon, 1953. Read by Ogden Nash from his poems.

M492 *Ogden Nash's Parents Keep Out.* (Phonograph record or cassette) Caedmon, n.d.

M493 *Ola.* (Filmstrip with record or cassette) Weston Woods, 1970. Based on a book by Ingri and Edgar Parin d'Aulaire.

M494 *The Old Bullfrog.* (Filmstrip with record or cassette; individual cassette) Miller-Brody, n.d. Based on a book by Berniece Freschet.

M495 *Old Mother Hubbard and Her Dog.* (Filmstrip with cassette) Viking, 1962. Based on a picture book illustrated by Evaline Ness.

M496 ————. (Filmstrip with cassette or text booklet; individual cassette) Weston Woods, n.d. 34 fr. 4 min. Based on a picture book illustrated by Paul Galdone.

M497 *The Old Woman and her Pig.* (Filmstrip with cassette or text booklet; individual cassette) Weston Woods, 1962. 51 fr. 7 min. Based on a book illus by Paul Galdone.

M498 *Once a Mouse...* (Filmstrip with cassette; individual cassette) Miller-Brody, n.d. Based on a book by Marcia Brown.

M499 *One Fine Day.* (Filmstrip with cassette or text booklet; individual cassette) Weston Woods, 1973. 27 fr. 5 min. Based on a book by Nonny Hogrogian.

M500 *One Fish, Two Fish, Red Fish, Blue Fish.* (Filmstrip with record or cassette; individual cassette) Random House, n.d. Based on a book by Dr. Seuss.

M501 *One Monday Morning.* (8mm and 16mm film) Weston Woods, 1972. 10 min. Iconographic. Color. Based on a book by Uri Shulevitz.

M502 ————. (Filmstrip with cassette or text booklet; individual cassette) Weston Woods, 1971. 31 fr. 7 min. Based on a book by U. Shulevitz.

M503 *One Morning in Maine.* (Filmstrip with cassette) Viking, n.d. Based on a book by Robert McCloskey.

M504 *One Was Johnny.* (16mm film) Weston Woods, 1978. 3 min. Animated. Color. Based on a book by Maurice Sendak.

M505 ————. (Filmstrip with cassette or text booklet; individual cassette) Weston Woods, 1977. 26 fr. 3 min. Based on a book by M. Sendak.

M506 *One Wide River to Cross.* (Filmstrip with record or cassette) Teaching Resource Films, an Educational Division of the New York Times, n.d. Based on a song illustrated by Ed Emberley, from a book by Barbara Emberley.

M507 *Opera Hits.* (Phonograph record) Arthur Fiedler conducting the Boston Pops.

M508 *Our Nation's Flag.* (2 filmstrips with record or cassette) BFA, 1970.

M509 *Our Veronica Goes to Petunia's Farm.* (Filmstrip with record or cassette) Random House, n.d. Based on a book by Roger Duvoisin.

M510 *Over in the Meadow.* (8mm or 16mm film) Weston Woods, n.d. 9 min. Iconographic. Color. Based on a song illustrated by John Langstaff.

M511 ————. (Filmstrip with cassette or text booklet; individual cassette) Weston Woods, 1965. 45 fr. 9 min. Based on a song illus by J. Langstaff.

M512 *Overtures; Tannhauser, Tristan and Isolde, Die Meistersinger, Lohengrin.* (Phonograph record) Seraphim, n.d. From operas by Richard Wagner.

M513 *The Owl and the Leming, an Eskimo Legend.* (Filmstrip with cassette) National Film Board of Canada. 1976.

M514 *The Owl and the Pussy Cat.* (16mm film) Weston Woods, n.d. 3 min. Iconographic. Color. Illus by Barbara Cooney. Based on a poem by Edward Lear.

M515 *The Owl and the Pussy-Cat*. (Filmstrip with cassette or text booklet; individual cassette) Weston Woods, 1967. 18 fr. 3 min. (Including *Wynken, Blynken and Nod*). Illus by B. Cooney. Based on poems by Edward Lear and Eugene Field.

M516 *Paddington Hits the Jackpot*. (16mm film) Film Fair, 1977. 5½ min. Animated. Color. Based on a book by Michael Bond.

M517 *Paddle to the Sea*. (16mm film) McGraw-Hill, 1968. 28 min. Color. Based on a book by Holling C. Holling.

M518 *Paint All Kinds of Pictures*. (Filmstrip with cassette or text booklet; individual cassette) Weston Woods, 1968. Based on a book by Arnold Spilka.

M519 *Paul Bunyan in Story and Song*. (Phonograph record or cassette) Caedmon, n.d. Read by Ed Begley, sung by Oscar Brand.

M520 *Perilous Road*. (2 Filmstrips with record or cassette; individual cassette) Miller-Brody, n.d. Based on a book by William O. Steele

M521 *Peter and the Wolf and Nutcracker*. (Phonograph Record) Columbia, n.d. Music by Prokofief and Tschaikovsky. The New York Philharmonic conducted by Leonard Bernstein.

M522 *Peter Rabbit and Tales of Beatrix Potter*. (16mm film) Britain, 1971. 90 min. Live action ballet. Color. Based on a book by Beatrix Potter.

M523 *Peter's Chair*. (16mm film) Weston Woods, 1971. 6 min. Iconographic. Color. Based on a book by E. J. Keats.

M524 ———. (Filmstrip with cassette or text booklet; individual cassette) Weston Woods, 1968. 4 min. 27 fr. Based on a book by E. J. Keats.

M525 *Petunia*. (16mm film) Weston Woods, 1971. 10 min. Animated. Color. Based on a book by Roger Duvoisin.

M526 ———. (Filmstrip with cassette or text booklet; individual cassette) Weston Woods, 1962. 11 min. 50 fr. Based on a book by R. Duvoisin.

M527 ———. (Phonograph record or cassette) Caedmon, n.d. Read and sung by Julie Harris. Based on books by Roger Duvoisin.

M528 *Petunia Beware!* (Filmstrip with record or cassette) Random, n.d. Based on a book by Roger Duvoisin.

M529 *Petunia Takes a Trip*. (Filmstrip with record or cassette) Random, n.d. Based on a book by Roger Duvoisin.

M530 *A Picture for Harold's Room*. (8mm and 16mm film) Weston Woods, 1971. 6 min. Animated. Color. Based on a book by Crockett Johnson.

M531 ———. (Filmstrip with cassette or text booklet; individual cassette) Weston Woods, 1972. Based on a book by C. Johnson.

M532 *A Picture Has a Special Look*. (Filmstrip with record or cassette) Weston Woods, n.d. Based on a book by Helen Borten.

M533 *Pierre*. (16mm film) Weston Woods, 1978. 6 min. Animated. Color. Based on a book by Maurice Sendak.

M534 ———. (Filmstrip with cassette or text booklet; individual cassette) Weston Woods, 1972. 6 min. 33 fr. Based on a book by M. Sendak.

M535 *Pilgrim Saga, the Story of the Pilgrims from Their European Origin to their Establishment of a Permanent Colony in America*. (Phonograph record or cassette) Caedmon, 1971.

M536 *Pinky Pye*. (Phonograph record or cassette) Miller-Brody, 1977. Based on a book by Eleanor Estes.

M537 *Pinocchio*. (Photograph record or cassette) Caedmon, 1969. Read by Cyril Ritchard. Based on a book by Carlo Collodi.

M538 *Pippi Longstocking*. (3 phonograph records or cassettes and paperbacks) Viking, n.d. Narrated by Esther Benson. Based on a book by Astrid Lindgren.

M539 *A Place of Our Own*. (Phonograph Record) Woodbury, NY: Pickwick International, Inc., n.d. Sung by Fred Rogers.

M540 *The Planet of Junior Brown*. (2 filmstrips with record or cassette; individual cassette) Miller-Brody, 1978. Based on a book by Virginia Hamilton.

M541 *Play Ball, Amelia Bedelia*. (Filmstrip with record or cassette) Teaching Resource Films, an Educational Division of the New York Times, n.d. 54 fr. Based on a book by Peggy Parish.

M542 *Play with Me*. (Filmstrip with cassette or text booklet; individual cassette) Weston Woods, 1962. 6 min 30 fr. Based on a book by Marie Hall Ets.

M543 *Plays: The Drama Magazine*. (Periodical) Plays, Inc. 8 Arlington St. Boston, MA 02116.

M544 *A Pocketful of Cricket*. (2 filmstrips with cassette; individual cassette) Miller-Brody, n.d. Based on a book by Rebecca Caudill.

M545 *Poems and Letters of Emily Dickinson*. (Phonograph record or cassette) Caedmon, n.d. Narrated by Julie Harris from the poems of Emily Dickinson.

M546 *Poems and Songs of Middle Earth*. (Phonograph record or cassette) Caedmon, n.d. Narrated by J.R.R. Tolkien, William Elvin and Donald Swann. Based on poems and stories of J.R.R. Tolkien.

M547 *Poems by a Little Girl*. (Phonograph record or cassette) Caedmon, n.d. Narrated from her poems by Hilda Conkling.

M548 *The Poetry of Benet*. (Phonograph record or cassette) Caedmon, n.d. Read by Joseph Wiseman and the poet Stephen Vincent Benet.

M549 *The Poetry of Countee Cullen*. (Phonograph record or cassette) Caedmon, n.d. Narrated by Ruby Dee and Ossie Davis. Based on poems of Countee Cullen.

M550 *The Poetry of Langston Hughes*. (Phonograph record or cassette) Caedmon, n.d. Narrated by Ruby Dee and Ossie Davis. Based on poems by Langston Hughes.

M551 *Pooh: His Art Gallery*. (8 Posters) Dutton, 1962. Illus by Ernest Shepard from *The World of Pooh* and *The World of Christopher Robin* by A. A. Milne.

M552 *Portrait of a Whale*. (16mm film or videocassette) National Geographic, 1976. 12 min. Live action. Color. Produced for TV.

M553 *Previews: News and Reviews of Non-print Media*. (Periodical) R. R. Bowker, 1180

Avenue of the Americas, New York, NY. 10036.

M554 *Puppets.* (16mm film) ACEI, 1967. 15 min. Color.

M555 *Puss in Boots.* (Filmstrip with cassette; individual cassette) Miller-Brody, n.d. Based on a book by Marcia Brown.

M556 *Puzzles.* (Filmstrip with record or cassette) Weston Woods, n.d. Based on a book by Brian Wildsmith.

M557 *The Queen of Hearts.* (Filmstrip with record or cassette) Weston Woods, n.d. (Also includes *Sing a Song for Sixpence.*) Based on rhymes illustrated by Randolph Caldecott.

M558 *The Queen Who Couldn't Bake Gingerbread.* (Filmstrip with record or cassette) Random, n.d. Based on a book by Dorothy Van Woerkom.

M559 *Rabbi Leib and the Witch Cunegunde/ Shrewd Todie and Lyzer the Mizer.* (2 filmstrips with record or cassette) Miller Brody, n.d. Based on stories by Isaac Bashevis Singer.

M560 *Rabbit Hill.* (16mm film) McGraw-Hill, 1968. 53 min. Color. Based on a book by Robert Lawson.

M561 ———. (Phonograph record or cassette) Viking, 1972. Played by the High Tor Repertory Players. Based on a book by Robert Lawson.

M562 *A Rainbow of My Own.* (Filmstrip with cassette) Viking, n.d. Based on a book by Don Freeman.

M563 *Rascal.* (Phonograph record or cassette) Miller-Brody, n.d. Based on a book by Sterling North.

M564 *Rain Drop Splash.* (Filmstrip with record or cassette) Weston Woods, 1968. Illus by Leonard Weisgard. Based on a book by Alvin Tresselt.

M565 *The Raven and Other Works. Phonograph record or cassette)* Caedmon, n.d. Narrated by Basil Rathbone from the poems of Edgar Allan Poe.

M566 *Reading for the Fun of it: Adventure.* (Filmstrip with record or cassette and guide) NY: Guidance Associates, 1976. 14 min.

M567 *Reading for the Fun of it: Fantasy.* (Filmstrip with record or cassette and guide) NY: Guidance Associates, 1976. 17 min.

M568 *Reading for the Fun of it: Many Lands.* (Filmstrip with record or cassette and guide) NY: Guidance Associates, 1976. 16 min.

M569 *Reading for the Fun of it: Mystery.* (Filmstrip with record or cassette and guide) NY: Guidance Associates, 1976. 15 min.

M570 *Reading for the Fun of it: Realistic Fiction.* (Filmstrip with record or cassette and guide) NY: Guidance Associates, 1976. 15 min.

M571 *Reading for the Fun of it: Science Fiction.* (Filmstrip with record or cassette and guide) NY: Guidance Associates, 1976. 17 min.

M572 *The Reading Teacher.* (Periodical) International Reading Association, 800 Barksdale, Rd., P. O. Box 8139, Newark, Delaware. 19711.

M573 *Really Rosie.* (8mm or 16mm film) Weston Woods, 1976. 26 min. Animated. Color. From a television program based on the Nutshell books: *One Was Johnny, Pierre, Alligators All Around,* and *Chicken Soup With Rice* by Maurice Sendak.

M574 ———. (Phonograph record) Weston Woods, n.d. Sung by Carole King. From a television program based on the Nutshell books by Maurice Sendak.

M575 *The Red Carpet.* (16mm film) Weston Woods, 1955. 9 min. Iconographic. Color. Based on a book by Rex Parkin.

M576 ———. (Filmstrip with record or cassette; individual cassette) Weston Woods, 1957. 8 min. 57 fr. Based on a book by R. Parkin.

M577 *Red Hawk's Account of Custer's Last Battle.* (Phonograph record or cassette) Caedmon, n.d. Narrated by Arthur S. Junaluska. Based on a book by Paul and Dorothy Goble.

M578 *The Reluctant Dragon.* (Phonograph record or cassette) Caedmon, n.d. Narrated by Boris Karloff. Based on a book by Kenneth Grahame.

M579 *Rifles for Watie.* (2 filmstrips with record or cassette; individual cassette) Miller-Brody, n.d. Based on a book by Harold Keith.

M580 *The Right Whale: An Endangered Species.* (16mm film or videocassette) National Geographic, 1976. 23 min. Live action. Color. Produced for TV.

M581 *Robert Frost Reads The Road Not Taken and Other Poems.* (Phonograph record or cassette) Caedmon, 1956. Narrated by Robert Frost from his poems.

M582 *Robinson Crusoe.* (2 filmstrips with record or cassette) Teaching Resource Films, an Educational Division of the New York Times, n.d. 140 fr. Based on a book by Daniel Defoe.

M583 ———. (Phonograph record or cassette) Caedmon, n.d. Narrated by Ian Richardson. Based on a book by Daniel Defoe.

M584 *Robert McCloskey.* (16mm film) Weston Woods, 1965. 18 min. Live action. Color. Interview with R. McCloskey.

M585 *Rogues in Music.* (Phonograph record) Bowmar, n.d.

M586 *Roots.* (12 MovieStrips with cassettes and guides) Films, Inc., 1977. Included are: *Roots I, the Making of a Slave; Roots II, Adjusting to Plantation Life; Roots III, Masters and Slaves;* and *Roots IV, Civil War and Emancipation.* From the David L. Wolper Television Production based on a book by Alex Haley.

M587 *Rosie's Walk.* (8mm or 16mm film) Weston Woods, n.d. 26 min. Animated. Color. Based on a book by Pat Hutchins.

M588 ———. (Filmstrip with record or cassette; individual cassette) 3 min. 29 fr. Based on a book by P. Hutchins.

M589 *Ruby Throat: The Story of a Hummingbird.* (4 paperbacks with a cassette) Morrow, n.d. Based on a book by Robert McClung.

M590 *Salt.* Filmstrip with record or cassette; individual cassette) Weston Woods, 1967. 12 min. 40 fr. Illus by Margot Zemach. Based on a book by Harve Zemach.

M591 *Sam and the Firefly.* (Filmstrip with record or cassette) Random, n.d. Based on a book by P. D. Eastman.

M592 *Sam, Bangs and Moonshine.* (Filmstrip with

record or cassette; individual cassette) Miller-Brody, n.d. Narrated by Rosemary Harris. Based on a book by Evaline Ness.

M593   *Scenes from Winnie the Pooh.* (3 posters) Young Reader's Press, n.d.

M594   *Scholastic Teacher.* (Periodical) Scholastic Magazines, Inc. 50 W. 44th St. New York, NY 10036.

M595   *School Library Journal.* (Periodical) R.R. Bowker, 1180 Ave. of the Americas, New York, NY 10036.

M596   *School Library Media Quarterly, Journal of the American Association of School Librarians.* (Periodical) American Library Association, 50 E. Huron St., Chicago, IL 60611.

M597   *Science Books and Films.* (Periodical) the American Association for the Advancement of Science, 1515 Massachusetts Avenue, NW, Washington, DC. 20005.

M598   *Sea Star: Orphan of Chincoteague.* (Phonograph record or cassette) Miller-Brody, n.d. Based on a book by Marguerite Henry.

M599   *Search for Stegosarus.* (2 filmstrips) Educational Dimensions, 1975. 59 fr. each.

M600   *Seasons of Poetry.* (4 filmstrips with records or cassettes) Chicago: Singer Society for Visual Education, n.d.

M601   *Secrets of Sleep.* (16mm film or videocassette) WGBH and BBC, 1976. 52 min. Live action. Color. Produced for TV.

M602   *See and Say.* (Filmstrip with record or cassette) Weston Woods, 1964. Based on a book by Antonio Frasconi.

M603   *The Selfish Giant.* (16mm film) Weston Woods, n.d. 14 min. Animated. Color. Based on a book by Oscar Wilde.

M604   ———. (Filmstrip with record or cassette; individual cassette) Weston Woods, 1971. 12 min. 41 fr. Illus by Gertraud and Walter Reiner. Based on a book by O. Wilde.

M605   *Sesame Street.* (Periodical) Children's Television Workshop. One Lincoln Plaza, New York, NY 10023.

M606   *Shadow of a Bull.* (Phonograph record or cassette) Miller-Brody, n.d. Based on a book by Mia Wojciechowska.

M607   *She'll Be Comin' Round the Mountain.* (Filmstrip with record or cassette; individual cassette) Weston Woods, 1975. 7 min. 40 fr. Based on a book by Robert Quackenbush.

M607   *Shrewd Todie and Lyzer the Miser.* (Filmstrip with record or cassette; individual cassette) Miller-Brody, n.d. Based on a book by Isaac Bashevis Singer.

M609   *The Shoemaker and the Elves.* (Filmstrip with record or cassette; individual cassette) Scribner/Miller-Brody, n.d. Based on a book by Adrienne Adams retold from the Brothers Grimm.

M610   *Silver Pennies.* (Phonograph record or cassette) Caedmon, n.d. Narrated by Claire Bloom and Cyril Ritchard. Based on a book edited by Blanche Jennings Thompson.

M611   *The Silver Pony.* (Filmstrip and study guide) Weston Woods, n.d. 92 fr. Based on a book by Lynd Ward.

M612   *Simon's Song.* (Filmstrip with record or cassette) Teaching Resource Films, an Educational Division of the New York Times, n.d. Sung by Tom Glazer. Based on a book illus by Ed Emberley.

M613   *Sing a Song for Sixpence.* (Filmstrip with record or cassette) Weston Woods, 1962. Includes *The Queen of Hearts.* Based on rhymes illustrated by Randolph Caldecott.

M614   *Sing Down the Moon.* (2 filmstrips with record or cassette; individual cassette) Miller-Brody, 1973. Narrated by Paulette Rubinstein. 45 min. Based on a book by Scott O'Dell.

M615   *Six Penguins.* (16mm film) McGraw-Hill, 1971. 5 min. Animated. Color. Another version of *The Lion and the Mouse* by Aesop.

M616   *Sleepy Book.* (Filmstrip with record or cassette; individual cassette) Weston Woods, n.d. 3 min. 18 fr. Includes *It Looked Like Spilt Milk.* Illus by Vladimir Bobri. Based on a book by Charlotte Zolotow.

M617   *The Snowy Day.* (8mm and 16mm film) Weston Woods, 1964. 6 min. Animated. Color. Based on a book by Ezra Jack Keats.

M618   ———. (Filmstrip with record or cassette; individual cassette) Weston Woods, 1965. 6 min. 27 fr. Based on a book by E. J. Keats.

M619   ———. (Poster) Horn Book Poster Set #1. Horn Book, n.d. From the book by Ezra Jack Keats.

M620   *Song of the Swallows.* (Filmstrip with record or cassette; individual cassette) Miller-Brody, n.d. Based on a book by Leo Politi.

M621   ———. (Poster) Horn Book Poster Set #1. Horn Book, n.d. From the book by Leo Politi.

M622   *Songs from Alice.* (Cassette) New York: Holiday, 1978. Based on *Alice in Wonderland* and *Through the Looking Glass* by Lewis Carroll.

M623   *Songs of the American Negro Slaves.* (Phonograph record) Scholastic, n.d.

M624   *Songs of the Humpback Whale.* (Phonograph record) Capitol Records, 1970. Voices of live whales.

M625   *The Sorcerer's Apprentice, a Musical Fantasy.* (16mm film) Coronet, 1970. 14 min. Color. Music by Dukas.

M626   *Sounder.* (16mm film) Twentieth Century Fox, 1972. 105 min. Live action. Color. Based on a book by William Armstrong.

M627   *Sparkle and Spin.* (Filmstrip with record or cassette) Weston Woods, n.d. (Includes *I Know a Lot of Things*) Based on a book by Ann and Paul Rand.

M628   *Springtime for Jeanne-Marie.* (Filmstrip with record or cassette; individual cassette) Miller-Brody, n.d. Based on a book by Francoise.

M629   *Squawk to the Moon, Little Goose.* (Filmstrip with cassette) Viking, n.d. Based on a book by Edna Mitchell Preston.

M630   *The Star Spangled Banner.* (8mm and 16mm film) Weston Woods, 1975. 5 min. Iconographic. Color. Based on a book by Peter Spier.

M631   ———. (Filmstrip with record or cassette; individual cassette) Weston Woods, 1975. 8 min. 43 fr. Based on a book by Peter Spier.

M632   *The Stonecutter.* (8mm and 16mm film)

Weston Woods, 1975. 6 min. Animated. Color. Based on a book by Gerald McDermott.

M633 ———. (Filmstrip with record or cassette; individual cassette) Weston Woods, n.d. 7 min. 33 fr. Based on a book by G. McDermott.

M634 *Stone Soup.* (16mm film) Weston Woods, 1955. 11 min. Iconographic. Color. Based on a book by Marcia Brown.

M635 ———. (Filmstrip with record or cassette; individual cassette) Weston Woods, 1957. 11 min. 46 fr. Based on a book by M. Brown.

M636 *Stories in Ballet and Opera.* (Phonograph record) Bowmar, n.d. Includes: *Amahl and the Night Visitors* by Menotti, *Hansel and Gretel Overture* by Humperdinck, and *The Nutcracker Suite Overture* by Tchaikovsky.

M637 *Stories in Motion.* (16mm film) Vermont Dept. of Libraries, 1973. 22 min. Live action. Color.

M638 *Stories of Sherlock Holmes: The Adventure of the Speckled Band and the Final Problem.* (Phonograph record or cassette) Caedmon, n.d. Narrated by Basil Rathbone. Based on a book by Sir Arthur Conon Doyle.

M639 *Stories of Sherlock Holmes: The Redheaded League.* (Phonograph record or cassette) Caedmon, n.d. Narrated by Basil Rathbone. Based on a book by Sir Arthur Conon Doyle.

M640 *Stories of Sherlock Holmes: Silver Blaze.* (Phonograph record or cassette) Caedmon, n.d. Narrated by Basil Rathbone. Based on a book by Sir Arthur Conon Doyle.

M641 *A Story, a Story.* (8mm and 16mm film) Weston Woods, 1973. 10 min. Animated. Color. Based on a book by Gail E. Haley.

M642 ———. (Filmstrip with record or cassette; individual cassette) Weston Woods, n.d. 10 min. 40 fr. Based on a book by G. E. Haley.

M643 *The Story About Ping.* (8mm and 16mm film) Weston Woods, 1955. 10 min. Iconographic. Color. Illus by Kurt Wiese. Based on a book by Marjorie Flack.

M644 ———. (Filmstrip with record or cassette; individual cassette) Weston Woods, n.d. Illus by K. Weise. Based on a book by M. Flack.

M645 *The Story of a Book.* (Filmstrip with cassette) Verdugo City, CA: Pied Piper Productions, 1970. How Holling C. Holling's *Pagoo* was written.

M646 *The Story of Babar.* (Filmstrip with record or cassette) Random, n.d. Based on a book by Jean De Brunhoff.

M647 *The Story of Ferdinand.* (Cassette with 8 paperbacks) Viking Seafarer Reading Chest, n.d. Illus by Robert Lawson. Based on a book by Munro Leaf.

M648 *The Story of Paul Bunyan.* (Filmstrip with record) Teaching Resource Films, An Educational Division of the New York Times, n.d. Sung by Tom Glazer. Based on a book by Barbara Emberley.

M649 *Strange Sleep.* (16mm film or videocassette) WGBH, 1976. 49 min. Live action. Color. Produced for TV. NOVA.

M650 *Strega Nonna.* (16mm film) Weston Woods, n.d. 9 min. Animated. Color. Based on a book by Tomie de Paola.

M651 ———. (Filmstrip with record or cassette; individual cassette) Weston Woods, n.d.

Based on a book by T. de Paola.

M652 *Stripe, the Story of a Chipmunk.* (Cassette with 4 paperbacks) Morrow, n.d. Based on a book by Robert McClung.

M653 *Stuart Little.* (2 phonograph records and 12 paperbacks) Miller-Brody, n.d. Narrated by Julie Harris. Based on a book by E.B. White.

M654 ———. (12 filmstrips with records or cassettes and guide) Cambridge, MA: Pathways of Sound, n.d. Read by E. B. White from his own book.

M655 *Suho and the White Horse.* (Filmstrip with record or cassette; individual cassette) Weston Woods, n.d. 10 min. 39 fr. Illus by Suekichi Akaba. Based on a book by Yuzo Otsuka.

M656 *Summer of My German Soldier.* (Phonograph record or cassette) Miller-Brody, n.d. Based on a book by Bette Greene.

M657 *Summer of the Swans.* (Phonograph record or cassette) Miller-Brody, n.d. Based on a book by Betsy Byars.

M658 *Sun Up.* (Filmstrip with record or cassette) Weston Woods, 1968. Illus by Roger Duvoisin. Based on a book by Alvin Tresselt.

M659 *The Sunspot Mystery; Sunspots Explained.* (16mm film or videocassette) WGBH, 1977. 31 min. Live action. Color. Produced for TV.

M660 *The Sunspot Mystery: The Sun-Weather Connection.* (16mm film or videocassette) WGBH, 1977. 30 min. Live action. Color. Produced for TV. NOVA.

M661 *The Surprise Party.* (Filmstrip with record or cassette; individual cassette) Weston Woods, 1972. 6 min. 30 fr. Based on a book by Pat Hutchins.

M662 *Sweet Betsy from Pike.* (Filmstrip with record) Teaching Resource Films, an Educational Division of the New York Times, n.d. Based on a book by Glen Rounds.

M663 *Swimmy.* (Filmstrip with record or cassette; individual cassette) Random, 1973. Based on a book by Leo Lionni.

M664 *The Swineherd.* (8mm and 16mm film) Weston Woods, n.d. 13 min. Animated. Color. Illus by Bjorn Wiinblad. Based on a story by Hans Christian Andersen.

M665 ———. (Filmstrip with record or cassette; individual cassette) Weston Woods, n.d. 12 min. 47 fr. Illus by B. Wiinblad. Based on a story by H. C. Andersen.

M666 *Swiss Family Robinson.* (Phonograph record or cassette) Caedmon, 1975. Based on a book by Johann Wyss.

M667 *The Tale of Benjamin Bunny.* (Filmstrip with cassette) Spoken Arts, 1974. Based on a book by Beatrix Potter.

M668 *The Tale of Benjamin Bunny.* (Filmstrip with record or cassette; individual cassette) Weston Woods, 1967. 8 min. 30 fr. Based on a book by B. Potter.

M669 *The Tale of Mr. Jeremy Fisher.* (Filmstrip with cassette) Spoken Arts, 1974. Based on a book by B. Potter.

M670 ———. (Filmstrip with record or cassette; individual cassette) Weston Woods, 1967. 6 min. 30 fr. Based on a book by B. Potter.

M671 *The Tale of Peter Rabbit.* (Filmstrip with

cassette) Spoken Arts, 1974. Based on a book by Beatrix Potter.

M672 ———. (Filmstrip with record or cassette; individual cassette) Weston Woods, 1962. 7 min. 33 fr. Based on a book by B. Potter.

M673 *The Tale of Squirrel Nutkin.* (Filmstrip with cassette) Spoken Arts, 1974. Based on a book by Beatrix Potter.

M674 *The Tale of Tom Kitten.* (Filmstrip with record or cassette; individual cassette) Weston Woods, n.d. 5 min. 30 fr. Based on a book by Beatrix Potter.

M675 *The Tale of Two Bad Mice.* (Filmstrip with record or cassette; individual cassette) Weston Woods, 1967. 6 min. 30 fr. Based on a book by Beatrix Potter.

M676 *Tales of Hiawatha.* (16mm film) Sterling Films, 1972. 19 min. Animated. Color. Selections from a poem by Henry Wadsworth Longfellow.

M677 *Talking Without Words.* (Filmstrip with record or cassette) Viking, n.d. Based on a book by Marie Hall Ets.

M678 *Teacher.* (Periodical) 77 Bedford St., Stamford, CT 06901.

M679 *Ten What?* (Filmstrip with record or cassette; individual cassette) Weston Woods, n.d. 4 min. 23 fr. Based on a book by Russell Hoban and Sylvie Selig.

M680 *Texas Folk Songs.* (Phonograph record) Tradition, n.d. Collected by Alan Lomax.

M681 *Thank You, Amelia Bedelia.* (Filmstrip with record or cassette) Teaching Resource Films, an Educational Division of the New York Times, 1974. 54 fr. Based on a book by Peggy Parish.

M682 *Theodore and the Talking Mushroom.* (Filmstrip with record or cassette; individual cassette) Random, n.d. Based on a book by Leo Lionni.

M683 *Theodore Roethke Reads His Poetry.* (Phonograph record or cassette) Caedmon, n.d. Read by Theodore Roethke from his poems.

M684 *They Were Strong and Good.* (Filmstrip with record or cassette; individual cassette) Weston Woods, 1968. 13 min. 38 fr. Based on a book by Robert Lawson.

M685 *This Britain: Heritage of the Sea.* (16mm film or videocassette) National Geographic, 1975. 52 min. Live action. Color. Produced for TV.

M686 *This is New York.* (16mm film) Weston Woods, 1962. 12 min. Iconographic. Color. Based on a book by M. Sasek.

M687 *The Three Billy Goats Gruff.* (Filmstrip with record or cassette; individual cassette) Weston Woods, 1962. 28 fr. 4 min. Based on a book illus by Marcia Brown.

M688 *The Three Poor Tailors.* (Filmstrip with record or cassette; individual cassette) Weston Woods, n.d. Includes *The Great Big Enormous Turnip.* Based on a book by Victor G. Ambrus.

M689 *Three Posters by Ezra Keats.* (Posters) Macmillan, 1972.

M690 *The Three Robbers.* (8mm or 16mm film) Weston Woods, n.d. 6 min. Animated. Color. Based on a book by Tomi Ungerer.

M691 ———. (Filmstrip with record or cassette; individual cassette) Weston Woods, 1965. 5 min. 31 fr. Based on a book by T. Ungerer.

M692 *Through the Looking Glass.* (Phonograph record or cassette) Caedmon, 1958. Narrated by Stanley Holloway, et al. Based on a book by Lewis Carroll.

M693 *Thy Friend Obadiah.* (Filmstrip with record or cassette) Viking, n.d. Narrated by Brinton Turkle from his book.

M694 *Tiger: The Story of a Swallowtail Butterfly.* (Cassette with 4 paperbacks) Morrow, n.d. Based on a book by Robert McClung.

M695 *Tikki Tikki Tembo.* (8mm and 16mm film) Weston Woods, n.d. 9 min. Iconographic. Color. Illus by Blair Lent. Based on a book by Arlene Mosel.

M696 ———. (Filmstrip with cassette or text booklet; individual cassette) Weston Woods, 1970. 8 min. 32 fr. Illus by Blair Lent. Based on a book by A. Mosel.

M697 *Tim All Alone.* (Filmstrip with cassette or text booklet; individual cassette) Weston Woods, n.d. 18 min. 64 fr. Based on a book by Edward Ardizzone.

M698 *The Time Machine.* (Cassette and paperback) Troll Associates, 1973. Based on a book by H.G. Wells.

M699 ———. (16mm film) MGM, 1960. 103 min. Live action. Color. Based on a book by H.G. Wells.

M700 *Time of Wonder.* (16mm film) Weston Woods, 1961. 13 min. Iconographic. Color. Based on a book by Robert McCloskey.

M701 ———. (Filmstrip with cassette or text booklet; individual cassette) Weston Woods, n.d. 13 min. 59 fr. Based on a book by R. McCloskey.

M702 *The Tombs of Atuan.* (Phonograph record or cassette) Miller-Brody, 1977. Based on a book by Ursula LeGuin.

M703 *The Tomten.* (Filmstrip with cassette or text booklet; individual cassette) Weston Woods, 1965. 7 min. 18 fr. Includes *Christmas in the Stable.* Illus by Harald Wiberg. Based on a book by Astrid Lindgren.

M704 *The Tompten and the Fox.* (Filmstrip with cassette or text booklet; individual cassette) Weston Woods, 1972. 5 min. 18 fr. Illus by H. Wiberg. Based on a book by A. Lindgren.

M705 *Top of the News.* (Periodical) American Library Association, 50 E. Huron St., Chicago, IL 60611.

M706 *The Tortoise and the Hare.* (16mm film) Disney, 1954. 10 min. Cartoon. Color. Based on a fable by Aesop.

M707a *The Tower of Babel.* (Filmstrip with record or cassette) Viking, 1970. Based on a book by William Wiesner.

M707b *Tracing a Legend: The Story of the Green Man.* (Filmstrip with cassette) Weston Woods, n.d. 66 fr. 15 min.

M708 *Transport 7-41-R.* (Phonograph record or cassette) Viking, n.d. Based on a book by T. Degens.

M709 *Travels of Babar.* (Filmstrip with record or cassette) Random n.d. Based on a book by De Brunhoff.

M710 *Treasure!* (16mm film or videocassette) National Geographic, 1976. 59 min. Live action. Color. Produced for TV.

M711 *Treasure Island.* (Cassette and Paperback) Troll Associates, 1973. Based on a book by Robert Louis Stevenson.

M712 ———. (16mm film) Walt Disney, 1950. 96 min. Live action. Color. Based on a book by R. L. Stevenson.

M713 *A Tree is Nice.* (Filmstrip with cassette or text booklet; individual cassette) Weston Woods, 1960. 4 min. 31 fr. Illus by Marc Simont. Based on a book by Janice Udry.

M714 *The Trip.* (16mm film) Weston Woods, 1980. 5 min. Iconographic and Animated. Color. Based on a book by Ezra Jack Keats.

M715 ———. (Filmstrip with cassette or text booklet; individual cassette) Weston Woods, 1980. 5 min. 27 fr. Based on a book by E.J. Keats.

M716 *Truck.* (Filmstrip with cassette) Somers, NY: Live Oak Media, 1981. 6½ min. 32 fr. Based on a book by Donald Crews.

M717 *Tucker's Countryside.* (Phonograph record or cassette) Miller-Brody, n.d. Based on a book by George Selden.

M718 *The Twenty-One Balloons.* (Phonograph record or cassette) Viking, n.d. Based on a book by William Pene du Bois.

M719 *The Twelve Days of Christmas.* (16mm film) Weston Woods, 1971. 6 min. Iconographic. Color. Based on a traditional song illus by Robert Broomfield.

M720 ———. (Filmstrip with cassette or text booklet; individual cassette) Weston Woods, n.d. 5 min. 16 fr. Based on a song illus by R. Broomfield.

M721 *The Ugly Duckling.* (8mm and 16mm film) Weston Woods, n.d. 15 min. Animated. Color. Illus by Svend Otto S. Based on a story by Hans Christian Andersen.

M722 ———. (Filmstrip with cassette or text booklet; individual cassette) Weston Woods, n.d. 17 min. 55 fr. Illus by Svend S. Otto Based on a story by H. C. Andersen.

M723 *Umbrella.* (Filmstrip with cassette or text booklet; individual cassette) Weston Woods, 1968. 5 min. 22 fr. Based on a book by Taro Yashima.

M724 *United States Flag.* (Filmstrip with record or cassette) Society for Visual Education, 1965. 45 fr.

M725 *The Upstairs Room.* (2 filmstrips with record or cassette) Miller-Brody, n.d. Based on a book by Johanna Reiss.

M726 *Urashima Taro, a Japanese Folktale.* (Filmstrip with cassette) NY: Guidance Associates, 1974.

M727 *Vampires Die at Midnight.* (4 filmstrips) Wayne, NJ: Leonard Peck Productions, 1974.

M728 *The Velveteen Rabbit.* (2 filmstrips with record or cassette) Miller-Brody, 1976. Based on a book by Marjorie Williams.

M729 ———. (Phonograph record or cassette with 8 paperbacks) Miller-Brody, 1976. Based on a book by M. Williams.

M730 *The Voyages of Doctor Doolittle.* (2 filmstrips with records or cassette; individual cassette) Miller-Brody, n.d. Based on a book by Hugh Lofting.

M731 *Waltzing Matilda.* (Filmstrip with cassette or text booklet; individual cassette) Weston Woods, n.d. 7 min. 32 fr. Illus by Desmond Digby. Based on a song by A. B. Paterson.

M732 *Whales.* (Pictures, cassette with 30 read-along copies, duplicating master and teacher's guide) National Geographic, 1978.

M733 *Whales, Dolphins and Men.* (16mm film or videocassette) BBC, 1973. 52 min. Live action. Color. Produced for TV. NOVA.

M734 *What Do You Do, Dear?* (Filmstrip with cassette or text booklet; individual cassette) Weston Woods, n.d. 5 min. 27 fr. Illus by Maurice Sendak. Based on a book by Sesyle Joslin.

M735 *What Do You Say, Dear?* (Filmstrip with cassette or text booklet; individual cassette) Weston Woods, 1963. 5 min. 27 fr. Illus by M. Sendak. Based on a book by S. Joslin.

M736 *What's the Big Idea, Ben Franklin?* (Cassette) Weston Woods, n.d. 39 min. Narrated by Jean Fritz from her book.

M737 *When Shlemiel Went to Warsaw.* (2 filmstrips with record or cassette) Miller-Brody, n.d. Based on a book by Isaac Bashevis Singer.

M738 *Where Does the Butterfly Go When it Rains?* (Filmstrip with record or cassette; individual cassette) Weston Woods, n.d. 3 min. 19 fr. Including *The Happy Day.* Illus by Leonard Weisgard. Based on a book by May Garelick.

M739 *Where the Wild Things Are.* (8mm and 16mm film) Weston Woods, 1975. 8 min. Animated. Color. Based on a book by Maurice Sendak.

M740 ———. (Filmstrip with cassette or text booklet; individual cassette) Weston Woods, 1968. 5 min. 38 fr. Based on a book by M. Sendak.

M741 *Where Was Patrick Henry on the 29th of May?* (Cassette) Weston Woods, n.d. 36 min. Narrated by Jean Fritz from her book.

M742 *Whispers and Other Poems.* (Filmstrip with cassette) McGraw Learning About Literature, Set 6, n.d. Based on a book by Myra Cohn Livingston.

M743 *Whistle for Willie.* (8mm and 16mm film) Weston Woods, 1965. 6 min. Animated. Color. Based on a book by Ezra Jack Keats.

M744 ———. (Filmstrip with cassette or text booklet; individual cassette) Weston Woods, 1965. 5 min. 28 fr. Based on a book by E.J. Keats.

M745 *White Snow, Bright Snow.* (Filmstrip with cassette or text booklet; individual cassette) Weston Woods, 1959. 7 min. 36 fr. Illus by Roger Duvoisin. Based on a book by Alvin Tresselt.

M746 *Whitefoot, the Story of a Wood Mouse.* (Cassette and 4 paperbacks) Morrow, n.d. Based on a book by Robert McClung.

M747 *Who's Dr. Seuss? Meet Ted Geisel.* (Filmstrip with cassette) Random House/Miller-Brody, 1980.

M748 *Whose Mouse are You?* (Filmstrip with cassette or text booklet; individual cassette) Weston Woods, 1972. 4 min. 26 fr. Illus by Jose Aruego. Based on a book by Robert Kraus.

M749 Why Do Birds Sing? (16mm film or video-cassette) WGBH, 1976. 27 min. Live action. Color. Produced for TV. NOVA.

M750 Why Don't You Get a Horse, Sam Adams? (Cassette) Weston Woods, n.d. Narrated by Jean Fritz from her book.

M751 Why Mosquitoes Buzz in People's Ears. (Filmstrip with cassette or text booklet; individual cassette) Weston Woods, 1976. 11 min. 46 fr. Illus by Leo and Diane Dillon. Based on a story retold by Verna Aardema.

M752 ———. (Phonograph record or cassette with book) Miller-Brody, n.d. Illus by L. and D. Dillon. Based on a story retold by V. Aardema.

M753 Why Noah Chose the Dove. (Filmstrip with cassette or text booklet; individual cassette) Miller-Brody, n.d. Based on a book by Isaac Bashevis Singer.

M754 Wild River. (16mm film or videocassette) National Geographic, 1970. 52 min. Live action. Color. Produced for TV.

M755 Wild Robin. (Filmstrip with cassette or text booklet; individual cassette) Weston Woods, n.d. 7 min. 34 fr. Based on a book retold and illus by Susan Jeffers.

M756 Will You Sign Here, John Hancock? (Cassette) Weston Woods, n.d. 34 min. Narrated by Jean Fritz from her book.

M757 William Tell and the Barber of Seville. (Phonograph record) Columbia, n.d. The New York Philharmonic conducted by Leonard Bernstein. Operas by Rossini.

M758 A Wind in the Door. (2 filmstrips with record or cassette; individual record or cassette) Miller-Brody, 1977. Based on a book by Madeleine L'Engle.

M759 Wind in the Willows. (Phonograph record or cassette) Caedmon, 1973. Narrated by David McCallum. Based on a book by Kenneth Grahame.

M760 Wind in the Willows. (4 phonograph records or 3 cassettes) Listening Library, 1974. Narrated by Jack Whitaker. Based on a book by K. Grahame.

M761 ———. (4 phonograph records) Pathways of Sound, n.d. Narrated by Robert Brooks, Jessica Tandy and Hume Cronyn. Based on a book by K. Grahame.

M762 The Wing on a Flea. (Filmstrip with cassette or text booklet; individual cassette) Weston Woods, 1963. 4 min. 27 fr. Based on a book by Ed Emberley.

M763 Winnie-the-Pooh. (Phonograph record or cassette) Caedmon, n.d. Read and sung by Carol Channing. Based on a book by A.A. Milne.

M764 ———. (Phonograph record) Cambridge, MA: Pathways of Sound, n.d. Narrated by Maurice Evans. Based on a book by A.A. Milne.

M765 ———. (9 cassettes) RCA/Pathways of Sound, 1975. 12 min. each. Read by A.A. Milne from his book.

M766 The Witch of Blackbird Pond. (Phonograph record or cassette) Miller-Brody, 1970. Based on a book by Elizabeth Speare.

M767 The Wizard of Oz. (16mm film) MGM, 1939. 101 min. Live action. Color. Based on a book by L. Frank Baum.

M768 A Woggle of Witches. (Filmstrip with record or cassette; individual cassette) Miller-Brody, n.d. Based on a book by Adrienne Adams.

M769 The World of Jacques-Yves Cousteau. (16mm film or videocassette) National Geographic, 1966. 52 min. Live action. Color. Produced for TV.

M770 Won't You Be My Neighbor? (Phonograph record) Woodbury, NY: Pickwick Int'l., n.d. Sung by Fred Rogers.

M771 A Wrinkle in Time. (2 filmstrips with record or cassette; individual record or cassette) Miller-Brody, n.d. Based on a book by Madeleine L'Engle.

M772 Wynken, Blynken and Nod. (16mm film) Weston Woods, n.d. 4 min. Iconographic. Color. Illus by Barbara Cooney. Based on a poem by Eugene Field.

M773 ———. (Filmstrip with cassette or text booklet; individual cassette) Weston Woods, n.d. 3 min. 19 fr. Includes The Owl and the Pussy Cat. Illus by Barbara Cooney. Based on poems by Eugene Field and Edward Lear.

M774 Wynken, Blynken and Nod and Other Poems. (Phonograph record or cassette) Caedmon, n.d. Read by Julie Harris. Based on a poem by E. Field.

M775 Yankee Doodle. (8mm and 16mm film) Weston Woods, 1976. 10 min. Iconographic. Color. Illus by Steven Kellogg. Based on a book by Edward Bangs.

M776 ———. (Filmstrip with cassette or text booklet; individual cassette) Weston Woods, 1976. 10 min. 53 fr. Illus by S. Kellogg. Based on a book by E. Bangs.

M777 The Yearling. (16mm film) MGM, 1946. 135 min. Live action. Color. Based on a book by Marjorie Rawlings.

M778 ———. (3 MovieStrips with cassettes and guide) Films, Inc., 1975. 252 fr. from the MGM movie which was based on a book by M. Rawlings.

M779 ———. (2 phonograph records or cassettes) Caedmon, 1974. Narrated by David Wayne, et al. Based on a book by M. Rawlings.

M780 You Are Special! (Phonograph record) Pickwick Int'l., n.d. Sung by Fred Rogers.

M781 Yukon Passage. (16mm film or videocassette) National Geographic, 1977. 59 min. Live action. Color. Prepared for TV.

M782 Zeely. (Phonograph record or cassette) Caedmon, n.d. Narrated and sung by Virginia Hamilton from her book.

M783 Zia. (Phonograph record or cassette) Miller-Brody, 1977. Based on a book by Scott O'Dell.

M784 Zlateh the Goat. (8mm and 16mm film) Weston Woods, n.d. 20 min. Live action. Color. Illus by Maurice Sendak. Based on a book by Isaac Bashevis Singer.

M785 Zlateh the Goat/The First Shlemiel. (2 filmstrips with record or cassette; individual record or cassette) Miller-Brody, n.d. Based on stories by I.B. Singer.

Title Index

ferent as Night and Day. Hanson. p. 352
The Ants Go Marching. Freschet. pp. 245, 265
Apartment 3. Keats. p. 208
Ape in a Cape, an Alphabet of Odd Animals. Eichenberg. pp. 220, 240, 242, 243
Apple and the Arrow. Buff. p. 290
Apples. Hogrogian. pp. 224, 249
Apples to Zippers, an Alphabet Book. Reuben. pp. 213, 239
Appleseed Farm. Douglas. pp. 127, 314
Appolonia's Valentine. Milhous. p. 224
Apricot ABC. Miles. pp. 240, 242
April Fools. Krahn. p. 249
April's Kittens. Newberry. p. 285
The Arabian Nights. Lang. pp. 112, 343, 367, 411, 519, 530, 536
The Arabian Nights, Ali Baba and the Forty Thieves. (Multimedia) pp. 519, 530
Arbuthnot Anthology of Children's LIterature. Sutherland. pp. 32, 53, 104, 106, 123, 124, 197, 198, 199, 313, 315, 346, 427, 430, 433, 457, 459, 487, 489–90, 491, 493, 523, 525, 526, 527, 528
The Arctic Sealer. Catherall. p. 145
Are You My Mother? Eastman. pp. 209, 415
Are You Square? Kessler. p. 173
Are You There God, It's Me Margaret. Blume. pp. 83, 103
Arion and the Dolphin. Anderson. p. 53
The Ark. Angel. p. 250
The Ark. Benary-Isbert. p. 105
An Arkful of Animals. Cole. p. 348
Arithmetic in Verse and Rhyme. Jacobs. p. 311
The Armadillo Who Had No Shell. Simon. p. 175
Around the House That Jack Built. Abish. p. 227
Around the Seasons. Farjeon. p. 339
Around the Year. Tudor. p. 225
The Arrow Book of Science Riddles. Wyler. pp. 474, 476
Arrow to the Sun. McDermottt. pp. 44, 192, 221
Art for Teachers of Children. Montgomery. p. 438
Art is Everywhere. Kessler. p. 172
Art is for You. Abish and Kaplan. p. 234
The Art of Art for Children's Books, a Contemporary Survey. Klemin. pp. 188, 192, 216
The Art of Color. Itten. p. 194
The Art of Hand Shadows. Almaznino. pp. 442–43
The Art of Making Cloth Toys. Roth. pp. 58, 238, 304
The Art of Making Puppets and Marionettes. Roth. pp. 438, 441, 444, 456
The Art of Making Wooden Toys. Stevenson. p. 238
Art of Mosaics. Currier. p. 233
The Art of Papier Mâché. Kenny. p. 235
The Art of Photography. Glubok. p. 214
The Art of the Eskimo. Glubok. p. 320
Art Techniques for Children. Tritten. pp. 237, 449
The Arthur Rackham Fairy Book. Rackham. pp. 196, 422, 433, 459, 520, 525, 536
Arthur's Christmas Cookies. Hoban. p. 180
As I Was Crossing Boston Common. Farber. pp. 177, 240
As Right As Can Be. Rose. p. 393
Ashanti to Zulu: African Traditions. Musgrove. pp. 185, 241
Ask Mr. Bear. Flack. pp. 79, 97, 394
The Astonishing Adventures of Patrick the Mouse. Beskow. p. 66
Attic of the Wind. Lund. pp. 48, 312
Audum and His Bear. Schiller. p. 43

Australian Legendary Tales. Parker. p. 538
Away and Ago. Behn. p. 301
Away and Go. McCord. p. 337
Away in a Manger, A Story of the Nativity. Nussbaumer. pp. 269, 349–50
Away Went Balloons. Haywood. p. 34
The Awful Mess. Rockwell. pp. 222, 341

B is for Betsy. Haywood. pp. 27, 34
Babar and Father Christmas. De Brunhoff. p. 220
Babar the King. (Multimedia) p. 74
Babar's Birthday Surprise. De Brunhoff. p. 74
Baboushka and the Three Kings. Robbins. pp. 192, 226, 268, 377, 452, 522
A Baby Sister for Frances. Hoban. pp. 48, 97, 190, 313
Baby's Song Book. Poston. pp. 276, 279, 286, 299
Back to School with Betsy. Haywood. p. 34
Backbone of the King: the Story of Paka'a and His Son Ku. Brown. p. 217
The Bad Child's Book of Beasts. Belloc. p. 306
Baker's Clay. Williamson. p. 234
Ballad of America. Scott. p. 271
The Ballad of William Sycamore. Benet. p. 333
Ballooning Adventures of Paddy Pork. Goodall. pp. 43, 221, 250
Ballpoint Bananas and Other Jokes for Kids. Keller. p. 464
Bam Zam Boom! Merriam. p. 212
Banner Forward! The Pictorial Biography of a Guide Dog. Rappaport. pp. 56, 104
Barbara Frietchie. Whittier. p. 316
The Barber of Seville. Johnston. p. 289
A Bargain for Frances. Hoban. p. 48
Barkis. Newberry. p. 221
Barkley. Hoff. pp. 444–445
The Baseball Trick. Corbett. pp. 307, 380
Basil and the Pygmy Cats. Titus. pp. 65, 132
Basil Bush of the Beach. Firmin. p. 211
Basil of Baker Street. Titus. pp. 65, 132, 279
A Basket in the Reeds. Saporta. p. 348
The Bat Poet. Jarrell. pp. 309, 310
Batik as a Hobby. Stein. p. 189
Batik for Beginners. Martin. p. 189
The Battle for the Kegs. Hopkinson. p. 315
The Bayeux Tapestry, the Story of the Norman Conquest, 1066. Denny. p. 237.
Be a Puppeteer. Worrell. pp. 437, 439, 440, 441, 455, 456
Be Nice to Spiders. Graham. p. 211
Beachcomber's Book. Kohn. p. 234
The Bear and the Fly. Winter. pp. 37, 251
A Bear Called Paddington. Bond. pp. 47, 76, 234
Bear Mouse. Freschet. pp. 68, 73
Bear Scouts. Berenstain. p. 243
The Bears Almanac. Berenstain. pp. 243, 333
The Bears Are Sleeping. Ylla. p. 283
The Bear's Bicycle. McLeod. p. 369
The Bears' Christmas. Berenstain. p. 243
Bears in the Night. Berenstain. p. 243
Bears on Wheels. Berenstain. pp. 243, 333
The Bears' Picnic. Berenstain. p. 243
Bear's Picture. Pinkwater. p. 187
The Bears' Vacation. Berenstain. p. 243
The Beast in Holger's Woods. Derleth. p. 139
The Beast of Monsieur. Ungerer. p. 178
Beasts, an Alphabet of Fine Prints. Fuller. pp. 177, 239, 240

Subject Index